ENCYCLOPEDIA
OF POLICY STUDIES

PUBLIC ADMINISTRATION AND PUBLIC POLICY

A Comprehensive Publication Program

Executive Editor

JACK RABIN
Graduate Program for Administrators
Rider College
Lawrenceville, New Jersey

Other volumes in preparation

ENCYCLOPEDIA OF POLICY STUDIES

edited by *STUART S. NAGEL*

University of Illinois at Urbana-Champaign
Urbana, Illinois

MARCEL DEKKER, INC.   New York and Basel

H
97
.E6
1983

Library of Congress Cataloging in Publication Data

Main entry under title:

Encyclopedia of policy studies.

    (Public administration and public policy ; 13)
    Includes bibliographical references and indexes.
    1. Policy sciences. I. Nagel, Stuart S., [date]
II. Series
H97.E6 1983   361.6'1   82-22111
ISBN 0-8247-1199-8

MARCEL DEKKER, INC.
270 Madison Avenue, New York, New York 10016

Current printing (Last digit):
10 9 8 7 6 5 4 3 2 1

PRINTED IN THE UNITED STATES OF AMERICA

Contributors

James E. Anderson Department of Political Science, University of Houston, Houston, Texas

Douglas E. Ashford Department of Government, University of Pittsburgh, Pittsburgh, Pennsylvania

Robert H. Blank Department of Political Science, University of Idaho, Moscow, Idaho

Charles Bulmer Department of Political Science, University of Alabama in Birmingham, Birmingham, Alabama

John L. Carmichael, Jr. Department of Political Science, University of Alabama in Birmingham, Birmingham, Alabama

Larry J. Cohen Department of Political Science, University of Illinois, Chicago, Illinois

Fred S. Coombs College of Education, University of Illinois, Urbana-Champaign, Illinois

Yehezkel Dror Department of Political Science, The Hebrew University of Jerusalem, Jerusalem, Israel

James A. Dunn, Jr. Department of Political Science, and Graduate Public Policy Program, Rutgers University-Camden, Camden, New Jersey

William N. Dunn Graduate School of Public and International Affairs, University of Pittsburgh, Pittsburgh, Pennsylvania

David J. Falcone Departments of Health Administration and Political Science, Duke University Medical Center, Durham, North Carolina

Neal M. Goldsmith* Woodrow Wilson School of Public and International Affairs, Princeton University, Princeton, New Jersey

Don F. Hadwiger Department of Political Science, Iowa State University, Ames, Iowa

Charles F. Hermann Mershon Center and Department of Political Science, Ohio State University, Columbus, Ohio

Helen M. Ingram[†] Department of Political Science, Utah State University, Logan, Utah

Charles O. Jones Department of Government and Foreign Affairs, University of Virginia, Charlottesville, Virginia

Dennis R. Judd Department of Political Science, University of Denver, Denver, Colorado

Richard S. Katz Department of Political Science, The Johns Hopkins University, Baltimore, Maryland

Edward A. Kolodziej Department of Political Science, University of Illinois, Urbana-Champaign, Illinois

Michael E. Kraft Department of Public and Environmental Administration, University of Wisconsin, Green Bay, Wisconsin

Robert M. Lawrence Department of Political Science, Colorado State University, Fort Collins, Colorado

George J. McCall Department of Sociology, University of Missouri-St. Louis, St. Louis, Missouri

Jarol B. Manheim Department of Political Science, Virginia Polytechnic Institute and State University, Blacksburg, Virginia

Dean E. Mann Department of Political Science, University of California, Santa Barbara, California

Dieter Matthes Department of Political Science and Geography, Francis Marion College, Florence, South Carolina

Daniel A. Mazmanian Department of Government, and Program in Public Policy Analysis, Pomona College, Claremont, California

Present affiliations:
*School of Urban and Public Affairs, Carnegie-Mellon University, Pittsburgh, Pennsylvania
†Department of Political Science, University of Arizona, Tucson, Arizona

Stuart S. Nagel Department of Political Science, University of Illinois, Urbana-Champaign, Illinois

Marian Lief Palley Department of Political Science, University of Delaware, Newark, Delaware

Dianne M. Pinderhughes Department of Government, Dartmouth College, Hanover, New Hampshire

Alan L. Porter Department of Industrial and Systems Engineering, Georgia Institute of Technology, Atlanta, Georgia

Robert F. Rich* Woodrow Wilson School of Public and International Affairs, Princeton University, Princeton, New Jersey

Leroy N. Rieselbach Department of Political Science, Indiana University, Bloomington, Indiana

Harrell R. Rodgers, Jr. Department of Political Science, University of Houston, Houston, Texas

Frederick A. Rossini Technology and Science Policy Program, Georgia Institute of Technology, Atlanta, Georgia

Paul A. Sabatier[†] Division of Environmental Studies and School of Administration, University of California, Davis, California

Warren J. Samuels Department of Economics, Michigan State University, East Lansing, Michigan

Larry L. Wade Department of Political Science, University of California, Davis, California

Stephen L. Wasby Department of Political Science, State University of New York, Albany, New York

George H. Weber[‡] Department of Health and Human Services, National Institute of Mental Health, Rockville, Maryland

Norman Wengert Department of Political Science, Colorado State University, Fort Collins, Colorado

Michael J. White School of Public Administration, University of Southern California, Los Angeles, California

Linda F. Williams Department of Political Science, Howard University, Washington, District of Columbia

Present affiliations:
*School of Urban and Public Affairs, Carnegie-Mellon University, Pittsburgh, Pennsylvania
†Center for Interdisciplinary Studies, University of Bielefeld, Federal Republic of Germany
‡National Catholic School of Social Services, The Catholic University of America, Washington, District of Columbia

Contents

Introduction

The purpose of this introduction to the *Encyclopedia of Policy Studies* is to describe briefly the general nature and background of policy studies, the institutions of the field, its substance/process/methods, its future, and the purpose/organization of this Encyclopedia.[1]

I. THE GENERAL NATURE AND BACKGROUND OF POLICY STUDIES

The field of policy studies can be broadly defined as the study of the nature, causes, and effects of alternative public policies for dealing with specific social problems. Some people in the field, such as Duncan MacRae and Yehezkel Dror, prefer to emphasize policy effects and the evaluation or optimization of these effects; others, such as Thomas Dye and Charles Jones, prefer to emphasize causal determinants and processes. Those who emphasize prescription, however, recognize that one cannot prescribe policies without an awareness of what policies are likely to be adopted and effectively implemented. Likewise, those who emphasize causes recognize that the effects of policies are often an important causal factor in shaping policies.

Policy studies is a field in itself and also an approach that is applicable to all fields of political science and all social science disciplines. Policy studies differs from what political scientists generally do in that most political scientists traditionally have not been concerned with specific policy problems such as environment, poverty, crime, and so on, although many now are. Policy studies also differs in its emphasis on the relations between policies and effects, whereas most political scientists have been concerned almost exclusively with government structures, processes, and behavior. Policy

---

[1] For further details on many of these subjects, see S. Nagel (1980), *The Policy Studies Handbook* (Lexington-Heath, Lexington, MA).

studies draws on the classical political science concern for controversial policy issues and normative evaluation. It also draws on the behavioral political science concern for using quantitative methods, although applied to policy problems. As such, policy studies tends to provide a kind of synthesis between classical and behavioral political science.

Although political science has played an important part in the development of policy studies, the field is truly interdisciplinary. Political science contributes a concern for the political and administrative feasibility aspects of alternative public policies. Economics contributes a concern for benefits, costs, and maximizing benefits minus costs, with an emphasis on deducing prescriptive conclusions from given goals and intuitively or empirically accepted relations. Psychology emphasizes the relevance of rewards and punishments in motivating people, and it provides a research paradigm emphasizing pretests and posttests of experimental and control groups. Sociology is concerned with social problems, social classes, and social statistics. Anthropology, geography, and history provide broadening perspectives across places and times. Natural science contributes a concern for the physical and biological factors that are often important in such policy problems as energy and health. Mathematics provides quantitative tools for measuring, analyzing, and evaluating the effects of alternative public policies. Philosophy shows a special concern for the values toward which public policies are directed and the ultimate logic of policy analysis.

The field of policy studies and its orientation have changed tremendously since 1970, as indicated by the rapidly expanding list of relevant journals, organizations, articles, books, book series, convention papers, conference themes, courses, schools, grants, and academic and government job openings. What has caused these changes? One early stimulus was the general public's concern for civil rights, the war on poverty, peace, women's liberation, environmental protection, and other social problems of the late 1960s and early 1970s. The scholarly implementation of those concerns among academics was facilitated by the development of new statistical and mathematical methods, the spread of computer software, and the development of relevant interdisciplinary relations. The relative attractiveness of the government as an employer and research sponsor also increased, as the role of universities in employment and research funding decreased. A more recent stimulus has been the concern for obtaining more government output from reduced tax dollars. In that regard, government retrenchment has decreased government prosperity, but it has increased the prosperity of policy analysts.

II. INSTITUTIONS OF POLICY STUDIES

The basic institutions of an academic field include training programs, research centers, funding sources, publishing outlets, associations, and placement opportunities. *Training programs* associated with policy studies can be classified in various categories, but it is quite possible to put programs in more than one category. The categories include whether the program is emphasizing (1) graduate or undergraduate work, (2) training for government teaching, (3) multiple disciplines or one discipline, (4) methodology or substance, (5) classroom or field experience, (6) university budget money or grants and contracts, (7) policy processes or evaluation of policy alternatives, (8) federal or state and local, (9) cross-national or national, and (10) questioning general societal goals or accepting them. Perhaps the most distinguishing characteristic of various programs relevant to the interests of political scientists is whether they emphasize a political science approach, as in the Berkeley Graduate School of Public Affairs; an economics approach, as in the Harvard Kennedy School; or a social-psychological approach as in Northwestern's

Evaluation Research Program. Those diverse orientations are increasingly coming together in recognition that each has a unique and valuable contribution to make. Political science emphasizes process and feasibility; economics emphasizes deduction and optimizing; and social psychology emphasizes experimentation and attitudes.

Many political science departments or universities could develop interdisciplinary training programs by simply cross-listing courses, faculty, and students. Benefits from developing a policies studies program include increased job opportunities, grants, program funding, intellectual stimulation, policy relevance, publishing opportunities, enrollment, faculty recruitment, and the opportunity to build on relevant departments and people. The incremental costs of a policy studies program are quite low given the existing people and facilities at nearly all universities. What may be especially needed is to get university administrators to show more recognition of the opportunities that exist if they can pull together some of their existing resources in a coherent policy studies training program.

Nongovernmental *research centers* in the policy studies field can be divided into those at universities (such as the Yale Institution for Social and Policy Studies or the UCLA Institute for Social Science Research) and those not at universities (such as Brookings, Abt Associates, Urban Institute, Mitre, and The American Enterprise Institute). Like training programs, research centers can also be classified in terms of quality, but that is much more difficult to do. There does seem to be some consensus that university research centers are good on general principles and creativity, but nonuniversity centers are generally better on following detailed specifications and meeting time constraints. What may be needed are more research centers that can draw upon academic creativity while still being effective in responding to government requests for proposals.

Funding sources in the policy studies field include both government agencies and private funding sources. Leading government sources with a broad orientation include the National Science Foundation (especially the Division of Applied Research and the Division of Policy Analysis) and the National Institutes of Mental Health. Virtually every government agency has the authority to issue a purchase order to buy research products relevant to the interests of the agency, including Defense, Energy, Housing and Urban Development (HUD), Health and Human Services (HHS), Justice, Agriculture, Transportation, Commerce, Labor, and Education. Leading private sources with broad orientation include the Ford Foundation (especially the National Affairs Division and the Committee on Public Policy), Rockefeller, and Russell Sage. Numerous private foundations have specialized interests in various policy problems, as indicated by the *Foundation Directory.*

On the matter of *publishing outlets,* there are a number of new journals in the field, including *Policy Analysis, Policy Sciences, Public Policy, Public Interest,* and the *Policy Studies Journal.* Although there is substantial overlap among those journals, each has a somewhat separate focus as reflected in their titles. *Policy Analysis* is concerned especially with the methodology of policy studies, with an emphasis on economic reasoning in program evaluation. *Policy Sciences* is also concerned especially with methodology, but with more emphasis on operations research, management science, and cross-national authors. *Public Policy* has focused more on substance than method, but its former political emphasis is moving toward economics. *Public Interest* is concerned mainly with substance and values, particularly from the perspective of nonmathematical sociology. The *Policy Studies Journal* tries to combine substance and method, although mainly with a political science or political orientation and a symposium format.

Other general policy-oriented scholarly journals include *Evaluation Quarterly,* the *Journal of the American Institute of Planners,* the *Journal of Legal Studies,* the

Journal of Political Economy, the *Journal of Public Economics,* the *Journal of Social Issues,* the *Journal of Urban Analysis, Law and Contemporary Problems, Law and Society Review, Policy and Politics, Public Administration Review, Public Choice, Social Indicators Research, Social Policy, Social Problems, Society, Socio-Economic Planning Sciences,* and *Urban Affairs Quarterly.* Disciplinary social science journals such as the *American Political Science Review* are increasingly publishing articles with a policy orientation. A number of scholarly publishers have established a book series or a set of books that deals with policy studies. These include Lexington, Sage, Ballinger, Duxbury, Elsevier, Goodyear, Marcel Dekker, Pergamon, Praeger, St. Martin's, and Academic Press. Some of the better-known series include the Sage Yearbooks in Politics and Public Policy, the Sage Policy Studies Review Annual, the Lexington-PSO series, and the Elsevier Policy Sciences Book Series.

There are now a number of new *associations* in the policy studies field. Like training programs and journals, they can be partly classified in terms of whether they are associated with political science, economics, or sociology-psychology. The Policy Studies Organization (founded in 1972) is associated especially with political science. The Association for Policy Analysis and Management (founded in 1979) is associated especially with economics, although so is the more mathematical Public Choice Society. The Evaluation Research Society (founded in 1977) represents especially psychology and sociology, and it is in the process of merging with the Evaluation Network and the Council for Applied Social Research. Psychologists and sociologists are also represented by units within the APA and ASA, namely, the Society for the Psychological Study of Social Issues and the Society for the Study of Social Problems. There may be a need for a more interaction and coordination among these associations in order to promote more interdisciplinary projects such as joint symposia, publications, research, convention panels, legislative testimony, and other activities.

Placement opportunities include the training programs and research centers mentioned previously. For many academic fields, placement opportunities include private business. The counterpart in policy studies is mainly government agencies. They represent the heart of policy studies, since there would be no government policies without government agencies. In other words, they represent not only an outlet for placing students and placing ideas, but also a reciprocal source of ideas relevant to improving the work of the training programs and research centers. Some government agencies, however, are more actively involved in planning and evaluating alternative policies than are other agencies. Federal agencies are especially active, but state and local agencies are becoming more so with the passage of legislation requiring more evaluation and the need to stretch tighter budgets. Among federal agencies, the planning and evaluation units at HUD, HHS, Labor, and Defense are generally well regarded, along with the executive office agencies such as the Office of Management and Budget (OMB) and the Domestic Council. In doing policy evaluation, Congress has the help of the General Accounting Office, the Congressional Budget Office, the Office of Technology Assessment, and the Congressional Reference Service. A survey of political scientists in government mentioned the need for more policy research by academic political scientists, more exchange of information between academics and practitioners, and more training on how government agencies actually function.

III. SUBSTANCE, PROCESS, AND METHODS OF POLICY STUDIES

Core courses in policy studies programs generally cover substance, process, and methods. A key issue in discussing policy studies *substance* is determining the social problems that are important to policy studies training and research. The answer is generally those social problems to which governments devote a substantial amount of resources. That is a descriptive approach to clarifying policy studies substance. A prescriptive approach points to the social problems on which governments should devote a substantial amount of resources, regardless of whether they do or not. For example, is family policy a subject for active government involvement with regard to husband-wife relations and parent-child relations? Is religious policy such a subject, with regard to facilitating parochial schools, contributions to religious institutions, and some forms of religious behavior? Closely related is the question of the relative importance of different policy problems in a policy studies program. Another key issue in the realm of policy studies substance is how to classify substantive policy problems. One approach classifies problems in terms of the disciplines with which they are most often associated, including problems especially related to political science (e.g., civil liberties or defense), economics (e.g., economic regulation or taxing-spending), sociology-psychology (e.g., race relations or population), planning (e.g., land use or transportation), and physical or biological science (e.g., energy or health).

Key issues in discussing the policy *process* include the following:

1. Do policies get made more by rational analysis of the relations between alternative policies and goals, or by incremental trial and error?
2. In studying policy adoption and implementation, how much emphasis should be placed on process analysis, as contrasted to the determinants and effects of policy variation?
3. In policy studies training, how much emphasis should be placed on process, as contrasted to methods and substance?
4. To what extent does the process change when we talk about different substantive issues such as crime policy versus environmental policy?
5. How does the policy adoption and implementation process differ across levels of government, branches of government, and across nations?
6. To what extent should the process be an evaluative goal in itself with regard to such matters as public participation, fair procedure, openness, and predictability?
7. To what extent should policy analysts consider political and administrative feasibility in evaluating alternative policies?
8. What is a good policy process in terms of effectiveness, efficiency, and equity on such dimensions as federalism, separation of powers, judicial review, the two-party system, and majority rule with minority rights?

Some issues in discussing policy analysis *methods* include:

1. How is policy analysis similar to and different from business analysis?
2. How can policy analysts become more sensitive to social values and more questioning of goals when evaluating alternative policies?
3. How can one predict the effects of alternative policies, as contrasted to reacting to policies that have already been adopted?

4. How can one accept goals as given and attempt to determine what policies will maximize them, rather than accepting policies as given and merely attempt to determine what are their effects?

5. How may analysts be given a good grounding in social science research methods, including a concern for meaningful measurement, sampling, determination of relations, and causal analysis?

6. How may analysts be given a good grounding in both finite math and calculus-oriented marginal analysis?

7. How can we keep analysts from going overboard in seeking precision methods when less precise techniques give the same results, or from suffering the opportunity cost of not taking advantage of precision that might be easily available?

8. How can we get analysts to be more sensitive to the subject matter with which they are working, as contrasted to using mechanical quantification without thinking through the implications?

9. How can we get analysts to analyze questions that have relatively broad significance, rather than unduly narrowly focused questions?

IV. THE FUTURE OF POLICY STUDIES

The future direction of policy studies is likely to be toward more growth, or a stabilizing at a high level of academic and government activity. Growth is likely to continue, since the causal forces responsible are still continuing. Those causal forces include the public concern for important policy problems, although the nature of the problem keeps changing. In the late 1960s and early 1970s, the problems related to civil rights, poverty, Vietnam, women's liberation, and environmental protection. In the early 1980s they related more to inflation, energy, and the Middle East. The causal forces also include improved quantitative methods, increased attractiveness of government as a social science employer and research sponsor, and increased government concern for stretching scarce resources.

Deeper causal forces relate to factors that explain increased government involvement and growth over the last 80 years. Those factors are of three kinds. First, there are socio-economic forces such as (1) in the increased severity of world conflicts, (2) the growing importance of public education, (3) the growth of large interstate and multinational business, (4) the growth of big labor and other pressure groups that seek aid and require regulation, (5) increased urbanization and the resulting loss of self-sufficiency, (6) increased severity of periods of inflation and recession, (7) competition with foreign ideologies, and (8) the fact that regulation and government activity generate more regulation and activity. Second, there are certain enabling factors, such as (1) expanded sources of government revenue necessary for carrying on increased government programs, (2) improved managerial techniques for handling large-scale government operations, and (3) changing constitutional interpretations. Third is the ideological shift from a prevailing attitude favoring minimal government toward an attitude that government has many positive responsibilities.

Within the field of policy studies, one might predict more specific increases in the following:

1. Training programs (undergraduate and graduate, disciplinary and interdisciplinary, and academic-oriented and practitioner-oriented)

2. Policy research centers (university, governmental, and nonuniversity private)
3. Funding sources (government line agencies such as HHS, government research agencies such as the National Science Foundation, and private foundations such as the Ford Foundation)
4. Publishing outlets (both journals and book publishers)
5. Policy-oriented scholarly associations (disciplinary, interdisciplinary, professional, and problem-focused)

Within the social sciences, one might predict increases in the following:

1. The percentage of social scientists who identify with policy studies
2. Emphasis on policy evaluation and implementation rather than just explaining variation across decisions
3. Use of microeconomic reasoning, rather that just statistical data processing
4. Concern for a wider variety of policy problems
5. The concern across subfields within each social science discipline for the nature, causes, and effects of relevant public policies
6. Synthesis between the traditional philosophical concern for normative evaluation and the scientific or behavioral concern for quantitative analysis
7. Interaction between social science academics and practitioners in training programs and in government
8. Reaching out to other disciplines in view of the interdisciplinary nature of policy problems

In general, policy studies seems to be a boom industry as a subdiscipline, an interdiscipline, and a developing new discipline. Policy studies also seems to be providing some new vitality to political and social science, while political and social science provide the foundation for policy studies.

V. PURPOSE AND ORGANIZATION OF THE ENCYCLOPEDIA

The purpose of this Encyclopedia is to bring together a set of chapters that analyze the basic issues and references dealing with each major aspect of the field of policy studies. The aspects of the field can be organized into general approaches to policy studies and specific policy problems. The general approaches cover matters that cut across the specific problems. Each specific problem deals with an area of government activity in which there is a general consensus that government ought to be involved, but controversy as to what forms that involvement should take. The general approaches include stages in policy studies research such as basic conceptualizing, research methodology, and research utilization. The approaches also include stages in the policy process such as policy formation and implementation. At the general level, one might also be concerned with policy analysis across nations and across disciplines, and concerned with the special policy problems of different levels of government, including state and urban government.

A meaningful way of classifying specific policy problems is in terms of the scholarly discipline with which they are most often associated. All policy problems are inherently multidisciplinary. The disciplinary classification used in this Encyclopedia merely indicates what discipline tends to offer the most courses of journal articles on the policy problem from among the basic disciplines of political science, sociology, psychology, planning, natural science, and engineering. The problem of poverty, for example, clearly involves economic, political, psychological, and planning aspects, but it is classified under sociology because sociology and social work departments tend to offer more courses on the subject than do other departments. The disciplines of law and operations research are relevant to nearly all policy fields, since policy often manifests itself in laws, and since operations research provides general methodologies for arriving at means for maximizing given goals. Having a set of categories helps to make the Encyclopedia more organized, rather than an A-to-Z "laundry list" of policy approaches and problems. Using a disciplinary classification also brings out the fact that many disciplines are relevant to policy studies.

Problems with a political science emphasis include foreign policy, defense, electoral matters, legislative reform, and civil liberties. Problems with an economics emphasis include economic regulation, labor, consumer protection, communications, taxing/spending, and agriculture. Problems with a sociology-psychology emphasis include poverty, minorities, crime, education, and population. Problems with an urban and regional planning emphasis include housing, land use, transportation, and environmental protection. Problems with a natural science or engineering emphasis include science/technology policy, health, energy, and biomedical policy. For each of those 23 specific policy problems and each of the nine previously mentioned general approaches, an expert social scientist has been chosen to draft for the Encyclopedia a comprehensive survey of the subject. Contributors have been requested to emphasize the basic issues and references so as better to inform nonexperts as to the nature of each aspect of the policy studies field.

This work is referred to as an encyclopedia rather than as a handbook, partly because there is already a *Handbook of Policy Studies,* edited by Stuart Nagel and published by Lexington Books in 1980. That Handbook is a short summary of the professional aspects of the field, rather than an intensive analysis of general policy approaches and specific policy problems, as this Encyclopedia is. A more important reason for using the word "encyclopedia" is the fact that the word "handbook" is defined in the *American College Dictionary* as "a small book or treatise serving for guidance as in an occupation or study." This volume is not small and not just vocational. Rather it is large and broadly conceived from a scholarly perspective. The separate chapters, however, can be considered as modules in their respective fields, and the Encyclopedia also has considerable practical policy relevance. According to the *American College Dictionary,* the word "encyclopedia" does not necessarily involve an alphabetic arrangement, although that might often be the case. Literally, the word "encyclopedia" means taking a walk around a subject. That is the purpose of this Encyclopedia, namely, to provide a grand tour of the field of policy studies.

Many people deserve credit for the massive amount of work that went into developing this Encyclopedia. They include the 41 chapter authors or co-authors who have communicated their expert knowledge by drafting detailed chapters covering their specialties. Thanks are also owed to Marcel Dekker (as publisher of the Encyclopedia) and to Jack Rabin (as editor of the series) for having inspired this work. Credit is also due to the numerous authors of papers, articles, book chapters, and books that are referred to in these Encyclopedia chapters. Most of that literature has been written within the last 10 or so years. The policy studies field is young but is growing rapidly. It is hoped that this Encyclopedia will record well that past growth and help stimulate future growth regarding the applications of political and social science to important policy programs.

Stuart S. Nagel
University of Illinois

ENCYCLOPEDIA
OF POLICY STUDIES

Unit One

GENERAL APPROACHES TO POLICY STUDIES

1

Basic Concepts in Policy Studies

Yehezkel Dror / The Hebrew University of Jerusalem, Jerusalem, Israel

Policy studies are presumptuous: They aim at supplying a scientific dimension to the most ambitious of all human activities—to try and influence the future according to our desires through conscious collective choice and action. Any look at history reveals the near hopelessness of this task: Policies have seldom been successful in terms of their ambitions and objectives; revolutions never achieved their dreams; and ordinary, incremental policies have had little impact on the main streams of history. True, deliberate action has influenced human history—but in unintended directions and nonplanned aggregations through heroic interventions or accumulative steps that, from a scientific point of view, are either random events or jumps resulting from little-understood deep social transformations.

If, nevertheless, we are to take policy studies seriously, this must be done in a self-conscious and sophisticated way, recognizing the difficulties of the mission as well as its critical importance. The very least we must do is to approach policy studies with a mixture of enthusiasm and skepticism and with a tough moral commitment to do the very best that we as human beings and scientists can, without expecting much in return—neither from traditional scientists nor from policy makers and rulers, nor from stubborn reality. Bearing in mind this admonition and recognition of inherent inadequacy, let us explore concisely some basic concepts fundamental to the very idea of policy studies and some of its underlying paradigms.

I. THE IDEA OF POLICY STUDIES

The unique core of policy studies is policy making as a subject for study and improvement. This includes both policy making as a pervasive process as well as specific policy issues and policy areas. Understanding how policies evolve and improving policy making in general and specific policies in particular are the scope, content, and mission of policy studies. Clearly, such an idea of policy studies includes a broad array of subjects, issues, approaches, methods, methodologies, and interests. Clearly also, as indicated above, policy studies are very demanding in the sense that a large range of objective and subjective knowledges are essential for any real progress, needs reaching far beyond the by-now conventional demand for "interdisciplinarity" to a really integrative view of policy making and policy as a dominant dimension of societal problem-handling capabilities and of the capacity to govern. The borders of policy studies are fuzzy and open-ended, leaving scope for different opinions and varieties of understandings. To the true policy scientist, however, nothing concerning policy making and policies can be strange—and this is a very tough requirement indeed.

Policy studies, in their pure form, are distinguished by an additional hard-to-achieve characteristic, namely, the capability to take clinical views of matters that are emotionally charged. Being in part prescriptive makes it all the harder to maintain ice-cold perception in arenas where red-hot attitudes rule. But the unique idea of policy studies as offering a scientific attitude as its special contribution to the improvement of policy making does require a maximum effort to distinguish between advocate and policy analyst, between social critic and policy scientist, between political activism and policy-professional contributions, between value analysis as an intellectual activity and value commitment as a moral human demand. The need to keep a careful and dynamic balance between personal values and attachment to particular policies on one hand and becoming a servant to power on the other hand characterizes policy studies not less so than does its unique subject matter. Becoming a novel bridge between knowledge and power is an essential and very difficult element of the idea of policy studies.

I have already mentioned several times the fusion, in policy studies, of researching and understanding policy-making reality and improving policy making and policies. This apparent duality creates serious, almost unique, tensions in policy studies. (Economics, the only other social science that combines behavioral and prescriptive approaches, is much simpler in its positivistic assumptions and single-dimensional criteria.) Striving for understanding of reality makes policy studies a part of the social and behavioral sciences, from psychology (and even neurology) through anthropology to organizational theory, political science, and sociology. The particular behavioral perspectives of policy studies require domains of study and research methodologies of their own (e.g., actor-observer and processing of policy makers' experiences as necessary methodologies and defense-intelligence failures as a subject for research); but, in principle, the research philosophies of social sciences apply fully to this side of policy studies.

It is the prescriptive side of policy studies that both creates harsh difficulties and makes policy studies a potentially very important artifact of human endeavors to increase influence on human futures: Part of the difficulty stems from the necessity of differentiating normative, value-derived, imperatives from instrumental, value-dependent but value-sensitivity-tested and value-assumption-explicated prescriptions. Furthermore, all prescriptions depend either on models of preferable reality (e.g., models of "perfect" decision making) or on contextual values taken for granted (e.g., democracy) and usually on an undefined and mainly tacit mix of both of these. The minimum requirement from policy studies is to try and explicate implicit values and positivistic assumptions, to sensitivity-test all recommendations, and to assure pluralism and positive redundancy in underlying values and assumptions. No perfect solution to the "value/value-free" dilemma is conceivable, but progress is possible if policy scientists are self-conscious and self-critical in their assumptions and values, strive for an external look at themselves, and insist on clinical detachment in the face of value-intense and emotion-arousing issues, without abandoning their own moral commitments.

Another difficulty of policy studies resulting from its prescriptive dimension is the necessity for prescriptive methodologies. This is a major problem, mainly for the following reasons:

1. Many policy studies scholars come from the social sciences, such as political science, which are distinguished by the absence of prescriptive methodology that can serve as a guide for moving from facts to recommendations.
2. Most available prescriptive methodologies have been developed in the context of relatively simple problems or simplified assumptions, as in economics, operations research, and decision sciences. Therefore, most contemporary texts in policy analysis are quite useless for all but the most simple policy issues, and problems tend to be selected according to their ability to fit available methodologies rather than their importance, or are handled in much too oversimplified a manner. More advanced prescriptive methodologies do exist, but more in the form of skills and craftsmanship than in explicated and directly teachable form.
3. Development of appropriate prescriptive methodologies fitting the needs of policy studies in the context of real-life problems is intellectually very difficult and requires special institutional contexts different from the usual university milieu (to be discussed soon).

Therefore, as well as for additional problems that require more extensive treatment, the absence of prescriptive methodologies fitting complex problems constitutes a main weakness of contemporary policy studies and constitutes a main gap between the idea of policy studies and the present state of the art.

Despite real tensions between the behavioral and prescriptive aspects of policy studies, both constitute facets of one whole, with close interdependencies. Thus, problem formulation and fact perception depend on cognitive maps based on the prescriptive interests of policy studies; prescriptive applications constitute an essential laboratory for advancing understanding of policy realities; and good understanding of policy realities is essential for developing effective recommendations.

These are only some of the complexities and challenges of the idea of policy studies. But this partial exploration conveys some taste of the special flavor of policy studies. Additional features of policy studies are brought out by brief consideration of some sociology-of-knowledge features of their modern development and by looking at some specific institutional features of policy studies.

II. SOCIOLOGY OF KNOWLEDGE OF POLICY STUDIES

As advisors, who are among the oldest of human professions and accompanied the emergence of government as a human artifact, so the search for aid from knowledge in handling problems goes back into prehistory. Certainly, the development of modern social sciences has been accompanied by interest in its applications. Work in prescriptive decision-making models is more recent, though it has antecedents in German Kammeralism and in Polish praxeology. It is a pity that a comprehensive history of attempts at systematic utilization of knowledge for human decision making is still sorely missing.

Moving on to the contemporary scene, the development of modern policy studies seems to be the aggregate product of interaction among quite a number of variables, including the following:

The maturation of "Think Tanks" such as the RAND Corporation and the Brookings Institution, which are the main laboratories in which useful policy studies, including their unique methodologies, have developed

A growing sense of the gravity of policy problems, including more concern with social issues by scientists and a demand for "relevance"

The shock of nuclear weapons, which served as a main drive in the search for better policy knowledge and pushed policy interests by scientists

A deep belief that science can make contributions to the solution of difficult policy problems, not only by technological inputs but by application of a "scientific attitude" and scientific methodologies

A growing uneasiness by policy makers, who sense inadequacy in the face of very difficult problems and seek help wherever they can get it

The demonstration effect of economics, which at some time provided very important policy knowledge, leading other social scientists and policy makers to seek similar inputs from a broader array of knowledge.

To complete this indicative list, the following observations are in order:

1. The trend toward policy studies originated and is still best developed in the United States, but there is increasing diffusion of interests and activities to other countries.
2. The upswing of interests and activities in policy studies is pronounced, but easily reversible. Disappointment, changes in social acceptance of "science," transformations in the delicate relations between intellectuals and governments and shifts in political culture are but some possible developments that may stop policy studies.
3. There is a clear trend for policy studies to become a "flag of convenience" for researches with a cause, for academic drifters, and for grant seekers. This is a major danger facing policy studies, aggravated by fuzzy borders and diffuse contents.

Whatever one's view of the genesis of policy studies, there is no doubt that its development has been and will be closely related to specific institutional designs, which characterize policy studies. To these we now turn.

III. INSTITUTIONAL FEATURES

Policy studies is closely related to four interrelated institutional innovations: "Think Tanks;" policy professionals; policy teaching programs; and policy studies discipline. Understanding of these institutional innovations is essential for an understanding overview of policy studies concepts.

"Think Tanks," in the sense of distinct policy research and analysis institutions, constitute both one of the more interesting inventions of governmental designs and the main breeding ground of policy studies. Going back more than 30 years, the unique features of think tanks include a critical mass of full-time, highly qualified professionals and scientists applying interdisciplinary knowledge to policy and policy-making issues, relatively protected from pressures, with good opportunities to incorporate their findings into policy making. Nowadays there exists quite a range of think tanks, in the United States and a growing number of other countries. From the perspective of policy studies, the critical roles of think tanks are development of policy studies methodologies, especially prescriptive ones such as systems analysis and other components of policy analysis; a pilot testing facility for applying policy studies to reality; the best training facility for applied policy students, who require clinical learning opportunities; a critical location for the professionalization of policy scholars, between academia and executive departments; a crystallizer for policy studies as a distinct discipline; and a main credit producer for the acceptability of policy studies. In this author's opinion, Think Tanks are the purest institutional expression of policy studies, for better and also for worse (e.g., in the dilemma between establishment demands and social critic functions). I think that every policy scientist should spend part of his or her working life in at least one think tank, developing the capacity to handle the interfaces between policy sciences knowledge and policy-making realities.

Policy professionalism as a recognized career is a more recent development, still in status nascendi. But there are growing numbers of workers classified as "policy analysts" and similar categories in federal, state, and local governments in the United States, in addition to the recognized think tankers and the policy teaching staffs. In other countries there is as yet little movement in that direction, exceptions being increasingly professionalized "policy planning" and "socioeconomic planning" careers in some countries. Emerging characteristics of the policy profession bring out additional features of policy studies: A need for movement among inside-bureaucracy policy analysis positions, Think Tank policy research periods, and study/teaching activities at appropriate university programs; problems of professional ethics because of tensions between "servants to power" and "free, critical, intellectuals"; unease about relations with traditional policy-advisory professions, such as economists; growing possibilities for international movement, as United Nations advisors, and soon, to meet increasing interest in policy professionals and broaden personal experiences; and in-built frustrations caused by at least two unavoidable contraries, namely, between the endless need for new knowledge and very limited time, most of which is devoted to down-to-earth policy studies, and between a hope-presumption to reform or at least improve reality and both very stubborn facts and inadequate knowledge.

Policy teaching programs signify the maturation of policy studies as a distinct academic-professional discipline. Going back about 12 years, the establishment of separate public policy schools and programs at top-level universities signifies the transition of policy studies from a cluster of interests into an integrated though open-ended scientific and professional entity. But the move from a craft to a domain of teaching carries with it great dangers, as illustrated by the history of "operations research." In particular, importance may be sacrificed for teachability, with economic and mathematical techniques driving out of consideration much more important though "softer" knowledge and methods. Also, being at present a popular theme, "policy programs" may become an overused term. Because of its presumptions and difficulties, any worthwhile policy teaching program must be very tough, very selective, and very demanding. The large number of self-titled "policy teaching programs" must, therefore, be regarded with some doubts and may well endanger the advancement of policy studies as a high-quality endeavor. Thus, some recent moves to merge policy studies with classical public administration and even business management, in part under the cloak of "implementation," may overdilute the quintessence of policy studies. A new area, such as policy studies can easily be taken over and serve as a fashionable cover for activities that may be important, but should not be mixed up with policy studies.

The last institutional I wish to mention here is the crystallization of a policy studies discipline, characterized by special publications, conferences, professional associations and similar symbols and substances of a discipline. Again, care must be taken not to sacrifice quality and uniqueness for quantity and acceptance. In general, however, the movement toward a policy studies discipline complements well other institutional developments and adds another essential foundation to policy studies.

IV. THE SUBSTANCE OF POLICY STUDIES

So far we have been looking at policy studies from the outside, taking an external view of its characteristics, history, and institutionalization. To complete exploration of basic policy studies concepts, our perspective must now change to look at the contents of policy studies.

Other chapters in this Encyclopedia deal with the substance of policy studies by policy areas and by methods. I propose to adopt a different perspective that should bring out fundamental policy studies concepts, by analytically characterizing policy making with the help of nine dimensions, to be concisely examined for their policy studies implications, behaviorally as well as prescriptively. These nine dimensions are reality and problem perception; grand policy and critical choice; transincrementalism; complexity; fuzzy betting; learning; policy architecture; tragic choice; and meta-policy.

Reality and problem perception is fundamental for policy making. Behaviorally it raises the epistemological and perceptual issues of how humans and human organizations form reality perceptions, formulate problems, and establish decision agenda. It is enough to mention the regularity of serious defense intelligence failings to indicate the difficulties of the matter. Prescriptively, the need is for a philosophically sound approach to problem formulation and situation diagnosis and for usable methods to achieve less distorted reality perception and to make decisions in ways less sensitive to irreduceable image distortions.

Grand policies and critical choices refer to fundamental policy decisions in which the very paradigms of policies are explored and reconsidered, as contrasted with the usual tendency to take policy curves as given and improve on them a little. Behaviorally, the need is to study and explicate the basic policies, which are usually implicit, and their underlying assumptions. Similarly, the variables that freeze grand policies and repress critical choices are an important domain for behavioral research. Prescriptively, ways to pose grand policy and critical choices as policy subjects are urgently needed. Not less important and even more difficult is the search after methods for grand policy analysis.

The problem is that for such issues quantification is of little use even as a metaphor, and certainly not as an analogue or model. Qualitative policy exploration methods are a must for improving grand policy decisions and critical choice—and are solely missing and not even intensely searched for in contemporary policy studies.

Transincrementalism refers to the behavioral issue: When do policies follow an incremental or a transincremental form? The assumption, still widespread in the United States literature, that policy making is usually incremental is a misperception, in urgent need of innovative research. Prescriptively, the need is for guidelines on the conditions under which more innovative, transincremental policies are preferable and those when incrementalism is acceptable. Then, prescriptive policy design and analysis methods are needed to handle transincremental and, when appropriate, trend-mutation policy-making needs. This is closely related to the grand policy and critical choice dimension mentioned above, and to some additional dimensions to be discussed soon.

Complexity, in the sense of close and dynamic interaction among a large number of components with much variety, is a main feature of policy making. Behaviorally, the problem is a double one: to understand the policy-relevant systems and to study the reaction of policy-making institutions to complexity, such as its repression and simplification. Prescriptively, the task again is a double one: to develop methods for managing complexity and to overcome institutional inabilities to face complexity.

"Fuzzy betting" is a very important concept, referring to the fact that all decisions face uncertainty and the important ones face ignorance. This implies that all decisions involve a choice between bundles of results with various degrees of uncertainty and with many of them having unknowable parameters and probabilities. Behaviorally, we need methods for mapping degrees of uncertainty and for understanding organizational reactions to uncertainty, such as displacement of objective uncertainty with subjective certainty-illusions and inconsistent attitudes to risk ("lottery values," in technical terminology). Prescriptively, methods are needed to reduce and pattern uncertainty, decision strategies to absorb irreduceable uncertainty must be developed, and policy-making designs that reduce uncertainty-mishandling should be developed, tested, and institutionalized.

Learning is a basic policy-making dimension, again with behavioral and prescriptive aspects. Behaviorally, actual learning/nonlearning/mislearning must be studied and explained. Prescriptively, methods and designs for accelerating and improving learning, such as evaluation methods and policy experimentation techniques, are needed.

Policy architecture introduces the element of creativity, especially in invention and design of novel policy alternatives. It also brings out the need to relate policy studies to planning, a neglected issue which requires much attention. Creativity becomes an increasingly important policy dimension because new issues, conditions, and values often require new policies (this is closely related to the transincrementalism dimension, mentioned above). Behaviorally, the subject of creativity-influencing variables is one of the most interesting and difficult ones, because of the essentially extrarational nature of creativity. Prescriptively, the problem is how to encourage policy creativity. The needs for policy architecture pose serious issues before prescriptive policy studies, as "policy analysis" usually focuses on choice between given or easily derived alternatives. Whether and how one can push policy creativity and how to include this requirement in the domain and development of policy professionals is an open question.

Tragic choice refers to the bitter fact that all policies involve value choice and the establishment of (usually tacit) rates of exchange between very dear values, often through organizational subdividing objectives between different units. Behaviorally, this dimension involves value mapping and research on the mechanisms by which the choice is made, including the dynamic tendency to hide the choice itself. Prescriptively, the tragic choice dimension involves a number of difficult issues: (1) The proper roles of professionals versus politicians and other strata in value choice; (2) possibilities to improve value choice without interfering with the value judgment process itself; (3) increasing the capability of policy-making systems to engage in value choices without prohibitive consensus disruption; and (4) designs for involving additional strata, such as the public or impacted groups, in value choice without ruining the policy quality. This is one of the most neglected areas of policy studies, in part because of its many taboos and emotional aspects as well as its ideological assumptions, in addition to research and prescription methodology scarcities.

Meta-policy is a short term that includes a lot, as it refers to "policies on policy making," that is, the overall operation and improvement of the policy-making system. This institutional dimension constitutes a dividing line between narrow policy analysis which, behaviorally, studies the evolution of specific policies, and, prescriptively, tries to improve specific policies on one hand, and policy studies in their broad sense, looking on policy making as a whole, behaviorally as well as prescriptively, on the other hand. Large sets of issues are included here, such as the roles of different policy-making units, information and feedback models of policy making, impacts of basic political structures on policy contents, and much more. This is a crucial perspective for looking on nearly all of political science and large segments of other social sciences such as sociology and psychology. It is these institutional and systems dimensions that characterize policy studies as a broad discipline, in contrast with the technical narrowness of many present "policy analysis" approaches.

V. SYNTHESIS

No short chapter can hope to reflect all the concepts of policy studies and to explore their challenges, difficulties, and promises, as well as their pitfalls and dangers. Even an Encyclopedia cannot do more at best than illuminate some aspects of so complex an endeavor as policy studies and guide the interested to further studies, while providing a frame of reference and whetting appetite. Policy studies is a pluralistic endeavor, multifaceted as well and multiopinionated. But there are common denominators, such as the aim to apply systematic knowledge to policy problems through tough thinking and clinical attitudes. Also shared are some basic concepts. These can be labeled under different verbal terms and looked at from multiple angles, sometimes contradicting one another, at least in appearance. But all of policy studies must face and handle some basic concepts, including those presented in this explorative and introductory chapter.

2

Policy Analysis and Management Science

Michael J. White / University of Southern California, Los Angeles, California

Policy analysis is a complex social process of creating and applying knowledge to public policy. Few policy choices are final, unambiguous, or fully articulated; and few policies are independent, self-contained, unquestioned, or consensually understood. Policy analysis, as a result, is turbulent and open-ended rather than neat and easy. Decisive studies are very much the exception rather than the rule. Problems throw at analysts more variables for consideration and interests for accommodation than single studies can encompass. The task of policy analysis is not to produce that decisive recommendation, but, instead, to contribute toward consensual understanding of actualities, possibilities, and desirabilities. Properly understood, policy analysis does produce, in Wildavsky's (1979) terms, new patterns of social interaction. Equally important, policy analysis produces new "psychosocial" forms, new collective understandings relevant to the specific functions of government. One consequence of these understandings is convergence of activity or behavior, and reduction of conflict among political groups. Policy analysis, in creating shared understandings, makes it possible to "get on with the task," to quarrel over details rather than over large questions.

This is not to presume, of course, that all questions can be brought to consensual resolution. Where value conflicts are irreducible, however, the role of knowledge may be small. Further, policy analysis will not necessarily lead toward a monotonic reduction in disagreement. Policy analysis may further the disintegration of an old consensus regarding understandings that are no longer feasible or valid. If analysis continues to be applied, however, it can help shape or validate a new and more suitable consensus.

Viewed in this larger frame, it should be apparent that policy analysis is not simply a collection of tools, techniques, or models of analytical nature. Likewise, policy analysis must be more than a study of consensus formation and dissolution. Rather, policy analysis lies somewhat between these two familiar poles. It is the production with those tools of understandings that affect consensus formation and dissolution. Unless methods of policy analysis are understood in this manner, confusions will surely result: Policy will be seen as failing because one's preferred study recommendation is ignored in a specific instance; techniques will override purposes; the social process of knowledge cumulation will be unrecognized; the social system of policy analysts will be ignored or improperly perceived; cynicisms about the place of knowledge in policy making will abound.

All of these shortcomings are common in the literature of policy analysis, and they retard the advance of the field. Further, these shortcomings, or misunderstandings, encourage a view of policy analysis as an easy, and primary technical task in which individuals or research teams produce studies, the results of which are often ignored by easily scapegoated policy makers. This convenient view offers the policy analyst ready excuses for frustrated ambition. It also places the analyst and the specific study at the center of attention, elevating the analyst to rather heroic proportions.

In this chapter, that view will be opposed by a social conception in which evolving bodies of knowledge and the social aggregate of analysts are the centers of attention. This chapter is, in that sense, a prolegomenon to a sociology of policy analysis. It is also an antidote to misconceptions, and has the specific aims of encouraging a realistic appreciation of the possibilities of policy analysis in the specific case, and of providing a foundation for further appraisal of the political and social impact of policy analysis. If this is accomplished, then a foundation has been established for the *use* of the technology as well, not simply by analysts but, more important, by policy makers.

This chapter takes as its focus not social science policy analysis, but management science. Management science, as a technology, has been applied to a wide, if not complete, range of public policy issues. It has also been applied extensively to public sector operations, to business problems, and to problems of war. It differs from social science in a number of ways; one of the more important is that management science studies often result in implemented *systems*, not just in policy recommendations. Management science has a more clearly articulated and coherent technological core than social science. The latter includes such diversity as cultural anthropology, econometrics, interpretive sociology, and attitude surveys. The former involves, as we shall see in the next chapter, some behavioral methods; for the most part, however, the technology is formal and mathematical. Definition of management science will not be offered here, however. Extensive perusal of major scholarly journals is recommended for those who do not find the following chapter adequate as an extended definition.

This chapter will consider the sociology of management science and the role of management science in policy analysis. Therefore, although not a direct consideration of all methods of policy analysis, it still will serve as a preliminary step toward a sociology of policy analysis. The first part of the chapter advances a conception of problem formulation for policy analysis, and, along with it, a view of the objectives of management science in policy analysis. This conception leads to a consideration of rationality in simple and complex forms, and to a formulation of management science as cumulative rather than atomized. The second part of the chapter considers the history and sociology of the profession of management science. That its history shapes our perceptions of its possibilities needs emphasis. That management scientists are a social entity of consequence for understanding management science technology is not usually appreciated. Looking at management science this way, it will turn out to offer substantial possibilities for those willing to take a long view of policy improvement, and not very much for those who seek (or fear) short-term impacts. This chapter considers the broader questions of appreciation and social context within which the application of techniques takes place. The next chapter considers specific models of management science and policy analysis.

I. FORMULATING PROBLEMS FOR POLICY ANALYSIS THROUGH MANAGEMENT SCIENCE

In using management science for policy analysis, the problems to be analyzed should be understood in a specific way consistent with the management sciences. Commonly, problems are viewed as involving discrepancies between desired and observed conditions (March and Simon, 1958). This view can lead to interventions proximal to the perceived discrepancies, instead of to effective adjustments informed by more thorough understanding. In management science, rather than viewing problems in this way, systems are more likely to be seen as exhibiting behavioral characteristics or outputs capable of improvement according to some specified criterion. Pattern, not discrepancy, is the focus.

A. System, Not Symptom

Fundamental to a management science approach to public policy analysis is the notion of system. The phenomena of interest are considered as exhibiting organization. Attributes, properties, and quantities are identified. Relations among them are sought, and convenient groupings are made. Boundaries are considered explicitly. Simplifications are pursued self-consciously. Goals are postulated and performance criteria examined. Only in the context of this methodical specification are outputs and performance characteristics considered for improvement.

Systems are usually considered to be dynamic, and social systems are viewed as having tendencies, when well functioning, toward survival rather than self-destruction. Dynamic systems have forward temporal linkages: The future states of the system are partially determined by the past states. Current outputs and performance characteristics are observed for the purpose of present and future adjustments. Influence also runs from future to present in the sense that anticipations affect current behavior. These dynamic loops exist in great number for any large system. Their recognition and analysis are major distinguishing features of problem definition by management science.

Failure to recognize dynamic linkages is common to a wide range of social policies. In health policy, for example, we are beginning to recognize the dynamic linkages among reimbursement, entitlement, demand for service, and service capacity. A review of U.S. federal health policies in recent decades makes it clear that efforts to meet need have led to expanded notions of need (Russell, 1980). In another area of policy, Feldstein (1976) argues that U.S. unemployment compensation policies increase unemployment. Approaching the point from the opposite side, hospital cost-containment efforts may be noted. Regulations aimed at reducing investment in hospital capacity were associated with unexpected increases in investment in hospital equipment (Salkever and Bice, 1979). By responding to symptom rather than to system, the desired objective of cost containment was not achieved.

Common to a management science approach to policy analysis is the assumption of general laws of organization. Whereas other approaches to policy analysis tend to seek the regularities in the phenomena of immediate interest (e.g., regularities in hospital capital investment or regularities in tested student achievement), the management science approach seeks also to include regularities common to all dynamic systems. These regularities are often stated at a very abstract level. In terms of designing public policies, one of the most important laws is Ashby's law of requisite variety. A discussion of this law and its implications will further clarify a view of policy analysis that provides a context for the use of management science.

B. The Law of Requisite Variety

The following exposition of the law of requisite variety is taken from Beer (1974). Through the law of requisite variety, he develops an analysis of common policy failings and a view of policy design into which management science readily fits. The basic concepts are "variety," "variety controller," and "relaxation time." The law, which Beer argues is a general law of nature, states that *only variety can absorb variety*. From this a search for pattern follows.

Variety is the number of possible states of a system, and is a measure of system complexity. If variety increases without a corresponding increase in our ability to understand and respond appropriately to it, the system will become unstable and tend toward catastrophic collapse (rapid and discontinuous reorganization). The instability results because the system, lacking control, is unable to adjust to the disturbances that it experiences in a way that tends toward an equilibrium rather than toward some form of collapse. New disturbances arrive faster than the "relaxation time" of the system—the time it takes to reach equilibrium after a disturbance. As equilibrium is never approached, it ceases to be envisioned. Without a view of what to adapt toward, adaptation itself ceases and catastrophe follows.

System variety increases, in social systems, with the range and frequency of impinging disturbances, with increases in system scale, and even with natural population growth. In order to avert catastrophe, systems are subject to regulation by "variety controllers" or regulators. A variety controller is "the mode of organization adopted for the system" (Beer, 1974: 11).

Beer (1974) argues that four common ways in which governments often control variety contribute to system breakdown. (1) Every government department makes a model of the country. However, these models rarely change; new departments are created for new variety, and old departments ignore new variety. (2) Each department has models of the domain for which it is responsible. However, these models tend to treat these domains not as "dynamic surviving systems" but as static entities. (3) As data are collected in great number, aggregation becomes essential. However, aggregation rarely proceeds according to the principles of cybernetic control. Essential information for variety control is therefore lost. (4) Governments may seek to control variety by using information that is dated. Delay is inherent in collecting and processing information for decision. The information about the most recent variety, although of crucial importance, is hardest to obtain. Often, this means that interventions are made that are out of phase with the system's actual state. Further, delay may mean that system variety has increased beyond that of the variety controller, making control theoretically impossible.

Two strategies present themselves for consideration. Each is the mirror image of the other. First, system variety can be decreased. Second, controller variety can be increased. Among the means of reducing variety are (1) hierarchical clustering, (2) rules, and (3) interference with the exogenous distrubances of the system (Beer, 1974: 11).

Often, our attempts at control run counter to these strategies. Computers, Beer observes, (1974: 26) may be adopted in ways that increase system variety rather than regulative variety. Without a clear understanding of the implications of Ashby's law of requisite variety, policy analysis efforts may become preoccupied with symptoms rather than with system.

Control of complex systems requires identification of the "patterns by which variety in the system is deployed" (Beer, 1974: 29). Further, the patterns must be identified for each component or level of a dynamic surviving system (Beer, 1974: 42). Patterns are identified in models of the dynamic surviving system. Useful models discriminate between disturbances that call for a response and those that do not; reduce the need for data; and specify "levels of recursion." Levels of recursion are the "boxes within boxes" by which parts of the system are aggregated for modeling. For example, government budgeting can be modeled as involving the behavior of individuals; but these individuals can be aggregated into agencies and agency behavior studied as well. "The law of requisite variety has to be satisfied at each level of recursion so that stability is induced" (Beer, 1974: 42). "The critical mistake we make is to take variety attenuating decisions at the wrong level of recursion" (Beer, 1974: 79).

C. The Place of Management Science and the Law of Requisite Variety

The preceding analysis locates, by use of the law of requisite variety, the place of management science in policy analysis. Two specific tasks have been identified: specifying dynamic models at a given level of recursion, and specifying dynamic models that link levels of recursion. Management science is a branch of knowledge and an intellectual discipline that includes a large number of generic models, expressable in mathematical/symbolic terms and adaptable to specific situations. It also includes methodologies for developing large-scale, dynamic, multilevel, multiperiod models. In the next chapter, examples of both will be given, and an attempt will be made to demonstrate how a concern for variety attenuation, expressed through management science models, can lead to effective policy analysis. So far, admittedly, the analysis has been abstract.

The analysis implies a view of policy analysis: that policy analysis is an activity concerned with understanding the behavior of systems in order better to control their behavior and performance. Other views are available.

One alternative is that policy analysis is a search for ultimate values and the means for attaining them. This is a view that I impute to many who write about policy analysis from the perspective of critical theory or phenomenology, such as Fischer (1980). In this alternative, the objective of policy analysis is the development of a logic of policy evaluation (Fischer, 1980: 183). The emphasis is retrospective, rather than prospective: The route to right values lies in the critical analysis of the ideas of others.

Wildavsky (1979) argues that an objective of policy analysis is the creation of new patterns of social interaction. This view represents an important advance over more conventional views of policy analysis as some kind of problem solving technology. Wildavsky puts the "social" at the forefront and provides an opportunity to develop linkages between technological visions of policy analysis and utopian concerns. A criterion for new patterns of social interaction is that they help citizens solve their own problems. The law of requisite variety contributes further criteria for the selection of these new social forms. In turn, Wildavsky's analysis suggests that the attenuation of variety is, in public policy analysis, inseparable from the control of social interaction.

The conventional social science view of policy analysis appears to be one of identifying needs and proposing remedies. In addition, policy analysis in the social sciences involves extensive efforts to describe social patterns, though often without attention to dynamic aspects. These descriptive efforts often lead to the development of new concepts, and thus to new ways of seeing social phenomena. Abundant examples of this are available in any volume of the *Policy Studies Review Annual* (Raven, 1980; Haveman and Zellner, 1979; Freeman, 1978; Nagel, 1977). Much of the social science concern with needs and remedies has led to conflicting and ambiguous results. A review of 58 studies of "work experiments" based on the premise that "restructuring the content and conditions of work" can improve worker attitude and performance (Cummings, et al., in Freeman, 1978) finds conflicting results and widespread methodological inadequacy. An equally wide-ranging review of studies of the academic achievements of black students in desegregated schools (Bradley and Bradley, in Freeman, 1978) finds the same confusion and inadequacy. These two examples illustrate the preoccupation of many social science policy analyses with means rather than with ends: The motivating question appears to be "does this mean produce the desired end," rather than "what is the system producing the observed performance and how might its variety be controlled to improve performance."

Explicit attention to the relative advantages of management science over social science in policy analysis have been considered elsewhere (White, 1979). Here, alternatives to management science approaches have been mentioned for ulterior motives. Each approach to policy analysis has distinct methods, and each can make a distinct contribution. Although this chapter takes management science as its focus, it tries to do so in the context of an explicitly formulated view of the place of management science in policy analysis. Other approaches make overlapping, but largely different contributions to policy analysis. Tolerance of different approaches is a first step toward constructive use of each. Clearer understanding of the contributions of one approach or technique not only sharpens its own use, but also sharpens the use of all other approaches and techniques.

The law of requisite variety, and the idea of dynamic systems, provide a context for the use of management science in policy analysis. The idea of dynamic systems encourages attention to feedback loops, anticipation, the effects of outputs on inputs, and levels of recursion. It also mitigates against a too-hasty fixing upon means, or a simplistic focus on symptoms. The law of requisite variety encourages an attention to pattern and a search for powerful and economical formulations of pattern as a means both of attenuating system variety and of increasing regulative variety. Management science methods, concepts, and techniques help in this search for control-augmenting pattern. In theory, management science is more consistent with the idea of dynamic surviving systems than other approaches to policy analysis, although in practice this consistency is not always realized.

D. Management Science and Rationality

By now, it should be clear that this chapter does not equate management science and rationality in any simple way. Some further comments on the notion of rationality will clarify the nature of management science. Management science should be seen as working toward cumulative and shared understandings that align system and regulative variety, thereby resulting in increased human options. Exposition of specific techniques or concepts can only be misleading unless the contrast between management science and simple rationality is clear.

Simple Rationality: Individual and Discontinuous. Commonly, management science is viewed as congruent with a simple notion of rationality. Since simple rationality is inadequate for policy analysis both in cognitive and in social terms, acceptance of this ascribed congruence would terminate this chapter. Majone (1980) equates management science and simple rationality through what he calls the "received view" of policy analysis. This view, which he claims was synthesized at the RAND Corporation and similar research institutes, holds that "ideal policymaking, rational decisionmaking, rational problem solving, and policy analysis are synonymous" (Majone, 1980: 163). In this view, the synonym is the common foundation of goal—model—hypothesis—prediction—correction of hypothesis or goal, iterated through to optimality according to some, usually utilitarian, criterion. This stereotype of management science can certainly find conformation in the writings of management scientists, particularly in introductory textbooks. However, sophisticated management scientists have for many years argued against such a simple formulation (Eilon, 1969). This formulation of steps in a rational decision is, at best, a logic for reconstruction (White, 1972a). Unfortunately it continues to find expression in both the textbook and professional literature (MacRae, 1980; MacRae and Wilde, 1977).

A further problem with simple rationality is that it equates policy making with individual decision (Majone, 1980). Such a view places policy makers in a commanding position with respect to policy change that few will admit to occupying. Lloyd Nigro, in conversation, calls this the "cowboy view of decision making." The degree of certainty, control, and intentionality implied varies considerably from that documented repeatedly in the case study literature. Majone (1980) notes Wildavsky's concept of "policy as its own cause" to argue against the equivalence of policy and individual decision (see also Wildavsky, 1979).

Majone (1980) clarifies a further weakness of this "received view." It presumes that policy analysis is only prospectively oriented toward decisions yet to be made, rather than used also in the rationalization of decisions, however taken, to those whose cooperation is needed for ratification or implementation. If policy making is seen as a social process taking place in the face of inadequate data and other substantial uncertainties and in spite of fuzzy and conflicting values, then rationalization of choices in terms responsive to the needs of significant others becomes another aspect of variety attenuation. In this more complex view of rationality, analysis, and implementation become not simply joined, but seamless.

Occasionally, policy choice may represent abrupt discontinuity. More commonly, however, step-function changes do not result from political choice. Matters are, to use an overworked term, changed incrementally. The same holds true for policy knowledge.

A More Complex Formulation: Cumulative and Social.   Except in very well-defined or otherwise unusual situations, rational decision is not the objective of management science. Neither is it the objective of policy analysis. For the most part, both management science and policy analysis are concerned with increased understanding of complex systems. This understanding, whether obtained through management science or through other approaches, enables system regulation and, less frequently, significant system change. For example, recent American legislation deregulating substantially several formerly regulated transportation industries followed years of careful research by many economists and management scientists. The regulation of transportation industries happens to be a well-studied subject. Other important and sizable policy domains, for example, social services for children (Kirst et al., 1980), have hardly begun to enter our consciousness as fields of study. These two subjects represent extremes in our social cumulation of policy knowledge.

The cumulative nature of policy knowledge has been recognized by management scientists. Blumstein (1979), a past president of the Operations Research Society of America, writes:

> The fact that the criminal justice system is now looking for approaches other than rehabilitation is a tribute to the accumulated credibility of rehabilitation research. This development suggests that research can become useful to policy makers only by accumulating a number of separate, independent studies that are individually valid and show consistent results. No single study can or ever should be sufficient to bring about a direct policy action.

Blumstein's caution about single studies should be kept in mind by analysts who complain of policy makers' ignoring their work, and by those who criticize management science or policy analysis on much the same grounds.

Rather than seeking single, decisive studies, management scientists work in a cumulative, social situation. Their knowledge builds on past accomplishments, and is shared with other researchers through professional channels. In some cases, particular issues have a long tradition of study. Balintfy, who has devoted much of his career to identifying low-cost alternatives for decent nutrition, traces a 35-year history of management science attention to this topic (Balintfy, 1979), with the seminal article being a 1945 piece by Stigler (1945). It is through cumulative and shared traditions like this that management science influences public policy. If a single decisive study can be identified, behind it will be found the preceding work that ties up many of the loose ends.

When a cumulative, shared tradition offers substantial understanding of a system for which policies are desired, that understanding is likely to be invoked. The effects of changes in welfare programs and the effects of changes in the U.S. federal personal income tax are two areas that have been the subject of extensive formal modeling efforts. These models are routinely consulted in exploring policy changes (Haveman and Hollenbeck, 1980).

A corollary to the proposition that management science involves cumulative, shared knowledge deserves mention here. If neither single studies nor single decision makers will normally be determining, and knowledge is cumulative and shared, one possible inference is that relevant knowledge is dispersed and no one holds all the parts. Even the most complete management science studies or systems will require that details be worked out on site, and contingencies be adjusted in process. Sowell (1980) emphasizes the dispersion of knowledge, and the various ways that costs of knowledge gathering and authentication are reduced through social processes. Management science may provide a centripetal tendency for much knowledge relevant to system regulation. But the cumulative social nature of management science should alert us to its imperfection and incompleteness for any single analyst or decision maker. The consequences of this locational incompleteness are hardly explored by either the critics or the advocates of management science (see, however, Beer, 1974, Churchman, 1979, and Ackoff, 1979a,b).

Policy and Operations in Management Science. Management science produces two kinds of knowledge which it is useful to keep distinct. On the one hand it produces knowledge about specific public systems that may be used in policy making. On the other hand, it produces knowledge about "operations," patterns of behavior or organization that usefully describe many different situations. Much of the insight into the former is based on insight into the latter. The latter, recurring patterns, are represented in the familiar techniques or models of operations research, such as queueing or inventory theory. These models are employed at high levels of generality in the study of large public systems, but also are used as building blocks in the creation of large-scale simulations.

Koopman identifies these recurring patterns as central to theory in operations research (OR). He writes that, "a theoretical advance in OR is the increased understanding of the structure of some type of *operation* regarded as a particular *phenomenon of nature*" (Koopman, 1974). Koopman here affirms the postulation, also attributed earlier in this chapter to Beer (1974), that management science is concerned with laws of organization that hold with some generality. From this perspective, management science, when used in policy analysis, seeks to identify, through cumulative and shared efforts with respect both to abstract models and to a particular system, patterns in that system, the understanding of which leads to a better alignment of system and regulative variety.

A second meaning of the word "operation" is also helpful here in understanding management science. Whether drawing on classical OR models, general cybernetic laws, or observed regularities, management science tends to be concerned with "operations" of systems in a more mundane sense: the "what is going on" of ongoing systems. The effort is to understand this in order to design system improvements. Policy, in this view, follows from operations either practically or theoretically understood, for policy is designed to control operation variety. Pollution control policies presume an ongoing system generating and regulating pollutants; welfare policies presume a payments system and clientele; hospital cost containment presumes a system of hospitals.

Policies, in this context, are hypotheses about the regulation of systems, usually ongoing systems but sometimes systems of only a theoretical existence. They are hypotheses because system boundaries are always to some degree arbitrary, and future disturbances of the system cannot be specified in advance (else they would not be disturbances!). Churchman (1979) has pointed out, in the context of corporate inventories, that inventory optimization presumes optimization of the environment as well. Policies chosen to regulate and improve systems are merely hypotheses because, as Churchman implies, they have not been extensionalized to all impinging circumstances. But here we complete another circle: This extensionalizing takes place, from the perspective of management science, in the cumulative and social processes of knowledge development.

Rationality of the simplistic, steps-in-a-rational-decision variety cannot adequately describe or prescribe for management science. Management science, and likewise policy analysis, is cumulative, social, and constantly extensionalized. When management science is understood as a cumulative, social process, oriented toward the alignment of system and regulative variety, two things happen: Simple criticisms fall to the side, and the place of the management science approach to policy analysis becomes more clearly delimited.

E. Management Science Delimited

Management science contributes to policy analysis by specifying pattern in systems of interest to policy makers. These patterns may be descriptive or normative, with either capable of stimulating system reorganization for improved performance. Whether performance actually improves will depend not only on the effectiveness of the improvement efforts on their own terms, but also on the extensionalization of these efforts to considerations not included in the analysis.

The focus of these pattern specifications, if shaped by the law of requisite variety, will be on aligning system and regulative variety by contracting the former, expanding the latter, or other possible combinations that have the consequence of satisfying that law. Large-scale models as well as classical operations research techniques are well-developed ways of developing and validating such patterns. For effective regulation, the patterns identified should usually be dynamic, that is, incorporate feedback and anticipation loops.

Given the attention to regulation and pattern specification, management science may not pay as much attention to certain issues as its critics desire. Specifically, it may be argued that management science is not particularly well suited for the identification of new human rights or areas of spiritual growth. These are areas of inquiry for which it is hard to identify existing "systems" for improvement. Denial to some rights enjoyed by others lends itself more readily to a management science approach.

Understood as presented here, the management science approach to policy analysis encourages modesty regarding the implications of single studies or isolated results. Specifying patterns in complex social systems is always difficult, tentative, and the consequence of a cumulative social process. Many management science studies are concerned with improving theoretical models. Those that are not tend to focus on some specific operations or system, and recommend for that specific setting only. In contrast, social scientists appear more ready to claim generality for their findings.

Classic management science models, when they can be shown to apply, offer great regulatory power. The normative as well as positive aspects of these models should be recognized. One reason for identifying, or perhaps postulating, pattern is to make it self-realizing. Practical applications of these generic models are usually much more complex than suggested by textbook discussions: Large computer programs and computational capacity, extensive data collection, and years of analyst effort will normally be required even when pioneering research has already been successfully completed for a similar system elsewhere. Straightforward applications to interesting problems are likely to be available only when practice has already converged substantially, because of prior management science efforts, toward patterns implied in the management science model. This is another dimension of management science as a cumulative social process. It places specific applications, straightforward as well as pioneering, in a developmental context.

With these contextualizing ideas in mind, it is now possible to proceed with a more direct discussion of management science as technology and as social movement. Misleading claims, of either proponents or opponents of management science in policy analysis, can be anticipated and discounted. The next section presumes that the reader has some superficial familiarity with management science as well as some misconceptions about its nature as a social phenomenon. In that section, the history of management science is sketched in an attempt to display a different way of looking at it. This alternative view represents an attempt to consider management science as a social fact, a social phenomenon having properties somewhat different from those of the individual units of which it is composed.

II. THE BACKGROUND OF MANAGEMENT SCIENCE

The methods of management science are subject to four common historical misinterpretations. First, and most common, management science is viewed as historically ineffective, especially with respect to public policy.[1] This view is a result of an expectation that single studies, rather than cumulative research, will be decisive in policy debate. It is also a result of expecting organizational or policy decisions to bring step-function changes from past decisions, rather than seeing change as incremental. When these two views are corrected, management science can be seen as producing traditions of research that influence decision premises and problem formulations of various decision or policy makers at various times and over time. No study or set of studies can consider all the practical contingencies that occur to the full range of political participants and that eventuate in claims upon policy makers. The more visible and discontinuous a policy decision, the less likely it is that management science can critically determine the decision. That, however, should not lead us to ignore all the preparatory analysis and debate that create the setting in which discontinuous change occurs.

The second common historical misinterpretation is that at some other time, for some other set of institutions, management science caused discontinuous policy changes with little effort. This erroneous view results from misinformation, albeit to a large degree due to the advocacy of management scientists themselves. The experience of wartime operations research has been repeatedly cited to justify the application of management science to other settings. Yet the extent of wartime operations research is not often appreciated and will be emphasized and documented here.

A third misconception also needs some attention. Management science is usually viewed as a technology, not as people; as disembodied studies rather than as efforts of formally chartered organizational staffs, consulting firms, and/or sponsored academics; and as a constant bag of techniques rather than as a dynamic field of applied mathematics constantly developing and differentiating its intellectual foundations.

Finally, management science is seen as unsuccessful at dealing with governmental problems. Even while documented instances of adopted management science recommendations have become more common, this criticism persists unabated. For the most part, reports of documented implementation will be left for the journals. However, the explosive growth of public sector management science will be indicated in this chapter. It seems evident that this criticism can be maintained only by continually elevating the level of policy to which the criticism refers, and by ignoring large areas of public policy that are not normally of interest to the critics (e.g., forest management, waste disposal, or hydroelectric projects).

A proper historical appreciation of management science is essential for its intelligent use; such an appreciation will also encourage a balanced appreciation of the possibilities of rational analysis of public policy in general. In order to discourage vain hopes and encourage an integrated sociotechnical understanding of management science and other methods of policy analysis, the social history of management science will be presented in greater detail than might otherwise be done. This corrective perspective is not readily available elsewhere, and is certainly not available in a single source from as many perspectives as will be covered here. The historical review will cover early origins, wartime military experiences, experiences in U.S. industries, experiences in government agencies, the growth of professional societies in the United States, some information on the extent of management science abroad, and a summary review of current applications areas in civilian government.

Management science does not exist apart from its social and historical context. Its application and use, and the likelihood of beneficial consequences, are improved by widespread appreciation of social and historical factors. Explications of techniques that ignore these background experiences and considerations have encouraged a narrow, harmful view of the practice of management science.

A. Origins of Management Science

Foundations for contemporary management science were established in mathematics in the nineteenth century and earlier. As this is not a mathematical exposition of management science, attention here will be given to more practical and immediate antecedents. Some of these antecedents foreshadow the distinctive character of later management science successes.

One of the earliest direct antecedents of contemporary management science is the work of A. K. Erlang on telephone switching for the Copenhagen telephone company. This work earned Erlang later recognition as the pioneer of "queueing theory," an important branch of operations research (Marshall, 1954). Frederick W. Lanchester opened many matters of military operations to mathematical analysis when, "as a hobby" he produced, during World War I, papers on the "relationships between victory, numerical superiority, and the superiority of firepower" (Trefethen, 1954; also, McCloskey, 1956, and Engel, 1954). Thomas A. Edison applied his talents to U.S. Navy operations during World War I as chairman of the Naval Consulting Board, directly under Navy Secretary Josephus Daniels. With several assistants he studied submarine problems and, true to form for an operations research analyst, redefined the problem. He focused on saving ships rather than destroying enemy submarines. His imaginative recommendations were entirely ignored by British as well as American officials (Whitmore, 1952).

The interwar period did not see further practical development of the interesting initiatives of Lanchester and Edison. However, theoretical foundations of importance were laid. In economics, mathematical economics developed in ways that later proved relevant to management science (Burkhead, 1956). John von Neumann's original scholarly paper on game theory appeared in 1928 (von Neumann, 1928). The Russian mathematician, L. V. Kantorovich, published seminal work on linear programming in the 1930s (Kantorovich, 1960; Moiseev, 1973).

B. Military Operations Research

The flowering of management science occurred with World War II. Ackoff (1978) attributes its development at that time to the fact that development in military technology had occurred faster than it could be incorporated into military tactics and strategy during the interwar years. In order to cope with this changing technology without battlefield testing, operations research substituted for experiential learning.

The wartime history of operations research is worth considering at some length for two reasons. First, it promotes an appreciation of the scale of effort necessary, even under these favorable conditions of urgency, to produce usable knowledge. Second, it makes clear the extent of institutional articulation achieved during the war.

British Wartime Operational Research. Prior to the outbreak of conflict, anti-aircraft studies were conducted under A. P. Rowe at the Bawdsley Research Station. There G. A. Roberts sought to improve detection system efficiency by integrating radar detection with efforts of the British Observor Corps. E. C. Williams studied early warning systems. Later, under H. C. Larnder, these researchers used data from German air attacks to study ground control interception (Trefethan, 1954).

Nobel laureate P. M. S. Blackett formed the Anti-Aircraft Command Research Group in 1940. This group is credited with establishing the value of interdisciplinary teams of scientists and operations specialists (Trefethan, 1954). Later Blackett moved to the Coastal Command and studied ship and submarine detection. J. D. Bernal and Sir Solly Zuckerman analyzed bomb damage through observations and experiments for the Civil Defense Research Committee. Among the staff of this committee were Americans later involved with operations research in the U.S. Air Force. Some of these research staffs became quite large—as many as 40 analysts—and turned into permanent staffs after the war.

The successes of the British efforts were frequently retold as the management sciences expanded after the war, both within government and into industry. Among the success stories noted by Trefethen (1954) (1) changes in detonation depths for air-dropped depth charges, which led the German military to conclude that the British had developed new weapons; (2) demonstrations that convoy losses were independent of convoy size; (3) doubled radar detection efficiency; (4) bomb damage studies that were also used for offensive plans; and (5) studies that led to increased size of bombing formations.

Trefethen attributes the success of British military operations research to the use of both headquarters and field research units; the use of interdisciplinary teams; the practice of considering problems in relation to the entire operations of which the problems were a part ("the one achievement which most distinguished World War II operational research from earlier research activities," Trefethan, 1954; 11); researcher independence in problem definition; and freedom from traditional features of the military bureaucracy. By the end of the war, more than 350 scientists were engaged in operational research for the British Army alone.

American Wartime Operations Research and After. In the United States, some management science activities have been identified in prewar industry (Levinson, 1954; Roy, 1954). Wartime work began under Ellis Johnson, who formed an operations research group at the Naval Ordnance Laboratory to study the use of mines as offensive weapons. The work of this group represented a shift from optimizing existing systems to projecting results of proposed courses of action. The group begun by Johnson ended up reporting to the Chief of Naval Operations, and its members dispersed throughout the Pacific as well as into headquarters.

In the Atlantic, antisubmarine warfare research began under Philip Morse, later first president of the Operations Research Society of America and author of the first American text on operations research (Morse and Kimball, 1951). The research group that Morse founded grew to include 70 scientists and had a continuous existence after the war. Stimulated by reports from James B. Conant and Vannevar Bush, Secretary of War Stimson supported the initiation of OR in the Air Force. With further support from Generals Arnold and Spaatz, each of the 26 combat air forces had "operations analysis groups" by the end of the war, employing more than 400 persons. The U.S. Army was much slower to adopt operations research.

American successes with operations research paralleled the British experiences: new patterns of search patrols for detection of ships by planes; alternative ways of sighting for range in bomber formations; mine-laying tactics; and other areas relevant to newer military technologies.

The wartime experience produced more than militarily useful studies. A new technology for influencing decisions had been developed and tested, and a cadre of several hundred specialists had gained experience in its use. The technology had been proven useful in carefully monitored implementation. Organizational experience as well as technical skill had been acquired. Yet some important lessons remained for the most part unlearned by both analysts and the wider community. From the missionary way that operations research was advocated after the war, it appears that few people recognized the scale of collective effort—under very favorable circumstances—that was required to produce a modest number of important understandings and then extend—or customize—them to specific practical settings. The accomplishments of wartime operations research are certainly striking, but even today the scale of effort remains unappreciated. Certainly today there are few civilian policies receiving continuous, urgent, and centrally coordinated and protected attention from a research staff the size of those that studied British air defense or American mine laying.

The wartime experiences established the basis for operations research and management science efforts that have continued to the present. Philip Morse's Operations Research Group in the Navy became, in 1947, the Operations Evaluation Group in a contract between the Office of Naval Research and the Massachusetts Institute of Technology. Operations analysis groups were established throughout the reorganized U.S. Air Force after the war. General Arnold, who had been instrumental in establishing operations research in the Army Air Force, initiated Project RAND in 1946. This later became the RAND Corporation, the first of the nonprofit "think tanks." Army interest in operations research was concentrated in logistics. Ellis Johnson became director of the Army's Operations Research Office, administered by the Johns Hopkins University. In the 1960s this office severed its formal ties with Hopkins and became the Research Analysis Corporation (RAC). Under prodding from both the first Hoover Commission and Defense Secretary Forrestal, a Weapons System Evaluation Group was established in the Office of the Secretary. Philip Morse became its first technical director. These staffs studied a wide range of problems from air combat attrition to seaport capacity to postwar economic and military aid. As interest grew regarding longer time horizons, social and political factors found a greater place in the efforts of these groups. RAND Corporation in particular has been innovative in the field of political assessment and futures research techniques.

Economics became more important in postwar management science, especially at RAND. With wartime urgency absent, cost became a constraint that had to be considered. In the military, as currently in medical care, resources are often viewed as essentially free given the unambiguous nature of the mission (win the war or save the patient, respectively). One particularly important study emphasized the importance of economic considerations and, at the same time, showed the analytical power that can result when analysts redefine a policy problem creatively.

Congress authorized $1.5 billion for overseas airbase construction in fiscal 1952. RAND was asked for help in determining how to spend the money. Quade (1964; 26) writes:

> Preliminary analysis soon showed, however, that the important problem was not how to acquire, construct, and maintain air bases in foreign countries but *where and how to base the strategic Air Force and how to operate this force in conjunction with the base system chosen.*

This new question opened a wider range of costs to scrutiny. Quade continues:

> One had to take into account what a base decision means to the total cost of the entire strategic force—how, for example, it affects the costs of extending the range of bombers which cannot reach the target unrefueled, the routes they must fly through enemy territory, the consequent losses they may suffer to the defense en route, and the difficulties the bases may have in recuperating from attack.

Substantively, the results of this study had a seminal impact on American defense policy that is still strongly felt today. "This study, originally conceived as a logistics exercise, became in the end a study of U.S. strategic deterrent policy" (Quade, 1964; 62). Quade might have said that this study raised many of the questions and offered many of the options that comprise strategic policy to this day. Yet this study employed no sophisticated mathematical techniques. Methodologically, it is distinct for its concentration on sensitivity and contingency, rather than on optimization (Quade, 1965; 63). Contemporary analysts of civilian policies neglect important traditions of management science when they concentrate on optimization rather than on such factors as those emphasized in the strategic air base study of almost three decades ago.

The review of military operations research need not be taken further: Essential lessons are clear. Military operations research had established by the early 1950s that military operations could be improved through careful analysis of the type that came to be called operations research and management science. Second, interdisciplinary teams were valuable. Third, large efforts were associated with the discovery and general use of major insights, and not all such efforts would bear fruit of this kind. Fourth, some break-throughs were as much the product of conceptual innovation and problem redefinition as they were of mathematical models. Fifth, the military experience provided both tech-nical tools and the beginnings of a new profession, the latter carrying the former into new areas of application. Finally, the area of military operations research continues to this day to be vigorous. Bonder (1979) estimates "conservatively" that between 10,000 and 15,000 persons are currently engaged in defense operations research in the United States alone.

C. Institutional Accommodation in Business and Government

Following World War II, operations research and management science began to penetrate American business. In Britain, operational research staffs were commonly organized to serve entire industries. In the United States, staffs were begun in individual corporations and, later, in individual government agencies. These staffs were usually small, in comparison to those established during the war. Further, these staffs did not face the same urgency that worked to the advantage of the wartime efforts. In both business and government, processes of institutional accommodation developed between management science staffs and the executives whom they were to serve. The accommodation that resulted over the years is instructive not just for structured situations such as agencies and corporations, but also for less structured but still organized social aggregates such as those concerned with a particular domain of public policy. It should be kept in mind, however, that even though the political network seems relatively unstructured compared to the internal corporate network, most management science work on public policy problems is spon-sored by some client. The sponsor/client will almost always be an interested participant in the debate, and most likely will be a government agency with some power to act in the matter. In many cases the work will be performed by an in-house staff or at least contracted for and monitered by such a staff. The development of long-term accommo-dations and confidences between management scientists and executives is important in government as well as business.

Management Science in U.S. Business Corporations.   Industry experiences in the United States offer insight into the organizational dynamics relevant to the use of management science in policy analysis. The perspective taken here is one that accepts that the tech-nology of management science is appropriate for many tasks of policy analysis when understood as presented in Sec. I of this chapter. Yet the realization of that potential requires developments in social expectations and relations that take *at least a decade* to work out. Industry experience demonstrates clearly that one does not just go out and "do" management science in policy analysis; nor, for that matter, can one just go out and "do" policy analysis. Not only, as already argued, does significant work depend on carefully coordinated intellectual development over several years. The recognition and use of that work also depends on a lengthy process of institutional learning and accom-modation between the analyst community and the consumers (top managers, policy makers). This process of institutional accommodation and development has been docu-mented by Radnor et al. (1968) in their study of management science in 66 large U.S. corporations from the late 1940s into the middle 1960s. They find that management science had a turbulent history and experienced in this period significant shifts in its characteristic organizational patterns.

Many early industrial management science activities began within the research and development divisions of the larger firm, and often began without a carefully worked out charter. Often, these early efforts terminated with the dismissal of the management scientists or research scientists involved in management science work, or with a complete reorganization of the management science effort. In some firms, such reorganizations happened several times in succession. This turbulence came to the attention of Rubenstein (1960) through his studies on the management of corporate R&D. He proposed that management science staffs tend to experience a sequence of "life cycle" phases from birth, through maturity, to death. Rubenstein et al. (1967) identified in a pilot study critical factors that appeared to affect the organizational fate of corporate management science staffs, including staff leadership, project portfolio characteristics, top management attitudes, staff researcher backgrounds, and client relationships.

Radnor et al. (1968) took this analysis one step further in a field study of 66 large U.S. corporations known to have ongoing management science activities. They traced the history of the management science staffs in each corporation through interviews and records. The chemical, food processing, pharmaceutical, and petroleum industries, among others, were well represented in their sample, and were among the early leaders in the use of management science. They found strong evidence of the increasing integration of management science into these firms. Although the early years, particularly in the early adopting firms, in each industry tended to be quite turbulent for management science, within 10 to 15 years experiences were for the most part smoother.

Several organizational changes accompanied this mitigation of conflict and more harmonious organizational existence. First, over the period from the late 1940s to the middle 1960s the backgrounds of the staff leaders changed. In the early years, staffs tended to be led by former military operations researchers, or by people formally trained in a management science area before entering the business world. In the middle part of this time span, research scientists and engineers led approximately half the staffs identified. In the latter part of this time span, the trend was toward experienced managers who had lately acquired management science abilities, and toward younger managers with formal management training (e.g., MBA degrees) that included quantitative coursework. In general, the trend over the 20-year period was away from management science specialists, whatever their training, and toward management specialists with quantitative skills. Among staff personnel, the trend was clearly away from the professional scientist or engineer and toward the young, quantitatively trained management specialist or toward the young management scientist with business experience. For both staff leaders and staff analysts, the trend was clearly away from "professionals" and toward "organizationals."

Clear trends were observed in other matters as well. Over the period, the location of management science staffs shifted away from the R&D or engineering divisions, and toward the finance division or the offices of top management and planning. These locational shifts can be accounted for, in part, by the availability of computers and data in finance divisions and planning offices.

With movement away from R&D and engineering divisions, the mission of management science staffs also changed. Limited missions (small-scale projects, short time horizon) predominate throughout the 20-year period. In the latter half of the period, staffs with missions to perform large-scale, long time-horizon projects decline proportionately and staffs with a "mixed" mission, combining some short-range with some long-range projects, grow proportionately and absolutely. Mixed missions are particularly associated with activities located in finance divisions. This trend might also be seen as a trend away from "grand optimization" schemes and toward a more pragmatic posture. Radnor et al. (1968) note, however, that these location and mission trends are not always well received by the professionally oriented management scientist.

Radnor et al. (1968) also identify a sharp trend upward in the use of formal liaison activities between the management science staff and its in-house clients. They confirm an earlier finding that the staff's sponsorship by a specific top manager contributes to staff stability. They note that the growing availability of computers, and the visibility of competitors' management science staffs are both incentives for a company to adopt management science. They comment that relations with other staffs can be difficult and competitive. Finally, they note in passing the possibility that personality conflicts are particularly salient for the management science activities they studied.

The research of Radnor et al. (1968) was replicated for a larger sample by Radnor and Neal (1973; see also Neal and Radnor, 1973), and many of these findings were confirmed. In addition, Radnor and Neal (1973) found evidence of wider diffusion of management science in industry and of the growing development of satellite management science staffs at decentralized corporate locations.

The work of Radnor and his colleagues discussed above establishes that management science became, between about 1950 and 1970, a well-accepted function in many large U.S. corporations. This process of adoption and diffusion was accompanied by substantial organizational conflict, and many early management science efforts were terminated as failures. Over the years, changes in personnel backgrounds, staff missions, and organizational location took place that represent an accommodation of professional and organizational needs. Less evident in the studies of Radnor and his colleagues are the technical developments in management science: the successful inventory, scheduling, and mathematical programming models that emerged from the interaction of mathematical developments, organizational experience, and cumulative knowledge.

Much of industrial management science began with two illusions: Organizational acceptance would come easily, and practical results would come soon. The 20-year path toward integration and utilization of management science in U.S. industry suggests that both take longer than is expected by the optimists and advocates. Few would deny today the contributions of the management sciences to industry. Likewise, although critics of the military may on occasion decry military operations research as well, its position is well established. Only in civilian government does the issue remain open. Here, however, the management sciences are also making contributions. In U.S. civilian government, however, the status today lags that of industry by a decade or more, just as the penetration of management science into federal civilian agencies lagged that into industry by a decade or more.

Management Science in Federal Civilian Agencies. White (1975) studied management science in federal agencies and identified patterns similar to those studied by Radnor, Rubenstein, and Bean (1968). He focused particularly on the patterns taken by management science activities in civilian agencies and found that, for the most part, the situation was characterized by less turbulence than the industrial experience. The small number of early adopters often experienced extreme conflict, but the more common experience was for gradual, evolutionary development. One possible explanation for this finding is that in the private business world, little learning was transferred among different industries, whereas federal civilian agencies were better able to share their management science experiences. The existence of most federal civilian agency management science efforts in a single city, as well as the existence of well-developed local professional associations, adds plausibility to this interpretation.

Among federal civilian agencies, early management science efforts can be traced to about 1960 in several agencies. The major period of growth for the management sciences is associated with the mandating of civilian agency Planning-Programming-Budgeting Systems (PPBS) in 1965. However, these activities did not fade into oblivion as PPBS did. In general, federal civilian agency management science drew more heavily on experienced managers and emphasized more limited missions than did industrial management science in its early years. "Death" rates are very low, even in the 1960s. Economists and mathematical statisticians ("math-stats") are commonly found performing management science work and staffs frequently drew heavily on in-house personnel with these backgrounds, rather than relying exclusively on external hiring. Consulting firms were widely used for technical support when demand did not justify hiring full-time, career specialists. In addition, the use of consultants resolved certain political problems and made it possible to obtain expertise that might not otherwise survive the delays of the federal personnel process. In some cases, the in-house staff served largely to design, negotiate, and monitor contract work, as well as to maintain the complex computer programs designed on contract (White, 1975). By the early 1970's White (1975) had identified 46 federal civilian agency management science staffs and studied in some depth 33 of them.

By the late 1970s, management scientists from such diverse agencies as the Farm Credit Banks, the U.S. Geological Survey, the New York City Human Resources Department, and the Tennessee Valley Authority were appearing on the program of the Institute of Management Science (TIMS) and the Operations Research Society of America (ORSA) Joint National Conference. At the November 1980 Joint National Meeting, more than 1980). An even larger proportion were of interest to civilian government agencies because they concerned subject matter with which one or another agency has responsibilities.

The history of management science in civilian agencies, like its history in industry, must be seen in the long view. Otherwise, judgments will be made about the applicability and impact of management science for public policy analysis, or about policy analysis itself, based on a slice of time. That kind of cross-sectional view, of course, will probably ignore what has happened before, which is likely to be less encouraging than the present. It is also likely to inhibit future-oriented theorizing that might contribute to informed projections of experiences to come. Cross-sectional appraisals of management science offer the convenience of fitting a curve to one data point. In taking the longer view, situational dynamics must be considered.

Although the organizational dynamics differ somewhat, with civilian agencies showing the effects of governmental personnel systems, agency size, and locational concentration, the main message is the same. The adoption and integration of management science into federal civilian agencies has taken about two decades so far, and is not yet a process at steady state.

Today, a large number of agency, consulting firm, and university personnel have developed expertise in applying management science to specific civilian problem areas and institutional settings. These analysts, in the aggregate, have an inner dynamic as individuals seek to expand their knowledge, explore new challenges, and advance professionally. Any realistic assessment of management science must take into account the social system of professionals practicing this craft, as well as acknowledge the extended time span and process of accommodation necessary for the integration of management science into a new institutional setting. The next subsection will focus on the profession in order to articulate management science more clearly as a social as well as technical phenomenon.

D. Professional Associations

The professional associations are dynamic social institutions that both shape and reflect developments in management science. The major associations are almost 30 years old in 1981. Their origins are of some interest here because the comparable organization for public policy analysis as an autonomous discipline (the Association for Public Policy Analysis and Management, APPAM) was formed only in 1979. Those concerned with the development of a methodologically sound and institutionally distinct discipline of policy analysis might find the experience of management science societies useful in speculating about the future of associations such as APPAM.

Four themes will be used to organize the discussion: diversification, diffusion, differentiation, and professionalization. Most of the illustrations of these themes will advance an additional argument: that management science has been applied with increasing frequency to civilian government problems, and public-sector management science is a well-accepted group of specializations within management science.

Birth of Professional Associations.   Professional associations grew up with the spread of management science into nonmilitary organizations. The two major associations are the Operations Research Society of America and The Institute for Management Science (ORSA and TIMS, respectively). Over the years, people affiliated with other professional associations and societies have also begun doing studies and using techniques quite similar to, or even identical with, those used by members of ORSA and TIMS. Not surprisingly, ORSA and TIMS members occasionally poach on the territory of other disciplines. Some members of the American Economics Association or the Public Choice Society, for example, would be comfortable at an ORSA/TIMS national meeting. More directly, associations such as the American Institute for Decision Sciences, the Military Operations Research Society, the American Institute of Industrial Engineers, the Institute of Electrical and Electronics Engineers, the various associations concerned with electronic computing, and umbrella associations such as the International Federation of Operations Research Societies and the U.S. National Research Council, all overlap with the functions and interests of these two lead societies. Attention here will be limited to the Operations Research Society of America (ORSA) and the Institute of Management Sciences (TIMS). These two societies were formed by people with distinct interests and have developed along different paths. In recent years, however, they have run joint meetings and shared publication responsibilities. The discussion of these two associations will also include some data on educational programs in management science.

Professional societies followed the initiation of educational programs in universities. Trefethen (1954) reports that courses in operations research emphasizing nonmilitary applications were offered at Massachusetts Institute of Technology in 1948, and in British universities shortly thereafter. The Case Institute of Technology offered the first U.S. master's degree in operations research shortly after holding a conference on business applications of operations research in 1951. Columbia and Johns Hopkins began regular course work in 1952.

ORSA was conceived at a meeting chaired by Philip Morse in 1952, and founded at Arden House in May of that year. Its founding was preceded by several years of activity by a committee of the National Research Council established to encourage nonmilitary operations research and training programs (Trefethan, 1954; Morse, 1952). The organizing meeting was attended by about 75 people, half with military organizations and another quarter with universities. The meeting was a professional one; papers were presented on mathematical matters as well as on applications in a variety of industries. The program even included a paper on problems of doing OR in business settings (Levinson, 1954), establishing ORSA's enduring concern with the behavioral side of the profession. A second meeting was held in November 1952. ORSA has continued to hold national meetings in the spring and fall since that time.

The society and the profession have developed hand in hand. ORSA had almost 900 members within 2 years of its founding (White, 1972b)[2]. By 1956 there were 10 degree programs, all at major universities, and 23 more universities were offering formal course work in operations research. In that year, ORSA had grown to more than 1500 members. By its sixth anniversary it had 2330 members.

The Institute of Management Sciences developed out of a meeting held at UCLA in 1954 in response to invitations by Melvin Salveson (Cooper, 1955). TIMS was founded at Columbia University in December of that year. From the start, it represented a set of concerns different from those that led to the founding of ORSA. Rather than representing a concern for the nonmilitary application of operations research, TIMS was founded by people with backgrounds in large corporations and major universities. At its first two national meetings, in 1954 and 1955, there were practically no papers on military problems or by military operations researchers.

TIMS differed from ORSA by drawing its active participants from corporate-oriented consulting firms and corporations themselves to a large degree. It also has maintained a clear international focus, generally having some officers or editors from abroad. TIMS has also pursued an interest in the behavioral sciences beyond the study of the profession and its problems. In this area, the work published in the pages of its journal, *Management Science,* is similar to that which appears in journals such as *Behavioral Science.*

Diversification, Diffusion, and Differentiation in ORSA and TIMS.   The same categorical framework can be applied to the development of either society or the profession. They can be viewed as developing along three lines: diffusion, differentiation, and diversification. *Diffusion* refers to the spread of management science within a set of institutions such as universities, consulting firms, or government agencies. *Differentiation* refers to the subdividing or specialization of the profession, its societies, its areas of application, or its

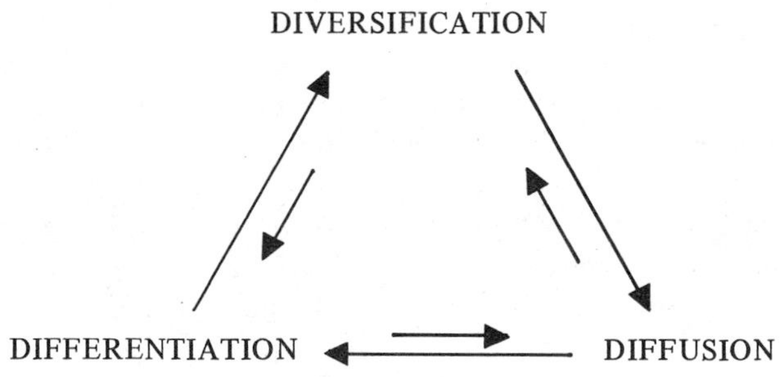

DIVERSIFICATION

DIFFERENTIATION ⟵⟶ DIFFUSION

Figure 1. Relations among diversification, diffusion, and differentiation in the development of management science.

technology. *Diversification* refers to the establishment of new horizons or beachheads for management science, with respect to new fields, new institutions, new technologies, or new approaches. The three types of development are related in a circular fashion as suggested in Figure 1. In this scheme, management science first diversifies into a new area (e.g., civilian government), then diffuses into a growing number of agencies, and finally differentiates as special competencies develop around the problems of particular agencies. These new specializations may then allow new diversification. For example, large-scale management science models completed for energy policy analysis may become the basis for large-scale models of other social sectors and encourage the diversification of management science into problem areas that it currently neglects.

On the other hand, the direction of development can also go the other way. Finer differentiation of technology, or of training programs, may encourage diffusion. For example, a management science training program that emphasized local government applications might facilitate applications in cities. As management science diversifies, it also automatically differentiates: As military operations research diversified into private industry, it also differentiated the profession into two parts. To some extent, TIMS and ORSA still reflect these two parts. Diffusion becomes diversification when management science crosses levels of recursion. For example, as applications in the natural resource area diffuse from federal to state agencies with similar functional responsibilities, management is also diversifying into state government.

Diversification.   Some other examples of these three lines of development further clarify the growth of the profession and its professional societies. The major examples of diversification are from military to private industry to civilian government applications. Among other prominent diversifications have been, in recent years, the development of large-scale simulation models and planning technologies as alternatives to traditional optimization techniques. Substantively, energy policy simulations have come to occupy a significant amount of the profession's collective effort. Health, criminal justice, natural resource, and transportation policy have been areas of substantial development in recent years. Bidding, decision support systems, risk assessment, and preference articulation and ordering (Saaty, 1980) are all subjects that appear to be destined for increasing attention in coming years. Management science also continues to diversify into new lands. Machol

(1980a) reports on the operations research societies of Egypt and Greece; Ansio et al. (1980) trace the history of management science in Finland. Small European countries, such as Denmark, have extensive operations research activity. Machol (1980b) reports that operations research is taught at all Danish universities and the Danish association has 250 members. At a recent TIMS-ORSA Joint National Conference, papers were presented by management scientists from Kuwait and Turkey as well as from more familiar countries such as India, Belgium, Japan, Denmark, Mexico, Venezuela, Chile, and Israel, among others (ORSA-TIMS, 1980).

On the other hand, there are substantive areas into which management science has not yet diversified to any great extent. Of particular interest to social scientists interested in public policy studies is the fact that management scientists have so far not applied their skills to welfare and social services to anywhere near the degree they have to many other policy areas. This situation may not be an enduring one, however. Evidence from Britain, where registers of operational research (as it is called there) projects are maintained, suggests favorable changes in the way welfare services questions are approached by management scientists. Boldy and Clayden conclude, from an examination of 1972 and 1977 registers, that projects involving simulation as a technique and strategy as a concern are increasing proportionately. Conversely, projects studying hospital tactics and using optimization techniques are decreasing proportionately (Boldy and Clayden, 1979). Housing and mental health are two other policy areas that represent frontiers for management science.

Diffusion.   Diffusion of management science has occurred rapidly during the last 30 years. In June 1956, 10 American universities offered graduate degrees in operations research, and 23 more offered some course work. By 1980, it no longer made sense to count the universities that offered course work in management science. Rather, it was more informative to note the variety of academic departments with which were affiliated authors of papers at the national convention. Among the expected departments of management science, operations research, managerial economics, statistics, business, economics, and such were mixed various engineering fields, a sprinkling of public administration and public policy programs, several geography departments, and a liberal assortment of medical departments, including ophthalmology and anesthesiology.

A further indication of the diffusion within universities is given by the number of referees used by the leading journals. *Management Science,* for example, used more than 550 university professors as referees between November 1978 and December 1979. This represented only about two-thirds of the total number of people involved. More than 100 referees were from outside the United States.

Of particular interest here is evidence of the diffusion of management science into government agencies. The most readily available data sources on this are the programs of the national meetings. These programs suggest a steady growth of civilian government management science.

At the founding meeting of ORSA in May 1952, no civilian government personnel are identifiable. The situation is marginally better at the Fourth National ORSA Meeting in 1956; two of some 70 paper presenters are affiliated with federal civilian agencies, the Census Bureau and the Public Health Service. By 1961, ORSA is recognizing article referees from NASA, the FAA, the National Bureau of Standards, and the Port of New York

Authority. At the May 1963 ORSA National Meeting, 12 of approximately 100 paper presenters were affiliated with civilian government agencies, half from local government. This relatively high proportion reflects several panels on urban planning. A few years later, at the Spring 1966 TIMS Conference, the proportion is half that for the same number of papers.

The 1970s saw much wider civilian agency participation. The 39th National ORSA Conference, in Spring 1971, had representation from 20 civilian government agencies including several at the local level. The president of ORSA for that year, W. E. Cushen, was the director during much of the 1960s and 1970s of a very large staff of civilian government management scientists at the National Bureau of Standards. Cushen's staff performed studies for a large number of government agencies at the federal level, and performed work for state and local agencies as well. By 1980, at the November 1980, TIMS-ORSA Joint National Meeting, papers were presented by 77 authors affiliated with civilian government agencies. Almost one-third of these were from agencies of the U.S. Department of Energy. One or more agencies of seven other federal departments, the Office of Management and Budget, the General Accounting Office, and several independent agencies were also represented in the group. Six authors came from state and local agencies in spite of the effects of the tax revolt on travel.

Civilian agency personnel have also made substantial advances in the hierarchies of professional associations. The 1977-1978 ORSA officers and council included among the list of 13, operations researchers from the National Bureau of Standards, the Federal Energy Administration, and the Consumer Products Safety Commission. The president for that year was Alfred Blumstein, a pioneer in application of management science to criminal justice and law enforcement, from Carnegie-Mellon University's School of Urban and Public Affairs. TIMS at that time, though having a slightly larger number of officers and board members, had only one person affiliated with a civilian government agency. Two years later, however, TIMS had officers or council members from the Federal Emergency Management Agency and the U.S. Fire Administration. Given the general dominance by university-affiliated personnel of scholarly and research associations, as well as the extensive networks of corporate and consulting management scientists, the appearance of any government officials among the officers and councils of TIMS and ORSA is strong indication of the integration of management science into government.

Differentiation.   For differentiation, the societies themselves can be examined. The internal specialization of TIMS and ORSA gives some indication of the concerns of these societies and their profession. One recurring issue of differentiation is that of theory and practice. ORSA instituted separate sections in its journals, *Operations Research,* for applications and mathematical articles in 1956. During the middle 1960s, TIMS published two separate series of its journal, *Management Science* A: Theory, and B: Applications. About 1970, TIMS began *Interfaces*, a nontechnical journal reporting interesting implemented studies, and presenting innovative papers on systems theory, management philosophy, and the practice of management science. ORSA began *OR/MS Today*, a somewhat more "newsy" publication, several years later. In the 1970s the two societies began to sponsor jointly an explicitly mathematical journal, *Mathematics of Operations Research.* ORSA began a book series in 1958, and TIMS began a series of edited monographs around 1970.

Each society began internal differentiation in the 1950s. ORSA developed a large number of geographic chapters, but also developed substantive sections on military, health, and transportation applications as well as on cost effectiveness. TIMS developed a geographic differentiation more slowly, but eventually had chapters abroad as well as in the United States. TIMS chose the term "colleges" for its substantive sections. By the 1970s these colleges covered management functions such as marketing, research and development, logistics, control systems, planning, organization, and management philosophy, and others. Additional sections for information systems, simulation and gaming, local government, and the practice of management science were also operating by that time. By 1980, TIMS had added sections on energy and natural resources, engineering management, and the management of technological change; a college of public programs and processes had replaced the one on local government. ORSA had "technical sections" and "special interest groups" in 1980 for corporate planning, crime and justice, educational science, energy applications, social science, applied probability, business applications, and computer science, in addition to those already mentioned. Cost effectiveness was no longer on the roster. This list of sections suggests a sizable interest in public and public-related policy issues on the part of TIMS and ORSA members. Journal departments support this conclusion. For example, during 1979, *Operations Research* had nine "area editors," three of which were for "energy and environment," "health and welfare," and "social sciences, defense, criminal justice, and other public sector applications."

This is not surprising when surveys of reader interest are considered. King et al. (1979) and Cattin (1979), in an exchange on the matter, present and interpret evidence suggesting that academic readers are most interested in articles about research methodology and public sector applications. "Practitioner" readers, on the other hand, "express primary interest in futuristic (planning, investment, corporate modeling), qualitative (project and crisis management), personnel-related and information-related (information systems, assessing organizational effectiveness, cost-benefit) topics" (King et al., 1979: 297). There is also a difference between readers and authors. The former prefer articles dealing with strategy, futures, effectiveness, and qualitiative matters. The latter prefer articles dealing with technique, algorithms, theory, and computability.

Professionalization. Diversification, diffusion, and differentiation are three themes through which the dynamic and expanding nature of management science can be appreciated as a social as well as technical phenomenon. Management science should also be appreciated as a professionalizing social entity. Three aspects of professionalization can be briefly noted. First, in response to charges by Alfred Wohlstetter that operations research had been misused by some of the participants in the public debate over the antiballistic missile system, ORSA President Thomas Caywood appointed a special committee that developed and published guidelines for the practice of operations research. The resulting debate suggests substantial disagreement about the role of operations research in public policy controversies (Washington Operations Research Council, 1972). One can infer from the guidelines (ORSA Ad Hoc Committee on Professional Standards, 1971) that the committee viewed the profession as one of advice givers rooted in esoteric knowledge, rather than as a bureaucratic profession as the two are distinguished by Carter (1967).

A second dimension of professionalizing is in the reporting of results in journals. *Operations Research* has published detailed guidelines on reporting computational details of an operations research application or of computer experiments testing the efficiency of an algorithm (Florian et al., 1979). Standards have also been developed for attesting to the implementation of reported applications. *Interfaces* requires a testimonial letter verifying the use of a public-sector application, and the verification of cost savings for a private-sector application (Editor's Note, 1980). *Operations Research* requires a report of the degree of implementation in the text of a submitted article. In spite of continuing concern over implementation, proper testimonials for public-sector applications are common where required.

III. CONCLUSIONS

The nature and history and social system of management science have been presented in this chapter for a single purpose: to encourage a proper appreciation of management science or any other rational approach to public policy analysis. The critical literature far too extensive even for cursory summary, ignores the cumulative, social nature of management science and instead concentrates on individual studies and recommendations. The social dimension, if noted at all, is usually noted in terms of a researcher-client dyadic relation. The consequence of this view is that management science is seen as an additive sum of its parts, even though the parts are not imaginatively conceived. The social history of management science points us in other directions and toward other data sources for an appreciation of what and how management science can contribute to policy analysis. Some conclusions may be offered on the basis of this review.

Management science is being applied extensively to a wide, but not universal, range of public policy problems.

The application of management science to particular policy domains occurs along the full range of the continuum between theory and practice, from purely theoretical advances that result in practical applications sometime later, to immediate work within agencies on short-range problems.

The profession of management science, with strong roots in academic institutions, is not dependent for its advance on the adoption by political officials of the recommendations of specific analyses. Rather, the profession has many channels for contributing policy-relevant information.

Within an operating agency, it is important to consider not the official adoption of specific project recommendations but instead the integration of the management science staff into ongoing policy-making systems. The former consideration is only a part of the latter and, over any brief time span, possibly a very misleading aspect of the latter.

The scale of management science effort necessary to make an impact on policy is larger than commonly understood. It takes several years and many studies to conceptualize a policy area for management science study and analysis. The World War II experience has been presented in a misleading way; it is actually a strong argument for a generous time horizon and investment.

The purpose of management science studies, in other than the most well-developed and well-structured areas, should not be to produce implementable recommendations. Rather, a realistic objective for individual studies is to build cumulative knowledge and understanding of complex social systems in ways that contribute to the alignment of system and regulative variety. Even where management science is pursued in a utopian mode, it still is involved with the discovery and use of order.

The technical skills of management science are rapidly spreading among the practitioners of other fields. Although some people foresee the death of operations research, an alternate view is that this represents further diversification, diffusion, and differentiation of operations research and management science. Those who see management science as a social system will therefore be looking for the core professional groups to establish new differentiation in order that these groups can be maintained. One possibility will be further elaboration of technology along the lines suggested by Ackoff (1979b), who advocates greater attention to planning and participation technologies. Alternatively, the core may become even more mathematical. In either case, the core will be the source of technology eventually to be widely diffused to others.

The organization of the practice of management science is neither unitary nor fixed. Great diversity exists, and new forms are likely to develop for new circumstances. The past 30 years have seen the development of in-house staffs, both centralized and decentralized; of different types of leadership and personnel backgrounds; of many different types of consulting firms and contract research firms; of various not-for-profit institutes and university centers; and of many kinds of researcher-client relationship.

In this chapter, management science has been considered a "social fact," the understanding of which requires multiple perspectives of appreciation. Management science, in this view, is much more than the collection of tools and techniques usually presented in texts. These tools and techniques are *one* set of building blocks, to be sure. But their understanding, even when thorough, is only a first step toward the use of management science in public policy analysis. This chapter has been an attempt to provide the perspectives necessary for understanding management science as methods of policy analysis. The next chapter will consider in a simple way many of the methods and concepts of management science presented in elementary textbooks. With the cumulative, historical, social, and institutional materials offered in this chapter, the reader should not fall victim to the traps common to most considerations of the place of rationality in public policy making.

NOTES

1. At this point, a note on terminology is at least politic. The term "management science" is a fairly recent one, and it is preceded in the literature by a decade or more by the term "operations (or, for the British, operational) research." Each term has a professional society adhering to its use. Often, writers about the topics considered here employ some acronym such as "OR/MS" in deference to the various institutional interests and terminological controversies. The major professional associations are converging as each diversifies into what were formerly areas of special emphasis of

another. One consequence may be the emergence of a generic term, "operational sciences." However, that term is not yet widely used, so is not employed here. The acronym, "OR/MS," while used in previous work by this author, seems obscure in this context. At the risk of offending those with strong alternative preferences or identifications, "management science" will generally be used here. Those in a position to quarrel seriously over this selection will also be able to appreciate its use as a generic term. I hope that no one will infer that I mean to diminish anyone's preferred identification. Where historical circumstances make other terms particularly appropriate, they are used instead.

2. Much of the historical information and the data about professional associations and journals that is given in this section is taken from White (1972b), an unpublished manuscript. Data otherwise unreferenced is usually taken from such sources as programs of professional conferences or rosters of officers appearing as front matter of journals. Specific citations not otherwise provided are available upon request.

REFERENCES

Ackoff, R. L. (1978). Operations research. In *International Encyclopedia of Statistics,* William H. Hruskal and Judith M. Tanur (Eds.). Free Press, New York, pp. 667–671.

—— (1979a). The future of operational research is past. *Journal of the Operational Research Society, 30*: 93-104.

—— (1979b). Resurrecting the future of operational research. *Journal of the Operational Research Society 30*: 189–199.

Ansio, T., Kiuigarvi, H., and Suisman, M. (1980). The past, present, and future of operations research at the Helsinki School of Economics and Business Administration. *Interfaces 10–3*: 83–96.

Balintfy, J. L. (1979). The cost of decent subsistence. *Management Science 25*: 980–989.

Beer, S. (1974). *Designing Freedom.* Wiley, New York and London.

Blumstein, A. (1979). The positive values of negative research. In *Evaluation Studies Review Annual,* vol. 4, L. Seechrest and Associates (Eds.). Sage, Beverly Hills, CA, pp. 727–728.

Boldy, D., and Clayden, D. (1979). Operational research projects in health and welfare services in the United Kingdom and Ireland. *Journal of the Operational Research Society 30*: 505–511.

Bonder, S. (1979). Changing the future of operations research. *Operations Research 27*: 209–224.

Bradley, L. A., and Bradley, G. W. (1978). The academic achievement of black students in desegregated schools: A critical review. In *Policy Studies Review Annual,* vol. 2, H. Freeman (Ed.). Sage, Beverly Hills, CA, pp. 643–693.

Burkhead, J. V. (1956). *Government Budgeting.* Wiley, New York.

Carter, B. (1967). Some problems in the sociology of the professions. In *The Professions in America,* K. S. Lynn (Ed.). Beacon, Boston.

Cattin, P. (1979). Comment on designing scientific journals. *Management Science 25*: 295–296.

Churchman, C. W. (1979). *The Systems Approach and Its Enemies.* Basic Books, New York.

Cooper, W. W. (1955). Presidential address to TIMS, delivered at the First National TIMS Meeting, October 21-22, 1954. Reprinted in part in *Management Science 1*: 2 183-186.

Cummings, T. G., Mulloy, E. S., and Glen, R. (1978). A methodological critique of fifty-eight selected work experiments. In *Policy Studies Review Annual,* vol. 2, H. Freeman (Ed.). Sage, Beverly Hills, CA, pp. 424-457.

Editor's Note (1980). *Interfaces 10-3*: 56.

Eilon, S. (1969). What is a rational decision. *Management Science 16*: B172-B189.

Engel, J. H. (1954). A verification of Lanchester's laws. *Operations Research 2*: 163-171.

Feldstein, M. (1976). Unemployment compensation: Its effects on unemployment. *Monthly Labor Review 99*: 39-41.

Fischer, F. (1980). *Politics, Values, and Public Policy: The Problem of Methodology.* Westview, Boulder, CO.

Florian, M., Fox, B., Crowder, H., Dembo, R., and Mulvey, J. (1979). Reporting computational experiences in *Operations Research. Operations Research 27*: vii-x.

Freeman, H. (Ed.). (1978). *Policy Studies Review Annual,* vol. 2. Sage, Beverly Hills, CA.

Haveman, R. H., and Hollenbeck, K. (Eds.) (1980). *Microeconomic Simulation Models for Public Policy Analysis* (2 vols.). Academic, New York.

Haveman, R. H., and Zellner, B. B. (Eds.) (1979). *Policy Studies Review Annual,* vol. 3. Sage, Beverly Hills, CA.

Kantorovich, L. V. (1960). Mathematical methods of organizing and planning production. *Management Science 6*: 366-422.

King, W. R., Kilmann, R. H., and Sochats, K. (1979). On analyzing survey data for journal design. *Management Science 25*: 296-298.

Kirst, M. W., Garms, W., and Oppermann, T. (1980). State services for children: An exploration of who benefits, who governs. In *Policy Studies Review Annual,* vol. 4, B. Raven (Ed.). Sage, Beverly Hills, CA, pp. 682-703.

Koopman, B. O. (1974). Recent U.S. advances in OR theory. In *Operational Research '72: Proceedings of the Sixth IFORS Conference on Operations Research, Dublin, Ireland, August 21-25, 1972*, M. Ross (Ed.). North-Holland, Amsterdam and London; American Elsevier, New York, pp. 561-570.

Levinson, H. C. (1954). Experiences in commercial operation-research. In *Operations Research for Management*, 2 vols., J. F. McCloskey and F. N. Trefethen (Eds.). Johns Hopkins Press, Baltimore, pp. 265-288.

Machol, R. E. (1980a). European notes: A continental OR round-up. *Interfaces 10-3*: 57-58.

—— (1980b). More notes on OR in Europe. *Interfaces 10-4*: 93-94.

MacRae, D., Jr. (1980). Concepts and methods of policy analysis. In *Policy Studies Review Annual,* vol. 4, B. Raven (Ed.). Sage, Beverly Hills, CA, pp. 74-80.

MacRae, D., Jr., and Wilde, J. (1977). *Policy Analysis for Public Decisions.* Duxbury, North Scituate, MA.

Majone, G. (1980). The uses of policy analysis. In *Policy Studies Review Annual,* vol. 4, B. Raven (Ed.). Sage, Beverly Hills, CA, pp. 161-180.

March, J. G., and Simon, H. A. (1958). *Organizations.* Wiley, New York.

Marshall, B. O., Jr. (1954). Queueing theory. In *Operations Research for Management*, 2 vols., J. F. McCloskey and F. N. Trefethen (Eds.). Johns Hopkins Press, Baltimore, pp. 134-148.

McCloskey, J. F. (1956). Of horseless carriages, flying machines, and operations research:

A tribute to Frederic William Lanchester (1868–1946). *Operations Research 4*: 141–147.

Moiseev, N. N. (1973). Operations research in the USSR: Development and perspectives. In *Operational Research '72, Proceedings of the Sixth IFORS International Conference on Operational Research, Dublin, Ireland, August 21–25, 1972,* M. Rodd (Ed.), North Holland, Amsterdam, and American Elsevier, New York.

Morse, P. (1952). The Operations Research Society of America. *Operations Research 1*: 1–2.

Morse, P., and Kimball, G. (1951). *Methods of Operations Research.* Wiley, New York.

Nagel, Stuart S. (Ed.) (1977). *Policy Studies Review Annual,* vol. 1. Sage, Beverly Hills, CA.

Neal, R., and Radnor, M. (1973). The relation between formal procedures for pursuing OR/MS activities and OR/MS group success. *Operations Research 21*: 451–474.

ORSA Ad Hoc Committee on Professional Standards (1971). Guidelines for the practice of operations research. *Operations Research* 19-5.

ORSA-TIMS (1980). November 1980 Joint National Meeting program. *ORSA/TIMS Bulletin 10.*

Quade, E. S. (1964). The selection and use of strategic air bases: A case history. In *Analysis for Military Decisions,* E. S. Quade (Ed.). Rand McNally, Chicago, pp. 24–63.

Radnor, M., and Neal, R. (1973). The progress of management science in large U.S. industrial corporations. *Operations Research 21*: 427-450.

Radnor, M., Rubenstein, A. H., and Bean, A. S. (1968). Integration and utilization of management science activities in organizations. *Operational Research Quarterly 19*: 117–141.

Raven, B. (Ed.) (1980). *Policy Studies Review Annual,* vol. 4. Sage, Beverly Hills, CA.

Rubenstein, A. H. (1960). Integration of operations research into the firm. *Journal of Industrial Engineers 11*: 421–428.

Rubenstein, A. H., Radnor, M., Baker, N. H., Heiman, D. R., and McColley, J. B. (1967). Some organizational factors related to the effectiveness of management science groups in industry. *Management Science 13*: B508–B519.

Russell, L. (1980). Medical care. In *Setting National Priorities: Agenda for the 1980's,* J. Pechman (Ed.). Brookings Institution, Washington, DC, pp. 169–203.

Saaty, T. L. (1980). *The Analytic Hierarchy Process.* McGraw-Hill, New York.

Salkever, D. S., and Bice, T. W. (1979). *Hospital Certificate of Need Controls: Impact on Investment, Costs, and Use.* American Enterprise Institute for Public Policy Research, Washington, DC.

Seechrest, L., and Associates (Eds.) (1979). *Evaluation Studies Review Annual,* vol. 4. Sage, Beverly Hills, CA.

Sowell, T. (1980). *Knowledge and Decisions.* Basic Books, New York.

Stigler, G. J. (1945). The cost of subsistence. *Journal of Farm Economics 27*: 303–314.

Trefethen, F. N. (1954). A history of operations research. In *Operations Research for Management,* 2 vols., J. F. McCloskey and F. N. Trefethen (Eds.). Johns Hopkins Press, Baltimore, pp. 3-35.

von Neumann, J. (1928). Zur Theorie der Gesell Schaftsspiele. *Math. Ann. 100*: 295–320.

Washingtons Operational Research Council (1972). ORSA guidelines report debated by Bergen and Stone. *WORC Newsletter 11-5*: 2–3.

White, M. J. (1972a). The impact of management science on political decision making. In *Planning-Programming-Budgeting: A Systems Approach to Management,* rev. ed., F. J. Lyden and E. G. Miller (Eds.). Rand McNally, Chicago.
—— (1972b). Definition and history of OR/MS. typescript, 81 pp.
—— (1975). *Management Science in Federal Civilian Agencies: Adoption and Diffusion of a Sociotechnical Innovation.* Heath, Lexington, MA.
—— (1979). Observations on management science in government. *Policy Studies Journal* *8:* 127–134.
Whitmore, W. F. (1952). Edison and operations research. *Operations Research 1:* 83–85.
Wildavsky, A. (1979). *Speaking Truth to Power: The Art and Craft of Policy Analysis.* Little, Brown, Boston.

3

Policy Analysis Models

Michael J. White / University of Southern California, Los Angeles, California

Methods of policy analysis are a subject of book-length exposition elsewhere and so can only be suggested here (Nagel and Neef, 1979; Quade, 1975; Stokey and Zeckhauser, 1978; White et al., 1980). Entire professional careers of distinction have been constructed around a single mathematical method such as queueing theory, linear programming, or multi-attribute utility analysis; book-length treatments of individual topics are common. This chapter presents an approach to policy analysis and a discussion of rational methods, brief definitions of important concepts of modeling and management science, and short expositions of some management science and operations research models.

For the most part, the chapter is strongly oriented toward the management sciences. Overlapping with the management sciences is the discipline of economic analysis, offering well-established observed regularities and battle-tested analytical methods and models. Equally important but more often neglected is the legal approach to policy analysis, which is important not least because it is the method of training of so many policy makers (Sigler and Beede, 1977). The social sciences offer a variety of investigative methods. These methods produce findings that are often embedded in theories or claims of generality extending beyond what is necessary for dealing with the situation immediately at the policy maker's hand. The social sciences, excluding economics, lack in practice the unifying methodology and terminology of management science, and thus are difficult to present as method for policy analysis. Public administration offers little in the way of method for policy analysis but does offer appreciations of governmental operations that policy analysts ignore at their peril (Nagel, 1979; a particularly important example is Shapek, 1981, or Seidman, 1980). In looking to social science or public administration, the policy analyst must exercise careful judgment regarding the validity and relevance of findings and the usefulness of conceptual frameworks.

I. AN APPROACH TO METHOD IN POLICY ANALYSIS

Today there are two alternative approaches to method in policy analysis. The common one views method as an elaboration of the rational decision paradigm (Hartle and Halpern, 1980), in which goals are specified, alternatives suggested, criteria for choice selected and applied, and a decision produced. These steps are offered in varying degrees of elaboration. For example, Quade in one formulation adds forecasting the future environment of the choice to be made, the estimation of costs, attention to timing and sensitivity analysis, careful examination of assumptions regarding factors omitted, and documentation of the work completed (Quade, 1968). Walker also adds implementation and monitoring of study results (Walker, 1979). Each, however, shares a common core of problem formulation, goal clarification, selection of criteria, generation and examination of alternatives, comparison, and choice. This set of steps, recognized often as iterative and nonsequential in practice, yet remains deductive in spirit: choice depends on prior establishment of goals.

An alternative approach turns deduction on its head. Wildavsky writes of the "strategic retreat from objectives," a political phase following upon "the age of design" and "the era of implementation" (Wildavsky, 1979: chap. 2). Instead, he proposes that problem formulation be the end of analysis. He writes:

> A first clue came from an unusual aspect of our teaching experience: policy analysis is better taught backward. Instead of beginning by formulating a problem, considering alternative solutions, developing criteria, applying criteria to data, and so on, students' work improved when exercises went the other way around. The best way to begin learning was to apply strong criteria to good data, go on to create strong criteria and discover alternatives, and, after numerous trials, formulate a problem at the very end. Why did anxiety decline and confidence rise when entering through the back door? Possibly, formulating the problem was more like the end than the beginning of analysis (Wildavsky, 1979: 2-3).

Wildavsky suggests that the realistic approach to policy analysis connects "what might be wanted with what can be provided" (Wildavsky, 1979: 3).

That approach is recommended here. Policies, and public problems in general, are embedded in complex, dimly perceived institutional and historical contexts. Stakeholders are numerous, and their interests not obvious. Any given situation will have meanings to some that can hardly be imagined by others of different background, training, or social location. On such shoals, policy analysis regularly founders. Defining or formulating "the problem" itself presumes an intolerant view of any presenting situation.

Policy analysis may be both art and craft, as Wildavsky asserts. However, it is also *persuasion or rhetoric*. Majone emphasizes rationalization of choices to others whose cooperation is needed, and Wildavsky writes of "retrospection" in policy analysis (Majone, 1980; Wildavsky, 1979: 135 ff). Using the preceding as an orientation, an alternative to the "rational paradigm" can be outlined in more detail.

To begin with, when presented with a policy "problem," several tasks should be begun. Although it may seem obvious, the first task is to study existing policies: statutes, cases, administrative practices, regulations, and constellations of interests. Second, the available literature on the subject should be reviewed, including legislative hearings. Interests have claims to benefits or access that are enforceable in court as well as through politics. The analyst's client may not understand the law and regulations properly. Any policy change is likely to require some legal means or instrumentality. Without a thorough grounding in the law, these cannot be chosen widely. Statutory draftsmanship cannot be ignored by the policy analyst.

Next, whenever possible, comes a search for data. At a simple level, the presenting problem may result from misinterpreted facts. Development of perspective through time series may force redefinition of the symptoms being presented. Often, surprising insights can be gained from the liberal employment of long division. Students analyzing policy case studies are regularly advised to "check the totals" in exhibits, and to compute freely available rates and proportions. The same advice holds for policy analysts: Absolute magnitudes are usually misleading, and even rates gain meaning only from comparison.

Data also allow the estimation of parameters such as contribution rates, elasticities, variances, and trade-off coefficients for observed systems. Available or easily collected data may allow the specification of frequency distributions and the determination of threshold levels. In turn this may bound and reduce what seemed a priori to be a large problem. For example, where rent control is advocated on the basis of relief for the elderly poor, the joint distribution of rent, income, and age may reveal the problem to be of a different size than the one claimed by advocates of policy change.

As data are collected and examined, frequency distributions and parameters estimated, existing policies and interests articulated, and previous research reviewed, the archaeology of the current situation will begin to become clear. By this term, which I adapt from Foucault (1973, 1975), I refer to the origin of existing policies and perceptions in interests and compromises from the past. One major task of policy analysis is persuasion: Some of the parties on whom change depends will be attached to existing policies and perceptions as these have served their interests well; change requires "unfreezing" these past attachments and reforming them along new lines (Schein and Bennis, 1965; Bennis et al., 1964); an important method of unfreezing involves demonstrating that attitudes no longer serve the functions once served (Katz, 1963a,b). An understanding of the archaeology of the current situation reveals the pathways to persuasion.

Recognizing the task of persuasion allows attention to possible adversary argument. Alternative theories to the analyst's, conceivable misinterpretations of the data, and weak. points in the analysis can all be used to attract important participants to an adversary's preferred policy. The critical piece of analysis may not be the one that faithfully models the policy situation; instead it may be the piece that defends the larger study against a threatening argument or diverts an unanswerable, because perspective-shifting, charge.

Focus on political dynamics complements focus on adversary arguments. If policy analysis is to become integral with its implementation, rather than isolated from it, policy analysts have to recognize that the nature of their task shifts from arena to arena, and with the vagaries of attention and segmented participation (March and Olson, 1976). Analyses should be conducted with an eye to their use in the succeeding as well as instant arena. This is a logical extension of the notion of policy analysis as persuasion or argument, rather than exclusively as objective research. Audiences shift as arenas change. A change of a single person in a group can change the group's receptivity to a fact or theory.

What may be called "cultural factors," for lack of a better word, must also be considered. For example, in American culture, notions of "fair share" and "hold harmless" are both prevalent. Persons who are poor and elderly, or who have a physical handicap, are normally regarded as deserving some degree of "protection." These kinds of considerations might better be considered constraints in the analysis, rather than irrationalities on the part of nonanalysts. Such factors serve to emphasize to the analyst that multiple meanings are attached to single events or facts.

If the problem is better formulated at the end than at the beginning of the analysis, then the analyst must recognize that many things remain beyond control. In policy analysis, the most important considerations may be the ones that no one could anticipate. Sometimes these may take the form of the inventive responses of those who turn a policy to their own end, in the process distorting the outcomes expected by those who choose the policy. Alternately, the policy, as implemented, may be affected by developments external to and independent from it: new technologies, demographic shifts, changed weather patterns, bizarre social movements, or international events, for example. The common rational paradigm for policy analysis is rarely sensitive to these kinds of contrary developments, the attention of systems analysts to analytic assumptions notwithstanding.

To deal with this reality of policy making and policy analysis, David Collingridge has advanced the "fallibilist theory" of decision making, based on choice in the face of "ignorance" (Collingridge, 1980). He uses the term *ignorance* to denote a situation where not only is it impossible to estimate probabilities of future events, but it is also impossible to enumerate or articulate what these events will be. Given this limitation, the guideline for choice becomes buffering against unforseen contingencies rather than calculation of preferable options. Collingridge identifies several ways to deal with ignorance, involving the *"buying of flexibility, controllibility, corrigibility or insensitivity of performance to error"* (Collingridge, 1980: 141, emphasis in original). His theory and his applications of it to specific controversies make it clear that the policy analyst deals not simply with multiple goals and constraints, but also with unknowns that become qualifications to any recommendation and, ultimately, universal constraints on all but the narrowest policy analysis.

Interdisciplinary teams, a feature of operations research at its beginning, become advisable if the rest of this approach is taken seriously. The value of interdisciplinary thinking is evident in such thorough research programs as the New York City Rand Institute Fire Project (Walker, et al., 1979). That project included, besides specialists in operations research, computer programming, and information systems, specialists in planning, management, statistics, and neighborhood studies. In addition, the project drew on Fire Department officials and an advisory panel. As appreciation of the persuasion task, and ignorance constraints, of policy analysis increases, the advisability of even more diverse project teams will become more evident. Economic pressures of the government contracts business tends to limit diversity in research teams, however (Biderman and Sharpe, 1972). Although no research team can anticipate all contingencies or assume the full range of adversary views, increasing diversity should help keep analyses from becoming too narrowly focused on the technical strengths of the analysts or the political preferences of their sponsors.

This view of method in policy analysis represents an attempt to deal with the two faces of analysis: learning and persuasion. Each face has a different audience. As learning, the audience is the analysts and their sponsors. For this audience analysts can admit, with Gohagan, that it is "completely unrealistic" to expect analysis to produce " 'the answer' " or even an "unequivaocal recommendation" (Gohagan, 1980: 1). As learning, analysis involves the cumulative, shared, formal understandings of similar problems or structures, conjectured, tested, and extended in the instant case.

As persuasion, however, the focus of analysis shifts. The beliefs and resources of the adverse or uncommitted are of interest equal to the phenomena under study. For persuasion, analysis must be presented *as if* it were far less equivocal than the analyst and sponsor know it to be. For the task of persuasion, the "rational decision paradigm" provides a useful and confidence-inspiring format. The paradigm also provides a means of displaying the logical consistency and completeness to analyst and audience alike.

The models and techniques of management science and policy analysis are more readily presented in rational, instrumental terms than they are in terms of learning and persuasion. "Rational" terms will be adopted freely in the rest of this chapter, in spite of the danger that the reader will take these terms as procedural guidelines.

II. CONCEPTS OF MANAGEMENT SCIENCE

Management science offers concepts and mathematical methods useful for configuring confusing data, experiences, and ideas into cumulative, shared intellectual constructs that are helpful for learning and persuading. The resulting intellectual constructs may be new ideas, calculation routines, algorithms, or computer programs. In this section, some of the concepts and techniques will be considered. Taken in the aggregate, these concepts and techniques comprise much of the "methods" available to the policy analyst.

A. Model

The concept of *model* is basic to the methods of management science. Other central concepts for the more formal techniques of management science are optimization, objective function, constraints, parameters, validity, feedback, boundaries, aggregation, trade-offs, sensitivity, and system. Other concepts that could be discussed are numerous. Some, however, will arise in discussions of specific techniques.

Model is the basic notion of management science. In the method outlined in the previous section, it is a model that provides the "strong criteria" and demands the "good data" Wildavsky desires.

Models are "compromises between reality and manageability" (Koreisha and Stobaugh, 1980: 64). Quade sees models as "any procedure that is meant to help a policy or decision maker . . . predict the consequences of prospective courses of action" (Quade, 1980: 31). These definitional statements can be further restricted and analyzed.

Models are simplified representations of some other, referent, system. They are explicit rather than tacit. Particularly for a chapter of this sort, they might be restricted to representations that are explicit enough to be testable. Greenberger et al. offer a definition (1976: 49):

> A formal model of a given reference system is another system expressed in a formal
> language and synthesized from representations of select elements of the reference
> system and their assumed interrelationships.

Sisson sees a model as a way of "abstracting the real world" so that time-dependent as
well as static relations are represented (Sisson, 1975: 7).

Models are composed of variables and relationships. Variables include changing
measures of quantities that vary with time or other condition(s). They also include codes
that identify items in a list or optional states (such as "on–off" or "funded–unfunded")
(Sisson, 1975: 7). "The *relationships* . . . are expressed as procedures for computing the
values of certain variables, given the values of others . . . " (Sisson, 1975: 7).

Greenberger et al. (1976: 54) also distinguish *parameters* and *coefficients.* Both are
constants, in that their values will not change during a given calculation with the model.
Parameters are, however, those constants the values of which are set by the analyst; and
coefficients are constants the values of which must be estimated on the basis of observations.

Sisson identifies four types of variables. His *controllable* and *uncontrollable* variables
correspond to the parameters and coefficients above. *Results or output variables* are normally what we desire to find. *Utility or value variables* represent the values we place on
those results (Sisson, 1975: 8).

This discussion of constituent parts implies, correctly in the view of Greenberger
et al. (1976), that models are distinguished from other aids to thinking by breaking down
phenomena self-consciously into parts and then reassembling the parts into wholes. The
parts are the various variables; identification of these parts is a major task of analysis.
Synthesis involves the assembly of the chosen parts through specification of the relations
among them. It is the self-awareness of the analysis/synthesis process as well as the for-
mality and disconfirmability of the results that distinguish formal from mental models.

Several types of models are useful in management science and policy analysis. Greenberger et al. (1976) discuss schematic, physical, role, and symbolic models. *Schematic
models,* unfortunately, are largely neglected in discussions of policy analysis. The term
refers to pictoral representations, of which blueprints are a familiar example. However,
two other types of pictoral representation should become more familiar. One is *flow
charts* and the other is *arrow diagrams.* Engineers frequently begin an analysis by pictur-
ing seemingly important variables in boxes and drawing causal arrows between pairs of
variables. This is an important first step in *systems dynamics,* a modeling approach associated with Jay Forrester (Roberts, 1978). Flow charts and associated representations
are the basic techniques of classical management analysis. They are used to define the
flow of work, communication, or materials. This widely diffused technology is essential
for organizational control. Many policy-relevant processes can be represented as flow diagrams. Caiden et al. (1978), for example, have analyzed state civil commitment proceedings in terms of flow diagrams. Siegel illustrates flow charting with examples not only
from office forms and materials handling, but also from property acquisition, commodity
marketing in Columbia, and the processing of criminal defendents (Siegel, 1980). Flow
charting is particularly useful because (1) it illustrates temporal sequences, thus inhibits
static analysis; (2) it encourages explicit attention to values of due process in a method
otherwise concerned largely with economic and instrumental values; and (3) it can

produce, in the hands of trained analysts, large amounts of reliable and useful data on operations.

Physical models also play a larger role in policy analysis than generally recognized by those unfamiliar with their special areas of applications. Physical models involve actual physical representations of variables and relationships. The similarity of form of equations for fluid dynamics, electricity, and other transport phenomena allow one physical system to be modeled by another in an analogue computer. Alternatively, a physical system may be modeled by its own miniature. Physical models are particularly common in the study of river basins, tidal estuaries, harbors, and other hydraulic systems (see Greenberger et al., 1976: 79–84). Analogue models are also employed to study ongoing operations such as traffic control, particularly in conjunction with digital computers (Greenberger et al., 1976: 51).

Role-playing models are used particularly for instruction, for identifying possible political options or unpredictable developments, or for systematically eliciting nonformalized inputs.

Symbolic models, particularly those represented mathematically or in computer languages, will be the major focus here. This most important class of models need to be differentiated further for discussion. These distinctions can be applied to the other classes as well, but are clearer here.

The familiar techniques of operations research and the widely discussed large-scale models come in several different varieties. These models may be either *static* or *dynamic*. In dynamic models, time is represented and considered explicitly. Some dynamic models are driven by events (such as arrivals in a waiting line), and some are driven by periods (calculations are performed to represent fixed periods of time) (Greenberger et al., 1976: 57). Static models do not take explicit account of time. Linear programming, for example, need not involve a time variable.

Models may be *stochastic* or *deterministic*. The latter allow the calculation of all outcome variables from known controllable and uncontrollable variables. In stochastic models some of the variables are known only in terms of their probability distributions, thus their values cannot be specified exactly by the analyst. Sometimes, important output variables can be calculated if the probability density functions can be expressed mathematically, but often the mathematics is too complex.

Micro and *macro* models differ in level of *aggregation,* about which more will be said later. The basic distinction is between models based on the behavior of individuals and models based on average or collective properties, properties quite different from those of individual units.

When a formal model cannot be solved mathematically or when the reference system has not yielded a familiar standard model as an adequate representation, analysts turn to simulation models. For this reason, Wagner (1970) introduces his chapter on simulation with the phrase, "when all else fails." Simulations come in too many varieties for easy summary here. Most large scale models are simulation models. The term is hard to pin down, however. One rather broad definition would simply be to stress that the more the parameters and coefficients are manipulated in order to explore the behavior of the model outputs, the more the term simulation is deserved. In a strict sense, otherwise, all models are simulations and it is just the referent system that makes management science simulations different.

B. Features of Models

All models involve *aggregation,* the level of which must be carefully selected. Aggregation is the grouping of quantities with common properties together and treating them as a whole. Particularly when dealing with statistical phenomena, such as birth and death or consumer behavior, aggregation may allow statements that could not be made with any certainty about individuals (House and McLeod, 1977: 159). House and McLeod argue that no system can be understood adequately at a single level of aggregation. Also, models should be developed at a high degree of aggregation first and detail added later as necessary (House and McLeod, 1977: 159–160). A related consideration is *decomposition,* which refers to analyzing a system into relatively noninteracting subsystems. Interactions among subsystems are then modeled in terms of aggregate properties of the subsystems while the subsystems themselves may be represented in greater detail (see Alexander, 1964).

Each model involves a decision about *boundaries,* in two senses. First the analyst must decide what to include and what to exclude. Second, many models involve a division of included variables into *exogenous* and *endogenous.* The latter distinction is often made in terms of interaction frequencies (Siegel et al., 1980: 31). The choice of what to include is a fundamental one. Neglect of important causal factors will preclude adequate prediction with the model. No easy guidelines exist.

Model *validation* implies some comparison with the referent system. Greenberger et al. (1976: 70) argue that validation can never be thorough, and has no uniform procedures. Each model is validated in terms of its adequacy for intended purposes. Comparison of model output with historical data, comparison of model predictions with future events, logical analysis of underlying theories, or exploration of model response to interesting inputs or parameter changes all can serve only to invalidate a model. It is important to emphasize that the ability of a model to predict past outcomes is not validation of the model for future prediction. This is, however, an issue dividing two major schools of modeling, systems dynamics and econometrics (Greenberger et al., 1976).

Some models are *descriptive,* in that they are used largely for exploring relations among variables. Some are *predictive,* in that they are used to project specific consequences and/or future values of important variables. Models are also used for *normative* purposes, for recommending preferable courses of action. *Optimization* models allow the calculation of a best choice, *given specified assumptions and constraints.* The term "optimize" is used very loosely, but should be carefully qualified. An optimum solution or choice need not be a good choice—it is simply the choice that satisfies particular mathematical requirements of a given mathematical model. Only if the model itself is accepted can the choice recommended be credited.

An optimum is either a maximum or a minimum of some function, the function's highest or lowest possible value. In calculus, one takes the first derivative of a function, equates it to zero, and solves for the variable one desires to optimize. The sign of the second derivative reveals whether the optimum is a maximum or a minimum. These determinations are internal to the mathematics. They do not necessarily reveal anything about the referent system. For well-structured problems, and when the validity of the particular model is well established, the identified optima may well be reliable guides to action.

However, far too often, the term "optimum" is used as if it refers not to the model but to the referent system.

In order to calculate an optimum, a model requires an objective function to be optimized. An *objective function* is a mathematical statement of the functional relationship between the desired output (or objective) and the factors that produce it. *Linear objective functions* are found in linear programming, goal programming, and related techniques that are solved by methods of linear algebra. The form of the objective function is given by $Z = aX_1 + bX_2 + \ldots + kX_n$, where Z is the quantity to be optimized, the X's are controllable variables, and $a, b, \ldots, k$ are parameters that represent the contribution of one unit of X_n to the objective, Z. Nonlinear objective functions, if differentiable, may allow easy calculation of an optimum. However, many functions do not yield an easily solved equation. Sometimes, nonlinear functions can be approximated by linear functions in the range of interest, or by successive linear "pieces." There are important conditions for such approximations to be valid, however.

Optimization of linear objective functions is mathematically interesting because of *constraints* on the controllable, or decision variables not present. A constraint is a mathematical function limiting the values that can be assumed by one or more decision variables. For linear models, the constraints are usually expressed as inequalities. For example, a common textbook problem involves a least-cost dietary mix of two or more foods. In such a problem, one food might be subject to the constraint that its amount, X_1, cannot exceed a value of K ($X_1 \leqslant K$). Another might be subject to the constraint that its value, X_2, must be equal to or greater than M ($X_2 \geqslant M$). A third constraint might be that X_1 plus X_2 must be less than or equal to N ($X_1 + X_2 \geqslant N$). Finally, both X_1 and X_2 would have to be greater than zero ($X_1, X_2 > 0$). Constraints can take many functional forms. When they are not linear, the mathematics becomes more complex.

A weakness of standard management science models is their *single-valued objective functions*. Most public problems of interest involve several objectives that must be considered simultaneously. Usually these objectives cannot be reduced to a common denominator. In some situations, analysis can proceed without heroic assumptions. For example, if the problem involves selection from a set of alternatives, and the alternatives can be ranked ordinally with respect to each of several objectives, a "trade-off analysis" can guide the selection of a preferable alternative (Fisher, 1980). *Goal programming* is a linear optimization technique in which goals are ranked, and then satisfied in order. The rankings can then be rearranged and the consequences of this reranking investigated. Sometimes, the original ranking will be replaced (Karwan and Wallace, 1980; McKenna, 1980). The analytical methods of public choice theory (Mueller, 1980) have been developed and refined to deal with problems of conflicting values and political, rather than market, choice.

Essential to the intelligent use of any complex model is *sensitivity testing*. Suing (1980: 171) writes:

> A model is normally tested for sensitivity (1) by determining if realistic changes in the model's components might lead to the selection of another strategy or (2) by determining what changes will be required in order to make another strategy more desirable.

Sensitivity analysis gains importance from the fact that parameters and coefficients are almost never as certain as physical constants. For example, in analyzing a job training program, outcomes are sensitive to the assumed discount rate, the drop-out rate, and long-term unemployment rate (Chapman and Thomas, 1980). For well-developed models such as linear programming, sensitivity analysis follows well-developed patterns (McKenna, 1980: chap. 9; Gohagan, 1980: chap. 16). Particularly, for this model, sensitivity is not simply ad hoc, but rather has a theoretical basis in the *dual theorem* (Wagner, 1970: chap. 5). Sensitivity testing is an idea relevant to any optimization, prediction, or descriptive model, however. The calculation of an optimum solution or other recommended course of action should be seen as an intermediate step in a management science or policy analysis.

C. Summary

The preceding sections hardly exhaust the concepts relevant to methods of policy analysis. Important ideas, such as feedback, have been left for later discussion or for further readings. Here, the attention has been largely on modeling and its attributes. *Model* has been defined generally and types of models discussed. The constituent parts of models have been noted. Essential features of optimization have been outlined. Some aspects of model building, sensitivity testing and validation, have been introduced. Specific types of models have been mentioned in passing. The next section describes a number of specific types in greater detail.

III. SOME REPRESENTATIVE MODELS

Nine methodologies for policy modeling have been articulated by Greenberger et al. (1976: 86–87). Their classification scheme can be adapted here. The types are (1) input-output analysis; (2) linear programming; (3) game theory; (4) probabilistic models; (5) algebraic models other than linear programming; (6) econometric models; (7) microanalytic models; (8) land-use models; and (9) systems dynamics. Discussion here will be restricted largely to (2), (4), (5), (7), and (9). The coverage is necessarily selective.

A different classification is offered by Sisson (1975: 12) on the basis of decision problems. He identifies the following general situations: (1) "waiting for service"; (2) "facilities that wear out"; (3) "items stored for future use" (inventories); (4) "allocation of resources to activities"; (5) "market place distribution"; (6) desirability of further information; and (7) "competition for limited resources."

Buffa and Dyer (1981) group management science models according to the categories of "optimization," "prediction of risk," and "evaluation." The first group includes linear programming, network analysis, integer programming, and inventory models. The second group includes queueing (waiting line), Monte Carlo simulation, and Markov chain models. The final group includes decision trees and utility functions. Only a few specific models or modeling methods can be explored here, however. For the most part, economic models such as benefit-cost analysis will be left for further reading. Decision analysis will be slighted, but see Baird (1978) and Keeney and Raiffa (1976). A promising modeling method not ordinarily discussed is *graph theory*, one of a number of less common discrete mathematical models discussed by Roberts (1976).

In the remainder of this section, several types of models are briefly described.

A. Mathematical Programming

The oldest technique of mathematical programming is linear programming. It was developed independently by Kantorovich in the Soviet Union in 1939, and by Dantzig in the United States in 1947. Both were working on problems of production planning (Greenberger et al., 1976: 93ff). Other techniques of mathematical programming include integer programming, dynamic programming, and network analysis.

Linear Programming. A linear programming problem is one in which several limited resources can be assigned in varying amounts to alternative uses that contribute to a common objective. The objective can be either to maximize return (output) or minimize cost (input). All equations and inequalities must be linear functions, that is, involve terms in which all exponents are equal to unity.

A linear programming problem has decision variables, the levels of the scarce resources, and an objective function relating chosen levels to the objective. It also has constraints that set limits on the values that can be assumed by the decision variables. In addition, a linear programming problem requires the specification of constants relating the contribution of a unit of a resource to the objective desired, and relating a unit of a resource to a given use of that resource (Stokey and Zeckhauser, 1978: 192).

Efficient algorithms have been developed for the solution of linear programming problems. Wagner (1970: 79) could safely assert a decade ago that his readers were not likely ever to solve a linear programming problem by hand. Computer programs exist that can handle several thousand variables and constraints.

Linear programming has been widely applied in business and government. It should be kept in mind that the two sectors share many common problems, and that many policy problems facing government are problems of regulating private sector activity. Accordingly, policy analysts need to understand business applications of linear programming and other management science models. Among the interesting public applications are those for low-cost adequate nutrition and for animal feed mixes; for bussing for racial integration; for sports training; for manpower planning and training; for control of airborne pollutants, for cash management, for nurse scheduling, for planning political campaign efforts, for state budget planning and cutback management; for police patrols; for water pollution control; and for postal operations.[1] Many more applications could be listed, and can be found in modern texts such as Baffa and Dyer (1981), McKenna (1980), or Gohagan (1980).

Integer Programming. Integer programming has been developed to handle problems where the decision variables cannot assume fractional values. Ralph Gomory is credited with discovering an algorithm for solving integer programming problems in 1958 (Greenberger et al., 1976: 103). Integer programming problems are similar to linear programming problems in their setup. Although it may seem that optimization of an integer programming problem can be approximated by a linear programming solution, this is not the case. In some cases, linear programming solutions cannot be rounded to produce even a *feasible* integer programming solution (Buffa and Dyer, 1981: 344). In a *mixed* integer programming problem, only some of the decision variables are restricted to integer values.

This might be the case where, for example, some of the decision variables are numbers of machines or service facilities. One cannot have half a machine or half an office. Facility location and capital budgeting problems are both common applications of integer programming.

Public-sector applications of integer programming are not common. Until recently, computational costs of solutions have been very expensive. No single solution algorithm is generally adequate. Buffa and Dyer recommend using integer models only where the decision variables involve significant unit costs, and note that many integer problems can be solved adequately by network analysis methods (1981: 368).

Dynamic Programming.   Dynamic programming has no standard mathematical formulation. Particular equations must be developed for each situation. Nonetheless, such problems do have common elements, as given by Hillier and Lieberman (1974). Dynamic programming problems are divided into *stages,* each requiring a policy decision. Each stage has a number of alternative *states* associated with it. The stages may be temporal divisions, but could also represent the decomposition of a problem into sequentially solved parts. The states are alternative conditions in which the system might be in a given stage. A *policy decision* transforms "a current state into a state associated with the next stage" (p. 252; italics omitted). The optimal policy for the remaining stages is not dependent on the decisions from the previous stages. Solution proceeds by solving for the last stage first and working backward.

Thierauf says that dynamic programming can be applied to such problems as employment smoothing, scheduling equipment (or facility) overhaul, equipment replacement, and capital investment (Thierauf, 1978: 252). Hillier and Lieberman illustrate it with applications to the assignment of medical teams to countries, and of additional research labor to parallel research efforts in order to reduce the probability of simultaneous failure. These examples suggest many potential applications in governments having major capital facility replacement requirements, for example, for highways, water supply systems, or office complexes.

Goal Programming.   Goal programming introduces multiple objectives. It was developed in the 1960s by A. Charnes and W. W. Cooper (Karwan and Wallace, 1980: 208). Its application to public-sector problems has been led by W. A. Wallace. The basic components of a goal programming model are similar to those of a linear programming model: decision variables, constraints, and numerical coefficients. Additionally, there are *deviational variables,* which measure the positive or negative deviation from each goal or constraint. "Rather than minimizing or maximizing the objective criterion directly in terms of decision variables, the deviations from the prescribed goals are minimized on the basis of priority assignments established by the administrator for each goal or subgoal" (Karwan and Wallace, 1980: 209). McKenna notes that computerized solutions to goal programming are not always available, and that the theory of goal programming is still "relatively young" (McKenna, 1980: 248). Applications have been made to marine environmental protection (Karwan and Wallace, 1980), to university planning, to forest management, and to manpower planning.

Network Analysis Models.   Network analysis models come in two kinds. Both kinds are special cases of linear programming. Buffa and Dyer (1981) call *transhipment models* those network models that are used to analyze distribution systems of origins and destinations. These models can also be used to assign workers to jobs. These models have helpful visual representations. Efficient computer programs are available for their solution (Buffa and Dyer, 1981: 282). *Shortest path models,* in which the path can be time, distance, or cost, are widely used in management. Where the path is measured by cost, these models can be applied to equipment replacement. Where time is used, the models can be used to schedule complex projects. Scheduling applications have a long history in the public sector, particularly in the management of weapons procurement. However, civilian applications are also common in construction management, and Buffa and Dyer (1981: 331) note that these methods have been used for moving a hospital. They also note that many experts feel that the major value of the application of network scheduling models is obtained in their development, not in their solution.

B. Probability Models

Queueing theory, or waiting line models, are the most familiar probabilistic models. These were developed by Morse and others during World War II, based in part on early work by Erlang and others (see the previous chapter, p. 22). Probabilistic models are mathematically complex, something that can be traced in part to the complexity of the density functions used to describe observed frequency distributions.[2] Accordingly, discussion is usually restricted to waiting lines which can be described by easy-to-use distributions, the Poisson and the negative exponential.

Waiting lines are ubiquitous features of life. People wait in lines, but so do forms, telephone calls, work orders, and equipment needing service. The general structure of a waiting line problem has several parts: a population from which arrive customers requiring service (calling population); an arrival distribution; one or more service facilities; a service distribution; a policy determining the order in which arriving customers will be served. Of interest are such descriptive attributes as the average length of the waiting line, the average waiting time, and the proportion of time that the service facility is occupied. Arrival rates often can be approximated by the Poisson distribution, and service times by the negative exponential. For textbook problems, plug-in formulas or easy-to-use tables are available. More realistic situations are handled more readily by simulation on a computer.

Among the decisions that may be considered in the analysis of waiting lines are the cost of waiting time for customers and of idle time for service personnel; the desirability of pooling service facilities or maintaining independent waiting lines; the desirability of adding or deleting service capacity; the desirability of changing the service time, the policy for customer service orders, or service hours; and the benefits of smoothing or otherwise attempting to regulate arrivals. Many of these concerns seem to be with operations rather than with policy at a grand level. Nonetheless, poorly functioning waiting line systems can cause sizable amounts of individual hardship, as when benefit checks are delayed because of processing foulups. Good management can be a very difficult policy to implement.

Many mathematical programming problems can have probabilistic components. Stochastic linear programming models tend to present difficult computational problems, but stochastic dynamic programming models are "*not* much more difficult to solve than their deterministic counterparts" (Wagner, 1970: 375). Probabilistic inventory models are also treated in the literature. In all cases, the mathematics of probabilistic models is very advanced for any beyond pedagogical examples.

C. Systems Dynamics

Systems dynamics is a modeling method developed by Jay Forrester for the analysis of industrial production and later applied by Forrester and his associates to a wide range of social problems (Forrester, 1975). The method got wide publicity with the publication of *Limits to Growth* in 1972 (Meadows et al., 1972). This study forecast a difficult transition to a world of steady-state resource depletion and economics. The method has been criticized frequently but offers some important advantages not readily available in other management science methods. Greenberger et al. (1976), in a thorough review of criticism of systems dynamics models to that time, find much of the criticism to be emotional or based on a poor understanding of the method. Some of this lack of understanding, however, they attribute to the fact that this modeling method is quite different from others.

"Systems dynamics is," according to Roberts (1978: 3), "the application of feedback control systems principles and techniques to managerial, organizational, and socioeconomic problems. Both positive and negative feedback is employed in systems dynamics models to link the variables together into a dynamic (time dependent) system. A system is viewed not as a collection of functional parts, but as a collection of flow processes. The system's structure is instead composed of "sources of amplification, time lags, and information feedback similar to those found in complex engineering systems" (Roberts, 1978: 4) involving the flow and accumulation of "people, money, materials, orders, capital equipment, [and] integrating flows of information."

Feedback always involves the effect of one variable on another in a closed loop and across a time delay. For example, interest rates affect the level of investment in the opportunity affording that rate, which in turn affects the interest rate. These effects are somewhat delayed, rather than instantaneous, as investors will generally have to extract their funds from some other investments, and the interest rates will not be adjusted until some trend in investment is identified. This particular loop is a negative feedback loop, in that the variables adjust in opposite directions: An increase in interest rate will result from decreased investment. Positive feedback loops can also be observed. For example, increased income maintenance benefits may call forth increased numbers of applications, which in turn lead to further pressure for benefit increases; the same may hold for business subsidies.

The time delays are essential to systems dynamics models. Effects can be delayed by a fixed amount or with an average amount but distributed in effect across several periods. When feedback loops involve several, rather than two variables, the delays can become quite complicated, as (illustratively) the delay of the effects of "A" upon "C" involves the delay of the effects of "A" on "B" mediated by the delay of the effect of "B" on "C." These loops can grow to include quite a number of steps, and can become nested into several levels. Roberts writes that, "the longer the time delays 'around the loop' and the less direct the consequences, the more difficulties will be encountered in recognizing feedback structures" (Roberts, 1978: 7). The complexity of feedback in referent systems makes these systems impossible to understand with conventional models, according to the presumptions of systems dynamics.

Systems dynamics models are composed of two main types of variables, levels and rates. *Levels* are the accumulation of flows in and out of some reservoir over time. Inventories, cash balances, housing stocks, labor pools, and populations are all levels. A *rate* is "a flow, decision, or behavior that changes over time as a function of the influence upon it" (Roberts, 1978: 19). Receipts, deliveries, expenditures, hiring, and learning are all rates. The distinction between the two is easily made: Rates disappear when all action stops.

Additionally, a systems dynamics model has *auxiliary variables,* which are nontangible information inputs such as "desired inventory" or "inventory deficiency" (desired minus actual). There are also *constants,* parameters that are not allowed to change during a simulation run.

Systems dynamics models are constructed and run on a computer. They require a special language and compiler, which is made available at a small cost by a firm long associated with systems dynamics modeling. Models are constructed first in terms of block-and-arrow diagrams, then represented in flow charts employing symbols developed for systems dynamics. Finally, relationships are expressed mathematically and programmed in the DYNAMO simulation language.

Systems dynamics does not emphasize historical time series or other extensive data collection. Rather, the emphasis is on articulation of the feedback loops, and their expression in "systems of equations—linear and nonlinear, algebraic and differential" (Roberts, 1978: 5). Systems dynamics is a *continuous* simulation. Sisson writes that in this type of simulation, time is "always advanced in equal steps, small compared to the phenomena under study, and the computations assume that all variables change by a small amount each period" (Sisson, 1975: 18). Many of the variables used in systems dynamics models do not have clear operational referents, and the relationships may not be evaluated statistically in any straightforward manner. Greenberger et al. (1976: 188) write that systems dynamics:

> tends toward the Kantian rationalist school of thought that believed in inescapable structures of knowledge that "transcend" empirical observation. Forrester argues that the best gauge of a model is not how well it reproduces a set of data from the past, but how well its internal structure resembles real mechanisms in the referent system.

Critics of systems dynamics often come from a different epistemological position, that of "logical positivism and Humean empiricism."

Regardless of these epistemological issues, systems dynamics deserves more attention from policy modelers because of its unusual attention to closed-loop feedback and delay consideration. Without more attention to delayed responses and feedback, policy models risk being only elegant calculations.

D. Optimal Control Theory

Another model that deals with time directly is optimal control theory. The mathematics here is advanced, but basic ideas fortunately do not require comparable skill.[3] Optimal control theory comes to policy analysis from enginnering and is related to the calculus of variations. It will be briefly explained through an illustration.

Optimal control theory came to the attention of policy modelers when Pontryagin, a Russian mathematician, developed mathematically more tractable solution methods to dynamic control problems. An early application was to rocket landings. The problem is as follows: Given that you are landing a rocket in a gravitational field, you must use the engines to slow the rocket's fall so that it lands softly. Since weight is expensive in spacecraft, you want to begin with the smallest possible amount of fuel. If you fail to use it properly, two things can happen. Either the fuel will run out before landing, allowing gravity to accelerate the spacecraft into a crash landing, or the fuel will be used too slowly and the spacecraft will not be slowed enough for a soft landing. Optimal control theory deals with problems of this sort.

A more relevant policy problem is posed by the management of fisheries or similar natural resources. The following draws from Peterson and Fisher (1976).

Optimal control problems have a stock variable, a growth function, a decision variable, and an objective function. The stock variable represents the amount of some "stock." In this example, it is the number of the fish species at a given time and location. But the stock could be capital, inventory, some other resource such as timber, or a fuel supply. The growth function represents the natural rate of change of that stock. For example, the growth rate could be a function exclusively of the stock:

$$\frac{d(X)}{d(t)} = g(X) \tag{1}$$

The decision variable relates to intentional changes in the stock: how much capital to invest in a period, how much timber to cut, or, in this example, how much fishing effort to permit. The objective in natural resource examples usually is to maximuze the present value of the resource. In groundwater management, for example, if the price is set too high, the water will not be used and will have little present value. If the price is set too low, the supply will be depleted too quickly for natural replenishment. The analysis, then, should lead to a choice of decision variable *at an instant of time* that maximizes the objective function. Decisions in this kind of model are continuous rather than episodic.

Pontryagin's *maximum principle* (Pontryagin et al., 1962) allows these kinds of problems to be set up in a way that is easy to solve and interpret.

The objective function is a function of the value of the resources extracted minus the cost of extraction, all discounted to present value. Equation (2) represents this objective.

$$Z = \int_0^\infty [P \cdot f(E, X, t) - WE] \, e^{-rt} \, d(t) \tag{2}$$

This objective is subject to a constraint of the growth function:

$$\frac{d(X)}{d(t)} = g(X) - f(E, X, t) \tag{3}$$

In these equations,

P	=	the unit price of the fish
E	=	a measure of fishing effort
X	=	the stock measure
t	=	time
W	=	unit cost of fishing
r	=	discount rate
e^{-rt}	=	the continuous discounting term
$g(X)$	=	natural rate of change in the stock
$f(E, X, t)$	=	the chosen depletion

The equation to be maximized is given by Eq. (4),

$$H = P \cdot f(E, X, t) - WE + q\,[g(X) - f(E, X, t)] \qquad (4)$$

and is called a Hamiltonian. Essentially, the second term of Eq. (4) is the constraint term times a multiplier, (given by Eq. 3), to be interpreted later. Optimization involves taking the partial derivatives of H with respect to E, X, and t. This yields three simultaneous equations, which represent three decision rules. These rules hold at every point in time for which the formulation is valid.

$\partial(H)/\partial(E)$ gives the depletion rate as a function of X and t.

$\partial(H)/\partial(X)$ gives the stock one should have, given E and t.

$\partial(H)/\partial(t)$ yields the value that should be put on the stock at a point in time. The interpretation of this rule is not as clear as the interpretation of the other two. The term q, a constant, is the marginal cost of the next unit of stock added or withdrawn.

The implications of application of optimal control theory to a wide range of public resources is rather astounding. All natural resources, including energy resources, are amenable to this type of model. Population or urban growth management might also be subjects for this model. The model might also be used for planning scarce labor resources such as nurses. Currently, applications outside of natural resources are rare.

E. Microanalytic Models

Whereas macroeconomic models have received a great deal of public attention, microanalytic models have not. Microanalytic models are based on a population of decision units, rather than on aggregated economic sectors and variables. This allows them to consider distributional consequences for the individuals, households, or other decision units of the model (Greenberger et al., 1976: 108). Decision units are represented by "operating characteristics," usually "statistical regression equations that define the probability of a decision unit's taking some step, such as a married couple's deciding to get a divorce or a manufacturing firm's expanding production capacity" (Greenberger et al., 1976: 109). Microanalytic models are dynamic, with forward motion requiring that probabilities be calculated for each period from the "operating characteristics," and then random numbers generated to determine which events occur. Microanalytic models, they note, are time-consuming and expensive for two reasons: The number of decision units requires many calculations; and, because of the amount of variance inherent in the Monte Carlo technique of simulation, simulation runs must be repeated to produce a distribution of outcomes that can be averaged or otherwise analyzed.

Early applications of microanalytic simulation included models of the poor, models of the American electorate, and models of the federal-income-tax-paying population. Greenberger et al. (1976) also trace out the development of income maintenance program models for studies of welfare reform by the Heineman Commission, DHEW, and several research institutes. They note that Daniel Moynihan credits this work with improving the quality of debate on income maintenance reform in the early 1970s. The Social Security Administration also developed a microanalytic model of welfare reform. Pension fund models have been developed at the Treasury Department and the Railroad Retirement Board. Much of this work receives an up-to-date discussion in Havemann and Hollenbeck (1980), a two-volume compendium that also includes papers on models of food stamp policy, the health care sector, and housing. Haveman and Hollenbeck acknowledge substantial diversity in current microanalytic models. Some use historical data from longitudinal surveys, whereas others use constructed data. Some are national and some regional. Some are dynamic, but some primarily estimate the impact of policy changes on a population in a static context (Haveman and Hollenbeck, 1980: xxiv). They also comment on the cost of microanalytic models and note their large opportunity for serious programming and calculation errors. Key parameters are many, and estimates for them may vary significantly, requiring extensive sensitivity analysis. The underlying data, even if taken from high-quality surveys, still leaves much to be desired. In spite of these problems, microanalytic models have established a record of influence in policy controversies that is reflected in the Haveman and Hollenbeck (1980) volumes.

IV. SUMMARY AND CONCLUSION

Any brief exposition of methods of policy analysis must slight both coverage and detail. This chapter has certainly done both, in the interest of presenting some nonstandard views of modeling approaches and some less familiar model types.

The first part of the chapter presented an alternative to the rational paradigm for model building and analysis. This alternative view emphasizes problem formation as an end of analysis rather than as its beginning, and persuasion as a concern throughout the analysis.

The second part of the chapter presented a selection of terms and concepts relevant to models and modeling. The concepts show the diversity of models and the importance of explicitness about model parts. A discussion of sensitivity testing concluded that optimization is an intermediate stage of analysis.

The third part of the chapter presented brief looks at five different types of model: mathematical programming in some of its many forms, probability models, systems dynamics, optimal control theory, and microanalytic simulation. Neglected were econometric models, forecasting techniques and large forecasting models, cost-benefit analysis, decision analysis, and public choice models. Each of these types is considered in one or more of the references for this chapter. Since only some types of models could be discussed, the choice has been to emphasize not only the less familiar but also the model types that promise much for policy analysis. Systems dynamics and optimal control theory, as well as some of the newer wrinkles in mathematical programming, all deserve more attention from policy studies advocates than they normally receive. The analysis of public policy issues should be improved as dynamic models are more commonly employed.

As a methodology for policy analysis, management science offers a much larger repertory of techniques and models than may at first be recognized. Some of these techniques and models are still new and being worked out. The models of management science offer a capability of handling large numbers of variables and large data sets, dynamic features and dynamic control strategies, and demanding precision in specification. The controversy which can engulf management science models is itself a good indication of the benefits they offer. For it is better to recognize and acknowledge error in policy analysis and formulation, than it is to have to correct it once policies are embedded (Collingridge, 1980).

NOTES

1. Most of the items on this list have been drawn from Buffa and Dyer (1981), but similar lists can be compiled by perusing recent professional journals, specialty texts, or bibliographic services.
2. I would be surprised if more than a few social scientists had ever seen the mathematical expression of the beta, F, or Student's-t distributions, for example; see Hillier and Lieberman (1974: 332 and Chapter 8), generally, or any advanced mathematical statistics text.
3. This section is made possible by the generous advice of my colleague, David Weitzel, who bears no responsibility for my errors.

REFERENCES

Alexander, C. (1964). *Notes on the Synthesis of Form.* Harvard University Press, Cambridge, MA.

Baird, B. F. (1978). *Introduction to Decision Analysis.* Duxbury, North Scituate, MA.

Bennis, W. G., Schein, E. H., Berlew, D. E., and Steele, F. I. (1964). *Interpersonal Dynamics.* Dorsey, Homewood, IL.

Biderman, A. D., and Sharpe, L. M. (1972). *The Competitive Evaluation Research Industry.* Bureau of Social Science Research, Washington, DC.

Buffa, E. S., and Dyer, J. S. (1981). *Management Science/Operations Research,* 2nd ed. Wiley, New York.

Caiden, N. J., Pollack, S., and White, M. J. (1978). *Evaluating Civil Commitments: A Policy Case Study.* Regional Institutes in Law and Mental Health, Institute for Psychiatry and Law, Department of Psychiatry, School of Medicine, University of Southern California, Los Angeles, CA.

Chapman, J. I., and Thomas, H. B. (1980). Cost-benefit analysis: Theory and use. In *Managing Public Systems,* M. J. White, T. R. Clayton, R. C. Myrtle, G. B. Siegel, and A. Rose (Eds.). Duxbury, North Scituate, MA, pp. 291–318.

Collingridge, David (1980). *Social Control of Technology*. St. Martins, London and New York.

Fisher, F. (1980). Trade-off analysis. In *Managing Public Systems,* M. White, T. R. Clayton, R. C. Myrtle, G. B. Siegel, and A. Rose (Eds.). Duxbury, North Scituate, MA, pp. 319–335.

Forrester, J. W. (1975). *Collected Papers of Jay W. Forrester*. Wright-Allen, Cambridge, MA.

Foucault, M. (1973). *Madness and Civilization: A History of Insanity in the Age of Reason*. Vintage, New York.

—— (1975). *The Birth of the Clinic*. Vintage Books, New York.

Gass, S. I., and Sisson, R. L. (1975). *A Guide to Models in Government Planning and Operations*. Sauger, Potomac, MD.

Gohagen, J. K. (1980). *Quantitative Analysis for Public Policy*. McGraw-Hill, New York.

Greenberger, M., Crenson, M. A., and Crissey, B. L. (1976). *Models in the Policy Process*. Russell Sage Foundation, New York.

Hartle, Terry W., and Michael J. Halperin (1980). Rational and Incremental Decision Making. In *Managing Public Systems,* M. White, T. R. Clayton, R. C. Myrtle, G. B. Siegel, and A. Rose (Eds.). Duxbury, North Scituate, MA, pp. 125-144.

Haveman, R. H., and Hollenbeck, K. (Eds.) (1980). *Microeconomic Simulation Models for Public Policy Analysis* (2 vols.). Academic, New York.

Hillier, F. S., and Lieberman, G. J. (1974). *Operations Research,* 2nd ed. Holden-Day, San Francisco.

House, Peter W., and John McLeod (1977). *Large Scale Models for Policy Evaluation*. Wiley, New York.

Karwan, K., and Wallace, W. A. (1980). Multiple-objective decision making: The use of goal programming. In *Managing Public Systems,* M. White, T. R. Clayton, R. C. Myrtle, G. B. Siegel, and A. Rose (Eds.). Duxbury, North Scituate, MA, pp. 205–223.

Katz, D. (1963). The functional approach to the study of attitudes. In *Psychology in Administration,* T. W. Costello and S. S. Zalkind (Eds.). Prentice-Hall, Englewood Cliffs, NJ, pp. 250–263.

—— (1963b). Determinants of attitude arousal and attitude change. In *Psychology in Administration,* T. W. Costello and S. S. Zalkind (Eds.). Prentice-Hall, Englewood Cliffs, NJ, pp. 265–274.

Keeney, R., and Raiffa, H. (1976). *Decision Analysis with Multiple Objectives*. Wiley, New York.

Koreisha, S., and Stobaugh, R. (1980). Modeling: Selective attention institutionalized. *Technology Review 83*: 64–66.

Majone, G. (1980). The use of policy analysis. In *Policy Studies Review Annual.* vol. 4, B. Raven (Ed.). Sage, Beverly Hills, CA, pp. 161-180.

March, J. G., and Olson, J. (1976). *Ambiguity and Choice in Organizations*. Universitaatsforlag, Oslo.

McKenna, C. K. (1980). *Quantitative Methods for Public Decision Making*. McGraw-Hill, New York.

Meadows, D., Meadows, D. L., Randers, J., and Behrens, W. W. III (1972). *The Limits to Growth*. New American Library, New York.

Mueller, D. (1980). *Public Choice*. Cambridge University Press, New York.

Nagel, S. S. (1979). Public administration and political science as key elements in policy analysis. In *Improving Policy Analysis,* S. Nagel (Ed.). Sage, Beverly Hills, CA, pp. 91–100.

Nagel, S. S., and Neef, M. (1979). *Policy Analysis in Social Science Research.* Sage, Beverly Hills, CA.

Peterson, F. M., and Fisher, A. C. (1976). The economics of natural resources. University of Maryland.

Pontryagin, L. S., Boltyanskii, V. G., Gamkrelidge, R. V., and Mischenko, E. F. (1962). *The Mathematical Theory of Optimal Processes,* K. N. Trirogoff (Trans.). Wiley-Interscience, New York.

Quade, E. S. (1968). Principles and procedures of systems analysis. In *Systems Analysis and Policy Planning: Applications to Defense,* E. S. Quade and W. I. Boucher (Eds.). American Elsevier, New York, pp. 30–53.

—— (1975). *Analysis for Public Decisions.* American Elsevier, New York.

—— (1980). Pitfalls in formulation and modeling. In *Pitfalls of Analysis,* G. Majone and E. S. Quade (Eds.). Wiley, New York, pp. 23–43.

Roberts, F. S. (1976). *Discrete Mathematical Models with Applications to Social, Biological and Environmental Problems.* Prentice-Hall, Englewood Cliffs, NJ.

—— (1978). Systems dynamics: An introduction. In *Managerial Applications of Systems Dynamics,* E. Roberts (Ed.). MIT Press, Cambridge, MA, pp. 3–35.

Schein, E. H., and Bennis, W. G. (1965). *Personal and Organizational Change Through Group Methods.* Wiley, New York.

Seidman, H. (1980). *Politics, Position and Power: The Dynamics of Federal Organization,* 3rd ed. Oxford University Press, New York.

Shapek, R. A. (1981). *Managing Federalism: Evolution and Development of the Grant-in-Aid System.* Community Collaborators, Chalottesville, VA.

Siegel, G. B. (1980). Seeing the problem systematically: Flow charging. In *Managing Public Systems,* M. White, T. R. Clayton, R. C. Myrtle, G. B. Siegel, and A. Rose (Eds.). Duxbury, North Scituate, MA, pp. 47–85.

Siegel, G. B., Petak, W. J., Rose, A., and White, M. J. (1980). Classical and systems theories. In *Managing Public Systems,* M. White, T. R. Clayton, R. C. Myrtle, G. B. Siegel, and A. Rose (Eds.). Duxbury, North Scituate, MA, pp. 15–46.

Sigler, J. A., and Beede, B. R. (1977). *The Legal Sources of Public Policy.* Heath, Lexington, MA.

Sisson, R. L. (1975). Introduction to decision models. In *A Guide to Models in Governmental Planning and Operations,* S. I. Gass and R. L. Sisson (Eds.). Sauger, Potomac, MD, pp. 1–38.

Stokey, E., and Zeckhauser, R. (1978). *A Primer for Policy Analysis.* Norton, New York.

Suing, David E. (1980). The creation and use of a payoff matrix. In *Managing Public Systems,* M. White, T. R. Clayton, R. C. Myrtle, G. B. Siegel, and A. Rose (Eds.). Duxbury, North Scituate, MA.

Thierauf, Robert (1978). *An Introductory Approach to Operations Research.* Wiley-Interscience, New York.

Wagner, H. M. (1970). *Principles of Management Science with Applications to Executive Decisions.* Prentice-Hall, Englewood Cliffs, NJ.

Walker, W. E. (1979). An introduction to deployment analysis. In *Fire Department Deployment Analysis,* W. E. Walker, J. M. Chaiken, and E. J. Ignall (Eds.). North Holland, New York, pp. 68–99.

White, M. J., Clayton, R., Myrtle, R. C., Siegel, G. B., and Rose, A. (1980). *Managing Public Systems: Analytical Techniques for Public Administrators.* Duxbury, North Scituate, MA.

Wildavsky, A. B. (1979). *Speaking Truth to Power: The Art and Craft of Policy Analysis.* Little, Brown, Boston.

4

Policy Evaluation Methods

Stuart S. Nagel / University of Illinois, Urbana-Champaign, Illinois

Policy evaluation methods can be defined as the set of skills associated with making a determination as to which of various alternative public policies will maximize benefits minus costs in achieving a given set of goals.

Policy evaluation can be thought of as combining the fields of policy analysis and program evaluation. Policy analysis tends to be characterized by association with:

1. Political science and economics
2. Foreign policy, civil liberties, inflation/unemployment, and economic regulation, which are the problems emphasized in political science and economics
3. Policies across places and times
4. Taking goals as givens and determining what policies will maximize or achieve them
5. Evaluating policies before they are adopted

Program evaluation tends to be characterized by association with:

1. Psychology and sociology
2. Health, education, and welfare problems
3. Policies as of a given time and place
4. Taking policies as givens and determining their effects
5. Evaluating policies after they are adopted

The concept of policy evaluation is meant to combine policy analysis and program evaluation across those five dimensions. The field of crime and criminal justice tends to cut across both political science/economics and psychology/sociology. It will frequently be used for illustrative purposes in this chapter.

In defining policy evaluation, we mention maximizing benefits minus costs. That tends to be the overall criterion for judging alternative public policies. It is the overall criterion because maximizing it tends to maximize the favorable change in society's net worth or its assets minus its liabilities as a result of adopting one policy rather than another. Other criteria that are sometimes also considered include:

1. Efficiency (benefits/costs, or costs/benefits)
2. Effectiveness (benefits achieved)
3. Cost saving (costs incurred)
4. Equity (fair distribution of benefits and costs across groups)
5. Elasticity or percentage slope (percent change in benefits/percent change in costs)
6. Marginal rate of return of absolute slope (change in benefits/changes in costs)
7. Detriments/costs
8. Public participation
9. Predictability
10. Procedural due process

Policy evaluation methods tend to fall into five categories:

1. Benefit-cost analysis (optimum choice among discrete alternatives without probabilities)
2. Decision theory (optimum choice with contingent probabilities)
3. Optimum level analysis (finding an optimum policy where doing too much or too little is undesirable)
4. Allocation theory (optimum mix analysis)
5. Time optimization models (optimum choice, level, or mix applied to time minimization)

This chapter is organized in terms of these five sets of skills or methods. Within each of those five sections is a discussion of one or more illustrative examples, interspersed with and followed by relevant general principles.[1]

I. CHOOSING AMONG DISCRETE ALTERNATIVES

The simplest kind of policy evaluation involves a set of discrete alternatives that have no inherent order. That is the case in choosing among alternative legislative redistricting patterns. It is also the case in choosing among alternative ways of providing legal counsel to the poor, and in deciding whether or not to adopt a policy of excluding illegally seized evidence from criminal proceedings.

A. Evaluating Alternative Programs for Delivering Legal Counsel to the Poor

How to provide legal counsel to the poor is a good example of optimum choice without probabilities. There are basically three alternative policies. The poor can be serviced through (1) volunteer attorneys, (2) attorneys who provide services to the poor by way of a government salary, or (3) a judicare system whereby poor people go to private attorneys

Goals	Weights	Policies and relations		
		Volunteer (X_1)	Salaried (X_2)	Judicare (X_3)
Ya. Inexpensive	less (0)	+	–	–
Yb. Visible and accessible	more (1)	–	+	–
Yc. Politically feasible	less (0)	+	–	+
Yd. Specialized competence and aggressive representation	more (1)	–	+	–
Unweighted sum of pluses		2	2	1
Weighted sum of pluses		2–	2+	1–

+ = Yes, relative to the other alternative policies (or 1)
– = No, relative to the other alternative policies (or 0)

Figure 1. Evaluating alternative programs for delivering legal counsel to the poor.

who represent them with the government providing reimbursement. There are basically four criteria for evaluating the policies. The policy chosen should be (1) relatively inexpensive, (2) visible and accessible, (3) politically feasible, and (4) staffed by attorneys who have specialized competence and aggressive representation.

Policy evaluation in this context involves determining (1) the relevant policies, (2) the relevant goals, (3) the relations between the policies and the goals, and (4) the policy that is best in light of those relations. For each goal, we can indicate the policy alternative that is relatively more positive, meaning the alternative that most achieves the goal. These relations are summarized in Figure 1. On being inexpensive, the volunteer system gets a plus, whereas the salaried attorney and especially the judicare system receive relative minuses. On being visible and accessible, the salaried attorney gets a relative plus, with judicare and especially the volunteer attorney system getting relative minuses. On being politically feasible, both the volunteer and judicare systems create no substantial political problems, especially the volunteer system which might thus be scored pluses, but the salaried attorney system has had political problems, which gives it a minus. The salaried attorney system, though, tends to result in specialized competence and more aggressive representation, which gives it a plus, with minuses to the volunteer and judicare systems on that goal.

With that information, one can say that the volunteer and salaried systems seem to be tied, with two pluses apiece. The volunteer system scores well on being inexpensive and politically feasible, whereas the salaried system scores well on being visible/accessible and being specialized/aggressive. To resolve that tie, those goals need relative weights. A conservative evaluator or policy maker would probably place relatively more weight on being inexpensive and politically feasible, and would thus tend to favor a volunteer system. A liberal evaluator would place more weight on being visible/accessible and specialized/aggressive, and would thus tend to favor the government-salaried system. Like most policy analysis, no conclusions can be reached without specifying the relative weights of the goals, even if there is agreement on what the goals are. The policy analyst can, however, clarify what policy is best in light of given goals and value weights. The important thing in this context is that insights can sometimes be obtained concerning what policy is best by working with relations between policies and goals that are expressed in terms of relative direction without specifying the exact magnitude of the relations.

This right-to-counsel problem can be viewed as a problem of determining which policy has the highest score on benefits minus costs, or the highest score by summing algebraically the weighted positive or negative effects of each policy. Each effect can be expressed as a quantity times price relative to each goal. In this context, each quantity is either a 1 or a 0. For example, on being inexpensive, the volunteer system gets a 1 and the other two policies get 0's. In this context, each value or price is also a 1 or a 0. Thus, the value of being inexpensive gets a relative 0 to liberals, and a 1 to conservatives. Thus, each of the three policies (X_1, X_2, and X_3) can be given a total score equal to $(QP)_a + (QP)_b + (QP)_c + (QP)_d$, which shows the benefits or costs that the policy achieves on each of the four goals. The policy that has the highest total score is the best policy, assuming that the Q scores are accurate and that one accepts the value of the P scores. One could probably move without difficulty from a binary 0 and 1 scoring to a rank-order scoring. The Q scores can then receive ranks of 1, 2, or 3, depending on how well each policy scores relative to the other two policies. The P scores can then receive ranks of 1, 2, 3, or 4, depending on how well each goal scores relative to the other three goals.

B. Evaluating Alternative Policies for Increasing Police Adherence to Legality in Searches

The right-to-counsel problem is especially simple because the relations are each expressed as 1's and 0's (or relatively low versus relatively high) and the weights for each goal are also expressed as 1's and 0's (or relatively less or more). The problem of excluding illegally seized evidence from the courtroom is an example of an optimum choice problem in which the relations can take a greater variety of positions. In 1961 the U.S. Supreme Court, in the case of *Mapp v. Ohio,* declared that the fourth amendment required that illegally seized evidence be inadmissible in all American criminal cases, at least when objected to by defense counsel.

In 1963, a mailed-questionnaire survey was made of one randomly selected police chief, prosecuting attorney, judge, defense attorney, and American Civil Liberties Union (ACLU) official in each of the 50 states to determine, among other things, their perceptions of changes in police behavior before and after *Mapp v. Ohio.* The experiment was aided by the fact that 24 of the 50 states had already adopted the exclusionary rule before *Mapp v. Ohio,* and respondents from those states could thus serve as a control group. Twenty-three states were newly forced to adopt the rule at that time, and respondents from those states could thus serve as an experimental group. Three states had partially adopted it, and they were not used in the analysis.

Figure 2 shows that 57 percent of the respondents from the control group of states reported an increase in police adherence to legality in making searches since 1961, whereas 75 percent of the respondents from the experimental group of newly adopting states reported an increase. This 18 percentage point difference cannot be readily attributed to a chance fluke in the sample of respondents, since there is less than a 5-out-of-100

(a) The relation between adopting the exclusionary rule and increased police adherence to legality in making searches

Exclusionary Rule

		Had all along (Control group)	Newly adopted (Experimental group	
Police adherence to legality	Increase since 1961	57%	75%	+18 percentage points difference
	No change	34%	21%	
	Decrease	9%	4%	
	Number of respondents	48	56	104

(b) Alternative policies and goals involved in increasing police adherence to legality in making searches

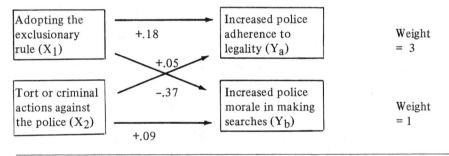

Figure 2. Evaluating alternative policies for increasing police adherence to the legality of making searches.

probability that one could distribute 104 respondents over the six cells in Figure 2 purely by chance and come out with a +.18 relation. This +.18 relation is also not readily attributable to a misperception of reality on the part of the respondents, since there was such a high agreement among the different kinds of respondents from the same state or type of states on the empirical question of police adherence to legality, even though there was great disagreement on the normative question of the desirability of the exclusionary rule. The +.18 relation between newly adopting the exclusionary rule and increased police adherence to legality in searches seems to be attributable largely to the fact that the states that newly adopted the exclusionary rule also disproportionately reported an increase in programs designed to educate the police as to search-and-seizure law, which in turn correlates highly with increased police adherence to legality. States that already had the exclusionary rule also often underwent an increase in police adherence to legality, possibly because of the stimulus of the publicity given to *Mapp v. Ohio*, and because of long-term public opinion trends demanding higher standards of police behavior.

Figure 2b shows the relation between alternative policies and alternative goals involved in the problem of increasing police adherence to legality in making searches. The top part of Figure 2b shows that the exclusionary rule (X_1) should be adopted if increased police adherence to legality (Y_a) is one's only goal, since there is a positive relation between X_1 and Y_a. Many judges and others (including Felix Frankfurter, in his dissenting opinion in *Mapp v. Ohio*) have argued that damages and criminal actions against the police are more effective than adopting the exclusionary rule as a means of increasing police adherence to legality. The questionnaire asked the respondents how often damages or criminal actions had occurred against the police in their communities for making illegal searches. If one divides the respondents into those relatively few who said that there had been at least one such action in recent years versus those who said that there had been none, then there is only a +.05 relation between the occurrence of such actions and increased police adherence to legality. The low relation and the low occurrence of such actions may be attributable to the fact that prosecutors are reluctant to prosecute the police who have been aiding them, and searched individuals are reluctant to sue because of the time, cost, embarrassment, unsympathetic juries, police discretion, and difficulty of assessing collectible damages. Thus, the exclusionary rule (X_1) should be preferred over damages or criminal actions (X_2), if increased adherence to legality (Y_a) is one's only goal, and if the decision maker cannot adopt both policies. This is so because there is a greater positive relation between X_1 and Y_a than there is between X_2 and Y_a.

An additional goal one might have in dealing with the problem of increasing police adherence to legality in making searches is the goal of simultaneously increasing police morale, or at least not decreasing it. The mailed questionnaire asked the respondents about changes in police morale before and after *Mapp v. Ohio*. The relation between being a respondent from a state that had newly adopted the exclusionary rule (X_1) and reporting increased police morale (Y_b) in making searches was -.37. The negative relation may be attributable to the fact that when evidence is thrown out that the police have worked hard to obtain through what they may have considered a lawful search, it is demoralizing to their enthusiasm for making future searches. If the relation between X_1 and Y_b had been positive, like the relation between X_1 and Y_a, then it would be easy to decide in favor of adopting X_1. However, since the relation between X_1 and Y_b is negative, one must decide whether that negative relation is enough to offset the positive relation between X_1 and Y_a. The matter is not resolved simply by noting that the X_1 and Y_b relation is greater than the X_1 and Y_a relation. This is so because it is unlikely that one would weight Y_a and Y_b equally. If the Y_a goal has a weight of three times or more than the Y_b goal, then the -.37 relation would not be enough to offset the +.18 relation in view of the fact that 3 times .18 is greater than 1 times .37. On the other hand, if the Y_a goal has a weight of two times or less than the Y_b goal, then the -.37 relation would be enough to offset the +.18 relation. In other words, if the relation between X_1 and Y_a (times the weight of Y_a) plus the relation between X_1 and Y_b

(times the weight of Y_b) is greater than zero, then X_1 should be adopted if Y_a and Y_b are one's only goals.

The most complicated problem situation involves both multiple policies and multiple goals, but even this situation is simple to resolve conceptually after going through the above problem situations. Suppose that the weight of Y_a is three times greater than the weight of Y_b as determined by a survey of public, legislative, or judicial opinions. Note also that the relation between the occasional occurrence of damages or criminal actions against the police and increased police morale was -.09. Thus, the exclusionary rule (X_1) should be preferred over damages or criminal actions (X_2), if increased adherence to legality (Y_a) and increased police morale (Y_b) are one's only goals, and if the decision-maker cannot adopt both policies. This is so because, in Figure 2, +.18 × 3 plus -.37 × 1 is greater than +.05 × 3 plus -.09 × 1. In other words, .54 plus -.37 is greater than +.15 plus -.09.

The weight of each goal can be considered a price. The regression coefficients between each policy and each goal can be interpreted like a marginal rate of return (MRR), or a quantity of goal units to be achieved as a result of a one unit increase in the policy. Thus, the total revenue from policy X_1 is equal to P times Q on goal Y_a, and the total cost from policy X_1 is equal to P times Q on goal Y_b. The relation between X_1 and Y_a is a benefit, since the MRR or Q is positive, but it is a cost on Y_b since the MRR or Q there is negative. To compare X_1 with X_2, one logically compares the benefits minus costs that each policy produces. Instead of talking in terms of benefits and costs, one could simply talk in terms of effects. Policy X_1 has some positive effects and some negative effects. One can determine the algebraic sum of the positive effects (P × Q for Y_a) and the negative effects (P × Q for Y_b). One can do likewise for X_2, and then compare the net effects of X_1 and X_2 to determine which is better if they are mutually exclusive, or which is more profitable if they can both be adopted.

One can determine the relative value of one goal versus another by conducting a survey of relevant segments of the public or the government, or by doing a content analysis of relevant commentators. One can also attempt to relate each goal to a higher goal and use those relational coefficients to indicate the relative value of the intermediate goals. One can also tentatively use the values of the researcher, supplemented by a sensitivity analysis to show how the conclusions would change with other values.[2]

II. MAKING DECISIONS UNDER CONDITIONS OF RISK

Sometimes one cannot simply decide among alternative policies by picking the policy that scores best on benefits minus costs, because the benefits and/or the costs are contingent on the occurrence of some event. The benefits and/or the costs then have to be discounted or multiplied by the probability that the event will occur. This may be the case for an administrative agency in deciding whether or not to gather certain data for future reference.

A. Data Gathering as an Example

Virtually everyone is probably opposed to excessive gathering of data by federal agencies. The key issue on that subject, however, is what is "excessive"? One purpose of this

Alternative decisions	Data would not be used (1–P)	Data would be used (P)	Expected benefits and cost
Gather the data (g)	C_g –10 Costs of gathering unused data	B_g +100 Benefits of gathering used data	$(B_g)\,(P) + (C_g)$ $(+100)\,(.60) + (-10) = +50$
Do not gather the data (n)	B_n +10 Costs saved by not gathering unused data	C_n –100 Benefits missed by not gathering used data	$(B_n)+(C_n)(P)$ $(+10)+(-100)(.60) = -50$

Abbreviations: P = probability of use; B = benefits, C = costs, g = gathering the data,
n = not gathering the data.

Rules for applying the above figure:
1. Determine the alternative decisions (i.e., what is the data to be gathered or not gathered). One can have multiple rows.

2. Determine the alternative occurrences (i.e., what is the potential use that will occur or not occur). One can have multiple tables.

3. Determine the ratio of the costs of gathering the data to the benefits of gathering the data, but ignore the positive and negative signs.

4. If P is greater than that ratio, then gather the data. If less, do not gather the data.

Alternatives to Rules 3 and 4:
3. Determine the probability that the data will be used.

4. If the cost/benefit ratio is greater than that probability, then gather the data. If less, do not gather the data.

Figure 3. Deciding whether or not to gather data that may or may not be used.

example is to try to give that concept some operational meaning. The meaning should make sense in light of the expected benefits and costs of gathering or not gathering data. "Expected" benefits and costs refer to the benefits and costs of using (or not using) the data, discounted by the probability of their being used (or not used). In other words, this is a decision problem under conditions of risk or uncertainty. As such, we may be able to gain some substantial insights into what is involved by analyzing the problem in terms of a simple decision theory table.

Figure 3 provides a decision theory table for analyzing a data-gathering problem. There are basically two alternatives available. One either gathers the data or a certain amount, or one does not gather the data. We could, however, make things more complicated by talking in terms of gathering multiple quantities or percentages of data, and thus have many rows in our table. Such an extension can logically be made after clarifying the simpler choice between two alternatives. Likewise, there are basically two outcome possibilities. Either the data get used in a certain way, or they do not get used. Again, we could later complicate things by talking in terms of multiple uses, with a separate expected benefit for each use.

With two alternative decisions and two alternative occurrences, there are four possible outcomes. Two are clearly undesirable or costly, namely, to gather the data and not have it used (cell C_g), or not to gather the data when it would have been used if it had been gathered (cell C_n). Two outcomes are clearly desirable or beneficial, namely, to gather data that subsequently gets used (cell B_g), and not to gather data that would not have been used if it had been gathered (cell B_n). Of the two undesirable outcomes, it is normally worse not to gather data that would have been used, although sometimes the other undesirable outcome may be worse.

If cell C_n is considered the worse of the two costs, then for convenience we can anchor it at a value of –100. For the sake of consistency, we could then also anchor cell B_n at +100 as the better of the two beneficial outcomes. Now all we have to do is determine how many times worse a cell C_n outcome is as compared to cell C_g. If failing to gather needed data in a given situation would be 10 times as bad or as costly as gathering the data and not having it used, then the value of cell C_g on our scale of –100 to +100 would be –10. Likewise, for the sake of consistency, the value of cell B_n would be +10. In this context, many people would find it simpler to work with the benefit/cost ratio of 100/10, or 10/1. Likewise, instead of talking in terms of a scale of 0 to 100, or 1 to 10, one could insert dollar amounts (or other units) into the cells for the benefits and the costs.

Now, with that information for our hypothetical situation, we can determine the expected values of gathering or not gathering the data. The expected value of gathering the data equals (+100) (P) + (–10), where P is the probability that the data will be used. In other words, the expected value of gathering the data equals the benefits and the costs of the gathering, discounted by the probabilities of the benefits and costs occurring. Likewise, the expected value of not gathering the data equals (+10) + (–100) (P), which equals the benefits and the costs of not gathering, discounted by their respective probabilities. Note that the cost of gathering the data is not discounted by any probability, since we must bear that cost when the data is gathered regardless of whether or not it is used. Likewise, we save that cost when we do not gather the data regardless of whether or not the data would have been used. We could take into consideration an amount for embarrassment cost, which would have to be discounted by 1 – P, since it is incurred only if the data are not used.

Logically, what we now want to do is to determine how high P has to be before the expected value of gathering the data will exceed the expected value of not gathering the data. To do that, all we have to do is set those two expected values equal to each other and solve for P. Doing so will give us the threshold probability above which we should gather the data and below which we should not gather the data. One can show algebraically that the threshold value of P (or P*) equals C_g/B_g, ignoring the plus and minus signs. That means the threshold probability with this data is 10/100 or .10. In other words, if there is better than a .10 probability that the data will be used, then we should gather it. Otherwise, it's not worth the trouble.

The above analysis can be applied without requiring users to be capable of translating costs or benefits into dollars, satisfaction units, or any kind of absolute units. All the users have to do is determine which of the two undesirable outcomes is more undesirable, and the rough ratio of the undesirability of the more undesirable outcome to the less undesirable outcome, taking the facts of the specific situation into consideration. Users can then apply the simple formulas of C_g/B_g or the cost/benefit ratio to determine the threshold probability. They should then ask whether the actual or perceived probability in this specific situation is greater or less than the threshold probability. If it is greater, gather the data; if it is less, don't.

B. Variations on the Basic Example

If the cost of gathering the data is greater than the benefits even before the benefits are discounted by the probability of their occurring, then we of course would not want to gather the data no matter how high the probability is that the data will be used.

The same type of analysis could also be used to determine what the cost/benefit ratio has to be in order to justify gathering the data. Suppose we know that the data has a .60 probability of being used. We have previously determined that the threshold probability is equal to the cost/benefit ratio. Therefore, if P equals .60, the cost/benefit ratio has to be less than .60 to justify gathering the data. If the cost/benefit ratio is greater than .60 and there is only a .60 probability of the data being used, the data should not be gathered.

This alternative type of analysis provides us with an alternative definition of "excessive" data gathering. It is excessive or nonrational to gather data where the opportunity cost of not gathering data that would be used is less than R^* times as great as the cost of gathering unused data. In that definition, R^* is the threshold ratio between the C_g and B_g costs when we know or think we know what the probability is of the data being used.

Another use of this type of analysis is to suggest that if we want to make data gathering more rational, we should concentrate on doing one of three things. First, we should try to increase the probability (P) that the data will be used, possibly by increasing its visibility. Second, we should try to decrease the relative cost of gathering data (C_g), possibly by providing for more automatic data-gathering routines. Third, we should try to increase the benefits of gathering the data when the data could have been used (B_g), possibly by providing more opportunities or ways in which data can serve as inputs into governmental decision making.

Still another set of insights that this type of analysis might generate is a better appreciation of the value of data gathering. That purpose is harder to justify than the above-mentioned purposes, which logically follow from the simple logic of the decision theory table. Saying that the table is supportive of data gathering is based on a feeling that if the analysis is applied, one will generally discover that the threshold probability (P^*) does not have to be very high (relative to reality) to justify most data gathering, given the relative costs of the cell C_g and B_g outcomes. Likewise, the threshold ratio (R^*) of Cell C_g to B_g probably does not have to be very high (relative to what it is likely to be in most factual situations) to justify gathering the data in question, given the probability of the data being used.

C. Other Purposes and Examples

The same type of analysis can be applied to a great variety of administrative and policy problems that involve decision making under conditions or risk. The problems can be classified in various ways. One classification emphasizes the purpose of the analysis, although that same classification could be applied to other policy evaluation methods. One purpose is to aid in making decisions. That purpose is illustrated by the above example of whether or not to gather data for future reference. A second purpose is to influence decisions. That purpose can be illustrated by applying the above analysis to a would-be wrongdoer who is trying to decide whether to violate an administrative regulation in light of the probability of being detected, adjudicated as a wrongdoer, and negatively sanctioned (P), the error costs of committing the violation and being negatively sanctioned (A), and the error costs of not committing the violation when one could have gotten away with it (B). That analysis tells us that if we want to reduce violations of administrative regulations, we should develop means of increasing P, increasing A, and decreasing B. If we can evaluate P, A, and B numerically, we can calculate a threshold probability (P*) and a threshold trade-off ratio (R*) between A and B.

A third purpose is to make predictions rather than to make or influence decisions. That purpose can be illustrated by the example of trying to predict nonhearing settlements of workers' comepnsation cases or other kinds of claims. The claimant is likely to settle if the defendant offers more than the claimant's perception of the expected value of going through a hearing. That expected value equals the perceived award (A_1), discounted by the probability of the claimant winning the hearing on the liability issue (P_1), plus a discount that the claimant is willing to take off to avoid the expense of a hearing (X_1). Likewise, the defendant is likely to settle if the plaintiff is willing to accept less than the defendant's perception of the expected value of going to a hearing. That expected value equals the defendant's perception of the award (A_2), discounted by the probability of the claimant winning (P_2), plus a bonus that the defendant is willing to add on to avoid the expense of a hearing (X_2). One can predict the effect of system changes on the direction and possibly the magnitude of the likelihood and level of a settlement by knowing how these system changes influence A_1, P_1, X_1, A_2, P_2, and/or X_2.[3]

III. MAKING DECISIONS WHEN DOING TOO MUCH OR TOO LITTLE IS UNDESIRABLE

A common public policy problem involves deciding how much of a policy to adopt when doing too much or too little may be undesirable. That kind of optimum level analysis can be illustrated with the problems of arriving at an optimum level of delay in administrative or judicial proceedings.

A. Measuring Delay Costs in Finding an Optimum Delay Level

Delay is a common problem in public administration, including judicial administration. Delay can sometimes be reduced through better allocation of resources, better sequencing

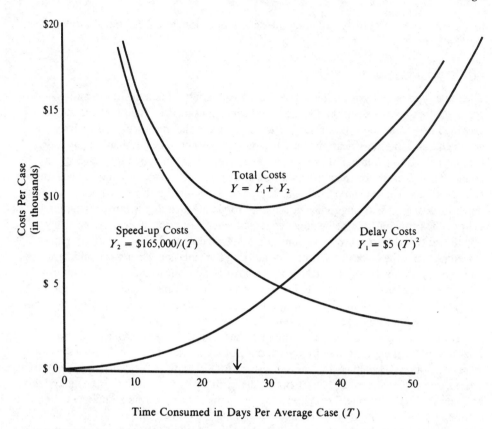

Figure 4. Finding an optimum level of delay in judicial administration. [From S. Nagel and M. Neef (1980), "Time-oriented models and the legal process: Reducing delay and forecasting the future," *Washington University Law Quarterly*, pp. 467–527.]

of the way in which cases are heard, the use of a decision theory perspective to influence decision makers to make time-saving rather than time-lengthening decisions, and other management science methods. Before reaching any decisions on how to reduce delay, it might be desirable to determine the level of delay that one should seek to achieve. One approach to doing this is to determine how fast it is possible to process whatever is being processed. That kind of approach can be referred to as *capability analysis,* because it emphasizes what one is capable of doing, regardless of the benefits or costs. One can determine how fast cases could be processed by looking to see how fast they have been processed at prior times, how fast they have been processed by other agencies, or by setting the average time as the time that all cases should take after adjusting for some measures of complexity.

Optimum level analysis represents an alternative approach. It recognizes that sometimes the speed-up costs may be greater than the delay costs, such that we may be better off with some delay. Optimum level analysis in the context of optimum time consumption is designed to determine the optimum level of delay in the sense of minimizing the sum of the delay costs (Y_1) and the speed-up costs (Y_2). Figure 4 shows what is involved in optimum level analysis for a hypothetical metropolitan court system. To apply the analysis, we need to develop an equation showing the relation between delay costs and time consumed. A survey and an accounting analysis might show that every extra day of time consumed in completing a criminal case is worth about $7 per jailed defendant to the system. The $7 represents waste in holding those defendants in jail who will receive an acquittal, dismissal, or probation when their case is tried. Of that $7, about $2 represents wasted jail maintenance costs, and $5 represents lost gross national product (GNP) that could have been earned. The $2 is calculated by noting that it costs $6 per day to maintain a defendant in jail, and one-third of them receive nonjail dispositions upon trial, meaning that $2 per day is wasted by delaying the nonjail disposition. The $5 is calculated by noting that defendants can earn about $15 a day if they are not in jail, and that about one-third of them would not be in jail if their acquitted or dismissed cases came up sooner, meaning that an additional $5 per day is wasted by delay.

There might also be about $3 per day wasted per released defendant. The $3 represents waste in releasing those defendants who will be jailed when they are eventually tried and convicted, but who during the delay commit a crime or have to be rearrested for failure to appear in court. That $3 is determined by calculating (1) the crime-committing cost or the rearresting cost for the average released defendant, (2) multiplied by the low probability of the occurrence of crime-committing or rearresting, (3) multiplied by the middling probability of being convicted and jailed if the case were to come to disposition, and (4) divided by the number of days released. If we assume that half the arrested defendants are jailed and half are released, then the $7 delay cost per day per jailed defendant becomes $3.50, and the $3 delay cost per day per released defendant becomes $1.50. Thus the total cost per day per case would be $5 (or $3.50 plus $1.50). If the $5 per day were a constant figure, we could say delay costs (Y_1) equal $5 times T days, or $Y_1 = \$5(T)$.

Since the likelihood of crime committing and the need for rearresting increase as delay increases, the relation between Y_1 and T might be better expressed by an equation of the form $Y_1 = \$5(T)^2$. That equation tells us that when T is 1 day, Y_1 is $5; but when T is X days, Y_1 is not $5 times X, but rather Y_1 increases at an increasing rate. More specifically, as T goes up 1 percent, Y_1 goes up 2 percent. The values of the multiplier of T and the exponent of T can be determined by performing what is known as a log-linear regression analysis if one has data showing for a set of cases (1) how much time was consumed by each case, (2) how much each case roughly costs in terms of jail maintenance and lost GNP for those held, and crime committing and rearresting costs for those released, and (3) the proportion or probability of cases in which nonjail sentences were handed down and the proportion of crime committing and rearresting of released defendants.

B. Measuring Speed-up Costs in Finding an Optimum Delay Level

The more time that is consumed, the higher the delay costs become at a possibly increasing rate. However, the more we rush cases to a disposition, the greater the speed-up costs might be. These costs mainly include the monetary cost of hiring additional personnel or introducing new facilities or procedures. Suppose that either through deductive queueing theory or through the compilation of empirical data, we find that with only 20 judges, cases average 75 days per case; with 40 judges, 38 days; with 60 judges, 25 days; with 80 judges, 19 days. We can meaningfully assume that with zero judges, the number of days would rise to infinity, and in order to get the number of days down to zero, we would have to have an infinite number of judges.

The speed-up costs curve shown in Figure 4 incorporates that data and those assumptions. A curve of that kind can be expressed by the equation $J = a/T$, where J stands for the number of judges, and T stands for time in days per average case. If $J = a/T$, then $T = a/J$. The a in the $J = a/T$ equation is the number of judges needed to get time down to 1 day per case (i.e., $T = 1$), and the a in the $T = a/J$ equation is the number of days consumed when there is only one judge (i.e., $J = 1$), if the relationships are carried out to their logical extremes even though at the extremes the empirical data does not apply. From the above data and a computerized regression analysis, we can determine that $a = 1500$. This means, according to our data, that $J = 1500/T$ and $T = 1500/J$.

Instead of talking in terms of the relation between the number of judges and the number of days consumed, we should be talking in terms of the cost of judges and the number of days consumed. If one judge costs \$40,000 a year, that means \$110 per day for a 365-day year. Thus the equation $J = 1500/T$ should be changed to $Y_2 = \$165,000/T$. The Y_2 is the speed-up costs or the additional judge costs, and the \$165,000 is simply \$110 times the previous a (also called the scale coefficient) of 1500 to show we have increased the scale by \$100 per judge per day. Our equation of $Y_2 = 165,000/T$ is algebraically the equivalent of the equation shown in Figure 4 of $Y_2 = 165,000(T)^{-1}$. This equation perfectly fits the above data, although in real life the equation fitting might provide a good fit, but not a perfect fit.

C. Minimizing the Sum of the Costs

Given the relationship between delay costs and time consumed of $Y_2 = \$5(T)^2$ and the relation between speed-up costs and time consumed of $Y_1 = \$165,000 (T)^{-1}$, the relation between total costs (Y) and time consumed is logically $Y = \$5(T)^2 + \$165,000(T)^{-1}$. We are now ready to calculate the optimum level of time consumed, which is graphically the value of T where the total costs curve hits bottom. Doing so involves recognizing that the total cost curve has a negative slope before it hits bottom, a positive slope after it hits bottom, and a zero slope when it bottoms out. Therefore, what we need to know is what is the slope of Y to T. We can then set that slope equal to zero and solve for T. In elementary calculus, one learns that in an equation of the form $Y = aX^b$, the slope of Y to X is baX^{b-1}. Therefore, in our total cost equation, the slope of Y to T is (2) (\$5) $(T)^{2-1}$ + (-1) (\$165,000) $(T)^{-1-1}$. If we set that expression equal to zero and solve for T, we get $10(T) - 165,000/(T)^2 = 0$, or $T = (16,500)^{.33}$, which means $T = 25$ days where the total costs hit bottom.

This means that 25 days or about one month is the optimum level of time consumption in order to minimize the sum of the delay costs and the speed-up costs as we have calculated them. We could also say that the optimum level of judges to have is 60 judges, since $J = 1500/T$, or $60 = 1500/25$. This means that our court system would be minimizing its total costs if we have about 60 full-time judges. We could make this optimum level analysis more accurate by taking into consideration that speed-up costs (Y_2) may only be accurately indicated as a combination of the cost of judges, prosecutors, public defenders, other personnel, courtrooms, and other costs, rather than just judges. The methodology, however, is basically the same, namely, (1) obtaining empirical equations relating speed-up costs to time and delay costs to time, (2) finding the slope of the sum of those two equations, (3) setting that slope equal to zero and solving for T to determine the optimum number of days per average case for minimizing total costs, and (4) thereby indirectly determining the optimum number of judges, prosecutors, public defenders, other personnel, courtrooms, and other costs.

D. Other Examples

Optimum level analysis can be applied to a great variety of administrative problems where doing too much or too little is undesirable. The same general model and methods can be used to obtain a better understanding of how much due process should be provided in administrative proceedings. By "due process" in this context we mean safeguards for the innocent, such as rights to have an attorney, present witnesses, cross-examine one's accusers, receive reasons for the decisions reached, be able to take an appeal, and other such rights. If too much due process is provided, it may become too difficult to establish wrongdoing where wrongdoing has occurred. If, however, too little due process is provided, it may be too easy to establish wrongdoing where wrongdoing has not occurred. Along related lines, optimum level analysis has been applied to attempting to determine an optimum jury size. With large juries, prosecutors may be unable to obtain unanimous convictions of too many truly guilty defendants, whereas with small juries, prosecutors may be able to obtain unanimous convictions of too many truly innocent defendants.

The same general model and methods can also be used to obtain a better understanding of how much enforcement should be applied in administrative regulation. By "enforcement" in this context, we mean how much money might be spent to secure compliance with administrative regulations, how severe the negative sanctions, fines, or jail sentences might be, or how high the standards of compliance might be set. If too much compliance is demanded, the enforcement costs may exceed the benefits. If too little compliance is demanded, great damage might be done that could have been prevented, as for example in the field of environmental regulation. To be more specific, demanding zero water pollution with regard to biodegradable wastes may be extremely expensive, with little harm done from small amounts of such pollution. On the other hand, allowing water pollution to the extent it was allowed prior to 1970 may jeopardize public health, commercial fishing, water recreation, industrial water uses, and other water uses, when only a small effort could have made a big difference. Optimum water pollution is thus somewhere between zero pollution and 100 percent pollution. Likewise, the optimum level of jail sentences for wrongdoers is somewhere between zero and life imprisonment. Excessively long sentences involve high holding costs of defendants who may no longer be dangerous and no longer serve as a deterrent example. Excessively short sentences involve high releasing costs of defendants who may still be quite dangerous and who if released early can represent a missed opportunity to deter others.

The a and b parameters in the equations of the form $Y = aX^b$ can be determined by statistical regression analysis, surveying knowledgeable people, deducing from accepted premises, or making reasonable assumptions. If knowledgeable people are surveyed, they should be asked questions that are relatively easy to answer, such as: "If there is a 100 percent increase on X (i.e., a doubling of X), then by what percent do you think Y would increase or decrease?" Likewise one can ask: "If X were only one unit, then how much of Y do you think there would be?" The first question aids in arriving at a value of b, and the second question aids in arriving at a value for a. If assumed values are used, then show for various values of b or a how X^* would change.[4]

IV. ALLOCATING SCARCE RESOURCES

Another common policy problem involves allocating a budget of dollars or effort across various activities or places. That kind of optimizing analysis can be illustrated by allocating the budget of the Legal Services Program of the Office of Economic Opportunity to various activities, or by allocating the budget of the Law Enforcement Assistance Administration to various places.

A. Allocating Legal Services Dollars to Activities

In 1970, the Auerbach management consulting firm was asked to develop teams of attorneys and other persons to evaluate the approximately 200 Office of Economic Opportunity (OEO) legal services programs across the country. Each program was evaluated on 113 different dimensions. The 114th dimension referred to overall satisfaction of the evaluators. That dimension was scored on a scale from 1 to 12, with a 1 being as bad as possible, a 12 being as good as possible, and a 7 being acceptable. A key controversy in providing legal services to the poor has been how to allocate time, effort, and money between routine case-handling and law reform work. Law reform mainly involves taking appeals designed to establish new precedents with regard to enforcing the legal rights of the poor. The percent of the budget devoted to law reform was determined for each legal services program, with the complement of that percent being devoted to routine case handling. Those percentages were then translated into dollars per client, and a statistical analysis was made to determine the relation between satisfaction and expenditures for law reform and case handling.

The average legal service agency spent $68.34 per client, of which $6.16 went to law reform and $62.18 went to case handling. The average agency also received a satisfaction score of only 6.51, just below the acceptable level. We can plot on a three-dimensional surface a dot for each legal service agency showing (1) its satisfaction score, (2) its law reform expenditures per client, and (3) its case-handling expenditures per client. We can then fit a line or a plane to those dots in order to minimize the squared distances from the dots to the line. Doing so produces results like those shown in Figure 5. The top left of the figure shows that as law reform expenditures increase, satisfaction also increases. When there is an increase of $1 for law reform per client in the average legal services agency, satisfaction scores go up one-third or .34 of a unit. On the other hand, there is virtually no relation between an increase in case-handling dollars and an increase in satisfaction. The top right of the figure shows that as case-handling expenditures increase by $1, satisfaction goes down by .03 of a unit, which amounts to almost no change.

Given this information, how would one logically allocate the $68 budget of the average legal services agency between those two activities? If there were no minimum or maximum constraints on law reform or case handling, one would allocate the whole $68 to

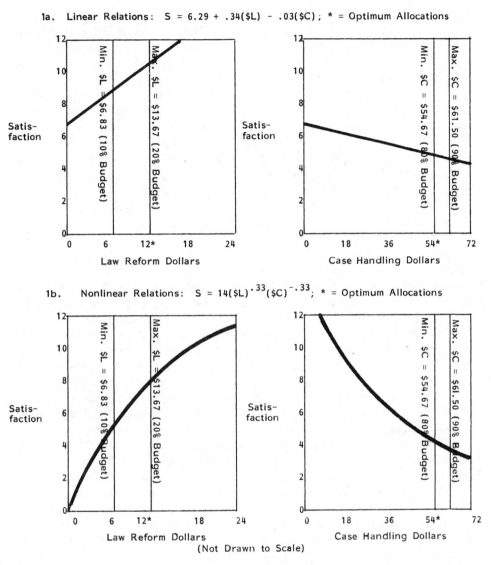

1a. Linear Relations: $S = 6.29 + .34(\$L) - .03(\$C)$; * = Optimum Allocations

1b. Nonlinear Relations: $S = 14(\$L)^{.33}(\$C)^{-.33}$; * = Optimum Allocations

(Not Drawn to Scale)

Figure 5. Allocating legal service dollars across activities. S = Satisfaction score of each legal services agency as determined by a team of evaluators; $L = dollars allocated to law reform activities, as determined by multiplying the total agency budget by the percent spent on law reform and dividing by the number of clients; $C = Dollars allocated to routine case handling activities, as determined by multiplying the total agency budget by the percent spent on case handling and dividing by the number of clients.

law reform, since it has a higher marginal rate of return than case handling in producing additional satisfaction per incremental dollar. The Office of Economic Opportunity, however, had issued evaluation guidelines that imply legal service agencies should spend no more than about 20 percent of their budget on law reform, and no less than 10 percent. That means expenditures for case handling should be no more than 90 percent of an agency budget, and no less than 80 percent. If those constraints are imposed on the two graphs in the upper part of Figure 5, one can readily see that the optimum allocation to law reform dollars would be 20 percent of the $68 budget, and the optimum allocation to case-handling dollars would be 80 percent of the $68 budget. In other words, when one assumes linear relations between policy inputs and goals for different activities, one should allocate all the budget to whatever activity has the best slope or marginal rate of return up to whatever maximum constraint needs to be recognized, and then switch to the next to the best activity, and so on. Before making those allocations, however, one should give each activity whatever the minimum constraints provide for.

The lower part of Figure 5 involves a more realistic fitting of curves to data. It recognizes that as one increases the policy inputs, satisfaction may increase, but probably at a diminishing rate of increase (rather than a constant rate), as shown in the lower left. Likewise, the lower right part of the figure recognizes that as one increases an input that lowers satisfaction, the decrease is also likely to occur at a diminishing or plateauing rate, rather than a constant rate. The numerical parameters for the nonlinear equation can be obtained through the same kind of statistical analysis that is used to obtain the numerical parameters for the linear equation, except that one instructs the computer to arrive at a best-fitting curve rather than a straight line. In this context, recognizing those diminishing returns does not affect the optimum allocation. This is so because case handling has a slightly negative marginal rate of return (MRR), and law reform has a positive MRR. Thus one would want to give the maximum possible to law reform and the minimum possible to case handling, regardless of whether the relations are linear or nonlinear.

If, however, case handling would have produced a positive-shaped curve like that in the lower left corner, but not rising so high, then the optimum allocation might have involved giving less than the maximum to law reform and more than the minimum to case handling. If we give the maximum to law reform, we may be wasting some of our money as we approach that maximum where the law reform curve gets relatively flat, relative to the beginning part of the case-handling curve or the part just above the case-handling minimum. Although the law reform curve may be steeper at any given dollar figure than the case-handling curve, the law reform curve may not be steeper at its maximum constraint than the case-handling curve is at its minimum constraint. Under those circumstances, the optimum allocation would involve first giving each activity its minimum allocation, which is $6.83 for law reform and $54.67 for case handling, or a total of $61.50. The remaining $6.84 should then be allocated to the two activities in proportion to their elasticity coefficients. That means that when the relation between satisfaction, law reform, and case handling is $S = a(\$L)^b(\$C)^B$, then law reform should receive $b/(b + B)$ part of $6.84, and case handling should receive $B/(b + B)$. One can prove algebraically that with both those nonlinear relations being positive (i.e., having positive exponents), the optimum allocation involves allocating in proportion to those exponents after satisfying the minimum and maximum constraints.

	Crime Occurrence (Y)			Anticrime Dollars (X)		
State	1972	1970	Change	1972	1970	Change
Wisconsin	10	20	−10	$35	$15	$20
Illinois	60	100	−40	$75	$25	$50

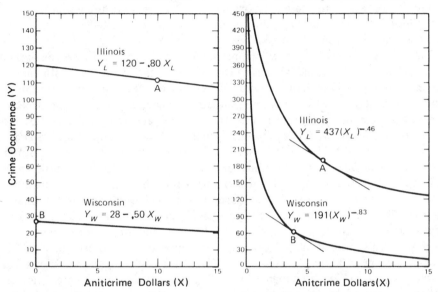

Point A is the point of otpimum allocation to Illinois.

At that point in the linear graph:
X = $10, Y = 112 crimes, slope = −.8

At that point in the nonlinear graph:
X = $6.21, Y = 189 crimes, slope = −14.
Tangent line is $Y_L = 276 - 14X_L$

Point B is the point of optimum allocated to Wisconsin.

At that point in the linear graph:
X = $0, Y = 28 crimes, slope - −.5

At that point in the nonlinear graph:
X = $3.79, Y = 63 crimes, slope = −14.
Tangent line is $Y_W = 116 - 14X_W$

Figure 6.   Allocating anticrime dollars across places.

B. Allocating Anticrime Dollars to Places

Suppose that the state of Wisconsin had 20 crimes in 1970 and 10 crimes in 1972, and it spent $15 in 1970 and $35 in 1972. Likewise, suppose that the state of Illinois had 100 crimes in 1970 and 60 in 1972, and it spent $25 in 1970 and $75 in 1972. How might one use that information in order to develop an optimum allocation of a $10 budget between those two places? At first glance, one might say give more money to Wisconsin because there crime was reduced by half between 1970 and 1972, or else give more to Illinois because there is more of a crime problem there. One might also say give more to Illinois because the state is making more of an effort to fight crime in view of the tripling of their anticrime expenditures there, or else give more to Wisconsin because that state has less money to spend.

Figure 6 shows graphically how that information can be used to arrive at an optimum allocation between Illinois and Wisconsin. The left side of the figure works with linear relations. It shows that as Illinois went up $50 between the two years, crime came down 40 units. That means that a $1 increase in anticrime expenditures in Illinois produces a .80 reduction in crime, assuming that other variables are statistically controlled for. Wisconsin, on the other hand, went up $20 in expenditures between those two years and dropped 10 crime units. That means that a $1 increase in anticrime expenditures in Wisconsin produces a .50 reduction in crime. Therefore, it is better to invest an anticrime dollar in Illinois than in Wisconsin if one is trying to minimize total crime across both states, as might be the case for a federal agency such as the Law Enforcement Assistance Administration. Thus the whole $10 budget would be given to Illinois, unless there are some minimum constraints with regard to what has to be allocated to each state (although we can assume that the $10 in this context represents discretionary money after the minimum constraints have been satisfied). The left side of the figure also shows that if nothing is given to Wisconsin, there will be 28 crimes in Wisconsin (or a prediction of 28 crimes) in light of the data that in effect extrapolate from the two data points of 10 crimes with $35 and 20 crimes with $15. Likewise, if zero dollars are given to Illinois, the extrapolation or projection of a line through its two data points shows a prediction of 120 crimes. With the equations for those two lines, one can optimally allocate between the two places, and also arrive at a predicted crime score for each place in light of those optimum allocations.

The right side of Figure 6 works with the same two data points for each state, but this time a curved line rather than a straight line is fitted to the Illinois pair of data points, and another curved line is fitted to the Wisconsin pair of data points. The numerical parameters for those curves can be determined with a hand calculator that provides for nonlinear curve fitting, or with a statistical analysis program available at virtually all computing centers. Working with such a calculator or computer tells us that the equation for the Illinois data is $Y = 437(X)^{-.46}$. This means that an increase of 1 percent in Illinois expenditures will mean a decrease of .46 in Illinois crime. The equation for Wisconsin shows that a 1 percent increase in Wisconsin expenditures will mean a decrease of .83 in Wisconsin crime. For a given number of dollars, Illinois is still a better investment, because it is operating at a higher level of crime, as indicated by the multiplier of 437. That multiplier indicates that if only $1 were spent in Illinois, there would be 437 crimes as contrasted to 191 in Wisconsin. In other words, a 10 percent reduction in a state that has 1000 crimes is much better than a 20 percent reduction in a state that has only 100 crimes. We do not, however, want to give the whole $10 to Illinois, because there is not much of a reduction when we move from $9 to $10 with Illinois. That tenth dollar would be better spent as the first dollar for Wisconsin, where there is a relatively big crime drop in going from $0 to $1.

We will be in a state of equilibrium or optimum allocation when we divide the $10 between Illinois and Wisconsin so as to satisfy simultaneously the equation that says $X_L + X_W = \$10$ and the equation that says $ba(X_2)^{b-1} = BA(X_W)^{B-1}$. That second equation says the marginal rates of return of both states should be equal to each other when we are in an optimum position so that nothing can be gained by switching dollars from one state to the other. The second equation recognizes that with a relation of the form $Y = aX^b$, the marginal rate of return or slope of Y to X is baX^{b-1}. The slope of Y to X is thus influenced by the value of X. Solving for X_L and X_W in that pair of equations informs us that the optimum allocation between Illinois and Wisconsin when one works with more realistic diminishing returns relations is $6.21 to Illinois and $3.79 to Wisconsin. One can logically extend that analysis to any number of places. Note that with places, each place has its own output/input equation. With activities, however, there is one equation with output shown on the left side of the equation, and the activities shown as interacting variables on the right side of the equation.[5]

V. TIME-ORIENTED OPTIMIZING MODELS

A common kind of policy optimization, especially in the realm of public administration, involves choosing among alternative policies in order to minimize the occurrence of unnecessary delay. Such choosing often involves finding an optimum choice, level, or mix among alternative policies, which means using the methods discussed previously but with time minimization as a goal. Time optimization or minimization models may also involve special methods other than finding an optimum choice, level, or mix. Those methods include variations on (1) queueing theory to predict the effects of system changes on backlog and delay, (2) optimum sequencing to reduce the amount of waiting time, and (3) critical path theory to determine where delay reduction efforts should be concentrated.

To illustrate how queueing theory can help see things more clearly, we might look at the corrections problem of overcrowded jails. To reduce such overcrowding, one might recommend increased pretrial release. The opposite effect might, however, occur, as is illustrated in Figure 7. This is so because increased pretrial release decreases the vulnerability of many defendants to the prosecutor's offer to reduce the sentence to time served or probation in return for a guilty plea. If increased pretrial release thereby decreases guilty pleas, then the queueing backlog model tells us to expect increased trials assuming that other variables remain constant. Likewise, the queueing delay model tells us to expect increased delay from the increased trials. If there is increased delay, then defendants sitting in jail awaiting trial probably will be there longer. That in turn means the pretrial jail population may increase, even though fewer defendants are being sent to jail to await trial in view of the increased pretrial release.

Queueing theory and other models not only provide a better understanding of the causal relations, they also indicate ways of decreasing the frequency of those relations. Thus, increased pretrial release need not result in decreased guilty pleas if the prosecutor

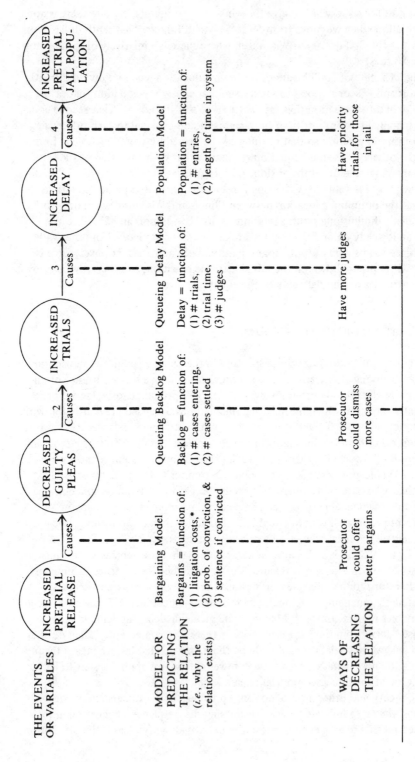

Figure 7. Time-oriented models for predicting and reducing backlogs and delay. [From S. Nagel and M. Neef (1980). "Time oriented models and the legal process: Reducing delay and forecasting the future," *Washington University Law Quarterly*, pp. 467–527.]

offers better bargains (such as probation) to defendants out of jail who otherwise would receive jail sentences. Even when there are fewer guilty pleas, they need not result in increased trials if the prosecutor dismisses more cases to offset the decrease in cases settled. Likewise, more trials need not result in increased delay if the system offsets extra trials with more judges. Finally, increased delay need not result in an increased pretrial jail population if priority trials are provided for those defendants who are in jail, even though that might mean even more delay for defendants out of jail.

Optimum sequencing models can be illustrated by noting that if one has two cases to process and one case takes 20 days to process and the other takes 15 days to process, then the average amount of waiting time plus processing time will be affected by the order in which they are heard. If the 20-day case is heard first, it will have zero waiting time, plus 20 days processing time, for a total of 20 days. The 15-day case will then have 20 days waiting time and 15 days processing time, for a total of 35 days. The sum of those two total amounts for the two cases is 55 days, or about 28 days per case. On the other hand, if the 15-day case is heard first, it will have zero waiting time, plus 15 days processing time, for a total of 15 days. The 20-day case will then have 15 days waiting time and 20 days processing time, for a total of 35 days. The sum of those two total amounts is 50 days, or about 25 days per case. That is three days less than the original order, which might be the first-come, first-served order. The difference would be even larger with more cases and more variety among the cases. This simple example leads to the general rule that reordering the cases to hear shorter cases first will minimize the average total time per case, although one may have to comply with a constraint that sets a maximum on the waiting time to which a case can be subject.

Critical path analysis can be illustrated in administrative proceedings that involve the government regulating or being sued by private parties. Suppose that the government tends to consume six weeks in preparation from the filing of a complaint initiating a proceeding until the time of administrative hearing, and the private parties tend to average four weeks for that same time period. The path from filing to hearing along the government route is then the critical path on which to concentrate one's time-reduction efforts. No time reduction will be achieved in processing cases if private parties reduce their average from four weeks downward, so long as the government is continuing to consume six weeks in preparation. More complicated sets of paths from start to finish could be described, but this simple example illustrates what is involved in critical path analysis.[6]

VI. SOME CONCLUSIONS

A. Trends in Policy Evaluation Methods

There are a number of trends in the development of policy evaluation methods that cut across the more specific techniques that relate to finding an optimum choice, level, or mix in policy evaluation. Different people in the field would be likely to see the trends differently, but some trends that do seem fairly clear are the following:

1. Policy analysis is building on business analysis, but it is developing its own methodology. Policy analysis builds on the basic business principle of maximizing income minus expenses, although in public-sector analysis, the words get converted to benefits

minus costs. Since benefits are usually nonmonetary in policy analysis, this means developing methods for summing benefits and costs in such a way that the benefits are weighted to take into consideration (a) their normative importance relative to the costs and (b) the differences in the measurement units used. Policy analysis also relies more on statistical inputs and less on accounting inputs. Policy analysis is more sensitive to the reactions of the people affected by the policies, which may necessitate considering special psychological and political constraints, as well as the more traditional economic ones.

2. Policy analysts have traditionally taken policies as givens in attempting to determine their effects, especially their effects on the intended goals. There is, however, a trend toward taking goals as givens, and then attempting to determine what policies will maximize or optimize these goals. The former approach is associated more with program evaluation in psychology and sociology. The latter approach is associated more with optimizing analysis from economics and operations research.

3. Policy analysts are becoming more sensitive to social values, with more questioning of goals when evaluating alternative policies. There are now a number of policy studies programs that emphasize the analysis of goals, rather than or in addition to the achievement of goals, such as those at Notre Dame University, the University of Maryland, Georgetown University, Duke University, and the Hastings Institute. Goals can be analyzed through survey research to see to what extent they are supported, through relational analysis to determine how achieving them would affect higher values, or through philosophical analysis to determine how they fit into more general philosophical systems.

4. Policy evaluation is becoming increasingly pro-active or pre-adoption, rather than reactive or post-adoption. Too often the effects of an adopted policy cannot be meaningfully determined because of (a) the lack of availability of a meaningful control group, or (b) the lack of availability of before-data or after-data. Waiting for policies to be adopted before they are evaluated may also lead to harm being done before the unsatisfactory policies can be changed, and it can lead to inertia and vested interests that resist needed changes. As a result, there is an increasing trend toward using pre-adoption projections or deductive modeling, rather than just post-adoption, before-and-after analysis.

5. Policy evaluation is becoming increasingly interdisciplinary in its methods. All the social sciences now offer courses, textbooks, journals, and other disciplinary communication media that emphasize policy or program evaluation methods from both a disciplinary and an interdisciplinary perspective. There is particularly an increasing synthesis of statistical methodology and deductive mathematical models.

6. Policy evaluation is showing increasing sophistication with regard to considering political and administrative feasibility. In the past, policy evaluation has often resulted in recommendations that did not adequately consider the likelihood of the recommendations being adopted by political decision makers or what might happen when it came to implementing or administering policy recommendations. The concern for political and administrative feasibility reflects the increasing role of political science and public administration in policy evaluation.

7. Policy evaluation is developing increased precision in its methods, but at the same time is increasingly recognizing that simple methods may be enough for many policy problems. This is especially so since the typical policy problem asks which policy is best, not how much better it is than the second-best policy, and not how all the policies compare with each other on an interval scale or even a rank-order scale.

8. Systematic policy evaluation is being used increasingly in government at the federal, state, and local levels and in the executive, legislative, and judicial branches. That utilization reflects an increased sensitivity among policy analysts to dealing with actual data, not just abstractions. At the same time, policy analysis is developing broad principles that cut across specific subject matters.

9. There is substantial growth occurring in policy evaluation training programs, research centers, funding sources, publishing outlets, scholarly associations, and other policy evaluation institutions.

B. The Benefits and Costs of Policy Evaluation

These trends all add up to making the field of policy evaluation an exciting one to be in, particularly in these formative times. What may be especially needed are more public administrators who can apply and understand the policy evaluation methods discussed in this chapter. The chapter frequently mentions maximizing benefits minus costs. What, however, are some of the benefits and the costs of applying policy evaluation methods to public administration problems? The benefits include (1) arriving at decisions that are more effective and efficient, (2) acquiring insights that might enable one to make recommendations for more favorably influencing the decision making of others, (3) predicting what decisions are likely to be reached by knowing how system changes influence perceptions of benefits and costs, and (4) understanding better why actual decisions differ from the alleged optimum decisions and then either attempting to change the actual decisions or adjusting one's criteria as to what constitutes optimum decisions.

The costs of applying policy evaluation methods include hard work in gathering and processing data, and hard thinking in deciding what data to gather and how to process it. Although a number of applications of policy evaluation methods have been and can be given, the field is still almost virgin territory. With that low level of development, a small quantity of effort may have a high marginal rate of return before the occurrence of substantial diminishing returns. It is hoped that this chapter will help stimulate further effort in applying policy evaluation methods to public administration problems.

NOTES

1. *On policy evaluation methods in general*:
    White, M., Clayton, R., Myrtle, R., Siegel, G., and Rose, A. (1980). *Managing Public Systems: Analytic Techniques for Public Administration.* Duxbury, North Scituate, MA.
    Stokey, S., and Zeckhauser, R. (1978). *A Primer for Policy Analysis.* Norton, New York.
    Dunn, W. (1981). *Public Policy Analysis: An Introduction.* Prentice-Hall, Englewood Cliffs, NJ.
    Quade, E. (1975). *Analysis for Public Decisions.* Elsevier, New York.
    Nagel, S. (1981). *Policy Evaluation: Making Optimum Decisions.* Praeger, New York.
2A. *On choosing among discrete alternatives*:
    Thompson, M. (1980). *Benefit-Cost Analysis for Program Evaluation.* Sage, Beverly Hills, CA.

Gohagan, J. (1980). *Quantitative Analysis for Public Policy*. McGraw-Hill, New York.

Black, G. (1968). *The Application of Systems Analysis to Government Operations*. Praeger, New York.

B. *On choosing among alternative programs for providing legal services to the poor*:
    Legal Services Corporation (1980). *The Delivery Systems Study*, LSC, Washington, DC.

    Nagel, S. (1975). How to provide legal counsel for the poor: Decision theory. In *Analyzing Poverty Policy*, D. James (Ed.). Lexington-Heath, Lexington, MA.

C. *On choosing among alternative policies for increasing police adherence to legality in searches*:
    Oaks, D. (1970). Studying the exclusionary rule in search and seizure. *University of Chicago Law Review 27*: 665–757.

    Nagel, S. (1975). Choosing among alternative public policies. In *Public Policy Evaluation*, K. Dolbeare (Ed.). Sage, Beverly Hills, CA.

3A. *On making decisions under conditions of risk*:
    Mack, R. (1971). *Planning on Uncertainty: Decision Making in Business and Government Administration*. Wiley, New York.

    Lee, W. (1971). *Decision Theory and Human Behavior*. Wiley, New York.

    Holloway, C. (1979). *Decision Making Under Uncertainty: Models and Choices*. Prentice-Hall, Englewood Cliffs, NJ.

    Nagel, S., and Neef, M. (1979). *Decision Theory and the Legal Process*. Lexington-Heath, Lexington, MA.

B. *On deciding whether to gather data that may be unused*:
    General Accounting Office (1978). *Data Collected from Non-Federal Sources: Statistical and Paperwork Implications*. GAO, Washington, DC.

    Nagel, S. (1978). Determining when data is worth gathering. *Society 16*:20–23. (Symposium on "Paperwork Control").

4A. *On making decisions where doing too much or too little is undesirable*:
    Brennan, M. (1973). *Preface to Econometrics: An Introduction to Quantitative Methods in Economics*. South-Western, Cincinnati, OH.

    Shockley, J. (1971). *The Brief Calculus: With Applications in the Social Sciences*. Holt, New York.

    Starr, M., and Miller, D. (1962). *Inventory Control: Theory and Practice*. Prentice-Hall, Englewood Cliffs, NJ.

    Nagel, S., and Neef, M. (1977). *Legal Policy Analysis: Finding an Optimum Level or Mix*. Lexington-Heath, Lexington, MA.

B. *On finding an optimum level of delay in judicial administration*:
    Nagel, S., and Neef, M. (1978). Time-oriented models and the legal process: Reducing delay and forecasting the future. *Washington University Law Quarterly*, pp. 467–528, especially pp. 490–494, 520–521, and 525.

5A. *On allocating scarce resources in general*:
    Kotler, P. (1971). *Marketing Decision Making: A Model Building Approach*. Holt, New York.

    Lee, S. (1976). *Linear Optimization in Management*. Petrocelli/Charter, Princeton, NJ.

    McMillen, C., Jr. (1970). *Mathematical Programming: An Introduction to the Design and Applications of Optimal Decision Machines*. Wiley, New York.

B. *On allocating anticrime dollars to places*:
Nagel, S. (1975). Minimizing costs and maximizing benefits in providing legal services to the poor. Chapter 13 in *Improving the Legal Process: Effects of Alternatives*. Lexington-Heath, Lexington, MA.

C. On allocating anticrime dollars to places:
Nagel, S. (1981). Allocating anti-crime dollars across places and activities. Chapter 12 in *Policy Evaluation: Making Optimum Decisions*. Praeger, New York.

6A. *On time-oriented optimizing models*:
Bohigian, H. (1971). *The Foundations and Mathematical Models of Operations Research with Extensions to the Criminal Justice System*. Gazette, North Tarrytown, NY.

Byrd, J. Jr. (1975). *Operations Research Models for Public Administration*. Lexington-Heath, Lexington, MA.

Baker, K. (1974). *Introduction to Sequencing and Scheduling*. Wiley, New York.

Gross, D., and Harris, C. (1974). *Fundamentals of Queueing Theory*. Wiley, New York.

B. *On the use of queueing backlog and queueing delay models in governmental case processing*:
Nagel, S. (1981). Predicting and Reducing Court-Case Time through Simple Logic, *North Carolina Law Review*, pp. 103–144.

5

The Utilization of Policy Research

Robert F. Rich* and Neal M. Goldsmith* / Princeton University, Princeton, New Jersey

Although it has been an issue of long-standing concern (Lynd, 1939), during the 1960s the perceived lack of utilization of social research results became an issue of direct relevance for managers of public service programs and for those responsible for the funding of research and development activities. Policy research had been conceived of as being meant for immediate and direct use in improving the quality of social and economic programming. In practice, however, some types of policy research information were seen as "generally not exerting significant influence on program decisions" (Weiss, 1972b: 10–11). The limited successes of big government intervention, from the New Deal to the New Frontier and the Great Society (Aaron, 1978), presented a dilemma for program managers: Could they rely on the social sciences to guide their work? Is social science information—qualitative or quantitative—relevant to the needs of public-sector officials?

Blue ribbon commissions (e.g., the National Academy of Sciences' Panel on Federal Investment in Social R&D, the Brim Commission, the Commission on Federal Paperwork) have concentrated on problems of translating research into action as well as on problems of "over" and "under" utilization of social science-related information.

Within the scientific community, some researchers responded to this perceived under-utilization by recommending that the social sciences be less involved in such applied activities as program evaluation (Zusman, 1976). Others began studying the *process* of applying research information to public policy (Halpert, 1966; Lippitt, 1965; Nagi, 1965; Sadofsky, 1966; Watson and Glaser, 1965), and results have begun to reflect the fact that the utilization of research may in fact be substantial, but also diffuse, indirect, and difficult to track (Cohen, 1977; Knorr, 1977; Patton et al., 1975; Rich, 1975, 1977; Weiss, 1977b, 1980).

In this chapter we (1) present a historical perspective on knowledge use and its societal applications; (2) analyze how various classes of theories relate to knowledge util-

*Present affiliation: Carnegie-Mellon University, Pittsburgh, Pennsylvania

ization; (3) critically review the literature regarding the process of applying policy research to public policy making; and (4) point to critical issues of concern for researchers and practitioners involved in this field.

I. MODELS OF KNOWLEDGE IN SOCIETY: A HISTORICAL PERSPECTIVE

A. Knowledge and Society

Historians and philosophers generally believe that the advancement of society/civilization is related directly to the advancement of knowledge and the way in which knowledge is used by members of society. The fundamental bases for societal actions are formed from what is "known"—"known" because it is accepted as valid/true by society as a whole.

This belief that knowledge is central to the advancement of the individual in society antedates our own Anglo-American culture. In ancient Greece a "higher level of education" was deemed necessary for a "successful career in a democratic government." This type of education included training in "humanistic studies, the arts, and public speaking" (Rich, 1979).

In most Western countries, this conception was extended to the training of civil servants, who were assumed to be highly educated and, even, learned individuals. At a minimum, the civil servant was thought to be a generalist capable of making *informed* judgments on a wide variety of topics/issues.

As the demands made on bureaucrats increased and as public-sector decision making became increasingly complex, expectations changed. Generalists were transformed into specialists or learned to rely on policy analysts to provide the "scientific basis" for decision making.

It has only been since World War II, however, that those responsible for public policy have come to view policy analysis as a subset of scientific research, subject to the laws, procedures, and potential for "certainty" of scientific methodology. Indeed, the field called "policy sciences" evolved in this period. It is only more recently, perhaps since the 1960s, that we have fully begun to view science policy and social policy as inextricably linked, with social policy amenable to the laws of scientific inquiry and with science policy having a direct and fundamental influence on the quality of our lives.

B. The Use of Policy Research in Organizations.

Policy research can be seen as having many different functions over time. Its unique feature relates to the expectation that it will directly aid in the policy-making process. Policy research information is meant to "provide feedback which can be used for program development . . . [as] part of a cycle of planning, implementing, observing, and correcting" (Rapp, 1969).

The dynamic nature of the organizational system warrants a brief discussion here of the concept of systemic "change." The concern in the field of utilization is in following the impact of research information through modes of change within a system. Such a conscious and systematic study of the change process may be seen as the foundation of efforts at *planned change*: the "conscious, deliberate, and collaborative effort to improve the operations of a human system, whether it be self-system, social system, or cultural system, through the utilization of scientific knowledge" (Bennis et al., 1969: 4).

The investigation of the phenomena of utilization from an empirical perspective has been dominated by individuals concerned with planned change (Havelock, 1972; Havelock and Lingwood, 1973; Lippitt, 1965; Rogers, 1962; Larsen, 1980; Zaltman, 1979). These individuals have focused on the process of diffusion, and have assumed that their analyses of specific innovations could be applied more broadly to utilization (Larsen, 1980). Consequently, "the term innovation [has become] central to [the] knowledge utilization phenomena" (Zaltman, 1979).

From this perspective, "use" can be seen as being a component of or synonymous with change or innovation. This is one historical root that is a very important part of the field. It should also be clear, however, that "use" has a very *concrete, instrumental* orientation in this context: It refers to the reinvention, adoption, adaptation, or rejection of specific technologies or ideas.

C. Is Policy Research Utilized?

Those groups involved in studying the research utilization process—applied social researchers, practitioners, and policy makers—based on different disciplinary biases and professional needs, have employed differing concepts and units of analysis in searching for factors that influence utilization. Thus, when more than one discipline is examined, we often find a great diversity of seemingly conflicting research; in terms of definitions or utilization as well as factors seen to influence it.

To quote Patton (1978: 24) in the context of evaluation research; in his search for a utilization definition:

> Most of the literature on evaluation research never explicitly defines utilization. But there is an implicit definition: utilization occurs when there is an immediate, concrete, and observable effect on specific decisions and program activities resulting directly from evaluation research findings. This definition stems from the stated purpose of evaluation research, which is to gather data that can be used to make judgments about program effectiveness. If such data is gathered, then a judgment ought to follow. That judgment leads somewhat directly to concrete action and specific decisions.

Employing this definition, many researchers have concluded that applied research is underutilized (Agarwala-Rogers, 1977; Bruce, 1972; May, 1975; Parsell, 1966; Sadofsky, 1966; Schulberg and Baker, 1968; Weiss, 1971, 1972b, 1972c; Cox, 1976).

Recently a less pessimistic outlook on utilization has emerged. As Cohen (1977: 527) stated:

> A decision maker who decided to pursue some course of action that is inconsistent with evaluation findings may still be employing the research if it provided some input for his/her decision . . . it seems unrealistic for an evaluator to expect his/her findings to be automatically converted into policy (i.e., implemented). However, it does not seem unrealistic to expect evaluation research findings to have some bearing on . . . policy decisions.

Knorr (1977: 180) also found that utilization may be indirect and diffuse:

> utilization does *not* follow the pattern of technical implementation of results estab-
> lished in the natural or technological sciences. Rather the main area of utilization
> consists of an *indirect* (bound to undergo further decision processes), *diffuse* (taken
> into account to various degrees and at different positions), *difficult to localize* util-
> ization responsibility (distributed over various decision levels), and possibly *delayed*
> *discursive processing* of the result in the stage of program development and decision
> preparation. The low visibility of this kind of utilization and the far too high expec-
> tations contribute to the popularity of the thesis that little utilization takes place.
> Its plausibility should be reexamined in the light of the present data and arguments.

Clearly, utilization, as seen in this perspective by Patton, Knorr, Cohen, Weiss, and
Rich, is different from the adoption of technologies as seen by those concerned with
planned change. "Use" in this case is not as clearly defined, and it does not have the
direct, concrete, documentable application that the planned-change field can and does
claim.

Beyond the traditions represented by Zaltman and Knorr, there are other perspectives on how to conceptualize and measure utilization within a policy context:

> The economist would advise us to examine the "value" of knowledge. As Machlup (1979)
> notes: "Readers acquainted with theories of value, especially in economics, will
> remember that 'use value' has long been a favorite expression. . . ." Generally, the
> economic approach has been one of measuring the "tangible or intangible good" of a
> use or application of knowledge (Machlup, 1979). They have also been concerned
> with questions of who pays and who benefits from a use of knowledge.
>
> The sociologist, social psychologist, and information scientist have focused on the "rela-
> tionship between social and psychological structures." "The success of social science
> can be measured by the extent to which it expands the boundaries between our
> private orbits of direct experience and the social and psychological structures that
> shape them from a distance" (Gregg et al., 1979). Social structures are seen as being
> reflected in the ways in which social problems are defined by researchers and policy
> makers. "The nature of problems—and the question of the social processes that struc-
> ture them"—are particularly important from this point of view (Holzner and Fisher,
> 1979). Here social structures are examined through citation analysis and through
> coding procedures that assess problem definitions—including whether the author
> concentrates on "person-centered, "milieu"-centered, or "system"-centered charac-
> teristics (Gregg et al., 1979).

These historical roots illustrate that the knowledge utilization field has a long and
multifaceted past.

II. THEORIES OF KNOWLEDGE USE IN ORGANIZATIONS

As part of exploring the diverse historical roots of this field, it seems appropriate to explore how social theories have defined and analyzed the problem of information utiliza-

tion. It is not surprising that many social theories posit that information/knowledge plays an important role in explaining cognitive, social, and political-economic behavior.

Each approach to theory has put forward a conception of what types of information are important, what significance they have in explaining bureaucratic behavior, and how they are used. In examining each of these theories, one is in the position of analyzing many different meanings of knowledge and knowledge utilization.

In explaining how organizations work and prosper, information/knowledge has been assumed to play an important role. In this case, information takes the form of the expertise of public officials.

The bureaucratic literature of the Weberian tradition identifies expertise as the primary source of bureaucratic power. "Weber contends that the power of executive officials is rooted in the technical or professional skills that distinguish administrators from amateur politicians. Bureaucratic power thus reflects the technological revolution and the growing influence of specialized knowledge in modern civilization" (Rourke, 1972).

Weber conceives of several distinct types of significant knowledge:

Training and skills that an individual brings to the bureaucracy—in other words, between-the-ears kinds of knowledge
That which confers the ability to produce and process information
That which confers the ability to apply information to problem-solving situations (a very general skill)

Having specified these different conceptions of knowledge, the Weberians go on to point out that expertise has served as the foundation for an independent/autonomous position of bureaucratic power.

This proposition sets the stage for understanding how organizations process and use information. As long as a bureaucracy has a monopoly on the technical skills, expertise, and other forms of information it provides to decision makers, its position is not contested and it is protected. Given this situation, one of the bureaucratic responses is an attempt to create an artificial monopoly through the use of secrecy. Along these lines, Weber (1968) suggests:

This superiority of the professional insider every bureaucracy seeks to further increase through the means of keeping secret its knowledge and incentives. Bureaucratic administration always tends to exclude the public to hide his knowledge and action from criticism as well as it can.

A large element of how knowledge is used or not used is the strong preference among career officials to defer to expertise:

Their own involvement and influence depend in large part on other officials deferring to their expertise. To challenge the expertise of another career group is to risk retaliation. Thus, Foreign Service Officers have been extremely reluctant to challenge the military on strategic questions or to challenge Treasury officials on economic matters (Halperin, 1974).

Officials defer to expertise in the expectation that they will be likewise deferred to in what is considered to be their specialty.

In the case of bureaucratic theory, it is clear that the judgment of what constitutes "meaningful knowledge" is more closely related to questions of values and insulation of power than it is to science or the "objective, technical" quality of information. *The usefulness of information has more to do with the characteristics of the person who possesses it (i.e., an expert) than it does with the substance of the message that is being conveyed.*

A. Classical Approaches to Organizational Behavior

The most frequently discussed construct/model of human behavior in organizations has traditionally been the "rational actor model" (Allison, 1971). The rational actor is engaged in the process of "optimizing." The optimizing strategy advocates selecting the course of action with the highest payoff. This strategy requires estimating the comparative value of every viable act in terms of expected benefits and costs.

All rational actor theories call for systematic canvassing of possible alternatives, for a systematic analysis of the consequences of each alternative in light of the values/goals that one wants to maximize, and for possible choices to be guided by this analysis (Braybrooke and Lindblom, 1963). There is some disagreement among those writing about "rationality," but all writers/scholars seem to agree that comprehensive and prospective analysis is essential. "Comprehensiveness is often seen as logically necessary for rational choice; in fact, rational choice comes close to being defined as a choice that, *inter alia,* responds to a comprehensive consideration of all relevant variables" (Braybrooke and Lindblom, 1963).

The limitations of rationality as a method of problem solving have been thoroughly indexed in the literature:

Herbert Simon (1976) has pointed out that human beings rarely adopt this decision-making approach. "Part of the problem is that determining all the possible favorable or unfavorable consequences of all the feasible courses of action would require the decision maker to process so much information that impossible demands would be made on his resources and mental capabilities" (quoted in Janis and Mann, 1977). Others argue that one can certainly be rational without engaging in a comprehensive search through all relevant and available information resources (Downs, 1967). Eulau et al. (1970) argue that highly accurate, reliable, and complete information resources are not ipso facto conducive to rational decision making in a representative democracy. "On the contrary, from the societal perspective, it may actually be so costly as not to be a rational instrument of government at all. . . ."

In other words, the rational actor theory has the following conceptions of knowledge and knowledge use:

1. All relevant information will be searched and used in human decision-making processes—in this case, types of knowledge or information are not differentiated.
2. It is assumed that the human mind is capable of processing *all* sources of available knowledge.
3. It is assumed that all relevant sources of available knowledge should be applied to a given problem.

4. "Use" is loosely defined in terms of considering all available sources of knowledge in weighing alternative courses of action. Presumably, the available knowledge will dictate the action ultimately taken.

B. Psychosocial Approaches to Organizational Behavior.

Psychosocial theories teach us that the "psychological nature of the interactions between . . . two parties is of paramount importance. . . . We are saying that in order for effective knowledge utilization to occur a rather complex set of psychological and social relationships is needed. We ignore considerations of psychology at the expense of endlessly repeating our misunderstandings of ourselves and others" (Mitroff and Mitroff, 1979). In essence, we have learned that as far as knowledge utilization is concerned, we should be focusing on "between-the-ears" processes and complex social relations that influence how information will be processed and used.

Because of the limitations of the rational actor model, decision makers are prone to adopt suboptimizing solutions (Miller and Starr, 1967). According to March and Simon (1958), the decision maker *satisfices* rather than maximizes: He looks for the course of action that is "good enough" and that meets a minimal set of requirements.

Herbert Simon (1976) argues that the *satisficing* approach best describes decision making because it reflects the limitations and constraints placed on human beings in organizations. Decision makers can be characterized as being subject to "bounded or limited rationality," which makes them prone to gross simplifications when dealing with complex decision-making problems.

Simon's work has been very influential in offering an alternative to the rational actor model. He argues rather forcibly that the satisficing approach best fits the limited information processing capabilities of human beings (Janis and Mann, 1977).

> Man's limited ability to foresee further consequences and to obtain information about the variety of available alternatives inclines him to settle for a barely "acceptable" course of action that is better than the way things are now. He is not inclined to collect information about the complicated factors that might affect the outcome of his choice, to estimate probabilities, or to work out preferred orderings from many different alternatives. He is content to rely on a drastically simplified model of the buzzing, blooming confusion that constitutes the real world (Simon, 1976); (discussed in Janis and Mann, 1977).

Social theorists have come to accept the power of the satisficing approach (Etzioni, 1968; Young, 1966; Miller and Starr, 1967; Johnson, 1974). Cyert and March (1963) point out that policy decisions are likely to be made on the basis of short-term acceptability within an organization.

The satisficing theories make it clear that:

Use is limited to the most relevant information as opposed to all of the information. Relevant use is self-defined in terms of the needs of the decision makers.
Use is loosely defined—there is no particular differentiation between types of use or types of information. Unlike theories where there is a distinction between types of information (e.g., cost-benefit theories), the satisficing theories give us only a very loose conception of information and types of utilization.

Psychosocial theories make an important contribution to our understanding of what constitutes usable knowledge and of the need for conceptualizations of the definitions of utilization. In these theories, we are reminded that information is processed through the mind, and that psychological/cognitive processes are essential to understanding different conceptions of use and different forms of information.

C. Contextual Approaches to Organizational Behavior

Other approaches to organizational theory attempt to understand the organization in terms of its broader cultural and political-economic environment (Meld, 1974; Scott, 1966). Bennis and Slater (1968), for example, have approached the reality of fluctuating environmental demands on organizations by proposing an organization as composed of temporary task- (rather than rule-) oriented groups, being formed and re-formed to respond to the organizational need of the moment. Such task forces would gather individuals with the skills necessary to meet an environmental challenge and would disband when the need abated. This approach acknowledges the impact of, and the need for, flexible responses to a dynamic environment, and is applicable to a wide variety of regulatory, funding, community, or professional demands. However, there is a question as to the durability of the solutions of such temporary task forces once disbanded; preexisting patterns of organizational response may tend to reemerge once the crisis is over (Katz and Kahn, 1978: 283).

Another contextual approach to organizational theory may be found in the field of economics. As Pugh (1966: 247) puts it:

> The facts that all organizations operate in an economic environment and the success or failure of many is judged on economic terms mean that the study of the context and the performance of organizations must rely primarily on economic concepts.

In this view, the organization is seen as an "active participant in economic decisions, rather than as a passive resultant of market forces" (Pugh, 1966: 246). These contextual approaches then, in their recognition of extraorganizational influences, add to other attempts at explaining organizational behavior.

Whereas the classical and psychosocial approaches discussed above involve the flow of objective information through the program's formal structure and subjective intrapsychic/interpersonal dynamics, respectively, contextual variables involve the less proximal and manipulable arena of program context. For Meld (1974: 453),

> choices that involve public versus private benefits are generally acknowledged to be political. However, when program choices affect different groups in the population differentially—in taxes, benefits, services, and so on—is not public policy also being made? Are not different political values being assigned to the various groups? The issue then is political—an issue of "who wins, who loses?" in the collection and distribution of resources. It is not a question of analysis and evaluation. Planners often make such decisions on the basis of negotiation, rather than on the basis of research data.

Cohen (1977) agrees, stating that "decision-making, of course, is a euphemism for the allocation of resources—money, position, authority, etc. Thus to the extent that information is an instrument, basis, or excuse for changing power relationships within or among institutions, [organizational research] is a political activity" (p. 139). The relevant context for program operation and policy research utilization includes two components: (1) *administration,* involving program enabling and regulatory legislation, as well as funding sources; and (2) *culture,* involving the program's community and clients, and the professional "culture" or values of program policy makers and staff as well as of the policy research enterprise itself.

Administrative policy making in large part depends on political and economic value judgments by policy makers. When the stakes are high (Cohen, 1977), research procedure and findings are apt to be subject to political manipulation (Cook et al., 1980; Meld, 1974; Weiss, 1972d) reflecting the perceived feasibility of utilizing findings (Cook et al., 1980; Weiss, 1972b, 1972c) as seen by policy makers, funders, and politicians subject to the pressures of competing influences (Weiss, 1973, 1975). The political uses of research, which, like the psychosocial reactions of program staff, serve to maintain program existence (Weiss, 1972b) include (1) commissioning a study to delay undesirable policy making, (2) providing ammunition to gain support for a successful program, (3) ducking responsibility by using evidence to make a decision for a policy maker, (4) discrediting opposition, (5) gaining prestige and improved public relations through the commissioning of a blue ribbon panel of researchers, and (6) fulfilling mandated program grant requirements and justifying budget requests (Weiss, 1972a, 1977b). In addition, the fact that funding for policy research is often controlled by the agency or program in question further implicates the role of economic context in the policy research endeavor (Suchman, 1967).

The cultural context of community groups and service consumers also may influence the use of policy research and its findings. Information regarding a study and its findings may be withheld from the public or manipulated by policy makers (Weiss, 1972c; Stufflebeam, 1974) in the light of the community's response to a popular program negatively assessed, the need to withhold certain treatments for the sake of an experiment, or the need for program support and voluntary cooperation of clients in research procedures (Suchman, 1967). In fact, research findings may be used by consumer groups to support their own interest in a program (Weiss, 1972a), in particular through the use of media attention (Riecken and Boruch, 1974).

Finally, it must be noted that the professional values of the program policy makers and program staff and of the research "community" represent yet another cultural context of the policy research endeavor. Researchers, because of their professional backgrounds and often nonprogram institutional bases (Schatzman and Strauss, 1973), enter the research field with biases and values that, practically speaking, constitute a political stance implicitly endorsing certain program goals, research methods, or policy outcomes (Weiss, 1973, 1975; Stufflebeam, 1974). At times, these professional orientations differ from values and ideological doctrines of the program policy maker or staff, and conflicts resulting in the lack of utilization of policy research findings may ensue (Berk and Rossi, 1976; Caplan, 1979; Caplan and Rich, 1976; Rich, 1977; Suchman, 1967; Weiss, 1972c).

The contextually constrained nature of the policy research system does not, however, imply a hopelessly subjective and unscientific course of events. A researcher's "knowledge of community structure and function . . . may provide for a substantive contribution . . . as great, and perhaps even more telling than his methodological skills in conducting [policy] research" (Suchman, 1967: 166). The acceptance of the influence of political values on research utilization (Argyris, 1971) may lead to their employment in methodology which takes values and biases into scientific account (Berk and Rossi, 1976; Guttentag, 1973; Riecken and Boruch, 1974; Scriven, 1976).

D. The "Two-Communities" Metaphor

Although we do not consider the "two communities" metaphor to be a distinct organizational theory (Dunn, 1980), it has been treated as such in much of the knowledge utilization literature. As a result, we are treating it here as a separate approach to theory, although it would be more appropriately conceived of under the contextual approaches to organizational behavior.

In the broadest sense, knowledge utilization has been thought by many to be a problem of *linkage*: building links between the knowledge production and knowledge utilization processes (Havelock, 1969). The nature of the linkages or mechanisms of knowledge transfer advocated depends to a great extent on one's diagnosis of what the problem is:

Many sociologists and communication scientists have expressed the belief that there is a "gap" between the culture of science and the culture of government. The problem is to bridge this gap so that greater and more effective utilization of science and technological information can follow (Rich, 1979). The nature of the problem is often assumed to be one of "communication failure or lack of organized effort to systematically introduce social science knowledge in usable form where it will most likely be used" (Caplan, 1979).

Others have observed that the problem may be one of "breaking down the hostility between researchers, program managers, federal policy makers, and third-party users" (National Research Council, 1978). In this case, the gap that exists, and the bridge that must be built, may be functions of politics (the rules and procedures of the public problem-solving process). Another way of conceptualizing this issue is in terms of the bureaucratic problems associated with the interactions among knowledge production and utilization processes (Rich, 1977; Caplan and Rich, 1976). In this perspective, the problem has to do with overcoming or finding ways to bypass standard operating procedures. According to this view, one could effect change in the knowledge utilization process by influencing regular or traditional bureaucratic rules and procedures. The "bridge" in this case would be in gaining an increased understanding of how bureaucracies work and how their standard operating procedures affect the production and utilization of knowledge.

A "gap" may also reflect alternative or competing incentives or reward systems (Lingwood, 1979). Program managers are rewarded for providing concrete results; in many cases, they are responsible for program implementation and must focus on the nuts and bolts of "how to do it." They may, indeed, appreciate research much as a connoisseur appreciates good food; it may likewise be viewed as a luxury. Researchers and research administrators, on the other hand, often hold the same values as the academic or scientific community, who reward the productivity of scholarship for the sake of scholarship. Neither set of values is better, more rational, or intrinsically "correct." The 1978 National Research Council Study Project, entitled *The Federal*

Investment in Knowledge of Social Problems, stated: "we noted considerable tension between program officials, who feel that they receive little help from research, and research administrators, who are weary of anti-intellectual program managers and their demands for how-to-do-it manuals" (p. 44). The nature of the need for constructing a bridge in this case seems to be related to educating officials who "have a limited understanding of how new information can foster innovation and change" (p. 53). Presumably, this education would be in the nature of rewards and incentives, as well as in the politics of problem solving in the public sector.

III. THE LITERATURE ON INFORMATION USE: WAYS OF VIEWING UTILIZATION

This chapter argues that utilization is a process; not simply one goal to be attained at one point in time, but a series of less than discrete "events" varying over time and area of application, and dependent on the type of information in question. We realize that all information is not the same. In daily life we regularly employ information gathered during schooling and professional training, from colleagues and friends, from the media and other more diffuse sources of information in our environment; these are the foundations of the data and facts we all store in our brains. "Mundane" types of information (Machlup, 1980) join with more particularly organizational sources of information, for example, policy analyses, demonstration project and evaluation research results, financing models, cost-efficiency studies, and structural and demographic statistics, to comprise the spectrum of types of information potentially used by a policy maker. In the realm of organizational decision making, it is generally assumed that the possession of information distinguishes the "expert" as "knower" from the policy maker as "user" of information. However, these varying types of information are generally not distinguished from each other in the research utilization literature; when they are, there is generally no attempt made to place the type of information studied for use on a reference classification of types of information. It seems apparent that different types of information will be used in different ways, and that the literature leaves this source of potential variance in utilization largely untapped, much to the detriment of a theory of policy research utilization.

We may also conceive of these sources of information as being differentially utilized depending on the information needs of the user. Certainly, a budget director in need of information relating to financing decisions, for example, might very well underutilize demonstration project results. This is not to say that another type of user—for example, a director of services—would not utilize such information if appropriate to specific problem-solving needs. Thus the needs of the user in specific areas of application are important to understanding and assessing information utilization, and may be seen as another perspective on variation in use largely ignored in the utilization research literature.

There have been exceptions to this lack of a framework. In terms of information use, one approach has been to distinguish between "instrumental" (immediate and directly observable) and "conceptual" (potentially having delayed and diffused impact, and therefore less readily observable) types of information use in policy making (Knorr, 1977; Rich, 1975; Caplan et al., 1975; Weiss, 1977a).

The problem addressed by this approach to types of use (and in need of more attention in the realm of types of users and information) becomes one of specification. If we agree that all forms of information and types of use are not the same (nor equally important for varying policy problem-solving needs), then we must begin to specify typologies of information and use, and the conditions and circumstances under which various types of information will be employed for varying types of use.

However, an even cursory review of the literature on knowledge utilization reveals a dearth of studies employing these crucial distinctions in their research designs. Even in those studies that (though not employing an information typology) do clearly delineate the type of information being investigated, we still find a lack of *precision* in specifications of levels and types of use and delineations of decision-making contexts (Larsen, 1980).

In an attempt to specify the relationships among types of information, types of institutional problem-solving needs and types of use, we shall review selected utilization literature, explicating ways of thinking about use through an ordering scheme based on concrete approaches to the assessment of use. To reiterate: In reviewing studies of utilization, we have looked for both breadth of scope in specifying forms of information that in varying situations will result in different types of use, as well as precision of measurement of use.

Although we concentrate here primarily on survey research, we do recognize the influence of other, more qualitative methods. Social framework analyses (Coleman, 1980; Nelkin, 1979; Rich, 1979), intellectual histories (Lindblom and Cohen, 1979; Pollak, 1980), and case studies (Deitchman, 1976; Horowitz, 1967), for example, have each made their unique contribution to our understanding of the use of information in society.

By far the most common way of viewing policy research utilization has been through the use of survey methods. In these investigations, structured observations, interviews, and questionnaires are the primary tools; often used in conjunction with relevant documents and research reports to obtain a fuller picture of the research utilization process.

A. Structured Observations

When used in a structured manner (i.e., with predetermined categories within which to place observations), observational methods can offer precision of measurement as well as a breadth of specification unbiased by respondent self-report. However, with this mode of inquiry, we find the potential for biases based on a loss of objectivity on the part of the researcher. In a field situation entailing direct observation, researchers may tend to identify with subjects under study. Furthermore, blind spots may develop as the investigator becomes accustomed to more common or subtle organizational behaviors. A structured checklist of observations to be made and categories within which to code observed behaviors may be helpful in this regard (Larsen, 1980; Selltiz et al., 1959) Another bias, which may be more difficult to control, can be introduced through reactivity of the subject to the phenomenon of being observed. However, this reactivity often fades after familiarity is established, and in any event is a problem shared with most other methods of inquiry. A further means of avoiding subject reactivity would be to observe subjects unobtrusively, or entirely without their awareness; however, with research on policy makers in public organizations such stealth would be impractical and quite likely unethical as well.

The literature on structured observational methods as applied to utilization research in public service organizations is just beginning to emerge. One innovative example may be found in an unpublished doctoral dissertation (Daillak, 1981) growing out of Alkin's work on the utilization of educational evaluation (Alkin et al., 1979). Daillak followed educational evaluators over a six-month period, sitting in on meetings, making structured observations, and conducting postmeeting-in-depth interviews. Daillak's study offered a detailed, first-hand analysis of evaluator styles and holds promise as an alternative mode of investigating the policy-making process.

An exciting example of the potential for precision of structured observations and of the analytical power of a design that clearly specifies several types and levels of variables may be found in Larsen and Werner's study, "Measuring Utilization of Mental Health Program Consultation" (1981). In this work, trained observers carefully recorded data regarding recommendations and suggestions made during 39 two-day mental health program consultations. Characteristics of the recommendations measured and a large number of consultation characteristics were rated. Use was conceptualized as occurring on both the individual suggestion ($N = 788$) level and on the level of the consultation as a whole ($N = 39$) and was measured on a seven-point scale ranging from several degrees of utilization, through simple interest in an idea, to several degrees of nonutilization. Measurements were taken at four-month and eight-month follow-up sessions after consultation.

Although the sample of consultations in this study appears to have been self-selected by community mental health centers specifying an interest in expert consultation on program change, and the levels of use were self-reported through follow-up interviews, Larsen and Werner's use of structured observations highlights the potential for precision of this approach in the specification of variables important to the research utilization process.

B. Sample Surveys

In an attempt to identify instances of empirically based social science knowledge influencing policy decisions, Caplan (Caplan, 1977; Caplan et al., 1975) conducted interviews with 204 federal-level officials. Caplan's landmark study presented a foundation for understanding and how and why social science information is used at the national level. However, the types of use and forms of research were broadly conceived; thus, it was not possible to differentiate among various types of applications. Furthermore, the study is biased in focusing on empirically grounded sources of social science information, and on utilization for which the respondent had to recall specific details of the study (including the name of the investigator).

Knorr (1977) provides another example of the application of survey methods to discern utilization. In a study conducted in Austria (offering one of the few cross-cultural validations of the research utilization phenomena), Knorr interviewed 70 federal and municipal decision makers and sent questionnaires to 628 social scientists. In this instance, several different policy areas were investigated, four functions of social science knowledge were identified, and subjective and objective forms of data were distinguished. Knorr concludes that instrumental utilization does occur (albeit with legitimating or motivating purposes) more often than had been suspected, but that such use may be indirect, diffuse, difficult to localize, and subject to delayed discursive processing (i.e., symbolic uses), rather than straightforward and easily measurable.

Although most research has held forms of information or types of utilization constant, some research has attempted systematically to sample user situations. Some of the earliest attempts to assess research utilization in this manner may be found in the work of Ronald G. Havelock and his associates at the Center for Research on Utilization of Scientific Knowledge at the University of Michigan's Institute for Social Research (Havelock, 1973; Havelock and Mann, 1968). Havelock (1973) selected a stratified national sample of school districts and administered a questionnaire asking for information on various uses of resources and on characteristics of school districts that might relate to their utilization of innovations (including research and ideas).

Patton et al. (1975) also employed a stratified sampling technique to select 20 evaluations randomly from five strata based on "nature of program." Three levels of respondents were interviewed for each of the 20 evaluations studied. In this research, however, utilization was still broadly defined, and the form of information (evaluation) was held essentially constant.

In a study of information behavior in German complex organizations, Badura and Waltz (1980) clearly specify types of information, user characteristics and situations, and characteristics related to the utilization of social science knowledge. The researchers used a stratified sample based on "organizational culture" of more than 400 law graduates, scientists, and engineers, and behavioral and social scientists selected from eight private-sector firms and four policy-related departments of the federal government. Types of information were specified as (1) economic, (2) scientific-technical, (3) legal, (4) linguistic, and (5) social scientific.

Although Badura and Waltz take care to specify the variables under consideration, their dependent measures are of attitudes toward and perceived need for social science knowledge. As a result, they measure attitudes (potentially) related to the utilization of social science knowledge and not utilization behavior itself. A further difficulty with Badura and Waltz's dependent measure is one shared with most survey research—that is, the self-report nature of questionnaire measurement. However, although self-reported behaviors are subject to many of the same potentials for distortion as are self-reported attitudes, self-reported behaviors are more readily subject to objective verification (through the archival record) than are self-reports of attitude or behavioral intent.

An example of a study that considers all three dimensions under scrutiny here (form of information, type of use, and user situation or need) can be found in a recent Weiss and Bucuvalas (1977) project measuring characteristics of social science research deemed useful for policy making. Weiss and Bucuvalas selected a stratified sample of 250 federal, state, and local mental health policy makers and applied social researchers. The respondents were instructed to assess 50 abstracts of studies selected for representativeness as to type of study, sampling characteristics, and clarity of results. The abstracts were varied systematically on the basis of manipulability of major explanatory variables, administrative feasibility of the implications, and degree of congruence with prevailing beliefs in the mental health field. Finally, respondents were interviewed and asked to rate the abstacts based on two questions regarding usefulness and 29 descriptive characteristics related to the types of purposes the study results might serve. By systematically varying forms of information and policy maker's situation, and by measuring use on the basis of several measures, the Weiss and Bucuvalas study comes close to capturing the variation inherent in the utilization process. However, it is not clear whether the measures of potential utility or usefulness would be the same as actual utilization. Weiss and Bucuvalas are asking what respondents *would do* if confronted with a given study—not what they *actually have done.*

In a study of utilization in mental health policy research currently in progress, Rich (in press) attempts to overcome these difficulties by approaching each of these sources of variation in utilization. A stratified sample of federal and state-level mental health policy makers responded to questionnaires and structured personal interviews. Area of application was varied based on service-oriented versus financial policy needs. Form of information was varied as to service-oriented information (program evaluation, demonstration project results, statistical data, and expert advice), or finance-oriented information (cost-efficiency studies, financing models, statistical data, and expert advice). Type of use was varied across both area of application and form of information, and attempts were made to assess the effect of various nonresearch extraneous factors for each type of information in both the service-oriented and finance areas of application. Preliminary results indicate different levels of use for different types of information depending on the characteristics of the policy maker and on the type of institutional need for problem-solving information.

C. Time-Series Analyses

This last study brings us to an additional source of variance in the utilization process; that is, differences in the level of utilization over time. Traditionally, utilization research has been conducted in the information science tradition; that is, research information is conceived of as "input" and utilization as "output" (in terms of research-based policy). Generally a direct one-to-one correspondence between input and output is assumed. In attempting to investigate a less straightforward relationship between information and utilization, formidable methodological difficulties present themselves. First, bits of knowledge tend to accumulate and congeal to a point where it is difficult to discern discrete, identifiable inputs. Second, because the process of making policy decisions is multiply determined, it is often impossible to trace the specific knowledge bases for specific decisions, even in cases where the population of bits of applicable knowledge may be discretely identified (Caplan and Rich, 1976). That much having been said, and keeping in mind the distortions of self-report techniques that plague most survey research, attempts have been made to trace degrees of utilization seen over time.

In Rich's (1975, 1977, 1981) study of the National Opinion Research Center's Continuous National Survey, which looked at the utilization process over time, the phenomena of delayed use and of "waves of utilization" were identified. Generally, during the first wave of measurement, "instrumental" (or concrete and directly identifiable) use was seen to a greater extent than was "conceptual" (or diffuse and less straightforwardly identifiable) use. During the second wave, the reverse was found to be true, with conceptual uses outnumbering instrumental uses. The first wave, which included many of the uses intended in collecting the data, seemed to occur from the point of the receipt of the information through approximately three months thereafter, and was oriented toward information inputs with policy-action implications. The second wave of use generally occurred from three to six months after the information was received, and was oriented toward information inputs offering understanding of the policy context within which decision making took place. In addition to its other advantages, this research points to the importance of studying types of use over time if one is to attain a clear picture of the utilization process. (Results of Rich's current project, when available, will offer another set of data illuminating the process of policy research utilization over time.)

Although the survey studies reviewed above deal to varying extents with issues of *specification* and *precision,* they all share, at least in part, sources of bias related to self-report (self-definition, memory, and social desirability distortions, for example), which limit the validity of conclusions drawn. Experimental designs ultimately offer a powerful research tool. Currently, however, practical difficulties limit the broad applicability of experimental methods to the real-world settings essential for research on the process of policy research utilization. As a result, we may look toward other methods, based on more objectively measurable data, which might reduce some of the threats to validity encountered when information is collected indirectly or secondhand.

D. Citation Analyses

A more precisely quantifiable method of assessing the impact of knowledge, and one that is not subject to respondent reactivity (although still subject to researcher selection bias) is that of social framework analysis based on citation analysis. Taking samples of the literature from the years 1936, 1956, and 1976, Gregg et al. (1979) read and coded 698 articles in six social problem areas taken from a wide variety of both pure and applied journals. More than 80 pieces of information were coded for each article, including type of journal, type of article, independent variables, causal attributions, relevance to theory or practice, and type of theory or practice under consideration. Each article was further analyzed on the basis of a more particular coding of the independent variables, causal attributions, and patterns of attributions studied. Results indicated complex relations among the causal attributions and among the attributional patterns that characterized each article. The data also revealed significant differences when examined by problem area, type of article, and type of journal. In addition, the authors discussed the role of political and nonscientific factors in social science and extrapolate from their data to predict future trends for the development of the social science.

Of particular significance to the present methodological discussion is the power of ths research method for specifying (with the precision of measurement offered by the citation analyses) complex interactions among forms of information and types of use (as seen through the journal analyses). In this study we do not, however, find "user situations" assessed. Furthermore, this research method was applied by Gregg and associates on the broadest of social science "cultural" levels. The potential clearly exists, however, for the specification of types of social science research users, and the application of the method to the assessment of institutional use of research reports.

E. A Note on Experimental Designs

The specification of information, situation, and use, and the precision with which they are measured are crucial to the development of utilization studies. However, through the control of extraneous influences and the purposive manipulation of "treatments," experimental and quasi-experimental research designs offer the potential elimination of certain threats to validity and reliability, thereby increasing the logical certainty with which we can answer the sorts of questions we have been asking here (Campbell and Stanley, 1966). Whereas the field of utilization research has not developed to the point where true experiments have been tried on a systematic basis, there have been preliminary attempts to utilize experimental and quasi-experimental techniques to isolate and assess influences on knowledge use. A well-developed example of the potential for experimental investigation of research utilization is given by a recent Pelz and Horsley (1981) study. The investigators measured outcome of a research utilization program designed to "disseminate current research findings and facilitate organizational modifications required for sound implementation in nursing departments of a sample of Michigan hospitals." Under stratification by size of hospitals within geographic and institutional clusters, hospitals were randomly assigned to 13 "treatment" and 15 comparison groups. Type of treatment was specified as to presence or absence of an Innovation Team (IT) (or of an "artificial" Innovation Team for the control situations) at the hospital. Variation in situation was controlled for through the use of the stratified random sampling employed. Levels of use were specified through five direct and five indirect measures of research utilization as a result of the Innovation Team training program intervention. In addition, observations were made at three times: prior to intervention, one year postintervention, and, in one-half of the treatment groups, two years postintervention. On the average, the results of the direct measures indicated that the Innovation Team intervention was more effective than either non- or artificial Innovation Team groups, with gains decreasing over the next year.

Although the geographic and institution stratification categories did not play a role in Pelz and Horsley's analysis of effects, this study does specify type of intervention to be utilized and type and degree of utilization over time. The sophistication of this design, however, offers a most promising direction for further research.

Again, the point of relevance for our present purposes is that experimental designs *can* be employed in the study of the research utilization process with attendant increases in the logical certainty of findings obtained.

IV. CONCLUSIONS

This chapter has attempted to place selected literature on utilization of policy research into a broad historical context. The interests of individuals and society in the application of knowledge/science/information to meet human needs dates back to the Greeks. Moreover, the importance of the use of information in social problem solving is a critical component recognized in almost every major social, economic, and political theory. It is clear that the creation, diffusion, and use of information plays a significant role in explaining individual and organizational behavior.

We feel that studies of research utilization have been unnecessarily burdened with narrow conceptions and measures of the process of research utilization:

The assumption seems to be that when speaking of the use of information, one is naturally referring to "new knowledge," as opposed to what is already known and stored in the human brain;

"New knowledge" usually refers to empirically grounded information, as opposed to "intuition," "hunches," "traditions," or many other forms of information.

"Use" is usually referred to as if all types of applications can be treated equally and as if there are no significant differences among the various types of information that might be used.

Use is generally examined as a "dependent" variable as opposed to thinking of it as an intervening variable: use for what, and for what purpose?

These are confining assumptions that constrain the process of linking utilization studies to the crucial question that has continued to be posed by major social theorists over time: What are the most significant factors in explaining human and organizational behavior over time?

Once placed in historical and theoretical perspective, a broad range of dependent variables (forms utilization may take) and independent variables (types of information to be utilized, and types of users of, needs for, areas of application for information, and factors affecting utilization) begins to emerge.

Although only touched upon in this chapter, several classes of utilization variables can be identified and should, in future research, be given further attention.

In terms of specifying forms of utilization (and in addition to the distinction between instrumental and conceptual use), the classes of abuse/misuse, premature use, and valid nonuse (Cook et al., 1980; Larsen, 1980; Weiss, 1972a, 1977b) should be included in the design of future utilization studies. Furthermore, utilization is an ongoing process; hence, it is not easy to identify where utilization begins and where it ends. We need to distinguish among the adoption, implementation or diffusion of information, and the durability of such uses over time needs to be traced (Beckhard, 1975; Glaser and Backer, 1977; Lehman, 1975; Seashore and Bowers, 1970).

We also need to specify clearly what it is we are attempting to utilize. Distinctions need to be drawn among general organizational information, research-based information, and innovative programs and technologies, for example. In addition, the various contexts within which utilization occurs and the variety of users of information need to be examined. For example, we may differentiate between public and private sectors, legislative, administrative and community, as well as administrative and service-oriented users.

Finally, we need to be sensitive to the problem of distinguishing between instances where utilization of social science information should be facilitated and instances where one may want to counsel deliberate nonutilization of the available studies. Not all utilization is good, and not all nonutilization is harmful. It is tautological to maintain that information is used. The crucial point seems to lie in identifying that policy-related information which will benefit society and then to develop the mechanisms that will facilitate its effective application.

REFERENCES

Aaron, H. J. (1978). *Politics and the Professors.* The Brookings Institution, Washington, DC.

Agarwala-Rogers, R. (1977). Why is evaluation research not utilized? In *Evaluation Studies Review Annual,* M. Guttentag (Ed.). Vol. 2, Sage, Beverly Hills, CA.

Alkin, M. C., Daillak, R., and White, P. (1979). *Using Evaluations: Does Evaluation Make a Difference?* Sage, Beverly Hills, CA.

Allison, G. T. (1971). *Essence of Decision: Explaining the Cuban Missile Crisis.* Little, Brown, Boston.

Argyris, C. (1971). Creating effective research relationships in organizations. In *Readings in Evaluation Research,* F. G. Caro (Ed.). Russell Sage Foundation, New York.

Badura, B., and Waltz, M. (1980). Information behavior in the German Federal Government: The case of the social sciences. *Knowledge: Creation, Diffusion, Utilization 1*(3): 351–279.

Beckhard, R. (1975). Strategies for large system change. *Sloan Management Review 16* (Winter): 43–55.

Bennis, W. G., Benne, K. D., and Chin, R. (1969). *The Planning of Change.* Holt, New York.

Bennis, W. G., and Slater, P. E. (1968). *The Temporary Society.* Harper & Row, New York.

Berk, R. A., and Rossi, P. H. (1976). Doing good or worse: Evaluation research politically re-examined. In *Evaluation Studies Review Annual,* G. V. Glass (Ed.). Vol. 1, Sage, Beverly Hills, CA.

Braybrook, D., and Lindblom, C. E. (1963). *A Strategy for Decision.* Free Press, New York.

Bruce, R. G. (1972). What goes wrong with evaluation and how to prevent it. *Human Needs 1*: 10–11.

Campbell, D. T., and Stanley, J. C. (1966). *Experimental and Quasi-experimental Designs for Research.* Rand McNally, Chicago.

Caplan, N. (1977). A minimal set of conditions necessary for the utilization of social science knowledge in policy formulation at the national level. In *Using Social Research in Public Policy Making,* C. H. Weiss (Ed.). Lexington Books, Lexington, MA.

—— (1979). The two communities theory. *American Behavioral Scientist, 22*: 459–470.

Caplan, N., Morrison, A., and Stambaugh, R. J. (1975). *The Use of Social Science Knowledge in Policy Decisions at the National Level.* Institute for Social Research, Ann Arbor, MI.

Caplan, N., and Rich, R. F. (1976). Open and closed knowledge inquiry systems: The process and consequences of bureaucratization of information policy at the national level. Presented at the Meeting of the OECD Conference on Dissemination of Economic and Social Development Research Results, Bogota, Colombia.

Cohen, L. H. (1977). Factors affecting the utilization of mental health evaluation research findings. *Professional Psychology* (*Nov.*): 526–534.

Coleman, J. S. (1980). The structure of society and the nature of social research. *Knowledge, Creation, Diffusion, Utilization 1*(3): 333–350.

Cook, T. D., Levinson-Rose, J., and Pollard, W. E. (1980). The misutilization of evaluation research: Some pitfalls of definition. *Knowledge: Creation, Diffusion, Utilization 1*(4): 477–498.

Cox, G. B. (1976). Managerial style: Implications for the utilization of program evaluation information. Paper read at the 84th annual American Psychological Association convention, Washington, D.C., September 1976. Manuscript submitted for publication.

Cyert, R. M., and March, J. G. (1963). *A Behavioral Theory of the Firm.* Prentice-Hall, Englewood Cliffs, NJ.

Daillak, R. (1981). *A Field Study of Evaluators At Work* (CSE Report No. 154). Center for the Study of Evaluation, Los Angeles.

Deitchman, S. J. (1976). *The Best-Laid Schemes: A Tale of Social Research and Bureaucracy.* M.I.T. Press, Cambridge, MA.

Downs, A. (1967). *Inside Bureaucracy.* Little, Brown, Boston.

Dunn, W. E. (1980). The two-communities metaphor and models of knowledge use: An exploratory case survey. *Knowledge: Creation, Diffusion, Utilization 1*(4): 515–536.

Etzioni, A. (1968). *The Active Society.* Free Press, New York.

Eulau, H., Sackman, N., and Nien, M. (1970). *Information Utility.* AFIPS Press, Montvale, NJ.

Glaser, E. M., and Backer, T. E. (1977). Innovation redefined: Durability and local adaption. *Evaluation 4*:131–135.

Gregg, G., Preston, T., Geist, A., and Caplan, N. (1979). The caravan rolls on: Forty years of social problem research. *Knowledge: Creation, Diffusion, Utilization 1*(1): 31–61.

Guttentag, M. (1973). Subjectivity and its use in evaluation research. *Evaluation 1*(2): 60–65.

Halperin, M. (1974). *Bureaucratic Politics and Foreign Policy.* Brookings Institution, Washington, DC.

Halpert, H. P. (1966). Communications as a basic tool in promoting utilization of research findings. *Community Mental Health Journal 2*(3): 231–236.

Havelock, R. G. (1969). *Planning for Innovation Through Dissemination and Utilization of Knowledge.* Institute for Social Research, Ann Arbor, MI.

—— (1972). *Training for Change Agents.* Institute for Social Research, Ann Arbor, MI.

—— (1973). Resource linkage in innovative educational and problem solving: Ideal vs. actual. *Journal of Research and Development in Education 6*: 76–87.

Havelock, R. G., and Lingwood, D. A. (1973). *R & D Utilization Strategies and Functions: An Analytical Comparison of Four Systems.* Institute for Social Research, Ann Arbor, MI.

Havelock, R. G., and Mann, F. C. (1968). *Research and Development Laboratory Management Knowledge Utilization Study.* Institute for Social Research, Ann Arbor, MI.

Holzner, B., and Fisher, E. (1979). Knowledge in use: Considerations in the sociology of knowledge application. *Knowledge: Creation, Diffusion, Utilization 1*(2): 219–244.

Horowitz, I. L. (1967). *The Rise and Fall of Project Camelot: Studies in the Relationship between Social Science and Practical Politics.* M.I.T. Press, Cambridge, MA.

Janis, I. L., and Mann, L. (1977). *Decision-Making.* Free Press, New York

Johnson, R. J. (1974). Conflict avoidance through acceptable decisions. *Human Relations 27*: 71–82.

Katz, D., and Kahn, R. L. (1978). *The Social Psychology of Organizations,* 2nd ed. Wiley, New York.

Knorr, D. (1977). Policymakers' use of social science knowledge: Symbolic or instrumental? In *Using Social Research in Public Policy Making,* C. H. Weiss (Ed.). Lexington Books, Lexington, MA.

Larsen, J. K. (1980). Knowledge utilization: What is it?" *Knowledge: Creation, Diffusion, Utilization 1*(3): 421–442.

Larsen, J. K., and Werner, P. D. (1981). Measuring utilization of mental health program consultation. In *Utilizing Evaluation: Concepts and Measurement Techniques,* J. A. Ciarlo (Ed.). Sage, Beverly Hills, CA.

Lehman, S. (1975). Psychology, ecology and community: A setting for evaluation research. In *Handbook of Evaluation Research,* vol. 1, E. Struening and M. Guttentag, (Eds.). Sage, Beverly Hills, CA.

Lindblom, C., and Cohen, D. (1979). *Useable Knowledge.* Yale University Press, New Haven, CT.

Lingwood, D. A. (1979). Producing useable knowledge. *American Behavioral Scientist 22*: 339–362.

Lippitt, R. (1965). The use of social research to improve social practice. *American Journal of Orthopsychiatry 35*: 663–669.

Lynd, R. (1939). *Knowledge for What?* Princeton University Press, Princeton, NJ.

Machlup, F. (1979). Uses, values, and benefits of knowledge. *Knowledge: Creation, Diffusion, Utilization 1*:(1) 62–81.

Machlup, F. (1980). *Knowledge and Knowledge Production.* Princeton University Press, Princeton, NJ.

March, J. G., and Simon, H. (1958). *Organizations.* Wiley, New York.

May, J. (1975). Symposium: The policy uses of research. *Inquiry 12*(3): 228-233.

Meld, M. B. (1974). The politics of evaluation of social programs. *Social Work (July)*: 448-455.

Miller, D. W., and Starr, M. K. (1967). *The Structure of Human Decisions.* Prentice-Hall, Englewood Cliffs, NJ.

Mitroff, I., and Mitroff, D. (1979). Interpersonal communication for knowledge utilization. *Knowledge: Creation, Diffusion, Utilization 1*(2): 203–217.

Nagi, S. (1965). The practitioner as a partner in research. *Rehabilitation Record (July/Aug.)*: 1–4.

National Research Council (1978). Study project on social research and development (Stokes, D. E., Chairman, et al.), Vol. 1. *The Federal Investment in Knowledge of Social Problems.* National Academy of Sciences, Washington, DC.

Nelkin, D. (1979). Scientific knowledge, public policy, and democracy. *Knowledge: Creation, Diffusion, Utilization 1*(1): 106–122.

Parsell, A. P. (1966). *Dynamic Evaluation: The Systems Approach to Action Research* (Report No. SP-2423, Systems Development Corporation, Santa Monica, CA). Paper presented at the 61st annual meeting of the American Sociological Society, Miami Beach, Florida, 9/1/1966. Systems Development Corporation, Santa Monica, CA.

Patton, M. Q. (1978). *Utilization-Focused Evaluation.* Sage, Beverly Hills, CA.

Patton, M. Q., Grimes, P. S., Guthrie, K. M., Brennan, N. J., French, B. D., and Blyth, D. A. (1975). *In Search of Impact: An Analysis of the Utilization of Federal Health Evaluation Research.* Minnesota Center for Social Research, University of Minnesota, Minneapolis, MN.

Pelz, D. C., and Horsley, J. A. (1981). Measuring utilization of nursing research. In *Utilization Evaluation: Concepts and Measurement Techniques,* J. A. Ciarlo (Ed.). Sage, Beverly Hills, CA.

Pollak, M. (1980). Paul F. Lazarsfeld: A sociological biography. *Knowledge: Creation, Diffusion, Utilization 2*(2): 157-177.

Pugh, D. S. (1966). Modern organizational theory: A psychological and sociological study. *Psychological Bulletin 66*(4): 235–251.

Rapp, M. L. (1969). *Evaluation as Feedback in the Program Development Cycle.* Rand Corporation, Santa Monica, CA.

Rich, R. F. (1975). An investigation of information gathering and handling in seven federal bureaucracies: A case study of the Continuous National Survey. Unpublished doctoral dissertation, University of Chicago.

—— (1977). Uses of social science information by federal bureaucrats: Knowledge for action vs. knowledge for understanding. In *Using Social Research in Public Policy Making.* C. H. Weiss (Ed.). Lexington Books, Lexington, MA.

—— (1979). The pursuit of knowledge. *Knowledge: Creation, Diffusion, Utilization.* *1*(1): 6–30.

—— (1981). *Social Science Information and Public Policy Making.* Jossey-Bass, San Francisco.

Rich, R. F. (in press). *The Politics of Public Sector Problem Solving: Mental Health Policy Making in an Intergovernmental Setting.*

Riecken, H. W., and Boruch, R. F. (1974). *Social Experimentation: A Method For Planning and Evaluating Social Intervention.* Academic, New York.

Rogers, E. M. (1962). *Diffusion of Innovations.* Free Press, New York.

Rourke, F. (1972). *Bureaucratic Power in National Politics.* Little, Brown, Boston.

Sadofsky, S. (1966). Utilization of evaluation results: Feedback into the action program. In *Learning in Action,* J. L. Schmelzer (Ed.). U.S. Government Printing Office, Washington, DC.

Schatzman, L., and Strauss, A. L. (1973). *Field Research: Strategies for a Natural Sociology.* Prentice-Hall, Englewood Cliffs, NJ.

Schulberg, H. C., and Baker, F. (1968). Program evaluation models and the implementation of research findings. *American Journal of Public Health 58*: 1248–1255.

Scott, W. R. (1966). Some implications of organization theory for research on health services. *Milbank Memorial Fund Quarterly 44* (Oct., Pt. 2): 35–64.

Scriven, M. (1976). Evaluation bias and its control. In *Evaluation Studies Review Annual,* G. V. Glass (Ed.). Vol. 1, Sage, Beverly Hills, CA.

Seashore, S. E., and Bowers, D. G. (1970). Durability of organizational change. *American Psychologist 25*: 227–233.

Selltiz, C., Jahoda, M., Deutsch, M., and Cook, S. W. (1959). *Research Methods in Social Relations,* Rev. ed. Holt, New York.

Simon, H. A. (1976). *Administrative Behavior: A Study of Decision-Making Processes in Administrative Organizations,* 3rd ed. Free Press, New York.

Stufflebeam, D. L. (1974). An administrative checklist for reviewing evaluation plans. Personal communication.

Suchman, E. A. (Ed.) (1967). *Evaluation Research.* Russell Sage Foundation, New York.

Watson, G., and Glaser, E. M. (1965). What we have learned about planning for change. *Management Review 54* (Nov.): 34–36.

Weber, M. (1968). *Economy and Society* (G. Roth and C. Wittich, Eds.). Bedminster, New York.

Weiss, C. H. (1971). *Organizational Constraints on Evaluation Research* (Report of Contract HSM-42-69-82, NIMH, 6/71). Bureau of Applied Social Research, New York. [Also published in condensed form as: Between the cup and the lip. *Evaluation 1*(2): 49–55.]

—— (1972a). Introduction. *Evaluation Research: Methods for Assessing Program Effectiveness.* Prentice-Hall, Englewood Cliffs, NJ.

—— (1972b). Evaluating educational and social action programs: A treeful of owls. In *Evaluating Action Programs: Readings in Social Action and Education,* C. H. Weiss (Ed.). Allyn & Bacon, Boston.

—— (1972c). Utilization of evaluation: Toward comparative study. In *Evaluation Action Programs: Readings in Social Action and Education,* C. H. Weiss (Ed.). Allyn & Bacon, Boston

—— (1972d). The politicization of evaluation research. *Journal of Social Issues 26*(4): 57–68.

—— (1973). Where politics and evaluation research meet. *Evaluation 1*(3): 37–45.

—— (1975). Evaluation research in the political context. In *Handbook of Evaluation Research,* E. L. Struening and M. Guttentag (Eds.). Sage, Beverly Hills, CA.

—— (1977a). Research for policy's sake: The enlightenment function of social research. *Policy Analysis 3*: 531–545.

—— (1977b). Introduction. In *Using Social Research in Public Policy Making,* C. H. Weiss (Ed.). Lexington Books, Lexington, MA.

—— (1980). Knowledge creep and decision accretion. *Knowledge: Creation, Diffusion, Utilization 1*(3): 381–404.

Weiss, C. H., and Bucuvalas, M. J. (1977). The challenge of social research to decision making. In *Using Social Research in Public Policy Making,* C. H. Weiss (Ed.). Lexington Books, Lexington, MA.

Young, S. (1966). *Management: A Systems Analysis.* Scott Forsman, Glenview, IL.

Zaltman, G. (1979). Knowledge utilization as planned social change. *Knowledge: Creation, Diffusion, Utilization 1*(1): 82–105.

Zusman, J. (1976). Can program evaluation be saved from its enthusiasts? *American Journal of Psychiatry 133*: 1300–1305.

6

Policy Formation

Charles O. Jones / University of Virginia, Charlottesville, Virginia
Dieter Matthes / Francis Marion College, Florence, South Carolina

In his thought-provoking essay on the impact of "issue networks" on the policy process, Hugh Heclo concludes by noting the following trend in American politics:

> Imagine trying to govern in a situation where the short-term political resources you need are stacked around a changing series of discrete issues, and where people overseeing these issues have nothing to prevent their pressing claims beyond any resources that they can offer in return. Imagine too that the more they do, the more you lose understanding and support from public backers who have the long-term resources that you need. Whipsawed between cynics and true believers, policy would always tend to evolve to levels of insolubility. It is not easy for a society to politicize itself and at the same time depoliticize government leadership. But we in the United States may be managing to do just that (Heclo, 1978: 123–124).

Implied in this statement is a policy process more confusing and unpredictable than in the past, one that has been altered significantly by the changing nature of the American political system. In this chapter we seek to present an overview of those activities associated with policy formation in this country. Table 1 indicates those significant activities that make up this part of the policy process. These activities will serve as an outline for the chapter; that is, we focused on those actions that lead from awareness of a problem to the development and approval of a plan for dealing with it.

What are the sources of problems treated in government? How are priorities set? How do issues change over time? Who is involved in formulating proposals, and how do they do it? How is support developed for policy proposals? What is the effect of institutional processes on program development? What cross-institutional devices emerge to facilitate program development? These questions are discussed in this chapter. Whenever possible, we define key concepts, identify characteristic behavior or actions associated with each activity, provide relevant examples, and note significant trends.

Table 1. Policy Formation Activities

Phase	Activities	Initial Product
Problem to government	Perception Definition	Problem
	Aggregation Organization Representation	Demand
	Agenda setting	Priorities

	Formation
	  Research
	  Review
	  Projection
	  Selection
		Proposal

Action in government	Legitimation Identification of interests Communication Bargaining Compromise	Program
	Appropriation Formation Legitimation	Budget

Source: Adapted from C. O. Jones, *An Introduction to the Study of Public Policy,* 2nd ed., Table 9.1. Copyright © 1977 by Wadsworth Publishing Company, Inc. Reprinted by permission of Brooks/Cole Publishing Company, Monterey, CA 93940.

Conclusions drawn in this chapter tend to be consistent with Heclo's analysis. Subtle but significant changes in the American political system have altered the policy process. For example, participation at the grass-roots level, as well as among single-issue politics, continues to increase. Characteristically, this participation is intense and uncompromising in nature. A policy process designed to facilitate compromise is severely tested by the policy demands of those unwilling to bargain. This condition of increased public participation in policy formation, therefore, leads to more uncertainty than in the past, both for predicting outcomes and for analyzing behavior.

I. SOURCES OF PROBLEMS TREATED IN GOVERNMENT

A multitude of public problems continuously compete for government attention. What happens to those few that reach government depends on those conditions responsible for getting them there. How a certain event affects people, who perceives and defines problems resulting from the events, which organizations arise to place their demands before government to alleviate the problem, and which key decision makers respond to demands all help shape the context and boundaries of the policy process for acting on any one public problem.

What makes a problem public? How do public problems differ from private problems? John Dewey (1927: 15–16) defines *public* as consisting "of all those who are affected by the indirect consequences of transactions to such an extent that it is deemed necessary to have those consequences cared for." Public problems, then, "are those that have a broad effect, including consequences for persons not directly involved" (Anderson, 1975: 57). Typically, the resolution of public problems requires a contribution by those not likely to profit—e.g., through taxation. Thus such problems may escalate participation unless the public is indifferent. Many events do not affect a large number of people and do not seem to hold consequences for those not directly involved. These are private problems.

Issues are created when counter demands are made on government to solve perceived problems. The original event or situation may be perceived differently by participants or observers, thereby leading to various definitions, demands, and strategies to deal with problems resulting from the event. Much of what government does represents efforts to deal with contradictory and conflictual definitions of and solutions to society's problems. What is referred to as the "energy problem," for example, consists of many issues affecting people in all areas of life. An event such as the Arab oil embargo leads to various perceptions and definitions with regard to the problems that result from the event and how they should be resolved. Demands made on government normally reflect such diversity. James E. Anderson (1975: 55) correctly notes that "[t]he nature of the problem ... helps determine the nature of the policy process."

The extent of participation in problem definition and agenda setting by government and private individuals varies considerably, as does the degree of cooperation between the two. The following four situations provide useful illustrative cases for discussion purposes.

Type 1: Private development with only limited government involvement
Type 2: Government development with only limited private involvement
Type 3: Combination of government and private development
Type 4: Neither government nor private development

Type 1 refers to those situations in which the private sector places public problems before government. This process may be a result of activities undertaken by private citizens on behalf of other citizens who have been affected by a certain event or situation. Or this process may be initiated by organized private groups attempting to represent others who have perceived and defined a particular public problem. The Ralph Nader crusade on behalf of automobile safety standards is a case in point. It was only after his constant and well-publicized pressure that government took action to deal with a major public problem in this country: the lack of adequate automobile safety protection for passengers. This does not mean, however, that those in the private sphere petitioning government perceive and define the problem in the same way. On the contrary, one would expect competition and conflict. Automobile manufacturers, for example, resisted the attempt by Nader and other groups to force them to improve safety features in their automobiles.

In the area of energy, coal operators and the United Mine Workers (UMW) have been at odds for decades. When a major mine disaster occurs and focuses public attention on safety problems, coal operators have generally perceived and defined the problem to be one of ignorance on the part of the miner, whereas the UMW has consistently blamed profit-hungry coal operators cutting costs in the safety area (Matthes, 1978). In short, multiple definitions of public problems affect the chances of government attention on the one hand and the type of government action on the other.

There may be a number of explanations for limited government involvement in defining problems that are perceived to be important in the private sphere. It may be that policy makers simply are not aware of the existence of these problems, or perhaps policy makers are aware of these problems yet feel that they lack authority to deal with them, or they may simply refuse to deal with a recognized problem because of other priorities. Prior to the 1930s, the private sector played a central role in problem identification, either by petitioning government to act or by attempting to act without government. More recently, government has been much more involved in defining problems in the private sphere. For example, the petroleum industry has been in a position in recent years to control the flow of petroleum-related problems to the government agenda. This pattern came to a dramatic end when the Arab nations cut off the flow of oil to the United States in the fall of 1973. Since then, government has become much more active in regulating the oil industry and therefore in defining the problems associated with the industry. This case illustrates that an event of significant proportion may dramatically alter the manner in which public problems are developed. The current trend is away from purely private development. In recent decades, government has been much more active in perceiving and defining public problems resulting from societal events and situations.

Type 2 depicts the processes in which government develops public problems with limited private participation. In this case public policy makers perceive and define problems without necessarily waiting for private initiative. It may be that those affected by a certain event or situation lack the resources to demand government relief. E. E. Schatt-schneider (1960) talks about a "bias" in our political system, by which those with the greatest need for government attention lack the time and money to petition government for that relief. Consequently, government policy makers themselves may become involved in defining problems for this group and attempt to legislate relief. Sometimes this involvement is quite circumstantial. For example, a presidential primary campaign through West Virginia contributed to John F. Kennedy's recognition that a myriad of problems confronted the poor in this country of affluence. What he witnessed as he toured the mountains of Appalachia significantly affected his priorities as President of the United States, priorities that were continued by his successor in the White House, Lyndon B. Johnson. As a matter of fact, that bundle of programs known as the "War on Poverty" represented a case where government took the initiative; that is, the federal government perceived and defined what the problems were, and on that basis developed programs to deal with them (Donovan, 1967; Moynihan, 1969).

As with type 1, multiple definitions of what problems exist may also occur frequently when the government is the principal source of problem definition. Various policy makers may differ in the perception of what problems exist, and these differing perceptions may affect efforts to develop acceptable solutions. Also like type 1, it is difficult to find many "pure" cases where government develops problems totally without private interaction. When this does occur, however, it may be that government initially recognizes the problem in order to allow private groups to enter the policy process and make demands. Type 2 cases may also include relatively noncontroversial issues that can be acted on with little publicity. In summary, this discussion leads one to conclude that the more common type of problem development includes a mix of private and public activities, a topic we turn to next.

Those processes associated with type 3 probably lead to the most interesting policy situations. Most problem development activities occur as a result of interaction between government and private actors. As government extends its scope of authority, problem definition activities have become more involved, complex, and time-consuming. Also, one may expect even greater variations in problem definition when so many different actors are involved. Therefore, conflict may surface at this early stage. However, even if conflict does not characterize problem definition, it may develop at later stages in the policy process. Thus, for example, disagreements may be postponed until the formulation or legitimation stages of the policy process. Even more so than with types 1 and 2, multiple definitions, whether conflictual or harmonious, will be the rule rather than the exception. In the late 1960s and early 1970s, a Democratic Congress allied with well-organized environmental groups fought a Republican Administration allied with energy-related industries over the problems associated with the recognition that the environment was being abused in this country.

The more publicized the event or situation, the more likely it is that both private and public actors will be active in defining public problems. Parallel activities, however, do not necessarily lead to conflict. Rather, they may simply require coordination to make the process more efficient. As single-issue groups become more and more involved in the policy process, and as political participation in general increases, multiple perception and definition activities will continue to characterize problem development processes. This outcome will require greater efforts by policy makers to find compromises that avoid polarization and conflicts.

Type 4 recognizes the possibility that neither public nor private problem development may occur, yet problems may in fact exist. This situation may be the result of a lack of resources available to those affected by a certain event, a lack of organization to petition government, or simply a lack of urgency compared to other public problems competing for government attention. It may also be that there is a conscious effort by private groups or policy makers to keep problems from being defined, a process defined by some scholars as "non-decision making" (Bachrach and Baratz, 1970). In his study of air pollution policy development, Matthew A. Crenson argues that the automobile industries consciously attempted to prevent government development of this particular issue (Crenson, 1971). Attempts to define those problems resulting from racial segregation in the 1950s throughout the South seem also to have been thwarted by Southern politicians at all levels of government (Dye, 1971).

The preceding discussion regarding the four types of problem development indicates the complexities inherent in this phase of the policy process. It becomes obvious that this phase entails a myriad of combinations between the private and public sectors that scholars need to anticipate when analyzing the policy process.

II. SETTING PRIORITIES IN GOVERNMENT

How are priorities set? According to David B. Truman, the existence of group loyalties determines what problems are acted on in government (Truman, 1951). Since so many groups exist and competition among them for government attention is intense, and since group life is characterized by overlapping and multiple memberships, no one group consistently determines which problems government will act on over a period of time. Policy makers actively participate in this group conflict, and as Roger W. Cobb and Charles D. Elder point out: "[a] primary function of government . . . is to manage group conflict" (1972: 33).

Robert A. Dahl has also suggested that organized groups have the capacity to be heard in our political system, thereby influencing what problems reach the policy agenda (Dahl, 1956). The major criticism directed at this group approach, and the pluralist interpretation of politics in general, is the inherent bias resulting from the exclusion of those who cannot organize their concerns. As noted earlier, Schattschneider has identified a bias inherent in this system of policy making (1960). Without prescribing how one may solve this problem of the "semisovereign people," the fact remains that policy makers interact continuously with those with resources to organize and voice demands. Consequently, a bias will certainly result, leading one scholar to characterize our system as one of "preferential pluralism" (Jones, 1977: 38).

It is important to go beyond those guidelines outlined by group theorists when discussing priority-setting activities. Problems reach the policy agenda in various ways. Table 2 provides an inventory of events that may elevate the consequent problem or problems onto the policy agenda. The important task for policy analysts is to identify which problems resulted from these events, who defined them in what manner, who organized to remedy the problem, and which key policy makers took an active role in attempting to alleviate the problem. Data on these matters permit the analyst to judge the extent to which the nature of the policy process is shaped by problem development and agenda-setting processes.

A problem must have the sympathy and command the support of key decision makers to attain agenda status. In general, policy makers actively participate in priority setting, and they are not bystanders by any means. Cobb and Elder identify factors that may give certain groups greater access than others. These include: (1) the decision maker may be indebted to that group, (2) some groups have more resources than others or are better able to mobilize their resources, (3) some groups are located so strategically in the social and economic structure that their interests cannot be ignored, and (4) some groups are held in greater esteem by the public than others and thus command greater access to decision makers (1972: 90).

Similarly, Charles O. Jones notes that agenda-setting strategies differ along dimensions of groups organization and pattern of access. He cites the following variations (1977: 42):

1. A well-organized group with established access
2. A well-organized group without established access
3. A poorly organized group with established access
4. A poorly organized group without established access

Table 2. How Problems Reach the Policy Agenda

Anderson (1975: 60–62)	Cobb and Elder (1972: 84)	Jones (1977: 27–32)
Political leadership Crisis/spectacular event Protest activity Media concerns	Internal: Natural catastrophe Unanticipated human event Technological change Civil rights protest Union strikes Ecological change External: Act of war (U.S. involvement) Innovation in weapons technology International conflict without U.S. Changing world alignment	Political campaign Immediate threats to a a significant number of persons Considerable publicity Efforts of single individual Previous policy application

Each group will employ whatever advantages it possesses, whether it be extensive organization, continuous access, or both.

Not all public problems resulting from events within society are acted on in government, and not all public problems acted on in government receive equal attention. Priorities must be set given the competition for government attention. The context within which priorities are set is a relevant factor. During times of prosperity, when resources are expanding, setting priorities simply means dividing an ever-growing pie. Such a situation existed after World War II in this country. Economic growth allowed government revenues to increase at a pace where new programs could be funded and old programs maintained. Recently, however, policy makers have had to cope with funding large government programs in a period of reduced economic growth. Efforts are now being directed toward making existing programs more efficient rather than initiating new programs.

President Jimmy Carter asked the Congress in 1980 to approve a "prudent and responsible" fiscal plan, one that would be "part of his blueprint to shrink the size of government and balance the budget by 1981" (*Congressional Quarterly Weekly Report*, February 2, 1980, p. 235). Pressures to be more fiscally conservative also exist in the Congress, reflecting the public mood to cut the size of government and streamline, perhaps even eliminate, some government programs. All of these developments influence contemporary priority setting. Relationships that have existed for years may have to adjust to new uncertainties as programs may be in danger of losing the support enjoyed in the past. One would expect the policies of priority setting to be more intense and complex with this reduction of available resources.

Policy scholars also need to comprehend the dynamics associated with setting priorities in government. Truman (1951: 105–106) notes that there is an inevitable expansion of government, since priorities seem to lead to other priorities. A major event can produce ripple effects for priority setting at all levels of government, as well as in the private sphere. The Great Depression, for example, significantly altered priority setting in both public and private spheres. More recently, the oil embargo of 1973 has had a significant expansion effect. This event elevated problems associated with energy supplies to the top of the government agenda. Other items were relegated to lower-priority status. Prior to the oil embargo, for example, environmental forces were scoring major political victories in most areas of environmental concern, especially air and water pollution concerns. The oil embargo changed the entire context within which these activities occurred, leading to a gradual reconsideration of environmental goals.

In addition to this process of displacing one issue with another on the list of priorities, an expansion process may occur within the new issue. For example, the oil embargo quickly led to initial debates concerning petroleum shortages and long gas lines, and how to deal with this immediate problem. Soon, however, other problems related to the initial event became quite apparent, problems such as dependence on foreign oil, military priorities in the Middle East, and economic concerns such as the increasing costs of imported crude oil. In short, one event not only displaced existing government priorities, it also led to ripple effects that make plain the problems that can result from one event.

This expansion will continue to occur as government acts on these new problems. Priorities of state and local governments may also be affected. These governments may have to adjust their own work in the light of activities at the federal level. For example, the federal law to conserve fuel by reducing speed limits on interstate highways resulted in law enforcement adjustments at both state and local levels. Federal energy efficiency standards for federal buildings, including thermostat controls, have also affected state and local governments. This ripple effect goes beyond government. Private industry and individuals will also have to adjust priorities. The oil embargo has affected the automobile industry. Individuals have had to adjust their driving habits since gasoline has become either scarce or expensive. Demands for smaller cars increased significantly, forcing manufacturers to shift priorities from luxury to fuel-efficient cars. Their lack of foresight and competition from abroad have resulted in further problems: The automobile industry needs help from government, illustrating the time dimension inherent in priority-setting dynamics. Ripple effects may occur several years after the initial event takes place.

It may also be the case that an event that has an expansive effect may reintroduce priorities that were displaced earlier. One example would be the 1980 riots in Miami, Florida, which vividly pointed to the existence of employment and economic problems in black communities across the country. Black leaders used this event to remind elected officials that the war on poverty of the 1960s had not been won. Coal mine safety also illustrates this dimension of priority setting. When a major mine disaster occurs, such as the one in Farmington, West Virginia, in 1968, policy makers are anxious to deal with the problems of safety in underground coal mines (Matthes, 1978). After a period of symbolic or substantive governmental activities, other, more pressing events displace the safety problem on the list of governmental priorities, until another mine disaster occurs. In summary, the dynamics of priority setting deserve attention due to the constant and complex interaction between perceptions and definitions of events at all levels of government, in both the private and public sphere. The result is an everchanging, unpredictable change in governmental priorities and the consequent ripple effects influencing all areas of society.

Governmental priorities are often referred to as agendas. Cobb and Elder identify two agendas. The first is the systemic agenda consisting of "all issues that are commonly perceived by members of the political community as meriting public attention and as involving matters within the legitimate jurisdiction of existing government authority" (1972: 85). The second is the institutional agenda, defined as "that set of items explicitly up for active and serious consideration of authoritative decision makers" (1972: 86). This second agenda refers to those problems perceived by decision makers to be important enough to warrant serious attention and efforts to develop a course of action. The systemic agenda suggests the existence of general boundaries that define what legitimate priorities may be considered by government. This concept indicates that in certain political systems certain kinds of issues cannot come before government because of the nature of the ideology or political structure. It also seems to indicate that these parameters change over time. What was possible before the 1930s in this country, for example, is quite different from what is possible today in government.

In moving beyond these broad concepts, agenda setting becomes even more complicated. In the first place, the founding fathers presented us with a system of separation of powers and federalism to disperse policy-making activities throughout the political system. Consequently, it should come as no surprise to find that a particular problem can be perceived and acted on by decision makers in one institution at one level of government while not being perceived at all in another. In short, multiple agendas may exist within and among various institutions at different levels of government.

Second, along with the institutional or systemic breakdown, policy agenda can also be defined along a dimension of functional policy activities: (1) problem definition agenda for "items receiving 'active and serious' research and definition," (2) a proposal agenda "where a shift has been made from defining the problem to finding a solution," (3) a bargaining agenda for "proposals for which support is 'actively and seriously' developed," and (4) continuing agenda for "items receiving continuous examination" (Jones, 1977: 40–41).

Table 3 combines these two dimensions of the policy agenda concept and illustrates that various types of policy agenda may exist within and vary throughout governmental institutions. One can expand this table further by including regional, state, and local governmental bodies. All institutions, however, do not necessarily deal with all problems that come before government. Along with other factors, the issue itself will determine which institutions become involved and at what stage of the policy process. One can also analyze agenda setting in terms of formal and informal agendas. In government there are at all times formal listings of work to be handled; this may include the daily schedule for the Senate and House. This formal agenda may differ from one's personal view of events and the problems emanating from those events. Others may differ in their interpretation of problems before government, illustrating how subjective agendas and agenda setting may be.

In a democracy, government may engage in a number of agenda-setting strategies. Government may play a very limited role in agenda-setting activities. This strategy would

Table 3. Initial Breakdown of Policy Agenda Concept

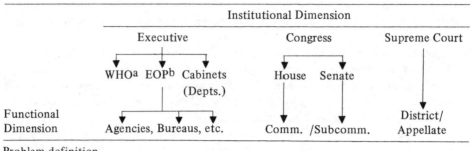

	Institutional Dimension		
	Executive	Congress	Supreme Court
	WHO[a] EOP[b] Cabinets (Depts.)	House Senate	
Functional Dimension	Agencies, Bureaus, etc.	Comm. /Subcomm.	District/ Appellate
Problem-definition agenda			
Proposal agenda			
Bargaining agenda			
Continuing agenda			

Source: Developed from Jones, 1977, pp. 40–41.
[a]White House Office.
[b]Executive Office of the President.

coincide with type 1 of the problem development activities discussed earlier; that is, private problem development activities, whether harmonious or conflictual, will determine priorities. This competition tends to favor those interests that can organize quickly and effectively. Those groups in most need of government attention, without resources necessary to compete for agenda status, will be ignored under this hands-off approach. As was mentioned earlier, the trend seems to be toward more active government involvement in agenda-setting activities.

A second agenda-setting strategy is for government to encourage broad involvement in problem definition. In this strategy government becomes less passive in perceiving and defining public problems. Government does not, however, identify problems for others, but only aids those acknowledged to lack the resources. In the third agenda-setting strategy, government takes the initiative and defines problems. Policy priorities are set by government, as described in the type 2 problem development situations. Jones notes that this strategy "places an enormous burden on government. Surveying events, judging the consequences, and setting priorities in a complex society are difficult and demanding responsibilities" (Jones, 1977: 38).

Each strategy entails certain biases. In general, the hands-off approach allows the inequalities in society to be perpetuated in government, whereas the more active strategies question if government has relevant capabilities to deal with societal problems. These approaches are also relevant to any discussion of non-decision making. It may be that this first strategy facilitates non-decision making, since private interests can mobilize enough resources to keep certain problems off the governmental agenda. However, it may be more useful to control government to keep certain problems from being discussed. The more centralized the political structures, the more likely that those who control these structures will be successful in controlling agendas. Thus, non-decision making may occur under all three strategies, again illustrating the complexity of the concept.

The trend appears to be toward more active government involvement in the agenda-setting phase of the policy process. This demanding activity carries with it the enormous responsibility of judging whose problems deserve attention and resources. However intense the conflicts over priorities in the past, we may expect even greater competition in the future.

III. CHANGING ISSUES OVER TIME

Once issues have been accepted as legitimate concerns for government, they undergo changes over periods of time. As new events occur and priorities change, certain issues receive varying degrees of attention from policy makers, as well as from the public itself. These events help dictate the manner in which issues change over time. For example, in the late 1960s and early 1970s, foreign policy issues were high on the government's action agendas (primarily as a consequence of the problems associated with the Vietnam war). More recently, emphasis has changed to domestic issues: for example, inflation, the environment, energy shortages, and unemployment. This is not to say that foreign policy issues have been ignored, especially since all of these domestic issues have foreign policy implications. The point is that changes in issue emphasis, or tendencies, occur in government.

One general trend with an impact on the policy process is the nationalization of issues. Policy makers recognize that national solutions must be formulated to deal with particular problems. The bundle of problems associated with energy is a case in point. Ever since 1973, there have been efforts in the White House and in the halls of Congress to come up with a "national energy policy." The recognition that energy problems are highly interrelated has forced policy makers to try and determine national interest. This process has been long, frustrating, and inconclusive as of the present time. Efforts to develop national policy for any major domestic issue typically involve lengthy, spirited debate and large-scale compromising. Despite these difficulties, however, the trend seems to be in the direction of greater comprehensiveness in public policy.

Another general trend in the area of issue changes is the internationalization of issues. It seems that the familiar dichotomy of "domestic" versus "foreign" issues is not as useful today as it has been in the past. In fact, most of the so-called domestic issues—inflation, unemployment, environmental degradation—are tied to international problems and questions. The world has become a smaller and more interdependent place to live. Actions taken by the Organization of Petroleum Exporting Countries (OPEC) will affect the rate of inflation in this country as we continue to pay billions for imported oil. Monetary adjustments by European allies will also affect our balance of payments as well as monetary policy in this country. Consequently, broader considerations will characterize policy-making activities as issues become more internationalized, perhaps leading to a more conflictual decision-making structure as strains between local, parochial ties and international considerations become more pronounced.

It is useful to identify three types of issues, in terms of demands made on government—expansive, consolidative, and contracting. Some issues are expansive in nature, that is, government expansion is virtually inevitable. We have already discussed the "inevitable gravitation to government" as well as the ripple effects inherent in policy-making activities. Many social welfare issues, for example,will expand as a consequence of government action itself. That is, once government has acted, further action is inevitable. These issues feed on themselves, since the initial demands will continue to grow until all those eligible to receive benefits in an expanding population are included. Consequently, demands will occur continuously, leading to constant reconsideration and adjustment. Those not included will demand to be included, whereas those already covered will demand more coverage. Programs that give direct benefits or make direct payments to individuals are particularly vulnerable to these types of policy activities.

Defense policy also fits under the category of expansive issues, especially during times of strained relations with the Soviet Union. The constant need to modernize weaponry and intelligence-gathering devices leads to an expansion of demands concerning defense-related issues. There are, of course, degrees of expansion. During wartime, the demands naturally increase significantly as all resources are mobilized to conclude the war as quickly as possible. After the war has ended, demands continue but at a lesser pace. As long as confrontation with the Soviet Union is a reality, defense-related demands will continue to expand. Under contracting resources, however, these tendencies will undoubtedly come under attack. The current debate surrounding efforts to balance the federal budget illustrates this point.

Consolidative demands constitute the second type of demand leading to issue changes. These demands urge efficiency and effectiveness through reorganization, evaluation, and analysis. Much more emphasis is being placed on these types of activities in government today. As resources contract, policy makers will increase their search for more efficiency and less waste in governmental programs. Virtually all presidential candidates in 1980 emphasized efficiency in government, recognizing that the pie is not expanding at the rate it was in the 1960s. Consolidative demands are very threatening to those benefiting from entitlement or other naturally expanding programs. Thus, it is to be expected that both the Executive and Congress have equipped themselves with agencies and procedures to develop more efficient evaluation of what is working and what is not. To become more exact in evaluation of programs is one aim of consolidative demands. It is not surprising, therefore that we have witnessed a virtual explosion of program evaluation in recent years.

The third type of demand leading to issue change is that to withdraw. These contracting demands indicate to government that enough has been done in an area and activity should be terminated. It may be that a general mood over the expansion of government into all phases of society will provide the context for more specific demands within certain issue areas. Government is urged to cut back, to reevaluate its priorities, perhaps to allow state and local governments to assume responsibilities for programs. These demands may, of course, be made by private groups or by policy makers themselves. The efforts to reevaluate the relevance of the space program after the moon project had been successfully completed resulted in demands that funding be cut back. Terminating a large program is not easy. Those who have an interest in the program, whether an interest group, an administrative agency, or a congressional subcommittee, will fight to keep the program intact and expand its scope of authority. The current trend indicates, however, that demands to reduce or eliminate programs will become more frequent in the future, perhaps fueled by more effective evaluation techniques.

All three demands may be made for a single issue at any one time. For example, federal subsidy programs to farmers, such as tobacco farmers, will generate expansive demands as subsidy increases occur year after year to help the American tobacco farmer. Nonfarming groups, or farming groups representing different crops, will undoubtedly argue against such increases, calling instead for a more consolidative approach in providing federal aid to farmers. Antismoking groups may call for an end to subsidies to an industry that produces cigarettes, which in turn cause cancer. This mix of demands must be weighed and evaluated by policy makers as they make their decisions. The trend is in the direction of more varied demands in our political system as increasing emphasis is placed on evaluation and efficiency, perhaps leading to demands to terminate government programs that are not working. Under conditions of contracting resources, these types of demands will increase, complicating the policy process even more. The public demands reductions in government, decision makers respond by seeking to consolidate programs, and yet such moves adversely affect the demands for expansiveness by groups currently benefiting. Several layers of conflict result and decision makers are faced with having to resolve what are basically incompatible requests.

IV. THE SOURCE, METHODS, AND STYLES OF PROGRAM FORMATION

We come now to consider the actual birth of proposals for government action to solve public problems. Who is involved in these activities? And what are the various methods used to formulate proposals? Before addressing those questions directly, it is useful to clarify what we mean by the term "program formulation" by distinguishing it from the term "planning."

Herbert J. Gans (1968: 129) defines "social planning" as

> . . . a method of decision making that proposes or identifies goals or ends, determines the means or programs which achieve or are thought to achieve these ends, and does so by the application of analytical techniques to discover the fit between ends and means and the consequences of implementing alternative ends and means.

Note the implicit emphasis on systematic methods in this definition. As used here, formulation is a more encompassing term. It includes the kind of methodical or systematic planning cited by Gans, but it also includes much less rigorous and much more subjective efforts to resolve public problems. This definition of formulation permits us to include, perhaps even be tolerant of, the work of politicians as they seek to satisfy constituents or seek reelection. Seldom thought of as planners, elected officials nevertheless do react to issues and almost instinctively formulate proposals for treating these issues. Often these proposals are filtered through a screen of personal political experience.

Policy proposals may emanate from various sources, depending on the interest, authority, and resources of persons in and out of government. The number of proposals for treating a public problem may vary from several to a few or just one. Proposals may be competitive or complementary. Typically, size and significance of the issue determine how many competitive proposals are forthcoming. For example, the problem of equalizing health services may be expected to involve many formulators producing ideas and plans that are highly competitive. On the other hand, the problem of inoculating a group of school children normally will involve very few persons and will elicit a single proposal. Conflict frequently increases as the problem itself is more visible. Literally thousands of problems are treated by governments every day without questions being raised or counterproposals being developed. Bureaucrats apply standard solutions or use their discretion to find means for handling a new situation. However, when an issue commands the attention of elected officials, it is often because it has become publicly visible. And when an issue is taken up in the political arenas, greater conflict is typically the result.

The precise sources of proposals are many and varied. From within government one may expect them to emanate from the following persons or groups, either singly or in combinations:

1. Political executives. Presidents, governors, mayors, and their appointees may personally generate proposals, but more commonly they stimulate, command, or direct others to do so. Because of their positions of authority, they may also be the recipients of unsolicited proposals.

2. Bureaucrats. Many bureaucrats are career planners. But those bureaucrats with other responsibilities may also become involved in formulating proposals as an outgrowth of their administrative work.

3. Consultants. Consulting groups are now very active in the early stages of program development. They may do much of the research that is required, and they may identify the options for treating the issue at hand. Many consultants have at one time worked for government.

4. Research agencies. The national government relies on its own research laboratories, supports quasi-government research institutions such as the RAND Corporation, and provides grants to universities and private research agencies. The research product is often used as the basis for proposals.

5. Legislators and their staffs. As with political executives, legislators have ideas about what ought to be done to solve a public problem. Until recently they had less staff than political executives, and thus were more likely to be directly involved in reviewing, not preparing, options. Recent expansions of congressional staff have changed this situation, making the relationship more like that between political executives and bureaucrats.

The sources of proposals from *outside government* may be just as varied:

1. Interest groups and associations. Businesses, labor unions, farmers, and professionals of various kinds are but a few of the social and economic groups that organize to influence government action. Many of these organizations have resources to do the research and analysis necessary to prepare proposals.

2. Clientele groups. Government programs often create clienteles, which then organize to preserve and expand benefits. In formulating new proposals, these groups often work closely with the government agency administering the program.

3. Citizen groups. Active citizen groups have been making demands on government for a very long time. The 1960s, however, produced a great deal more direct involvement

by such groups. Groups such as those organized by Ralph Nader, Common Cause, and various environmental and energy organizations actively participated in identifying problems and proposing solutions.

4. Political parties. The rise of citizen group participation in program development contrasts with the decline of political party involvement. Parties were an important source of proposals at one time, at least at the state and local level. They are less significant today.

5. The media. Newspapers and magazines continue to be a source for identifying public problems and suggesting means for solving them. But the important development in recent decades is the widespread impact of television, particularly on agenda setting. Television documentaries can draw attention to and promote public issues, often with the result that the issue becomes a priority matter in government.

Several points should be emphasized in thinking about these various sources of proposals. First, several of these sources may work cooperatively in developing proposals— as a team in all activities or by dividing up the work (e.g., certain sources primarily involved in identifying a problem, others primarily involved in analyzing options, still others in selecting one course of action over others). Second, governments themselves may be the source of proposals for other governments—either within the same political system or between political systems. Increasingly, it seems, the national government has influenced the agendas of state and local governments, with some reciprocation. And attention is increasingly paid to how other nations solve the common problems associated with energy, environment, labor management relations, trade, and so on. Third, the development of a proposal by one source (or a combination of sources) may stimulate competitive proposals. This competition in program formulation may eventually result in cooperation and a melding of proposals, complete victory for one group over another, or stalemate. Fourth, one may observe an escalation of proposals when an issue rises quickly in public awareness. For example, the Arab oil embargo dramatically raised the consciousness of the public regarding energy shortages, and the publication of Rachel Carson's *Silent Spring* had a similar impact with regard to environmental issues. With both, we witnessed an outpouring of short-term responses and longer-term planning.

The methods and styles of program formulation also vary considerably. Methods may be comprehensive or segmental, systematic or unsystematic, projective or reactive. The first distinction is often the most difficult to explain. One hears a great deal about the importance of being comprehensive. Thus, for example, the President and Congress are frequently criticized for failing to promote a comprehensive policy for energy, the environment, and the economy. Unfortunately, the requirements for comprehensiveness are never fully explicated. What does it mean to be comprehensive in developing energy proposals? The following elements should be considered in responding to that question.

1. The number of issues or problems treated: whether the universe of all issues, a sample (more than one), or just one
2. The extent of the analysis: whether synoptic (treating all aspects of the issue or issues), or segmental (treating selected aspects)
3. The estimation of effects: whether judging the effects to all others, from one issue to all those within the issue area, or just those within a single issue

Clearly, these elements introduce many permutations of comprehensive planning or formulation. The most idealistic, and therefore the least probable, is the universal, synoptic, cross-issue approach, by which one attempts to treat all aspects of all energy problems, including estimating the effects of any proposals on all other issues. Actually, what is frequently labeled "comprehensive" is no more than an approach that draws a sample of problems, treats selected aspects of these problems, and estimates the effects of proposals within each of the problems treated. Even more common is the purely segmental approach, which considers selected aspects of just one issue or problem and may or may not estimate the effects of proposals. Thus, in common usage the difference between the comprehensive and the segmental approaches to program formulation turns on whether those involved go beyond the narrowest possible analysis. If they do, then the effort may be popularly labeled "comprehensive."

The difference between systematic and unsystematic methods requires less discussion. Often it is a distinction between who is participating in formulation and what resources are available. Thus, for example, one may expect a scientist or technician in an agency with ample research funds to be highly systematic. On the other hand, a member of Congress campaigning in the district is likely to be quite unsystematic in gathering information about problems and drawing conclusions about what ought to be done about them.

The projective/reactive dichotomy is related to the earlier distinction between agenda-setting strategies designed to "make it happen" versus those designed to "let it happen." That is, the projective method is forward-looking. It attempts to estimate future problems as effects of existing and proposed government programs. The knowledge gained from this effort is fed into present program formulation. Often the projective method has the effect of expanding the agenda of government, since it leads to a kind of "cover the waterfront" mentality—if five outcomes are possible, then one should prepare for all five. By comparison, those content with the reactive method are less anxious and perhaps also less confident. In this mode, those with the interest and authority to formulate proposals for government action wait for the buildup of demands, responding when the pressure is great. The reactive method is based on quite a different philosophy of government than is the projective method. Those taking this approach view government as a corrective for problems that resist private solution.

Styles of program formulation refer to what one relies on in preparing proposals. *Routine formulation* relies on what was done in the past—turning to precedent or the standard response for a particular set of circumstances. *Analogous formulation* examines what was done to treat a problem judged to be similar in characteristics to the present problem. *Creative formulation* is not bound by the past or by analogies. Rather, an effort is made to develop imaginative proposals suited to the unique characteristics of the problem at hand.

Source, method, and style may be determined in part by the time available to propose solutions and whether or not a problem is foreseen. An emergency or crisis may be defined as an unforeseen problem requiring immediate action. Under these circumstances, participation may be limited to top executives who have no time for systematic analysis and who may be forced to rely on available routines or analogies. Conversely, futurism may be defined as an effort to foresee the emergence of problems in the long term (20 to 50 years). If taken seriously, such efforts may be expected to attract widespread participation in and out of government and result in demands for systematic analysis and maximum creativity. Finally, it should be noted that seldom is the immediate neatly separable from either the past or the future. Today's emergency may be only the first signal of tomorrow's permanent agenda. Yet the unsystematically developed, short-term response by a few persons may create the routine or analogies on which future programs rely.

V. BUILDING SUPPORT FOR PROPOSALS

The next activities to consider are those associated with having one's proposal accepted. What is involved in gaining acceptance? Basically, it is a process of getting the approval of those who count. And who counts? The specific answer to that question will vary from one proposal to the next. In general, however, one can say that those persons count who have the authority to say "yes" or "no" and who have the interest, organization, and resources to be heard on the subject. Getting approval, then, typically requires getting support from those with authority and interest. Those touched in some way by the proposal may have been involved in its development. If so, they may be relied on for building support with others. But it is not always a simple matter to be all-inclusive in program formulation. Some effected groups intentionally or unintentionally ignored in the development phase may then actively oppose the proposal as it is set before those with authority. The point is that in program development politics one should be prepared for interaction between and among those with authority and interest.

Getting the approval of those who count is, by definition, a complex matter in a democracy of such large scale as that in the United States. We have established rather elaborate processes at all levels of government—processes typically involving majority coalition building in legislatures (normally in two houses), executive approval, and, often, considerable bureaucratic discretion. It would be an overstatement to say that all proposals are subjected to long and tedious approval processes. Even complicated proposals with major policy implications may win quick approval from those in authority (e.g., the Economic Opportunity Act of 1964). But the potential for a long, drawn-out controversy is always there because of the elaborateness of formal methods for getting agreement. Further, getting the approval of those in authority does not always ensure acceptance of the program by those effected. The latter may have very little advance information about the proposal, or not be prepared to form an opinion even if they do have the information. Their reactions may not develop until they see the program in operation, but at that point, they may become quite vocal in opposition to or in favor of modification. In fact, it is exactly this postapproval review and analysis that characterizes the ongoing policy process associated with specific government programs.

The civil rights, antiwar, feminist, and environmental movements of the 1960s and 1970s significantly altered the approval processes at all levels of government. Dissatisfaction with those in positions of authority appeared to lead to a demand for more direct involvement by citizen groups. For many persons, elections were no longer producing effective decision makers. As a consequence, voting turnout declined, but more direct forms of policy participation increased. As Richard A. Brody puts it: "Cynicism has increased and turnout has declined, but other forms of political activity, including activities directly related to the electoral process, have trended upward. . ." (1978: 323). These developments have had an impact on policy approval processes. Reduced turnout in elections reduces the legitimacy of elected officials, and greater direct participation by citizen groups in coalition building may prolong that process. In some instances these groups claim greater legitimacy for themselves than they are willing to attribute to those in official government positions. "There is little question that in recent years public interest groups have gained a growing acceptance as legitimate representatives of significant constituencies or 'interests' within the polity" (Berry, 1977: 3). This trend toward expanded participation means that building support for a proposal may take longer in the past—or may not be possible at all.

What are the various types of approval processes? We tend to think only of those associated with legislatures. Certainly majority coalition building in law making is an important type of approval process. But there are others—those associated with hierarchies, professionalism, efficiency, and direct citizen participation. Each deserves a brief discussion.

A. Building Majorities in a Legislature

As the most familiar approval process, legislative majority building requires the least description. The process of gaining and maintaining support through several stages of legislative action is described and analyzed in countless books and articles (see references). It is worth noting, however, that the democratic structure requires that legislatures authorize other approval processes. Often, in fact, proposals are subjected to a two-or-more-tiered approval process, beginning with the legislature but extending to the bureaucracy because of the discretion granted to administrators.

B. Hierarchical Authority

The right to say "yes" or "no" may be granted to a person because of his or her position in a hierarchy. Those subordinate to and affected by hierarchical authority may accept a decision because they judge hierarchy as rational and effective. As Max Weber explained (Gerth and Mills, 1948: 197):

> The principles of office hierarchy and of levels of graded authority mean a firmly ordered system of super- and subordination in which there is a supervision of the lower offices by the higher ones. Such a system offers the governed the possibility of appealing the decision of a lower office to its higher authority, in a definitely regulated manner. With the full development of the bureaucratic type, the office hierarchy is monocratically organized.

There are political as well as bureaucratic hierarchies, and an effort is made to integrate the two in the United States—not always successfully. Thus, getting approval for a proposal may require attention to both types of hierarchies. Accepting the legitimacy of hierarchy often is the consequence of training—of civil servants, politicians, the military, the public at large. Both political and bureaucratic hierarchies have been challenged in recent years, directly through criticism of this means for approving proposals and indirectly as a consequence of the high turnover among public officials.

C. Professionalism

Related to hierarchical approval processes are those associated with professional expertise. Complex hierarchies are created to ensure rational decision making, in part by dividing work among specialists. Although it is true in principle that those at the peak of the hierarchy have the formal authority to make the decision, it is often true in fact that they may do no more than ratify the proposals offered by professionals.

The trend appears to be toward professionalism. The greater complexity of issues demands expert analysis, as does the expansion of social and economic programs. But there are more subtle forces at work too. Single-issue politics tends to break down the reliance on hierarchy by political executives and legislators and forces them to hire their own experts. Often the environmentalists, pro- or anti-abortionists, feminists, pro- and anti-nuclear power advocates, welfare groups, and so on, are intolerant of a politician's reliance on system specialization, demanding that each one develop a position on the issue at hand. The result frequently has been an expansion of personal staffs. We have also witnessed an expansion in the use of consulting groups by bureaucratic agencies. This development too is related to the growing complexity of issues, but it so happens that use of consultants tends to obscure responsibility. The legislator avoids responsibility by permitting administrative discretion. Administrators contract out the responsibility to a consulting group. Program development and approval may end up being very distant from those making the demand.

D. Efficiency

An approval process relying on efficiency or cost effectiveness is of a different order than those discussed so far. Reference here is to a particular criterion to be applied. In its purest form, efficiency consists of "meeting the objective at the lowest cost or in obtaining the maximum amount of the objective for a specified amount of resources" (Wildavsky, 1971: 184). In a process dominated by the rule of efficiency, those with the authority to say "yes" or "no" presumably must justify their approval by reference to the criteria above. Typically, where efficiency is demanded, an analytical system is designed to achieve the desired goal, for example, some form of cost-benefit analysis or program budgeting. Although these systems may be prompted as value-free, Aaron Wildavsky, among others, warns that they are not:

> A straightforward description of cost-benefit analysis cannot do justice to the powerful assumptions that underlie it or to the many conditions limiting its usefulness. The assumptions involve value judgments that are not always recognized and, when recognized, are not easily handled in practice. The limiting conditions arise partly out of the assumptions and partly out of severe computational difficulties in estimating costs and especially benefits (Wildavsky, 1971: 185).

E. Citizen Participation

Citizen participation is basic to legitimizing a government program in a democracy. But it may take many forms. Indirect involvement is said to occur in elections. Citizens vote for their representative who, in turn, reads the election for its issue content and acts for citizens as proposals are presented. As noted earlier, dissatisfaction, even disillusionment, with political representation has led to demands for other forms of involvement. More direct policy contact with decision makers has become commonplace—for example, in writing and calling them, in testifying, in demonstrating, in meeting with them. The direct lobbying on Capitol Hill by citizen groups has increased dramatically in the last 20 years.

But these groups have become active in the second or third tier of approval processes as well. They no longer cease activity with the passage of law. And, in fact, legal requirements for public involvement in administrative decisions are not uncommon (in setting standards, issuing licenses, selecting sites, etc.). Then one also observes increased attention to direct legislation—particularly in the west. In his study of initiatives in California, Eugene C. Lee concludes that "the initiative has become so deeply rooted in the political culture of the state that no public figure in memory has suggested that it be eliminated. . . and none is likely soon to do so" (Butler and Ranney, 1978: 120). On the other hand, "the United States is one of the very few democratic countries that has never had a referendum at the national level" (Butler and Ranney, 1978: 67).

In summary, getting a proposal approved appears to be more challenging today due to an increase in demands for government action, the greater technical complexity of issues, and reduced public confidence in representative institutions. In particular, there appears to be a trend away from exclusive reliance on majority coalition building and hierarchical authority for program approval in all its phases; and a trend toward greater reliance on professionalism, efficiency, and citizen participation. Interestingly, these trends will make it more difficult in the future to identify who is responsible for approving what. Whatever the problems associated with approval by a legislature or within a hierarchy, one can, in most cases, identify responsibility for the decision.

VI. THE EFFECT OF INSTITUTIONAL PROCESSES ON PROGRAM DEVELOPMENT

Separation of powers has traditionally been cited as a principal characteristic of our political system, but it does not, in fact, describe our working government. Ripley and Franklin, among others, refer to "separate institutions, shared powers" in their analysis of the American national government (1980: 14). Their description applies as well to the state and local levels of government. Separated institutions tend quite naturally to develop formal processes to channel policy activities. Examples within the executive branch are the development of the budget, clearance of all legislative proposals, the preparation of messages by the executive (e.g., the State of the Union message), and the writing of annual reports. Examples within the legislative branch are committee hearings, preparation of reports, scheduling of legislation on the floor, floor procedures, and conference committees.

These institutional processes provide formal decision points which serve as foci for policy activities. They therefore help to organize and direct the flow of these activities and thus provide a public means for coordination. Agreements reached by those primarily involved in program development are displayed in institutional processes. In fact, most law-making processes are composed of a succession of agreements that are then displayed before larger and larger audiences (in the subcommittee, committee, the full chamber).

The display typically elicits support or opposition, and the agreement is then displayed in a different arena or adjustments are made to garner more support.

It is frequently the case that proposals are fed routinely into institutional processes with little or no negative feedback. But the very existence of successive display points may influence program development. The rational policy formulator will look ahead to forces likely to be affected by a proposal and calculate when and if these forces will react. Adjustments may be made in the proposal, depending on these analytical projections.

Theodore J. Lowi is concerned about the lessening of influence of these institutional processes. In particular, he believes that Congress has delegated much of its power to the Executive. He refers to "policy without law" and identifies interest group liberalism as the culprit:

> It [interest group liberalism] renders formalism impossible. It impairs legitimacy by converting government from a moralistic to a mechanistic institution. It impairs the self-correctiveness of positive law by the very flexibility of its broad policies and by the bargaining, co-optation, and incrementalism of its implementing processes. It impairs the very process of administration itself by delegating to administration alien materials—policies that are not laws (Lowi, 1969: 96–97).

In a sense, what Lowi is arguing is that the institutional processes have come to be no more than pro forma means for ratifying either the specific needs of special interests or a set of private or barely visible means by which these needs will be met.

Lowi's argument is interesting in its own right, but it also raises the important issue of the continuing relationship between policy and institutional processes. If the latter fail to accommodate the former, then one may expect reform. That is, if the formal structure impedes rather than facilitates program development, one may expect demands for change. Of course, Lowi identifies the interesting situation in which institutional processes are *too* accommodative to a pluralistic set of policy processes. It appears that reform is more difficult to achieve under these circumstances.

VII. CROSS-INSTITUTIONAL PROGRAM DEVELOPMENT

Earlier we reviewed the sources for policy proposals, noting the several possibilities from within and outside government. The many policy activities associated with program development (problem identification, interest organization, formulation of proposals, seeking approval) may be participated in by an almost limitless combination of public and private actors. Students of public policy have found it useful to speak of these combinations as "subgovernments" (Cater, 1964), "policy-making subsystems" (Freeman, 1955), "whirlpools" (Griffith, 1939), "cozy little triangles" (James, 1974; Davidson, 1977), and "issue networks" (Heclo, 1978). Although all used these labels to refer to cross-institutional and public/private combinations of policy participants, few made distinctions among combinations. Most were content to record the important observation that many policy issues are treated by networks of public officials and private citizens rather than solely by institutional units (bureaucratic agencies, legislative committees). Hugh Heclo, however, did distinguish between the policy triangle or subgovernment and what he called an "issue network":

Iron triangles or subgovernments suggest a stable set of participants coalesced to control fairly narrow public programs which are in the direct economic interest of each party to the alliance. Issue networks are almost the reverse image in each respect. Participants move in and out of the networks constantly. Rather than groups united in dominance over a program, no one, as far as one can tell, is in control of the policies and issues (Heclo, 1978: 102).

This interesting observation suggests that different types of issues may produce combinations with quite different characteristics. Emmette S. Redford has provided the most elaborate framework for analyzing these differences. He distinguishes among micropolitics, subsystem politics, and macropolitics—citing the different connections or associations associated with each.

Micropolitics is that in which individuals, companies, and communities seek benefits from the larger polity for themselves. Subsystem or intermediary politics is the politics of function, involving the interrelations of bureaus and other administrative operating agencies, the counterpart congressional committee structure, and the interest organizations, trade press, and lobbyists concerned with a particular area of program specialization. Macropolitics is produced when the community at large and the leaders of the government as a whole are brought into the discussion and determination of policy (Redford, 1969: 83).

Jones (1982) characterizes these three sets of association respectively as "cozy little connections," "cozy little triangles," and "sloppy large hexagons." He observes that issues vary in the number of and interactions among program formulators. Having connections with the right people may be all that is necessary to deal with some issues—for example, getting a contract or grant. A more stable and continuing set of associations in the executive and legislature may be necessary with more important issues—for example, renewing a subsidy program, maintaining a set of regulations. And virtually uncontrolled participation may characterize certain major issues—for example, developing a comprehensive energy program, reforming welfare programs.

No set of associations will necessarily stay the same throughout the life of an issue. Micropolitical connections may lead to intermediary political triangles and even macropolitical hexagons. Thus, for example, the cozy connections and triangles maintained by the oil industry for so many decades no longer determine government program development with regard to oil supply, distribution, and use. Participation in decision making for this vital issue has expanded greatly—within officialdom and among public interest groups. The point is that program development may vary across issues and over time within a particular issue.

The present trend in program development appears to be toward macropolitics. At least two popular demands contribute to this trend. First is the dissatisfaction with subsystem politics—characterized by the kind of complaints registered by Lowi (1969) that pluralistic government lacks substance. In this view, no effort is made in our own government even to identify the public interest, let alone establish standards by which it is realized. Thus, certain persons and groups (e.g., the Nader Task Groups and Common Cause) are anxious to break up those cozy triangles. Second is the demand that new programs be measured for their effects on other programs. The environmental impact statement is a major example of this type of demand. But many of the provisions for citizen involvement in planning are also predicated on the same idea. If program development is to proceed only when all effects are measured or projected, then almost by definition all issues are raised to the level of macropolitics. After all, everything is ultimately connected to everything else.

The trend toward macropolitics has the potential for inducing stalemate. Expanding the number of participants in program development normally delays the decision, since time and resource constraints simply limit how much can be done. Thus, either the political system develops decisional sclerosis or means are developed for reestablishing connections and triangles. We appear to be at this particular crossroads in the early 1980s.

VIII. SUMMARY

Changes in the American political system over the past two decades have significantly altered the processes associated with developing public policies. We have attempted to identify those changes affecting the activities associated with developing policies, and speculate about the trends likely to dominate these activities in the future. Changes in the policy development phase undoubtedly will have consequences for activities in other phases of the policy process, including implementation. What trends seem to be most significant for those seeking to understand the policy process?

A. Increase in Participation

Probably the most significant trend treated in this chapter deals with the increase in participation for all activities within this phase of the policy process. The American political system has always offered access points to those interested in making demands on government, thereby allowing citizen participation during all phases of the policy process. Many individuals in the past, however, did not take advantage of the opportunities for participation. Consequently, patterns of interaction were established that made policy-making activities fairly predictable, removing much of the uncertainty from the policy process. The late 1960s and 1970s, however, ushered in a period of increased citizen participation in all stages of the policy process. This participation has included mass demonstrations, direct petitioning to decision makers, campaign and election activity, testimony before official groups, monitoring of program implementation. Existing patterns of policy formation have thereby been altered. More demands, in numbers and variety, have led to crowded agendas and greater uncertainty among traditional policy actors. This increase in the complexity of demands also affects formulation and legitimation activities, leading to greater efforts to effect compromise among groups or individuals not always willing to bargain. This process results in more time-consuming activities, which may be more conflicting in nature. In summary, this increase in participation, hailed by some as a democratization process in American politics, has altered the activities associated with developing policies, indicating less predictability and more uncertainty for the future.

B. More Complex Issues

Without a doubt, those issues being brought before the governmental agenda are more complex now than they ever have been, requiring more expertise in government. This trend has led to more professionalism in government, as experts are hired to develop programs to deal with highly complex and technical problems. One of the reasons that government has grown significantly in the past decade is the increase in experts, especially in the executive and legislative branches of government.

C. Nationalization and Internationalization of Issues

There is a trend to formulate "national" programs to deal with problems that affect many Americans in all parts of the country; for example, problems associated with energy, environment, and the economy. This trend has led to a more centralized decision-making system, as the federal government preempts state and local governments in various areas of decision-making responsibilities. Also, issues are becoming more international in the sense that actions taken by other governments or organizations, such as OPEC, have a significant impact on the American policy process. Thus, policy makers have to look abroad and speculate about the effects of international actions and reactions to American domestic and foreign policies.

D. More Evaluation and Efficiency

As resources level off or actually decline, government will focus on the efficiency and effectiveness of present programs rather than formulate new ones. It has already become evident that this trend will dominate policy making in the near future as cost-benefit analysis and other methods of program evaluation become a normal part of the policy process. There is also an effort to be more "comprehensive," efforts that, as we have discussed, promise more than they deliver.

In addition to others mentioned in this chapter, these trends will dominate policy formation activities in the future. We can only speculate what effects they will have on these processes. What is certain is that large-scale changes in the American political system have altered those activities associated with the important policy formation phase of the policy process.

REFERENCES

Anderson, J. E. (1975). *Public Policy Making.* Praeger, New York.

Bachrach, P., and Baratz, M. (1970). *Power and Poverty: Theory and Practice.* Oxford University Press, New York.

Berry, J. (1977). *Lobbying for the People.* Princeton University Press, Princeton, NJ.

Brody, R. A. (1978). The puzzle of political participation in America. In *The New American Political System,* A. King (Ed.). American Enterprise Institute, Washington, DC.

Butler, D., and Ranney, A. (Eds.). (1978). *Referendums: A Comparative Study of Practice and Theory.* American Enterprise Institute, Washington, DC.

Cater, D. (1964). *Power in Washington.* Random House, New York.

Cobb, R. W., and Elder, C. D. (1972). *Participation in American Politics: The Dynamics of Agenda-Building.* Allyn & Bacon, Boston.

Crenson, M. A. (1971). *The Un-Politics of Air Pollution.* Johns Hopkins Press, Baltimore.

Dahl, R. A. (1956). *A Preface to Democratic Theory.* University of Chicago Press, Chicago.

Davidson, R. H. (1977). Breaking up those "cozy triangles": An impossible dream? In *Legislative Reform and Public Policy,* S. Welch and J. G. Peters (Eds.). Praeger, New York.

Dewey, J. (1927). *The Public and Its Problems.* Holt, New York.

Donovan, J. (1967). *The Politics of Poverty.* Pegasus, New York.

Dye, T. (1971). *The Politics of Equality.* Bobbs-Merrill, Indianapolis, IN.

Freeman, J. L. (1955). *The Political Process.* Random House, New York.

Gans, H. J. (1968). Regional and urban planning. In *International Encyclopedia of the Social Sciences,* D. L. Sills (Ed.). Macmillan, New York.

Gerth, H., and Wright, M. C. (1948). *From Max Weber: Essays in Sociology.* Routledge and Kegan Paul, London

Griffith, E. (1939). *The Impasse of Democracy.* Harrison-Hilton Books, New York.

Heclo, H. (1968). Issue networks and the executive establishment. In *The New American Political System.* American Enterprise Institute, Washington, DC.

James, D. B. (1974). *The Contemporary Presidency.* Bobbs-Merrill, Indianapolis, IN.

Jones, C. O. (1977). *An Introduction to the Study of Public Policy.* Duxbury, North Scituate, MA.

—— (1982). *The United States Congress: People, Place, and Policy.* Dorsey, Homewood, IL.

Lowi, T. J. (1969). *The End of Liberalism.* Norton, New York.

Matthes, D. (1978). Regulating the coal industry: Federal coal mine health and safety and surface mining policy development. Unpublished Ph.D. dissertation, University of Pittsburgh.

Moynihan, D. P. (1969). *Maximum Feasible Misunderstanding.* Free Press, New York.

Redford, E. S. (1969). *Democracy in the Administrative State.* Oxford University Press, New York.

Ripley, R. B., and Franklin, G. (1980). *Congress, the Bureaucracy, and Public Policy.* Dorsey, Homewood, IL.

Schattschneider, E. E. (1960). *The Semi-Sovereign People.* Holt, New York.

Truman, D. B. (1951). *The Governmental Process.* Knopf, New York.

Wildavsky, A. (1971). *The Revolt Against the Masses.* Basic Books, New York.

7

Policy Implementation

Paul A. Sabatier* / University of California, Davis, California
Daniel A. Mazmanian / Pomona College, Claremont, California

"To implement," according to *Webster's,* is "to provide the means for carrying out; to give practical effect to." From this starting point, then, policy implementation can tentatively be viewed as the process of carrying out a basic policy decision in the form of a law, appellate court decision, executive order, or, in parliamentary regimes, cabinet or ministerial decree.

Although implementation as a distinctive field of study did not emerge until the early 1970s,[1] it owes a heavy debt to a least two bodies of theory and empirical research. The first is public administration. This is hardly surprising, as "to administer" is, in many respects, a synonym of "to implement." Although there may well have been a period of innocence in which the administration of a statute was viewed as nonproblematic, as simply a matter of handing over a settled legislative decision to civil servants to be carried out faithfully and efficiently,[2] such a view did not long withstand serious scrutiny. On the one hand, a number of major studies in the decade before and after World War II (Herring, 1936; Leiserson, 1942; Selznick, 1949; Long, 1949; Bernstein, 1955; Freeman, 1955) clearly revealed that administrative agencies were affected not only by their legal mandates but also by the strength of various interest groups concerned with their activities, by the intervention of legislators in their policy subsystem, and by a variety of other factors in their political environments. In addition, organization theorists in the 1950s and early 1960s cast serious doubts about the degree of hierarchical control in even private bureaucracies operating in relatively stable environments. They identified the now-familiar phenomena of subunit loyalty, cognitive limits on rationality, distorted communication flows, difficulties in monitoring subordinates' behavior, and so on (March and Simon, 1958; Kats and Kahn, 1966; Downs, 1967; Wilensky, 1967; Kaufman, 1960).

Present affiliation: University of Bielefeld, Bielefeld, Federal Republic of Germany

The second body of theory important in the genesis of a distinctive literature on policy implementation was, quite simply, the development of a systems approach to political life (Easton, 1965; Jones, 1970; Dye, 1972: chap. 11). For it enabled policy scientists to break out of the organizational perspective of public administration and start thinking in terms of environmental inputs, legislative and administrative policy outputs (decisions), impacts/outcomes, and feedback loops. This, in turn, directed attention to what have become some of the standard questions of implementation analysis: To what extent are (1) the policy outputs of the administrative agencies and (2) the subsequent outcomes of these decisions consistent with the original policy objectives? What effects, in turn, do these outcomes have on subsequent legislative decisions, that is, on policy reformulation or the feedback loop?

These two literatures (and others, e.g., on intergovernmental relations) provided many of the conceptual and empirical insights on which implementation research was to be built.[3] But it was the perceived failure of many Great Society programs—and the related phenomenon of problematic compliance with the Supreme Court's desegregation and school prayer decisions—that provided much of the intellectual, emotional, and financial spur to investigate the relationships between original decision and subsequent performance. Just as much of the best empirical work in the years around World War II had sought to explain the tendency of New Deal regulatory agencies to become dominated by their clientele (Herring, 1936; Leiserson, 1942; Bernstein, 1955), so it was the desire to investigate the anatomy of failure that gave birth to the vast majority of early implementation studies: Title I of ESEA (Bailey and Mosher, 1968; Murphy, 1971); President Johnson's cherished "new towns" program (Derthick, 1972); job creation programs (Pressman and Wildavsky, 1973); and Southern desegregation (Wirt, 1970). Indeed, some of the emerging European interest in implementation (Cerych, 1979) has been motivated by a similar concern with explaining performance gaps.

One of these early studies—Pressman and Wildavsky's analysis of the reasons behind the federal government's total inability to attain its stated objective of 3000 new jobs for unemployed inner city residents of Oakland—so set the tone for much of implementation analysis that it deserves to be considered a classic in the same mold as Selznick (1949) or Kaufman (1960). In particular, it illustrated many of the features that were to distinguish the mainstream of implementation analysis from the antecedent literature on public administration: (1) an explicit concern with policy evaluation as well as with political behavior, with examining the extent to which various policy objectives were achieved as well as the reasons for that performance; (2) a focus on what they termed "the complexity of joint action," that is, the myriad of actors in various public and private institutions involved in the implementation of a decision rather than the more limited traditional concern with the actors within a single agency and its immediate political environment; and (3) careful analysis of the (often implicit) causal assumptions behind the original policy decision, which would have to be met if its goals were to be attained.

Nevertheless, as will soon be evident, there is no one "correct" paradigm for implementation analysis. In fact, the first part of this chapter discusses a variety of critical issues dividing recognized scholars in the field. The next section attempts to summarize briefly several substantive propositions on which there is fairly wide consensus. And the final section presents some tentative observations concerning the ability of various political systems and policy subsystems (areas/domains) to implement legal objectives effectively.

I. ALTERNATIVE APPROACHES TO THE STUDY OF POLICY IMPLEMENTATION

Although policy implementation as a distinct area of inquiry is barely a decade old, the literature is now sufficiently developed to identify a number of different orientations. In this section we first identify some critical questions that have emerged and then suggest how choices on these issues have generally tended to cluster into a limited number of major approaches to the field.

A. Critical Issues

The Relationship Between Formulation and Implementation. Certainly most scholars have assumed that a reasonably clear distinction can be made between (1) the formulation/adoption of a policy, usually in the form of a statute or a landmark court decision, such as *Brown v. Board of Education*; (2) its implementation by one or more administrative agencies and perhaps the courts and subordinate/peripheral legislatures; and in many recent studies, (3) its reformulation by the original policy maker based, in part, on the successes and difficulties of the implementation experience (Pressman and Wildavsky, 1973; Murphy, 1971; Derthick, 1972; Jones, 1975; Hargrove, 1975; Lieber, 1975; Rodgers and Bullock, 1976; Bardach, 1977; Van Horn, 1979; Cerych, 1979; Goodwin and Moen, 1981; Bullock, 1981; Sabatier and Mazmanian, 1979a, and 1981). This view, based on the very meaning of implementation as the carrying out of a prior decision, is reaffirmed by Americans' traditional notions of the separate functions of legislatures and administrative agencies and by the general practice in Congress and several states of thoroughly reexamining major legislation every four to six years—a pattern that is likely to be strengthened by the current fascination with "sunset laws." It is also the approach taken in several studies of the implementation of various innovations by public bureaucracies (Nelson and Yates, 1978). Finally, although Rabinovitz et al. (1976) have called attention to the need to distinguish the development of general guidelines (regulations) from their "routine" administration and enforcement, they view these as substages in the implementation of major statutes (see also Rein and Rabinovitz, 1977; Berman, 1978: 167).

The conceptual distinction between formulation and implementation has been at least implicitly challenged from two sources. First are what have been termed "adaptive" or "interactive" approaches to implementation, which emphasize the mutual adjustment of goals and strategies among various actors throughout the process—perhaps best illustrated by Bardach (1977) and by the RAND study of the adoption and implementation of educational innovations in local school districts (Berman and McLaughlin, 1976). The second challenge comes from Majone and Wildavsky (1978). Although they regard as illegitimate any effort by implementing officials to alter basic goals and strategies, they nevertheless advocate a view of policy making in which goals and programs are continuously modified to adjust to constraints and to changing circumstances (Majone and Wildavsky, 1978: 109, 111, 114):

> Policies are continuously transformed by implementing actions that simultaneously alter resources and objectives. . . . It is not policy design but redesign that goes on most of the time. Who is to say, then, whether implementation consists of altering objectives to correspond with available resources or of mobilizing new resources to accomplish old objectives? . . . Implementation is evolution. . . . When we act to implement a policy, we change it.[4]

These views serve as reminders that important statutes and appellate court decisions are elaborated and often modified as they go through the implementation process. Moreover, there may well be occasions in which the distinction between formulation and implementation proves rather tenuous. These include cases in which the original policy decision (e.g., by the legislature) is so ambiguous as to be vacuous—"regulate in the public interest"—thereby forcing implementing officials actually to formulate any "policy" that is to evolve. Other problematic cases involve those occasions in which the formulation of a reasonably coherent policy involves numerous interchanges among courts/legislators and administrative agencies over a number of years—as has recently been the case between the District of Columbia Court of Appeals and the Environmental Protection Agency in the development of regulations for initiating formal safety reviews of pesticides (MacIntyre, 1980)—or when a small experimental program gradually evolves into a major policy innovation, such as the 25/5 Scheme in Swedish higher education (Cerych and Sabatier, 1981).

Nevertheless, it strikes us that any effort to blur the distinction between formulation and implementation should be resisted on several grounds. First, the fact that the vast majority of implementation scholars have made the distinction suggests that the problematic cases are the exception rather than the rule. Second, if we accept Majone and Wildavsky's argument that objectives evolve *continuously* as a result of the interaction among a myriad of actors or as a response to new constraints, then evaluation of goal attainment becomes impossible. Third, and perhaps the most important, viewing policy making as a seamless web obscures one of the principal normative and empirical concerns of scholars interested in public policy, namely, the division of authority between elected public officials (principally legislators), on the one hand, and appointed and career administrative officials, on the other (Davis, 1969; Lowi, 1969).

Moreover, it is not at all necessary to vitiate the formulation-implementation distinction in order to incorporate Majone and Wildavsky's legitimate concern with the evolution of policy over time as value priorities change, more effective instruments for attaining goals become available, causal theories of the factors affecting goal attainment improve, evaluation studies reveal performance gaps, and so on. In fact, the division into three basic stages of formulation, implementation, and reformulation directs attention to this area of inquiry by focusing on the extent to which the legislature (or appellate court) modifies its original policy as a result of the implementation experience. For example, a recent analysis of the implementation of the automotive-related provisions of the 1970 Clean Air Act reveals that the 1977 Amendments essentially retained the original goal of a 90 percent reduction in new car emissions but (1) reduced it to 75 percent in the problematic area of nitrogen oxides, (2) extended the unrealistic timetables in the original legislation, (3) clarified the originally implicit constraints on the efforts of the Environmental Protection Agency (EPA) to reduce vehicle miles traveled through transportation control plans, and (4) greatly increased the sanctions available to EPA in its efforts to convince states to enact automobile inspection and maintenance programs (Mazmanian and Sabatier, 1981). Similarly, the recent analysis of U.S. welfare policy over the last four decades by Goodwin and Moen (1981) demonstrates, first, how the 1936 Social Security Act's initial concern with aiding children with deceased fathers became submerged by the dramatic increase in the number of families with fathers who had either left or had never been part of the family unit and, then, how legislative and administrative officials gradually became aware of, and sought to address, the variety of factors affecting family economic dependency: from the focus on the provisions of social and psychological services in the 1962 welfare amendments to the emphasis in the 1967 Amendments on forced work training to the reluctant recognition in the 1971 Talmadge Amendments and the Carter administration's 1978 welfare reform proposals of the labor market context (e.g., the need to create additional public service jobs).

Likewise, viewing policy making as an iterative process of formulation, implementation, and reformulation—rather than as a seamless web of continuous evolution—helps focus on the traditional concern with administrative discretion. For one can ask such questions as the following: (1) At what substage of the implementation process did the important discretionary decisions occur? During guideline writing by central authorities? During the subsequent processing of cases? As a result of performance gaps revealed by audits, formal evaluation studies, or other feedback mechanisms? (2) Did the exercise of discretion involve (a) efforts to make sense out of conflicting statutory mandates (Rein and Rabinovitz, 1977: 12)? (b) modification of statutory intent in order to accommodate the objections of important political actors (Lazin, 1973; Altman and Sapolsky, 1976; Lieber, 1975)? (c) the development of policy initiatives in an area on which the original statute was silent (Sabatier and Klosterman, 1981)? (3) How significant was the discretionary authority exercised by implementing officials? Did it functionally modify the basic objectives of the legislation or merely the strategies for achieving them? (4) Were the policy adjustments made during implementation the result of administrative discretion or rather a response to court decisions or to legislative oversight? Finally, (5) to what extent were these adjustments subsequently affirmed, modified, or rejected by the original policy maker (usually the legislature) in the course of formal reformulation?

In short, although the formulation-implementation-reformulation distinction may be difficult to apply in some instances, it can certainly incorporate different authors' concern with policy evolution. On the other hand, its abolition risks jeopardizing the ability to assess both the extent of goal attainment and the distribution of authority between elected and appointed officials.

Focus and Criteria of Program Evaluation. Although almost all implementation studies have sought to evaluate program performance, there have been a wide variety of approaches concerning (1) the evaluative criteria employed and (2) whether one focuses on policy outputs or eventual outcomes (or both).

In terms of evaluative criteria, the starting point in most research has been the formal objectives enunciated in the original statute or appellate court decision (Murphy, 1971;

have missed the program's inherently limited ability to achieve its basic goal of reducing the welfare rolls because it would have ignored the program's inability to affect the number occupation of much of implementation research with assessing the extent, and the reasons for, the inability of major policy initiatives actually to attain their stated objectives. This focus on legal objectives has also revealed their frequent ambiguity and inconsistency and the consequent adjustments made during the implementation process. Finally, in focusing on the original policy makers' intent, one can ask both (1) to what extent were the (preferably quantitative) objectives attained? and (2) even if not attained, did the program result in more of those values than would have been the case in its absence? Although the latter approach involves some thorny methodological problems in specifying the counterfactuals, it may nevertheless be precisely the sort of analysis that policy makers want in a world where optimal solutions are few and far between.

Another frequently employed approach, particularly in regulatory policy, is benefit-cost analysis. In most cases, the benefits of the program are calculated in terms of the legislation's stated goals (e.g., the effects of reduced pollution emissions on health and property values), whereas the costs involve both administrative expenses and the time and monetary costs borne by target groups. Although such studies sometimes seek simply to arrive at a net benefit/cost figure (National Academy of Sciences, 1974), they frequently also compare the present program against an alternative, such as deregulation or a system of emissions fees (Phillips, 1975; Friedlaender, 1978). Although such approaches invariably run into problems of accurately estimating benefits and costs—and, in the latter case, of estimating the uncertain effects of alternative programs—they have the advantage of incorporating the fiscal constraints that are at least implicitly part of most policy decisions.

Finally, studies sometimes use evaluative criteria only partially related to statutorily prescribed goals. These may be taken from the researcher's own value preferences, such as program effects on the poor (Levy et al., 1974; Browning et al., 1981), or concerned with their effects on other societal goals. For example, Ingram and Mann (1980: 15) suggest that, although U.S. immigration policy has obviously failed to reach its stated objective of stemming the flow of illegal aliens from Mexico, it also should be evaluated in terms of its overall effect on maintaining friendly relations with that country.

A second, and related, topic concerns whether the focus of analysis is on policy outputs or the ultimate outcomes of a program. On the one hand, Van Horn (1979: 9–10) argues that implementation analysis should be concerned only with measuring the extent to which the policy outputs of the implementing agencies conform to various objectives—with, for example, the extent to which Comprehensive Employment and Training Act (CETA) agencies provide jobs for the hard-core unemployed—rather than with the policy's ultimate impacts on target groups, such as the extent to which the long-term employment or earnings potential of low-income people are affected by enrollment in CETA programs.[5]

We would disagree on the grounds that such a circumscribed approach often precludes some of the most interesting and important aspects of implementation analysis, namely, the adequacy of the underlying causal theory and, in regulatory programs, the degree of (private) target group compliance with agency decisions. For example, an inquiry confined to the extent to which various social services were delivered to Aid for Families with Dependent Children (AFDC) recipients under the 1962 welfare amendments would have missed the program's inherently limited ability to achieve its basic goal of reducing the welfare rolls because it would have ignored the program's inability to affect the number of jobs available (Goodwin and Moen, 1981)—that is, one of the fundamental short-comings of its underlying causal theory. Similarly, a study of the California coastal com-missions' ability to attain their legal objective of significantly increasing public access to the ocean, which focused merely on the extent to which the commissions' *permit decis-ions* conformed with this objective, would never have seen that the commissions were actually able to provide very little access despite legally correct permit decisions. This shortfall was due to problematic compliance by landowners with those decisions and to the commissions' inability to provide either the necessary maintenance and liability services before accessways could actually be opened or funds to purchase additional parks (Sabatier and Mazmanian, 1979a: chap. 7). Of course, there are certainly instances in which statutes make absolutely no pretense of doing anything more than delivering a specific service or regulating a specific type of behavior. But where they also seek to at-tain an objective, it is entirely appropriate for implementation analysis to ask if the stat-ute incorporates an adequate understanding of the factors affecting that objective and gives implementing officials sufficient jurisdiction at least to have the possibility of attaining it. For it is precisely in revealing the inadequacy of the underlying causal theory or the limited ability of regulatory agencies to bring target groups into compliance that implementation studies can often make their greatest contributions.

This wider view is accepted by many, if not most, people in the field, including Pressman and Wildavsky (1973), Bardach (1977), Majone and Wildavsky (1978), Brown-ing et al. (1981). In addition, there may be a rough consensus that implementation anal-ysis should examine (1) the extent to which major legal objectives have been achieved and (2) any other program impacts—intended and otherwise—that affect the amount of support and opposition to the program and eventually the reformulation process. Finally, one should consider examining the role of formal evaluation studies—as opposed to more informal feedback mechanisms such as legislative case work—in the reformulation process, as there is now a fairly extensive (and, on the whole, discouraging) literature on the util-ization of formal impact assessment in the policy process (McLaughlin, 1975; Primack and von Hippel, 1974; Rhoads, 1974; Nelkin, 1975; Meltsner, 1976; Rein and White, 1977; Weiss, 1977; Sabatier, 1978; Patton, 1978; Mazmanian and Sabatier, 1980a).

From Whose Perspective: Center, Periphery, and/or Target Group?   The implementa-tion of any program involves the efforts of some policy maker to affect the behavior of what Lipsky (1971) has termed "street level bureaucrats" in order to provide a service to, or regulate the behavior of, one or more target groups. Among the conceptually simplest cases, as it involves a single organization, would be the efforts of a local school board to alter the practices of classroom teachers. Of course, most implementation efforts involve more than one organization, for example, a city council and local bureaucracies, and many involve more than one level of government. In fact, probably the majority of im-plementation studies have dealt with the most horrendously complex intergovernmental cases, that is, the efforts of the U.S. Congress or federal appellate courts to affect the be-havior of classroom teachers, local social service case workers, or private industrial firms throughout the entire country.

Thus the implementation of any program—but particularly those involving multiple organizations or several levels of government—can be viewed from three quite different perspectives: (1) the initial policy maker (the Center), (2) field-level implementing officials (the Periphery), (3) or the private actors at whom the program is directed (the Target Group). From the standpoint of the Center, implementation involves the efforts of hierarchically superior officials or institutions to obtain compliance from peripheral institutions and officials in order to provide a service or directly change behavior. If the program is not working, then either adjustments have to be made in the program, or sanctions have to be invoked, or the basic policy has to be reformulated. But the basic concerns from the Center's perspective are, first, the extent to which official policy objectives have been attained and, second, the reasons for attainment or nonattainment. Probably the dominant approach in implementation research, this perspective is reflected in the studies of Bailey and Mosher (1968), Murphy (1971), Derthick (1972), Swanson (1975), Rodgers and Bullock (1976), Bardach (1977), Szanton (1978), Van Horn (1979), Johnson et al. (1978), Sabatier and Mazmanian (1979a), Hargrove and Dean (1980), Bullock (1981), and Goodwin and Moen (1981).

From the standpoint of the Periphery, however, implementation focuses on the manner in which local implementing officials and institutions respond to the perturbations in their environment caused by the efforts of outside officials to achieve central policy. For example, the study by Browning et al. (1981) of the implementation of three federal programs (general revenue sharing, community development bloc grants, and model cities) in 10 Bay Area cities focuses on the extent to which local political officials and groups use federal funds to pursue their own goals. Similarly, the RAND study of the implementation of educational innovations dealt primarily with variables affecting the adoption of federally sponsored innovations in local school districts and, even more so, with the manner in which those innovations were modified by local school officials and classroom teachers in order to meet the exigencies of their specific situation. Other examples of this approach include the Huron Institute's study of the experimental school voucher program in Alum Rock, California (Cohen and Farrar, 1977), and the analysis by Weatherly and Lipsky (1977) of the coping behavior of local school officials involved in the implementation of a Massachesetts special education law.

Finally, implementation can be viewed from the perspective of the Target Group— for example, the poor in social welfare programs or emission sources in pollution control programs. When Target Groups are supposed to be the principal beneficiaries, their perspective may be quite similar to those of central authorities: To what extent are the intended services actually delivered (Burby and Weiss, 1976: chap. 19)? But they are likely to be even more concerned with whether the services make any real difference in their lives; that is, does participation in CETA significantly improve long-term income flows? In regulatory programs, by contrast, the Target Group perspective is likely to focus on the difficulties encountered in complying with program mandates. Understanding the perspective of Target Groups is also likely to be useful to central authorities, both in terms of anticipating political feedback and in enabling them to test the behavioral (causal) assumptions on which the program is based. For example, a study of welfare recipients in New York and Chicago concludes that the work incentive program is based on the erroneous assumption that AFDC mothers do not perceive any negative status to being on welfare and thus need to be prodded into seeking work; although this may be true of some, for many others their expectations of remaining economically dependent are a function of past inability to find work and/or an unwillingness to leave small children in day care centers (Goodwin and Moen, 1981).

Detailed case studies of the implementation of local programs (Mechling, 1978; Feeley, 1978) or of intergovernmental programs in a few selected areas (Wirt, 1970; Pressman and Wildavsky, 1973) have been able to combine two or more of these perspectives. Unfortunately, the ideal research design involving (1) a comprehensive evaluation of the extent to which central objectives were attained and (2) an analysis of the activities and perspectives of central authorities, local implementing officials, and target groups is usually precluded by resource constraints.[6] When choices have to be made, it would appear that the Center-focused perspective is appropriate, first, when the researcher wishes simply to obtain a general idea of the extent to which, and the reasons for which, official objectives were attained and, second, in cases where the basic policy decision provides reasonably clear objectives and coherently structures the implementation process (Sabatier and Mazmanian, 1979b). But it becomes more crucial to understand the perspectives of the Periphery the more ambiguous are central objectives and/or the more discretion accorded peripheral officials (Berman, 1980). Likewise, an appreciation of Target Group perspective becomes critical when the program is based on assumptions concerning their motivational patterns.

B. Principal Approaches to Implementation Research

Choices on the three issues discussed in Sec. I.A have tended to cluster into a few principal orientations to implementation analysis.

The first, pioneered by Derthick (1972) and probably best represented by Pressman and Wildavsky (1973), Van Horn (1979), Sabatier and Mazmanian (1979a), and Bullock (1981), is the most comprehensive approach in that it focuses on all three of what we feel should be the principal topics of implementation analysis:

1. To what extent were the policy outputs of the implementing agencies and/or the eventual impacts of the implementation process consistent with the official objectives enunciated in the original statute, appellate court case, or other basic decision? In addition, were there other politically significant impacts?
2. To what extent were the objectives and basic strategies in the original decision modified during the course of implementation and/or during the period of policy reformulation by the original policy maker?
3. What were the principal factors affecting the extent of goal attainment, the modifications in goals and strategies, and any other politically significant impacts?

This approach usually combines the perspectives of Center, Pheriphery, and Target Group, although the emphasis tends to be on the first. That depends, however, on the nature of the program. For example, Van Horn's (1979) analysis of three programs (general revenue sharing, CETA, and community development block grants) that made only modest efforts to change the behavior of field-level officials, understandably had to focus on the Periphery in order to understand variation in program outcomes across local jurisdictions.

A second approach is concerned less with the extent to which official (Central) goals are attained and more with how the Periphery (e.g., street-level bureaucrats and/or local governments and interest groups) respond to the perturbation in their ongoing systems. This orientation is best represented by the Browning et al. (1981) study of Bay Area cities and the Weatherly and Lipsky (1977) study of the implementation of a state special education reform in several Boston-area schools. It is also represented by studies of the implementation of innovations within large organizations that share the Argyris-Bennis preoccupation with meeting subordinate officials' psychological needs for autonomy and participation (Elmore, 1978: 209–217). Although many of these studies are concerned with the effects of participation in obtaining peripheral officials' commitment to policies roughly consistent with legal intent (Mosher, 1967; Berman and McLaughlin, 1976), a focus on meeting the psychological needs of implementing officials runs the risk of ignoring the critical topic of the degree of democratic accountability in the implementation of governmental policy (Majone and Wildavsky, 1978: 107).

A third approach, represented by Goodwin and Moen (1981) and by Kirst and Jung (1980) but also including Altenstetter and Bjorkman (1977), focuses on the formulation-implementation-reformulation cycle. It is less interested than the first two orientations in understanding the details of policy implementation and more concerned with policy making as an evolutionary or learning process in which goals within a policy area are clarified over time or revised to meet changes in social priorities and in which various strategies are attempted and modified to see which "work." For example, a longitudinal study of the implementation of Title I of the 1965 Elementary and Secondary Education Act (ESEA) over a 13-year period reveals that (1) the original ambiguity in congressional intent over whether the program was to focus on disadvantaged pupils or be general aid to school districts has been rather clearly resolved by Congress and the Office of Education in favor of the former goal; (2) this has been a process marked by cumulative incrementalism in which changes in both the statute and program regulations have consistently expanded federal efforts to target the funds to disadvantaged children; and (3) the most important causal factors have probably been the emergence of an active constituency in favor of compensatory education and the publication of numerous evaluation studies documenting early abuses in the program and periodically monitoring compliance by state and local agencies (Kirst and Jung, 1980).

Additional approaches may, of course, emerge in the future. It is worth noting, for example, that the field thus far has had a strong inductive orientation, with numerous case studies and most of the conceptual work consisting of loosely linked hypotheses and identification of critical variables derived from the case materials (Van Meter and Van Horn, 1975; Van Horn, 1979; Sabatier and Mazmanian, 1979b, 1981). Perhaps in the future there will be more interest in deductive approaches drawn from, for example, exchange theory (Heath, 1976; Nagel and Neef, 1979). Although Luft (1976) and Bardach (1977) have adopted the individual strategizing assumptions that form the basis of exchange theory, no one has yet been able parsimoniously to incorporate into individuals' behavior the legal, political, and economic constraints that often strongly affect the implementation process.

II. WHAT HAVE WE LEARNED THUS FAR?

Following are some of the principal conclusions that have emerged from the decade of empirical research focused specifically on policy implementation. Although not intended to be exhaustive, the list provides at least a reasonable introduction to the field.[7]

A. The Importance of Assignment to a Sympathetic Implementing Agency with Slack Resources

There is little question that most public bureaucracies develop a general policy orientation over time through the socialization and self-recruitment of personnel and through pressures from the dominant interest groups and legislative sovereigns within their respective subsystems (Kaufman, 1960; Downs, 1967: chap. 18). Although significant changes in an agency's external environment can lead to a modification in its basic orientation, such evolution is normally slowed by resistance from personnel with civil service protection, by a variety of sunk costs, and by the continued presence of resistant actors in its subsystem (Kaufman, 1971; Mazmanian and Nienaber, 1979). Thus to assign implementation of a policy to an agency with an inconsistent general orientation is to beg for trouble, as the means of monitoring and controlling the behavior of personnel hostile to the policy will almost certainly be inadequate (March and Simon, 1958; Downs, 1967, Heclo, 1977; Elmore, 1978: 191–199) and as the policy will almost certainly be opposed by the traditional interest groups and legislators within its subsystem. For example, several studies of the regulation of pesticide safety have revealed a historical pattern of rather lax regulation and enforcement by federal and state departments of agriculture, followed by a notable change in orientation when responsibility at the federal level was transferred from the Department of Agriculture to the Environmental Protection Agency in 1970 (Whorton, 1974; Blodgett, 1974; MacIntyre, 1980).[8]

But assignment to a sympathetic agency is not sufficient. The implementing agency must also have slack resources (or be given substantial new ones) if one is to avoid the problems associated with the coping behaviors of overworked street-level bureaucrats and if the energy is to be expended to alter operating procedures without substantial delay (Weatherly and Lipsky, 1977).

Thus it is hardly surprising that successful implementation tends to be associated with assignment either to (1) sympathetic existing agencies with slack resources that are looking for new programs or to (2) new agencies created after a vigorous political campaign. In the latter case, the program will necessarily be given high priority within the agency, and the creation of a large number of new positions provides the opportunity for the infusion of new personnel who are strongly committed to the new program (Downs, 1967; Sabatier and Mazmanian, 1979a; Cerych and Sabatier, 1981). When neither strategy is feasible—as is often the case—implementation is likely to be marked by considerable delay and by polity outputs that reflect a compromise between legal directives and the preferences of agency officials.

B. Problems in Center-Periphery Cooperation

Although peripheral officials seldom will flagrantly violate (central) legal norms, numerous studies have shown that they will seek aggressively to exercise any discretionary authority in order to pursue their own agendas, in keeping with the perspectives of their organization and/or the exigencies of the local political situation. This is particularly true in intergovernmental programs, where local officials feel little loyalty to the externally imposed norms, where they are often dependent on local institutions for critical resources and political support, and where, in any event, their discretion is usually considerable (Lazin, 1973; Lieber, 1975; Van Horn, 1979; Williams, 1980). For example, the Browning et al. (1981) study found substantial variation in the implementation of the Model

Cities law among Bay Area cities, depending on whether or not it accorded with the preferences of the dominant coalition in the particular jurisdiction. Berke and Kirst (1972)
and Berman and McLaughlin (1976) came to similar conclusions in their studies of the
implementation of federal education programs. But responsiveness to local conditions and
consequent interjurisdictional variation in policy outputs occur even within a single
agency (Selznick, 1949; Foss, 1960). This was clearly demonstrated in a recent study of
the California coastal commissions, which found substantial differences in the policies
pursued by different regional commissions (within the same state agency) and which, in
turn, were strongly correlated with the policy preferences of implementing officials and
with variations in the local/regional political and economic situation (Sabatier and Mazmanian, 1979a).

   To the extent that such interjurisdictional variations in compliance with central
directives are deemed undesirable, they can be significantly reduced through clear program goals and through placing substantial sanctions and/or incentives in the hands of
central authorities. For example, the coastal commission study found that interregional
variations in the policies eventually pursued could be reduced substantially through appeals to a state commission dominated by supporters of statutory objectives (Sabatier
and Mazmanian, 1979a). Even more significantly, Rodgers and Bullock (1976) show
clearly that the massive resistance by Southern school districts to federal desegregation
orders all but ceased when sanctions became great enough, that is, the cutoff of not only
federal but also state funds.

C. Implementation as an Extension of the Conflicts
of the Formulation Stage

Although there are instances in which skillful mobilization of support during the formulation stage produces genuine agreement among all interested parties on the program to be
pursued,[9] implementation is normally a continuation and elaboration of the conflicts of
the formulation phase (Mayntz, 1976; Bardach, 1977). Sometimes the legislative product
is the result of compromises in which the parties agree on little except to pass an ambiguous bill, thereby leaving much of the real policy making to the implementation stage
(Lowi, 1969; Majone and Wildavsky, 1978). When decisions are made, they often involve
trade-offs—for example, restrictive policies but weak enforcement mechanisms (Rosenbaum, 1981)—that leave nobody satisfied and thus encourage everyone to continue the
fight before the implementing agencies, the courts, and subsequent legislatures. And even
in those instances when legislators make a reasonably clear and coherent decision—for
example, the provisions in the 1970 Clean Air Amendments calling for a 90 percent
reduction in automotive emissions from new cars by 1975—the losers in the formulation
stage will normally continue the fight in the hope that application of the policy can be
delayed or modified through appeal to hostile leverage points, that the emergence of undesirable side effects will force revisions, and/or that changing economic or political conditions will lead to a reformulation of the original policy.

   Of course, the ability of a specific interest to continue its struggle is dependent on its
capacity to monitor the process, to intervene periodically before implementing agencies,
and to appeal agency decisions to the courts, the legislature, and/or the mass media at
critical junctures. Murphy (1971) has argued that the outcome of the struggle between
the formal objectives of Title I of the 1965 ESEA to help disadvantaged (poor) children

and the preferences of most implementing officials for general aid was critically affected during the 1965–1972 period by the limited ability of the poor to develop organizations that could monitor the details of the process and intervene effectively before local school boards and the Office of Education—particularly in contrast to the influence wielded by school officials, parents, and members of Congress representing the more affluent majority. And the oft-remarked tendency of many regulatory agencies gradually (or periodically) to become dominated by the industries they are supposedly regulating has been at least partially attributed to the greater financial and technical resources of regulated groups vis-a-vis consumer and environmental interests (Bernstein, 1955; Sabatier, 1975). In fact, variation in the strength of competing interest groups and peer agencies in different jurisdictions probably explains much of the interjurisdictional variation in the policy outputs of implementing agencies, as agency officials have to be sensitive to the balance of support in their area.

D. The Importance of Background Socioeconomic Conditions

More than a decade of research by political demographers (Sharkansky, 1970; Eulau and Prewitt, 1973; Hofferbert, 1974)—to say nothing of the much older Marxist tradition—has repeatedly demonstrated the association between changes over time and jurisdiction in social and economic conditions on the one hand, and the policy outputs of public agencies on the other. Although the precise linkages are not always clear, few people would argue that such conditions can affect the perceived needs of local populations and officials, the strength of competing interest groups, the financial resources of various jurisdictions, and many other factors.

For example, Nathan and Adams (1977) found that probably the most important factor affecting the expenditures of general revenue sharing funds in various jurisdictions was local fiscal pressure, with jurisdictions facing potential deficits or cutbacks utilizing the federal funds to maintain existing programs, whereas more fortunate local governments tended to use the funds for capital expenditures and to establish new programs. Similarly, regression and path analyses by Mazmanian and Sabatier (1980b) found that more than half of the variation in the voting records of regional coastal commissioners could be explained in terms of the socioeconomic characteristics of their respective jurisdictions.

Changes in socioeconomic conditions over time can also critically affect the implementation process. For example, the implementation of the automotive provisions of the 1970 Clean Air Amendments was strongly influenced by the dramatic rise in gasoline prices following the 1973–1974 Arab oil boycott, as the United Auto Workers (UAW) and Congress became much more concerned with the (allegedly) negative effects of pollution control systems on fuel efficiency and, in turn, with the impacts of increased public concern with fuel efficiency on the sale of domestic automobiles. As a result, the UAW and many Democrats who had been strong proponents of stringent controls in 1970 successfully sought to soften the economic impacts on the troubled industry, such as by pushing back the deadlines for compliance (Mazmanian and Sabatier, 1982).

E. The Complexity of Joint Action

One of the greatest contributions of the Pressman and Wildavsky (1973) study was the attention it drew to the multiplicity of clearance points involved in the implementation of virtually any program and thus the difficulty of organizing cooperative activity among numerous semiautonomous actors (see also Bardach, 1977; Berman, 1978: 165). In the implementation of the EDA public works projects in Oakland, for example, they counted 30 important decisions with an average of about 2.5 actors per decision—thus requiring a cumulative total of about 70 assents for the program to succeed. A similar, but less detailed, analysis of the implementation of the access requirements of the 1972 California coastal law revealed a minimum of seven major decision points involving nine different institutions in order to open a coastal accessway or park (Sabatier and Mazmanian, 1979a).

Even given agreement among all actors on basic objectives, the multiplicity of clearance points offers numerous occasions for delay and the breakdown of consensus as participants negotiate specific agreements. In the absence of such goal consensus, there is every likelihood that opponents or lukewarm supporters of program objectives will be able to control sufficient clearance points to demand important concessions and potentially to scuttle the program as it applies to them. This is particularly likely in intergovernmental programs, where there will normally be substantial variation in the attitudes of implementing officials in various jurisdictions (Hucke, 1978).

The number of clearance points would not be so critical if central officials had sufficient sanctions and inducements at their disposal to bring about compliance from the multitude of actors involved. In such cases, negotiating the necessary clearances might involve delay but not significant program modifications. Since *very* few statutes provide such incentives for anything more than a small minority of clearance points, however, it is hardly surprising that one usually finds substantial interjurisdictional variations in policy outputs—if not significant changes in overall program design (Berman and McLaughlin, 1976; Ingram, 1977; Van Horn, 1979).

F. Financial and Technical Resources

A minimum level of financial and technical resources is necessary if a program is to have any possibility of being effectively implemented. This is most obviously the case when the distribution of funds is at the heart of the program. For example, the "new towns" provisions of the 1970 Urban and New Communities Act were effectively killed when, under President Nixon, the Office of Management and Budget (OMB) impounded most of the funding that Congress had approved for grants, loans, and other front-end costs associated with developing large-scale new communities (Mazmanian and Sabatier, 1982). It is also quite clear that the creation of new programs requires additional funds for hiring new personnel, and so on. Weatherly and Lipsky (1977) note, for example, that the legislature's failure to fund new positions to help implement the special education law placed enormous strains on existing school personnel who, although strongly committed to the new program, nevertheless found it impossible to carry through on some of its more time-consuming features, such as extended consultation with parents.

Although inadequate funding is often noted as a problem in labor-intensive and/or fund-dispersal programs in education, housing, welfare, and other social services, it can pose substantial constraints on regulatory programs as well. For example, Radian and Sharkansky (1979) demonstrate how a reform of Israel's income tax law requiring additional scrutiny of self-employed persons' tax returns was severely impaired not only by the failure to hire additional personnel but also by a net *decline in the number of tax* agency accountants brought on by a public-sector salary freeze at the same time that the new law increased the demand for such personnel in the private sector. And Jacoby and Steinbruner (1973) argue that the EPA's efforts to implement the automotive provisions of the 1970 Clean Air Act were significantly affected by the underfunding of its research and development program into alternative engine technologies, thereby hindering its ability to develop alternatives to the problematic catalyst technology chosen by the American automobile companies.

Although adequate financial and technical resources are a necessary condition for effective implementation, they are certainly not a sufficient one. Moreover, they are critically dependent on other variables, particularly the level of political support for the program in the legislature. In fact, a recent analysis of the implementation of eight higher education reforms in six European countries has tentatively concluded that inadequate funding was not an important factor in explaining nonattainment of program objectives, whereas two of the new programs—the British Open University and the University of Tromsø in northern Norway—were able substantially to surpass original budget estimates because of their extensive political support (Cerych and Sabatier, 1981).

G. The Importance of the Underlying Causal Theory

"It's tough to get to Poughkeepsie without a good map." Pressman and Wildavsky's (1973) contention that a policy decision should be viewed as a hypothesis, "if *a, b,* then *x*," or, alternatively, as a map for getting from the present situation to the designated objective(s), is certainly one of the foundations of implementation analysis. In the case of the EDA's jobs program in Oakland, for example, they argued that—even had the program not been hampered by the multitude of clearance points and the lack of support from numerous participants—it may well have fallen short of its objective of providing 3000 new jobs for the hard-core unemployed, or certainly would have done so very inefficiently. The program was based on the erroneous assumption that the trickle-down effect from public works projects, which is relatively successful in providing such jobs in underdeveloped regions (e.g., Appalachia), will be equally effective in targeting jobs in fully developed, relatively prosperous regions such as San Francisco–Oakland.

Although the concept of causal theory has been central to much of the implementation literature, not all authors have agreed on precisely what it means. Both Pressman and Wildavsky (1973) and Bardach (1977) have focused on the (often implicit) cognitive theory behind a reform and have often been concerned with the relative efficiency of various approaches—hence their argument that providing benefits directly to target groups, for example, via a negative income tax, is likely to be more effective and certainly more efficient than relying on enormous welfare and social service bureaucracies (Bardach, 1977: 250–254). The long-standing debate in pollution control policy over the relative efficacy and efficiency of detailed regulations versus emission taxes would also fall within this tradition (Friedlander, 1977; Majone, 1976; Wenner, 1978).

A somewhat different conception of causal theory can be found in Berman (1978: 163). Forsaking any explicit concern with efficiency, he divides the causal assumptions underlying a program into two components: one dealing with "implementation effectiveness" (i.e., with the ability of the program to provide the policy outputs consistently with legal objectives), the other with what he terms "technical validity," that is, the ability of those outputs to lead to the desired outcomes. In pollution control, for example, the former would be concerned with the factors affecting the consistency of agency permit decisions with legal objectives (and perhaps the compliance of target groups with those decisions), whereas the latter would be concerned with the extent to which legally correct permit decisions actually led to improvements in ambient air quality and ultimately to the desired effects on human health and property.[10]

In their recent work, Mazmanian and Sabatier (1981; 1982) have developed a third version of causal theory, which focuses on two questions:

1. To what extent did the policy formulators understand the principal factors and causal linkages affecting goal attainment? (the cognitive component)
2. To what extent did they give implementing agencies jurisdiction over sufficient linkages to have at least the potential of attaining legal goals? (the jurisdictional component)

Their emphasis, then, is on the theory actually *incorporated into* the statute (or other authoritative policy decision) rather than on the one that some policy formulators may have had in mind. For example, the 1972 California Coastal Initiative incorporated a much more valid theory with respect to visual than to physical access. On the former, the authority given the coastal agencies to regulate all development within 1000 yards of the coast was clearly sufficient to protect view corridors from the coastal highway to the ocean. On the latter, however, the commissions' permit review authority would only enable them to require applicants to allocate land for accessways or to deny developments pending possible acquisition of the land for park purposes. But the commissions were not given authority actually to manage accessways or to purchase land for park purposes (Sabatier and Mazmanian, 1979a).

No matter how one cares to conceptualize causal theory, one of the most fascinating aspects of implementation analysis is the extent to which deficiencies in the original theory become known and are subsequently corrected. In the California case, for example, the 1976 reformulation of the Coastal Act addressed many of the inadequacies in the original legislation by (1) creating a new agency (the Coastal Conservancy) with some responsibility for acquiring and managing accessways and (2) authorizing a $100 million bond issue for coastal park acquisitions.

H. The Twin Imperatives of Political Support and Managerial Skill

It should be apparent by now that the effective implementation of any nonincremental policy will normally be contingent on overcoming a variety of obstacles, including (1) the indifference and perhaps even hostility of many implementing officials, particularly in intergovernmental programs; (2) harassment from interest groups and legislators who had originally opposed the reform; (3) the problems of negotiating agreements from numerous agencies (often in different levels of government), all of them extremely sensitive to invasions of their "turf" and to the preferences of interest groups and sovereigns in *their* subsystems; (4) the yearly threat of debilitating restrictions in legal authority or cuts in funding during executive and legislative budget review; (5) the need to correct deficiencies in the causal theory underlying the original policy decision; and (6) the possibility that change in relevant socioeconomic conditions will undermine that theory and/or the program's political support.

The ability of a program to overcome the pressures for delay and for compromising fundamental objectives—while at the same time retaining the capacity to respond to weaknesses in the original design or to changes in background conditions—is contingent on both (1) continuous political support from some key interest groups and legislative (and/or executive) sovereigns throughout the implementation process and (2) substantial commitment and at least average managerial and political skill from top implementing officials. Without the latter, the program is likely to be beset by scandal, internal dissension, continuous conflicts with peer and subordinate agencies, and/or an inability to develop creative solutions to inadequacies in the underlying causal theory. Without political support from interest groups and key sovereigns, the program is likely to be severely damaged by attacks from opponents within the legislature and to be unable to reformulate the original legislation so as to improve the underlying causal theory and implementing mechanisms consistent with the original objectives.

We have already noted the arguments by Murphy (1971) and by Kirst and Jung (1980) that implementation of Title I of ESEA has been critically affected by the absence of an effective constituency in favor of compensatory education during the 1960s and then its gradual emergence beginning in 1969. Likewise, Bullock (1981) has shown that the degree of support from executive, legislative, and judicial sovereigns and, to a slightly lesser extent, the presence of a strong supportive constituency are some of the critical factors explaining variation in the extent to which four civil rights policies have attained their objectives. Finally, Levin's (1980) analysis of 10 effective programs reveals that "strong leadership"—which combines both the mobilization of diffuse support and Bardach's administrative "fixer"—was one of the elements characteristic of all 10.[11]

I. The Extent of Behavioral or System Change

Several authors have begun with the common sense premise that implementation difficulties will be roughly proportional to the extent of system or behavioral change mandated by a policy reform (Van Meter and Van Horn, 1975; Sabatier and Mazmanian, 1981; Cerych and Sabatier, 1981). The reasoning is quite straightforward: Other things being equal, the amount of resistance encountered from implementing officials and target groups will be proportional to the amount of change demanded of them. In addition, insofar as the amount of change requires traversing new ground, there are likely to be numerous false starts until implementing officials learn to coordinate the various program elements.

Although basic hypothesis has generally been supported by the available evidence, it is nevertheless subject to a number of caveats or conditional propositions. First, if there is widespread consensus about the desirability of the change—as was the case with the Peace Corps or the moonshot program (at least initially)—there is no reason to expect opposition (Van Meter and Van Horn, 1975). Second, and often related to the first, insofar as the reform affects only an easily isolated part of a system in which participation is voluntary, resistance will likely be minimal. For example, the British Open University represented a rather dramatic change in teaching methods but encountered little opposition because participation was entirely voluntary and the reform was carefully designed so as not to affect the traditional universities adversely (Cerych and Sabatier, 1981).[12] Finally, the RAND study of educational innovations found that "projects demanding little change in teacher behavior were likely to be implemented in a pro forma fashion, whereas ambitious change efforts that engaged the sense of professionalism among teachers could be made to work with appropriate [i.e., participatory] implementation strategies" (Berman, 1980: 215). The explanation would seem to lie in the fact that the reforms did not challenge the basic objectives (or perhaps even strategies) of teachers, but instead dealt with the tactics or means for reaching those goals, such as improving students' reading ability.

J.   Overview of the Implementation Process

Anyone reviewing the implementation literature of the 1970s has to be struck by the difficulties involved in meeting legal objectives. Among the cases of substantial shortfall in goal attainment are the following: (1) the EDA jobs program in Oakland, California (Pressman and Wildavsky, 1973); (2) a variety of "new towns" schemes in the United States (Derthick, 1972; Burby and Weiss, 1976); (3) Title I of ESEA (Murphy, 1971); (3) Northern and Latino school desegregation (Bullock, 1981); (4) model cities (Williams and Elmore, 1976; Browning et al., 1981); (5) the automotive provisions of the 1970 Clean Air Amendments (Mazmanian and Sabatier, 1982); (6) pollution control legislation in the German Federal Republic (Hucke, 1978); (7) attempts to reform the treatment of pretrial inmates in New Haven, Connecticut (Feeley, 1978); (8) federal efforts to prevent racial discrimination in public housing in Chicago (Lazin, 1973); (9) federal welfare programs (Goodwin and Moen, 1981); (10) a 1974 Israeli income tax reform (Radian and Sharkansky, 1979); (11) the 1974 Comprehensive Employment and Training Act (Van Horn, 1978; Hargrove and Dean, 1980); and, in all likelihood, (12) the 1972 Water Pollution Control Amendments (Lieber, 1975).

In contrast, the cases of substantial attainment of nonincremental goals tend to be fewer, although not as infrequent as the current American preoccupation with the ineffectiveness of government would lead one to conclude: (1) the 1972 California Coastal Initiative (Sabatier and Mazmanian, 1979a); (2) the 1965 Voting Rights Act (Rodgers and Bullock, 1972); (3) the San Francisco Bay Conservation and Development Commission (Swanson, 1975; Sabatier and Klosterman, 1981); (4) reforms in sanitation practices in New York City (Mechling, 1978); (5) restrictions on urban expansion in Sacramento County, California (Johnston et al., 1978); (6) the 1972 Massachusetts Special Education Law (Weatherly and Lipsky, 1977); (7) the British Open University (Cerych and Sabatier, 1981); and, after years of failure, (8) Southern school desegregation (Rodgers and Bullock, 1976; Bullock, 1981).

Any attempt to explain these variations in program success must begin with the degree of system or behavioral change envisaged by the reform. It is easier to reduce dramatically the rate of filling of San Francisco Bay than to increase substantially the earnings of millions of low-income, one-parent families. But that is only part of the explanation, as some programs calling for rather massive system change—most notably, Southern school desegregation—have largely attained their legal objectives.[13]

Within this context, Mazmanian and Sabatier (1981; 1982) argue that the extent to which the objectives of a statute or other authoritative policy decision are attained will be a function of (1) the clarity and consistency of its objectives; (2) the adequacy of the underlying causal theory; (3) the extent to which the policy decision structures the implementation process by, for example, assigning implementation to sympathetic agencies and providing adequate sanctions and incentives to induce compliance from recalcitrant actors; (4) the political and management skill of the principal implementing officials; (5) the extent of support for the program from constituency groups and critical sovereigns; and (6) the absence of substantial shifts in socioeconomic conditions undermining the statute's causal theory or political support. To the extent that these conditions are not met—as will frequently be the case, in appellate court decisions even more than with legislatively enacted statutes (Baum, 1981)—one would anticipate shortfalls in goal attainment. In such cases the authors suggest a number of adaptive strategies to increase future conformity between intent and outcomes. In the case of an underlying cognitive theory of dubious validity, for example, one can encourage experimental programs, participation by field-level professionals, and periodic formal evaluations (Sabatier and Mazmanian, 1979a). And there is some evidence that both bureaucratic rationality and recent decisions of the federal courts encourage a gradual clarification of program objectives over time (Schapiro, 1968; Davis, 1969; Rein and Rabinovitz, 1977; Horowitz, 1977; MacIntyre, 1980).

In contrast to the authors' approach—which suggests that goal achievement is basically a function of meeting a set of necessary and sufficient conditions, either initially or progressively over time—Berman (1980) has argued that different implementation strategies are appropriate in different situations. He suggests, for example, that a "programmed" approach involving clear goals, detailed program specifications, few program participants, and so on, is appropriate when there is minimal goal conflict, an adequate causal theory, few agencies involved, and a stable political environment. To the extent that these situational parameters are not met, a more "adaptive" implementation strategy involving bargaining and mutual adaptation among multiple participants is called for. The "adaptive" approach, however, makes it difficult to evaluate implementation by reference to the statutorily prescribed goals. It also assumes that the behavior of recalcitrants probably will not be changed over time through the clarification of goals, the incorporation of more adequate sanctions, or efforts to circumvent them (e.g., through the creation of a new agency).

III. THE PROSPECTS OF EFFECTIVE IMPLEMENTATION: A COMPARATIVE ASSESSMENT

In this final section, we would like to offer some tentative observations concerning the probability of effective implementation of legally prescribed objectives in different political systems and, to a lesser extent, in different policy areas. We make no pretense of being either comprehensive or definitive, but instead seek to stimulate interest in the largely unchartered waters of comparative policy implementation.

A comparison of the list of implementation "successes" and "failures" among U.S. programs, as discussed earlier, reveals a rather high percentage of federal programs among the latter, whereas the list of "successes" tends to be disproportionately state or local initiatives. Although neither list constitutes anything like a random sample of the implementation studies at each level, there are sound reasons for expecting federal programs to be, on the whole, less successfully implemented than state or local ones. First, federal programs almost always involve more implementing officials and more people in target groups and thus, *ceteris paribus,* a greater amount of mandated behavioral change. It's more difficult to change the behavior of several million people than that of several hundred or of several thousand. Second, most federal programs are actually implemented through state and local governments, which drastically increases the number of clearance points over which top implementing officials have little control. Although many state porgrams are likewise administered by local authorities, local governments generally have less constitutional and fiscal autonomy vis-a-vis state officials than do the states vis-a-vis Washington (Kaufman, 1963). Third, there is almost always much greater variety in the social, economic, and political situations confronting peripheral implementing officials involved in federal than in state, and certainly than in local, programs. Consequently, almost any federal program (outside of national defense and perhaps the income tax) will ultimately be dependent on the behavior of officials with widely varying policy preferences confronting quite different situations—which, given the usual limits of federal authority, almost guarantees somewhat comparable variation in policies actually pursued. In contrast, the situations in most towns and even in many states are more homogeneous. Fourth, the greater heterogeneity confronting federal policy makers means that they have a much more difficult task framing clear policies and regulations than do their counterparts in most states and virtually all local governments. To what extent does it make sense to have the same rules for Wyoming as for New York, for Mississippi as for Massachusetts? Finally, the greater financial resources of the federal government and the traditional fear of states and localities of placing themselves at a competitive disadvantage with their counterparts elsewhere means that a higher percentage of the most vexing social problems—pollution control, industrial health and safety, transportation regulation, welfare, energy—have been passed up to the federal government for resolution, with the "lower" levels subsequently often striving covertly to reap a competitive advantage through differential enforcement during the implementation phase.

Although one would thus expect a higher rate of effective implementation of legal objectives of local than of federal programs, local governments are not without their problems in this sphere. In particular, implementation of local programs is often frustrated by events largely beyond the control of local authorities, namely, (1) national/state economic trends and (2) competing legal mandates emanating from Washington or state capitals. In fact, we would hypothesize that the rate of effective implementation is probably highest at the state level, which affords a happy mean between the horrendous size and diversity problems confronting federal officials and the lack of economic and political autonomy bedeviling their local counterparts.

Turning to other countries, it would seem, first of all, that effective implementation requires a minimum level of administrative competence that may well be lacking in many Third World nations and even in some European systems, such as Italy. Second, one might expect implementation to be easier in relatively homogeneous, middle-sized countries, such as Norway and Sweden, than in either very large and diverse ones (e.g., the Soviet Union, Brazil) or in nations that are so small (e.g., the Netherlands and New Zealand) as to be at the mercy of economic and strategic circumstances largely beyond their control. Third, one might argue that the incidence of effective implementation would be higher in countries with a strong tradition of civil servant deference to the cabinet than in systems, such as that in the United States, with a relatively autonomous and/or "politicized" bureaucracy. Fourth, one might hypothesize that implementation would be easier in countries such as Britain, France, or South Africa with a heavily centralized legal system than in otherwise comparable federal systems, such as the German Federal Republic, Canada, or Australia.[14] Finally, one would expect effective implementation to be correlated with governmental stability—except perhaps in the extreme case where governments are so ephemeral that the bureaucracy reaches a stable compromise with important interest groups and perhaps some parliamentarians and then applies the negotiated settlement over time irrespective of the comings and goings of specific governments.

In addition to comparative analyses across political systems, more attention needs to be directed at the implementation of governmental programs in different policy areas. Given the complexity of joint action, for example, one might hypothesize that implementation of legal objectives would be more effective in policy areas such as national defense, which are relatively autonomous and involve relatively few actors than those such as energy, which are connected with virtually everything in a modern industrial society. Likewise, there may be some areas, such as higher education or land use, in which field-level implementors traditionally enjoy unusually great autonomy from central government authorities.

Although extremely tentative at this stage of implementation research, these (and like) hypotheses can begin to direct attention to what is likely to become the focus of the field in its second decade: systematic comparative policy implementation.[15]

ACKNOWLEDGMENTS

The authors would like to thank Paul Berman, Martin Levin, Angus MacIntyre, Dale Rogers Marshall, and Carl Van Horn for taking the time to comment on an earlier draft of this chapter.

NOTES

1. For the growth in the (American) literature on policy implementation, compare the appendix of the original (1973) edition of Pressman and Wildavsky's *Implementation* with that of the revised edition, released in 1979. The original literature review did, however, slight some early implementation studies, for example, Mayhew (1968).
2. For an exposition of this view, see Nakamura and Smallwood (1980: chap. 1).
3. For example, Van Meter and Van Horn (1975) list three bodies of literature that contributed to their understanding of the implementation process: (1) organization theory, (2) compliance with appellate court decisions, and (3) intergovernmental relations.
4. Although these extracts incorporate one of the central arguments running throughout the article, they cannot reflect all the subtleties of the Majone-Wildavsky position.

5. This is not to imply that Van Horn totally neglects such topics. He simply prefers to assign them to the field of "impact analysis," which he views as quite separate from "implementation analysis"—both conceptually (1979: 9–10) and in his empircal work on CETA (1979: 88).

6. To the best of our knowledge, all of the studies of the nonlocal programs that have approached this level of comprehensiveness—the Rand study of educational innovations, the Ohio State study of CETA, the Rodgers-Bullock work on Southern school desegregation, the Browning et al. research in Bay Area cities, and our own work on the California coastal commissions—have all involved grants of at least $200,000.

7. For another list, see Williams (1980: chap. 2).

8. In a more subtle example, Pressman and Wildavsky (1973) show how an urban jobs program assigned to a rural development agency (EDA) lost any momentum it had when the few urban enthusiasts who had started the program left the agency after a few years.

9. Examples of the formulation stage resolving all major conflicts include most pork barrel programs, much of U.S. tax policy (Surrey, 1976), and the creation of the British Open University (Cerych and Sabatier, 1981).

10. Although we have no serious quarrel with Berman's approach—and, in fact, adopted it at one time (Sabatier and Mazmanian, 1979b)—we decided to drop it (1) because of his lack of clarity about where to look to "find" the causal theory and (2) the confusion that the term "technical validity" seemed to arouse (somewhat mysteriously to us) in the minds of a high percentage of people.

11. According to Bardach (1977: 273–283), a "fixer" is an official—often a leader on one of the relevant legislative committees—with the (staff) resources to monitor closely the implementation effort, the desire to intervene on a virtually continuous basis, and the authority to affect seriously the decisions of legislative and/or executive sovereigns concerning the agency's budget or legal authority. An example would be Senator Edmund Muskie, the principal author of the 1970 Clean Air Amendments and, as chairman of the Senate pollution subcommittee, the acknowledged congressional expert on air and water pollution control (Asbell, 1978).

12. For example, proponents of the Open University made it clear (1) that the new institution would not sacrifice academic quality in an effort to attract students and (2) that it would not take students under 21 years of age, thereby drastically reducing potential competition with the traditional institutions (Cerych and Sabatier, 1981).

13. This assumes that the goal of desegregation was the elimination of dual schools (rather than the much more difficult task of improving the educational achievements or self-image of black students).

14. Although this hypothesis may eventually be supported by the evidence, it is also quite clear that France, at least, is much less centralized in practice than a reading of the legal code would lead one to expect (Crozier and Friedberg, 1977: 218–234).

15. One might cite the following as the first wave of this trend: (1) the study of the regulation of sulfur dioxide emissions in 10 Western European countries by scholars at the Center for Environment and Society in Berlin (Knoepfel et al., 1980); (2) the work by Cerych and Sabatier (1981) on the implementation of higher education reforms in several European countries; and (3) the application of each author's conceptual framework to a variety of programs in different policy areas by Van Horn (1979) and by Mazmanian and Sabatier (1982).

REFERENCES

Altenstetter, C., and Bjorkman, J. W. (1977). *Implementation of a Federal-State Health Program*. International Institute for Management, Berlin.

Altman, D., and Sapolsky, H. M. (1976). Writing the regulations for health. *Policy Sciences 7*: 417–437.

Asbell, B. (1978). *The Senate Nobody Knows*. Random House, New York.

Bailey, S. K., and Mosher, E. K. (1968). *ESEA: The Office of Education Administers a Law*. Syracuse University Press, Syracuse, NY.

Bardach, E. (1976). Policy termination as a political process. *Policy Sciences 7*: 123–131.

—— (1977). *The Implementation Game*. M.I.T. Press, Cambridge, MA.

—— (1980). Implementation studies and the study of implements. Paper presented to 1980 Annual Meeting of the American Political Science Association, Washington, DC.

Baum, L. (1981). The influence of legislatures and appellate courts over the policy implementation process. In *Effective Policy Implementation*, D. A. Mazmanian and P. A. Sabatier (Eds.). Heath, Lexington, MA.

Berke, J. S., and Kirst, M. W. (1972). *Federal Aid to Education*. Heath, Lexington, MA.

Berman, P. (1978). The study of macro- and micro-implementation. *Public Policy 26*: 157–184.

—— (1980). Thinking about programmed and adaptive implementation: Matching strategies to situations. In *Why Policies Succeed or Fail*, Sage Yearbooks in Politics and Public Policy, Vol. 8, H. M. Ingram and E. D. Mann (Eds.). Sage, Beverly Hills, CA.

Berman, P., and McLaughlin, M. W. (1976). Implementation of educational innovation. *Educational Forum 40*: 345–370.

Bernstein, M. (1955). *Regulating Business by Independent Commission*. Princeton University Press, Princeton, NJ.

Blodgett, J. E. (1974). Pesticides: Regulation of an evolving technology. In *Consumer Health and Product Hazards*, Vol. II, S. S. Epstein and R. D. Grundy (Eds.). M.I.T. Press, Cambridge, MA.

Browning, R. F., Marshall, D. R., and Tabb, D. H. (1981). Implementations and political change: Sources of local variations in federal social programs. In *Effective Policy Implementation*, D. A. Mazmanian and P. A. Sabatier (Eds.). Heath, Lexington, MA.

Bullock, C. S. (1981). The Office for Civil Rights and implementation of desegregation programs in the public schools. In *Effective Policy Implementation*, D. A. Mazmanian and P. A. Sabatier (Eds.). Heath, Lexington, MA.

Burby, R., and Weiss, C. (1976). *New Communities U.S.A.* Heath, Lexington, MA.

Cerych, L. (1979). Higher education reform: The process of implementation. *Education Policy Bulletin 7*: 5–21.

Cerych, L., and Sabatier, P. A. (1981). *The Implementation of Higher Education Reforms*. Institute of Education, Paris.

Cohen, D., and Farrar, E. (1977). Power to the parents? The story of education vouchers. *Public Interest 48*: 72–97.

Crozier, M., and Friedberg, E. (1977). *L'acteur et le systeme*. Seuil, Paris.

Davis, K. C. (1969). *Discretionary Justice*. University of Illinois Press, Urbana.

Derthick, M. (1972). *New Towns In-Town*. Urban Institute, Washington, DC.

Downs, A. (1967). *Inside Bureaucracy*. Little, Brown, Boston.

Dye, T. (1972). *Understanding Public Policy*. Prentice-Hall, Englewood Cliffs, NJ.

Easton, D. (1965). *A Systems Analysis of Political Life.* Wiley, New York.

Elmore, R. E. (1978). Organizational models of social program implementation. *Public Policy 26*: 185–228.

Eulau, H., and Prewitt, K. (1973). *Labyrinths of Democracy.* Bobbs-Merrill, Indianapolis, IN.

Feeley, M. M. (1978). The New Haven redirection center. In *Innovation and Implementation in Public Organization,* R. R. Nelson and D. Yates (Eds.). Heath, Lexington, MA.

Foss, P. O. (1960). *Politics and Grass.* Greenwood, New York.

Friedlander, A. F. (1978). *Approaches to Controlling Air Pollution.* M.I.T. Press, Cambridge, MA.

Goodwin, L., and Moen, P. (1981). The evolution and implementation of family welfare policy. In *Effective Policy Implementation,* D. A. Mazmanian and P. A. Sabatier (Eds.). Heath, Lexington, MA.

Hanf, K., and Scarpf, F. W. (Eds.) (1978). *Interorganizational Policy-Making.* Sage, Beverly Hills, CA.

Hargrove, E. (1975). *The Missing Link.* Urban Institute, Washington, DC.

Hargrove, E., and Dean G. (1980). Federal authority and grass-roots accountability: The case of CETA. *Policy Analysis 6*: 127–149.

Heath, A. (1976). *Rational Choice and Social Exchange.* Cambridge University Press, Cambridge.

Heclo, H. (1977). *A Government of Strangers.* Brookings Institute, Washington, DC.

Herring, P. (1936). *Public Adminstration and the Public Interest.* Russell and Russell, New York.

Hjern, B., and Porter, D. O. (1980). The organizational society and organizational analysis. Discussion paper 80–48. International Institute of Management Science Center, Berlin.

Hofferbert, R. I. (1974). *The Study of Public Policy.* Bobbs-Merrill, Indianapolis, IN.

Horowitz, D. L. (1977). *The Courts and Social Policy.* Brookings Institution, Washington, DC.

Hucke, J. (1978). Bargaining in regulative policy implementation: The case of air and water pollution control. *Environmental Policy and Law 4*: 109–115.

Ingram, H. M. (1977). Policy implementation through bargaining: The case of federal grants-in-aid. *Public Policy 25*: 499–526.

Ingram, H. M., and Mann, D. E. (1980). *Why Policies Succeed or Fail.* Sage, Beverly Hills, CA.

Jacoby, H., and Steinbruner, I. S. (1973). *Clearing the Air.* Ballinger, Cambridge, MA.

Johnston, R. A., Schwartz, S. I., and Klinkner, T. (1978). Successful plan implementation: The growth phasing program of Sacramento County. *AIP Journal 44*: 412–423.

Jones, C. O. (1970). *An Introduction to the Study of Public Policy.* Wadsworth, Belmont, CA.

—— (1975). *Clean Air.* Pittsburgh University Press, Pittsburgh.

Katz, D., and Kahn, R. L. (1966). *The Social Psychology of Organizations.* Wiley, New York.

Kaufman, H. (1960). *The Forest Ranger.* Johns Hopkins Press, Baltimore.

—— (1963). *Politics and Policies in State and Local Governments.* Prentice Hall, Englewood Cliffs, NJ.

—— (1971). *The Limits of Organizational Change.* University of Alabama Press, University, Alabama.

Kirst, M. W., and Jung, R. (1980). The utility of a longitudinal approach in assessing implementation: A thirteen-year view of Title I, ESEA. *Educational Evaluation and Policy Analysis 2*: 17–34.

Knoepfel, P., Weidner, H., and Hanf, K. (1980). Analytical framework and research guidelines for the national research teams. International comparative analysis of program formulation and implementation in SO_2 air pollution control in the EEC countries and Switzerland. International Institute for Environment and Society, Berlin.

Lazin, F. A. (1973). The failure of federal enforcement of civil rights regulations in public housing, 1963–1971. *Policy Sciences 4*: 263–274.

Leiserson, A. (1942). *Administrative Regulation.* University of Chicago Press, Chicago.

Levin, M. A. (1980). Conditions contributing to effective implementation and their limits. *Proceedings of the Association for Public Policy Analysis and Management,* Boston.

Levy, F. S., Meltsner, A. J., and Wildavsky, A. (1974). *Urban Outcomes.* University of California Press, Berkeley.

Lieber, H. (1975). *Federalism and Clean Waters.* Heath, Lexington, MA.

Lipsky, M. (1971). Street level bureaucracy and the analysis of urban reform. *Urban Affairs Quarterly 6*: 391–409.

Long, N. E. (1949). Power and administration. *Public Administration Review 9*: 257–264.

Lowi, T. (1969). *The End of Liberalism.* Norton, New York.

Luft, H. S. (1976). Benefit-cost analysis and public policy implementation. *Public Policy 24*: 437–462.

MacIntyre, A. A. (1980). The politics of nonincremental domestic change: Major reform in federal pesticide and predator control policy. Unpublished Ph.D. dissertation, University of California, Davis.

Majone, G. (1976). Choice among policy instruments for pollution control. *Policy Analysis 2*: 589–613.

Majone, G., and Wildavsky, A. (1978). Implementation as evolution. In *Policy Studies Review Annual–1978,* H. Freeman (Ed.). Sage, Beverly Hills, CA.

March, J. G., and Simon, H. A. (1958). *Organizations.* Wiley, New York.

Mayhew, L. H. (1968). *Law and Equal Opportunity.* Harvard University Press, Cambridge, MA.

Mayntz, R. (1976). Environmental policy conflicts: The case of the German Federal Republic. *Policy Analysis 2*: 577–587.

—— (ed.) (1980). *Implementation Politischer Programme: Empirische Forschungsberichte.* Athenaum, Konigstein, FRG.

Mayntz, R., and Scharpf, F. W. (Eds.). (1975). *Policy-Making in the German Federal Bureaucracy.* Elsevier, New York.

Mazmanian, D. A., and Nienaber, J. (1979). *Can Organization Change?* Brookings Institution, Washington, DC.

Mazmanian, D. A., and Sabatier, P. A. (Eds.) (1981). *Effective Policy Implementation.* Heath, Lexington, MA.

—— (1980a). The role of attitudes and perceptions in policy evaluation by attentive elites. In *Why Policies Succeed or Fail,* H. M. Ingram and D. E. Mann (Eds.). Sage, Beverly Hills, CA.

—— (1980b). A multivariate model of public policy making. *American Journal of Political Science 24*: 439–468.

—— (1982). *Implementation and Public Policy.* Scott, Foresman, Glenview, IL.

McLaughlin, M. W. (1975). *Evaluation and Reform: The Case of ESEA, Title I.* Ballinger, Cambridge, MA.

Mechling, J. (1978). Analysis and implementation: Sanitation policies in New York City. *Public Policy 26*: 263–284.

Meltsner, A. (1976). *Policy Analysts in the Bureaucracy.* University of California Press, Berkeley.

Moore, M. H. (1978). Reorganization Plan #2 revisited. *Public Policy 26*: 229–262.

Mosher, F. (1967). *Governmental Reorganization.* Bobbs-Merrill, Indianapolis, IN.

Murphy, J. T. (1971). Title I of ESEA. *Harvard Education Review 41*: 36–63.

Nagel, S., and Neef, M. (1979). *Policy Analysis in Social Science Research.* Sage Library of Social Research, Vol. 72. Sage, Beverly Hills, CA.

Nakamura, R. T., and Smallwood, F. (1980). *The Politics of Policy Implementation.* St. Martin's New York.

Nathan, R. P., and Adams, C. F. (1977). *Revenue Sharing: The Second Round.* Brookings Institution, Washington, DC.

National Academy of Sciences (1974). *Air Quality and Automobile Emission Control.* Report prepared for the Senate Committee on Public Works. U.S. Government Printing Office.

Nelkin, D. (1975). The political impacts of technical expertise. *Social Studies of Science 5*: 40–54.

Nelson, R. R., and Yates, D. (1978). *Innovation and Implementation in Public Organizations.* Heath, Lexington, MA.

Patton, M. Q. (1978). *Utilization-Focused Evaluation.* Sage, Beverly Hills, CA.

Phillips, A. (1975). *Promoting Competition in Regulated Markets.* Brookings Institution, Washington, DC.

Pressman, J., and Wildavsky, A. (1973, 1979). *Implementation.* University of California Press, Berkeley.

Primack, J., and von Hippel, F. (1974). *Advice and Dissent.* Basic Books, New York.

Rabinovitz, F., Pressman, J., and Rein, M. (1976). Guidelines: A plethora of forms, authors, and functions. *Policy Sciences 7*: 399–416.

Radian, A., and Sharkansky, I. (1979). Tax reform in Israel: Partial implementation of ambitious goals. *Policy Analysis 5*: 351–366.

Rein, M., and Rabinovitz, F. (1977). Implementation: A theoretical perspective. Working Paper No. 43. M.I.T.-Harvard Joint Center for Urban Studies.

Rein, M., and White, S. (1977). Policy research: Belief and doubt. *Policy Analysis 3*: 239–271.

Rhoads, S. E. (1974). *Policy Analysis in the Federal Aviation Administration.* Heath, Lexington, MA.

Rodgers, H. R., and Bullock, C. S. (1972). *Law and Social Change.* McGraw-Hill, New York.

—— (1976). *Coercion to Compliance.* Heath, Lexington, MA.

Rosenbaum, N. (1981). Statutory structure and policy implementation: The case of wetlands regulation. In *Effective Policy Implementation,* D. A. Mazmanian and P. A. Sabatier (Eds.). Heath, Lexington, MA.

Sabatier, P. A. (1975). Social movements and regulatory agencies. *Policy Sciences 6*: 301–312.

—— (1978). The acquisition and utilization of technical information by administrative agencies. *Administrative Science Quarterly 23*: 396–417.

Sabatier, P. A., and Klosterman, B. J. (1981). A comparative analysis of policy implementation under different statutory regimes. In *Effective Policy Implementation,* D. A. Mazmanian and P. A. Sabatier (Eds.). Heath, Lexington, MA.

Sabatier, P. A., and Mazmanian, D. A. (1979a). *Can Regulation Work? The Implementation of the 1972 California Coastal Initiative.* Final report to N.S.F. [A revised version will be published in 1982 by Plenum.]

—— (1979b). The conditions of effective implementation. *Policy Analysis 5*: 481–504.

—— (1981). The implementation of public policy: A framework of analysis. In *Effective Policy Implementation,* D. A. Mazmanian and P. A. Sabatier (Eds.). Heath, Lexington, MA.

Shapiro, M. (1968). *The Supreme Court and Administrative Agencies.* Macmillan, New York.

Schultz, R. L., and Slevin, O. P. (Eds.) (1975). *Implementing Operations Research/ Management Science.* American Elsevier, New York.

Selznick, P. (1949). *TVA and the Grass Roots.* University of California Press, Berkeley.

Sharkansky, I. (1970). *Policy Analysis in Political Science.* Markham, Chicago.

Surrey, S. S. (1976). Treasury Department regulatory material under the tax code. *Policy Sciences 7*: 505–518.

Swanson, G. (1975). Coastal zone management from an administrative perspective. Coastal Zone Management Journal 2: 81–102.

Szanton, P. L. (1978). Urban public services: Ten case studies. In *Innovation and Implementation in Public Organizations,* R. R. Nelson and D. Yates (Eds.). Heath, Lexington, MA.

Tobin, R. J. (1979). *The Social Gamble: Determining Acceptable Levels of Air Quality.* Heath, Lexington, MA.

Van Gunsteren, H. R. (1976). *The Quest for Control.* Wiley, New York.

Van Horn, C. E. (1978). Implementing CETA: The federal role. *Policy Analysis 4*: 159–183.

—— (1979). *Policy Implementation in the Federal System.* Heath, Lexington, MA.

Van Meter, D. S., and Van Horn, C. E. (1975). The policy implementation process: A conceptual framework. *Administration and Society 6*: 445–488.

Weatherly, R., and Lipsky, M. (1977). Street-level bureaucrats and institutional innovation: Implementing special-education reform. *Harvard Education Review 47*: 171–197.

Weiss, C. H. (1977). *Using Social Research in Public Policy Making.* Heath, Lexington, MA.

Wenner, L. M. (1978). Pollution control: Implementation alternatives. *Policy Analysis 4*: 47–65.

Whorton, F. (1974). *Before Silent Spring.* Princeton University Press, Princeton, NJ.

Wilensky, H. L. (1967). *Organizational Intelligence.* Basic Books, New York.

Williams W. (1980). *The Implementation Perspective.* University of California Press, Berkeley.

Williams, W., and Elmore, R. F. (1976). *Social Program Implementation.* Academic, New York.

Wirt, F. M. (1970). *Politics of Southern Equality.* Aldine, Chicago.

Yin, R. K. (1980). Studying the implementation of public programs. Discussion paper. Solar Energy Research Institute, Golden, CO.

8

Comparing Policies Across Nations and Cultures

Douglas E. Ashford / University of Pittsburgh, Pittsburgh, Pennsylvania

I. INTRODUCTION: THE COMPARATIVE METHOD

Although there have been a number of departures to link policy studies to comparative politics (Ashford, 1978b; Rose, 1976; Heidenheimer et al., 1975; Gywn and Edwards, 1975; Smith, 1975, Wiatr, 1977), most scholars would agree that the theories and concepts that relate policy studies to comparative politics are weak. In outlining the development of comparative policy studies over the past several decades, the aim of this chapter is to show that the disjunction between empirical analysis of policies and the general body of comparative politics theory is not as serious as may be presumed, and that policy studies provide promising ways of refining and testing the theories and concepts often used in comparative politics. Indeed, there are reasons to think that comparative policy studies may contribute to building better theories and concepts for comparing nations, societies, and cultures.

If comparative policy studies are to be seen as an aspect of comparative politics more generally, it is important to begin with a brief survey of how the general field of comparative political inquiry has developed over the past generation, and to put current disputes about comparative politics into perspective by noting developments in other disciplines. Possibly the most important intellectual force since World War II has been the enormous development of behavioral and quantitative research, which influenced all the social sciences, and, in particular, comparative politics. Wars are often thresholds in our thinking about society and politics. During World War II a number of highly talented social scientists worked together (Social Science Research Council, SSRC, 1949-1950), who were both intellectually and methodologically armed to make a major new attack on our understanding of human behavior at the close of the war.

The effect on comparative research was a curious one because the underlying behavior model greatly simplified comparison, but at the same time ignored many critically important problems of comparative research of all kinds. The behavioral model of man was and remains a powerful conceptual tool because it reduces a wide variety of historical, social, and political circumstances to individual behavior. If the individual is studied in isolation from other generalizations about social and political change, then one of the essential tasks of comparative inquiry is simply eliminated. Within the definitions of a behavioral design, observations about Swedes, Turks, and Indians are presumed to be equivalent. In this way, the behavioral model simultaneously facilitated cross-national research by greatly simplifying the theoretical and conceptual foundations of comparison itself. Like many critically important discoveries, the behavioral model was a tremendous stimulus to research as the paradigm was elaborated and as methodologies were refined. The secondary effect, of more immediate importance to this chapter, was the ease with which the setting of human behavior could be standardized. How individual acts were located in relation to cultural, social, and political processes of change and choice was of relatively little significance. Although there is no necessary bias against policy studies in behavioral studies (in fact, important applied areas developed, such as marketing research and opinion polls), the contextual meaning of how people vote, work, or play made little difference to the basic concepts and theories of behavioral science.

The second major intellectual shift that leads us to the relation of comparative politics and policy studies took place over the 1960s. The behavioral model was never critically assessed, but there were perhaps three main theoretical formulations that promised to revive comparison as an important field of inquiry. The first, and probably the most influential, was the work of Almond and Coleman (1960), which was later elaborated and imprinted on comparative studies by the Comparative Politics Committee of the SSRC. The aim was to develop a model of the political system that would be universally applicable. The key definitional problem was how to separate "political" from other activities in every society. The ease with which Almond's model can be attacked as thinly veiled pluralist politics often blinds us to the conceptual importance of the distinction he was trying to make, which intentionally or unintentionally runs counter to the behavioral stance. Political systems were to be differentiated from society by the monopoly of coercion assigned to the state. In retrospect, it is perhaps unfortunate that Almond's collaborators were more concerned with the various components of his model than with its validity. The immense practical effect of this departure, which as we shall see opened the way for a wide variety of comparative policy studies, was to embrace the developing countries, the Western democracies, and the communist states in a single framework. Because Almond's model emphasized the nature of participation (and implied certain advantages of pluralist democratic politics), it was readily converted into behavioral terms and in fact inspired some major cross-national surveys.

The second major figure in redirecting comparative theory was Easton (1965), although he was not concerned primarily with comparison. Nonetheless, he devised a general model of political systems that naturally attracted comparativists, and one where policies seemed to have more importance. For Almond the performance of political systems was relatively unimportant, because authoritative decisions were the expected result of the successful monopolization of coercion. Working essentially from the more sophisticated systems analysis of natural sciences, Easton sees the equilibrium between inputs and outputs as the defining characteristic of political systems. Again, it is easy to attack Easton for the wrong reasons. There is certainly a conservative emphasis in any equilibrium model, but an equilibrium is not necessarily static, and the same kind of reasoning has been a powerful conceptual tool in developing economic analysis. His thinking placed importance on what political systems do and made the reciprocal relationship between performance and support for political systems much clearer than it had been. Although there is a recognition of interdependence of policies and political support within political systems, behavioral research could be easily related to his model because the individual remains the appropriate unit of analysis.

The third important contributor in diverting comparative politics from the behavioral tradition was Deutsch, who has been heavily influenced by information theory and whose interest in policy studies is evident. His important work on the flow and aggregation of information in political systems (1963) more firmly breaks with the behavioral tradition and calls directly for policy analysis. The cybernetic underpinnings of his theory enable him to differentiate levels of complexity of policy making and to underscore the importance of learning capacities in political systems, both of which lead to policy studies. His work can be readily linked to organizational analysis and cognitive psychology, which are also important tools of policy analysis. Unlike Almond and Easton, Deutsch specifies the normative implications of his theory and differentiates how choices among values affect the flow of information. In this respect, he parts dramatically from more narrowly conceived behavioral theory.

Thus, comparative political theory over the past decade has been enriched by these and other ideas that implied, if they did not achieve, radical departures from the dominant social science tradition. If the proposals of Almond, Easton, and Deutsch have not been widely applied, it is because it is extremely difficult to disaggregate their highly abstract propositions. With the possible exception of Almond, they were not concerned specifically with comparative methods nor with differentiating comparison from other forms of political or social inquiry. To see this particular gap in the study of comparative politics, and possibly in the study of politics generally, it is worth noting how other disciplines simultaneously developed both macro- and microtheories. Less committed to a single paradigm of human behavior, economics has developed an obvious interplay between general theories about economic and industrial development and the application of economic analysis to decisions. There has been a steady accumulation of comparative analysis of economies by such scholars as Kuznets (1946), Kindleberger (1964), and Clapham (1936), while microeconomics has also been refined. Likewise, in sociology, one can easily point to major efforts to redefine the context of sociological research in broad comparative terms (Etzioni, 1968; Kornhauser, 1959; Merton, 1968) while a variety of empirical and applied sociological research was being done.

The explanation for this curious gap in the comparative study of politics and policy is twofold. On the one hand, the prevailing behavioral model of man did not encourage rethinking the contextual and historical issues that confront the analysis of political systems (Bendix, 1964; Moore, 1966). There was an immense amount of valuable quantitative work done (Merritt and Rokkan, 1966), and still to be done, on the most easily separable components of political systems, such as elections, parties, and voting behavior. Much of this work is distinctly cross-national (Allardt and Littunen, 1964; Lipset and Rokkan, 1965; and Rokkan et al., 1970), but it has little bearing on the performance of political systems, nor does it depart from the dominant behavioral mode of analysis. Although one can find a distinct policy connection in the use of aggregate measures of performance (Deutsch, 1961), the internal dynamics and differences that account for different performance were not investigated, and the primary concern was to explain patterns of mobilization and participation. The methodology was dictated by the behavioral paradigm itself, and the possibility that the explanations for similar aggregate levels of performance might in fact be very different among countries tended to be ignored. In short, the validity of the comparison was seldom called into question, and more cross-national policy analysis did not seem important.

The second element in explaining the relative neglect was that political science tended to cut itself off from policy studies (Tribe, 1972). It is now often forgotten that many of those most active in invigorating American political science in the 1930s (Merriam, 1945) were heavily committed to understanding the processes and choices of government. But the study of public administration and public law tended to gravitate to separate faculties, so that the source of applied knowledge was divorced from the theory and concepts of political science. These tendencies were even more pronounced in most European universities, although the urgent problems of developing countries often set the stage to bring applied and theoretical interests back into common focus. There were, of course, such stalwarts as Schattschneider (1960), who saw the control and manipulation of decisions as crucial to understanding politics in one country, but the time was not ripe for a cross-national effort. Until the limits of the prevailing paradigm were recognized and until there was a promising body of data and experience from several countries, comparative policy studies could not advance. The important conceptual change was to begin to differentiate systemic and subsystemic level variation.

II. SYSTEM VARIATION

Until the validity of cross-national comparisons was called into question, it was unlikely that comparative policy studies would achieve importance. There are many strands to the growing accumulation of research and findings during the 1960s that paved the way for this change, but a variety of controversies arose in conducting comparative studies within a single country that led political scientists to examine policies more carefully. The community power debate in the United States, for example, began primarily as a methodological controversy between Dahl and his colleagues at Yale (Dahl, 1961), and sociologists such as Hunter (1953), who used very different methods. There was also a major effort made to analyze aggregate data in order to understand state and local politics by Dye (1966) and others. Out of closer examination of how communities and states behaved grew the awareness, first, that there might be considerable diversity within one country in solving problems, and, second, that policy research might become an important factor in understanding the enormous importance attributed to social and economic conditions. Once the diverse meanings of political variables were investigated more carefully, for example, by Presthus (1979), and the roots of the socioeconomic differences were broken down in terms of policy (Clark, 1974), comparison within one system indicated how cross-national comparative analysis might benefit from policy research.

Concern with variation within political systems was, then, a product of empirical research in the 1960s, although comparative theory is most often associated with systemic-level analysis. Thus, comparative policy studies takes its clue from the most fundamental theoretical issue of comparative politics more generally: how intrasystemic differences relate to systemic differences. If we wish to compare events or behavior within political systems, it is important that systemic variation be minimal. Conversely, if national characteristics vary greatly, then inferences made from intrasystemic differences may be misleading, because systemic variations may account for the results. Concern with the logic of comparison (Przeworski and Teune, 1971) grew from criticisms of the validity of survey research methods and from similar analytical problems of ecological research methods (Schwirian, 1973). The implication was that if one wished to study behavior within systems, they should be as near "alike" as possible, whereas if one wished to study more general, systemic characteristics, then validity would be enhanced if subsystemic characteristics were as different as possible. As we shall see, realization that the context and meaning of aggregate variables might differ radically from one country to another was, and remains, a major stimulus to comparative policy studies.

In fact, the research designs that would meet fully the standards of validity are extremely difficult to construct. If the pitfalls of comparative analysis have been neglected in drawing conclusions from much early cross-national behavioral research, it should be remembered that these same problems complicate policy research. Although some features of policy research increase the chances that the investigator will be more sensitive to the contextual and structural differences among countries (if the person indeed pursues his or her work in two or more countries), the most interesting theoretical possibility of cross-national policy studies is that it may help refine and test systemic-level theories. Although it does not fully satisfy the problem of cross-national validity, showing that performance or outputs are similar among several systems reassures us that conclusions about participation or inputs are valid. From this perspective, it makes little difference whether one is more interested in inputs or outputs. If similar inputs produce very different outputs across countries, then one should be cautious in drawing conclusions about the political system generally without examining closely the historical, institutional, and organizational factors that link the two activities in each country. Conversely, if outputs are similar across countries, then caution should be exercised in concluding cross-national similarities at the systemic level without finding out how similar inputs are.

Thus, one of the exciting possibilities that comparative policy studies raises is that we may refine both our ability to compare systems as a whole, and simultaneously add validity to comparisons of interdependence of inputs and outputs. The emphasis on behavioral research during the 1960s failed to exploit this possibility. There was a great deal of research using the individual as the unit of analysis on voting, elections, and parties. New theories explaining party systems and party coalitions multiplied, with relatively little concern about whether the policy processes and policy options confronting various party systems were similar or different. Political science developed new concepts about parties and democratic participation, starting from the development of pluralist theory by Dahl (1961) and continuing with the consociational theories (Lijphart, 1968), without using policy as a way of comparing within or between political systems. The omission is all the more striking because the growth of government during the 1970s produced a flood of policy-related studies on national planning, center-local politics, and urban politics, most of which was initially assigned to a theoretical limbo.

The growing specialization within the field of comparative politics also meant that important changes in the study of developing countries was neglected. Although some important surveys were carried out in developing countries (Verba et al., 1971; Jacob, et al., 1971), behavioral methods were not readily applicable to many problems facing the Third World. More important, perhaps, scholars of developing countries were aware that there were important differences in the performance of developing countries, and that important policy choices have been embodied in early efforts to modernize. The most striking cases were the "early modernizers," Turkey and Japan, whose rapid advance stimulated historical and institutional research. In Latin America, economic dependence and colonialism produced new theories based on their deprivation and poverty. In Africa and Asia, the turbulence of nationalist movements and military governments led many scholars to see performance as a causal factor and to reexamine how regimes might be affected by difficult policy choices. Thus, unlike comparative studies of Europe and North America, in the Third World there were strong stimuli to analyze politics as a function of policy constraints and opportunities.

By the late 1970s, there were two promising avenues for comparative policy studies. Most closely related to the more conventional theories of comparative politics was the possibility of using policy materials to validate comparisons of inputs and participation. A second possibility, stimulated by the growing number of important case studies and by a small number of scholars who never subscribed to the very abstract theories of political systems, was to treat policy initiatives, implementation, and evaluation as independent factors. In the United States, structural changes linked to performance were analyzed by Lowi (1969) and McConnell (1966), and renewed interest in the policy constraints of federalism on American politics. In Europe, the impetus came from organizational sociologists such as Crozier (1964). But there were still few general frameworks by which to handle the fundamental problems of comparison, and by means of which the disconnected studies of policies and politics in single countries might be compared across systems. Comparative policy analysis was established in the 1970s, but it was not quite clear what direction it might take. There were, in fact, (and are) three such general concepts at work. Each proposes slightly different theoretical frameworks for integrating and comparing the performance of the modern state.

A. The Welfare State

Possibly the most influential idea that spawned new theories on the interdependence of policies and politics was the "welfare state." From the turn of the century, it had been evident that an increasing proportion of national income was being devoted to new programs for education, social assistance, housing, unemployment, and so on. For reasons that have been noted, it was not political scientists but economic historians who first began the search for an explanation to the growing importance of the public sector. One of the early studies (Peacock and Wiseman, 1967) arrived at the essentially historical explanation that wars generated large increments in public spending. Wilensky (1975) produced a careful study of how economic development resulted in increased welfare expenditure, and suggested that age structure and the time of initiating welfare programs were important mediating factors in the growth of public expenditure. In a study of both communist and noncommunist countries, Pryor (1968) showed that ideology had less to do with increased welfare expenditures than the age of various welfare programs.

Although based on aggregate data, studies of this kind brought the importance of changing governmental structure and institutions to the attention of comparative political studies. But like much of earlier research using developmental theories of Almond and others, the explanations remained statistical. Now important approaches can be derived from the aggregate analysis. First, they can be used to establish typologies. Typologies are not really explanations, but a conceptual device to sort out in a rather crude way what appear to be the clustering of important variables around obvious differences. Hopefully, the definitions used for the distinctions made in typologies will be mutually exclusive, and the range will be all-inclusive. When aggregate statistical data are used for constructing typologies, this is necessarily the case. As such, they provide provoking questions and help integrate detailed policy studies across countries. For example, a comparison of total welfare spending among European countries shows France and West Germany, two more aggressively capitalist governments, spending more on welfare than Britain, often considered to be one of the countries most intent on enlarging welfare expenditures since 1945.

Perhaps less widely recognized, typologies also help locate explanatory factors where we are dealing with complex patterns of interaction and long time periods involving many actors and institutions. One can proceed, as Peters (1978) has done, to introduce structural variables statistically in order to extricate political and social effects on welfare. A second possibility that has as yet to be more widely applied is to use independent variables concerning structural features of the political and social system (Heclo, 1974). In this situation, one is not necessarily adhering to the typology, but testing associations suggested by the typology. For example, the complexity and size of bureaucracy is often associated with enhancing or inhibiting the expansion of the welfare state, and one can easily devise such hypotheses against contrasting levels of welfare expenditure (Peters, 1978).

If one is to see comparative policy studies as directed toward developing better comparative theory, as is argued in this essay, the second alternative may be more promising. There are, for example, a number of country-specific generalizations, such as Kesselman's (1970) argument concerning "over-institutionalization" in France. The typologies established by aggregate data provide ways of extending his argument to other countries, and possibly transforming his insight into a single country into a more general theory about governmental and institutional change as political systems achieve increasingly higher levels of welfare expenditure. Similar broad distinctions about party systems can be treated in the same way, as can fundamental institutional distinctions such as federal and unitary systems of government (Ashford, 1977).

B. Governability

The argument over "governability" emerged from analysis of the welfare state, but puts the growth of the modern state in a very different context. During the 1970s it became apparent that some of the European countries were increasing public spending at faster rates than economic growth (Rose and Peters, 1978). The excessive burdens undertaken are not related in a linear order to size of welfare spending, so in this respect the governability argument can be seen as either a rejection or possibly an elaboration of the investigations into the welfare state. From a methodological perspective, the advance was to see governance (Rose, 1976) as a distinct problem rather than as an ambiguous product of increasing welfare. The concept captures the notion of dynamic change, which is essential to policy studies, and also permits one to make rough relative measurements across countries. Governability is not necessarily a problem of being rich or poor, but a function of keeping policy commitments and obligations in balance with social and economic capabilities.

Although amenable to statistical treatment, seeing political systems in terms of their governability returned to many of the classical problems of political science: the viability of democracy, the succession of leadership, and the ability of political systems to aggregate public preferences and priorities. Governability bears some relationship to earlier theories of institutionalization advanced by Huntingdon (1968), who saw that institutional relationships between demands on government and its ability to perform could be dislocated at many levels of socioeconomic development. In this respect, the notion of governability is a more dynamic concept than the earlier abstract theories of comparative politics; and also introduces a concern with structural requisites of democratic government that is missing in behavioral research.

The opportunities for comparative policy studies are spelled out more clearly in relation to governability. There are, first, a number of neglected questions to be studied in relation to the role of government in the aggregation and disaggregation of decisions and choices. The growth of the welfare state certainly made political scientists more aware of administrative influence over government, as suggested, for example by Self (1977), but more precise comparisons across countries of differing governmental organization and administrative structures might account for the different balance of demands and obligations. For example, there is some evidence that federal systems might have more capacity than unitary systems to expand social benefits rapidly (Derthick, 1975) and to adjust the locational pattern of national assistance to industry and the economy (Sundquist, 1975). The ability to change both the areal and functional focus of policies is an important measure of the capacity of government to meet new demands while honoring previous commitments and obligations. Although there remains much to be done, governability leads directly to a concern with the "capacity" of political systems to redefine their objectives, to adapt to external stresses and opportunities, and to learn from the earlier policy experience. For example, Rose (1977) has made a promising attempt to translate the organization of policy-making activities into more general concepts about how states transform their capacities.

The concept of governance shifts our thinking from policy as a dependent variable, as it has most often been treated in analyzing the welfare state, to policy as an independent variable. But before more ambitious comparative policy studies can be made, better indicators and measurement will be needed to compare capacity across nations. Some possibilities are comparative analysis of innovation diffusion in the administration, time spans between initiation and implementation of new policies or directives, and, perhaps most ambitious of all, more precise analysis of internal governmental disputes over redefinition of policy aims. Such inquiry is likely to be carried out initially on a country-by-country basis and would begin to identify what kinds of policy changes appear to characterize different political systems. For example, longitudinal analysis of the distribution of local subsidies in France (Ashford, 1978a) shows that although French policy-making operates under comparatively strong absolute constraints (the total amount of subsidies is controlled), there is considerable capacity to shift resources from one area or problem to another; and there is also capacity to reformulate the conditions and procedures for administering local investment support policies.

Research of this kind provides a more rigorous (though still nominal) measurement to compare what kinds of policies are open to change and innovation across countries, and also opens the way for more explicit hypotheses relating inputs and outputs. For example, if it appears in a number of policy areas that France displays high flexibility in dealing with policies having a spatial or territorial dimension, then the multiple and localized party structure, for example, is more easily explained. Conversely, in countries where the policy process appears less able or less responsive in handling policies with territorial implications, one might hypothesize that rigidities and nationalization of the party structure resist territorial dispersion of decision making.

C. Sectoral Politics

As the economic role of the modern state expanded, it was natural that attention should shift to relations between the public and private sectors. Political science seems to have been slow to pick up the challenge. Important in-depth studies began to appear from other scholars, for example, Scott and McArthur (1969), and comparisons were made by economists interested in industrial policy, for example, Vernon (1973). There were important exceptions, often for countries such as France, where the interdependence of the private economy and politics is pronounced (Ehrmann, 1957), but there are also significant exceptions. Sweden, for example, was often analyzed as a pioneer welfare state, but less attention was given to the intriguing fact that the Swedish economy remained preponderantly in private hands. Few are surprised today by interpretations of the close links among banking, industry, and government in Japan and West Germany, but there are few detailed studies. In many respects, it was inquiry into the Third World, where scholars became sensitive to the impact of the world economy on development and where the concentration of wealth was most visible, that shifted attention to sectoral analysis.

As investigation of the private sector grew, comparative policy studies acquired new importance. First, abstract theories of political systems tended to assume that public-private distinctions were easily made; and, second, the prevailing mode of behavioral analysis was not easily transferred to questions based on fundamental structural differences between sectors. An entirely new theoretical framework was needed and emerged from two quarters. There was first the effort to generate theories about decision making that would span both private- and public-sector behavior, and which came, not surprisingly, from political scientists who had learned economics and followed the rapid development of decisional theories in that discipline. Lindblom (1965, 1969) is certainly the leading figure, but there was also a spillover into areas that had long been the preserve of behavioral research (Downs, 1957), and there were important applications to policy questions facing developing countries (Hirschman, 1963). These scholars were the most important in reviving policy studies in the United States, although they did not initially see their work as having comparative implications.

The second impulse was the revival of neo-Marxist theory, not surprisingly, from Europe. The prosperity of the 1950s and 1960s saw the eclipse of socialist parties in the major European countries. The initial reaction was to construct theories of class politics to fit the realities of European politics. Important contributors were Dahrendorf (1959,

1968), who saw how the transformation of economic power in the modern state had implications for Marxist theory; and Miliband (1961), who saw how representative government and parliamentary politics might divert class politics from its avowed Marxist objectives. Although their work was an important stimulus for more careful examination of specific policies in relation to class conflict and its suppression, the policy implications were (and in many respects remain) unclear. But more than any single group of scholars, they shattered the assumption that the private sector could be reasonably excluded from comparative political studies. Paradoxically, the second wave of neo-Marxist scholars in the 1970s were divided by an ideological dispute over the historical and political conditions to achieve socialism (Pickvance, 1977), but there are now a variety of neo-Marxist policy studies on labor relations, social welfare, and urban government.

Although it is impossible to unravel here the intense and sometimes polemic debate between the neo-liberal and neo-Marxist departures to link the private and public sectors, the main conceptual differences and similarities can be noted. First, both decisional and class theories have helped to restore the importance of institutional structures in comparing how policies are made, implemented, and revised. Oddly enough, both groups consider institutions an impediment to social change, but are also agreed that the organized structure of the state is primordial in our understanding of policy making. Second, in converse ways the two groups have underscored the perplexing analytical problem that is the keystone of comparative policy analysis: how we aggregate (for decisional theory) and how we disaggregate (for neo-Marxists) decisions. If the two groups often appear to be racing past each other, it is because they begin from opposite ends of the methodological racetrack surrounding empirical research. As we have learned from earlier abstract comparative political theories, the methodology of aggregation is easier than disaggregation, so it is not surprising that there has been more notable progress as decisional theorists explore ways to generate higher-order generalizations (Olson, 1965; Hirsch, 1976; Breton, 1974). Third, and also stemming from the methodological advantage of the decisional theorists, is their ability to demarcate the public sector and gradually to extend their findings and concepts into private-sector behavior, whereas the neo-Marxists (oddly enough, like nineteenth-century liberals) tend to see the private sector as the focal point in understanding public-sector decisions. The immense importance of both approaches was to free political science from the constraint of treating policy as an independent variable because in rather different ways, as we shall see, both adopted an interaction framework and recognized mutual dependence so that outputs were no longer easily distinguished from inputs.

III. SUBSYSTEMIC VARIATION

There is probably nothing more than taste to differentiate those who prefer systemic-level cross-national comparison from those who are more fascinated by subsystemic comparison. Both inquiries raise the same problems of validation. Subsystemic generalizations risk becoming mired in methodological problems of research methods, and the leap to more abstract analysis can be delayed. Systemic generalizations may have difficulty defining operational terms and may avoid the issue of validation, which is inescapable in subsystemic-level comparisons.

A. Comparative Elites

Whatever our theoretical predispositions, one can always identify those at the top of the formal power structure. There are many respects in which the formal and informal influence attached to high elected and administrative positions are important contributions to comparative policy studies. These persons are key figures in determining the priority and design given new policies, and, thus, provide us with a direct measure of innovative intentions and capacities of the policy process. For nearly every advanced industrial country there are continuing controversies about the reform of the higher civil service, the regulation of political patronage, and the social background and recruitment of political and administrative leaders. All of these materials are potentially convertible into larger generalizations about the institutional and political foundations of policy making. For example, the alleged failure of British leaders to exploit technical and industrial opportunities is often attributed to their generalist background, whereas the centralizing tendencies attributed to French policy making is often attributed to their high levels of technical competence and elitist education.

Perhaps the most important contribution of comparative elite studies to comparative policy studies is that it provides the building blocks for intermediate-level theory. Before we can develop new theory and concepts about policy making cross-nationally, it is essential to have accurate data and generalizations about key components in individual countries. Many doctrinaire assumptions about the policy process arise from abstract political models or have been inferred from behavioral research with little testing against actual behavior in political and administrative roles. For example, Suleiman's (1974) study of French top officials shows a complex pattern of interdepartmental communication and mutual dependence in French government, which, in turn, questions generalizations about the individual behavior of policy makers as formulated by Crozier (1964); and also provides us with a rich base from which to explore how French politicians and administrators influence the policy process.

More difficult to relate to cross-national policy studies are the many studies of social background and attitudes, although the extension of more sociological investigation into policy-related research is a promising avenue of inquiry, both to validate the cross-national findings of behavior and to refine elite theory so that it may more easily be integrated into theories and concepts about policy making itself. For example, Putnam's (1973) attitudinal survey of British and Italian elites could be extended to see if differing perceptions influence how policies are designed, implemented, and evaluated. Very similar problems arise in trying to see how the often extensive analysis of the social background of leaders (Dogan, 1975; Armstrong, 1973) may or may not influence policy making. Not the least of complications for comparative elite studies is that the evolution of the welfare state and the complexity of governance, as has been outlined, have radically changed the setting within which elites function.

B. Comparative Administration

As the task of reconstructing the links between political science and public administration began in the 1960s, a major contributing force was concern with bureaucracy in developing countries. At that time administrative studies of European countries were largely the province of administrative law and formal administrative studies. But the demise of colonialism meant that nearly every country of Africa, Asia, and, to a some-what lesser extent, Latin America faced enormous problems in organizing new services and undertaking economic development. In some respects, the literature of comparative administration had, and continues to have, more theoretical concern than similar studies in advanced industrial societies. There was, first, a good historical literature on the colonial impact and its administration, which provided a comparative dimension. Second, scholars of the Third World could not affort to indulge in the aversion toward adminis-tration that then characterized political science. For developing countries, administration had obvious importance to political, economic, and social change in the societies. Third, there were a variety of intervening administrative problems, such as the transfer of tech-nology and the training of new officials, that led Third World scholars to explore inter-mediate-level theories of communication, learning, innovation, and organization, all of which became tools in building higher-order generalizations.

The result was that relatively early in the extension of comparative politics to the developing countries, comparative administration became an acknowledged and respec-ted avenue of inquiry. Early efforts were made by Siffin (1957), LaPalombara (1963), and Heady and Stokes (1962). More ambitious theoretical offshoots by Riggs (1964) linked administrative behavior to the structure of society. Perhaps the most ambitious effort was Eisenstadt's extensive writings on the history and transformation of bureau-cracy (1966, 1973), which rivaled Weber's classical studies of the historical develop-ment of administration and politics. Political development was soon linked to new the-ories of political economy (Ilchman and Uphoff, 1969), to variants of decisional theory (Schaffer, 1973), and to anthropological theory (Geertz, 1963a). Unlike the compara-tive analysis of the advanced industrial states at that time, rapid change imposed a strong policy content and explicit concern with performance. As the neo-Marxists ex-tended their theory to include economic imperialism and dependence in the Third World, another theoretical dimension was added that has strong policy implications.

The failure of mainstream political science to respond to the advances being made in comparative administration is more surprising when one recalls that much of the very early comparative studies of European politics was indeed about bureaucracy, its rela-tion to democracy and to parliamentary government. In addition to Weber, Ostrogroski (1910) and Michels (1962) were deeply concerned that the growing administration of European countries would entrench elites and dampen participation. The growth of European government renewed interest in comparing administrative elites and struc-tures, both along more conventional lines (Dogan, 1975) and along neo-Marxist lines (Birnbaum, 1977). But compared to advances made in other forms of comparative inquiry, the concepts to define and locate how administration relates to policy making and performance in advanced industrial states is relatively undeveloped and has been stimulated by sociologists. The gap in our conceptual equipment is a serious one, be-cause it means that comparison is likely to fall back on very abstract theories of soci-ety, and therefore become difficult to line to performance. Alternatively, administrative studies may be geared so completely to organizational theory that they are difficult to use to improve the validity and reliability of cross-national policy studies.

The failure to pursue administrative theories is due perhaps to the tendency of ad-ministrative experts to treat administration as a self-contained problem of government, whereas politics, on the other hand, tends to treat administration in very general neo-Weberian or neo-Marxist terms. There are a number of fairly simple hypotheses and questions that would link administrative theory to comparative policy studies, much of which could be carried out with the analysis and case studies that exist for most industrial and less developed countries. For example, do federal as opposed to unitary administrative systems display significant differences in the initiation, implementation, and evaluation of public policies? How does political influence over the administrative system vary with major policy areas and across countries? The more detailed literature on social, industrial, and labor policies within many countries, particularly for Europe and North America, is highly developed and specialized, but has still to be integrated around comparative concepts of administration.

C. Comparative Organizations

Of the various suggestions for dealing with subsystemic units of analysis, perhaps the field of organizational theory and behavior is the most developed, and, with notable exceptions, not widely applied in comparative policy studies or even in comparative politics more generally. In fact, organizational theorists as such are not particularly concerned with systemic-level comparison, although it is easy to find organizational theory applied both to social (La Porte, 1975) and political (Presthus, 1979) systems. Dyson (1976) thinks that the reluctance of organizational theorists to tackle more institutional aspects of politics, which would imply a comparative dimension, is an important oversight in their work.

At the risk of oversimplifying the conceptual controversies that go on among organizational theorists (Perrow, 1972), their work provides a number of distinct advantages over other attempts to disaggregate complex social and political systems into components that can be observed and analyzed with relative ease. First, the environment of an organization can be more easily defined so that hypotheses about innovation, adaptation, and defensive tactics can be formed. Second, the goals of organizations are also usually identifiable even though they may range from the highly ambiguous goals of research organizations to the fairly specific goals of routinized organizations. Third, the ability to distinguish individual motives and needs within organizations from the behavior of the organization, although hotly disputed, enables many students of organizational behavior to circumvent the pitfalls and complexities of dealing simultaneously with subjective and objective measurement. Fourth, if organizational theory does not aspire to replace more general theories of society and politics, it provides us with operational handles that are closely related to the more abstract theories discussed in Sec. II.

The important breakthrough in organizational theory in the 1960s was to depart from the highly formalized and more mechanical thinking of the early organizational writers. The most important work was done by Simon and March (Simon, 1957; March and Simon, 1958), which suggested that rationality in organizations and the rationality of individuals are conceptually separable. Related to the theories of the marketplace and decision making used by Lindblom, they developed the concept of "satisficing" to describe how individual need for information and knowledge of the organization may be less than the requirements of the organization. Thus, in what is essentially a neo-Weberian view of the world, hierarchy and conflict are not dealt with by rules and simple control mechanisms, but by developing organizational capacities to handle uncertainty in the environment and to assemble information in appropriate ways. As developed later in Deutsch's attempt to relate information theory to political systems, goals are seldom specific or singular, and therefore cannot be maximized (Cyert and March, 1963).

Though not directly contradicting the work of March and Simon, Selznick (1949) and others were more inclined to treat organizations as organic wholes, and to use sociological theory to search out their unintended and unanticipated consequences. From this perspective, there is more concern with how organizational self-interest and survival affect the selection of organizational goals, the recruitment of members, and the role of leaders, although the concepts are equally applicable to organizational extinction. The analysis tends to focus on the consequences of deviance and interdependence within organizations, which, in turn, stimulates interest in organizational complexity (Brunner and Brewer, 1971). As the foundations for comparative policy studies, both the operational and conceptual attractions of these ideas are manifold.

Because the ideas of complexity and interdependence figure so heavily in systemic-level theories of the modern state, the insights provided by organizational theory are especially valuable. The more abstract theories of the welfare state were, in part, generated by the growing complexity of social and economic policies. The general problem of governance reflects the difficulty of isolating problems and choices in the modern state, which, in turn creates distance between citizens and officials in modern democracies. Although contemporary organizational theory is often based on neo-Weberian assumptions, there is no reason why it cannot be applied to major policy failures, such as the Concorde, and to various instances of neglect or miscalculation in major policy areas, of which there are numerous examples among social and health policies. Comparative analysis with pronounced organizational dimensions is contained with corporatist theories of the state (Schmitter, 1977) as well as its more obvious association with pluralist theories of the state. Organizational concepts figure heavily in some foreign policy analysis (Allison, 1971), urban policy (Danziger, 1978), and local politics (Dearlove, 1979). There are numerous studies of labor-management relations with strong organizational foundations (McCarthy and Ellis, 1973; Adam and Reynaud, 1978), but they most often remain country studies.

But the immense value of organizational theory to comparative politics generally as well as to comparative policy studies is that it provides us with provocative, but yet operational, intermediate-level generalizations by which we can validate and compare findings across countries, while also indirectly testing various abstract theories (Hanf and Scharpf, 1978). For example, one might hypothesize that multiparty systems are more likely to perform the synthesis and aggregation of information about performance necessary in complex organizations, whereas the capacity for the synthesis and aggregation of information would be less in more competitive, two-party systems, where partisan behavior may produce perceptual inattention and more concern with the tactics of winning elections. Using policy materials as an independent variable, one might pursue ideas already developed by Lowi (1978), that particular types of decisions lead to particular kinds of political behavior or that the organizational structure of administrative systems creates a policy environment eliciting distinguishably different political reactions and behavior. Both within and across a number of policy areas of any one country, it would be fairly easy to design ways of comparing how rapidly goals are redefined, whether multiple goal seeking is common, and how readily conflicting feedback information is reconciled with previous commitments. These ideas are well grounded in organizational theory, and, in turn, could be compared to political inputs and participation.

D. Comparative Ideologies

There are numerous approaches to the comparative study of ideologies, but as yet most of these studies have not been linked directly to the performance of the political system. The basic reason, noted by a leading psychologist some years ago (Miller, 1956), is that it is extremely difficult to show that attitudes account for behavior. Generally speaking, the more rigorous the behavioral controls one places on comparative analysis of attitudes and values, the more difficult it becomes to demonstrate that perceptual differences have consequences. Much of the early cross-national survey research did not attempt even indirect measures of the behavioral consequences of attitudinal differences (Almond and Verba, 1963; Rokkan et al., 1969). One of the reasons for declining interest in political socialization, despite the empirical refinement and methodological sophistication, was that it is unclear how the different values and perceptions instilled at an early age affect a person's behavior in later years. One of the unexplored, though indirect, ways of demonstrating that these studies do have social and political consequences is to see whether differing values and perceptions do in fact alter the individual's choices and behavior when making policy choices.

Ideologies are also observable in the patterns of beliefs and the cognitive structure of learning, which have been explored more by psychologists and anthropologists than by political scientists. As has been noted, these approaches have been used most often in developing countries, where the exacting (and to some extent limiting) standards of behavioral research are difficult to meet. Early attempts were made by Hagen (1962) and Apter (1964) to relate more sophisticated personality theories to developmental problems of the Third World, which, in turn, encouraged application cross-nationally to problems of communication and innovation in developing countries. There have also been a number of more ambitious efforts to conduct cross-national studies of perception, often based on theories of cognition and learning, of which the work of Triandis (1972) is typical. The great advantage of cognitive and learning theory is that it deals directly with the individual's capacity to manipulate and to understand the environment, which, in turn, can be clearly linked to performance.

For several reasons it is unfortunate that political science has tended to ignore anthropological theory, not only because it provides an entirely different approach from the prevailing paradigm of behavioral research, but also because anthropologists are aware of the problem of working simultaneously with systemic and subsystemic variance (Smith, 1956). They often have to reconstruct the societies they are studying, and for the most part are concerned with social integration and cohesion against formidable external conditions (Ashford, 1973). Although anthropologists engage in many of the same fundamental conceptual disputes as other social scientists, some of the most provocative work has been done by Geertz using linguistic analysis (1964), and later using the linguistic imagery to compare several countries (1963a). Much of the work done by Bailey (1960) and Lynch (1969) on the differential adaptation of various caste structures to modernization relates changing belief systems to profound social and political changes.

Less concerned with beliefs, but readily intelligible to an organizational theorist, is the comparative work on how tribes adapt to threatening and precarious environments (Leach, 1954; Evans-Pritcahrd, 1949). In this general sense, anthropologists have been more aware of the interdependence of outputs and inputs than have political scientists. Well before political science took the Third World seriously, Kluckholn wrote an article on administration and culture (1943).

IV. STRUCTURAL ANALYSIS AND CROSS-NATIONAL POLICY STUDIES

Thus far I have discussed comparison and its relation to cross-national policy studies in the conventional language of social science. Comparison has been most often conceived along the dimensions outlined in Table 1. Inputs and outputs have been regarded as fairly easily distinguished from each other, both in the more abstract theories discussed in Sec. II and the subsystemic analyses discussed in Sec. III. The argument of this section will be that these conceptual distinctions impose severe limits on both the design and the theoretical development of comparative theory and, more specifically, of its subtopic, comparative policy studies. Indeed, the most exciting challenge of comparative policy studies is to forge the concepts and theories that will enable us to escape from the self-imposed constraints of input-output and systemic-subsystemic paradigm.

The task of comparative policy studies is, first, to test the accuracy and usefulness of the concepts and theories that the basic paradigm provides. As I have suggested, much of the discussion has been about units of analysis, and heavily influenced by behavioral social science that prefers the individual as the unit of analysis. As Table 1 indicates, the conventional paradigm in fact attaches relatively little importance to policy studies, and, most often within the rather limited context of how authoritative or collective decisions respond directly to individual preferences and expectations. The second task of comparative policy studies is to assist in the revision of the conventional paradigm, and some suggestions on how structural analysis may contribute to this task will be given in Sec. IV.B.

A. Limits of the Conventional Paradigm

A crude test of the force of new ideas is how easily they provide us with new hypotheses and enable us to redefine the world in new ways. As Kuhn has suggested, the patterns of discovery, exploration, and criticism become rough cycles in the redesign of knowledge. Perhaps the most intriguing aspect of comparative policy studies is the way in which they have questioned the conventional paradigm and made us more sensitive to its limitations.

Table 1. The Conventional Comparative Paradigm

	Systemic	Subsystemic
Inputs	Elections and parties	Voting participation
Outputs	Aggregate performance	Policy impact and efficiency

For many years the relationship of inputs at systemic and subsystemic levels to policy was simply ignored. Conventional political science was heavily occupied studying electoral and voting behavior, and applying sociological analysis to see how social characteristics, attitudes, and the environment related to these connections (Dogan and Rokkan, 1969; Merritt and Rokkan, 1966). Although sometimes invoking theories of personality to provide explanations of individual behavior, there was less interest in how issues, performance, and interests affected politics. Although the policies and performance of states would seem to be an obvious channel for microanalysis of political systems, it is interesting to note that an authoritative book on cross-national microanalysis published as late as 1972 had no policy articles (Pierce and Pride, 1972). Although it has now become fashionable to vilify the pluralist assumptions that were presumed to link participation to performance, it should be noted that this oversight was in fact shared by most scholars of the period. There were, of course, notable exceptions (Key and Cummings, 1966), but the community power debate, even if it did generate more heat than light, made a wide variety of scholars aware that participation has (or should have) consequences, and that policy materials are a rich source of data about national and subnational participation.

The relationship between policy at the systemic and subsystemic levels was, not surprisingly, analyzed most often using analysis of variance, multivariable analysis, and so on, which could manipulate increasingly large data banks and which could readily convert performance data into continuous variables. Just as those most concerned with inputs turned to sociology, so those occupied with outputs found a haven in economic theory. Out of this venture grew the various approaches to political economy that, not surprisingly, seem to reflect the assumptions of whatever economic theory one chooses to apply. The range of choice is as large as the entire field of economics, running from the clearly laissez-faire ideas of the Ostroms, Tullock, and Buchanan, to the neo-Marxist writers. Although the efforts to apply economic concepts and theory to the links between systemic and subsystemic performance have done much to invigorate comparative policy studies, one runs the risk of simply rehashing debates that economists have already held and, of course, becoming the victim of their assumptions, methodology, and preoccupations. The curious result was that both systemic and subsystemic inquiry were distracted from, if not uninterested in, devising new political concepts, and questioning the validity and assumptions implicit in their analysis.

True, the aggregate data could be arranged in ways to compare highly generalized concepts of performance with levels of political development, party competition, electoral patterns, and so on, and in this way, a rudimentary link was made between the systemic-level study of inputs and outputs. But these studies remained extremely vulnerable to the criticism that they were assuming comparability of highly different systems. Nonetheless, more sophisticated methodology and more longitudinal data has made it possible to refine this approach. Until the entire paradigm is replaced, macroanalysis of this kind will continue to provide comparative insights into the overall relationships between inputs and outputs at the systemic level. However, it is possible to introduce cross-national policy differences into the existing methodology and concepts of comparison, as done, for example, by Heidenheimer (1973) for social policy and by Hibbs (1978) for labor politics. Important as the systemic level is, it does not represent a major departure from the existing paradigm but does add methodological sophistication and the conceptual range to aggregate analysis.

The direct linkages between inputs and outputs at the subsystemic level are perhaps the most neglected in the conventional paradigm, which helps explain some of the conceptual problems of linking policy studies to comparative theory. There are, in fact, numerous policy studies by other social science disciplines into the activity and performance of lower-level activities. The literature on prisons, hospitals, community services, local government, and so on, is immense, but poorly integrated into the conventional comparative analysis of systems and subsystems. Part of the explanation is, of course, neglect of policy studies, and even at the systemic level, links between inputs and outputs are of very recent interest. The price of the prevalence of systemic-level concerns is that the contradictions and complexities of the behavior of smaller groups are assumed to have similar constraints across systems.

The 1960s and 1970s saw an entirely new array of governmental policies and programs directed toward citizens and issues at lower levels of government, but for some time this activity was not related to comparative theory. Disinterest was, on the whole, reciprocated by the applied social scientists working in communities, with families, and so on, even though they had in their grasp a rich body of policy materials and studies. Their concern was (and remains) helping people, not systems, and their immediate objectives were to have an impact and to find ways of directing limited resources to relieve social problems. In countries where social services achieved organizational strength and identity, such as Britain, more general concepts about expanded services and the underlying political choices emerged (Titmuss, 1962), but on the whole, both sociology and economics had more attractions for applied social science than politics. For obvious reasons, the equalitarian aims of neo-Marxist thinkers were more appealing to them. Political science generally was slow to respond, although it is significant that some of the early articles on using case studies began to appear (Lijphart, 1975). On the whole, political science was slow to perceive the rapid changes in political and social relationships created by the advanced welfare state. If the neo-Marxists were often more sensitive to the needs of the poor and to the social costs of highly industrialized societies, they, too, had difficulty converting their abstract social theory into applied knowledge. But rather like the unanticipated effects of the pluralists of the 1960s, the Marxists of the 1970s began to show how structural theories could be useful, and possibly more than any other conceptual innovation, this opened the way to integrate policy studies with comparative theory.

B. Structural Theories and Comparing Policies

Structural comparisons of entire political systems or the important activities within political systems are constructed very differently from the deductive empirical theories used in earlier cross-national studies. A structuralist looks for concepts that capture the particular dynamic of the relationships under investigation. Rather than concentrating on the limits to variability, the concern is with the contextual or relational regularities of behavior. The procedure is virtually the opposite of linear and multilinear models often used in more rigorous empirical research. One of the most devastating attacks on linear concepts, and on the abstraction of properties from the events or objects they are used to analyze, is Nadel's analysis (1957) of role theory. What the structuralists lose in methodological rigor, they gain in devising concepts that deal better with the configuration of social and political structures. Because the definitions themselves are descriptions of a desirable relationship and of the requisites for their achievement in the society or polity, structural concepts usually have normative implications. Boudon (1971), for example, speaks of "intentional definitions" as basic to structural analysis of many kinds.

Structural or possibly quasi-structural concepts might be placed along a continuum from the most rigorous and positivist forms of behavioral investigation to the very abstract structural concepts of information theory, organizational theory, and Marxist social theories. Lerner's (1960) use of "thresholds" in the development of communication capacities in developing countries is, for example, a combination of conventional empirical methods with concepts of how fundamental structural change takes places as literacy, media, and information converge in the modernization process. In much the same way as Marxist social theorists would argue about class relationships, Lerner argues that as information flows become more dense and more specialized, fundamental social and political relationships are changed. One could, of course, build linear variables from the more complex communication patterns, but the structuralist would argue that such analysis might fail to observe more basic change. A great deal of historical longitudinal and diachronic analysis is structural. Economic analysis of structures composed of primary, secondary, and tertiary production is a simple structural concept. Anthropologists have been deeply immersed in structural analysis to link lineage and family systems to social systems. In all these problems, one is studying activity whose properties resist transformation into interval variables, and, the structuralist would argue, transformation into continuous variables would limit our understanding of the events under investigation.

Structural concepts reduce, and possibly eliminate, reliance on the systemic-sub-systemic and the input-output dimensions of the conventional comparative paradigm. An exception is, of course, Marxist social theory, which must operate at the level of entire societies and thereby risks being tautological. It has become commonplace to treat many behavioral properties of class such as income, occupation, and education as though their interrelations across and within systems are invariant as hypothesized by Marxist social theory. For Marxist theories, the issue is less damaging because in a socialist world, social solidarity eliminates the conflicts and confusions of the various subunits of social systems. Liberation from materialist constraints would abolish the distinction between inputs and outputs. Of course all this is extremely abstract and not open to empirical demonstration, which is why applying Marxist concepts to problems within and among mixed economies can be extremely misleading, and also why the Marxists themselves carry on a heated, but as yet unresolved, debate over how the organization and policies of advanced capitalist societies relate to their ideal society.

The importance of structural analysis to comparative policy studies is more limited. Structural concepts are particularly appropriate to policy problems, because they begin (rather than end) with definitions of the dynamic relationships of special concern. The requisite conditions for changes are usually specified, and their relationship within systems is of primary importance. The analysis of center-local relationships is a good illustration. The initial aggregate analysis of states and communities was limited to statistical explanation. The debate between the pluralist and elite methods then introduced a quasi-structural choice, namely, the "marketplace" of local group politics of the pluralists weighed against the exclusion and manipulation found by some sociological analysts. Oddly enough, both were reacting against the limitations of behavioral assumptions. The interesting question is why such a vigorous debate dwindled away, and how so much valuable empirical research might be used comparatively.

The stalemate is important for comparative theory, and was quite possibly a loss for comparative policy studies in particular. Indeed, there was one article (Sharpe, 1973) which suggested that comparison no longer made sense because the liberal tradition remains so embedded in American society. Sharpe's position seems curious because there are so many important similarities between national and local democracy. In part, the failure was due to the strength of the behavioral tradition itself; that is, if American towns and cities behave differently, their relationship to the system must be different. This assumption easily lapses into saying that the systems are completely different and, thereby, defy comparison. In short, the system-subsystem distinction was not only accepted uncritically, but without an attempt to see how comparison might be done. In fact, there are many important similarities, both within British and American cities, and in their relationship to the political system. For example, in both countries, localities actually dispense huge sums of mcney and employ more persons than the national government. In relation to the political system, both serve as a training ground for national leaders, as subordinate organizations to political parties, and as vital conduits for the implementation of national policies.

Put somewhat differently, local government and local politics have immense importance to the politics of both countries, but self-imposed conceptual limits retarded the development of more useful and persuasive comparative theory. There were more studies of attitudes and values of national and local elites on the one hand, and the complexities of national and local spending and taxation, on the other hand. But the conceptual price was arbitrarily (by definition) to separate two avenues of research as dictated by assumptions about the input-output distinction. The interdependence of national and local government is a much more complex relationship than these early studies assume within and across systems, and the input-output distinction has many permutations and combinations. For example, the massive increase in benefits and services administered at the local level in the United States from the 1960s very likely restored confidence in national government (Derthick, 1975). Most European countries and North America were experiencing large movements of population from one part of the country to another (Sundquist, 1975), and most were undergoing substantial changes in the fiscal and financial relationships between industry and government. These significant policy changes were neglected because they did not conveniently fit the paradigm of conventional social research and, more important, because they were embedded in structural relationships that existing theories and methods were not well equipped to handle.

My point is not that more limited and more rigorous forms of analysis are misleading as much as that, in the absence of structural analysis, their full value cannot be extracted. Quite clearly, comparative policy involves a variety of structural issues, but recognition of the diverse patterns of performance is the first step toward integrating policy studies and comparative theory. More limiting functional definitions of policy are appropriate for single countries, because one can assume that the cultural and social context for any particular activity is widely understood (if not shared) and that the interdependence of any particular activity across various levels of government and among political organization is roughly the same throughout the system. But an increasing number of policy studies show that even within one system this may be a misleading assumption, and that across systems this may be simply wrong.

As comparative policy studies grow, perhaps the greatest risk to improving compara-tive theory is that policy analysis will become so specialized that it is difficult to link findings to larger questions. Within the compartmentalized structure of universities, and in an even greater number in specialized research agencies of government and industry, we are now accumulating an enormous data bank of policy research. For the comparativ-ist the specific findings may not be as important as the vast amount of information at our disposal to explore similarities and differences of political systems. The traditional con-cepts of policy studies, such as efficiency, rationality, and even effectiveness, tend to be specific to the nature of the policy itself and understandably phrased in such concrete language that those interested in building new concepts rarely have the patience and ener-gy to sift through this vast reservoir of information. There are many possible departures to build structural concepts which, in turn, help describe how comparative policy studies can become an integral part in comparative political theory.

V. CONCLUSION: RETHINKING COMPARATIVE POLICY RESEARCH

For those concerned with theory formation in comparative political studies, as opposed to comparing societies or individuals, the stumbling block can often be distinguishing politics from other kinds of activities. For this reason, the very abstract comparative theories discussed in Sec. II began with very general definitions of politics. The result is that those interested in relating policy studies to comparative theory are left with an unhappy choice. First, they can pursue the well-developed fields of policy evaluation, impact studies, and market research, which spring from behavioral research, and forego generalization. From the perspective of most consumers of policy analysis, this makes little difference. Second, they can devise better typologies to make sense of the bewil-dering number of policy studies, hoping that comparison along functional similarities will suffice. This is an important step in building theory and, as we have seen in Sec. III, cross-national studies of health, social welfare, planning, and many other activities have begun to develop this option. Third, they can seek ways of integrating comparative policy studies with comparative political theory, perhaps the most exciting, but also the most precarious avenue of developing comparative policy studies.

Space permits only two illustrations, but it should first be made clear that such an undertaking would not subsume the politics of policy making to other disciplines, as, for example, is generally done in most political economy and public choice models, nor would it answer the usual questions asked about policies in input-output terms. Some of these limitations have already been noted by Eckstein in outlining his more axiomatic comparative theory. As he notes (1973: 1144), focusing on the distinctly political means that we forego functional definitions of politics, and by implication define policies so that we broaden "the scope of the field at the cost of virtually eliminating its boundaries altogether." A cost of viewing comparative policy studies as part of the more general com-parative study of politics is that we are not likely to enhance our ability to tell policy makers how to do things. On the other hand, the functional definition of politics has been extremely damaging to theory formation, not the least because it so vastly simpli-fied the activities of government in the advanced industrial state. If one sacrifices the functional approach, then the existing input-output paradigm either dissolves as a useful conceptual tool or must be radically reformulated.

Important theoretical departures occur because scholars are persuaded that their understanding is inadequate to explain events and relationships. The reasons for rethinking comparative policy studies are numerous. First, the relationship between inputs and outputs has not led to a fruitful connection with the traditional and normative concerns of politics, nor, as has been noted, is it readily adapted to test and to elaborate the various thories of participation, party competition, and so on, that have been developed by those most concerned with inputs. Second, there is widespread prima facie evidence that the discipline is looking for ways of reformulating the highly abstract comparative theories of the 1960s. Behavioral influence on theory formation made the deductive and axiomatic theories attractive because the goal was simply to insert behavioral findings in the abstract design, much as many neo-Marxists now argue in extending a version of class politics to all policy problems. But the institutional and organizational complexities that in fact limit political change are too important and too diverse to be subsumed by macro theories, many of them embedded in the policy process in various ways, that seem to contradict the general theories or describe important events that are unaccounted for. Much of the interest in neo-Marxist theories can be traced to this problem, although the neo-Marxists themselves do not agree on how best to relate policy analysis to politics. Fourth, and perhaps the most persuasive stimulus, is that we have great difficulty deciding on the important subsystemic units of analysis for both general comparative analysis and comparative policy studies. By default more than intent, policy analysis within countries adopts whatever organizational or institutional unit is found, thereby further delaying and complicating the problem of aggregating case studies into comparative generalizations.

A. The Policy Content of Consensus

Survey research and content analysis tell us much about the subjective nature of social support for government, but they do not take into account that these measures over time and across functions relate to an expanded and more complex government. When citizens express confidence in the political system, they are obviously not approving the same things. If one is interested only in inputs, this constraint is of less importance. But the constraint also makes less and less sense as the activities of government expand. From this perspective, the findings that people express roughly the same levels of support for government as they did a generation ago is surprising, because the intricate and often obscure processes of policy making in the advanced industrial states has not incurred higher costs in popular disenchantment and distrust. Nor do the various forms of professionalization and specialization that have restructured relationships among the consumers, clients, and groups in the policy process seem to have caused strong popular reactions (Anton, 1975).

Even a crude comparison of attitudes toward major policy areas across countries would probably show that there are major differences in the patterns of support. Many major activities of the welfare state have been sustained as part of political consensus. In effect, the substantive content of political consensus (widespread and shared expectations about government) has vastly increased with the amount of public goods and services now routinely provided. Neo-liberals and neo-Marxists are alike in feeling (for very different reasons) that the existing consensus is inadequate, and both have difficulty accepting that the expansion of benefits may have restructured political consensus. An important aim of cross-national policy research is to develop a clearer understanding of the diversity and intricacy of the actual choices, programs, and procedures that understandably confound the more abstract theories.

There are several promising avenues to blend cross-national policy studies with the simultaneous transformation of inputs and outputs over recent decades. Within countries, comparison could be made of the ease with which agreement and approval have shifted from one area of concern to another; the "lag time" between initiation and acceptance; and the importance of popular resistance due to earlier commitments and obligations. To use Banfield's notion of the "two-step flow" of communications (1961), it seems likely that opinions differ in the extent to which policy areas are well or poorly organized. Agriculture, for example, is an area of choice where government frequently finds that consensus is well formed and well organized, whereas some of the specialized social welfare needs often lack support and understanding.

The possibilities to refine and update our ideas about consensus are many. First, we would be taking more explicitly into account the historical experience of each country in redefining benefits and services. An obvious example is the predominance of family allowances in the French social security system compared with the concern for unemployment relief in Britain. We may find that the substantive content of consensus varies across countries. Policy materials could provide an independent check on how rapidly change can be made. It might also appear that our concept of consensus can be broken down into policy-related areas in order to compare countries. There are, for example, many reasons to think that the German people place more emphasis on economic growth, whereas the British emphasize social welfare. The concern with inputs would not necessarily be abandoned, but it might well be that the type of party system or form of party organization have little bearing on those differences.

Because neither neo-liberals nor neo-Marxists are eager to abandon their more doctrinaire claims, cross-national comparison has often been limited to very generalized aggregations of opinions and attitudes. Comparative policy studies offer a relatively simple way to test the assumptions of more general theories, while also providing us with intriguing opportunities to compare directly how states redefine policy objectives and reallocate resources. For example, Eckstein (1961) has suggested for Britain that the congruence of social and elite attitudes has produced political stability. An alternative view is that congruence permits British leaders to engage in "stop-and-go" policies at very low political cost. Compared to many countries, there is much less need to demarcate policy areas where agreement exists or where political intervention is appropriate. If one analyzes the interdependence between inputs and outputs rather than the distinguishing behavior associated with each in the political system, admiration for British political stability must be weighed against the sometimes abrupt dislocations and reversals of policy making (Ashford, 1980). A policy perspective on British consensus might arrive at quite different conclusions on how political stability is reconciled with the complexities of policy making.

B. Institutional Variance and the Policy Process

Policy materials can also help us formulate concepts that restore the importance of institutionalized behavior in cross-national comparison. Encouraged by the functionalist approach to government and the difficulties of making systemic-subsystemic distinctions for comparative purposes, the input-output distinction neglected institutionalized influence in political systems. Institutions have most often been examined in relation to *either* inputs (election, voting, and legislative behavior) *or* outputs. For different reasons, both concerns require that the institutional limits to change be specified, but the concepts for establishing institutional invariance remain disconnected in much political research. Neither approach grasps how institutionalization itself is part of the policy process and in many ways represents how each political system has forged an acceptable compromise between demands and performance, which is, in turn, imprinted on the entire process of government. Put simply, there is a great deal of institutionalized behavior that is not obviously related to the scope of inputs or outputs, but to reconciliation of demands and resources and to the routinization of expanded governmental activity.

Preoccupation with individual behavior no doubt accounts for the reluctance to integrate policy analysis with comparative theory. Although we have diverse concepts to describe roughly the structure of inputs (pluralist, consociational, clientelist), we lack similar concepts that characterize how outputs are structured. The tendency, then, is to superimpose a very general social theory (neo-liberal or neo-Marxist) derived from theories and concepts about inputs to provide a link to governmental performance. Such theoretical interpretations may have little or no bearing on the actual institutional relationships and policy process of the country is in question. Great violence may be done to both the complexity and the diversity of institutional structures. For example, very little attention may be paid to the fact that few, if any, political and administrative actors share the norms attributed to them by more general theories.

The shortcomings of this approach are increasingly in evidence as cross-national comparisons of policy areas multiply. Policy studies create numerous alternative possibilities to analyze the independent role of institutions in modern political systems. From such studies one might gradually build a comparison of institutional variance in relation to policies. For example, one can demonstrate the periods in the development of most policies when critical choices are left to the recognized institutions of a country. Institutionalized routinization is generally seen as a weakness from both neo-liberal and neo-Marxist perspectives, yet the modern state could not function without such support. To assess institutional effects requires better measures of how much and in what way decisions are affected by the policy process. Some of the efforts made at comparing legislatures and legal systems have made progress in this direction (Loewenberg, 1979; Schwartz and Wade, 1972). A wide variety of measures could be developed from organizational theory such as the time lapse between initiation and decision, the complexity of the internal process of coordination and consultation, and contrasts in selecting and weighing relevant information. Though not as yet extended to make cross-national comparison, recent administrative theory (van Gunsteren, 1976; Hood, 1976) also provides the groundwork for organizational comparisons.

Cross-national comparison has much to accomplish in developing more concrete and more specific concepts relating policies to the institutional context of political systems. One suggestive step in this direction is Hayward's essay on the inertial effects of political institutions in Britain and France (1976). Cross-national comparison would lead to very different kinds of hypotheses. For example, in federal systems, political intervention in policy is based on penetration of the institutional structure itself; in unitary systems, it appears that selective choice and administrative conflicts figure more heavily in policy making. One of the important initial tasks of policy analysis applied to institutional differences across countries is to test many of the well-worn generalizations that are part of the national political folklore of individual countries. Though a much less glamorous undertaking than singling out the obvious weaknesses and shortcomings of specific policies in a more partisan and often more ideological framework, there are a host of untested clichés about the institutional behavior of nearly every modern state.

Analyzing institutional variance using policy materials initially means disencumbering ourselves of much of the inherited abstract theory and essentially behavioral models used in the past. Even if the concepts used to study institutions and policy making were more developed, comparativists would not be studying policies for the same reasons or in the same ways as those commonly associated with policy studies in a single country. The initial cross-national differences would very likely take the form of structural concepts based on the underlying and persisting normative priorities of the institutions. Like many of the functionally defined cross-national policy comparisons we now have, much of the early investigation would still be directed at the assumptions and weaknesses of the policy process, but the results would not be linked solely to inputs or outputs of political systems. The aim to improve our concepts and theories dealing with the interstitial and interconnecting activity that affects policy making across a number of areas. In turn, the results would provide a more solid springboard to test the assumptions of abstract theories, and to assess the validity of much research that has dealt only with how demands are placed on government.

From a comparative policy perspective, possibly the greatest danger to developing new concepts and theories is quite simply that fascination with tilling this neglected field, combined with the growing need of both public and private agencies for advice, may dilute the intellectual effort needed to devise promising cross-national theories and concepts. Comparative policy studies are intriguing because they open possibilities of improving comparative theory and question many of the assumptions of political science as it has developed over the past generation. Steering a balanced course between applied research and oversimplification of modern government is the true challenge of confronting cross-national policy studies.

ACKNOWLEDGMENTS

I am indebted to Professor Charles Anderson, Arnold Heidenheimer, Peter Katzenstein, and Theodore Marmor for comments on this chapter.

REFERENCES

Adam, G., and Reynaud, J. D. (1978). *Labor Conflict and Social Change* (in French). Presses Universitaires de France, Paris.

Allardt, E., and Littunen, Y. (Eds.) (1964). *Clevages Ideologies and Party System.* Westermarck Society, Helsinki.

Allison, G. T. (1971). *Essence of Decision.* Little, Brown, Boston.

Almond, G., and Coleman, J. A. (Eds.) (1960). *The Politics of Developing Areas.* Princeton University Press, Princeton, NJ.

Almond, G., and Verba, S. (1963). *Civic Culture.* Princeton University Press, Princeton, NJ.

Anton, T. J. (1975). Conceptual premises in the study of complex policy processes: Critiques and new directions. *Journal of Policy Studies 3*: 225–233.

Apter, D. E. (Ed.). (1964). *Ideology and Discontent.* Free Press, New York.

Armstrong, J. A. (1973). *The European Administrative Elite.* Princeton University Press, Princeton, NJ.

Ashford, D. E. (1973). *Ideology and Participation.* Sage, Beverly Hills, CA.

—— (1977). Are Britain and France "Unitary"? *Comparative Politics 9*: 483–499.

—— (1978a). French pragmatism and British idealism: Financial aspects of local reorganization. *Comparative Political Studies 11*: 231–254.

—— (1980). *Politics and Policy in Britain: The Limits of Consensus.* Temple University Press, Philadelphia, and B. H. Blackwells, Oxford.

Ashford, D. E. (Ed.). (1978b). *Comparing Public Policies: New Concepts and Methods.* Sage, Beverly Hills, CA.

Ashford, D. E., Katzenstein, P., and Pempel, T. J. (1978). *Comparative Public Policy: A Cross-National Bibliography.* Sage, Beverly Hills, CA.

Bailey, F. (1960). *Tribe, Caste and Nation.* Manchester University Press, Manchester.

Banfield, E. (1961). *Political Influence,* Free Press, New York.

Bendix, R. (1964). *Nation Building and Citizenship.* Wiley, New York.

Birnbaum, P. (1977). *The Summit of the State* (in French) Seuil, Paris.

Boudon, R. (1971). *The Uses of Structuralism.* Heinemann, London.

Breton, A. (1974). *The Economic Theory of Representation.* Aldine, Chicago.

Brunner, R. D., and Brewer, G. D. (1971). *Organizational Complexity: Empirical Theories of Development.* Free Press, New York.

Clapham, J. H. (1936). *The Economic Development of France and Germany 1815–1914,* 4th ed. Cambridge University Press, Cambridge.

Clark, T. N. (1974). *Comparative Community Politics.* Halsted, New York.

Crozier, M. (1964). *The Bureaucratic Phenomenon.* University of Chicago Press, Chicago.

Cyert, R., and March, J. A. (1963). *A Behavioral Theory of the Firm.* Prentice-Hall, Englewood Cliffs, NJ.

Dahl, R. A. (1961). *Who Governs? Democracy and Power in an American City.* Yale University Press, New Haven, CT.

Dahrendorf, R. (1959). *Class and Class Conflict in Industrial Society.* Stanford University Press, Stanford, CA.

—— (1968). *Essays in the Theory of Society.* Stanford University Press, Stanford, CA.

Danziger, J. N. (1978). *Making Budgets: Public Resource Allocation.* Sage, Beverly Hills, CA.

Dearlove, J. (1979). *The Reorganisation of British Local Government.* Cambridge University Press, Cambridge.

Derthick, M. (1975). *Uncontrollable Spending for Social Services Grants.* Brookings Institution, Washington, DC.

Deutsch, K. W. (1961). Social mobilization and political development. *American Political Science Review 55*: 493–514.

—— (1963). *The Nerves of Government: Models of Political Communication and Control.* Free Press, New York.

Dogan, M. (Ed.) (1975). *The Mandarins of Europe.* Halsted, New York.

Dogan, M., and Rokkan, S. (Eds.) (1969). *Quantitative Ecological Analysis in the Social Sciences.* M.I.T. Press, Cambridge, MA.

Downs, A. (1957). *An Economic Theory of Democracy.* Harper & Row, New York.

Dye, T. R. (1966). *Politics, Economics and the Public.* Rand McNally, Chicago.

Dyson, K. H. F. (1976). Institutional government: A new perspective in organizational theory, *Journal of Management Studies 13*: 131–151.

Easton, D. (1975). *A System Analysis of Political Life.* Wiley, New York.

Eckstein, H. (1961). *A Theory of Stable Democracy.* Center of International Studies, Princeton, NJ.

—— (1973). Authority patterns: A structural basis for political inquiry. *American Political Science Review 67*: 1142–1161.

Ehrmann, H. W. (1957). *Organized Business in France.* Princeton University Press, Princeton, NJ.

Eisenstadt, S. N. (1966). *Modernization, Protest and Change.* Wiley, New York.

—— (1973). *Tradition, Change and Modernity.* Prentice-Hall, Englewood Cliffs, NJ.

Etzioni, A. (1968). *The Active Society.* Free Press, New York.

Geertz, C. (1963a). *Peddlars and Princes.* University of Chicago Press, Chicago.

—— (1964). Ideology as a cultural system. In *Ideology and Discontent,* D. E. Apter, (Ed.). Free Press, New York.

Geertz, C. E. (Ed.) (1963b). *Old Societies and New States.* Free Press, New York.

Gywn, W. B., and Edwards, G. C., III (Eds.) (1975). *Perspectives on Public Policy-Making.* Tulane Studies in Political Science, New Orleans.

Hagen, E. E. (1962). *On Theory of Social Change.* Dorsey, Homewood, IL.

Hanf, K., and Scharpf, F. (1978). *Interorganizational Policy Making: Limits to Coordination and Central Control.* Sage, Beverly Hills, CA.

Hayward, J. (1976). Institutional inertia and political impetus in France and Britain. *European Journal of Political Research 4*: 341–359.

Heady, F., and Stokes, S. L. (Eds.) (1962). *Papers in Comparative Administration.* University of Michigan, Institute of Public Administration, Ann Arbor.

Heclo, H. (1974). *Modern Social Politics in Britain and Sweden.* Yale University Press, New Haven, CT.

Heidenheimer, A. J. (1973). The politics of public education, health and welfare in the USA and Western Europe: How growth and reform potentials have differed. *British Journal of Political Science 3*: 315–340.

Heidenheimer, A., Heclo, H., and Adams, C. T. (1975). *Comparative Public Policy: The Politics of Social Choice in Europe and America.* St. Martins, New York.

Hibbs, D. A., Jr. (1978). On the political economy of long-run trends in strike activity. *British Journal of Political Science 8*: 153–177.

Hirsch, F. (1976). *Social Limits to Growth.* Harvard University Press, Cambridge, MA.

Hirschman, A. O. (1963). *Journeys Toward Progress.* Twentieth Century Fund, New York.

Hood, C. C. (1976). *The Limits of Administration.* Wiley, New York.

Hunter, F. (1953). *Community Power Structure.* University of North Carolina Press, Chapel Hill.

Huntingdon, S. P. (1968). *Political Order in Changing Societies.* New Haven, Yale University Press, New Haven, CT.

Ilchman, W. F., and Uphoff, N. (1969). *The Political Economy of Change.* University of California Press, Berkeley.

Jacob, P. E. (1971). *Values and the Active Community.* Free Press, New York.

Kesselman, M. (1970). Over institutionalization and political constraint. *Comparative Politics 3*: (October) 21–44.

Key, V. O., and Cummings, M. C. (1966). *The Responsible Electorate.* Harvard University Press, Cambridge, MA.

Kindleberger, C. P. (1964). *Economic Growth in France and Britain.* Harvard University Press, Cambridge, MA.

Kluckholn, C. (1943). Covert culture and administrative problems. *American Anthropologist 45*: 213–227.

Kornhauser, W. (1959). *The Politics of Mass Society.* Free Press, Glencoe, IL.

Kuznets, S. S. (1946). *National Income.* National Bureau of Economic Research, New York.

LaPalombara, J. (1963). *Bureaucracy and Political Developments.* Princeton University Press, Princeton, NJ.

La Porte, T. (Ed.) (1975). *Organized Social Complexity: Challenge to Politics and Policy.* Princeton University Press, Princeton, NJ.

Leach, E. R. (1954). *Political Systems of Highland Burma.* London School of Economics, London.

Lerner, D. (1960). *The Passing of Traditional Society.* Free Press, New York.

Lijphart, A. (1968). *The Politics of Accommodation: Pluralism and Democracy in the Netherlands.* University of California Press, Berkeley.

—— (1975). The comparable-cases strategy in comparative research. *Comparative Political Studies 8*: 158–177.

Lindblom, C. E. (1965). *The Intelligence of Democracy.* Free Press, New York.

—— (1969). The science of muddling through. *Public Administration Review 19*: 79–88.

Lipset, S. M., and Rokkan, S. (Eds.) (1965). *Party Systems and Voter Alignments.* Free Press, New York.

Loewenberg, G., and Patterson, S. (1979). *Comparing Legislatures.* Little, Brown, Boston.

Lowi, T. J. (1969). *The End of Liberalism.* Norton, New York.

—— (1978). Public policy and bureaucracy in the United States and France. In *Comparing Public Policies,* D. E. Ashford (Ed.). Sage, Beverly Hills, CA.

Lynch, O. M. (1969). *The Politics of Untouchability.* Columbia University Press, New York.

March, J. A., and Simon, H. A. (1958). *Organizations.* Wiley, New York.

McCarthy, W. E. J., and Ellis, N. D. (1973). *Management by Agreement.* Hutchinson, London.

McConnell, G. (1966). *Private Power and American Democracy.* Knopf, New York.

Merriam, C. E. (1945). *Systematic Politics.* University of Chicago Press, Chicago.

Merritt, R. L., and Rokkan, S. (Eds.) (1966). *Comparative Nations: The Use of Quantitative Data in Cross-National Research.* Yale University Press, New Haven and London.

Merton, R. K. (1968). *Social Theory and Social Structure.* Free Press, New York.

Michels, R. (1962). *Political Parties.* Collier Books, New York.

Miliband, R. (1961). *Parliamentary Socialism.* Allen and Unwin, London.

Miller, G. (1956). The magical number seven, plus or minus two. *Psychological Review 63*: 81–97.

Mitchell, W. C. (1969). The shape of political theory to come: From political sociology to political economy. In *Politics and the Social Sciences,* S. M. Lipset (Ed.). Oxford University Press, Oxford.

Moore, B. F. (1966). *Social Origins of Dictatorship and Democracy.* Beacon, Boston.

Nadel, S. F. (1957). *The Theory of Social Structure.* Free Press, Glencoe, IL.

Olson, M. (1965). *The Logic of Collective Action.* Harvard University Press, Cambridge, MA.

Ostrogorski, M. I. (1910). *Democracy and the Party System.* Macmillan, New York.

Peacock, A. T., and Wiseman, J. (1967). *The Growth of Public Expenditure in the United Kingdom,* 2nd ed. Allen and Unwin, London.

Perrow, C. (1972). *Complex Organizations: A Critical Essay.* Scott, Foresman, Glenview, IL.

Peters, B. G. (1978). *The Politics of Bureaucracy: A Comparative Perspective.* Loufman, New York.

Pickvance, C. G. (1977). Marxist approaches to the study of urban politics. *International Journal of Urban and Regional Research 2*: 219–255.

Pierce, J. C., and Pride, R. A. (1972). *Cross-National Micro-Analysis.* Sage, Beverly Hills, CA.

Presthus, R. (1979). *The Organizational Society.* St. Martin's, New York.

Pryor, F. L. (1968). *Public Expenditures in Communist and Capitalist Nations.* Dorsey, Homewood, IL.

Przeworski, A., and Teune, H. (1971). *The Logic of Comparative Social Inquiry.* Wiley, New York.

Putnam, R. D. (1973). *The Beliefs of Politicians.* New Haven, Yale University Press, New Haven, CT.

Riggs, F. (1964). *Administration in Developing Countries.* Houghton Mifflin, Boston.

Rokkan, S., Campbell, A., Torsvik, P., and Valen, H. (1970). *Citizen, Elections and Parties.* McKay, New York.

Rokkan, S., Verba, S., et al. (1969). *Comparative Survey Analysis.* Mouton, The Hague.

Rose, R. (1977). The evolution of public policy in the european states. in *Comparing Public Policies,* J. Waitr and R. Rose (Eds.). Political Academy of Science, Warsaw.

Rose, R. (Ed.) (1976). *The Dynamics of Public Policy: A Comparative Analysis.* Sage, Beverly Hills, CA.

Rose, R., and Peters, B. G. (1978). *Can Government Go Bankrupt?* Basic Books, New York.

Schaffer, B. B. (1973). *The Administrative Factor.* Cass, London.

Schattshneider, E. (1960). *Semi-Sovereign People.* Holt, New York.

Schmitter, P. C. (1977). Corporatism and policy-making in contemporary Western Europe. *Comparative Political Studies 10* (special issue, April).

Schwarts, B., and Wade, H. W. R. (1972). *Legal Control of Government: Administrative Law in Britain and the United States.* Clarendon, Oxford.

Schwirian, K. P. (1973). *Some analytical problems in the comparative treatment of ecological theories. In Comparative Social Research,* M. Armen and A. D. Grimshaw (Eds.). Wiley, New York.

Scott, B. R., and McArthur, J. H. (1969). *Industrial Planning in France.* Harvard University Press, Cambridge, MA.

Self, P. (1977). *Administration Theories and Politics.* Allen and Unwin, London.

Selznick, P. (1949). *TVA and the Grass Roots.* University of California Press, Berkeley.

Sharpe, L. J. (1973). American democracy reconsidered. *British Journal of Political Science 3*: 1–28, 129–168.

Siffin, W. (Ed.) (1957). *Toward the Comparative Study of Public Administration.* Indiana University Press, Bloomington.

Simon, H. A. (1957). *Administrative Behavior.* Knopf, New York.

Smith, M. G. (1956). On segmentary lineage systems. *Journal of the Royal Anthropological Society 86*: 39–80.

Smith, T. (1975). *The Comparative Policy Process.* ABC Clio, Santa Barbara and Oxford.

Social Science Research Council (1949–1950). *The American Soldier.* SSRC, New York.

Suleiman, E. (1974). *Power, Politics and Bureaucracy in France.* Princeton University Press, Princeton, NJ.

Sundquist, J. L. (1975). *Dispersing Population: What America Can Learn from Europe.* Brookings Institution, Washington, DC.

Titmuss, R. M. (1962). *Income Distribution and Social Change.* Allen and Unwin, London.

Triandis, H. (1972). *The Analysis of Subjective Culture.* Wiley, New York.

Tribe, L. H. (1972). Policy science: Analysis or ideology? *Philosophy and Public Affairs* 2: 66–110.

van Gunsteren, H. R. (1976). *The Quest for Control.* Wiley, New York.

Verba, S., Nie, N., and Kim, F. (1971). *Models of Democratic Participation,* Sage, Beverly Hills, CA.

Vernon, R. (1973). *Big Business and the State.* Harvard University Press, Cambridge, MA.

Wiatr, J. L., and Rose, R. (Eds.) (1977). *Comparing Public Policies.* Polish Academy of Sciences, Committee on Political Sciences, Warsaw.

Wilensky, H. L. (1975). *The Welfare State and Equality: Structural and Ideological Roots of Public Expenditure.* University of California Press, Berkeley.

9

Policy Analysis Across Academic Disciplines

George J. McCall / University of Missouri-St Louis, St. Louis, Missouri
George H. Weber* / National Institute of Mental Health, Rockville, Maryland

Nagel (1979: 9) considers that "policy analysis can be broadly defined as the study of the nature, causes and effects of alternative public policies. All fields of scientific knowledge, but especially the social sciences, are relevant to such a study."

In this chapter we seek to analyze the multidisciplinary character of policy analysis to identify the distinctive contributions made to this enterprise by a wide variety of academic fields. In the first section, a rudimentary framework for classifying types of contributions to policy analysis is set forth. The second section delimits the fields to be reviewed and analyzes the differing structural relations of professions and disciplines to the peculiarly multidisciplinary nature of policy research. The third and fourth sections, respectively, consider the distinctive contributions of various professions and of various social science disciplines to policy analysis.

I. A FRAMEWORK OF POLICY ANALYSIS

According to *A Dictionary of the Social Sciences* (Gould and Kolb, 1964: 509), "the most common social and political usage of the term *policy* refers to a course of action or intended course of action conceived as deliberately adopted, after a review of possible alternatives, and pursued, or intended to be pursued."

One common distinction in policy analysis is between the study of policy *content* and the study of policy *process*. Policy content (Ranney, 1968: 8) includes "the particular object or set of objects the policy is intended to affect, the particular course of events desired, the particular line of action chosen, the particular declaration [of intent] made, and the particular actions taken—in all cases as actually chosen from among the alternative objects, courses of events, lines of action, declarations, and actions that might have

Present affiliation: The Catholic University of America, Washington, DC

been chosen." Policy process, on the other hand, includes "the actions and interactions that produce the authorities' ultimate choice of a particular policy content over its rivals" (Ranney, 1968: 8), and, in many conceptions, the consequences and assessments of the policy as well.

A second common distinction in policy analysis (Golembiewski, 1975) is that between the *prescriptive* study of policy (in which normative principles are centrally employed and which yields policy recommendations) and the *descriptive* study of policy (which purports to be "value-free" and eventuates in descriptive and/or explanatory accounts).

Historically, prescriptive policy studies have focused primarily on the content of policies, whereas descriptive policy studies have focused largely on the policy process. However, we consider that these two dimensions are fully crossed, yielding four major types of policy studies: prescriptive/content, descriptive/content, prescriptive/process, and descriptive/process.

Prescriptive studies of policy *contents* seem largely to deal with substantive (rather than procedural) policies. Froman discerns two traditions within this type:

> The first, and older, tradition may be called "normative" studies of public policy. These studies attempt to analyze, usually in a critical fashion, a particular public policy. . . and generally will also suggest either reforms in the existing policy or a new type of policy altogether. . . . The criteria for evaluating these critiques of ongoing programs are usually certain stated goals that the authors feel are, or ought to be, highly valued. Often authors will suggest that if certain steps are taken, programs can be developed which will lead to "solutions" of the problems under examination. The major point of argument, however, is generally the extent to which ongoing policies deviate from important values or goals (Froman, 1968: 42).

The second, and newer, tradition in the prescriptive study of policy content has been one of "future analysis," examining either the future consequences of current policies or the kinds of policies that would be appropriate in some forecast future. In either case, such studies may be regarded as "problem-oriented" in that they concern some particular problem and the policies that are appropriate to dealing with it. Studies of this type still predominate in many serious policy periodicals, such as *The Public Interest* and *Social Policy*, and are frequently encountered in policy journals.

The second of our four major types of policy analysis is the *descriptive* study of policy *content*. In this type, one or more attributes of policy content is examined as a dependent variable (or, less commonly, as an independent variable) in relation to policy process (Spadaro et al., 1975). For example, a variety of scholars have examined the influence of political system characteristics of cities, states, and nations on the content of public policy (Dye, 1975). Policy attributes include, first of all, various traditional content categories: substantive policy area, institutional categories, target categories, time periods, ideological categories, value categories, extent of support, and governmental level (Froman, 1968). More abstract attributes include distinctions between "style" and "position" issues; between "material" and "symbolic" satisfactions; between "strategic" and "structural" issues; among distributive, regulatory, and redistributive policies; and between "areal" and "segmental" policies (see Froman, 1968).

The third major type of policy analysis is the *prescriptive* study of policy *process*— critical analyses of procedural policies suggesting either reforms in existing policy procedures or an altogether new type of procedural policy. Recent studies of this type tend to employ formalized deductive models of "rational choice"—systems analysis, operations research, program-planning-budgeting systems, strategic analysis, and so on—optimizing decisions with respect to such normative principles as efficiency or equity (Golembiewski, 1975).

The fourth type of policy analysis is the *descriptive* study of policy *process.* Such studies generally examine one or more of the stages of the so-called policy cycle. Although conceptualizations of the policy cycle vary in the number and nature of stages discerned (e.g., Lasswell, 1956; Mitchell and Mitchell, 1969; Kahn, 1969), all would include at least the stages of formulation, decision making, implementation, effects, and feedback. Perhaps the greatest number of descriptive studies of policy process have centered on either the stage of policy formulation (e.g., studies of the nature, extent, perceptions, and causes of a policy problem or issue) or on the stage of policy effects (e.g., impact assessments, effectiveness evaluations, and cost-benefit analyses).

II. THE MULTIDISCIPLINARY CHARACTER OF POLICY ANALYSIS

In their seminal volume, Lerner and Laswell (1951) introduced the concept of "the policy sciences." Which fields of learning comprise the policy sciences? "Virtually all academic disciplines are currently experiencing an increased concern for being relevant to important governmental policy problems" (Nagel, 1979: 9), a trend stemming from the societal unrest of the 1960s, facilitated by the computer revolution, and nurtured by the increasing attractiveness of the government as an employer and sponsor.

Indeed, various reviews (Nagel, 1975; Dror, 1971) make a strong case for the policy relevance of perhaps the majority of fields listed in the catalogue of any major university. From among the professional schools of such a university, the schools of management (public or business administration), social work, urban planning, law, engineering, and medicine are reasonably viewed as being more or less policy-relevant. From within the core college of liberal arts and sciences, a wide range of fields is considered policy-relevant. Central are the social and behavioral sciences, particularly political science, economics, sociology, psychology, anthropology, and geography. Less centrally relevant are some of the natural sciences: mathematics, biology, chemistry, and physics. From among the humanities, history (as a sometimes social science) is most frequently cited, and a strong case is made for the policy relevance of philosophy.

The contributions made to policy analysis by these many fields of learning differ rather widely in accordance not only with their varying interests but also significantly with their inner constitutions.

Any field of learning contains the potential for developing any of three somewhat distinct foci—academic (or discipline) research, applied research, and/or practice (Weber and McCall, 1978a). *Discipline research* is that research designed to advance knowledge within an academic discipline and addressed to the members of that discipline (Coleman,

1972). *Applied research* is that research undertaken for application to some practical purpose beyond the academic concerns of a discipline (Lazarsfeld and Reitz, 1975). [Applied research thus includes, but is not exhausted by, *policy research*: research designed as a guide to social action in specific policies and addressed to an audience of political actors (Coleman, 1972).] *Practice,* on the other hand, is the provision of a more or less esoteric service—advice and/or action—to an individual or organizational client (Hughes, 1963b).

These simple distinctions afford us bases for accomplishing three of our major tasks in this chapter.

First, they provide a workable criterion for discerning which are the policy sciences. The criterion we propose is that within the applied research activity of any field, much of this activity be of the type we have defined as policy research. By this criterion, in our rough judgment, from the initial list of relevant fields only the social and behavioral sciences, the management sciences, urban planning, social work, and law would qualify as core policy sciences.

Second, the simple distinctions among the three potential foci of any field cast important light on the differing relations to policy analysis of those fields that are professions (in which practice is the central activity) and those that are academic disciplines (in which discipline research is central). Both theory and research differ characteristically between these opposing models for organizing a field of knowledge. Disciplines endeavor to develop *theories of fact*; professions strive to develop *theories of practice*, which define for the client desirable and undesirable conditions in relation to putative techniques for manipulating such conditions (e.g., the disease model in medicine). In either case, applied research (including policy research) is only a secondary focus. However, in a professional field, knowledge is pursued (i.e., research is undertaken) in order to improve practice; applied research is therefore rewarded by one's peers, a situation not to be found within a discipline (Price, 1965). It is for this reason, among others (Hughes, 1963b, 1952), that academic disciplines with substantial segments engaged in applied research or practice— such as psychology, sociology, and political science—experience considerable internal strain toward the "professionalization" of their fields.

Third, these distinctions among discipline research, applied research, and practice help make clear why it is that "policy science" is, and must be, a multidisciplinary field of learning more closely akin to a profession than to an academic discipline, as many have contended (Dror, 1971; Lasswell, 1971; Lazarsfeld and Reitz, 1975; MacRae, 1976; Charlesworth, 1972). Put simply, the fact that policy research is a variety of applied research entails that any substantial and reliable academic rewards for its sustained pursuit cannot be obtained within a discipline model of organization.

The alternative model—an independent, "professionalized" field of policy science, devoted to the systematic improvement of public policy making—can, of course, fit relatively comfortably into a university structure, drawing many of its faculty, courses, concepts, facts, principles, and methods from the whole range of policy-relevant fields [see, e.g., the special issues of *Policy Sciences* (1971-1972), vol. 1, no. 4, and vol. 2, no. 1]. In the remainder of this chapter we elaborate the preceding arguments and review the distinctive contributions of concepts, facts, principles, and methods made to policy science by these various fields.

III. PROFESSIONAL FIELDS AND POLICY SCIENCE

If the emergent field of policy science is to be a "professionalized" one, the question arises as to why it is that the existing policy relevant professions have not already subsumed policy science.

One general reason is their one-sided emphasis on prescriptive studies to the relative neglect of descriptive studies. Since the core of any professional field of learning is its theory of practice, and such theories of practice are inherently prescriptive in nature, it is scarcely coincidental that the primary contributions of these fields to policy analysis have been prescriptive studies of policy content and process.

A second general reason has to do with the domains of validity of these theories of practice, a matter that is in turn closely related to the nature of the clients of the existing policy-relevant professions. The fact is that these clients are (at best) *managers* rather than policy makers; not surprisingly, therefore, the existing theories of practice are really theories for improving *managerial decision making* rather than for improving policy making (cf. Dror, 1971).

A. Management Science

The field of management (or administrative science, considered to include both public administration and business administration) strives to identify and apply generic "management principles" based on analysis of administrative processes, dynamics, and activities within a wide range of large-scale organizations. Its clients are to be found within the ranks of top-level and middle management in business firms and bureaucracies, rather than within the policy-making ranks of those organizations. At the theoretical core of this field lies a concern for improved administrative decision making (Simon, 1957), a concern grounded in social psychology but relying centrally on the information and decision sciences (including operations research, systems analysis, managerial economics, and systems engineering).

Perhaps the greatest contribution of the field of management to policy analysis (Dror, 1971) is its proclivity for a "systems approach" to problems, stressing the complex interrelatedness among a large number of conditions and events, and emphasizing the impossibility of judging the desirability of a single intervention without examining its ramifications in the operations of the entire system. Application of this approach to any concrete decision problem depends on the availability of some adequate model of the system permitting the (at least probabilistic) prediction of system effects through simulation. Such models are generally either mathematical models or computer programs; particularly important have been linear and dynamic programming, network analysis, game theory, and decision analysis. Recently, the utter dependence of the systems approach on strictly quantitative data and models has eased somewhat, incorporating such developments as gaming and the Delphi method.

The potential applicability to policy making of this management approach has been clearly recognized (e.g., Radnor, 1971). Others, however, doubt that such an approach is usefully transferable from managerial decision making to policy making, citing a variety of limitations in the existing practice of management:

1. Management sciences try to propose optimal policies while neglecting the institutional contexts of both the problems and the policy-making and policy-implementation process.
2. Management sciences are unable to handle political needs, such as consensus maintenance and coalition building.
3. Management sciences are unable to deal with irrational phenomena, such as ideologies, charisma, high-risk commitments, self-sacrifice, and unconventional styles of life.
4. Management sciences are unable to deal with basic value issues and often inadequately explicate the value assumptions of analysis.
5. Management sciences deal with identifying optimal alternatives among available or easily synthesized ones. The invention of basically new alternatives is beyond their scope, although they can sometimes help by showing the inadequacy of all available alternatives.
6. Management sciences require some predictability in respect to alternatives. Situations of "primary uncertainty" (when not only the probabilities of various outcomes but the dimensions of the possible outcomes are unknown) cannot be handled by them.
7. Management sciences depend on significant quantification of main relevant variables and the availability of models permitting "exercising" of these variables. Therefore, complex social issues cannot be dealt with and most behavioral sciences knowledge is ignored (Dror, 1971: 14–15).

Indeed, improvement of managerial decisions, when the governing policies are in need of formulation or reformulation, may even be counterproductive, leading to more efficient pursuit of the wrong objectives.

B. Urban Planning

A not dissimilar emphasis on a systems approach together with quantitative modeling techniques characterizes the profession of urban planning, whose clients, too, tend to be managerial decision makers—in municipal and metropolitan governments. When the term "planning" began to acquire a pejorative connotation during the "red scare" hysteria of the 1920s, the originally substantial social ameliorationism of this field was abandoned in favor of a narrower and safer centering on the arrangement and regulation of land use and land occupancy (Hubin, 1971). During this period, city planning became more closely associated with natural science fields (chemistry, physics, engineering, architecture, etc.) than with the social sciences.

It was not until about 1960 that this trend began to reverse itself and the field of city planning reconverged with social planning [a specialization within social work (Kahn, 1969)] to form the more comprehensive field of urban planning (Frieden and Morris, 1968). This broader approach, acquiring momentum through the twin forces of the war on poverty and the civil rights movement, rested on several related criteria: A decent modern environment includes not only physical comfort and work, but education, services, and social relationships that open opportunity for all; physical elements are not sufficient to establish the urban environment, and social measures are not powerful enough either; change that occurs by chance is not necessarily suitable for human needs.

Unlike the field of management, urban planning during the 1960s became quite concerned over the possibility of technocratic dictation—the substitution of technical for political decision making in the reshaping of urban America (Frieden and Morris, 1968; Gans, 1968). A great deal of professional debate developed regarding who is, or should be, the planner's client, and the concept of advocacy planning emerged as one device for reconciling professional practice with representative democracy (Davidoff, 1965).

C. Social Work

The domain of social work is *social welfare*, primarily "those programs implementing access to benefits, entitlements and services by other than market criteria" (Kahn, 1975). According to Meyer (1968: 495), "the objectives of social work are to help individuals, families, communities, and groups of persons who are socially disadvantaged and to contribute to the creation of conditions that will enhance social functioning and prevent breakdown."

The three principal divisions of social work practice are case work, group work, and community organization, and are differentiated most clearly on the basis of type of client served—individuals, groups, and associations, respectively. Ancillary activities include social welfare administration and planning, social welfare research, and social action (Friedlander, 1961).

It is through the ancillary activity of social welfare administration and planning that the field of social work attains its principal policy relevance (Kahn, 1973). Social planning includes not only "welfare planning" (in the sense of allocative decisions regarding transfer payments within the social sector, akin to welfare economics), but also *service coordination* within the bewildering system of agencies for distributing social services (and is thus concerned with the resulting problems of discontinuity, fragmentation, inundation, access, procurement, and resource competition). Once again, the clients of this professional activity are primarily agency administrators engaged in managerial decision making, rather than policy makers.

Since these clients are themselves social service providers, it is not surprising that (in comparison with the field of management) social planning is less concerned to maximize economic efficiency at the possible expense of such social welfare principles as human dignity, social justice, and the good life. Similarly, as a branch of social work, social planning is much more intimately grounded in sociology and psychology than in the rationalistic and utilitarian models of microeconomics, mathematics, and engineering. As an intermediate composite of these two prescriptive approaches (cf. Sec. III. B), urban planning may represent the "middle way" for the 1980s.

D. Law

Since laws constitute one very significant instrument of public policy, it is to be expected that the legal profession is of considerable policy relevance. Lawyers play unique roles both in the making and interpretation of law and in the advocacy of clients (individuals, government agencies, corporations, voluntary associations, and occasionally social categories or classes) within legal arenas. The legal profession greatly influences statute formulation through its disproportionate representation among legislators, and quite directly controls the processes of case law (Horowitz, 1977). Legal advocacy has provided to the other fields the prototype of the advocacy model of practice and has contributed much to policy making, particularly within the area of public-interest legal practice (Patner, 1978).

However, neither the methodology of legal research (Sigler and Beede, 1977) nor the methodology of legal practice (Hart and McNaughton, 1971) is scientific in character, thus greatly limiting the profession's contribution to policy analysis. Legal research is primarily documentary analysis aimed at clarifying the historical development, overt intent, and subsequent legal interpretations of particular public policies (Sigler and Beede, 1977). Advocacy practice in the legal profession remains largely a rhetorical art (despite some growing use of social scientists in jury selection and in expert testimony). Similarly, the practice modality of legislative drafting remains oriented to developing legal language that is acceptable to legislatures and courts rather than specifically framed to achieve complex public policy goals. [However, the emergent school of experimental jurisprudence (Beutel, 1975) seeks to remedy just this situation, through scientific experimentation on the drafting, effects, and subsequent revision of legal statutes.]

In any case, the effectiveness of law making as a policy instrument is rather sharply limited. Effecting social change through laws involves overcoming a large component of inertial resistance; one interest group may prevail in the arena of formulation, whereas a countervailing interest group may win out in the arena of enforcement (Mayhew, 1971). "Law, by building in a possibility for defense, builds in the possibility of evasion" (p. 480).

E. Engineering

If law holds forth the attractive possibility of a "legal quick fix" of many policy problems, engineering (Perrucci and Gerstl, 1969) offers the comparably attractive and elusive prospect of a "technological fix"—the development and application of some new material product or process designed to solve a policy problem (e.g., the universal use of metal detectors in airports in response to the skyjacking problem). Although the benefits of technology are unquestionable, technological responses to policy problems—being more readily implementable than basic social reforms—too often fail (Spicer, 1954) for overlooking fundamental social causes, undesirable side effects (generating new problems while solving an earlier one), or the likelihood of technological countermeasures. (In fact, the example of antiskyjacking metal detectors can be seen to have displayed each of these flaws).

The contributions of civil engineering to policy science by way of urban planning have already been noted, as have those of systems engineering through the management sciences (indeed, in the wake of the space program cutbacks during the 1960s, many systems engineers found employment in management consultation and in policy planning and evaluation firms). Not at all facetiously, it may be said that the greatest contribution of engineering to policy science surely stems from electronic engineering in the form of the large-scale computer, which has made possible highly elaborate manipulations of very large masses of policy-relevant data.

On the other side, perhaps the greatest disservice of engineering to policy science has been the dangerously misleading but ever-popular idea that policy science can be to the social sciences what engineering is to the natural sciences. Engineering rests on a base of ancient pragmatic knowledge, can take for granted a continuous flow of relevant basic and applied scientific research, operates on tangible and tractable material objects, and can utilize a clear-cut organizational model for research/development/testing/production. None of these conditions applies to policy science (Dror, 1971; Lazarsfeld and Reitz, 1975).

F. Medicine

Even more than in the field of law, the clients of medical practice tend to be ordinary individual citizens, with the major exception of the specialization of public health (or community medicine). Indeed, public health practice has always been closely linked with governmental activity, relying heavily on public law and public agencies of health care as instrumentalities.

Although the policy concerns of this branch of medicine are concerned mainly with health policy, this concern has traditionally been quite broadly construed, as including sufficient and acceptable supplies of food and water, control of physical environmental hazards, prevention and control of epidemic and endemic diseases, wide provision of health care services, and the relief of physical and social disability (Rosen, 1968). Since midcentury, social disability has been taken to include mental health problems of individual adjustment to the stresses of social living (Mechanic, 1969). Thus the concerns of public health closely resemble those of urban planning and social work, although its practice modalities rest more heavily on medical research and technology.

Medicine, like engineering, too often offers the prospect of a technological fix to policy issues and problems—for example, methadone maintenance as a solution to heroin addiction, or tranquilizers as a solution to mental illness.

IV. ACADEMIC DISCIPLINES AND POLICY SCIENCE

A field of learning is a discipline to the extent that it offers "a single order of phenomena which, when observed and/or manipulated in a systematic way, yield a body of consistent theory" (Hughes, 1963a). A discipline is, in this sense, a science rather than an art.

> Scientists, in the purest case, do not have clients. They discover, systematize, and communicate knowledge about some order of phenomena. They will be guided by faith that the society at large and in the long run will benefit from continued increase of knowledge about nature; but the various actions of the scientist, *qua* scientist, are undertaken because they add to knowledge, not because of any immediate benefit to any individual or group which may be considered his client. The test of the scientist's work lies in convincing communication of it to colleagues, communication so full and so precise that any of them can undertake to test the validity of claimed findings by following the same procedures. Scientists chafe under secrecy. If laymen do not receive full report of work done, it is simply because they are not sophisticated enough to understand the report. The great point in the scientist's code is full and honest reporting to his colleagues, and, with it, willingness to submit to full criticism. Since this is so, and since no client is involved, scientists ordinarily do not seek the protection of state license. Informal controls are sufficient (Hughes, 1952: 441; cf. Price, 1965).

Discipline research, in this mode, is the core activity within such academic disciplines. Not being undertaken for purposes of any application, discipline research is rarely applicable to improving policy making, even though it is not infrequently policy relevant (Davis, 1975) in the sense of being addressed to a matter of general social concern. Instead, the policy fruits of discipline research are to be found largely in its fueling effects on the professions and on applied research (including policy research) conducted by members of the same or another discipline.

Applied research, within a discipline, is very much an ancillary and rather poorly rewarded activity. Policy research efforts, as a type of disciplinary applied research, are generally policy-relevant but only sometimes applicable (Dror, 1971; Demerath et al., 1975; Scott and Shore, 1979).

Complex policy problems tend to be formulated quite narrowly, to fit within the domain of a single discipline, and to be analyzed only through the limiting (and sometimes distorting) lens of its own theoretical framework. Policy recommendations, then, tend to be restricted to policy instruments natural to the discipline; policy research within a discipline tends to lack an adequate appreciation of the necessity for social invention and experimentation and for the search for plausible points of policy leverage.

Disciplinary frameworks lack any established criteria for evaluating the significance of various policy issues or problems, and thus disciplinary policy research is characteristically vulnerable to issue fads and fashions and to over- or underreaction (including sensationalism). Such frameworks also generally fail to provide any perspective on the political realities of policy making, so that disciplinary policy researchers are often led to either utter naivete or profound cynicism in their development of policy recommendations.

Disciplinary policy research lacks the requisite flexibility in work arrangements to permit timely research response, and its norms of methodological perfectionism constitute a further obstacle to timely completion of policy studies. It tends also to ignore limitations on available policy resources and the consequent need for comparative cost-benefit analysis of policy alternatives.

It is scarcely surprising, then, that many research-based policy recommendations from the academic disciplines prove impractical or useless, if not actually counterproductive.

A. Natural Sciences

Such limitations on the applicability of disciplinary policy research are perhaps least unexpected in the case of the natural sciences, since the order of phenomena with which they are distinctively familiar is radically different from the intricate social dynamics of policy making. The policy-relevant contributions of the physical science and life science disciplines are likely to be indirect—through the professions of engineering, urban planning, and medicine—as a consequence of discipline and applied (nonpolicy) research efforts, generating knowledge and providing a basis for new technologies.

Mathematics presents a somewhat different situation, however, in that many branches of applied mathematics—particularly statistics—provide both fundamental theoretical models (Greenberger et al., 1976) and research tools (Fairley and Mosteller, 1977) to a wide variety of the policy sciences.

B. Philosophy

Philosophy represents a somewhat oblique case, since it does not purport to be an empirical science and members of this discipline undertake very little applied research. Yet philosophy, as the "mother discipline," exerts considerable influence on the core policy sciences. Its contributions effectively straddle those of the natural and the social sciences.

Logic, as one branch of philosophy, closely parallels applied mathematics, in contributing fundamental theoretical models and research tools (axiomatic systems, rules of inference, etc.). Of special relevance is the recent work in modal logic on possible worlds, importantly underlying "future analysis." Analytic philosophy is of considerable value in the clarification of fundamental concepts in all the policy-relevant disciplines, and the philosophy of science has made great strides in the "postpositivist" era.

In the realm of social philosophy, normative philosophical analysis provides useful prescriptive principles. The field of ethics, revitalized by the work on justice stimulated by Rawls (1971), has substantial bearing on policy analysis (Ladd, 1975), as does legal philosophy (Golding, 1975).

More than either philosophy or the natural sciences, the social and behavioral sciences—as disciplines oriented toward the understanding of society and social behavior—both expect and are expected to prove useful in the improvement of policy making. Although policy research remains very much an ancillary activity within these disciplines, it is an increasingly common and debated activity (e.g., van de Vall and Bolas, 1980).

A number of favorable trends in applied social science are often cited in these debates. First, more explicitly policy-oriented methodologies have been developed, such as social indicators and social reporting, evaluation research, and social experimentation. Second, new applied roles have emerged, including advocacy roles (Weber and McCall, 1978b). Third, greater attention is devoted to social change and anticipated consequences. Fourth, more research is being conducted on policy making (including the role of scientists in this process) and on specific policies. And finally, applied social science is said to have exerted crucial substantive influence on some important policy recommendations and decisions (e.g., regarding pornography, riots, and desegregation).

Other commentators, however, find very limited progress made by applied social science research in the policy realm, particularly at the national level (Scott and Shore, 1979; Demerath et al., 1975; Dror, 1971; Lazarsfeld and Reitz, 1975). These commentators find that a very large proportion of applied social science studies fail to derive any policy action implications whatsoever. Furthermore, they find the purported cases of national policy input to be more illusory than real. In the first place, these inputs have been much more into policy recommendations (e.g., of presidential commissions) than into enacted policies. Second, most of these recommendations have been rejected by policy makers as being impractical or politically infeasible. ["Various reasons have been given for the irrelevance of much of the work done for policy. . . . One is that it tends to be too piecemeal, specialized and partial in scope to ever be applicable to policy-making. . . . A second reason is that the research has implications that are so far-reaching and revolutionary as to virtually assure inaction" (Scott and Shore, 1971: 29)]. And finally, even where social science research is reputed to have influenced enacted policy (e.g., the Supreme Court desegregation rulings), it is contended that the research merely supported decisions arrived at on other grounds. In short, policy research within the social and behavioral science disciplines is seen as still suffering all the limitations of discipline-based research in general, as reviewed above.

These revealing criticisms, though quite generally applicable, tend to obscure key differences within this group of disciplines. For example, these disciplines vary rather sharply in their domains of interest (i.e., the single orders of phenomena with which they are concerned). In some cases the domain is relatively restricted; economics and political science deal only with economic systems and political systems, respectively, and geography deals only with spatial distributions. In other cases the domain is relatively encompassing, dealing in some ways with the entire sweep of society and of human behavior (e.g., sociology, anthropology, history, psychology).

These disciplines vary also in the nature of their theoretical frameworks. Some (such as economics and some branches of political science) deal in normative theory, whereas others confine themselves to explanatory theory. [Even the latter fields, however, contain within their theoretical frameworks distinctive value premises and normative principles, such as anthropology's commitment to cultural relativism. MacRae (1976) provides an insightful analysis of the distinctive "ethic" respectively characteristic of economics, of political science, of psychology, and of sociology.] Whether normative or explanatory, the theoretical framework of a discipline represents a distinctive intellectual perspective, resting on interrelated concepts, assumptions, and working principles of analysis.

Closely associated with these, of course, are distinctive modes of inquiry, or research methods, tailored to the types of data of interest. Some disciplines, such as history and anthropology, rely predominantly on qualitative data and analysis. But even between the relatively quantitative disciplines, the mix of particular quantitative methods used varies characteristically.

In reviewing the policy science contributions of the social and behavioral sciences, then, we shall also take note of the special character of each of them, drawing heavily on the comparative analysis in Smelser (1967).

C. Economics

Samuelson (1961) defines economics as "the study of how men and society *choose,* with or without the use of money, to employ *scarce* productive resources to produce various commodities over time and distribute them for consumption, now and in the future, among people and groups in society." Out of all the many factors that may determine such allocation patterns, economics essentially selects as independent variables only the factors of market supply and demand. By means of the simplifying assumptions of economic man and economic rationality, the highly normative theoretical framework of economics gives rise to often quite elegant theoretical solutions to a wide range of economic problems.

It is this simplistic and highly quantifiable theoretical framework that is both the principal strength and the major weakness of economics as a contributor to policy research (Amacher et al., 1976). Microeconomic analyses of the allocation of scarce resources among alternative uses are among the most successful instances of prescriptive study of policy contents (Phillips and Votey, 1977; Haveman and Hamrin, 1973). Macroeconomic analyses of money, income, and price level in achieving the full use of resources (as in Keynesian economics) cast considerable prescriptive light on the contents of national economic policy. Public choice economics (Wade, 1975) and economic theories of firms and bureaucracies have deeply explored certain procedural policies, as key contributions to the prescriptive study of policy process.

Yet large parts of economics are quite weak in their knowledge of the behavior of individuals and institutions and therefore yield incorrect policy recommendations when such behavior does not correspond to the simplified assumptions of its framework, as in modernizing and in postindustrial societies.

Such gaps in behavioral knowledge can be traced in part to the relative weakness of descriptive research methods within economics. The discipline makes virtually no use of experimental method, and very little use of comparative method or the case study method. Survey research is not a major tradition in economics. However, the discipline has been a leading force in the redefined application of statistical methods (especially within econometrics) and of deductive mathematical modeling.

These tools, including cost-benefit analysis, are among the key contributions of economics to the professions of management, urban planning, and social work.

D. Political Science

The domain of political science is the political system, that is, those institutions and behaviors that are concerned primarily with the creation and exercise of *power*.

"Traditional" political science was (and is) essentially normative in nature, concerned with the institutional structure and philosophical justification of government. Conceptualization of public policy within this tradition stems largely from political economy (i.e., institutional and market economics) and from public law (stressing the procedural and structural aspects of government) (Lowi, 1975). Research methods are more closely akin to those of the historian and the philosopher than those of the other social sciences, and emphasize the prescriptive study of policy content and process.

"Behavioral" political science, arising after World War II in reaction to these limitations of the traditional approach, focuses on the empirical descriptive study of the political behavior of individuals and political organizations. In its search for explanatory (rather than normative) theory, behavioral political science turned to sociology and to psychology. From these same sources were borrowed appropriate quantitative research methods, particularly the survey method. Policy analysis here predominantly takes the form of descriptive studies of policy process—particularly the explanation of individual decisionmaking.

"Postbehavioral" political science (Graham and Carey, 1972) arose in the societal unrest of the 1960s in response to the alleged aridity and social irrelevance of the behavioral approach. The quantitative and explanatory emphases of behavioral political science were to be retained, while seeking to link the descriptive study of policy processes and behaviors with the content of public policy (Dye, 1975). Indeed, the "policy science" model ranks as the leading candidate for defining what is to be the nature of postbehavioral political science, a possibility not totally favored by all prominent political scientists (Simon, 1974; Van Dyke, 1968; Sharkansky, 1970). At any rate, prescriptive study of policy process (drawing on the mathematical deductive models of microeconomics and the management sciences) has become more common within political science research.

Whether discipline research within postbehavioral political science can successfully embody the policy science model has been seriously questioned (e.g., Lowi, 1975; Dye, 1975). Political science is disciplinarily preoccupied with the importance of political system characteristics as policy determinants, to the relative exclusion of economic, social, cultural, historical, and technological factors as influential policy determinants. More specifically (Dye, 1975), the discipline's ideological commitment to pluralism disposes it to presume that political values (such as participation, competition, and equality) are key determinants of public policy. On the other hand, it is charged that postbehavioral political science represents a return to macropolitics without inclusion of the macropolitical perspective and knowledge of "traditional" political science (Lowi, 1975). For example, the currently fashionable "rational choice" prescriptive models seem unable to incorporate any truly political perspective (cf. Sec. III.A).

Political science has long enjoyed an intimate, though ever-changing, association with the field of management through that branch known as public administration (Golembiewski, 1975). The discipline also has a special association with urban planning (based on their common interest in municipal regulations) and with law (Jones, 1975), as noted in the discussion above of "traditional" political science.

E. Geography

The discipline of geography is concerned with the "man-land" relationship, particularly the spatial distribution of human populations and social functions (Haggett, 1972). In the United States, however, these central topics were significantly preempted by human ecology and demography (as specializations within sociology). At the core of the theoretical framework of geography lie location theory (a rational choice model of optimum location of social functions, drawing heavily on economics) and the concept of the urban hierarchy (differentiating levels of human settlements and the varying service zones these serve). Modern geography is substantially quantitative, relying heavily on census data, mapping, and household survey research.

Geography was quite late in affording attention to social problems of any kind, even though human ecologists of the Chicago school of sociology had been undertaking spatial analysis of a wide variety of social problems since very early in this century. Applied research in American geography dates only from the 1930s, and it was not until the late 1960s that the quest for policy relevance emerged, spawning a considerable body of work on the spatial dimensions of social justice and, to a lesser extent, on environmental impact studies (O'Loughlin, 1975).

Geography, of course, enjoys a special association with the profession of urban planning. Indeed, it is largely through this profession that geography's sophisticated algorithms for optimizing location-allocation influence public policy through planning of service zones for medical, school, and social service facilities (as well as electoral districts). In this prescriptive mode, applied geography fully embraces urban planning's guiding values of efficiency and equity, particularly in its analyses of sociospatial justice (O' Loughlin, 1975).

We turn now from the restricted-domain disciplines to the more encompassing social and behavioral sciences.

F. Sociology

Smelser (1967: 9) regards sociology as being centrally interested in "the *units of social structure* and in *variation of human behavior oriented to social structure*." The concept of social structure refers to any pattern of social interaction that is selective, recurrent, regularized, and regulated by various social controls. The basic units of social structure are social roles (i.e., structured clusters of social norms and expectations) and social organizations (i.e., structured clusters of roles, such as small groups, associations, diffuse collectivities, institutions, and societies). "Behavior oriented to social structure" refers centrally to the broad categories of conformity to and deviance from social roles, and is the province of the major sociological specialization of social psychology.

The theoretical framework of sociology includes a variety of explanatory models: static models (organizing a number of variables to account for structural characteristics), process models (explaining changes in variables within a social structure), and change models (explaining changes of a structure itself). All such models tend to presume substantial multiple causation. Accordingly, sociology has pioneered in the social science application of multivariate statistical analysis procedures, particularly in the form of "path analysis" and related procedures for the causal modeling of nonexperimental (or "correlational") data (Blalock, 1971), and of the survey research method.

The policy relevance of sociology derives chiefly from its special disciplinary interests in social problems, deviant behavior, criminology, and social change. Policy research in sociology (Demarath et al., 1975; Lazarsfeld and Reitz, 1975) is almost entirely descriptive rather than prescriptive, and has heavily concentrated on policy process (particularly on the formulation, implementation, and effects stages) rather than on policy content. However, such research has been of limited applicability (Scott and Shore, 1979), owing in good part to the structural emphasis of the sociological framework, directing attention to variables scarcely amenable to manipulation through practical policies (Davis, 1975; Lazarsfeld and Reitz, 1975).

Sociology contributes most directly to the professions of management (through organizational theory and research) and social work. Some influence of sociology is to be found on urban planning (through human ecology and demography), law (through criminology and the sociology of law), and medicine (through medical sociology).

G. Anthropology

Of all the social science disciplinary domains, anthropology's is the most encompassing—"the science of man." But in this analysis, we must reluctantly leave aside two of anthropology's grand divisions—physical anthropology and archaeology—to focus on the more commensurable division of social and cultural anthropology.

Although anthropology (in this restricted sense) shares sociology's concern with social structure and behavior oriented toward social structure, the distinguishing feature of anthropology's theoretical framework is its preoccupation with *culture*—those meaning systems, norms, rules, standards, and patterns implicit in the social structure, behavior, and artifacts of society. Despite a growing interest in nomothetic comparative studies of societies, anthropology retains a fundamental proclivity for the holistic and idiographic analysis of societies as unique sociocultural patterns. This proclivity stems from the discipline's traditional focus on small, isolated, and "exotic" societies, and gives rise to its doctrinal principle of "cultural relativism." Similarly, this proclivity for holistic and idiographic analysis conditions the characteristic research method of the discipline, namely, ethnographic field work. This ethnographic case study method involves the participative immersion of the investigator in the culture under study, in order that qualitative data gleaned through direct observation and informant and respondent interviewing can be interpreted more faithfully within the broader meaning context of social behavior (a method also employed by some sociologists, but referred to as "participant observation"). Quantitative methods have only slowly gained ground within anthropology.

Applied anthropology arose early in this century in response to the cross-cultural problems of colonial administration (Barnett, 1956), matured within international technical aid and development programs (Spicer, 1954), and has recently focused on inter-ethnic problems in urbanized societies (Redfield, 1973), with particular attention to cultural barriers to effective and equitable service programming. Perhaps the chief contributions of applied anthropology to policy analysis have been (1) its qualitative descriptive method and (2) its identification of cultural ethnocentrism and the difficulties of cross-cultural communication as factors that frequently undermine public policies and programs.

Contributions of applied anthropology to the professions are currently most extensive within medicine and urban planning.

H. Psychology

Of the core policy sciences disciplines, only psychology is not, strictly speaking, a social science but is instead a behavioral science. Although the domain of psychology is comparably encompassing, its conceptual focus is on the *person* rather than on some social or interpersonal unit of analysis. The theoretical framework of psychology focuses on "the individual person as a system of needs, feelings, aptitudes, skills, defenses, and such, or on one or more [personal] processes, such as the learning of skills" (Smelser, 1967: 34).

The professionalization of psychology has gone further than any of the other liberal arts fields (Hughes, 1952), but perhaps only clinical psychology merits designation as a profession. The specializations of experimental and social psychology remain essentially academic disciplines and, therefore, the principal focus of this subsection of our chapter. Psychological social psychology examines the influence of other persons and of social organizations on the individual (as system) and on personal processes. Experimental psychology examines the influence of largely nonsocial environmental factors on personal processes. Nonclinical psychology of these sorts has led the way in the behavioral science application of experimental design and analysis (as a branch of statistics) and in the development of behaviorally based measurement of quantitative variables.

The earliest applied research of some policy relevance in social psychology was Lewinian group dynamics and behavior change (Marrow, 1969); more recent has been the development of community psychology (Mann, 1978), which takes the community as its client. Some psychological applied research, quite like behavioral political science, has examined factors in the behavior of decision makers as individuals. Perhaps the most significant psychological contribution to policy research (Korten et al., 1969) has been the development of the methodology of planned social experimentation and quasi-experimental design (Cook and Campbell, 1979).

Psychology contributes to the professions of social work and medicine (i.e., psychiatry), principally through the branches cf developmental and clinical psychology, but also more recently through behavior modification techniques based on Skinnerian experimental psychology. The discipline also contributes to the profession of management, through the personnel selection and training research of industrial and organizational psychology.

I. History

History, too, is not in the strict sense a social science, even though its subject matter is genuinely social (unlike psychology) and its approach is empirical and explanatory (unlike, say, philosophy). In its study of social life, history is not nomothetic (like, say, sociology) but is idiographic (Gardiner, 1959). This idiographic thrust differs from that of anthropology, however, in that it is generally unguided by the selective ordering principles of any coherent and distinctive theoretical framework. Consequently, a research problem within the discipline of history is one inherent in the logic of events within a particular place and period rather than deriving from a theoretical framework. The research methods of history are generally qualitative and, like those of archaeology, involve drawing defensible interpretative inferences from surviving fragmentary evidence; the discipline has evolved a highly self-critical methodology of historiography to guide such inferences (Kitson Clark, 1967).

Discipline research within this field has traditionally devoted substantial attention to examination of the historical causes and consequences of both particular policies and specific policy-making mechanisms. Indeed, historical causes and consequences are so important in policy analysis that these are typically examined even in descriptive policy studies undertaken by nonhistorians, though too often without benefit of the methodological principles of historiography. The very eclecticism of historical research can itself prove advantageous, encouraging the analyst to seek pertinent causes and consequences from among a wide variety of political, economic, social, cultural, and technological determinants.

V. CONCLUSIONS

Through this review we have shown that *policy analysis*—the study of the nature, causes, and/or consequences of public policies—is an activity engaged in to varying degrees by a very wide range of fields of learning. Professional fields, organized around theories of practice, tend to emphasize prescriptive studies of policy content and process, whereas academic disciplines, organized around theories of fact, more frequently engage in descriptive studies.

For reasons intrinsic to the social organization of fields of learning, *policy research*—as that type of applied research aimed at influencing policy makers—is found to be more prevalent within professional fields than within academic disciplines.

We are led to conclude that *policy science*—as a field of learning devoted to the scientific improvement of policy making—is best conceptualized as an emergent profession that might profitably draw pertinent facts, concepts, principles, theories, and methods from many disciplines (especially economics, political science, sociology, anthropology, and psychology) and from a number of related professions (especially management, urban planning, social work, and law).

REFERENCES

Amacher, R., Tollison, R. D., and Willett, T. D. (Eds.) (1976). *The Economic Approach to Public Policy.* Cornell University Press, Ithaca, NY.

Barnett, H. (1956). *Anthropology in Administration.* Row, Peterson, Chicago.

Beutel, F. K. (1975). *Experimental Jurisprudence and the Scienstate.* Rothman, Littleton, CT.

Blalock, H. M. (Ed.) (1971). *Causal Models in the Social Sciences.* Aldine, Chicago.

Charlesworth, J. (Ed.) (1972). *Integration of the Social Sciences Through Policy Analysis.* American Academy of Political and Social Science, Philadelphia.

Coleman, J. S. (1972). *Policy Research in the Social Sciences.* General Learning Press, Morristown, NJ.

Cook, T. D., and Campbell, D. T. (1979). *Quasi-Experimentation: Design and Analysis Issues for Field Settings.* Rand McNally, Chicago.

Davidoff, P. (1965). Advocacy and pluralism in planning. *Journal of the American Institute of Planners 31* (January): 12–21.

Davis, J. A. (1975). On the remarkable absence of nonacademic implications in academic research: An example from ethnic studies. In *Social Policy and Sociology,* N. J. Demerath, O. Larsen, and K. F. Schuessler (Eds.). Academic, New York.

Demerath, N. J., Larsen, O., and Schuessler, K. F. (Eds.) (1975). *Social Policy and Sociology.* Academic, New York.

Dror, Y. (1971). *Design for Policy Sciences.* Elsevier, New York.

Dye, T. R. (1975). Political science and public policy: Challenge to a discipline. In *The Policy Vacuum,* R. N. Spadaro, T. R. Dye, R. T. Golembiewski, M. S. Stedman, and L. H. Ziegler (Eds.). Lexington Books, Lexington, MA.

Fairley, W., and Mosteller, F. (Eds.) (1977). *Statistics and Public Policy.* Addison-Wesley, Reading, MA.

Frieden, B. J., and Morris, R. (Eds.) (1968). *Urban Planning and Social Policy.* Basic Books, New York.

Friedlander, W. A. (1961). *Introduction to Social Welfare,* 2nd ed. Prentice-Hall, Englewood Cliffs, NJ.

Froman, L. A. (1968). The categorization of policy contents. In *Political Science and Public Policy,* A. Ranney (Ed.). Markham, Chicago.

Gans, H. J. (1968). *People and Plans.* Basic Books, New York.

Gardiner, P. (Ed.) (1959). *Theories of History.* Free Press, New York.

Golding, M. R. (1975). Legal philosophy and policy studies. In *Policy Studies and the Social Sciences,* S. S. Nagel (Ed.). Lexington Books, Lexington, MA.

Golembiewski, R. T. (1975). Public administration and public policy: An analysis of developmental phases. In *The Policy Vacuum,* R. N. Spadaro, T. R. Dye, R. T. Golembiewski, M. S. Stedman, and L. H. Ziegler (Eds.). Lexington Books, Lexington, MA.

Gould, J., and Kolb, W. L. (Eds.) (1964). *A Dictionary of the Social Sciences.* Free Press, New York.

Graham, G. J., and Carey, G. W. (1972). *The Post-Behavioral Era: Perspectives on Political Science.* McKay, New York.

Greenberger, M., Crenson, M., and Crissey, B. (Eds.) (1976). *Models in the Policy Process.* Russell Sage Foundation, New York.

Haggett, P. (1972). *Geography: A Modern Synthesis.* Harper & Row, New York.

Hart, H. M., and McNaughton, J. T. (1971). Some aspects of evidence and inference in the law. In *Evidence and Inference,* D. Lerner (Ed.). Free Press, New York.

Haveman, R., and Hamrin, R. (Eds.) (1973). *The Political Economy of Federal Policy.* Harper & Row, New York.

Horowitz, D. L. (1977). *The Courts and Social Policy.* Brookings Institution, Washington, DC.

Hubin, D. (1971). The people who work at solving social problems. In *Handbook on the Study of Social Problems,* E. O. Smigel (Ed.). Rand McNally, Chicago.

Hughes, E. C. (1952). Psychology: science or profession? *The American Psychologist 7*: 441–443.

—— (1963a). Is education a discipline? In *The Discipline of Education,* J. Walton and J. L. Kuethe (Eds.). University of Wisconsin Press, Madison.

—— (1963b). Professions. *Daedalus 92*: 655–668.

Jones, E. (1975). Law, political science, and policy studies. In *Policy Studies and the Social Sciences,* S. S. Nagel (Ed.). Lexington Books, Lexington, MA.

Kahn, A. J. (1969). *Theory and Practice of Social Planning.* Russell Sage Foundation, New York.

—— (1973). *Social Policy and Social Services.* Random House, New York.

—— (1975). Social work and policy studies. In *Policy Studies and the Social Sciences,* S. S. Nagel (Ed.). Lexington Books, Lexington, MA.

Kitson Clark, G. (1967). *The Critical Historian.* Basic Books, New York.

Korten, F., Cook, S., and Lacey, J. (Eds.) (1969). *Psychology and the Problems of Society.* American Psychological Association, Washington, DC.

Ladd, J. (1975). Policy studies and ethics. In *Policy Studies and the Social Sciences,* S. S. Nagel (Ed.). Lexington Books, Lexington, MA.

Lasswell, H. D. (1956). *The Decision Process.* University of Maryland Press, College Park.

—— (1971). *A Pre-View of Policy Sciences.* Elsevier, New York.

Lazarsfeld, P. F., and Reitz, J. (1975). *An Introduction to Applied Sociology.* Elsevier, New York.

Lerner, D., and Lasswell, H. D. (Eds.) (1951). *The Policy Sciences.* Stanford University Press, Stanford, CA.

Lowi, T. J. (1975). What political scientists don't need to ask about policy analysis. In *Policy Studies and the Social Sciences,* S. S. Nagel (Ed.). Lexington Books, Lexington, MA.

MacRae, D. (1976). *The Social Function of Social Science.* Yale University Press, New Haven, CT.

Mann, P. A. (1978). *Community Psychology.* Free Press, New York.

Marrow, A. J. (1969). *The Practical Theorist: The Life and Works of Kurt Lewin.* Basic Books, New York.

Mayhew, L. H. (1971). Social planning, social control and the law. In *Handbook on the Study of Social Problems,* E. O. Smigel (Ed.). Rand McNally, Chicago.

Mechanic, D. (1969). *Mental Health and Social Policy.* Prentice-Hall, Englewood Cliffs, NJ.

Meyer, H. J. (1968). Social work. In *International Encyclopedia of the Social Sciences*, vol. 14, D. L. Sills (Ed.). Macmillan and Free Press, New York.

Mitchell, J. M., and Mitchell, W. C. (1969). *Political Analysis and Public Policy*. Rand McNally, Chicago.

Nagel, S. S. (Ed.) (1975). *Policy Studies and the Social Sciences*. Lexington Books, Lexington, MA.

—— (1979). Policy studies across the social sciences. *National Forum 69*(1): 9–11.

O'Loughlin, J. (1975). Geographic contributions to policy studies. In *Policy Studies and the Social Sciences*, S. S. Nagel (Ed.). Lexington Books, Lexington, MA.

Patner, M. (1978). Advocacy and the public interest lawyer. In *Social Scientists as Advocates*, G. H. Weber and G. J. McCall (Eds.). Sage, Beverly Hills, CA.

Perrucci, R., and Gerstl, J. E. (1969). *The Engineers and the Social System*. Wiley, New York.

Phillips, L., and Votey, H. (Eds.) (1977). *Economic Analysis of Pressing Social Problems*. Rand McNally, Chicago.

Price, D. K. (1965). *The Scientific Estate*. Harvard University Press, Cambridge, MA.

Radnor, M. (1971). Management sciences and the policy sciences. *Policy Sciences 2*: 447–456.

Ranney, A. (1968). The study of policy content: A framework for choice. In *Political Science and Public Policy*, A. Ranney (Ed.). Markham, Chicago.

Rawls, J. (1971). *A Theory of Justice*. Belknap, Cambridge, MA.

Redfield, A. (Ed.) (1973). *Anthropology Beyond the University*. University of Georgia Press, Athens.

Rosen, G. (1968). Public health. In *International Encyclopedia of the Social Sciences*, vol. 13, D. L. Sills (Ed.). Free Press, New York.

Samuelson, P. A. (1961). *Economics*, 5th ed. McGraw-Hill, New York.

Scott, R. A., and Shore, A. R. (1979). *Why Sociology Does Not Apply: A Study of the Use of Sociology in Public Policy*. Elsevier, New York.

Sharkansky, I. (Ed.) (1970). *Policy Analysis in Political Science*. Markham, Chicago.

Sigler, J., and Beede, B. (1977). *The Legal Sources of Public Policy*. Lexington Books, Lexington, MA.

Simon, H. A. (1947). A comment on "the science of public administration." *Public Administration Review 7*: 202.

—— (1957). *Administrative Behavior: A Study of Decision-Making Processes in Administrative Organization*, 2nd ed. Macmillan, New York.

Smelser, N. J. (1967). Sociology and the other social sciences. In *The Uses of Sociology*, P. F. Lazarsfeld, W. H. Sewell, and H. L. Wilensky (Eds.). Basic Books, New York.

Spadaro, R. N., Dye, T. R., Golembiewski, R. T., Stedman, M. S., and Zeigler, L. H. (Eds.) (1975). *The Policy Vacuum: Toward a More Professional Political Science*. Lexington Books, Lexington, MA.

Spicer, E. (1954). *Human Problems in Technological Change*. Russell Sage Foundation, New York.

van de Vall, M., and Bolas, C. (1980). Applied social discipline research or social policy research: The emergence of a professional paradigm in sociological research. *The American Sociologist 15*: 128–137.

Van Dyke, V. (1968). Process and policy as focal concepts in political research. In *Political Science and Public Policy*, A. Ranney (Ed.). Markham, Chicago.

Wade, L. L. (1975). The public choice approach to policy analysis. In *Policy Studies and the Social Sciences*, S. S. Nagel (Ed.). Lexington Books, Lexington, MA.

Weber, G. H., and McCall, G. J. (1978a). Applied sociology: issues and questions. Paper presented to Southwestern Sociological Association, Houston, Texas.

Weber, G. H., and McCall, G. J. (Eds.) (1978b). *Social Scientists as Advocates: Views from the Applied Disciplines.* Sage, Beverly Hills, CA.

10

The States in the Federal System

Dennis R. Judd / University of Denver, Denver, Colorado

I. WHY STUDY STATE GOVERNMENT?

The allocation of governmental authority within the federal system has long been central to most disputes in our politics. It is difficult to identify an important government service or public policy that has not involved fights over the role of the federal government versus the states and localities. A perceptive observer would be puzzled over the apparent obsession with the *structure* and *form* of making public decisions, as opposed to the *content* of public decisions. As an example, in congressional hearings on the 1963 Clean Air Act, the National Association of Manufacturers, the Manufacturing Chemists Association, the National Coal Association, and the American Iron and Steel Institute sent spokesmen to testify that federal legislation was not necessary; the states and localities should take responsibility for air pollution. The representative for the Manufacturing Chemists Association said that "the general health laws on the books of communities, our cities, our states, are sufficient to deal with air pollution to the degree that it effects health."[1]

Although it might seem that the chemists were motivated by concerns about the structure of federalism, they were, in fact, arguing for state and local control only because they knew that this would guarantee weak air pollution laws. The apparent concern about structure was actually a concern about the substance of air pollution policy. One of the senators present expressed this connection very succinctly: "Are you really concerned with the health of the people? This whole testimony indicates that you think that you as an organization has some closer boring process with the municipal and state government than you do with the vast federal government that represents all the people."[2]

A review of the history of intergovernmental relations reveals that debates over the locus of power in the federal system always are surrogates for the real issue: policy substance. If decisions are made by state and local governments, different groups are represented than if those decisions are made at the national level. That is why it is important to examine the role that state governments play in the federal system.

II. THE STATES' ROLE IN THE EVOLVING FEDERAL SYSTEM

A. The Constitutional Framework

In 1937, the U.S. Supreme Court upheld the constitutionality of the National Labor Relations Act. In embracing the political philosophy of the New Deal, the high court dealt a lethal blow to a constitutional construct that had long overshadowed intergovernmental relations in the United States. The doctrine of "dual federalism" had been maintained by the Court through numerous decisions over the previous 100 years—at least since the death of Chief Justice John Marshall in 1835. The doctrine had been used by constitutional conservatives to justify an extremely circumscribed domestic role for the national government and an enhanced role for the states. Dual federalism held that the national government was sovereign in its sphere, and that the states were also sovereign in the implementation of their functions. Although from our present perspective it might seem difficult to differentiate so clearly national from state concerns—their governmental activities overlap in such complex ways that it is difficult to separate the two— the early constitutional theorists did not find the task so difficult.

The constitution that created our federal system granted the national government rather limited powers. The principal tasks of the federal government seemed largely limited to the national defense, to foreign policy and trade, and to control of the currency. The Tenth Amendment specified that "the Powers not delegated to the United States by the Constitution, nor prohibited by it to the States, are reserved to the States respectively, or to the people." The framers of the Constitution obviously intended this amendment as a check against the powers of the federal government; it is the only amendment of the first 10 which does not guarantee specific rights to individuals.

The powers of the federal government are enumerated in Article I, Section 8. It is important to note that the basic services that governments provide—police, education, public health, relief, and so on—are not mentioned in the Constitution. The provision of these services are left to the states. Local governments are not mentioned at all in the Constitution. In sum, states were sovereign governments that agreed to cooperate in the creation of the federal government, which was also a sovereign government with enumerated powers. Local governments were not sovereign at all. If there was any doubt about this, it was cleared up in 1918 by the Supreme Court, which held in the *Dartmouth College* case that cities were nothing but creatures of the states, whose charters could be amended (or even rescinded) at will.[3] Thus the term dual federalism: The states and the federal government were granted separate constitutional status. Since local governments did not figure in the constitutional scheme, it was a two-tier federal system.

B. The Evolution of Federal Relations

In his classic work, *The American Partnership*, Daniel J. Elazar convincingly demonstrated that although the ideology of dual federalism had dominated political thought on intergovernmental relations up to the New Deal period, the evidence of government activity clearly demonstrated that it was often violated.[4] Elazar closely detailed myriad ways in which the national government had influenced policies at the state and local level. For example, Congress promoted national expansion through a massive program of internal improvements. The creation of the Corps of Engineers (1802) and the Board of

Internal Improvements (1924) were evidence of congressional intentions to secure new territory. The Corps of Engineers was used extensively to assist in the construction of numerous canals and navigable waterways.

The national government utilized land grants to promote many of its purposes. Over the years, the federal government conveyed nearly 13.1 million acres of land to the state of Minnesota for the purpose of aiding railroad construction—fully one-fourth of the land area of the state. In this case, even the general routes of the railroads were dictated by Congress, underscoring its active role in directing national expansion. These and other railways were crucial in opening the frontier west of the Mississippi and in populating the Great Plains.

In attempting to open up the western territories, the national government ultimately gave away about one-sixth of the total land area of the United States to states or to private corporations. It should be noted that this was not always in strict pursuit of a conscious policy to promote westward expansion. As detailed in much of the literature on railroad building in the nineteenth century—most notably Dee Brown's book, *Hear the Lonesome Whistle Blow*, part of the government's keen desire to aid the railroads was fueled by corruption on a scale that has probably never been approached since.[5]

Several pieces of congressional legislation had the express or implied intention of populating the nation's frontier. In 1788, the national government provided grants of land to veterans of the Revolution who had been in the national service. Although primarily a payment for services rendered, this action had the obvious effect of encouraging the population of the territory beyond the Ohio. Several homestead and preemption acts, tree culture acts, and townsite election acts facilitated the disposal of national lands in a manner designed to populate the interior and expand the nation. Best known is the Homestead Act of 1862, through which a million families received title to more than 240,000 acres of national land.[6]

Despite the obviously cooperative nature of the federal system, the doctrine of dual federalism was kept very much alive. The national government was constrained from effectively regulating economic activity and refrained from participating in "social" policy. It was said that the federal government dealt with foreign governments and with the states, not with individuals. It was only the availability of public lands that had given the federal government a strong influence over national policy. Federal budgets remained so small for most of the nineteenth century that the federal treasury ran surpluses even though duties and tariffs supplied most of its income. Between 1816 and 1836, there were only three deficits in the federal budget, and these were insignificant and probably inadvertent.[7] Budget surpluses were a chronic problem. In 1836, Congress passed legislation to distribute some of the surplus federal money to the states. It was not conceived that the national government ought to spend more or take on increased responsibilities in order to use up its surpluses. Rather, the distribution measure—the first "revenue sharing" scheme to be implemented in the United States—was designed to help the states finance internal improvements.

Following the Civil War, the limited realm of federal responsibility again made it difficult for the national government to spend its limited funds. From 1866 to 1893, one budgetary surplus followed another, with only the exception of a minor deficit in 1874.[8] Despite the repeal of one tax after another, the problem of too much income

Table 1. Federal Grant-in-Aid Expenditures, 1915–1931 (in thousands of dollars)

Program	1915	1920	1925	1929	1931
Highways		62,535	95,750	82,097	135,593
Agricultural experiment stations	1438	1,440	1,440	3,840	4,340
Agricultural extension work	480	4,472	5,879	7,151	8,650
Agricultural and mechanical colleges	2500	2,500	2,550	2,550	2,550
Forestry aids	70	95	399	1,393	1,779
Vocational education		2,477	5,615	6,879	7,879
Public health		2,324	611	650	887
Maternal and child health			933	777	

Source: Adapted from M. Grodzins, *The American System: A New View of Government in the United States* (Rand McNally, Chicago, 1966), p. 49.

continued to plague the Treasury Department. But the political philosophy of time did not allow an expansion in the responsibilities of the federal government.

The only serious attempt to intrude the national government directly into social policy came in 1854, when Congress approved legislation to use income from sales of federal land to help the states provide for support of the indigent insane. The legislation was vetoed by President Franklin Pierce, on the ground that it would set the precedent "to transfer to the Federal Government the charge of all the poor in all the States," which would subvert "the whole theory upon which the Union of these States is founded."[9] Like the Presidents before him, President Pierce believed that "the minimum of federal government should afford the rule and measure of construction of our powers under the general clauses of the Constitution."[10]

After the turn of the century, the federal government ventured into some grant-in-aid programs, but by any modern standard—or, for that matter, any standard at all—these were small indeed. In 1914, Congress passed legislation that allowed the Department of Agriculture to hire agricultural extension agents to work with land grant colleges. These agents later were granted the responsibility of working with individual farmers and with rural governments. In 1916, Congress passed the Federal Aid Road Act. This legislation provided grants-in-aid to state highway departments for the purpose of building and improving rural roads. Designed to "get the farmer out of the mud," the road funds were administered through the Department of Agriculture. Finally, Congress passed a Vocational Education Act in 1917, which authorized the federal government to help pay teachers' salaries and other personnel in state vocational education institutions. A small vocational rehabilitation program to help retrain injured workers was passed in 1920. By 1931, highway grants-in-aid accounted for 83 percent of grant-in-aid expenditures of the federal government (refer to Table 1). Agriculture (9.5 percent) and vocational education (5.4 percent) made up most of the rest. From 1915 to 1931, grant-in-aid expenditures by the government increased from $5.5 million to $163 million. But in the latter year, the grant-in-aid expenditures still constituted less than 3 percent of all federal expenditures.[11] In 1890, the national government had spent 36.2 percent of the public monies in the United States. The rest was accounted for by state and local governments. By 1932, the federal proportion had actually declined, to 35.4 percent.[12]

Thus, until the early 1930s, the federal government remained far removed from any significant participation in social policy. Education, housing, health, welfare, and nearly all other areas of policy were chiefly local, and often private, but with increasing state participation between 1900 and 1930. In the first thirty years of the 20th century, several states undertook programs to provide relief for dependent children, orphans, the mentally ill, and the aged. The states expanded and consolidated their influence over education policy, passing statutes specifying minimum teacher education requirements, and passing truancy laws and minimum education laws. The states also moved to regulate medical and legal education. In fact, nearly all of the literature that refers to the states as "laboratories of reform" cite this period; not before or since have the states been so active in exploring new policy options.

C. The Alleged Decline of the States

One of the earliest scholarly studies of the New Deal began with the observation that "increasing activities of the federal government under the New Deal have made the issue of centralization one of sharply increasing importance in the last decade. The New Deal has been savagely attacked for undermining the essentials of American government."[13] This observation was founded upon the fact that the federal government had vastly expanded its powers during the Great Depression. The old principals of constitutional federalism had been challenged. The Social Security Act of 1935 created a permanent federal involvement in unemployment insurance and welfare policy. The Federal Emergency Relief Act, Works Progress Administration (WPA) and other programs provided relief and jobs to millions of citizens. When state governments were unable or unwilling to implement these programs under federal guidance, the federal administrators set up their own offices and did it themselves, or worked with local officials.

There was widespread disillusionment concerning the ability or willingness of the states to respond to the economic emergency. By March 1933, when Franklin Delano Roosevelt was inaugurated as President, the Depression had reached such crisis proportions that the tradition of the decentralized government seemed to be an inadequate or irrelevant historical anachronism. The popular mood favored revolutionary change. Al Smith, the Democratic candidate for President in 1928, compared the Depression to a wartime emergency, and gave this advice: "In the world war we took our constitution, wrapped it up and laid it on the shelf, and left it there until it was over."[14] Many of the nation's business and political leaders were ready to cast aside "outdated" constitutional principles.

State governments were thought to be, in general, corrupt, ineffectual, or unconcerned. They were often considered so irrelevant that they would cease to play any significant role in the intergovernmental system at all. For example, in 1933, a well-known political scientist asked the question, "Is the state the appropriate instrumentality for the discharge of . . . sovereign functions?" His answer was that: "The answer is not a matter of conjecture or delicate appraisal. It is a matter of brutal record. The American State is finished. I do not predict that the States will go, but affirm that they have gone."[15]

The attitude expressed in this statement was based on the observation than in important new policy areas, the states had, in most instances, a relatively minor role to play. During the early years of the Depression, while municipal governments' expenditures for jobs and relief skyrocketed, the states cut expenses: "As tax revenues dwindled, and unemployment increased, economy in government became the magic word."[16] As state tax revenues declined, wholesale reductions were made in public works and construction programs. The states compounded the unemployment crisis. In other governmental areas as well, the states failed to respond to the economic crisis. Local officials petitioned the states for employment, public works, and relief programs, but their pleas fell on deaf ears. Except in a very few states, no response was forthcoming. For the most part, governors were unconcerned about what state government might do to alleviate the problems of the Depression. For example, at the 1930 Governors' Conference in Salt Lake City, the major topics of discussion included such weighty matters as "The Essentials of a Model State Constitution," "The Need for Constitutional Revisions," "Constitutional Versus Legislative Home Rule for Cities," and "The Extent of Legislative Control of City Government."[17]

The frustrations felt by local officials led them to seek direct ties with the federal government. Local officials found a ready ally. The Roosevelt administration had encountered a multitude of problems in attempting to administer the WPA and other programs through state governors' offices. State legislatures refused to appropriate matching funds. Politicians attempted to use public works money to enrich themselves and their friends. Partly as a result of problems like these, the New Deal often bypassed the states and dealt with the cities. The Civil Works Administration, the Public Works Administration, and especially the WPA operated with federal-city lines of communication. This startling development prompted one observer to note that "municipalities in this country are no longer mere political subdivisions of the several states. We are now entering upon a recognized new relation of the urban citizenry with the citizenry of the nation itself."[18] The establishment of federal-local ties provided the model for important subsequent legislation. For example, the United States Housing Act of 1937 established federal grants-in-aid to local governments. This example was followed in the 1949 Housing and Urban Development Act, which was administered through local housing authorities and local public housing authorities.

But these developments—the expansion of national authority, and the federal-city linkage—did not spell doom for the states. In fact, New Deal administrators undoubtedly strengthened the states in critical respects. Administration of government programs strictly through federal agencies was a rarity, even during the New Deal. The Social Security Trust Fund for the aged was the only important contribution by the New Deal to direct national administration. All other important programs were administered as grants-in-aid to state and local governments—and the 1937 Housing Act, and public works, were the only ones with direct federal-local connections. And in most cases, even the WPA programs depended on state and local officials (very frequently state officials) to screen applicants and identify public projects. Cooperative state governments had close relationships with federal officials; only recalcitrant officials found themselves left out.

Most of the New Deal programs proceeded through grants-in-aid to state and local governments. Usually these required state matching funds. For example, the Federal Emergency Relief Act, passed in May 1933, required $3 in state funds for each $1

Table 2. Federal Grant-in-Aid Expenditures, 1933–1941 (in thousands of dollars)

Program	1933	1935	1937	1939	1941
Highways	101,266	12,657	86,602	181,084	165,900
Agricultural experiment stations	4,359	4,384	5,611	6,538	6,861
Agricultural extension work	8,607	8,580	16,343	17,822	18,477
Agricultural and mechanical colleges	2,550	2,550	4,030	5,030	5,030
Forestry aids	1,817	1,547	1,737	1,883	1,081
Vocational education	7,726	9,997	9,695	19,533	20,068
Vocational rehabilitation	993	1,029	1,585	1,799	2,217
Public health	421	264	7,765	10,346	16,236
Maternal and child health			3,002	3,739	5,471
Crippled children			1,991	3,029	3,928
Child welfare			969	1,521	1,532
Assistance for the elderly			124,585	210,160	259,781
Aid to dependent children			14,789	31,467	62,991
Aid to the blind			4,560	5,272	7,073
Employment security		1,927	12,243	62,338	66,199
Annual contributions, public housing					4,764

Source: Adapted from M. Grodzins, *The American System: A New View of Government in the United States* (Rand McNally, Chicago: 1966), pp. 49–50.

granted to a state by the federal government. When most states refused or were unable to come up with matching grants, the legislation was amended to allow grants-in-aid without matching state funds.

Most of the programs included in the Social Security Act of 1935—Aid to Dependent Children, Assistance to the Aged, Aid to the Blind, and Employment Security (unemployment insurance)—were administered by state administrative agencies which received specified grants from the federal government. Although the federal government did require centralized state administration and uniform auditing practices, the states were free to set most eligibility criteria to determine levels of aid, and to determine the minimum and maximum support levels. Like most grant-in-aid programs, the welfare and unemployment insurance programs were highly decentralized in operation.

Table 2 reveals the popularity of the grant-in-aid device. With only the exception of public housing, *all* of the programs listed in the table were administered through state agencies. As a result of the Social Security Act programs, the state became heavily involved in welfare programs—these programs, in fact, became a major aspect of state budgets. Using the states as primary implementors of social policy did more to strengthen the states than any other development in American history.

Programs adopted after World War II followed the grant-in-aid precedent. The 1949 Housing and Urban Development Act provided grants-in-aid to local urban renewal authorities, housing authorities and public housing authorities. In the Urban Renewal Program, local urban renewal administrators were given authority over site selection, selection of contractors, and the planning of new developments. All of this took place under general federal guidelines dictating that most new development had to be residential. The essentially local nature of the public housing program is illustrated by the political problems involved in site selection. Between 1949 and the end of 1952, public housing programs were rejected by referenda in 40 communities, including several of the largest cities: Akron, Houston, and Los Angeles.[19] Urban renewal was the pre-1960s program that confirmed the direct tie between the federal government and local communities.

Other programs confirmed the grant-in-aid relationship between the federal government and the states. For example, the 1956 National Defense Highway Act was implemented through grants-in-aid to state highway departments. Under the terms of the act, the federal contribution toward the construction of interstate highways was 90 percent, with a 10 percent matching share required of the states. Although the federal government retained primary influence over route selection, most administrative decisions were left to the highway departments.

D. Social Policy in the 1960s: The Attempts to Dismantle Traditional Federalism

During the 1960s, there was a purposeful attempt to reform and change the intergovernmental system. Presidents Kennedy and Johnson were impatient for implementation of the New Frontier and the Great Society: They would not brook opposition or foot-dragging simply because states and localities were captured by conservative political elements. Virtually every piece of legislation called for new institutional arrangements. Ninety percent of the legislation administered by HEW in 1968, for example, made non-profit organizations, special districts, or newly created government entities chiefly responsible for implementation, thus bypassing city hall and the State House.[20]

Another distinguishing characteristic of the Democratic administrations was the preoccupation with issues of equality and equity. There is scarcely a piece of social legislation enacted between 1964 and 1968 that was not specifically addressed to the issues of poverty, race, and equality of opportunity. The social and political conditions were ripe for the rapid enactment of major domestic reforms. Under the close personal leadership of President Lyndon Johnson there

> . . . was a massive breakthrough in domestic legislation directed at states, local governments, and other public-private instrumentalities for the purpose of achieving national programs and goals.[21]

This legislative outpouring produced a great many programs and policies that were to have a lasting impact on the pattern of intergovernmental relations in America. The first of four such major developments was a dramatic change in the nature of grants-in-aid. Project grants increasingly became the primary tool of achieving national intent. By 1969, project grants represented 83 percent of all aid actually given.[22] The significance of the project-type grant over the previously dominant formula-type grant lay in the discretionary manner in which allocations could be made. This forced competition among the potential recipients, reducing cooperation among them while at the same time increasing the administrative leverage of the national bureaucracy over state and local authorities—significantly affecting the nature and quality of intergovernmental relations.

A second major change dealt with the substantive nature of the exploding grant-in-aid system. The authority of the national government was, for the first time, injected into some of the most sacred areas of local and state control. Education, elections, and law enforcement, for example, were made subjects of national intent through the Elementary and Secondary Education Act, Voting Rights Act, and Safe Streets and Crime Control Act, respectively. Both the Economic Opportunity Act and the Model Cities legislation attempted to alter the social and political structure by creating local programs independent of established political elites.

Heretofore, the policy norm was for the national government to utilize state and local administrative agencies to implement national programs. Now these governments were frequently bypassed. The impact was dramatic. States and localities no longer implemented their own policies, but were called upon to implement those of the national government. And the national government, in search of effective means of implementation, went so far as to circumvent these governments altogether and utilize special purpose and private instrumentalities for promulgation of the national intent. This new posture—the national purpose through the most efficient or appropriate means—was to have a dramatic impact on the nature of intergovernmental relations. It was the most important development marking the 1960s as a unique era in intergovernmental relations.

E. The Reaction to Federal Activism: "Return Power to State and Local Governments"

Immediately following his 1968 election victory, President Nixon emphasized his desire to decentralize governmental domestic programs, and he became more outspoken on the subject during 1971 and 1972. In his 1969 revenue sharing message, he spoke of the grant programs as producing a "gathering of the reins of power in Washington," which he saw as "a radical departure from the vision of federal-state relations the nation's founders had in mind." He referred to his proposal as "a turning point in federal-state relations, a beginning of decentralized relations of governmental power, the restoration of a rightful balance between the state capitol and the national capitol."[23] This was a rather modest statement of the theme to which he was to turn many times, perhaps most pointedly in his October 21, 1972 radio address on "The Philosophy of Government":

> Do we want to turn more power over to bureaucrats in Washington in the hope that they will do what is best for all the people? Or do we want to return more power to the people and to the state and local governments so that people can decide what is best for themselves? It is time that good, decent people stopped letting themselves be bulldozed by anybody who presumes to be the self-righteous moral judge of our society. In the next four years, as in the past four, I will continue to direct the flow of power away from Washington and back to the people.[24]

Nixon's philosophy was implemented through the New Federalism, which had the expressed objective of decentralizing the political authority and financial capacity of the federal government and dismantling the intergovernmental system of the Great Society.

Through the State and Local Fiscal Assistance Act of 1972 (revenue sharing), an attempt was made to simplify procedures under which state and local governments were given authority to spend federal revenues. The revenue sharing program was accompanied by a strong effort to dismantle many of the Great Society programs. In 1973 and 1974, many of the important social programs—including the antipoverty program and model cities, urban renewal, and housing legislation—were folded into broad bloc grants carrying relatively few restrictions with regard to purpose or method. State and local governments found, for example, that under the Community Development Act of 1974, they were able to devise and implement plans tailored to their own priorities, and to escape the constraints of stringent oversight previously characteristic of the federal grant-in-aid process.

The Nixon reaction had the support of a very large political coalition. By the 1976 presidential campaign, politicians of all political persuasions had rallied around the new political issue. During the 1960s, conservatives had railed against the growth and size of the federal bureaucracy, whereas liberals had defended the expansion of federal power to accomplish national objectives. By 1976, both Ford and Carter campaigned on promises that they would seek cutbacks and reform in the federal bureaucracy and that they would continue to decentralize governmental power. In his speeches about the national bureaucracy, Carter sounded very much like the Nixon of 1968. But Carter's programs failed to go far enough. The Reagan landslide of 1980 represented, in part, a continuation of the "anti-big government" reaction to the 1960s.

III. THE PUSH FOR DECENTRALIZATION: WILL IT IMPROVE GOVERNMENT PERFORMANCE?

An observer of intergovernmental relations over the past 30 years might conclude that our politics move in cycles. In 1957, President Eisenhower appointed a joint Federal-State Action Committee, whose purpose was to find federal programs that could be turned back to the states. The President had the impression that the New Deal had centralized a great many programs at the federal level. The committee could come up with only two programs that they thought should be turned back to the states: vocational education and waste treatment grants. Nevertheless, the intention to decentralize the governmental system was there. Soon after, under the Kennedy and Johnson administrations, the power gravitated to the federal bureaucracies. This phase lasted about eight years; first President Nixon, then all of the subsequent Presidents, campaigned against a federal Establishment. The finishing touch was put on by the results of the 1980 election, with promises by the Republican presidential candidate, Ronald Reagan, to abolish the Education and Energy Departments, and drastically to curtail federal domestic spending. It might appear that we had gone full circle, and returned to the Eisenhower years.

Despite the superficial evidence, intergovernmental relations are not strictly cyclical. There is no returning to "dual federalism," if it ever existed. There is no possibility, in fact, of even returning to a pre-New Deal federalism. And it is not plausible to think that the national government will disinvest itself of social problems such as Social Security, welfare, and unemployment insurance. By now, Medicaid and Medicare are too legitimated. Air and water pollution control are well established, even though some funding levels may drop. Aid for the cities has the backing of a very large coalition of Democratic and Republican members of Congress, mayors, civil rights leaders, and other groups. Methods of administration and funding levels are the subject of very lively debate, but it is highly unlikely that the federal government will abandon its social welfare responsibilities.

Nevertheless, there has been a very strong reaction to federal bureaucracy, and it has enjoyed a considerable staying power. Most government programs have been decentralized over the past several years, by converting them into bloc grant arrangements, or by reducing funding requirements.

A. The Intricacies of the Federal System

The concept of decentralization can be looked at in two principal ways. First, it is often used as a code word for reducing overall spending by the federal government, thus moving the burden or providing government services to state and local governments. Second, it is typically used to describe a process whereby the federal government exerts less direct influence over the content of programs, even if federal funds are involved. Clearly, it is possible to decentralize programs without reducing overall federal expenditures. However, in the last few presidential campaigns, politicians have used the term to describe both a reduced federal financial commitment *and* lesser federal influence.

The intricacies of the federal system practically guarantee that states and localities will continue to be central in the provision of most government services, regardless of the extent of the federal role. The same intricacies guarantee that the federal government is not likely to withdraw from most of its major commitments. There are several reasons

Table 3. Major Sources of Federal, State, and Local Tax Revenue, 1948 and 1978

	General tax revenue					
	Federal		State		Local	
Type of tax	1948	1978[a]	1948	1978[a]	1948	1978[a]
	Percent					
Individual income	51.0	65.8	7.4	26.1	9.7	5.3[b]
Corporate income	25.6	21.7	8.7	9.0		
General sales			21.9	30.3	3.2	7.7
Selective sales and excise	20.2[c]	9.9[c]	34.2	17.9	2.9	3.3
Property			4.1	2.0	88.6	80.1
Estate and gift	2.3	2.1	2.7	1.8		
Motor vehicle			8.8	4.3		
Other	0.9	0.6	12.3	8.6	4.6	3.6
	Billions of dollars					
Total amount	37.9	271.8	6.7	114.0	6.6	81.5

[a]Estimate.
[b]Includes minor amounts of corporation income tax revenue.
[c]Includes custom duties.
Source: G. F. Break, *Financing Government in a Federal System* (Brookings Institution, Washington, DC, 1980), p. 10.

Table 4.   Role of State Grants-in-Aid in Local Finance, Selected Fiscal Years, 1902–77

Fiscal year	Total grants (billions of dollars)	Percent of total local revenue	Percent of aid used to finance			
			Education	Public welfare	Highways	General government
1902	0.1	6.1	86		4	10
1922	0.3	8.1	65	1	22	11
1927	0.6	10.1	49	1	33	16
1932	0.8	14.1	50	4	29	18
1942	1.8	25.0	44	22	19	13
1950	4.2	30.1	49	19	14	11
1952	5.0	29.8	50	19	14	11
1957	7.4	29.1	57	15	15	9
1962	10.9	28.4	59	16	12	8
1967	19.1	32.7	62	15	10	8
1970	28.9	35.7	59	17	8	10
1972	36.8	33.4	58	19	7	10
1977	61.1	34.1	60	14	6	10

Source: G. F. Break, *Financing Government in a Federal System* (Brookings Institution, Washington, DC, 1980), p. 180.

why this is the case. One important reason is that state and local governments have a very large built-in reliance on the infusion of federal funds to help them provide services which, though federal monies are involved, are labeled "state and local" in character. Approximately one dollar out of every three in state and local budgets has come from the federal treasury. Much of this money flows to the states to assist in relief programs, highway construction, public health, and education. Between 1963 and 1973, state and local tax collections rose 147 percent, from $234 per capita to $577 per capita. But federal grants to these governments increased by 361 percent, and by 1973 federal grants constituted 32.6 percent of state and local tax collections, up from 18.9 percent in 1963.[25] A powerful constituency made up of governors, mayors and hundreds of local officials, Democrat and Republican alike, defend continuance of the grant system.

During the 1980 campaign, Ronald Reagan talked about reducing federal taxation in order that state and local governments would have a greater ability to raise tax revenues and therefore finance government services on their own. Such a proposal is not very realistic. If one considers the tax capacity of the federal government in comparison to state and local governments, it is obvious that the national government has a much greater capacity to collect taxes. Table 3 shows the sources of tax revenues for federal, state, and local governments. Obviously, the federal government has the lion's share of individual and corporate income taxes. States rely to a much greater extent on other sources of taxation, especially sales and excise taxes. Local governments are especially reliant on property taxes. Even if the federal government were to reduce the level of personal and corporate taxation, it is very doubtful that taxpayers would be willing to allow an increase in the tax burden imposed by state and local governments. The tax revolt of the last several years has insured that state and local governments will find it difficult to resist actual reductions in tax revenue and tax rates.

Already, states and localities are providing a great many services. In 1973, 75.8 percent of all government expenditures in the United States occurred at the state and local levels—if federal intergovernmental programs that are "built into" state and local budgets are included. Even if the federal share of these budgets is completely excluded, 58.4 percent of all government expenditures in 1973 were dispersed by state and local governments.[26] If federal spending for social insurance programs is not counted, state and local governments spend more than 80 percent of government budgets in the United States.[27]

As George Break has indicated, "state governments are deeply involved in the intergovernmental grant business"[28]—so involved, in fact, that the system could not operate without them. The states play three primary roles: They receive federal funds for their own programs; they transfer federal funds to localities; and they dispense grants directly to local governments. In 1977, the states sent $62 billion in grants to localities. This was almost as much as the $68.4 billion in intergovernmental grants provided by the federal government.[29]

Most of the federal money passed through by states to localities are targeted for public welfare and education. But the grant system is so intricate that it is nearly impossible to trace the precise amount of money that has been generated by the states and then passed to localities, and how much of it is indirectly traced to federal funds.

The dependence on the federal government by the states is very large, and the dependence by local government on both federal and state governments is overwhelming. A look at Table 4 clarifies the degree of dependence. By 1977, 34 percent of local revenues came from state grants. Combined with direct federal grants to localities, it is very commonly the case that large cities derive more than half of their budgets through intergovernmental revenues.

Table 5 indicates the major purposes of state grants to local governments. Education takes by far the largest proportion—an average of 57 percent for all the states—and public welfare comes second. Education, public welfare, and highways account for more than 80 percent of all state payments to local governments.

All these data indicate that the intergovernmental system is so complex that it defies accurate description. Nearly all governmental services are financed by all levels of government. Even when it appears that the bulk of financing originates at state and local levels, the federal government is often involved indirectly through revenue sharing or other transfer payments. Local governments are extraordinarily dependent on the states. In turn, the states receive a very high proportion of their budgets from the federal government.

Even if the federal grant-in-aid role does not appreciably decline, obviously decentralization can be accomplished by removing compliance requirements. Up to now, federal intergovernmental aid has often come in the form of project grants, which carry specific oversight procedures from administrative bureaucracies, require application for specific projects, such as airport construction, highway building, and the like. Project grants carry a great many rules and regulations regarding the expenditure of monies. In contrast, 87 percent of all state grants to localities in 1972 were formula-type grants.[30] If the federal government were to abandon project grants in favor of formula grants, bloc grants, or

Table 5. State Intergovernmental Payments, by Purpose, 1973

	Transfer payments	
Purpose	Millions of dollars	Percentage of total
Specific		
Education	23,316	57.1
Public welfare	7,532	18.5
Highways	2,953	7.2
Other	2,742	6.7
Total	36,542	89.5
General	4,280	10.5
Total	40,822	100.0

Source: Census Bureau, *State Government Finances in 1973,* p. 38, as presented in James A. Maxwell and J. Richard Aronson, *Financing State and Local Governments,* 3rd ed. (The Brookings Institution, Washington, DC, 1977), p. 85.

revenue sharing procedures, the federal government would continue to play a very large fiscal role in the intergovernmental system, but a much smaller policy role. This is, in fact, the direction that the Reagan administration can be expected to pursue.

B. Do States Do Better Than the Feds?

The idea that the federal system should be decentralized is supported by several assumptions regarding the ability of state and local governments to provide services efficiently and effectively. It is very difficult to compare the various levels of government by these criteria, which is one of the reasons why politicians typically resort to dramatic examples to prove their point. It may be useful to consider some evidence regarding the premises underlying the arguments for decentralization.

Critics of the federal government have often argued that the states are the policy innovators in the federal system. They cite many examples: In 1911, Wisconsin became the first state to adopt an income tax, two years before the federal income tax law. The states during the progressive period adopted streamlined budgeting accounting systems, which preceded the Federal Budget and Accounting Act of 1921. The states provided old age insurance, unemployment insurance, and categorical public assistance during the progressive period, but the federal government did not participate in such programs until the Social Security Act of 1935.[31]

Other scholars have argued that state government is closer to the people, and therefore more responsive.[32] They have also argued that states compete with each other in the provision of government services, and thus encourage maximum experimentation.

Although many examples of state innovation can be found, it is easy to find examples in which control of policy by the states has led to rather perverse policy results. Public assistance and employment insurance is a good example. In 1911 Illinois and Missouri became the first states to adopt mothers' aid. California and Colorado followed in 1912, and in 1913, 14 more states passed mothers' aid legislation.[33] Many states also adopted categorical aid programs for the aged, the blind, and the disabled. Wisconsin

established the first aid-to-the-blind program in 1907. By 1934, 24 of the states had enacted aid-to-the-blind programs. Arizona passed a pension program in 1915, but a state
court subsequently declared it unconstitutional. Montana and Nevada were the first
states to adopt official old age assistance programs in 1923. By 1934, 28 states had adopted assistance for the elderly.[34]

But state enactment of legislation was not usually followed by a widespread extension of funded programs. As late as 1934, one year before the Congress passed the Social
Security Act, only 11 of the 24 states that had programs for the blind provided any state
financial role.[35] In most of the states, the legislatures had simply empowered counties
or local governments to provide categorical aid to the blind. In four of the 24 states, no
funds at all were spent, even by the local governments. Of the 28 states with assistance
for the elderly, only 16 had ever appropriated any money for these programs. And although 45 states had enacted mothers'-aid legislation by 1934, the number of persons
receiving aid was very small. New Mexico, Arkansas, and Mississippi had not enacted any
mothers'-aid legislation at all. In Alabama, Georgia, and South Carolina, there was no
state financial role. In the other 42 states that had enacted mothers' aid, only half of the
counties participated in the program.

The fact that only three or four states provided relief to any appreciable degree, and
that most states did not even have an administrative structure that could distribute large
amounts of relief, helped to lead to the Social Security Act. The purposes of the Social
Security Act went beyond fiscal aid to the states. The legislation forced a degree of administrative competence. To participate, states were required to establish state welfare
agencies which would coordinate and supervise activities of the local offices. They also
were required to adopt uniform accounting procedures.

Nevertheless, states were granted wide discretion in the administration of federally
assisted relief and unemployment insurance. They retained authority to adopt their own
residency requirements, benefit levels, and to impose their own definition of "need."
The states were not required to supply a minimum level of relief or unemployment insurance. The effect of this structure was to guarantee wide variations in benefit levels and eligibility requirements. In 1941, benefit levels for unemployment insurance ranged from
$5.90 in the state with lowest benefits, to $14.57 in the state with the highest.[36] In
June 1947, the average payment for a family in aid to dependent children programs was
$101.47 in California, but $31.60 in neighboring Nevada.[37] In Mississippi the average
grant was $26.43. Assistance for the elderly ranged from $7.18 in Colorado to $16.38
in Mississippi.[38]

Although many liberals had argued that the problems of unemployment and poverty
were national in scope, and thus that a national program was required, the Social Security
Act created state programs with federal assistance. The consequence was to create a
patchwork system of great inequity, which maximized the potential for abuse by Southern states to enforce racist standards, and by many states that used public aid as a way
to discipline the poor and keep them in their place.

Civil rights provides another example in which state "innovation" led to perverse
policy results. From the passage of the Civil Rights Act of 1875, which was subsequently
declared unconstitutional by the Supreme Court, Congress enacted no civil rights legislation until 1957. For most of this period, the Supreme Court generally upheld the legal

right of the states to enact legislation that discriminated against blacks. The absence of a federal role gave carte blanche to Southern and border states to devise comprehensive systems of legal segregation, to deny blacks equal education, service on juries, and basic protection from violence and intimidation. When the federal government began to assert greater authority, especially following the *Brown vs. Topeka Board of Education* decision of 1954, state authorities adamantly resisted. Federal marshalls and federal troops were repeatedly resisted by governors, state legislators, and by mobs encouraged by the state officials. It is clear that without federal intervention, hundreds of black and white civil rights activists would have lost their lives in the civil rights protests of the 1950s and 1960s. It is also clear that without the Civil Rights Act of 1964, blacks would not have gained basic constitutional guarantees. It is clear that the states could not be relied upon for "innovation" in civil rights.

Although it can be argued that civil rights is an extreme and atypical case, recent evidence indicates that the states are usually quicker to adopt new policies or policy innovations if the federal government is involved. When two political scientists measured how long it took the states to adopt 63 different policies or policy innovations, they found that the states consistently were quicker in adopting policies if the federal government led the way by providing grant programs.[39] Further, they found that policies which carried substantial penalties for nonparticipation were most widely adopted.

When the federal government is not involved, the rate of policy diffusion among the states varies greatly. States with higher income levels and more advanced economic development adopt policy innovations faster than poorer and less economically developed states.[40] Left on their own, some states will innovate, although many or most will not; with the encouragement of the federal government, policy becomes more uniform across the nation.

The history of legislation on clean air and clean water illustrate these points. In 1948, Congress passed the first legislation governing water pollution. The Water Pollution Control Act provided temporary authority for the federal government to give loans to states and localities for waste treatment plant construction. In 1956, Congress passed the Water Pollution Control Act amendments, which granted permanent authority to the federal government to make outright grants (instead of loans) for treatment plant construction. The states were left as the primary enforcers of water pollution control. Over the subsequent history of water pollution legislation, one of the foremost issues was federal versus state control. When the states were the primary enforcers, enforcement was weak or practically nonexistent.

The nation went through the same experience with regard to clean air legislation. For example, the 1967 Clean Air Act was crippled in its enforcement provisions. The obstacles to enforcement have been described as follows:

> . . . those seeking industry action to reduce polluting discharges had an impossible task. They had to demonstrate benefit impossible to assess on a plant by plant basis; often lengthy and detailed health studies taking years of work were necessary to provide data adequate to defeat arguments by high paid lawyers hired by the industry. An industry was always able to document the cost of control in excruciating detail. Since under these . . . laws a new plant had to meet only locally determined environmental regulations, industries would shop around and locate where the

pollution-abatement requirements were the most permissive. Each community was truly faced with the growth versus no-growth choice.[41]

Communities were put into a competitive position, and so were the states.

Without the entrance of the federal government, air pollution policy enforcement would not have gone forward to any great extent, because the states were doing so little. In 1963, there was air pollution legislation on the books in only 16 states.[42] In 1961, 33 of the 50 states spent less than a total of $5000 each on air pollution. The state expenditures increased from $2 million in 1961, to $26 million in 1968—almost entirely because of the federal presence. The number of full-time officials employed to combat air pollution increased from 148 in 1961 to 587 in 1967. Even with the increases, the states did very little. As of May 1967, 16 states still spent no funds whatsoever on air pollution control, and 28 states spent either nothing or less than $40,000.[43] Only California, New York, and New Jersey were spending enough on air pollution to go significantly beyond research.

In fact, the maintenance of state and local control of pollution policy was an important strategy for industrial polluters. In this case, the argument that the intergovernmental system should remain decentralized helped serve the interests of powerful private institutions. A larger federal role became politically possible following the Santa Barbara oil leak in January 1969. The National Environmental Policy Act, signed into law on January 1, 1970, ended years of frustration with enforcement mechanisms that relied on a decentralized federal system.

This discussion illustrates, but certainly does not prove, that decentralization is fraught with many difficulties. There are many reasons why the nation went through a period in which it assessed "national purposes." Several of these national purposes have survived in legislation. Civil rights requirements are contained in nearly all programs at every level of government. Environmental protection clauses are inserted into any legislation that has anything to do with air, water, or land. Other influential national policies include "planning and project coordination, wage rate and procurement standards, public employee standards, access to government information to decision processes, and obligations to provide relocation assistance and make acquisition of real property."[44] All of these policies emerged because it was judged that they were national problems that could not be addressed by states or local governments. Indeed, this continues to be the case. Do the states do better than the federal government? In many cases, it is obvious that they have not done so.

But it may well be that the states are more appropriate than the federal government in addressing many societal problems, and in providing some government functions. In the construction of highways, in the provision of education, in the adoption of zoning laws, and in other programs, the federal bureaucracies are probably too large and too far away from local constituencies to be sufficiently sensitive or efficient in the allocation of societal resources.

C. Current Issues Facing the States

One of the most significant recent developments facing state governments is the reemergence of sectional rivalries. In 1976, the New England Governor's Conference was formed

Table 6. States with the Highest and Lowest per Capita General Expenditure, Excluding Federal Grants, 1973

Highest states	Per capita expenditure in dollars	Lowest states	Per capita expenditure in dollars
Alaska	1759	North Carolina	439
Hawaii	1061	Kentucky	437
New York	1058	South Carolina	425
Delaware	906	Alabama	413
Nevada	871	Mississippi	368
Washington	816	Arkansas	313

Source: Adapted from J. A. Maxwell and J. R. Aronson, *Financing State and Local Governments*, 3rd ed. (Brookings Institution, Washington, DC, 1977), p. 34.

to fight for the political interests represented in those states. The Southern Growth Policy Board was organized in 1977 to promote Southern industry.[45] A comparison of the population growth rates among the states reveals why the sectional rivalries are intensifying. From 1973 to 1980, according to Bureau of Census estimates made in 1973, Nevada was expected to grow by almost 40 percent compared to a 31 percent population increase in Arizona.[46] The Bureau predicted an actual loss in population in Wyoming and Montana, and only modest growth of 13 percent in Utah. By 1980, it is clear that the Census Bureau estimates were wildly in error; most of the mountain states are now anticipating huge population increases as a result of energy development.

Even before the huge infusion of public and private funds into energy development, the nation was undergoing unequal regional development. Between 1960 and 1977, the northeast region of the nation grew by 10 percent compared to 39 percent in the West and 27 percent in the South.[47] Cities in the West and South were undergoing rapid population growth, while the cities of the northeast and midwest continued to empty out and to undergo a social crisis. Between 1960 and 1970, the metropolitan area of Anaheim, California, grew by more than 100 percent. The Phoenix metropolitan area grew by 46 percent, and the metropolitan areas encompassing Dallas and Houston, Texas, grew by 40 percent. Pittsburgh's metropolitan area, meanwhile, lost two-tenths of one percent of its population, and Boston's grew by only 6 percent.[48] The contrast among major cities was even more startling. In the decade of the 1960s, St. Louis lost 17 percent of its population, Cleveland lost 14 percent, Boston 8 percent, and Chicago 5 percent. In contrast, Los Angeles added 14 percent to its base population. While urban areas of the midwest and northeast were beset by the problems associated with population and economic decline, the sunbelt cities of Dallas, Houston, Phoenix and Denver, were also beset by problems, but they were problems associated with runaway growth.

There are many issues associated with unequal economic development. Battles are developing over the severance tax collected on oil development in states such as Wyoming and Alaska; residents living in northeastern cities must pay more for their oil when the severance taxes levied by the producing states have been added to the price of oil. The energy-producing states are able to reduce taxes and to invest in better public services, whereas the energy-dependent states continue to lose population and industry, and to increase taxes and cut back public services.

Already, states differ greatly in their ability and willingness to provide services. Alaska, in 1973, spent $1759 per capita, compared to Arkansas, which spent $313 per capita. As Table 6 indicates, there is great variation among the states in general expenditures. States in slow-growth regions of the country will find it difficult to maintain adequate public services. Other states, such as Alaska, will be able to draw on large tax revenues resulting from oil exploration to provide both tax relief to residents, and a very high level of services.

D. The States' Future

The states need not fear that they will become expendable in the federal system. They are crucial to the everyday workings of nearly all public policies. Federal funds of every kind go to the states, or through the states, to be distributed to local governments. Federal bureaucracies are extremely dependent on state governments as a result. Aid for dependent children, highways, regional planning, unemployment insurance, hazardous waste disposal—a complete list of federally assisted programs administered by the states would be very long.

Local governments are even more dependent. A large proportion of their budgets come from state formula grants. But local governments are dependent in a strictly legal sense, too. They depend for their charters and their governmental powers on the states. They are able to zone, educate children, build sewers, hold elections, only at the permission of the states.

What now seems anachronistic are not the states, but the predictions of their demise. In a 1966 interview, NBC newscaster David Brinkley observed that "states are pretty much disappearing as a political force. They're almost through. I think in another generation they will be, politically speaking, just about insignificant."[49] For better or for worse, Brinkley's prediction has proved to be somewhat incorrect.

E. The Reagan Counterrevolution

At the beginning of 1982, Americans were embroiled in a national debate about the purposes and organization of government. On January 27, 1982, President Reagan unveiled a revolutionary "New Federalism" which would, he said, return power back to the people in their states and communities. After his speech, he asserted that "Those who still advocate far removed federal solutions are dinosaurs mindlessly carrying on as they always have, unaware that times have changed."[50]

President Reagan's New Federalism is counterrevolutionary, in the strict sense that it is attempting to recreate a federal government which existed before the New Deal. In his State of the Union address, delivered on January 27, 1982, he outlined a 10-year program for turning over to the states $47 billion in federal programs, all to be accomplished by 1991.

In fiscal year 1984, Aid to Families with Dependent Children and Food Stamps, at a combined cost of $16.5 billion, would be turned over to the states. As a "bribe," the federal government, in turn, would assume all costs of the Medicaid program, saving the

Table 7. Rating Capabilities of the States

	A	B	C	D	E	F	G
Ala.	28	65%	11	Y	N	N	R
Alaska	5	71%	8	Y	Y	N	N.A.
Ariz.	25	55%	10	N	Y	Y	R
Ark.	21	68%	8	N	Y	N	B
Calif.	18	63%	4	Y	Y	Y	B
Colo.	42	51%	6	Y	Y	Y	B
Conn.	4	55%	1	Y	Y	N	R
Del.	9	80%	9	N	N	Y	B
Fla.	26	52%	6	Y	N	N	R
Ga.	30	57%	7	N	N	N	B
Hawaii	40	85%	8	Y	Y	Y	N.A.
Idaho	50	63%	11	N	N	Y	P
Ill.	12	54%	2	Y	N	N	R
Ind.	37	61%	7	Y	N	N	R
Iowa	44	60%	7	Y	Y	N	R
Kan.	14	53%	9	Y	N	N	R
Ky.	29	76%	8	Y	Y	N	R
La.	10	66%	9	Y	Y	Y	R
Me.	2	65%	8	Y	Y	N	R
Md.	6	60%	8	Y	Y	N	B
Mass.	43	54%	3	Y	Y	N	R
Mich.	16	57%	4	Y	N	Y	P
Minn.	17	64%	5	Y	Y	N	P
Miss.	45	66%	12	Y	Y	N	R
Mo.	19	52%	6	Y	N	Y	R
Mont.	31	53%	9	Y	Y	N	B
Neb.	41	49%	10	Y	Y	N	B
Nev.	46	46%	9	N	Y	Y	R
N.H.	22	51%	12	Y	N	N	R
N.J.	36	51%	2	Y	Y	Y	R
N.M.	48	76%	9	Y	Y	N	B
N.Y.	35	45%	5	Y	Y	N	P
N.C.	3	68%	11	Y	Y	N	B
N.D.	24	65%	10	Y	Y	N	B
Ohio	27	53%	8	Y	Y	N	R
Okla.	13	64%	11	Y	N	N	B
Ore.	1	53%	9	Y	Y	Y	P
Pa.	7	56%	4	Y	N	N	R
R.I.	38	65%	9	Y	N	Y	R
S.C.	15	60%	7	Y	N	Y	B
S.D.	47	54%	7	Y	N	N	R
Tenn.	34	55%	5	Y	N	Y	R
Texas	11	50%	6	Y	Y	Y	R
Utah	20	53%	7	N	Y	Y	B
Vt.	39	69%	10	N	Y	N	P
Va.	8	59%	8	Y	N	N	B

Table 7. (Continued)

	A	B	C	D	E	F	G
Wash.	32	61%	5	Y	Y	Y	B
W. Va.	49	76%	9	Y	Y	N	B
Wis.	23	61%	6	Y	Y	N	B
Wyo.	33	55%	9	N	Y	N	B

A. Rank of states by the degree to which they permit local governments to have discretionary authority free from state interference.

B. Percentage of the total that states provide for functions they share with the local governments, such as schools, highways, welfare and health. The national average is 57 percent.

C. Rank of states by the number of assistance programs they have to help distressed communities.

D. States whose legislatures have laws barring conflict of interest or requiring financial disclosure by members.

E. States that enacted reductions in income and/or sales taxes from 1977 through 1980.

F. States that enacted limits on taxing and spending from 1976 through 1980.

G. States with a progressive (P), regressive (R) or balanced (B) income tax base, 1976.

Source: U.S. Advisory Commission on Intergovernmental Relations; *New York Times*, September, 27, 1981.

states $19.1 billion. From fiscal 1984 through fiscal 1988, the states would go through a voluntary transition period, taking on up to 43 grant programs. To help them pay for the new responsibilities, a trust fund composed of federal excise taxes on gasoline, tobacco, alcohol, and telephones, plus part of the federal "excess profits" tax on oil, would be established. After fiscal 1988, a four-year phase-out of the trust fund would occur, leaving the states with full responsibility for the programs.

The prospect that states and localities may not be able to cope with returned federal programs is very real. First, we are still in the midst of a nationwide tax revolt which had its beginnings during the Reagan years in California. Governor Richard Lamm of Colorado has noted that Reagan is not cutting taxes but rather shifting them as he did in California.[51] When Reagan was governor of California, he de facto shifted taxes to the counties and cities. This eventually resulted in Proposition 13, which spread across the country. Now Reagan is attempting to shift taxes to state and local governments. It is absolutely certain that some of those governments will be unable or unwilling to assume the larger burdens placed on them, as Table 7 indicates.

David Cohen, the former president of Common Cause, has also noted that about half of the state legislatures do not have the staff and expertise that are needed for the type of programs which they are being asked to assume. Based upon all prior experiences, the states will not do well at all. A recent Conference of Mayors report stated: "The history of city-state relations has too often been one of neglect of city needs by the state."[52] A former Atlanta Mayor points out that "at best, there are only four states—Massachusetts, Michigan, Minnesota, and California—that have shown responsibility on urban issues. The other 46 have shown either neglect or downright hostility."[53]

The states' abilities to generate sufficient revenues to meet their future obligations or maintain their old ones is hampered by the traditional usurpation of the federal income tax, but other measures may emerge from the Reagan administration. One which may be particularly restrictive and which has the preliminary approval of the Reagan administration is a tax bill sponsored by Senator Charles Mathias of Maryland. The bill would prevent states from using "unitary apportionment methods" to collect taxes from multinational corporations. This method permits a state to receive the proportion of the corporation's tax obligations measured by the actual activity within the state as indicated by payroll, sales, and property. California stands to lose the greatest amount of revenue if this tax bill is passed—$485 million. California Controller Kenneth Cory has stated:

> If Congress passes the Mathias bill, the multinational corporations will be free to play a shell game with their profits, using a variety of accounting devices to transfer them to foreign subsidiaries.[54]

With less than full funding of present programs plus possible restrictions of state tax programs—and the current anti-tax sentiment that exists in many states—it is not feasible to believe that the programs returned to the states will be maintained to any significant degree.

We are currently in a period in which decentralization is strictly *de rigeure*. Nobody, but nobody, talks about *increased* federal spending and responsibility. States and local governments are enjoying more and more autonomy from federal bureaucrats. This probably has some advantages; but only the federal government can lay down national standards for program administration. States and localities cannot, in the nature of things, address national issues. When national issues again come to the forefront, as they did during the Great Depression, and during the Great Society, then the pendulum will swing back toward a stronger federal role.

NOTES

1. R. B. Ripley, "Congress and air pollution," in *Pollution and Public Policy: A Book of Readings,* D. F. Paulsen and R. B. Denhardt (Eds.), Dodd, Mead, New York, 1973), p. 184.
2. Ibid.
3. See *Dartmouth College v. Woodward,* 4 Wheat. 518 (1819). In 1868, Iowa Judge John F. Dillon reinforced this doctrine so strongly that the complete dependence of local governments on the states became known as "Dillon's rule." Cities, i.e., municipal corporations, he said, are "mere tenants of the will of the legislature." Cf. *City of Clinton v. Cedar Rapids and Missouri River Railroad Co.,* 13 Iowa 455, 475 (1868).
4. D. S. Elazar, *The American Partnership: Intergovernmental Co-operation in the Nineteenth Century United States* (University of Chicago Press, Chicago, 1962).
5. D. Brown, *Hear That Lonesome Whistle Blow: Railroads in the West* (Holt, New York, 1977).
6. Elazar, *The American Partnership.*
7. J. A. Maxwell, *The Fiscal Impact of Federalism in the United States* (Harvard University Press, Cambridge, MA, 1946), p. 12.
8. Ibid, p. 21.
9. Ibid, p. 20.
10. Ibid, p. 20.

11. M. Grodzins, in *The American System: A New View of Government in the United States,* D. J. Elazar (Ed.) (Rand McNally, Chicago, 1966), pp. 49, 54.

12. Ibid, p. 51.

13. G. C. S. Benson, *The New Centralization: A Study of Intergovernmental Relationships in the United States* (Farrow and Rinehart, New York, 1941), Preface, ix, x.

14. A. M. Schlesinger, Jr., *The Coming of the New Deal* (Houghton Mifflin, Boston, 1957), p. 5.

15. L. C. Gulick, "Reorganization of the state," *Civil Engineering* (August 1933), 420–421; as cited in T. Sanford, *Storm Over the States* (McGraw-Hill, New York, 1967), p. 21.

16. J. T. Patterson, *The New Deal and the States: Federalism in Transition* (Princeton University Press, Princeton, NJ, 1969), p. 39.

17. Ibid, p. 45.

18. L. Brownlow, quoted in American Municipal Association, *Proceedings 1931–1935,* p. 198; as quoted in M. I. Gelfand, *A Nation of Cities: The Federal Government and Urban America 1933–1965* (Oxford University Press, New York, 1975), p. 65.

19. L. Freedman, *Public Housing: The Politics of Poverty* (Holt, New York, 1969), p. 55.

20. J. L. Sundquist and D. W. Davis, *Making Federalism Work: A Study of Program Coordination at the Community Level* (Brookings Institution, Washington, DC, 1969).

21. D. H. Harder, *When Governments Come to Washington: Governors, Mayors, and Intergovernmental Lobbying* (Free Press, New York, 1974), p. 53.

22. Ibid, p. 55.

23. Quoted in M. Reagan, *The New Federalism* (Oxford University Press, New York, 1972), p. 97.

24. Quoted in T. B. Clark, J. K. Iglehart, and W. Lilly, III, "The new federalism I: Return of power to states and cities looms as theme of Nixon's second-term domestic policy," *National Journal: The Weekly on Politics and Government,* December 16, 1972, p. 1911.

25. J. A. Maxwell and J. R. Aronson, *Financing State and Local Governments,* 3rd ed. (Brookings Institution, Washington, DC, 1977), p. 47.

26. Ibid, p. 15.

27. M. Schneider and D. Swinton, "Policy analysis in state and local government," *Public Administration Review 39* (January–February 1979), no. 1: 12.

28. G. F. Break, *Financing Government in a Federal System* (Brookings Institution, Washington, DC, 1980), p. 179.

29. Ibid.

30. Ibid, p. 181.

31. For examples of programs adopted by the states, cf. Maxwell and Aronson, *Financing State and Local Government,* p. 27.

32. For discussion of this argument, see Break, *Financing Government in a Federal System,* p. 14.

33. I. M. Rubinow, *Social Insurance* (Holt, New York, 1913), p. 36.

34. J. C. Brown, *Public Relief 1929–1939* (Holt, New York, 1940), p. 27.

35. Ibid.

36. J. T. Patterson, *The New Deal and the States,* p. 92.

37. J. A. Maxwell, *Federal Grants and the Business Cycle* (National Bureau of Economic Research, New York, 1952), p. 47.

38. Ibid, p. 43.

39. S. Welch and K. Thompson, "The impact of federal incentives on state policy innovation," *American Journal of Political Science 24* (November 1980), no. 4: 715–779.

40. J. Walker, "The diffusion of innovations among the American states," *American Political Science Review 63* (September 1969), 880–899.

41. R. L. Sansom, *The New American Dream Machine: Toward a Simpler Lifestyle in an Environmental Age* (Anchor Press/Doubleday, Garden City, NY, 1976), pp. 68-69.

42. D. M. Rohrer, D. C. Montgomery, M. E. Montgomery, D. J. Eaton, and M. G. Arnold, *The Environment Crisis: A Basic Overview of the Problem of Pollution* (National Textbook, Skokie, IL, 1970), p. 146. Subsequent statistics are also from this source.

43. Ibid, pp. 142–144.

44. Break, *Financing Government in a Federal System*, p. 138.

45. J. J. Harrigan, *Politics and Policy in States and Communities* (Little, Brown, Boston, 1980), p. 49.

46. U.S. Bureau of Census Statistics; as presented in M. S. Stedman, Jr., *State and Local Governments*, 2nd Ed. (Winthrop, Cambridge, MA, 1979), p. 10.

47. U.S. Bureau of Census; as calculated by Harrigan, *Politics and Policy*, p. 50.

48. D. R. Judd, *The Politics of American Cities: Private Power and Public Policy* (Little, Brown, Boston, 1979), p. 160.

49. J. F. Fixx, "An Anniversary talk with Huntley and Brinkley," *McCall's* (October, 1966), p. 176, as cited in T. Sanford, *Storm Over the States* (McGraw-Hill, New York, 1967), p. 37.

50. *Rocky Mountain News,* January 28, 1982, p. 3.

51. News broadcast, January 21, 1982.

52. *New York Times,* June 21, 1981.

53. Ibid.

54. *Rocky Mountain News,* January 3, 1982, p. B1.

11

Urban Government Policy

Dianne M. Pinderhughes / Dartmouth College, Hanover, New Hampshire
Linda F. Williams / Howard University, Washington, District of Columbia

I. INTRODUCTION

To some observers, urban politics is simply a microcosm of state and national politics. We contend, however, that urban politics is different in some important ways from these other levels of government. They are, after all, legally subordinate to both of their larger partners in American federalism. As Mayor Coleman Young puts it, "State legislatures can practically eliminate cities if they want" (*Nation,* June 1975). Even more important, this juridical dependence is only symptomatic of the broader substantive dependence of most cities (Katznelson and Kesselman, 1975). Mayor Richard Hatcher of Gary pointed to the problem:

> I am mayor of a city of roughly 90,000 Black people but we do not control the possibilities of jobs for them or money for their schools, or state funded social services. These things are in the hands of the U.S. Steel Corporation, the county department of welfare, the state of Indiana and the federal government. . . . The resources are not available to the cities to do the job that needs doing (Allen, I 1970: 111).

Parallels with state and national governments are, of course, much in evidence. Each level of government is concerned with such policy areas as employment, housing, transportation, education, health care, civil rights, welfare policy, and so on. But as Stone et al. (I1979) point out, more than the others, local government is on the service-delivery firing line. That is, it is city government and city officials who are blamed if housing stock declines and housing costs rise; if schools are of inferior quality and segregated by race; if unemployment and underemployment are high; if health care services are poor and county hospitals are closing; if transportation services are uncomfortable and expensive;

if the industries are deserting the cities and the jobless rate is increasing. Local governments are sites of public demands, supports, and protests regarding how good most of our services are, although, as one theme of this chapter purports, urban problems cannot be resolved by urban governments alone, forcing broadening of decision-making on policies beyond the borders of central cities.

A second theme is that in the postwar era there has been an increasing federalization of urban policy as a consequence of the perpetual financial squeeze of the cities and their growing dependency. Since the New Deal, the issues have been what kind of national policy would alleviate urban problems, how much aid, and with what conditions. With the property tax becoming an increasingly unpopular source of revenue, urban governments are likely to become even more dependent on federal and state aid.

The third theme is the increasing significance of race and poverty in American cities due to white flight from older American cities and large-scale black in-migrations. Some 4 million blacks migrated to American cities between 1940 and 1970. Blacks now make up 24 percent of central city population as opposed to 11 percent of overall population. Urban policy has increasingly reflected a concern with, though not a solution for, the problems of this massive black population in employment, housing, education, and so on.

Obviously, we cannot discuss the full list or trace out all the areas of policy making in one chapter. Instead, we shall focus on six policy areas of increasing importance for large urban areas: employment, housing, education, crime, health care, and transportation.

II. SUMMARY OF MAJOR ISSUES IN URBAN GOVERNMENT POLICY

A. Structure

Federally, state and locally initiated adjustments in the structure of governmental relations in urban areas exert important influence on urban public policy. Three major forces have affected internal and external relationships between inner cities and their surrounding jurisdictions: maintenance of political control, creation of policy-specific metropolitan planning or administrative commissions, and federal aid supplied in a way that maximizes the likelihood of metropolitan or regional planning.

Concern about race and income are important in explaining the significance of the first factor; national dissatisfaction with increasing urban political discord based on the reluctance of local political jurisdictions to deal with the arrival of new racial and economic groups, and federal concern with overlapping jurisdictions and planning duplication, explain the second and third factors. Discussion of these three areas follows.

Maintenance of Political Control.   Political leaders in urban areas have attempted to block the acquisition of political power by increasing black or hispanic populations. In cases where blacks equal 50 percent or less of the city's total population, city officials, such as those in Richmond, Virginia, moved to absorb suburban districts with predominantly white populations (Murphy, I11978). In other cases, if the black population already dominates the city, suburban districts may resist absorption in order to avoid increased financial costs of resource-poor inner city areas, and political domination by large black voting populations.

Policy-Specific Metropolitan Planning or Administrative Commissions. In 1962 the Federal Highway Act, and subsequent environmental, health, housing, and urban development legislation, Congress has required regional and metropolitan planning as a prerequisite for federal grants. Transportation systems (e.g., METRO in Washington, D.C., BART in San Francisco, MARTA in Atlanta) have been planned, developed, and governed by independent boards composed of representatives of the participating political jurisdictions. Consequently, the political, economic, and administrative control over regional growth enjoyed by cities in the early and middle portions of the century has eroded in the wake of suburbanization of large portions of the population in the years since World War II.

A second type of regional commission has developed based on concern for maximizing efficiency, economies of scale, and cost reduction. Fire, sanitary, and police districts have been combined, especially in Western states, in order to avoid duplication of services and high capital costs.

Metropolitan and Regional Planning. Finally, federal aid has been supplied in a way that maximizes intergovernmental as well as intragovernmental planning and consultation. From the 1960s through the 1970s, federal aid has undergone a dramatic shift from direct categorical aid to cities, or in the case of the War on Poverty, to urban nongovernmental neighborhood units, to the broader state grants known generally as revenue sharing. The shift from specific urban grants to broader state grants has increased cooperation in part because of the structural qualities of the format, but also because federal and state legislation has attached specific requirements to the recipients.

The initial profusion of programs generated by the War on Poverty, the Elementary and Secondary Education Act of 1965, and the creation of the Department of Housing and Urban Development was also followed by the Model Cities program, which included requirements of increased interdepartmental as well as citywide and multineighborhood consultation on program activity. Federal programs have thus resulted in greater cooperation between cities and the surrounding jurisdictions, and greater coordination and development of political support within urban jurisdictions.

The overall impact of these structural developments has been to shift the locus of policy making away from popularly elected political units toward appointive, regionally based, suburban-dominated, specialized policy arenas. Although costs, efficiency, and coordinated planning are important explanations for implementing such structural changes, such revisions also reduce the influence of urban centers newly dominated by racial or ethnic groups.

B. Employment

Today, even the casual observer of the American economy recognizes that millions of workers in American cities are burdened by different kinds of employment problems—with varying symptoms and causes. Public concern and public policy in the postwar era, however, have focused on two main sets of problems: unemployment and underemployment.

In practically any discussion of either unemployment or underemployment, race should be brought to the center of analysis, given the constantly greater problems blacks have had historically in the labor market. A quick glance at a few Bureau of Labor statistics bear out this conclusion.[1] In most metropolitan areas, black unemployment ranged from 1½ times to 3½ times that of white unemployment.

Teenage unemployment rates were significantly higher and showed even greater racial differentials. In older metropolitan areas, the central city unemployment rates were also higher and demonstrated greater racial inequality.[2] In short, unemployment is presently massive and growing in urban areas. Moreover, racial differentials in the unemployment rates coupled with the greater representation of blacks in the lower-paying occupations partly explain racial inequality in income, poverty rates, and other economic and social indicators.

Just as the significance of race stands at the forefront in any examination of employment in urban areas, so does the impotence of local governments in generating employment. Urban mayors in older cities such as Detroit complain bitterly of their lack of power to stem the flow of industries and jobs from their cities. They cannot offer cheaper land, new technology, cheaper labor, a better natural climate, or a more favorable business climate made up of business-oriented labor, and zoning laws. Nor can they significantly alter taxes, although mayors, such as Coleman Young of Detroit, have been instrumental in securing tax cuts for corporations, such as Chrysler. Thus city governments are extremely limited in their policy-making capacities in the area of employment. Although one should be careful not to overestimate the constrictions placed on local authorities, it is scarcely an exaggeration to note that city mayors are judged on the basis of their ability to exploit federal policies and secure federal funds to generate jobs and maintain income levels in their cities.

The growing dependency of the cities on the federal government for employment policy has been a long-term process. Federalization of employment policy was legally institutionalized in the Employment Act of 1946, a landmark piece of legislation contributing to the transformation of the presidency into an agency responsible for the overall direction of the economy. The Employment Act instructs the President to take steps to maintain high employment and production, combat inflation, and satisfy economic needs. More practically, however, federalization began with the existing system of income maintenance programs, which originated in the Depression of the 1930s when millions were unemployed.[3] As income maintenance programs evolved over 35 years, they have been based on a three-pronged strategy of employment, social insurance, and public assistance. The assumption was that in our society the great majority of people obtain their income and social status through employment. The strategy thus assumed that monetary and fiscal policies would guarantee sufficient employment at adequate wages for most people, while education and training programs would assist others in developing their employment potential. If there were enough jobs, adequate education would assure young people a place in the labor force. In addition, a family or individual would need protection against changes in the unemployment rate and against the crippling losses of income when the breadwinner retires, dies, or becomes disabled. Finally, public assistance would be necessary as a "residual program" to aid those considered unable to enter the labor force.

The strategy behind the income maintenance programs of the 1930s was aimed at the lack or loss of employment—those who wanted to work but could not find a job. Those who were employed seemed satisfied, at least, and those who were not looking for work seemed incapable of working for health or family reasons. The unemployment rate seemed a perfectly adequate measure of the severity of employment problems.

Several developments during the decade of the 1960s, however, forced attention on a new set of problems. Greater prosperity had solved the employment problems of many workers who had been formerly unemployed.[4] The civil rights movement and ghetto riots had focused concern on the difficulties of blacks, especially those in the central cities.[5] The continuing evolution and frequent failure of manpower programs produced new impressions of success and failure, which affected objectives and priorities (Levitan and Mangum, IIA1969).

By the end of the 1960s, analysts and government officials tended to use the concept of "underemployment" to evoke the new set of problems with which they had become preoccupied. The concept intended to reflect the problems of a large group of disadvantaged workers, often described as "secondary workers" or the "underclass," who were frequently able to find work but earned low wages, worked intermittently, and could rarely hope for occupational advancement. While unemployment rates, measured by traditional statistical categories, were often around 8 or 9 percent in central city ghettos by the end of the decade, underemployment rates soared as high as 30 to 35 percent.[6]

This evolving concern with underemployment involved several important changes in traditional perceptions of the labor market (Thurow, IIA1965). From a policy standpoint, the most important of these changes was that policy paid increasing attention to the effects of extralabor market institutions on labor market problems, particularly the effects of housing segregation. And finally, the discussion of underemployment became permeated with a concern for the causes and effects of labor market discrimination, not only against racial minorities, but also against women and teenagers.

This change of emphasis helped stimulate most of the innovations in manpower programs during the 1960s. Wide varieties of public efforts were designed to stimulate training: institutional vocational training; financial incentives to firms to provide more on-the-job training to disadvantaged workers; job referral services to steer workers toward the most stable job opportunities; various programs to improve worker motivation and stability; and additional programs to open up new job opportunities (Levitan and Mangum, IIA1969).

Sharing many of the same basic concerns and analytic assumptions underlying these programs, the more conservative Nixon and Ford administrations did not move to change these programs when they assumed power. Befitting their more conservative suspicions about the potential of government programs, they intended simply to slow down the pace of innovation, hopefully improving coordination and management of all the different programs.

The Carter administration promised, however, to reverse these trends. It designed a national urban policy whose chief focus was to restore the economy of distressed areas through massive job programs, incentives to business for training programs, and in general other programs much like the Great Society programs of the 1960s. These programs were for the most part never implemented, and immediately prior to leaving office, the Carter administration allowed its Presidential Commission for a National Agenda for the 80s to produce a report belittling hope for employment in older industrial states and cities and suggesting instead that Washington assist able-bodied workers to find jobs in the Sunbelt cities. In short, the Presidential Commission advocated "benign neglect" toward

Frostbelt cities and their peoples, whose taxes made possible the federal growth subsidies that had triggered the Sunbelt boom. This was a total repudiation of the Carter urban policy. Thus President Carter was forced to repudiate his own commission—a highly unusual occurrence.

At this writing, the Reagan administration's urban policy is still being formulated. According to a number of newspaper articles, it would embrace a concept labeled "urban enterprise zones," which will be sent to Congress as the Kemp-Garcia bill.[7] The Kemp-Garcia bill would designate 10 to 15 square blocks as "urban enterprise zones." It would reduce federal and local taxes and social security in these zones. It would give business breaks in depreciation and accounting rules. On the other hand, it would cut CETA, urban renewal, model cities, and urban development action grants as well as relax environmental laws, the minimum wage, and occupational safety standards. In general, the emphasis would be almost entirely on aiding business, especially small businesses, rather than directly guaranteeing needy individuals a decent job and standard of living.

In sum, while policies have helped the poor, the unemployed, and the underemployed, we have not developed a national program that provides economic security to all those in need; provides aid in an efficient dignified, consistent fashion; and preserves the incentives that have provided much of American growth as a nation and as individuals. The results of this failure are the massive unemployment and underemployment problems plaguing American cities today.

C. Housing

Housing policy is a clear case of the intersection of the overarching issues we have outlined as affecting urban policy: its federalization, the structural limitations of policy making within urban areas, and finally the increasing significance of race and poverty in the third quarter of the twentieth century. From the late 1940s through the beginning of the 1980s, urban governments and policy makers have wrestled with the severe shortage and declining conditions of the urban housing stock, and the complex set of housing problems resulting from a rapid increase in the number and proportion of the urban black and poor population, as the white middle class moved to the suburbs.

In the opening years of the era, local officials used the federal urban renewal program to attempt to compensate for the two-decade-long drought in housing construction imposed by the Depression and World War II. Although proposed as a program to provide replacement for "slum housing," it was revised to enable the clearance of land for use by developers of commercial or upper-middle-income housing. As legislated, and as implemented, the program attempted to stabilize the middle-class and white sectors of urban areas by dispersing and/or consolidating black and lower-income groups.

The 1949 Housing Act's goal of "a decent home and suitable environment for every American family" had not been reached by 1965 when the Department of Housing and Urban Development (HUD) was created. The advent of HUD masked the simultaneous success and failure of the urban renewal program. Cities had effected marked changes within specific urban renewal areas, but the massive migration of blacks from the south overwhelmed even the large projects that had been undertaken in the 1950s. As the urban black and poor grew numerically and proportionately in the 1960s, whites fled the cities on federally funded highways to suburban housing subsidized by the Federal Housing Authority (FHA) and Veterans Administration (VA) programs.

In the 1960s racial segregation, and with it the increased deterioration of urban housing stock, became important issues. However, because much of the white population with discretionary income moved to newer suburban areas outside the cities, where racial distinctions might be more effectively maintained by explicit racial exclusion and/or economic limitations, it was structurally difficult and politically counterproductive for urban governments to encourage racial integration of housing. Under these circumstances, the maintenance of existing housing stock, the access of poor and of blacks to home ownership, and the support and the development of existing economic activities became important if conflicting priorities on urban political agendas.

Bankers and real estate agents had long withheld credit and service from blacks on an individual level (the 1968 Civil Rights Act outlawed housing discrimination against individuals), but in the 1970s local activists discovered related practices that limited mortgage funds to specifically designated geographic areas within the city. Mortgage money was invested in neighborhoods with new housing and where the population was predominantly upper income and white. Because the black population of many cities increased dramatically, was disproportionately low-income, and was confined to older areas, housing deterioration accelerated rather than declined by the mid-1960s. With credit unavailable from the private market, HUD redirected FHA and other mortgage-subsidy programs toward urban areas and low-income purchasers. In the mid-1970s Congress required banks to collect information on the race, sex, and religion of its mortgagees and also to cease discriminatory practices such as "red lining."

Large, visible, publicly owned housing projects experienced overwhelming financial and maintenance costs. Pruitt-Igoe in St. Louis was dynamited out of existence in a symbolic conclusion to the public housing program as a national solution to the deficit in low-income housing. Federal policy moved toward increasing emphasis on public subsidy of privately constructed and privately owned housing; the programs moved toward an economically heterogeneous mix of tenants subsidized through an income-based formula.

Finally, in the mid-1970s cities began to confront the accumulated problems of the 1950s and 1960s by private rather than public action; this encouraged revitalization in the economic and housing sectors. Rather than direct grants to the poor, or attempts to integrate the city by opening the areas on the borders of black areas, cities began to develop programs to support the small "back-to-the-city" movement; the increased attractiveness of inner city areas was prompted by a combination of depreciated housing values in central city areas and high and increasing transportation costs to suburban neighborhoods. Inflation and high interest rates resulted in a temporary slowdown in housing changes in the early 1980s.

D. Education

When we turn to education policy, we again find that racial, economic, and structural issues are among the most important concerns faced by policy makers in the postwar era. Racial and economic issues encouraged a variety of structural innovations as urban school systems attempted to respond to the problems produced by an increasingly black school-age population.

The explosion in the total black population in urban areas was outpaced by the upward shift in the black school-age population. School districts faced very serious problems in educating the black school-age population, because a number of additional variables interacted to complicate and structure events inside the classroom. Because blacks are disproportionately lower-income, they are less likely to complete high school or college or attain high achievement scores; because income and educational achievement are strongly correlated, classroom performance of black school children is problematical.

Civil rights groups and associations of black parents attacked racial segregation within school districts, differential expenditures across racial lines, and differing achievement and performance levels. In the early 1960s, when there were large and increasing black populations within cities, the emphasis both on the part of local groups and federal officials was on techniques for desegregation within districts.

In cities such as New York and Los Angeles, school boards and superintendents faced groups of citizens' conflicts on these three issues. The *Brown v. Board of Education* desegregation decision assumed that physical separation, which was frequently accompanied by spending differences, had a negative psychological impact on black children resulting in an inherently unequal educational experience. Civil rights groups raised the issue of equalizing achievement levels through an equalization of expenditures; they argued that this would in turn be accomplished most effectively by the redesignation of school district boundaries and the racial integration of the school population.

Attempts to redraw boundaries met with resistance by local PTAs and white groups, and most important, the support or enforcement of desegregation policy in northern cities was dealt a severe blow by Lyndon Johnson's refusal to continue the Office for Civil Rights' fund cutoff to Chicago, allowed in Title VI of the 1964 Civil Rights Act.

Because desegregation, racial change, and redistributive issues involve relatively dramatic, comprehensive policy reform, the large urban bureaucracies that were linked to specific constituencies within the schools and neighborhoods were much more likely to seek maintenance of the status quo or to make relatively small, incremental policy changes. With weak federal enforcement, strong local resistance, and the incremental tendencies of urban educational bureaucracies at work, few systems were voluntarily desegregated, and those under court order. In the mid-1960s civil rights and neighborhood groups began to concede the issue of desegregation and place more emphasis on redistribution of educational funding and administrative jurisdiction to the local communities.[8] Intertwined with the development of black power, some areas emphasized direct control over personnel, spending, and curriculum through popularly elected community boards.

New York City underwent the most public, controversial debate over the issue, which was strongly resisted by desegregation opponents and the professional unions. The consequences have been mixed, based on the model by La Noue and Smith (IIC1973: 26) (see Chart 1). The political conflict generated about the issue emphasized increased participatory aspects and administrative responsibility, but the boards and superintendents had the discretion to disaggregate the demand into a consensus about community participation or to concerns about the degree of administrative centralization. In some cases boards have delegated administrative responsibility to professionals in a newly decentralized system without addressing the issue of participation (administrative delegation). In others they have retained professional centralized control of school affairs (bureaucratic monopoly), or added grass roots representatives to school board committees (lay participation). Under the most favorable circumstances, such as the case of Washington,

Chart 1

Degree of Concentration		Locus of Influence	
Administrative responsibility		Community	Professional
	Centralized	Lay participation	Bureaucratic monopoly
	Decentralized	Community control	Administrative delegation

Source: Adapted from G. R. La Noue and B. L. R. Smith (IIC1973), *The Politics of School Decentralization* (Heath, Lexington, MA).

D.C., where community control was activated by a supportive federal bureaucracy, and professional unions encountered a politically neutral local school apparatus, implementation of community control was a long, complex, and conflict-filled process.[9] But even in cases where community boards were recognized, funded, and elected, citizen involvement in elections was typically low, as is generally the case in local elections; elected representatives "have had backgrounds in anti-poverty organizations . . . and in most cases the policies for black students will still be made by whites . . . [who] represent neighborhood power bases, parishes or congregations, homeowners and taxpayers associations, and small businessmen" (La Noue and Smith, IIC1973: 230) rather than those groups represented in the reform era of the 1950s and 1960s.

At present administrative and structural reform and racial issues have been displaced by the adjustments to inflationary price rises.

E. Criminal Justice

Since at least the 1960s, crime has been identified as one of the top three urban problems in a number of public opinion polls. Clearly this is not just misperception, for FBI studies reveal that many kinds of crime (street, white collar, and organized) have increased rapidly in American cities, especially in minority communities in central cities. For example, the FBI's index crimes [willful homicide, forcible rape, aggravated assault, robbery, burglary, larceny (of $50 or more), and motor vehicle theft] are committed twice as frequently in cities with more than 1 million people as on the average throughout the country.

In addition, as other sections of this chapter demonstrate, the socioeconomic and demographic conditions associated with rising crime are increasing rather than disappearing—for example, high unemployment, poverty, poor health care, overcrowded housing, and high-density neighborhoods.

That the issue of the increasing significance of race and poverty, the structural limitations of policy making and federalization of the urban policy-making process cut across any consideration of this policy area is also evident. Especially, the significance of race in relationship to policies seeking to minimize crime has been openly recognized. In fact, by the late 1960s, "law and order" had become little more than a battle cry against minorities, especially blacks, who, according to FBI statistics, tend to commit crimes much more frequently than whites.[10] It should also be pointed out that minorities are disproportionately the victims of crime. According to Reasons, most crime in fact tends to be committed against members of one's own group (Reasons and Kuykendall, IID1972).

At the same time, minorities and the poor are treated from arrest through detention in much harsher ways than whites charged with similar crimes. They are disproportionately arrested, arraigned, and serve longer sentences than do whites. That crime rates and criminal justice are related to other policy areas appears clear. For example, the numbers of black and other minorities locked into the pattern of prison and recidivism are by no means insubstantial in relation to the numbers of blacks who are unemployed.

Local government officials have tried a number of policy alternatives to combat crime and inequality in the criminal justice system. As urban citizens struggled for greater "community control" of the police, for example, a number of cities instituted police review boards, neighborhood police (that is, requiring that police live in the neighborhood they patrol), and smaller police districts. Efforts to secure more minority-group police officers have also been instituted in cities such as Atlanta, Detroit, and Washington, D.C. Public defender systems, although far from adequately funded, have been instituted.

On the other hand, many local governments sought stricter police control and better-equipped police departments as means to deter crime. For example, cities such as Kansas City instituted practices of "stop-and-frisk" and "no-knock" laws.

In some areas, crime rates did decline in the early and mid-1970s—for example, in Atlanta, Detroit, and Gary, Indiana. Several analysts have argued that these declining crime rates have demonstrated that urban black political officials in these cities have proven both their considerable seriousness about a "war on crime" and their more than adequate abilities in reducing crime (Greer, IID1980). On the other hand, crime rates have begun to rise again in these black-led cities as well as in white-led cities throughout the nation. In cities such as Washington, D.C., the crime rate is presently higher than it has been in 10 years. As rising crime statistics reveal, local policies do not appear to be adequate for the prevention and deterrence of crime in light of recession and rising unemployment.

The attempt at federalization of policies to deter crime has also occurred. The chief federal instrument to date was the creation of the Law Enforcement Assistance Administration (LEAA). The LEAA was an outgrowth of the policy recommendations of the Johnson administration's Presidential Commission on Crime. This commission recommended the use of scientific techniques for further rationalization of the system of law enforcement and administration of justice. The LEAA was composed of several components—research, technology, community crime prevention, juvenile crime, and so on. Millions of dollars were given by the LEAA to local police departments to improve their methods. According to Quinney (IID1978) and other analysts, most of the money given to the cities by the LEAA was spent on equipment—especially riot control equipment. This equipment has already been used selectively against demonstrators in such cities as New Orleans and Jackson, Mississippi, to quell civil discontent.

In a number of cities, such as Washington, D.C., Seattle, and Chicago, community crime prevention programs were instituted through grants from the LEAA. The methods and purposes of these programs remained greatly varied. At this point their potential success seems likely to remain unfulfilled, given the creation of the Organization of Justice Administration and Research Statistics (OJARS) and the almost total disbanding of the LEAA. Although higher crime waves are occurring, only the national research arm of the LEAA has received continued funding by Congress.

F. Transportation

In this section, we first sketch the sequence of events that have brought about the crisis in urban transportation. Then we describe the heavy reliance on technology fostered by federal policy that has dominated efforts to revitalize public transportation.

For most suburbanites, enjoying the benefits of urban transportation services is a simple matter of walking out of their suburban homes, getting into their automobiles, and driving where they want to go with minimal delay caused by congestion. In the past several years, however, the realization has grown that transportation in the contemporary metropolis must be more than automobility. Now the specter of an energy shortage has heightened that realization.

In 1962 President Kennedy issued a transportation message to Congress, calling for a system of model urban transportation, balanced between the use of private automobiles and modern mass transportation. This signaled a rebirth of public transportation after a half-century of decline. As diagnoses were made of civil disorders in the mid-1960s, one conclusion was that the lack of mobility for inner city residents—especially their isolation from the new job market on the suburban rings—was an important cause of discontent. Again, the significance of race, given the great proportion of blacks in the inner city, should be noted. Out of these and other concerns came the passage of federal and state legislation designed to improve public transportation.

Each of a host of policy choices and personal choices has played its part in affecting public transportation—most notably, the strong automotive lobby in Congress, residential and employment locations, and economic subsidies for highway construction.

One problem that proponents of mass transportation cite repeatedly is the absence at the federal level of any comprehensive, coherent statement as to just what our national posture toward urban mass transit is or ought to be. The federal approach to mass transportation has been piecemeal, an amalgam of approaches that attempt to respond to a given set of pressures or crises and often work at cross-purposes with each other. The federal urban transportation effort consists of a long and expensive series of programs—the Interstate Highway System; federal research, development, and technical studies; and grants to build personal transit systems—and only recently has it been refocused toward mass transit.

One of the first statements of transportation policy for urban areas came with the passage of the Transportation Act of 1940. This act called for the improvement and development of all modes of transportation—including rail, highway, and water (Smerk, IIE1965: 174). Next, and probably more important, came the Federal Highway Act of 1956. The most visible consequence of this act is the Interstate Highway System of almost 40,000 miles that criss-cross the United States and has made automobile travel the dominant means of travel. From a policy perspective, the most important feature of that act was the creation of the Highway Trust Fund, which earmarks revenues from taxes on the sale of gasoline, tires, and auto parts and supplies for the construction and improvement of the interstate network. As a result, the highway lobby, with funds ever available from the automotive industry, can pursue its aims without having to worry about how new highways will be paid for. As Castells points out, no other interest group in the history of the United States has been given such special financial tratment (see Castells, I1979).

Mass transportation, on the other hand, gets no such special treatment, though many interest groups have lobbied for one. After a major struggle in Congress, recent legislation has made it possible for states to use some of their federal highways funds for mass transportation purposes, but few have elected to do so because of the great outcry from the automotive industry that even suggestion of such a policy generates. Urban travel continues to be dominated by the auto.

Urban governments have found that federal dollars are available only generally for new buses and rail vehicles and only very limited funds are available for experiments in service improvement that do not focus on hardware technology. This is due to the federal government's tilt toward technological solutions—that is, federal money is generally tagged for capital grants and technical studies programs. Until the passage of the National Mass Transportation Assistant Act of 1974, no funds were available to local governments to cover operating deficits. In sum, by its choice of what to subsidize, the federal government has actually encouraged local governments to take a hardware approach to the solution of their transportation problems, while ignoring the social aspects of the problem.

Meanwhile, some local governments have sought to comply with citizens' increased demands and built public transportation systems—for example, San Francisco's Bay Area Rapid Transit system (BART) and Washington, D.C.'s METRO system. But these systems have been beset with problems. For example, in Washington, D.C., METRO is still to be completed after several years of delay, and capital costs for the regional plan have risen dramatically from the $2.1 billion projected in 1967 to more than $7 billion in an urban economy suffering from massive deficits and making necessary cutbacks in public employment. Citizen complaints are already being voiced. These complaints involve such issues as these: Low-income riders must pay the same fare as higher-income riders, even though in many cases they travel shorter distances and thus use less energy; and more comfortable, cleaner public transportation is reserved for the suburbs.

In sum, the transportation policy that exists today is a patchwork of three decades of decisions that reflect the biases and values of those who made them. The net effect has been to favor automobiles over the movement of people and goods. The domination of automotive transportation is not accidental. It is due to the strong automotive lobby in Congress and the expansion of highways at the public's expense in the post-World War II era. These highways in turn made the suburbs feasible even as the FHA gave credit to the middle class to build surburban housing. This in turn further increased the need for the two-car family. There was little public choice in this process. The result is that citizens must provide their own means of transportation in most situations. To base urban transportation policy on the assumption that everyone owns a car is to inflict hardship on the many poor and black Americans who do not. Twenty percent of all American households and one-third of households in the central city do not own automobiles. Even for the affluent who have private automobiles, we need a process for working our way toward a road system and a system of mass transportation that provide more benefits of urban mobility.

G. Health Care

Race and economic status have a significant impact on the development of health policy in urban areas. Rates of infant mortality, maternal mortality in childbirth, and life expectancy are consistently and considerably higher for nonwhites and for low-income groups than for the middle- and upper-income groups and whites within metropolitan areas. Blacks and the low-income population also "suffer a disproportionate share of heart conditions, mental and nervous conditions, arthritis and rheumatism, high blood pressure, orthopedic impairments and visual impairments" (Palley and Palley, IIF1977: 192).

The cumulative interactions of the racial and economic variables inhibits lower-income and especially black access to medical care and facilities on two levels. Blacks have less to spend on health care because housing and other consumer items cost more for them than for whites of the same income level. On a metropolitan level, physicians, hospitals, and other privately employed individuals in health care seek out the most profitable locations—that is, away from the black and low-income population.

Thus urban and rural areas with high black and/or poor populations also experience the greatest scarcity of medical professionals. Blacks and the poor have fewer personal resources to invest in health care, and fewer and less well distributed resources/facilities when they reach the point of requiring service. These difficulties are aggravated by the orientation toward the private sector, or profit-making institutions, which emphasize the capital-intensive, profitable aspects of medical care. Care for serious or complex illness is available for those who can pay, whereas inexpensive, consistent routine health maintenance has been emphasized only recently. Acceptance of the "fee-for-service" concept has pushed health care costs upward and has encouraged treatment of illness rather than maintenance of health.

Federal programs have reinforced rather than reorganized the elements of this system. Medicare, Title XVIII of the 1965 amendment to the Social Security Act, and Medicaid, Title XIX, subsidize health care for the poor and the elderly. Medicaid is a state program with subsidies provided on a fee-for-service basis. Urban areas, in the largest, "more progressive states are the largest recipients of Medicaid benefits" (Palley and Palley, IIF1977: 196).

The issues of increased coordination and intergovernmental cooperation were also felt in health policy. The 1966 Comprehensive Health Planning and Public Health Services Amendments limited eligibility for federal funds to those states that established a state-level health planning agency, and a consumer-dominated advisory council. In 1974 the Health Planning Resources Development Act set up state and local agencies responsible for approving and coordinating health care plans. Federal expenditures for places that do not fit the overall arrangements can be blocked by local groups. Health systems agencies are much more likely to handle hardware issues, such as construction and equipment.

As Greer (II1979) notes, the attempt to increase health care accessibility through Medicare, Medicaid and the Neighborhood Health Centers, National Health Service Corps scholarships, was not accompanied by a reexamination of the fee-for-service concept. Payments were not linked to scarce medical resources or personnel. Programs were detached from the conventional economic model: Payments did not rise in areas where physicians and other medical professionals were in greatest demand, nor fall in areas where there was a surplus. The new programs made no attempt to relate payment to normal market demand. Thus costs rose, but no real or significant shift in services occurred. Although some improvements in black mortality statistics have been achieved in recent years, the shift of large portions of the black population to urban areas and the rising costs of service may overwhelm the improvements that have been made.

III. CONCLUSION

We have viewed several problematic urban policy areas separately. We chose this format merely for heuristic and analytical reasons, but part of the problem of past urban policy has been that for several decades (at least in liberal administrations), the federal government has formulated policy in fragmented arenas, each designed to ameliorate a specific problem as though it were unrelated to others in the social or economic system. Results have been disappointing, and this has led to debate. Is it that we do not know enough and have only "thrown money at problems"?

Our view, as we have tried to bring out at various points, is that it will be virtually impossible to remedy urban ills without a fundamental understanding of the underlying systemic connections between these urban problems. Unemployment and underemployment produce lower incomes, which in turn produce the inability to afford better housing, health care, education, and transportation. As we have pointed out, it is an important cause as well of the motivation for criminal activities. The problems cities now face are symptomatic of deep-seated tensions between races and classes in American society.

These issues—race, poverty, and federalization—will be more and less serious in the future. The black population will become slightly more economically differentiated in the future, which will pull the small middle and upper classes from the central city and toward the periphery of the city and into the suburbs. Evidence of this can be found in cities such as Washington, D.C., and Chicago, where the number of black children enrolled has declined within city schools and has risen in suburban jurisdictions. In some cases the poorest blacks will move along with them, but because they can no longer afford to live within the revitalizing city.

A final issue, which we have not addressed specifically but which will affect urban areas, and the issues of race and poverty, is the national problem of inflation coupled with its impact on areas of declining economic growth such as the cities of the Northeast and Midwest. As inflation persists and cities find their economic bases eroding, they have and are finding it increasingly difficult to fund the demands placed on them. As cities with large black and poor populations with expanded services during the urban crisis of the 1960s have come to represent profligacy and waste to the suburban and rural areas of the nation, taxpayer revolts have developed, limiting tax resources at the same time that inflation pushes up the cost of city services. The contraction of the national economy sharply increases the already high levels of unemployment in the black population, thereby complicating and aggravating the already great economic and political responsibilities of the cities.

NOTES

1. U.S. Department of Labor, Bureau of Labor Statistics, September 1979, Report 571, *Geographic Profile of Employment and Unemployment: States, 1978, Metropolitan Areas, 1977–78.*
2. Unemployment is defined as the percentage of the total labor force that is not employed. The labor force includes those who are employed and those who say that they are looking for work. Those who are neither employed nor looking for work, even if they are simply too discouraged to do so, are considered "not in the labor force." For further discussion of these categories and their historical justification, see Wolfbein (IIA1694).
3. The President's Commission on Income Maintenance Programs (IIA1969). *Poverty Amid Plenty: The American Paradox.*
4. During the 1960s, for instance, the unemployment rate had dropped from nearly 7 percent to roughtly 3.5 percent before it began to rise again in 1969.
5. The "Riot Commission Report" crystallized many of these influences. See *Report of the National Advisory Commission on Civil Disorders* (IIA1968).
6. For a discussion of the first use of this concept and its statistical embodiment, see *Manpower Report of the President, 1967* (IIA1967: 74–75).
7. See *The New York Times,* November 23, 1980, Section E, p. 23.
8. See R. T. Nakamura and D. M. Pinderhughes (1977). Federal education projects in Anacostia 1967–1977, unpublished manuscript completed under NIE contract for Gibboney Associates.
9. Nakamura and Pinderhughes, op. cit.
10. For a discussion of this phenomenon, see Graham (IID1970).

REFERENCES

I. General

Allen, R. L. (1970). *Black Awakening in Capitalist America.* Anchor Doubleday, Garden City, NY.

Banfield, E. (1961). *Political Influence.* Free Press, Glencoe, IL.

—— (1974). *The Unheavenly City Revisited.* Little, Brown, Boston.

Castels, M. (1979). *The Urban Question.* M.I.T. Press, Cambridge, MA.

Gordon, D. (1971). *Problems in Political Economy: An Urban Perspective.* Heath, Lexington, MA.

Katznelson, I., and Kesselman, M. (1975). *The Politics of Power.* Harcourt, Brace, New York.

Lineberry, R. L. (1977). *Equality and Urban Policy, the Distribution of Municipal Public Services.* Sage, Beverly Hills, CA.

Lineberry, R. L., and Masotti, L. (1975). *Urban Problems and Public Policy.* Lexington, Lexington, MA.

Lineberry, R. L., and Sharkansky, I. (1971). *Urban Politics and Public Policy.* Harper & Row, New York.

Palley, M. L., and Palley, H. A. (1977). *Urban American and Public Policies.* Heath, Lexington, MA.

Palumbo, D. J., and Taylor, G. (1979). *Urban Policy: A Guide to Information Sources.* Gale Research Co., Detroit.

Shank, A. (1970). *Political Power and the Urban Crisis.* Holbrook Press, Boston.
Sharkansky, I. (1972). *Public Administration: Policymaking in Government Agencies.* Markham, Chicago.
Stone, C., Whelan, R., and Munin, W. (1979). *Urban Policy and Politics.* Prentice-Hall, Englewood Cliffs, NJ.
Williams, L. F. (in press). *Race, Class and Politics: The Impact of American Political Economy on Detroit's Blacks.* University of Wisconsin Press, Madison.
Wilson, J. Q., and Banfield, E. (1963). *City Politics.* Harvard University Press, Cambridge, MA.

II. Structure

Bahl, R., and Vogt, W. (1976). State and regional government financing of urban public services. In *State and Local Government: The Political Economy of Reform,* A. K. Campbell and R. Bahl (Eds.). Free Press, New York.
Campbell, A. K., and Bahl, R. (Eds.) (1976). *State and Local Government: The Political Economy of Reform.* Free Press, New York.
Collins, J. N., and Downes, B. T. (1976). The effect of size on the provision of public service. *Urban Affairs Quarterly 12*: 333–348.
Greenstone, J. D., and Peterson, P. E. (1973). *Race and Authority in Urban Politics.* University of Chicago Press, Chicago.
Merriam, R. E. (1976). Multipurpose districts, modernized. In *State and Local Government: The Political Economy of Reform,* A. K. Campbell and R. Bahl (Eds.). Free Press, New York.
Mogulof, M. B. (1972). *Five Metropolitan Governments: An Exploratory Comparison.* Urban Institute, Washington, D.C.
Murphy, T. P. (1978). Race-base accounting. *Urban Affairs Quarterly 14*: 169–194.
Nathan, R. (1977). *Revenue Sharing: The Second Round.* Brookings Institution, Washington, DC.
Sundquist, J. (1969). *Making Federalism Work.* Brookings Institution, Washington, DC.
Turk, H. (1973). Comparative urban structure from an interorganizational perspective. *Administrative Science Quarterly,* March 1973: 37–55.

A. Employment

Levitan, S., and Mangum, G. (1969). *Federal Training and Work Programs in the Sixties.* Institute of Labor and Industrial Relations, Ann Arbor, MI.
Manpower Report of the President, 1967 (1967). U.S. Government Printing Office, Washington, D.C.
President's Commission on Income Maintenance Programs (1969). *Poverty Amid Plenty: The American Paradox.* U.S. Government Printing Office, Washington, DC.
Report of the National Advisory Commission on Civil Disorders (1968). Bantam, New York.
Thurow, L. (1965). *Poverty and Discrimination.* Brookings Institution, Washington, DC.
Wolfbein, S. (1964). *Employment and Unemployment in the United States.* Science Research Associates, New York.

B. Housing

Aaron, H. (1972). *Shelters and Subsidies: Who Benefits from Federal Housing Policies.* Brookings Institution, Washington, DC.

Bellush, J., and Hausknecht, M. (1967). *Urban Renewal: People, Politics and Planning.* Doubleday Anchor, New York.

Clay, P. (1979). *The Neighborhood Renewal Game: Middle Class Resettlement and Incumbent Upgrading in the 1970's.* Lexington, Lexington, MA.

Danielson, M. N. (1976). *The Politics of Exclusion.* Columbia University Press, New York.

Downs, A. (1973). *Opening Up the Suburbs.* Yale University Press, New Haven, CT.

Federal Housing Policy: Current Programs and Recurring Issues (1978). Background Paper, Congressional Budget Office, Washington, DC.

Helper, R. (1969). *Racial Policies and Practices of Real Estate Brokers.* University of Minnesota Press, Minneapolis.

Housing in the 70's Working Paper (1976). Department of Housing and Urban Development, Washington, DC.

Kain, J., and Quigley, J. (1975). *Housing Markets and Racial Discrimination: A Microeconomic Analysis.* National Bureau of Economic Research, Columbia University Press, New York.

Lowi, T. J. (1979). *The End of Liberalism.* Norton, New York.

Meehan, E. J. (1979). *The Quality of Federal Policymaking: Programmed Failure in Public Housing.* University of Missouri Press, Columbia, MO.

Mendelson, R. E., and Quinn, M. A. (Eds.) (1976). *The Politics of Housing in Older Urban Areas.* Praeger, New York.

Meyerson, M., and Banfield, E. (1955). *Politics, Planning and the Public Interest: The Case of Public Housing in Chicago.* Free Press of Glencoe, London.

Pynoos, J., Schafer, R., and Hartman, C. W. (1973). *Housing Urban America.* Aldine, Chicago.

Rossi, P., and Dentler, R. (1961). *The Politics of Urban Renewal.* Free Press of Glencoe, New York.

Sawers, L., and Wachtel, H. M. (1977). Who benefits from federal housing policies? In *Problems in Political Economy, An Urban Perspective,* David Gordon (Ed.). Heath, Lexington, MA.

Wellfeld, I. (1970). Toward a new federal housing policy. *Public Interest 19*: 31–43.

Wilson, J. Q. (Ed.) (1966). *Urban Renewal.* M.I.T. Press, Cambridge, MA.

C. Education

Bailey, S. K., and Mosher, E. K. (1968). *ESEA The Office of Education Administers a Law.* Syracuse University Press, Syracuse, NY.

Crain, R. (1969). *The Politics of School Desegregation.* Doubleday, New York.

Fantini, M., and Gittel, M. (1973). *Decentralization: Achieving Reform.* Praeger, New York.

Gintis, H., and Bowles, S. (1976). *Schooling in Capitalist America: Educational Reform and the Contradictions of Economic Life.* Basic Books, New York.

Gittell, M., and Fantini, M. (1970). *Community Control and the Urban School.* Praeger, New York.

Jencks, C. (1972). *Inequality.* Harper & Row, New York.

La Noue, G. R., and Smith, B. L. R. (1973). *The Politics of School Decentralization.* Heath, Lexington, MA.

Lehne, R. (1978). *The Politics of School Finance Reform.* Longman, New York.

Morris, L. (1980). *Elusive Equality.* Howard University Press, Washington, DC.

Nakamura, R. T., and Smallwood, F. (1980). *The Politics of Implementation.* St. Martin's New York.

Orfield, G. (1978). *Must We Bus? Segregated Schools and National Policy*. Brookings Institution, Washington, DC.

Persell, C. (1977). *Education and Inequality*. Free Press, New York.

Peterson, P. E. (1976). *School Politics Chicago Style*. University of Chicago Press, Chicago.

Rist, R. C. (1970). Student social class and teacher expectations: The self-fulfilling prophecy in ghetto education. *Harvard Educational Review 40*: 411–451.

―― (1979). *Desegregated Schools*. Academic Press, New York.

Rogers, D. (1968). *110 Livingston Street, Politics and Bureaucracy in the New York City Schools*. Random House, New York.

Sexton, P. (1964). *Education and Income*. Viking Press, New York.

Timpane, M. (1978). *The Federal Interest in Financing Schooling*. Ballinger, Cambridge, MA.

Willie, C. V. (1978). *The Sociology of Urban Education*. Heath, Lexington, MA.

D. Crime

Graham, F. (1970). Black crime: The lawless image. *Harper's,* December 1970: 64–65.

Greer, E. (1980). *Big Steal, Little Steal.* Monthly Review Press, New York.

President's Commission on Law Enforcement and the Administration of Justice (1967). *The Challenge of Crime in a Free Society*. U.S. Government Printing Office, Washington, DC.

Quinney, R. (1978). *Social Class and Crime*. McGraw-Hill, New York.

Reasons, C., and Kuykendall, J. L. (Eds.) (1972). *Race, Crime and Justice*. Goodyear, Pacific Palisades, CA.

E. Transportation

Hilton, G. W. (1974). *Federal Transit Subsidies*. American Enterprise Institute. Washington, DC.

Kendrick, R. J. (1975). Urban transportation policy: Politics, planning and people. *Policy Studies Journal 3*: 376.

Lupo, A., Colcand, F., and Fowler, E. P. (1971). *Rites of Way: The Politics of Transportation in Boston and the U.S. City*. Little, Brown, Boston.

Owen, W. (1966). *The Metropolitan Transportation Problem*. Anchor, Garden City, NY.

Smerk, G. (1965). *Urban Transportation: The Federal Role*. Indiana University Press, Bloomington.

F. Health

Alford, R. A. (1975). *Health Care Politics*. University of Chicago Press, Chicago.

Blair, J. P., and Nachmias, D. (Eds.) (1977). *Fiscal Retrenchment and Urban Policy*. Sage, Beverly Hills, CA.

Conant, R. W. (1968). *The Politics of Community Health*. Public Affairs Press, Washington, DC.

Darity, W. A. (1977). Health care for blacks. *Focus 19*: 4–5.

Greer, A. L. (1979). Health care policy: Disillusion and confusion. In *Fiscal Retrenchment and Urban Policy*, J. P. Blair and D. Nachmias (Eds.). Sage, Beverly Hills, CA.

Greer, S. (1978). Professional self-regulation in the public interest: The intellectual politics of psro. In *Accountability in Urban Society: Public Agencies Under Fire*, S. Greer, R. Hedlund, and J. Gibson (Eds.). Urban Affairs Annual Review, Sage, Beverly Hills, CA.

Kane, R. L., Kasteter, J. M., and Gray, R. (Eds.) (1976). *The Health Gap: Medical Services and the Poor.* Springer, New York.

Klarman, H. (1965). *The Economics of Health.* Columbia University Press, New York.

Koleda, M., and Bloom, S. S. (1978). The impact of health systems agencies on urban ambulatory health centers. *Urban Health 7:* 16.

Lassiter, H. B. (1973). HMO's and the inner city practice. *Urban Health 2:* 18.

Miller, C. A. (1975). Issues of health policy: Local government and the public health. *American Journal of Public Health 65:* 1330–1331.

Mustalish, A., Eidsvold, G., and Novick, L. F. (1976). Decentralization in the New York City Department of Health: Reorganization of a public health agency. *American Journal of Public Health 66:* 1149–1154.

Palley, M. L., and Palley, H. A. (1977). *Urban America and Public Policies.* Heath, Lexington, MA.

Unit Two

SPECIFIC POLICY PROBLEMS

12

Foreign Policy

Charles F. Hermann / Ohio State University, Columbus, Ohio

Today two quite distinctive kinds of foreign policy studies exist side by side. One type involves description, evaluation, and prescription of specific, current foreign policy issues. It addresses—usually in an idiographic manner—problems confronting particular governments or other foreign policy actors. The other type of study involves the search for explanation, interpretation, and perhaps prediction of certain recurrent features of foreign policy. Using primarily a nomothetic orientation, it concerns the development of generalizable assertions about foreign policy and the conditions under which they are likely to occur. The boundaries between the two kinds of studies overlap, and seldom are individual analysts interested only in questions found in one area. The main thrust of each, however, remains distinctive. This chapter examines the second class of foreign policy studies.[1]

I. THE ELUSIVE NATURE OF FOREIGN POLICY: REVELATIONS ABOUT THE STATE OF INQUIRY

A. Challenges to Traditional Definitions

Foreign policy consists of the plans, goals, and actions of national governments directed at entities outside the nation. Not long ago that statement might have passed for an acceptable textbook definition of foreign policy.[2] Challenges to such definitions reveal some of the ferment in the theory-oriented field of foreign policy studies. Consider these questions. If foreign policy comprises plans and actions, what about deliberate decisions not to act in a given international situation? How do the extemporaneous remarks of a visiting head of state constitute foreign policy if they are inconsistent with previous declarations of his government and if they are later "reinterpreted" by a press secretary? When a provincial government or other subnational government conducts a trade mission or establishes offices abroad to promote trade, investment, and tourism in its particular jurisdiction, is it conducting foreign policy? What about the multinational corporation that conducts negotiations with various governments and seeks to arrange policies favorable to its interests? Are other nongovernmental groups and private individuals who try to mediate a dispute between governments or who deal directly with private groups and individuals in other countries conducting foreign policy? Even the idea that foreign policy is deliberately directed to entities outside a country has been questioned. If a large, internationally active country suffers an economic recession or other major changes in its economic condition, the results could be felt strongly in those countries that have extensive economic interactions with it. Is that foreign policy? Or what about the case of a deliberate policy action taken strictly for domestic reasons, but which has severe implications for those outside the country. Illustrations might include the termination of the research and development, for reasons of costs or inadequate technology, of a weapon system that foreign governments also had planned to purchase as a key element of their own defense. Is that foreign policy? What about a metropolitan government that refuses landing rights to all supersonic commercial jet aircraft because of pressure from domestic groups about noise pollution, which nevertheless bankrupts a foreign air carrier that had invested heavily in such aircraft for that specific route? Is it meaningful to refer to a given state's foreign policy if its actions are determined by a foreign government or international corporation or if its actions are countermanded by domestic guerrillas holding sizable parts of the country?

B. Orientations Minimizing the Need to Characterize Foreign Policy

For over a decade questions such as these have seriously eroded easy and simple definitions of foreign policy and have even led a number of observers to suggest that the distinction between domestic and foreign policy is no longer useful (e.g., Friedrich, 1966; Rosenau, 1969; Hanrieder, 1971; Katzenstein, 1978). Though that conclusion can be argued as premature, what is noteworthy is that the conceptualization of foreign policy is under scrutiny. Remarkable as it might seem to thoughtful individuals who do not normally attend to foreign policy as an era of research, those who do study foreign policy have tended in the past to treat the concept as a "given" or "undefined" term. The challenging questions have awakened the field from its indifferent slumber about the nature of the concept and the implications of any particular definition.

How can it be that until recently the meaning of foreign policy, beyond simplistic textbook statements, has been ignored? The answer to that question reveals a good deal about the nature of foreign policy research. It seems possible to classify most foreign policy research into one of five categories: single case studies, internal institution and process descriptions, independent variable studies, relational chronologies, and conflict analyses. These categories are not mutually exclusive, but a very large portion of research usually classified as concerning foreign policy can be assigned to one or more of these categories. Each one contains its own logic for making unnecessary any consideration of the nature of the concept of foreign policy and its implications.

Single Case Studies. Single case studies likely constitute the most numerous kind of foreign policy research.[3] The author examines the development or evolution of a set of activities undertaken by a collective actor (usually a national government) in response to a particular historical problem in world affairs. The researcher asks how did the government cope or fail to cope with a particular problem at a given point in time. Although the investigators need not be historians and frequently address cases in very recent history—the last 10 to 15 years—many of the research techniques are familiar to the historian. They include the search for and evaluation of original materials, the construction of a plausible set of inferences and interpretations consistent with all the available evidence of what happened and, at least to a degree, why it happened. Because the author of a single case study focuses on a discrete issue in time and space, the research design does not require him or her to ask seriously of what class of phenomena is this particular episode an instance? What are the defining properties that make this an example of one kind of behavior rather than another? In short, it is unnecessary to locate the case as representing a particular kind of foreign policy.

Internal Institution and Process Studies. Internal institution and process studies, as the name implies, examine the organizations and procedures by which foreign policy is made. Often case studies concentrate on the foreign policy machinery involved in the specific episode examined. Many process studies, however, do not invoke the case format. Some are primarily descriptive and concentrate on the operation of, for example, a single ministry (e.g., Bacchus, 1974), a type of policy (e.g., Destler, 1980), a branch of government (e.g., Robinson, 1962), or a survey of an entire government's foreign policy machinery (e.g., Wallace, 1975). Other process studies have an evaluative orientation dedicated to the development of recommendations for improving foreign policy procedures. Destler (1972), in his own study recommending modifications in governmental operations for the conduct of foreign policy, notes that no less than 11 major studies have been performed on the foreign policy procedures of the U.S. government since World War II. The latest in this apparently favorite American pastime (Murphy et al., 1975) consists of a one-volume summary report and seven oversized volumes of supporting research. Evaluative studies of this kind share a premise that the organizations and procedures by which policies are made can affect the quality of the resulting foreign activities.

Organization and process studies can be extremely informative in the descriptive mode, and in the prescriptive mode they provide a necessary foundation for any proposals for the modification of foreign policy procedures. Nevertheless, they permit the analyst to concentrate on small group, organizational, and administrative issues without any particular attention to the kind of public policy that the organizations and processes are designed to formulate. At least, a review of institution and process studies suggests that a careful examination of the nature of foreign policy and its distinctive qualities is almost never considered.

Independent Variable Studies. What factors shape the nature and quality of foreign policy? This question lies at the core of most independent variable studies. Much scholarly work as well as textbook material in foreign policy has centered on the investigation of independent or explanatory variables that can be used to account for foreign policy. As will be examined more fully in the second major section of this chapter, a large number of variables or clusters of variables have been identified and explored, including public opinion (Almond, 1950; Hughes, 1978), ideology (Ulam, 1971), national attributes and power capabilities (Sullivan, 1976, especially Chapters 4 and 5), leader personalities (de Rivera, 1968), types of political regimes (Brzezinski and Huntington, 1963; Waltz, 1967), the national interests (Krasner, 1978), and the organizational decision process (e.g., Huntington, 1960; Allison, 1971), to name but a few. Some analyses of independent variables have considered only one class of factors, but others have enumerated many candidates (e.g., Thomson and Macridis, 1976), and some have engaged in systematic comparison of multiple sets of independent variables (e.g., Rosenau, 1966, 1974).

Studies of this kind serve an undeniable function in guiding explanations of foreign policy at a more generalized level than the discrete case study. They provide clues as to where to look for the cause or source of foreign policy activity. What is extraordinary about these studies is that—like the other categories noted above—they pay scant attention to the specification of the dependent variable that they seek to understand—foreign policy. To the outside observer such neglect in these studies may seem incredible. How is it possible to describe the effect of one kind of variable—such as public opinion or class structure—on another without being quite specific about exactly what that other variable is? The fact remains that many of these studies exclude any systematic consideration of the nature or kinds of foreign policy.

Relational Chronologies.   Relational chronologies, the fourth category of foreign policy studies, consider the exchanges over a period of years between a pair of countries or a larger set located in the same geographic region or in a common military or economic alliance. Examples of this kind of study include the policies of China and the Soviet Union toward one another (Griffith, 1964), or relations among North Vietnam, China, and the Soviet Union (Zagoria, 1967), or the member states in the European Economic Community (Camps, 1966). In sharp contrast to the independent variable studies, relational chronologies do not omit mention of foreign policy. Instead they tend to describe in serial form the stream of discrete foreign activities, the reasons they were initiated, the effect they had on the recipients, and the foreign policy activities they triggered in response. As with case studies, however, relational chronologies tend to enumerate specific decisions and actions at a concrete level and in historical context without the critical examination of the more general kinds of policy these occurrences represented and, indeed, what properties make them "foreign." To the extent that they group or cluster such activities, they tend to use the categories selected by the policy makers themselves or those offered by journalists (e.g., Truman Doctrine, *Ostpolitic*).[4] Though analysts constructing a relational chronology may estimate the effects of policies and their success in achieving intended objectives, few have challenged the actor's assertions as to what activities were foreign policies and what labels should be used to describe them.

Conflict Analyses.   Conflict analyses have generally been more attentive to the nature of foreign policy behavior than the other four types. The distinctive feature of these studies is their concentration on a broad class of foreign policy activities that manifest some form of conflict (e.g., Holsti, 1972; Singer et al., 1972; Haas, 1974). Important differences exist among the concepts of crisis, war, aggression, hostility, and violence. Yet they have in common the investigator's concern with those actions of governments and other international actors that are designed to harm or to threaten harm to the objectives if not the actual existence of other foreign entities. A number of these studies have been quite rigorous in their conceptual definition, their measurement, and their classification of types of conflict.

Much of this conflict research has sought to associate particular factors to war or other forms of hostility in a systematic fashion. Certainly a strong case can be made that this class of literature has contributed to our understanding of one broad area of foreign activity. In one sense, therefore, it is incorrect to suggest that most of these studies have ignored the concept of foreign policy. In another sense, they have contributed to the neglect. For whereas they have generally been conscientious about defining conflict, they have tended to ignore setting such activity in a larger context. In the spectrum of all foreign policies, where do conflict and hostility fit? If conflicts are a recurrent phenomena in foreign policy, how should we understand the vast domain of subjects over which various kinds of conflicts arise? Rather than seeing conflict as one kind of expression of foreign policy, the concept of conflict and associated concepts of collective violence and expressions of hostility have replaced the concept of foreign policy.

Until very recently, many Western foreign policy and international relations scholars have seen war prevention as the paramount value to be addressed in their scholarship. The importance of social justice, economic development, and equality as other values realized or deprived through foreign policy activities is only now beginning to receive broad attention. The growing awareness of other values and dimensions of foreign policy makes it less acceptable to collapse all foreign policy into a continuum of conflict.

A number of reasons can be offered for the frequent failure to come to terms with the concept of foreign policy. There may have been a sense that every thoughtful person knew what foreign policy was and, accordingly, an unarticulated assumption of consensus about the concept prevailed. Furthermore, many particular questions of widely recognized importance do not require direct examination of the umbrella term, foreign policy. The causes of war offer an unambiguous illustration. So, too, on a more micro scale do questions posed by other kinds of studies, such as why a nation whose economy is still struggling to recover from the ravages of World War II commits itself to the Marshall Plan—the largest foreign assistance program in its history (Jones, 1955). In short, agreement as to the meaning of foreign policy was either frequently assumed or the concept's explication seemed unnecessary for the research task of interest.

C. Status of the Field as Revealed by the Definition Issue

From this review a number of characteristics of the study of foreign policy should be evident. Some of the major features can be summarized as follows:

1. Over the years a quite substantial number of single case studies have been conducted that consist of large quantities of descriptive material and some evaluative analysis of various actors' discrete policy activities—usually the subject is the United States or another country for which information about policy-making is accessible to Western scholars. Single case studies are a frequent subject of doctoral dissertations in foreign policy and are augmented by the occasional production of new studies by more senior scholars.
2. For Western nations and to a lesser degree for selected other countries, considerable descriptive and some evaluative material has been produced about the organizations and processes involved in the formulation of policies that would be widely regarded as "foreign" policies.

3. An extensive cataloging has been performed of the various factors or clusters of independent variables that plausibly might be expected to influence some kinds of unspecified foreign policy. A good deal of descriptive work has been performed with these variables, including some empirical analysis, usually using conflict data or U.N. voting as the dependent variable.

4. For some countries and time periods, descriptive accounts have been prepared of the declared foreign policies of two, three, or a larger grouping of governments toward one another and the effects of these policies.

5. A vigorous subset of studies using a variety of perspectives and research methods has analyzed the nature of war and other kinds of international conflict and hostility as one form of behavior in which nations engage across national boundaries.

6. In many of the kinds of research noted above there has been a rather close connection between scholarship and the policy community in the borrowing of the definition of problems and the selection of concepts, although the research results have often seemed to have had little recognizable utility to the policy community.

7. For much of the noted research it has not been necessary to delve into the meaning of the umbrella concept of foreign policy and the various forms it might take. Useful closure on the established research problem could normally be achieved without it, or it could be assumed that most researchers shared some common understanding of the undefined term.

8. The inattentiveness to the concept of foreign policy and to its implications is disappearing as the result of a series of challenging questions asked from various quarters about the actors who engage in foreign policy, the continued utility of distinguishing domestic from foreign policy, the appropriate way to treat unintended external effects of various actions or inactions, and the apparent breakdown of sovereignty as it has been assumed to exist for many states.

It should not be surprising that one conclusion from this review is that the cohesion of foreign policy studies as a field or area of inquiry has not been strong and that it is in considerable flux. There is a good chance that the field may look considerably different in the not too distant future from the way it looks today if consensus begins to emerge about the meaning of foreign policy, the units into which it can be classified or dimensionalized, and the basic questions about it that establish the core concerns of the field. Such a state does not exist today, but the questions noted earlier are producing a stream of literature grappling with various aspects of the issue concerning the nature of foreign policy (Meehan, 1971; Hermann, 1972; Rummel, 1972; Kegley, 1973; Kegley et al., 1974; Salmore and Munton, 1974; O'Leary, 1976; Callahan et al., 1982).

D. Toward a Definition of Foreign Policy

The fluidity of foreign policy studies at the present time makes any attempt at the definition of the concept of foreign policy a most provisional and personal exercise. Yet it may be unfair to end this section without the author stipulating one possible definition for consideration and use as a benchmark for examining others.

To begin, a distinction will be drawn between foreign policy and foreign policy behavior. Foreign policy consists of the development and conscious pursuit of some preferred goal or goals of an actor through the selective use of foreign policy behavior.

Foreign policy behavior is purposeful action resulting from the implementation of a political-level decision to act so as to attempt to influence attitudes, beliefs, and/or actions of one or more other actors where entities external to the political jurisdiction of the decision makers are either (1) the subject of the influence attempt or (2) the channel through which a message is conveyed to domestic individuals of collectivities.

Some basic terms in these definitions need elaboration. International actors are entities that have the resources and the motivation to undertake regularly influence attempts to or through entities residing outside the political jurisdiction of the nation they rule or in which they are chartered or otherwise established legally (e.g., citizens) or by continued residency (e.g., Palestinians in Lebanon). Goals are the preferred states of affairs that do not exist and are sought or that do exist and are desired to be retained. In the latter form, goals may be boundaries within which certain phenomena are desired to be kept. Collective entities may act in a goal-seeking manner when all members accept the same goals through consensus or when the goals are those of one or more leaders who obtained the necessary support of members through side payments of rewards or punishments. Political-level decisions are choices made by individuals with the authority to commit the resources of the government, ruling party, corporation, or other international entity. Finally, behavior is purposeful, as contrasted with unintended or unconscious, action. Actions undertaken in an attempt to influence others are, therefore, behaviors.

Of the numerous implications of these stipulated definitions, several should be noted at once. First, not all foreign policy behavior is in the service of foreign policy; that is, it need not be behavior initiated in pursuit of some clearly established goals. For many actors communication and influence attempts may be undertaken for momentary advantage against a traditional adversary or in support of a traditional ally. In short, they may be reflexive or habitual behavior that seems dictated by immediate circumstance. Such behavior can still be intentional and, hence, rightly labeled foreign policy behavior even without explicit, accepted goals. In short, the purpose of influence is present even if the reason for it is not. When, however, action has no intention to influence a foreign entity or a domestic one through a foreign entity, it is not foreign policy behavior. Both isolated behaviors and goal-seeking policies must be undertaken with the expectation that external entities will enable the transmission of a signal to someone else or will themselves be susceptible to influence. Unintended foreign effects of actions or domestic behavior do not constitute foreign policy of foreign policy behavior, but such unintended actions may trigger another entity to engage in foreign policy or foreign policy behavior.

The proposed definitions permit a distinction between domestic and foreign policy. Foreign policy and behavior require a deliberate attempt to use or affect entities outside one's own political jurisdiction. This distinction may yield sharp differences in the behavior of at least some kinds of international actors who may be expected to have different types of control within their own jurisdiction, may be affected by different laws and norms, and may enjoy different status and power domestically as compared to abroad. (Notice that the emphasis is on differences internally and externally and not on the assumption of sovereignty or more power domestically.) These differences usually are a matter of degree and apply more to some actors than others.

It should also be apparent that states, national government, and ruling political parties are not envisioned as the only entities capable of initiating foreign policy and foreign policy behavior. Subnational governments, private voluntary organizations, and corporations are among the other candidates. Accordingly, it becomes extremely important to specify the kinds of international actors that a study program dictates should be investigated to explore particular research questions. Stating that one is studying foreign policy does not automatically reveal the actors included or excluded from the research.

Determining the goals of individuals, to say nothing of complex social entities such as governments, poses an extremely difficult task (Hermann, 1978b). They are often a matter of conjecture and frequently are not subject to direct examination. Foreign policy behaviors, by contrast, are observable, although governments may attempt to shield them from the scrutiny of outside parties. In every case there must be an actor and a recipient and the behavior should in most instances be evident to both (although the motives may not be). Such circumstances create a basis for observation in the contemporary world. Foreign policy behaviors often leave a trace in the form of written records. In the distinction between foreign policy and foreign policy behavior, the effort is made to create for foreign policy researchers a unit of observation that the traditional definitions which incorporate goals and plans frequently deny.

II. THEORETICAL FRAMEWORKS AND CONCEPTUAL APPROACHES

The current unsettled state of the field of foreign policy studies is further revealed through the diversity of theoretical frameworks and conceptual approaches that characterize research. Some social scientists have given considerable attention to the role of paradigms in the development of various areas of scientific inquiry following the work of Kuhn (1963). If by a field or disciplinary paradigm one means a set of widely accepted, fundamental, and critical assumptions that characterize the phenomena being studied and that also indicate what questions, problems, and modes of inquiry appropriately constitute the frontier of knowledge, then foreign policy studies have no accepted paradigm. A subset of scholars concerned with the cross-national study of foreign policy using the scientific method have come close to adopting a paradigm based primarily on the works of Rosenau (1966, 1971, 1974), but that too seems in disarray (Kegley, 1979).

Lack of serious examination of the concept of foreign policy has not prevented its use in general orientations to foreign policy studies. The variety of current frameworks and approaches can be organized by the relationship envisioned between the usually undefined term, foreign policy, and other components in the framework. The five categories in the previous section used widely recognized features of research to suggest reasons in each set why the concept of foreign policy has seldom been seriously investigated. If one of the trends for the future is the fuller explication of the meaning and properties of foreign policy, we need to classify the existing designs in a different fashion to propose how foreign policy is incorporated and the functions it is expected to play.

The most pervasive orientation, which generates various approaches, views foreign policy as the dependent variable—that which is to be understood and explained. Some frameworks, however, assign foreign policy as the independent variable and consider its effects on other factors. Finally, there are approaches that interpret foreign policy as a mediating variable, usually in a continuous or cyclical process in which the distinction between independent and dependent variables may not be useful. Representative frameworks developed in each of these three broader orientations will be reviewed.

A. Foreign Policy as a Dependent Variable

Individual Characteristics. A number of quite distinctive research designs have been developed around a basic question dealing with what differences in the substance of foreign policy or in the orientation to foreign policy might be attributable to variation in the characteristics of an individual participant in the policy process (Kelman, 1965; de Rivera, 1968). One approach has sought to construct the cognitive maps of decision makers. The research focuses on the cognitive structures and processes of the mind involved in a person's set of causal assertions about the things in his or her environment and the relations that affect their operations. Such mental maps become the basis for processing information and calculating appropriate action (see Bonham and Shapiro, 1973; Holsti, 1976). Another effort centers on the political beliefs of policy makers and the means for assessing their effects on behavior. Pioneering work by Leites (1951) has been developed further by George (1969) and applied to a number of individuals such as Senator Frank Church (Johnson, 1977). Other research has pursued psychobiographies (Edinger, 1965; Wolfenstein, 1971) or has stressed social background experiences (e.g., Beck et al., 1973). Recently more integrative approaches to psychological factors have been advanced that take into account beliefs and attitudes, motives, background experiences, and interpersonal and decision styles (e.g., Hermann, 1980).

One of the continuing concerns about the search for explanation of foreign policy in terms of the psychological characteristics of individuals is the question of whether individual properties make any difference in complex social phenomena such as governmental policy making (e.g., Rosenau, 1968). The contention is that the effects of individual characteristics depend on a number of conditions such as the nature of the problem (routine versus crisis), the location of the individual (head of state versus middle-level bureaucrat), the decision-making process (numerous people involved versus one or a few people), or the style of the individual (passive versus active).

Bureaucratic Politics. Few volumes in the last two decades devoted to the explication of a conceptual framework in foreign policy have received the widespread attention given Allison's (1971) *Essence of Decision.* Allison offers three distinctive interpretations of the Cuban missile crisis depending on which of three frameworks is applied. Although the volume deserves examination on several grounds (e.g., the critique of the national, unified actor model of decision making), its explication of a bureaucratic politics framework comprises a dominant feature. A number of analysts contributed to the development of a bureaucratic politics framework prior to Allison, including Neustadt (1970), Huntington (1960), Hilsman (1967), and Schilling et al., (1962). It has been further articulated by Allison and Halperin (1972), Halperin and Kanter (1973), and Halperin (1974) among others. This orientation views foreign policy as the result of bargaining and persuasion among leaders or their representatives from different governmental organizations or bureaucracies. Each bureaucracy has its own interests and missions and interprets the national interests of the government so as to advance its own welfare. The resulting conflict among competing interests and the inability of any one individual to assert effectively his agency's preferences over all the others necessitates "log rolling," compromises, and other bargaining strategies that produce an agreed-upon foreign policy that is often the hybrid of many positions and not an effective strategy for the realization of any of them. Bureaucratic politics clearly asserts that the primary sources for explaining foreign policy are within the government itself and tends to minimize the effects of other domestic factors as well as the behavior of international actors. It also highlights the implementation of policy as much as the acts of choice by high-level officials. It contends that considerable discrepancy can arise between decision and execution (if any) as a result of further bureaucratic politics. A basic question in the bureaucratic politics framework is what organizational actors or players have which skills and resources to shape in part a given policy, and how does the result reflect the tradeoffs made among the key actors?

The bureaucratic politics approach has attracted its share of critiques (e.g., Krasner, 1972; Art, 1973). Among the points that have been made are that it seems applicable only to the United States and perhaps a few other societies with modern bureaucracies and considerable distribution of power. Even in the United States it overlooks the distinctive role of the President in many major issues. Furthermore, key actors who are transitory political appointees may not have strong ties to the ministries they lead, and indeed, may have loyalties to one another that produce very different behaviors. (See the discussion of small group behavior below.) Nevertheless, the bureaucratic politics perspective has proven an attractive interpretative framework for many case studies of policy making. Additionally, it does what many approaches fail to do by developing clear linkages between independent variables (e.g., bargaining, compromising) and kinds of foreign policy (e.g., "paperclip" policies, deferred action, lowest-common-denominator agreements, etc.).

Small Decision Groups.   Whereas bureaucratic politics postulates foreign policy as the result of conflict between major participants in the decision process, a major proponent of the small group perspective finds not group conflict but an excessive concern for consensus within the group as a source of danger to quality decision making. Janis (1972) contends that some groups of decision makers become so concerned with maintaining the well-being and the good feeling among fellow policy makers that they will distort information processing, banish alternative options, and engage in various forms of "group think" that significantly erode the likelihood of quality decisions. Empirical research has begun to sharpen the conditions under which such behavior occurs (Tetlock, 1979).

From a somewhat different perspective, George (1972) also has noted that the premature closure on a single interpretation of the situation and prescription for dealing with it can lead a group to poorer decisions. He proposes the deliberate introduction of "multiple advocates," who argue the merits of competing options to prevent consensus without careful examination of various alternatives. Elsewhere, George (1974) has summarized the extensive literature on the effects of stress on small group decision making and applied it to the political process. Quick consensus and stress both may be problems in small decision groups, but equally important can be the various methods used to resolve substantive disagreement. Different conflict management techniques employed in a group can yield different results (Hermann, 1978a). At the core of research sharing this approach is an assumption that the processes used in small groups for processing information and handling conflict can influence the policies adopted. The difficulty of accessibility to the procedures of decision groups is an apparent criticism. So is the problem of distinguishing the reasons for consensus (e.g., "yes men" yielding to the preferences of a strong leader, excessive concurrence seeking to preserve the group's well-being, or a genuinely shared conclusion based on a thorough examination of the evidence). Variability in the process and motives for consensus may have an effect on the quality of the decision. Despite unresolved issues, the small group perspective reminds us that at the point of choice the decision unit in foreign policy is often a small, face-to-face group.

Political System—Collective Beliefs and Organization.   It may be stretching a point to suggest that anything approximating a unified framework exists to deal with the effect of the political system on foreign policy. Certainly a stream of research addresses the effects of the nature of government or regime types on foreign affairs. A long-standing issue for study has been the relative merits of democracies versus authoritarian systems (e.g., Long, 1966; Farrell, 1966), with the general argument being that authoritarian systems have greater flexibility and capacity to respond to changes in their external environment. The foreign policies of presidential and parliamentary systems also have been compared (Waltz, 1967). More recently, regime characteristics such as the degree of opposition, the amount of cohesion, and the responsiveness to political elites have been treated as variables applicable to any regime and as influencing foreign policy (Salmore and Salmore, 1978).

Normally, a regime is thought to include not only the rulers but also the politically relevant aspects of the entire society. These other aspects of a polity can be assumed to affect foreign policy. At various times scholars have sought to explain foreign policy by means of national character, political culture, public opinion, interest groups, and political elites, to mention a few of the elements that can be distilled from the umbrella construct of political system. These efforts can be divided between those who have focused on the collective beliefs, attitudes, and expressed opinions of politically salient members of societies and those who have concentrated on the organized representation of various elements of the public in the form of interest groups, political parties, and political elites.

World War II provided impetus to American scholars concerned with national character research. Studies were prompted by the need to understand the adversaries. Through national character, the investigator seeks to describe the enduring personality characteristics, unique life styles, and cultural behavior patterns shared by all, or most, members of a nation. At their core the national character studies proposed that culturally determined practices such as child rearing, acceptable patterns of interpersonal relationships, and cognitive-perceptual-reasoning practices promoted by language structure all resulted in shared attitudes toward authority or variations in values that found expression in many aspects of public behavior, including foreign policy (e.g., Leites, 1948; Klineberg, 1950; Brodersen, 1961).

Although the attempt to attribute foreign policy to a modal national character seems to hold less interest in recent scholarship, the concern with a society's collective efforts to shape political beliefs—political socialization (Renshon, 1977)—and the effect on foreign policy remains an active area of inquiry. For example, Inglehart (1967) found that young people in four Western European countries had more positive attitudes toward political integration than did older generations. He attributed the difference to changes in early socialization practices in those countries and forecasted that as those youngsters became the majority of the voting-age population, the foreign policies of their countries would reflect that increased commitment to European integration. A recent major study of Chinese foreign policy (Bobrow et al., 1979) seeks to establish the "national decision culture" of China as manifested in basic beliefs and decision logics that can be applied in dealing with foreign policy. In contrast to the previously noted work on belief systems of individuals (e.g., George, 1969), Bobrow and his associates search for the shared beliefs that can be the bases for decision rules of an entire elite.

An influential book by Almond (1950) suggested that the American society could be conceived as a pyramid with the mass public as the large base, a small attentive public near the top and, at the apex, the policy and opinion elites who include among them the actual policy makers. With respect to foreign policy, he noted the differing role of each group, the mobility between strata, and the interaction in terms of policy influence and mobilization of the public. That book and the continuing advances in survey methodology have triggered an extensive literature—both conceptual and empirical—on the role of public opinion (e.g., Rosenau, 1964; Cohen, 1973; Mueller, 1973; Deutsch et al., 1967). Though not lending itself readily to the type of aggregate data analysis found in many public opinion studies, research on interest groups in American foreign policy has been continuous (Bauer et al., 1963; Cohen, 1963; Chittick, 1970; Trice, 1976). Following the lead of scholars in American and comparative politics, efforts to discern the role of interest groups in the foreign policies of other countries also has become a subject of inquiry (Hellmann, 1969; Spielmann, 1978).

To date no major effort has been made to conceptualize how such components of the political system as interest groups, public opinion, political parties, and political elites interact to affect foreign policy in other kinds of societies, but several efforts have been made for the United States. Cohen (1957) traced through their interaction in a case study of the American decision to conclude a peace treaty with Japan years after World War II. More recently, Hughes (1978) characterized six alternative models of the foreign policy decision process (e.g., pluralist, power elite, rational actor). Based on a review of various case studies and data from opinion surveys, Hughes concluded that the extent and nature of public and group influence on foreign policy decision making depends on issue type (economic, security, and diplomatic), the locus of decision within the government (executive versus legislative), and the speed with which a decision is made. He contends that the adequacy of the various decision models to account for the role of nongovernmental components of the political system depends on the configuration of the issue, decision locus, and decision time variables.

The frameworks and approaches that take elements of the political system as independent variables suggest that foreign policy decision makers are influenced by the political system of which they are a part. They are affected both as a result of values and beliefs that were acquired as part of their own political socialization and as a result of explicit preferences and direct influence attempts of those outside of the government or ruling party. A problem that is hardly unique to these approaches, but which they dramatically illustrate, is one of causality. It has been difficult to demonstrate empirically that public opinion or interest group activities are responsible for observed policy actions. Furthermore, the problem of assessing effect becomes acute when—as often happens—collective beliefs or organizational positions are divided.

National Attributes. Explanations of a nation's foreign policy have long been attributed to the variety and quality of its national attributes, which often are interpreted as elements of capability or power. For example, this has been a key element in the realist perspective on foreign policy and international relations (see Morgenthau, 1967; Krasner,

1978). Whereas the political system frameworks discussed previously concentrate on aspects of society that pertain consciously and directly to governance, national attribute approaches deal with human and nonhuman resources that can be used for many different purposes and that have no intrinsic political intent. The emergence of aggregate data on national attributes—properties applicable to an entire nation but variable across nations—has encouraged numerous empirical studies that seek to correlate attributes with behavior (e.g., Clark et al., 1971; Kean and McGowan, 1973; East and Hermann, 1974). Indicators of wealth and size frequently have been found to be associated with such foreign policy behaviors as general conflict or the total amount of international activity. The most extensive effort to interpret foreign policy in terms of national attributes has been conducted by Rummel (1972, 1977, 1979), who has sought to use national attributes in his development of field theory. Numerous attributes are reduced statistically to a set of underlying components. The distance between the values of these components for pairs of nations is theorized to represent social forces that determine foreign policy behavior. Another major attribute approach to account for war as one kind of foreign policy behavior proposes that as the population and technology of a society increase relative to its internal resources, the nation will engage in "lateral pressure"—external actions that can lead to war (North and Lagerstrom, 1971; Choucri and North, 1975).

All attribute studies assume that there are identifiable properties of an entire nation that shape much of its foreign policy. Empirical analyses generally support correlations between certain behaviors and classes of attributes, but why? Realists have suggested that some attributes provide power capabilities; Rummel suggests that the difference between two countries' attributes creates status differentials and generates social forces that drive policy. The development of the underlying logic for the relationship, the chain of reasoning, and the necessary conditions for the greater or lesser effects of attributes still remains to be done. One effort in that direction by East (1978) contends that attributes generate variation in the policy makers' "capacity to act." The absence of certain attributes would constrain certain actions, but their existence does not impel their use. Thus, unanswered from a national attributes perspective is when available resources will be used.

External and Systemic Factors. The frameworks and approaches reviewed up to this point have sought to explain foreign policy as a consequence of various domestic factors located inside the jurisdiction or territory of the nation state or other actor. It would seem logical that parallel frameworks would have been developed to consider sources outside the jurisdiction or boundaries of an international actor. Remarkably few undertakings have been built around the identification of specific types of external and systemic variables as independent variables that treat foreign policy exclusively as the *dependent variable.* Rosenau (1972) and Hanrieder (1967, 1971) have speculated on the reasons for this neglect and cite difficulties in levels of analysis, availability of data, and conceptual development. Without specifying kinds of variables, the Sprouts (Sprout and Sprout, 1965) have stressed that the environment can influence the foreign policy choices of policy makers only through the perceptions of those in the decision-making process.

Harf and his associates (1974) have advanced a now widely acknowledged distinction between external and systemic variables. External variables are qualities that are (1) exogenous to the acting nation or other actor and (2) dependent on their relationship with that actor for their meaning and assignable value. Thus, the concept "alliance

partners" would be an external variable, the nature and number of which would vary
from country to country. Systemic variables refer to characteristics of the entire international system and have the same value (although not necessarily the same implications)
for all members of the system (e.g., the amount of conflict occurring in the world at any
given time). East (1978) has provided an explicit systemic framework for examining foreign policy that is keyed on five systemic, independent variables that characterize the
complexity of the international system and the resources available in it. This singular effort to date involves no empirical analysis.

Somewhat more has been done with external variables and foreign policy. Deutsch
(1966b) has proposed how external variable effects can be transmitted through domestic
groups who act as receivers and conveyers of inputs. A different focus has been adopted
by Brady (1978), who emphasizes the properties of transitory international situations as
sources of foreign policy. One specific set of situational variables can be stipulated as
crises that when perceived by policy makers as having certain features (e.g., short time,
high threat, and surprise) can substantially affect the foreign policy process and the resulting behavior (Hermann, 1969). The previously cited study by Harf et al. (1974)
offers some preliminary empirical evidence for several external variables concerning a
nation's likelihood of becoming involved in war. Actually, the amount of attention to
external variables is greater than indicated by the survey in this section, as will be evident
when the relationship between external variables and foreign policy is cast in other than
the independent-to-dependent variable format. It appears that when investigators conceptualize the relationship between an international actor and its external environment,
they find the postulation of foreign policy as a dependent variable a less intriguing perspective. Why this should be so is a matter for conjecture.

Multilevel, Integrated Analyses.   Not surprisingly, after a review of approaches such as
those described in the six previous sections, there have been repeated calls for a more
holistic or integrated perspective in the efforts to account for foreign policy behavior.
A series of frameworks have been advanced suggesting that foreign policy must be seen
as the interaction of multiple variables at different analytical levels—the individual, the
group, the organization, the entire society, and so on. It should also not be startling that
such overviews find gaps in the array of explanatory factors usually considered (Mc
Gowan, 1976a).

One effort at a more comprehensive framework has been undertaken by Brecher
and his associates (Brecher et al., 1969; Brecher, 1972), who organize explanatory variables as operational environment components (subdivided into domestic and external)
connected by communication through decision elites to a psychological environment (attitudinal prism and elite images), which, in turn, lead to the formulation and implementation process that yields foreign policy outputs. Though differing in some details, the
broad set of categories proposed by Cohen and Harris (1975) seems generally similar.

Yet the question may be asked here as it was of national attribute research: Where
is the connective tissue—the underlying logic that provides the reasoning for suggesting
how various categories of explanatory variables are to be combined and the conditions
under which specific interactions occur with particular policy results? Rosenau (1966),
in a conceptualization that has inspired much subsequent work (e.g., Rosenau, 1974),[5]
has proposed that the basic question is not how the variables interact, but the circum-

stances under which one class of variables prevails over others in accounting for foreign policy. In other words, which category of explanatory variables is more "potent"? As a beginning, he proposes that a set of genotypic categories of nations and types of issue areas might be used as conditions for ordering the salience of explanatory variables in accounting for foreign policy.[6] As an alternative, a group of investigators (Salmore, M. G. Hermann, Salmore, and C. F. Hermann, 1978) have proposed that specific causal linkages might be established among particular kinds of variables, thus permitting new interaction effects rather than the override of one kind of variable by another. That approach introduces considerable complexity and has yet to be investigated empirically.

The most ambitious empirical investigation of an integrated framework reported to date has been conducted by the Interstate Behavior Analysis (IBA) Project (Wilkenfeld, et al., 1980). Using a partial least-squares model of analysis, the investigators apply their framework to data on 56 countries. The framework itself groups explanatory variables into five major clusters ranging from psychological to global components and seeks to account for six dimensions of foreign policy behavior. Rather than treat all nations in an undifferentiated fashion, the IBA analysis follows Rosenau in grouping nations into categories based on three dimensions. This research represents an important advance in developing comprehensive models of foreign policy susceptible to empirical investigation. It still leaves to the future the task of constructing models that advance the conceptual logic for the interaction of various categories of independent and mediating variables in explaining foreign policy (as opposed to interaction stipulated by the statistical model used in the analysis).

B. Foreign Policy as an Independent or Mediating Variable

Most—but certainly not all—of the frameworks that treat foreign policy as a dependent variable concentrate on domestic sources of explanation; that is, they seek to account for differences in foreign policy by examining differences within the society or other unit that is the policy-initiating entity. Furthermore, most such approaches have a certain static quality. Conditions exist in the factors assumed to be relevant, and certain kinds of foreign policy are assumed to result. That is the end of the conceptualization. The approaches examined in this section tend to view foreign policy in a different manner. With a few exceptions, they concentrate on the environment outside the actor, and they are more oriented to a continuous process of action-reaction or interaction. In that context the distinction between independent and dependent variable becomes much less useful as an analytic device. The first two approaches reviewed do not explicitly introduce a closed cyclical process, but they do emphasize interaction. They are linkage politics and dependency theories.

Linkage Politics. The phrase "linkage politics" was advanced by Rosenau (1969) in part as a result of his observation of a gap in political science research between scholars dealing with comparative politics and those dealing with international relations. The former normally concern themselves only with the effects of domestic politics that are experienced within that political system and ignore the external consequences of domestic political system factors. International relations specialists tend to ignore the effects of international politics on domestic politics. Rosenau noted that thoughtful observation of actual politics offered numerous illustrations of the effects occurring across the gap created by the self-imposed boundaries of the two fields. He urged that attention be given to this neglected linkage. Rosenau imposed no direction of causality to the continuous cycle of interaction between domestic actors and their international environment. Instead he noted that there were many cases that ought to be studied in which domestic politics generated international political consequences and vice versa.

Beyond the contributors to his initial volume, the scholars who responded most vigorously to the Rosenau (1969) appeal were those interested in the relationship between domestic and international conflict. Early empirical studies (e.g., Rummel, 1963; Tanter, 1966, Haas, 1968) found little support for the "scapegoat hypothesis" that internal violence produces external violence because policy makers seek to reduce domestic disruptions by public appeals for support against external dangers often interpreted as the cause of domestic difficulties. Associating themselves with the linkage approach, Wilkenfeld (1973a) and several of his contributors sought to show that a relationship between internal and external violence did occur in certain types of political regimes. Such analysis, while addressing the gap noted by James Rosenau, appears to have drawn little of its explanatory reasoning from the linkage perspective. Indeed it might be argued that linkage politics is less a framework that suggests how classes of variables interact than the observation of an important gap in knowledge.

Dependency Theories. Whereas the research on the "scapegoat hypothesis" examines the effect of domestic politics on foreign policy, dependency research considers the effects of one or more countries' (or corporations') foreign policy on the domestic conditions in another society. It seems inappropriate, however, to associate this work with linkage politics, because some significant contributions substantially predate the linkage conceptualization and little of it explicitly draws on linkage politics. In general, dependency frameworks advance a relationship between a country's asymmetrical reliance on an external entity and its internal development. Although both Marxist and non-Marxist interpretations of dependency abound, the seminal works of Marx and Engels with their focus on imperialism of capitalist countries and the effects on the economic development of satellites or colonies has provided the conceptual foundation. New scholarship has expanded the various forms of dependence (e.g., dependency on a single foreign source; amount of foreign penetration of domestic markets) and on types of dependency (e.g., trade, assistance, investment). Recent conceptual developments and arguments by Frank (1970), Bodenheimer (1971), Sunkel (1972), and Moran (1978) have been complemented by increasingly sophisticated empirical research. The effects of foreign dependency on economic growth remain unclear. Galtung (1971), Chase-Dunn (1975), Alschuler (1976), and Bornschier (1977) find that greater dependence is associated with lower economic growth. Kaufman and associates (1975), McGowan (1976b), and Ray and Webster (1978) tend to find either no relationship or a positive one. The smaller number of studies of the effects of dependency on internal inequality (e.g., in land or income distribution) have found a small positive association (e.g., Galtung, 1971; Rubinson, 1976, 1977). As with the "scapegoat" hypothesis, the possibility that critical mediating conditions have a significant influence seems worth investigation. Gobalet and Diamond (1979) consider the conditioning effect of the recipient's own internal strength. Other considerations worth investigation as intervening conditions might include regional differences, various time lags, the status of the overall world economy, and the effects of different operationalizations. Finally, it should be noted that whereas the problem of economic development becomes a major—if not the major—task of foreign policy for most third and fourth world countries (see for example, Weinstein, 1976), the concept of dependency can be applied to nations that for other than economic development reasons are at the periphery rather than the center of an international system. Thus, for example, a source of international weakness that causes peripheral status on some issues could be dependency on external sources of energy. Dependency also can be viewed not only as influencing domestic factors (e.g., overall rate of economic growth, internal inequality in land or income), but also the dependent state's foreign policy (e.g., Richardson and Kegley, 1980).

Stimulus-Response Mediated by Perception.   As applied to foreign policy, the basic stimulus-response model would suggest that government A's response behavior toward government B can best be estimated based on government B's prior behavior toward A. Arms race models in their basic form follow this precept (Busch, 1970; Zinnes, 1976, especially Chapter 14). In the 1960s the Stanford Conflict and Integration Project (Holsti et al., 1964, 1968) advanced what they called a two-step, mediated stimulus-response model—S-r:s-R—as a modification of the basic formulation. In continuous interaction, state A's actual behavior toward state B would constitute a stimulus (S), which would be perceived and interpreted as a response (r) by state B, which in turn would perceive its own new action toward A as a new stimulus (s), which when manifested as behavior would become the "actual" response (R) to the initial stimulus (S). This response of state B would become a stimulus for state A and the process would recycle. The important features were (1) the introduction of the perceptions of other's behavior and the actor's own response, (2) the combination in empirical research of perceptual data with objective indicators, and (3) the view that this interaction of foreign policy behavior and perception among states was a continuous process of international communication. Snyder and his associates (1962) had earlier emphasized the decision makers' subjective definition of the situation that is rather equivalent to the "r" in the Stanford studies of the foreign policy process. This attention to the perception of behavior directed toward an actor as an important indicator of the actor's own actions has been a major component in research by Zinnes (1966, 1968; Zinnes et al., 1972) as well as that of others (Gamson and Modigliani, 1971, Jervis, 1976). The model advanced by the Stanford group has been modified by Phillips (see Phillips and Crain, 1974; and Phillips, 1978). He contends that when policy makers cannot identify a clear signal in the behavior addressed to them by others, they tend to repeat their own prior responses; when the stimulus is perceived (accurately or not) by all key decision makers as unambiguous, then they reciprocate and respond with the same kind of behavior as that which they interpreted was addressed to them.

The introduction of the actor's perceptions to an action-reaction framework introduces a decision-making perspective and, it can be argued, transforms an international relations orientation into one involving foreign policy processes. Having permitted the camel's nose under the tent, so to speak, do these analysts provide an adequate representation of the role of foreign policy decision making? As we have seen, the policy process in many independent-dependent variable frameworks entails more than interpreting behavior from external entities. Must domestic pressures and capabilities be considered?

What about the actual process of decision making with multiple participants and the possible slippage in implementation? Even if the analysis is limited to perceptions, is it adequate to confine them to those indicators of collective official perceptions found in government documents? Many of these issues appear susceptible to further empirical analysis.

Cybernetics and Adaptation. Both of the last two frameworks reviewed address the effects of one entity's behavior on another. In one the dominant and asymmetrical power relationship of a given state or corporation influenced the economic development of another society. In the other framework, the behavioral interaction of two or more foreign policy-producing entities was seen to be dependent on each side's perception of those behaviors. In this last framework to be considered, the focus shifts from two or more interacting entities to the decision-making process in a single entity interacting with a complex and rather unspecified external environment. Both the cybernetic and adaptive approaches posit a goal-seeking entity that constantly adjusts its foreign policy behavior in the pursuit of its goals based on a continuous monitoring of selected features of its environment. The feedback from the environment stimulates either continuation of existing policy or some corrective if the policy goals seem to be becoming less obtainable. Deutsch (1966a) and Steinbruner (1974) have proposed the most extensive explications of the cybernetic approach applied to foreign policy using a systems and decision-making orientation, respectively. Steinbruner (1974) offers the cybernetic approach as an alternative to the rational or analytic model for explaining decision making. He suggests that the requirements of the analytic approach are unrealistic for complex decision making under conditions of uncertainty. His cybernetic alternative contends that decision makers or their representatives focus on a few indicators flowing from the environment to monitor the status of a goal. The monitoring activity moves to finer or more macro sets of indicators depending on the stability of the feedback received.

As advanced by Rosenau (1970a, 1970b), adaptation can be regarded as a cybernetic framework in which the goals are specified. He posits that all national societies are shaped by four essential structures (physical, political, economic, and social) and that maintaining these structures within certain boundaries becomes the task (goal) of both foreign and domestic policies. Because a given configuration of the structures defines any given society, if the status of any structure exceeds its critical limits, then the society is transformed. Policy makers, because of their power stake in the existing configuration, act to prevent transformation. Depending on a regime's responsiveness to the mix of internal and external demands, it will pursue one of several different strategies in its foreign policy —always adjusting to retain the configuration of structures. Using some modifications of Rosenau's ideas, McGowan (1974a, 1974b; and O'Leary, 1974) has sought to operationalize some of the key concepts in Rosenau's adaptation framework. An alternative perspective on adaptation has been proposed by Thorson (1974a, 1974b), who introduces an artificial system perspective following the developmental work in other contexts by Simon (1969).

Central to all cybernetic or adaptation frameworks is the positing of goals for foreign policy entities. Although Thorson (1974b) stresses that foreign policy goals can be constraints and Rosenau (1970a) views goals as boundaries or limits not to be exceeded, the idea of a complex, collective entity behaving in a goal-seeking manner requires careful examination. At conceptual level, what it means for a state or organization to pursue goals can be a difficult problem. Agreement on goals may not exist or be so vague as to be useless. Equally troublesome is the task of empirically determining goals for particular actors in a valid manner that again avoids the vague and broad definitions that provide few clues as to appropriate associated behaviors.[7]

C. Illustrative Findings from Research Frameworks

Before we draw implications from the frameworks reviewed, it may be useful to examine some representative propositions suggested by the various approaches. These examples permit insight into what the frameworks tell us at the present time about the observable world of foreign policy. They also suggest the kinds of questions and problems each framework investigates. Of course, the evidence for the propositions varies from conclusions generalized from one or two case studies to results confirmed by several separate statistical analyses using aggregate data. The reader is cautioned that none of the illustrated relationships should be regarded as strongly substantiated for any specifiable conditions.

Individual Characteristics. When predominant leaders lack training in foreign policy, the personal characteristics of degree of distrust of others, need for power, and nationalism have a greater effect on foreign policy behavior (Hermann, 1980).

Bureaucratic Politics. The more dependent officials are for promotion, status, and other career rewards on the bureaucratic organization of which they are a part, the more likely they are to interpret the foreign policy interests of the entire government in terms of the welfare of their organization and insist on the recognition of this interpretation in the formulation of foreign policy (Allison and Halperin, 1972).

Small Decision Groups. The more members of a decision group are concerned with the well-being and maintenance of the group, the more likely they are to resist the introduction into the group of new information or analysis when consensus begins to emerge in the group on a preferred alternative (Janis, 1972; Flowers, 1977).

Political System. The less the importance of a foreign policy issue to the general public, the greater is the likelihood of any concerned interest group's influence on the outcome of the issue (Milbrath, 1967).

National Attributes. The more economically developed and larger the nation, the greater is its participation in international affairs (Rummel, 1972).

External and Systemic Factors. A national government is more likely to make new proposals, concessions, or agreements in international negotiation with another state if that other state displays cooperation toward the acting country on issues external and unrelated to negotiations (Hopmann, 1972).

Multilevel, Integrated Analyses. Global, interstate economic, and societal factors together account for most of the variance in constructive diplomatic behaviors, with no additional contribution from the prior interactions of the parties (i.e., sequences of action-reaction) (Wilkenfeld et al., 1980).

Linkage Politics. In nations having dictatorial and highly centralized regimes, there is a greater tendency than in nations not having such regimes for domestic conflict to be followed by external conflict (Wilkenfeld, 1973b).

Dependency Theories.   Direct investment and foreign aid dependence increase domestic inequality (Bornschier, 1977).

Stimulus-Response Mediated by Perception.   The more the policy makers of a state perceive their country to be the subject of another country's hostility, the more likely those policy makers are to express hostility toward that source (Zinnes, 1966).

Cybernetics and Adaptation.   Small, closed, poor political systems tend to pursue a promotive foreign policy in which the policy makers are equally unresponsive to signals from their country's external environment and to those concerning domestic structures (McGowan, 1974b).

A much larger number of propositions of this type could be presented (see Jones and Singer, 1972; McGowan and Shapiro, (1973), although a few of the frameworks would account for a disproportionately large percentage of the available results. It can be argued, however, that the list above is generally representative. They reveal the kinds of issues at the core of the considered materials.

D. Observations About Frameworks and Approaches

Compatibility.   As one reviews the array of frameworks, it is reasonable to speculate whether these diverse pieces could be fitted together into a more comprehensive mosaic. Some of the approaches do seem complementary and even compatible in a more fundamental sense. For example, the mediated stimulus-response approach with its concern about policy makers' perceptions appears to complement developments at the level of individual characteristics that address how perceptions are shaped (e.g., cognitive mapping or operational codes). Similarly, the bureaucratic politics approach invites consideration of the way membership in a government ministry structures a person's world view. It introduces an organizational element indicating that under some conditions the perceptions of governmental policy makers will conflict depending on the different bureau memberships represented among participants.

Between other frameworks the proposed dynamics appear to be in conflict. The group processes advanced by Janis (1972) result in a reduction in the quality of decision making when the concern for concurrence among members becomes too great. The reverse is argued in bureaucratic politics because conflict among representatives of competing bureaucratic interests is viewed as the potential source of reduced performance. Cybernetic models assume that policy makers sufficiently share goals to permit their behavior to be guided by monitoring indicators that reveal unequivocally whether the nation is moving toward or away from its goals. Bureaucratic politics would suggest concurrence on goals in a specific fashion would be quite difficult. Accordingly, agreement on the status of goals and indicators of them might prove impossible. Dependency theory would propose that for a nation locked in an asymmetrical relationship, the corrective goal-seeking actions of the government would have no effect on those aspects of its national life (e.g., economic development) that are controlled externally. Thus, policy makers operating according to the cybernetic model would be unable to affect any changes in the goal of economic development.

Taken at face value, some frameworks seem more congenial with one another than do others. Significantly, the underlying assumptions regarding the dynamics and logic of many approaches are not sufficiently explicated to make reliable judgments about their compatibility.

Incomplete Development. The suggested lack of explication of the underlying assumptions in various frameworks may be part of a larger pattern that results from the involvement of a limited number of investigators whose efforts are spread across a diversity of theoretical frameworks. Thus, research on most approaches depends on the efforts of a very few scholars. When propositions are investigated, the luxury of multiple tests by independent investigators using varying techniques and data is beyond reach. A fair number of scholars have examined the internal-external conflict hypothesis, and perhaps an even larger number from more diverse theoretical orientations are currently concerned with empirical research on dependency theory. Although they have to date produced little systematic inquiry, a substantial group of academics and practitioners have been attracted to the bureaucratic politics model. Similarly, parts of Rosenau's multilevel analysis have captured the attention of a set of investigators, many of whom have tended to examine separate features. Even in these four cases, the actual number of people contributing to the framework at any one time may be no more than 10 or 12. With respect to the other approaches the committed human resources are even less. Under the circumstances, perhaps one should marvel at how much has been done. It does mean, however, that in considering the findings of the field such as the illustrative propositions presented above, we must constantly remember that most are based on one or two unreplicated studies.

III. BRIEF CONCLUSIONS

"Waiting for Kepler" was the title used by Munton (1973) to characterize the present state of foreign policy studies. His phrase captures important qualities about the pre-paradigm state of inquiry in the field of foreign policy. Though no one has yet provided the critical assumptions and organizing theory that most can share, one senses a certain collective anticipation.

Considerable conceptual and empirical mapping has been performed as the diversity of frameworks testify. If foreign policy—which should have been a key organizing concept—has for too long remained an undefined term, that too is changing.[8] Recent theoretical statements such as those by Bobrow and associates (1979) and Wilkenfeld and associates (1980) move forward on the task of developing more integrated explanations that incorporate features from clusters of variables at various analytic levels. New sophistication about such long-established techniques as the case study [now treated in a systematic, comparative fashion, for example, George and Smoke (1974)] parallel the sophistication in the application of new techniques such as computer simulations (Howard, 1973; Bremer, 1977). An increasing comprehension of the merits and problems of the comparative approach to the study of foreign policy—both cross-nationally and longitudinally—seems evident. Comparative analysis has become more than a code word for the application of the scientific method to foreign policy and certainly more than the serial and unrelated examination of the foreign policies of selected countries.

If the foreign policy field needs a Kepler equivalent or, more exactly, an individual or group who can establish in a compelling way the critical assumptions needed to organize the field, the conditions to facilitate such a development have substantially improved over the past 15 years. Undoubtedly further improvements can be made in creating an environment for inquiry that encourages major advances. One possible candidate might be greater consciousness in framework development concerning the underlying assumptions, explanatory dynamics, and necessary conditions for the postulated relationships to hold. Another condition to encourage is the increased identification of puzzles that exist in the observable world of foreign policy and the contradictory hypotheses and findings about that world. Highlighting these features might sharpen the focus on potentially key theoretical mechanisms.

   If the number of committed investigators in the foreign policy field does not diminish, these and other aids to improved explanation seem likely. In fact, perhaps the most concise summary statement about the field of foreign policy is that the present fluidity and diversity contain many of the features needed for significant theoretical development over the next decade or so.

NOTES

1. The concerns of the other domain of foreign policy studies are reflected in such
    journals as *Foreign Affairs, Foreign Policy, Journal of International Affairs, Orbis,*
    and in surveys such as *The International Yearbook of Foreign Policy Analysis* (e.g.,
    Jones, 1975) and *The United States and World Development* (e.g., Sewell, 1977).
2. It is revealing that most foreign policy textbooks offer a more extensive treatment of
    the concept of foreign policy than do most research materials on the subject. Presumably, unlike students, professionals in the field know what foreign policy is, its
    dimensions, and implications. Representative of definitions found in textbooks are
    the following: Lentner (1974: 3–10); Berkowitz et al. (1977: 1–3); Spainer (1960:
    1–4).
3. Because single case studies are so numerous, it is impossible to cite even a small
    sample to suggest the volume and scope. Several well-known foreign policy cases that
    are frequently cited are Jones (1955), Paige (1968), and Newhouse (1973). These
    three show the continuing popularity of single case studies throughout the postwar
    period and the diversity of backgrounds of the authors. In the three cited examples,
    one author is a policy maker, another an academic, and the third a journalist.
4. Of course, there is no reason why policy makers and journalists cannot construct useful categories of foreign policy. Their purposes, however, may differ from the researcher, who seeks classifications that are mutually exclusive, exhaustive, and theoretically useful (i.e., the categories participate in relationships with other variables).
    Policy makers may wish to create symbolic categories for political purposes or to organize their understanding. Journalists may provide their audiences with categories
    to organize and to simplify diverse events. These are worthy purposes, but may not
    produce useful categories for scholarship.
5. It is the work of James Rosenau (see References) and its subsequent elaboration,
    described elsewhere in this chapter, that may comprise the closest approximation to
    a paradigm for some scholars interested in the comparative study of foreign policy.
    An effective summary of Rosenau's framework as developed over a period of years
    is offered by McGowan (1974a), and the problems with its continuation as a paradigm are reviewed by Kegley (1979). Allison (1971) and Steinbruner (1974) suggest

that the rational actor or analytic model may have been a prevailing paradigm in international politics, but, if so, they also note its demise as a set of critical assumptions nearly universally shared.

6. As an individual who has worked intensively with the factors involved in the foreign policy of one nation, Weinstein (1976: 25–26) stresses the severe difficulty in sorting out the relative importance of explanatory variables on a conceptual basis as contrasted with a statistical process. Representative of the careful efforts to differentiate the relative role of explanatory variables in a statistical manner (i.e., amount of variance explained) is the research of Moore (1974).

7. For a further discussion of the use of the concept of foreign policy goals, see Hermann (1978b).

8. Nowhere is the current concern for exploring the dimensions and categories of foreign policy more clearly evident than in the work on foreign policy issue areas; e.g., see the review of Potter (1980).

REFERENCES

Allison, G. T. (1971). *Essence of Decision.* Little, Brown, Boston.

Allison, G. T., and Halperin, M. H. (1972). Bureaucratic politics: A paradigm and some policy implications. *World Politics 24*: 40–79.

Almond, G. A. (1950). *The American People and Foreign Policy.* Harcourt, Brace, New York.

Alschuler, L. R. (1976). Satellization and stagnation in Latin America. *International Studies Quarterly 20*: 39–83.

Art, R. J. (1973). Bureaucratic politics and American foreign policy: A critique. *Policy Sciences 4*: 467–490.

Bacchus, W. I. (1974). *Foreign Policy and the Bureaucratic Process.* Princeton University Press, Princeton, NJ.

Bauer, R. A., Pool, I. D., and Dexter, L. A. (1963). *American Business and Public Policy.* Atherton Press, New York.

Beck, C., Fleron, E. F., Jr., Lodge, M., Waller, D. J., Welsh, W. A., and Zaninovich, M. G. (1973). *Comparative Communist Political Leadership.* McKay, New York.

Berkowitz, M., Bock, P. G., and Fuccillo, V. J. (1977). *The Politics of American Foreign Policy.* Prentice-Hall, Englewood Cliffs, NJ.

Bobrow, D. B., Chan, S., and Kringen, J. A. (1979). *Understanding Foreign Policy Decisions.* Free Press, New York.

Bodenheimer, S. (1971). Dependency and imperialism: The roots of Latin American underdevelopment. In *Readings in U.S. Imperialism,* K. T. Fann and D. C. Hodges (Eds.). F. Porter Sargent, Boston.

Bonham, G. M., and Shapiro, M. J. (1973). Simulation in the development of a theory of foreign policy decision-making. In *SAGE Yearbook of Foreign Policy,* vol. I, P. J. McGowan (Ed.). Sage, Beverly Hills, CA, pp. 55–71.

Bornschier, V. (1975). The effects of international economic dependence on development and inequality: A cross-national study. *American Sociological Review 40*: 720–738.

—— (1977). Multinational corporations in the world economy and national development. *Bulletin of the Social Institute of the University of Zurich,* No. 32.

Brady, L. P. (1978). The situation and foreign policy. In *Why Nations Act,* M. A. East, S. A. Salmore, and C. F. Hermann (Eds.). Sage, Beverly Hills, CA, pp. 173–190.

Brecher, M. (1972). *The Foreign Policy System of Israel.* Yale University Press, New Haven, CT.

Brecher, M., Steinberg, B., and Stein, J. (1969). A framework for research on foreign policy behavior. *Journal of Conflict Resolution 13*: 75–101.

Bremer, S. A. (1977). *Simulated Worlds.* Princeton University Press, Princeton, NJ.

Brodersen, A. (1961). National character: An old problem re-examined. In *International Politics and Foreign Policy*, J. N. Rosenau, (Ed.). Free Press of Glencoe, Glencoe, IL, pp. 300–308.

Brzezinski, Z., and Huntington, S. P. (1963–1964). *Political Power: USA/USSR.* Viking Press, New York.

Busch, P. A. (1970). Appendix: Mathematical models of arms races. In *What Price Vigilance?* B. M. Russett (Ed.). Yale University Press, New Haven, CT, pp. 193–233.

Callahan, P., Brady, L. P., and Hermann, M. G. (1982). *Describing Foreign Policy Behavior.* Sage, Beverly Hills, CA.

Camps, M. (1966). *European Unification in the Sixties.* McGraw-Hill, New York.

Chase-Dunn, C. (1975). The effects of international economic dependence on development and inequality: A cross-national study. *American Sociological Review 40*: 720–738.

Chittick, W. O. (1970). *State Department Press, and Pressure Groups.* Wiley, New York.

Choucri, N., and North, R. (1975). *Nations in Conflict.* Freeman Press, San Francisco.

Clark, J. F., O'Leary, M. K., and Wittkopf, E. R. (1971). National attributes associated with dimensions of support for the United Nations. *International Organization 25*: 1–25.

Cohen, E. C. (1957). *The Political Process and Foreign Policy.* Princeton University Press, Princeton, NJ.

—— (1963). *The Press and Foreign Policy.* Princeton University Press, Princeton, NJ.

—— (1973). *The Public Impact on Foreign Policy.* Little, Brown, Boston.

Cohen, B. C., and Harris, S. A. (1975). Foreign policy. In *Handbook of Political Science*, vol. 6. Addison-Wesley, Reading, MA.

de Rivera, J. H. (1968). *The Psychological Dimension of Foreign Policy.* Merrill, Columbus, OH.

Destler, I. M. (1972). *Presidents, Bureaucrats, and Foreign Policy.* Princeton University Press, Princeton, NJ.

—— (1980). *Making Foreign Economic Policy.* The Brookings Institution, Washington, D.C.

Deutsch, K. W. (1966a). *The Nerves of Government.* Free Press, New York.

—— (1966b). External influences on the internal behavior of states. In *Approaches to Comparative and International Politics*, R. B. Farrell (Ed.). Northwestern University Press, Evanston, IL, pp. 5–26.

Deutsch, K. W., Edinger, L. J., Macridis, R. C., and Merritt, R. L. (1967). *France, Germany and the Western Alliance.* Scribner's, New York.

East, M. A. (1978). The international system perspective and foreign policy. In *Why Nations Act*, M. A. East, S. A. Salmore, and C. F. Hermann (Eds.). Sage, Beverly Hills, CA, pp. 143–160.

East, M. A., and Hermann, C. F. (1974). Do nation-types account for foreign policy behavior? In *Comparing Foreign Policies*, J. N. Rosenau (Ed.). Sage-Halsted Press, New York, pp. 269–303.

Edinger, L. J. (1965). *Kurt Schumacher.* Stanford University Press, Stanford, CA.

Farrell, R. B. (1966). Foreign policies of open and closed political societies. In *Approaches to Comparative and International Politics*, R. B. Farrell (Ed.). Northwestern University Press, Evanston, IL, pp. 167–208.

Flowers, M. L. (1977). A laboratory test of some implications of Janis' groupthink hypotheses. *Journal of Personality and Social Psychology 35*: 888–895.

Frank, A. G. (1970). The development of underdevelopment. In *Imperialism and Underdevelopment*, R. I. Rhodes (Ed.). Monthly Review Press, New York, pp. 4–17.

Friedrich, C. J. (1966). International politics and foreign policy in developed (Western) systems. In *Approaches to Comparative and International Politics*, R. B. Farrell (Ed.). Northwestern University Press, Evanston, IL, pp. 97–119.

Galtung, J. (1971). A structural theory of imperialism. *Journal of Peace Research 8*: 81–117.

Gamson, W. A., and Modigliani, A. (1971). *Untangling the Cold War*. Little, Brown, Boston.

George, A. L. (1972). The case for multiple advocacy in making foreign policy. *American Political Science Review. 66*, 3 (September): 751–790.

George, A. L. (1969). The operational code: A neglected approach. *International Studies Quarterly 13* (June): 190–222.

—— (1974). Adaptation to stress in political decision making: The individual, small group, and organizational contexts. In *Coping and Adaptation*, G. V. Coelho, D. A. Hamburg, and J. E. Adams (Eds.). Basic Books, New York, pp. 167–245.

George, A. L., and Smoke, R. (1974). *Deterrence in American Foreign Policy*. Columbia University Press, New York.

Gobalet, J. G., and Diamond, L. J. (1979). Effects of investment dependence on economic growth. *International Studies Quarterly 23*: 412–422.

Griffith, W. E. (1964). *The Sino-Soviet Rift*. M. I. T. Press, Cambridge, MA.

Haas, M. (1968). Social change and national aggressiveness, 1900–1960. In *Quantitative International Politics*, J. D. Singer (Ed.). Free Press, New York, pp. 215–244.

—— (1974). *International Conflict*. Bobbs-Merrill, Columbus, OH.

Halperin, M. H. (1974). *Bureaucratic Politics and Foreign Policy*. Brookings Institution, Washington, DC.

Halperin, M. H., and Kanter, A. (1973). The bureaucratic perspective: A preliminary framework. In *Readings in American Foreign Policy: A Bureaucratic Perspective*, M. H. Halperin and A. Kanter (Eds.). Little, Brown, Boston.

Hanrieder, W. F. (1967). Compatibility, consensus, and an emerging political science of adaptation. *American Political Science Review 61*, 4 (December: 971–982.

—— (1971). *Foreign Policies and the International System: A Theoretical Introduction*. General Learning Press, Morristown, NJ, pp. 1–24.

Harf, J. E., Hoovler, D. G., and James, T. E., Jr. (1974). Systemic and external attributes in foreign policy analysis. In *Comparing Foreign Policies: Theories, Findings, and Methods*, J. N. Rosenau (Ed.). Sage, Beverly Hills, CA, pp. 235–267.

Hellmann, D. (1969). *Japanese Foreign Policy and Domestic Politics*. University of California Press, Berkeley.

Hermann, C. F. (1969). International crisis as a situational variable. In *International Politics and Foreign Policy*, rev. ed. J. N. Rosenau (Ed.). Free Press, New York, pp. 409–421.

—— (1972). Policy classification: A key to the comparative study of foreign policy. In *The Analysis of International Politics*, J. N. Rosenau, V. Davis, and M. A. East (Eds.). Free Press, New York, pp. 58–79.

—— (1978a). Decision structure and process influences on foreign policy. In *Why Nations Act*, M. A. East, S. A. Salmore, and C. F. Hermann (Eds.). Sage, Beverly Hills, CA, pp. 69–102.

—— (1978b). Foreign policy behavior: That which is to be explained. In *Why Nations Act*, M. A. East, S. A. Salmore, and C. F. Hermann (Eds.). Sage, Beverly Hills, CA, pp. 25–47.

—— (1980). Explaining foreign policy behavior using the personal characteristics of political leaders. *International Studies Quarterly 24*, 1 (March): 7–46.

Hilsman, R. (1967). *To Move a Nation*. Doubleday, New York.

Holsti, O. R. (1972). *Crisis, Escalation, and War*. McGill University Press, Montreal, Quebec, Canada.

—— (1976). Foreign policy decision makers viewed psychologically: "Cognitive process" approaches. In *In Search of Global Patterns*, J. N. Rosenau (Ed.). Free Press, New York, pp. 120–144.

Holsti, O. R., Brody, R. A., and North, R. C. (1964). Measuring affect and action in international reaction models. *Journal of Peace Research 3-4*: 170–190.

Holsti, O. R., North, R. C., and Brody, R. A. (1968). Preception and action in the 1914 crisis. In *Quantitative International Politics*, J. D. Singer (Ed.). Free Press, New York, pp. 123–258.

Hopmann, P. T. (1972). Internal and external influences on bargaining in arms control negotiations. In *Peace, War, and Numbers*, B. M. Russett (Ed.). Sage, Beverly Hills, CA, pp. 213–237.

Howard, N. (1973). A computer science system for foreign policy decision making. *Journal of Peace Science 1* (Autumn): 61–68.

Hughes, B. B. (1978). *The Domestic Context of American Foreign Policy*. Freeman, San Francisco.

Huntington, S. P. (1960). Strategic planning and the political process. *Foreign Affairs 38*, (2): 285–299.

Inglehart, R. (1967). An end to European integration? *American Political Science Review 61*(1): 91–105.

Janis, I. L. (1972). *Victims of Groupthink*. Houghton-Mifflin, Boston.

Jervis, R. (1976). *Perception and Misperception in International Politics*. Princeton University Press, Princeton, NJ.

Johnson, L. K. (1977). Operational codes and the prediction of leadership behavior: Senator Frank Church ad midcareer. In *A Psychological Examination of Political Leaders*, M. G. Hermann (Ed.). Free Press, New York, pp. 80–119.

Jones, J. M. (1955). *The Fifteen Weeks*. Harbinger Press, New York.

Jones, P. (Ed.). (1975). *The International Yearbook of Foreign Policy Analysis*, vol. 2. Crane and Russak, Oberlin, OH.

Jones, S. D., and Singer, J. D. (1972). *Beyond Conjecture in International Politics*. Peacock Press, Itasca, IL.

Katzenstein, P. J. (1978). *Between Power and Plenty*. University of Wisconsin Press, Madison.

Kaufman, R. H., Chernotsky, H., and Geller, D. (1975). A preliminary test of the theory of dependency. *Comparative Politics 7*: 303–330.

Kean, J. G., and McGowan, P. J. (1973). National attributes and foreign policy participation: A path analysis. In *Sage International Yearbook of Foreign Policy Studies*, vol. I, P. J. McGowan (Ed.). Sage, Beverly Hills, CA, pp. 219–252.

Kegley, C. W., Jr. (1973). A general empirical typology of foreign policy behavior. In *Sage Professional Papers in International Studies 2*, Sage, Beverly Hills, CA, pp. 02–014.

—— (1979). The comparative study of foreign policy: Paradigm lost? Unpublished paper presented at conference on the future of International Studies and the ISA at the Institute of International Studies, University of South Carolina, Columbia, SC, November 29–December 1.

Kegley, C. W., Jr., Salmore, S. A., and Rosen, O. J. (1974). Convergences in the measurement of interstate behavior. In *Sage International Yearbook of Foreign Policy Studies,* vol. II, P. J. McGowan (Ed.). Sage, Beverly Hills, CA, pp. 309–339.

Kelman, H. C. (1965). Social-psychological approaches to the study of international relations: Definition of scope. In *International Behavior,* H. C. Kelman (Ed.). Holt, Rinehart and Winston, New York, pp. 3–39.

Klineberg, O. (1950). *Tensions Affecting International Understanding.* Social Science Research Council, New York.

Krasner, S. D. (1972). Are bureaucracies important? *Foreign Policy* 7 (Summer): 159–179.

—— (1978). *Defending the National Interest.* Princeton University Press, Princeton, NJ.

Kuhn, T. S. (1963). *The Structure of Scientific Revolutions.* University of Chicago Press, Chicago.

Leites, N. (1948). Psycho-cultural hypothese about political acts. *World Politics:* Vol. I, No. I, pps. 102–119.

—— (1951). *The Operational Code of the Politburo.* McGraw-Hill, New York.

Lentner, H. H. (1974). *Foreign Policy Analysis.* Charles E. Merrill, Columbus, OH.

Long, N. E. (1966). Open and closed systems. In *Approaches to Comparative and International Politics,* R. B. Farrell (Ed.). Northwestern University Press, Evanston, IL, pp. 155–166.

McGowan, P. J. (1974a). Problems in the construction of positive foreign policy theory. In *Comparing Foreign Policies,* J. N. Rosenau (Ed.). Sage, Beverly Hills, CA, pp. 25–44.

—— (1974b). Adaptive foreign policy behavior. In *Comparing Foreign Policies,* J. N. Rosenau (Ed.). Sage, Beverly Hills, CA, pp. 45–54.

—— (1976a). The future of comparative studies: An evangelical plea. In *In Search of Global Patterns,* J. N. Rosenau (Ed.). Free Press, New York, pp. 217–235.

—— (1976b). Economic dependence and economic performance in Black Africa. *Journal of Modern African Studies 14*: 25–40.

McGowan, P. J., and Shapiro, H. B. (1973). *The Comparative Study of Foreign Policy: A Survey of Scientific Findings.* Sage, Beverly Hills, CA.

Meehan, E. J. (1971). The concept of "foreign policy." In *Comparative Foreign Policy,* W. F. Hanrieder (Ed.). David McKay, New York, pp. 265–294.

Milbrath, L. W. (1967). Interest groups and foreign policy. In *Domestic Sources of Foreign Policy,* J. N. Rosenau (Ed.). Free Press, New York, pp. 231–251.

Moore, D. W. (1974). Governmental and societal influences on foreign policy in open and closed nations. In *Comparing Foreign Policies,* J. N. Rosenau (Ed.). Sage, Beverly Hills, CA, pp. 171–200.

Moran, T. H. (1978). Multinational corporations and dependency: A dialogue for dependistas and non-dependistas. *International Organization 32*: 1. pps. 79–100.

Morgenthau, H. J. (1967). *Politics Among Nations,* 4th ed., Knopf, New York.

Mueller, J. E. (1973). *War, Presidents and Public Opinion.* Wiley, New York.

Munton, D. (1973). Waiting for Kepler. Paper prepared for the International Studies Association meeting in New York.

Murphy, R. D., and Commission Members (1975). *Commission on the Organization of the Government for the Conduct of Foreign Policy.* U.S. Government Printing Office Washington, DC, 022-000-00108-6.

Neustadt, R. E. (1970). *Alliance Politics.* Columbia University Press, New York.

Newhouse, J. (1973). *Cold Dawn: The Story of SALT.* Holt, Rinehart and Winston, New York.

North, R. C., and Lagerstrom, R. (1971). *War and Domination: A Theory of Lateral Pressure.* General Learning Press, Morristown, NJ.

O'Leary, M. K. (1974). Foreign policy and bureaucratic adaptation. In *Comparing Foreign Policies,* J. N. Rosenau (Ed.). Sage, Beverly Hills, CA, pp. 55–70.

—— (1976). The role of issues. In *In Search of Global Patterns,* J. N. Rosenau (Ed.). Free Press, New York, pp. 318–325.

Paige, G. D. (1968). *The Korean Decision.* Free Press, New York.

Phillips, W. R. (1978). Prior behavior as an explanation of foreign policy. In *Why Nations Act,* M. A. East, S. A. Salmore, and C. F. Hermann (Eds.). Sage, Beverly Hills, CA, pp. 161–172.

Phillips, W. R., and Crain, R. C. (1974). Reciprocity and uncertainty in foreign study. In *Sage International Yearbook of Foreign Policy Studies,* vol. II, P. J. McGowan (Ed.). Sage, Beverly Hills, CA, pp. 227–268.

Potter, W. C. (1980). Issue area and foreign policy analysis. *International Organization 34*(4): 405–427.

Ray, J. L., and Webster, T. (1978). Dependency and economic growth in Latin America. *International Studies Quarterly 22*: 409–434.

Renshon, S. A. (Ed.) (1977). *Handbook of Political Socialization.* Free Press, New York.

Richardson, N. R., and Kegley, C. W. (1980). Trade dependence and foreign policy compliance. *International Studies Quarterly 24*: 191–222.

Robinson, J. A. (1962). *Congress and Foreign Policy Making.* The Dorsey Press, Inc., Homewood, IL.

Rosenau, J. N. (1964). *Public Opinion and Foreign Policy.* Random House, New York.

—— (1966). Pre-theories and theories of foreign policy. In *Approaches to Comparative and International Politics,* R. B. Farrell (Ed.). Northwestern University Press, Evanston, IL, pp. 27–92.

—— (1968). Private preferences and political responsibilities: The relative potency of individual and role variables in the behavior of U.S. Senators. In *Quantitative International Politics,* J. D. Singer (Ed.). Free Press, New York, pp. 17–50.

—— (1969). *Linkage Politics.* Free Press, New York.

—— (1970a). Foreign policy as adaptive behavior. *Comparative Politics 2*: 365–387.

—— (1970b). *The Adaptation of National Societies.* McCaleb-Seiler, New York.

—— (1971). *The Scientific Study of Foreign Policy.* Free Press, New York.

—— (1972). The external environment as a variable in foreign policy analysis. In *The Analysis of International Politics,* J. N. Rosenau, V. Davis, and M. A. East (Eds.). Free Press, New York, pp. 145–165.

—— (Ed.) (1974). *Comparing Foreign Policies.* Sage-Halsted Press, New York.

Rubinson, R. (1977). Dependence, government, revenue, and economic growth, 1950–70. *Studies in Comparative International Development 12*: 3–28.

Rummel, R. J. (1963). Dimensions of conflict behavior within and between nations. *Yearbook of the Society for General Systems 8*: 1–50.

—— (1972). *The Dimensions of Nations.* Sage, Beverly Hills, CA.

—— (1977). *Field Theory Evolving.* Sage, Beverly Hills, CA.

—— (1979). *National Attributes and Behavior.* Sage, Beverly Hills, CA.

Salmore, B. G., and Salmore, S. A. (1978). Political regimes and foreign policy. In *Why Nations Act,* M. A. East, S. A. Salmore, and C. F. Hermann (Eds.). Sage, Beverly Hills, CA, pp. 103–122.

Salmore, S. A., and Munton, D. (1974). An empirically based typology of foreign policy behavior. In *Comparing Foreign Policy*, J. N. Rosenau (Ed.). Sage, Beverly Hills, CA, pp. 329–352.

Salmore, S. A., Hermann, M. G., Hermann, C. F., and Salmore, B. G. (1978). Conclusion: Toward integrating the perspectives. In *Why Nations Act*, M. A. East, S. A. Salmore, and C. F. Hermann (Eds.). Sage, Beverly Hills, CA, pp. 191–209.

Schilling, W. R., Hammond, P. Y., and Snyder, G. H. (1962). *Strategy, Politics, and Defense Budgets.* Columbia University Press, New York.

Sewell, J. W. (1977). *The United States and World Development.* Praeger, New York.

Simon, H. (1969). *The Sciences of the Artificial.* M.I.T. Press, Cambridge, MA.

Singer, J. D., Bremer, S., and Stuckey, J. (1972). Capability distribution, uncertainty, and major power war, 1820–1965. In *Peace, War and Numbers*, B. M. Russett (Ed.). Sage, Beverly Hills, CA, pp. 19–48.

Snyder, R. C., Bruck, H. W., and Sapin, B. (1962). *Foreign Policy Decision Making.* Free Press, New York.

Spanier, J. (1960). *American Foreign Policy Since World War II*, 8th ed. Holt, Rinehart and Winston, New York.

Spielmann, K. F. (1978). *Analyzing Soviet Strategic Arms Decisions.* Westview Press, Boulder, CO.

Sprout, H., and Sprout, M. (1965). *Ecological Perspective on Human Affairs.* Princeton University Press, Princeton, NJ.

Steinbruner, J. D. (1974). *The Cybernetic Theory of Decision.* Princeton University Press, Princeton, NJ

Sullivan, M. P. (1976). *International Relations: Theories and Evidence.* Prentice-Hall, Englewood Cliffs, NJ.

Sunkel, O. (1972). Big business and dependencia: A Latin American view. *Foreign Affairs 50*: 517–531.

Tanter, R. (1966). Dimensions of conflict behavior within and between nations, 1958–60. *Journal of Conflict Resolution 10*(1): 41–64.

Tetlock, P. E. (1979). Identifying victims of groupthink from public statements of decision-makers. *Journal of Personality and Social Psychology 37*: 1314–1324.

Thomson, T. W., and Macridis, R. C. (1976). The comparative study of foreign policy. In *Foreign Policy in World Politics*, R. C. Macridis (Ed.). Prentice Hall, Englewood Cliffs, NJ, pp. 1–31.

Thorson, S. J. (1974b). Adaptation and foreign policy theory. In *Sage International Yearbook of Foreign Policy Studies*, Vol. II, P. J. McGowan (Ed.). Sage, Beverly Hills, CA, pps. 123–139.

Thorson, S. J. (1974a). National political adaptation. In *Comparing Foreign Policies*, J. N. Rosenau (Ed.). Sage-Halsted Press, New York, pp. 71–116.

Trice, R. H. (1976). *Interest Groups and the Foreign Policy Process: U.S. Policy in the Middle East.* Sage International Studies Series 02-027. Sage, Beverly Hills, CA.

Ulam, A. B. (1971). Soviet ideology and Soviet foreign policy. In *The Conduct of Soviet Foreign Policy*, E. P. Hoffmann and F. J. Fleron, Jr. (Eds.). Aldine-Atherton, Chicago, pp. 136–153.

Wallace, W. (1975). *The Foreign Policy Process in Britain.* The Royal Institute of International Affairs, London.

Waltz, K. N. (1967). *Foreign Policy and Democratic Politics.* Little, Brown, Boston.

Weinstein, F. B. (1976). *Indonesian Foreign Policy and the Dilemma of Dependence.* Cornell University Press, Ithaca, NY.

Wilkenfeld, J. (1973a). *Conflict Behavior and Linkage Politics.* McKay, New York.

—— (1973b). Domestic and foreign conflict. In *Conflict Behavior and Linkage Politics.* J. Wilkenfeld (Ed.). MacKay, New York, pp. 107-123.

Wilkenfeld, J., Hopple, G. W., Rossa, P. J., and Andriole, S. J. (1980). *Foreign Policy Behavior.* Sage, Beverly Hills, CA.

Wolfenstein, V. E. (1971). *The Revolutionary Personality.* Princeton University Press, Princeton, NJ.

Zagoria, D. S. (1967). *Vietnam Triangle.* Pegasus Press, Indianapolis, IN.

Zinnes, D. A. (1966). A comparison of hostile behavior of decision-makers in simulate and historical data. *World Politics 18*(3): 474–502.

—— (1968). The expression and perception of hostility in prewar crisis: 1914. In *Quantitative International Politics,* J. D. Singer (Ed.). Free Press, New York, pp. 85-122.

—— (1976). *Contemporary Research in International Relations.* Free Press, New York.

Zinnes, D. A., Zinnes, J. L., and McClure, R. D. (1972). Hostility in diplomatic communications. In *International Crisis,* C. F. Hermann (Ed.). Free Press, New York, pp. 139–164.

13

Military Policy: The Use, Threat, and Control of Force

Edward A. Kolodziej / University of Illinois, Urbana-Champaign, Illinois

I. INTRODUCTION

Military policy refers to the use, threat, and control of organized violence by states and their ruling elite to influence either the behavior of other states, elites, and groups beyond the state's boundaries or of internal groups and individuals, or both, in ways that are considered desirable by governmental authorities. This definition focuses on the decisions and actions of governments and the dominant coalitions within them that have the authority and capacity to employ the state's coercive instruments. Although this definition emphasizes the key role of nation-states in using, threatening, and controlling the physical means of coercion, it views nation-state behavior in the domain of security apart from the perspective, interests, and values of any particular political regime, whether authoritarian or democratic.

The definition of military policy used in this chapter assumes that the nation-state is the principal political unit of global politics. Peoples and nations are seen to be organized in separate states that claim to be sovereign. Those in control of these state structures assert the right to decide the authoritative values of the people inhabiting the territorial space over which the state holds sway. The divergent claims of states, backed by the physical violence at their disposal, create the conditions of anarchy that characterize much of international relations. In the absence of shared values or an appeal to higher moral or legal authority to resolve differences, military force or its threatened use is still the ultimate arbiter in disputes between states and peoples. Military policy is, therefore, a fundamental imperative of all states. The survival of the state, the successful pursuit of its objectives, and the legitimacy and credibility of its authoritative claims, to arbitrate disputes between its citizens, between them and other states, or between itself and other states, depend critically on the effectiveness of its military policies.

The systematic study of the dependence of a political community's survival and its objectives on "organized violence" or military force has a long history. Contemporary concern for effective use and control of military power is but the latest installment in attempts by decision makers and their advisors to understand and define this elusive relation in terms advantageous to their communities and themselves. In the brief space that is available, it may be useful to sketch this line of policy analysis as background to the discussion of current policy problems. If such an outline suggests the mutable character of policy issues raised by the play of force or its threat in human affairs, it also crystallizes the underlying unity between the past and the present, and presumably the future, in the efforts of political communities to employ yet discipline force in governing themselves and their relations with other peoples.

Such diverse writers as Sun Tzu in China, Kautilya in India, Thucydides in Greece, and Caesar in Rome probed the role of force in their society's affairs long before the development of the modern state. Machiavelli's *The Prince* and the *Discourses* are the first modern effort to examine systematically the crucial and continuing need of governing authorities to rely on force to survive and to work their will. Machiavelli's broad political and psychological conception of force tended, subsequently, to be narrowed by military analysts to the organization, deployment, and use of force. The French writer Vauban and later Jomini treated military policy as much as a science as an art. The return to Machiavelli's sweeping perspective can be traced to Carl von Clausewitz's monumental *On War*. Written to explain the success of Napoleonic warfare, it has become the touchstone of all serious contemporary analysts of state policy and military force.[1] For Clausewitz, war was a political act and an extension of state politics as well as an instrument of state policy. Seen in this light, it had neither moral justification nor instrumental meaning unless it were directed as a political act and as a tool of policy. This conception prompted his celebrated and much-quoted definition: "War is not merely a political act, but also a political instrument, a continuation of political commerce, a carryout of the same by other means."[2] Although there is a tendency of many military officers, whom Huntington calls "managers of violence," to distinguish between political and military dimensions of strategy and to concentrate on the latter to the exclusion of the former,[3] Clausewitz's frame of reference bound one to the other. Partly for this reason, his views about military force have enjoyed wide currency across ideological or regime divisions, having had impact on such diverse individuals as Schlieffen in Imperial Germany, Lenin in Russia, and Mao Tse-Tung in China. Drawing on Lenin's approval of Clausewitz's grasp of the interdependence of politics and violence, Mao Tse-Tung offered his own equally well circulated view: "It can therefore be said that politics is war without bloodshed while war is politics with bloodshed."[4]

Clausewitz was also the beginning point of a generation of American and European writers who, after the devastation of World War II, the emergence of the cold war, and the rising destruction of modern weapons, sought to develop a theory of warfare that would calibrate military force to political purpose. The two appeared to be increasingly incompatible, because the physical damage that adversaries could inflict on each other exceeded the limits of most political needs or aims. The writings of P. M. S. Blackett in Great Britain,[5] André Beaufre[6] and Raymond Aron [7] in France, and Robert Osgood,[8] Henry Kissinger,[9] Herman Kahn,[10] Thomas Schelling,[11] and Bernard Brodie[12] in the United States, as well as V. D. Sokolovskii and his associates in the Soviet Union,[13] took as their point of departure Clausewitz's dictum that war was a continuation of politics by other means. However much these writers may have differed, they agreed with

Clausewitz that war is a complex form of politics with "its own language, but not its own logic."[14] Much of their attention has been directed at specifying the "language" of military force under contemporary conditions of warfare, implying in many cases, and certainly between the superpowers, the use of threat of nuclear weapons and how these uses do, can, or should comply with political logic and discourse. In this light it is no accident that Herman Kahn should title his controversial book on nuclear weapons *On Thermonuclear War.* In adding an adjective Kahn drew attention to the need to update Clausewitz without abandoning his fundamental policy premises.[15]

The discussion below discusses some of the major concerns, issues, and concepts of military policy. The point of view is primarily that of policy makers and analysts interested in relating modern war and weapons to the foreign policy goals of the governments they serve or of which they are a part. To lend coherence to the discussion, military policy will be approached from the perspective of the practitioner and serious student of military strategy directed by political purpose. Narrow questions of military tactics, supply, logistics, communication and transportation, operations and maintenance, recruitment, training, and leadership—staples of military professionalism—are not treated. Although the resolution of many of these problems bear significantly on the political results sought by military power, they pose a different order or level of interest than the political objectives and orientations presumably guiding military force.

The discussion will be divided into two major parts. The first identifies the immediate purposes of exercising military power that serve a wide variety of political aims. In this way we can proceed independently of the substantive claims of states and elites and focus on the outcomes that are viewed as the military-strategic preconditions of varied desirable political objectives. The second stipulates nine dimensions of contemporary military policy making that in greater or lesser measure characterize the national policies of states and their ruling regimes. The notes throughout are copious and are designed to provide an initial working bibliography that by no means purports to be complete.

II. MILITARY POLICY AND POLITICAL PURPOSE

In using, threatening, and controlling military force, a state's governing elite seeks to produce certain outcomes. These concern primarily the behavior of other groups and regimes which are explicitly or implicitly threatened or compelled to act in ways that they would not otherwise have chosen but for the coercion, real or threatened, exercised upon them. These outcomes imply patterned and sustained responses that are considered beneficial by the elites applying such means. They may be classed into at least seven analytically separable but operationally overlapping groupings. These include defense, deterrence, directed behavior, dominance, destruction, display, and exchange. These results of the application or, more broadly, the manipulation of military forces are distinguishable from the aims that may be attributed to state action in the abstract, as realist or systemic school[16] writers have assumed, or elite behavior as a function of its composition and domestic political setting.[17] The outcomes, keyed to the play or possibility of organized violence, may simultaneously serve several consistent or competing state or regime objectives. The immediate aim of military policy may be conceived as the effort to produce or promote one or more of these patterned outcomes.

A. Outcomes of Force and Forced Outcomes

Defense. The traditional concern of military force is with the defense of territory or with whatever object has strategic or political value. This concern has usually been identified with the use of force to prevent the investure or control by invading armies of a nation's territory, its citizens, or its physical resources; it implies the ability to hold, to fend off attack, and to expel invaders.[18] This territorial conception of national defense has been put into question by the destructive nature of modern warfare and the increasing economic, military, and political interdependencies of states. A modern military establishment requires the ability to project force at long distances to forestall adverse military actions. This condition, created by the devastating character of modern weapons—nuclear and conventional—and by the capacity of states to deliver them over vast distances with accuracy approaching several hundred feet, has generated a need for global communication and detection systems (e.g., spy satellites), foreign bases to monitor opponent moves to pre-position supplies and to conduct military operations abroad, and clients and allies to furnish these requirements as well as their own military forces. Seen in this light, defense encompasses the possibility of military operation far from a nation's shores and potentially deep within the territory of allies and adversaries. One could plausibly speak of a forward defense strategy for the United States on the Elbe against the Soviet Union rather than on the Atlantic Ocean as some statesmen, such as Robert Taft and Herbert Hoover, might have preferred.[19] Russian leaders after World War II similarly acted on the assumption that their nation's vital interests extended beyond the immediate borders of the Soviet Union and indeed to the control of the governments of Eastern Europe.[20]

Given the ability of many states suddenly to deliver large amounts of military hardware and firepower against specified military and civilian targets over long stretches with relative ease against an unsuspecting adversary, the concept of defense has tended to merge with preemptive and preventive attacks and offensive warfare.[21] The distinction between preemption and prevention turns largely on timing and perceptions of opponent military and political moves and intentions. In preempting, a state and its allies attack first in anticipation of a coming blow that is calculated in hours, days, or a few weeks at most. Or a client may trigger a first strike to commit an otherwise reluctant ally to support it against an impending assault aimed exclusively at it. Lacking discriminating information about the variable disposition of alliance partners to use force, the adversary whose mobilization prompted the client attack may then be forced to launch its counterstrikes against the alliance as a whole, including those states that might have stood apart.

Preventive warfare is measured in months and even years. A state initiates a preventive military attack because its regime is convinced that time is working against it or that the attacked state is determined to launch an aggression as soon as its military capabilities are sufficient to assure victory. The Israeli attack against Egypt in 1956 appears to have been a preventive action; the Six Day War in 1967 illustrates a preemptive attack.[22]

Determining whether preemption or prevention constitutes defensive behavior or offensive warfare is very difficult. It requires knowledge of the subjective values and inner psychological condition of the adversaries. Because these are not easily (if ever) known—

even to the principals themselves—defense, as suggested below, can be a surrogate for directed response or the destruction of an adversary as exemplified in Cato's often-quoted declamation: "Carthago delanda est" (Carthage must be destroyed).

Deterrence. Deterrence contrasts with defense because control is exercised in most instances through threats of hostile action rather than through the direct application of coercion or military force. Deterrence exists when one party threatens to invoke some sanction against another party if some forbidden act is committed. A coercive or military sanction is only one subcategory of the spectrum of deterrent situations that can be identified in terms of the cost of acting to the deterred party. In coercive cases, one threatens to hurt, maim, kill, or destroy, or to inflict pain in some form if the deterred party acts in an untoward manner specified by the deterrer. From this perspective, deterrence, as one analyst suggests, "involves the manipulating of someone's behavior by threatening him with harm."[23] Other analysts use a broader definition of deterrence. General André Beaufre, for example, speaks of a "dialectic of conflict" in defining deterrence.[24] From this broader perspective, a sanction may be coercive or noncoercive. The key element in the dialectical chain is the potential loss of some desired value if the deterred party refuses to heed a threat. "In short," as one analyst observes, "deterrence may follow, first, from any form of control which one has over an opponent's present and prospective 'value inventory'; secondly, from the communication of a credible threat or promise to decrease or increase that inventory; and, thirdly, from the opponent's degree of confidence that one intends to fulfill the threat or promise."[25]

The conditions that produce viable deterrent outcomes, based on threats of violence, are in dispute among theorists. Much of the difficulty of specifying these conditions arises from the fundamentally psychological and subjective character of the deterrent relationship. Deterrence is either bilateral or multilateral and may occur as much between allies as adversaries. Under different circumstances, the behavior of an ally may pose more costs and risks than the feared actions of the adversary. If an ally precipitately launches a nuclear strike against a common adversary, all alliance parties may suffer damage when accommodation may have been the preferred course for some or all other alliance partners.[26] Deterrence effectiveness depends on the value priorities of the deterred and deterring parties which, as often as not, hold each other hostage to what each, paradoxically, holds dear. Knowledge of those respective value structures is very hard to acquire; there is usually some residual that escapes determination. The conflicting parties may not be fully aware of their respective value scales or the contradictions within them. The values registered on these scales change in composition over time, as do the relative priorities between continuing values. The mutual bargaining between opponents may prompt adversaries and allies to shift the weights that each attaches to the values of its respective scale, increasing the importance of some objects (say, the protection extended to a client) and decreasing others (cutting arms aid or transfers). New conditions may strengthen or weaken a deterrent field between adversaries: The unavailability of crucial resources, such as oil or bases, may create new concerns and vulnerabilities that may be threatened, or bloc assignments may be reshuffled because of a regime change (e.g., Ethiopia's shift from American to Soviet client status). Carried to a logical conclusion, tending toward limitless regression, deterrence hinges on the estimates that an adversary has of the value calculus held by his opponent of his value calculus and of his ability and will to carry out reprisal if his threats fail to deter.

There exists no agreement, moreover, on what factors—physical or psychological—will assure desired deterrent results. Practitioners and theorists of nuclear deterrence, for example, differ widely in their methodological approaches and findings about the factors that enhance or diminish deterrence.[27] Some stress the manipulation by physical means;[28] others emphasize assertions of will and signals to an adversary of a determination to carry out a deterrent threat.[29] It is very difficult to test if the moves made by a player are linked to the behavior of the deterred party. Given the conflict of the adversaries (and divergent values of allies), none of the parties is disposed to reveal preferences or moves or to verify the effectiveness of an opponent's threat projections.

Communicating a threat also poses formidable problems for the stability of deterrence. Messages must normally be mediated through the established pattern of misunderstandings and grievances of the conflicting parties. Their perceptions of reality also filter and distort signals sent by an opponent.[30] The historical experience of a people and its leadership shape their perceptions of the international environment. A country with a long history of invasions is likely to place considerable emphasis on external security and to be sensitive to hostile or threatening signs from other states. This disposition can lead to self-fulfilling prophecies, in which the state's defense preparations are so extensive that they appear to be motivated by aggressive intent and designed for offensive strikes. The sets of expectations that each has of the other's motives and behavior, accumulated over the course of their conflict, condition what meaning and credibility each will attribute to the statements or actions of each other.[31]

Even if these perceptual and psychological, not to mention substantive, valuational barriers could be overcome and a clear passage created for communication, the problems associated with effective and efficient oral, written, or electronic messages would not necessarily be resolved.[32] Official messages vary in their impact, depending on the source of a statement and the status and power enjoyed by the communicator in the government. Or the message may be vaguely attributable to high-ranking members of a government. The communication of a threat may also be general or specific. General statements have the advantage of covering a wide range of aggressive moves, but their very breadth diminishes their credibility. The American doctrine of massive retaliation, announced by Secretary of State John Foster Dulles in 1954, suffered this shortcoming. It was implausible that the United States would use nuclear weapons in retribution for unspecified acts by an adversary. Although specific threats avoid these problems, they carry their own hazards. Although certain opponent moves may be deterred, others not covered by the deterrer's threat may be judged to be permissable, or the likelihood of effective and costly reprisal may be discounted.

Messages may assume many forms other than oral, written, or electronic communications. Military maneuvers, large (or small) expenditures for defense, the development of new weapon systems, the dispatch of advisors to another country, or a step-up in military assistance convey intentions, however ambiguously. These can shape the perceptions of adversaries, often in unintended ways. Under conditions of doubt and suspicion, conveying the real significance of nonverbal actions is difficult. Credence is not readily extended. The problem of interpreting adversary deterrent signals is compounded when the adversary also resorts to dissimulation. If signals issuing from a government are ambiguous or contradictory, which are to be considered relevant and operational? To what degree are the actions aimed at domestic audiences for home consumption or at allies with the intent of garnering support or dissuading some anticipated initiative by an allied or client state? The perceptual and informational problems, puzzling to adversaries, are transferred to interchanges between allies and to the flow of communication, commands, and control procedures between individuals and groups within the government of a nation and between them and nongovernmental elites and the public. The "rational man" models of decision making, in which information is linked to preferences and to the costs and benefits of maximizing desired outcomes, are often of doubtful relevance or explanatory power.

To assure that messages are received as intended by the communicator, the study of communications, command, and control structures—"C^3" systems in the jargon of specialists—has become an important subbranch of strategic analysis. Both the content and the medium of a message are critical to its reception and controlled response. Failure to fashion a workable C^3 system risks severing or weakening the link between governmental aims and policy. Under these conditions messages can easily be misunderstood, miscalculations encouraged, inadvertent and unintended provocations initiated, and unauthorized actions taken by subordinates.[33]

Distinguishing between defense and deterrence is often more useful for analytic than operational purposes. In keeping with the ancient aphorism—if you want peace, prepare for war—a strong defensive posture may be a major deterrent. So long as a bargaining relation exists between rival parties, wherever both have leverage over the other (measured in costs that each incurs in coercively imposing solutions on his opponent), deterrence is working. The outbreak of hostilities does not signal the end of deterrence. As logical analysis suggests and as the experience of the Korean War or World War II reveal, states engaged in combat, even as total as that conducted by the Nazi regime, hesitate to employ all of the destructive means at their disposal. Herman Kahn sketches an elaborate escalation ladder of increasingly devastating military power at each ascending rung.[34] Nuclear war need not involve a mutual spasm of annihilation, because each opponent has an incentive of keeping losses down and of terminating hostilities on a basis most favorable to his interests. Despite Chinese vulnerability to American nuclear attack, the Truman administration refrained from employing this advantage out of fear of widening the war and perhaps precipitating Soviet counterreaction in Europe or elsewhere against American allies and clients.[35] Hitler's Germany could have used poison gas, but appeared deterred by the fear of counter Allied use.

Directed Behavior. Deterrence seeks to forestall some undesired behavior or action within the capacity of another state or group to take. The deterrer hopes to prevent something from happening. In directed behavior a state threatens or uses military force to induce or compel another government or group to behave in a desirable way. This may involve stopping an action already undertaken or performing some action that the opponent or ally might otherwise refrain from doing in the absence of coercive incentives.

The expectation that military force can direct the decisions and actions of those against whom it is targeted is pervasive. In an informal 1980 poll of European leaders, many felt that the U.S. government under President Carter was slow in responding to growing Soviety military power. According to the report, they feared that the Soviet Union was in a position to expand its diplomatic influence because of the perceived military-strategic advantage that it enjoyed.[36] President Charles de Gaulle justified his government's development of a nuclear strike force on grounds of the increased weight that France would gain in diplomatic negotiations with the superpowers and other nuclear states, President Nixon's order to resume bombing of North Vietnam in December 1972 was calculated to bring Hanoi to the bargaining table to sign a peace treaty with the Saigon regime. America's European allies also agreed to impose economic sanctions against Iran because they feared that the Carter administration might take even harsher and potentially more costly and riskier actions against the Iranian government and terrorists holding the American hostages.[37] Moscow's disenchantment with the government in Afghanistan prompted its initiation of a coup d'état, the subsequent invasion by Russian troops, and the installation of a puppet regime under Babrak Karmal.

As these examples suggest, the problems of effectively directing an opponent's or ally's behavior are many and complex. The requirements of each operation cannot be reduced to a simple formula. They vary with the actors involved, their relative military power, the nonmilitary factors influencing their behavior, the stakes at issue, and the costs incurred in invoking threats or force to position the target state in a desirable mode. The kind of military power that would have to be projected to launch a successful offensive against an opponent—say, the Warsaw Pact against the NATO states—is obviously of quite a different order than shifting a vote in the United Nations. Military intervention in the affairs of another state, on the level of the American effort in Vietnam or the Soviet campaign in Afghanistan, demands still other military capabilities and political skills. Some of these differences will become clearer in the discussion below of military doctrine and the different rules of warfare appropriate to nuclear, conventional, guerrilla, or terrorist forms of forceful action.

Applications of force in a directed behavior mode raise as many problems as those in defense and deterrence. The use of violence against another state requires the expenditure of blood and treasure. This poses the possibility that costs may well exceed the anticipated benefits from the action. Neither is subject to precise calculation. Costs and benefits will almost inevitably be evaluated differently over time. What may have been a tempting opportunity (the Soviet closing of Berlin in 1948) or a relatively low-cost intervention (initial U.S. intervention in Vietnam) may gradually increase out of all proportion to the gain that was originally anticipated. The defending party may also be capable of exerting its will either to neutralize and even to overcome its disadvantage. The American airlift to Berlin in 1948–1949, which did not engage Soviet military forces but implied a determination to meet Soviet military actions to stop or hinder flights into and out of the city, eventually convinced Moscow to lift the blockade. If North Vietnam's troops were unable to defeat American ground forces in direct clashes, Hanoi's resilience in carrying on the war despite substantial American bombing raids and its ability to inflict casualties on American troops eventually eroded popular support for the war.

The Berlin Blockade and Vietnamese reaction to U.S. intervention illustrate two different strategies of directed behavior in which force was actively threatened or used to compel a foe to behave in a desirable manner or to accept terms that would otherwise have been unpalatable. A strategy of attrition is another course that a state might adopt to control the behavior of another state. The limited wars of the eighteenth century aimed principally at weakening the opponent's will and capacity to sustain a war rather than to annihilate military forces.[38] In the modern period, wars of attrition have assumed a new meaning previously unparalleled in human warfare. The destructiveness of today's weapons and the wide expanse over which they can be used make a war of attrition highly damaging to the participants. These novel conditions increase incentives for a breakthrough strategy of rapid victory. This implies overwhelming superiority at the points of military engagement. The Japanese attack on Pearl Harbor was designed to deliver a knockout blow against American military power in the Pacific. The disarming raid was intended to achieve a rapid tactical victory in the region and induce the United States to sue for peace on terms favorable to the Tokyo government. What American military officials conceived was a deterrent—the presence of the American fleet in Hawaii —was evaluated by the Japanese as an attractive target. American shock and outrage ill-disposed the American people or their government to a settlement. The Japanese attack prompted a full mobilization of American military power, which over three years of bitter fighting led to the collapse of Japanese military power and the destruction of two Japanese cities by nuclear weapons.

The German Schlieffen Plan to destroy first the French army and then the Russian armies in swift succession also illustrates the search for a decisive battle or engagement that will effectively disarm the opponent and permit peace terms to be dictated.[39] Both the German and the Japanese plans failed, although initiative and, to some degree, surprise were enjoyed by the aggressor power. Planners miscalculated their adversaries' capabilities. Japan crippled only part of the military power of the United States; its industrial production base was untouched; its officer cadres remained intact; and the determination of the American people to win the war was forged by the sudden and unexpected attack. The German violation of Belgium's neutrality in World War I partly tipped British reluctance to intervene in war. The weakening of the German invasion force against France because of the battle at Tannenberg against Russian troops nullified the possibility of rapid victory. Japan in World War II and Germany in World War I were ensnared in a war of attrition beyond their means to win.[40]

A strategy of attrition may, paradoxically, be more appropriate to a developing than to a developed state. Vietnam defeated an opponent vastly superior in economic resources and military capabilities. Its low level of economic development left little to be destroyed by American military power. Amply supplied by the Soviet Union and Communist China, it had sufficient means to carry on the war indefinitely. The inflexible commitment of the Hanoi government to see the war to a successful conclusion and its ability to command the loyalty of its population and armed forces—qualities absent in Saigon's rule—afforded it decisive leverage in the long struggle. Mao Tse-Tung relied on the same steadfastness of his government and the Chinese people in ultimately defeating Japan. Mao is clear on this point:

> The mobilization of the common people throughout the country will create a vast sea in which to drown the enemy, create the conditions that will make up for our inferiority in arms and other things, and create the prerequisites for overcoming every difficulty in the war. To win victory, we must persevere in the War of Resistance, in the united front and in the protracted war. But all these are inseparable from the mobilization of the common people.[41]

Because a war of attrition lacks definite limits and affects the entire population, whether through mobilization, taxation, or adverse impact, it is very difficult to control or to justify. Because it assumes large-scale human and material costs, the losses engendered compete in importance with the values pursued in the struggle. Whose behavior is being directed in the struggle is increasingly difficult to distinguish as the opponents exhaust themselves. Modern firepower is so deadly and home populations so vulnerable that the attrition rate of warfare can be speeded up substantially. Four years passed before the antagonists in World War I reduced each other to ruins. The Middle East wars in 1967 and 1973 required only days to ruin the military forces of one or both sides.

Coercive diplomacy differs from the search for a quick, decisive victory and a war of attrition. These latter tacts carry great political risks. Victory makes military success a precondition for a political solution; attrition entails such high costs that the proportion between military means and political aims risk being adversely unbalanced. Coercive diplomacy seeks to calibrate military costs and political benefits more precisely. Emphasis is placed on the aims of policy. Force is subordinated to these claims. It is integrated within the framework of the conflict that groups coercive and noncoercive incentives in manipulating the behavior of the opponent. It is a stick, and not necessarily a very large one, added to an array of other sticks and carrots that may be visited upon the targeted party if it does or does not act in a prescribed way. Alexander George, a leading analyst of coercive diplomacy, summarizes its principal features:

> . . . Coercive strategy focuses upon affecting the enemy's will rather than upon negating his capabilities. It does not rely on ample or quick use of force to achieve political objectives. Rather, if threats alone do not suffice and force is actually used, it is employed in a more limited, selective manner than in the quick, decisive strategy. That is, force is used in an exemplary, demonstrative manner, in discrete and controlled increments, to induce the opponent to revise his calculations and agree to a mutually acceptable termination of the conflict.[42]

Theorists have not been able to specify the conditions for the successful application of coercive diplomacy. The American intervention in Vietnam illustrates the problem. Strategists initially applied a strategy of coercive diplomacy in intervening, only to have Hanoi raise the ante with each increase in American military power. Each mounting of the escalation ladder intensified and extended the conflict over time in which the Vietnam strategy of attrition undid American coercive diplomacy.[43] This reversal suggests at least eight preconditions for the successful application of coercive diplomacy: (1) strength of the initiator's motivation; (2) asymmetry of motivation favoring initiator; (3) clarity of objectives; (4) sense of urgency to achieve objectives; (5) adequacy of domestic support; (6) usable military options; (7) opponent's fear of unacceptable motivation; and (8) precision concerning the terms of settlement.[44]

Directed behavior also implies the manipulation of threats to elicit desired behavior before, during, and even after a temporary respite in the application of force. Threats to compel or induce behavior pose more problems than those designed to deter. To compel actions one must make the first move. One's initiative is "intrusive, hostile, or provocative," whereas the converse tends to be true for the party ignoring a deterring threat.[45] The compeller is tagged with an aggressor's label.

Deterrence is indefinite in time although not necessarily in place. "Cross this line and we attack your cities!" This is a threat that is operative for as long as the deterred opponent may be perceived to desire to commit an action distasteful to the deterrer. No time limit is presumably set to protect the defined interest, such as the protection of an ally's frontiers or regime. Compellence and inducement require specification in time and space; otherwise the target of coercion would not know how or when to render a threat "harmless." Timing in issuing and executing the threat are also important. If one acts too quickly in implementing a threat, the target may be unable to comply. If one waits too long, the threat may lose credibility and may require an escalation of threat or a greater application of violence to compensate for previous inaction or hesitancy. Compliance may not be easy, take longer than the compelling power can wait for a satisfactory response, or may even be beyond the capacity of the threat recipient to comply. All of these limitations were at play in the mutual demands for satisfaction and threats preceding World War I. Deterrence broke down; compellent threats were communicated and subsequently executed, with the unforeseen outcome of disaster for all of the adversaries.[46]

Deterrence and compellence differ in the degree to which the recipient of the threat can be assured that compliance will be rewarded. In deterrence, the threat recipient can rely on accumulated experience that if he does not commit a prescribed act, nothing will happen. No penalty will be incurred. In complying with a demand to avoid execution of a threat, the recipient cannot be sure that his positive response will release him from additional ultimata to act in accordance with the threatener's wishes. Compellence may give way to blackmail, and the recipient's independence of maneuver may be constrained and his resources ransomed to the deterrer's whims. The recipient's prestige may become publicly engaged and hinder a positive response. Domestic pressures may resist compliance, and a potentially pliable regime may be stiffened to resist by the objectional manner, timing, or makeup of a threat and the action to be performed.

Destruction of the Opponent. To direct the behavior of an opponent through the use or threat of military force implies limits. The aims of a directing party may be circumscribed or the means available to impose one's views will be checked by the opponent's countervailing forces, lack of resources to overcome the latter's resistance, the absence of national will to impose wider sanctions or compellent power, or the threat that successfully asserting one's demands on a particular opponent may galvanize an adverse coalition against one of even more formidable military capacity than the opponent's. The latter possibility is hardly farfetched. Bismarck labored for more than a generation to prevent such an alignment against Prussia only to see his efforts nullified by his successor's indiscretion. The expansion of American military and economic power had a similar effect of prompting the formation of state groupings to counterbalance what many perceived as the development of a unifocal, American-dominated international system.[47]

What might be termed the limiting or extreme case of directed behavior is the destruction not only of the opponent's armed forces and physical means of defense but also the state's regime. War or military conflict under these circumstances approaches in intent, if not always in actual levels of combat, Clausewitz's notion of pure war, in which the opponents seek total victory over each other and employ all available means to accomplish this goal. Bargaining and diplomacy as tools of accommodation lose much of their meaning as the antagonists are driven to increasingly desperate military measures.

Civil wars, not surprisingly, tend to be conflicts of destruction, whether measured in physical or regime terms. Recent strife in Vietnam, Cambodia, Sudan, Chad, Zaire, and Nigeria suggest the dimensions of such warfare. The opponents are unable to reach any compromise on the fundamental divisions between them. Temporary accords, such as the 1973 Paris agreements halting hostilities between the two Vietnams and paving the way for American military withdrawal, become merely tactical moves to gain time or advantage. The aim of warfare is still total, terminating only with the overthrow of the rival regime or, under the most extreme circumstances, the annihilation or dispersal of the rival nation. The wholesale dismantling of the Cambodian social and economic structure by Pol Pot and his followers and the elimination of all effective internal opposition provide additional evidence that this total form of warfare can be conducted with relatively primitive military means. Nuclear weapons, if used, would speed the rate of destruction, but they would not necessarily be more thorough than the modest military capabilities implied by revolutionary warfare. Calls by the Palestine Liberation Front and several Arab states for the elimination of the Jewish state suggest that a war of destruction is possible between nations or races, as in the case of South Africa.

Demonstration. Contrasting with the aim of destruction is the need of some states or regimes and their peoples to demonstrate or flaunt their military capabilities. Such prestige or status goals are pervasive—and have always been. The military requirements to satisfy these needs are significantly different from those that would be responsive to imperatives of defense, deterrence, or the other provisional aims of military force. Developing states appear to be particularly driven by this motive in acquiring weapons. The sale of F-15's to Saudi Arabia was partly, if tacitly, justified by the determination of the ruling Saudi regime to have the latest in military equipment although it does not possess indigenous forces or cadres to fly or to maintain them. These prestige factors figured in arms sales to Iran under the Shah, Russian dispatch of naval equipment and vessels, including submarines, to Sukarno's Indonesia, and France's sale of 110 Mirage aircraft to Libya in the early 1970s.

The psychic need to display military prowess also operates at the nuclear level. It was no accident that France under Charles de Gaulle identified a foreign policy of *grandeur* with the possession of nuclear weapons.[48] This same prestige factor cannot be discounted in the thinking and feeling of other elites. The Pakistani military are actively pursuing a military nuclear program although there exists no developed doctrine for its use or threat. That India has displayed such a capability appears sufficient reason to go ahead,[49] notwithstanding New Delhi's claim that its explosion was a peaceful device. Rationales for using nuclear weapons appear to follow in the wake of their creation, because psychic income is perceived to be earned simply in displaying a capability to produce a bomb.

Distinguishing between prestige or demonstration purposes and other objectives is very difficult and may be impossible in many instances. The search for status through marshall displays may be harmless enough and may be tolerated by potential opponents. When linked to other strategic and political objectives, the stakes rise accordingly. Analysts have not devised ways of isolating these motives or of determining accurately what are the implications of different weapons acquisition strategies.

Domination. To this point the discussion has focused primarily on armed interstate conflict. Somewhat obscured from view, but no less compelling as a motive, is the drive of a ruling regime to dominate its internal opponents. Many military systems, ostensibly designed for use against foreign threats, are really aimed at stilling domestic adversaries. The forces, weapons, command, control, and communication structures needed for domestic domination are different from those that a defensive or deterrent purpose would require. Latin America states, such as Argentina and Brazil, have almost no exterior security threats confronting them. The military or quasi-military cast of these regimes puts a premium on counterinsurgency and policy capabilities and preparedness that extends to the production of indigenous arms.

The dialectic of violence changes, too. The control of the civilian population is the aim of military force. Maintaining tight direction over military forces to prevent coups becomes an important subsidiary goal. Civil-military relations cannot be taken for granted, because the existence of the regime depends on its access to reliable and loyal military units. The kind of freedom and initiative required by local military commanders in dealing with a foreign invasion or incursion is likely to be an invitation to intrigue for a regime based on the exercise of military and police power. The ideological and personal loyalty of the officer corps consequently becomes an important concern. Political allegiance, not military competence, counts most. From an analyst's perspective the study of civil-military relations, the organization, recruitment, and promotion policies of the military, and C_3 systems for internal use become more relevant objects of study than strategic doctrine or weapons system development and deployment.

Exchange. A final dimension of military policy may, paradoxically, not be aimed at the use or threat of violence. Acquiring, producing, transferring, selling, and deploying arms, matériel, and military forces may be in exchange for other valued objects. These may be far removed from using or threatening force, however indirectly they may be related to these objects. The most obvious and prominent example is arms sales. Once engaged in the independent production of arms for security purposes, the incentives to sell arms abroad to support a viable weapons complex become increasingly strong. These include reduced unit costs through series production, a greater number of weapons for national forces for the same expenditure, lowered research and development costs per number of arms produced, and the potentiality of substantial profits for domestic arms producers. All of the major arms manufacturers, including the Soviet Union, have relied on arms sales to offset rising oil prices. The economic imperative of access to sufficient amounts of oil to service industrial and commercial needs has overridden concerns that an increase in the quantity and quality of arms to the region will destabilize delicate military and diplomatic balances and increase prospects of armed conflict. Involvement in upheavals in the Middle East for a supplier, such as France, for example, threatens to disrupt the flow of oil, force cuts in domestic production and economic growth, increase unemployment and social unrest, and damage lucrative markets.[50]

There is also an important body of literature that relates arms production and sales to economic development. Policy analysts, however, are split in their views about the impact of arms manufacture on economic growth. The traditional view pits one against the other and poses the issue in terms of guns versus butter. Military spending is considered a burden on the public treasury and largely a drag on a nation's economy. This result is posited of developed and developing societies that consecrate large amounts of their wealth and productive capacity to arms. The American economy is not spared criticism. One notable analyst concludes "that the war economy caused substantial modifications in the capitalist system, from the firm on up, and that [the] war economy has become a major source of corrosion of the productive competence of the American economy as a whole."[51] The same skepticism is voiced about the tendency of developing states to maintain high levels of defense spending.[52] Continued high levels of military spending are often attributed to the pressures of a nation's military-industrial complex or to "arms merchants" bent on making profits at the public expense and safety.[53]

Other analysts assume a more optimistic attitude toward arms manufacture. In countries as disparate as France and India, advocates can be found who see important economic and social gains in stimulating weapons production.[54] For these analysts, one must speak of butter *because* of guns. The high technological development associated with modern weapons is portrayed as a significant contributor to economic development. Defense production is a means of marshalling a nation's resources, of justifying large expenditures for research and development, including basic science, and of creating a large and diverse technological-industrial structure needed to sustain new findings and to translate them rapidly into desirable capital and consumer products. Military spending is portrayed as a prod to the civilian economy and as a source for expanding markets abroad.[55]

III. DIMENSIONS OF MILITARY POLICY: USE, THREAT, AND CONTROL

Seven policy outcomes of using and threatening military force have been identified. Each may serve a variety of specific political purposes. Achieving these identified outcomes or conditional states depends on the development of coherent national security policies. This requires the governmental integration of nine levels of decision and action which comprise the key components of the security policy of any state. These include:

1. Assumptions about the international system within which national military forces must operate; whether, for example, the structure is constraining or permissive or hostile or benign
2. The definition of military (and nonmilitary) threats to the regime or nation or both and the national and regime objectives to be supported by the use or threat of military force
3. The military doctrinal response to these threats and opportunities, requiring the use or threat of force
4. The force levels and weapon systems organized to respond to the previous three functions
5. The announced strategies to communicate to, or to conceal policies from, allies, adversaries, and neutrals as well as subordinates (military elites, functionaries, et al.)
6. The human and material resources, including advanced technology, needed to respond to security imperatives while addressing internal socioeconomic demands
7. The marshalling of public opinion, political parties, and interest groups to support regime and national objectives and policies
8. The creation of political incentives and controls to direct the military establishment to support defined objectives
9. Alignment strategies with allies and adversaries to maximize security objectives, including arms control and disarmament measures

A. Assumptions About the International System

Whether a state will rely primarily on military means in contrast to political or economic measures to achieve its security objectives hinges to an appreciable degree on the perceptions of governmental elites of the protection and support afforded by the regional and global system within which the state must act. If conflicts between other states threaten to envelop a state or if some states appear to be expanding their traditional range of interests and exercise of power, a menaced state may be led to increase its military capabilities for defense and deterrence or the state may be encouraged to appease the ascending power or join with other states to resist subjugation. On the other hand, if international intercourse is conducted in an atmosphere of mutual confidence and respect, incentives to use coercion to get one's way may not be strong because less costly and riskier means are available.

Analysts are deeply divided over the question of what global structure of political and military strategic relations is likely to be stable or unstable, defined by the system's inclination toward armed hostilities or war. Many believe that the bipolar system arising from World War II between the United States and the Soviet Union and resting on a mutual balance of nuclear terror is essentially stable.[56] One prominent theorist argues that despite mutual threats and recriminations the superpowers have preserved an uneasy peace between them. Each has adjusted to the rise of the Third World and the nonaligned movement. Each has also had to adjust to dissent from within its own bloc.

Other analysts and decision makers are persuaded that a more diffuse system is stabler,[57] more responsive to individual national needs, and more appropriate as a principle of political organization for global politics.[58] The nonaligned movement has been predicated on these assumptions. The cold war was viewed as fundamentally destabilizing and illegitimate. On the one hand, the superpowers were led to organize separate global blocs. The ideological struggle between Washington and Moscow and the arms race spurred by their split tended to be extended to other states and to polarize them along bloc lines. Local and regional differences between small states were subsequently magnified to global proportions as these more circumscribed issues were absorbed into the cold war vortex. The number of flashpoints between the superpowers that might lead to nuclear war were increased. Smaller states thus risked being drawn into a nuclear conflagration against their interests or desires and over which they had little or no influence. Such a bleak prospect weakens the principle of national independence, because the decision of peace or war is effectively transferred to the superpowers. To the degree that a state is captive of one of the superpowers, including entrapment in a nuclear war not of its own choosing, it is unable to fashion its own security and foreign policies. If the cold war robbed the nation-state of its raison d'être, then it followed that the system of international politics built on the superpower struggle was also flawed and illegitimate. Added to these criticisms of the East-West split was the view shared by most developing states that the Soviet-American conflict deflected needed resources from economic development. A global order that led to a diversion of scarce economic resources to military purposes was deemed fundamentally inequitable.

The response of superpower allies and neutrals to these lines of criticism has been to search for greater national independence and maneuver and, as a consequence, to create a more decentralized and diffuse system. At an economic level the Western European states have created their own trading bloc and increasingly strive, as in the Middle

Table 1. Number of Third World Countries with Advanced Military Systems, 1950, 1960, 1970, 1977

	1950	1960	1970	1977
Supersonic aircraft		1	28	47
Missiles		6	25	42
Armored fighting vehicles	1	38	72	83
Modern warships	4	26	56	67

Source: Stockholm International Peace Research Institute, *World Armaments and Disarmament: 1978* (Crane, Russak, New York, 1978), pp. 238–253). Military systems refer to postwar production.

East, to develop common regional positions. Similar efforts have been launched in other regions. The U.N. Group of 77, composed of developing states, was formed to lobby the developed states for more aid and to focus attention on the problem of the growing economic gap between North and South as a key security issue in the broadest sense of that term.

Militarily, states outside the NATO and Warsaw alliances have increased their military expenditures over the past 10 years at a faster rate than the developed states. Between 1968 and 1978 the developing world increased its defense spending in constant 1976 dollars by more than 70 percent, from $54 billion to $92 billion. The military expenditures of the developed state grew only 4.6 percent, from $305 billion to $319 billion.[59] These increases are for increasingly sophisticated equipment. Table 1 summarizes inventory acquisitions of advance weapons by Third World states from 1950 to 1977. Substantial increases are registered at each 10-year period, in supersonic aircraft, missiles, armed fighting equipment, and modern warships.

This expansion is now being pressed beyond conventional arms into nuclear weapons. India's "peaceful" explosion of a nuclear device enlarged the official nuclear club to six. There is considerable evidence that Israel is also a nuclear power.[60] Other states, including Pakistan, South Africa, Taiwan, South Korea, Iraq, Argentina, and Brazil, are strong candidates to become nuclear states in the future. The politico-strategic motivations of these states, unlike those of Britain, France, and China, appear to be more regionally than globally directed. Nuclear weapons respond to local needs for defense against close and definable adversaries. The military implications of a proliferated world are still unclear, and their study forms an important part of contemporary military policy analysis.[61]

B. Perception of Threats and Opportunities

Perhaps nothing more difficult than communicating a threat, as noted earlier, is perceiving a threat (or opportunity) requiring a military response. If an adversary is preparing to use force, he has every incentive to hide his moves to maximize his chances for surprise. When an adversary wishes to communicate a threat, it is normally for purposes of deterrence or directed behavior. Even under these circumstances, in which there is some incentive to make sure the opponent is notified of a threat to do or to refrain from some action, concealment and reservation may be at play. A threat that leaves something to chance or that is general may have a greater impact than one that is concrete and pointed.

Determining the credibility of a threat involves a host of imponderables and uncertainties. It depends on the form, source, importance, and manner of communicating the threat and the likelihood and impact of the threat if it is carried out. Analysts tend to use two basic approaches. Either they stress adversary capabilities or intentions or attempt to mix these perspectives to develop a composite view of what an adversary might do. The most prevalent fault of analysis is to posit the worst case: either to argue that the enemy *will* do something damaging because he has the ability to do so, or that his motives are so insidious that he is preparing to do the worst. The first line of analysis fosters an atmosphere of preemption and preventive warfare; the second encourages arms races. Both risk becoming a self-fulfilling prophecy. This may be understood as "a false definition of a situation which makes the originally false conception come true."[62] A significant part of the evolution of the struggle and military strategic balance of the superpowers can be plausibly explained in mirror image terms in which policy makers tended to see the worst in the statements and behavior of the opponent.[63] Arms races between India and Pakistan or between Israel and the Arab states assume the same character.[64]

Part of the problem of detecting threats arises from the meaning of intelligence itself. It has at least three dimensions: information, organization, and activity.[65] The first refers to information collection and evaluation. But what kind of information does one seek to gather? In what context is it to be interpreted? For what purpose? Information or data are infinite in their possibilities. The collection of material is blind outside of context and purpose. Even if these questions can be provisionally resolved, there are still others that need answering. Should information be gathered in terms of traditional categories, like an almanac or travel book? Or should data be collected in terms of problem areas? The former is comprehensive but unfocused; the latter is focused but risks overlooking important material. In either case there is also the problem of "noise," the detection of information that appears important but deflects attention from an adversary's true intentions and developing moves.

These informational problems are paralleled by organizational issues. Who should receive information? When? How much? In what form? How should security be handled?[66] The failure of American intelligence to detect the Japanese attack on Pearl Harbor was attributed largely to the decentralization of American intelligence services among rival armed services and the State, Navy, and War departments.[67] Although U.S. experts had broken the Japanese diplomatic code, they were unable to use this breakthrough. In retrospect, there appears to have been enough information available in the intelligence network to have foreseen a Japanese attack. The data were so dispersed, the process of evaluation and interpretation so diffuse and decentralized, and the potential users so insulated from each other that no one person or unit could bring these diverse pieces of information about the impeding attack into focus and alert relevant decision makers to take appropriate defensive moves.

To these problems must be added the problem of checking the accuracy and interpretation of intelligence evaluations and the activity of operatives. The first is fundamental. The pictures or images one has of adversary intentions and behavior shapes responses. If the intelligence service is centralized, other governmental groups and top decision makers may be prompted to take actions consciously or unwittingly suggested in intelligence reports. This risk becomes greater when the agencies charged with gathering information also have responsibility for executing governmental policy. They may thus present selected information or make evaluations to bias anticipated decisions by higher governmental officials in directions they favor. The Japanese military in China during the 1930s doctored information to appear that aggression had been committed against Japanese forces, and not that the reverse was true. U.S. intelligence reports from Vietnam were similarly distorted to present an optimistic picture of the fighting in Vietnam or, as in the case of the Tonkin incident, to label an attack by North Vietnamese gunboats against American destroyers as "unprovoked" aggression without mentioning South Vietnamese infiltration attempts in the period preceding the raid.[68] Maintaining tight political control over clandestine operations is also difficult, as evidenced by Senate disclosures of foiled assassination attempts by CIA operatives of Fidel Castro, unauthorized intervention in the Angolan civil war, and the conduct of intelligence surveillance in the United States in violation of domestic law.[69]

C. Development of Military Doctrine

How weapons will be used for what tactical and strategic purposes is the domain of military doctrine. The object of military doctrine is to develop a set of rules of behavior or operational code for the efficient and effective use of weapons and personnel. Different rules will apply to different situations. In the absence of such rules, the officer corps and political leadership of a state would be obliged to treat each contingency requiring the use or threat of force anew. Contradictions, lapses, and ambiguities in command, with resulting confusion and disorientation in execution, would be the inevitable result. Training and integration of new personnel in the ranks would be impossible. Maintaining the cohesion of the armed forces, especially the officer corps, would present insuperable problems.

The need for coherent and consistent military doctrine is easier to stipulate than to achieve. The history of warfare is strewn with the wreckage of military doctrine overtaken by new ideas to use men and weapons, political and ideological movements, socioeconomic forces, and technological change. The static, defensive warfare of the eighteenth century, codified in Vauban's writings,[70] was destroyed by the use of massed artillery and military forces, inspired by revolutionary ideology, during the Napoleonic wars.[71] Military art gave way to military science with the rise of the general staff whose principal task was the development of doctrine that would coordinate military operations, weapons development, procurement, supply, recruitment, and training and link these to the political objectives of the state. These efforts in the nineteenth century culminated, albeit disastrously, in the German Schlieffen Plan and the French Plan 17. Both were based on an offensive strategy aimed at enveloping the forces of the rival army. The deadly firepower of the machine gun and field artillery, particularly the French 75-mm cannon, and the obstacles posed by barbed wire and defense forces protected by trenches produced unimagined casualties, measured in millions. Neither plan nor the strategic doctrine on which they were based foresaw these implications of modern warfare.[72] The machine gun, for example, was viewed initially as an offensive weapon. Based on a notion of quick victory, neither side could adjust its doctrine to the conditions of a war of attrition. Nor were the adversaries, especially Germany, sensitive to the political and socioeconomic context in which military doctrine was to be applied. The German front collapse arose from two unforeseen developments: domestic opposition to the war and American intervention brought about by the policy of unrestricted submarine warfare, which had been launched to extricate Germany from its precarious military predicament. Contrariwise, French doctrine ossified after World War I. As Germany developed a *Blitzkreig* strategy, based on the coordinated use of massed armor and airpower, French generals placed their faith on a defensive posture founded on the Maginot Line.[73]

Contemporary military doctrine falls into three main groupings: nuclear, conventional, and revolutionary or guerrilla warfare. Nuclear doctrine has stressed deterrence over defensive or offensive use of these deadly weapons. Deterrence depends on credibility, which has two components: the ability of the deterrer to convince his opponent that he has the will and the material capacity to carry out his threat. Because deterrence is essentially psychological, the projection and the manipulation of the adversary's will are critical in the dialectic between deterrer and deterred. This can be accomplished in a variety of ways: making threats that bind one to an automatic response; developing a reputation for keeping one's commitments; or acting irrationally to convey the impression that one may lose control in a conflict as tensions mount.[74]

The material side of deterrence is no less complex. At issue are the number, size, type, reliability, and accuracy of delivery vehicles, the explosive power to be transported, the vulnerability of weapons systems (concealed, dispersed, hardened, secret), the level of alert to launch weapons, the effectiveness of C^3 systems, and the preparedness of active and defense efforts to defeat or nullify incoming attacks.[75]

Two general tendencies have emerged among analysts of nuclear deterrence warfare.[76] The first is a minimalist position. It stresses the ability of a state to destroy an opponent's cities and socioeconomic structure. Such a threat is considered to be sufficiently potent to deter aggression against one's homeland and those values that are of vital importance. The weapons needed for a finite or minimalist position are usually small in number (although of relatively high destructive power), invulnerable, and capable of penetrating an opponent's defense system. Strong concern for arms control and minimum mutual assured destruction postures on both sides are added features of this position.

The second or maximalist position argues for sufficient amounts of delivery vehicles, warheads, and explosive throw-weight as well as active and defensive systems to fight a nuclear war, if deterrence breaks down. This implies an ability to limit damage to one's homeland, allies, and armed forces and to sustain a credible deterrent and defense effort in the midst of hostilities to bring war to a swift conclusion on advantageous terms. Aside from resource and technological capabilities, limits on a state's nuclear preparations are a function of its opponent's military posture. Proponents of a maximalist approach stress further that the ability to "win" or "prevent" a nuclear exchange is essential if deterrence is to be credible in defending allies or in protecting important, yet peripheral, values of the deterring state. Arms races are discounted as less destabilizing than the appearance of inferiority. So also are the costs of arms competition. The political stakes at issue are considered to be of sufficient importance to justify the expense.

The debate over Senate ratification of the SALT II treaty at the end of the 1970s is but the latest episode in the debate of proponents of one or the other of these orientations.[77] Issues concerned verification of Soviet nuclear forces, the surveillance of nuclear development programs, the vulnerability of American Minuteman missiles, the development of a new land-based MX force, the increasing growth of Soviet nuclear forces, symbolized by the development of heavy missiles such as the SS-18, and the alleged attachment of Soviet strategists to a nuclear war-fighting doctrine. The withdrawal of the SALT treaty from Senate consideration in the wake of the Soviet invasion of Afghanistan in 1979 has shifted the focus of the debate to the evaluation of the nuclear balance between the United States and the Soviet Union in Europe. Soviet modernization of its nuclear forces in Eastern Europe and its introduction of the SS-20 missile, capable of carrying multiple warheads, prompted NATO ministers, under U.S. prodding, to propose deploying Cruise missiles and Pershing II intermediate-range ballistic missiles (IRBM) to counter the Soviet threat.[78] The theatre nuclear balance in Europe is thus linked to the global strategic balance between the two superpowers.

A separate but related level of analysis is conventional, or what analysts often refer to as limited war. Whether tactical nuclear weapons can be plausibly included within discussion of limited war is a hotly contested point.[79] A limited war is generally conceived to be a war fought for limited purposes with circumscribed means with the immediate aim of a termination of hostilities through a bargained accord.[80]

What counts in determining whether a war is limited or not are the means used on the battlefield and the scope and intensity of combat, not the announced intentions or the exaggerated threats of the adversaries. Weapons may be variously classified according to firepower, precision, accuracy, viability, vulnerability, and reliability. How these weapons mixes and personnel are deployed affect the degree to which a conflict will be limited. The geographic extent of the battle, whether there are sanctuaries or not, and the degree to which an area is mutually agreed upon as a limited combat zone (e.g., bombing goes on but invasion is ruled out) define other factors controlling the level of violence. To these limits should be added the length and intensity of combat, the number of casualties, the material damage suffered by armed forces and civilians, and the extent of national mobilization. What may be a limited war for one opponent (the United States in Vietnam or the Soviet Union in Afghanistan) may be total for the other (Hanoi and the Afghan rebels, respectively). These asymmetries play a role in the bargaining between the adversaries and the prospects of termination. If one opponent is taxed to his physical limits, he may also be a more determined foe because the stakes are presumably total, whereas the less engaged ally may have more incentive to find a compromise solution.

In contrast to nuclear deterrence, conventional deterrence is fundamentally unstable. The latter conforms to traditional notions of the relation of military force and diplomacy. Despite the higher firepower now possible with nonnuclear munitions, there still appears to be a closer balance between costs and risks, on one hand, and gains or benefits, on the other, to tempt states to employ force.[81] These positive incentives of use can be overstated. The five Middle East wars since World War II suggest that the antagonists are quickly spent during an outbreak of hostilities, and must rely on massive external transfusions of arms. The same may be said of Indian-Pakistani clashes or of the Indian-Chinese war. In all of these instances, the belligerents' ability to prevail depended not only on the arms in being, which were rapidly exhausted, but also on their access to outside suppliers. If the geographic scope of hostilities is limited, the strategic-diplomatic context within which the conflict is played out may well be extraregional and even global.

Guerrilla warfare represents a third order of armed conflict. It has its own rules and order of operation. These are defined by the essential asymmetry of the power balance on both sides and the immediate aim of combat when it occurs. Samuel Huntington's definition and description of guerrilla warfare remains apt:

> Guerrilla warfare is a form of warfare by which the strategically weaker side assumes the tactical offensive in selected forms, times, and places. Guerrilla warfare is the weapon of the weak. It is never chosen in preference to regular warfare; it is employed only when and where the possibilities of regular warfare have been foreclosed.[82]

The guerrilla is by definition in a weaker military position. To survive, guerrilla forces can engage superior government or foreign troops where they hold the tactical advantage of terrain, personnel, and firepower. The object of these encounters is control over certain areas and the civilian populations within them. It is possible for the control to be dual, with the guerrillas controlling night movements and regular forces exercising authority during the day. Strategists such as Mao Tse-Tung and Che Guevara[83] have contributed to the romance of guerrilla warfare and to the body of rules and doctrine governing this mode of conflict.

Guerrilla warfare, however, should be distinguished from *revolutionary warfare*. Whereas guerrilla warfare is a *form* of military engagement, revolutionary warfare is a type of war. A government ousted by a foreign invader may well use guerrilla warfare tactics to regain ascendancy, trading space for time, or maintaining a war of attrition that weakens the aggressor's political will to persist in the struggle. It implies no particular ideological bent. Conservative and liberal forces may equally avail themselves of guerrilla warfare. The term "guerrilla" derives from Spanish resistance, composed largely of monarchist supporters, to French invasion forces propelled by the ideology of the French revolution. In contrast to guerrilla warfare as a mode of armed conflict, revolutionary war "is a struggle between a nongovernmental group and a government in which the latter attempts to destroy the former by some or all means at its command, and the governmental group attempts by all means at its command to replace the government in some or all of its territory."[84] This kind of conflict tends to be without limit, because the contending forces seek to replace each other.

Revolutionary war, as its name implies, has been usually associated with the socioeconomic and political transformation of a nation. These motives tend to influence the domestic struggle and encourage progressively more destructive and extreme forms of coercion characterized by random acts of terrorism, genocide, or unremitting class warfare suggested by the mass executions conducted by the Pol Pot regime in Cambodia.[85]

D. Force Levels and Weapon Systems

The relation of military doctrine to weapon systems and available personnel is clearer in logic than in the behavior of states. Examining the decision making of states in military policy suggests that the weapons systems, indigenously produced or imported by a state, as much dictate its military doctrine as its strategy directs the development and acquisition of its arms. Nuclear weapons heavily influenced American doctrine after World War

II and gave a new lease on life to strategic bombing, which had been given low marks for effectiveness in World War II.[86] A case can be made that the technical capacity of a state to produce a weapon has generated a presumption in favor of its development. While this inclination to produce what can be created does not always transpire because of competing costs (e.g., nuclear versus conventionally driven aircraft carriers) or competing claims (the B-1 bomber versus cruise missiles), the history of arms acquisition by states has been heavily influenced by the pressure of military elites to demand the latest in military equipment. The growth in sophistication of the weapons inventories of Third World states, noted in Table 1, reflects these upward pressures.

Matching force levels and weapons systems to strategic doctrine and reconciling them with scarce technical and economic resources and competing political objectives are not easy tasks. SALT II illustrates the problem. There has been considerable dispute over what mix of air, sea, and ground launched missiles and bombers would furnish an adequate deterrent posture on a basis of parity with the Soviet Union. The perceived vulnerability of American land-based missiles (Minutemen) sparked in the early 1980s a major debate over the composition of the American triad—and whether the triad should be continued.[87] The Carter administration's proposal of an MX system of movable missiles in concrete silos was subsequently rejected by the Reagan regime. Many strategists, while conceding the need for a replacement of Minutemen, prefer to strengthen other systems, such as sea-based systems, or seek reactivation of the B-1 bomber program. These proposals are related to calls for the deployment of cruise and intermediary-range missiles in Europe to supplement alliance capabilities. Finally, others would scrap entirely the entire SALT process as ill-conceived. They view with alarm both the impressive increase of Soviet strategic nuclear capability and the persistence of the Soviet military strategists in developing what they believe is a war-fighting capability.

E. Announced and Operational Strategies: Bargaining with Allies, Adversaries, and Neutrals

Policy makers also face difficulties in reconciling the competing demands and expectations of allies, adversaries, and neutrals. Strategies conceived to deter an adversary may be considered provocative by allies. Or strategies calculated to respond to neutral sentiment may appear weak and vacillating to hard-pressed allies. The American doctrine of "massive retaliation," announced by Secretary of State John Foster Dulles in 1954, was supposed to counter Soviet and Communist aggression against the United States and its allies with nuclear weapons of America's choosing in time, place, and degree of nuclear retaliatory response. The American strategy was widely criticized as lacking credibility, particularly as the Soviet nuclear force expanded. The U.S. declaration that it would initiate nuclear war in response to even minor Communist military probes did not appear plausible. To the extent that Washington was prepared to employ such weapons, allies felt threatened that they would be dragged into a war against their will and interest. On the other hand, the Kennedy administration's replacement of "massive retaliation" with "flexible response" worried allies that the superpowers would make their homelands sanctuaries and that a war between them would be fought on allied territory. Deterrence against Soviet conventional attack might be strengthened by the ability of NATO forces to respond in kind, but even such an exchange might be devastating for the European states. The unwillingness of either European or American public opinion to pay the costs of ample defense and deterrence to meet Soviet and Communist military actions at all levels of possible military provocation further weakened the credibility of a flexible response strategy.

The same problems face strategists elsewhere. The Brezhnev doctrine, announced in 1968 to justify Soviet and Warsaw Pact invasion of Czechoslovakia, can be interpreted as a conservative stance. Moscow's claim that it has a right to protect established Communist regimes could be rationalized as a partially legitimate response to Soviet security needs. But what is the status of the doctrine when it is used to justify maintenance of a Communist government that was installed by a coup d'état to expand Moscow's sphere of interest? The doctrine is transformed into a forward strategy in which the distinction between defending what has been gained and expanding to defend what one has secured through intervention becomes blurred.

F. Resources, Technology and Socioeconomic Demands

At this dimension of decision, policy makers face several dilemmas. First, there is the traditional problem of balancing security and socioeconomic imperatives. This issue has grown far more complex today than in the past because the competing possibilities of weapons purchases are so varied and costly that no state has enough resources to purchase all of the equipment that could be supplied. These tensions in decision making are deepened when substantial differences arise over the kind and seriousness of the threat that a state confronts. Even those who might agree that a state faces a military threat may differ sharply over the dimensions and scope of the menace. The American debate over SALT II and the defense budget reflect these differences of view among analysts. Decision makers may agree on large defense spending, but are in less accord on priorities. When discord turns on whether a threat exists at all or whether internal conflict may be the more imminent danger, policy differences can be expected to be more sharp and less easily resolved.[88]

The marriage of military weapons development with the almost infinite possibilities of scientific and technological discovery has added new strains to the resource allocation question. Choices among weapons also imply choices in industrial strategies to produce them. One can usefully distinguish, therefore, two sets of different but related decisions. The first are strategic and involve the various aspects of military policy already discussed above. The second refers to structured decisions. These refer to:

> (1) budget decisions concerning the size and distribution of funds made available to the armed forces; (2) personnel decisions concerning the number, procurement, retention, pay, and working conditions of members of the military services; (3) material decisions concerning the amount, procurement, and distribution of supplies to the armed forces; and (4) organizational decisions concerning the methods and forms by which the military services are organized and administered.[89]

A wrong decision at any of these decisional levels not only will be costly but may also undermine a nation's defense system—perhaps irretrievably. Complex weapon systems, such as advanced aircraft or nuclear submarines, require a decade or more to develop. Parallel developments in counterweapons design may negate a system laboriously perfected over a long period. The introduction of precision-guided munitions (PGMs) challenges the superiority of heavy armor and the tank on conventional battlefields.[90] Small, mobile units, armed with accurate, high explosives—deliverable at high rates of reliability against moving targets—dilute massed armor without the necessity of quick resort to nuclear weapons to stem defeat. Arms races are thus frought with great uncertainty and cost: either high, even prohibitive, expenditures for weapons that may not yield an advantage (offset by the adversary's production of the same weapons or countering devices), or greater risks for both sides, or the creation of weapons gaps that give a decisive advantage to one side.[91]

G. Political Support and the Politics of Military Policy

In greater or lesser measure, no government can escape the problem of mobilizing domestic support for its military policies. Authoritarian regimes must rely on manipulative and coercive means of eliciting support. These can be impressive. Nondemocratic regimes in Japan, Nazi Germany, and the Soviet Union fielded massive armies and spurred their populations to the limits of human endurance. Hanoi was able to prevail over the vastly superior resources of the United States. With little respite, it replenished its losses with fresh, highly motivated troops. Public opinion in the United States was less steadfast, and withdrawal of American troops became increasingly a touchstone of domestic cohesion.

Developing consent in a democratic framework poses special problems. It is not always easy to convince a majority of a distracted citizenry, when beset by economic and social problems, to support costly defense programs or to maintain a large standing army. As the French Third Republic discovered, national consensus may be at a level adequate for uneasy social cohesion but be at a level below what is needed to deter or defend against enemy attack. American preparedness was similarly impaired before World War II. Only the shock of the attack on Pearl Harbor galvanized a majority of the population to support a world war. The cold war rationalized continued American commitment to a global strategy. The French and American experiences raise again the central question of whether democratic governments are capable of providing an adequate defense of national interests over time. Students and practitioners are fundamentally divided on this issue.[92]

The process of generating domestic support in a democracy varies from one government to another. In the United States, consensus building is focused on legislative-executive relations and, specifically, on Congress and the President.[93] This relationship has undergone major changes since the inception of the republic. Now Congress may be in the ascendancy; under crisis conditions the President may again seize the upper hand. The American constitution was quite deliberately written to induce the President and Congress to cooperate or to be in perpetual conflict over military policy. The President is Commander-in-Chief of the Armed Forces. Only the President can direct the armed services, appoint officers, and deploy the nation's military forces. But only Congress has the authority to raise and support armed forces, approve military commissions, define the organizational structure of the defense system, and declare war. As in foreign policy, the Constitution is an invitation to a struggle over which branch of government will control military policy.

The battle over military policy is centered in the annual budget process.[94] The lines of consensus and cleavage between the Congress and the President are far more complex and confused than may initially strike the casual observer. Within Congress there are often sharp differences between committees, the two houses, or the membership. This tapestry of cross-cutting patterns is overlaid by those between groups and committees in Congress and segments of the executive branch that may be more responsive to legislative cues than to presidential directives. The success of Admiral Hyman Rickover in gaining congressional support for the nuclear submarine program over 20 years, often over official Navy and presidential opposition, provides a glimpse of the fluid and diffuse character of the military policy process.[95] As President Eisenhower discovered, the President may be unable to control the top officer corps, and end-runs to the public or Congress may become more the rule than the exception.

H. Control of the Military Establishment

It is difficult to underestimate this dimension of military policy. The large number of military regimes around the world suggest the difficulty of preserving civilian control. Four problem levels exist. The first is managerial. It is focused on efficient and effective direction of a politically loyal military. Issues turn on technical command, communication, and control systems. Coordinating the diverse activities of millions of personnel poses enormous and exacting managerial tasks whose difficulty is heightened by frictions and resistances within the system.

The second order of problem arises from the creation of a military bureaucracy. To assure the resources it needs, the officer corps has incentive to influence top decision makers and the public in support of their requests. Rather than an instrument of policy, the military bureaucracy has a tendency to become its own object. Modern weapons development has also spurred the creation of military industrial systems within modernized states. Thus, civilian control is complicated by the interest of important segments of the civilian leadership to maintain and enlarge these arms-producing systems.

The issue of internal influence leads to a third order of problem—the development of independent security policies. President Harry Truman's dismissal of General Douglas MacArthur as the American commander in Korea highlighted this issue. Soldiers in the field often have their own ideas about how a war should be fought. In MacArthur's case, he not only issued public criticism of the Truman administration's management of the war, but advocated an expansion of hostilities. [96]

The influence of military thinking on national policy may be more subtle and unconscious than the MacArthur episode suggests. The German Schlieffen Plan narrowed the political options available to the Prussian crown. Mobilization was dictated more by the schedule for moving troops by train to the battlefield than by clear political objectives. Imprisoned by prevailing war plans, German authorities stumbled into a world war that proved disastrous to their nation and rule.

The possibility of a military takeover caps the problems of controlling the military. In developing states this outcome has become as much the rule as the exception. In Africa and Latin America, military regimes are the most common form of rule. Latin America's three major states—Argentina, Brazil, and Chile—are all under military rule. Many governments, ostensibly ruled by civilians, as in Syria or Iraq, owe much of their existence to sustained support from the military establishment.

I. Alliances and Arms Control

Security alliances are characteristic features of the nation-state system. Since no state, including the superpowers, is able to provide unilaterally for its own defense or security needs, allies are required. Allies, however, play varied roles whose value to a state will inevitably change over time. The value of an ally will therefore be assessed in terms of one or more evaluative scales that are by no means mutually exclusive or necessarily compatible. Traditionally, the most important value has been the degree to which a state increases another's power through alliance. States have joined with other nations against another state or alliance because they do not possess the means alone to confront a rival or its allies. This notion underlies the historic operation of the balance of power where a combination of states joins together against another state or grouping to prevent either one or the other from gaining a hegemonial position.

The traditional role of alliances—to increase member power—has had to be redefined by the rise of two superpowers and the development of nuclear weapons. Theoretically, neither superpower can be defeated militarily by any combination of states that does not involve the other superpower. This circumstance weakens superpower incentives for allies. Offsetting this consideration, however, is the view that the loss of an ally is a gain for an adversary or, in the words of game theory, that the superpowers are in a zero-sum game. Allies assume a different value than that of an extension of superpower influence. They become strategic assets in their own right, valued as an object of the superpower struggle and not just as a means. Viewed from still a third perspective, the ability to control the behavior of an ally may assume under certain conditions more importance than collective action against the common adversary. Allies possessing nuclear weapons, for example, pose problems for allied cohesion since independently acting allies can potentially involve an ally in a nuclear war against the latter's own interests and will. Incentives arise, inducing allies to seek control over each other's behavior involving the use or threat of nuclear weapons. For these various reasons, alliances remain conditional, and the degree of cooperation that one can expect of allies depends on the specific interests and objectives that the alliance serves or, alternately, the risks and costs of remaining loyal to allies which may act contrary to one's interests. One way to lower dependency on allies is to relax some of the constraints of the international environment that prompt the need for security alliances. Arms control, therefore, assumes an increasingly important part of alliance bargaining.

Arms control implies stabilization of the military environment between opponents or opposing alliances in order to reduce the real or potential costs and risks of using arms, especially weapons of high destruction. These actions may be unilateral, such as the dismantling of obsolete missiles, or they may be implemented in cooperation with allies and adversaries. Exchanging information about troop movement, for example, to dampen incentive for preemptive war would constitute an arms control measure.

Cooperating with an opponent to lower the costs and risks of using military power or to regulate the rate and scope of an arms race is the principal focus of contemporary arms control policy. A wide number of measures or initiatives fall under this heading: the test ban and the nonproliferation treaties, the prohibition on nuclear weapons in space or the sea bed, restrictions on gas or bacteriological weapons, the creation of "red alert" phones to provide direct communications between the American President and the Soviet Premier, and SALT I and II.

The concept of arms control, especially as a means to promote cooperation between antagonists, has aroused considerable controversy in policy circles. On its face the prospect of agreement to limit conflict between adversaries appears contradictory. This view of arms control is based on the premise of potentially mutual advantage—or less disadvantage—to foes if they cooperate in specified areas of military policies rather than act independently in response to the perceived aggressive moves of the other. The danger grows of the use of force arising from miscalculation, misperception, accident, or inadvertence. Arms control has a compelling attraction if the alternative is a devastating nuclear war that no one wants. It then becomes another bargaining mechanism between the adversaries in which they attempt to manage their conflict pursuing efforts to gain a decisive advantage.

On the other hand, as long as the adversaries are irreconcilable and the military environment—thanks to new discoveries and technological breakthroughs—remains unstable, arms control will suffer as a tool of diplomacy. These concerns have led some to reject arms control measures. Those focused on the expanding capabilities and imputed deceit of the adversary view arms control as a snare. Those interested in disarmament see arms control as an illusion. Arms control does not automatically result in a decrease in military spending or a prohibition on the introduction of new weapons in the arsenals of states. To maintain or create military balances and stability more, not less, arms may be advised from an arms control perspective. Weaker states also argue that superpower attempts to impose the nonproliferation treaty on other states is designed to preserve their domination while their struggle unabatedly continues. A more moderate position between these hard and soft line stances views arms control as a device leading to still more arms control and modest disarmament measures. In an atmosphere of increased arms cooperation, political agreement would then be formulated.

IV. CONCLUDING REMARKS

Using and controlling military force are among the most critical problems facing governments today. The range of strategic outcomes, discussed in Sec. II, and the complexities of rational decision making in strategic planning and operations, outlined in Sec. III, suggest the difficulty of the problem. Whether military policy will remain disciplined to political purpose is by no means certain. Whether it can be controlled and calibrated to serve national and international security needs is a question that cannot be confidently answered affirmatively. Sensitivity to the dimensions of the military problems confronting decision makers and the populations to whom they are responsible is a key starting point in resolving, or at least managing, the dilemmas of threatening, using, and controlling force.

NOTES

1. A useful sampling of the thinking of modern strategists beginning with Machiavelli is found in Edward Mead Earle (Ed.), *Makers of Modern Strategy* (Atheneum, New York, 1941). Space limitations preclude extensive bibliographic references. What appear are representative works of a richer literature than can only be suggested here.

2. Carl von Clausewitz, *On War*, J. J. Graham (Trans.) (Routledge and Kegan Paul, London, 1962), vol. I, p. 23.
3. Samuel P. Huntington, Jr., *The Soldier and the State* (Belknap Press, Cambridge, MA, 1957).
4. Mao Tse-Tung, *Selected Military Writings of Mao Tse-Tung* (Foreign Languages Press, Peking, 1968), p. 227.
5. P. M. S. Blackett, *Studies of War* (Hill and Wang, New York, 1962).
6. André Beaufre, *An Introduction to Strategy*, R. H. Barry (Trans.) (Praeger, New York, 1965), and *Deterrence and Strategy*, R. H. Barry (Trans.) (Praeger, New York, 1966), and *Strategy of Action*, R. H. Barry (Trans.) (Faber and Faber, London, 1966).
7. Raymond Aron, *The Great Debate*, E. Powell (Trans.) (Doubleday, Garden City, NY, 1965), and *Peace and War*, R. Howard and A. Fox (Trans.) (Doubleday, Garden City, NY, 1966).
8. Robert E. Osgood, *Limited War* (University of Chicago Press, Chicago, 1956).
9. Henry A. Kissinger, *Nuclear Weapons and Foreign Policy* (Doubleday, Garden City, NY, 1957), and *The Necessity for Choice* (Doubleday, Garden City, NY, 1960).
10. Herman Kahn, *On Thermonuclear War* (Princeton University Press, Princeton, NJ, 1960).
11. Thomas C. Schelling, *The Strategy of Conflict* (Oxford University Press, New York, 1960), and *Arms and Influence* (Yale University Press, New Haven, CT, 1966).
12. Bernard Brodie, *War and Politics* (Macmillan, New York, 1973), and *Strategy in the Missile Age* (Princeton University Press, Princeton, NJ, 1959).
13. Marshall, V. D. Sokolovskii (Ed.), *Soviet Military Strategy* (Prentice-Hall, Englewood Cliffs, NJ, 1963), and *Military Strategy* (Praeger, New York, 1963).
14. Clausewitz, quoted by Brodie, *War and Politics*, p. 1.
15. Kahn, *On Thermonuclear War*.
16. Realist writer and writings include the following: Nicholas J. Spykman, *America's Strategy in World Politics: The United States and the Balance of Power* (Harcourt, Brace, New York, 1942; Reinhold Niebuhr, *Moral Man and Immoral Society* (Scribner's, New York, 1947); and Hans Morgenthau, *In Defense of National Interest* (Knopf, New York, 1951). Representative writers of a systemic persuasion are Richard Rosecrance, *Action and Reaction in World Politics* (Little, Brown, Boston, 1963), and Morton Kaplan, *System and Process in International Politics* (Wiley, New York, 1957).
17. See, for example, James Rosenau, *Domestic Sources of Foreign Policy* (Free Press, New York, 1967).
18. Schelling, *Arms and Influence,* elaborates on this point. The typology of outcomes adopted in this review was suggested in part by the stimulating essay of Robert J. Art, "To What Ends Military," *International Security 4*, (Spring, 1980): 3–25.
19. See Robert Taft, *A Foreign Policy for Americans* (Doubleday, New York, 1951), and Herbert Hoover, *The Challenge to Liberty* (Scribner's, New York, 1934).
20. The vast literature on the cold war cannot be rehearsed here. Useful are Louis Halle's *The Cold War as History* (Harper & Row, New York, 1967), and Thomas W. Wolfe, *Soviet Power and Europe: 1945–1970* (Johns Hopkins Press, Baltimore, 1970).
21. Brodie's discussion, *Strategy in the Missile Age*, pp. 241–248, 227–239, is relevant.
22. For a discussion of the latter case, see Randolph and Winston Churchill, *The Six Day War* (Heinemann, London, 1967).
23. Patrick M. Morgan, *Deterrence: A Conceptual Analysis* (Sage, Beverly Hills, CA, 1977), p. 9.

24. See n. 6.
25. Glenn H. Snyder, *Deterrence and Defense* (Princeton University Press, Princeton, NJ, 1961). See his more recent *Conflict Among Nations,* written in collaboration with Paul Diesing (Princeton University Press, Princeton, NJ, 1977).
26. Nuclear blackmail is argued to be a virtue in alliance cohesion: see Beaufre's *Deterrence and Strategy.*
27. For contrasting methodological approaches to understanding deterrence, see Schelling, *Strategy of Conflict,* and Alexander George and Richard Smoke, *Deterrence in American Foreign Policy* (Columbia University Press, New York, 1974).
28. Albert Wohlstetter, The delicate balance of terror, *Foreign Affairs 37,* 2 (January 1959); 211-234.
29. See the approach of Charles de Gaulle to foreign and security policy: Edward A. Kolodziej, *French International Policy under De Gaulle and Pompidou* (Cornell University Press, Ithaca, NY, 1947), especially pp. 19-175.
30. A brief but probing discussion of the impact of images on decision making is Kenneth Boulding's *The Image* (University of Michigan Press, Ann Arbor, 1956).
31. A comprehensive review of the relation of perception to international relations is Robert Jervis' *Perception and Misperception in International Politics* (Princeton University Press, Princeton, NJ, 1976).
32. For a sketch of some of the problems associated with communicating meaning and intent between governments, consult Snyder, *Deterrence and Defense,* chap. 5, pp. 239-258.
33. Some of the problems of C^3 systems in using and controlling force are reviewed in two articles by Davis B. Bobrow: "Communications, Command and Control: The Nerves of Intervention," in *The Limits of Military Intervention,* Ellen P. Stern (Ed.) (Sage, Beverly Hills, CA, 1977), pp. 101-120, and "Arms Control Through Communication and Information Regimes," in *American Security Policy and Policy-Making,* Robert Harkavy and Edward A. Kolodziej (Lexington Books, Lexington, MA, 1980), pp. 115-128.
34. Herman Kahn, *On Escalation* (Praeger, New York, 1966).
35. See, for example, Morton Halperin, *LimitedWar in the Nuclear Age* (Wiley, New York, 1963).
36. *The New York Times,* June 6, 1980, Sec. I, p. 3.
37. Current European security policy problems are reviewed in Edward A. Kolodziej, Europe: The partial partner, *International Security 5,* 3 (Written 1980/81):104-131.
38. Osgood, *Limited War,* pp. 61-87, offers a valuable review of the characteristics of eighteenth-century warfare.
39. Hajo Holborn reviews the failures of the Schlieffen Plan in Earle (Ed.), *Makers of Modern Strategy,* pp. 172-205.
40. Some insight into Japanese thinking may be found in Roberta Wohlstetter, *Pearl Harbor* (Stanford University Press, Stanford, CA, 1962); background material on Japanese naval strategy is presented by Alexander Kiralfy in Earle (Ed.), *Makers of Modern Strategy,* pp. 457-484.
41. Mao Tse-Tung, *Selected Military Writings,* p. 228.
42. Alexander George, David K. Hall, and William R. Simons, *The Limits of Coercive Diplomacy* (Little, Brown, Boston, 1971), p. 19. This is an excellent treatment of this form of strategic behavior.
43. There are a host of studies recounting the American entrapment in Vietnam. The most inclusive is *The Pentagon Papers.* Among the most readable are David Halberstam, *The Best and the Brightest* (Random House, New York, 1972), and Frances Fitzgerald, *Fire in the Lake* (Atlantic-Little, Brown, Boston, 1972).

44. George et al., *Limits,* pp. 215–216.

45. Much of this discussion contrasting deterrence and compellence is drawn from Schelling, *Arms and Influence,* especially pp. 69–78.

46. These chains of unfortunate circumstances are traced in Barbara Tuchman's *The Guns of August* (Macmillan, New York, 1962).

47. George Liska's *Imperial America: The International Politics of Primacy* (Johns Hopkins Press, Baltimore, 1967) suggests this possibility. The Western European perception of the United States as a super-superpower is described in Robert Gilpin, *France in the Age of the Scientific State* (Princeton University Press, Princeton, NJ, 1968).

48. See Kolodziej, *French International Policy,* pp. 69–175.

49. Stephen Cohen, Identity, survival, security: Pakistan's defense policy, in *The Security Policies of Developing Countries,* Edward A. Kolodziej and Robert Harkavy (Eds.) (Lexington Books, Lexington, MA, 1980).

50. See Stephanie Neuman and Robert Harkavy (Eds.), *Arms Transfers in the Modern World,* (Praeger, New York, 1979), for a review of arms transfers and international politics.

51. Seymour Melman, *The Permanent War Economy* (Simon and Schuster, New York, 1974), p. 260.

52. Emile Benoit, *Defense and Economic Growth in Developing Countries* (Lexington Books, Lexington, MA, 1973). Ruth Leger Sivard contrasts military and socioeconomic spending in *World Military and Social Expenditures: 1978* (WMSE Publications, Leesburg, VA, 1978).

53. The early "merchants of death" literature is ably reviewed in Robert Harkavy, *The Arms Trade and the International System* (Ballinger, Cambridge, MA, 1975), p. 251, n. 20.

54. See, for example, the French White Paper on defense written by then Minister of Defense Michel Debré, *Le Livre Blanc sur la Défense Nationale,* and the writings of analysts close to the Indian military-industrial system: K. Subrahmanyam, *Defence and Development* (Minerva Associates, Calcutta, 1973), and Rajesh K. Agarwall, *Defence Production and Development* (Arnold Heinemann, New Delhi, 1978).

55. Gilpin, *France,* describes in detail how French elites drew this lesson from American economic development after World War II.

56. Kenneth Waltz, The stability of a bipolar world, *Daedalus,* Summer 1964, pp. 881–909.

57. Karl Deutsch and J. David Singer, Multipolar power systems and international stability, *World Politics 16,* 3 (April 1964): 390–406.

58. Among the more comprehensive and trenchant critiques of the cold war is that developed over a decade by President Charles de Gaulle. See Kolodziej, *French International Policy,* especially pp. 19ff.

59. U.S. Arms Control and Disarmament Agency, *World Military Expenditures and Arms Transfers: 1968–1977* (U.S. Government Printing Office, Washington, DC, 1979), pp. 27–31.

60. Robert Harkavy, *Spectre of a Middle Eastern Holocaust* (University of Denver Press, Denver, CO, 1977).

61. A recent useful discussion of the proliferation problem is John Kerry King (Ed.), *International Political Effects of the Spread of Nuclear Weapons* (U.S. Government Printing Office, Washington, DC, 1979).

62. Quoted in Jervis, *Perception and Misperception,* pp. 76–77.

63. Two books of widely different purpose that rely on a "mirror image" interpretation of American-Soviet behavior are Halle, *The Cold War as History,* and Charles Osgood, *An Alternative to War and Surrender* (University of Illinois Press, Urbana, 1962).

64. The literature on arms races is rich and abundant. Most prominently cited are Quincy Wright, *Study of War* (University of Chicago Press, Chicago, 1964), 2 vols., and the more specialized attempt at quantification first developed by L. F. Richardson, *Arms and Insecurity: A Mathematical Study of the Causes and Origins of War* (Boxwood, Pittsburgh, 1960). Shorter and more easily read and absorbed in Samuel P. Huntington, Arms races: Prerequisites and results, in *Public Policy* (Belknap Press, Cambridge, MA, 1958), pp. 41–83.

65. This threefold division is drawn from Sherman Kent's classic study of intelligence, *Strategic Intelligence for American World Policy* (Princeton University Press, Princeton, NJ, 1949).

66. Still useful is Roger Hilsman, Intelligence and policy-making in foreign affairs, *World Politics 5,* (October 1952): 1–25.

67. The most authoritative study of the Pearl Harbor disaster and of the breakdown of intelligence is Roberta Wohlstetter, *Pearl Harbor.*

68. See n. 43 above.

69. See the hearings and report of the Church Committee, Ninety-Fifth Congress, 1st and 2nd sessions, hearings held December 27, 1977, to April 20, 1978 (U.S. Government Printing Office, Washington, DC, 1978).

70. Henry Guerlac, Vauban: The impact of science on war, in Earle (Ed.), *Makers of Modern Strategy,* pp. 26–48.

71. Ibid, pp. 77–166.

72. A major exception was I. S. Block, *The Future of War in Its Technical, Economic, and Political Relations* (Ginn, New York, 1902).

73. Two general treaties on war that discuss briefly the evolution of warfare and military doctrine are Richard A. Preston and Sydney F. Wise, *Men in Arms* (Holt, Rinehart, and Winston, New York, 1979), and J. F. C. Fuller, *The Conduct of War, 1789-1961* (Rutgers University Press, New Brunswick, NJ, 1961).

74. Schelling, *Arms andInfluence,* explores these dimensions of deterrence at length. See also Beaufre, *Deterrence and Strategy,* passim, and Snyder, *Defense.* Recent analyses of note are Patrick Morgan, *Deterrence: A Conceptual Analysis* (Sage, Beverly Hills, CA, 1977), and Robert Jervis, Deterrence theory revisited, *World Politics 31,* 2 (January 1979): 289–324.

75. The number and variety of books and articles bearing on nuclear deterrence are too large and extensive to cite here. Many have already been cited above, in notes 5–13, 23, 25.

76. The schools that are depicted are a composite of the views of many analysts grouped loosely under two divergent and opposing headings to facilitate discussion.

77. This debate is too extensive to permit exhaustive citation. A useful review is found in the Senate report on SALT II, U.S., Cong., Senate, Committee on Foreign Relations, *The Salt II Treaty,* 96th Cong., 1st Sess., 1979.

78. This debate is still joined and heated at this writing. See the symposium in *Foreign Policy,* Summer 1980, pp. 14–73.

79. Many change their minds, too. Henry Kissinger first advocated their use in the middle 1950s as a response to Soviet conventional superiority in Europe and then shifted to a defense of the flexible response strategy four years later. See his *Nuclear Weapons and Foreign Policy,* and *The Necessity for Choice.*

80. For current thinking about limited war, see Robert E. Osgood, *Limited War Revisited* (Westview, Boulder, CO, 1979).

81. Beaufre, *Deterrence,* discusses these incentives at length.

82. Quoted in Franklin Mark Osanka, *Modern Guerrilla Warfare* (Free Press, Glencoe, IL, 1962), p. xvi.

83. See Mao Tse-Tung, *Selected Military Writings,* and Edward L. Katzenbach, Jr., and Gene Z. Hanrahan, The revolutionary strategy of Mao Tse Tung, in Osanka, *Modern Guerrilla Warfare,* pp. 131–146.

84. Samuel P. Huntington, Jr. in Osanka, *Modern Guerrilla Warfare,* p. xvi.

85. For a behavioral discussion of revolutionary war, consult David Wilkinson, *Revolutionary Civil War* (Page-Ficklin, Palo Alto, CA, 1975), and Martha Crenshaw Hutchinson, *Revolutionary Terrorism* (Hoover Institution Press, Stanford, CA, 1978), chap. 2, pp. 18–39, and citation noted therein.

86. The father of strategic bombing doctrine is Guilio Douhet, *The Command of the Air,* Dino Ferrari (Trans.) (Coward-McCann, New York, 1942).

87. See n. 69 above. Critical commentary of current American strategic nuclear policies include William R. Van Cleave and W. Scott Thompson, *Strategic Options for the Early Eighties: What Can Be Done?* (National Strategy Information Center, New York, 1979), and Colin S. Gray, "The strategic forces triad," *Foreign Affairs, 61,* 4 (July 1978): 771–789.

88. An able discussion of the resource allocation problem is Bruce Russett, *What Price Vigilance* (Yale University Press, New Haven, CT, 1970).

89. Samuel P. Huntington, Jr. *Common Defense,* (Columbia University Press, New York, 1961), p. 4.

90. A provocative discussion of one impact of new weapons on military tactics and strategy is James Digby, *Precision-Guided Weapons,* Adelphi Paper No. 118 (International Institute for Strategic Studies, London, 1975).

91. A useful discussion of technology and resource allocation is Juddith Reppy, Military research and development: Institutions, output, and arms control," in Harkavy and Kolodziej, *American Security Policy-Making,* pp. 165–180.

92. Huntington, *Common Defense,* ends on an optimistic note in contrast to his conclusion in *Soldier and the State.* Skepticism about the prospects of developing democratic and effective foreign and security policies are concisely treated in Henry Kissinger, *American Foreign Policy* (W. W. Norton, New York, 1974): Expanded edition, pp. 9–50.

93. Edward J. Laurence, The congressional role in defense policy making: The evolution of the literature, *Armed Forces and Society 6,* 3 (Spring 1980): 431–454, reviews the literature in this field.

94. For the early postwar period, see Huntington, *Common Defense,* and Edward A. Kolodziej, *The Uncommon Defense and Congress* (Ohio State University Press, Columbus, 1966). A recent notable study is Arnold Kanter, *Defense Politics* (University of Chicago Press, Chicago, 1979).

95. This decentralized process is sometimes characterized as bureaucratic politics. This view is exposed at length in Graham Allison, *Essence of Decision* (Little, Brown, Boston, 1971). For a critique, see Robert Art, Bureaucratic politics and American foreign policy, *Policy Sciences 6* (December 1973): 467–489.

96. John Spanier, *The Truman-MacArthur Controversy and the Korean War* ((Belknap Press, Cambridge, MA, 1959); Richard H. Rovere and Arthur Schlesinger, Jr., *The MacArthur Controversy and American Foreign Policy* (Farrar, Straus and Giroux, New York, 1965).

14

Electoral Policy

Richard S. Katz / The Johns Hopkins University, Baltimore, Maryland

I. APPROACHES TO ELECTORAL POLICY

The conduct of elections is one of the oldest and most continuously contested areas of policy. Aristotle, Cicero, leaders of the medieval Catholic church, Machiavelli, Peel, and Disraeli, to name only a few from previous centuries, were all concerned with the politics of election, as well as with electoral politics. In America, electoral reform was often a subject of debate in the colonial legislatures. Elections, or more properly lack of elections, provided a central focus for the American Revolution under the banner "no taxation without representation." Since independence, electoral policy has remained a lively issue; fully half the constitutional amendments ratified since the Bill of Rights have been concerned with the conduct of elections, as have large volumes of legislation and litigation.

That most major offices should be filled by election is now generally accepted, in the nondemocratic world as well as in the democracies. Precisely who should be allowed to vote, what kind of choices they should be given, what candidates and parties should be allowed to do to influence their votes, how individual votes should be aggregated into a list of elected candidates, and many other questions involved in the definition and operation of electoral systems remain unsettled, even within individual democratic countries.

As a policy area, electoral policy has two interrelated but analytically separable focuses. One has stressed the centrality of elections to democracy. Although the relative importance of such goals as equality, personal development, popular participation, and popular sovereignty, and indeed even their meanings, is not universally agreed, those taking this approach evaluate electoral systems and proposed reforms in terms of function and process and on normative grounds without explicit attention to the particular policies likely to be adopted in other areas. From this point of view, policies adopted on the basis of appropriate elections would be desirable or legitimate because of the legitimacy of the electoral process (e.g., Schumpeter, 1950).

The other approach to electoral policy reverses this statement, defending elections in general and evaluating particular electoral policies based on the desirability of their likely impact in other fields. Changing the rules of the electoral game may make it more or less likely that a specific group will have its interests attended to by government, more or less likely that certain candidates or types of candidates will be elected, more or less likely that identifiable resources, tactics, or decision criteria will be influential in determining the results (Finer, 1975). Thus one might evaluate the direct primary based on the type of candidates it produces and its impact on party organizations (and the impact of that on government in general) rather than on the "democratic" grounds of direct popular participation.

These two approaches are related. Reforms that "democratize" elections are likely to have policy consequences in many fields. And because those who favor elections on democratic grounds usually also have an idea of what democratic policy is, this may lead to conflicts. On the other hand, in democratic societies, elections are the great legitimizers. There is something generally unacceptable about partisan manipulation of the electoral system. Thus reforms actually designed to influence policy or alter the intergroup balance of power are likely to be defended on more high-minded grounds. Nonetheless, many electoral reforms have had significant and sometimes counterproductive unintended consequences because the connections between normative concerns and practical results have been ignored.

A. Functions of Elections

In functional or normative terms, there are a number of criteria by which electoral policies may be evaluated (Rose and Mossawir, 1967). The first is often forgotten in its simplicity, but exercises a controlling influence nonetheless. The fundamental purpose of an election is to select from among a group of contenders the candidate or candidates, party or coalition, or policy that is "the voters' choice." To be acceptable, any electoral process must produce a determinate winner. For example, systems requiring an absolute majority of the votes cast must provide for the possibility that with three or more candidates none will achieve a majority.[1]

In a democracy, elections confer legitimacy on those chosen to wield government power. Procedures such as plurality rather than majority elections may be criticized as illegitimately granting power to someone chosen by less than half the people. Similarly, it is often on this ground that parliamentary elections that fail to produce a clear majority party are criticized and because of its capacity to "manufacture" majorities that the American electoral college is supported.[2]

Elections are also expected to impose popular control over the government. Exactly what this means is subject to debate. To some, popular control, or popular sovereignty, demands that the will of the people be translated into public policy. Elections give the people a choice among candidates standing for alternative policy programs; the winner thus has a mandate to carry a platform into effect and by so doing gives effect to the popular will. Others take a less active view of the role played by public opinion in policy making. Rather than prospectively determining the direction of policy, this veto-group view sees public opinion as retrospectively judging the result of government. Elections give the people the opportunity to turn out of office politicians whose stewardship of government has failed to produce acceptable results (Dahl, 1956; Ranney, 1962).

Popular sovereignty and popularly imposed restraint in mass societies are exercised through representatives rather than directly (with the partial and infrequently used exceptions of recall, initiative, and referendum[3]). Another function of elections is to create a representative relationship between those holding public office, particularly in the legislature, and their constituents. How a particular electoral system is judged often depends on the meaning of representation preferred and the nature of the groups that one believes ought to be represented. Representation can be either real or virtual. "Real" representation involves a direct relationship between the constituent and the representative; one can be "really" represented only by someone elected from one's own district. Virtual representation, on the other hand, requires only that there be a representative, whether from the constituent's district or not, who can speak for his or her interests (Pitkin, 1967). Thus a black voter in New Jersey might be "virtually" represented by a black congressman from New York but would not be "really" represented by him. Only multi-member systems can provide real representation for local minorities. Is virtual representation adequate?

The second question concerning representation is the object of the relationship. Traditionally, the things represented were communities as organic wholes. As democracy spread, the object of representation became people in their capacity as residents of communities. This style of representation is reflected in plurality and majority electoral systems. But there are other aspects to people that might also deserve representation. For example, people might be represented as holders of opinions or supporters of particular parties. This is the logic of proportional representation. Alternatively, they might be regarded as primarily members of specific occupational or economic strata (corporatistic representation) or as members of distinct ethnic or racial groups. Attention to any one of these can alter one's evaluation of an electoral system.

Equality is yet another democratic virtue that elections may be expected both to reflect and to further. Until quite recently this was often not the case either in theory—with second and even third votes or votes in additional districts allowed on the basis of property or educational qualifications in several countries or more simply with large segments of the population excluded from voting at all—or in fact—with gross disparities in district populations. Now, and especially in the United States since the series of court decisions beginning with *Baker v. Carr,* equality has become more important in the evaluation of electoral systems.

Finally, elections may be valued because popular participation in public affairs is seen as a value in itself. Active involvement in government may be necessary to the citizen's intellectual and moral development. Patriotism and public spirit may be built from participation in public life (Bachrach, 1967). From the point of view of the rulers rather than the ruled, loyalty and voluntary compliance may be furthered by at least the illusion of participation (Swearer, 1961; Ginsberg and Weissberg, 1978). And if direct participation, either real or illusory, is impossible in societies with millions of voters, elections provide a more manageable substitute.

In addition to all of these, of course, one also wants elections to produce wise, just, and efficacious results: to choose worthy office holders and good policies (Einaudi, 1954). The problem arises because in the real world the desiderata may be incompatible with one another. The choice of electoral policy often reflects a choice among these competing values.

B. Impact on Other Policies

If electoral policy is important because of its impact on these fundamental values, it is also important because of its potential impact on all other policy fields. In democratic societies, basic decisions are made by individuals who have been elected by the people. Any policy that changes the identity of public office holders is likely to change the decisions made. Make it easier for politicians representing the poor to be elected, for example by eliminating property qualifications for voting, and it becomes more likely that policies favoring the poor will be adopted. This influence can extend beyond those directly elected, to the bureaucracy as well. Knowing that their actions are subject to review by those elected and that their departments are ultimately dependent on those elected, bureaucrats try to anticipate the reactions of their elected masters (Crossman, 1972). Thus even in areas of secondary importance, election outcomes may have an impact as civil servants attempt to go along in order to get along.

Electoral policy can significantly alter the balance of power among competing interests, either by altering the balance of their votes (as through suffrage expansion) or voting power (as through reapportionment of legislative seats), or by altering the importance of resources that they control. For example, campaign finance has been regulated in many countries with the intention of lessening the political influence of big contributors.

Beyond these direct effects of electoral policy, there may be indirect effects. It is often said that the first job of a politician is to be reelected. Electoral policy can have a substantial impact on the whole policy-making process and even more generally on the whole style of politics by determining the kinds of behavior that are likely to be rewarded with reelection (Mayhew, 1974). Some electoral systems (plurality election and especially the single transferrable vote) encourage localism and patronage, whereas others (large district proportional representation) encourage ideological politics (Katz, 1980). The electoral system can influence the number of political parties and hence the ease with which a majority is formed and the stability of government (Rae, 1971); it may also, by denying some interests legitimate representation, encourage extraparliamentary activity such as demonstrations, strikes, or violence.

II. ELECTORAL SYSTEMS

One set of electoral policy questions concerns the operation of the formal electoral system, that is, the way in which voters' preferences will be expressed and then aggregated to produce a list of elected and defeated candidates. A number of specific decisions are involved here. First, there is the choice of electoral formula. Second, and related, where more than one official is to be chosen, there is the choice of district size: How many individuals should be elected from each district, and how large should the electorate of each district be? Third, should each office be filled by direct election, or should some officials be elected indirectly either by a specially constituted electoral college or by individuals already elected to some other office? Additional questions, more important in some systems than others, involve nomination and the degree to which voters rather than party organizations should be allowed to choose the particular individuals to be elected from among a party's candidates, the layout of the ballot and the information it should contain, and the drawing and redrawing of constituency boundaries.

A. Electoral Formula

Plurality Election. With variations within each subtype, there are four basic electoral formulas. The most common in the Anglo-American world is plurality election. Members of Congress, all 50 state legislatures, the 50 state governors, and the lower house of the British, Canadian, and New Zealand parliaments are elected in this way. In its simplest form, single-member plurality election, each district returns one representative and each voter has a single vote, which must be given to a single candidate. At the end of the polling, the votes for each candidate are counted and the one with the most votes wins, regardless of how well other candidates may have done and regardless of how narrow the margin between the first- and second-ranked candidates. An essentially similar system is multimember plurality election, in which more than one representative is returned from each district, and the voter casts as many votes for as many candidates as there are seats to be filled.[4] Before 1885, the British House of Commons involved many two-seat districts (the last was not abolished until 1950), whereas, for example, most members of the Maryland House of Delegates are elected from three-member districts. When all the representatives are chosen from a single district, the election is said to be "at large."

Plurality election is particularly suited to the representation of communities or of majorities within them. It tends to underrepresent, often dramatically, minorities, especially minorities whose strength is geographically dispersed. Even with equal district populations, it is always theoretically possible to draw boundaries that will give a favored party a share of the representatives roughly twice as large as its share of the votes, up to giving a party with 51 percent of the vote all of the seats (Loosemore and Hanby, 1971). And if this is the theoretical limit, actual experience is often only a little more encouraging. For example, in one election in Prince Edward Island, the Conservative party won 42 percent of the vote but no seats, whereas in another election the United Farmers of Alberta won 67 percent of the seats with less than 40 percent of the vote. The degree to which minorities are underrepresented depends on the way in which the districts are drawn, but often approximates the "cube law" that the ratio of the two parties' share of the seats will equal the cube of the ratio of their votes (Kendall and Stuart, 1950; Tufte, 1973).

The winner-take-all character of plurality election can be used to exclude racial or other minorities by creating large multimember districts or ultimately by at-large election. In this way a geographically concentrated group, which might be in the majority in a few areas but is an overall minority, can be totally excluded from representation. Although the U.S. Supreme Court has forbidden the courts from ordering reapportionment plans with multimember districts and has banned at-large election adopted for the purpose of excluding minorities, the courts have sometimes ordered at-large election in the absence of any acceptable apportionment plan and have allowed at-large systems to stand where the intent was not discriminatory even if the effect is to deny blacks representation they might otherwise have won.

Because it results in the underrepresentation of small parties, and particularly of third parties, plurality election encourages two-party competition. This tendency, however, applies particularly at the district level. There is no guarantee that the same two parties will compete in every district. Although plurality election in general discriminates against minor parties, it is actually the most advantageous system for small parties whose support is concentrated in only a few districts, because it has the lowest threshold of representation. Thus, whereas the Liberal party has been dramatically underrepresented in the British Parliament, the Scottish and Welsh nationalists have been unscathed or even aided. Such national pressure to two-party competition as there is appears to come rather from the majority election of the head of government.

One way of describing the underrepresentation of minorities by plurality electoral systems is to say that they involve large numbers of wasted votes, that is, votes that contribute to no one's election. One attempt to minimize the problem of wasted votes while retaining plurality election's focus on votes for individuals rather than parties is the single transferrable vote system discussed below. Another, used for elections to the Illinois House of Representatives, is to use three-member districts and give each voter only two votes but to allow these votes to be cumulated (given to the same candidate). This allows a minority with between 25 and 50 percent of the vote to elect one of the three representatives (provided that all votes are cast as efficiently as possible).

Majority Election.   With plurality election, candidates may win with far less than half the votes. Although they will be the most popular candidates of those running, this means that far more people will have voted against them than for them. Moreover, there is no guarantee that such minority winners could defeat any, let alone all, competitors in a head-to-head election. This problem is particularly vexing when a minority candidate wins only because of a schism in the natural majority party. In part to avoid this difficulty, some electoral systems require an absolute majority rather than a simple plurality for election. In the event that no candidate obtains a majority, a runoff election is held. In this election, either a majority is assured by restricting entry to the two top vote winners in the preliminary round, or else a plurality suffices for election. In either case, candidates may withdraw between rounds.

Majority election allows a majority party to factionalize without losing an election because its supporters have the opportunity to coalesce behind their strongest candidate in the second round. This property made majority elections attractive to Southern whites in Democratic primaries, because even if a black finished first in the first round as a result of fragmentation of the white vote, he or she could be defeated in the runoff. It often meant, however, that a candidate would have to fight three campaigns in order to be elected. To avoid this, Louisiana adopted a nonpartisan majority electoral system in which the top two candidates from an all-party primary compete in the general election (unless, of course, one candidate achieves an absolute majority in the primary, in which case that candidate is elected without a general election runoff). Although it was suggested that this reform was aimed at destroying the Republican party because it would often mean Democrat facing Democrat in the general election with no Republican candidate at all, there is no evidence that the Republicans have actually been hurt.

In multiparty systems, majority election tends to discriminate against extreme parties. After an initial trial of strength in the first round of voting, parties often form alliances by withdrawing in complementary districts and instructing their supporters to vote for the remaining candidate of the alliance. In making such alliances, moderate parties are in a far stronger bargaining position, because they have a choice of allies whereas extreme parties typically do not. Moreover, once a deal is struck, the extreme party is more likely to deliver its supporters in the districts where it has withdrawn. This system has been used in France particularly to undermine the strength of the Communist party (Campbell, 1965).

Like plurality election, the majority system assumes representation of communities. It aims to create an immediate, personal relationship between representative and represented. The representative is to represent the entire constituency, even those who voted for other candidates. This naturally presents a problem, since as many as half the voters may have supported the loser. Nonetheless, this is the price that must be paid for single-member districts.

Single Transferrable Vote. A modification of the majority system, the alternative vote, used in Australia, allows majority election with a single round of voting. Instead of voting for a single candidate, the voter ranks all the candidates. The first preference votes are counted, and if any candidate has a majority, he or she is elected. Otherwise the candidate with the fewest votes is eliminated and his or her votes are transferred to the candidates ranked second by his or her supporters—presumably the candidates they would have supported had their first choice not run. This process continues until some candidate achieves an absolute majority.

When the alternative vote system is used in multimember constituencies, it is the single transferrable vote (STV) system, often called proportional representation but actually a variety of majority election. Now instead of requiring a majority for election, a candidate needs a quota that, if *n* seats are to be filled, is the smallest number of votes each of *n* candidates could have while assuring that no other candidate could have as many. If a candidate receives more votes than the quota, then the surplus is transferred to other candidates in proportion to the second-place votes expressed in his or her ballots.

STV is used in the national elections of Ireland and Malta, to elect the Northern Ireland assembly, and in many local elections (for example, elections of the Cambridge, Massachusetts city council and local school boards in New York City). It was also used at one time to elect the New York City council; it was abandoned because its low electoral threshold coupled with large districts allowed Communist candidates to be elected. As with list proportional representation, the more representatives are to be elected from each district, the smaller the proportion of votes a minor party needs to win a seat. The Irish have steadily reduced the average size of their districts with the intention of driving out small parties and making the formation of a parliamentary majority easier.

The system is, in fact, reasonably proportional in its results so long as voters rank candidates strictly within parties. Its aim, however, is simply to maximize the number of voters who supported a candidate who won over a candidate who lost, and like plurality and majority systems, it is oriented toward candidates rather than parties. Although STV districts are naturally larger than single-member plurality or majority districts would be, there is a strong tendency apparent for parties to distribute their nominations throughout the district and for candidates to divide the district into personal bailiwicks, thus preserving something of the territorial representation typical of single-member districts. There is also a marked tendency toward personalism and patronage in politics (Sacks, 1976).

List Proportional Representation. If the aim of elections is to produce a legislature that accurately reflects the distribution of opinions in society, representing each party in proportion to its voting strength, then all the candidate-oriented systems have serious weaknesses. Instead, the best electoral system is proportional representation (PR) based on party lists. This is the system used to elect most of the parliaments of continental Europe and in modified form for the election of delegates to the Democratic national convention. Most often, list PR was adopted after a multiparty system had developed under a plurality or majority system. These generally involved a single socialist party competing against several older liberal and conservative parties. PR allowed the bourgeois parties to maintain their separate identities without suffering the consequences of fragmentation in single-member districts.

For PR, the country may be divided into constituencies or (as in the Netherlands and Israel) the entire country may be regarded as a single constituency. In each district, the parties present lists of nominees. In the simplest case, the voter chooses only one list. In the case of systems with *panachage* (see below), the voter actually selects a number of individual candidates without regard to list, but for the purposes of assigning seats to parties, these are counted as fractional votes for the lists. The representation for the district is divided among the lists in rough proportion to their voting strength. There are a number of specific ways in which this may be done, some slightly more favorable to small parties (e.g., largest remainder) and others (e.g., d'Hondt) more favorable to large parties. In all cases, the more representatives elected from each district, the easier it is to win a seat and the more proportional the overall result (Rae, 1971).

In order to maximize proportionality while avoiding excessive splintering of parties, some PR systems impose a minimum vote test in excess of the normal vote share required to win one seat before a party receives any representation. In West Germany, for example, only parties with at least 5 percent of the vote are entitled to any seats. Another possibility, used in Italy, is to require a party to win at least one seat in a local consituency before becoming eligible to participate in a national distribution of remainders. In this way the representation of locally strong minorities is protected while national splinter parties are avoided.

This is important because one effect of PR is to lower the cost of exit from a party for dissatisfied minorities. Where in majority or STV systems a schism is likely to be costly, and where in plurality systems it would almost certainly result in severe losses, in PR systems a schism may be nearly costless. Conversely, PR seems to discourage alliances formed in the electoral arena. Instead, it encourages ideological competition in which similar parties maximize their apparent differences (Katz, 1980). The result is that where plurality systems encourage compromise early, and a choice by the voters among a sharply reduced set of "packaged" alternatives, PR offers the voters a wider choice but often with a less direct link between electoral outcomes and public policy (Milnor, 1969).

B. Apportionment and District Boundaries

In list PR systems with large districts, the actual district boundaries make little difference. Coupling a small province with a large one or transferring a small area from one district to another may disadvantage a few politicians, but with multimember districts, it is easy to maintain proportionality between population and district representation by manipulating the number of deputies per district, and so long as this proportionality is maintained actual boundaries will make little difference to the party balance.

In smaller districts, and particularly in single-member districts, however, the drawing of constituency boundaries can be crucial. Here, there are two general classes of problems —malapportionment and gerrymandering. Malapportionment refers to significant disparitites in the number of people represented by each deputy, a possibility that when systematic can lead to significant overrepresentation of some interests. Gerrymandering refers to the drawing of district lines for partisan advantage, even within the stricture of equal district populations (see Polsby, 1971).

Malapportionments can result either from failure to redistrict after shifts in population or from application of principles other than equality in the drawing of district lines. One of the most malapportioned legislatures was the British House of Commons before 1832. Each of the English counties (special provision was made for Scotland) had equal representation, while the boroughs were represented on the basis of their population and importance several hundred years before. The result was that whereas some large industrial cities, such as Manchester, had no separate representation in the House, "rotten boroughs" with no people at all continued to send members. Since 1832, although the British have recognized population as one important basis of representation, major disparities in district populations are allowed to exist in deference to other principles. Reflecting the notion of community representation, for example, local boundaries are respected. Where a district would otherwise be unmanageably large or difficult to travel (the Shetland and Orkney Islands), it is permitted to continue with below-average population. Scotland and Wales are systematically overrepresented in compensation for their former independence. In 1970, the population of British districts ranged from 18,309 to 113,452. Given the generally greater strength of the Conservatives in the rural areas and the concentration of Labour voters in heavily working-class constituencies, this pattern slightly favors the Conservatives.

Although not as badly apportioned as the unreformed House of Commons, the trend in pre-1960 America was roughly what it had been in Britain. Although the Constitution requires periodic redistribution of congressional representation among the states, states would often adjust to the loss of a congressional seat by combining two adjoining districts or to a gain in Congress by dividing their most populous district. In 1960, for example, the largest congressional district in Texas had a population of 951,527, whereas the smallest had only 216,371. State legislatures were similarly malapportioned. In some cases, one house would represent counties rather than people. Even the "popular" houses often had not been reapportioned in many years. Also in 1960, more than half of the lower house of the legislature was elected by less than 20 percent of the voters in Connecticut, Delaware, Florida, Kansas, and Vermont. This led to a series of court challenges beginning with *Baker v. Carr* and *Reynolds v. Sims* that have imposed strict limits on allowable population disparities for congressional districts, districts for both houses of state legislatures, city and county councils, and so forth.

Reapportionments were (and are) often resisted for quite obvious reasons. In many cases, what is asked is that the current majority reduce its own representation. Given usual population trends, the effect of malapportionment has generally been to overrepresent rural interests. This is also the case when representation of communities or local government units is stressed. Though contrary to the norm of equality, this is sometimes defended on the ground that rural voters are particularly virtuous or worthy of representation because they embody the backbone and spirit of the country.

Changes in district boundaries are unsettling to existing party and personal campaign organizations. They may force incumbents to compete against one another in the new districts, or reduce some incumbents' margins of victory. In any event, they add to electoral uncertainty. The requirement of equal population also forces local boundaries to be violated, sacrificing community representation and leading to a crazy-quilt pattern of district boundaries. Two areas in the same state legislative district may be in different congressional districts, leading to complicated career patterns and campaign arrangements.

Gerrymanders differ from malapportionments in that they are conscious attempts to manipulate the results of elections by changing the district boundaries and can coexist with perfectly equal district sizes. Indeed, some observers believe that by making local government boundaries irrelevant to the district-drawing process, the "reapportionment revolution" simply made gerrymandering easier. Although the term is American, the process of gerrymandering is quite ancient, having been used, for example, in the Roman Republic. It is also usually associated with single-member plurality systems, but the Irish reapportionment before the 1977 election was an attempt to gerrymander in an STV system.

Although gerrymanders, like the Irish, can be aimed at the general advantage of a party, they can also be directed for or against particular individuals. In some cases, the results can be quite bizarre, as the California congressional district created in an attempt to defeat Paul McCloskey that was contiguous only at low tide. Another example is provided by Congressman Sam Stratton of New York, who had his district in Schenectady abolished. He then moved to Amsterdam, only to have that district abolished as well; ultimately he was elected from Albany. There can also be bipartisan gerrymanders, in which incumbents of both parties conspire to protect their own seats.

Equal-size districts say nothing about fairness with respect to parties. They also say nothing about the representation of minorities. Although gerrymanders designed to exclude minorities have been outlawed, those designed to ensure their representation have been approved. The problem is that what benefits one minority may harm another (see *United Jewish Organizations of Williamsburgh, Inc. v. Carey, La.*).

C. District Size

District size interacts with election formula. In PR and STV systems, increasing the number of representatives per district increases the proportionality of the overall result while making it easier for minorities to achieve representation. Large districts thus may also increase the fragmentation of the party system. In plurality systems, however, the result is just the reverse. By making local majorities into regional minorities, multimember plurality election extends that system's tendency to underrepresent small groups that are geographically dispersed to those that are concentrated as well. (The Illinois system is, of course, an exception.)

Small districts also tend to increase the importance of candidates and the personal link between represented and representative, whereas large districts lead to greater stress on party, both as a mediator in the representative relationship and in defining the role of representative. In large districts (almost always PR) there are many candidates, and voters tend to identify them by party rather than personality. Many parties are likely to win seats. Elected candidates represent primarily their party's supporters. Supporters of other parties are represented by candidates of their parties. Ties to party that cut across district lines are emphasized over ties to community. In single-member districts, on the other hand, the eventual winner must represent all constituents, because they have no other representatives. Ties to community and the representation of community interests are more important.

D. Intraparty Choice

The above discussion has been based on the tacit assumption that parties are important. System-wide underrepresentation of minority parties by plurality systems or the discrimination against extreme parties in national alliance formation typical of majority systems make sense only if party is a meaningful concept in national politics. Proportionality, of course, is intelligible only to the extent that party is meaningful. The proportionality of STV and the exclusion of minorities in multimember plurality systems depend on party-line voting. Even where party is terribly important, however, the distribution of representation among the parties is not the only important concern. Also important is the question of which particular individuals from those parties are elected. Not all Republicans are alike; neither are all Conservatives nor all Communists.

Electoral policy regarding the selection of elected individuals may go in one of two broadly different directions, with a gray area in between. On one hand, the choice of individuals may be left entirely to the parties, although they must exercise their discretion before the election takes place. In single-member districts this is done when the party organization puts up a single candidate without prior consultation with the voters. A vote for the party is thus a vote for its candidate, and a vote for the candidate is a vote for the party; if the party wins, the candidate is elected. In multimember plurality or STV systems, the same effect would be achieved if each party nominated a number of candidates exactly equal to the number of seats it could win. In list PR systems, each party submits an ordered list of candidates with the proviso that its share of the seats will be filled by the appropriate number of candidates from the top of its list.

This system gives great power to the party organization. If it refuses to nominate an individual or gives him a unfavorable list position, he has no chance of election, or, in the case of incumbents who might equally be punished, no chance of reelection, regardless of the people's views. The specter of a few party tyrants deciding among whom the people can choose has seemed unacceptably antidemocratic to some reformers, who have insisted on greater popular involvement in the choice of candidates.

In single-member systems, intraparty choice comes, if at all, when party nominees are selected, because it is to a party's clear advantage to have only one candidate in the final election. In the United States, an intraparty choice is provided by the direct primary.

In PR and STV systems, however, parties ordinarily nominate more candidates than they can elect. With STV, this automatically means that the choice of representatives from among each party's nominees is left to those who vote for its candidates. In PR systems, although list order may determine order of election, it need not do so. Instead, the party's voters may be allowed to influence or determine the order of election by use of a personal preference vote.

The simplest form of preference voting allows each voter to single out one (or more) of the candidates of the list for which he or she has just voted for personal support. Candidates from each list are then declared elected in the order of their personal voting strength. In this case, those of each party's voters who cast explicit personal preference votes completely determine the order in which candidates are elected and preference voting may be a primary cause of parliamentary turnover (Katz and Bardi, 1980). In other systems, although a personal preference vote is permitted, the party is able to influence the order of election more substantially. Greatest control is given to the party when its list order prevails unless changed by a substantial percentage of its voters. Because only a minority of voters cast preference votes even where this is the sole determiner of order of election, this kind of preference voting is usually in fact illusory (Campbell, 1965). Alternatively, each constituency may be divided into nominating districts, with votes not cast explicitly for someone else counted as preference votes for the party's nominee associated with the voter's home district. Although the preference votes then determine the order of election, the party, by nominating its preferred candidates in those districts within the constituency where it expects many party votes, can greatly increase their chance of election (Pedersen, 1966).

All these systems restrict the voter to selecting candidates of one party. A wider choice is allowed with *panachage,* used in Switzerland and Luxembourg. Each voter has as many votes as there are seats to be filled from the district, and each voter may give them to any candidates, regardless of party. The voter may also give more than one vote to a single candidate. Rather than running as individuals, however, the candidates run as members of party lists. In assigning seats, the votes for all candidates of each list are totaled and seats are assigned to a list in proportion to its total vote. Individuals are then declared elected in order of their personal votes within their list. A party can influence the order of election by including an individual's name more than once in its list so that unmodified party votes (usually the vast majority) involve cumulation for him. This has the perverse effect that a split vote for one candidate may primarily contribute to the election of one of his co-partisans instead.

One of the motivations for the direct primary and preference voting was to undermine the power of central party bosses. The illegitimacy of the smoke-filled room, coupled with a distaste for party discipline that punished a representative for preferring his constituents to his party leader, led some advocates of democracy to insist that the voters choose people as well as parties. In this attempt, the reformers were quite successful. Central party control has been undermined in systems with effective preference voting. This reform has had a variety of other effects, however, not all of which are necessarily desirable.

If preference voting has weakened a candidate's need for the support of a central party organization, it has not lessened the importance of organization in general. Instead, it has made candidates dependent on personal organizations that can be mobilized to ward off intraparty challenges as well as to fight a general election. Because the resources needed to maintain such an organization cannot be mobilized through the party, this often makes candidates dependent on special interests. The vitality of the party organization, and its ability to perform other functions such as mobilizing mass support, channeling demands, and coordinating government is sapped, as personal organizations become more important to candidates and the party less important. One frequent result is factionalism in the party; another is fragmentation (Zariski, 1965; Thayer, 1969; Mayhew, 1974; Katz, 1980).

Preference voting also has an impact on the type of candidate who is likely to be successful. For professional politicians, the most important thing in an election is to win and keep winning. This gives them a strong incentive, especially in single-member plurality systems, to choose candidates who will be attractive to the electorate as a whole and who will perform well in office so that the party will be returned to power at the next election. Moderate, capable, responsible, if perhaps uninspiring, candidates, and a balanced ticket are likely results. Individual voters, however, lack both the knowledge and the incentive to select this kind of candidate. In a primary, instead of supporting the candidate they think is best able to win the general election, knowledgeable voters choose the candidate they would most *like* to have win the general election. But because the distribution of opinion, and particularly of active and informed opinion, within a single party is likely to be far different from that of the general electorate, this may lead to extremist candidates. For most voters, intraparty voting, which is divorced from the anchoring cue of party labels, is a contest among relative unknowns. Any candidate who can grab their attention is likely to have a great advantage in securing their votes. This naturally gives an advantage to incumbents. It also encourages image builders, flashy campaigners, irresponsible promises, and demagoguery over quiet competence.

E. Indirect Election

The elections discussed so far have all been direct elections: The votes of ordinary people directly determine the winners. In some cases and for some offices, however, societies have opted for indirect elections; rather than choosing their officials themselves, the people choose a group of choosers to make the final decision. This kind of election was quite common in medieval Europe. In more modern times, indirect election is sometimes used to select a head of state or one house of a national legislature.

Indirect election is justified on any of three grounds. Most commonly, indirect election of one house of the national legislature is a reflection of a federal state. Whereas one house represents the people, and is directly elected by them, the other house represents the federated governments, and so is elected by them. Examples are the Bundesrat in West Germany, the U.S. Senate before 1913, and the parliamentary assembly of the European Economic Community (EEC) before 1979.

A second justification, particularly relevant to the election of a head of state, is the desire to deny the person elected the legitimacy conferred by direct election. In parliamentary systems, this is important in that it assures that the prime minister rather than the president is the effective head of government. In reverse, this is one of the arguments advanced by European integrationists in favor of direct election of the EEC parliament.

Finally, one might favor indirect election because of doubts about the ability of the people to make a wise choice. This was one argument in favor of the electoral college in the United States. The people, unfamiliar with candidates from other states, might vote for demagogues. They could be trusted, however, to select local men of judgment to choose a President for them. As things have developed, the American electoral college has been reduced to registering, in weighted form, the result of popular election, thus eliminating much of the indirectness of presidential elections. They retain, however, enough of the features of selection by a true electoral college to make discussion of them relevant to this topic.

Although not logically necessary, most electoral colleges overrepresent less populous areas. The American system of giving each state a number of electoral votes equal to the sum of its senators and representatives is no exception, and the procedure of voting by states in the House of Representatives in case there is no majority in the electoral college is even more heavily weighted toward the small states. In practice, however, the winner-take-all system (multimember plurality) by which each state's electors are chosen has forced candidates to pay most attention to states with closely contested elections and a large number of electoral votes (Longley and Braun, 1972).

By eliminating local minorities before the votes are counted, the electoral college tends to produce majorities where they might not otherwise exist. As in all plurality elections, this operates at two levels (Downs, 1957; Duverger, 1959). First, third parties and independents are discouraged from contesting the election and voters from supporting them by the knowledge that they are unlikely to win and so votes for them will be wasted. This increases the two-party proportion of the votes cast. Second, because unless he has a plurality in a state, a candidate gets no electoral votes, the vote in the electoral college is even more strongly two-party than the popular vote. For example, in the elections of 1960, 1968, and 1976, clear majorities in the electoral college were won by candidates with less than 50 percent of the popular vote.

Finally, the electoral college presents the problem of the "faithless elector." Because the electoral college originally assumed that electors were to exercise independent judgment, there is no constitutional requirement that they actually support the candidate they were elected to support. Although some states have passed laws requiring loyalty, none has been tested in court; and because they are obviously contrary to the original spirit of the Constitution, it is doubtful whether they would survive a court challenge. Although there have been occasional defections by individual electors, these would be significant only in the case of a very close election. Defections have been more significant in the indirect election of the Italian president.

F. Ballot Format

Finally, the format of the ballot may play an important role. The first question is whether there is an officially printed ballot. Before about the 1890s in the United States, and even today in Norway and Sweden, there is no official ballot. Instead, voters may indicate their selections on a plain sheet of paper. More commonly, they use ballots printed by the parties, but of course each party's ballot lists only its own candidates. In the United States, this made casting a split-ticket vote far more difficult than necessary (Rusk, 1970), whereas in Scandinavia it makes it extremely difficult to change the party's list order to cast a personal preference vote.

If there is an official ballot, what should it contain and how should it be laid out? In list PR systems, the only question is the ease with which party list order can be changed. The Italian ballot, for example, does not list candidates' names, so to cast a preference vote the voter must remember the names or numbers of the candidates he wishes to support. This gives a great advantage to the candidate with the number 1. In other systems, the local or party-preferred candidate may be given an advantageous position, or it may be made far easier to cast a ballot maintaining than one changing the party's list order.

In plurality, majority, and STV systems, one question is whether party designations should appear on the ballot. When they do not, one has a nonpartisan ballot. Until 1974, Britain used nonpartisan ballots in parliamentary elections. They continue to be used in some American local elections. Similarly, in multimember districts, should all of a party's candidates be listed together? In the Irish STV system they are not, whereas in the Maltese STV system they are. Grouping candidates by party has a strong impact on the level of interparty transfer votes in STV systems, whereas simply including party labels seems to have a more marginal influence on the level of party voting.

A related question concerns the order in which candidates should be listed. Except where the party column format (see below) dictates otherwise, candidates may be listed alphabetically, randomly, or in rotation, either overall or within party. This is particularly important when there are many candidates and, in STV systems especially with regard to transfer votes, candidates at the top of a list tend to do better than those at the bottom, who do better than those in the middle (Bain and Hecock, 1957; Mueller, 1970).

In the United States, where several offices are filled at each election, these questions compound into the distinction between the party-line and office block ballots. In a party-line ballot, the names of the candidates are arranged in a grid, with party defining one dimension and office the other. Often there is a single box or lever to cast a straight party vote. An office block ballot, on the other hand, sorts the candidates only by office. The party-line ballot discourages split-ticket voting by making a straight ticket far easier to cast (Walker, 1966). It also tends to suggest that one "ought" to think of politics in partisan terms (Rusk, 1974). The party-line ballot moreover puts independents and third-party candidates at an obvious disadvantage, both emphasizing their differentness and relegating them to the bottom of the ballot paper or voting machine.

III. NOMINATIONS

These dimensions of electoral policy all concern the conduct of elections after a set of candidates has been chosen. A second area of electoral policy concerns the choice and qualification of candidates. Free elections must allow reasonable access to the ballot. To deny candidates access to the ballot is to force their supporters to adopt extraelectoral means of expressing demands. If candidates who might win significant fractions of the vote cannot compete, the legitimacy of the actual result is undermined. At the same time, there are a variety of reasons why one would like to restrict access.

First, the more choice the voters are given, the more complicated is their decision. If access to the ballot were unrestricted, voters might be confronted by 20 or 30 contenders for each office, many differing only marginally from each other. To evaluate all these candidates would strain the resources of a full-time analyst. Second, the meaning of the result would be similarly in doubt. Even with the forgiving second round of majority electoral systems, the legitimacy of the winner would be questionable. In PR systems, the result would be a totally fragmented parliament in which stable coalition formation would be difficult. Worst of all, in plurality systems there would almost certainly be many candidates elected with very small vote totals. Third, restricting access is vital in systems where legally qualified candidates are entitled to some public resource, such as campaign funding or media access. Otherwise, many individuals might run for office solely to use these resources in order to publicize either their views or themselves without any hope of, or real interest in, winning.

In the United States, access to the ballot is regulated by the states in one of two ways. First, recognized parties whose candidates secured a minimum percentage of the vote in the previous election generally are entitled automatically to have their nominees appear on the ballot. Often, previous success also determines their relative placement on the ballot. For independent and minor or new party candidates, and for candidates seeking to contest a primary, the requirement is usually the filing of petitions signed by a percentage of the qualified voters in the jurisdiction. In the case of statewide offices, there is often also a requirement of geographic distribution for the nominating petitions.

Additionally, there is a question of timing. A state clearly may require the filing of petitions in good time to allow certification of signatures. Some states have also used filing dates as a means of discouraging third-party and independent candidacies. An extremely early filing date may make it hard to recruit sufficient volunteers to circulate petitions. It may also force a candidate to choose between entering a major party primary and running as an independent. This is especially troublesome in the case of the presidency, where primary results in one state may affect a candidate's choice of how to run in others. In this case, the justification for "sore loser laws" (so-called because they aim to keep the losers of primaries from running as independents in the general election) is less clear. The campaign of John Anderson in 1980 led to the challenge of early filing deadlines in many states.

In the United States, concern with popular participation and a desire to undermine the power of party bosses have led to the nearly universal employment of the direct primary to select party nominees. In some states, anyone filing a certain number of petition signatures may run in a primary; in others, a minimum level of support at a party nominating convention is required to force a primary. Most Northern and Western primaries are conducted under the plurality system, Southern primaries tend to use majority election; some Democratic presidential primaries use a system akin to list PR.

In some states, the right to participate in a party's primary is restricted to people registered in that party. Although Southern Democrats at one time tried to claim that their primaries were private party elections and not subject to constitutional prohibitions against racial discrimination, they are now considered public elections so that the only consequence of this "closed primary" system is to compel would-be primary voters to declare their party well in advance of the election. In other states, with "open primaries," any registered voter can vote in either primary simply by declaring a preference at the polls. The voter still can vote in only one primary. The Washington state "open-open primary" allows the voter to vote in either party's primary for each office. Finally, as already mentioned, Louisiana now has nonparty primaries in which all the candidates compete with one another.

The use of primaries in presidential nominations presents some special problems. First, the length of the primary season, beginning with the New Hampshire primary in February, when added to the general election campaign, makes the overall formal presidential campaign nearly a full year long. One could well argue that when politicians spend so much time running for office, they have too little to devote to the offices they already hold. As well, decisions made for their short-run electoral impact may not be in the long-term interest of the country, a particularly acute problem when an incumbent

President is running for reelection. The drawn-out nature of the primaries, coupled with the media's obsession with the "horse race" character of elections, make the early primaries extremely important, yet they are often held in small and atypical states. Because candidates need early wins to give their campaigns "momentum," they are led to make commitments to appeal to voters in the first few primaries that can come to haunt them later on. The undue influence thus given to voters in New Hampshire led several states to move their primaries up, only to have New Hampshire advance its own even further. Moreover, the proliferation of early binding primaries forces candidates to declare early and may leave a party irrevocably committed to a candidate before challengers' campaigns are fully organized, only to find later that he or she is not an attractive standard bearer. At the same time, even attractive challengers may find that they have missed filing dates to run as independents by the time it is clear they will not win their party's nomination.

These difficulties, among others, have led to a number of proposed reforms. The simplest would be to have a single national primary. The first problem is that because there could be no early trials of strength, all prospective candidates would have to enter, making a confused race and a minority winner the usual results. Second, relatively unknown candidates would not be able, as they are now, to concentrate their resources in a limited area while gaining exposure. Another possibility would be a series of regional primaries. If they were close together, however, this would be little different from a national primary, and if more separated it would not differ substantially from the current system. A final reform would be to decrease the importance of presidential primaries by making them nonbinding and/or fewer in number. Those who endorse this view argue that what is important for democracy is that voters be given a choice between two attractive candidates in the general election, not that the highly atypical group who votes in primaries decide who the nominees will be.

Outside the United States, and for some local offices in the United States, the requirement for access to the ballot is more often the posting of a monetary deposit and nomination by a purely nominal number of local voters. Frivolous candidacies are discouraged because the candidate's deposit is forfeit unless he or she obtains a minimum percentage of the votes. In Britain, for example, a deposit of £150 is lost unless the candidate posts at least one-eighth of the vote.

Finally, candidates may be excluded from the ballot because of their political beliefs. To counter the Sinn Fein policy of abstention, the government of the Irish Free State required candidates to pledge that they would take their seats if elected before they could appear on the ballot. In a similar vein, the Constitutional Court in West Germany can ban a party judged to be antidemocratic. This procedure was used, for example, to prevent neo-Nazis from competing in German elections.

IV. SUFFRAGE

Along with access to the ballot, access to the ballot box must also be regulated. Historically, this was a question of great importance. In the early nineteenth century, suffrage was greatly restricted on the basis of wealth and gender so that, for example, in Britain in 1830, less than 5 percent of the adult population could vote. Property requirements were generally eliminated in the United States by the early nineteenth century and in Europe by the early twentieth century.

The timing of this reform had a great impact on future politics. Where the working class was enfranchised early (relative to industrialization) and gradually, the tendency was for a moderate socialist party to develop in a moderate bipolar system. Where working-class votes came more rapidly and later, more extreme socialist or communist parties emerged in a far more fragmented party system.

The last major holdout against women voting was Switzerland, which granted female suffrage only in 1971. In the 1960s and 1970s, the minimum age for voting was nearly everywhere lowered to 18.

Although these reforms set the basic parameters of universal adult suffrage for citizens, they did not end debate over access to the ballot box. One set of questions concerns the registration of voters. Advance preparation of a list of voters allows timely resolution of disputes over voter eligibility and was introduced to counter the wholesale corruption reputed to be typical of nineteenth-century elections (Mackenzie, 1958). The problem is that significant numbers of otherwise qualified voters may be denied the vote solely because they are not registered, and this may significantly influence the balance of political power (Kelley et al., 1967).

In most of the world, this problem is minimized by laying the burden of seeing that citizens are duly registered on the government. On the European continent, registration of voters is usually a side process in the general registration of citizens for identity cards, national insurance, and internal passports. In Britain, a postal canvass is conducted annually to produce a register for that year; although this register is nearly totally accurate when it is prepared, its accuracy decays through the year as people move, die, or come of age. The Canadians instead conduct a door-to-door canvass just before each parliamentary election. In the United States, however, the burden of registration is placed on the citizen. In the early days of registration, voters were often required to appear personally before every election. More recently, this has been widely replaced with permanent registration (voters remain registered so long as they vote at least once every two or four years) and frequently can be handled by mail. Nonetheless, registration must still be performed well in advance of the elections, and only 73.8 percent of the voting-age population were registered in 1976.

This situation has led to the suggestion that voters be allowed to register at the polls on the day of an election. In the 1976 election, this was permitted in four states—Maine, Minnesota, Oregon, and Wisconsin. The results were somewhat mixed. Turnout was not greatly increased; election-day registration basically compensated for a decline in preelection (voters remain registered so long as they vote at least once every two or four years) nificant errors in the registrations, including large numbers of registrants permitted to vote in the wrong jurisdictions, there were no reports of significant fraud. On the other hand, these states traditionally have had extremely high turnout and honest politics, so the relevance of their experience to other states can be doubted. If election-day registration were adopted, it would benefit candidates of the lower classes and minorities, whose registration rate is lowest. Candidates running against those with stronger organizations would also be aided, because organizations can be used to ensure that likely supporters are registered whereas a challenger who must use the excitement of the campaign to lure supporters to the polls often finds that once they are interested it is already too late for them to register. This is especially a problem in primary elections.

A second set of problems involves the imposition of additional requirements for voting. If community interests are to be represented, then some period of residence in the community is a reasonable requirement, and in any case some residency requirement is needed to prevent voters from being "bussed in" to flood the polls in a close race. Likewise, some literacy or education test might be imposed to guarantee a minimal level of electoral competence. Additionally, a poll tax was required in some states. Each of these requirements is justifiable in theory, but is also subject to abuse. Primarily with the purpose of disenfranchising poor and especially minority citizens, these tests were often imposed in a discriminatory or unreasonable fashion. The Supreme Court has banned any residency requirement longer than 30 days for voting in a federal election. The poll tax was outlawed by the 24th Amendment to the Constitution. Finally, literacy tests and discriminatory enforcement of registration requirements were dealt with in the Civil Rights Act of 1964, which established a sixth-grade education as presumptive evidence of literacy, and the Voting Rights Act of 1965, which allowed the Attorney General to suspend local registration requirements and disapprove of new ones or ultimately to supplant local election officials with federal examiners. In 1975, Congress banned literacy tests altogether.

Of course, even if registration is made fair and easy, some potential voters will abstain, either through disinterest or distaste for all candidates. (Some will be sick or out of town, but they are of little consequence.) Based on a presumption that voting is a civic duty rather than a privilege, some countries (e.g., Australia) have made voting compulsory. Naturally, this increases turnout, although one might argue that the electorate is better able to decide without benefit of those brought to the polls only by the threat of a fine. In partisan terms, compulsory voting is like election-day registration; it benefits candidates with poor organizations and those appealing to voters with higher abstention rates. In the longer term, compulsory voting, election-day registration, and public financing of campaigns (see below) may all have the effect of undermining party organization by making it less necessary. To the extent that parties are a means for popular involvement in political life, this would mean less democracy rather than more.

V. CONDUCT OF CAMPAIGNS

Finally, a fourth complex of electoral policy questions concerns the conduct of campaigns. In particular, the three major questions are (1) the regulation and limitation of campaign spending; (2) fundraising and provision of financial resources to candidates; and (3) terms of access to mass media, particularly television and radio. In each case, the problem is to balance equality for the sake of fairness with the right of candidates and their supporters to use whatever resources they can to advance their views.

A. Finance

The original impetus to control campaign spending was a desire to prevent the outright purchase of victory by bribing the voters.[5] In the United States, this led first to prohibition of certain specific types of expenditures and then to requirements of reporting expenditures. In the same vein, gifts of alcohol in exchange for votes were banned by closing bars and liquor stores on election day. With the exception of a few problems, such as liquor, however, none of these specific regulations was terribly effective.

More generally, regulation of spending is based on considerations of fairness. If one point of view or party can so outspend its rivals as to drown their arguments in counter-propaganda, can the electorate reach a reasonable judgment? Attempts to limit total spending, however, have presented several difficulties, at least in the United States, and especially with regard to senatorial, gubernatorial, and presidential elections. In particular, proposed regulations have run afoul of candidates' rights to spend their own money in support of their candidacies. In the case of very rich candidates, personal fortunes can make a significant difference, especially in primaries. Moreover, although candidates and their parties or official organizations may be limited, it is far more difficult to regulate the spinning off of ostensibly independent committees, all supporting the same candidate. These problems are illustrated by federal regulation of presidential campaign spending.

Early regulations (1907–1944) prohibited contributions from corporations, public utilities, and labor unions either to parties or to candidates. They could not stop funds being channeled through individuals for subsequent donation to a political campaign, nor could they prevent the establishment of formally independent "political action committees." Later efforts to restrict individual contributions and the spending of campaign committees were similarly easy to circumvent. In 1971, Congress moved to limit television and radio spending, require disclosure of contributions over $100, and set up public subsidies of presidential campaigns. (The disclosure requirement did not become effective until April 1972, leading to a rush of last-minute anonymous contributions. Public subsidies, as a result of President Nixon's opposition, did not become effective until 1976.) This law was amended in 1974 to limit contributions and total spending. The amendments also established a Federal Election Commission. After a court challenge claiming that the limits imposed abridged freedom of speech, that the act discriminated against independents and third-party candidates, and that the composition of the commission (two members appointed by the President and four by Congress) was unconstitutional (*Buckley v. Valeo*), the act was again amended in 1976.

After the 1976 amendments, individuals were limited to a total political contribution of $25,000 per year; all individual contributions over $100 must be reported. Candidates who accept public funding are limited in both their primary and general election expenses. Major party candidates who raise at least $5000 in contributions of $250 or less in each of 20 states can have up to $250 of each contribution matched by the government. Candidates of minor parties (between 5 and 25 percent of the vote at the previous election) are eligible for dramatically lower subsidies; independents get no federal money. The 1971 media spending limits have been repealed.

Enactment of these regulations has obviously been influenced by partisan considerations. President Nixon insisted that public subsidies not start until after the 1972 election; in that year he outspent his Democratic challenger by more than 2 to 1. After the original composition of the Federal Election Commission was overturned, Congress delayed establishing a new board (appointed by the President with the advice and consent of the Senate) long enough to cause severe financial problems for some candidates. They have also undercut the financial advantage traditionally enjoyed by Republicans. The limitations placed on individual contributions have made it harder for relatively unknown ideologues to mount challenges; often these would be funded by only one or two individuals until public recognition was built up. On the other hand, once the threshold for public subsidy has been reached, candidates are encouraged to stay in the presidential race. If individual contributors have been made less important, political action committees and mass fund raisers have become more important. Moreover, many restrictions apply only to declared candidates during the campaign period; wealthy individuals can spend as much as they want to promote their own candidacies before the primary season begins. (On American campaign finance, see Adamany, 1975; Alexander, 1976.)

Unfettered by the letter of the First Amendment, many other countries have effectively limited total spending. In Britain, for example, spending for any purpose in support of an individual's candidacy for the House of Commons must be authorized by his or her agent (thus eliminating the possibility of unauthorized committees), and is strictly limited based on constituency population. Still unregulated, however, is central spending for the party in general and spending between elections. Canada has adopted similar restrictions coupled with direct and indirect public subsidies. Spending by both candidates and parties is limited. All contributions of more than $100 must be reported with the name of the donor, but there are no limits on donations. Parties are reimbursed for half of their expenses in buying television and radio time from a pool that broadcasters are required to make available. Candidates can also be reimbursed for a portion of their expenses provided they win at least 15 percent of the vote. Individual contributions are encouraged by a tax credit of 75 percent of the first $100, declining to a maximum credit of $500 on donations over $1150 (as opposed to the $1 federal election checkoff and a credit of 50 percent of contributions up to a total of $50 allowed in the United States).

B. Media Access

All these policies are aimed at providing a measure of equality among candidates, although the American policies are heavily weighted in favor of the major parties and all leave candidates who cannot raise adequate funds unprovided for. Another area in which the problem of equality arises is in broadcasting. This is a particularly vexing problem, both because of the great importance of radio and television in influencing voters and because of the government's involvement in the licensing and operation of broadcast facilities. Especially where broadcasting is noncommercial, some form of rationing is necessary.

The basic provisions of American law regarding media access are in the Federal Communications Act. The law requires that equal access be given to all legally qualified candidates for elective office. Since 1959, bona fide news events have been excepted. Until 1975, this was interpreted very narrowly, so that special legislation was required to allow Nixon and Kennedy to debate in 1960 without minor candidates. Since then, the Federal Communications Commission has taken a broader view. For nonnews events and advertising, the requirement is equal opportunity, not equal time; candidates can still be limited by lack of funds. The other requirement is that all candidates for federal office be given "reasonable access." This obligation is often satisfied by late-night spots for minor candidates. Finally, if a station endorses a candidate or editorializes in favor of a specific policy position, the "fairness doctrine" requires that opponents be given an opportunity to reply (Schmidt, 1976).

In France, Denmark, and Italy, the rule is strict equality of time. In the 1976 Italian election, each party was given two 45-minute programs, one in the format of a press conference, the other to be used as the party decided. In the 1974 French presidential election, each candidate had 65 minutes in six programs before the first ballot. The policy of equal time ruled out face-to-face debates until after the first round of voting. The British and Canadians have adopted a policy of allocating time roughly in proportion to vote. In Canada, free time is allocated in proportion to seats in the House of Commons, whereas in Britain, a formula agreed by the parties of equality for Labour and Conservatives, somewhat less time for the Liberals, and time within their countries for Welsh and Scottish nationalists is used. In both cases, any party with a minimum number of candidates is entitled to some time. In Canada, there is also a pool of commercial television and radio time available for sale in proportions set by the Canadian Radio-Television Commission. In all these cases, the trade-off is obvious. Equality among candidates encourages frivolous candidacies and makes head-to-head debates impossible. Proportionality or commercial rationing, however, stacks the system in favor of currently strong parties. Not surprisingly, the latter idea is generally adopted where there are two parties that dominate national politics.

VI. POLICY MAKING

Electoral policy is preeminently political. What is at stake is the fundamental distribution of political power and office. The values at issue are not mere matters of taste but the basic norms of free democratic societies. The ramifications of electoral policy decisions extend to all areas of policy made by elected officials. This presents a serious paradox. On the one hand, electoral policy is too basic and too important to be made by officials who are not politically responsible. On the other hand, however, can elected officials be trusted to make policy in an area that so vitally and immediately affects their own personal interests as incumbents as well as the partisan interests they were elected to represent?

With the exception of a few questions, such as the FCC's jurisdiction over broadcasting, electoral policy in the United States is made by the legislative branch of government —usually Congress or the state legislature—although, as with many other policy areas, intervention by the courts is becoming more and more common. Until the 1960s, federal involvement in electoral policy was minimal. The Constitution established direct election of the House of Representatives and the electoral college, but left the method of selection to the states. Later, the Seventeenth Amendment mandated direct election of senators as well. Suffrage was likewise a state matter; all that was required was that suffrage for federal elections be no more restrictive than for elections of the more numerous house of the state legislature. Subsequent amendments required that the vote not be denied on the basis of race, sex, or age over 18, or on the basis of failure to pay a poll tax. The date of federal elections was also established by Congress. Court involvement was directed primarily against racial discrimination in the South.

Since 1964, Congress has taken a more active role in establishing electoral policy. In order to protect the rights of minorities, the Voting Rights Act of 1965 and subsequent amendments gave the Attorney General substantial powers to review state actions affecting elections, including registration of voters, the actual conduct of the election, and reapportionment. Congress has also taken a more active role in regulating campaign finances. These rules are overseen by the Federal Election Commission. As this body establishes a case law tradition, it will become an increasingly important policy maker. Already its decision in 1976 to deny Eugene McCarthy's campaign for the presidency the status of a political party, thus barring his receipt of federal funds, may have contributed significantly to the outcome of one election.

Most other policy questions are decided by the state legislatures. Nominating procedures and deadlines, registration requirements, finance of nonfederal elections are all state matters. Most significantly, the drawing of district boundaries, for both state offices and for the House of Representatives, is done by the state legislature. Naturally, this makes control of the legislature in the years immediately following a census particularly important.

For the most part, court involvement, although pervasive, has been reactive, judging the constitutionality of both federal and state actions. Although some finance regulations have been overturned, the courts have generally allowed great leeway in regulating elections. One area of electoral policy in which the courts have been quite active, however, is legislative redistricting. Not only have they, through judicial review, established standards for population equality that must be met when state legislatures draw district lines, they have also imposed reapportionment plans of their own when the states failed to act. In doing this, the courts have imposed even more restrictions on themselves, in the name of avoiding politics,than they have imposed on the legislatures. Although states may adopt multimember districts, a court-ordered plan can only have single-member districts. Court-ordered plans must also conform more closely to strict population equality than legislatively devised plans (*Connor v. Finch*). This total attention to equal population means, of course, that other criteria are given little or no weight.

In an effort to avoid the conflict of interest inherent in allowing legislatures to draw the districts from which their own members will be elected, some countries have set up nonpartisan commissions. The British, for example, have constituency boundary commissions for England, Wales, Scotland, and Northern Ireland that periodically suggest modification of district lines. A similar plan is used in Canada. This requires a political culture in which boards of distinguished citizens can be expected to "rise above party politics." Whether such a system could be adopted in the United States is very doubtful. To date, although the Federal Election Commission has been bipartisan in the sense of having members from both parties, party-line votes have been significant.

VII. CONCLUSIONS

Partisan concerns are always central to electoral policy. Although electoral systems are openly adopted or supported precisely because they will aid one party over another only rarely, it is inescapable that the choice of an electoral system will aid some parties and hurt others. Reforms proposed and defended on the basis of lofty principles are often little more than attempts by those temporarily in power to ensure their continued advantage. This is not to say that normative concerns are irrelevant to electoral policy making, even when viewed strictly from the viewpoint of the self-interest of policy makers. To win an election is valuable primarily because of the legitimacy it confers. Unless the electoral process is perceived by the vast majority of citizens to be fair, so that they ought to submit voluntarily to the decisions of those elected, electoral victory is worth very little.

If reforms are adopted either for partisan advantage or for normative reasons, one of history's clear lessons is that they can have unintended consequences. Rather than making parties more democratic, preference voting has often increased the power of oligarchs within the party or interest-group systems. Although American campaign finance reform has decreased the importance of individual wealthy contributors, it has made candidates more dependent on special interest groups with their political action committees and on media consultants and fund raisers. One key to understanding the likely impact of a reform is to ask how candidates seeking election can adapt themselves to it.

This points, in particular, to the importance of organization. Many reforms directed against parties have had precisely the opposite effect from that intended because organization allowed the party to adapt better than its less organized opponents. Early registration schemes often aided the urban machines they were supposed to combat because the ward heeler got people to the registrar's office while the reformers, relying on civic spirit, did not (McCormick, 1953). Preference voting has a different effect for the Italian Communists with a disciplined organization than it has for the Christian Democrats without one. Often reforms supported in the name of democracy and popular participation redound to the benefit or organized interests. In each case, it is not the reform itself but the way parties, politicians, interest groups, and voters adapt to it that determines the result.

VIII. ORGANIZATIONS AND ELECTORAL POLICY

A variety of organizations take an active part in the formulation and study of electoral policy. The Federal Election Commission, aside from being an active participant in the regulatory process, publishes valuable compendia of electoral law reforms and electoral case law at federal, state, and local levels. Also at the official level, the League of State Governments has periodically published studies of state electoral systems. Among private organizations, the National Municipal League (publisher of the *National Municipal Review*) and groups such as Common Cause and the Ralph Nader groups have been active in pressing for "democratic" reforms such as finance control and for openness and probity in the conduct of elections. At the level of more scholarly organizations, both the Brookings Institution and the American Enterprise Institute have been leaders in electoral policy research. *Congressional Quarterly* has also published many reports on proposed electoral reforms.

In Europe, the Inter-Parliamentary Union has sponsored compilations of electoral practice in member countries (e.g., Herman and Mendel, 1976). The Commission of the European Communities has been active in sponsoring research into electoral systems, particularly with an eye to the establishment of an electoral system for the European parliament. Much of the current research is centered at the University of Mannheim. As in the United States, there are as well many private groups sponsoring reforms. The best known of these is the British Proportional Representation Society, which advocates replacing the British single-member plurality system with STV; an analogous organization exists in Ireland to push for the replacement of STV by plurality election.

NOTES

1. In majority electoral systems, this is a common occurrence in the first round of voting, so a procedure for dealing with it will be well institutionalized. Plurality systems, with no second round of voting and only infrequent ties, use more ad hoc procedures. Often ties are resolved by the drawing of lots. Especially in parliamentary elections, this may be acceptable because if a single seat changes hands it will have little effect on such questions as cabinet formation. In Sweden for a time, however, the Riksdag was tied. It was then agreed among the parties that tie votes would be resolved by the toss of a coin, with the provision that no coin toss would be regarded as a vote of no confidence.
2. Whether a "manufactured" majority really confers legitimacy depends on the gullibility of the people. To the extent that plurality systems discourage votes for third parties, they probably do contribute to the legitimacy of the result. If a candidate with only 40 to 45 percent of the vote were to win a decisive majority in the American electoral college, it is unlikely that the legitimacy of the election would be increased by the institutional creation of a majority, especially if, as is possible, one of the winner's opponents had more popular votes.
3. The use of the referendum is becoming more common in Europe, where it resolved the question of divorce in Italy, entry into the European Economic Community in Britain, Ireland, Norway, and Denmark, and devolution of power in Scotland and Wales. Especially in Britain, this has engendered significant debate over the appropriateness of direct public policy making without the mediation of parliament.
4. A related system that is quite different in operation is the single nontransferrable vote method used to elect members of the House of Representatives of the Japanese Diet. Each voter has one vote in a multimember district, and the top candidates are declared elected. This means that an especially popular candidate can actually be a liability to the party and leads to very intense intraparty conflict (Curtis, 1971).
5. In pre-reform Britain with its restricted electorate, parliamentary constituencies were often bought and sold, sometimes even with newspaper advertising.

REFERENCES

Adamany, D. W. (1975). *Political Money: A Strategy for Campaign Financing in America.* Johns Hopkins University Press, Baltimore.

Alexander, H. E. (1976). *Financing Politics: Money Elections and Political Reform.* Congressional Quarterly Press, Washington, DC.

Bachrach, P. (1967). *The Theory of Democratic Elitism.* Little, Brown, Boston.

Bain, H. M., and Hecock, D. S. (1957). *Ballot Position and Voter's Choice.* Wayne State University Press, Detroit.

Campbell, P. (1965). *French Electoral Systems.* Faber and Faber, London.

Crossman, R. H. S. (1972). *The Myths of Cabinet Government.* Harvard University Press, Cambridge, MA.

Curtis, G. (1971). *Election Campaigning Japanese Style.* Columbia University Press, New York.

Dahl, R. A. (1956). *A Preface to Democratic Theory.* University of Chicago Press, Chicago.

Downs, A. (1957). *An Economic Theory of Democracy.* Harper & Row, New York.

Duverger, M. (1959). *Political Parties*. Wiley, New York.

Einaudi, L. (1954). *Il buongoverno*. Editori Laterza, Bari.

Finer, S. (1975). *Adversary Politics and Electoral Reform*. Anthony Wigram, London.

Ginsberg, B., and Weissberg, R. (1978). Elections and the mobilization of popular support. *American Journal of Political Science 22*: 31–55.

Herman, V., and Mendel, F. (1976). *Parliaments of the World*. Macmillan, London.

Katz, R. S. (1980). *A Theory of Parties and Electoral Systems*. Johns Hopkins University Press, Baltimore.

Katz, R. S., and Bardi, L. (1980). Preference voting and turnover in Italian parliamentary elections. *American Journal of Political Science 24*: 97–114.

Kelley, S., Ayers, R., and Bowen, W. (1967). Registration and voting: Putting first things first. *American Political Science Review 61*: 359-379.

Kendall, M. G., and Stuart, A. (1950). The law of the cubic proportion in electoral results. *British Journal of Sociology 1*: 183-197.

Longley, L. D., and Braun, A. G. (1972). *The Politics of Electoral College Reform*. Yale University Press, New Haven, CT.

Loosemore, J., and Hanby, V. J. (1971). The theoretical limits of maximum distortion: Some analytic expressions for electoral systems. *British Journal of Political Science 1*: 467–477.

McCormick, R. P. (1953). *The History of Voting in New Jersey*. Rutgers University Press, New Brunswick, NJ.

Mackenzie, W. J. M. (1958). *Free Elections*. George Allen and Unwin, London.

Mayhew, D. R. (1974). *Congress: The Electoral Connection*. Yale University Press, New Haven, CT.

Milnor, A. J. (1969). *Elections and Political Stability*. Little, Brown, Boston.

Mueller, J. E. (1970). Choosing among 133 candidates. *Public Opinion Quarterly 34*: 395-402.

Pedersen, M. W. (1966). Preferential voting in Denmark. *Scandinavian Political Studies 1*: 167–187.

Pitkin, H. (1967). *The Concept of Representation*. University of California Press, Berkeley.

Polsby, N. W. (1971). *Reapportionment in the 1970s*. University of California Press, Berkeley.

Rae, D. W. (1971). *The Political Consequences of Electoral Laws*. Yale University Press, New Haven, CT.

Ranney, A. (1962). *The Doctrine of Responsible Party Government*. University of Illinois Press, Urbana.

Rose, R., and Mossawir, H. (1967). Voting and elections: A functional analysis. *Political Studies 15*: 173–201.

Rusk, J. G. (1970). The effect of the Australian ballot reform on split ticket voting: 1876-1908. *American Political Science Review 64*: 1220-1238.

—— (1974). The American electoral universe: Speculation and evidence. *American Political Science Review 78*: 1028-1049.

Sacks, P. M. (1976). *The Donegal Mafia*. Yale University Press, New Haven, CT.

Schmidt, B. C., Jr. (1976). *Freedom of the Press vs. Public Access*. Praeger, New York.

Schumpeter, J. A. (1950). *Capitalism, Socialism and Democracy*. Harper & Row, New York.

Swearer, H. (1961). The function of Soviet local elections. *Midwest Journal of Political Science 5*: 129–149.

Thayer, N. B. (1969). *How the Conservatives Rule Japan*. Princeton University Press, Princeton, NJ.

Tufte, E. R. (1973). The relationship between seats and votes in two-party systems. *American Political Science Review 67*: 540–554.

Walker, J. (1966). Ballot forms and voter fatigue: An analysis of the office block and party column ballots. *Midwest Journal of Political Science 10*: 448–463.

Zariski, R. (1965). Intra-party conflict in a dominant party: The experience of Italian Christian Democracy. *Journal of Politics 27*: 3–34.

15

Legislative Change, Reform, and Public Policy

Leroy N. Rieselbach / Indiana University, Bloomington, Indiana

Process profoundly influences policy. The structure of institutions, including legislatures, that produce policy will affect, perhaps decisively, the content of that policy. In consequence, those who care about programs will have a stake in the organizational features of the institutions that enact them; when dissatisfied with programmatic results, they may well seek to change the structures and processes in the hope of inducing different outcomes. The unhappy, in short, will become "reformers," endeavoring to create a "more effective" institution that produces "better" policies.

Some such process has taken place, since the late 1960s, in American legislatures, particularly in the U.S. Congress.[1] Vietnam, Watergate, the "energy crisis" of the 1970s, and severe economic dislocations revealed the relative weakness of representative assemblies. Lawmakers, reacting to a variety of supposed shortcomings, adopted a series of wide-ranging changes in the legislative institution. This chapter attempts to put these alterations in theoretical and historical context, to describe them briefly, and to assess their impact on legislative policy making.[2]

I. CHANGE, REFORM, AND POLICY: SOME DEFINITIONS

Reform, defined as *intentional* efforts to reshape institutional structures and processes, is only one, and perhaps not even the most important, source of organizational alteration. *Change*, more broadly conceived as *any* shift—intended or inadvertent, evolutionary or revolutionary—in basic institutional patterns or procedures, may occur more randomly and unobtrusively. In addition, the content of *public policy*, the values—money, power, symbolic preferment—that statutes or other organizational (here legislative) activities confer, may reflect either reform or change, as defined, or both. Thus, change appears basic; a variety of causes may stimulate new forms of organization and action and lead to new institutional outcomes. In this light, *reform* is best seen as a type of change, an *explicit* effort to bring about preferable (and perhaps particular) results through specific structural or procedural alterations. The analyst's task is to sort out the causes and shape of change, including reform, and to assess the impact, if any, of change on the legislature's policy enactments.

This is a complicated task, for as Rohde and Shepsle (1978) make clear, change may flow from a multiplicity of forces. For one thing, *events* outside the assembly may impinge directly on it. Domestic recession or international crisis may pose problems that highlight congressional deficiencies. Second, *membership turnover* may bring new personnel, with different backgrounds, experiences, and perspectives, to the legislature; newcomers may operate the existing machinery in ways quite at variance with old routines or may seek to rebuild the legislative engine to produce more efficient performance (see Clausen and Van Horn, 1977; Burstein and Freudenberg, 1977; Deckard, 1976; Burstein, 1979; Asher and Weisberg, 1978). Alternatively, events may compel incumbents to reassess their views, leading to either policy change or reform efforts, or both. For example, the frustrations of the Vietnam-Watergate decade and the major infusion of new blood into Congress, particularly in the 1964 and 1974 elections, contributed directly to the period of major change of the early and mid-1970s (Uslaner, 1978; Cavanaugh, 1980; Loomis, 1980; Rohde et al., 1974). In short, events and new members, neither planned nor predictable, may contribute as much or more to legislative change than any self-conscious reform movement.

II. REFORM IN THEORY

Given the complexity of the change phenomenon, and the number of interests and individuals involved in large, bicameral legislatures, it is not surprising to find that reform, when it comes, is seldom guided by broad visions of a "better" state of affairs. Rather, reformers have most frequently followed an incremental strategy, singling out prime targets —for example, the arbitrary power of committee chairpersons or the role of "unlimited debate" (filibuster)—and seeking to remove them, in piecemeal fashion, as barriers to a "more effective" legislature. Ad hoc, shifting coalitions of reformers act to modify structural failings as they perceive them; support for one set of changes implies nothing about backing other, subsequent sets. Reform, in toto, over any given period—as the history of congressional reform in the 1970s so abundantly illustrates—may well, and often does, consist of contradictory, incompatible elements.

A. Some Broad Perspectives on Legislatures

This is not to argue, however, that there are no sweeping visions of what legislatures, Congress in particular, might be in the best of all possible political worlds. Indeed, Davidson et al. (1966:15–36; see also Saloma, 1969; chaps. 1–2) outline three such views of the national assembly.

The Executive Force Theory. Proponents of the executive force model (Burns, 1949, 1963; Clark, 1964) are pessimistic about congressional capacity to govern. They stress the need to solve pressing political, economic, and social problems, and despair that the legislature can contribute meaningfully to policy formulation. The executive, by contrast, is likely to be the catalyst for progress; Congress, given its basic structures and processes, can only impede innovation. As a decentralized, fragmented institution, representing multiple interests, especially the rural, small town, "conservative" constituencies of Middle America, the legislature is incapable of acting decisively. It is better suited to oppose than to create, to react than to invent.

In consequence, if policy making is to meet the nation's needs, the President must be permitted to lead, unobstructed by a recalcitrant Congress. Executive initiatives must pass and be implemented. Reform should reduce legislative ability to frustrate presidential policy making. Independent sources of power—committees and subcommittees, for instance—should be curbed. Rules of procedure, which permit minorities to block action, require modification. In general, the path of presidential proposals through Congress needs to be smoothed substantially. This executive supremacy view, in sum, stresses presidential leadership and reduces Congress' role to legitimation, perhaps modification, and review after the fact (Huntington, 1973). The President proposes and the legislature disposes according to his wishes.

The Responsible Parties Model. An alternative avenue to escaping congressional obstructionism is through the use of disciplined, cohesive, "responsible" political parties. If the majority party, given its command of the legislative terrain as the chief organizational mechanism of the assembly, marched smartly and decisively forward in rank, its policy proposals would triumph at each and every stage of the law-making process. If, moreover, the President commanded the party troops, they would advance his (desirable and progressive) programs without risk of rear-guard delay or defeat.

Proponents of responsible parties (e.g., American Political Science Association, 1950; Bolling, 1965) promote reforms to enlist rank-and-file members of Congress in the partisan armies. In general, they would empower the respective party national committees to manage the electoral process. With the ability to control the nomination, using a legal monopoly of campaign finance, for example, the central committees could compel their elected representatives: To break ranks would, in effect, end the deserter's political career; the nomination would be given to a new, more loyal, recruit. Inside Congress, the rules would be rewritten to ensure that disciplined majorities could more easily carry the legislative day. In sum, in the responsible parties view, the President proposes and his loyal partisan army disposes consistently with his marching orders. Here, too, Congress would eschew policy making, emphasizing instead legitimizing and nonpolicy representational (e.g., constituent service) activities.

The "Literary" Theory. What appear as Congress' vices to the proponents of executive force and responsible parties models become virtues to adherents of the literary theory (Burnham, 1959). The latter pay homage to "constitutional tradition," to checks and balances, to separation of powers. In their view, Congress should restrain the power-seeking executive, during both policy formulation and implementation. Policy departures should come slowly, only after careful deliberation that considers all alternatives, and only after a genuine national consensus emerges. Thus, a decentralized legislature, to which multiple interests have access, and that can act only cautiously, is highly desirable.

These virtues have been lost in the twentieth century, the so-called age of executives, and reform is required to restore the status quo ante. To that end, literary theorists resist

all centralizing mechanisms: They prefer an election system that protects legislators'
independence; they fear disciplined political parties that might run roughshod over citizen
sentiments; they distrust executive leadership in any form; and, most important, they are
predisposed to congressional procedures that protect the power of individual legislators
to speak, slow action, promote deliberation, and oversee the administration. Overall, they
want Congress to propose *and* dispose—to make policy, to represent citizens, to police the
bureaucracy—to countervail the executive. They seek to restore Congress to what they see
as its rightful, legitimate place at the very center of the political process.

The Congressional Supremacy ("Whig") Model.   The literary view shades off into a vision
that stresses to an even greater extent the centrality of Congress. Legislative supremicists
see Congress as "the first branch of government" (de Grazia, 1965, 1966b), the prime
mover in national affairs. They favor all the reforms that the literary theorists advocate as
well as other changes intended, in effect, to strip the chief executive of most major bases
of authority. This "whig" view envisages a Congress that proposes and an administration,
President and bureaucracy, that disposes in strict accordance with legislative desires. A
supreme Congress will both make policy—explicit, and on its own terms—and oversee
the implementation of that policy.

Overall, then, there are broad visions of Congress, each of which entails its own particular set of structural and procedural reforms. Each view could, theoretically, provide a
model against which to evaluate specific reform proposals: Does the given suggestion
move the legislature, or is likely to do so, toward a clearly stated objective? Central to
such assessment is a general question about the obligation of government and a narrower
issue relating to the role of Congress in policy making. Both executive force and responsible parties proponents stress action; government must find prompt and effective solutions to national problems. In stark contrast, the literary and congressional supremacy
views focus on caution and consensus; policy initiatives should come slowly, after due deliberation leads to wide agreement that new programs are needed.

These considerations carry concomitant organizational requisites, which revolve
around the centralization of Congress. Those who desire to foster active policy making,
the executive force and responsible parties theorists, seek to subordinate Congress in a
centralized set of structural arrangements. Dominant executives, sustained by an accom-
modating legislature, formulate and implement (presumably) innovative public policies.
Those who prefer inaction look favorably on a decentralized legislature—with numerous,
autonomous decision-making centers—that can move only after attending to many points
of view and melding them into widely acceptable programs. In other words, the pro-
executive visions seek to minimize independent congressional policy influence, whereas
pro-legislative views seek to maximize it.[3]

B. Evaluating Reform: Some Criteria

These visionaries paint more or less coherent pictures of what the legislature should be.
Reformers, in practice, are less often moved by such comprehensiveness; they tend to be
legislators who seek to alter their institution in ways that advance their own, relatively
narrow causes (Jones, 1977a). They have, in recent years, in response to a series of legis-

lative "crises," imposed a wide variety of changes on themselves (see Sec. III), without much conscious effort to justify them as integral parts of any far-reaching plan to create a Congress of clear design. Observers of these structural shifts have, nonetheless, discerned some central tendencies in them, which provide some criteria with which to categorize and assess these developments.

For instance, Davidson and Oleszek (1976) distinguish between *adaptation* and *consolidation.* The former consists of reforms intended to permit more efficacious, from the legislative vantage point, relationships with external actors—executives in particular, but also judges, interest-group clienteles, and citizens more generally. Consolidative reforms seek to relieve internal stresses, to reduce tensions that occur within the assembly. Thus, frustrated career expectations of junior lawmakers led them to attack the entrenched (as they saw it) power structure of Congress to make legislative service more meaningful and satisfying for themselves.

Similarly, reforms impinge on legislative functions. Some (e.g., enhancing the ability of party leaders to centralize congressional operations and move programs ahead more effectively) seek to enhance legislative *responsibility,* to make Congress better able to define, impose, and implement its own policy priorities. Other reforms (e.g., "democratizing" the assembly through a more equitable allocation of authority) aim to promote legislative *responsiveness,* to make the assembly more representative of citizen viewpoints. Still others (e.g., financial disclosure statutes) are intended to increase Congress' visibility, to improve its *accountability* to the public (Rieselbach, 1977a).

Jones (1977b) proposes a more sophisticated category scheme. He distinguishes among the content of *reforms enacted* (do they affect the legislature's electoral arrangements, its internal procedures, its distribution of power, its analytical capacity, or its authority relative to external actors?), the *change accomplished* (in personnel, allocation of authority, in the legislative process itself, or in the actual output of Congress), the *functions served* by reforms (following Davidson and Oleszek, 1976, whether they reflect adaptation or consolidation), and the *institutional effects realized* by the reforms (the extent to which they move the assembly toward a legislative supremacy, executive force, or party responsibility model of Congress). Jones' ambitious integrative effort makes clear the extraordinary difficulties inherent in sorting out reformers' intentions, actions, and accomplishments.

In sum, such theorizing as exists about legislative reform does little more than raise some general, but pertinent, questions. The visionaries pose the central question: What sort of legislature is most desirable? Literary theorists and legislative supremicists envision Congress as a potent, if cautious, policy maker; executive force and responsible parties proponents prefer to keep Congress at the periphery of the policy process. The more pragmatic observers of reform present a series of subsidiary questions about specific reforms: At what *aspect*—internal structures or external relationships—of Congress is reform aimed? What is the *intent* of reform proposals? Is the intent realized? What is the overall effect of reform on the legislative institution? (For other efforts to pose equivalent questions, see Oleszek, 1977; Patterson, 1977; and Rieselbach, 1975). In the real world, the basic issue has been ignored, and the secondary questions answered only after the fact of reform. Change has occurred without much guidance from theory in any form.

III. REFORM IN REALITY: THE 1970s

This is not to suggest, however, that reform has been implemented purposelessly. The conclusion is only that reform—and there has been an exceptional period of reform in the 1970s—has proceeded pragmatically and incrementally, intended to deal directly with discrete matters, not to restructure the assembly in keeping with some grand design. Indeed, a singular combination of developments, beginning with the mid-1960s emergence of the anti-Vietnam war protests, produced a barrage of criticism of legislative performance and some extraordinary steps to remedy the exposed shortcomings. These steps were halting and taken in different and not always compatible directions, with little conscious thought about their long-run implications.[4]

Events and new members created conditions in which Congress considered reform seriously. The legislature's inability to influence the conduct of the Indochina conflict and its confrontation with the Nixon administration over impoundment, which revealed with extraordinary clarity the chaotic character of the congressional budgetary process (Wildavsky, 1979; Ippolito, 1978; LeLoup, 1977), made obvious the assembly's weakness relative to the executive branch.[5] Simultaneously, the electoral process—in consequence of the Goldwater candidacy of 1964, the Nixon resignation (and his successor's controversial pardon of the "disgraced" ex-President) in 1973-1974, and an increasing tide of retirements from Congress in the 1970s—brought a "new breed" of lawmaker to Capitol Hill. The newcomers recognized Congress' failings; they were younger, more policy-oriented, more independent-minded, and as a result less predisposed to adhere to the ordinary modus operandi. Moreover, many of these new members found it electorally advantageous to run "against" Congress (Fenno, 1975, 1978) and were thus prepared to make reform a major part of their personal agendas. Reform became possible under these propitious circumstances.

This singular combination of events and personnel turnover stirred up a wave of congressional self-evaluation and analysis; without these elements of basic change, it is doubtful that reform would have followed. In any case, Congress, goaded by the liberal Democratic Study Group (Stevens et al., 1974) adopted the Legislative Reorganization Act of 1970. Congressional introspection grew apace thereafter. The House conducted three separate self-studies: The (Bolling) Select Committee on Committees in 1973-1974 (see U.S. House, 1973, 1974; Davidson and Oleszek, 1977); the (Obey) Commission on Administrative Review in 1977 (U.S. House, 1977a, 1977b); and another Select (Patterson) Committee on Committees during the 96th Congress (U.S. House, 1980). Not to be outdone, during the same period, the Senate launched the (Hughes) Commission on the Operation of the Senate (U.S. Senate, 1976a) and, in 1976-1977, the temporary Select (Stevenson) Committee to Study the Senate Committee System (U.S. Senate, 1976c; Parris, 1979). An extraordinarily varied welter of ideas emerged from these assessments; many were adopted (more were not!). For convenience, we identify four separate sets of reforms, but in fact the proposals were implemented piecemeal and seriatim, without reference to broad theorizing or even to one another.

A. Reform for External Influence

One group of reforms, in many ways the most visible and dramatic, aimed to shore up Congress' position relative to the executive. If the national legislature could impose its own policy preferences, even in the face of executive opposition, it would recapture its ability to act as a responsible policy maker. In fact, the argument, which "liberals" most commonly advanced, made sense only when a perhaps atypical conservative Republican President sat in the Oval Office. A reinvigorated Congress could indeed save the Great Society from decimation (Orfield, 1975), but in the long-run an independent legislature would be more in keeping with the literary or whig theorists' views than with the policy goals of those who led the reform battles in the 1970s.

However, short-run considerations proved decisive. Congress moved against the President in 1973, passing the War Powers Resolution to circumscribe the Commander-in Chief's authority to commit American military forces to combat, as in Korea and Indo-china. The legislation, enacted over President Nixon's veto, gave Congress the ability to compel[6] the executive to withdraw any troops sent into the field within 60 days (90 days under special conditions) (see Franck and Weisband, 1979; Pious, 1979; Holt, 1978). In theory at least, the executive should cultivate congressional approval before commiting troops or risk legislative reversal of his military leadership.

Budgetary reform is a second congressional effort to enhance the legislature's authority. Acknowledging past failure to exercise effective control over federal expenditures, Congress adopted a major reform package—the Budget and Impoundment Control Act of 1974. The law created new budget committees in each chamber; provided them with a powerful analytic agency, the Congressional Budget Office, capable of competing with the Office of Management and Budget; and charged them with imposing fiscal discipline on an archiac budgetary process (Havemann, 1978; Ellwood and Thurber, 1977a, 1977b; Steinman, 1977; Finley, 1975). The product of the new scheme is, potentially, a coherent, unified budget that compares revenues and expenditures, and does so on a fixed (though in practice flexible) timetable. The act sought to enable Congress to centralize and coordinate its consideration of the budget, and thus to compete on even terms with the executive for fiscal supremacy. Tacked on to the budget reforms were major restrictions on the President's power to impound—to delay spending or to decline to spend entirely—funds that Congress had duly authorized and appropriated (Munselle, 1978; Dodd and Schott, 1979: 133–135; Fisher, 1975, chaps. 7–8). Enacted specifically in response to Richard Nixon's aggressive, and often illegal, use of impoundment, these new provisions made it considerably more difficult for the President to control the flow of federal funds.[7]

Third, on the institutional level, Congress has moved to strengthen its informational resources. The legislature has created new research agencies—the Congressional Budget Office and the Office of Technology Assessment, the latter to analyze the potential impact of various scientific programs. It has refurbished and strengthened old ones. The General Accounting Office has moved well beyond simply auditing the federal books to become a powerful agency for systematic policy analysis. The Congressional Research (formerly the Legislative Reference) Service of the Library of Congress is larger, more skilled, and well staffed; it produces serious research for congressional committees and individual members. (On these developments, see U.S. Senate, 1976b; *Congressional Quarterly Weekly Report*, 1979, *37*: 2631–2654; Gilmour, 1980.) Congress also has sought to harness computers to legislative needs (Frantzich, 1979); numerous information systems help representatives know more about more issues. Staff resources—capable experts on individual and committee payrolls—have expanded enormously during the

1970s, providing members with specialists to assign to policy formulation and assessment (Fox and Hammond, 1977; Malbin, 1980). To the extent that useful and usable data flow from such innovations, Congress is able to counterpoise its programmatic preferences to those of the executive; it need no longer defer so readily to an administration presumed to possess superior information.[8]

Finally, Congress began to assert, far more forcefully than previously, powers already well established. The Legislative Reorganization Act of 1946 had formalized the legislature's obligation to oversee the executive branch; Congress was to exert "continuous watchfulness" over administrative agencies and bureaus (Harris, 1965; Ogul, 1976). Greater informational resources, coupled with an enlarged number of vantage points—particularly in subcommittees (see Sec. III.C)—stimulated an upsurge of congressional surveillance of the executive (Aberbach, 1979; Dodd and Schott, 1979, chap. 6; Regens and Stein, 1979). Even the seemingly sacrosanct Central Intelligence Agency came in for substantial scrutiny. Watergate revelations triggered major investigations of the CIA, which led directly to House and Senate creation of Intelligence Committees, charged to oversee the intelligence community. In addition, a 1974 amendment to the foreign aid bill (the Hughes-Ryan amendment) required the CIA to report "covert operations" that it conducted, or had carried out on its behalf, to "the appropriate committees of the Congress," perhaps as many as four in each chamber.[9]

More generally applicable as a policy control device is the legislative veto, which Congress came increasingly to employ in the 1970s. Though found in a variety of forms,[10] the legislative, or congressional, veto reserves to Congress the opportunity to block executive actions—reorganizations, arms sales, agency regulations—within a specified time period. Fundamentally, the veto permits the legislature to prevent executives from acting, though they are authorized by law to do so, when some significant number of lawmakers disagrees with the substance of administrative policy (Gilmour, 1980; Bolton, 1977). Both the War Powers Resolution and the Impoundment title of the 1974 Budget Act contain congressional veto provisions, as do more than 150 other statutes, many enacted since 1975 (Gilmour, 1980: 13; Dodd and Schott, 1979: 231-232, Cohen, 1980).

B. Reform for Internal Efficiency: Centralization

If the first set of congressional reforms sought to redress a perceived imbalance between the legislature and the executive, the second—directed at centralizing legislative procedures—contributed to the same end, at least to a limited extent. The House of Representatives, aware that its fragmented, decentralized decision-making structure impeded coherent policy formulation, took a few halting steps toward strengthening the capacity of the majority party to impose some discipline on its members and, thus, on the institution. These were consolidative reforms, efforts to improve internal organization, enhancing responsibility, making Congress a more effective policy maker. The long-run implications were scarcely considered, and indeed are difficult to fathom. If reforms create a centralized legislature that can impose its favored programs on a hostile president, they are compatible with the literary and congressional supremacy views. If, on the other hand, reforms permit presidential partisans to move his programs ahead without serious opposition, the new procedures would please the proponents of executive force and responsible party positions.

Specifically, the reforms adopted sought to enable the majority party, the Democrats, to move its legislative programs ahead more efficaciously. The party—the Caucus and its leader, the Speaker—were made stronger, while the committees, the chief roadblocks to legislative responsibility, were in some ways brought to heel. (On these developments, see Jones, 1980; Dodd and Oppenheimer, 1977b; and the sources cited in note 2.) Party power was enlarged in several ways. The caucus met in December, before each new Congress, to organize. Its members claimed for themselves the right to pass on committee assignments and to approve committee chairpersons. The latter step undermined the hoary "seniority rule" (at least in principle) and, in fact, led to the ouster in 1975 of three elderly Southern oligarchs (Hinckley, 1976a; on seniority generally, see Hinckley, 1970, and Ornstein and Rohde, 1975). Appropriations *sub*committee chairs were also subject to caucus scrutiny. In addition, the caucus created a Steering and Policy Committee, and eventually empowered it to make committee assignments.

The Speaker also received additional authority. He (or she) was granted power to regulate the flow of legislation to committees: to make multiple or serial referrals, impose time limits on committee consideration, and create ad hoc (select) committees to facilitate coherent treatment of complex policy issues (Vogler, 1978). The Speaker was also given a major voice in the new Steering and Policy Committee; in effect, 12 of the 24 members are the Speaker's appointees and, presumably, allies. Finally, the Speaker was empowered to appoint, on his own authority, Democrats to serve on the Committee on Rules; selecting loyal party members has contributed to the firm yoking of that panel, a major obstacle to liberal legislation in the 1950s and 1960s, to the party leadership (Oppenheimer, 1978, 1980a).

A few other reforms, with implications for centralization, were adopted during the decade of the 1970s. The new budget process, noted previously, contains the seeds of centralization: If the new budget committees succeed in imposing control over the disparate standing committees and appropriations subcommittees, they will be poised to dictate the congressional budget. A series of rules changes, directed largely to eliminate dilatory tactics, were designed to ease the path of legislation, to curtail the minority's ability to subvert the majority. The most significant of these changes is the weakening of the Senate filibuster: The number of votes needed to end debate was reduced from two-thirds of those present (64 or 65 under ordinary circumstances) to a constitutional three-fifths majority (60 votes); the possibilities for a postcloture "filibuster by amendment" were largely eliminated by a 1979 change that mandated that the vote on final passage must come within 100 hours after cloture is invoked (see *Congressional Quarterly Weekly Report,* 1975, *33*: 2721–2722, and 1979, *37*: 319–320). In sum, stronger party leadership and limitations on minority power position the parties to centralize policy making to a greater degree than was the case in the prereform period.

C. Reform and Internal Influence: Decentralization

Congressional reformers tended to view committees as the major locus of the legislature's difficulties. Liberals, mostly Democrats, and junior members of both parties viewed all-powerful panels with displeasure. The former found their policy preferences frustrated in committees where conservative Southerners were safely ensconced in the chair, protected by the seniority rule. The latter felt deprived of the opportunity to participate fully: The chairperson, frequently in collaboration with the ranking minority member, dominated the committee's internal life. Strengthening the parties was one way to circumvent recalcitrant committee leaders, but the reformers, and their number increased in the 1970s as an unusually large contingent of newcomers was elected, were unwilling to pass up the opportunity to improve their own individual circumstances.

Thus, the reformers pushed successfully for a series of consolidative changes, which relieved the internal stresses that strong committees created. Because these alterations were decentralizing, opening positions of influence to many members previously powerless, the changes increased Congress' responsiveness; they established a legislative process more accessible to greater numbers of outside interests—citizens, organized groups, and governmental personnel. More basically, though the reformers seem to have given little conscious consideration to the matter, these decentralizing changes appear to be most compatible with the literary theory. By diffusing influence more widely, the alterations create conditions that exacerbate the problems in assembling majorities; a legislature that can integrate policy only with great difficulty, through complex bargaining and negotiating processes, is likely to act as neither a supreme policy formulator nor a pushover for powerful presidents. Rather, it will be most effective in blocking action, in requiring compromise as the price of even modest policy departures.

Specifically, the reform movement undercut the dominant position of committee chairpersons, effectively devolving their authority to autonomous subcommittees. As noted, the effort to enhance the position of the political parties produced steps to curb the committee chairs, but only part of their power was assigned to the parties. More significantly, substantial portions were reallocated to the rank and file, mainly junior members. Such shifts were particularly pronounced in the House, where, first of all, members were limited to one subcommittee chair each. In addition, no individual could select a second subcommittee assignment until each full panel member had chosen one subcommittee position. Similar changes in the Senate effectively guaranteed that members of both chambers could secure a "piece of the action," in subcommittee, earlier in their congressional careers (Congressional Quarterly, 1977: 743-794, and the sources cited in note 2).

The House went further: The Democratic Caucus, in 1973, adopted a series of changes, collectively known as the "subcommittee bill of rights," to protect the independence of subcommittees (Rohde, 1974; Freed, 1975; Ornstein, 1975b; Dodd and Oppenheimer, 1977b). The bill of rights required that subcommittees have fixed jurisdictions and that legislation on these subjects be referred automatically to them; it permitted subcommittees to meet at the pleasure of their members, to write their own rules, and to control their own budgets and staffs. Moreover, two years later, the Caucus mandated that all committees with more than 20 members create a minimum of four subcommittees. The upshot of these changes has been to establish an "institutionalized" subcommittee system, with active, permanent, and independent panels (Haeberle, 1978). Subcommittee members are strategically located to exert considerable influence over matters in its jurisdiction (though such areas may be quite narrow).

In sum, these changes have made the House more like the Senate (Ripley, 1969). Both chambers are decentralized: Committee chairpersons must, under threat of ouster, share their authority with full committee majorities and subcommittee leaders. In general, more people, operating from more secure power bases, now have the potential to shape legislative policy making.[11]

D. Reform for External Consumption

A final set of changes sought to counter an increasingly hostile public opinion. Along with all governmental institutions, and politicians generally, Congress fell into public disfavor in the 1960s and 1970s (Ripley, 1978: 387–390; Parker, 1977). While citizens had continuing confidence in their own members of Congress, they considered Congress collectively to be performing poorly (Parker and Davidson, 1979; Cook, 1979). To remedy this situation and restore public approbation, Congress imposed on its members a series of reforms, adaptive in character, designed to expose its operations to public scrutiny. To the extent that citizens (and voters) could discover what their representatives were doing, and satisfy themselves that these activities were ethically beyond suspicion, the populace could hold Congress accountable and accept the legislature's policy making as legitimate and untainted. The need to reassure a skeptical public stimulated these reforms; as usual, little if any consideration of their long-range impact was visible. In fact, if these accountability alterations have any effects, they are likely to promote the literary theory, at the margins at least. If the reforms, by making congressional politics more visible, place obstacles in the path of party leaders—"open" decisions openly arrived at will involve more participants and, in turn, weaken the power of any set, including the party apparatus (Froman and Ripley, 1965)—they will undercut the potential for executive force or party responsibility models. Conversely, if these reforms permit opponents of policy change to identify and exploit legislative "veto points," they make it more difficult for Congress to act, limiting the legislature to blocking or modifying policy initiatives, as the literary theorists prefer.

In any event, three broad programs, intended to expose members and congressional operations to the glare of publicity, were implemented in the 1970s. First, the Federal Election Campaign Act of 1971, as amended in 1974, 1976, and 1979, and as interpreted by the Supreme Court in *Buckley v. Valeo* (1976), established a congressional election system in which contributors' donations are limited and candidates' expenditures are not. What the latter spend, however, and the sources of these funds must be disclosed (Alexander, 1980; Congressional Quarterly, 1976: 544–557). In general, the laws both limit large gifts and record even more modest ones on the public record.[12]

Second, both the House and Senate adopted codes of ethics, including financial disclosure provisions, designed to deter or expose conflicts of interest (Bullock, 1978). Members were required to report gifts they (and their employees) receive; their property holdings, their investments in securities, and their debts; and their income from all sources. Such disclosures should enable concerned citizens, or enterprising journalists, to discover to whom, if anyone, members of Congress are in any way financially beholden, and to assess the extent, if any, to which members' personal interests impinge on matters about which they must, as legislators, vote or otherwise become involved.

Finally, members of Congress concluded that they should carry on their internal operations in the "sunshine" (Bullock, 1978). The Legislative Reorganization Act of 1970 decreed that legislators vote publicly in committee and on the floor: Committee roll calls are to be recorded and made available; new requirements for recording teller votes reduce the possibility that members can avoid going "on the record," as individuals, during debate and preliminary floor consideration of legislation (Ornstein and Rohde, 1974). The committee process was opened up as well: All sessions, including "markups" and conference committee meetings, are to be public, unless a majority votes, in public, to close them. Although executive sessions on secret or controversial matters remain possible, the burden of proof now lies with those who would exclude outside observers. In all these ways, the people can find out not only what their representatives are doing but also if the conduct is in any way ethically suspect. A satisfied citizenry should come, once again, to hold its national legislature in high regard.

IV. THE IMPACT OF REFORM ON POLICY

That substantial and significant legislative reform has occurred is incontrovertible; the problem, of course, is to assess the consequences that change and reform have wrought. Because reform has been undertaken in response to many influences—political and personal—and because it has not been guided by any broad, long-term, widely shared vision of desirable legislative structure, its effects seem inconsistent and uncertain. Indeed, because reform has been so recent, its impact, and especially that on the content of policy, is most difficult to decipher. Yet some, admittedly incomplete and impressionistic, evidence is at hand to suggest that the results of reform have been many and varied. Reformers' intentions have sometimes been realized, and sometimes not; on other occasions, quite unintended, and often undesirable, consequences seem to have followed from reform efforts. And whatever the outcome, intended or otherwise, it may be impossible ever to ascertain definitively whether the reform or other factors—turnover and events—explain the observed results.[13]

A. The Challenge to the Executive

Nowhere is the difficulty in disentangling the effects of reform from those of more general change more visible than in the effort to evaluate the impact of the congressional challenge to the executive branch. The War Powers and Budget Acts passed during a period of popular discontent, rapid turnover in Congress, and a scandal-ridden and politically vulnerable presidency. Moreover, there has been (fortunately!) no clear test of the war powers provisions, and the new budget process has not yet fallen into a clearly established pattern.

Nevertheless, the available evidence suggests that Congress has not yet used its newly claimed authority to impose its will on the executive, especially in the military realm. On five occasions, the President has felt obliged to report to Congress in compliance with the War Powers Resolution; only two were controversial: Ford's recapture of the ship *Mayaguez,* seized by Cambodia, and Carter's abortive effort to rescue the American hostages held in Iran. Each episode lasted only a few hours; neither really offered Congress a chance to act in any meaningful fashion. Each President complied with the letter, if not the spirit, of the statute, though opponents of the Iranian rescue mission asserted that, given the planning that went into the operation, the Administration should have consulted in advance with relevant members of Congress. In each instance, protests in Congress were short-lived: It was hard to quarrel with a widely applauded "success" (in Ford's case) or to indulge in recriminations about an embarrassing failure (in Carter's actions).

In reality, Congress has the opportunity to participate in military policy making only when troops remain in the field for substantial periods. In these circumstances, Congress *can* act decisively, ordering the troops home if it wishes, or by default, doing nothing and thus requiring the President to cease military operations. The issue, of course, is whether the legislature *will* act, imposing its preferences on the Commander in Chief, who will most certainly invoke the "national interest," the nation's prestige and honor, and the gravity of the situation. There is no cause to believe with certainty that members of Congress would, in such circumstances, be prepared to run the risk or assume the responsibility for overruling the Chief Executive.

More speculatively, the War Powers Act may be significant less after the fact of military involvement than as a prior deterrent to precipitous, or difficult to justify, armed intervention. Presidents can never be entirely certain that Congress will approve their actions, and they may calculate carefully about congressional response before commiting troops. For example, there was widespread speculation, in the press and elsewhere, that the Ford administration was considering direct intervention, in 1974, in the civil war in Angola. The foreign policy committees of Congress, especially the Senate Foreign Relations panel, became increasingly concerned, given the perceived lessons of our Indochina involvement, that American commitment of money and military supplies might escalate into military support of our favored faction. Such forthright expression of concern may well have contributed to executive caution: No use of U.S. troops was ever publicly proposed.[14] Whether such actions truly constrain the President is difficult to determine; if they do, whether this is desirable depends on the observer's view of the President and/or the policy that military intervention would seek to pursue.

Finally, and more generally, the record to date on general congressional success in asserting its will against the executive is mixed. On the one hand, Congress has imposed its preferences, at least negatively, on frequent occasions. It refused to ratify SALT II, the strategic arms limitations treaty with the Soviet Union, and it has repeatedly delayed or blocked arms sales to various foreign governments, using the legislative veto. (For a full treatment of recent congressional-executive relations in foreign affairs, see Crabb and Holt, 1980). On the other hand, some signs point to a revival of legislative deference to executive international relations leadership. Heightened international tensions increase risk to the country, and incline legislators to accept the views of the professional military. For instance, Congress not only has failed to enact a comprehensive "charter" to control intelligence agencies but also has backed away from the Hughes-Ryan oversight provisions, moving to reduce the number of committees entitled to know what activities the CIA undertakes overseas. Similarly, domestic problems—recession or the "energy crisis," for example—with their obvious electoral implications, may require members to redirect their attention to the home front, leaving international matters to the executive. In sum, although presidents can no longer count on customary congressional acquiesence to their foreign policy initiatives, the legislature's assertiveness may reflect less structural reform than more basic, evolutionary change: more members more willing, under the stimulus of political circumstances, to use basic legislative prerogatives to challenge the administration. Should membership and situations alter, the old pattern of congressional subordination might readily recur.

Assessment of the new budget process, as a token of legislative revival, yields a similarly cloudy picture, complicated because the reforms have led to somewhat different results in the House and Senate. On the whole, Congress has observed the form of the new scheme: It has for the most part formulated a coherent budget, specifying revenues, outlays, and the size of the deficit, and has done so with only minimal departures from the prescribed timetable. Moreover, the Congressional Budget Office, "now considered the best source of budget numbers in Washington" (Wildavsky, 1979: 246), provides the lawmakers with invaluable data with which to formulate independent budget proposals (see also Thurber, 1978). At a minimum, Congress now looks at the federal budget from a far broader perspective than it did previously.

The Senate seems particularly well positioned to make the process work. Its Budget Committee, a permanent panel, prospered under bipartisan leadership from Senators Edmund Muskie (D., Me.), the chair, and Henry Bellmon (R., Okla.), the ranking minority member.[15] The committee has been cautious, careful to conform to the chambers' norms, to accommodate Senate power centers (LeLoup, 1979a), and to avoid posing direct challenges to the existing committees.[16] The full chamber, in consequence, seems satisfied with the operation of the new process (Wildavsky, 1979; Thurber, 1978).

The situation in the House is more problematic. The House Budget Committee differs dramatically from other panels: It restricts its members to three (originally two) terms of service; it represents other revenue-related committees (Appropriations, and Ways and Means) and the party leadership in its ranks. These unique membership requirements reflect marked disagreement about the substantive purposes of the new process: Some members hoped that more effective procedures would rationalize legislative budgeting, but others sought to influence the substance of fiscal outcomes. Liberals, for example, expected the new process to provide more funds for social programs and less for defense; conservatives hoped for the reverse. The latter, in addition, were eager to see the Budget Committee control "backdoor spending," mostly for social welfare, that otherwise escaped legislative management. Thus, committee assignments tended to go to liberal Democrats and conservative Republicans, leaving the panel polarized and volatile (LeLoup, 1979b; Fisher, 1977a). Partisanship has, in fact, threatened the process in the House, which has been hard pressed to comply with the Act, often passing the required resolutions late and by slender margins.

In the final analysis, of course, the question is whether the revised procedures influence budgetary decisions, and here the evidence is neither clear nor consistent. Pfiffner (1977) and Thurber (1978) suggest that congressional budgets for fiscal years 1976-1977 differed "significantly" from President Ford's proposals, but to what extent the variance reflects natural enmity between branches controlled by opposing political parties rather than the budget process itself remains difficult to determine. In contrast, several observers (Wildavsky, 1979: 254–262; LeLoup, 1979a, 1979b; Huddleston, 1979), looking at later years, find congressional impact moderate to low during the Democratic Carter administration; as Huddleston (1979: 24) puts it, the act has produced "no major shifts in spending priorities." Since it is impossible to divine "what might have been" without the reforms, the most reasonable conclusion seems to be that the new procedures have put Congress in a better position to assert and sustain its positions if, and when, it chooses to do so.

More important, perhaps, the ability of the budget committees to impose their preferences on the standing committees, and thus to centralize the budget process, may be increasing. In attempting, admittedly for election-year political purposes, to balance the fiscal 1981 budget, the committees used a "reconciliation" procedure, never previously invoked, to force eight substantive committees in each house to reduce expenditures. When the House Education and Labor Committee balked, the Senate budget panel successfully urged the upper chamber to reject a conference report on higher-education legislation, forcing the House to make the cut (*Congressional Quarterly Weekly Report*, 1980, *38*: 2758). Should such precedent become firmly established, Budget Committee superiority to the authorizing bodies might enable the former to dominate the budget decisions both within Congress and against the executive. Until this incident, however, the budget committees have walked softly, seeking to appease the other committees rather to impose on them.

With respect to impoundment, the Budget Act has had a clear and pronounced effect. The President is now considerably less able to regulate the flow of federal funds. Impoundment for policy purposes, as Richard Nixon practiced it, is now virtually impossible without legislative acquiesence, and the burden has been transferred to the executive to win that approval (Munselle, 1978). When Congress appropriates, it is far more probable that the funds will be spent. Yet the anti-impoundment provisions have had unintended consequences as well. Traditionally, impoundment was a useful, and noncontroversial, device that promoted efficient administration. Now, all matters, even the most routine deferrals, must be reported to Congress; members have complained that many hours are wasted on relatively trivial items, a concern that bureaucrats share (Pfiffner, 1977; Wildavsky, 1979: 240).[17] Once again, it seems clear that reforms have enabled Congress to act and to win, if it has the determination to do so. Whether the legislature does, and what the long-term effect of such decisiveness will be, remain open questions.

Similar uncertainties appear about the results of the "information revolution." From one perspective, it is incontrovertible that members of Congress (and of state legislatures; see Balutis, 1977) have substantially greater quantities of data than ever before. Enlarged staff resources, new agencies (CBO and OTA), more effective old support facilities (GAO and CRS), and increasing computer technology (see Sec. III.A) combine to expand enormously the congressional capacity to engage in serious analysis, which can sustain legislative alternatives to executive initiatives. These developments, however, are not necessarily an unmixed blessing.

For one thing, members of Congress may not have adequate incentives to seize these new opportunities. Fundamentally, in some, perhaps most, circumstances, senators and representatives are politicians rather than objective analysts. They may well be searching less for optimal policies than for programs that will serve their political purposes. They want ideas that will satisfy their constituents—voters and supporting interest groups. They need solutions that will survive the bargaining and compromising policy process of a decentralized legislature. Policy analysts who do not recognize the political needs of their principals will find their advice ignored. Where politics and analysis merge, the latter may be of considerable use to legislators; where they diverge, analysis is likely to receive low priority (on these matters, see Jones, 1976; Schick, 1976).

Moreover, information that these reforms make available may actually distract lawmakers from programmatic activities. Too much data, "information overload," may overwhelm members. They may not know how to cope with what is available to them and they may be increasingly inclined to look to staff for substantive guidance (Malbin, 1980). Conversely, staff personnel who are prepared to be "entrepreneurs" rather than impartial "professionals" (Price, 1971) may come to play powerful policy roles. Dependence on the experts may undercut the members' ability to exercise genuinely independent policy judgments. Finally, there is an information management problem; members may

spend more time and energy administering large staffs than they do using the data that
their information resources supply. Although some offices now employ professional
managers (Hammond, 1978), the risk remains that organizational confusion and chaos
will intrude on legislators' ability to engage the substance of policy questions.

In sum, Congress in the 1980s is better equipped institutionally to challenge presidential policy leadership. The reforms it has adopted—the War Powers Act, the Budget
Act, strengthened analytic capacity—have placed the national legislature in a strong position to define and fight for its own priorities. But capability and its use are not necessarily synonymous: Whether Congress will, in fact, employ its weapons against the executive depends equally on both member willingness to do so and events encouraging them
to seize the initiative. What this suggests, of course, is that Congress can, but only sometimes will, be the more forceful policy advocate that reform has enabled it to be.

B. Policy and Internal Power Considerations

Congressional reformers not only sought to rearm the legislature against the executive,
but also to reallocate authority internally. The standing committees, and their supposedly
autocratic chairpersons, were the chief targets of the reform revolution of the 1970s (see
Secs. III.B and III.C). Committee power was reassigned outward to the party leaders
and downward to the subcommittees and their leaders, an incremental set of often in compatible reforms. Here, too, the evidence is partial and hard to assess, but on balance it
indicates that fragmenting forces have triumphed over those leading to centralization. The
result, overall, seems to be a Congress that has more rather than less difficulty integrating
and enacting coherent public policies.

Strengthening the Parties.   Despite some specific successes, there is little evidence that
reform has significantly strengthened the political parties in Congress. The House Democratic Caucus did oust three elderly and allegedly arbitrary committee chairmen—W. R.
Poage (Tex.) of Agriculture, Edward Hebert (La.) of Armed Services, and Wright Patman
(Tex.) of Banking and Currency—from their posts, but little or no change in committee
factional alignments, leadership patterns, or policy outcomes seems to have followed;
most committees, even with new leaders, seem to have acted in customary fashion (Unekis and Rieselbach, 1979, 1980; Berg, 1978). About all that can be said is that committee
chairs are now on notice that they have no guarantee of retaining their positions, which
may shape the ways in which they use the powers available to them. The Caucus also won
one significant policy victory: It voted to instruct the Rules Committee to permit an
amendment, previously defeated in the Ways and Means Committee, to repeal the oil
depletion allowance to be offered on the floor, where it passed and eventually became
law. But in general the Caucus has been unwilling or unable to impose discipline on its
majority, leaving policy individualism to flourish.

The Speaker, too, has made successful but infrequent use of his new powers. Although the Rules Committee, whose majority membership the Speaker controls, most
often supports the party leadership (Oppenheimer, 1978, 1980a), even it balks from time
to time; for example, in 1980, the panel refused to comply with Speaker O'Neill's request
for restrictions on amendments to the 1981 fiscal budget reconciliation bill. Similarly,
the Speaker used his power to establish ad hoc committees to promote passage of an
Outer Continental Shelf bill (in 1975–1976) and President Carter's energy package (in

1977) when committee conflict threatened to make concerted and comprehensive action impossible (Uslaner, 1980; Oppenheimer, 1980b). More commonly, such intrusion into standing committee jurisdictions and authority has seemed too risky, too unlikely to overcome the divisive and divergent preferences of numerous individual members.

The Speaker's enlarged bill referral powers may even have had counterproductive consequences. Although he can (and did, 4148 times in the 95th Congress; Uslaner, 1980: 12) refer bills to several committees and impose time limits on their consideration of the bills, multiple referrals greatly exacerbated the problem of coordinating congressional activity. Uslaner (1980: 13) reports that multiply referred legislation lingered substantially longer in committee and was significantly more likely to be amended and less likely to pass if it did reach the floor. Far from providing centralization, the Speaker's referral authority seemingly encouraged House committees to assert their authority; indeed, Oppenheimer (1980b) argues that pressing jurisdictional claims provided full committee chairpersons with an opportunity to compensate for their otherwise declining influence. In any case, party leaders' new powers appear inadequate to overcome the decentralizing forces that the reform movement also unleashed.[18]

Finally, procedural reforms have produced only minimal effects; and entangled in broader changes, some of those have been unanticipated. Dilatory tactics are more difficult to use, and legislation is somewhat less likely to get enmeshed in parliamentary thickets in the House. In the Senate, however, the new cloture procedures have not facilitated more rapid processing of bills. This is not because cloture has not been invoked; it has been used more successfully in recent years (see Congressional Quarterly *Almanacs* for 1977: 813, and 1979: 13, and *Congressional Quarterly Weekly Report 38*: 1618, 2252, 2247, and 2453). Rather the norms governing the conduct of filibusters have changed markedly. Historically, unlimited debate was reserved for major matters, those about which an intense minority felt passionately (Wolfinger, 1971). At present, by contrast, any topic, however minor, seems fair game for extended debate, led by a handful of Senators, or on occasion a single member. Norm changes, condoning seemingly frivolous filibusters, have undercut the intended effect of rules reforms.

Unleashing the Subcommittees. Basic to leadership failure to centralize congressional operations, even with its enlarged authority, is the devolution of influence, formerly lodged in full committees, to subcommittees. The reformers, especially the junior members within their ranks, chafed under the restrictions that the old committee regime imposed on them: an inability to participate fully in committee affairs, much less to contribute meaningfully to the policy content of committee legislation. They took advantage of full committee vulnerability to create new opportunities for themselves: The limits on subcommittee chairmanship and the subcommittee bill of rights, in particular, were designed to open up new avenues of participation and influence. Viewed narrowly, these reforms accomplished their purpose, but from a broader perspective their proponents may have won the battle but lost the war.

At the most fundamental level, the subcommittee reforms did enable more (and junior) members to accede to positions of potential power. Limiting individuals to a single subcommittee chair did open up at least 16 leadership positions to those previously denied such posts (Ornstein, 1975b; Stanga and Farnsworth, 1978). Moreover, the number of subcommittees has grown—from 116 in the House in the 92nd Congress to 134 in the 96th—providing additional positions for still more majority members (Deering and

Smith, 1980). Finally, the new subcommittee chairpersons are more liberal, more typical Democrats, making the House leadership more representative of the party (Deering and Smith, 1980). Yet there are limits to the impact of reform here: Stanga and Farnsworth (1978) suggest that, though wounded, seniority survives, and much of the reform-induced change is concentrated on a few committees. That is, exclusive House committees remain the province of senior members, and on other panels there has been at best only modest reduction in the seniority of subcommittee chairpersons. Within these limits, however, it seems safe to say that more members have some subcommittee seat from which to seek influence over the substance of policy than was the case in the prereform period.

More important, perhaps, the vast array of subcommittees are independent. Subcommittees are often active; they are frequently expert—with their own staffs; and they are protected from outside interference—with guarantees of jurisdiction, control over their own rules, and adequate budgets. Indeed, Deering and Smith (1980) find that party leaders do not often seek to impose discipline on the subcommittees; they most regularly confer with subcommittee chairs on procedural matters, such as scheduling, and only rarely "lobby" the subcommittees with respect to the content of policy. In fact, the most common communications between party and subcommittee leaders find the latter placing demands on the former. Such policy-related contact as the party leaders choose to initiate is limited to issues of major significance and often takes place after the subcommittee has completed action.[19] In general, the leadership "neither desires to influence nor is capable of influencing the specific legislative outcomes of the vast majority of subcommittee deliberations . . ." (Deering and Smith, 1980: 36).

Such subcommittee autonomy—though the evidence remains sketchy—suggests that structural change has produced more fragmentation than centralization. Party leaders simply cannot impose their preferences on independent subcommittees. In consequence, there are at present more individuals and power centers to deal with in coordinating congressional policy-making activities. Concomitantly, the legislature's ability to act at all, much less decisively, may have declined as a result of reform. A decentralized institution further fragmented, for whatever motives, may find it nearly impossible to integrate small increments of power sufficiently to produce meaningful policy innovations.

Variations on the Theme. Because explicit structural reform coexists with a variety of other changes, all of which impinge differentially on the various elements of legislative organization, it is hardly surprising to discover that reform and change combine in numerous ways within different units of Congress. Fenno (1973) has made clear that congressional committees vary along a number of dimensions—the members' personal goals, the environmental context within which the committee works, a panel's "strategic premises" (decision rules or norms), and its decision-making process (specialization, partisanship, participation)—that together shape the policy decisions they make. In short, committees differ, and changes—events that alter environmental forces, the rise and fall of leaders, membership turnover, and the like—have a differential impact on them.

For instance, Ornstein and Rohde (1977) find that the explicit reforms of the 1970s combine with membership turnover in distinctive ways. The House Agriculture Committee "implemented the full array of subcommittee-strengthening reforms," experienced major personnel change, and got a new chairperson, in the process becoming ideologically more moderate and regionally more balanced. Yet despite these major alterations, because the new members' goals varied little from the motivations of the members they replaced, "little overt change in behavior or policy outputs occurred . . ." (1977: 227-229). These authors also find that reforms have increased the autonomy of most, and the activity of many, subcommittees on the House Commerce and Government Operations Committees *without* significantly altering policy-making behavior. Indeed, on the former, the shifts have, if anything, inhibited policy activities (1977: 237-252). On House Foreign Affairs (sometimes International Relations), new members and new rules put liberal members into prominent positions in subcommittee, and pressured the committee chair into joining the more active panel members in placing more restrictions on presidential foreign policy leadership (Ornstein and Rohde, 1977: 252-261; see also Kaiser, 1978). In short, change and reform in varying forms and combinations produced some policy shifts in some committees and none in others (see also Berg, 1978, and Deering, 1980).

House Ways and Means offers a clear instance of unintended and negative consequences of reform. Long a target of liberal hostility (or jealousy) during Wilbur Mills' lengthy and successful tenure as chairperson, the committee suffered the wrath of the reformers when circumstances were conducive, when Mills' personal problems left him, and his panel, vulnerable. Mills was, in effect, forced from the chair and Ways and Means was stripped of its committee assignment powers, required to create subcommittees, enlarged from 25 to 37 members, and deprived of some procedural protection (the "closed rule") for the legislation it reported. The upshot was that the new Ways and Means chairperson, Al Ullman (D., Ore.), failed to sustain the bipartisan consensus that had characterized the committee (Manley, 1970; Unekis and Rieselbach, 1980), the panel began to split along party lines (Parker and Parker, 1979; Unekis and Rieselbach, 1979), and it suffered a series of humiliating defeats on the floor (Rudder, 1977b, 1978; Oppenheimer, 1980b).[20] Rudder (1978) concludes that Ways and Means' ability to carry its proposals on the floor has been seriously impaired.

Planned reform and other elements of change mix in distinctive fashions to influence performance at the subcommittee level as well. Price (1978), examining the variety of changes that affected the House Commerce Committee, attributes the shift in behavior of that body's Subcommittee on Oversight and Investigations to the accession of John Moss (D., Cal.) to the subcommittee chair. Though replacing the sitting chairperson was one part of a thoroughgoing reform—the parent Commerce Committee rewrote its rules and reallocated its resources to accommodate its subcommittees—Price concludes that Moss was responsible for significant change: his "goals and methods as a leader . . . made for alterations in the subcommittee's product and performance" (1978: 154). Malbin (1978) reaches a similar conclusion: Subcommittee activity reflected Moss' legislative interests; reform per se was less critical. Again, the moral seems clear: Reform and more general change combine distinctively to influence subcommittees and full committees differently.

On balance, insofar as fragmentary evidence permits generalization, the overall effect of congressional reallocation of internal authority appears to favor decentralization. Although party power has won an occasional dramatic victory, subcommittee autonomy more often carries the day. Committees and subcommittees are distinctive units in an increasingly decentralized structure, and on the whole they have claimed and jealously guarded independent authority. By multiplying the number of power centers involved in policy formulation, reform and change have both increased the need for complicated bargaining and compromise to reach policy agreement and made that agreement more difficult to attain.

C. Accountability and Policy

On the face of it, reforms intended to permit the public to inform itself about congressional commitments and deliberations, and thus to hold members to account more easily, have attained their purposes. All three sets of reforms have opened legislators' accounts and activity to citizen, and media, scrutiny: The Federal Election Commission collects and disseminates candidates' campaign finance data; members file their financial disclosure information and the media publicize it (the number of millionaires in the Senate, for instance, makes good copy); the vast majority, more than 95 percent, of congressional sub- and full committee meetings are open sessions. Yet beneath the surface, the picture is more cloudy. Each set of reforms has seemingly produced one or more unforeseen, and undesirable, consequences.

Campaign finance reform, for example, has led to paradoxical results. On one hand, the new election system—with limits on contributions, but none on expenditures, and with full disclosure provisions—has seemingly helped to entrench incumbents, especially in the House. With presidential campaigns now federally funded in full, private groups, particularly the newly legitimized political action committees (PACs), have channeled their resources into congressional contests. Federal Election Commission and Common Cause studies (see Jacobson, 1980; Alexander, 1980) suggest that these donors prefer the safe course of contributing to incumbents, who hold potentially powerful positions in Congress, to the riskier strategy of funding challengers, who might someday hold prominent posts.[21] Incumbents start with sizable advantages, inherent in the perquisites of office (Mayhew, 1974; Cover, 1977; Fiorina, 1977), and unless their opponents can raise and spend significant sums—at least $150,000 and probably more than $200,000 (Copeland and Patterson, 1978; Jacobson, 1980)—their prospects range from dismal to nil. In the reform period, more than 90 percent of House incumbents seeking reelection held their seats. Senate contests, by contrast, tend to be more visible; in more hetereogeneous, state-wide constituencies, attractive challengers are more likely to emerge and to collect adequate campaign funds. In consequence, Senate incumbent success averaged 77 percent in the 1970s, but fell to 64 and 60 percent, respectively, in 1976 and 1978 (Hinckley, 1980).

On the other hand, public scrutiny—the combination of campaign finance and personal disclosure requirements—has made life more difficult for members of Congress, and record numbers have chosen to retire rather than risk the relentless exposure of their daily routines, and those of their families, to popular examination. Moreover, many of those leaving are relatively young—in their fifties—and have substantial seniority—already holding positions of some prominence and power in Congress. The rise of aggressive investigative reporting in the wake of Watergate no doubt accounts, in part at least, for the increase in attention to the personal lives of legislators; events formerly left unreported— alcoholism, family problems, financial dealings, even brushes with the law—are now "fair game" for the media. In any case, many lawmakers have found the rewards of legislative service lacking and have chosen to pursue careers elsewhere.[22]

Nor has financial disclosure, which House and Senate ethics codes mandated, had much visible effect. There is no evidence to indicate that members are forced to think twice before they act in ways that might leave them vulnerable to charges of conflict of interest. There has been no diminution in the frequency of ethical problems that representatives and senators have encountered since the codes were adopted. In the recent period, the House has censured Charles Diggs and Charles Wilson for their financial dealings, and expelled Michael Myers, snared in the FBI's "Abscam" net; the Senate "denounced" Herman Talmadge. Voters retired Wilson and Richard Kelly, also trapped by Abscam, but renominated others—for example, John Murphy and John Jenrette, alleged Abscam conspirators, and Talmadge. There has been, in short, no reduction in legislators' malfeasance in the postreform period.

Public congressional operations have also had some repercussions that some observers find discomforting. With committee proceedings and voting now matters of public record, lawmakers can no longer hide behind closed-session doors and unrecorded votes; they must act in the open. With constituents and campaign contributors watching, they must take care to protect their electoral flanks. As single-interest groups and PACs become more numerous and more forceful, sitting legislators may be less willing to risk offending any potentially decisive electoral force. Prudence dictates caution, and lawmakers may feel obliged to resist party or presidential calls for policy support. Where previously members could help out undetected, in the quiet of the committee room or on a standing or teller vote on the floor (Froman and Ripley, 1965), at present there are dangers in doing so. The observant, more likely an organized interest than an ordinary citizen, have more influence in the more public setting of contemporary congressional politics. Members may be loath to act at all, preferring to entrench themselves electorally by acting as ombudsmen (Fiorina, 1977), by claiming credit for serving the district, or by limiting their policy making to "position taking" (Mayhew, 1974), choosing sides on substantive questions only when it is safe to do so or obfuscating their stands to minimize the risk of being caught on the wrong side of a policy issue that turns out to be controversial.

In sum, although congressional activity is certainly more accessible to citizens, the fragmentary evidence accumulated in the short time the "sunshine" reforms have been in effect suggests that the public is not really more aware of members of Congress, their activities, or their policy performance. Citizens seem no better able to *recall* their representative (Ferejohn, 1977), though many can *recognize* the incumbent's name when it is presented to them (Mann, 1978; Tedin and Murray, 1979); there has been no visible increase in issue-based voting in congressional elections (Hinckley, 1976b; Mann and Wolfinger, 1980). Incumbency and partisanship more than policy positions shape voter consideration of Congress and congressional candidates. The *potential* for citizen-enforced accountability is real, but to date unrealized. In fact, visibility may contribute to legislative inertia: Rather than acting publicly, lawmakers may find it safer not to act at all.

D. Reform and Policy: The Experience in the States

Congressional reform has attracted most of scholars' recent attention, but reform has proceeded apace in the states as well. Indeed, the state experience in many ways provides a clearer, comparative, opportunity to assess the impact of reform on policy. Some research has, in fact, been directed to the question of whether "reformed" legislatures produce policies superior to those that "unreformed" assemblies enact (or fail to enact). The Citizens Conference on State Legislatures (CCSL) ratings (1971; Burns, 1971) of legislatures —along five dimensions: functionality, accountability, informational capacity, independence, and representativeness—provide a convenient starting place.[23] Legislatures strong on these measures are believed to be "professional" bodies (modeled admittedly after the U.S. Congress) and to possess the capacity to act effectively.

Tests of the relationships between CCSL measures and state legislative policy products have led to divergent conclusions. For example, Ritt (1973, 1977) and Karnig and Sigelman (1975) find little to suggest that "reformed" or "professional" legislatures perform differently, enact significantly different policies, than assemblies of lesser quality. More qualitative studies (Gove, 1973, 1977; Wyner, 1973; Flinn, 1973; Balutis and Butler, 1975) reach comparable conclusions. In short, as Ritt (1977: 199) puts it: ". . . the burden of proof is still on the reformers to show that the changes they advocate . . . influence public policy."

Alternatively, Tatalovich (1978) and Roeder (1979) provide more optimistic, if qualified, results. Although each author agrees that reform (or capacity) taken alone is insufficient to guarantee quality public policies, each finds that in conjunction with facilitating conditions reform may matter. Tatalovich, for example, discovers that legislative quality, though less significant than state socioeconomic conditions or party competition, does have an independent effect on policy outputs, suggesting that reforms that "increase . . . professionalism should have beneficial effects on the quality of public policies enacted" (1978: 231; see also Carmines, 1974). Roeder (1979) draws a similar moral: Where legislative reform occurs in response to state socioeconomic change and income inequality, and together with reform of the executive branch, it has a separate if indirect influence on state policy. In sum, the evidence is mixed: Reform that increases legislative quality (capacity, professionalism) cannot hurt, but it may not help much either.[24]

V. CONCLUSION: WHAT HATH REFORM WROUGHT (OR WREAKED)?

This review of developments and consequences of an unprecedented period of reform makes clear, at the very least, that conscious effort to redesign legislatures is part of, and quite similar to, the general pattern of American politics. Both as a substantive issue and as a means to an end—a revised and presumably "better" policy process—reform is best understood as an integral element of an ongoing political system, characterized as much by unplanned change, or evolution, as by any revolutionary recasting of legislative institutions. This central fact goes far to explain both the nature of the reforms adopted and the consequences of those reforms for policy formation, enactment, and implementation.

As a subject of the legislative process, reform looks very much like most other policy domains. Legislators—motivated by power, policy, and reelection goals—are the prime movers for reform, and they tend to treat it, as a substantive issue, in much the same way as they deal with other matters. Reforms have been incremental not wholesale, individually modest not radical reactions to events and "crises," not products of comprehensive planning. Specifically, there was little talk of the relative merits of a Congress compatible with the executive force, literary, or legislative supremacy notions. To the contrary, members came to recognize their inability to cope with the dominant executive, to formulate successful programs, or to meet the public's ethical expectations. Citizen concerns complemented these member perceptions, leading the legislators to act, in response to internal and external pressures, as circumstances dictated. Policy failure in Vietnam—the product of executive leadership and legislative acquiescence—inspired the War Powers Act. Congressional ineffectiveness led lawmakers, liberals and conservatives, to reform the budget process and induced Democrats to move to curb the committees. Given the opportunity that these developments offered, junior members, lacking in power, leaped in to reallocate authority not only to their party leaders but also to themselves. The dramatic decline in popular approbation for government in general, and Congress in particular, rooted in Watergate and legislative scandals, created the climate for campaign finance, financial disclosure, and "sunshine" reforms. Reforms, in short, were adaptive and consolidative, intended to enhance congressional responsibility, responsiveness, and accountability, but simultaneously were political, pragmatic, and more-or-less spontaneous responses to seemingly irresistable forces.

The fate of the reform impetus, when the conditions that precipitated it faded in intensity and receded into history, makes clear the incremental nature and ephemeral quality of reformism. After 1977, members seemed to feel that enough had been done To be sure, some conditions demanded response. A loophole in the Senate filibuster rule, which permitted postcloture "filibusters by amendment," was quickly closed in 1979. When ethical failings surfaced, the members moved rapidly to "censure," "denounce," or even expel their wayward colleagues. But on the whole the reform spirit flagged. A series of proposals—from the House (Obey) Commission on Administrative Review (1977) and the (Patterson) Select Committee on Committees (1979-1980)—designed to clarify the confusing committee jurisdictions, to create an Energy Committee, and in general to make the House more efficient, and more effective, was brushed aside after perfunctory consideration. Similar, but even more modest, moves in the Senate received the same treatment. In the absence of numerous facilitating conditions—supportive members, the press of public opinion, the stimulus of national and international events—reform is likely to founder. Such conditions were present between 1970 and 1977, but faded rapidly thereafter; the tide of congressional reform ebbed with them.[25]

Given that reform programs resemble other policy areas in terms of their incremental content and mode of adoption, it is not surprising that their impact has been uncertain and unpredictable. The numerous reforms adopted in Congress have often been incompatible with one another. Reformers have won some victories, attaining their goals; suffered some reverses, failing to achieve their purposes; and often discovered that their alterations have led to quite unexpected and frequently undesirable results. Indeed, such is the case with each set of reforms Congress enacted.

Specifically, Congress is most certainly positioned to oppose the President, but given the rapid change in membership and the shifting push of events, it is not clear that there will be steady pressure on the members to use their potentially powerful weapons. The ultimate consequences of the War Powers and Budget Acts, coupled with the increase in Congress' analytic capacity, remain impossible to predict; the legislature may, or may not, be a more responsible policy maker.

Similarly, it is equally certain that it is easier to hold Congress accountable since the passage of campaign finance, financial disclosure, and public operations standards. More *can* be known about congressional deliberations, but there is no reason to believe that more actually *is* known, at least by ordinary citizens. Finally, structural change has produced a mixed pattern of results. The new party and leadership powers are in place, but seldom employed decisively. Junior members have secured advantageous legislative terrain, but have used it differently in different committees (and subcommittees) and on different policy questions.

On balance, Congress has become more decentralized, more responsive to a multitude of forces inside and outside its halls, and as a result more hard pressed to formulate and enact coherent, responsible public policies. Structural change has enlarged the number of power centers, in particular the subcommittees, involved in policy making, and party power cannot mobilize them in support of programs that either challenge or sustain the President. "Sunshine" changes have left members visible and vulnerable to attentive publics, most often organized interests. More independent members, faced with more difficult policy choices—the "politics of scarcity" requires allocation of sacrifice rather than permitting dispensation of largesse—on issues that evoke great emotion—abortion and energy, for example—find it politically expedient to avoid risky actions. To do so, of course, is to duck controversy: to defer to others, to delay, or to obfuscate. In consequence, Congress enters the 1980s seemingly less willing or able to frame and fight for its policy preferences. Paradoxically, greater individual influence somehow sums to reduced institutional authority.

In short, Congress, and in all likelihood state legislatures as well, reform themselves in much the same way, and with much the same results, as they make public policy on more substantive matters. In the absence of any overarching vision of what the legislature should be, reform, when it comes, is piecemeal and episodic, swept along by powerful tides of more general political change. As long as this situation persists, and there is scant reason to suspect that circumstances will alter, reform will remain an uncertain activity. Legislatures may well, for lack of a viable alternative, continue to "muddle through" as part of the characteristic and classic pattern of American politics and policy making.[26]

NOTES

1. The most dramatic instances of reform have occurred in Congress, although change has restructured state legislatures as well. Moreover, most systematic investigations of reform have focused on the national legislature; the literature on the states is fragmentary and inconclusive. Thus, major attention here is devoted to Congress.
2. For an overview of these events and their consequences, see Davidson et al. (1966); Ornstein (1976); Dodd (1977); Rieselbach (1977a); Ornstein and Rohde (1978); and Patterson (1978). A number of collections—de Grazia (1966a); Ornstein (1974, 1975a); Dodd and Oppenheimer (1977a); Welch and Peters (1977); and Rieselbach (1977b, 1978)—contain much useful material on these issues.
3. Huntington (1973: 7) captures the dilemma precisely: "If Congress legislates, it subordinates itself to the executive; if it refuses to legislate, it alienates itself from

public opinion. Congress can assert its power or it can pass laws; but it cannot do both." Reforms, at least those guided by a broad view of Congress' place in national politics, make this choice explicitly.

4. Much writing on reform reflects this short-term focus (e.g., Clark, 1965; McInnis, 1966; Committee for Economic Development, 1970; New York City Bar Association, 1970; Twentieth Century Fund, 1974). So, too, does almost all testimony before congressional committees (see, inter alia, U.S. House, 1973). Finally, two studies of state legislative reform (Hedlund and Hamm, 1976; Moncrief and Jewell, 1980) find no consensus among lawmakers about either the intent or accomplishments of reform.

5. Some events, however, produce few or even quite unexpected consequences. Court-enforced reapportionment—following the "one person, one vote" principle applied to the states in *Reynolds v. Sims* (1964) and to Congress in *Wesberry v. Sanders* (1964) and *Kirkpatrick v. Preisler* (1969)—surely altered the population characteristics of legislative districts (see Noragon, 1972; *Congressional Quarterly Weekly Report,* 1978, *36:* 973) but produced rather modest effects on legislative politics and policies (e.g., Hacker, 1964; Erikson, 1971; Bullock, 1975; Bicker, 1971; Hanson and Crew, 1973; but cf. Feig, 1978).

6. Congress apparently had so little faith in its capacity to oppose the President that it wrote the law in such a way that legislative *inaction* triggers the troop withdrawal. That is, although the chief executive can introduce forces into hostilities on his own initiative, he is obligated to withdraw them unless Congress acts positively—by declaring war or enacting some legislative authorization of the conflict—to approve the commitment.

7. As with the war powers procedures, the anti-impoundment provisions were written to permit Congress to get its way with a minimum of effort. To rescind, that is, cancel, appropriations, the President must secure an approving resolution from both houses; inaction by either house obligates the chief executive to spend the money. To defer, that is, delay, expenditures is less difficult; a presidential request to defer is approved automatically unless either house votes a resolution of disapproval.

8. Similar developments have occurred in a number of states; see Bradley (1980); Balutis (1975); Wissel et al. (1976); Worthley (1976, 1977).

9. The committees were Foreign Relations in the Senate, Foreign Affairs in the House, and the Armed Services, Appropriations, and Intelligence panels in each chamber.

10. Both chambers, either house, or even a single committee—through requirements that an agency "come into agreement" with it before acting—can exercise the veto, usually by enacting resolutions of disapproval (although the statute may permit inaction to indicate disapproval) within a specified (usually between 30 and 90 days) period. The one-house veto, providing for either House or Senate to block executive action, remains controversial; all recent Presidents have resisted it, as an unconstitutional derogation of the separation-of-powers principle, but the courts have steadfastly refused to resolve the issue (Bolton, 1977).

11. A considerable quantity of reform, or "experimentation," has been proposed, or adopted, to improve legislative structure and performance in the states. These are summarized in the leading legislative process texts (Keefe and Ogul, 1977; Jewell and Patterson, 1977; Van Der Slik, 1977) and treated in greater detail in a number of more specialized works (Herzberg and Rosenthal, 1971; Robinson, 1973; Hedlund and Hamm, 1977; Lyons and Thomas, 1978; Rosenthal 1974a). Jewell (1981) provides a comprehensive review of "the state of state legislative research."

12. For a summary of state experiments with control of campaign finance, see Alexander (1980, chap. 7).
13. For an imaginative, but largely ignored to date, plea to treat "reforms as experiments," as hypotheses to be tested scientifically and abandoned if disconfirmed, see Campbell (1969).
14. Just to be certain, Congress added an amendment, by overwhelming margins in each chamber, to the Defense Department (DOD) appropriations bill forbidding the expenditure of any funds for "any activities involving Angola directly or indirectly." Since CIA funds were hidden in the DOD appropriation, this action effectively removed the legal basis for either overt or covert intervention in Angola.
15. The future remains uncertain, however. Ernest Hollings (D., S.C.) replaced Muskie, departing to become Secretary of State, in the chair in 1980. Bellman announced his retirement at roughly the same time. The relationship the new leadership establishes within the committee and with the full Senate will determine whether the panel can retain its favorable position.
16. This is not to suggest that there was no conflict between the budget and other committees (see, for example, Fisher 1977a, 1977b; Rudder, 1977a; Havemann, 1978; Schick, 1974), but rather to note that the Senate panel sought accommodation rather than confrontation during the early phases of the new process.
17. In addition, some critics have speculated that the law inadvertently gives the President the power to rescind funds, temporarily, for policy purposes, authority never previously acknowledged. That is, the chief executive can propose recessions that effectively withhold funds for the 45 days until congressional inaction compels him to release the monies.
18. Peabody (1980) finds a similar decline in Senate leaders' ability to manage the upper chamber. Current congressional leaders—House Speaker O'Neill and Senate Majority Leader Byrd—freely acknowledge their weaknesses; see Arieff (1980).
19. Such sweeping generalizations, of course, disguise wide variations among subcommittees. See Sec. III.B.
20. For example, dissident member Democrats, abetted by a Caucus decision to instruct the Rules Committee, reversed the committee on the floor and repealed the oil depletion allowance. More devastating still, the committee's major 1977 energy tax bill was destroyed by amendments on the floor, exposed under an open rule.
21. This concentration of contributions to sitting members may alter in the 1980s. The rise of ideological groups, such as the National Conservative Political Action Committee (NCPAC) and the evangelical Christian movement's Moral Majority (see the four-part series, *The New York Times,* August 17–20, 1980), that support challengers, or at least oppose incumbents, became visible in 1980.
22. For example, Rep. John J. Cavanaugh (D., Neb.), 35 years old, well regarded in his district and in the House, retired in 1980 after two terms, in part because the "continuous campaigning is debilitating and the campaign financing is corrupting" (quoted in Gamarekian, 1980). See also Rep. Otis Pike's (D., N.Y.) "retirement speech" (*Congressional Quarterly Weekly Report,* 1978, *36:* 528–529).
23. There is considerable conceptual confusion in this literature. The CCSL indicators actually seem to measure legislative quality or capacity rather than "reform" or "effectiveness" (see Tatalovich, 1978). Nonetheless, to the extent that the attributes of quality or professionalism are associated with particular policy outcomes, reformers seeking to promote such results may discover which structural changes are worth working for.

24. For instance, observers (e.g., Ray, 1974; Rosenthal, 1974b) believe that rapid personnel turnover undercuts legislative professionalism. Bernick and Wiggins (1978), however, find that personal problems—family and financial—far outweigh professional considerations—low pay, poor facilities, inadequate support—in lawmakers' decisions to retire from office. Thus, reformers' proposals, which look to the latter difficulties, may be misguided.

25. State legislative reform similarly seems to be the product of numerous forces, from inside and outside the assembly, and to have had various effects, from consequential to trivial. See, for instance, Winters (1977) and McDowell (1977).

26. It may seem that congressional policy making in the first year of the Reagan administration belies this line of argument. Actually, the events of 1981 buttress a central pillar of this analysis of legislative change: Congress remains a powerful institution that *can,* and will, do what its members want to do. And it is obvious that a determined majority was eager to enact the Reagan economic vision in the early days of the 97th Congress.

    However, despite the dramatic and skillfully engineered administration victories, it seems premature to conclude that the old, prereform mode of conducting congressional business has revived on Capitol Hill. If Reagan's solid electoral victory in 1980 conferred any mandate, it was surely that new economic policies, to remedy the conspicuous failures of the Carter programs, were worth trying. The election, moreover, gave the new administration working majorities in both chambers, and the triumphant Republicans were particularly eager to solidify their party's status in the nation, and in consequence to support their President. Against this backdrop, Reagan's personal attractiveness and ability as a "communicator;" a virtually exclusive focus on the economy, the issue most likely to maximize support for the administration; an innovative use of the 1974 Budget Act's reconciliation procedure; and adept use of good, old-fashioned political bargaining enabled the President to assemble a winning coalition on economic issues.

    The conditions that facilitated this virtuoso performance are unlikely to recur readily in so pure a form. Indeed, by late 1981, the congressional response to administration initiatives—on Social Security, on a second round of budget cuts, on arms sales to Saudi Arabia, and on tax exemptions for private schools that discriminate—suggested a more likely, and more assertive, legislative performance. As social (abortion, busing), environmental (Clean Air Act revisions), international (East-West relations) and the "New Federalism" issues—which split each party, arouse strong ideological passion, and pit "Snowbelt" against "Sunbelt"—have risen on the political agenda, reelection concerns, committee rivalries, and policy individualism seem closer to the surface in Congress.

    In short, it is too soon to discount the effect of reform and change on congressional policy making. The legislature remains a representative institution. Where there is consensus in the country, Congress will reflect it; institutional structures and processes cannot deter its actions when a majority of its members, for whatever motives, want to act. Where agreement is lacking, as it most often is, the sort of congressional politics projected here is likely to appear. On these divisive issues, recent change (whether evolutionary or reform-induced), especially increased decentralization and greater member independence, seem likely to make congressional action more difficult. Thus, the odds continue to favor instability and uncertainty in Congress's policy formulation; if such is the case, reform and change will have contributed significantly to the shape of legislative politics.

REFERENCES

Aberbach, J. D. (1979). Changes in congressional oversight. *American Behavioral Scientist 22*: 493-515.

Alexander, H. E. (1980). *Financing Politics: Money, Elections and Political Reform,* 2nd ed. Congressional Quarterly Press, Washington, DC.

American Political Science Association, Committee on Political Parties (1950). *Toward a More Responsible Two-Party System.* Rinehart, New York.

Arieff, I. B. (1980). House, Senate chiefs attempt to lead a changed Congress. *Congressional Quarterly Weekly Report 38*: 2695-2700.

Asher, H. B., and Weisberg, H. F. (1978). Voting change in Congress: Some dynamic perspectives on an evolutionary process. *American Journal of Political Science 22*: 391-425.

Balutis, A. P. (1975). Legislative staffing: A view from the states. In *Legislative Staffing: A Comparative Perspective,* J. Heaphey and A. Balutis (Eds.). Halstead Press, New York, pp. 106-137.

—— (1977). Legislative staffing: Does it make a difference? In *Legislative Reform and Public Policy,* S. Welch and J. G. Peters (Eds.). Praeger, New York, pp. 128-143.

Balutis, A. P., and Butler, D. K. (Eds.). (1975). *The Political Pursestrings: The Role of the Legislature in the Budgetary Process.* Wiley, New York.

Berg, J. (1978). The effects of seniority reform on three House committees. In *Legislative Reform: The Policy Impact,* L. N. Rieselbach (Ed.). Lexington Books, Lexington, MA, pp. 49-59.

Bernick, E. L., and Wiggins, C. W. (1978). Legislative reform and legislative turnover. In *Legislative Reform: The Policy Impact,* L. N. Rieselbach (Ed.). Lexington Books, Lexington, MA, pp. 23-34.

Bicker, W. E. (1971). The effects of malapportionment in the states—a mistrial. In *Reapportionment in the 1970s,* N. W. Polsby (Ed.). University of California Press, Berkeley, pp. 151-210.

Bolling, R. (1965). *House Out of Order.* Dutton, New York.

Bolton, J. R. (1977). *The Legislative Veto: Unseparating the Powers.* American Enterprise Institute, Washington, DC.

Bradley, R. B. (1980). Motivations in legislative information use. *Legislative Studies Quarterly 5*: 393-406.

Bullock, C. S., III (1975). Redistricting and congressional stability, 1962-1972. *Journal of Politics 37*: 569-575.

—— (1978). Congress in the sunshine. In *Legislative Reform: The Policy Impact,* L. N. Rieselbach (Ed.). Lexington Books, Lexington, MA, pp. 209-221.

Burnham, J. (1959). *Congress and the American Tradition.* Regnery, Chicago.

Burns, J. M. (1949). *Congress on Trial.* Harper, New York.

—— (1963). *The Deadlock of Democracy.* Prentice-Hall, Englewood Cliffs, NJ.

Burns, J. (1971). *The Sometime Governments.* Bantam, New York.

Burstein, P. (1979). Party balance, replacement of legislators, and federal government expenditures, 1941-1976. *Western Political Quarterly 32*: 203-208.

Burstein, P., and Freudenberg, W. (1977). Ending the Vietnam war: Components of change in Senate voting on Vietnam war bills. *American Journal of Sociology 82*: 991-1006.

Campbell, D. T. (1969). Reforms as experiments. *American Psychologist 24*: 409-429.

Carmines, E. G. (1974). The mediating influence of state legislatures on the linkage between intraparty competition and welfare policies. *American Political Science Review 68*: 1118-1124.

Cavanagh, T. E. (1980). The deinstitutionalization of the House. Paper presented to the Everett McKinley Dirksen Congressional Leadership Research Center–Sam Rayburn Library Conference, Understanding Congressional Leadership: The State of the Art, Washington, D.C., June 10–11.

Citizens Conference on State Legislatures (1971). *State Legislatures: An Evaluation of Their Effectiveness.* Praeger, New York.

Clark, J. S. (1964). *Congress: The Sapless Branch.* Harper & Row, New York.

—— (Ed.) (1965). *Congressional Reform: Problems and Prospects.* Crowell, New York.

Clausen, A. R., and Van Horn, C. E. (1977). The congressional response to a decade of change, 1963-1972. *Journal of Politics 39*: 624-666.

Cohen, R. E. (1980). Congress steps up use of the legislative veto. *National Journal 12*: 1473-1477.

Committee for Economic Development (1970). *Making Congress More Effective.* Committee for Economic Development, New York.

Congressional Quarterly (1976). *Guide to Congress,* 2nd ed. Congressional Quarterly, Washington, DC.

—— (1977). *Congress and the Nation,* vol. IV. Congressional Quarterly, Washington, DC.

Cook, T. E. (1979). Legislature vs. legislator: A note on the paradox of congressional support. *Legislative Studies Quarterly 4*: 43-52.

Copeland, G. W., and Patterson, S. C. (1978). Money in congressional elections. In *Legislative Reform: The Policy Impact,* L. N. Rieselbach (Ed.). Lexington Books, Lexington, MA, pp. 195-208.

Cover, A. D. (1977). One good term deserves another: The advantage of incumbency in congressional elections. *American Journal of Political Science 21*: 523-541.

Crabb, C. V., Jr., and Holt, P. M. (1980). *Invitation to Struggle: Congress, the President and Foreign Policy.* Congressional Quarterly Press, Washington, DC.

Davidson, R. H., Kovenock, D. M., and O'Leary, M. K. (1966). *Congress in Crisis: Politics and Congressional Reform.* Wadsworth, Belmont, CA.

Davidson, R. H., and Oleszek, W. J. (1976). Adaptation and consolidation: Structural innovation in the House of Representatives. *Legislative Studies Quarterly 1*: 37-65.

—— (1977). *Congress Against Itself.* Indiana University Press, Bloomington.

de Grazia, A. (1965). *Republic in Crisis.* Federal Legal Publications, New York.

—— (Coord.) (1966a). *Congress: The First Branch of Government.* American Enterprise Institute, Washington, DC.

—— (1966b). Toward a new model of Congress. In *Congress: The First Branch of Government,* A. de Grazia (Coord.). American Enterprise Institute, Washington, DC.

Deckard, B. S. (1976). Political upheaval and congressional voting: The effects of the 1960's on voting patterns in the House of Representatives. *Journal of Politics 38*: 326-345.

Deering, C. J. (1980). Adaptation and consolidation in Congress's foreign policy committees: Evolution in the seventies. Paper presented to the Annual Meeting of the Midwest Political Science Association, Chicago, April 24-26.

Deering, C. J., and Smith, S. S. (1980). Majority party leadership and the effects of decentralization. Paper presented to the Everett McKinley Dirksen Congressional Leadership Research Center–Sam Rayburn Library Conference, Understanding Congressional Leadership: The State of the Art, Washington, DC, June 10-11.

Dodd, L. C. (1977). Congress and the quest for power. In *Congress Reconsidered,* L. C. Dodd and B. I. Oppenheimer (Eds.). Praeger, New York, pp. 269-307.

Dodd, L. C., and Oppenheimer, B. I. (Eds.) (1977a). *Congress Reconsidered.* Praeger, New York.

—— (1977b). The House in Transition. In *Congress Reconsidered,* L. C. Dodd and B. I. Oppenheimer (Eds.). Praeger, New York, pp. 21–53.

Dodd, L. C., and Schott, R. L. (1979). *Congress and the Administrative State.* Wiley, New York.

Ellwood, J. W., and Thurber, J. A. (1977a). The new congressional budget process: Its causes, consequences, and possible success. In *Legislative Reform and Public Policy,* S. Welch and J. G. Peters (Eds.). Praeger, New York, pp. 82–97.

—— (1977b). The new congressional budget process: The hows and whys of House-Senate differences. In *Congress Reconsidered,* L. C. Dodd and B. I. Oppehneimer (Eds.). Praeger, New York, pp. 163-192.

Erikson, R. S. (1971). The partisan impact of reapportionment. *Midwest Journal of Political Science 15:* 57-71.

Feig, D. G. (1978). Expenditures in the American states: The impact of court-ordered legislative reapportionment. *American Politics Quarterly 6:* 309-324.

Fenno, R. F., Jr. (1973). *Congressmen in Committees.* Little, Brown, Boston.

—— (1975). If, as Ralph Nader says, Congress is "the broken branch," how come we love our congressmen so much? In *Congress in Change: Evolution and Reform,* N. J. Ornstein (Ed.). Praeger, New York, pp. 277-287.

—— (1978). *Home style: Representatives in their districts.* Little, Brown, Boston.

Ferejohn, J. A. (1977). On the decline of competition in congressional elections. *American Political Science Review 71:* 166-176.

Finley, J. J. (1975). The 1974 congressional initiative in budget making. *Public Administration Review 35:* 270-278.

Fiorina, M. P. (1977). *Congress—Keystone of the Washington Establishment.* Yale University Press, New Haven, CT.

Fisher, L. (1975). *Presidential Spending Power.* Princeton University Press, Princeton, NJ.

—— (1977a). Congressional budget reform: Committee conflicts. Paper presented to the Annual Meeting of the Midwest Political Science Association, Chicago, April 21-23.

—— (1977b). Congressional budget reform: The first two years. *Harvard Journal on Legislation 14:* 413-457.

Flinn, T. A. (1973). The Ohio General Assembly: A developmental analysis. In *State Legislative Innovation,* J. A. Robinson (Ed.). Praeger, New York, pp. 226-278.

Fox, H. W., Jr., and Hammond, S. W. (1977). *Congressional staffs: The invisible force in American lawmaking.* Free Press, New York.

Franck, T., and Weisband, E. (1979). *Foreign Policy by Congress.* Oxford University Press, New York.

Frantzich, S. E. (1979). Computerized information technology in the U.S. House of Representatives. *Legislative Studies Quarterly 4:* 255-280.

Freed, B. F. (1975). House reforms enhance subcommittee power. *Congressional Quarterly Weekly Report 33:* 2407-2412.

Froman, L. A., Jr., and Ripley, R. B. (1965). Conditions for party leadership: The case of the House Democrats. *American Political Science Review 59:* 52-63.

Gamarekian, B. (1980). A congressman who's going home again. *The New York Times,* August 31, 1980, p. 20.

Gilmour, R. S. (1980). The new congressional oversight and administrative leadership. Paper presented to the Everett McKinley Dirksen Congressional Leadership Research Center–Sam Rayburn Library Conference, Understanding Congressional Leadership: The State of the Art, Washington, DC, June 10-11.

Gove, S. K. (1973). Policy implications of legislative reform in Illinois. In *State Legislative Innovation,* J. A. Robinson (Ed.). Praeger, New York, pp. 101-135.

—— (1977). The implications of legislative reform in Illinois. In *Legislative Reform and Public Policy,* S. Welch and J. G. Peters (Eds.). Praeger, New York, pp. 174-188.

Hacker, A. (1964). *Congressional Districting,* rev. ed. Brookings Institution, Washington, DC.

Haeberle, S. H. (1978). The institutionalization of the subcommittee in the U. S. House of Representatives. *Journal of Politics 40*: 1054-1065.

Hammond, S. W. (1978). Congressional change and reform: Staffing the Congress. In *Legislative Reform: The Policy Impact,* L. N. Rieselbach (Ed.). Lexington Books, Lexington, MA, pp. 183-193.

Hanson, R. A., and Crew, R. E., Jr. (1973). The policy impact of reapportionment. *Law and Society Review 8*: 69-93.

Harris, J. P. (1965). *Congressional Control of Administration.* Doubleday Anchor, Garden City, NY.

Havemann, J. (1978). *Congress and the Budget.* Indiana University Press, Bloomington.

Hedlund, R. D., and Hamm, K. E. (1976). Conflict and perceived group benefits from legislative rules changes. *Legislative Studies Quarterly 1*: 181-199.

—— (1977). Institutional development and legislative effectiveness: Rules changes in the Wisconsin Assembly. In *Comparative Legislative Reforms and Innovations,* A. Baaklini and J. Heaphey (Eds.). State University of New York Press, New York, pp. 173-213.

Herzberg, D. G., and Rosenthal, A. (Eds.) (1971). *Strengthening the States: Essays on Legislative Reform.* Doubleday, Garden City, NY.

Hinckley, B. (1970). *The Seniority System in Congress.* Indiana University Press, Bloomington.

—— (1976a). Seniority, 1975: Old theories confront new facts. *British Journal of Political Science 6*: 383-399.

—— (1976b). Issues, information costs and congressional elections. *American Politics Quarterly 4*: 131-152.

—— (1980). House reelections and Senate defeats: The role of the challenger. *British Journal of Political Science 10*: 441-460.

Holt, P. (1978). *The War Powers Resolution.* American Enterprise Institute, Washington, DC.

Huddleston, M. W. (1979). Thraining lobsters to fly: Assessing the impacts of the 1974 congressional budget reform. Paper presented to the Annual Meeting of the Midwest Political Science Association, Chicago, April 19-21.

Huntington, S. P. (1973). Congressional responses to the twentieth century. In *The Congress and America's Future,* 2nd ed., D. B. Truman (Ed.). Prentice-Hall, Englewood Cliffs, NJ, pp. 6-38.

Ippolito, D. S. (1978). *The Budget and National Politics.* Freeman, San Francisco.

Jacobson, G. C. (1980). *Money in Congressional Elections.* Yale University Press, New Haven, CT.

Jewell, M. E. (1981). The state of U.S. state legislative research. *Legislative Studies Quarterly 6*: 1-25.

Jewell, M. E., and Patterson, S. C. (1977). *The Legislative Process in the United States,* 3rd ed. Random House, New York.

Jones, C. O. (1976). Why Congress can't do policy analysis (or words to that effect). *Policy Analysis 2*: 251-264.

—— (1977a). Will reform change Congress? In *Congress Reconsidered,* L. C. Dodd and B. I. Oppenheimer (Eds.). Praeger, New York, pp. 247-260.

—— (1977b). How reform changes Congress. In *Legislative Reform and Public Policy*, S. Welch and J. G. Peters (Eds.). Praeger, New York, pp. 11-29.

—— (1980). House leadership in an age of reform. Paper presented to the Everett McKinley Dirksen Congressional Leadership Research Center–Sam Rayburn Library Conference, Understanding Congressional Leadership: The State of the Art. Washington, DC, June 10-11.

Kaiser, F. M. (1978). Congressional change and foreign policy: The House Committee on International Relations. In *Legislative Reform: The Policy Impact*, L. N. Rieselbach (Ed.). Lexington Books, Lexington, MA, pp. 61-71.

Karnig, A. K., and Sigelman, L. (1975). State legislative reform and public policy: Another look. *Western Political Quarterly 28*: 548-552.

Keefe, W. J., and Ogul, M. S. (1977). *The American Legislative Process*, 4th ed. Prentice-Hall, Englewood Cliffs, NJ.

LeLoup, L. T. (1977). *Budgetary Politics*. King's Court Press, Brunswick, OH.

—— (1979a). Budgeting in the U.S. Senate: Old ways of doing new things. Paper presented to the Annual Meeting of the Midwest Political Science Association, Chicago, April 19-21.

—— (1979b). Process versus policy: The U.S. House Budget Committee. *Legislative Studies Quarterly 4*: 227-254.

Loomis, B. A. (1980). The "me" decade and the changing context of House leadership. Paper presented to the Everett McKinley Dirksen Congressional Leadership Research Center–Sam Rayburn Library Conference, Understanding Congressional Leadership: The State of the Art, Washington, DC, June 10-11.

Lyons, W., and Thomas, L. W. (1978). *Legislative Oversight: A Three State Study*. University of Tennessee–Bureau of Public Administration, Knoxville, TN.

McDowell, J. L. (1977). Legislative reform in Indiana: The promise and the product. In *Legislative Reform and Public Policy*, S. Welch and J. G. Peters (Eds.). Praeger, New York, pp. 157–173.

McInnis, M. (Ed.) (1966). *We Propose: A Modern Congress*. McGraw-Hill, New York.

Malbin, M. J. (1978). The Bolling Committee revisited: Energy oversight on an investigative subcommittee. Paper presented to the Annual Meeting of the American Political Science Association, New York, Aug. 31-Sept. 3.

—— (1980). *Unelected Representatives: Congressional Staff and the Future of Representative Government*. Basic Books, New York.

Manley, J. F. (1970). *The Politics of Finance*. Little, Brown, Boston.

Mann, T. E. (1978). *Unsafe at Any Margin: Interpreting Congressional Elections*. American Enterprise Institute, Washington, DC.

Mann, T. E., and Wolfinger, R. E. (1980). Candidates and parties in congressional elections. *American Political Science Review 74*: 617-632.

Mayhew, D. R. (1974). *Congress: The Electoral Connection*. Yale University Press, New Haven, CT.

Moncrief, G., and Jewell, M. E. (1980). Legislators' perceptions of reform in three states. *American Politics Quarterly 8*: 106-127.

Munselle, W. G. (1978). Presidential impoundment and congressional reform. In *Legislative Reform: The Policy Impact*, L. N. Rieselbach (Ed.). Lexington Books, Lexington, MA, pp. 173-181.

New York City Bar Association (1970). *Congress and the Public Trust*. Atheneum, New York.

Noragon, J. L. (1972). Congressional redistricting and population composition, 1964–1970. *Midwest Journal of Political Science 16*: 295-302.

Ogul, M. S. (1976). *Congress Oversees the Bureaucracy: Studies in Legislative Supervision.* University of Pittsburgh Press, Pittsburgh, PA.

Oleszek, W. J. (1977). A perspective on congressional reform. In *Legislative Reform and Public Policy,* S. Welch and J. G. Peters (Eds.). Praeger, New York, pp. 3-10.

Oppenheimer, B. I. (1978). Policy implications of Rules Committee reforms. In *Legislative Reform: The Policy Impact,* L. N. Rieselbach (Ed.). Lexington Books, Lexington, MA, pp. 91-104.

—— (1980a). The changing relationship between House leadership and the Committee on Rules. Paper presented to the Everett McKinley Dirksen Congressional Leadership Research Center–Sam Rayburn Library Conference, Understanding Congressional Leadership: The State of the Art, Washington, DC, June 10-11.

—— (1980b). Policy effects of U.S. House reform: Decentralization and the capacity to resolve energy issues. *Legislative Studies Quarterly 5*: 5-30.

Orfield, G. (1975). *Congressional Power: Congress and Social Change.* Harcourt Brace Jovanovich, New York.

Ornstein, N. J. (Ed.) (1974). Changing Congress: The committee system. *Annals of the American Academy of Political and Social Science 411*: 1-176.

—— (Ed.) (1975a). *Congress in Change: Evolution and Reform.* Praeger, New York.

—— (1975b). Causes and consequences of congressional change: Subcommittee reforms in the House of Representatives, 1970-1973. In *Congress in Change: Evolution and Reform,* N. J. Ornstein (Ed.). Praeger, New York, pp. 88-114.

—— (1976). The Democrats reform power in the House of Representatives, 1969-1975. In *America in the Seventies,* A. Sindler (Ed.). Little, Brown, Boston, pp. 1-48.

Ornstein, N. J., and Rohde, D. W. (1974). The strategy of reform: Recorded teller voting in the House of Representatives. Paper presented to the Annual Meeting of the Midwest Political Science Association, Chicago, April 25-27.

—— (1975). Seniority and future power in Congress. In *Congress in Change: Evolution and Reform,* N. J. Ornstein (Ed.). Praeger, New York, pp. 72-87.

—— (1977). Shifting forces, changing rules and political outcomes: The impact of congressional change on four House committees. In *New Perspectives on the House of Representatives,* 3rd ed., R. L. Peabody and N. W. Polsby (Eds.). Rand McNally, Chicago, pp. 186-269.

—— (1978). Political parties and congressional reform. In *Parties and Elections in an Anti-Party Age,* J. Fishel (Ed.). Indiana University Press, Bloomington, pp. 280-294.

Parker, G. R. (1977). Some themes in congressional unpopularity. *American Journal of Political Science 21*: 93-109.

Parker, G. R., and Davidson, R. H. (1979). Why do Americans love their congressmen so much more than their Congress? *Legislative Studies Quarterly 4*: 53-61.

Parker, G. R., and Parker, S. L. (1979). Factions in committees: The U.S. House of Representatives. *American Political Science Review 73*: 85-102.

Parris, J. H. (1979). The Senate reorganizes its committees, 1977. *Political Science Quarterly 94*: 319-337.

Patterson, S. C. (1977). Conclusions: On the study of legislative reform. In *Legislative Reform and Public Policy,* S. Welch and J. G. Peters (Eds.). Praeger, New York, pp. 214-222.

—— (1978). The semi-sovereign Congress. In *The New American Political System,* A. King (Ed.). American Enterprise Institute, Washington, DC, pp. 125-177.

Peabody, R. L. (1980). Senate party leadership: From the 1950s to the 1980s. Paper presented to the Everett McKinley Dirksen Congressional Leadership Research

Center–Sam Rayburn Library Conference, Understanding Congressional Leadership: The State of the Art, Washington, DC, June 10-11.

Pfiffner, J. P. (1977). Executive control and the congressional budget. Paper presented to the Annual Meeting of the Midwest Political Science Association, Chicago, April 21-23.

Pious, R. M. (1979). *The American Presidency.* Basic Books, New York.

Price, D. E. (1971). Professionals and "entrepreneurs": Staff orientations and policy making on three Senate committees. *Journal of Politics 33*: 316-336.

—— (1978). The impact of reform: The House Subcommittee on Oversight and Investigations. In *Legislative Reform: The Policy Impact,* L. N. Rieselbach (Ed.). Lexington Books, Lexington, MA, pp. 133-157.

Ray, D. (1974). Membership stability in three state legislatures: 1893-1969. *American Political Science Review 68*: 106-113.

Regens, J. L., and Stein, R. M. (1979). Congressional oversight behavior: Components of committee-based activity. Paper presented to the Annual Meeting of the American Political Science Association, Washington, DC, Aug. 31-Sept. 3.

Rieselbach, L. N. (1975). Congressional reform: Some policy implications. *Policy Studies Journal 4*: 180-188.

—— (1977a). *Congressional Reform in the Seventies.* General Learning Press, Morristown, NJ.

—— (Ed.) (1977b). Symposium on legislative reform. *Policy Studies Journal 5*: 394-497.

—— (Ed.) (1978). *Congressional Reform: The Policy Impact.* Lexington Books, Lexington, MA.

Ripley, R. B. (1969). *Power in the Senate.* St. Martin's Press, New York.

—— (1978). *Congress: Process and Policy,* 2nd ed. Norton, New York.

Ritt, L. G. (1973). State legislative reform: Does it matter? *American Politics Quarterly 1*: 499-510.

—— (1977). The policy impact of state legislative reform: A 50-state analysis. In *Legislative Reform and Public Policy,* S. Welch and J. G. Peters (Eds.). Praeger, New York, pp. 189-200.

Robinson, J. A. (Ed) (1973). *State Legislative Innovation.* Praeger, New York.

Roeder, P. W. (1979). State legislative reform: Determinants and policy consequences. *American Politics Quarterly 7*: 51-70.

Rohde, D. W. (1974). Committee reform in the House of Representatives and the subcommittee bill of rights. *Annals 411*: 39-47.

Rohde, D. W., Ornstein, N. J., and Peabody, R. L. (1974). Political change and legislative norms in the United States Senate. Paper presented to the Annual Meeting of the American Political Science Association, Chicago, Aug. 29–Sept. 2.

Rohde, D. W., and Shepsle, K. A. (1978). Thinking about legislative reform. In *Legislative Reform: The Policy Impact,* L. N. Rieselbach (Ed.). Lexington Books, Lexington, MA, pp. 9-21.

Rosenthal, A. (1974a). *Legislative Performance in the States: Explorations of Committee Behavior.* Free Press, New York.

—— (1974b). Turnover in state legislatures. *American Journal of Political Science 18*: 609-616.

Rudder, C. (1977a). The impact of the Budget and Impoundment Control Act of 1974 on the revenue committees of the U.S. Congress. Paper presented to the Annual Meeting of the Midwest Political Science Association, Chicago, April 21-23.

—— (1977b). Committee reform and the revenue process. In *Congress Reconsidered,* L. C. Dodd and B. I. Oppenheimer (Eds.). Praeger, New York, pp. 117-139.

—— (1978). The policy impact of reform of the Committee on Ways and Means. In *Legislative Reform: The Policy Impact*, L. N. Rieselbach (Ed.). Lexington Books, Lexington, MA, pp. 73-89.

Saloma, J. S., III (1969). *Congress and the New Politics*. Little, Brown, Boston.

Schick, A. (1974). Budget reform legislation: Reorganizing congressional centers of fiscal power. *Harvard Journal on Legislation 11*: 303-350.

—— (1976). The supply and demand for analysis on Capitol Hill. *Policy Analysis 2*: 215-234.

Stanga, J. E., and Farnsworth, D. N. (1978). Seniority and democratic reforms in the House of Representatives: Committees and subcommittees. In *Legislative Reform: The Policy Impact*, L. N. Rieselbach (Ed.). Lexington Books, Lexington, MA, pp. 35-47.

Steinman, M. (1977). Congressional budget reform: Prospects. In *Legislative Reform and Public Policy*, S. Welch and J. G. Peters (Eds.). Praeger, New York, pp. 73-81.

Stevens, A. G., Jr., Miller, A. H., and Mann, T. E. (1974). Mobilization of liberal strength in the House, 1955-1970: The Democratic Study Group. *American Political Science Review 68*: 667-681.

Tatalovich, R. (1978). Legislative quality and legislative policy making: Some implications for reform. In *Legislative Reform: The Policy Impact*, L. N. Rieselbach (Ed.). Lexington Books, Lexington, MA, pp. 223-231.

Tedin, K. L., and Murray, R. W. (1979). Public awareness of congressional representatives: Recall versus recognition. *American Politics Quarterly 7*: 509-517.

Thurber, J. A. (1978). New powers of the purse: An assessment of congressional budget reform. In *Legislative Reform: The Policy Impact*, L. N. Rieselbach (Ed.). Lexington Books, Lexington, MA, pp. 159-172.

Twentieth Century Fund (1974). *Openly Arrived At: Report of the Twentieth Century Fund Task Force on Broadcasting and the Legislature*. Twentieth Century Fund, New York.

Unekis, J. K., and Rieselbach, L. N. (1979). The structure of congressional committee decision making. Paper presented to the Annual Meeting of the American Political Science Association, Washington, DC, Aug. 31-Sept. 3.

—— (1980). Congressional committee leadership: Stability and change, 1971-78. Paper presented to the Everett McKinley Dirksen Congressional Leadership Research Center–Sam Rayburn Library Conference, Understanding Congressional Leadership: The State of the Art, Washington, DC, June 10-11.

U.S. House of Representatives, Commission on Administrative Review (1977a). *Administrative Reorganization and Legislative Management*, 2 vols. U.S. Government Printing Office, Washington, DC.

—— (1977b). *Final Report*, 2 vols. U.S. Government Printing Office, Washington, DC.

U.S. House of Representatives, Select Committee on Committees (1973). *Hearings on the Subject of Committee Organization in the House*, 3 vols. U.S. Government Printing Office, Washington, DC.

—— (1974). *Committee Reform Amendments of 1974*. U.S. Government Printing Office, Washington, DC.

—— (1980). *Final Report*. U.S. Government Printing Office, Washington, DC.

U.S. Senate, Commission on the Operation of the Senate (1976a). *Toward A Modern Senate: Final Report*. U.S. Government Printing Office, Washington, DC.

—— (1976b). *Congressional Support Agencies: A Compilation of Papers*. U.S. Government Printing Office, Washington, DC.

U.S. Senate, Temporary Select Committee to Study the Senate Committee System (1976c). *The Senate Committee System.* U.S. Government Printing Office, Washington, DC.

Uslaner, E. M. (1978). Policy entrepreneurs and amateur democrats in the House of Representatives: Toward a more policy-oriented Congress? In *Legislative Reform: The Policy Impact,* L. N. Rieselbach (Ed.). Lexington Books, Lexington, MA, pp. 105-116.

—— (1980). The congressional war on energy: The moral equivalent of leadership? Paper presented to the Everett McKinley Dirksen Congressional Leadership Research Center–Sam Rayburn Library Conference, Understanding Congressional Leadership: The State of the Art, Washington, DC, June 10-11.

Van Der Slik, J. R. (1977). *American Legislative Processes.* Crowell, New York.

Vogler, D. (1978). The rise of ad hoc committees in the House of Representatives: An application of new research perspectives. Paper presented to the Annual Meeting of the American Political Science Association, New York, Aug. 31-Sept. 3.

Welch, S., and Peters, J. G. (Eds.) (1977). *Legislative Reform and Public Policy.* Praeger, New York.

Wildavsky, A. (1979). *The Politics of the Budgetary Process,* 3rd ed. Little, Brown, Boston.

Winters, R. (1977). Legislative reform and legislative cleavages. In *Legislative Reform and Public Policy,* S. Welch and J. G. Peters (Eds.). Praeger, New York, pp. 111-127.

Wissel, P., O'Connor, R., and King, M. (1976). The hunting of the legislative snark: Information searches and reforms in the U.S. state legislatures. *Legislative Studies Quarterly 1*: 254-267.

Wolfinger, R. E. (1971). Filibusters: Majority rule, presidential leadership, and Senate norms. In *Congressional Behavior,* N. W. Polsby (Ed.). Random House, New York, pp. 111-127.

Worthley, J. A. (Ed.). (1976). *Comparative Legislative Information Systems: The Use of Computer Technology in the Public Policy Process.* National Science Foundation, Washington, DC.

—— (1977). Legislative information systems: A review and analysis of recent experience. *Western Political Quarterly 30*: 418-430.

Wyner, A. J. (1973). Legislative reform and politics in California: What happened, why, and so what? In *State Legislative Innovation,* J. A. Robinson (Ed.). Praeger, New York, pp. 46-99.

16

Free Speech and Civil Liberties Policy

Stephen L. Wasby / State University of New York–Albany, Albany, New York

Congress shall make no law respecting an establishment of religion, or prohibiting the free exercise thereof; or abridging the freedom of speech, or of the press; or the right of the people peaceably to assemble, and to petition the Government for a redress of grievances (First Amendment).

This chapter explores the fundamental aspects of civil liberties policy. Scholars have from time to time attempted to distinguish *civil liberties* from *civil rights*. The latter are defined as the rights of minorities, such as the right to vote and to equal treatment, deriving largely from citizenship. In the organization of this Encyclopedia, such civil rights matters as voting and other equal protection issues are considered to fall under the rubric of "Blacks, Women, and Other Minorities," also a more relevant place for discussion of issues relating to sex roles and sex, such as abortion and use of contraceptives. *Civil liberties* is usually considered to include freedom of speech and religion and fair and proper treatment at the hands of the law. The latter, *due process*, is most visible in connection with criminal procedure and is therefore more appropriately discussed under the heading of "Crime and Criminal Justice."

In this chapter, attention is given predominantly to First Amendment freedoms of speech, press, assembly, and petition, and to the directly derivative freedom of association; limited attention is given to aspects of free exercise of religion assimilatable to freedom of speech. Because of the Establishment Clause's effects on attempts to aid sectarian education, that portion of the First Amendment is more appropriately treated in connection with education policy. A central focus on First Amendment protections for speech and closely related rights is justified by the particular importance of communication in a democracy and of speech-related rights in making other rights and liberties meaningful—by protecting communication to others about how those rights are being violated and how they can be better protected. Such an emphasis can be seen in the judicially created doctrine of a "preferred position" for First Amendment rights.

The brief first portion of the chapter deals with development of the scholarly analysis of civil liberties policy and its independence from more general developments in policy analysis. Some contextual matters—threats to and support for civil liberties, the purposes behind free speech, and conflicts of values in civil liberties policy—are discussed next. In the third and major portion of this chapter, the basic theme is whether public policy in the United States favors free speech or limitations on speech. After examination of the quintessential limitation on free speech—prior restraint—and limits on access to information, attention is turned to limits on sedition, obscenity, and libel, to "time, place, and circumstance" limitations, and to the right of association. From time to time, we note shifts from the Warren Court's policy to that of the Burger Court (Wasby, 1976a).

I. CIVIL LIBERTIES AND POLICY ANALYSIS

The literature on civil liberties—defined to exclude civil rights—has been quite separate from other literature in the policy analysis field. Although constitutional law scholars' law review articles and treatises analyzing the doctrinal bases of Supreme Court decisions are a type of policy analysis, the term "policy analysis" has only recently been found in conjunction with the study of civil liberties. For many years, there was little attention either to the process by which the Court's decisions came about or, except for speculation about possible doctrinal effects, to postdecisional matters. Many of the articles in a volume on civil liberties policy (Wasby, 1976b), indicative of the state of work in the area, were analyses of judicial decisions (and statutes) on civil liberties. Significantly, more sophisticated policy analysis work—studies of television and socialization to violence (Robinson, 1976; Watts, 1976)—was contributed to that volume by those whose principal interest was not constitutional law or even civil liberties.

Why is civil liberties policy literature still so distant from other policy analysis? The answer seems to be scholars' focus on the courts. For a long time, most scholars rejected the notion that the Supreme Court's decisions were "policy": In the traditional formulation, the Congress and the President made policy, whereas the Supreme Court found law. Scholars could thus describe the law found by the Supreme Court without having to recognize it as "policy," or, if policy, as policy laid down by the Founding Fathers or framers of the amendments. Even when there was recognition, and acceptance, of the Supreme Court's making of policy, attention remained limited largely to the substance of policy.

This court focus resulted from the Supreme Court's role until the 1960s as a "solo actor" with respect to civil liberties and civil rights, coupled with constitutional law scholars' lack of training in the policy analysis methods to which others were beginning to turn. Despite the voting rights statutes of 1957 and 1960, policy analysts interested in the implementation of statutes by the executive branch had little with which to work until the "shared decision process," which occurred when the Civil Rights Act of 1964 was passed and the HEW school desegregation guidelines were developed (Orfield, 1969; Radin, 1976). Continued legislative involvement in matters of discrimination—see the EEOC Amendments of 1972 and the Education Act Amendments of the same year, with its Title IX—has led to further implementation studies (Stewart, 1981; Conway, 1981).

On most civil *liberties* matters, the Supreme Court remained a "solo actor," with congressional action sporadic and defensive, as in threats to remove the Court's appellate jurisdiction over internal security cases (Murphy, 1962), or efforts to initiate constitutional amendments to overturn school prayer and reapportionment rulings. Increasing statutory civil liberties policy making in the 1970s has been restricted largely to policy on access to information and informational privacy for the individual (Morgan, 1976; Hanus, 1976). This increased statutory participation has not, however, thus far produced very much additional civil liberties policy-analytic research.

When public law scholars began to focus on the process by which judicial decisions were made and the effect of those decisions, they often turned to study the civil liberties area. Students of judicial behavior had focused heavily on the Supreme Court's non-unanimous civil liberties decisions in their studies of voting blocs and attitudinal distribution in the Court (see Pritchett, 1948; Schubert, 1965). Their attention, stimulated by their liberal personal inclinations, was attracted by the highly favorable disposition of civil liberties claims by the Warren Court, starting with the school desegregation cases and continuing with internal security, obscenity, criminal procedure, reapportionment, and school prayer. That attention did not abate during the transition from the Warren Court to the Burger Court, with its more conservative stance (Wasby, 1976a).

Studies of the civil liberties/civil rights policy process include examinations of the role of interest groups in the development of judicial policy, with attention given both to the NAACP (Vose, 1959; Kluger, 1976) and to the ACLU's emphasis on precedent-setting rather than implementing cases (Halpern, 1976); when and how lawyers came to be involved in civil liberties cases (Casper, 1972); and individual and group litigants in Establishment Clause cases (Sorauf, 1976).

Policy analysis came most obviously to the civil liberties area through studies of the impact of Supreme Court decisions (Wasby, 1970). The focus of most such studies on civil liberties was affected by scholars' values when they saw an increasing disjuncture between "law on the books" (the Court's liberal decisions) and "law in action" (noncompliance). Most early examination of impact, which focused on desegregation, was not particularly analytical. Later studies were, however, more sophisticated, turning to law's ability to produce social change (Grossman and Grossman, 1971). In one of the few studies not adopting a "top down" (Supreme Court to community) approach, school districts' compliance with school desegregation was explained (Rodgers and Bullock, 1976). The racial equality area has also seen broad applications of policy analysis (Dye, 1971; Bullock and Rodgers, 1972, 1975; Rodgers, 1980) not yet seen on civil liberties topics.

On the latter, of particular note are studies of the school prayer rulings, where social psychological theory was applied to explain attitudinal reaction and change (Johnson, 1967; Muir, 1967) and researchers penetrated beyond school administrators' reports to actual classroom prayer observance (Dolbeare and Hammond, 1971). Studies of criminal procedure decisions' impact brought attention to communication of judicial decisions to the police (Wasby, 1976c) and to relationships between compliance and agency professionalism (Milner, 1971). Studies of the effect of the exclusionary rule (see particularly Canon, 1973-1974) have become central to policy debate because of Chief Justice Burger's call for repeal of the rule because of its "costs" in freeing guilty persons.

As this discussion suggests, policy analysis with respect to civil liberties has been focused almost solely on the United States. Attention to the cross-national study of human rights (see Claude, 1976; Bayley, 1964; Van Dyke, 1970), given added impetus by President Carter's human rights concerns (see Molineu, 1981), is beginning to change this emphasis somewhat. Studies of human rights have attracted scholars of comparative politics and international relations to studies of civil liberties matters; this supplements the work of international law experts, whose examination of human rights subjects was particularly stimulated by U.S. involvement in Vietnam (see Falk, 1968).

II. FREE SPEECH: SOME CONTEXTUAL MATTERS

The context of free speech/civil liberties policy includes threats to civil liberties from multiple sources and support for civil liberties, particularly for the right of the unpopular to speak out. The purposes to be served by free speech, often taken for granted, are then discussed to provide a basis for policy distinctions courts have made. Conflicting goals or values are discussed at the conclusion of this section.

A. Threats to Civil Liberties

Allowing people free speech or unfettered access to material is a highly emotional matter, as could be seen starkly in the response to the President's Commission on Obscenity and Pornography (1970). The Commission, while recommending that limits be placed on the sale of sexually explicit pictorial materials to young persons and that people be protected from having such material thrust upon them through the mails or in open public discussion, had proposed that government not interfere with adults who wished to read or view such materials. Not only did Congress refuse to adopt the recommendations, but, without having read the report—which was based on considerable policy-relevant research undertaken at the Commission's direction—voted to reject its work.

The Bill of Rights, although its free speech protections now extend to the states, was adopted as a restraint on the national level of government, and the First Amendment is the only one that talks specifically of the national legislature: "*Congress* shall make no law . . ." (emphasis supplied). Despite the First Amendment's focus on the national government, threats to civil liberties in general and free speech in particular have come predominantly at the community level from repressive homogeneous majorities or intense minorities acting while the majority remains passive, seen in removal of "obscene" or "subversive" books from libraries and in obstacles to group demonstrations.

Action at the national level is, however, of substantial importance. National leaders' statements, such as Vice President Agnew's attacks on the media or President Lyndon Johnson's attacks on opponents of his Vietnam policy, do not create an atmosphere conducive to free speech. The national government's actions directed at the media, including the "Pentagon Papers" and *Progressive* cases, as well as the "Houston plan," FBI surveillance, and CIA use of journalists, may have far more a "chilling effect" than state or local officials' actions.

Traditionally we have viewed civil liberties, seen as "freedom from government interference," as likely to be restricted only by the government. Yet decisions by the television networks not to show certain programs may have a greater effect than government censorship, and private individuals limit civil liberties by shouting down speakers (the "heckler's veto"). Private censorship, because more erratic and more direct, may indeed result in more severe "self-censorship" than limits government would impose (Randall, 1968).

B. Support for Civil Liberties

Surveys over an extended period attest to Americans' generally low level of knowledge of civil liberties—in part a function of the inadequacies of public schools, where civil liberties is a "controversial" topic. For adults, Watergate appears not to have been the "large adult education course in civil liberties" some wished it to be, with a recent Gallup Poll indicating that almost 4 out of 10 respondents felt that restrictions on the press were "not strict enough" (*The New York Times,* January 18, 1980). *Support* for civil liberties is generally not high, although elites and those of higher income and education are more supportive of civil liberties than is the general public (see Stouffer, 1955; Prothro and Grigg, 1960). Strong agreement on basic principles of democracy has not been matched by consensus about specifics: Disagreement has exceeded consensus on the extension of freedoms to Communists and the right to criticize churches and religion. Later use of the same questions showed apparent increases in political tolerance. When people identified groups they most opposed, however, such tolerance proved illusory; intolerance had been directed toward new targets. Only one-third of those responding in a recent study were willing not to outlaw their least-liked group; even fewer would allow members of such groups to teach in schools (Sullivan et al., 1979).

The most widely publicized recent civil liberties test at the community level was the Nazi effort to march in Skokie, Illinois, where many survivors of the Holocaust or their relatives live. Such a situation provided a test of the "degree of threat" as a contextual variable to explain commitment to civil liberties. A study of members of the American Civil Liberties Union (ACLU)—some of whom left the organization over its support for Nazis' rights—showed that they had highly libertarian attitudes in terms of groups they would allow to speak; however, a significant percentage would bar speeches that advocated overthrow of the government or that might produce audience violence and would support police's stopping demonstrations under some "heckler's veto" conditions. The study showed a general consistency between attitudes and reported behavior (Gibson and Bingham, 1979).

C. The Purposes of Free Speech

Why free speech? Is it for the speaker, the listener, or the larger community? Does the listener have only the limited right to listen to others' speech or an independent right to acquire information? The latter may mean that the right to information "may entail no correlative right in any particular source to originate the communication" (Tribe, 1978: 676). Is speech an end in itself or a means to an end, an instrumental device? Some see speech's effects in cognitive, intellectual terms; others place greater value on speech's emotion and affective functions. Recognition of the latter should not obscure the importance of "dialogue" or exchange which, if emphasized, might lead to limiting "fighting words" used "as projectiles" where harm might be caused before a response is possible (Tribe, 1978: 605,651). Some find speech important for self-expressive purposes independent of its "social value" as an important part of personal autonomy. Others view free speech as intended to contribute to a democratic polity, a view leading to restriction on non-"political" speech. Recognizing that information can be communicated in advertisements, which allow consumers to make more intelligent decisions, as well as through "pure speech," the Supreme Court has, however, eliminated many restrictions once placed on "commercial speech," and has also sustained First Amendment rights for corporations (banks and public utilities).

Related to self-expression are questions of a right to silence, often ignored outside the context of the Fifth Amendment right not to incriminate oneself. The assertion, by reluctant witnesses in legislative investigations, of a First Amendment right to silence has not been honored but others, who did not wish to participate in public displays—a compulsory flag salute or use of license plates bearing the "Live Free or Die" motto—have been protected from being compelled to state beliefs with which they do not agree, in cases that also implicated the free exercise of religion (*West Virginia Board of Education v. Barnette,* 1943; *Wooley v. Maynard,* 1977).[1] On the question of how people must *present* themselves, the Court has sustained dress codes for certain employees (police), although it has consistently refused to decide the question of school "long hair" regulations.

D. Conflicts in Values

Other considerations regularly compete with free speech concerns. In one sense, there is always a "conflict of values" question when regulation of free speech is proposed—between the speech, or speech-related activity, and the broader "rights" of government or society to control the material or activity in question, even when the government is pursuing legitimate regulatory goals. Thus the state's interest in regulating door-to-door solicitation has regularly failed in the face of First Amendment claims, particularly where religious solicitation implicates the "free exercise of religion." As to campaign finance, with the government's interest in preventing corruption or its appearance, congressional limits on contributions to candidates have been upheld but limits on individuals' independent expenditures in political campaigns were struck down, in part, because of the close relation between discussion of candidates and discussion of issues (*Buckley v. Valeo,* 1976).

Conflicts of values particularly difficult to resolve are those pitting communication interests against other civil liberties values, for example, free press—fair trial and freedom of press—privacy. Where the question is how the media shall obtain information rather than whether they may report information already obtained, conflicts are quite likely. If the media have obtained information, even sensitive personal information, such as the name of a rape victim, from public (court) records, the courts will not prevent publication (*Cox Broadcasting v. Cohn,* 1976).

Justice Brennan (1979) has distinguished the two situations of publishing and information gathering in terms of two models of the press's role. In the "speech" model, where self-expression is at issue, there should be an absolute prohibition on any interference with freedom of expression. In the "structural" model, involving "the structure of communications necessary for the existence of our democracy" and thus "all the myriad tasks necessary for [the press] to gather and disseminate the news," balancing

---

[1] Full references for cases cited are given in Table of Cases.

is necessary and the press's claim to independence may have to be subordinated, for example, to a plaintiff's interest in ascertaining the process by which a reporter prepared an allegedly libelous story (*Herbert v. Lando,* 1979).

Similar to Justice Brennan's two models are Tribe's (1978: 580-582) "two tracks" of First Amendment constitutional analysis. The first track applies to government efforts to suppress particular speech because of its content or its effect, whereas the second track, where balancing is needed, applies to limitations on certain *non*communicative activities that may lead to restrictions on the flow of communication, as when reporters are asked to reveal confidential sources to a grand jury.

Of great contemporaneous controversy is the conflict between the First Amendment and the Sixth Amendment's "public trial" requirement. The Court first held that this could be met without television's presence (*Estes v. Texas,* 1965), a position it did not alter even after a large number of states allowed television in court (Wasby, 1979); the Court did, however, finally agree that states could constitutionally allow radio, television, and still photographic coverage of criminal trials for public broadcast, even over defendant's objections (*Chandler v. Florida,* 1980). In deciding, shortly after initially dealing with cameras in the courtroom, that excessive publicity prior to and during trial was a basis for reversing a criminal conviction, the Court ruled that the judge could bar certain statements by lawyers, the parties to the case, witnesses, or court officials (*Sheppard v. Maxwell,* 1966), a ruling that became the basis for American Bar Association fair trial-free press guidelines. Over a decade later, after striking down limitations a judge could place on the publication of materials from an open court hearing, the Court had to deal with judges' closing of pretrial hearings and trials themselves. The Court ruled that the Sixth Amendment public trial rights attached to *defendant,* not the *media,* and struck the balance against the press (*Gannett v. DePasquale,* 1979). Whether that ruling was restricted to pretrial proceedings was, however, unclear, and it led to a substantial increase in judicial closings of both hearings and trials. Only a year later, the Court, in a ruling sustaining First Amendment rights for the press to attend a trial in order to report on it to the public, shifted its position and held that trials could not be closed (*Richmond Newspapers v. Virginia,* 1980).

Another civil liberties conflict of values involves religion—the potential conflict between the "free exercise" and "establishment" clauses of the First Amendment itself. The two clauses are said to be "at least compatible and at best mutually supportive," with both reinforcing religious liberty and thus supporting the value of "voluntarism" (Tribe, 1978: 814,818). Conflicts in policy certainly arise, however, seen most readily in the application of Sunday closing laws to those whose religions require observation of a Saturday sabbath or the denial of unemployment compensation benefits to a Seventh Day Adventist who would not accept Saturday work. The Court's policy has not been fully consistent, the Sunday closing laws being sustained as involving only a secular, not sectarian, day of rest whereas payment of the unemployment compensation was required (*Braunfeld v. Brown,* 1961; *Sherbert v. Verner,* 1963). Called on later to interpret a congressional requirement of "reasonable accommodations" to employees' religious choices, the Court ruled that an employer did not have to arrange Saturdays off for Saturday sabbatarians where additional costs would be involved for the employer or where violations of seniority would occur in substituting other employees, whose interests also had to be considered (*Trans-World Airlines v. Hardison,* 1977). These cases show that the breadth of the definition of "religion" can be narrow for

Establishment Clause purposes to avoid striking down governmental enactments on the ground that they embody religious principles; it can also be expanded for purposes of "free exercise of religion," seen in the Conscientious Objector cases (Tribe, 1978: 828-833).

III. FREE SPEECH POLICY

A. Free Speech or Limited Speech

Although we are accustomed to characterizing our polity as having freedom of speech, incidents abound of efforts to restrict that freedom which are not merely random or erratic. The Supreme Court does not lightly accept limitations on speech. Statutes trenching on free speech concerns do not share the presumption of validity attributed to statutes, for example, in the field of economic regulation, but are subjected to particularly close scrutiny. The possible "chilling effect" on speech that improperly drawn statutes affecting speech might have also produced considerable concern. Thus statutes touching upon free speech that are either overbroad, that is, encompassing more than can properly be controlled, or vague are particularly likely to be invalidated, although the Burger Court has been less likely than the Warren Court to strike down statutes containing imprecise language. (When a court rules a statute invalid as vague or overbroad, it is not saying that the legislature may not act, but only that the legislature must rethink its actions and write with greater precision; in effect the Court is initiating a dialogue with the legislature.) Yet there are subject matter areas and circumstances where speech has regularly been limited or controlled. We thus see that a general approach which makes considerable demands on statutes affecting free speech does not necessarily mean that civil liberties claims will invariably be sustained.

Rules concerning freedom of speech are to a considerable extent "neutral," that is, protecting not only liberals and radicals, whose rights are more frequently limited and thus more often become the subject of litigation, but also rights of conservatives and reactionaries, whether Nazis wishing to demonstrate in Skokie or the National States Rights Party wishing to be freed from a ban on demonstrations opposing civil rights for blacks (*Carroll v. Princess Anne*, 1968). That a free speech limitation—the banning of "for sale" signs—is enacted with liberal goals in mind, for example, protecting an integrated community from "blockbusting" and "panic selling," will not save it from invalidation (*Linmark v. Willingboro*, 1977).

B. Prior Restraint

Whatever else freedom of speech may mean, it appears to mean an absence of government interference with the act of publishing, that is, restrictions that prevent material from seeing the light of day—whatever other action (such as a civil libel suit or a criminal prosecution) might occur later. When people talk of "censorship," they refer to such restrictions, known as *prior restraint*, which also includes restrictions enforced before a judge has had an appropriate opportunity to determine whether the material questioned is subject to First Amendment protections (Tribe, 1978:725).

Judge-imposed "gag orders," even if permissible as applied to court officials and lawyers, are improper if they bar the media from using material they already possess

(*Nebraska Press Association v. Stuart,* 1976). To bar a subsequent issue of a periodical because of distaste for previous issues is forbidden (*Near v. Minnesota,* 1942); for the government to obtain an injunction against publication of particular stories, even where matters of national security are involved, a particularly high threshhold has been set by the courts (*New York Times v. U.S.,* 1971). The issuance of an injunction against *The Progressive's* publishing an article about nuclear weapons was the first federal district court injunction issued against a periodical; because the government dropped the case, policy as to prior restraint about such sensitive matters remains ambiguous. The Supreme Court's upholding contracts that compel present and former CIA employees to obtain clearance of material they write, whether or not classified material is used, subject to the penalty of having to forfeit all profits (*Snepp v. U.S.,* 1980), raises still further questions about the degree to which the Courts avoid prior restraint. The print media also cannot be made to publish certain material, such as responses by candidates to editorial criticism (*Tornillo v. Miami Herald,* 1974). However, the Court has been willing to put aside prior restraint objections in sustaining orders affecting the composition of help wanted advertisements in newspapers (*Pittsburgh Press,* 1973).

If prepublication restrictions on print media are disfavored, the picture is different for movies and electronic media. If we look at print and electronic media and movies together, as we should to develop a "collective" standard encompassing both print media and movies and the broadcast media, we find less concern about prohibiting prior restraint than if we look only at print media, or print media and movies (Bonnicksen, 1980: 263,290-291). "Licensing"—the need to obtain official permission before publishing—has been the most hated form of prior restraint. This type of censorship has, however, long been allowed in the United States for movies. Only in 1965 did the Supreme Court shift the burden from the exhibitor (to show why questioned material was not improper) to the censor (to demonstrate that the material to be removed was obscene) (*Freedman v. Maryland,* 1965). This ruling eliminated most remaining official censorship boards, leaving officials to proceed against movies through criminal prosecution or by means of "classification" of films as fit for "adults only." The Court has also limited seizure of movies before a judge's preliminary determination that the movie is obscene, because to do otherwise would be a prior restraint; requirements of a judicial determination prior to issuance of a warrant also extend to seizure of printed material. (Attempts to use morality commissions that label materials as improper have run afoul of problems of lack of standards and law enforcement officials' "informal" use of lists to threaten sanctions.)

Congress—and the Supreme Court—have predicated government regulation of radio and television on the limited number of channels, which must be allocated if interference is to be avoided. (It has also been assumed that entry into the newspaper field is easier than entry into electronic media, an assumption no longer valid if the comparison is between newspapers and radio.) Regulation of stations is to take place through review of programming when a station's license is to be renewed, but the power of the Federal Communication Commission (FCC) to impose fines for the broadcast of certain language including "dirty words" has been sustained, and FCC procedures for dealing with indecent speech are less strict than those demanded of local officials in censoring movies under *Freedman* (see Bonnicksen, 1980: 290-291). The FCC's rules have clear implications for political debate; best known is that an appearance by one candidate requires a station to provide equivalent time at comparable rates ("equal opportunity," more commonly known as "equal time") and that a person attacked in a radio or television pro-

gram has a (free) right of reply. Sustaining the FCC, the Court has ruled that the First
Amendment does not require that stations allow individuals or groups to purchase time
for editorial advertisements (*C.B.S. v. Democratic National Committee,* 1973).

Usually not considered with prior restraint, restrictions on advertising are nonetheless
closely related; for many years the courts sustained such restrictions—imposed by legislative enactment, often at the behest of vocational groups—on the basis of a distinction
between "commercial speech" and other (political?) speech. That distinction was first
eroded and then almost totally eliminated, with the Court striking down bans on the advertising of abortions, advertising by lawyers, and advertising of the costs of drugs. The
informational content of advertisements was stressed, as were consumers' rights to receive
information. However, limitations on political advertising in other settings have recently
been sustained in the context of public transit, on the theory that advertising space in
buses is not a "public forum" to which the First Amendment applies (*Lehman v. Shaker
Heights,* 1974).

C. Access to Information

As Justice Brennan indicated, some freedom of speech cases involve the media's ability
to obtain information so that they can perform their communicative function. Although
the media invariably decry restrictions on obtaining information, such as "gag" orders
applied to court officials and lawyers and closings of pretrial proceedings, as "prior restraint" because they cannot publish information they do not have, a distinction between
these restrictions and straightforward bans on publication or broadcast seems tenable,
whatever one thinks of the Supreme Court's policy pronouncements.

Two closely related areas of policy that, in addition to the issue of closed hearings,
have particularly agitated media representatives have been demands that reporters reveal
confidential sources to grand juries (*Branzburg v. Hayes,* 1972)—leading some reporters
to go to jail rather than turn over their notes—and searches of media facilities (*Zurcher v.
Stanford Daily,* 1978), both of which lead to fears that the media will lose access to information. On both matters the Burger Court has failed to support media claims, using
the rationale that the press should have no more protection than ordinary citizens. Department of Justice guidelines requiring government to seek information for alternative
sources before subpoenas are issued to reporters have been more protective of media
rights than have the Court's rulings, which *permit* statutory enactment of "shield laws"
while saying that the First Amendment does not provide such protection. Such statutes
have been enacted in some states, but elsewhere, including at the national level, efforts
to enact them have been frustrated by disagreement over who is properly considered a
media representative and questions of qualified versus absolute immunity from subpoena.
(Nor have judges always interpreted the statutes to provide maximum press freedom.)
Legislation also has been introduced against search warrants for media facilities, although disagreement as to whether to cover only the media or all situations where material affecting third parties might be seized has deterred enactment.

The courts have also limited media access to information about prisons. Interviews
with specific prisoners, whether demanded by the media or the prisoners, can be barred
as long as some other mechanism (the mails) exists by which prisoners can communicate
grievances to those outside the prison (*Pell v. Procunier,* 1974). Rulings limiting availability of information also appear in an area of policy not normally viewed as involving

First Amendment issues—the Speech and Debate Clause, which immunizes members of Congress from "being questioned" about their "legislative acts" (Act. I, Sec. 6). For example, Senator Mike Gravel's efforts to obtain publication of the "Pentagon Papers" were said not to be part of his legislative work and thus he (and his aide) could be questioned before a grand jury about it (*Gravel v. U.S.,* 1972). Suits against subordinate congressional employees for circulation or potentially libelous committee documents have been allowed, and, more recently, Speech and Debate Clause protection was refused to senatorial press releases (*Hutchinson v. Proxmire,* 1979).

Efforts by citizens to seek access to points of view other than those usually heard have also encountered obstacles, particularly where the federal government has asserted its foreign policy powers. Thus the Attorney General's discretionary authority to deny entry to a Marxist scholar who was to give speeches has been sustained; the Court has also refused to uphold a First Amendment right to travel to foreign countries to obtain information for self-education (*Kleindeinst v. Mandel,* 1972; *Zemel v. Rusk,* 1965; see Mittlebeeler, 1976). The government has also used the postal power to hinder access to certain "subversive" materials, by requiring that the individual specifically request them once the Post Office had intercepted them, but the Court invalidated the statute (*Lamont v. Postmaster General,* 1965). If people cannot obtain what they wish to read, privacy rights to peruse what one wants within the confines of the home do not mean much, but "privacy" has not been held to provide a sufficient basis for obtaining the material. Congressional action to *assist* individuals who wish to prevent offensive material from being "thrust" into their homes, however, been sustained.

With increased attention to access to information have come major statutory initiatives concerning materials in the government's possession—the 1965 Freedom of Information Act (FOIA) and "sunshine" legislation, the latter to open up government agency meetings. Embodying a commitment to disclosure by the executive branch, the FOIA "requires publication of certain executive branch documents such as agency rules and procedural norms; . . . requires that 'final opinions' and 'statements of policy' must be made available to the public; and . . . provides for public access, on request, to other executive branch documents" (Morgan, 1976: 131) unless those documents are within the scope of the statute's exemptions. As a result of agency resistance, consideration litigation has developed over the exemptions, for example, over interagency or intraagency documents that were not "final opinions," and the Congress was led to tighten them in 1974. Immediate difficulty arose over whether executive branch classification of materials, release of which might adversely affect the national security, was determinative; after the Court would not question the executive's classification determination, Congress required that an executive order establish criteria for maintaining the secrecy of national security documents [5 U.S.C. §552(b)(1)].

Government control of information in the national security sphere is of particular sensitivity, shown as well by the "Pentagon Papers," *Progressive,* and *Snepp* cases. Part of the problem results from sloppiness in declassifying materials—which became available for use in *The Progressive*—but more from the tendency to "overclassify" material. In time of war, government control of information is particularly severe and has included application of the Sedition Acts, censorship of communications in and out of the United States, and application of the Trading with the Enemy Act. Further concern has developed from efforts to enact an omnibus federal criminal code bill (S. 1 and its progeny), because of limitations that might be placed on reporters' and "whistleblowers," use of government information—some have said moving us closer to an "Official Secrets Act."

Concern about access to government information also extends to the materials of highest government officials, particularly as a result of Watergate. Surrender of the Watergate tapes for use in a criminal trial did not end litigation over the tapes and President Nixon's papers. His agreement with the General Services Administration (GSA) was set aside on the basis of the Presidential Recordings and Materials Preservation Act (*Nixon v. Administrator of General Services*, 1977). Congressional legislation and judicial discretion has been found appropriate to deal with release of the tapes played at the Watergate cover-up trial; the Supreme Court has held that there is no First Amendment access to them (*Nixon v. Warner Communications*, 1978). Moreover, access to materials prepared by high officials while in office was severely decreased by the ruling that if someone placed documents outside the agency, they could not be reached by means of the Freedom of Information Act, which covered only documents in the government's possession (*Kissinger v. Reporters Committee*, 1980).

D. Access to Government Information II:
Privacy Concerns

The linkage between demands for access to information held by the government, in order that the public can be better informed, and personal privacy, entailing the right to prevent distribution of information about oneself, "to project one identity rather than another upon the public world"—an aspect different from "secrecy, sanctuary, or seclusion" (Tribe, 1978:887-888)—can be seen in the FOIA exemption for "personnel and medical files . . . the disclosure of which would constitute a clearly unwarranted invasion of personal privacy" [5 U.S.C. §552(b)(6)]. The Privacy Act's provisions are much tighter than the FOIA exemption. The Privacy Act (5 U.S.C. §522a) has the twofold purpose of barring most disclosure of records maintained by government agencies to those outside the agency and allowing an individual access to that person's records; there are also provisions for correcting erroneous records. Agencies are also directed to maintain only relevant information and to collect it in the most reliable practicable way (see Hanus, 1976).

Federal employees obtained access to their personnel records through the Privacy Act. That has produced pressure, to which the Privacy Protection Study Commission (established by the statute) has added, to allow access to personnel records to private-sector employees, although present policy is to rely on private employers' voluntary compliance. Largely as a result of revelations about psychological evaluations of elementary and secondary school students by school personnel, Congress passed the Buckley Amendment (the Family Educational Rights and Privacy Act of 1972) (20 U.S.C. §1232a), which gives parents (in the case of college students, the students themselves) access to records maintained by school officials and the right to challenge their accuracy. The provision applies to all educational institutions receiving federal funds, thus providing the potential (if infrequently used) sanction of a cutoff of federal funds under Title VI of the Civil Rights Act of 1964.

Of particular privacy concern has been the accuracy of and unregulated access to financial records; breadth of access has stimulated and reinforced concern about accuracy. Legislation to protect bank depositors' privacy illustrates policy making through interaction between Congress and the Supreme Court. Congress in 1970 had required banks to maintain records of checks and certain foreign and domestic transactions, with implementing regulations requiring reporting of some of those transactions. The Court upheld the record-keeping portions of the act, but deferred privacy challenges by banks, depositors, and the American Civil Liberties Union—which claimed infringement of associational rights (*California Bankers Association v. Schultz*, 1974). This meant that banks could respond to government subpoenas for information without having to notify the depositor; the records were the bank's, not the individual's. Responding to unabated privacy concerns, in 1978 Congress—in the Right to Financial Privacy Act (35 U.S.C. § 3401-3422)—provided for notification of government subpoenas to depositors, and an opportunity to oppose them. That the legislation has not been fully effective in protecting customers' privacy is suggested by the introduction of legislation to limit the availability of background information possessed by all types of private financial institutions.

Protection for information used in the obtaining of credit has been provided in the Fair Credit Reporting Act of 1970 (15 U.S.C. § 1681), which restricts both collectors of information and those who use it. Consumers must be notified that requests for credit investigations have been made, and are then able to obtain disclosure of the nature and scope of the investigation as well as the nature and sources of information in the reporting agency's files. As in other privacy-related statutes, opportunities are provided to correct or dispute information in the agency's records. This ability to correct or rebut information allows protection of personal reputation. The Supreme Court has, however, not otherwise aided in such protection, relegating individuals to state remedies even when maligned by public officers.

The government's need to maintain records in order to administer its programs, coupled with increased use of computers for this record keeping, has produced heightened civil liberties concern about decreased personal privacy (see Westin and Baker, 1972). Faced with a state statute requiring computer-bank record keeping of drug prescriptions, the Court sustained the statute, considering sufficient the protection it provided against release of patients' identities.

E. Sedition

Policy directed at seditious speech—that critical of the government—extends back to the Republic's early years; dissident editors were jailed under the Alien and Sedition Acts. In the twentieth century, however, sedition has become almost synonymous with advocacy of overthrow of the government. In this internal security area, which also clearly implicates the right of association, the courts have developed standards to be applied in determining whether or not to limit speech.

The "clear and present danger" test enunciated by Justice Holmes while upholding —in the context of our World War I efforts—a conviction of a man for distribution of antidraft pamphlets (*Schenck v. U.S.*, 1919) is the most famous of the speech-related standards. If that test requires that the danger created by speech be immediate and clear, not merely possible at some later date, the far more restrictive "bad tendency" test allows limits on speech that might have a tendency to create an evil at some future time (*Gitlow v. New York*, 1925). One test is, however, often enunciated when the other is meant, for example, when the Smith Act convictions of Communist party leaders were affirmed: "Clear and present danger" was stated, but "bad tendency" was really operative (*Dennis v. U.S.,* 1951). In this case, involving the teaching or advocacy of overthrow of the government by force and violence and conspiracy to carry out such acts, the court of appeals had used still another test, the "gravity of an evil discounted by the probability of its occurrence."

Faced with additional Smith Act convictions, the Court, ruling that abstract advocacy of overthrow of the government was protected although specific incitations to violence were not, definitely adopted the "clear and present danger" test (*Yates v. U.S.,* 1957). Its use was reaffirmed when a state criminal syndicalism law (outlawing advocacy of crime, sabotage, violence, and terrorism, and assembly to teach or advocate the same) was invalidated because mere advocacy and related assembly were punished (*Brandenburg v. Ohio,* 1969).

The Warren Court's "tight" reading of what types of seditious speech could be limited was carried over into rulings on disclaimer affidavits requiring an individual to deny past and present membership in organizations advocating overthrow of the government. Basic doctrine, also developed by the Warren Court, is that to restrict the activities of a member of an organization, the government must show that the individual belonged to an organization that advocated illegal acts and both knew about the illegal aims and intended to participate in them. Loyalty oaths, disclaimer affidavits, and similar inquiries concerning state employment for entrance to occupations containing broader language are invalid.

Use of standards such as "clear and present danger" and "bad tendency" has been restricted to seditious speech; obscene material, for example, may be prosecuted without a showing of dangerous effect. However, the Court has allowed school officials to prevent protests and demonstrations within the school only when "material disruption" (not merely fear of it) might result (*Tinker v. Des Moines School District,* 1968); such a standard, like the others, leaves school officials—and judges called upon to interpret them—much discretion.

F. Obscenity

Both national and state statutes have long barred obscenity. Only in 1957 did the Supreme Court begin to grapple with First Amendment issues relating to its definition; it has been trying, rather unsuccessfully, ever since to define its scope. The Court first made clear that obscenity was *not* subject to First Amendment protections and adopted a definition—cast in terms of the dominant theme of material taken as a whole and its appeal to the prurient interest of the community's average member (*Roth v. U.S.,* 1957)—that allowed more material to circulate than had been possible under earlier standards. Except for allowing prosecutions based solely on advertising about material, an aberration in terms of policy development, and making it easier to stop offensive material aimed at children, the Warren Court refined its definition in ways that made obscenity prosecutions even more difficult. The Court finally went as far as to rule that a person could maintain in the privacy of the home a collection of material regardless of its offensiveness (*Stanley v. Georgia,* 1969).

Regardless of what a person could do once material was obtained, the Burger Court reaffirmed the validity of long-standing statutes that, under the customs, postal, and interstate commerce powers, barred the movement and transfer of such materials. Thus access to sexually explicit materials, based on a privacy theory, was not to occur. The earlier-noted response to the Obscenity Commission's recommendations was given constitutional backing by the Burger Court when it gave greater weight in defining obscenity to material's appeal to prurient interest and focusedon community standards at the state or local—rather than national—level (*Miller v. California,* 1973), providing a formula "likely to be as unstable as it is unintelligible" (Tribe, 1978: 656). By allowing control by the FCC of indecent (but not obscene) speech, the Court has further muddied standards of what is acceptable and reinforced the idea of "variable obscenity" (Bonnicksen, 1980: 280-281).

Because state authority to bar obscene material is based on different grounds—the "police power" to regulate health, welfare, and morals—from those used to support federal regulation, obscenity policy raises questions of federalism. The Court has, however, generally rejected any differentiation in the level of restriction between federal and state levels: Whether federal or state prosecutions are involved, "contemporary standards" must be part of the criteria for evaluation at either level, with those standards applied by juries drawn from the locality. Recently, however, the Court did allow a federal mail statute prosecution in a state that had not outlawed the distribution of obscene materials to adults; the absence of such a state law was held not to be controlling on the matter of "community standards" (*Smith v. U.S.,* 1977).

Obscenity is a policy area in which considerable attention has been given to *mechanisms* for regulating material beyond the usual prosecution after material has been made available. For example, an *in rem* (against the thing) proceeding may be brought against a book or movie to obtain a declaration of its obscenity, after which those continuing to show or sell the item can be held in contempt of court. Such a device, however, requires examining challenged material outside the context in which it is sold or shown. As noted earlier, regulation of movies through classification has been attempted, but the movie industry's adoption of a rating scheme probably staved off more serious government intervention. Most recently, perhaps out of frustration with the problem of developing a clear definition of obscenity, some justices have advocated a "public nuisance" approach to the subject rather than one based on materials' content, and the Court has sustained local regulations that require either dispersal or consolidation of adult bookstores or moviehouses.

G. Libel

The area of libel law, once part of private law but now heavily constitutionalized, is another in which the Warren Court changed doctrine to encourage freedom of speech. If the Burger Court has made it easier to sue for libel, it is largely the result of efforts to accommodate the right of free speech/press with the right not to have one's character improperly defamed. Privacy rights have, however, generally been made secondary to those of free speech, perhaps a result of the later judicial recognition of the former.

In a nonincremental policy shift, the Supreme Court moved to limit libel suits by public officials. Common law doctrine allowing recovery if reputation had been damaged, with the burden on the defendant to show that the statements made were true, was replaced with the rule that such plaintiffs had to show that the allegedly defamatory statements were made with malice, defined as knowledge that the statements were false or were made with reckless disregard of their falsity (*New York Times v. Sullivan,* 1964). Although some states had given greater protection to statements in political campaigns ("fair comment"), the Court made clear that some inaccurate reporting was a price to be paid in a democracy to achieve full discussion; reporters were, however, held to at least minimum standards of their profession, particularly in reporting about public *figures* rather than public *officials*. The general tendency was clearly toward expanding statements protected unless made "with malice" (as defined); some members of a divided Court even held that someone brought into the public eye by a newsworthy arrest was a public figure (*Rosenbloom v. Metromedia,* 1973). (That a person's private life has become well known through a fictionalized, but only slightly veiled, account, is sufficient to strip the individual of privacy where the connection between the account and the "real-world" person is pointed out. However, a recent state decision allows a person defamed in such a fictionalized account to collect a libel judgment.)

Down the road to expanding protection for libelous statements the Court would not, however, proceed. Instead, the Court, while adhering to the rule that public officials and public figures could recover only under the malice standard, also to be used when private citizens sought *punitive* damages, stated that the latter could recover *actual* damages only upon a showing of negligence by the person making the statement (*Gertz v. Welch,* 1974). Because some states had earlier allowed recovery without any showing of fault, this ruling to some extent increased the amount of protected speech and limited privacy protections; furthermore, national policy replaced state policy as the framework for libel suits by private citizens, who have been assisted by a narrowing of the scope of "public figure."

H. Time, Place, and Circumstance: Free Speech Plus

Policy has also been developed to restrict conduct related to speech. The "speech"-"conduct" distinction is not easy to draw (see Tribe, 1978:599-601), but one may roughly separate printed materials and movies from picketing and demonstrations. The latter—at times called "free speech plus"—are the object of "time, place, and circumstance" restrictions, which the Supreme Court has been more willing to sustain than it has been to restrict the content of speech itself.

One basic rule is that local officials cannot have unfettered discretion to determine who may or may not speak, although they may be allowed, for example, to separate protestors from counterprotestors to limit the possibility of violence. One of the clearest statements limiting discretion came in a case also involving free exercise of religion claims, when Jehovah's Witnesses, without a license required for religious solicitation, had made anti-Catholic statements on the street to passers-by. To allow local officials to determine what was religion for purposes of the license, the Court said, was constitutionally improper (*Cantwell v. Connecticut,* 1940).

The question of limitations on protests and demonstrations, beyond those involving union picketing, came to the fore in the 1960s, as a result of the civil rights movement and anti-Vietnam war protests. This was the period when violence produced legislative reaction such as the 1968 Open Housing Act's "Rap Brown" provision banning the crossing of state lines to incite a riot (used in the Chicago Seven case). The proposed federal criminal code revisions not only carry forward such provisions but may add others that might restrict activities of those opposed to nuclear power or the draft.

At first affirming the right to demonstrate peacefully in order to petition one's government (a march to the state capitol), even the "liberal" Warren Court began to sustain limitations on picketing, particularly at courthouses and jails, even without a showing that operation of the facilities had been hindered. (*In* prisons, officials have been given considerable leeway in regulating those entrusted to their care, although First Amendment rights penetrate when asserted by those on the outside, as in the right to receive mail from prisoners.) In other contexts, however, the Court will not let officials impose prior restraints on peaceful demonstrations, for example, leafleting outside a realtor's home or Skokie's efforts to limit Nazi demonstrations.

A shift in approach from the Warren to Burger Courts became evident when shopping centers—"privately" owned but "public" in character—were the scene of activity. Union picketing in front of a store in a shopping center was first allowed, because the shopping center was like the "company towns" to which free speech protections had earlier been extended (*Food Employees v. Logan Valley Plaza,* 1968). The Burger Court, however, allowed shopping centers to ban general political leafletting (about the Vietnam war) (*Lloyd Center v. Tanner,* 1972) and indeed directly overruled the Warren Court a few years later. When it later sustained a state court ruling giving such protection to the same free speech rights under a state constitution (*Pruneyard Shopping Center v. Robins,* 1980), the Court illustrated that civil liberties may be more thoroughly protected at the state than at the federal level. Antiwar protest also took the form of flag desecration and draft card burning. In one of its more conservative decisions, the Warren Court, showing considerable deference to congressional action and ignoring Congress' motivation, sustained draft card burning convictions under statutes requiring that draft cards be carried at all times (*O'Brien v. U.S.,* 1965). The Burger Court, although some expected it to rule otherwise, protected flag desecration, for example, the wearing of flag emblems, because of statutory vagueness and the activity's symbolic aspects.

The Court did, however, make it extremely difficult to mount political activity at or near military bases. Giving considerable deference to military commanders' decision-making authority, the Court allowed those commanders to limit political activity on the base, in part because service personnel had access to political activities off the military base (*Greer v. Spock,* 1976). In a recent decision, the Court went so far as to allow banning of circulation of petitions to Congress with respect to complaints about military matters, giving short shrift to the associational rights of those trying to join the petition signing (*Brown v. Glines,* 1980). Perhaps most striking is the Court's explicitly stated position that free speech rights are indeed limited in the military context (*Parker v. Levy,* 1974).

I. Right of Association

Policy concerning the right of association must focus on interest groups, including political parties, as well as on individuals' broader right to associate, such as the right of unrelated individuals to live together. Religious freedom is also largely associational. The cases on the question of whether civil courts can decide disputes involving religious groups (yes, but only if they do not have to decide theological questions) directly involve the question of government impingement on religious association, as do tax exemptions for religious property, sustained because of the "excessive entanglement" between church and state that would otherwise result (*Walz v. Tax Commission,* 1970). These associational elements are also apparent in continuing policy controversy about whether government may regulate certain religious groups (e.g., the Worldwide Church of God) because they are perceived as "cults" that "kidnap" and "brainwash" young adults. Even the attempt to *investigate* such activities usually brings a strong objection that First Amendment freedoms—both "free exercise of religion" and the right of association—are being invaded. The issue of cults reveals a host of competing interests: an individual's right to make associational choices, parents' family rights to protect their children and values they have inculcated, and the government's interest in preventing decisions based on fraud or duress.

Perhaps most fundamental to the right of association is one's right to belong to certain groups. This issue arises directly with respect to government employees. The traditional doctrine that a government employee retains constitutional rights but has no constitutional right to remain a government employee has lost some of its force, but government employees do surrender some citizen rights, even as to free speech where "reasonably necessary to promote effective government" (*Brown v. Glines,* 1980: 600, n. 13). Although even a nontenured public university professor may not be discharged for exercising free speech rights, the Hatch Act's limitations on government employees' political activity have been sustained against a variety of attacks, including those focusing on freedom of expression and association (*Civil Service Commission v. Letter Carriers,* 1973).

Closely related is a group's right to withhold information about members. If the right not to sign a broadly worded disclaimer affidavit or not to have to list memberships as a condition of employment allows an individual a privacy interest to withhold information about personal activities, the right of an organization to "do business" without providing such lists (a right established in connection with the South's 1950s "counterattack" on the NAACP) protects the members themselves—from economic and physical harassment —and the organization, by making it easier for individuals to join. Nondisclosure issues also affect campaign finance regulation: General disclosure provisions have been upheld against a right of association claim, but minor parties need make only a limited showing of likely harassment to be exempt from the provisions (*Buckley v. Valeo,* 1976). Also affecting political parties as associations are rulings sustaining the national party organization's power to determine procedures by which convention delegates will be chosen and decisions limiting patronage firings as interfering with employees' associational rights.

Once the right to belong to groups has been established, the next policy issue is whether those groups can operate in certain contexts. For many years, government employees could not join unions or, if they could, "outside" unions could not operate among government employees. However, in a major change in policy, recognition of public employee unions has proceeded rapidly in recent years, and the right of those unions to bargain collectively with the public employer has also been established by statute in many jurisidctions (Britton, 1976). (When prison inmates attempted to form unions, the Court sharply limited the inmates' associational rights.) Whether certain dissident groups such as the Students for a Democratic Society (SDS)—and more recently gay liberation groups—should be recognized on campuses became an issue in the 1960s, but the Supreme Court told university officials that they could not deny recognition simply because of groups' political views, as long as the groups agreed to adhere to reasonable regulations (*Healy v. James,* 1972).

The degree to which the group's activities can be regulated is also of considerable importance. Most rulings in this area turn directly on the Constitution, but federal statutory provisions, such as those about labor unions' rights to solicit members prior to union recognition or a certification election under the Wagner (Labor Relations) Act, also have to be interpreted, most recently with respect to such rights in the context of solicitation in certain areas of hospitals. Both lobbying and litigative activities have been subject to regulation. Registration and disclosure requirements for activities aimed directly at legislators are considered legitimate, but efforts to regulate "indirect" or "grass roots" lobbying (even by disclosure) have met with more resistance. Attacks have been made on the litigative activities of the NAACP and ACLU, with states charging the organizations with barratry (solicitation of cases, usually for a financial consideration). As part of its effort to sustain both the NAACP's activities and general rights of association, the Court held that the right of association clearly entails the ability to assist members in asserting their constitutional rights through litigation *(NAACP v. Button,* 1963), policy recently reaffirmed. Other decisions have upheld the right of groups (labor unions) to assist their members in finding legal counsel or in bringing client and counsel together.

IV. CONCLUSION

Policy making with respect to free speech elements of civil liberties is made primarily through the courts, making Supreme Court pronouncements in this area of particular significance. Attention to legislative activity is likely to increase, but the Court is likely to remain the predominant policy actor for some time to come. It is also clear that, regardless of the character of new justices who may be appointed, our policy will continue to be one that, despite the First Amendment's apparently clear language, accepts numerous restrictions on freedom of speech, both in terms of content and the circumstances in which speech-related activities take place, although some of those limitations are almost inevitable because of the conflicts of values that must be resolved as civil liberties policy is made. That policy will also continue to be made in the context of continuing threats to civil liberties and a lack of support for granting civil liberties to disliked groups. It is hoped that this presentation of basic elements in civil liberties policy and policy making will stimulate work in this area and particularly that policy-analytic tools applied elsewhere will be brought to bear on this material.

REFERENCES

Bayley, D. (1964). *Public Liberties in the New States.* Rand McNally, Chicago.

Bonnicksen, A. L. (1980). Obscenity reconsidered: Bringing broadcasting into the mainstream commentary. *Valparaiso University Law Review 14*: 261-293.

Brennan, W. J., Jr. (1979). The symbiosis between the press and the court. *Rutgers Law Review 32*: 173-183.

Britton, T. C. (1976). Faculty rights to bargain collectively. In *Civil Liberties,* S. L. Wasby (Ed.). Lexington Books, Lexington, MA, pp. 37-48.

Bullock, C. S., III, and Rodgers, H. R., Jr. (1972). *Law and Social Change.* McGraw-Hill, New York.

—— (1975). *Racial Equality in America.* Goodyear, Pacific Palisades, CA.

Canon, B. C. (1973-1974). Is the exclusionary rule in failing health? Some new data and a plea against a precipitous conclusion. *Kentucky Law Journal 62*: 681-730.

Casper, J. (1972). *Lawyers Before the Warren Court.* University of Illinois Press, Urbana.

Claude, R. P. (Ed.) (1976). *Comparative Human Rights.* Johns Hopkins University Press, Baltimore.

Conway, M. M. (1981). Anti-discrimination laws and the problems of policy implementation. In *The Analysis of Policy Impact,* J. G. Grumm and S. L. Wasby (Eds.). Lexington Books, Lexington, MA.

Dolbeare, K., and Hammond, P. (1971). *The School Prayer Decisions: From Court Policy to Local Practice.* University of Chicago Press, Chicago.

Dye, T. (1971). *The Politics of Equality.* Bobbs-Merrill, Indianapolis, IN.

Falk, R. A. (Ed.) (1968-1976). *The Vietnam War and International Law,* 4 vols. Princeton University Press, Princeton, NJ.

Gibson, J. L., and Bingham, R. D. (1979). Conditions of commitment to civil liberties: Libertarian behavior of American elites. Paper presented to American Political Science Association, Washington, DC.

Grossman, J. B., and Grossman, M. A. (Eds.) (1971). *Law and Change in Modern America.* Goodyear, Pacific Palisades, CA.

Halpern, S. C. (1976). Assessing the litigative Role of ACLU Chapters. In *Civil Liberties,* S. L. Wasby (Ed.). Lexington Books, Lexington, MA, pp. 159-168.

Hanus, J. J. (1976). Informational privacy. In *Civil Liberties,* S. L. Wasby (Ed.). Lexington Books, Lexington, MA, pp. 119-128.

Johnson, R. (1967). *The Dynamics of Compliance.* Northwestern University Press, Evanston, IL.

Kluger, R. (1976). *Simple Justice.* Knopf, New York.

Milner, N. (1971). *The Supreme Court and Local Law Enforcement: The Impact of Miranda.* Sage, Beverly Hills, CA.

Mittlebeeler, E. V. (1976). Freedom to travel abroad. In *Civil Liberties,* S. L. Wasby (Ed.). Lexington Books, Lexington, MA, pp. 139-147.

Molineu, H. (1981). Human rights: Administrative impact of a symbolic policy. In *The Analysis of Policy Impact,* J. G. Grumm and S. L. Wasby (Eds.). Lexington Books, Lexington, MA.

Morgan, R. E. (1976). The right to know. In *Civil Liberties,* S. L. Wasby (Ed.). Lexington Books, Lexington, MA, pp. 129-138.

Muir, W. K. (1967). *Prayer in the Public Schools: Law and Attitude Change.* University of Chicago Press, Chicago.

Murphy, W. F. (1962). *Congress and the Court.* University of Chicago Press, Chicago.

Orfield, G. (1969). *The Reconstruction of Southern Education.* Wiley, New York.

President's Commission on Obscenity and Pornography (1970). *Report.* Bantam Books, New York.

Pritchett, C. H. (1948). *The Roosevelt Court: A Study in Judicial Politics and Values,* 1937-1947. McGraw-Hill, New York.

Prothro, J. W., and Grigg, C. W. (1960). Fundamental principles of democracy: bases of agreement and disagreement. *Journal of Politics 22*: 276-294.

Radin, B. A. (1976). *Implementation, Change, and the Federal Bureaucracy: School Desegregation Policy in H.E.W., 1964-1968.* Teachers College Press, New York.

Randall, R. S. (1968). *Censorship of the Movies.* University of Wisconsin Press, Madison.

Robinson, D. C. (1976). Television, children, and censorship. In *Civil Liberties,* S. L. Wasby (Ed.). Lexington Books, Lexington, MA, pp. 25-36.

Rodgers, H. R. (Ed.) (1980). *Racism and Inequality: The Policy Alternatives.* Freeman, San Francisco.

Rodgers, H. R., and Bullock, C. S. (1976). *Coercion to Compliance.* Lexington Books, Lexington, MA.

Schubert, G. (1965). *The Judicial Mind.* Northwestern University Press, Evanston, IL.

Sorauf, F. J. (1976). *The Wall of Separation: The Constitutional Politics of Church and State.* Princeton University Press, Princeton, NJ.

Stewart, D. (1981). Organizational variables and policy impact: Equal employment opportunity. In *The Analysis of Policy Impact,* J. G. Grumm and S. L. Wasby (Eds.). Lexington Books, Lexington, MA.

Stouffer, S. (1955). *Communism, Conformity, and Civil Liberties.* Doubleday, New York.

Sullivan, J. L., Piereson, J., and Marcus, G. E. (1979). An alternative conceptualization of political tolerance. *American Political Science Review 73:* 781-794.

Tribe, L. H. (1978). *American Constitutional Law.* Foundation Press, Mineola, NY.

Van Dyke, V. (1970). *Human Rights, The United States, and the World Community.* Oxford University Press, New York.

Vose, C. (1959). *Caucasians Only: The Supreme Court, The NAACP, and the Restrictive Covenant Cases.* University of California Press, Berkeley.

Wasby, S. L. (1970). *The Impact of the United States Supreme Court.* Dorsey, Homewood, IL.

—— (1976a). *Continuity and Change: From the Warren Court to the Burger Court.* Goodyear, Pacific Palisades, CA.

—— (Ed.) (1976b). *Civil Liberties: Policy and Policy-Making.* Lexington Books, Lexington, MA.

—— (1976c). *Small Town Police and the Supreme Court.* Lexington Books, Lexington, MA.

—— (1979). Laying *Estes* to rest: A case note. *Justice System Journal 5:* 58-69.

Watts, M. W. (1976). Television and socialization to violence: Policy implications of recent research. In *Civil Liberties,* S. L. Wasby (Ed.). Lexington Books, Lexington, MA, pp. 13-24.

Westin, A. F., and Baker, M. A. (1972). *Databanks in a Free Society: Computers, Record-Keeping and Privacy.* Quadrangle Books, New York.

Table of Cases

Cox Broadcasting Co. v. Cohn, 420 U.S. 469 (1975)

Dennis v. U.S., 341 U.S. 494 (1951)

Estes v. Texas, 381 U.S. 532 (1965)

Food Employees v. Logan Valley Plaza, 391 U.S. 308 (1968)

Gannett Co. v. DePasquale, 99 S.Ct. 2899 (1979)

Gertz v. Welch, 418 U.S. 323 (1974)

Gitlow v. New York, 268 U.S. 652 (1925)

Gravel v. U.S., 408 U.S. 606 (1972)

Greer v. Spock, 424 U.S. 828 (1976)

Healy v. James, 408 U.S. 169 (1972)

Herbert v. Lando, 99 S.Ct. 1635 (1979)

Hutchinson v. Proxmire, 99 S.Ct. 2675 (1979)

Kissinger v. Reporters Committee for Freedom of the Press, 100 S.Ct. 960 (1980)

Kleindeinst v. Mandel, 408 U.S. 753 (1972)

Lamont v. Postmaster General, 381 U.S. 301 (1965)

Lehman v. City of Shaker Heights, 418 U.S. 298 (1974)

Linmark v. Willingboro, 431 U.S. 85 (1977)

Lloyd Center v. Tanner, 407 U.S. 551 (1972)

Miller v. California, 413 U.S. 15 (1973)

NAACP v. Button, 371 U.S. 415 (1963)

Nebraska Press Association v. Stuart, 427 U.S. 539 (1976)

Near v. Minnesota, 283 U.S. 697 (1931)

New York Times v. Sullivan, 376 U.S. 254 (1964)

New York Times v. U.S., 403 U.S. 713 (1973)

Nixon v. Administrator, General Services, 433 U.S. 425 (1977)

Nixon v. Warner Communications, 98 S.Ct. 1306 (1978)

O'Brien v. U.S., 391 U.S. 367 (1968)

Parker v. Levy, 417 U.S. 733 (1974)

Pell v. Procunier, 417 U.S. 817 (1974)

Pittsburgh Press v. Pittsburgh Human Relations Commission, 413 U.S. 376 (1973)

Pruneyard Shopping Center v. Robins, 100 S.Ct. 2035 (1980)

Richmond Newspapers v. Virginia, 100 S.Ct. 2814 (1980)

Rosenbloom v. Metromedia, 403 U.S. 29 (1971)

Roth v. U.S., 354 U.S. 476 (1957)

Schenck v. U.S., 249 U.S. 47 (1919)

Sheppard v. Maxwell, 384 U.S. 333 (1966)

Sherbert v. Verner, 374 U.S. 398 (1963)

Smith v. U.S., 431 U.S. 291 (1977)

Snepp v. U.S., 100 S.Ct. 763 (1980)

Stanley v. Georgia, 394 U.S. 557 (1969)

Tinker v. Des Moines School District, 393 U.S. 503 (1969)

Trans-World Airlines v. Hardison, 423 U.S. 65 (1977)

Walz v. Tax Commission, 397 U.S. 664 (1970)

West Virginia Board of Education v. Barnette, 319 U.S. 624 (1943)

Wooley v. Maynard, 430 U.S. 705 (1977)

Yates v. U.S., 354 U.S. 298 (1957)

Zemel v. Rusk, 381 U.S. 1 (1965)

Zurcher v. Stanford Daily, 98 S.Ct. 1970 (1978)

17

Economic Regulation

James E. Anderson / University of Houston, Houston, Texas

The regulation of private economic activity is one of the primary tasks of governments in the United States. In this chapter the focus is largely on the regulation of business by the national government. Other chapters in this Encyclopedia, such as those concerned with energy, labor, transportation, and environmental policies, overlap somewhat with this one. There is no simple or clear-cut way to differentiate them from this chapter. However, my concern is with economic regulation of business generally, whereas they focus on particular functional areas. A person wanting to get a thorough view of business regulation should regard these several chapters as an interrelated unit.

Several aspects of the economic regulation of business are treated in this chapter. We begin with a discussion of the nature of regulation, moving from there to an examination of the development of economic regulation in the United States. An effort is then made to convey a good notion of the "expanse" of regulation—its extent and variety. Next comes a summary of some of the problems in and criticisms of economic regulation, which, in turn, is followed by a discussion of the regulatory reform movement of recent years. Some of the accomplishments in deregulation are the focus of the next section, along with a couple of conclusions concerning the future of economic regulation in the United States.

I. THE NATURE OF REGULATION

What is regulation? (In this chapter regulation should be taken to mean economic regulation, even when that adjective is not included.) A well-known text on public policies states that "Regulation is what regulators do" (Shepard and Wilcox, 1979). A definition of that sort is catchy, perhaps, but it aids little in understanding. Shepard and Wilcox do go on to provide some amplification:

To regulate has at least three definitions. One is tough and unilateral: "to govern or direct according to rule." Another refers to compromise and smoothing over: "to reduce to order . . . to regularize." And another is superficial, perhaps empty: "to make regulations." Actual regulation varies among these, sometimes strict, sometimes trivial or even a tool of corporate interests.

The third definition is logically deduced from their statement that "Regulation is what regulators do." There is, however, nothing to be gained from belaboring this. Something better is needed.

Lawyers and economists often make a distinction between antitrust activity, intended to maintain competitive conditions in the economy, and "regulation." What it is that really differentiates these two categories of action is not made clear. One is just left with the notion that there is something different between government action designed to maintain competition and regulatory action, such as regulation of railroads by the Interstate Commerce Commission (ICC). In an important sense there is. Antitrust lays down some basic rules of the economic game—for example, "Thou shalt not monopolize," "Thou shalt not conspire to restrain trade." Within this framework of rules, businesses are left free to act, to compete, as they choose. Regulation of the railroads by the ICC goes beyond this, however, and really involves the agency in the management of railroads. Decisions to raise rates, to abandon service, to issue stocks require approval by the ICC. Control, in short, is more intensive, more thorough, and ICC judgment may be substituted for railroad judgment.

In each of these instances, however, and in all of the others that are popularly designated as regulation, the common element that one finds is control or restraint by public officials and agencies *to limit the discretion,* the freedom of action, of persons involved in economic activity by proscribing some actions and prescribing other actions. Thus, companies are told that they cannot restrain trade, however strongly they might wish to do so; or railroads are informed that they cannot raise rates without ICC approval. Regulatory programs may, and do, differ in the extent or degree to which they limit the discretion of the regulated parties, but the fact that in some way they do is what puts them into the category of "regulation." To put it another way, this is what makes regulations "regulatory." (One should not fail to note, of course, that sanctions or penalties are typically provided for those who do not comply with regulations. This gives them some "zing.")

A number of different techniques are used to regulate businesses. Some of the major categories are noted and illustrated here.

Rule Making.   Most regulatory agencies are authorized to make rules, which, following the Administrative Procedure Act (1946), can be defined as agency actions of "general applicability and future effect." Rules are usually intended to fill in the details of the law, given that Congress tends to legislate in general terms. Thus, the Occupational Safety and Health Administration (OSHA) is authorized to make and enforce rules to protect against industrial illnesses and accidents, the Federal Aviation Agency (FAA) to make rules governing airline safety, and the Federal Trade Commission (FTC) to make rules about unfair or deceptive practices.

Adjudication.   Agency ajudication involves the application of a statutory provision or a rule to a particular situation. The output of a successful adjudication (from the agency perspective) is an order or directive telling someone to do or not do something; thus the FTC may direct a company to "cease and desist" using a particular advertising claim because it is deceptive, or the ICC may direct a railroad to make reparation to a shipper who was charged an unreasonable rate. Agency adjudication is akin to action by the courts, whereas rule making is essentially legislative in nature.

Price, Rate, and Profit Controls.   Agencies are often authorized to regulate the rates or prices charged by companies and, in the case of public utilities, their rates of returns or profit levels. Railroad rates are regulated by the ICC, the prices charged by gasoline stations by the Economic Regulatory Administration (Department of Energy), and interstate telephone rates by the Federal Communications Commission (FCC). In somewhat different fashion, employers are required to pay at least a minimum wage ($3.35 an hour in 1982) by the Fair Labor Standards Act, and banks were prohibited from paying interest on checking accounts by the Banking Act of 1933. In 1980 Congress passed banking legislation that lifted this prohibition in 1981.

Standard Setting (and Inspection).   Regulation often involves the setting and enforcement of standards, through inspections and related proceedings. Standards, which may be set by Congress itself or by administrative agencies, may involve such matters as industrial health and safety, automobile safety, control of air and water pollution, "sound" banking practices, or the quality of grains. In some instances, such as pollution control or automobile safety, a distinction may be made between performance and specification standards. A performance standard would set a goal for pollution reduction, with companies being left to exercise discretion as to how to meet the goal. In contrast, a specification standard would require the use of scrubbers to reduce smokestack emissions. Standards are often enforced through inspection—the examinations of premises, products, books and records, and so on,—to determine compliance or noncompliance.

Licensing.   Licensing, which may also be called enabling action, is another common regulatory technique. Licenses are sometimes called "licenses," but they also can be named franchises, permits, certificates of convenience and necessity, or charters. Whatever its name, a license typically permits someone to do something that is otherwise prohibited, whether to drive a car, use the corporate form of business organization, operate a television broadcast station, or practice medicine. Licensing may be used to allocate scarce resources, such as in the case of television broadcast stations; to ensure a level of competence, as in the licensing of automobile drivers and doctors; or to reduce or limit competition, as in the case of commercial banks and many occupations. Some 75 different trades, professions, and occupations are licensed by the various states, with the number ranging from 10 to 45 in a given state. It is, as was noted, a very widespread form of regulation.

Prohibition of Undesirable Practices.   Some practices or activities may be regarded as so undesirable, whether on moral or other grounds, that they are simply and completely banned. Of course, where standards are involved, those who do not meet the standards set either cannot engage in the pertinent activity or are subject to penalties, but there is at least the possibility of participation. Such does not exist when an activity is prohibited or banned, such as the private sale of liquor, the use of certain pesticides, or the conduct of business in an area zoned residential. The difference between standards and prohibition can be illustrated with banking regulation. There are standards for "sound" banking practices, such as those involving loans to officers, to which banks are required to comply. In contrast, many states ban the practice of branch banking. Here the foreclosure of activity is complete—no room at all is left for the exercise of private discretion.

Noncoercive Forms.   Efforts may be used to influence or shape the exercise of private discretion—to regulate—that are noncoercive in that no legal penalties or sanctions are attached to noncompliance. Examples include the use of mediation and conciliation in the settlement of labor disputes, voluntary standards (such as the Johnson administration's wage-price guideposts to control inflation), and "moral suasion" by the Federal Reserve Board to influence bank lending practices. Such techniques depend on a "consensus of purpose" for their effectiveness. It often does not develop.

Taxation.   The techniques discussed thus far are sometimes collectively referred to as traditional or classical regulation (Breyer, 1979). In the last several years, taxation as an alternative form of regulation has gained considerable popularity (but little actual usage). Thus, it has been proposed (Kneese and Schultze, 1975) that instead of standard setting and enforcement to control population, taxation could be used. A fee or tax would be imposed on each unit of a pollutant discharged sufficient to make it economically attractive for polluters to reduce their discharges and thereby avoid paying some or all of the tax. They would be left with discretion as to what means to use in cleaning up their operations. It is argued that the tax or fee system would be more effective than traditional regulation because it would utilize the incentives of the marketplace to achieve a public purpose. Opposition has come from those who are committed to traditional regulatory patterns, who believe that taxation should be reserved for revenue-raising purposes, and who envisage various administrative and political problems in the use of taxation for regulatory purposes (Commission on Law and the Economy, 1979).

Before moving to the next section, it seems advisable to compare regulation with the promotion of business and government ownership on the private discretion criterion. Promotion involves governmental encouragement or assistance to private business activities, whether through cash subsidies, tax benefits, the provision of free data and information, guarantee of loans, or construction of facilities (e.g., airports and harbors). This is done to induce businesses to undertake or continue involvement in desired activities by enhancing their profitability or the likelihood thereof. Businesses retain much discretion as to whether to engage in the promoted activities, although there is an element of control involved, but it is control through the carrot rather than the stick (Donkeys can be consulted to learn more about the comparative use of these techniques). To illustrate, assume government wants to bring about industrial plant modernization (to achieve what is now called reindustrialization). This could be done by making investment tax credits available to those who modernize. Or the government could set plant modernization standards and penalize those who failed to meet them. Which of the two businesses would prefer and which is likely to be most effective should be obvious.

The government might take the position, however, that private management is incapable of or unlikely to modernize a particular industry and decide that the only workable solution is to make it a government enterprise. If such were done, there would be no room left for the exercise of private managerial discretion; all would be governmentally determined. Although there are a variety of government enterprises in the United States, and many of them are more efficient than folklore would have it, there has been no strong urge to replace private enterprise with public enterprise. The Western European democracies rely considerably more on government enterprises than does the United States, especially in transportation and industrial production.

II. THE DEVELOPMENT OF THE REGULATORY STATE

Governments in the United States have always engaged in the regulation of private economic activity, although for the first century of our national history most regulations flowed from the various state governments. The experiences of three states are illustrative. The Handlins (1947) report that in the decades following the American Revolution, Massachusetts engaged in such regulatory activities as the setting of manufacturing standards, the licensing of lotteries, the licensing of mill sites (on condition that the millers agree to limits on their rates, among other things), and the setting of tolls charged by bridges and ferries licensed by the state. In Pennsylvania, Hartz (1948) found an extensive variety of regulatory programs, including regulation of creditor-debtor relations, control of liquor traffic, labor legislation, regulation of banks and insurance companies, and inspection and licensing programs. "The inspection program included such articles as flour, fish, beef, pork, hogslard, flaxseed, butter, biscuits, harness and leather, tobacco, shingles, potash and pearlash, staves, heading and lumber, ground black-oak bark, pickled fish, spiritous liquors and gunpowder." Licensing was applied to such occupations as "innkeepers, peddlers, retailers of foreign goods, liquor merchants, brokers of various kinds, wharfage pilots, and auctioneers." Missouri, a newer Western state, also was actively involved in the economy, including inspection and licensing programs, and labor regulation (Primm, 1954).

Throughout much of the nineteenth century, national regulatory activity was rather limited, being restricted to such matters as protective tariffs, regulation of trade with the Indian tribes, and steamboat inspection. In the years after the Civil War, as industrialization increased and the economy became more and more national in scope, pressures developed for the control of the railroads and large businesses ("trusts") spawned by the transformation of the economy. State regulation was first sought and, when this appeared ineffective or unavailable, attention turned to the national government. The enactment of the Interstate Commerce Act (1887) and the Sherman Act (1890) mark the beginning of a shift in political power and regulatory activity from the states to the national government. The twentieth century was to witness a tremendous expansion of national economic regulation.

National regulatory activity has continuously expanded since 1890, but it has been especially notable during three time periods—the Progressive Era, the New Deal years (especially the 1930s), and the 1960s and early 1970s. During the Progressive Era railroad and antitrust regulation was expanded, meat inspection and pure food and drug laws were enacted, and the Federal Reserve System was created. The Progressive Era saw regulation firmly established as the dominant method used by government in dealing with the problems of the new industrial society. As Musolf (1965) has remarked:

> In ideological terms, regulation has drawn strength from the general belief that it is a halfway house between laissez faire and socialism. If the former became increasingly inappropriate as the Industrial Revolution continued, the latter appeared equally inappropriate in an economy largely based on vigorous private enterprise. Certainly regulation lacks the ideological appeal of the other two, but America has not been fertile soil for elaborate ideologies. Regulation permits, and even invites, the piecemeal, pragmatic approach to specific public policy problems that seems to fit the American temperament.

After a period of comparative quiescence during the 1920s, the pace of regulatory expansion quickened markedly during the 1930s. The business community was in disarray and disfavor and the New Deal, dedicated to economic relief, recovery, and reform, produced a variety of major regulatory statutes. A partial listing of major statutes includes the two Agriculture Adjustment Acts, the Securities Exchange Act, the Public Utility Holding Company Act, the National Labor Relations Act, the Robinson-Patman Act, the Motor Carrier Act, the Communication Act of 1934, the Civil Aeronautics Act, the Natural Gas Act, the Fair Labor Standards Act, and the Food, Drug and Cosmetics Act of 1938. Some of this New Deal regulatory legislation, such as the National Labor Relations Act and the Food, Drug and Cosmetics Act, was intended primarily to protect the interests of disadvantaged groups in society, such as workers and consumers. Other statutes, while containing a protective element, were designed to help promote economic recovery and the interests of particular economic groups by restricting competition among their members. Here the Motor Carrier Act and the Civil Aeronautics Act are illustrative. Many of the independent regulatory commissions were products of New Deal legislation. By the end of the 1930s there was no doubt that, henceforth, a major role of the government would be that of regulator of the economy.

The third major period of regulatory expansion stretches from the mid-1960s to the mid-1970s. Much of the legislation enacted by Congress was concerned with protecting the environment and health and economic interests of consumers and workers. Some have characterized this legislation as being focused on protecting and improving the quality of life. Table 1 lists the various regulator statutes enacted during 1970-1980. Perusal of it will indicate that though there were some other concerns, such as economic stabilization and energy regulation, protection of consumers, workers, and the environment predominate.

Two aspects of this most recent surge in regulation merit brief notice. First, a number of major new regulatory agencies were created, including the Environmental Protection Agency, the Consumer Products Safety Commission, the Occupational Safety and Health Administration, and the National Highway Traffic Safety Administration. These agencies are organized along functional rather than industry lines. Second, the regulatory statutes are either quite lengthy and detailed in nature, such as the Employee Retirement Income Security Act (ERISA), or they confer broad discretion on the administering agency, such as the Consumer Product Safety Act. Detail, however, does not always reduce

Table 1. Federal Economic Regulatory Legislation: 1970–1980

Year enacted	Title of statute
1970	Clean Air Amendments
	Egg Products Inspection Act
	Occupational Safety and Health Act
	Poison Prevention Packaging Act
	Securities Investor Protection Act
	Economic Stabilization Act
	Fair Credit Reporting Act
1971	Economic Stabilization Act Amendments
	Federal Boat Safety Act
	Lead-Based Paint Poisoning Prevention Act
	Wholesome Fish and Fisheries Products Act
1972	Consumer Product Safety Act
	Motor Vehicle Information and Cost Savings Act
	Noise Control Act
	Equal Employment Opportunity Act
	Federal Environmental Pesticide Control Act
	Federal Water Pollution Control Act Amendments
	Ports and Waterways Safety Act
1973	Agriculture and Consumer Protection Act
	Emergency Petroleum Allocation Act
	Flood Disaster Protection Act
1974	Atomic Energy Act
	Commodity Futures Trading Commission Act
	Magnuson-Moss Warranty/FTC Improvement Act
	Council on Wage and Price Stability Act
	Employee Retirement Income Security Act
	Federal Energy Administration Act
	Transportation Safety Act
	Fair Labor Standards Act Amendments
	Safe Drinking Water Act
	Equal Credit Opportunity Act
	National Mobile Home Construction and Safety Standards Act
1975	Energy Policy and Conservation Act
	Securities Act Amendments
1976	Railroad Revitalization and Regulatory Reform Act
	Consumer Leasing Act
	Medical Devices Act
	Antitrust Improvements Act
	Consumer Product Safety Commission Improvement Act
	U.S. Grain Standards Act
	Toxic Substances Control Act

Table 1. (Continued)

Year enacted	Title of statute
1977	Surface Mining Control and Reclamation Act
	Clean Air Act Amendments
	Food and Agriculture Act
	Clean Water Act
	Fair Labor Standards Act Amendments
1978	Petroleum Marketing Practices Act
	Federal Pesticide Act
	Airline Deregulation Act
	Public Utility Regulatory Policies Act
	Futures Trading Act
	Natural Gas Policy Act
1979	Aviation Safety and Noise Abatement Act
	Pipeline Safety Act
	Trade Agreements Act
1980	Staggers Rail Act
	Regulatory Institutions Deregulation and Monetary Control Act
	Federal Trade Commission Improvement Act
	Motor Carrier Reform Act
	Solid Waste Disposal Act Amendments

administrative discretion, as the administration of the Internal Revenue Code by the Internal Revenue Service clearly indicates.

Many factors—political, economic, social, and philosophical—have contributed to the development of the American regulatory state. One could handle the task of explaining its development ideographically, accounting for first one statute and then another. This would require much time and space, and would be both tedious and redundant. More useful is a focus on general causes of regulation. Two explanatory schemes will be summarized here. One is Steiner's (1953) classification of the underlying causes of regulation. The other is the theory of "market failure," which is perhaps more a rationale for regulation than an explanation of its development.

Steiner suggests that there are several somewhat overlapping causes underlying the growth of economic regulation. These include the following.

Technological Change and the Breakdown of Laissez Faire.   The transformation of the United States from a rural agrarian society into an urban industrial society produced conditions that did not conform to laissez faire assumptions. In a modern industrial society, for example, the pursuance of self-interest does not always lead to harmony, competition does not always prevail, and the market does not always provide security for those willing to work hard. People were (and are) often disciplined to accept the action of the market mechanism as the decider of their economic fate. Moreover, people came to insist that social and ethical values as well as economic values should be reflected in the operation of the economy. Generally, the economy (the marketplace) was seen as a product of human activity, as something properly subject to control and improvement through government action when its results were thought unacceptable. Persons suffering economic distress or dislocation in the market have often sought governmental aid in dealing with their problems.

Problems of Resource Coordination.　Government action has often been viewed as necessary to bring about more efficient coordination and utilization of resources. Regulation often requires the disclosure of information designed to improve individual economic decisions, as in the purchase of products or the borrowing of money, and to prevent fraud, deception, or chicanery. Macroeconomic controls—fiscal and monetary *policies*— are used by government in an attempt to ensure full utilization of the economy's resources and an absence of inflation. The Employment Act of 1946 generally committed the national government to this course of action.

Pressures to Resolve Group Conflicts.　Economic activity has been a fertile source of conflicts in American society. Conflicts have developed between labor and management, big business and small business, bankers and bank depositors, farmers and the purchasers of farm products, sellers and consumers, and so on. Government programs to deal with group conflicts have involved efforts to equalize group power (the Wagner Act), to resolve conflicts that threaten the public interest (labor dispute settlement), to establish the "rules of the game" among groups (prohibition of unfair competition), and to protect the economically weak against the economically strong. The last item, says Steiner, "has always been a function of government in the American code of political morality." The resolution of conflict, indeed, is a basic reason for the existence of government.

The Socialization of Risk.　People have long been interested in shifting some or many of the risks of economic life from themselves to government. People have always been concerned with security. What has changed in the twentieth century is not so much the desire for security as the way security is defined and the means for achieving it. Much more reliance is now placed on government action to protect individuals against the hazards of old age, unemployment, industrial illness and accident, and low incomes. Many businesses have also successfully sought greater security through government action, whether in the form of protective tariffs to reduce foreign competition, restrictions on entry into businesses (such as commercial airlines and motor carriers) to reduce domestic competition, or subsidies to reduce the costs and risks of investment and entrepreneurship. What is it but a concern basically with security, a concern over the risks of competition, that caused many airline, motor carrier, and railroad officials to resist deregulation (albeit, perhaps, in the name of the need to maintain an adequate transportation system, the public interest, or some other higher goal)?

Factors such as these, it must be stressed, are *underlying* causes. They help explain why people often seek governmental assistance, in our case regulatory programs, in dealing with perceived economic problems. They do not explain why some succeed in this endeavor and others do not, why Congress established a Consumer Products Safety Commission but refused to authorize a few years later an Agency for Consumer Advocacy. Such discrete actions will depend on the configuration of political forces that exist at a particular time and focus on a particular issue. These factors, viewed in historical perspective, do help to explain (but not necessarily to justify) why regulatory programs were sought from government, and why the role of government, especially the national government, shifted from that of "watchman" to that of active and pervasive regulator.

In recent years, the theory of "market failure" has gained considerable acceptance as a rationale for government intervention in the economy and as a critique of current regulatory programs. The market is seen as the norm, as the best means of securing the efficient allocation of resources for a society and such other values as individual freedom and the minimization of governmental power. Only when the market does not work properly, when it "fails," should government intervene. When do these failures occur?

One is in the case of "natural monopolies." In some instances the economics of scale may be such that it is inefficient for more than one firm to supply a product such as eletrical power. In the absence of regulation, the firm could restrict its output and charge prices above the "competitive level." Regulation in such instances is seen as necessary to protect consumers against the exercise of monopoly power and to help secure allocative efficiency by setting rates for the monopolists at a "competitive level."

Regulation may also be justified when there are third-party or spillover effects that are not reflected in the price of a product. Thus the costs of air and water pollution resulting from the operation of a factory may not be reflected in the prices of its products. More of these products may be purchased than would be the case if their (higher) prices reflected the true costs of production. Regulation to require a reduction in pollution is then justified to ensure that the costs of pollution are not ignored. Another way to do this would be to levy a fee or tax on the discharge of pollutants by the factory. (Moreover, there is really no way to establish a market for clean air.)

Third, consumers may lack the information necessary for the market system to operate effectively. If they lack information on the quality of products, the true cost of interest, or the potential effectiveness of a drug, they will not be able to evaluate competing products effectively and make rational economic decisions. A misallocation of resources may again be the consequence. Government action here may be taken to ensure that buyers will have sufficient information or perhaps to reduce the costs of information that might conceivably be obtained by them acting alone. Market economists see this as the justification for truth-in-lending legislation. Others may see it as necessary to protect borrowers against deception.

Fourth, the government action may be necessary to maintain competition. Classical economics to the contrary, competition neither always prevails nor maintains itself. Many of those who prefer the market system to government regulation for allocation of resources and values see a need for antitrust action to maintain competitive conditions in the economy. Action may be necessary to block the development of monopolies, to break them up when they exist, or to prevent restrictions on competition, as through price-fixing agreements. Interestingly, price fixing is the most clear-cut and obvious violation of the Sherman Act's prohibition of restraints of trade; it is also the form of violation most frequently proceeded against by the Antitrust Division.

Although there may be other grounds for government intervention, these should amply illustrate the "market failutes" rationale for regulation. Articles analyzing the regulatory programs from this point of view appear with regularity in the *Journal of Law and Economics.* This perspective also undergirds the analysis of federal regulation done by the American Bar Association's Commission on Law and the Economy (1979). Those for whom the market failures rationale is appealing find many current regulatory programs to be undesirable. They have indeed helped give impetus to the current movement for deregulation in the transportation, banking, and natural gas industries. More reliance, it is said, should be placed on competition as a regulator of economic behavior.

III. THE "EXPANSE" OF REGULATION

That the national government is now engaged in a vast amount of regulatory activity is beyond question. It is not easy, however, to convey a good view, in limited space, of the extent and variety of existent regulation, let alone its impact on economy and society.

One rough way to provide a notion of the expanse of the regulatory state is to list, as is done in Table 2, the various national regulatory agencies. In developing the list, the definition of a regulatory agency developed by the Senate Committee on Government Operations (1977a) was used (except for the appointment criterion). It reads:

> A Federal regulatory agency . . . is one which (1) has decision-making authority, (2) establishes standards or guidelines conferring benefits and imposing restrictions on business conduct, (3) operates principally in the sphere of domestic business activity, (4) has its head and/or members appointed by the President . . . subject to Senate confirmation . . . and (5) has its legal procedures generally governed by the Administrative Procedure Act.

The list in Table 2, which totals 42, should encompass all of the major regulatory agencies and many of the lesser ones. In comparison, the General Accounting Offices says that there are 116 regulatory agencies, whereas President Jimmy Carter, in his March 1979 message on regulatory reform, said that there were 90. What one finds is determined partly by one's definition and one's purposes. (In campaigning for the Presidency in 1976, Carter stated that there were more than 1900 national administrative agencies. No one has apparently located them or the basis for his figure.) My list, although comparatively modest in number, should nonetheless indicate that there is a whole lot of regulating going on.

A technique that has gained some currency for depicting the growth in the volume of regulations is the comparison of the number of pages in the *Federal Register* for various years. Thus one might learn that the *Federal Register* expanded (as it did) from approximately 20,000 pages in 1970 to 61,000 pages in 1978, for a growth rate of slightly more than 300 percent! (The exclamation mark indicates that this is a startling fact.) In actuality, however, this is a very rough measure at best of the increase in regulation. Only a small portion of the *Federal Register's* pages are accounted for by the final rules issued by agencies. Much more is taken up by informational materials—announcements, proposed rules, descriptions of agency proceedings, and the like. A better measure would seem to be the growth of the *Code of Federal Regulations,* which expanded by about 40 percent during the 1970–1978 period, for a "solid" but less spectacular rate of growth. Does this, however, mean that the economy was 40 percent more controlled at the end of the period in question? I don't know. Much depends on such matters as the nature of the regulations, the number of persons affected by them, and the way in which they are enforced. Clearly, one should take statistics such as those in this paragraph with

Table 2. National Regulatory Agencies (1980)

Independent Regulatory Commissions
  Interstate Commerce Commission
  Federal Reserve Board
  Federal Trade Commission
  Federal Energy Regulatory Commission
  National Labor Relations Board
  Securities and Exchange Commission
  Federal Communications Commission
  Civil Aeronautics Board
  Federal Maritime Commission
  Consumer Products Safety Commission
  Nuclear Regulatory Commission
  Commodity Futures Trading Commission

Independent Agencies
  Environmental Protection Agency
  Federal Deposit Insurance Corporation
  Federal Mediation and Conciliation Service
  Equal Employment Opportunity Commission
  National Transportation Safety Board
  Federal Home Loan Bank Board
  National Mediation Board

Bureaus in Executive Departments
  Agricultural Stabilization and Conservation Service (USDA)
  Agricultural Marketing Service (USDA)
  Food Safety and Quality Service (USDA)
  Federal Grain Inspection Service (USDA)
  Animal and Plant Health Inspection Service (USDA)
  Food and Drug Administration (HHS)
  Antitrust Division (Justice)
  Drug Enforcement Administration (Justice)
  Wage and Hour Division (DOL)
  Office of Federal Contract Compliance (DOL)
  Mine Safety and Health Administration (DOL)
  Occupational Safety and Health Administration (DOL)
  Federal Aviation Administration (DOT)
  Federal Railroad Administration (DOT)
  National Highway Traffic Safety Administration (DOT)
  Economic Regulatory Administration (Energy)
  National Bureau of Standards (Commerce)
  Office of the Comptroller of the Currency (Treasury)
  U.S. Customs Service (Treasury)
  Bureau of Alcohol, Tobacco, and Firearms (Treasury)
  Office of Interstate Land Sales Registration (HUD)
  Office of Surface Mining Reclamation and Enforcement (Interior)
  U.S. Geological Survey (Interior)

---

a large grain of caution. Yet the number and variety of economic regulatory programs is obviously increasing. So, too, is the scope and complexity of the economy.

Regulatory programs differ considerably in terms of their purposes, control techniques, number of people affected, direct and indirect costs, economic impact, and other characteristics. Simply to lump them together under the heading of "regulation" is to gloss over such differences. A somewhat rudimentary classification scheme involving five categories of regulation, using general purpose as a distinguishing criterion, is presented here.

Competitive regulatory programs are concerned with maintaining competitive condition of the economy, with preventing monopolization and restrictions on competition. Antitrust legislation is the prime component of this category, and it has long been a cardinal feature of American regulatory policy.

Protective regulatory programs are intended to prevent or eliminate the existence of activities and conditions variously regarded as unfair, unsafe, unhealthy, undesirable, or, for good measure, immoral. Illustrative are programs to prevent air and water pollution, industrial illnesses and accidents, the sale of unsafe or ineffective drugs, the sale of unwholesome meat and poultry products, the use of deceptive trade practices, and to ensure commercial airline safety. Most programs for the protection of consumers and workers would fit into this category.

Promotional regulatory programs serve to protect or benefit the interests of those who are ostensibly regulated. Often this involves programs that limit entry into businesses or occupations or lessen competition in some manner among those in the field. Some would call much of what is involved here "self-regulation." A good set of illustrations are state occupational licensing programs, which are frequently dominated by members of the licensed groups. There is also a good measure of self-regulation in agricultural marketing orders for milk, fruits, and vegetables, and some of it in agricultural price support programs. Other examples in this category are tariffs, and other import-restriction programs, the Robinson-Patman Act (intended to lessen price competition for the benefit of small businesses), and "buy America" requirements for government purchasing.

Some regulatory programs, established for other purposes, may over time take on a promotional orientation. Railroad regulation by the ICC was initiated primarily to protect user interests. After enactment of the Transportation Act of 1920, which gave the ICC power to set *minimum* railroad rates, among other things, regulation became more and more responsive to and promotive of the railroads' interests. Motor carrier regulation is another example of this sort of regulatory metamorphosis.

Managerial regulatory programs, which could also be called public utility-type programs, are usually but not always applied to natural monopolies—for example, electric power, gas, and telephone companies—where it is thought that competition cannot be used as a regulatory mechanism. This type of regulation typically involves rate and service regulation, which means that the regulating agencies become participants in the making of basic managerial decisions. Controls may also be exercised over market entry and financial and accounting practices. This form of regulation is the most restrictive of the exercise of private discretion in economic activity. Examples include regulation of railroads and motor carriers by the ICC and shipping companies by the Federal Maritime Commission. Every state has a regulatory commission applying such regulation to various public utility industries. As these illustrations indicate, this variety of regulation tends to focus on particular industries, as does promotional regulation. Protective and competitive regulation, in contrast, are directed at various practices or activities throughout the economy, such as unfair methods of competition or unsafe working conditions.

Macroeconomic regulatory programs are intended to influence the overall operation of the economic system. Fiscal and monetary policies, and sometimes price and wage controls, are used to combat inflation and recession, and to encourage economic growth. The national government became fully committed to this sort of regulatory activity only after World War II. Although macroeconomic regulatory policies focus on the economy as a whole, with the partial exception of monetary policy, they are directed at the behavior of particular groups of persons—those whose taxes are raised or lowered, or those seeking to increase prices when restraints on prices are in effect, and so on. Monetary policy operates somewhat differently in that when, say, credit is tightened, no particular set of persons is the target. In the nature of things, however, some may find it more difficult to borrow money than others—small businesses may experience more difficulty than large businesses, for example, because of differing credit ratings. In one way or another, macroeconomic programs are intended to influence or control the exercise of private economic discretion.

Most regulatory programs can be placed into one or another of these categories, although some programs will overlap two or more categories. Thus, meat inspection may be viewed as protective in that it is designed to protect consumers against the sale of unwholesome meat; it may also be promotional in that, by incurring consumer confidence, it encourages the purchase of meat products to the benefit of business. It should not be surprising that a field of activity so complex and diverse as business regulation cannot be put neatly into a few pigeon holes.

However one measures the volume of regulation currently in effect in the United States—whether by number of regulatory agencies, volume of pages in the *Code of Federal Regulations* or *Federal Register,* budgetary costs, or societal costs—there is no doubt that it has increased greatly since the beginning of the New Deal years, let alone some earlier time. But it is also true that this increased volume of regulation has been imposed upon a larger, more diverse, more complex economy. If much economic activity is subject to government control, still more seems to be left to the exercise of private economic discretion. How much, though, is a splendid topic for conjecture and debate, as well as more systematic inquiry.

IV. REGULATORY PROBLEMS

Regulatory programs have generated a substantial variety and volume of problems, complaints, and alleged failures. Everyone seems to have a favorite regulatory anecdote or two involving the misuse, abuse, nonuse, or overuse of regulatory power. Whether one finds a particular regulatory program to be necessary and effective depends on a variety of factors—the nature of the program, the skill and zeal with which it is administered, the economic interests and ideological perspective of the person making the judgment, and so on. Very few, if any, persons would say that all regulatory programs are either necessary, desirable, or reasonably well administered. So, too, would few persons consider economic regulation generally unnecessary and inappropriate. (Some of the more devout followers of the "Chicago school of economics" do seem to approach this position.) However, both the general supporters and general critics cite a variety of problems (or shortcomings, or failures) in the conduct of regulatory programs. In this section some of these problems are surveyed in order to provide a perspective on regulatory performance as well as background for the next section on regulatory reform. None of the problems cited is relevant to all regulatory agencies or programs, nor are all relevant to a particular program or agency. Such is the case with generalizations. Some of the problems cited are more economic, others are more political or administrative in nature.

Price or rate regulation is often said to result in distortion of the market and interference with prices as allocators of resource. Thus, it has been contended that regulation of airline rates by the Civil Aeronautics Board (CAB) kept passenger rates too high, thereby discouraging air travel while stimulating competition among the airlines in terms of services and "frills." The result, from a market perspective, is a misallocation of resources. Conversely, it was also frequently contended that regulation of natural gas prices by the Federal Power Commission (the predecessor of the Federal Energy Regulatory Commission) kept prices too low, encouraging excess consumption of natural gas while discouraging exploration and development of additional supplies. The consequence was a shortage of natural gas in the mid-1970s. (All, it should be noted, do not agree with this viewpoint.) Generally, critics of rate or price regulation view the market as a better way of determining prices and bringing supply and demand into balance.

Regulation sometimes produces, intentionally or otherwise, a reduction in competition. This is typically the case when there is control of entry by firms into an industry (or by persons into an occupation or a profession). Examples include control of airline entry by the CAB, banking entry by the Comptroller of the Currency and others, and radio and television broadcast entry by the FCC. Regulatory programs have also been designed to reduce price competition, as in the regulation of foreign shipping rates by the Federal Maritime Commission or railroad rates by the ICC. The Robinson-Patman Act of 1936 was intended to lessen price competition between small businesses and their larger competitors to the benefit of the former. (Neither the Antitrust Division nor the FTC, who share jurisdiction under the Robinson-Patman Act, now do much to enforce it.) Those who prefer competition find such regulation objectionable. They do not accept the contention that regulation is necessary to prevent "excessive competition." If undesirable practices such as "predatory pricing" occur, these could be dealt with by such means as the antitrust laws or private judicial action.

Regulation is also claimed sometimes to cause a reduction or delay in scientific or technological progress. Thus it is contended that the requirement that new drugs be proven safe and effective, which is administered by the Food and Drug Administration, has resulted in a decline in the rate of introduction of new and desirable drugs (Peltzman, 1973). The ICC has been blamed for delaying the use of "big john" cars for grain transportation and "piggyback" cars for hauling truck trailers by the railroads. These innovations were put into effect only after some years of delay, caused partly by concern of the ICC (and some railroads) with the uncertainty they might cause in the railroad industry (Kohlmeier, 1969).

In recent years a frequent complaint has been that regulations, while often of some benefit, also often entail costs that exceed their benefits. In short, regulatory programs are sometimes characterized by an unfavorable cost-benefit ration. Thus it may be argued that some air and water pollution standards set by the Environmental Protection Agency reduce pollution but at a level of costs (including direct administrative costs and industry costs of compliance) that exceeds their benefits (reduced health hazards, aesthetic values, etc.). This assumes, of course, that the costs and benefits of programs can be quantified with reasonable accuracy. In 1980 the U.S. Supreme Court held that a new more stringent standard for benzene discharges set by the Occupational Safety and Health Administration exceeded its legal authority because the agency did not demonstrate that its benefits justified the additional costs that would be imposed on industry. The underlying contention of the cost-benefit argument is that if the costs of a regulation or regulatory program exceed its benefits, there is a net reduction in social welfare and, on this basis, the regulation should be eliminated. Economic efficiency is the underlying value here. An examination of the literature will indicate that far more attention has been paid to the costs than the benefits of regulation. This in part reflects the ideological proclivities and economic interests of those involved.

Moving now to more political or administrative problems, a familiar feature of regulatory lore has been the contention that regulatory agencies are often "captured" by the groups they are to regulate, and regulation then becomes a means for promoting group interests rather than protecting the public interest. Favorite examples include the "capture" of the ICC, the CAB, and the Federal Maritime Commission by the railroads, airlines, and shipping companies, respectively. Some would say that this happens because as agencies move through their life cycle, gestation, youth, maturity, and old age), they lose their vigor and more or less fall naturally into the clutches of the regulated (Bernstein, 1955). Others see capture as a consequence of the fact that the regulated industries have intense and concentrated interests in regulation, whereas the interests of the public are limited and diffuse. There are also other explanations. Typically, however, one finds that neither the meaning of capture nor the process by which it is done is very well or convincingly explained. And further, if the CAB and the ICC were the captives as alleged of the airlines and the railroads, why did these two agencies take initiatives in deregulation in the later 1970s that were strongly opposed by the regulated industries? If agencies appear to be too responsive to the interests of those they regulate, this is much more likely to be a function of their statutory mandates. Whether "captured" or not, it may well be that some agencies are too responsive to those whom they regulate. But then they may be pushed in this direction by their authorizing statutes, and by the exercise of official discretion.

When regulatory agencies have overlapping or competing jurisdictions, a lack of coordination may occur. Railroad regulation may be implemented without regard for the impact it may have on other competing forms of transportation. The Ash Council (1971) was especially concerned about the lack of coordination in transportation regulation and recommended a merger of the various national transportation regulatory agencies. When national and state regulatory agencies operate in the same area, such as environmental protection or banking regulation, conflict of divergence in their activities may occur. Banks, for instance, may shift from national to state charters in order to avoid some requirements or disabilities of federal policy.

Economic regulation in the twentieth century has become predominantly regulation by administrative agencies that often operate under rather broad, general statutory mandates. Administrative regulation is sometimes characterized by such problems as slowness and delay in proceedings, cumbersome and complex procedures, inadequate information (as on the costs and benefits of proposed actions), and a lack of qualified personnel. Here the focus is on the issue of delay. A recent study by the Senate Committee on Governmental Affairs (1977b) reported that administrative agency proceedings averaged more than 19 months for licensing, 21 months for rate making, and 36 months for enforcement actions. In a survey for the committee of more than a thousand lawyers who practiced before eight major regulatory commissions, "undue delay" was most frequently cited as a major problem of federal regulation. The causes of delay include the volume of cases, complex procedural requirements, poor agency leadership and management, uncertainty, and efforts by affected private parties to put off final agency action. Slowness and delay are not confined to administrative regulation; it also appears in regulation involving the courts. A classic illustration involves the government's antitrust suit against IBM Corporation, filed in January 1969, on the last day of the Johnson administration; in January of 1982 the case was still in the trial stage when the government decided to dismiss it. A dozen years of work on the case thus came to naught.

Finally, agencies are often accused of making unwise, ill-considered, or "bad" decisions. Such judgments may issue from persons who find particular agency actions to be inconvenient, inexpedient, or otherwise counter to their interests. In other instances such judgments may be more impartial, based on the merits of the actions or consideration of their societal effects. It would, for example, seem difficult to accuse a person of partiality for regarding the Occupational Safety and Health Administration rule prohibiting the use of ice in drinking water in workplaces as unnecessary, dumb, or something of that sort. The rule was a carryover from an earlier era, when there was a fear that the ice used to cool drinking water might be cut from polluted ponds. OSHA did repeal the rule (which was one of the consensus standards adopted soon after the agency was established), along with several hundred others in 1978.

No claim is made that this discussion of regulatory problems is either complete or exhaustive. It should indicate, however, that all is not seen as well in the regulatory state and that the regulatory reform movement, to which we now turn, is based on more than an inherent American urge to engage in political and administrative tinkering.

V. REGULATORY REFORM

Several major efforts at regulatory reform have been made in the past, usually with a primary focus on the independent regulatory commissions. They were based on studies by the President's Committee on Administrative Management (1937), famous for its depiction of the regulatory commissions as "a 'headless fourth branch' of the Government, a haphazard deposit of irresponsible agencies and uncoordinated powers"; the Attorney General's Committee on Administrative Procedure (1941); the Hoover Commission (1949 and 1955); James M. Landis' Report on Regulatory Agencies to the President-Elect (1960); and the President's Advisory Council on Executive Organization (1971). Most of these studies recommended changes in regulatory agency organization and procedures. Generally, they did not result in much basic change because of a lack of responsiveness in Congress to executive proposals for changes in the regulatory commissions, which have been viewed by Congress (especially liberal Democrats therein) with some affection and proprietary instinct.

The last several years, however, have seen a substantial broadening of both the interest in and the scope of regulatory reform. Both Presidents Ford and Carter gave considerable attention of a continuing sort to regulatory reform, popular interest in reform expanded, and Congress displayed considerable interest (beyond the always present rhetoric) in the operation and improvement of the regulatory process. All of this can be collectively described, with limited hyperbole, as a regulatory reform movement. It is not, however, a movement that is monolithic in nature. Rather, following the lead of Welborn (1977), three general orientations toward regulatory reform—the traditionalist, populist, and restrictivist—may be identified and described.

The *traditionalist* orientation long dominated thinking about economic regulation, which was viewed for the most part as basically sound and necessary to control the exercise of private economic power. The basic structural change advocated by those with a traditionalist orientation is stronger presidential control and leadership of the regulatory agencies to overcome the diversity and lack of coordination in their activities. Beyond that only limited changes are seen as necessary to make the regulatory system fully sound and effective. These include such actions as larger budgets, better personnel, improved procedures, clarification of statutory authority, and better definitions of standards and improved internal agency organization and management. In a way their view is that the problems of regulation can be corrected by more and better regulation.

Those with the *populist* orientation also accept the necessity of economic regulation. They view corporate power with considerable suspicion and see a need for more regulation to ensure that governmental power dominates over corporate power. Presently, however, their view is that, at the least, business has been able to use its political power to cause regulatory programs to be more responsive to business interests than to those of the public. To put it another way, regulation has failed because it does not adequately benefit the public; the cause of this failure is essentially political.

Persons who hold the populist orientation believe that regulatory reform should be designed to ensure the existence of "pervasive and direct democracy in governmental and economic affairs" (Lazarus, 1974). There are two general routes to this goal. One is to reduce the influence of regulated interests by such means as limitations on *ex parte* contracts with agencies, strong conflict-of-interests rules, and restrictions on the employment of officials by regulated companies. The other route is to enhance the influence of the public in agency proceedings. This be done by such means as open meeting ("sunshine") requirements, creation of offices of consumer or public counsel within agencies, subsidization of public participation in agency proceedings, and permitting outside groups to petition agencies for regulatory action.

Persons with a *restrictivist* orientation have a basic dislike for administrative regulation, viewing much of it as unnecessary or a burdensome interference with the operation of the market. Business people, economists, and conservatives are numerous in this category. Business people tend to view regulation as bothersome and as a limitation on profits. Economists see it as something that more often than not restricts rather than promotes competition and interferes with the efficient allocation of resources. The restrictivists have several preferred reforms. One is the elimination of regulations that restrict competition, together with reliance on antitrust action to prevent the misuse of economic power

(Commission on Law and the Economy, 1979). Another is the use of market incentives (e.g., fees or taxes) rather than administrative regulation, as proposed in the case of environmental pollution. A third is to use the techniques of economic analysis, especially cost-benefit analysis, in appraising the effects of regulation and, of course, to be guided by the use of the results in policy making.

The presence of these orientations in the regulatory reform movement and some of its adherents is illustrated in a statement by Welborn (1977):

> Each of the three major orientations to questions about regulation are represented in the regulatory reform process, including in the Congress. The strongest reflection of the traditionalist orientation is in the agencies themselves and among the regulated and their representatives. The restrictivist orientation is reflected by economists generally and by those institutions which they populate. In the government, these include the Council of Economic Advisers and the Council on Wage and Price Stability. It is also reflected in significant ways in places such as the Antitrust Division of the Department of Justice, the Department of Transportation and the Federal Trade Commission . . . it [also] appeared in potent form at the presidential level during past years. The populist orientation, of course, is reflected in the main by public interest organizations such as those compising the Nader group and Common Cause.

The regulatory movement reform has produced a variety of positive responses. In line with the populist orientation, the government in the sunshine act, which became law in 1976, required many agencies to conduct their business in open public proceedings. Some agencies, such as the Federal Trade Commission, finance public participation in some of their proceedings. Changes in line with the traditionalist orientation include efforts by some agencies to develop criteria for more systematic enforcement programs, increased if still somewhat episodic congressional oversight of regulatory agencies, and various efforts to improve agency management. The Regulatory Flexibility Act (1980) is intended to make agencies more considerate of the problems and circumstances of small businesses (including compliance costs) when they develop regulations. (It will also make regulatory activity more complex.)

The most dramatic changes that have occurred reflect the impact of the restrictivist orientation. Many persons have come to believe, without accepting, the total philosophy of the restrictivists, that regulation can be made less burdensome while continuing to be effective in the protection of public interests. Two areas of restrictivist impact are especially notable—one is the expanding usage of cost-benefit analysis in the appraisal of regulation, the other is deregulation. Here attention will be given only to some recent developments in deregulation.

The deregulation movement was given major impetus by President Gerald Ford, who made deregulation a major goal of his administration. Strong support for deregulation also characterized the years of the Carter administration. Initially, it was easy to be cynical about the prospects for deregulation because the effort appeared to lack, among other things, a clear focus. For many deregulation seemed to mean "get rid of the regulatory programs I don't like and keep the programs I do like." Approaches of this sort lack a persuasive quality. However, efforts at deregulation have come to be focused on the regulated industries, especially in transportation, where regulation often involves limitations on competition. Economists and others have long been critical of these regulatory programs. In the later 1970s these programs were also criticized as contributing to inflation, thereby adding to support for reform. The result has been some substantial success in deregulation.

The Railroad Revitalization and Regulatory Reform Act of 1976 provided that railroad rates could not be held to be too low by the ICC if they covered the variable costs of providing service. When competition existed with other railroads, a carrier could set maximum rates at any level it chose. Moreover, rates could be raised or lowered by 7 percent in either direction if they were not "predatory" in nature and if the railroad did not dominate the market involved. All of this was intended to open up opportunities for competition. In the fall of 1980 the enactment of additional railroad deregulation legislation gave the railroads still more freedom in setting rates. What this amounts to is a lessening of regulation. In the case of the commercial airlines, something more drastic is now in process.

In October 1978, Congress enacted legislation that, unless it should be amended, will entirely phase out airline regulation by the CAB over a period of several years. Although the transitional provisions are too complex to summarize here, the legislation included the following timetable: CAB authority over domestic routes will end on December 31, 1981; its authority over domestic fares and rates, mergers, and acquisitions will expire on January 1, 1983; and the board will be abolished on January 1, 1985, with its remaining functions, such as those involving foreign air transportation, being transferred to other agencies. Domestic air transportation, if things go according to plan, will then be an unregulated industry.

The motor carriers' turn at deregulation came in 1980. Trucking deregulation enacted by Congress made it easier for new companies to enter the business; permitted individual truckers greater freedom in setting rates in a "zone of rate freedom" (rates can be raised or lowered up to 10 percent annually without ICC approval, etc.); and eliminated the antitrust immunity, which had been provided by the Reed-Bulwinkle Act of 1948, for some collective rate making through industry rate bureaus. Also, restrictions on hauling food were loosened, and various products used in agricultural production were exempted from regulation. In all, the legislation provides for considerable loosening of ICC regulation of truckers, which was something the agency had been threatening to do on its own.

These deregulation efforts drew support from a variety of sources—the Ford and Carter administrations, as already mentioned; consumer and public interest groups; many economists and others with a restrictivist orientation; and substantial majorities in Congress. These regulatory programs, which had flowered during the New Deal years, or earlier in the case of railroads, reflected a notion that restrictions on entry and regulation of rates were appropriate governmental responses to industry problems. By the 1970s this viewpoint had come under strong attack and deregulation appeared, to use a cliche, as "an idea whose time had come." As Wilson (1980) has suggested, ideas, as well as interests, can have important effects on the course of regulatory activity. Should the attention of the "deregulators" turn next to some newer regulatory programs—such as those concerned with safety in the workplace, consumer protection, and environmental protection—the likelihood of success will be much slimmer. These programs, given their concern with the quality of life and the environment, are still much in vogue with large segments of population. Thus a survey conducted for the Union Carbide Corporation in 1979 found that, among a national population sample, 60 percent favored stricter water pollution regulations, 52 percent stronger air pollution regulations, and 56 percent stronger industrial accident regulations (Siskind and Shor, 1980). Most of the other persons polled believed that the regulations ought to remain about the same; only a small percentage favored easing regulation. Such an opinion context, although it does not auger well for deregulation, does not bar the possibility of other types of regulatory reform. And it certainly did not seem in the spring of 1981 that the regulatory reform movement had spent its force.

Indeed, the deregulation movement was given new strength when the conservative Reagan administration took office in 1981. Some of its initial actions included the early elimination of domestic petroleum price controls, the establishment of a unit in the Office of Management and Budget to review "major" proposed regulations, the creation of a Presidential Task Force on Regulatory Relief (chaired by the Vice President) to ride herd on the regulatory system, and the issuance of an executive order requiring agencies to use the least costly method of reaching their regulatory goals and to prepare a regulatory impact analysis (including a description of potential costs and benefits) for each "major" rule. Moreover, most of the persons appointed to major positions in regulatory agencies and commissions appeared committed to the view that deregulation was necessary and desirable. Administration officials frequently spoke with fervor of the need to reduce further the scope and weight of regulation in order to "get government off the people's back."

The Reagan administration did succeed in slowing down the expansion of regulation and secured the rescission of some existing administrative regulations. However, no major or drastic reductions were made in consumer protection, environmental, and industrial health and safety regulatory programs. If such efforts were attempted, they would be likely to encounter strong resistance, as the poll mentioned above indicates. Piecemeal elimination of particular agency rules and regulations, and the moderation of the process of regulatory implementation, can have an important effect, although they may be a less ideologically pleasing strategy. Apart from the energy area, really sweeping alterations in the contours of the regulatory state to not seem highly probable. This, however, does not mean that the actions of the Reagan administration will not have important consequences for both the subjects and the beneficiaries of regulation. They likely will.

REFERENCES

Ash Council (The President's Advisory Council on Executive Organization) (1971). *A New Regulatory Framework*. U.S. Government Printing Office, Washington, DC.

Bernstein, M. (1955). *Regulating Business by Independent Commission* Princeton University Press, Princeton, NJ.

Breyer, S. (1979). Analyzing regulatory failure: Mismatches, less restrictive alternatives, and reform.

Commission on Law and the Economy (1979). *Federal Regulation: Roads to Reform*. American Bar Association, Washington, DC.

Handlin, O., and Handlin, M. F. (1947). *Commonwealth: A Study of the Role of Government in the American Economy: Massachusetts, 1774-1861*. New York University Press, New York.

Hartz, L. (1948). *Economic Policy and Democratic Thought: Pennsylvania 1776–1780.* Harvard University Press, Cambridge, MA.

Knees, A. V., and Schultze, C. L. (1975). *Pollution, Prices, and Public Policy.* Brookings Institution, Washington, DC.

Kohlmeier, L. (1969). *The Regulators.* Harper & Row, New York.

Lazarus, S. (1974). *The Genteel Populists.* Holt, Rinehart and Winston, New York.

Lowi, T. J. (1979). *The End of Liberalism.* Norton, New York.

Musolf, L. D. (1965). *Government and the Economy.* Scott, Foresman, Chicago.

Peltzman, S. (1973). An evaluation of consumer protection legislation: The 1962 drug amendments. *Journal of Political Economy 81*: 1067.

Primm, J. N. (1954). *Economic Policy in the Development of a Western State: Missouri 1820–1860.* Harvard University Press, Cambridge, MA.

Senate Committee on Governmental Affairs (1977a). *The Regulatory Appointments Process.* 85th Cong., 1st Sess. U.S. Government Printing Office, Washington, DC.

—— (1977b). *Delay in the Regulatory Process.* 95th Cong., 1st Sess. U.S. Government Printing Office, Washington, DC.

Shepard, W. G., and Wilcox, C. (1979). *Public Policies Toward Business.* Richard D. Irwin, Homewood, IL.

Siskind, F. B., and Shor, G. M. (1980). Regulations that get public approval. *Houston Chronicle,* August 21, 1980.

Steiner, G. A. (1953). *Government's Role in Economic Life.* McGraw-Hill, New York.

Welborn, D. M. (1977). Taking stock of regulatory reform. Paper presented at the 1977 Annual Meeting of the American Political Science Association, Washington, DC.

Wilson, J. Q. (1980). *The Politics of Regulation.* Basic Books, New York.

18

Labor Policy

Charles Bulmer and John L. Carmichael, Jr. / University of Alabama in Birmingham,
Birmingham, Alabama

I. BACKGROUND

Government policy in support of the labor movement in the United States was slow to
develop. In its modern form government promotion of organized labor really began in
1935 with the passage by Congress of the National Labor Relations Act (Wagner Act).
This act as amended by the Taft-Hartley Act in 1947 and the Landrum-Griffin Act in
1959 constitutes major legislation affecting labor.

The right of workers to join together in unions was recognized in the United States
rather early. In 1842 a significant decision by the Supreme Court of Massachusetts,
Commonwealth v. Hunt, declared that labor unions were not illegal per se; it was only
when labor unions engaged in unlawful activity that their actions were proscribed. Although this was a decision by a single state court, it was generally accepted doctrine
throughout the United States. Nevertheless, activities of labor organizations were hindered by such devices as civil suits against their leaders for damages, and in the latter part
of the nineteenth century by the labor injunction. This latter weapon was most effective
and was used with increasing frequency in the twentieth century, attaining perhaps its
most widespread use in the 1920s.

In 1890 the Sherman Act was passed by Congress. Aimed at controlling the growth
of business trusts, the act was unclear with respect to its possible use against labor unions.
The act declared that any combination or trust in restraint of trade was illegal. Certainly
the intent of the drafters of the legislation was not to include labor unions in the prohibition; however, in 1908, in the "Danbury Hatters' Case," *Loewe v. Lawlor,* the U.S.
Supreme Court ruled that a labor union did fall within the intent of the act.

In 1914 Congress passed the Clayton Act, a comprehensive set of amendments to
the Sherman Act. This legislation attempted to clarify some of the ambiguities of the
Sherman Act, mainly by being more specific. With respect to labor it purported to
exempt unions from antitrust liability and attempted to circumscribe the situations in

441

which injunctions could be used against labor unions. This endeavor was not successful; labor unions were the object of efforts by the federal courts, particularly in the 1920s, to limit their actions. Again, in 1932 Congress attempted to reduce the use of the injunction by, among other things, providing that the injunction could not be employed to prevent a strike by unions. This was the Norris-La Guardia Act, which also outlawed the "yellow-dog contract" whereby a worker agreed, as a condition of employment, not to join a union.

In 1933, during the first year of the Roosevelt Administration, the National Industrial Recovery Act (NIRA) became law. Aimed mainly at bolstering business at a time of a nationwide depression by encouraging businesses to establish "codes of fair competition," this legislation also contained Section 7(a), which guaranteed workers the right to join labor unions and to engage in collective bargaining with management. Also, the National Industrial Recovery Act provided that no employee could be required to join a company union as a condition of employment.

Nevertheless, company unions, dominated by management, grew rapidly in the 1930s and reflected an attempt by employers to thwart the growth of employee unions after the enactment of Section 7(a) of the National Industrial Recovery Act. Company unions increased in number, in 1933, by almost 200 percent. An estimated 70 percent of all employer-promoted unions in existence when the National Labor Relations Act (1935) was passed were formed after the enactment of Section 7(a) of the National Industrial Recovery Act.

Following passage of the National Industrial Recovery Act, President Roosevelt in August 1933 by executive order created the National Labor Board to handle labor disputes threatening suspension of work. This was done without express legislative authority. Although this was not the first governmentally sponsored labor board to mediate labor disputes, it marked the first time such a board had been created, during a period of peace, with application industrywide. (In 1918 a National War Labor Board was created and was in operation for 16 months. The Transportation Act of 1920 created a Railroad Labor Board consisting of representatives of labor, industry, and the public. It had no enforcement powers but relied on public opinion to encourage compliance with its decisions. Its composition was similar to that of the Labor Board created in 1933. Railway workers had been the object of legislation specifically affecting them as early as 1916 when Congress, in the Adamson Act, limited their employment to an eight-hour day. Then in 1926 the Railway Labor Act created a U.S. Board of Mediation, whose purposes paralleled those of the Labor Board established in 1933.)

The National Labor Board (1933) was composed of three labor members, three employer representatives, and a seventh member, Senator Robert F. Wagner of New York, as chairman. (Senator Wagner was the author of the National Labor Relations Act of 1935.) The first task of the board was the handling of problems arising under Section 7(a) of the NIRA. The board, in a given case, attempted to determine the facts, define issues, and use its good offices to mediate a labor dispute.

If these attempts failed to resolve the dispute, measures to ensure compliance were available. The case could be referred to the Department of Justice and the Compliance Board of the National Recovery Administration. The Compliance Board might deprive an employer of the right to fly the "blue eagle" emblem, which would deny him the ability to sell goods to the government. The Department of Justice might prosecute, but the maximum fine for failure to comply was small ($500). The National Labor Board expired in 1934, but during its one-year existence settled approximately 1000 threatened strikes.

After several months as chairman of the National Labor Board, Senator Wagner introduced in the Senate, in early 1934, a bill similar to the Wagner Act passed in 1935 and designed to create a new and more powerful Labor Board. Instead of passing this bill, however, Congress passed a joint resolution authorizing the President to establish one or more boards to investigate labor disputes under Section 7(a) of the National Industrial Recovery Act and conduct elections among employees to determine their representatives for collective bargaining.

Under authority of this resolution, President Roosevelt appointed the National Labor Relations Board, which commenced operations in July 1934 and continued in existence until August 1935, at which time the National Labor Relations Board, established by the National Labor Relations Act (Wagner Act), came into existence.

The first National Labor Relations Board (1934) served an important function in protecting labor's right to bargain collectively. It had the power to investigate and to order and conduct elections. The board had to depend largely on voluntary compliance, however, and lacked really effective enforcement powers. Perhaps one of the board's outstanding accomplishments was the building up of a group of informed and experienced personnel. The National Labor Relations Act of 1935 preserved the existing staff of the National Labor Relations Board and directed that it be transferred to the newly created board.

Senator Wagner of New York was largely responsible for passage of the Act in 1935, and it is interesting to note that support for this legislation by the Roosevelt administration, initially, was less than enthusiastic. Before the Senate passed the bill, President Roosevelt had, in fact, invited Senator Wagner to a White House conference where, in Roosevelt's presence, two senators tried to persuade Senator Wagner to withdraw the bill. Only after the Senate passed the bill, and before the House considered it, did Roosevelt endorse the bill.

II. DEVELOPMENT OF MODERN LABOR LAW

A. National Labor Relations Act (Wagner Act) (1935)

This new law restated the basic language of Section 7(a) of the National Industrial Recovery Act, which had just been declared unconstitutional in the Supreme Court decision, *Schechter v. United States* (1935). The Wagner Act, in Section 8, defined certain unfair labor practices on the part of employers. These included the refusal of an employer to bargain collectively with employees' representatives. The new Labor Board had stronger enforcement powers than its predecessor. If an employer refused to comply with an order of the National Labor Relations Board (NLRB), the act contained no criminal penalties but authorized the NLRB to file the record of the proceedings with a federal Circuit Court of Appeals. The court would decide, after hearing argument, whether, on the record, there was evidence to sustain the NLRB's order. If there was, the court would issue its own order affirming the NLRB's order.

Opposition to the Labor Board, and to the Wagner Act itself, was intense in some quarters. For example, a conservative organization, the National Lawyers Committee of the American Liberty League, asserted that the act was definitely unconstitutional:

Considering the Act in the light of our history, the established form of government, and the decisions of our highest Court, we have no hesitancy in concluding that it is unconstitutional and that it constitutes a complete departure from our constitutional and traditional theories of government.

In addition to attacks on the constitutionality of the act, claims were made that the act was unfair. One criticism was directed at the fact that the act forbade interference by employers with the employees' right to self-organization and collective bargaining but did not forbid coercion of employees by labor nor, in fact, did the act define and prohibit any unfair practices by union organizers. The act was allegedly one-sided and discriminated against the employer.

Without question, the Wagner Act was directed at strengthening labor's position relative to that of employers. (Not until the passage of the Taft-Hartley Act in 1947 were unfair labor practices on the part of unions defined and prohibited.) The argument of the proponents of the act was that this was necessary to place labor in a more nearly equal position with employers for the purpose of bargaining.

Until the Supreme Court upheld the Wagner Act in 1937, a major part of the NLRB's efforts involved the fighting of injunction suits designed to prevent hearings. During this period of almost two years, nearly 100 injunction suits were filed to restrain the NLRB. Eventually, the Supreme Court ruled that the district courts did not have jurisdiction in the cases. Finally, the constitutionality of the act was upheld in a series of five cases decided by the Supreme Court in 1937, the most significant one being *National Labor Relations Board v. Jones and Laughlin Steel Corporation.* The NLRB determined that Jones and Laughlin had discharged some of its employees because of labor union activities, defined under Section 8 of the Wagner Act, as constituting an unfair labor practice. The company failed to comply with an order of the board to reinstate the employees and was sued by the board. The Supreme Court sustained the order of the board and further declared that the Wagner Act was constitutional because cessation of operations by industrial strife at Jones and Laughlin would have a most serious effect on interstate commerce, on which the act was based. This case had significance beyond its impact on labor relations because it was the first case declaring a major New Deal Law constitutional; it was a turning point for the Supreme Court, which since that time has taken a much more liberal position on major issues affecting American society, including labor relations.

No more important labor act has been passed by Congress than the Wagner Act; two other acts of major importance to labor are the Taft-Hartley Act (1947) and the Landrum-Griffin Act (1959), both of which are amendments to the Wagner Act. It will be useful to consider the provisions of the Wagner Act in some greater detail.

Section 3 created the NLRB, originally composed of three members, subsequently increased to five, whose terms of office are for five years. Members are appointed by the President, must be confirmed by the Senate, and can be removed by the President only for "neglect of duty of malfeasance in office." This is consistent with the rule established by the Supreme Court in *Humphrey's Executor v. United States* (1935), wherein the

Court declared that a member of a regulatory agency could be removed by the President only for good cause. Section 7 guaranteed the right of collective bargaining, in language identical to that in Section 7(a) of the NIRA, which was declared unconstitutional in 1935. Section 8 made it an unfair labor practice for an employer to interfere with employees' right to form unions, to dominate or interfere with the creation or administration of unions, to discriminate against employees seeking to join labor unions, to discharge or otherwise to discriminate against employees for filing unfair labor practice charges, and to refuse to engage in collective bargaining with union representatives.

Section 9 provided for the selection of the union to represent employees in a particular company. The union is determined by a majority vote of the employees; if a single employee so requests, the NLRB can conduct a representation election. The election may involve the selection of one union from among two or more unions, and the workers have the right to vote for no union.

Section 9(b) empowered the NLRB to determine the appropriate unit for collective bargaining purposes. This might be the employer unit, craft unit, plant unit, or some subdivision thereof. Although the Wagner Act did not specify how this determination was to be made, the NLRB developed certain guidelines. The board decided that in determining the appropriate unit, no rigid rule is to be applied but each case is to be considered on its own merits. The board considers the history of labor relations in the industry, the organization of the business in terms of function or geographic location, and the existing arrangements for employee representation. After the determination of the appropriate unit the NLRB may order an election.

Under Section 10 of the act, if a charge of an unfair labor practice has been filed with the NLRB, the board can conduct hearings to ascertain if such practice has occurred.

In spite of provisions in the Wagner Act granting the NLRB power to act to prevent unfair labor practices, the NLRB rendered relatively few decisions in its early history. In the first year the NLRB issued only 56 decisions finding unfair labor practices and ordering employers to cease and desist and three decisions dismissing charges. In the second year there were only 39 cease-and-desist orders and eight dismissals.

In 1935, a deep cleavage occurred in the labor movement with the formation of the Committee for Industrial Organization (CIO). The formation of this new labor organization followed the vote at the American Federation of Labor (AFL) 1935 convention against unrestricted industrial unionism in the mass production industries. This was to give rise to conflict within the ranks of labor and was to result in problems for the NLRB that had not been anticipated.

Although the controversy between those favoring the craft unit and those favoring the industrial unit had been a bitter and recurrent one throughout the history of the American labor movement, the conflict became particularly acute after formation of the Committee for Industrial Organization. Prior to 1936 the American Federation of Labor had been one of the main champions of the government's attempt to foster self-organization among employees. During the first year of the NLRB's existence the board was not disturbed by conflicts between AFL and CIO unions. The conflict, however, became rather severe in 1936-1937.

Section 9(b) of the Wagner Act, as previously noted, authorized the board to determine the appropriate unit. After the formation of the CIO, the craft unions of highly skilled workers were in danger of being included in larger units and being outvoted. The

AFL considered the CIO a rebel organization. The NLRB, so far as it was concerned, was faced with the problem of striking a balance between two conflicting demands: freedom of employees to choose their bargaining representative and stability of labor relations in the plant. If the NLRB were to grant representation to every group seeking it, chaos might result. On the other hand, if it never permitted representation, the legitimate special interests of groups with particular skills might be submerged in a plantwide unit.

Rather early the NLRB developed the "Globe" doctrine to help it decide. in the *Globe* case one union sought a single unit for all production and maintenance employees while two other unions sought to represent separately two small craft groups. After reviewing the collective bargaining history and nature of the employer's business, the NLRB concluded that either a single overall unit or three separate units might be appropriate and that where the considerations were so evenly balanced, the determining factors should be the desire of the employees themselves. The NLRB permitted the two craft groups to vote for separate representation or to become part of the larger industrial unit.

The NLRB in 1938 was faced with opposition from employers and was seeking to mediate dissension within the ranks of organized labor. The AFL accused the NLRB of showing favoritism toward the CIO, In 1938 statistics, in fact, showed that the CIO had won, since 1935, a much greater number of elections than had the AFL. The AFL appeared ready to join with business interests in an attempt to discredit, if not to destroy the labor board. President William Green of the AFL was quoted in the summer of 1938 as having said in a public speech that "we will mobilize all our political and economic strength in an uncompromising fight until the board is driven from power."

Newsweek magazine reported in 1938 that an attorney for the AFL was planning to file unfair practice charges against employers who dealt with CIO unions, even if the NLRB had certified the CIO as collective bargaining agent. Although it is extremely doubtful that any of the defined unfair labor practice charges in the Wagner Act would permit such a suit to be sustained, an attempt such as this demonstrates the dissatisfaction of the major labor organization with the NLRB. Opposition by the AFL continued, in spite of the fact that in the previous year, 1937, the Supreme Court had declared the Wagner Act, and the NLRB that it created, constitutional. Although competition between the two major labor organizations continued, the rift was healed when, in 1955, the two groups reunited to form the combined AFL-CIO.

Perhaps the greatest criticism directed at the Wagner Act after its passage was the omission of any unfair labor practices on the part of unions. Labor proponents argued that the limitation of such practices, to apply only to employers, was an attempt to place labor in a more equal bargaining position with management because of organized labor's weakened position in 1935. However, business interests continued to charge unfair treatment, and the Taft-Hartley Act in 1947 defined a number of unfair labor practices to apply to unions; the NLRB was now required to consider unfair labor practice charges against unions as well as against employers. The Wagner Act did not prohibit a union from making an agreement with an employer for a closed shop, whereby an employee was required to join a union before he or she could be employed. This was considered particularly unfair by business interests and was finally proscribed by the Taft-Hartley Act.

B. Fair Labor Standards Act

In 1938 Congress passed another important labor act, the Fair Labor Standards Act. In many respects it represented the culmination of efforts begun much earlier to prescribe minimum wages, maximum hours of employment, and to regulate child labor. The federal government, by presidential order or congressional enactment, had previously extended protection to workers on a selective basis by limiting hours of employment and requiring minimum wages. For example, as early as 1840 President Van Buren by executive order set a 10-hour work day for workers in Navy yards. In 1907 Congress limited the hours of employment for railroad workers engaged in interstate transportation to 16 hours, and the Adamson Act in 1916 reduced the maximum number of hours to 8 for such workers. The Davis-Bacon Act of 1931 required the payment of minimum wages equal to the prevailing rate in the locality for contractors employed by the federal government performing work in excess of a stated dollar amount. The Public Contracts (Walsh-Healey) Act (1936) provided the same basic minimum wage requirement for government contractors, with time and a half for overtime, and further stipulated a 40-hour work week. This act provided a model for the Fair Labor Standards Act, although the latter act was much broader in coverage, applying to employers engaged in interstate commerce (with certain exempted occupations). These originally included agricultural and domestic workers and certain retail employees. Today, the only major exempted occupation is that of workers employed in agriculture.

The Fair Labor Standards Act also limits or prohibits child labor for those industries engaged in interstate commerce. Labor of children under 14 years of age is regulated or prohibited, and the Department of Labor may limit hours and conditions of employment for workers between the ages of 14 and 16. No person under the age of 18 may perform work designated hazardous. Efforts had previously been made to regulate or prohibit child labor when Congress in 1916 passed the Owen-Keating Act prohibiting the shipment in interstate commerce of goods produced by child labor, but this act was struck down by the Supreme Court in *Hammer v. Dagenhart* (1918). Congress tried again in 1918 with the passage of a law placing a 10 percent federal tax on all goods produced by child labor, but in a 1922 decision, *Bailey v. Drexel Furniture Co.,* the Supreme Court struck down the law as involving an unconstitutional use of the taxing power. Then in 1924 Congress submitted to the states for ratification a constitutional amendment regulating child labor, but the amendment was never ratified by the necessary number of states. With the passage of the Fair Labor Standards Act the amendment was no longer needed. Child labor has ceased to be a real problem in labor relations.

C. Workmen's Compensation

Employers in all states must provide workmen's compensation insurance, secured either from the state or from private firms. States supervise the programs; coverage is limited, however, mainly to manufacturing. Furthermore, benefits have been inadequate and have not kept pace with inflation. A recent two-year study by the National Commission on State Workmen's Compensation Laws indicates that a substantial number of workers are excluded and that two-thirds of the states offer substandard benefits. A recent proposal has been introduced in Congress to provide federal standards. One of the major provisions is to extend coverage to all public and private employees not otherwise covered by statutes. Another proposal would provide for adjustment of benefits to reflect rises in average wage rates. A third recommendation calls for the extension of coverage to all work-related injuries and occupational diseases. There are other possible standards that need to be considered.

D. Labor Management Relations Act
(Taft-Hartley Act) (1947)

The Taft-Hartley Act of 1947 was passed in an attempt to reduce some of the imbalance in labor management relations that had been created by the passage of the National Labor Relations Act of 1935. The feeling in many quarters was that the 1935 law had created a disproportionate advantage for labor in order to encourage the growth of unions and the collective bargaining procedure. The strikes by John L. Lewis' coal miners during World War II and the postwar strikes by other workers convinced the public that something had to be done.

One of the main provisions of the Taft-Hartley Act provides for unfair labor practices on the part of the unions. The earlier Wagner Act had provided for unfair labor practices on the part of employers. These were included in Taft-Hartley, but in addition six unfair labor practices on the part of unions were defined. It became an unfair labor practice for labor leaders to restrain or coerce employees in organizing for collective bargaining. Second, it was an unfair labor practice for labor leaders to cause an employer to discriminate against an employee for not belonging to a union. A third unfair practice was for labor leaders to refuse to bargain collectively with the employer. Fourth, secondary boycotts were prohibited. Fifth, it was an unfair practice to require excessive initiation fees, and finally payment for work not performed was prohibited.

Other provisions of the act outlawed practices such as the closed shop, although the union shop was still permitted. Unions were required to file affidavits that their officers were not communists. Employers were permitted to sue unions for breach of contract. The size of the National Labor Relations Board was increased from three to five, with three constituting a quorum. It is interesting to note that, in the early years of the act, in spite of the fears of labor, most of the unfair labor complaints were against the employer.

The provisions of Taft-Hartley most strongly opposed by organized labor were the right-to-work section and the secondary boycott provision. A continuing debate in the labor-management field has been the right-to-work provision in the Taft-Hartley Act. Organized labor has sought its repeal ever since its passage in 1947. Title I, Section 14(h), of the Taft Hartley Act states that:

> Nothing in this Act shall be construed as authorizing the execution or application of agreements requiring membership in a labor organization as a condition of employment in any State or Territory in which such execution or application is prohibited by State or Territorial Law.

About half of the states have adopted right-to-work laws as a result of which union membership cannot be required of workers as a condition of employment. The union shop, which requires workers to join the union once they have been employed, is thus prohibited in these states, although they would otherwise be permitted under Taft-Hartley.

Strong arguments can be advanced both in support of and against right-to-work laws. For example, nonmembers do not pay a part of the expense involved in supporting union activities, yet they benefit from the improved working conditions that union activity makes possible. It is only fair that those who benefit from the union's activity should pay their share of the costs of running the union. On the other hand, one could argue that compulsory union membership violates the individual's freedom of choice. If, after weighing the factors involved, an individual chooses not to join a labor union, he should not be forced to act against his own judgment. The right not to join an organization should be respected. Making union membership a condition of employment violates this basic individual right and is an intolerable infringement on individual freedom. Also, not allowing required membership in unions states may encourage union leaders to be more responsive to membership views because members have the right to withdraw or withhold union membership.

The secondary boycott prohibition, Section 8 of the Taft-Hartley Act, has provided another area of controversy in the labor-management relations field. The main objective of Section 8 was to keep third parties from becoming unnecessarily involved in labor disputes that do not concern them. Unions are forbidden from instigating actions against employers who might be doing business with another employer with whom the union has a dispute. The object is to keep the disputes confined to the parties directly concerned.

Some labor union supporters argue that the prohibition of secondary boycotts limits the effectiveness of the tactics unions must necessarily use in dealing with employers and Section 8 should be modified or repealed altogether.

The problem has been particularly apparent in the construction industry. A major objective of organized labor has been the passage of legislation by Congress that would permit what is known as common-situs picketing. Common-situs picketing is not specifically prohibited in the Taft-Hartley Act, but decisions of the Supreme Court and the National Labor Relations Board have placed restrictions on it, by construing common-situs picketing to fall within the prohibition of the language in Section 8(b)(4)(B) banning secondary boycotts. Common-situs picketing usually involves union picketing of an entire area—a construction site would be the most obvious situation—the objective of which is to stop all work activity in the entire area. In the case of a construction site all contractors, whether involved in the labor dispute or not, would become objects of the picketing and would consequently suffer even though they could do little to affect the settlement.

Perhaps no union objective has generated such controversy as common-situs picketing. In 1977 organized labor launched a major effort to get a common-situs picketing bill passed by Congress. The unions argued that they needed the right of common-situs picketing to protect the right of workers in industries that are not heavily unionized and in which employment is seasonal. In spite of a tremendous lobbying effort, the bill was defeated in early 1977 and common-situs picketing is still prohibited under Taft-Hartley.

Some of the other provisions of Taft-Hartley were modified by the Landrum-Griffin Act, passed in 1959.

E. Labor-Management Reporting and Disclosure Act (Landrum-Griffin Act) (1959)

The Landrum-Griffin Act grew out of the investigations of the McClellan committee in the 1950s. The investigations revealed certain abuses in union practices, particularly the

Teamsters Union. Irregularities in the handling of pension, health, and welfare funds appeared to be widespread, and the membership seemed to have little control over the organization that was supposed to be representing their interest. One of the major goals of the act was to provide for greater membership control of labor organizations and to promote "democracy" within labor unions.

The act included what is known as the "bill of rights" for union members. These include the right of union members to participate in the running of the organization, to nominate and vote for officers in the union, the right to speak freely at and otherwise participate in union meetings, and to take an active part in the organization's activities.

The act also attempts to protect the financial integrity of labor organizations by preventing some of the abuses revealed by the McClellan committee investigations. The act requires detailed annual financial reports that include sources of income, expenditures, and salaries of union officers. The act also requires disclosure of loans to union employers and requires officers and employees of the union to file reports with the Secretary of Labor disclosing any financial activities that could create a conflict with their union responsibilities. The Landrum-Griffin Act was a major step in the direction of reforming labor organizations.

F. Occupational Safety and Health Act (1970)

The Occupational Safety and Health Act (OSHA) was passed by Congress in 1970. It was a landmark piece of legislation. The purpose of the act, in its own language, was to provide a "place of employment which is free from recognized hazards that are causing or likely to cause death or serious physical harm to his (the employer's) employees." To enforce the act and to develop proper safety and health standards, a National Institute for Occupational Safety and Health was created by the legislation. The agency was given broad powers to enforce the provisions of the legislation, including those requiring record keeping and allowing for inspections and investigations.

The legislation has been controversial ever since its passage. Some argue that the standards set by OSHA have been unrealistic and arbitrary and have not resulted in significant improvement in the work environment of the average American worker. The standards have been ineffective and are not the most efficient way to go about reducing accidents in most industries.

Although it has remained controversial, suggested changes in the approach to occupational safety and health have not received very much support.

G. Equal Employment Opportunity

Congress mandated equal employment opportunity in Title VII of the Civil Rights Act of 1964. The law forbids discrimination based on race, color, religion, sex, or national origin discrimination in employment practices by employers, employment agencies, or labor organizations. The act also created the Equal Employment Opportunity Commission (EEOC) to administer its provisions. Under the 1964 act, the commission had the responsibility of investigating charges of discrimination in employment practices, but it had virtually no enforcement authority. The EEOC had no authority to initiate action on its own and could intervene only if an individual filed a suit claiming unlawful discrimination. By 1972 the feeling was that the EEOC should be given some enforcement powers and authority to act in the area of unlawful discrimination. To accomplish these goals, the Equal Employment Opportunity Act of 1972 expanded the coverage of Title VII and provided the Equal Employment Opportunity Commission with powers to enforce fair employment practices.

Under the 1972 act, the EEOC is empowered to receive charges of unlawful employment practices from aggrieved persons. The commission then has the responsibility of notifying the parties concerned of the charges within 10 days after receiving them conducting an investigation to determine the validity of the alleged violations. If after the investigation, the commission discovers that the allegations are probably true, the law requires that the commission attempt to eliminate the offending practice by informal methods such as conference and persuasion. These informal procedures are kept private, and penalties are provided for individuals making any part of the informal process public. If these informal procedures do not produce results, no later than 120 days from the filing of the charge the commission is authorized to take direct action in the form of a civil suit with respect to the charge. Under the 1972 act the courts are instructed to hear cases involving unlawful employment practices at the earliest practicable date and "to cause such cases to be in every way expedited." In spite of the emphasis or concern with expediting the handling of complaints, the commission has experienced serious problems with the processing of alleged unlawful practices. The greatest problem the commission has had is dealing with the volume of complaints that have arisen under the act. The commission has been as much as two years behind in the processing of complaints.

Labor organizations are covered under the provisions of the act. Title VII defines a labor organization in language very similar to that used in the Landrum-Griffin Act. The language is broad enough to include independent unions, national unions, and international unions in the United States. To come under the provision of the act a union must be engaged in an industry affecting commerce. The union is considered to be in an industry affecting commerce if it maintains a hiring hall or office and obtains employees for employers or jobs for employees. A union also falls within the scope of the act if it has 15 or more members and is the certified bargaining agent for employees in an industry affecting commerce.

Under the act affected unions are forbidden to deny union membership to any individual because of race, color, religion, sex, or national origin or to cause any individual to be deprived of employment opportunities, or to cause, or even attempt to cause an employer unlawfully to discriminate against an individual. Unions are also prohibited from retaliating against anyone who should bring a complaint under the act.

Because of some of the problems related to enforcement, a move was undertaken at the federal level in 1978 to reorganize equal employment responsibilities and to streamline the procedures of the EEOC. In a major administrative reorganization, most of the responsibilities for equal employment enforcement were shifted from agencies such as the Department of Labor, the Civil Service Commission, and the Equal Employment Opportunity Coordinating Council to EEOC. The move thus consolidated equal employment policy in the one agency most concerned and suited to the task of enforcing the provision of the equal opportunity legislation. In addition, the EEOC has developed a "backlog charge processing system" that the commission hopes will help it reduce the severe backlog of complaints that has always plagued it in the past and enable it to permanently eliminate backlogs in the future. Also, a "rapid charge processing system" was established by all EEOC district offices in 1978 to negotiate settlements quickly by combining investigation, conciliation, and litigation activities into one process. The process consists primarily of promptly gathering evidence from all parties concerned as soon as a complaint is filed and then by face-to-face conference between the complainant and the accused attempting to resolve the dispute. If these and further attempts at resolution fail to bring about an agreement, the EEOC then files a suit in the federal courts if the evidence warrants such action.

The attempt to bring about equality of opportunity in the area of employment has not been totally effective. Only continued effort, particularly at the federal level, can achieve this elusive goal.

H. Affirmative Action

One of the most controversial subjects in the area of equal employment opportunity is what has come to be known as affirmative action. Affirmative action is based on the notion that because certain groups have been the victims of discriminatory actions in the past, practices that discriminate in favor of these same groups are now justified. They are justified because no other way is available to help disadvantaged groups overcome the effects of past discrimination. Affirmative action programs have been implemented in several areas, most particularly in the areas of education and employment practices. A variety of schemes have been developed to give special treatment to certain groups when considering admission to colleges and professional schools and, in the area of employment, special consideration has been given to disadvantaged groups in hiring and training policies. Either quotas have been established or preferential treatment has been given to individuals identified as members of a "disadvantaged" group. Conversely, individuals who are not members of recognized disadvantaged categories have, in effect, been discriminated against in order to accommodate the special treatment given to the recognized disadvantaged groups. How one discriminates in favor of certain individuals without discriminating against certain other individuals at the same time has not yet been discovered. Whether discrimination is justified in certain situations is at the heart of the issue. In any case the discrimination that takes place in the context of affirmative action has caused considerable controversy and debate, which is not likely to be resolved in the near future.

In 1979 the Supreme Court had to deal with the issue of affirmative action in the area of employment practices. A white worker at Kaiser Aluminum Company sued the company, which had turned him down for a training program established by the company, but accepted two black employees with less seniority. The program had been set up with an equal number of slots for black and white workers. Brian Weber, the white worker, claimed that Kaiser was discriminating against white employees in violation of the 1964 Civil Rights Act. In a complex ruling the Court ruled that programs such as the one at Kaiser were intended to correct the unfair practices of the past, were temporary in nature, and did not violate the intent of the Civil Rights Act. In spite of the decision in *Weber v. Kaiser Aluminum Company,* it is doubtful that the issue of what has been labeled by some as "reverse discrimination" has been settled.

I. Full Employment Policy

The Humphrey-Hawkins full employment bill provides for long-term economic planning designed to ensure full employment, defined as an adult unemployment rate of 3 percent.

It requires coordination among the President, Congress, and the Federal Reserve System. It obliges the Federal Reserve System to submit annual reports to the President and Congress of its monetary policies and how they would help to achieve full employment. The President is required to submit as a part of his economic report five-year plans that set annual goals for employment and unemployment as well as projections for production, real income, and prices. The act, if fully implemented, moves the free market economy several steps closer to the planned economies of the socialist systems. The government would assume the decision role in determining not only levels of unemployment but also production levels, income levels, and price levels.

The Full Employment and Balanced Growth Act or Humphrey-Hawkins Act was enacted into law in 1978. It represents the first major attempt on the part of the Congress to deal with the issue of full employment since the passage of the Employment Act of 1946.

Following World War II there was considerable concern about a possible return to the high levels of unemployment and depression that characterized the 1930s. The Employment Act of 1946 was designed to address this concern and to enlist the support of the government to achieve the goals of high employment and low unemployment. The act did not provide for the achieving of full employment by direct intervention on the part of the government as employee of last resort. Rather, the government was charged with the responsibility of creating the conditions under which maximum employment opportunities would be available for those actively seeking work.

In order to promote "maximum employment," the act created the Council of Economic Advisers and the Joint Economic Committee of Congress. The act also required an Annual Economic Report of the President. Although the Employment Act of 1946 attempts to promote full employment, it did not mandate the use of federal resources to assure that goal. The legislation thus fell far short of the desires of those who believed full employment to be the highest economic priority of government.

Following the passage of the Employment Act of 1946, the issue of full employment ceased to be a matter of great national concern. The much feared return of the high levels of unemployment that characterized the Great Depression of the 1930s failed to materialize. Even though the economy experienced periods of recession in the postwar period, the unemployment rate averaged 4.7 percent, not enough to cause serious national concern. It was not until the mid-1970s, when unemployment stayed around 7 percent, that serious interest in government policies designed to achieve full employment returned. The result was the enactment of Humphrey-Hawkins, which for the first time in American history set specific goals in the area of unemployment to be achieved by government intervention in the economy and which makes the reduction of unemployment the top economic goal of the federal government.

The debate over economic priorities was not ended with the passage of the Humphrey-Hawkins Act. Some have questioned whether the government could effectively coordinate fiscal, monetary, and employment policies with the result of creating jobs and providing stable economic growth in the manner called for by the Humphrey-Hawkins bill. For others the five-year plans called for in the legislation are disturbingly reminiscent of the planned economies of the communist bloc. Is this sort of policy really compatible with a free market economy?

Perhaps the biggest question of all concerning the unemployment goals of the Humphrey-Hawkins bill is the effect such a policy would have on the nation's other major

economic concern of the present era, namely, inflation. What will be the effect of govern-
ment-provided or -instigated programs designed to achieve full employment on an inflation rate that has shown an ever-increasing tendency to achieve double-digit levels? Can
the problem of unemployment or the achieving of full employment ever be solved or realized as long as the economy continues to be battered by prices rising at a level that only
a short time ago would have been unthinkable? Isn't a policy that demands that full employment be achieved regardless of the impact on the other major issues of the economy
an illusion doomed to failure?

These concerns were particularly evident at the end of the act's first year. The annual
economic report from the President, required by the act, which includes estimates for employment and unemployment, projected an unemployment goal of 6.2 percent, a rate 0.4
percent higher than the rate at the time the report was issued!

III. ORGANIZING THE PUBLIC SECTOR

A. Hatch Act Reform

Hatch Acts, passed by Congress in 1939 and 1940, prohibit partisan activity on the part
of public employees and seek to insulate them from coercion by political incumbents. A
1967 study commissioned by Congress recommended removing some of the restrictions
on political activities by public employees. In 1976 a bill was passed by Congress permitting government workers to participate in election campaigns and to run for office
themselves. The bill was also designed to strengthen further the protection against coercion of employees and would have established an independent board to assist in accomplishing this goal. However, the bill was vetoed by President Ford, and Congress failed to
muster the necessary votes to override.

The question remains: Does the Hatch Act, in its present form, limit the civil and
political rights of public employees? Would repeal of certain provisions of the act subject
the public employee to political pressures?

B. Public Employee Unions

The process of unionizing public employees was a slow one. In the 1950s public employees made up only about 5 percent of the total union membership in the United States.
Today that percentage has doubled.

There are several different types of labor organizations that represent the interests
of employees in the public sector. There are those organizations that limit their membership to public employees or to employees of quasi-public, nonprofit, charitable, or educational institutions. The most important of these is the American Federation of State,
County, and Municipal Employees (AFSCME). This all-public union is a member of the
AFL-CIO. The membership of the organization includes workers in almost every type of
government function and in both state and local government, with the exception of
teachers and fire fighters.

In addition to these organizations that limit their membership to public employees
or those working for quasi-public institutions, the public-sector employees are also represented by unions that represent workers in the private sector. Indeed, these mixed organizations are the most common type of union representing public employees. The three

largest unions of this type are the Service Employers International Union, the Laborer's International Union of North America, both members of the AFL-CIO, and the International Brotherhood of Teamsters, Chauffeurs, Warehousemen, and Helpers of America.

The Service Employees International Union represents primarily workers employed in maintenance, servicing, and security in both the public and the private sector. The Laborers' Union is made up of unskilled and semiskilled workers in the construction industry. The bulk of its members are in the private sector, but about 10 percent of the union is made up of public employees. Its main interest is the federal employee. The Teamsters have represented public employees of municipal, county, and state governments, particularly in the street, sanitation, and highway departments.

In addition to these major organizations there are many state and local employee associations representing public employees in different areas, including the Fraternal Order of Police and the International Conference of Police Associations. There are also many professional associations that have become collective bargaining agents for public professionals, such as the National Education Association and the American Nurses Association, two of the largest.

As a result of the organizing efforts of the last decade, a majority of public employees are now represented by unions, workers associations, or professional associations. The degree of organization varies from one area and geographic region to another. The large cities of the Middle Atlantic, Pacific, and North Central states show higher levels of union activity among public employees. However, organization in all regions have been substantial.

IV. LABOR LAW REFORM

Organized labor has pressed for modification of the basic labor law designed mainly to make the existing legislation more effective. Basically, the changes would expedite the work of the National Labor Relations Board and apply sanctions against employers who refuse to comply with decisions of the board. These changes were embodied in the Labor Reform Act of 1977, which passed the House of Representatives but failed in the Senate as a result of a filibuster.

Specifically, the Reform Act would accelerate the holding of elections to certify unions as bargaining representatives and disposition of cases involving unfair labor practice charges. The board would be required to streamline its procedures and the Reform Act provides incentives to employers not to hinder the process of union organization. In general, the act would enhance the ability of unions to organize workers.

A substantial change in the law would impose deadlines on the board to minimize delays in the calling of representation elections. This would be accomplished by amending Section 9(c) of the Wagner Act, which simply directs that a representation election be held without specifying any time limit. The amended Section 9(c) would require the board to call an election within 7 days after the filing of a petition for the election and to conduct the election no more than 15 days after the petition is filed.

In order to further expedite the work of the board, the Reform Act provides that the decision of an administrative law judge (formerly the hearing examiner), upon motion of the successful party, be final in unfair labor practice cases unless the board decides to take the case on appeal. A quorum of two members of the board can make this decision. Obviously, this amendment of the existing law would strengthen the position of the administrative law judge and potentially expedite procedures of the board by removing the necessity for review by the board; however, there is a safeguard in that, if two members of the board, comprising a quorum, should decide that the case merits further consideration, the board can consider the matter.

Arguably, the number of administrative law judges should be increased, because more decisions of these judges would likely be final than before. Presumably, more time would be required to dispose of the cases when the likelihood of appeal to the board is diminished. This would place a greater burden on the administrative law judges.

Membership of the Labor Board would be increased from five to seven under the proposed reform law. It is anticipated that this expansion in membership would expedite the handling of cases. Under Section 3(b) of the present law, the board is allowed to "delegate to any group of three or more members any or all of the powers which it may itself exercise." Under the present five-man board, only one such group would be possible and the workload potential of the board is not increased. However, if the number is expanded to seven members, then the board could divide itself into two working units and, conceivably, substantially speed up its handling of cases.

Critics of the proposed change in the law assert that by expanding the size of the board from five to seven, the result would be to produce further delays because agreement of seven rather than five would be required, and this would mean more discussion and consideration. However, the fact that the board could now consider cases in panels of three, and would probably do so except in the most serious cases, should increase the ability of the board to handle in a expeditious manner the cases that are appealed to it.

Under the present law, the Wagner Act (1935) as amended, Section 10(f) permits the filing of an appeal from an order of the board to the federal Court of Appeals in the circuit wherein an alleged unfair labor practice occurred. In the Labor Reform Act of 1977 this section would have been amended to provide for an appeal within 30 days from final order of the board; otherwise, the decision of the board would be final.

The intent of the amendment would be to hasten a final decision of the matter by preventing extended periods of delay, because theoretically the aggrieved party, at present, has an indefinite time in which to file the appeal. A potential problem exists, however, in that by requiring filing of an appeal within a short period of 30 days the result may be an increase in appeals and more cases in the federal court. Once the appeal has been filed, the court would have to rule, and the time in which the final ruling takes place typically involves an extended period. If the number of appeals increases, the time period for a final ruling by the court should increase as the case load of the court becomes larger. Furthermore, under the present law, voluntary compliance with the board's decision frequently takes place; speeding up the appeals process might obstruct the ability to secure such compliance although there would still be the possibility of out-of-court settlements.

Section 10(l) of the present act relating to unfair labor practices would be amended to include within the category of cases receiving priority treatment by the board those in which an employee has been fired in violation of Section 8(a) (3) or 8(b) (2) during a representation election or after a union has been certified as representative for the employees but before the first collective bargaining agreement.

If the board determines that the employer has discharged the worker because of membership in a union, then the board must go to the federal District Court to obtain an injunction reinstating the employee. A further protection to the worker is the amendment of Section 10(c), in the new act, providing for double wages during the period of discharge and until reinstatement. This new provision is designed to assure than an order of the of the board reinstating an employee will be effective. The board is required not to rely solely on its own enforcement powers, but to secure the added help of the federal court.

A major complaint of organized labor under the present law is that an employee who is illegally fired for engaging in union organization efforts is entitled only to the back pay that would have been received had the employee not been fired. The amount the employee received is also subject to reduction because any wages received during the period of illegal firing is deducted from the amount of back pay that would otherwise be received. In addition, the employer can raise objections to the amount of the settlement, claiming that the employee did not diligently seek comparable employment or exercised poor judgment in seeking other employment during the period of illegal firing. Section 10(c) of the present law would be amended to require "double the employee's wage rate" for the period of unemployment due to the unfair labor practice.

Also, if the employer refuses to bargain with the designated representative of the employees prior to the establishment of the first collective bargaining contract, the board may award to the employees compensation for the delay in bargaining based on the difference between what they received during the period of delay and the average increase in "wages and other benefits" obtained by other workers at the time of the negotiation of the collective bargaining agreement, to be determined by statistical measures available to the Bureau of Labor Statistics.

Another proposed change, similar to the above, would require that employers who refused to engage in "good faith" collective bargaining pay wage rates equal to the average rates prevailing industrywide. These "wage settlements" would be imposed on such employers.

A modification of Section 10(c) of the Wagner Act would deny government contracts to employers failing to comply with a final order of the board. A list would be prepared by the Comptroller General and circulated to all government agencies. No government contracts would be awarded to these employers during a three-year period. This is perhaps the most drastic sanction of any in the Reform Act, to secure compliance with orders of the Labor Board, and involves, in a sense, "blacklisting" of employers, a practice used by employers against workers seeking to join unions at an earlier time in labor history. This remedy could be viewed as an improper use of governmental power and might raise serious constitutional questions. Government procurement has grown tremendously in the twentieth century and accounts for a significant portion of many companies' business. Furthermore, the effectiveness of this sanction might be questioned because a company, particularly if the government contract accounted for a small portion of its total output, might forego the contract rather than comply with an order of the board. Workers might be intimidated by fear of losing their jobs. A reduction in the number of workers required would occur, and, ironically, the withholding of government contracts would reduce, rather than increase, protection to employees.

Complaints have been made by unions that their representatives do not have sufficient opportunity to solicit workers and that these organizers should be given an opportunity during the work day to do so. Employers have the opportunity to talk to their employees during working hours; unions would like to have "equal access." An amendment to Section 6 of the existing law would require this, but with the stipulation that organizing efforts be consistent with the maintenance of normal and orderly production. How this could be accomplished without disturbing production is subject to question. An argument can be made that unions already enjoy an advantage after working hours, and that "equal access" would give undue advantage to unions.

Perhaps no labor bill has provoked as much controversy as the Labor Reform Act of 1977. Supporters of the bill contend that it is necessary to make the basic labor law effective, to provide strong incentives to employers, who otherwise would resist compliance, to accept decisions of the Labor Board. Some employers view the proposal with alarm and consider it, essentially, as an attempt of labor to increase union membership at a time of decline in union strength as a percentage of the total working force.

RECENT LITERATURE AND REFERENCES

There are many excellent sources. Among those useful for further information are the following:

Morris, C. J. (Ed.) (1971). *The Developing Labor Law: The Board, the Courts, and the National Labor Relations Act.* Bureau of National Affairs, Washington, DC.
McAdams, A. K. (1964). *Power and Politics in Labor Legislation.* Columbia University Press, New York.

The latter is a thorough treatment of the legislative history of the Landrum-Griffin Act. Additional sources include:

Selznick, P. (1969). *Law, Society, and Industrial Justice.* Russell Sage Foundation, New York.
Williams, J. S. (1965). *Labor Relations and the Law.* Little, Brown, Boston.

Williams' book covers the early history and development of labor law, concentrating on the process of collective bargaining. A recent book covering many substantive areas in labor policy is

Bulmer, C., and Carmichael, J. L., Jr. (Eds.) (1980). *Employment and Labor-Relations Policy.* D. C. Heath, Lexington, MA.

A very useful source is *Labor Relations and Social Problems,* a series published by the Bureau of National Affairs in the 1970s. For example, particularly useful is

Grodin, J. R., and Wollett, D. H. (1975). *Collective Bargaining in Public Employment.* Bureau of National Affairs, Washington, DC.

Another volume in the Bureau of National Affairs' collection that would be appropriate is

Bureau of National Affairs (1973). *The Equal Employment Opportunity Act of 1972.* Bureau of National Affairs, Washington, DC.

For the early history of the labor movement and an analysis of major federal legislation, see

Wykstra, R., and Stevens, E. (1970). *Labor Law and Public Policy.* Odyssey Press, New York.

For specific information on the Labor Board, see

McCulloch, F., and Bornstein, T. (1974). *The National Labor Relations Board.* Praeger, New York.

On the subject of public employees,

Douglas, J. D., Horton, R. D., Kheel, T. W., Lewin, D., Lipset, S. M., Mansfield, H., Meany, G., Nisbet, R. A., Orr, D., Raskin, A. H., Uhlman, W., Wellington, H. H., Wheeler, C. B., Winter, R. K., Wurf, J. (1976). *Public Employee Unions: A Study of the Crisis in Public Sector Labor Relations.* Institute for Contemporary Studies, San Francisco, CA.

analyzes the nature of and suggests solutions for current problems in public labor relations.

Some excellent additional publications dealing with labor-management policy in a general way are the following:

Auerbach, J. S. (1969). *American Labor: The Twentieth Century.* Bobbs Merrill, Indianapolis, IN.
Backer, J. M. (1968). *Guaranteed Income for the Unemployed.* Johns Hopkins University Press, Baltimore.
Bailey, S. K. (1950). *Congress Makes a Law: The Story Behind the Employment Act of 1946.* Columbia University Press, New York.
Bowen, W. G. (Ed.). (1965). *Labor and the National Economy.* Norton, New York.
Burtt, E. J., Jr. (1963). *Labor Markets, Unions and Government Policies.* St. Martin Press, New York.
Dulles, F. R. (1966). *Labor in America.* Thomas Y. Crowell, New York.
Finley, J. E. (1975). *White Collar Union.* Octagon Books, New York.
Metz, H. W. (1945). *Labor Policy of the Federal Government.* Brookings Institution, Washington, DC.
Northrup, H. P., and Bloom, G. F. (1963). *Government and Labor* (Richard D. Irwin, Homewood, IL.
Rayback, J. G. (1966). *A History of American Labor,* Macmillan, New York.

There are many sources that deal with specific policy areas in labor-management relations. Some of the better ones listed by area are the following:

A. Collective Bargaining

Beal, E. F. (1967). *The Practice of Collective Bargaining.* Richard D. Irwin, Homewood, IL.

Chamberlain, N. W. (1965). *Collective Bargaining.* McGraw-Hill, New York.

Davey, H. W. (1959). *New Dimensions in Collective Bargaining.* Harper & Row, New York.

DeMenil, G. (1971). *Bargaining: Monopoly Power Versus Union Power.* M.I.T. Press, Cambridge, MA.

Dunlop, J. T., and Chamberlain, N. W. (1967). *Frontiers of Collective Bargaining.* Bureau of National Affairs, Washington, DC.

Peck, C. J. (1972). *Cases and Materials on Negotiation.* Bureau of National Affairs, Washington, DC.

Prasow, P., and Peters, E. (1970). *Arbitration and Collective Bargaining: Conflict Resolution in Labor Relations.* McGraw-Hill, New York.

Sherman, H. L. (1972). *Unionization and Collective Bargaining.* Bureau of National Affairs, Washington, DC.

B. Democratization of Unions

Bureau of National Affairs (1959). *The Labor Reform Law.* Bureau of National Affairs, Washington, DC.

Dunsford, J. E., Alleyne, R. H., Morris, C. J. (1973). *Individuals and Unions.* Bureau of National Affairs, Washington, DC.

Getman, J. G., Anderson, J., and Silverstein, E. (1973). *Allocation of Power and Individual Rights.* Bureau of National Affairs, Washington, DC.

Slovenko, R. (Ed.) (1961). *Symposium on LMRDA.* Claitor's Bookstore Publishers, Baton Rouge, LA.

C. Equal Employment Opportunity

Becker, G. S. (1957). *The Economics of Discrimination.* University of Chicago Press, Chicago.

Bracey, J. H. Jr. (Ed.) (1971). *Black Workers and Organized Labor.* Wadsworth, Belmont, CA.

Bureau of National Affairs (1973). *The Equal Employment Act of 1972.* Bureau of National Affairs, Washington, DC.

Foner, P. S. (1974). *Organized Labor and the Black Worker.* Praeger, New York.

Greer, S. (1949). *Last Man In: Racial Access to Union Power.* Free Press, New York.

Hughes, M. M. (1970). *The Sexual Barrier: Legal and Economic Aspects of Employment.* Hughes, Chicago.

MacNabb, R. R. (1969). *Equal Employment Opportunity.* Machinery and Allied Products Institute, Chicago.

Peskin, D. B. (1971). *The Building Blocks of EEO.* World, New York.

Sovern, M. I. (1966). *Legal Restraints on Racial Discrimination in Employment.* Twentieth Century Fund, New York.

D. Labor Economics

Barbash, J. (1972). *Trade Unions and National Economic Policy,* Johns Hopkins University Press, Baltimore.

Bloom, G. F., and Northrop, H. R. (1955). *Economics of Labor Relations.* Richard D. Irwin, Homewood, IL.

Blum, S. (1969). *Labor Economics.* Arno Press, New York.

Brown, E. H. P. (1962). *The Economics of Labor.* Yale University Press, New Haven, CT.

Douglas, P. H., Hitchcock, C. N., and Atkins, W. E. (1969). *The Worker in Modern Economic Society.* Arno Press, New York.

Fair, R. C. (1969). *The Short-Run Demand for Workers and Hours.* North-Holland, Amsterdam.

—— (1969). *Excess Labor and Aggregate Employment Functions.* Princeton University Press, Princeton, NJ.

Fisher, M. R. (1971). *The Economic Analysis of Labour.* Weidenfeld, and Nicolson, London, England.

Furniss, E. S. (1969). *Labor Problems.* Arno Press, New York.

Galenson, W. (1959). *Labor and Economic Development.* Wiley, New York.

Ginzberg, E. (1976). *The Human Economy.* McGraw-Hill, New York.

Gitlow, A. L. (1957). *Labor Economics and Industrial Relations.* Richard D. Irwin, Homewood, IL.

Gupta, R. D. (1971). *Wage Flexibility and Full Employment.* Vikas, Delhi, India.

Heneman, H. G., and Yoder, D. (1965). *Labor Economics.* South-Western, Cincinnati, OH.

Kuhn, A. (1967). *Labor Institutions and Economics.* Harcourt, Brace, New York.

Lester, R. A. (1964). *Economics of Labor.* Macmillan, New York.

McConnell, C. R. (1970). *Perspectives on Wage Determinations: A Book of Readings.* McGraw-Hill, New York.

Moore, H. L. (1967). *Laws of Wages.* Augustus M. Kelly, Clifton, NJ.

Morgan, C. A. (1966). *Labor Economics.* Dorsey Press, Homewood, IL.

Perlman, S. (1968). *A Theory of the Labor Movement.* Augustus M. Kelly, Clifton, NJ.

Phelps, E. S., Alchian, A. A., Holt, C. C., Mortensen, D. T., Archibald, G. C., Lucas, R. E., Rapping, L. A., Winter, S. G., Gould, J. P., Gordon, D. F., Hynes, A., Nichols, D. A., Taubman, P. J., Wilkinson, M. (1970). *Microeconomic Foundations of Employment and Inflation Theory.* Norton, New York.

Rees, A. (1973). *The Economics of Work and Pay.* Harper & Row, New York.

Reynolds, L. G. (1974). *Labor Economics and Labor Relations.* Prentice-Hall, Englewood Cliffs, NJ.

E. Occupational Safety and Health

Anderson, C. (1975). *OSHA and Accident Control Through Training.* Industrial Press, New York.

Bureau of National Affairs (1971). *The Job Safety and Health Act of 1970.* Bureau of National Affairs, Washington, DC.

Fellner, B. A., and Savelson, D. W. (1976). *Occupational Safety and Health Law and Practice.* Practicing Law Institute, New York.

McCulloch, F. W., and Bornstein, T. (1974). *The National Labor Relations Board.* Praeger, New York.

Morris, C. J. (Ed.) (1971). *The Developing Labor Law.* Bureau of National Affairs, Washington, DC.

F. Public Sector

Bradley, P. D. (1959). *The Public Stake in Union Power.* University Press of Virginia, Charlottesville.

Chauhan, D. S. (1976). *Public Labor Relations: A Comparative State Study.* Sage, Beverly Hills, CA.

Connery, R. A., and Farr, W. F. (1970). *Unionization of Municipal Employees.* Academy of Political Science, New York.

Godine, M. R. (1967). *The Labor Problem in the Public Service.* Russell and Russell, New York.

Grodin, J. R., and Wollett, D. H. (1975). *Collective Bargaining in Public Employment.* Bureau of National Affairs, Washington, DC.

Gunderson, M. (1975). *Collective Bargaining in the Essential and Public Service Sectors.* University of Toronto Press, Toronto.

Hamermesh, D. S. (Ed.) (1975). *Labor in the Public and Nonprofit Sectors.* Princeton University Press, Princeton, NJ.

Marx, H. L., Jr. (Ed.) (1969). *Collective Bargaining for Public Employees.* H. W. Wilson, Bronx, NY.

Murphy, R. J., and Sackman, M. (Eds.) (1970). *The Crisis in Public Employee Relations in the Decade of the Seventies.* Bureau of National Affairs, Washington, DC.

Nesbitt, M. B. (1976). *Labor Relations in the Federal Government Service.* Bureau of National Affairs, Washington, DC.

Schick, R. P., and Couturier, J. J. (1977). *The Public Interest in Government Labor Relations.* Ballinger, Cambridge, MA.

Warner, K. O., and Hennessy, M. L. (1967). *Public Management at the Bargaining Table.* Public Personnel Association, Chicago.

Wirtz, W. W. (1964). *Labor and the Public Interest.* Harper & Row, New York.

19

Communication Policy

Jarol B. Manheim / Virginia Polytechnic Institute and State University
Blacksburg, Virginia

To speak of "communication policy" is, in reality, to speak of an amalgam of several
more generic types of policy, for the communication process is, in a sense, merely an
object of regulatory, foreign, science and technology, and other policies that may best be
understood in the broader contexts described elsewhere in this Encyclopedia. Nevertheless, because communication is so fundamental a form of human interaction, and because
the unique policy problems it raises do require special attention and do generate more or
less unique solutions, communication policy deserves examination in its own right. In
this chapter we consider this policy area in terms of its historical development, the actors
involved in making communication policy both in the United States and internationally,
and the present and projected future directions of that policy.

I. THE HISTORY OF COMMUNICATION POLICY

Historically, one of the primary features of communication policy has been its pioneering
role in the regulatory process. In the United States, the broadcasting industry was the
first to eschew self-regulation and literally to demand the intervention of the federal government in its affairs. Internationally, the International Telegraph Union (now the International Telecommunication Union), established in 1865, is the oldest existing international administrative organization, and served as a prototype for many other international regulatory agencies. Yet at center, the widely recognized need for regulation has
resulted from a more basic concern of communication policy, the continuing need to
respond to rapid technological development, and both the accomplishments and the failures of communication policy makers are best judged with this in mind.

Leaving aside questions of the propriety or control of the substantive content of
communication (these are treated elsewhere in this Encyclopedia by Stephen Wasby), the
communication process emerged as a concern of government policy makers with the

earliest development and implementation of telecommunications technology, that employing electrical or, later, electronic devices. The first of these was the electric telegraph, a functioning model of which appeared in England in 1837 and in the United States in 1844. By the early 1850s electric telegraphy had spread throughout Europe as its commercial applications, its military value, and not least its contribution to the unification of nations became evident. Indeed, next to the railroad, whose operations it was used to control, the electric telegraph became one of the major forces contributing to the development and continuity of the nation-state on anything approaching contemporary terms. In the United States electric telegraphy was controlled by the private sector, whereas in Europe it was in government hands, a differential pattern that continues today.

The first international treaty linking the electric telegraph systems of two countries was signed by Prussia and Austria in 1849, and was followed by a series of multinational agreements that culminated in 1865 in the establishment of the International Telegraph Union. The purpose of this organization was to establish and update minimum technical standards for international telegraphy, to control access to the international wire network, and to set rates for international messages. In 1885 the union began to incorporate the second medium of electrical long-distance communication to be developed, the telephone, in its regulations, though because of technical, commercial, and other constraints full regulation of international telephony was delayed until 1903.[1] In that same year, conferees began work on a parallel organization, the International Radiotelegraph Union (IRTU), which was finally established in 1906, to control a third technology developing during this period, radio. The IRTU undertook the allocation of frequencies and setting of technical standards for international point-to-point (and later for broadcast) radio service. The sinking of the *Titanic* in 1912 gave impetus to strengthening maritime communication under IRTU auspices, a service that was later extended to air navigation. Finally, in 1932, these organizations were merged into the agency that survives to the present, the International Telecommunication Union (ITU) (Codding, 1972).

The ITU has been restructured or redirected on several occasions since 1932, most notably in 1947, 1959, 1965, and 1973. It consists of a Plenipotentiary Conference composed of all member nations, which meets more or less regularly to review the International Telecommunication Convention and the general policies of the organization; a broadly based Administrative Council, which oversees ITU activities in the interim; worldwide and regional Administrative Conferences, called as necessary to deal with such matters as the allocation of the electromagnetic spectrum among various services and users; an International Frequencies Registration Board (IFRB), which serves as a clearinghouse, registration bureau, and legitimizing agent for the assignment of frequencies consistent with ITU policy; and technical committees and study groups. In general, the Plenipotentiary Conference establishes organizational goals, structures, and relationships that are maintained by the Administrative Council; the Administrative Conferences set policy that, in the case of spectrum allocations, are implemented insofar as possible by the IFRB; and the technical committees and study groups, which are more open to private-sector participation than are other agencies of the ITU, develop and recommend equipment standards and specifications. Finally, a General Secretariat without policy-making authority oversees the day-to-day activities of the organization.

The functions of the ITU include, among others, allocation of the electromagnetic spectrum, coordination of efforts to reduce interference and make maximally efficient use of the spectrum, fostering the diffusion of telecommunications technology to less developed countries (LDCs), and gathering and publishing information about telecommunication and generating recommendations for telecommunication policy. ITU membership now extends to more than 140 nations. It is important to note, however, that throughout its history ITU has acted not as a quasi-government in its own right, but always as an agent of its nation members. Because of the compelling need for such an agency, it has endured wars both cold and hot, but it has never developed an independence of its own (Jacobson, 1972; Leive, 1972).

For its part, the United States, usually a reluctant partner in early international agreements when it participated at all, was developing its own regulatory structure and requirements for telecommunication policy during this period. As noted above, the U.S. government was more inclined than were its European and other counterparts to leave substantial control over communication in private hands. Thus, except for limited powers granted to the Interstate Commerce Commission under the Mann-Elkins Act of 1910 and antitrust action to force divestiture of Western Union by American Telephone and Telegraph (AT&T) in 1919, the wired common carriers (principally at that time AT&T, Western Union, and Postal Telegraph) were virtually unregulated during their developmental period. The Radio Corporation of America (RCA) was established with government encouragement in 1919 to provide domestic and international radio services (and, not incidentally, to avert the development of a British monopoly), and was joined in providing international voice communications by AT&T in 1927. A number of companies competed to provide international radiotelegraph service including several subsidiaries of International Telephone and Telegraph (ITT) (Goldberg, 1978).

It was maritime communication, or perhaps more accurately the absence of it, that first propelled Congress into promulgating regulations for radio service. In the Wireless Ship Act of 1910, for example, Congress required that any "oceangoing steamer" licensed to carry at least 50 persons could not leave any U.S. port unless it carried an efficient radio set capable of transmitting a signal at least 100 miles and a skilled, licensed operator (Codding, 1972). Then, in 1912, impelled by the *Titanic* disaster, Congress passed the first Radio Act, a comprehensive law specifying procedures to be followed in transmitting and receiving distress calls and requiring that every radio station in U.S. jurisdiction receive a license from the Secretary of Commerce for use of a radio frequency. The Radio Act of 1912 did not provide standards of operation or discretion in the granting of licenses, and indeed, conveyed to its administrator little real authority for action, but together with the 1910 legislation it did establish the precedent of situating the locus of authority for enforcing telecommunication policy in the Secretary of Commerce. In 1912 the United States participated in the London Conference of the IRTU that adopted similar maritime recommendations. The executive branch was granted further authority over telecommunications in the Cable Landing License Act of 1921, which authorized the President to license the landing operation (point of interconnection) of undersea telegraph cables (Will, 1978).

In that same year, acting under what he claimed to be authority granted in the Radio Act of 1912, then Secretary of Commerce Herbert Hoover designated 833 KHz as *the* frequency for radio broadcasting (he added a second frequency the following year) and made the first attempt to regulate the frequencies, schedules, and power utilization of broadcasters (Krasnow and Longley, 1978). By 1922, however, 322 stations were broadcasting on a more or less regular basis, and the airwaves were filled with a confusion of interwoven signals (Codding, 1972). In that year, at the behest of President Harding, Hoover convened the first of a series of conferences on the structure and control of radio use, the so-called First Radio Conference.

This conference, comprised of representatives of government and industry, unanimously resolved that radio was a public utility that should be regulated and controlled by the federal government, and specifically recommended the delegation of such authority to the Secretary of Commerce. Legislation to this effect was introduced in Congress, but stalled in committee. For his part, Secretary Hoover did in 1922 form the Interdepartment Radio Advisory Committee (IRAC), consisting of representatives of all executive branch and military radio users, to coordinate radio use by, and the radio policy of, the government itself, a function the committee continues to perform in expanded form today.

As the airwaves continued to fill with broadcasters, and as the courts began chiseling away at Hoover's claims of regulatory authority, pressure built for legislative action. So it was that Congress came to pass the Radio Act of 1927, establishing a five-member Federal Radio Commission (FRC) with authority to grant and review licenses, but authorizing the Secretary of Commerce to determine operator qualifications, inspect station equipment, and assign call letters. Congress, and most notably the Senate, was uncomfortable with this arrangement, however, and provided for the expiration of most FRC authority after one year. This limitation, which in the event merely provided for annual review of FRC activities pending extension of its life, together with inadequate appropriations and delays in confirmation of its members, assured the FRC of a stormy, highly politicized, relatively ineffective, and, as it turned out, brief existence. Finally, in 1934, President Franklin Roosevelt, supported by the report of an investigatory commission, prevailed upon Congress to pass the Communications Act, which, despite recent efforts at a fundamental revision, remains the primary statute governing the regulation of telecommunications in the United States.

The Communications Act of 1934 established a seven-member Federal Communications Commission (FCC) with authority to regulate all forms of telecommunication including telephony and telegraphy. It charged the FCC with studying new uses for radio, supporting experimentation, setting long-range goals for communication policy, and proposing legislation to meet those goals. The act also slightly broadened the President's appointive powers and gave him the authority to designate the allocation of frequencies for government use (a task actually performed by IRAC) and, upon his proclamation of a state of war or national emergency, to suspend all rules and regulations applicable to any station (Will, 1978; Krasnow and Longley, 1978).

The FCC today is organized along functional lines that reflect the various components of the telecommunications industry, including broadcasting, cable, common carriers, and safety and special services. Some 85 percent of the professional staff consists of lawyers and engineers, whereas economists and statisticians make up less than 5 percent (Robinson, 1978). The commissioners themselves serve an average of about four and one-half years (of a seven-year term), and are typically lawyers with prior government administrative experience who tend to see their roles as regulators in legal and administrative rather than social or political terms. Because of their short tenure and their dependence on support staff for advice and information, most commissioners have relatively little long-term impact on FCC policies. That is not to say, however, that the commission is not highly politicized. To the contrary, the FCC is continually pressured by Congress, which has on occasion used the appropriation process in a punitive manner and which has never adequately funded commission activities; by the industry, whose historic role in the origins of the commission and whose control over much needed technical information gives it substantial leverage; by the White House, through its control over FCC appointments as well as subsequent patronage, over budget requests, and over legislative initiatives; by the courts, most notably the U.S. Court of Appeals for the District of Columbia (specified in the Communications Act of 1934 as the court of last resort for many appeals of FCC decisions), which have been quite willing to reverse commission actions; and increasingly, by consumer, public, and other interest groups who, since a series of court decisions in the 1960s, have been granted a larger voice in FCC proceedings (Krasnow and Longley, 1978).

A number of other policy-making agencies have developed over the years both in the United States and internationally, and the range of issues in communication policy is, of course, substantially broader than our discussion to this point might suggest. Nevertheless, current approaches to communication policy making follow rather directly from these origins, and even this brief history should provide a general sense of the development of communication policy, and of those agencies that make it, which is essential to understanding contemporary issues in this field. Let us now turn our attention to these more current concerns.

II. ISSUES AND ACTORS IN DOMESTIC COMMUNICATION POLICY

Before examining the range of issues in U.S. domestic communications policy, let us survey the participants in the policy-making process. First and foremost, of course, is the FCC, whose origins and structure we have already considered. Leaving aside the regulation of program content through the "fairness doctrine," requirements for public affairs and news programming, and the like, most FCC policy decisions relate to questions of allocating and licensing spectrum use by nongovernmental agencies, structuring telecommunications-related industries, defining the boundaries and terms of common carrier service, and establishing standards of operation. With so broadly defined a role, the commission is a primary factor in setting U.S. communication policy. Still, because it is at heart a *regulatory* agency, because it generally aggregates interests rather than articulating them, and because, due to its staffing, budgeting, and information-gathering problems, it tends to be a reactive rather than a creative force in making policy, the Federal Communications Commission does not monopolize the formulation of domestic communication policy even within the government. Other agencies active on this front include the following:

Interdepartment Radio Advisory Committee (IRAC). We have already noted the origins of IRAC and suggested its general purpose, oversight of spectrum used by the government itself. In effect, IRAC performs many of the regulatory functions within the government that the FCC performs outside, a fact that leads to occasional conflicts between the two agencies, particularly over spectrum allocation. IRAC provides an important forum for the representation of military and other security interests in communication. Its meetings are closed to the public, and its activities receive little publicity. It is chaired by a representative of the Commerce Department, and heavily influenced by representatives of the Defense Department (Will, 1978; Mosco, 1979).

National Telecommunications and Information Administration, Department of Commerce (NTIA). NTIA was formed in the mid-1970s, and in 1977 took on most of the functions of the White House Office of Telecommunication Policy (OTP). OTP had been formed in 1970 to provide long-range planning within the executive branch on telecommunications issues, and, not incidentally, to counterbalance both the Congress *and* the FCC. It was given substantial authority to formulate international policy positions as well (Will, 1978; Goldberg, 1978; Miller, 1982). But OTP became mired in the politics of the Nixon and Ford administrations as well as in interagency battles involving the Departments of Justice and Defense, among others, and in 1977 President Carter merged it into the nascent NTIA. It is an NTIA representative who now chairs IRAC, an important function inherited from OTP. Despite the scope of its activities, however, NTIA is limited to an advisory role in many areas of policy making (Mosco, 1979).

United States Postal Service (USPS). Although much of our discussion to this point has focused on the use and control of telecommunications, we must keep in mind that other forms of communication are subject to policy making as well. A case in point is the Postal Service, whose rate making influences not only the cost of doing business throughout the economy, but the economic well-being of print journalism as well. A series of decisions over the last decade designed to eliminate subsidies for mailing publications has threatened those with weak subscriber bases much as an earlier policy of providing such subsidies had helped them. USPS was formed in 1971 in an effort to solve certain structural problems of the then Post Office Department, and has made some strides to streamline mail delivery. Since that time, however, the agency has lost some of its more lucrative business to such private corporations as United Parcel Service and Federal Express, and in the near future faces stiff competition for first-class service from electronic alternatives ranging from automatic money transfers (more than half of all first-class mail involves financial transactions) and satellite business communication systems (some 80 percent of first-class mail is business-related) to interactive cable or telephone systems. USPS response to this competition, including provision of electronic mail services, will help to determine the nature of interpersonal, and, to a degree, mass communication in the United States in the future (Geller and Brotman, 1978).

Although a number of lesser issues occupy the agenda of domestic communication policy makers, two major dimensions of policy predominate. The first pertains to the allocation and use of frequencies in the electromagnetic spectrum; the second to the structure of communications industries and markets. The two are, of course, not wholly independent of one another, but the distinction is useful for analytic purposes.

The issues of spectrum allocation arise from the fact that the spectrum is a limited resource. Indeed, whereas in the past our use of the spectrum was limited by the quality of our technology, particularly at the extreme ends, the finite physical availability of spectrum space is coming increasingly into play. This may best be understood by examining the nature of the spectrum itself.

In the simplest applications, electromagnetic waves are generated when electricity is passed through a coil of wire. By varying the length or compactness of the coil, or by inserting a magnetic core, one may vary the length of those waves. And because such waves travel at a constant speed (that of light, which is itself a part of the spectrum), variations in the length of the waves are inversely related to their frequency, which is to say the number of complete wave cycles to pass a given point in one second. The measure of frequency for electromagnetic waves is the hertz (named for an early pioneer of radio technology), abbreviated Hz. Waves of different frequencies display different propagation characteristics, and thus have different applications. These are summarized in Table 1.

Propagation refers to the way an electromagnetic signal travels. Groundwaves, those at the lowest frequencies, actually carry through the earth and into the lower atmosphere, and will bend to follow a path around the curvature of the planet beyond the horizon. At higher altitudes, however, they dissipate. Skywaves, on the other hand, will not penetrate the earth, but carry well through the atmosphere. Those toward the middle of the spectrum, especially medium frequency (MF), high frequency (HF), and very high frequency (VHF), literally bounce off the ionosphere, again permitting signals to follow the earth's curvature, sometimes over great distances. Those of higher frequency, however, travel only by line of sight, and are not reflected. Accordingly, they provide for more localized uses (satellite up- and down-links, for example) than the broadcasting (literally) typical of the midrange frequencies (Bennett, 1974).

Relatively recent technological developments have enabled us to make more and better use of the spectrum, particularly in the very low frequency (VLF), low frequency (LF), super high frequency (SHF), and extra high frequency (EHF) ranges. But the economic cost of access to extreme frequencies is substantial, with the result that most innovative uses are developed and controlled by the military (a control that IRAC has sometimes been reluctant to sanction). Still, the feasibility of commercial development of portions of the ultra high frequency (UHF) and SHF bands has led to some significant policy decisions over the last two decades. Two cases in point, both dating to 1962 but having very contemporary implications, were the legislation and rule making requiring that all television receivers traded in interstate commerce in the United States be equipped to receive UHF channels 14 to 83, and the decision to establish the quasi-governmental Communications Satellite Corporation (COMSAT) to provide interface between the domestic and international communications satellite systems. In the first instance the process leading up to the decision is illustrative of communication policy making, whereas in the second the shape and consequences of the policy itself are most revealing.

UHF television, operating in the range from 470 to 890 MHz, has long been the stepchild of American commercial broadcasting. Because of the technical challenges of broadcasting in the UHF band, transmission and reception of UHF signals was inferior to that of VHF signals from the inception of service in 1952. This technical weakness was compounded by an economic constraint that traced to an even earlier FCC decision. In 1945, the commission had determined that the 12 VHF channels were sufficient to meet then-current needs for television service, and that when UHF technology, with its multitude

Table 1. Components of the Electromagnetic Spectrum

Frequency range	Band designation (abbreviation)[a]	Other designation	Propagation	Uses
0–30 KHz[b]	Very low frequency (VLF)		Groundwaves ◄►	Experimental
30–300 KHz	Low frequency (LF)	Long wave		Submarine and other military communication, navigation
300–3000 KHz (3 MHz)	Medium frequency (MF)	Medium wave	Sky waves	Domestic broadcasting
3–30 MHz[c]	High frequency (HF)	Short wave	Reflected by ionosphere ◄‑‑‑‑‑►	International, marine, and amateur broadcasting and radiotelegraphy
30–300 MHz	Very high frequency (VHF)			Television and FM radio broadcasting, aircraft and public service
300–3000 MHz (3 GHz)	Ultra high frequency (UHF)	Microwave	Line-of-sight	Television broadcasting
3–30 GHz[d]	Super high frequency (SHF)			Radar, satellite transmissions, point-to-point communication, cooking
30 GHz–10¹⁸Hz	Extra high frequency (EHF)		Sky waves ►	Experimental
10¹⁸ Hz–300(10)²⁰ Hz	Light x-rays and gamma rays			Fiber optic communication

[a]Most of these designations were first established by the ITU in 1947.
[b]Kilohertz, or $(10)^3$ Hz.
[c]Megahertz, or $(10)^6$ Hz.
[d]Gigahertz, or $(10)^9$ Hz.

of channels, became more practical, it would either supplement or supplant VHF service. Accordingly, almost all early commercial broadcasting service developed on channels 2 through 13. Indeed, because the assignment of multiple stations in diverse locations to the same frequency is limited by the potential for signal interference, each area was limited to relatively few competing channels, and most of these were quickly exploited. In 1952 UHF service was introduced, and by 1954 some 125 UHF stations were operating. But by 1961 only 5.5 percent of all new receivers were equipped with UHF tuners, and UHF broadcasters, whose number had declined to about 75, were losing money consistently, in large measure because their substantially smaller audiences were unattractive to potential advertisers.[2]

Pursuant to its 1945 decision, the FCC acted on two fronts. First, it asked Congress for legislation requiring that all television sets sold in interstate commerce be equipped with UHF as well as VHF receivers. Second, it initiated a policy of "deintermixture" of UHF and VHF broadcasting in various markets. Under this policy, a given market would be served by either UHF or VHF television, but not by both. Existing VHF stations would be reassigned to UHF frequencies. The latter half of this policy was anathema to the vested economic interests in the broadcasting industry, and was the object of concerted and effective political action by a variety of industry groups. By contrast, the "all-channel" receiver requirement, which posed both the threat of increased competition (e.g., more stations in individual markets) and the promise of expansion (e.g., more stations in more markets meant larger audiences and revenues for the networks), looked more attractive. So it was that a compromise was struck. The FCC agreed to "postpone" its efforts at deintermixture, and the All-Channel Receiver Bill sailed through Congress with broad industry support. Not only has this legislation over the years reinvigorated commercial UHF service, but, by assuring a sizable potential audience, it cleared the way for the expansion of public broadcasting on the UHF band as well (Blakely, 1979; Krasnow and Longley, 1978). We can see, then, that frequency allocation policy decisions, though essentially technical in character, are shaped by political forces and are politically, economically, and even socially consequential.

Our second example, the establishment of COMSAT, reveals a more fundamental element of U.S. frequency allocation policy, though again one with a significant economic component. In this instance, the point at issue was government versus private control of access to international satellite communication, and the decision, while consistent with American precedent, was unique among nations. In January and February 1962, at a time when the feasibility of satellite communication was becoming apparent and the need to design agencies to control it manifest, three measures were introduced in Congress to this end. One called for creation of a communications satellite corporation wholly owned by U.S. common carriers. A second would have established a government-owned satellite system independent of the common carriers. The third, supported by the Kennedy administration, sought to divide ownership between the common carriers and the public and to allow for presidential appointment of a minority of directors of the new corporation. It was the Administration plan, more or less intact, that emerged victorious.

Initially, COMSAT was to be owned half by the common carriers and half by the public, and four common carriers, AT&T, ITT, General Telephone and Electronics (GTE), and RCA purchased more than 90 percent of the available stock. Later amendments to the act reduced the common carrier interest to 20 percent, and AT&T and ITT divested themselves of all holdings in the corporation. What has resulted, then, is essentially a private international common carrier, some of whose directors are presidential appointees.

The interesting thing about COMSAT is precisely this very limited degree of government participation in its activities. But where a similar pattern in American telegraphy and telephony had earlier led to some problems in the integration of U.S. telecommunications into the world system, in this instance it provided the nation with a unique opportunity. For it was COMSAT that provided the impetus for the international agreements on satellite communication that developed into INTELSAT, the International Telecommunications Satellite Organization.[3] And it was the inherently commercial nature of the American involvement that gave shape to the definitive INTELSAT agreements. Indeed, because of American near-monopoly in the technology of satellite communication, and because of COMSAT's initial monopoly over international common carrier service involving the United States, COMSAT was accepted at the outset as, in effect, the managing partner of INTELSAT, and COMSAT and the State Department have greatly influenced the organization's policies through the years. The result internationally has been an agency whose goals have been defined in economic rather than political terms (Pelton, 1974). The concomitant effect domestically has been that frequencies allocated for satellite use have by and large been exploited for commercial rather than governmental advantage.

Two other policies deserve mention before we turn to a consideration of more expressly economic decision making. The first, the FCC's decision in 1976 to expand from 23 channels of citizen's band (CB) radio to 40 in response to ballooning demand, was similarly concerned with spectrum allocation, but illustrates a more recent and consistent tendency of the commission, that toward deregulation of telecommunications on a broad scale. In the mid-1970s, the commission was literally overwhelmed by the sudden demand for CB licenses, and found itself without the means effectively to enforce its rules on licensing and station operation. Faced with a public clamor for access, the commission withdrew from rule enforcement, proclaimed itself merely a registration bureau, and urged CB users to police themselves. In a second decision in 1979, faced with a much smaller-scale expansion in the number of individually owned satellite television receiving systems, which threatened similarly to strain enforcement of restrictions on use of such equipment, the FCC again withdrew its constraints and provided registration services (this time at the option of the equipment owners). In each instance, rather than see its authority effectively challenged because of its limited ability to respond, and consistent with a mandate first put forward during the Nixon administration, the commission drew back from conflict by reducing its own function. The result in each instance was an expansion in public access to the spectrum and, incidentally, in the development and sale of related electronic equipment.

As these examples make clear, frequency allocations are not without economic consequences. Still, other decisions of communication policy makers are more directly economic in character, particularly those regarding the competitive structure of the communications industry and its components. Since about 1970, these have increasingly taken the form of reduced government regulation, especially by the FCC, and encouragement of increased industrial competition. Recent examples of such policies include the progressive enrichment of cable television services, the forced divestiture of cross-owned newspaper and broadcasting combinations, the dropping of increasingly artificial distinctions between electronic communication and data processing, and efforts to regulate differerentially different strata of common carriers. Let us look briefly at each in turn.

In the case of cable television, the commission faced an obvious conflict of economic interests. On the one hand, established broadcasters had developed local audiences in their respective markets whose maintenance was central to their economic well-being They feared competition from the cable because it would provide those audiences with more viewing options and would therefore dilute local advertising revenues. On the other hand, cable television offered more diverse programming, public access, and the eventual prospect of interactive services that promised to enhance the social value of television. Initially the FCC was very protective of so-called free TV, but as cable systems demonstrated their economic viability and as the technology was improved, the layers of protection have been progressively removed. In 1980, for example, the commission dropped its last restrictions on importing competing network and syndicated programs into local markets. The commission's clear purpose in these recent actions has been to nurture increased competition and to remove itself from the competitive process.[4]

In the cross-ownership decisions, the FCC's goal, albeit pursued more reluctantly, has been much the same, to foster competition and diversity. A common pattern of media ownership until the mid-1970s was for the single remaining newspaper and the sole, or a principal, television or radio station in a given city to be held by the same interests. In 1973 the Antitrust Division of the Justice Department began challenging license renewals of stations involved in cross-ownership on grounds that such arrangements controlled too much local advertising revenue. As the challenges mounted, the FCC was forced to deal with the issue of ownership patterns in its licensing proceedings (or face lengthy legal battles that might well result in limiting its authority). Accordingly, in 1975 it ordered divestiture of a number of newspaper-broadcast combinations and banned future same-city combinations in most instances. Although the effects of this decision have yet to be felt fully, at least one observer expects it to enhance not only economic competition in local markets, but the competition of ideas as well (Gormley, 1976).

Similar tendencies toward deregulation and enhanced competition are evident in recent common carrier decisions. Historically, for example, the commission has differentiated between communication and data processing services, and has imposed this distinction on the marketplace, as in its protection of AT&T's monopoly over communication services but its prohibition of the firm's participation in marketing computers. The merger of the two technologies in the late 1970s, however, forced a rethinking of this position, and in 1980 the commission removed its increasingly artifical distinction, allowing both AT&T's entry into data processing and the movement of data processing firms into communication, particularly by providing data transmissions by satellite. On a related front, the commission has moved to distinguish between "dominant" and "nondominant" common carriers (e.g., AT&T, which offers a wide range of services to a large number of customers, versus MCI Communications, which offers limited long-distance telephone service), and to reduce the regulatory burden on the lesser carriers. The effect would be to ease the entry of these secondary firms into the marketplace and to weaken AT&T's monopoly position. Indeed, the two decisions were hardly independent of one another, because on the one hand the commission opened some of the AT&T's most lucrative markets to competitors, while on the other it offered that company, or in reality an arms'-length subsidiary, entry to new and potentially lucrative markets as well. The 1982 settlement of antitrust litigation involving AT&T, however, has introduced considerable doubt as to the eventual outcome of this restructuring effort.

The consistent thread in all of these domestic policy decisions is the expansion of services within the private sector under conditions of increasing competition. And if the FCC, as principal policy maker, has not always been a willing and aggressive force in making these decisions (and indeed it has not), it has nevertheless, as a highly politicized agency, carried them forward.

III. ISSUES AND ACTORS IN U.S. FOREIGN COMMUNICATION POLICY

The principal agencies involved in making foreign communication policy in the United States are three in number. The first, NTIA, was described earlier. Its foreign policy responsibilities are carried out by an Office of International Affairs, and include coordinating economic, technical, and other preparations for U.S. participation in any conferences or negotiations regarding international telecommunications (such as the Administrative Conferences of ITU). In this regard, NTIA is limited to advising policy makers rather than actually formulating policy. Other important actors include the following:

Department of State (DOS).   The Office of International Communication Policy deals with ITU deliberations and advises on foreign policy implications of communications activity. The Bureau of International Organizations deals with issues of media content and operation such as those raised by UNESCO (see below). Other DOS agencies deal with issues in trans-border data flows and provide some guidance to the International Communication Agency. DOS is assigned primary responsibility for formulating U.S. foreign communication policy, but in general does not assign to this task a high order of priority.

International Communication Agency (ICA).   This agency, the product of a merger of the U.S. Information Agency, which operated the Voice of America and other overseas information services, and the State Department's Bureau of Educational and Cultural Affairs, which operated international exchange programs, is not really a policy maker in the fullest sense. Indeed, though it has some autonomy, its policy is guided by DOS. Still, ICA is the principal agent of international communication per se by the U.S. government, and the form and substance of its actions reflect the government's policies (Mosco, 1979). It is for this reason that we include it in the present discussion.

It is difficult to speak in isolation of U.S. foreign communication policy for two reasons. First, such issues do not exist in a vacuum. On the one hand, they are often extensions of domestic communication policy decisions, a case in point being the role of DOS in aiding the international operations of COMSAT. On the other, they are often extensions of more general directions in foreign policy, as, for example, in the initiation of Voice of America broadcasts in Farsi during the Iranian hostage crisis. At the same time,

American foreign communication policy must be understood in the context of international issues to which we have yet to address ourselves. Accordingly, let us confine the present discussion to a few underlying principles or directions of American policy without focusing too narrowly on details. As we shall see, these themes are strongly interrelated.

First and foremost among these principles, at least publicly, is the pursuit of a so-called free flow in information. The question here is one of access, access by others to information provided by the United States or its agents, and access by the United States and its agents to information about or provided by others. The first point is manifested in the U.S. position on direct broadcast satellites, those capable of beaming television transmissions directly into a country other than that of origin without interference and without the permission of the government of the receiving country. In contrast to more restrictive preferences expressed by the Soviet Union and its allies, by the LDCs, and even by a number of Western industrialized nations, the United States has argued that any specific limitations on such broadcasting are premature and unnecessary, and would have the effect of stifling the development of direct broadcast technology. In effect, the American position calls for a laissez faire approach with its attendant absence of controls over information flow (Dizard, 1980). The second point is evident in the U.S. position on remote sensing satellites, those capable of scanning and transmitting data about geological, agricultural, meteorological, and other characteristics of target countries. Although the LDCs are especially anxious to control and limit scanning of their territories, the United States has continued the practice while offering to share its data with the target countries (Yanchinski, 1980). And finally, both dimensions of access are reflected in the American position in the ongoing debate over the activities of Western news agencies, particularly in the LDCs. Many of these countries not only wish to control the flow of news about themselves to the outside world, but also wish to end what they perceive as their dependence on Western agencies (primarily Associated Press, United Press International, Reuters, and Agence France Presse) for news of the outside and, in some instances, news about themselves. They propose to do so by limiting, replacing, or even eliminating certain activities of the news agencies. Again the U.S. position is to permit free access by the news agencies to both news and news markets in these countries (Righter, 1979a).

Apparent in much of the debate over free flow, in fact if not in word, is a second principle of U.S. foreign communication policy, the maintenance of American hegemony. It is, for example, the United States that benefits most directly from remote scanning, because it is best equipped to conduct such scanning. It is the Western allies led by the United States who have the least to fear from direct satellite broadcasting and who are most likely to engage in it, and it is these same nations who dominate the flow of international news and would have the most at risk were that flow to be significantly altered. Thus, although a "free flow" of information is a potent symbol, its accomplishment is not necessarily value neutral or equivalent for all parties to it (Branscomb, 1979).

A third value espoused in American policy flows similarly from the concern with hegemony, that of progress with stability in the international communication system. In the World Administrative Radio Conference (WARC) of 1979, for instance, the United States and its allies argued that stability would be threatened by Third World demands for reassignment of short wave frequencies, and progress likewise threatened by demands to reserve geostationary satellite parking orbits for future LDC use. Progress with stability is also an element in the U.S. position on direct broadcast satellites as noted above. But again, stability, which is to say slowed and controlled change, benefits those parties who are best served by the status quo (McLeod, 1980).

A final element in American policy is commercialism. From the earliest international telegraphy to the point-specific decision to establish COMSAT in the private sector, American communication policy has centered on commercial exploitation. Especially in such areas as provision of news services, export of communication equipment, and export of programming, the United States has long enjoyed market preeminence with the support of policy makers (Tunstall, 1977). Moreover, commercialism helps to define the demands for international policies placed on policy makers by their domestic constituents. With regard to the allocation of both frequencies and satellite slots, for example, the support of a competitive commercial system requires that the United States work to obtain enough of each to accommodate multiple users, potentially an inefficient use of spectrum and orbital space (Whittaker, 1979). In this sense, then, U.S. foreign communication policy is very much a creature of the domestic communication system.

IV. ISSUES AND ACTORS IN INTERNATIONAL COMMUNICATION POLICY

The principal actor in international communication policy making is the ITU, whose development and functions we have already explored. Other important participants (excluding the national representatives of other countries) include the following:

United Nations Educational, Scientific and Cultural Organization (UNESCO). Whereas the ITU focuses primarily on technical considerations in international communication, UNESCO is a primary forum for the development, though not always the resolution, of expressly political issues. In recent years, it has been the center of two major controversies, one over direct broadcast satellites and the other over the role of international news agencies, both of which have focused on the question of free flow. In general, an alliance of communist and Third World nations has more or less controlled the agenda of UNESCO debates since about 1972, and the organization has often served as a sounding board for restrictive (or, depending on one's point of view, protective) policies. Because the United States contributes a substantial share of UNESCO's operating funds, however, it has generally been able to impose some restraints on UNESCO declarations. This was best exemplified by the extended (eight years) and often acrimonious debate over the United Nations Declaration of Fundamental Principles on the Media,[5] finally adopted in 1978, in which the United States and other Western nations were able to avert United Nations sanctioning of major restrictions on the gathering and dissemination of news. Still, UNESCO is frequently perceived as a locus of substantial threat to Western communication interests (Righter, 1979b).
United Nations Committee on Peaceful Uses of Outer Space. This group focuses on legal, scientific, and technical aspects of satellite communication, and is rather less politicized than UNESCO. The committee's work was instrumental in developing the 1967 Outer Space Treaty, which provided for both free access to space exploration

and exploitation by all nations and protection of national vehicles and personnel. Most recently it has been working on developing principles governing direct broadcast satellites, a task it took over from UNESCO in 1973 (Dizard, 1980; Brown et al., 1977).

International Telecommunications Satellite Organization (INTELSAT). INTELSAT is an international, and primarily Western,[6] consortium of nations that operates a network of satellites providing international and, on a concessionary basis, domestic commercial public communication services. Initially established in 1964 and made permanent in 1973, INTELSAT is the only international organization of governments operating as a commercial enterprise. The U.S. investment/voting share of some 20 to 30 percent (down from more than 50 percent initially) still provides for substantial influence, though COMSAT's role as system manager ended in 1973. But the current trend toward regional (Arab and European in particular) and domestic (in Canada, the Soviet Union, and Indonesia as well as the United States) satellite systems poses a serious threat to INTELSAT's viability (Snow, 1980).

The principal issues in international communication policy today have already been suggested by our discussion of U.S. foreign policy. They include the "free flow" of news and other information, remote sensing, direct broadcast satellites, definitions of equity in the allocation of spectrum space and orbital slots, control over trans-border data flows, and the transfer of communications technology.

As noted, debate over the free flow of news has emerged most pointedly in UNESCO, and has generally pitted communist and Third World nations against the industrial democracies, with the former arguing for substantial government control over in- and outflows of news in individual nations and the latter for freedom of movement. It is the contention of the LDCs that Western control of news gathering and dissemination to, from, and even within them, dominated as it is by Western definitions of news values, deprives those nations of the right to define their own goals and accomplishments in their own terms and, cumulatively, even threatens to destroy their separate indigenous cultures. Although they have been thwarted in many of their attempts to impose formal international constraints on news flows, they have by and large persuaded Westerners of the validity of some of their claims, and have, as well, begun an expansion of home-based news coverage of the Third World (Righter, 1979b).

Remote sensing emerged as an issue with the launching by the United States in 1972 of *Landsat 1,* a resource sensing satellite. Until that time nations had been able to control access to (information about) their natural resources, but under terms of the 1967 Outer Space Treaty, not to mention the absolute inability of nonspace powers to control satellite overflights, this capability was lost. The remote sensing satellites thus constitute an effective, if limited, threat to national sovereignty, and have become a matter of increasing concern to a number of nations, particularly LDCs, who fear that information gathered by satellite will be used to their economic, political, or military disadvantage (Brown et al., 1977).

The same question of sovereignty is raised by direct broadcasting from satellites, because technology now coming on-line in Japan and Western Europe, and soon to be deployed elsewhere, allows the transmission of television signals across national boundaries where they may then be received by relatively inexpensive equipment. Jamming of such signals by target states is difficult or impossible because, unlike more vulnerable short-wave broadcasts, line-of-sight microwave signals from satellites are, in effect, multiple point-to-point signals. Effective jamming would thus require either destroying the satellite emitting the signal or parking another satellite using the same frequency nearby so as to interfere with the transmission, both tactics available only to space powers or their allies. Accordingly, it is again the LDCs who feel most threatened, though communist states have often sided with them, at least publicly, in debates on the issue.

Like spectrum space, suitable parking orbits for communications satellites are limited in number. Geostationary orbits, those in which a satellite will orbit the earth but remain stationary over one geographic location, are possible only over the equator at an altitude of 22,300 miles. These positions offer substantial technical advantages over other orbital patterns. Because communication satellites must be able to "see" populated areas; because they must be separated by 3 to 4 degrees of arc to avoid interfering with one another's signals, because they are almost invariably parked over international waters so as to avoid claims of territorial sovereignty (no equatorial nations are themselves space powers), and because their frequency allocations are limited, the number of available and functional orbital slots is finite. And like ITU treatment of spectrum space, allocation of these positions has been on a first-come, first-served basis. In recent years, LDCs have argued that both spectrum space and orbital slots should be reserved for their future use, while major spectrum users and space powers have worked to preserve their own prerogatives by arguing that foregoing current use of these resources is wasteful. Development of new satellite frequencies, multi-use satellites, and better equipment allowing tighter spacing of parking orbits promise a compromise on these issues in the near term, perhaps as early as the ITU conferences on frequency and parking orbit allocations scheduled for 1985 and 1987, (McLeod, 1980).

The issues involved in trans-border data flows arise from the marriage of data processing and communication technologies, and again raise the question of national sovereignty, though not in quite the same way. Here the perceived threat to information- or technology-poor nations comes less from other governments than from multinational corporations, for it is these corporations that, by centralizing their record keeping in a relative few locations, import and export information electronically across national boundaries. This means that data about a country's banking, resources, and daily commerce may be routinely stored outside that country, where they are effectively beyond the control of its government. An international agency, the Intergovernmental Bureau for Informatics (IBI), has been formed to examine technological developments and policy in this area, and by 1979 some 60 countries had adopted their own policies, but this issue promises to increase in importance as the technology for electronic data transmissions becomes still more advanced (Freese, 1979; Pipe, 1979).

The transfer of communication technology to the LDCs is really only a part of larger issues of technology transfer generally. Put most simply, the LDCs are becoming more sophisticated in their demands, primarily by seeking not merely the transfer of externally selected and developed devices, but rather transfer as well of the expertise for determining which technologies are most appropriate to their needs and how best to employ them.

As is readily apparent, many of these issues tend to resolve themselves into a component of the larger North-South debate, that between industrialized and lesser developed countries. Indeed, the LDCs have propounded what they term a New World Information

Order, a call for enhanced respect for the needs of the LDCs on the part of the industrialized countries and for an assertion of common interest by the LDCs themselves. In effect, the argument is made that control over communications by outside nations, combined with an insensitivity to the consequences of that control for dependent nations, constitutes a form of informational colonialism whose dimensions, its proponents would argue, are apparent in the consistent divergence of interests we have outlined above. The neocolonial powers, that is, the technology-rich nations, it is claimed, have a responsibility to redress this circumstance, and the LDCs have an obligation to take both internally and externally directed corrective measures as well (Masmoudi, 1979; Lopez-Escobar, 1978). This call for a new order, which effectively integrates a number of outstanding issues, has attracted widespread attention and is likely to shape the international communication policy agenda for some time to come.

V. CONCLUSION

This review of domestic and international communication policy and policy makers has been necessarily brief and incomplete, and can only suggest the complexity of the issues involved. Nevertheless, three important points about these issues should be clear. First, both domestically and internationally, communication policy follows more than it directs technological development. That is, policy makers in this area tend to respond to changed circumstances more than they guide that change. To a point, of course, this is inevitable, because one cannot simply command that technologies develop according to some plan. It means, however, that much communication policy is made only after interests have become vested, with the result that otherwise attractive options may be foreclosed. Second, the distinction between domestic and international policy, particularly toward *tele*communications, is becoming increasingly artificial and the interdependence of the two more apparent. And third, the world is now involved in a fundamental clash of ideological and economic interests covering a wide range of issues of which communication is but one, albeit an important one. The resolution of that conflict, or the failure to resolve it, will bear heavily on U.S. communication policy in the years ahead.

Glossary of Agencies

AT&T	American Telephone and Telegraph
COMSAT	Communications Satellite Corporation
DOS	Department of State
FCC	Federal Communications Commission
FRC	Federal Radio Commission
GTE	General Telephone and Electronics
IBI	Intergovernmental Bureau for Informatics
ICA	International Communication Agency
IFRB	International Frequencies Registration Board
INTELSAT	International Telecommunications Satellite Organization
IRAC	Interdepartment Radio Advisory Committee
IRTU	International Radiotelegraph Union
ITT	International Telephone and Telegraph
ITU	International TelecommunicationUnion

Glossary of Agencies (Continued)

NTIA	National Telecommunications and Information Administration
OTP	Office of Telecommunications Policy
RCA	Radio Corporation of America
UNESCO	United Nations Educational, Scientific and Cultural Organization
USPS	United States Postal Service
WARC	World Administrative Radio Conference

NOTES

1. In part this was because those parties with heavy capital investments in telegraphy resisted the diffusion of the new technology.
2. This was compounded by the higher capital costs of providing UHF service equivalent to VHF and by substantially higher energy costs. Technology developed in 1980 promises to ease the energy cost burden on UHF broadcasters but to impose still higher capital costs.
3. Until 1973, the International Telecommunications Satellite *Consortium.*
4. It is worth noting that much regulation of cable services is in the hands of local governments through the granting of franchises and easements to cable operators, and while competition between cable and broadcasting has increased in the aggregate, competition *among* cable operators in particular established markets is the exception.
5. The correct title is "Declaration of Fundamental Principles Concerning the Contribution of the Mass Media to Strengthening Peace and International Understanding, the Promotion of Human Rights and to Countering Racialism, Apartheid and Incitement to War."
6. LDCs have, however, acquired increasing interests in recent years.

REFERENCES

Bennett, H. (1974). *The Complete Short Wave Listener's Handbook.* Tab Books, Blue Ridge Summit, PA.

Blakeley, R. J. (1979). *To Serve the Public Interest: Educational Broadcasting in the United States.* Syracuse University Press, Syracuse, NY.

Branscomb, A. W. (1979). Waves of the future: Making WARC work. *Foreign Policy 34:* 139-148.

Brown, S., Cornell, N. W., Fabian, L. L., and Weiss, E. B. (1977). *Regimes for the Ocean, Outer Space, and Weather.* Brookings Institution, Washington, DC.

Codding, G. A., Jr. (1972). *The International Telecommunication Union: An Experiment in International Cooperation,* reprinted. Arno Press, New York.

Dizard, W. P. (1980). The U.S. position: DBS and free flow. *Journal of Communication 30:* 157-168.

Frees, J. (1979). The dangers of non-regulation. *Journal of Communication 29:*135-137.

Geller, H., and Brotman, S. (1978). Electronic alternatives to postal service. In *Communications for Tomorrow: Policy Perspectives for the 1980s.* G. O. Robinson (Ed.). Praeger, New York, pp. 307-349.

Goldberg, H. (1978). International telecommunication regulation. In *Communications for Tomorrow: Policy Perspectives for the 1980s,* G. O. Robinson (Ed.). Praeger, New York, pp. 157-187.

Gormley, W. T., Jr. (1976). *The Effects of Newspaper-Television Cross-Ownership on News Homogeneity.* University of North Carolina Press, Chapel Hill.

Jacobson, H. K. (1972). The International Telecommunication Union: ITU's structure and functions. In *Global Communications in the Space Age: Toward a New ITU.* Twentieth Century Fund, New York.

Krasnow, E. G., and Longley, L. D. (1978). *The Politics of Broadcast Regulation,* 2nd ed. St. Martin's Press, New York.

Leive, D. M. (1972). *The Future of the International Telecommunication Union: A Report for the 1973 Plenipotentiary Conference.* American Society of International Law, Washington, DC.

Lopez-Escobar, E. (1978). *Analisis del "Nuevo Orden" Internacional de la Informacion.* Ediciones Universidad de Navarra, Pamplona, Spain.

Masmoudi, M. (1979). The new world information order. *Journal of Communication 29:* 172-179.

McLeod, N. (1980). Not so much a punch-up, more a WARC-in. *New Scientist,* January 24, pp. 246-248.

Miller, J. (1982). Policy planning and technocratic power: The significance of OTP. *Journal of Communication 32:* 53-60.

Mosco, V. (1979). Who makes U.S. government policy in world communications? *Journal of Communication 29:* 158-164.

Pelton, J. N. (1974). *Global Communications Satellite Policy: INTELSAT, Politics and Functionalism.* Lomond Books, Mt. Airy, MD.

Pipe, G. R. (1979). National policies, international debates. *Journal of Communication 29:* 114-123.

Righter, R. (1979a). Battle of the bias. *Foreign Policy 34:* 121-138.

—— (1979b). Who won? *Journal of Communication 29:* 192-194.

Robinson, G. O. (1978). The Federal Communications Commission. In *Communications for Tomorrow: Policy Perspectives for the 1980s,* G. O. Robinson (Ed.). Praeger, New York, pp. 353-400.

Snow, M. S. (1980). INTELSAT: An international example. *Journal of Communication 39:* 147-156.

Tunstall, J. (1977). *The Media are American: Anglo-American Media in the World.* Columbia University Press, New York.

Whittaker, P. N. (1979). To beat the band. *Foreign Policy 34:* 160-164.

Will, T. E. (1978). *Telecommunications Structure and Management in the Executive Branch of Government, 1900-1970.* Westview Press, Boulder, CO.

Yanchinski, S. (1980). Thorny questions over remote sensing. *New Scientist,* April 17, pp. 150-152.

20

Taxing and Spending Policy

Warren J. Samuels / Michigan State University, East Lansing, Michigan
Larry L. Wade / University of California, Davis, California

I. TAXES

A. Fiscal Federalism: Tax Structure and Perceptions

Taxes are mandatory contributions extracted from individuals and firms by governments for public purposes. The American federal system has produced marked differences in tax structures among national, state, and local governments. The federal government relies more heavily on individual income taxes (about 65 percent of all its tax revenues in the late 1970s) and the corporation income tax (23 percent in the same period). Local governments across the nation rely principally on the property tax (80 percent of all local tax revenue); state taxes display no obvious predominance of tax types, although in 1976-1977, sales and gross receipts taxes (including selective taxes on gasoline, tobacco, etc.) provided nearly 52 percent of all state tax revenue. Other substantial sources of state and local tax revenue include income taxes (13.5 percent) and service and license fees (11 percent). By 1976-1977, the federal government was collecting $384 billion in taxes compared to $338 billion by state and local governments. Any thorough consideration of national tax and expenditure policy must therefore take into account the great size of the state and local sector (see Bureau of the Census, 1977).

The question of the optimal mix of taxes in a federal system is an important if elusive subject (Oates, 1972; Musgrave, 1965). Assuming an acceptable distribution of income (an assumption typically ignored by policy makers), benefit pricing (by which consumers pay for benefits received) is an attractive principle, although in practice recourse is made to other types of taxes, sometimes based on the principle of ability to pay (Musgrave, 1959: chap. 5). A federal system, because it provides for the interjurisdictional movement of goods and productive factors, introduces serious complications bearing on income distribution and efficiency that are not present in a unitary system of government. At the same time, interjurisdictional variations in tax and service levels increase a consumer's range of choices: A market solution sometimes is said to be approximated that accommodates different tastes for public goods (Tiebout, 1956). Efficiency may be enhanced also by innovations in financing, organization, and type of public goods provided, as well as by a greater tendency to tie expenditure decisions closely to real resource costs. By the same token, "excessive" decentralization of the fisc introduces inefficiencies and limits the redistributive capacity of the society of the whole. Inefficiencies may arise with respect to government's stabilization function and its capacity to provide an optimal supply of public goods in those cases where taxpayer/beneficiary interests do not conform to jurisdictional boundaries (Oates, 1972: 4–13). The normative approach to fiscal federalism, however helpful, should be considered in the light of its actual operation. Bingham et al. (1978) have identified several particularly salient trends, including less federal spending in the declining Frostbelt and more in the developing Sunbelt, which has energized political forces around norms in which political interests appear to dominate over both efficiency and equity. Similarly, the adoption of state and local tax systems seems to yield to no obvious rule of economic rationality. Although total state and local taxes are regressive (if property taxes are so regarded), there is considerable variation among them: Some states are far more regressive than others; about 11 have proportional tax systems and several have progressive systems (Phares, 1973: 76–80). Even more important, perhaps, is the fact that political and socioeconomic variables have not been shown to be related decisively to different types of revenue devices in the states. Bingham et al. (1978: 155) conclude their astute empirical study of the influence of such factors with the words: "The prime explanatory variables are not those that describe current social, economic, or political divisions within a state. The strongest single variable is the time of adoption of the tax: the earlier a state's adoption of a tax, the greater the reliance on that tax." The authors quite appropriately call for historical studies that might reveal a closer connection between tax systems and sociopolitical tastes at the time of adoption, but such evidence would not change the fact that history rather than voter or economic logic often best explains current patterns.

An optimal tax system would require individual knowledge of tax incidence, and it has been reasonably argued that institutions often function to deny this knowledge. The real resource costs of public activity may be disguised through, among other ways, the use of the public domain to finance government, excise taxes hidden in consumer prices, deficit financing, and inflation. In addition, Buchanan (1967: 126–143) has identified as "fiscal illusions" income tax withholding, social security taxes (represented as "insurance"), and corporate income taxes.

Whether for reasons of fiscal illusion or otherwise, survey research data suggest that there is widespread public confusion about tax systems. Obler (1979: 524–540) analyzed responses from a 1969 national sample stratified along income, racial, and regional lines in which respondents were asked whether taxes should be based on "how much people spend," "how much people earn," or "the value of property people hold." The data revealed, contrary to conventional assumptions, that "either opinions vary little according to respondents' income, or when variation occurs, it challenges rather than confirms the assumption." Attitudes toward the income tax were as positive among the affluent as among the poor, and the sales tax was more popular among the poor than the affluent. (Obler's incidence data were from Tax Foundation, 1967).

Obler's data file may not, however, accurately reflect current opinion (illustrating the great need for replication of fiscal attitudes surveys). The Advisory Commission on Intergovernmental Relations (1977: 11) presented data showing that in 1972 only 19 percent of a national sample regarded the federal income tax as the "least fair" tax, compared to 28 percent in 1977. In 1972, the local property tax was regarded by 45 percent of the respondents as least fair, compared to 33 percent in 1977. State income taxes and sales taxes were each thought to be least fair by 13 percent in 1972, and by 11 and 17 percent, respectively, in 1977. These attitudes would seem to have less to do with whether a tax is progressive or regressive than with the share a tax occupies in one's total tax burden. Although they may be progressive, state income taxes are less onerous than the federal income tax, and regressive sales taxes less onerous than property taxes, however regarded.

B. Tax Incidence

Acceptable public policy requires knowledge of the incidence of taxes (where they finally rest) in order to assess their implications for both fairness and economic efficiency. This knowledge is often difficult to obtain (Peppard and Roberts, 1977). An excise tax on alcoholic beverages may be imposed on distilleries but shifted *forward* to consumers or, if demand is reduced because of the tax, *backward* to the producers of beverage ingredients. The tax's incidence will depend on the elasticities of demand and supply: If demand is inelastic and supply elastic, forward shifting is predicted; if demand is elastic and supply inelastic, backward shifting is expected. Similar shifting occurs with respect to indirect taxes generally, corporate income and property taxes being prime examples. In spite of impressive and sometimes fruitful efforts (Brown, 1974: 93-108), the waters are still muddied as to the precise conditions under which corporate income taxes are shifted to stockholders, employees, or consumers, as well as the tax's aggregate impact on income distribution. Property tax shifting also is a complex matter (Simon, 1943). Traditional theory held generally that taxes on unimproved land were borne by the property owner in the form of reduced property values; taxes on improved land would be shifted to renters or purchasers. This scheme is complicated, according to Oates (1972: 166-179), by the attractiveness of the services provided in particular jurisdictions, for example, if property tax increases go to finance better schools—themselves an inducement to accept a higher tax rate—the increase will not reduce property values. Property tax increases without an accompanying improvement in services would depress property values. Tax shifting and incidence are shown in Oates' important study to be inseparably linked to the provision and incidence of public goods.

The impact of taxes in America has not been such as to redistribute income significantly since World War II. Adding (under reasonable assumptions) the benefits received from government spending to both earned and unearned income and subtracting taxes, net income distributions have not changed greatly since 1950 (Reynolds and Smolensky, 1977). Nor does the tax system considered alone have all the progressive features sometimes assumed. Using variable assumptions of final tax incidence, Pechman and Okner (1974: 64-65) concluded that in the 1960s for the vast majority of households (87 percent), the total tax burden (about 25 percent of income) was either proportional or only slightly progressive. Inequality was reduced by only 5 percent under the most progressive assumptions and by only 0.25 percent under the least. Effective rates are somewhat higher for the highest population decile, but so are they also for the lowest decile. However, the tax rate of the lowest decile is probably overstated, because for some people membership has not been permanent (the retired) or lasting (the young). (But see

Peppard, 1976.) Federal taxes are progressive across the whole range. Property taxes are either regressive, or have a U-shaped pattern, depending on whether such taxes are treated as a tax on income or capital. (Redistribution through government may take several forms: taxation to provide goods and services, which varies from marginal benefit taxation; resource-exhausting expenditures, which are selectively beneficial and not based on efficiency criteria; and transfers.)

Regardless of the various incidence assumptions used, the greatest variation among tax rates stems from the structural characteristics of the personal income tax. Pechman and Okner (1974: 82-83) have shown that, among various groups, tax rates are lowest for "homeowners, rural-farm residents, families with transfers as their major sources of income, and large families." Rates are highest for "renters, urban residents, families whose major source of income is property or business, and single persons." These variable patterns are related to the incidence of tax deductions, which gives rise not only to the divergence of effective from nominal rates but to long-standing and intense political conflicts involving equity and social policy. The largest personal tax deductions, exemptions, and exclusions in the federal personal income tax are state and local tax deductions, mortgage interests on homes, pension contributions, charitable contributions, and capital gains (Break and Pechman, 1975: 14-15).

Some of these so-called loopholes, in addition to confering differential benefits on people otherwise similarly situated (and hence "inequitable" in various ethical value systems) can be defended either in terms of economic efficiency or social and political purposes. Others can be justified on equity grounds. Social purposes are presumably served by tax rules that encourage home ownership, charitable contributions, or family solvency. Efficiency is presumably enhanced by the preferential treatment of capital gains and investment tax credits; equity by the exclusion from taxation of social security benefits; and political objectives (federalism, local problem solving) by the treatment of interest on state and local bonds and the deductability of property and state taxes. The lack of ideological homogeneity perpetuates conflict concerning these matters that far transcends the capacities of policy analysts to resolve.

In any case, the tax burden on the American people as a whole is less onerous than in most other advanced liberal societies, as the data in Table 1 indicate. This is not to say that tax collections as a proportion of gross national product (GNP) are either too large, too small, or roughly "correct" in the United States. The answer to that question depends on either ideological predispositions or varying normative assumptions employed in the neoclassical or some other analytical framework. Presuming a "responsive" government, tax collections have been held to be excessive (accepting the assumptions of rationality and taxpayer/voter/consumer sovereignty) if costs are underestimated and benefits are appreciated. Collections would be too small if costs are visible and benefits underestimated. If costs and benefits are simultaneously and accurately understood, it is argued that collections will be "about right" (Musgrave and Musgrave, 1980: chaps 5, 6, 14). A close examination of the actual processes of fiscal decision making suggests that such grand assumptions need to be amended considerably in the interests of realism and meaningfulness.

The consequences of inflation both on income distribution and as a hidden tax are not known precisely, and conflicting hypotheses continue to be advocated. "Moderate" inflation of the sort experienced prior to the 1970s has been thought generally either to enhance profits at the expense of wages, interest, and rents, or to improve the position of

Table 1. Tax Revenue as Percent of
Gross National Product, 1973

United States	28.0
Canada	33.9
Japan	22.6
Australia	23.8
Austria	36.6
Belgium	36.6
Denmark	44.1
France	36.9
Germany	37.3
Italy	29.2
Norway	45.9
Sweden	43.5
Switzerland	26.4
United Kingdom	32.8

Source: *Revenue Statistics of OECD Member
Countries, 1965–1973.* Organization for
Economic Co-operation and Development,
Paris, 1975, p. 342.

debtors at the expense of creditors, although Bach and Ando (1957: 12-13) conducted empirical investigations that revealed more complex findings. They argue that the redistributional effects cut "across and through" broad income groups, and that to be effective ameliorative policy should focus more precisely on those adversely affected and less on broad income groups as such. The effects in the United States of "hyperinflation" on income distribution are yet to be thoroughly studied, say, in relation to the notion that high inflation in Latin America is a "substitute" for civil war.

It is a most troublesome fact that equity (income distribution) objectives of taxation cannot be well grounded in the absence of information on the benefits arising from the distribution of public goods. In much analysis, arbitrary assumptions have governed the imputation of public goods among income groups, even while information on consumer preferences for public goods is indispensible to a correct analysis (Aaron and McGuire, 1970). The collection of such data is one of the great future research tasks of the public finance community.

The ethical questions underlying tax policy are excruciating difficult, with alternative conceptions of justice promoting different tax bases and rates (Phelps, 1973: parts 4-5) or, indeed, no taxes at all in an extreme libertarian system (Rand, 1964: 116-120). The progressivity or regressivity of taxes has implications not only for various conceptions of justice but for economic productivity, a problem described by Okun (1975) as the "big tradeoff" between equality and efficiency. Pursuit of equality through progressive taxation entails losses in efficiency at some point, although efficiency itself is specific to distribution. The question of how progressive income taxes "should be" (Atkinson, 1973), assuming such a tax is normatively acceptable (Blum and Kalven, 1964), cannot be known without greater homogeneity of individual preferences than exists. Progressive taxation has often been justified by the norm of equal marginal sacrifices, itself based on the utilitarian principle that optimal social welfare consists in maximizing the sum of individual utilities. It has been argued (Mirrlees, 1971; Fair, 1971) that such a policy would have serious disincentive effects and that optimal tax rates should be set substantially below those suggested by the equal sacrifice theory. Acceptance of such a view, however, entails the rejection of the reasonably clear utilitarian norm. Rawls (1971) has proposed in its place a contractarian maximin principle—policy should maximize the welfare of the most disadvantaged—but which itself can be unhelpful or lead to absurd outcomes in identifiable instances (Harsanyi, 1975).

In an intriguing analysis, Reynolds and Smolensky (1976) suggest that taxation designed to alter the distribution of income may no longer be politically feasible. The history of the greatest redistributive programs—progressive income taxation and social security—indicates that their early impact (when income taxpayers were few and rich and when social security recipients were few and poor) has been dissipated and now tend toward distributional neutrality. As they argue, "It is the very scale of government programs which today militates against their capacity to sharply redistribute net income downward. . . . Under the mass taxation and spending of today, . . . even program changes with small extra benefits per recipient imply large aggregate benefits to recipients and large individual costs to nonrecipients." Ancillary reasons are also identified. Avoidance behavior has increased with tax rates, as shown by the growth of employee fringe benefits (now 10 percent of compensation compared to 1 percent in 1929). Heed is given (Lampman, 1974) to the view that redistribution has never in any case been broadly advocated in America, that Nozick's (1974) concern with the fairness of the game is more consistent with the culture (or the preferences of the median voter/taxpayer) than Rawl's interest in outcomes.

C. Some Political Determinants and Consequences

Traditional economics has sought to describe the fisc and to evaluate it within the canons of efficiency (albeit only roughly in the presence of public goods and externalities) and equity (however stipulated). The size and importance of government in the economy have in recent years encouraged efforts at explaining fiscal choices in democratic society, efforts that go beyond the traditional presumption that "government" was a rational, autonomous player in marketplace activity. (Ruling class or elite theories always have included efforts at explanation.) In this effort, economists and political scientists have operated from somewhat different vantage points. The economic, or public choice, approach to fiscal decision making rests on a methodology that normally takes the following form: Rational, welfare-maximizing individuals possess scarce resources and insatiable wants and occupy various, sometimes overlapping, roles in the society as voters, taxpayers, consumers of public and private goods, interest group members and leaders, incumbent and opposition politicians, bureaucrats, and so on. The properties of the system are identified; the rules of exit, entry, power, and decision are stipulated; and the goals of the participants are clarified and ranked. Formal models are then erected; that is, interactions are posited that give rise to expected outcomes (predictions, hypotheses), or outcomes are explained *post hoc* (sometimes *post hoc, ergo propter hoc*) by presumed prior interactions. Mitchell (1979) has noted that this approach has led to varying assessments of the relationship between the economy and polity. In the work of Downs (1957), a symbiosis of interests between vote-maximizing politicians and benefit-maximizing voters was held to produce tax/expenditure decisions that had broadly acceptable (if not always strictly efficient or equitable) consequences for social welfare. More recent work in this now large literature by Niskanen (1971), Wagner (1977), Tullock (1974), Breton (1974), and others (as in the volume edited by Buchanan and Tollison, 1972) points to the corrosive impact that political rules and behavior may have on both economic equity and efficiency.

Public choice analysis appears destined to assume increasing importance in the examination of fiscal (and other) issues. Future development would seem to require, however, that the extreme simplicity of most models advanced thus far yield to a keener appreciation of behavioral evidence (for example, the consequences of the fact that the actors in public choice are not situated symmetrically, as stressed by Bartlett, 1973). As Bingham et al. (1978: 194) note, "Development of these models requires constant checking against actual decisions. Where the fit is not satisfactory, there is need for changes in either the assumptions or the linkages the models posit." Examinations of misplaced argument and predictions in this literature have appeared (Wade, 1979: 81), although the need for a thoroughgoing critique remains. An illustration will make the general point. Tollison (1972) has sought to analyze the military draft, a subject normally approached by economists in terms of the inefficiencies associated with such an institution. Tollison advanced a number of simplifying assumptions about the real world, but, he wrote (p. 303): "As will be noted . . . the divergences between the individualistic model and the world are not large. The model should possess explanatory power." The model used generates a number of dubious assertions concerning the motivations of voters, interest group members and spokesmen, and politicians. Politicians are held to fear the economic solution of a volunteer military force because of the short-term money costs involved and the resulting loss of electoral support—thus the "stability" of the draft is "explained." The draft, of course, was ended in 1972, falsifying Tollison's prediction in the same year his study was reprinted in Buchanan and Tollison. The danger of working solely from assumptions and formal models is well shown in this instance. Such criticisms aside, the public choice approach may contribute importantly to a better understanding of taxing and spending as its practitioners show less attention to pure analytics and more to empirical data as well as proceed less on highly selective normative premises (Samuels, 1978). To the extent that this is done, however, the public choice approach will become indistinguishable from other social research—a healthy development for those who have sought a unified social science. A broader and more open-ended approach to public choice is provided, for example, in Schmid (1978).

Fortunately, Tollison has himself (Tollison et al., 1975) joined the growing ranks of those now investigating the empirical connections among economic and political factors relating to fiscal choices. This effort has accelerated greatly in recent years and shows every sign of generating more reliable statements about the determinants of fiscal choice as data sources increase and as analytical models mature. Thus far, the questions asked in this literature deal largely with the so-called political business cycles in democratic societies (but see Ames, 1981, for an extension to autocratic systems). In much of this literature, it is presumed that there is a relationship between the search for votes by elected officials in a competitive political order and their choice of tax/spending allocations (Nordhaus, 1975). It often is argued that politicians will seek to take advantage of the voter's short-term interest by offering fiscal policies that, at the time of election, will have induced periods of low unemployment and price stability, or that will have rewarded voters by tax reductions or selective expenditures. (For the argument that deficits lower the tax price and thereby increase public spending, see Buchanan and Wagner, 1977.) The economic position of the voter is thought to influence decisively his decision whether and for whom (what) to vote. In this scheme, it is not social welfare that motivates politicians, but a concern for their own political advantage. The voter's short-term interest, not society's long-term welfare, may be served by such a system. This is indeed a frustrating conclusion, for it suggests that both efficiency and equity goals may be of scant interest to democratic decision makers. Still, the evidence thus far is not entirely convincing on this point; indeed, it is quite perplexing as to its welfare implications.

Space does not allow for a full discussion of this continuing issue (but see Amacher et al., 1979; Tufte, 1978); however, one major area may be cited as a case in point. In 1971, Kramer published findings pointing to the importance that changes, during the year prior to the election, in general economic conditions (income, prices, unemployment) had on the popular vote for congressional candidates. Increases in income were found to be associated with increases in the vote for the "incumbent party," or the party in control of the White House. Inflation seemed to have little or no effect, as was also true of unemployment. Stigler (1973) subsequently took issue with these conclusions, arguing that general economic conditions had little impact on voting choices, although social welfare policies bearing on redistribution might do so. Other studies have appeared (Arcelus and Meltzer, 1975; Goodman and Kramer, 1975; Bloom and Price, 1975; McCallum, 1978) in which various model specifications and data bases have led to complicated and still unsettled results.

Several issues in this literature concerning economic conditions and voting choices have been put in useful perspective in an important study by Owens and Olson (1980). By disaggregating the national congressional vote to the district level and by examining local economic conditions (prices, income), their models showed no linear relationship between changes in the vote for individual candidates and changes in inflation and real income in 1972, 1974, and 1976. This was so even during a period when economic conditions were cited in opinion surveys as the greatest problem before the country. The aggregate congressional vote could not usefully be viewed as a national referendum, suggesting that Kramer's findings may have been spurious. Owens and Olson's evidence suggests that the "established" voting model (Campbell et al., 1960) continues to offer the most powerful explanation of voting behavior. That model emphasized the importance of both short-run (issues, personalities) and long-run forces (partisanship, a number of sociological and demographic variables) in voting choices. In such a model, calculated, short-run economic position is only one of many influences on voting. This reaffirmation suggests that the political fate of members of Congress is not tied to the need to manipulate the economy in order to provide a temporary "prosperity" at election time. It may be true that congressional politicians behave otherwise, but, if Owens and Olson are correct, and if politicians should learn as much, economic policy perhaps could be based more on long-term than short-term community welfare. But if the objective evidence indicates that congressional interests need not be incompatible with the broader public interest, the public choice approach, as used by Kramer and Nordhaus, suggests that a relationship should obtain between stop–go economic policies and presidential elections.

The empirical evidence for this is quite weak even in cross-national settings, if only because so few data points are available (Keynesian possibilities were not well understood until the mid-1930s). Nor, at least for the United States, does a rational choice model yield unambiguous hypotheses by considering only presidential elections. A self-interested incumbent President seeking a second term (Eisenhower in 1956, Johnson in 1964, Nixon in 1972, Carter in 1980) might be expected to engage in economic manipulation for personal political advantage. The incentives would presumably be less for retiring Presidents (for example, in 1952, 1960, 1968) to engage in such tactics unless extremely strong, and increasingly unrealistic, assumptions are made concerning team (party) loyalty. A retiring President might be concerned more with a historical reputation for "sound" economic policies than with manipulating the economy to someone else's advantage: Consider Eisenhower's attitude toward Nixon, or Johnson's toward Humphrey. In any case, presidential elections are complex affairs. Economic conditions are important, but so are other factors, as the seminal Campbell et al. study demonstrated.

Of course, there is a politics of spending and taxing policy, but its understanding must extend far beyond the connections between voters and politicians. The roles of political institutions, including public bureaucracies (Wildavsky, 1979); the Presidency (Pious, 1979; Fisher, 1975); the legislature (Fenno, 1966; Havemann, 1978; Ferejohn, 1974); and interest groups (Ornstein and Elder, 1978) in the formation of taxing and spending policy have been described in a literature far too vast to be cited fully here. The taxing/spending policy process does not yield easily to generalizations, although several schemes (Lowi, 1964; Wilson, 1973: 327-346; Bartlett, 1973) have proved useful in the organization of data and the generation of hypotheses. Wilson, for example, argues that the *perception* of the costs and benefits associated with different issues shapes political conflict (and Bartlett suggests how the manufacture of information can influence perceptions and policy). Actual costs and benefits are analytically and normatively but not always politically important. "Majoritarian" politics is said to emerge when *perceived* benefits and costs are both widely distributed. Economic issues involving, for example, inflation and social security are apt to be addressed electorally by the formation of popular majorities precisely because the promised benefits and necessary costs are understood to be broadly shared. "Interest group" politics is occasioned by perceptions of concentrated benefits and concentrated costs. Tariffs, cable television licenses, and NLRB decisions are perceived, in spite of their communitywide impacts, as involving conflicts between exporters and importers, over-the-air and cable TV operators, and labor and management. "Client" politics arises when benefits are perceived to be concentrated and costs diffused. Tax credits to solar homeowners bestow benefits on the solar industry at the expense of taxpayers generally. Farm price supports, subsidies to Chrysler Corporation or the merchant marine industry, and so on, create governmental clients. Oppositions to favored clients are not always well organized, because the costs of doing so on any particular occasion usually far outweigh the potential benefits. Finally, when benefits are perceived as widely distributed and costs as concentrated, the stage is set for "entrepreneurial" politics. Framing issues in this manner is a tactic of some "policy entrepreneurs": Howard Jarvis and Proposition 13 (eliminating a few wasteful practices or bureaucrats would bring benefits to everyone else); Ralph Nader and automobile safety (improve everyone's security at the expense of the few producers); and many politicians ("break up big oil" for its monopolistic pricing, thus conferring benefits on everyone else).

If economic policy decisions often deviate from what might be preferred on the basis of more ethically persuasive criteria, it is Wilson's view that the same sources may be sought in the diverse perceptions and elusive motivations of the political players. They also must be sought in the diverse and not always coordinated political institutions that choose and interact on the basis of formal and informal rules that are both complex and still inadequately understood. At the federal level, the executive agencies, the Office of Management and Budget, the Treasury, the Council of Economic Advisors (the latter three comprising the "troika" of executive fiscal decision making), the Federal Reserve Board, the Congressional Budget Office, the Joint Economic Committee, the budget committee in each house, the appropriations committee in each house, the Senate Finance Committee, and the House Ways and Means Committee are the principal but by no means only institutional actors. Each is itself a complex institution, with its own resources, culture, ideological tendencies, and constituencies. In such circumstances, insights rather than firmly grounded universals constitute current knowledge. Mitchell (1977) has noted that these institutions increased or broadened social security benefits in every election year between 1950 and 1976, that the payments typically are initiated between June and the November election, and that taxes to provide them are not usually extracted until the following January. Veterans' benefits usually have been increased much more in the third quarter of election years than at other times, and grants to states and local governments have followed a similar pattern (Tufte, 1978: 36-39,53). Various institutions are biased toward various perspectives: It will often be the case that Democrats will tend toward equity; Republicans, toward efficiency. Democrats will tend to emphasize full employment; Republicans, price stability. The executive agencies and the Senate Appropriations Committee will have a spending bias, the Office of Management and Budget and the House Appropriations Committee, a cutting bias; the State Department, a "liberal" foreign economic policy, the Treasury, a "conservative" one; the White House an "easy" money bent, the Federal Reserve, a "tight" money one. Presidents promise tax "reform," whereas Congress marches to its own drummer on tax legislation. But these are tendencies only: Events, personalities, strategic behavior, objective conditions often undercut them, as when President Nixon announced that "we are all Keynesians now," or when liberal politicans rushed to adopt a fictitious "balanced" budget in 1980 in the context of double-digit inflation and a recession obviously at hand.

II. SPENDING

A. Public Expenditure: Growth and Structure

There has been a gradual but enormous cumulative increase in public expenditures during the past century. Public expenditures as a percentage of gross national product in the United States increased from under 7 percent to about 33 percent between 1890 and 1975. Per capita, in 1958 dollars, the increase was from about $45 to approximately $1330. That public expenditure growth may be a correlate of economic and political modernization is suggested by the following: The ratio of public spending to gross national product in most (but not all) developed, non-Soviet bloc countries has reached the range of 35 ± 10 percent; in the less developed countries the range is approximately 17 ± 5 percent.

Changes in the structure of public spending in the United States have been no less remarkable. Intergovernmentally, although state-local spending increased relatively somewhat more rapidly in recent decades, the relative size of federal spending has been reversed: In 1900, approximately two-thirds of public expenditure was at the state-local

level; for some time after World War II, the federal proportion was two-thirds, and remains over 60 percent. On the state-local level, in 1900 local spending was almost five
times state spending; in 1975, state spending was 50 percent greater than local spending.
In terms of spending programs, although while substantially all have vastly increased both
absolutely and as a percentage of gross national product, social welfare and education
spending (on all levels of government) has increased enormously, constituting now some
two-thirds of civilian expenditures in contrast with one-third in the early twentieth century. Total civilian expenditure, as a percentage of total expenditures, has been unstable
but was 79.2 percent in 1902 and 79.5 percent in 1977, having been, for example, 62
percent in 1960 (Musgrave and Musgrave, 1980: 141ff, 542).

B. Approaches to Public Expenditure Analysis

Perceptions of the meaning and significance of public spending are profoundly influenced
by attitudes toward the economic role of government, the nature and source of social
problems, and conceptions of socioeconomic justice. Among public expenditure analysts,
at least four principal approaches are followed. The Pigovian approach emphasizes government as a corrective instrument to remedy perceived market failures, such as externalities
and instability, imbalances of economic power, and poverty. Beyond this the Pigovian
accepts reliance on private enterprise and markets. Such acceptance is even greater and
more thorough among Paretians. They would minimize government intervention, sanctioning only full specification of property rights to permit market exchange. Whereas Pig-
ovians tend to perceive underspending by government, Paretians see overspending. The
Marxists generally see government spending as a facet of the instrumental use of government by the dominant business class, functioning to facilitate private, corporate capital
accumulation and the ideological legitimation of the capitalist system (the latter in part
through welfare programs), in the face of perceived problems and crises of various sorts
(Miliband, 1969; O'Connor, 1973). The Institutionalists are interested principally in identifying the actual processes and consequences of public expenditure (and other government activities), including (and in common with others, especially but not solely the Pigo-
vians) analysis of alternative policy instruments and the relations among decision-making
structure, policy, and performance (Samuels and Schmid, 1980). Each approach tends
in practice to be a kaleidoscopic mix of positive and normative analysis. Finally, the conduct of public expenditure analysis, and policy analysis generally, is influenced by perceptions as to the relative importance in policy making of technical considerations and subjective judgments (contrast Musgrave and Musgrave, 1980: 5, with Burkhead and Miner,
1971: 98-99).

C. Some Further Determinants of Public Expenditures

Although there are a number of intractable interpretive problems in reaching a meaningful
understanding, including the respective weights, of the causes of the enormous increase in
public expenditure in the twentieth century, the causes themselves are generally straightforward, however often interconnected. First, there is the greater prevalence and costliness of war. This includes consideration of such factors as national security, control of
the domestic population, the inefficiencies of military procurement and related budgetary
processes, the military-industrial complex, the vested interests of the military establishment,

the needs of ideology and national identity, imperialism, and the greater capital intensiveness of modern warfare.

Second, there has been a complex set of changes in both the value system and the balance of political power in Western society. The state has been increasingly responsive to a wider array of organized interests who have not hesitated to use the state to advance their objectives. Thus the values of hitherto excluded groups have newly entered government decision making.

Third, there has been a growing consciousness of the policy (artifact) character of government and other institutional arrangements and a consequent orientation toward intervention in the sense of changing the interests to which government has been providing its support.

Fourth, there has been a great increase in perceived technical knowledge in the biological, physical, and social sciences. This has enhanced both the desire and the perceived ability to control individual and collective environments, adjustments, and evolution.

Fifth, there has been enhanced, albeit still selective, perception of externality problems and public good production possibilities (see below).

Sixth, although in one sense government has become a more readily available process of collective choice, in another, it has become more evidently both an arena and instrument of power play among economic and social interests. Substantially all groups have seen in government an avenue for redistribution of opportunity, income, and wealth, in part through the redetermination of legal rules and private rights.

Seventh, there are observable tendencies for government programs to be resistent to termination and, instead, to expand, in part through the efforts of cumulating beneficiaries.

Eighth, there has been a perception of lessened private capacity in an increasingly urban, industrial, and interdependent society, coupled with growing concerns over the distribution of personal welfare in a hierarchical society.

Ninth, the production of certain private goods, such as the automobile, has engendered the wide-ranging and expensive production of governmentally produced goods, such as roads and highways and traffic and other controls.

Tenth, budgetary decision making has been fractionalized in several respects: Decisions are made on several levels of government, in various committees of legislatures, and decisions as to taxation and expenditures are generally separated. In addition, only rarely has a deliberate decision been made by Congress as to its total budget; and many expenditure arrangements are reached through the trading of votes by legislatures.

Eleventh, there is a certain logic of politics that involves the offering of voters increased prospective rewards so as to secure votes, a process reinforced by budgetary deficits that lower the immediate tax price of public spending (Buchanan and Wagner, 1977).

Twelfth, certain demographic changes seem to have produced expenditure consequences: urbanization, industrialization, and changes in the age distribution of the population.

More specific and elaborate analysis of the determinants of public expenditure has focused on such topics as budgetary processes, voting rules, political pluralism, coalitions, politics, bureaucracy, ideology, political symbolism, and so on. A century ago, Adolph Wagner reached, on empirical grounds, a "law of rising public expenditures" and speculated that (on what in modern terms is) an increasing percentage of gross national product

going to (or through) government was due to pressure for socioeconomic programs consequent to and dependent on the interaction between private- and public-sector growth.
More recent empirical studies have (1) correlated total public spending growth with economic growth; population increase; technology producing increased income, urbanization, and industrialization; and value system changes (Fabricant, 1952); and (2) found
variances in municipal spending due principally to community size, housing density,
population age, and industrialization (Wood, 1962; Winfrey, 1973: 170-172).

The consequences of public spending have been felt throughout the economy, in part
through transfer payments, government purchasing, and the capitalization of the costs
and benefits affecting the value of both income and nonincome earning property, as well
as on employment, profit-making opportunities, and capital gains. Government spending
is a major factor in the determination of the distributions of individual income and
wealth but has not greatly affected the quintile or decile distribution patterns. It has
been found, for example, that the combination of state-local taxation and expenditure
has had a mildly equalizing affect on income distribution despite a regressive tax system
(Peppard and Roberts, 1977: 86-87); but that although explicit grants have redistributed
income toward the poor, implicit grants of various types have tended to greater inequality (Boulding and Pfaff, 1972: 2).

D. Public Expenditure Theory

Although the seminal and architectonic work of Musgrave (1959) established allocation,
distribution, and stabilization as the three principal dimensions of public finance, including public expenditures, most subsequent work concentrated on the interrelated (Samuels and Schmid, 1981) concepts of externality and public goods in what amounts to an
effort to understand interdependence among economic actors and the fundamentals of
public expenditure policy. Although both bodies of theory (as well as grants theory)
are of controversial applicability to questions of actual policy and neither attempts to
penetrate the actual processes of public expenditure decision making, together they articulate the elements of public choice ultimately encountered therein.

Externalities. The broadest analysis is the Institutionalist, although it is in the distinct
minority within economics. Externalities are defined broadly to cover all impacts on
second or third parties and are seen to arise ultimately from interdependence and to be
reciprocal in character. Externalities are ubiquitous, inevitable, and a function of power
structure, as are externality solutions, which also generate further externalities, including changes in power, opportunity sets, and costs and benefits. The externalities treated
by public policy are typically perceived selectively, especially given the reciprocal nature
of externalities: Pollutor and pollutee are so related, given geographic relationships and
technology, that pollution (the impact on the pollutee of the pollutor's actions) is inextricably related to the inhibition on the pollutor's actions if the pollutee is to be assured of clean air or water. In this view, the fundamental problem of externality policy
is which, or whose, externality, or whose interest is to be sacrificed to another's. The
Institutionalist also has broad and open-ended definitions of injury (benefit) and evidence of injury.

Quite different approaches are taken by the Pigovian and Paretian variants of neoclassical economics. Both, however, perceive markets as the preeminent mode of

internalization, differing on their normative (and to some extent positive) treatment of market failure, so-called. The Pigovian considers markets to work when marginal private and social costs (and benefits) are equated and to fail when marginal social costs exceed marginal private costs (thereby resulting in overproduction of the commodity in question because the producer—and ultimately the consumer—is not compelled to bear all the costs thereof) or when marginal social benefits exceed marginal private benefits (thereby resulting in underproduction). Thus the Pigovian seems to open the door to governmental corrective action although the mere identification of an externality is not sufficient to warrant such action, an additional normative premise being required to justify further government action in the area.

The Pigovian and general neoclassical approach also distinguishes between so-called pecuniary and technological externalities, the former comprising uncompensated impacts seen as taking place and priced within the market, and the latter as impacts not priced through the market. Institutionalists question the coherence (and policy significance) of the distinction: Impacts are impacts and even technological externalities have price consequences (the pollutee's costs are priced through the market).

If the pecuniary-technological distinction narrows the scope of externalities suitable for theory and policy, the Paretian approach narrows it much further. The Paretian, emphasizing the capacity of markets to internalize when rights are fully defined so as to permit trade, distinguishes between Pareto-relevant and -irrelevant externalities, the former involving impacts that give rise to trade (for example, the pollutee buying off the pollutor) and the latter not so. Although the psychodynamics of the distinction is that Pareto-irrelevant externalities are (or should be) irrelevant for policy, thereby closing the door to government corrective action, generally speaking, the set of Pareto-irrelevant externalities is relatively coextensive with the set of Pigovian inequality-condition externalities (say, once rights are fully defined so as to maximize opportunities for trade), thus leaving open in principle the possibility of government corrective action going beyond formal rights specification. Thus, from an Institutionalist perspective, in both cases the question remains as to which (whose) externalities, in a world of ubiquitous and inevitable externalities, are to be promoted and which (whose) inhibited.

Not all externality correction measures involve public spending, but their discussion generally comes within the ambit of public expenditure analysis. Among the available correction procedures are regulation (for example, pollution standards), property rights, liability rules, taxation (of pollution) or subsidy (of pollution control equipment), government production financed through either or both user charges or general taxation, education, and mergers. Governments, in general, can attempt either to produce a desired performance result or to promote further private action, independent of specific results. Policy making and execution are made complicated, however, by, *inter alia,* the naivetes of ideological wishful thinking; the fact that different rights or liability systems will produce different transaction cost situations, so that choice of system is tantamount to choosing performance result; and the practice of preference masking coupled with the realities of free and forced riders—which reintroduces the problem of externality per se.

Public Goods.   A somewhat different but not mutually exclusive set of insights is acquired through the theory of public goods, much of which is focused on the alternative variables by which public goods are defined. In contrast to the concept of private goods, in which individual solely enjoy consumption, goods have a "public" quality insofar as provision for one individual may constitute provision for others who may not be excluded from its enjoyment or only at some more or less substantial cost. This is the predominant conception and blends two separable definitional criteria: (1) joint supply, joint consumption, or provision with a zero marginal cost for an additional consumer; and (2) nonexclusion or costly exclusion. But there are still other definitional criteria, and one or more of these have been combined with either or both of the first two to provide a variety of taxonomies of public goods or spectra of private-public goods. These include nonappropriability, individual nonadjustment of quantity, transaction costs, indivisibility, increasing returns, and some notion of externality itself. (In this latter connection it should be noted that externalities may be benefits or costs—goods or bads—and that parallel to public goods are public bads. The practice of most economists and other analysts is to use public goods theory for the benefits or goods and externality theory for the costs or bads, although in principal both theories are symmetrical.)

All public goods analyses are further complicated by certain additional considerations. These include whether the group in question is large or small in number; whether the analysis is intended to be partial or general equilibrium; problems of access and exposure, to which are related problems of inequality or asymmetry; and so on. Thus, among the array of taxonomies, one focuses on the combination of nonmarketability and exclusion costs; another on degree of indivisibility and the size of the interacting group; another on the relative symmetry of externalities and the relative substitutability of the good in question with a conventional private good; and others on various combinations of the two principal criteria with one or more of the other criteria or considerations (Burkhead and Miner, 1971: chaps. 2, 3).

Public goods theory (usually in combination with still additional factors) has been addressed to the question of the magnitude of public spending, specifically whether there has been over- or underproduction of public goods or under- or overspending by government. Lines of reasoning have been adduced in support of each position. The net result is empirically uncertain, ultimately relying on narrow normative premises. The respective lines of reasoning tend to be supported by advocates of the obvious respective normative or political positions (Samuels, 1980).

Several problems clearly and inevitably emerge. First, theoretical public goods (to which the above discussion is directed) should not be confused with "public" goods actually governmentally (or, for that matter, privately) provided: For perhaps every good has at one time and place or another actually been provided by a government. Second, the analyst or policy maker has to choose which taxonomy with which to work (if, indeed, he/she chooses to work with one). Third, a fundamental choice must be made as to the category, in any particular taxonomy, in which a particular case is to be placed, that is, the particular line of reasoning (or definitional conception) with which to approach a particular case. (It is not absolutely conclusive, for example, that education, postal, police, and fire services, which clearly have public good qualities, must be provided publicly or even are to be categorically labeled as public goods, or some subsidiary classification thereof.) Fourth, an additional normative premise is necessary to move from the category of theoretical public good to support for actual government provision thereof.

Thus, although public goods theory, as in the case of externality theory, seems capable of enlightening both analysis and decision making as to the elements of problems of choice, there is considerable doubt as to whether or how much it provides the conclusive calculus or key to public choice. Individual taxonomic systems attempt to provide structure and, to some degree, closure, but considered as a whole, public expenditure theory cannot by itself determine for a policy maker the choices to be reached. Neither externality nor public goods theory provides a technical calculus for choice; and certainly neither explains how actual public choice with regard to public expenditures is conducted. But the two bodies of analysis have enabled analysts and policy makers to treat more abstractly, if not more objectively, the questions comprising the choices that they still have to make. These choices ultimately concern whose interests are to count. To some extent policy making (in part through benefit-cost analysis) has made use of public expenditure theory; but perhaps to a greater extent not; and the degree of greatest possible extent is itself an issue. The facts of the matter are that both public spending and taxation are facets of power play over the use of government with regard to the distribution of income, wealth, and opportunity, and that vast gulfs exist between ideology and reality, between private and public objectives, and between intentions and achievements.

REFERENCES

Aaron, H., and McGuire, M. (1970). Public goods and income distribution. *Econometrica* *38*: 907-920.

Advisory Commission on Intergovernmental Relations (1977). *Changing Public Attitudes on Government and Taxes.* U. S. Government Printing Office, Washington, DC.

Amacher, R., Boyes, W., Deaton, T., and Tollison, R. (1979). The political business cycle: Review of theoretical and empirical evidence. *ACES Bulletin 21*: 1-42.

Ames, B. (1981). A note on the political expenditure cycle in Latin America. In *Taxing and Spending Policy,* W. Samuels and L. Wade (Eds.). Lexington Books, Lexington, MA, chap. 6.

Arcelus, F., and Meltzer, A. (1975). The effects of aggregate economic variables on congressional elections. *American Political Science Review 69*: 1232-1239.

Atkinson, A. B. (1973). How progressive should income-tax be? In *Essays on Modern Economics,* M. Parkin (Ed.). Longman, London, pp. 90-109.

Bach, G. L., and Ando, A. (1957). The redistributional effects of inflation. *Review of Economics and Statistics 39*: 1-13.

Bartlett, R. (1973). *Economic Foundations of Political Power.* Free Press, New York.

Bingham, R., Hawkins, B., and Herbert, F. (1978). *The Politics of Raising State and Local Revenue.* Praeger, New York.

Bloom, H., and Price, H. (1975). Voter response to short-run economic conditions. *American Political Science Review 69*: 1240-1254.

Boulding, K. E., and Pfaff, M. (Eds.) (1972). *Redistribution to the Rich and the Poor.* Wadsworth, Belmont, CA.

Break, G. F., and Pechman, J. A. (1975). *Federal Tax Reform: The Impossible Dream?* Brookings Institution, Washington, DC.

Blum, W., and Kalven, H. (1963). *The Uneasy Case for Progressive Taxation.* University of Chicago Press, Chicago.

Breton, A. (1974). *The Economic Theory of Representative Government.* Aldine, Chicago.

Brown, E. (1974). Recent studies of the incidence of the corporate income tax. In *Public Finance and Stabilization Policy,* W. Smith and J. M. Culbertson (Eds.). North Holland, Amsterdam.

Buchanan, J. M. (1967). *Public Finance and Democratic Process.* University of North Carolina Press, Chapel Hill.

Buchanan, J. M., and Tollison, R. (Eds.) (1972). *Theory of Public Choice.* University of Michigan Press, Ann Arbor.

Buchanan, J. M., and Wagner, R. E. (1977). *Democracy in Deficit.* Academic Press, New York.

Bureau of the Census (1977). *Compendium of Governmental Finances,* vol. 4. U.S. Government Printing Office, Washington, DC.

Burkhead, J., and Miner, R. (1971). *Public Expenditure.* Aldine, Chicago.

Campbell, A., Converse, P., Miller, W., and Stokes, D. (1960). *The American Voter.* Wiley, New York.

Downs, A. (1957). *An Economic Theory of Democracy.* Harper, New York.

Fabricant, S. (1952). *The Trend of Government Activity in the United States Since 1900.* National Bureau of Economic Research, New York.

Fair, R. C. (1971). The optimal distribution of income. *Quarterly Journal of Economics 75*: 551-579.

Fenno, R. (1966). *The Power of the Purse.* Little, Brown, Boston.

Ferejohn, J. (1974). *Pork Barrel Politics: Rivers and Harbors Legislation, 1947-1968.* Stanford University Press, Stanford, CA.

Fisher, L. (1975). *Presidential Spending Power.* Princeton University Press, Princeton, NJ.

Goodman, S., and Kramer, G. (1975). Comment on Arvelus and Meltzer. *American Political Science Review 69*: 1255-1265.

Harsanyi, J. C. (1975). Can the maximim principle serve as a basis for morality? *American Political Science Review 69*: 594-606.

Havemann, J. (1978). *Congress and the Budget.* Indiana University Press, Bloomington.

Kramer, G. (1971). Short-term fluctuations in U.S. voting behavior, 1896-1964. *American Political Science Review 65*: 131-143.

Lampman, R. J. (1974). What does it do for the Poor? A new test for national policy. *The Public Interest 34*: 66-82.

Lowi, T. (1964). American business, public policy, case-studies, and political theory. *World Politics 16*: 677-715.

McCallum, B. R. (1978). The political business cycle: An empirical test. *Southern Economic Journal 44*: 504-515.

Miliband, R. (1969). *The State in Capitalist Society.* Basic Books, New York.

Mirrlees, J. A. (1971). An exploration in the theory of optimum income taxation. *Review of Economic Studies 38*: 175-208.

Mitchell, W. (1977). *The Popularity of Social Security: A Paradox of Public Choice.* American Enterprise Institute, Washington, DC.

—— (1979). The democratic state: Public choice and Marxist perspectives. Paper delivered at the Annual Meeting of the Public Choice Society.

Musgrave, R. (1959). *The Theory of Public Finance.* McGraw-Hill, New York.

—— (Ed.) (1965). *Essays in Fiscal Federalism.* Brookings Institution, Washington, DC.

Musgrave, R., and Musgrave, P. G. (1980). *Public Finance in Theory and Practice,* 3rd ed. McGraw-Hill, New York.

Niskanen, W. (1971). *Bureaucracy and Representative Government.* Aldine-Atherton, Chicago.

Nordhaus, W. (1975). The political business cycle. *Review of Economic Studies 42*: 169-190.

Nozick, R. (1974). *Anarchy, State, and Utopia.* Basic Books, New York.

Oates, W. E. (1972). *Fiscal Federalism.* Harcourt Brace Jovanovich, New York.

Obler, J. (1979). The odd compartmentalization: Public opinion, aggregate data, and policy analysis. *Policy Studies Journal 7*: 524-540.

O'Connor, J. (1973). *The Fiscal Crisis of the State.* St. Martin's Press, New York.

Okun, A. M. (1975). *Equality and Efficiency.* Brookings Institution, Washington, DC.

Ornstein, N., and Elder, S. (1978). *Interest Groups, Lobbying and Policymaking.* CQ Press, Washington, DC.

Owens, J., and Olson, E. (1980). Economic fluctuations and congressional elections. *American Journal of Political Science 24*: 464-488.

Pechman, J. A., and Okner, B. A. (1974). *Who Bears the Tax Burden?* Brookings Institution, Washington, DC.

Peppard, D. M. (1976). Toward a radical theory of fiscal incidence. *Review of Radical Political Economics 8*: 1-16.

Peppard, D. M., and Roberts, D. B. (1977). *Net Fiscal Incidence in Michigan: Who Pays and Who Benefits?* Division of Research, Graduate School of Business Administration, Michigan State University, East Lansing.

Phares, D. (1973). *State-Local Tax Equity: An Empirical Analysis of the Fifty States.* Lexington Books, Lexington, MA.

Phelps, E. S. (Ed.) (1973). *Economic Justice.* Penguin, Baltimore.

Pious, R. (1979). *The American Presidency.* Basic Books, New York.

Rand, A. (1964). *The Virtue of Selfishness.* New American Library, New York.

Rawls, J. (1971). *A Theory of Justice.* Harvard University Press, Cambridge, MA.

Revenue Statistics of OECD Member Countries (1975). Organization for Economic Cooperation and Development, Paris.

Reynolds, M., and Smolensky, E. (1976). Why changing the size distribution of income through the fisc is not more difficult. *Discussion Papers.* Institute for Research on Poverty, University of Wisconsin, Madison.

—— (1977). *Public Expenditures, Taxes, and the Distribution of Income.* Academic Press, New York.

Samuels, W. J. (1978). Normative premises in regulatory theory. *Journal of Post Keynesian Economics 1*: 100-114.

—— (1980). Toward positive public choice theory. *Review of Social Economy 38*: 55-64.

Samuels, W. J., and Schmid, A. A. (1980). *Law and Economics.* Martinus Nijhoff, Boston.

—— (1981). Interdependence and impacts: Toward the integration of externality, public goods and grants theories. In *Taxing and Spending Policy,* W. Samuels and L. Wade (Eds.). Lexington Books, Lexington, MA, chap. 16.

Schmid, A. A. (1978). *Property, Power, and Public Choice.* Praeger, New York.

Simon, H. (1943). The incidence of a tax on urban real property. *Quarterly Journal of Economics 57*: 398-420.

Stigler, G. J. (1973). General economic conditions and national elections. *American Economic Review, Papers and Proceedings 63*: 160-167.

Tax Foundation (1967). *Tax Benefits and Burdens of Government Expenditures by Income Class, 1961–1965.* Tax Foundation, New York.

Tiebout, C. (1956). A pure theory of local expenditures. *Journal of Political Economy 64*: 416-424.

Tollison, R. (1972). The political economy of the military draft. In *Theory of Public Choice,* J. M. Buchanan and R. Tollison (Eds.). University of Michigan Press, Ann Arbor, pp. 302-314.

Tollison, R., Crain, M., and Pautler, P. (1975). Information and voting: An empirical note. *Public Choice 24*: 43-49.

Tufte, E. (1978). *Political Control of the Economy.* Princeton University Press, Princeton, NJ.

Tullock, G. (1974). *The Social Dilemma.* University Publications, Blacksburg, VA.

Wade, L. (1979). Public administration, public choice, and the pathos of reform. *Review of Politics 41*: 344-374.

—— (1981). The political theory of public finance. In *Taxing and Spending Policy,* W. Samuels and L. Wade (Eds.). Lexington Books, Lexington, MA, chap. 17.

Wagner, R. (1977). Economic manipulation for political profit. *Kyklos 30*: 395-410.

Wildavsky, A. (1979). *The Politics of the Budgetary Process,* 3rd ed. Little, Brown, Boston.

Wilson, J. (1973). *Political Organizations.* Basic Books, New York.

Winfrey, J. C. (1973). *Public Finance.* Harper & Row, New York.

Wood, R. C. (1962). *1400 Governments.* Anchor, Garden City, NY.

21

Agricultural Policy

Don F. Hadwiger / Iowa State University, Ames, Iowa

U.S. policy for agriculture has been designed to serve influential interests within that sector, and often too, to serve a grand vision or scenario of what America is becoming. Protection of slavery in the Constitution was the first of many agricultural policies to serve a Southern landed aristocracy, and the incompatibility of this interest with the grand vision of agricultural fundamentalism became a major issue prompting the Civil War. The vision of egalitarian farmers as the pillar of a republic has been used to justify many agricultural policies since Jefferson first espoused it.[1]

I. U.S. PUBLIC POLICY AND AGRICULTURAL DEVELOPMENT

Although some agricultural policies have been concessions to contemporary reality, as the policy of continental expansionism legitimized the sweep of frontier farmers, other policies have had enormous developmental consequences, usually not wholly intended. Agricultural research and education and an array of other public services, which were justified as a way to permit farmers to survive in an economy populated by large units,[2] did not in the end preserve small farm agriculture but did help create a highly efficient agricultural industry. Multifaceted programs designed to moderate the risks of dryland farming helped swell the nation's cropland acreage and production per acre, and the favorable balance of international agricultural trade.[3] Other programs for marginal producers revealed the dead hand of government, such as those after World War II that delayed Southern diversification away from a cotton economy.

On the whole, federal policy has been one among many dynamic factors in U.S. agricultural development. Other factors included the social structure, technology, the natural environment, and major events such as the Civil War. In the United States, as in some other countries, farming developed under conditions of land abundance. Geographic expansion, however, often awaited new technology to accommodate natural environments.

Expansion in the South awaited the cotton gin; settlement beyond rivers awaited the development of alternative forms of freight transport; farm settlements west of the Mississippi awaited the development of barbed wire, windmills, binders, and gang plows. Farm settlement on the High Plains awaited the creation of irrigation systems and, in this century, the techniques of dryland farming.

The choice of farming structure and of the kinds of commodities to be produced, while frequently an object of policy, was determined by and large by cultural values and market demand, although structures and commodities in turn became powerful constraints on policy. Farming structures were originally of two major types—small freeholding farms and plantations using slave labor, with a few locations featuring corporate landholding and landed estates. The plantation economy that dominated Southern politics was always embarrassed by the national values of individualism and equality. Following the Civil War, the plantations were replaced by concentrated landholding, and then by large-scale industrial farms after technology drastically reduced labor needs.[4] Southern large-farm agriculture supported a structure of rural elites who were a presence in national politics, from the Virginians of the constitutional period to the current survivors in the ebbing congressional seniority system, such as Representative Jamie Whitten (D., Miss.), Chairman of the House Appropriations Committee.

Recognition of the interests of large landholders was a condition for Southern and Far Western participation in the coalitions that passed federal farm legislation. Although large-farm agriculture often exerted influence out of proportion to its economic significance, in the nation, farmer aristocrats, mostly from Southern states, were powerful political resonators during the nineteenth century on issues where large-farm and small-farm interests were perceived to coincide. These interests included monetary, credit, and tariff policies, and regulation of railroads and other middlemen. Other major agricultural regions subsequently played leading roles in the establishment of agricultural policy, particularly the Midwest, which was always a center of support for land policies favoring small-farm freeholding, and the Plains region, whose late-blooming, unstable commercial agriculture demanded direct government assistance, and which spawned the Populists and some other radical movements in American agriculture.

II. THE EVOLUTION OF AN AGRICULTURAL SYSTEM

In a political system responsive to popular elections, U.S. farmers were unable to mobilize the power which their numbers once offered them. Farmers comprised a majority of all Americans at least until 1870, when they were still 53 percent of all persons gainfully employed.[5] Their numbers increased absolutely up to World War I, at which time farming remained the largest single occupation of Americans. But numbers often proved a poor measure of power. During the constitutional period, for example, most rural freeholders could not or did not vote, although they comprised "the great mass of white Americans."[6]

And more important than legal constraints were social barriers to participation. As Lester Milbrath has commented, a major determinant of political participation is a person's distance from the centers of affairs.[7] Geographic, social, and psychological centers are loaded with stimuli, and those living within the centers are likely to be relatively well informed, highly involved, confident, and committed to the system. Those on the periphery, in contrast, do not have a strong sense of belonging or capacity to work within the system, as exemplified by the nineteenth-century farmer protest groups and the Populist party. The Populists, who tried to speak for a majority of small farmers and workers, perceived themselves as outsiders to the great party coalitions, the financial centers, corporations, government agencies, and the press.

As an additional handicap, farmers lacked respectability among other sectors of the population, which may have explained, in part, why the Democratic party was unable to win once it did embrace Populist programs: "In the context of their period of origin, it was not Populists' principles that were retrogressive—merely the fact that they were championed by and in the name of farmers and laborers. The path to reform could be made much smoother almost overnight if these same principles were embraced by urban, middle-class spokesmen and championed in the name of the middle class."[8]

Rural constituencies did have some effective spokesmen within the Congress and executive, buttressed in the twentieth century by a strong commercial farmer lobby. Federal policies facilitating farming proceeded through a number of stages. During the nineteenth century, according to Murray Benedict, agriculture was affected most directly by federal laws setting the mode for distributing public lands, also by the federal monetary system, and by protective tariffs.[9] At first land distribution policy had the goal of obtaining revenues for government, and land was sold in large segments. Pressure from Western spokesmen resulted in a succession of land laws, beginning in 1800 (the Homestead Act of 1862 is the most famous), which permitted small farm purchases and ultimately provided small farms free of charge to settlers.[10] Public research institutions for agriculture were created, in large measure, by nineteenth-century public interest lobbies composed of newspaper editors, gentleman farmers, and scientists seeking the improvement of agriculture and rural life. These research institutions included the U.S. Department of Agriculture, chartered in 1862 as an information-gathering agency; the state agriculture colleges, supported by federal land grants and subsidies after 1862; the agricultural experiment stations, after 1887; and the cooperative extension services, after 1914. The enormous impact of these institutions on farming was to be registered many decades later.

There seemed to be no governmental remedy for the farm depressions that added to the miseries of nineteenth-century farmers. The underlying economic problem was overproduction resulting from rapid expansion of cropland.[11] The geographic expansion of agriculture slowed after 1900, and with rising demand for farm products farmers enjoyed two decades of relative prosperity during which the more progressive farmers purchased a new mechanical technology.[12] Farmers reaped profits from World War I demand despite the government's efforts to hold farm prices down. But the innovative farmers, hastening to capitalize new technology, found themselves dangerously in debt with the return of low prices during the 1920s. It was these "successful farmers" who developed a new political structure and an impressive policy structure for agriculture. During the 1920s laws were enacted supporting cooperatives and regulating middlemen. Under the New Deal administration of the 1930s, commodity price supports and other types of direct federal subsidies were passed. The political structure developed as an agricultural subsystem with the following identifiable components:

1. It was based on a subculture with a socialization process whose norms sanctioned sub-system interaction and support. The major political elites shared farm backgrounds and often had attended land grant agricultural colleges, subsequently experiencing interaction in farm organizations and economic firms, through the media, and in governmental agencies.
2. A rough hierarchy of goals was agreed to. Farm income as an important political objective was to be achieved through a combination of production efficiency and adequate market prices.
3. Material and status incentives were provided to individuals contributing to subsystem goals. However, there were increasingly sharp status distinctions between the commercial farmers and technical service functionaries, on the one hand, and the subsistence farmers and farm workers on the other. The latter's interests were largely ignored.[13]
4. The subsystem featured a discrete and integrated economic system with its own monitoring agencies and market information mechanisms, and even its own "agricultural" economics.
5. The subsystem developed a set of remarkable political mechanisms including the following:
   a. A coalition of groups representing major commodities, coordinated within the congressional agricultural committees.[14]
   b. A cooperating bureaucracy that included the many bureaus of the U.S. Department of Agriculture (USDA) and the land grant institutions.[15]
   c. A rural electorate whose large swing votes (outside the South) were noticeably responsive to prices for principal commodities.[16]
   d. Client organizations that exercised grass roots controls over relevant federal bureaucracies as a vehicle for developing their own memberships.[17] Lowi called the agricultural subsystem "the new feudalism" because each of at least 10 bureaucracies was run by its own clientele.[18]

This has by no means been a stable subsystem during the past 40 years, nor has it exercised unchallenged control over agricultural policies. Its beginning is in the emergence of a "general" farm organization—The American Farm Bureau Federation,[19] formed from local farmer groups brought together for extension teaching during the 1910s, 1920s, and thereafter. The Farm Bureau organized a congressional coalition and mobilized other farm organizations for enactment of price support programs during the 1930s.[20] In recent times the general farm organizations including the Farm Bureau have yielded some power to organizations that represent specific commodities. It has been the commodity organization—for example, the National Association of Wheat Growers— that has had principal influence over a particular commodity's policies, such as those for controlling production, prices, and international trade in wheat.

There are several reasons for the shift of power. Farming has become more specialized, so that farmers have fewer common interests. Also, the general farm organizations, particularly the large Farm Bureau, have not been able to maintain a united front among farm groups. Another change favoring commodity groups is the development of large input and output industries, offering the opportunity for vertical organization, an early example being the National Cotton Council, with participation from cotton producers, cotton ginners, textile firms, and other cotton industries. Nowadays, the typical commodity organization is likely to be maintained by a nonfarm sector—particularly by a processing industry.

Finally, specialization that has consolidated interests vertically has also produced a need for specialized knowledge that commodity groups can best provide. Another set of groups whose influence on agricultural policy is based considerably on specialized knowledge are the trade organizations, such as the Fertilizer Institute.

Organization by commodity, however, has weakened political support for generalized bureaucracies such as the agricultural research institutions. There have been new efforts to achieve integration among "aggie" interests, including that of the National Farm Coalition, organized during the 1960s by some general and commodity organizations. The Farm Coalition, with about three dozen participating groups, provides a vehicle for consultation and joint action on major issues of wide interest to agriculture.[21] Another mode of cooperation is that of the informal or ad hoc coalition, such as that formed in 1978 to seek a priority for agricultural users of energy. Such coalitions are products of a specific need, and are formed by those organizations most interested in the issue (in the case of energy priority, the Fertilizer Institute was the organizer).

Another recent group phenomenon in farm politics is the American Agriculture Movement (AAM), which seeks a general farmer membership, mainly attracting farmers who have expanded rapidly and thereby have suffered the consequences of high interest rates, expensive technology, and periodically lower prices for commodities in which they specialize. AAM supporters are relatively young, with commercial farms that are still relatively small, and they are likely to have recently borrowed money and to have suffered financial hardship.[22]

The AAM is, in its attitudes, a successor to earlier farm protest movements that sometimes turned to violence. But it emulates tactics of the nonviolent civil rights movement, and other recent minority movements. The AAM has made strident calls for "parity"—a goal based on historical measures under which farmers would deserve high prices for production. AAM has engaged in "tractorcades" that snarled traffic in downtown Washington, D.C. Although its tactics were condemned and its goals repudiated as unrealistic, the AAM did capture national attention and is credited with having achieved slight increases in price support levels for various commodities.

III. NONAGRICULTURAL INFLUENCES ON AGRICULTURAL POLICY

The AAM seeks a clientele of farmers only, but farmers today are unlikely to achieve major concessions without the support of other members of the agricultural industry. Furthermore, a counterforce to the industry has developed, in large part as a result of efforts by environmentalist and consumer public interest groups, challenging the industry's lack of concern about the externalities or side effects resulting from agricultural production. These externalities include chemical additives and residues in food; malnutrition among the poor; damage to the natural environment from soil and soil-based chemical contaminants; mistreatment of rural minorities and farm workers; policy biases toward large farmers; technology that relies increasingly on nonrenewable resources; and soil erosion.

In the 1960s, notable critics of agriculture included environmentalist Rachel Carson, and a "hunger lobby" that succeeded in diverting agricultural funds to a large food stamp program for the poor.[23] In the 1970s, journalist Jim Hightower led an attack on the agricultural research institutions,[24] and then on food manufacturing corporations.[25] Other critics joined in, to produce a "new agenda" that would regulate the undesired side effects of food production and to press for alternative methods of production.

The basic strategy of these externalities/alternatives (ex/al) advocates has been to create concerned publics among the nonagricultural population, and to create jurisdictions for nonagricultural agencies and congressional committees. At their initiative, agricultural policy, earlier cultivated as an esoteric subject for subsystem eyes only, gained front pages in the media and became a favorite subject of oversight for congressional committees. In effect, the ex/al coalition instituted a new set of policies, most of which were enacted outside the usual agricultural policy process. Pesticide regulation, for example, was removed to a new Environmental Protection Agency (EPA), which helped write a new pesticide law. Regulatory outputs of EPA, those of the Food and Drug Administration and the Occupational Safety and Health Administration, and activities of investigatory agencies such as the General Accounting Office, were among many policy outputs not subject to influence from the agricultural industry, though the industry was obliged to adjust to the restrictive environment these policies created.

IV. CONTRASTING SCENARIOS FOR AGRICULTURAL POLICY

The industry subsystem and the ex/al coalition, each in response to the other's challenge, have constructed differing scenarios for the future of American and world food production, on the basis of which their respective policy positions are justified. A typical presentation of the subsystem scenario[26] reviews the industry's success in producing abundant food at low cost, in exporting both technology and food to forestall, and in time to nullify, doomsday prophesies of hunger, famine, and institutional collapse. The mission envisioned for the agricultural industry is to produce food enough for nutritionally adequate diets, and even luxurious diets for the increasing number who can afford them, during a period in which world population is stabilizing. The importance of this mission justifies the use of a technology dependent on nonrenewable resources in the form of fuel, fertilizers, and pesticides. It is argued that there are still adequate supplies of fossil energy, land, and water, and emerging technology will use them more efficiently.

In the industry scenario there is admittedly a major difficulty in distributing food to the poor people who comprise a majority of the world's population, many of whom will be removed from subsistence agriculture as a result of technology change and who may not be able to purchase adequate food. This immense adjustment problem is left for a political solution, short of moving to a socialist system.

In the scenario of alternative agriculture, by contrast, agriculture is invited to play a central role in our efforts to become reconciled with the environment in which we are obliged to live. Agriculture as the link between humanity and the ecosystem has been the theme of Dr. Barry Commoner, an exponent of the ex/al scenario. Commoner points out that agriculture is part of two systems—the ecological system that sustains life, and the system that produces humanity's goods. Agriculture must be constrained in that it can no longer regard energy as a cheap and abundant resource, nor can it any longer abuse the environment.

Commoner has stressed that agriculture plays a vital role in trapping abundant solar energy. Farmers need not be burdened by the increasing costs of fuel, electricity, and chemicals if they diversify their farming to include crops that can fix nitrogen in the soil, using animals whose manure is a necessary part of the energy-regenerating process. For Commoner, agriculture's crucial balance sheet could counterpose the energy gleaned from the farm and used efficiently against the energy that must be purchased and that is often inefficient.[27]

The approximate embodiment of Commoner's efficient farm is the "organic" farm, which minimizes the use of synthetic chemicals. There is an organic farming movement in the United States with a component of organized farmers as well as media organizations. The organic farming movement has an ideology and is a way of life. It has past and current prophets, and a large number of "true believers."[28]

Another of the prophets of alternative agriculture is the late British economist, E. F. Schumacher, whose book, *Small Is Beautiful,* has become a major document not only for organic farmers but for others who question the brashness of agricultural scientists, busily erecting their beaver dams against the forces of nature, heedless of whether the disequilibriums they create will multiply until they are impossible to maintain. Schumacher says that man no longer sees himself "as a part of nature but as an outside force destined to dominate and conquer it. He even talks of the battle with nature, forgetting that, if he won the battle, he would find himself on the losing side."[29]

The alternative agricultural scenario, though it seeks ecological and human values, still envisions a production process in which there is enough food for everybody. Frances Moore Lappé and Joseph Collins have argued that the world contains adequate food resources without use of the synthetic fertilizers on which the "green revolution" was based. They argued that even Bangladesh, a "basketcase" nation with its proliferating, malnourished population, can feed itself if its agriculture is fully developed, and is devoted to production for local people rather than to exports. In the ex/al scenario, the export of food and technology by governments of developed capitalist nations, or by multinational corporations, is turning developing country agriculture away from production from small plots for sale in local markets, toward large, capital-intensive farms that may not yield as much per acre despite large fertilizer inputs, and that tend to convert the land to crops profitable in export markets.[30]

The ex/al scenario offers an alternative world in which most countries are self-sufficient in food production and do not have to import expensive fertilizer and other inputs. The land and other natural resources are preserved rather than "mined."

A major problem for alternative agriculture is the demand that it makes on humans: that many humans should be willing to spend a lifetime in agricultural labor, indeed that they should gain pleasure and status from such labor; that humans who are now well off should be willing to accept simpler diets, and especially to reduce their demand for imported foods now grown on fertile lands in developing countries. Ex/al writer Wendell Berry grants that it will be difficult to manage "the vulnerabilities of the human personality," which seems inclined against farm work and simple food. Pessimism creeps in in any honest confrontation with the question: "Can we, believing in 'the effectiveness of

power,' see 'the disproportionately greater effectiveness of abstaining from its use'?"[31]
Berry admits that the only group he knows who have been willing adequately to restrain
themselves in energy use are the Amish. The ex/al scenario, like the industry scenario,
describes an interesting future based on dubious assumptions.

V. FOOD AND AGRICULTURE POLICY
MAKING IN CONGRESS

The industry subsystem has given high priority to programs that assure adequate returns
for specific agricultural commodities. Commodities such as wheat and cotton were particularly affected by unstable price and production, so the agricultural committees that
wrote farm bills tended to be dominated by representatives of cotton, wheat, and feed
grains. For some other products such as pork, price variability was desirable, although
pork producers clamored for government purchases during the low part of pork price
cycles.

There was a wide variety of devices for stabilizing markets. A successful program
for tobacco involved stringent acreage controls, which held production at levels assuring high prices. For cotton, too, producers were willing to accept mandatory controls
in exchange for high price guarantees. In wheat and feed grains, producers preferred
"voluntary" programs, in which those who limited production were rewarded with payments on idled acres, per bushel subsidies, and low-interest loans, as well as generous
fees for storing "surplus" products on the farm.

A variety of devices were developed for other products. Milk producers were allowed to form marketing agreements in which regional markets were to be served mainly
by local producers at fixed prices. For food and vegetable producers there were marketing agreements that utilized product grading to help weed out market surpluses. Sugar
producers preferred a system of import quotas under which a very adequate share of the
domestic market was reserved to domestic producers. For a number of commodities,
there was the option of government purchases of market surpluses, to be used for feeding
the armed forces, for school lunch programs, for subsidized exports to needy nations, and
for other purposes outside the regular markets. A large "Food-for-Peace" program
emerged under which as much as one-half of total U.S. foreign aid was in "surplus" agricultural products.

Programs for many commodities were reenacted frequently—typically, every three
to five years—in part because conditions continually changed and adjustments were
needed, in part because changes of administration and of congressional leadership, as well
as changes of policy within the farm organizations, tended to be reflected in the character
of the legislation. Omnibus commodity bills, which usually included some adjustments in
other agricultural services and a few nonagricultural provisions such as rural electrification, credit, or even research, and a number of symbolic offerings designed to make a bill
pleasing to nonfarm voters, were centerpieces of agricultural policy making. Extensive
congressional hearings on each bill attracted representatives of the various farm groups,
numerous members of Congress from farming regions, and representatives of the USDA.

At a time when rural population was large, and even into the 1960s, a strategy for
passing farm bills through committee and on the floor was to achieve a consensus among

the many commodity interests[32] and to assume little interest and no opposition from nonfarm legislators. However, opposition to these commodity bills developed within the Eisenhower and Nixon administrations and from the American Farm Bureau Federation, which mobilized some urban votes and conservative votes against the bills. It became necessary to mobilize nonfarm votes in behalf of farm bills. Coalitions were formed largely within the Democratic congressional party, most typical of which was a coalition of feed grains, wheat, and leaders of organized labor.[33] In seeking nonfarm votes, agricultural groups pursued two strategies or combinations thereof during the 1970s. One is the older strategy of subsystem policy making, seeking at the end to trade votes with nonfarm groups. The other strategy is to invite nonfarm groups to participate in framing bills that can then be supported on their merits. Vote trading has occurred on the minimum wage law to obtain labor union support, and on consumer food programs such as food stamps, which attract urban liberals. Farm bills in 1973,[34] 1975,[35] and 1977[36] benefited from vote trading, but these laws were also written to be somewhat attractive to nonfarm groups. Although industry groups preferred vote trading, both strategies have been necessary in recent years in order to obtain sufficient support, and because the coalition of ex/al groups has insisted that agricultural policy include environmental protection, food safety, and minority and farm worker provisions, among other objectives.

A combination of strategies was used to develop a large congressional majority in support of the 1977 farm bill. House leadership had shifted from the conservative Agriculture Committee Chairman Robert Poage to Representative Thomas Foley (D. Wash.), a wheat legislator who was also chairman of the liberal House Democratic Caucus. The 1972 and 1974 congressional elections had produced a large number of liberal Democrats from country and city who were interested in provisions other than the support of commodity prices. For example, there was renewed interest in preserving the family farm, with the result that the sugar program, primarily for the benefit of very large firms, could not achieve adequate support in Congress. A number of new liberals had taken seats on the House Agriculture Committee, including one urban member, Frederick Richmond (D., N.Y.), whose major role was to generate support for liberalizing the food stamp program. For consumer groups and environmental groups seeking research and other provisions in the 1977 bill, the strategy was to insert provisions within the commodity and other programs that made the bill attractive on its merits to progressive and liberal groups. In a sense, then, passage of the 1977 bill evidenced the development of a "grand coalition" that included ex/al groups concerned about environmental protection, nutrition, and energy conservation. As a result of support from urban Democrats and even from Republican legislators (48 percent voted for the 1977 bill), the bill passed by a comfortable margin,[37] in sharp contrast with the precarious majorities that had previously passed farm bills.

However, the grand coalition that passed the 1977 farm bill was not in charge of agricultural appropriations within the Congress, by which many provisions of legislation were implemented. The appropriations process for agriculture has been dominated over a period of 30 years by Jamie Whitten (D., Miss.), who has reluctantly engaged in vote trading on such matters as food stamps but has been unwilling to implement many of the liberal reforms such as those designed specifically to help small farm agriculture, and solar energy development in agriculture. Thus the two processes in Congress—the one for policy making and the one for appropriations—are very different in the case of agriculture. The result is that a great deal of agricultural legislation has not been fully implemented.

In 1981 another omnibus farm bill was passed, by the same coalition of commodity representatives and urban Democrats. Logrolling was made difficult in this case by budget constraints set by the Reagan administration and imposed through threat of veto. In addition, the food stamp program, which had been used to win urban votes, had become more controversial, and an effort was made to separate that program from the farm bill. During the 1970s commodity interests had, in any case, been moving away from dependence on government income supports, and seeking greater returns from enlarging world markets for America's efficiently produced farm output. There were predictions that the 1981 law was the "last farm bill."

Implementation of farm programs depends on support from within the executive branch, where much change has also occurred in the past decade.

VI. THE CHANGING DEPARTMENT OF AGRICULTURE

Historians Wayne Rasmussen and Gladys Baker, looking at the Department of Agriculture's history in its first century from 1862 to 1962, found an "old" and a "new" department. One can argue that there have now been two additional eras—one in the post-World War II period in which the USDA entered into the service of an industry clientele; and the present period in which it has lost its clientele identification, and is becoming responsible to a wider range of food interests.

The "old" U.S. Department of Agriculture, from its founding in 1862 until 1932, developed as an excellent scientific and statistical agency.[38] A "new" department developed during Secretary of Agriculture Henry A. Wallace's administration, in which the earlier functions of science and education shared importance with a host of new action programs, including commodity price supports and market development, and also major programs for soil conservation, rural electrification, farm workers relief and resettlement, as well as food assistance to needy families.

With these new functions, the size of the USDA increased from 22,000 full-time employees in 1932 to 79,000 in 1948, which is approximately its current level. As a large agency sprawling into many functional areas, the "new" USDA was viewed with some suspicion by President Roosevelt's Committee on Administrative Management. But according to a professional administrator, former USDA Undersecretary Paul Appleby, "They found, on examination, that if there is any fact of quality related to size of the agency, it was that the larger agencies were better administered. It was hinted that Agriculture was the convincing exhibit."[39]

This broad-ranging department entered a third stage in which its major programs were run by and for industry clients. Programs that had been constructed to permit farmer grass roots decision making, usually by means of administration under local farmer committees, became a means for client dominance. Farmer and industry clients exerted influence from the top through close relations with political and permanent USDA officials, and through congressional oversight and congressional appropriations by the agricultural and appropriations committees. By the 1960s, Theodore Lowi counted "at least ten separate autonomous local self-governing systems" within the agencies of the Department of Agriculture.[40]

Under governance by the farm organizations and legislators within the subsystem coalition, several USDA programs were phased out, including those for farm workers, rural communities, and food consumers. One USDA Secretary, Charles Brannan (1948–1952), made an unsuccessful effort to address the goals of human nutrition as well as small farmer equity, and in the 1960s Secretary Orville Freeman also announced some nonindustry goals such as "rural renewal," but the presidential Administrations in which Brannan and Freeman served felt obliged to yield the USDA to its industrial clientele, as the price for obtaining cooperation from conservative rural Democrats who were influential in the Congress. "Placate them!" President John Kennedy told Secretary Freeman, referring to the Southern chairmen of the agricultural and appropriations committees. As a result of this presidential strategy, the liberal Freeman's administration was unable to support a substantial expansion of food stamps.[41]

During this postwar period, the Republican Secretaries of Agriculture also made strong efforts to reduce clientele control over certain segments of USDA programs. Secretary of Agriculture Ezra Taft Benson tried to reduce federal involvement in controlling prices and production. Although periods of impasse between Benson and congressional leaders[42] usually resulted in compromises under which price support programs were continued at moderate levels, there was an accumulation of enormous surpluses of wheat and other grains under legislative programs ongoing in Secretary Benson's administration. Storage costs on these enormous supplies constituted a major portion of the USDA's enlarged budget at the time Benson left office. The "solution" for the problem of government surpluses was achieved under Freeman by using the storage budget to subsidize farmers voluntarily to reduce production.

A subsequent Republican Secretary of Agriculture, Earl Butz, was more successful in reducing dependence on federal price and income programs during the 1970s, largely because the world demand temporarily kept prices at acceptable levels. Butz, like Benson, wished to make the department a helpmate and service agency to the private agricultural industry, and in that sense a clientele department that would not be involved in programs for consumers such as the food stamp program. But his efforts to have food stamps and other consumer welfare programs transferred from the department were unsuccessful, in part because rural congressmen saw them as useful in trading for urban support of price programs, and in part because these food programs had found considerable support among minority, urban, and consumer legislators within Congress. Had Secretary Butz had his way, the USDA would have become a department concentrating on research, marketing, and other services to the agricultural industry. With a smaller budget, less political support would have been required, and certainly less would have been forthcoming in Congress. The USDA would have been one of several small clientele departments including Commerce and Labor. Indeed, the USDA would have been abolished under President Nixon's plan for reorganizing the executive branch, being redistributed to departments organized along functional lines such as the Department of Health, Education and Welfare.

We may postulate a fourth stage in the USDA's history, beginning in 1977 under Secretary Robert Bergland, in which the USDA has developed support among concerned publics favoring better nutrition, environmental protection, and rural community development. In 1977, Secretary Bergland, himself a farmer, chose his assistant secretaries from among leaders of these concerned publics, including Carole Tucker Foreman, who was formerly the director of the National Consumer Federation; also Rupert Cutler, a former editor of the National Wildlife Newsletter; Alex Mercure, formerly a grass roots leader among Mexican-Americans; and Howard Hjort, who had gained a reputation as a "populist" economist. These assistant secretaries maintained an "open door policy" toward nonagricultural public interest groups. They also made speeches and statements proclaiming new directions for the USDA; for example, a speech by Assistant Secretary Rupert Cutler called for reduction in the use of agricultural chemicals in the interest of environmental protection; the speech was hailed by the Environmental Defense Fund as "a basic shift in policy." Cutler's deputy assistant secretary, James Nielsen, speaking to senior administrators of the Agricultural Research Service, stated eight priorities of the new administration, among which the traditional mission of "productivity" was conspicuously listed last. Among the other priorities were human nutrition research, energy conservation, pest management, environmental protection, and service to special disadvantaged groups such as minorities and women. The Bergland administration was quick to challenge any effort to transfer out of the department those food, welfare, and developmental functions that had become the department's major budget items. The USDA sought and received the status of "lead agency" for nutrition research, thus reversing its posture of neglecting this research subject. The USDA's open door policy, and the strong statements of new direction, earned support from most consumer and conservation organizations. Meanwhile, some industry clients were confused and irritated by their loss of exclusive access to the department, but the new broader clientele seemed likely to be accepted as a permanent feature,[43] whose support would maintain the USDA as a major department within the federal government.

A sharp turn was taken by the Reagan administration, particularly with respect to a number of social programs within the USDA. The budget for rural housing, for example, was sharply reduced, and under Reagan's New Federalism the largest USDA program— food stamps—would be transferred from the federal government to the states.

VII. CONTINUING AND EMERGING CONCERNS
OF AGRICULTURAL POLICY

The environment of agricultural policy has been unstable, and rapidly changing. The transformation from a system of relatively isolated subsistence homesteads of the nineteenth century to an industrial system with constantly revised technology packages has required enormous adjustment. Currently, more large changes in the the environment may be occurring: the increasing scarcity of energy resources for inorganic fertilizers, pesticides, and mechanized agriculture; increasing demands for food both for domestic populations and for export; a new interest in human nutrition as a means to improve quality of life and to reduce medical and food costs; awareness of the increased loss of valuable topsoil and of its role as the major pollutant of surface waters; and increased interest in alternative agricultural structures that might reduce these problems. In these circumstances, however, both of the scenarios earlier discussed, on which current agricultural policies are based—the one stressing a rejuvenated small-farm system, the other stressing an energy-intensive, production-maximizing, profit-seeking, industrial system—

seem less than realistic. But the policy struggle between proponents of these scenarios promises to be more encompassing and more enlightening than that of previous agricultural eras.

NOTES

1. A. W. Griswold, *Farming and Democracy* Harcourt, Brace, New York, 1948), pp. 22-23.
2. H. E. Breimyer, *Individual Freedom and the Economic Organization of Agriculture* (University of Illinois Press, Urbana, 1965).
3. D. F. Hadwiger, *Federal Wheat Commodity Programs* (Iowa State University Press, Ames, 1970).
4. Richard Rodefeld coined the term "large-scale industrial farms" to describe those on which more than half of the work is performed by hired workers. See testimony of Richard D. Rodefeld, in Hearings on the Role of Giant Corporations in the American and World Economies, Part 3, before the Subcommittee on Monopoly of the U.S. Senate Select Committee on Small Business, 92d Congress, 2nd Session, 1972.
5. W. D. Rasmussen, American agriculture: A short history, mimeographed, based on Wayne D. Rasmussen, *A Documentary History of American Agriculture*, 4 vols. (Random House, New York, 1975).
6. T. R. Dye and L. H. Zeigler, *The Irony of Democracy: An Uncommon Introduction to American Politics* (Duxbury Press, Belmont, CA, 1972), p. 28.
7. L. W. Milbrath, *Political Participation: How and Why Do People Get Involved in Politics?* (Rand McNally, Chicago, 1965), pp. 113–114.
8. O. G. Clanton, *Kansas Populism: Ideas and Men* (University Press of Kansas, Lawrence, 1969), p. 243.
9. M. R. Benedict, *Farm Policies of the United States, 1790-1950* (Octagon, New York, 1966), pp. 3-60.
10. T. LeDuc, History and appraisal of U.S. land policy to 1862; and P. W. Gates, The Homestead Act: Free land policy in operation, 1862–1935; both in H. W. Ottoson (Ed.), *Land Use Policy and Problems in The United States* (University of Nebraska Press, Lincoln, 1963), pp. 1-46.
11. G. C. Fite, *American Agriculture and Farm Policy Since 1900* (Macmillan, New York, 1964), pp. 4-9.
12. Ibid.
13. G. McConnell, *The Decline of Agrarian Democracy* (University of California Press, Berkeley, 1953).
14. C. Jones, Representation in Congress: The case of the House Agriculture Committee, *American Political Science Review 55* (June 1961): 358-367.
15. Described by W. Rasmussen and G. Baker, in *The U.S. Department of Agriculture* (Praeger, New York, 1972), pp. 43-45, 125.
16. A. Campbell et al., *The American Voter* (Wiley, New York, 1960), p. 417.
17. C. M. Hardin, *The Politics of Agriculture: Soil Conservation and the Struggle for Power in Rural America* (Free Press, Glencoe, IL, 1953). See also R. B. Talbot and D. F. Hadwiger, *The Policy Process in American Agriculture* (Chandler, San Francisco, 1968).

18. T. Lowi, *The End of Liberalism* (Norton, New York, 1969).

19. J. H. Shideler, *Farm Crisis 1919–1923* (University of California Press, Berkeley and Los Angeles, 1957).

20. C. Campbell, *The Farm Bureau and the New Deal* (University of Illinois Press, Urbana, 1962).

21. G. Youngberg, The National Farm Coalition and the politics of food: New interest group strategies in a changing environment, in J. G. Peters (Ed.), *Issues and Agricultural Politics and Policy*

22. W. P. Brown, The American Agricultural Movement: What is it and why?, in J. G. Peters (Ed.), *Issues in Agricultural Polics and Policy*

23. N. Kotz, *Let Them Eat Promises* (Doubleday, Garden City, NY, 1971).

24. J. Hightower, *Hard Tomatoes Hard Times* (Agribusiness Accountability Project, Washington, DC, 1972).

25. J. Hightower, *Eat Your Heart Out: Food Profiteering in America* (Crown, New York, 1975).

26. See, for example, K. O. Campbell, *Food for the Future: How Agriculture Can Meet the Challenge* (University of Nebraska Press, Lincoln, 1979).

27. See B. Commoner, *The Poverty of Power: Energy and Economic Crisis* (Knopf, New York, 1976), especially pp. 155-175; and U.S. Congress, House Science and Technology Committee, *Special Oversight Review of Agricultural Research and Development*, 94th Congress, 2nd Session, 1975, pp. 513-549.

28. G. Youngberg, "The alternative agriculture movement, in D. F. Hadwiger and W. P. Browne (Eds.), *The New Politics of Food* (Lexington Heath, Lexington, MA, 1979), pp. 227-246.

29. E. F. Schumacher, *Small Is Beautiful: Economics as if People Mattered* (Harper & Row, New York, 1973), p. 14.

30. F. M. Lappé and J. Collins, *Food First: Beyond the Myth of Scarcity* (Houghton Mifflin, Boston, 1977), especially pp. 111-118.

31. W. Berry, *The Unsettling of American Agriculture* (Sierra Club, 1978), p. 95. Berry is quoting Ivan Illich.

32. D. F. Hadwiger and R. B. Talbot, *Pressures and Protests: The Kennedy Farm Program and the Wheat Referendum of 1963* (Chandler, San Francisco, 1965).

33. W. V. Barton, Coalition-building in the United States House of Representatives: Agricultural legislation in 1973, in J. E. Anderson (Ed.), *Cases in Public Policy Making* (Praeger, New York, 1976), pp. 141-161.

34. Ibid.

35. Agriculture/consumers, *Congressional Quarterly Weekly Report 33* (July 5, 1975): 1416.

36. J. G. Peters, The 1977 farm bill: Coalitions in Congress, in D. F. Hadwiger and W. P. Browne (Eds.), *The New Politics of Food* (Heath, Lexington, MA, 1978), pp. 23-25).

37. Ibid.

38. It was so characterized by L. D. White, *The Republican Era, 1869-1901* (Macmillan, New York, 1958), chap. 11.

39. G. L. Baker, W. D. Rasmussen, V. Wiser, and J. M. Porter, *Century of Service: The First One Hundred Years of the Department of Agriculture* (Centennial Committee –USDA, Washington, DC, 1963), p. 271.

40. T. Lowi, *The End of Liberalism* (Norton, New York, 1969), p. 110.

41. D. F. Hadwiger, Freeman and the poor, *Agricultural History 45* (January 1971): 22-23.

42. J. P. Heinz, The political impasse in farm support legislation, *Yale Law Review 71* (April 1962): 952-78; R. Fraenkel and D. F. Hadwiger, The agricultural policy process, *Policy Studies Journal 4* (Autumn 1975): 20-25.
43. D. Paarlberg, A new agenda for Agriculture, in D. F. Hadwiger and W. P. Browne (Eds), *The New Politics of Food* (Heath, Lexington, MA, 1978), pp. 135-140.

22

Poverty and Income Maintenance Programs

Harrell R. Rodgers, Jr. / University of Houston, Houston, Texas

Poverty remains a world plague—a spector that haunts even the richest nations in the Western industrial world. America, still by many measures the richest of all the world's nations, continues to suffer acute poverty. Every region of the country, every major city, and every ethnic group is afflicted by poverty.

No official attempt was made to measure American poverty until the mid-1960s. Backdating its standard, the Social Security Administration reported that some 40 million Americans lived in poverty in 1960 and 1961, a figure that declined to 33.2 million by 1965 (Rodgers, 1979: 17-38). By 1968 the number of official poor had declined to about 25 million, a level where it stabliized despite massive increases in welfare expenditures (Orshansky, 1963, 1965). Between 1968 and 1978 the official poverty rate averaged 24.6 million, with only rather modest yearly variations. In 1980 it leaped to 29.3 million.

Why has American poverty remained at a high and steady rate despite substantial increases in welfare expenditures? Some have contended that the poverty count remains high because of measurement error—that is, that the government simply overestimates poverty. A larger group of scholars maintain that the government actually underestimates poverty, and that welfare expenditures cannot further reduce poverty because the benefits are too modest, are unavailable to many of the poor, and are not designed to break the cycle of poverty by permanently ending the conditions that cause poverty.

This controversy suggests the topics that must be investigated to understand American poverty, poverty programs and their impact, and recent proposals for welfare reform. In the sections that follow the poor population are identified, the controversy over the measurement of poverty reviewed, the various theories of the causes of poverty examined, and American welfare programs and suggested reforms analyzed and compared to European income maintenance programs and antipoverty strategies.

I. MEASURING POVERTY: THE AMERICAN APPROACH

Poverty may be defined in absolute or relative terms. An absolute standard attempts to define some basic set of resources necessary for survival. A relative standard attempts to define poverty in relationship to the median living standard of the society. A relative standard shows not only how many people cannot hope to live close to the average standards in a society, but it also provides insight into how evenly income is distributed among the population. In 1969 the President's Commission on Income Maintenance in the United States (p. 8) concluded that:

> The community's decision as to what is "essential" is dictated in general by its social conscience. If society believes that people should not be permitted to die of starvation or exposure then it will define poverty as the lack of minimum food and shelter necessary to maintain life. . . . As society becomes more affluent it defines poverty as not only the lack of the components of a subsistence level of living, but also the lack of opportunity for persons with limited resources to achieve the quality of life enjoyed by persons with an average amount of resources. The definition of poverty progresses from one based on absolute standards to one based on relative standards.

The irony of the commission's reasoning is that although America is certainly an affluent nation, it still defines poverty in absolute subsistence terms.

The first poverty standard was formulated by the Council of Economic Advisors (CEA) in 1964. This standard attempted to estimate the minimal income needs of a four-person family, using an estimate of the cost of a nutritionally adequate diet for the family as a base (Rodgers, 1979: 18). In 1965, the Social Security Administration (SSA) attempted to improve upon the CEA standard, but decided to continue to base the standard on the estimated cost of an "adequate" diet for families of various sizes. Using an economy food budget formulated by the National Research Council, a poverty standard was computed for various family sizes, with an adjustment for urban or rural residence. It was assumed that food costs represented 33 percent of the total income needs of families of three or more, and 27 percent of the total income required by two-person households.

Table 1 shows the 1978 SSA poverty standard for various family sizes. Note that the standard varies by family size, the sex of the family head, and the family's place of residence. Farm families are presumed to need only 85 percent of the cash income required by nonfarm families (until 1969 they were presumed to need only 70 percent as much). The rate for single persons is adjusted up to compensate for the higher cost of living alone (the food budget is multiplied by 5.92 rather than by 3.0). The food budget for couples is multiplied by 3.88 to compensate for their higher costs. Female-headed families receive slightly less and two-person elderly families are presumed to need 8 percent less than nonelderly two-person families.

Table 2 shows the SSA poverty threshold for a nonfarm family of four backdated to 1959, and the number of persons counted as poor by year using the standard. Until 1969, the yearly changes in the poverty standard reflect changes in the cost of the economy food budget. Since 1969 the standard has been adjusted yearly according to changes in the Consumer Price Index. Taken at face value, the SSA standard suggests that substantial progress was made toward reducing poverty in the 1960s, with some reversals occurring

Table 1. Poverty Standard: 1978

		Nonfarm			Farm		
Size of family unit		Total	Male head	Female head	Total	Male head	Female head
1 person (unrelated individual)	$ 3,302	3,311	3,460	3,196	2,795	2,898	2,690
14–64 years	3,386	3,392	3,516	3,253	2,913	2,978	2,764
65 years and over	3,116	3,127	3,159	3,118	2,661	2,685	2,650
2 persons							
Head 14–64 years	4,363	4,383	4,407	4,286	3,731	3,737	3,614
Head 65 years and over	3,917	3,944	3,948	3,923	3,352	3,354	3,313
3 persons	5,178	5,201	5,231	5,065	4,413	4,430	4,216
4 persons	6,628	6,662	6,665	6,632	5,681	5,683	5,622
5 persons	7,833	7,880	7,888	7,806	6,714	6,714	6,700
6 persons	8,825	8,890	8,895	8,852	7,541	7,543	7,462
7 persons and more	10,926	11,002	11,038	10,765	9,373	9,386	8,813

Source: U.S. Bureau of the Census, Money income and poverty status of families and persons in the United States: 1978 (advanced report), *Current Population Reports,* Series P-60, No. 120, (U.S. Government Printing Office, Washington, DC, 1979).

Table 2. Poverty Schedule: Family of Four (Nonfarm): 1959–1980)

Year	Standard	Millions of poor	Percent of total pop.	Median family income	Standard as percent of median family income
1959	$2,973	39.5	22	$5,620	53.0
1960	3,022	39.9	22		
1961	3,054	39.9	22		
1962	3,089	38.6	21		
1963	3,128	36,4	19		
1964	3,169	36.1	19		
1965	3,223	33.2	17		
1966	3,317	30.4	16		
1966[a]	3,317	28,5	15		
1967	3,410	27.8	14		
1968	3,553	25,4	13		
1969	3,743	24,1	12		
1970	3,968	25.4	13	9,867	38.0
1971	4,137	25.6	12.5	10,285	40.2
1972	4,275	24.5	12	11,116	38.4
1973	4,540	23.0	11	12,051	37.6
1974	5,038	24.3	12	12,836	34.2
1974[a]	5,038	24.3	11.5	12,902	39.0
1975	5,500	25.9	12	13,719	40.0
1976	5,815	25.0	12	14,958	30.8
1977	6,200	24.7	12	16,009	38.7
1978	6,662	24.7	11.4	17,640	37.7
1979	7,412	26.1	11.7	19,680	37.6
1980	8,414	29.3	13	21,020	40.0

Source: Derived from U.S. Bureau of the Census, Characteristics of the low-income population, *Current Population Reports,* Series P-60, various years.
[a]Revision in Census calculations.

in the 1970s. In 1959 there were almost 40 million American poor, but the count dropped to 25.4 million by 1963. The count remained bascially steady until 1973 and 1974 (revised figures), when poverty declined to about 23 million. In 1975, however, poverty increased by 2.5 million persons and actually exceeded poverty for every year back to 1967. In 1976, 1977, and 1978 the count stabilized at about 25 million poor, but rose substantially in 1980.

An analysis of the actual computation of the official poverty standard for one family size is illustrative. In 1978 the poverty threshold for a nonfarm family of four was $6662. This standard allowed $1665.50 per person per year, or $4.56 a day, one-third being the allocation for food ($1.52). The family could spend a total of $2.03 per meal for all four persons, or $42.56 per week on food. A budget for a four-person family would look like this:

$2220.66 for Food: $1.52 a day (51¢ per meal) per person; $10.64 per week per person

$2220.66 for Shelter: $185.05 a month for rent or mortgage for four person
$2220.66 for Necessities: $46.26 a month per person for clothing, furniture, transportation, health care, utilities, taxes, entertainment, etc.

The first thing one notices about the standard is that the estimates are extremely low. It is highly doubtful that anyone could prepare a nutritious meal for four persons for $2.03, or that a family of four could be fed adequately on $42.56 a week. The allowances for rent or mortgage and other necessities are also extremely low. The same is true, of course, for other family sizes. Notice in Table 1 that an elderly urban residence is allowed only $3127. Clearly one intention of the SSA is to define poverty in a manner that keeps the poverty count as low as possible. Notice in Table 2 that the poverty standard has not increased at anything like the rate of growth in personal income. In 1959 the standard was 53 percent of median family income. By the 1970s it averaged only about 40 percent of family income. Much of the decline in the poverty count between 1959 and 1980 may be the result of the failure of the standard to keep pace with the growth of personal income, rather than from families actually escaping poverty. As the authors of a recent Organization for Economic Co-operation and Development (OECD) (1976: 63) study note:

> It is not surprising . . . that the percentage of the United States population that falls below the official poverty line has declined considerably over the last decade or more (from 22.4 percent of total population in 1959 to 11.9 percent in 1973). For, as long as poverty is defined in absolute terms, economic growth is likely to be enough to eliminate much of it without any special income maintenance programs. . . .

The unrealistic nature of the SSA standard is suggested by the research of another government agency (*The Houston Post,* 1979). The Bureau of Labor Statistics (BLS) annually estimates the income families need to live at a "lower-level" standard of living, a "middle-level" standard, and a "higher-level" standard. The BLS estimated that in 1978 an urban family of four would have had to gross $18,622 to live at a "middle-level" or moderate standard. This is almost three times the SSA poverty standard for a family of four. A "lower-level" standard of living, the BLS said, would have required $11,546—almost $5000 more than the poverty standard.

Thus by the BLS estimates the poverty standard is clearly a bare subsistence level, one that leaves the poor far below the living standards of even lower-income families, and far from a moderate standard of living. This would be true even if the poor had as much money as the poverty standard allows. However, the income figures collected yearly by the Census Bureau reveal that most poor families have incomes that fall considerably below the poverty level. For example, in 1978 the average poor family fell $1930 below the poverty threshold. For white families the median deficit was $1753; for black families it rose to $2306 (U.S. Bureau of the Census, 1979: 35).

Critics have raised a large number of additional criticisms about the SSA standard. The major ones are these:

Regional Variations.   There are no allowances in the index to compensate for the rather substantial variations in cost of living across the nation.

Rural Versus Urban.   The 15 percent reduction for farm families is not supported by empirical evidence. Although some persons in rural areas may be able to grow some of their own food and may incur lower housing costs, many necessities in rural areas are more expensive.

The Food Budget. Because the food plan is the base of the poverty standard, its calculation is critical. Quite clearly, SSA did not decide to use the economy budget as a base because it was deemed adequate for poor people's needs. Wilcox (1969: 27) reports that SSA originally designed the economy budget for temporary or emergency use only, but decided to use it permanently because more adequate budgets showed too much poverty. In July 1975 the SSA substituted a thrifty food budget for the economy budget. The new budget reflects changes in RDA food standards, in public purchasing habits, and food manufacturing (Peterkin, 1976). The new budget, however, will mean little as far as the poverty standard is concerned.

The Multiplication Rate. The assumption that food expenditures account for one-third of poor people's budgets is based on a 1955 study. More recent studies (Miller, 1971: 120) indicate that poor people spend about 28 percent of their income on food. Thus, critics argue, the food budget should be multiplied by a factor closer to 3.4 rather than 3. This would increase the poverty standard and count substantially.

Table 3 provides some examples based on a 1976 study by the Department of Health, Education and Welfare (since renamed the Department of Health and Human Services). The figures show that the poverty standard would be affected substantially by changing the food budget ratio and/or by substituting a more generous food budget. All the figures in Table 3 are based on a multiplier of 3.4 rather than 3. Notice that with this multiplier and the thrifty food budget, 39.9 million persons would have been counted among the poor in 1974 (the threshold for an urban family of four would have been $6360). If the food budget were based on only 80 percent of the more generous low-cost food plan, and a multiplier of 3.4 used, the poverty count would have been 41.4 million (the threshold would have been $6494 for an urban family of four). If the low-cost budget had been completely substituted for the thrifty food plan and a 3.4 multiplier used, the poverty threshold for an urban family of four would have been raised to $8118 and would have yielded a staggering poverty count of 55.4 million. Notice in Table 3 that changing only the multiplication factor increases the number of poor by 15.6 million persons. Changing both the budget and the multiplication factor increases the number of poor by 31.1 million persons.

Pretax Income. The poverty standard reflects gross not net income. An urban family of four with an income of $6675 in 1978 would not have been considered poor by the SSA standard, but their net pay would have been considerably less than the poverty standard after deductions for taxes, social security, retirement, and insurance.

In-Kind Benefits and Assets. Although cash income security payments (e.g., social security and unemployment compensation) and cash assistance benefits (e.g., AFDC, SSI, and general assistance) are included in SSA's measure of income, neither assets or in-kind benefits such as food stamps and Medicaid are included. Because it is conceivable that some families may have low incomes but assets they can draw on, the failure to include assets may distort poverty calculations to some extent (Weisbrod and Hansen, 1968).

The failure to include in-kind benefits is a more severe problem. In-kind benefits such as food stamps are quite expensive, go to a large number or people, and definitely

Table 3. Size of the Poor Population Under Current and Revised Poverty Cutoffs, 1974 (in millions)

			The poor			
				Using revised poverty cutoffs		
	U.S. population	Using official poverty cutoffs	80% of Low-cost plan condensed family size	Thrifty plan	80% of Low-cost plan	Low-cost plan
Persons	209.3	24.3	39.2	39.9	41.4	55.4
Families	55.7	5.1	8.8	8.7	9.0	12.8
Unrelated individuals	18.9	4.8	8.4	8.2	8.4	9.2
Children ages 5–17	49.8	7.5	10.4	11.1	11.6	15.4

Source: U.S. Department of Health, Education and Welfare, *The Measure of Poverty* (U.S. Government Printing Office, Washington, DC, 1975), p. 77.
aThe poverty level for a nonfarm family of four would be $6,494 under the 80% condensed family budget; $6,366 under the thrifty budget; $6,494 under the 80% of low-cost budget; $8,118 under the low-cost budget.

improve the life of recipients. A recent study by Sneeding concluded that if the poverty figures were adjusted for underreporting of income by the poor, taxes paid by the poor, and receipt of in-kind benefits, the number of persons below the poverty line would have been 8.7 percent of all persons in 1968 (rather than 13 percent), 8.0 percent in 1970 (rather than 13 percent), and 5.4 percent in 1972 (rather than 12 percent). This would have dropped the poverty count to around 17 million in 1968 and 1970, and some 11 million in 1972 (Sneeding, 1975).

A study of the Congressional Budget Office reached similar conclusions for fiscal year 1976 (see Table 4). Before any transfer income, 20.2 million households (25.5 percent of all households) were below the poverty threshold. Social insurance (social security) reduced the number of poor households to 11.2 million. Adding cash assistance reduced poor households to 9.1 million. In-kind aid reduced the number to 5.3 million, and adjustments for taxes paid raised the number slightly to 5.4 million households. This would leave 6.9 percent of all households, or about 14.2 million persons, in poverty in 1976.

Those critics of SSA's standard who believe that the government overestimates poverty base their argument on the failure of SSA to count in-kind benefits (Browning, 1976). Although the figures above clearly indicate that the failure to include in-kind benefits does distort the calculations, those who believe SSA's standards underestimate poverty make two points. First, whereas in-kind benefits, or some proportion of their value, should be included in the calculations, the poverty threshold should also be adjusted upward substantially. These scholars argue that the unrealistic poverty threshold underestimates poverty much more severely than the failure to consider in-kind benefits increases the count.

Table 4. Households Below the Poverty Level Under Alternative Income Definitions, Fiscal Year 1976

Households in poverty	Pre-tax/ pre-transfer income	Pre-tax/ post-social insurance income	Pre-tax/ post-money transfer income	Pre-tax/ post-in-kind transfer income		Pre-tax/ post-total transfer income
				I[a]	II	
Number in thousands	20,237	11,179	9,073	7,406	5,336	5,446
Percent of all families	25.5	14.1	11.4	9.3	6.7	6.9

Source: Congressional Budget Office, *Poverty Status of Families Under Alternative Definitions of Income* (U.S. Government Printing Office, Washington, DC, 1977), p. XV.
[a]Excludes Medicare and Medicaid Payments.

This seems to be a valid point. As noted above, when adjustments for in-kind benefits, unreported income, and taxes paid are made, the number of poor is reduced by about 10 to 15 million. Adjustments in food budgets and the multiplication factor, however, show that the poverty standard underestimates the poor by anywhere from 15 to 31 million. Because most in-kind benefits go to persons in the lowest income quintile, those persons not counted in the poverty estimates because of the low thresholds are unlikely to be receiving in-kind aid. Thus, many scholars (Harrington, 1977; Rodgers, 1978) argue, a much improved measure that considered in-kind benefits, taxes paid, underreporting of income, and raised the food budget and multiplication factor, would probably show anywhere from 5 to 20 million additional poor.

A second point often raised is that in-kind benefits should not be calculated at face value. The reasoning is that the value of the service or aid may not be equal to the government's cost. Medicaid services are a good example. Medicaid services, which are often dispensed by Medicaid mills, may be expensive yet worthless or even harmful to recipients. Additionally, a dying person who receives expensive Medicaid services would be pushed over the poverty threshold, perhaps even into some upper-income group. But, of course, the person could hardly be said to have escaped poverty because of an expensive illness or death.

II. ALTERNATIVE APPROACHES TO THE MEASUREMENT OF POVERTY

In most industrialized nations poverty is defined in a relative rather than an absolute manner. A relative standard defines poverty not in terms of the basic resources required for subsistence but in relationship to the model standards of living in a society. Townsend (1974: 15) describes the spirit of a relative standard: "Individuals, families and groups in the population can be said to be in poverty when they lack the resources to obtain the type of diets, participate in activities and have the living conditions and amenities which are customary, or are at least widely encouraged or approved, in the societies to which they belong."

The most usual manner of formulating a relative definition is by pegging it to median income (OECD, 1976: 64-67). The poor are defined as those who earn less than some percentage of the median income for their family size. The percentage is generally in the 50 to 66 percent range. If this approach was adopted in America, it would substantially raise the poverty standard and the poverty count. For example, in 1978 the official poverty threshold for an urban family of four was $6662. The median income for four-person families was $20,428. If half the median income was used as the poverty standard, the relative standard would have been $10,214—an increase in the poverty standard for four-person families of more than 50 percent. Roughly estimated, a relative standard of this type for all family sizes would yield a poverty count of 50 to 60 million American poor. The great increases in the poverty count explains in substantial part why the American government has resisted the adoption of such a standard.

A recent OECD (1976: 67) study formulated a much more modest, and basically very crude, relative standard, and compared it to private and public measures of poverty in 10 industrialized nations. Regardless of the measure used, the data revealed a significant amount of poverty in all but three nations [West Germany (3 percent), Denmark (5 percent), and Sweden (3.5 percent)]. The standardized data for eight of the nations shows the highest rates of poverty in Canada (11 percent), the United States (13 percent), and France (16 percent).

By far the most sophisticated attempt to measure poverty is Townsend's (1979) study of British poverty. Townsend altered the traditional measures in two important ways. First, he developed a measure of resources in place of cash income. Townsend's measure of resources consisted of five components: cash income, imputed as well as actual income from the ownership of wealth, and three types of in-kind assistance: employer welfare benefits, public social services, and private income. Townsend also measured style of living (rather than simple consumption) to determine the levels at which resources were so low as to constitute deprivation. Townsend's measure showed a great deal more poverty than official government statistics. The official British government measure of poverty (based on supplemental benefit levels) has in recent years shown that about 7 percent of all households live in poverty. Townsend's deprivation standard showed that about 25 percent of all British households are poor (1979: 272).

The measurement of poverty is, therefore, complex and highly political. Most industrialized nations have not given the matter serious consideration, and some that have manifest a clear bias toward measuring poverty in a manner that underestimates deprivation. No nation is more guilty of this than the United States. Townsend's research has set the standard for quality measurement of poverty, but his efforts are unlikely to be emulated by governments that would find serious studies of poverty embarrassing. There is little doubt that serious studies of American poverty would find that the problem is considerably more extensive than official figures indicate.

III. THE POOR

Knowing who the poor are provides insights into the causes of poverty and suggests the reforms necessary to alleviate it. In America poverty exists in all regions of the nation,

Table 5. Poverty Rates, 1978

Race

Percent of racial groups groups living in	Number of poor (in millions) by race		Percent of poor by race
White 8.7%	White	13,652	56%
Black 32.6%	Black	7,625	31%
Spanish origin 21.6%	Spanish Origin	2,607	11%
	Other	613	2%
		24,497 (million)	100%

Families: By race and sex of head

Percent of all families who are poor

Family composition: % poor

Race	*Female*	*Male*
White 6.9%	Female-headed 31.4%	Male-headed 5.2%
Black 27.5%	White female-headed 23.5%	White male-headed 4.7%
Spanish origin 20.4%	Black female-headed 50.4%	Black male-headed 11.3%

Percent of poor families headed by female: by race

Black families 74%
White families 39%

Age

Percent of all persons	Percent of the poor population
65 and over 14%	13%
18 and under 16%	40%

Region

Percent of the poor who live in	Percent of the population that is poor
Northeast 21%	10.4%
North central 21%	9.1%
South 42%	14.7%
West 16%	10.0%

Source: U.S. Bureau of the Census, Money income and poverty status of families and persons in the United States: 1978 (advance report), *Current Population Reports,* Series P-60, No. 120, (U.S. Government Printing Office, Washington, DC, 1979).

affects every racial and ethnic group, the young and the old, the employed and unemployed. Some persons, however, are much more likely to be poor than others. Table 5 provides an overview of the poor population in 1978. From a strictly numerical point of view, whites constitute by far the largest group among the poor. Fifty-six percent of the poor were white, 31 percent were black, and 11 percent were of Spanish origin. However, poverty is clearly a less severe hazard for whites than for minorities. Only 8.7 percent of all whites were poor in 1978, compared to 32.6 percent of all blacks and 21.6 percent of Spanish-origin citizens.

Female-headed families also have a very high potential for poverty. Female-headed families have increased rapidly in the last 15 years, reaching 15 percent of all families in 1978. Thirty-one percent of these female-headed families were poor in 1978: 23.5 percent of the white female-headed families, and 50.4 percent of all black female-headed families. Only 5.2 percent of all male-headed families were poor. Women headed 74 percent of all black poor families, and 39 percent of all white poor families.

A majority of all the poor in 1978 were either over 65 years of age or 18 or under. One aged person in seven lived in poverty, as did one out of every six children. Thirteen percent of all the poor were 65 or older, whereas 40 percent were 18 or under.

The South is by far the poorest region in America. Fifteen percent of the Southern population is poor, about 50 percent higher than the rate for other regions. Forty-two percent of all the poor live in the South. The major urban areas of the nation also have very high poverty rates, especially among urban blacks.

Thus, American poverty most acutely affects minorities, female-headed families, the young and old, residents of the South, and minorities concentrated in poverty pockets of major cities.

IV. CAUSES OF POVERTY

Scholars have long debated the causes of poverty. The debates have generally centered around a few basic theories. The four most prominent theories of poverty are described briefly and then a more comprehensive theory linking poverty to both the political and economic system is elaborated.

A. The Orthodox Economic Theory

The core of orthodox economic theory is the belief that the abilities of each worker determines his/her income (Gordon, 1972; Lydall, 1968). Working on the assumption of perfect competition and market equilibrium, this school of economics argues that there is a high correlation between wages and marginal productivity. Thus, if an individual's income is too low, it means that his productivity is too low. To increase the individual's income, his productivity must be increased. To these economists it is not the structure of the job market that determines productivity (either in whole or in part), but the abilities of individual workers.

Because this theory suggests that poverty is the outcome of variations in natural ability, it basically places the blame for poverty on the poor. Although the application of the theory varies, as applied by some economists the theory takes on distinctly racist and sexist tones in that it implies that the distribution of abilities naturally leaves a disproportionate percentage of minorities and women in low-income jobs.

B. Functionalist Explanations

Somewhat aligned with the orthodox economic interpretation is the functional explanation developed by sociologists, chiefly Talcott Parsons, Kingsley Davies, and W. E. Moore (Davies and Moore, 1945; Lipset, 1966). This theory argues that inequality results from variations in the attractiveness and functional importance of jobs. To ensure that all jobs will be done, the rewards for labor must vary. Jobs that require the most responsibility must pay the most and carry the most prestige to attract applicants and hold encumbents. The more menial and low-paying jobs go to those without the ambition or inclination to strive for a high-paying position.

Like the orthodox interpretation, this theory assumes that one's personal characteristics determine one's economic level. It fails entirely to consider the social factors that influence job ability, biases that evaluate some of the ambitious and hard-working and leave others behind, or the upper limits on good jobs. By implication, it also suggests that women and minorities are less ambitious.

C. The Subculture of Poverty

A number of anthropologists and sociologists have advanced the notion that the poor develop a deviant culture with values and habits that are so self-defeating they make poverty self-perpetuating. This theory was popularized by Oscar Lewis (1965: XXIV):

> In anthropological usage the term culture implies essentially a design for living which is passed down from generation to generation to generation. In applying this concept of culture to the understanding of poverty, I want to draw attention to the fact that poverty in modern nations is not only a state of economic deprivation, of disorganization, or of the absence of something. It is also something positive in the sense that it has structure, a rationale, and defense mechanisms without which the poor could hardly carry on. In short, it is a way of life, remarkably stable and persistent, passed down from generation to generation along family lines.

Some of the characteristics of this culture were unemployment or subemployment, little savings, apathy, fatalism, frequent use of violence to settle family quarrels and discipline children, an inability to defer gratification, and frequent abandonment of the family by the father. Lewis did not argue that all the poor manifested these beliefs and habits, but that the culture existed among some of the poor and was devastating enough to ensure their continuation in poverty. Lewis never argued that the culture of poverty was the initial cause of poverty, only that it was an adaptation to poverty that often aggravated attempts to end the condition.

The culture of poverty theory has been widely and heatedly debated. Some empirical tests have found that the condition is not as widespread as many believe. As Townsend (1979: 68) notes:

> A large number of sources might be cited to demonstrate that shantytown inhabitants and other poor individuals in different societies are part of complex forms of social organization, are generally in regular employment, uphold conventional values and develop cohesive family relationships.

Some scholars have altered the theory to a culture of deprivation (Harrington, 1962). This theory simply argues that poor schools, unhealthy housings, bad nutrition, and other aspects of poverty handicap many of the poor, making it more difficult for them to escape deprivation. Other, more conservative social scientists (Glazer and Moynihan, 1963; Moynihan, 1965; Banfield, 1968) have used the culture of poverty theory to justify characterizing the poor as mostly being unworthy.

D. The Dual Labor Market

The dual labor market theory directly challenges both the orthodox economic interpretation and the functionalist theory of poverty. Scholars who support this theory argue that market forces are more important than individual characteristics in determining wage levels. These economists argue that there are two job markets: the primary sector and the secondary sector. In the secondary sector, employment is unstable, pay is low, prospects for promotion poor, and unions of small importance.

The dual labor market theory has attracted many advocates (Tussing, 1975; Bosanquet and Doeringer, 1973) in the United States and other Western industrial nations, but some critics (Wachtel, 1971) have argued that the theory fails to link the job structure to the broader political and economic systems. The radical economic school has attempted to identify these links. Applying Marxism, these scholars have attempted to demonstrate that, just as in orthodox economics, the market price of a product affects the value of an individual's marginal product. Individual productivity is also affected by supply and demand, reinforced by competition. But, the radical theorists argue, the class division and distribution among classes will also affect the distribution of individual income (Townsend, 1979: 78). "An individual's class will ultimately affect both his productivity, through the differential access of different classes to different kinds of complementary capital, and his relative share of final product." The resulting stratified labor market also discourages a common consciousness among workers.

E. A Combined Explanation: The Subclass Theory

A number of scholars have suggested a multiple factor explanation of American poverty that draws on and supplements the above theories, especially the dual labor market theory. Rodgers (1979: 40–60), for example, has attempted to explain American poverty in terms of four factors: elite rule, welfare capitalism, racism and sexism, and geographic isolation.

Elite Rule. The concept of elite rule argues that the American political system with its separation of powers and system of checks and balances is designed to preserve the status quo. Given the structure of the system, all groups find it difficult to influence the political system. For a number of reasons, however, some groups find it easier to have their interests presented in the political system than others. Some groups, for example, have a vested interest in preserving the status quo. This is particularly true of the more affluent members of society. The poor, however, need to produce change, even if it is only the passage of policies such as full employment legislation. The need to produce change is a distinct disadvantage.

Some groups are also advantaged because the political system has a natural bias toward looking after their needs. Any administration, for example, be it Democratic or Republican, finds it necessary to keep business happy and prosperous. Thus business representatives can count on having their views and needs considered. Indeed, business representatives always serve in the cabinet and on the staff of the President. The needs, concerns, and wishes of the poor and economically deprived hardly carry this weight.

All interests, be they farmers, automakers, or labor unions, find political influence an expensive undertaking. Sophisticated influence requires full-time lobbying staffs, research departments, public relations specialists, legal staffs, and dozens of other experts.

The poor, including those groups who attempt to represent the poor, simply do not have the resources necessary to pursue political influence in a sophisticated manner.

For a variety of reasons, therefore, the poor have little power or representation in the political system. Periodic upheavals, such as the civil rights movement and urban riots, can elevate their influence temporarily, but these are unusual events, not persistent strategies.

Welfare Capitalism.   The economic system has two very important consequences for the poor. First, the philosophy of capitalism advances a number of widely accepted beliefs that are quite harmful to the poor. The three most obvious are the following:

1. The economic system is so viable that anyone who really wants to make a good living can do so. Anyone who fails is not trying.
2. The best motivator of people is economic self-interest. People will work harder if they know they will reap the benefits of their efforts and if they know that no one will help them if they do not work.
3. The economic system rewards people equitably (i.e., the salary one receives is a reflection on the value of one's labor).

These beliefs have a number of consequences. Most obviously, they create a very hostile attitude toward the poor. To be poor is to be almost automatically considered to be lazy, dishonest, even sinful. Aid to the poor is considered to be a defeating strategy, one that only encourages sloth. When aid is given, it is extended only to those among the poor who are considered the least objectionable—the aged, disabled, and mothers and their dependent children. Aid is kept low, and given in obvious forms that constantly remind the poor that they are on the dole, a shameful condition.

The second consequence of capitalism for the poor is that, despite beliefs to the contrary, even in relatively prosperous times the American economy provides inadequate opportunities and compensation for millions of citizens. Periodically the economy malfunctions severely enough to disadvantage millions more. Throughout American history the economy has been plagued by panics, depressions, periods of stagnation, cycles of inflation and recession, and recently by stagflation.

Since World War II the unemployment rate has averaged more than 5 percent, and in recent years has never been that low. The unemployment rate for black Americans has averaged more than twice that national rate. Millions of other Americans work only part time or part of the year while seeking full-time work, and millions more work full-time at jobs that pay an extremely low wage. These Americans are said to be subemployed—a condition that conservatively estimated affects 25 percent of the work force (Vietorisz et al., 1975).

Limited opportunities and poor wages cause millions of families to live on very low incomes. For example, in 1978, 31 percent of all families had incomes of $12,000 or less. Seventy-five percent of all single adults in 1978 had incomes below $12,000 (U.S. Bureau of the Census, 1979: 2). As in every year back to 1945, the top 40 percent of all earners received about 65 percent of all income in 1978, compared to about 17 percent for the bottom 40 percent.

The deficiencies of the American economy—combined with its suppressing ideology—contribute very substantially to poverty. As detailed below, recent welfare reform proposals have acknowledged the contribution of economic problems to poverty but have failed to recommend adequate remedies.

Racism and Sexism. America's long history of racism and sexism contributes very directly to the poverty problem. Poverty is most acute for those groups that have historically been discriminated against in America. Although many of the discriminatory barriers have been overcome, some discrimination continues. Millions of women and minorities who were psychologically programmed for subordination, and denied good educations and job skills, have no way of catching up now that the most overt barriers have been lowered. Millions more are in the process of catching up, a lengthy process at best. The result is that females and black families currently have earnings that average only about 60 percent of the earnings of white men and white families, respectively (Rodgers, 1979: 56-57). Not surprisingly, women and minorities head a majority of all the poor families in America.

Geographic Isolation. Millions of Americans live outside the social and economic mainstream of the nation (Tussing, 1975: 106-107). People isolated in rural areas, especially in the South and in Appalachia, have fewer job opportunities, the worst educational systems, and the worst health care, because these sections of the country have not shared fully in the prosperity and growth of the rest of the country. This creates a dual problem: large numbers of poor people and few funds to deal with them. As noted, the South is home to about 40 percent of the nation's poor, but it is also the least wealthy region. Thus welfare payments in the South are generally very low.

Rural poverty has also contributed very substantially to urban poverty. Most of the nation's urban poor migrated to the cities in an attempt to escape rural poverty. Unfortunately, most found opportunities in urban areas as bleak as those that launched their relocation. As noted below, recent poverty reform proposals have not given any consideration to the economic revitalization of rural areas.

In summary, the poor constitute a subclass created by discrimination and a deficient economic system. Their plight is worsened by their limited influence in the political system and by the myths of capitalism that blame the poor for their condition.

V. INCOME MAINTENANCE AND WELFARE PROGRAMS

In Western industrial nations the development of the welfare state is, for the most part, a post-World War II phenomenon. Although Germany, Norway, and New Zealand had the basis of a welfare state early in the twentieth century, most Western nations developed their programs over the last 40 years. The trend in most nations is toward greater state responsibility for health care, unemployment, and the needs of the aged.

The most popular type of social welfare program is social insurance. In return for regular contributions, citizens receive pensions, sickness benefits, medical care, and other benefits under social insurance schemes. The most popular type of outright welfare programs are means-tested. Those qualifying citizens falling below specified income and asset levels receive enough assistance to bring them up to the benefit, or cutoff point. A third type of program provides flat-rate benefits to all qualifying citizens—for example, parents —without concern for their income or assets. Flat-rate programs are found primarily in Norway, Sweden, and the Netherlands.

By 1980 the welfare state was well developed in all the major Western industrial nations, but the approaches used vary enough to make comparisons complex. A primary difference is that whereas some nations attempt to relieve certain conditions, other nations place more emphasis on trying to prevent the problem from arising. Sweden, for example, emphasizes full employment rather than unemployment benefits. Some nations also use educational expenditures as a method of preventing dependency. Another difference involves the use of tax programs as a substitute or supplement to welfare programs. Rather than a housing allowance, for example, a nation might provide tax breaks for homeowners.

A recent OECD study (1976: 17) found that in the early 1970s the average Western nation was spending about 25 percent of its total budget, or about 8½ percent of gross national product, on social welfare expenditures. France, Germany, Austria, Belgium, and the Netherlands were spending considerably more than the average, whereas the United Kingdom, Ireland, Canada, and the United States were spending less. Japan, the major nation with the least developed welfare state, spent only 2.8 percent of its GNP on social welfare expenditures in 1973.

The most costly expenditure in all the nations is old-age pensions (OECD, 1976: 20). In the early 1970s pensions for the aged constituted an average of 62 percent of all social welfare expenditures in Western nations. At 39 percent, Canada ranked at the bottom, whereas 73 percent of all social welfare expenditures in the United States involved social security expenditures. Children allowances were the next largest expenditure for most nations (a type of program that does not exist in the Untied States), followed by expenditures for sickness and health care.

A. American Programs and Their Impact

Table 6 shows the major social welfare programs in operation in recent years, the basic eligibility qualifications, the source of funds, the form of aid, the number of persons served by each program, and the yearly cost. The programs are of three types: social insurance, means-tested cash assistance, and means-tested in-kind aid. The social insurance programs are by far the most expensive. Social security cost $102.3 billion in 1979 and served an average of 34.5 million persons per month. Medicare, a health insurance program for the aged, cost $29.1 billion in 1979 while serving a monthly average of 26.7 million persons.

Only two of the programs provide cash assistance. Aid to Families with Dependent Children (AFDC) provides cash aid and services (such as job training programs and some child care). Most AFDC benefits go to female-headed families with dependent children. In 1979 AFDC cost approximately $11.2 billion, and served an average of 10.4 million persons per month in some 3.5 million families. Supplemental Security Income (SSI), a program that began in 1974, is a guaranteed income for the aged, disabled, and blind. Benefits from SSI are quite modest. In 1979 the average recipient received $133.58 per month. To be eligible for SSI a single person cannot have liquid assets worth more than $1500, and a couple cannot have liquid assets in excess of $2250. SSI was designed to supplement low social security payments and to replace many inadequate state and local programs for the aged, blind, and disabled. SSI cost $6.3 billion in 1979 and served a monthly average of 4.2 million persons.

Table 6. Social Welfare Programs

Programs	Basis of eligibility	Source of funding	Form of aid	Fiscal 1977		Fiscal 1978		Fiscal 1979	
				Expenditures (billions)	Beneficiaries (monthly ave. in millions)	Expenditures (billions)	Beneficiaries (monthly ave. in millions)	Expenditures (billions)	Beneficiaries (monthly ave. in millions)
Social insurance programs									
Old age Survivors and Dependent Insurance (OASDI)	Age, disability or death of parent or spouse, individual earnings	Federal payroll taxes on employers and employees	Cash	84.2	33.3	92.5	34.5	102.3	34.5
Unemployment compensation	Unemployment	State and federal payroll taxes on employers	Cash	14	11.0	12.3	11.1	10.3	9.5
Medicare	Age or disability	Federal payroll tax on employers and employees	Subsidized health insurance	21.2	25.2	26.0	25.3	29.1	26.7
Cash assistance (means tested)									
Aid to Families with Dependent Children (AFDC)	Certain families with children, income	Federal, state, and local revenues	Cash and services	11.4	10.3	11.0	10.7	11.4	10.4
Supplemental Security Income (SSI)	Age or disability income	Federal and state revenue	Cash	6.3	4.4	6.3	4.3	6.3	4.2
In-kind programs (means-tested)									
Medicaid	Persons eligible for AFDE, or SSI and medically indigent	Federal, state, and local revenues	Subsidized health service	17.2	10.4	20.0	10.7	22.7	11.0
Food stamps	Income	Federal revenues	Vouchers	5.0	17.7	6.3	17.1	7.0	17.4

Source: Social Security Bulletin, September 1979, pp. 35-104.
aThe Figures for 1979 are preliminary.

The Medicaid and food stamp programs provide noncash (in-kind) benefits to recipients. Medicaid is an assistance program for the medically needy. In 21 states, only AFDC and SSI recipients may receive medical assistance under Medicaid. In 28 states, AFDC, SSI, and some specifically defined needy persons can obtain some care. Arizona is the only state that does not participate in the Medicaid program. In 1979 the Medicaid program cost $22.7 billion and served a monthly average of 11 million persons.

The food stamp program is designed to help needy persons obtain enough food for a nutritious diet. The food stamp program provides families with net incomes below the poverty level with stamps that can be redeemed at food markets for groceries. The stamps can be used only for food items, not for tobacco, liquor, toilet articles, household cleaners, wax paper, toilet paper, soap, and other items.

The number of stamps a family can receive depends on income and family size. For example, as of early 1979, a four-person family with no income could receive $191.00 worth of stamps free. If the family had net earnings of $100 per month, it could receive $161.00 in stamps. If the family earned $389, it could receive $75.00 worth of stamps. If the family earned $553 or more, it would no longer be eligible for assistance. Additionally, families with liquid assets of $1750 or more are ineligible for food stamps (recreational homes and campers, boats, and expensive cars are considered liquid assets, as are cash, stocks, and bonds). Food stamps and AFDC recipients are required to register for employment or job training, with exemptions for mothers of preschool children. In 1979 the food stamp program cost $7 billion and served about 17 million persons per month.

The welfare programs serve a number of people. Social Security, SSI, and Medicare primarily serve the aged, with most of the aged receiving benefits from more than one of these programs. SSI, Medicaid, AFDC, and the food stamp program serve the needy, with AFDC recipients making up a significant proportion of all food stamp and Medicaid recipients. All the major social welfare programs cost $189 billion in 1979, with social security and Medicare accounting for 69 percent of the total costs. AFDC, SSI, food stamps, and Medicaid had a combined cost of $47.4 billion in 1979, or some 25 percent of the total cost of major social welfare programs.

Even with these large expenditures, poverty has certainly not been alleviated. An obvious reason for this is that most welfare benefits are so modest that all they can really do is supplement poverty income enough to push some of the poor over the poverty line, and provide minimal help to the most destitute among the poor. Thus, although welfare programs reduce the incidence of poverty, they are too modest to end it. Plotnick and Skidmore, for example, estimated that in 1974, 17.6 million households, including 39.5 million persons, were poor before cash welfare or social security. Cash welfare and social security reduced the number of poor to about 23 million persons, a 44 percent reduction in the pre-aid poor (Plotnick and Skidmore, 1975: 51). SSA's poverty count of 25 million for 1977 was after cash welfare and social security had been taken into account. Without this aid some 41.5 million persons would have fallen below the poverty level. Of the 25 million left in poverty in 1977, some received no assistance. Others received aid but too little to help them surpass the poverty level.

VI. WELFARE REFORM

It has become increasingly clear to public officials and much of the public that the current approach to welfare is expensive, but not very effective. Presidents Nixon, Ford, and Carter all recommended major reform proposals to Congress. Before these reforms are reviewed, it is instructive to note the major deficiencies of current welfare programs.

Extant programs suffer from the following major problems:

1. Welfare programs are far too numerous and often fail to mesh, thus creating duplication and even dysfunctional impacts on the poor.
2. Much of the overlap, waste, and ineffectiveness of welfare programs is attributable to the fact that they are administered by too many levels of government (federal, state, and local).
3. Because each state has considerable latitude over the number of state and federal dollars its poor will receive, there are extreme interstate variations in welfare aid.
4. Welfare assistance is narrow in coverage, unresponsive to the needs of many poor persons, and often detrimental in its impact. The most obvious example is the categorical nature of welfare programs, which allows the neglect of needy single persons, couples without children, and intact male-headed families. The result is not only inadequate response to the needs of many poor but also the frequent destruction of the family unit.
5. Multiple benefits, high tax rates on some earning, and exclusion of some working poor from in-kind programs such as Medicaid often discourages work.
6. Benefits under the major cash welfare program (AFDC) are generally inadequate and unresponsive to changes in the cost of living.
7. Welfare programs lack horizontal equity—those with the same need do not receive the same degree of aid.
8. Welfare programs lack vertical equity—those with the greatest need do not receive aid before those with less severe needs.

One option to all these deficiencies would be to try to revise existing programs. In the absence of more fundamental reform, even modest revisions would help. But it would be far from an ideal approach. Fundamental reform would require scraping most existing programs. An ideal approach would require:

1. The creation of economic conditions that would allow as many persons as possible to earn their own living in the job market
2. Simplifying and streamlining welfare programs, and designing them to prevent and break the cycle of poverty rather than just administer to the poor
3. Adequate provision for those who because of age, disability, motherhood, or economic deficiencies cannot care for themselves

Even the most comprehensive proposals submitted to Congress in recent years have fallen considerably short of these goals. Little emphasis has been placed on breaking the cycle of poverty (such as better educational and health care programs for poor children), and none of the major proposals has been tied to full employment legislation. The core of recent proposals has been the negative income tax (NIT), often supplemented with tax relief.

In recent years both Democratic and Republican administrations have proposed NIT plans as a method of streamlining welfare programs. NITs have been proposed in many forms (Green, 1967; Lampman, 1971), but the idea is basically a simple one. All NIT proposals recommend a guaranteed income that varies with family size, a cutoff point for aid, and a scheme called a tax rate designed to encourage family heads to work and achieve earnings above the guaranteed floor.

The NIT is attractive for several reasons. A NIT could replace all other cash aid programs; it would provide a national floor of income for all families, thereby eliminating the acute disparities that currently exist; it would assist all the poor, including male-headed families and single individuals; it would not penalize marriage or work; and it would be much simpler than current programs.

In 1969 Richard Nixon proposed to Congress a NIT plan for poor families with children. The bill passed the House twice, but failed to gain the necessary support in the Senate. The narrowness of the bill and its modest benefits doomed it. Congress formulated its own NIT proposal in 1974. The bill failed to gain much support, but the sophistication of the bill set the standard for future efforts (Adams, 1976). Gerald Ford also forwarded a NIT plan to Congress, but dropped the project when both unemployment and inflation became serious problems during his administration. President Carter introduced a reform plan in the fall of 1977 involving a NIT proposal entitled "The Better Jobs and Income Program."

Carter's plan emphasized a dual strategy: The poor would have been divided into those who could work and those who could not. Those designated as capable of work would have been expected to accept a public- or private-sector job that the government, using a NIT plan, would have supplemented if wages fell below levels established for varying family sizes. Many of these families would also have received some tax relief. Those judged unable to work would have been eligible for a guaranteed income based on family size. Carter's dual plan would have covered all the poor, including two-parent families, single persons, and childless couples.

To stimulate the job market, Carter proposed the creation of 1.4 million public-sector jobs. Poor workers in both the private and public sectors would have been eligible for subsidies based on family size. A family of four, for example, would have been eligible for a work benefit of up to $2300. For every dollar earned over $3800, the benefit would have been reduced 50 percent, disappearing when earnings reached $8400. If, then, the head of a four-person family earned $5000, he/she would have received a supplement of $1700 ($2300 minus 50 percent of earnings in excess of $3800), providing a total income of $6700. Additionally, many low-income workers would have received some tax breaks.

Those not expected to work would have received a monthly cash grant. The grants would have varied by family size and would have been quite modest. A family of four would have received a total grant of $4200, some $1615 less than the poverty threshold for a nonfarm family of four in 1977. An aged, blind, or disabled individual would have received $2500, a couple $3750. A single individual would have received only $1100. A couple without children would have received $2200. The states would not have been required to supplement the grants, but would have been encouraged to do so by federal cost sharing.

The attractions of Carter's proposal were numerous. The proposal would have achieved some important program consolidation, provided a base of uniform benefits, eventually federalized welfare, covered all the poor, simplified administration, and provided some tax relief for poor families. The negative features were that the grants to non-workers were very low, too few new jobs would have been stimulated, and the plan was not coupled directly to a comprehensive program designed to deal better with inflation, unemployment, and subemployment.

Carter's welfare reform proposal failed to attract much support in Congress. Many members of Congress were afraid that the proposal would substantially increase welfare costs, and many are opposed to any NIT or guaranteed income proposal. Of course, the proposal suffered from the fact that the power structure in Washington is such that there were few powerful groups to work on behalf of the reform, and powerful groups to work against it.

VII. CONCLUSIONS

Poverty is likely to be a serious problem in America for a long time to come. The reason is that the prerequisite to poverty alleviation in America is a much improved economy. Welfare programs are likely to be creative and generous enough to take care of the dependent poor only if everyone who can earn his/her own living does so. A full employment economy would greatly reduce the number of persons that government programs would need to help, and would provide the increased industrial growth and tax revenues necessary to deal adequately with the poor.

Most Western nations have found that a healthy, growing economy requires careful government management. Although American capitalism has not remotely resembled laissez faire capitalism for at least 100 years, there is still considerable resistance in America to sophisticated government management involving economic planning, wage and price controls, and public participation in major investment decisions. The recent failures of simple Keynesian economic strategies to deal with stagflation, an economic condition with which the strategies were never meant to deal, suggest that different and perhaps more sophisticated techniques will have to be employed. Given the nation's current economic problems, in the immediate future a more sophisticated approach will be necessary not to reduce poverty, but to keep it from growing.

REFERENCES

Adams, B. (1976). Welfare, poverty, and jobs: A practical approach. *Challenger,* September–October, pp. 6-12.

Banfield, E. C. (1968). *The Unheavenly City.* Little, Brown, Boston.

Bosanquet, N., and Doeringer, P. (1973). Is there a dual labour market in Britain? *Economic Journal 31:* 210-231.

Browning, E. K. (1976). How much more equality can we afford? *The Public Interest,* July, pp. 90-103.

U.S. Bureau of the Census (1979). Money income and poverty status of families and persons in the United States: 1978 (advance report). *Current Population Reports 120*: 35.

Davies, K., and Moore, W. E. (1945). Some principles of stratification. *American Sociological Review 32*: 101-119.

Glazer, N., and Moynihan, D. P. (1963). *Beyond the Melting Pot.* Harvard University Press, Cambridge, MA.

Gordon, D. M. (1972). *Theories of Poverty and Unemployment.* Lexington Books, Lexington, MA.

Green, C. (1967). *Negative Taxes and the Poverty Problem.* Brookings Institute, Washington, DC.

Harrington, M. (1962). *The Other America.* Penguin, New York.

—— (1977). Hiding the other America. *The New Republic,* February, pp. 15-17.

The Houston Post (1979). Cost of moderate living standard up 9%. April 29, p. 22A.

Lampman, R. J. (1971). *Ends and Means of Reducing Income Poverty.* Academic Press, New York.

Lewis, O. (1965). *The Children of Sanchez.* Penguin, Harmondsworth, England.

Lipset, S. M. (1966). *Class, Status and Power.* Free Press, New York.

Lydall, H. (1968). *The Structure of Earnings.* Oxford University Press, London.

Miller, H. P. (1971). *Rich Man, Poor Man.* Thomas Y. Crowell, New York.

Moynihan, D. P. (1965). *The Negro Family.* U.S. Department of Labor, Washington, DC.

The Organization for Economic Co-operation and Development (OECD) (1976). *Public Expenditure on Income Maintenance Programmes.* OECD, Paris.

Orshansky, M. (1963). Children of the poor. *Social Security Bulletin 25*: 2-21.

—— (1965). Counting the poor: Another look at the poverty profile. *Social Security Bulletin 27*: 3-39.

Peterkin, B. (1976). *The Measure of Poverty.* U.S. Department of Health, Education and Welfare, Washington, DC.

Plotnick, R. D., and Skidmore, F. (1975). *Progress Against Poverty: A Review of the 1964-74 Decade.* Academic Press, New York.

The President's Commission on Income Maintenance Programs (1969). *Poverty Amidst Plenty.* U.S. Government Printing Office, Washington, DC.

Rodgers, H. R. (1978). Hiding versus ending poverty. *Politics and Society 8*: 253-266.

—— (1979). *Poverty Amid Plenty: A Political and Economic Analysis.* Addison-Wesley, Reading, MA.

Sneeding, T. M. (1975). Measuring the economic welfare of low income households and the anti-poverty effectiveness of cash and non-cash transfer programs. Unpublished Ph.D. dissertation, University of Wisconsin, Madison.

Townsend, P. (1974). Poverty as relative deprivation: Resources and style of living. In *Poverty, Inequality, and Class Structure,* D. Wedderbuan (Ed.). Cambridge University Press, London.

—— (1979). *Poverty in the United Kingdom: A Survey of Household Resources and Standards of Living.* University of California Press, Berkeley.

Tussing, D. A. (1975). *Poverty in a Dual Economy.* St. Martin's Press, New York.

Vietorisz, T., and Mier, R., and Harrison, B. (1975). Full employment at living wages. *Annals of the American Academy of Political and Social Science 418*: 104.

Wachtel, H. M. (1971). Looking at poverty from a radical perspective. *Review of Radical Political Economics 13*: 20-31.

Weisbrod, B., and Hansen, W. L. (1968). An income-net worth approach to measuring economic welfare. *American Economic Review 58*: 1315-1329.

Wilcox, C. (1969). *Toward Social Welfare.* Irvin-Dorsey, Homewood, IL.

23

Blacks, Women, and Public Policy

Marian Lief Palley / University of Delaware, Newark, Delaware

One could discuss at length the problems of Hispanic Americans, Orientals (Chinese, Koreans, Vietnamese, and others), blacks, or American Indians. In this chapter, however, it is not possible to address the issues of importance to each of these groups and then to discuss the issues of significance to women. Therefore, inasmuch as women represent more than half of the population and blacks represent the largest "nonwhite" minority group in the United States today (more than 12 percent of the population), this chapter will consider only issues relating to women and blacks. More specifically, a brief discussion of the evolution of the contemporary black and womens' rights movement is followed by an assessment of the response of the political system to some of the articulated demands of these two population cohorts. Next the goals of the major rights organizations and their roles in their respective movements are considered. Finally, this chapter addresses several separate policy areas—employment opportunity, educational opportunity, and the special case of the Equal Rights Amendment and "free choice" regarding abortion—and assesses why "rights" groups have succeeded or failed in their attempts to bring about change.

It is important to begin with a brief statement on social change and the role of black and womens' rights groups regarding change. Both black and womens' rights movements are presented as somewhat monolithic in their goals. Certainly the major goals of most of the groups within the respective movements are akin to each other. The groups desire improved status for the members of the secondary group they represent. There are, however, differences in strategies and tactics displayed by different groups, which are glossed over in the pages that follow. Furthermore, special attention is paid to the mainstream of the two movements, which operates "within" the political system. That is, fringe groups that may want to topple existing institutions and replace them with new institutions are not discussed. These groups, at least at the present, are not deemed significant enough to consider in the context of contemporary politics. Finally, the differential impact of changes on different groups of blacks and women is considered.

I. THE SOCIAL CONDITIONS

The conditions that have led to the demands of women and blacks for changed status in society are well known to most Americans and thus will receive just a brief restatement. The black population in the United States has had since the Civil War disproportionately fewer income opportunities, poorer educational opportunities, unequal employment opportunities, and has suffered other general discrimination based on race. Even when examining recent unemployment data, such racial disparities are clear. According to the Bureau of Labor Statistics, in March 1977 black male unemployment was 12.6 percent and the comparable figure for white males was 6.2 percent. The figures for females were 12.7 percent and 7.5 percent, respectively. Minority youth unemployment (largely black) was more than 40 percent. Regarding education, in 1960, 42 percent of blacks completed high school, whereas 66 percent of whites completed high school. Twenty years later conditions had improved considerably, and comparable figures were 75 percent and 85 percent, respectively (Alexis, 1979). In response to these kinds of conditions, the black civil rights movement was born in the early years of the twentieth century. This movement expanded in the 1960s and 1970s as new black rights groups emerged in response to the gap between expectations and reality that arose in the years following the 1954 Supreme Court decision in *Brown v. The Board of Education of Topeka* (347 U.S. 483) (Barker and McCoy, 1976; Walton, 1972).

Women as a group also have been the object of discrimination. Traditionally, women received "second-class" status in the political, economic, and religious realms (Palley, 1976; Ruether, 1974). More recently, they too have demanded changes in their roles in society as expectations have been broadened in response to improved educational opportunities, technological advances that have effected a transformation in the role of women as mothers and homemakers, and increased participation in the labor force (Palley, 1976). Thus, from 1950 to 1970, female participation in the labor force almost doubled. Educated women grew up encountering the most contradictions in their lives. They had achievement-oriented values that were contradicted by the "traditional" female role. These women have become the leadership cadre of the womens' movement in the decades of the 1970s and 1980s. Some of the women activists of the 1960s responded to their secondary (i.e., subordinate) positions in the new left and civil rights movements of the early 1960s and were instrumental in fashioning the early feminist organizations (Gelb and Palley, 1982).

Though one can draw together the experiences of blacks and women and note the history of discrimination for both groups, it is important to distinguish between their experiences. Whereas blacks are disproportionately members of the lower classes in this nation, women have traditionally drawn their status from their fathers or their husbands. Thus, women are distributed more evenly than blacks across class groupings—though women are at a greater risk of being in poverty than are men (Schiller, 1980). Also, the black rights movement is older and more established than the womens' rights movement, which is less than 20 years old—though womens' groups such as the League of Women Voters and the Council of Jewish Women, though not feminist organizations, are older, well-established women's organizations (Costain, 1975).

To what extent has the political system been responsive to the demands of blacks and women? This is, of course, a very difficult question to answer. To the extent that the demands made by women and blacks to eliminate sexual and racial discrimination are becoming institutionalized, they have been successful. However, legislation, administrative guidelines, and judicial decisions have not eliminated all discrimination, though they have reduced the extent of discrimination in policy areas as disparate as education, employment, credit, housing, reproductive choice, and the awarding of government contracts (Palley and Preston, 1979). The courts have been particularly active in the areas of education and housing.[1] But it is notable that American urban public schools are more black today than they were 10 years ago and that, on the average, student achievement levels have not increased. The U.S. Civil Rights Commission found that three-quarters of the black children in the 26 largest U.S. cities attended schools that had between 90 and 100 percent minority enrollments (Friedman, 1980). As far as housing is concerned, despite Supreme Court decisions that deem many discriminatory housing practices unconstitutional, the vast majority of blacks still live in segregated neighborhoods (either by necessity or by choice) (Bryce et al., 1978). Thus, the Joint Center for Political Studies (Friedman, 1980) noted that in 23 of 26 medium and large cities with black majorities and heavily nonwhite populations, 16 ranked among the poorest cities in the nation; and nearly one-half had experienced sharp population declines in the previous decade and most of these cities had relatively old housing stock.

In addition, women and blacks on the average still earn considerably less than white men. On the average, women college graduates can expect to have lower earning capacities than male high school dropouts; also, the average earnings gap between blacks and whites has not changed in the past 20 years (Adams and Ratner, 1980). It is the case, too, that blacks and women have disproportionate risks of being in poverty, and that though there are more women doctors, lawyers, and other professionals than there were 10 or 20 years ago, the vast majority of women who hold low-skilled or nonskilled jobs are paid at rates lower than men who work in low-skilled or nonskilled jobs (Adams and Winston, 1980). Thus, beginning sanitation workers, who are working at low-skilled jobs, on the average earn more than waitresses. Put into an even starker perspective, these same sanitation workers on the average, earn more than skilled women who are beginning secretaries and nurses.

Finally, conflict among women and blacks can have the effect of lessening the impact of both groups. Consider for a moment the question of quotas and affirmative action. C. Douglas Ades, who was for 11 years a Chemical Bank vice president, was quoted as saying: "The women threw a monkey wrench into the affirmative action process—many were educated, well-to-do and militant, and when the barriers came down, they jumped in, head-to-head with blacks, and the women won." Gloria De Sole, Associate Director of Affirmative Action at the State University of New York at Albany, charged in response that the issue of white women taking jobs from blacks is a "red herring." "If we argue about who comes first, then the man has us fighting among ourselves. This is divisiveness in the extreme. It is also guilt-tripping" (*The New York Times*, 1980). This type of interchange, of course, tends to heighten intergroup conflict at a time when, as Barbara Rochman, Executive Director of the New York chapter of the National Organization for Women (NOW), notes, "the more groups you include, the more you reduce the opposition to all the protected classes" (*The New York Times*, 1980).

One final point should be noted before proceeding to discuss the two rights movements and specific issue areas. Though the policy effects seem relatively limited to some observers, blacks and women have made some significant headway in several areas. More blacks and women hold elective office than at any other time in American history (Smith, 1978); more blacks and women are succeeding in the professions and business (Adams and Winston, 1980); and the verbalization of hostility against these groups seems to have lessened over time.

II. THE NATURE OF THE RIGHTS MOVEMENTS

The manifest goals of both the black rights movement and the feminist movement are to improve life conditions for blacks and women, respectively. The different groups within each of the movements, of course, focus on different issues and utilize different tactics to try to achieve their goals.

The black groups that seem to be in the forefront of the black rights movement as the decade of the 1980s commences include the National Association for the Advancement of Colored People (NAACP), the National Urban League, People United to Save Humanity (PUSH), and the Southern Christian Leadership Conference (SCLC). These groups have been in existence for variable time periods, with the NAACP, now led by the Reverend Benjamin Hooks, and the Urban League, now led by John Jacob, being the oldest black rights groups. The SCLC is an organization that had its greatest influence in the 1950s and 1960s under the charismatic leadership of the Reverend Martin Luther King, Jr., and PUSH emerged in the 1970s under the leadership of the Reverend Jesse Jackson. Though these four organizations are the major mass membership organizations in the black civil rights movement (for example, the NAACP has 400,000 members), there are other smaller, oftentimes local, groups, too (*Sunday News Journal*, 1980). Also, and of special note, the NAACP Legal Defense and Educational Fund has been central to the gains made by blacks in the judicial process. The Legal Defense and Educational Fund has been responsible for many of the court battles regarding school integration, segregated housing, and affirmative action.

The womens' movement has no group comparable to the NAACP in terms of membership. In fact, not one of the feminist groups is a truly mass membership organization. The largest of these groups is the National Organization for Women (NOW). In 1978, NOW had 125,000 members. All of the other groups, with the exception of the National Abortion Rights League (NARAL) (which had 70,000 members in 1978), and the National Womens' Political Caucus (which had 11,000 members in 1978), are essentially nonmembership organizations. Thus, the Womens' Equity Action League, the Womens' Legal Defense Fund, the NOW Legal Defense and Education Fund, the Womens' Rights Project (WRP) and the Reproductive Freedom Project (RFP) of the American Civil Liberties Union (ACLU), the Center for Women Policy Studies, and the NOW Project on Equal Education Rights (PEER), to name just some of the feminist groups, are all important group actors in the feminist movement but are all leadership-based, not membership-based organizations (Gelb and Palley, 1982). Furthermore, not only are feminist organizations involved in trying to affect the goals of the womens' movement, some of the traditional womens' organizations— such as the League of Women Voters, the American Association of University Women, the National Council of Jewish Women, B'nai Brith Women, the National Federation of Business and Professional Women, and the United Methodist Women—all have supported the womens' movement on specific issues at different times (Gelb and Palley, 1982).

The womens' movement, given the proliferation of groups, does not have the visible leadership that the black movement has traditionally been able to maintain. Rather, coalitions based on specific issues ebb and flow in the feminist movement. There have been no charismatic leaders in the womens' movement akin to Martin Luther King or more recently Jesse Jackson in the black rights movement.

Most successful political drives require coalition development among disparate groups. The feminist groups have developed coalition building to a "science," having learned to build issue-specific coalitions to gain support from some groups on specific issues where these groups might be hesitant to be supportive on other issues of importance to women. For example, there are labor groups that have been supportive of feminist positions regarding equal employment laws, credit laws, and education regulations, but they disappear from feminist coalitions supporting free choice regarding abortion rights (Gelb and Palley, 1979).

Black civil rights groups have also learned to build coalitions. They too have been able to garner support from diverse groups on issues. Inasmuch as their organizations are mass-based, however, they do not have to generate complicated intramovement coalitions as a first step as do the womens' groups. On such issues as voting rights, school desegregation, fair housing, and equal employment opportunities, blacks have been able to generate support from nonblack rights organizations. Thus, the ACLU has provided support for school desegregation and fair housing, and some labor unions have joined blacks in the quest for equal employment opportunity. As noted earlier, there are occasions when women and blacks join together in common causes, but sometimes distrust can overcome what might appear as good political sense.

To be effective in influencing the political process, "out" groups in particular need to build coalitions. There are other useful conditions that seem to affect the success rates of emergent organizations. Gelb and Palley (1979) suggest that there are six "rules" that influence whether "out" groups will succeed or fail in the various attempts to bring about change:

1. Successful groups must maximize their image of broad-based support in order to demonstrate potential electoral impact to decision makers. Third-party support must be mobilized whenever possible.
2. Successful groups must select a narrow issue that does not challenge fundamental values and does not divide potential constituents into competing groups.
3. A policy network must be mobilized to work in conjunction with the group's goals in order to secure access to decision makers. Ongoing contacts must be maintained with the individuals and groups who comprise this "network" at all stages of the policy-making process. Relevant groups must "monitor" the process at all times to prevent erosion of their positions.
4. The successful group must provide technical and informational resources to members and bureaucrats at all stages of the policy-making process.
5. Successful groups must be willing to compromise both in dealing with constituent groups' demands and in the political process.
6. Success must be defined in terms of increments of change rather than total victory, although significant change may nonetheless be achieved.

In the remainder of this chapter, several problem areas for blacks and women are examined. Problems are defined, and then group demands and political/societal responses are discussed. The success or failure of the movements regarding these issues is considered within the six-point framework just outlined.

III. SOME MAJOR ISSUE AREAS

A. Employment Opportunity

In 1978, the Urban League published *The State of Black America, 1978*, in which it was charged that conditions for blacks had not improved since the urban conflicts of the 1960s. Rather, the study noted that employment among black men, women, and teenagers (see above for income data) was still a significant issue and that unless "some special arrangements" were made—in other words, an affirmative federal government policy to ensure opportunities for blacks—meaningful changes would not be forthcoming.

The relatively poor employment picture that emerges must be considered more fully because it does not make apparent the very real gains made by the black middle and upper classes. Opportunities for black professionals and business people have improved considerably in the past decade. William Julius Wilson (1979) has pointed out that in the 10 years between 1967 and 1977 the number of blacks with incomes between $15,000 and $24,999 increased and the percentage of black families with incomes in the "over $25,000 a year" category almost doubled. Taking this consideration one step further, Wilson estimated that about 35 percent of blacks are members of the "underclass," 30 percent are members of the working class, and about 35 percent are middle class. The 35 percent underclass figure is, however, disproportionately high for American society. [If one compares black income with white income, it is clear that despite black economic advances, income equality is a goal still to be achieved. According to the U. S. Bureau of the Census, the ratio of black median family income to white median family income in 1977 was 0.57 (1978).] Thomas F. Pettigrew has noted some very serious problems that have arisen as a result of these class differences within the black population. In particular, he has expressed a concern that: "This differential association process lends visible support to the widely held white contention that the critical aspects of racial injustice were corrected during the civil rights era of the 1960s. This sanguine fiction is further supported by the arguments of conservatives who wish to give racial change a low national priority" (Pettigrew, 1979).

It is appropriate to ask what government actions have been taken to try to redress the racial imbalance we have noted in employment opportunities. There is the Civil Rights Act of 1964, affirmative action programs, the Equal Pay Act and the Equal Employment Opportunity Act (EEOA), to name just a few of the most visible responses. In addition, there is the Civil Rights Commission, which is empowered to oversee the employment practices of both public- and private-sector units that receive federal dollars. Furthermore, special monetary incentives are provided to minority businesses by the Small Business Administration. Finally, though not a civil rights program, manpower training programs have been established to try to train poor, largely nonwhite people for jobs. These later programs, however, have often trained people for positions that do not materialize. This is a special problem during periods of high employment and rapid technological advance.

The case of women and the employment scene is somewhat different from the case of blacks, though both groups share disproportionately the poorest-paid employment. Women entered the workplace in increasing numbers in the decade of the 1970s. For example, their full-time participation in the labor force increased from 18 percent in 1970 to 35 percent in 1980 (The Roper Organization, 1980). The expected earning capacity of women relative to men, however, has not increased, and on the average, female earning capacity is less than 0.60 of male earning capacity. Women, like blacks, tend to be clustered in the poorest-paid jobs. Despite affirmative action programs, the EEOA, and the somewhat uneven activities of the Civil Rights Commission regarding women (the Civil Rights Commission has been criticized by some womens' group leaders as being at best uninterested in womens' rights issues), women have made very little headway economically in the employment area.

Just as blacks in the professions and in business have advanced in the environment of "racial and sexual opportunities" of the past decade, so too have professional and business women. There are more women lawyers and doctors than ever before in American history. However, women are sometimes symbolic—as are blacks—in their presence in both the public and nonpublic forums of decision making and power. Thus, one can count on the fingers of one hand the blacks or the women who sit on the boards of the 5 or 10 largest corporations; and though there are now black and women mayors and members of Congress (Barnett, 1977) and women governors, they too are relatively few in number. There have been fewer than 20 blacks and 20 women in Congress at any one time during the past two decades. Discussing blacks in particular, Mach H. Jones (1978), using the case of Atlanta, has noted that elected black leadership, which too often emerges without strong alliances and policy agendas, will have "no regular structure for political debate and deliberations between black officials and black rank and file. Political discussion of consequence continues to be monopolized by the white commercial and business elite and the elected officials. Under these circumstances, the political empowerment of the black community remains a goal to be attained rather than an already realized milestone."

Despite often very vocal pronouncements of concern by black and feminist leaders, very little has been done to alter conditions for the blacks and women who are most discriminated against. These are the vast majority of both groups who are not in the professions or in business. These are the people who tend to be located in the poorest-paying, often "dead-ended" employment positions. Often union training programs are opened only reluctantly and narrowly to members of these population groups. Other times, jobs are classified so that women in particular cannot enter, or if they enter, advance. For example, the U.S. Army will not permit women to serve in combat roles. However, advancement in the military has traditionally been tied to combat experience. Harassment too has often made moving into new employment areas very difficult, especially for women.

Inasmuch as the majority of employment opportunities in the United States are in the private sector, *active* government involvement is very difficult. Moreover, the records of governments in advancing blacks and women have been poor, too. Thus it has been found that women who work for state governments perceive discrimination in their workplaces (Hopkins, 1980). In the federal bureaucracy, women and blacks tend to be clustered at the bottom of the pay scale. If one looks at the population distribution in the federal civil service supergrades, the weak compliance by the federal government with its own policy pronouncements becomes very clear. Women and blacks are clustered disproportionately in the lower-grade government positions. Proportionately few blacks and women are in the better-paid supergrade jobs. Thus, of the nearly 200,000 black federal employees, more than 115,000 or almost 58 percent are clustered in the ranks between GS-4 and GS-7; there are 360 (or 0.018 percent) black employees in the much higher-paying supergrades, GS-16, 17, and 18. The picture for women is just as bleak. Of the slightly more than 634,000 female federal employees, almost 42 percent are clustered in the GS-4 and GS-5 ranks. There are 436 (or 0.00068 percent) women who hold supergrade positions. If figures for men are examined, the inequities become apparent. There is a clustering of men in the ranks between GS-11 and 13. Of the almost 997,000 men in the federal civil service, nearly 373,000 hold GS-11, 12, and 13 ranks. This represents 37 percent of the federal civilian employees. There are 8492 men in the supergrade positions or approximately 1 percent of the male civil servants. Only 6 percent (or 64,626) of men hold positions classified between GS-4 and GS-7 (Office of Personnel Management, 1980).

What can be done about these unequal employment opportunities raises an entirely different set of problems. The groups that represent women and blacks tend to represent middle-class blacks and women. They have not focused their attentions as strongly as they might on the problems of the less fortunate members of their race or sex. These groups have tended to focus more of their energies on the concerns of the middle and upper classes in their group cohorts. Thus access to professions for the educated has been a more central concern than working conditions for nonunion labor or day care facilities for woman who cannot afford in-home care for their children while they work at poorly paid jobs. This is not intended to suggest either lack of concern or lack of rhetoric. Rather it is a statement of where limited resources are channeled in the group processes of Washington and statehouses across the nation.

B. Educational Opportunities

An area that has received considerable attention from both black and feminist groups is education. In recent years, the focus has been on desegregation, affirmative action programs, quotas, and, for women in particular, equal opportunities in athletics.

Desegregation has been one of the central concerns of the black rights movement since World War II (Orfield, 1978). The first major success came when, in 1954, the NAACP Legal Defense and Educational Fund argued successfully before the Supreme Court in the Brown case that "separate is not equal." In the years since this landmark decision, numerous other court decisions have mandated the desegregation of public schools. It is not clear, however, to what extent these court rulings have been successful in bringing about school integration nor how one should define *success* in the context of an issue as sweeping as school desegregation. As noted earlier, the vast majority of black children still attend predominantly minority classes, and many urban school districts have largely nonwhite student bodies. These conditions reflect segregated residential housing patterns as well as "white flight" from desegregated school districts. "White flight" is usually accompanied by "black middle-class flight" out of the public schools. Thus the minority population that is often concentrated in the public schools is disproportionately in need. In 1965 Congress first enacted the Elementary and Secondary Education Act, which targets some federal funds to school districts with "problems." Insofar as such districts tend to be disproportionately nonwhite some federal dollars now flow to "educationally distressed" largely nonwhite school districts. Also, many of the states have responded to the funding problems confronted by largely nonwhite urban school districts by establishing formulas for the distribution of state funds that will work to the advantage of these districts.

When one assesses "success" from the vantage of achievement levels, it is necessary to be cautious. Figures are most often published for school districts, not for particular schools. It therefore is difficult for members of the public to disaggregate test scores by schools or by race. The available measures of central tendency—which themselves have limited utility— are thus further limited in their usefulness in discussing success because they tend to aggregate entire districts.

When nonwhites live in integrated neighborhoods, they go to integrated schools. But, given the relatively small portion of the population that lives in racially mixed neighborhoods, this is not a major question to ponder. For example, in 1976 black households represented just 5 percent of all suburban households (Lake, 1979)—and of course not all of these residences were in integrated neighborhoods.

In the previous discussion the term *desegregation* was used rather than the term *integration*. This use of terminology was deliberate in that despite legal efforts to mix children of all races in public schools (integration), to date only *de jure* desegregation has transpired in most jurisdictions. Given this reality, other kinds of efforts have been made by black leaders to try to improve educational opportunities for blacks.

The most recent efforts by black groups in the area of education have focused on the maintenance of affirmative action programs and special quotas for admission of black students to specialized professional programs. The attention focused on *Baake v. Regents of the University of California* (438 U.S. 265) reflects this concern with quotas. In deciding the Baake case in 1978, the Supreme Court did not uphold the right of educational institutions to maintain admissions quotas for minorities (i.e., to put a certain number of their openings "in reserve" for minority groups members). When an institution maintains such a pool of positions, the likelihood of acceptance into programs—such as medicine, law, business, and engineering—is enhanced. The Court did uphold, however, the right of institutions to use race as one of several criteria to determine admissions.

The attention that has been focused by the black rights groups on both postsecondary education and on school desegregation has been criticized by some blacks as evidence of the middle-class bias of the movement. For example, William Julius Wilson (Friedman, 1980) has noted:

> Whereas the Humphrey-Hawkins bill is so designed as to address the problems of the poor, affirmative-action programs are designed to improve the job prospects for trained and educated minority members. Whereas the black poor would gain from a shift in emphasis from race to economic dislocation, more privileged blacks tend to emphasize, and, . . . have, for the moment, vested interest in keeping race as the single most important issue in developing policies to promote black progress.

Women also have been concerned with affirmative action programs. Just as these programs have either led to expanded opportunities for blacks or occurred simultaneous to these chances for blacks, so have opportunities for women improved in the era of affirmative action—though the extent of their successes has been questioned (Palley, 1978). More women attend professional schools and thus there are now more female doctors, lawyers, and business executives. Unlike the black movement, womens' groups have not entered the foray over quotas. In fact, they have not endorsed these programs for women. In part this is rooted in the belief that if sex is eliminated as a criterion for selection such that women are given an equal chance with men, women will be accepted into academic programs without any "special" programs or designations. Rather, the women's movement has focused considerable energies on the implementation of Title 9 of the Education Amendments of 1972, which requires that educational opportunities for women be equal to those provided for men (Fishel and Pottker, 1977). In particular, attention has been placed on achieving parity with men for women in school athletics (Gelb and Palley, 1982).

The groups in the feminist movement operating in a coalition known as the National Coalition for Women and Girls in Education has been reasonably successful in improving athletic opportunities for women in all stages of their education. Women have also been successful in reducing sex role stereotyping in education. In particular, courses that were restricted to boys only or to girls only are now open to children of both sexes. Thus, boys now take cooking and sewing classes and girls learn shop skills.

Just as affirmative action and quotas are seen by some observers to be middle-class black issues, so too are affirmative action and educational equity issues perceived by some critics of the womens' movement to be middle-class issues. These feminist concerns do not address the working conditions of low-wage women nor do they address the poor pay opportunities (wage and salary discrimination) noted in the previous discussion of female employment opportunities.

C. The Special Case of ERA and "Free Choice" Regarding Abortion Rights

Though the successes of the black and womens' groups in the areas of employment and education may be questioned as reflecting upper-class and middle-class concerns, often to the exclusion of the concerns of the less affluent, these groups nonetheless have been reasonably successful in achieving *some* of their goals. When discussing the Equal Rights Amendment (ERA) (Boles, 1979) and free choice regarding abortion (Gelb and Palley, 1982; Mohr, 1978), the discussion must turn from considerations of success to considerations of failure. Though ERA passed in the Congress in 1972, the womens' movement has not been able to generate support in enough states for ERA to become an amendment to the Constitution. Similarly, in 1973, in *Roe v. Wade* (4106 U.S. 179), the Supreme Court denied the right of states to interfere with the rights of a woman to have an abortion during the first trimester of pregnancy (Gelb and Palley, 1982). Since 1976, however, the Department of Health, Education and Welfare and the Department of Labor appropriations bill has had an amendment attached to it that bans the use of Medicaid funds to pay for most abortions. This is known as the Hyde amendment, named after its initial promoter, Rep. Henry Hyde (R., Ill.) Since this early legislative incursion on the rights granted women by the Court, Congress has denied funds for abortions to Peace Corps volunteers and military women and the dependents of military personnel. In addition, in 1980, the Supreme Court, in *Harris v. McRae* (100 S.Ct. 2671), upheld the constitutionality of the Hyde amendment (Gelb and Palley, 1982).

Why have womens' groups experienced failure in these two areas? Several explanations seem plausible. First, both of these issues divide women themselves. Thus, there are women in the countermovements to ERA and free choice (Brody and Tendin, 1976). Also, both of these issues are emotionally charged, and the anti groups have built on the emotionality of the issues. The anti-ERA movement warns that ERA will bring the draft to women along with integrated public toilets. The anti-free choice groups discuss dead fetuses and the murder of babies. In both instances, fundamental values effecting role change for women are being challenged by the feminist organizations when they support ERA and free choice. Finally, these are issues that are difficult to compromise; whereas stages can be developed to expand job opportunities or athletic facilities, stages to implement equal protection of the law—which women already possess under the Fourteenth amendment (Goldstein, 1979)—cannot be staged. Similarly, decisions regarding motherhood cannot be phased in gradually to poor women Medicaid recipients.

D. Assessment

Briefly, consider the pluralist theorems introduced earlier. Even if one finds it difficult to quantify success or finds the success to have a middle- and upper-class bias, one can impressionistically note achievements in the areas of both employment and education for blacks and women. In both of these areas, coalitions were built to provide broad-based support. For example, in the case of school desegregation, many groups have provided *amicus curia* briefs when the desegregation cases have been in the courts. Similarly, women's groups have garnered support from education and labor groups as well as from the traditional womens' organizations in their drive for educational and athletic equity. In addition, the employment and education issues that have been selected by blacks and women have been both defined in their scope and limited in their potential for dividing group members into competing groups. Thus all blacks and women want to receive equal pay for equal work, regardless of their relative class status, or in the case of women, their current out-of-home employment status. Though it has not been addressed in this chapter because of the limitations of space, policy networks have been established by blacks and women, though women have been more diligent in the administrative monitoring stages. This has been especially true regarding Title 9, where much of the detail of implementation has been worked out by bureaucratic agencies. In conjunction with this observation, it is significant to note that both blacks and women have been most willing to provide technical and informational resources to government officials. The Urban League and the NAACP both maintain ongoing data analyses that are provided to public decision makers. Similarly, womens' groups have been diligent in providing technical materials and analyses to public officials. Thus, in education, it was a women's monitoring effort that provided the data about the limited compliance checks by the Office of Civil Rights on Title 9, which in turn led to an investigation of that office's compliance reviews. Certainly, it must be clear that in the areas of employment and education, blacks and women have compromised. Neither movement has been able to achieve optimum conditions for the group, but some progress has been made for members of both groups. Finally, inasmuch as women and blacks have defined their success in terms of increments of change rather than in terms of total victory, they have been able to achieve some successes and, over time, some significant changes that have benefited blacks and women. Regarding ERA and free choice on abortion—as noted previously, these issues have not surfaced as sucess stories for the women's movement because of a variety of interrelated factors.

IV. CONCLUSIONS

Certainly, the conditions for some blacks and for some women have improved in the past decade. The groups that have been influential in representing blacks and women have

operated very much within the mode of pluralist politics and, perhaps ironically sometimes, the criticisms leveled at these movements is in the form of the charge that they are
too much a "part of the system."

Both the scholarly critics and the more popular social critics who appeal to the broad
base of society tend to generalize about groups and their members. Thus blacks are perceived by too many Americans to share more than racial characteristics and women are
assumed to share more than sexual characteristics. Variations in education, income, occupation, and more generally social class identification are thus glossed over. Most of the successes for both blacks and women have not been for the majority of blacks and women.
Most of the achievements have benefited the upper- and middle-class members of these
groups. In part it is these people who have the skills to succeed if they are given the opportunities. However, often the rights groups that are dominated by middle- and upper-class
interests and that have represented blacks and women have not focused their attentions on
the issues that more directly affect their less fortunate group cohorts. In the quest for improved life chances for blacks and women, there seems to be an element of social class
politics that often overrides concerns for the problems of the poor and the working class.

NOTE

1. Among the landmark school desegregation decisions are the 1954 opinion in *Brown v.
    The Board of Education of Topeka* (347 U.S. 483); the 1971 Supreme Court decision
    in *Swann v. Charlotte-Mecklenburg Board of Education* (402 U.S. 1); and the 1974
    Supreme Court decision in *Milikan v. Bradley* (74 S.Ct. 3112). In the area of desegre-
    gating housing patterns, Supreme Court decisions in 1948 in *Shelley v. Kramer* (344
    U.S. 1), *Hills v. Gautreaux* (1976, 96 S.Ct. 1538), and *Gladstone Realtors v. Village of
    Belwood* (1979, 77 L.W. 1493) have all addressed discrimination in housing patterns.

REFERENCES

Adams, C. T., and Ratner, R. S. (1980). *Equal Employment Policy for Women*. Temple
    University Press, Philadelphia, pp. 12-23.
Adams, C. T., and Winston, T. W. (1980). *Mothers at Work*. Longman, New York, chap. 1.
Alexis, M. (1979). A view of the urban ghetto. In *The Declining Significance of Race*, J. R.
    Washington, Jr. (Ed.). University of Pennsylvania Press, Philadelphia, pp. 41-42.
Barker, L., and McCoy, W. (1976). *Black Americans and the Political System*. Winthrop,
    Boston, chap. 7.
Barnett, M. R. (1977). Congressional Black Caucus: Symbol, myth and reality. *The Black
    Scholar*.
Boles, J. (1979). *The Politics of the ERA*. Longman, New York.
Brody, D., and Tendin, K. (1976). Ladies in pink: Religion and political ideology in the
    anti-ERA movement. *Social Science Quarterly 56*: 72-82.
Bryce, H. J., Cousar, G. J., and McCoy, W. (1978). Housing problems of black mayor
    cities. *Annals of the American Academy of Political and Social Science 439*: 80-89.
Costain, A. (1975). A social movement lobbies: Women's liberation and pressure politics.
    Paper presented at Southwest Political Science Association.
Fishel, A., and Pottker, J. (1977). *National Politics and Sex Discrimination in Education*.
    Lexington Heath, Lexington, MA, chap. 5.

Friedman, M. (1980). The new black intellectuals. *Commentary 69:* 51.

Gelb, J., and Palley, M. L. (1979). Women and interest group politics. *Journal of Politics 41:* 363.

Gelb, J., and Palley, M. L. (1982). *Women and Public Policies.* Princeton University Press, Princeton, NJ.

Goldstein, L. (1979). *The Constitutional Rights of Women.* Longman, New York, pp. 66-98.

Hopkins, A. (1980). Perceptions of employment discrimination in the public sector. *Public Administration Review 40:* 131-137.

Jones, M. H. (1978). Black political empowerment in Atlanta: Myth or reality. *Annals of the American Academy of Political and Social Science 439:* 90-117.

Lake, R. W. (1979). Racial transition and black homeownership in American suburbs. *Annals of the American Academy of Political and Social Science 441:* 142-156.

Mohr, J. (1978). *Abortion in America.* Oxford University Press, New York.

The New York Times (1980). August 12, pp. B1, B6.

Office of Personnel Management (1980). Telephone interview.

Orfield, G. (1978). *Must We Bus?* Brookings Institution, Washington, DC.

Palley, H. (1979). Abortion policy since 1973: Political cleavage and its impact on policy outputs. In *Race, Sex and Policy Problems*, M. L. Palley and M. B. Preston (Eds.). Lexington Heath, Lexington, MA, pp. 131-144.

Palley, M. L. (1976). Women and the study of public policy. *Policy Studies Journal 4:* 288-296.

Palley, M. L. (1978). Women as academic administrators in the age of affirmative action. *Journal of the National Association of Women Deans, Administrators and Counselors 42:* 3-9.

Palley, M. L., and Preston, M. B. (1979). *Race, Sex and Policy Problems.* Lexington Heath, Lexington, MA, p. 261.

Pettigrew, T. (1979). Racial change and social policy. *Annals of the American Academy of Political and Social Science 441:* 117.

The Roper Organization (1980). *1980 Virginia Slims American Women's Opinion Poll.* Roper Organization, New York.

Ruether, R. R. (Ed.) (1974). *Religion and Sexism.* Simon and Schuster, New York.

Schiller, B. (1980). *The Economics of Poverty and Discrimination, 3rd ed.* Prentice-Hall, Englewood Cliffs, NJ, p. 31.

Sindler, A. P. (1978). *Baake, DeFunis, and Minority Admissions.* Longman, New York.

Smith, R. (1978). The changing shape of urban black politics. *Annals of the American Academy of Political and Social Science 439:* 16-28.

Sunday News Journal (Wilmington, DE) (1980). June 29, p. A6.

Urban League (1978). *The State of Black America, 1978.*

U.S. Bureau of the Census (1977). *Current Population Reports*, Series P-60. U.S. Government Printing Office, Washington, DC.

Walton, H. (1972). *Black Politics.* Lippincott, Philadelphia, pp. 140-160.

Wilson, W. J. (1979). The declining significance of race: Myth or reality? In *The Declining Significance of Race*, J. R. Washington (Ed.). University of Pennsylvania Press, Philadelphia, pp. 10-14.

24

Criminal Justice Policy

Larry J. Cohen / University of Illinois, Chicago, Illinois

Citizens may be willing to forgive their governments for many failings or inadequacies, but typically not for an inability to ensure public safety and security. Concern to alleviate the fear and reality of crime and disorder is among the most fundamental social instincts. Government officials wary of running afoul of such fear are continually seeking ways to address the events and the perceptions that stimulate it. The search is sometimes frantic, as in the mid- and late 1960s when the threat of disorder was felt widely across the nation. More commonly, as now, there is less immediate pressure, but still persisting, nagging reminders from media reports and law enforcement statistics that crime continues apace.

An observation on the persistence of crime is an appropriate starting point for an overview of criminal justice policy. The control and disposition of criminal behavior plainly does lie at the heart of any such policy framework. Yet it is important to realize from the beginning that controlling crime per se is only one of a variety of functions served by the criminal justice system. Others include such things as contributing to social justice, maintaining order, defining and administering due process, mediating disputes, providing for the public safety and acting to preserve dominant values (Ruth, 1977: 79). Furthermore, criminal justice institutions, like any organizations, develop internal maintenance goals as well (see, e.g., Blumberg, 1979; Eisenstein and Jacob, 1977), which may conflict with those already mentioned. An obvious example is plea bargaining, where prosecutors, judges, and defense attorneys all have an interest in lowering charges and reducing sentences in return for guilty pleas as a way of pushing cases through the process (Abel, 1980; Alschuler, 1968; Heumann, 1978; Rosett and Cressey, 1976). Finally, there is considerable ideological controversy over which goals ought to be pursued and then how they can be achieved (compare Wilson, 1975; Inciardi, 1980; and Clark, 1969).

Criminal justice is an institutionally complex process as well. It involves a vast array of agencies spanning a variety of functional activities across all layers of government. City police, county felony court judges, prosecutors and defense attorneys, and state correctional institutions receive most of the attention, and also account for the largest share of manpower. But there are a variety of other criminal justice institutions as well, some well known (such as the Federal Bureau of Investigation, federal district courts, and county sheriff's departments) and others barely visible at all [such as lower criminal courts (Feeley, 1979), state planning agencies (Feeley et al., 1977) and U.S. attorneys (Eisenstein, 1978)]. Additionally, there is a growing realm of quasi-public agencies designed to deal with disputes generally, including crime-related controversies. Neighborhood justice centers, for instance, reflect an effort by the state to make use of the skills, influence, and sensitivities of community groups and individuals in dealing with less serious civil and criminal troubles (McGillis and Mullen, 1977). Such mechanisms not only divert cases from the formal process, but may provide more lasting solutions to problems (Danzig and Lowy, 1975). There is also an enormous private sector directly involved in or at least bearing on the activities of the criminal justice process. This includes not only private police (O'Toole, 1978; Kakalik and Wildhorn, 1972; Becker, 1974; Jacobs and O'Meara, 1979), but also the private industries and individuals serving the criminal justice system with hardware, technical advice, scholarly opinion, and program guidance (White and Krislov, 1977).

The criminal justice system, in short, is a vast network of agencies performing a variety of social functions (Skoler, 1977). Similarly vast is the scholarly and journalistic literature that describes and assesses the behavior of agencies and actors in that system. Fortunately, there are some vehicles available for finding one's way through this literature to particular areas of interest.[1] There are also extended discussions that provide an overview on criminal justice processes (Cole, 1980; Jacob, 1973; Neubauer, 1977; Silberman, 1978) and on criminal justice policy as well (Levine et al., 1973; Rhodes, 1977).

The problem we face here is how to do justice to this literature, and to the agencies, actors, and policy issues with which it is concerned, all within the limited space of a chapter. The simplest solution might be to describe briefly the various parts of the criminal justicy policy process, and then discuss the main issues that presently are and shortly may be faced therein. This approach would satisfy the interests of readers who simply want to know about criminal justice policy as it is presently developed and carried out. By itself, however, a focus on such instrumental matters as agency functions, responsibilities, and problems would present an incomplete picture. By taking the present system as given, it would ignore more fundamental questions about how crime policy problems are defined, how agency responsibilities are set and allocated, and how goals are determined and evaluated. Such questions are often ignored in crime policy research and debates because they are at least temporarily resolved within present practices. Yet such resolutions are hardly uncontroversial and certainly not immutable, and thus must as well be part of our inquiry. We seek to merge these instrumental and reflective/critical concerns in what follows. Specifically, as we review present and likely future policy issues in the several main parts of the criminal justice process, we also consider some of the implicit assumptions reflecting particular interests and biases in that process. At the end such assumptions are drawn together in a broader discussion of the political dimension of this policy enterprise.

I. THE CRIME PROBLEM

Technically speaking, crime is simply "any act for which a court may lawfully impose punishment" (Glaser, 1978: 15). Those who refer to the "crime problem" or "crime crisis" normally have a much more specific referent in mind than that, however. Violent crimes, such as robbery, rape, assault, and homicide, and intrusions against private property, such as burglary, larceny, and auto theft, are what stimulate that "fear of crime" (Harris, 1969) which is purportedly so prevalent in American society today (Silberman, 1978). The most recent crisis surfaced in the early 1960s, when the two previously quiet decades were followed by dramatic reported increases in the above "street crime" categories (Cho, 1974). These increases have continued into the late 1970s (Block, 1977). Some categories will continue on this line, although some projections suggest a leveling or decreasing in some categories in the years ahead (Cohen et al., 1980; Fox, 1978).

In many important respects, the "crime problem" so defined is a pressing and significant public concern. Individual costs are high, both those incurred by the immediate victim (Gray, 1979; Barkas, 1978) and those of potential victims as well (Balch et al., 1978). Social costs are substantial, too, in the investment made for law enforcement services, in the loss of productivity due to changed or terminated behavior patterns, in the waste of scarce and irreplaceable resources (e.g., energy: Balkin, 1978), and in the damage done to social relationships, including especially the sense of alienation engendered (Conklin, 1975). Furthermore, crime is by no means distributed evenly across all groups in society. Certain classes of citizens are particularly susceptible to and especially harmed by victimization, including the elderly (Haber, 1976), women (Hursch, 1977; Chappell et al., 1979; Walker, 1979; Walker and Barofsky, 1976; Brownmiller, 1976; Hilberman, 1976), the poor (Reiman, 1979), and minority group members (Hindelang et al., 1977). Those most likely to be victimized are typically those least able to afford it, and also least able to make their problems and losses known.

Serious and real as the consequences of this view of the crime problem are, it hardly yields a complete or undistorted picture. First, it is important to recognize that the "crime problem" is by no means a strictly modern one. In numerical terms, there may now be more recorded crime than ever before, but violence and disorder were perceived as equally widespread and destructive, if not more so, in times past (Barnes, 1926, 1931; Boone, 1872; Fielding, 1751; Lydston, 1908). David Rothman contends that it was the sense of such pervasive lawlessness that gave rise to the modern penal movement (1971). Similar perceptions spurred the creation of the modern local police force (Rubinstein, 1973; Fogelson, 1977). Later, a concern that "respect for the law as law is fading from the sensibilities of our people" led President Hoover to support the first national crime commission. His charge to locate the "shortcomings of the administration of justice" and the "causes and remedies for them" (cited in Ruth, 1971: 6,8) would essentially be repeated with the 1967 Presidential Crime Commission and the 1973 National Advisory Commission on Criminal Justice Standards and Goals. Finally, a look at the cross-national data reveals crime perceived as a major dilemma in much of the rest of the developed (Radzinwicz and King, 1977; Gurr et al., 1977; Neumann, 1976; Nettler, 1974) and developing (Clinard and Abbott, 1973) world.

Second, one might well take issue with limiting the scope of the crime problem to street crime offenses. For all the genuine suffering associated with such offenses, it nonetheless has been argued that more harm is done overall to more people by illegal corporate practices (Conklin, 1977; Herlihy and Levine, 1976; Stone, 1971; Ermann and Lundman, 1978), government corruption (Rose-Ackerman, 1978; Gardiner and Olsen, 1974; Gardiner and Lyman, 1978; Reisman, 1979; Sherman, 1978), and various other white-collar criminal activities (Sheldon and Zweibel, 1975; Edelhertz, 1975; Katz, 1980; Parker, 1976; Berquai, 1978; Farr, 1975). There are several reasons why these offenses receive relatively less attention than do street crimes. For one, corporate bribes and government kickbacks do not bear so directly or leave such obvious scars as assaults and burglaries. Consequently, there is no perceived immediate or severe suffering with which citizens can identify. Second, the perpetrators are often influential elites who can hide their culpability or minimize any repercussions. Finally, as Henry Ruth has commented, "we are prisoners to a degree of what we have measured" (1977: 5). Police statistics, and their compilation by the Federal Bureau of Investigation in the UCRs, or *Uniform Crime Reports* (Federal Bureau of Investigation, 1930-present) focus on street crime offenses.[2] It is that set of data which is reported in the media, which is the basis for resource allocation decisions, and to which the public attends in its concern about crime.

Although these reported crime statistics are central to public debate and to criminal justice policy processes generally, their validity and reliability have been and continue to be matters of controversy. At issue is the so-called dark figure of crime (Oba, 1908, Radzinowicz and King, 1977), the widely recognized gap between criminal events officially recorded and actually occurring in society. Certainly part of the explanation for this gap lies in the "furtive nature" of crime, often leaving even the victim "unclear about what has happened, when, or by whom" (Skogan, 1977: 3). This hidden quality of crime entails an area of darkness that no amount of effort is likely to enlighten. More readily discoverable, and probably of greater significance in creating the "dark figure" are such factors as the disjunction between personal and legal definitions of an event as criminal,[3] the failure of victims to report acknowledged criminal offenses, and the manipulation of the data by police and other public officials to serve their own personal, political, and organizational ends (Black, 1970).

It is impossible, at least at this point, to know just how seriously flawed these official data may be. Surely the inaccuracies are more serious for some offenses—for example, assaults—than for others—for example, murder and auto theft—but in the absence of a measure that compensates for the errors in official rates, we cannot know very precisely just how great the inaccuracies are. Furthermore, as Richard Sparks (1977) and others have observed, the gap probably fluctuates over time and place. As a result, comparative analyses are inevitably beset with serious deficiencies when they use official data.

Recognition of the problems with official data spurred the development of an alternative measurement device, the victimization survey. In this approach, population sample members are asked to report any victimization experiences that occurred during a reference period. Crime incidence rates are then estimated using standard statistical estimation techniques. The approach is a justifiable improvement on theoretical grounds because it records the criminal event directly from a participant, avoiding the aberrations produced

Table 1. Official Statistics (Uniform Crime Reports) and Victimization Surveys
(National Crime Survey): Means, Standard Deviations, and Ranges for 26 Selected Cities[a]

Category	Means			Standard Deviations			Ranges		
	UCR	NCS	NCS/ UCR	UCR	NCS	NCS/ UCR	UCR	NCS	NCS/ UCR
Auto theft	1,180	1,279	1.1	498	464	0.2	2,227	2,261	1.1
Robbery	690	1,993	3.3	302	582	1.4	1,198	2,216	8.4
Burglary	2,279	6,395	3.1	790	1,528	1.1	3,292	6,493	6.1
Larceny	3,156	10,860	3.7	1,102	3,760	1.5	4,584	14,634	7.0
Rape	58	153	2.9	18	55	1.4	64	233	6.0
Assault	423	1,102	3.4	178	354	2.5	799	1,478	11.6

[a]All estimates are per 100,000 population. See Cohen and Lichbach (1982).

in organizational processes and organizational/individual interactions (Monkonnen, 1977, 1979).

As expected, the surveys point to considerably more crime than has been reported in the official police data. Note, though, that the differences between the two measures are not consistent across offense types (see Table 1). These inconsistencies are due in part to the nature of the offenses, with their respective psychological and material costs and benefits in reporting. Embarrassment, for instance, undoubtedly inhibits rape reporting by victims, whereas availability of insurance claims boosts the reporting of auto thefts. Yet it is also possible that the variations observed are methodological artifacts, due in part to differences in the definition of an incident in each and in part to differences in the jurisdictional reference points. Thus, whereas the police record only those incidents that occur within their area of responsibility, the surveys record any victimizations experienced anywhere by the respondent.[4] Finally, all surveys are unreliable to some degree, because of memory problems, falsification, ambiguity in wording, coding problems and, when one generalizes statistical estimation limitations (Mendenhall et al., 1971).

Still, the survey is an invaluable tool for policy research, providing not only better insight on the level of crime, but also the opportunity to address previously inaccessible questions about the problems and experiences of the victim, the all-too-often forgotten link in the chain of criminal events (McDonald, 1979a). Survey-based research has made it possible to confirm, for instance, the particular susceptibility of the poor, and especially the poor black male youth, to victimization (Hindelang et al., 1978). As for the fear of crime, the evidence indicates that it is very often those who are less likely to be victimized who are more likely to be fearful. This suggests that success in crime control efforts alone may not greatly affect the public's concern about crime (Garofalo, 1979). Policies aimed at dealing with that fear are also needed (Skogan and Klecka, 1977). As for the victimization experience, the surveys indicate, for instance, that only about 10 percent of personal crime victims are seriously injured, that self-protection efforts by victims increase the likelihood of injury, and that this likelihood is less when the offender has a gun than with any other weapon. Finally, the surveys speak to the law enforcement process too, with Skogan and Antunes (1979) demonstrating that the frequency of reporting crime experiences to the police and the usefulness of the information provided for solving crimes vary tremendously among crime categories. Given the importance of information supplied by the victim in clearing cases (Bloch and Bell, 1976), there are severe limitations on what government agencies alone can do about most serious crimes. Skogan and Antunes conclude with a discussion of ways to enhance the role of citizens as "co-producers of police outputs" (p. 232).

If the greatest advantage of the victim survey lies in its redefinition of the crime problem as a problem that individual citizens face, therein too lies its greatest potential danger. With crime viewed from the victim's perspective, we risk seeing the victim as responsible by virtue of a failure to modify behavior in such a way as to reduce susceptibility to criminal experiences (Ryan, 1969; Crawford, 1977). The problem becomes exacerbated to the extent that we expect the individual to absorb the cost of that behavior change, or assess costs (as with insurance claims) after the incident has occurred. The issue here is not the wisdom of individuals taking precautions to protect themselves, but rather the burden imposed, both material and psychological, when society makes the victim's actions an issue in crime control.

There are other definitional problems in the surveys too, as with their focus on street crimes and their inattention to what George Cole calls "upperworld" and "organized" crime (1980: 5). In this, however, surveys are no worse than the police reports discussed earlier. The answer, in the end, is not simply one of how we may better measure particular events. It is that to be sure, but is even more fundamentally a question of what we decide to measure, and ultimately what we choose to include in the "crime problem." Later in this chapter we explore the political dimension of crime definition further.

II. CRIMINAL JUSTICE POLICY PROCESSES

Before reviewing the specific institutions of criminal justice policy, some general comments are in order to place the broader process in context. The demographics alone are fairly overwhelming. There are 56,339 state and local and 967 federal criminal justice agencies, including prosecutorial, defense, law enforcement, adjudication, and correctional functions. This state and especially local domination is mirrored in the personnel and expenditure figures. Thus, of the more than 1 million criminal justice employees, 10 percent are federal, 28 percent state, and 62 percent local officials. The nearly $20 billion annual expenditures reflect 12.5 percent federal, 26.4 percent state, and 61.1 percent local dollars (U.S. Department of Justice, 1979). Law enforcement dominates these resource commitments at the federal and local levels, but policing is second to correctional processes at the state level.

Although a decentralized system has many advantages, especially in allowing a close connection between local culture and crime policy (Ostrom et al., 1978), it entails some problems as well. Chief among these is a lack of consistency in treatment across jurisdictions, both for defendants in their adjudication and the citizenry in their protection. There are also limitations on the potential for innovation, arising from the lack of external knowledge and the shortage of experimental funds. These last two problems were the dominant force behind the federal effort during the past 15 years to redirect the course of criminal justice policy at all levels. Looking back, it is now clear that those efforts have largely failed (Cohen, 1979), and with the proposed dismantling of the Law Enforcement Assistance Administration the present fractionalized practices will likely continue.

This fractionalization also has consequences for comprehending the criminal justice system. On the one hand, procedural due process requirements in the law and professional norms and traditions set a framework for behavior common to all jurisdictions. On the other hand, various constraints impinge on that framework, producing a range of specific practices in and outcomes of social control activity. Chief among these constraints is a disjunction between the resources available to and demands for the services of criminal justice agencies. The size and shape of this disjunction, and the way in which criminal justice actors respond to it reflect the political, social, economic, and cultural environments in which their agencies are located. Other constraints similarly affected by the environment include the variable competence of the actors in the process; the interests, expectations, and needs of these actors; demands by influential individuals and groups outside the process; and the problem of relating ambiguous laws to specific actions.

One recent effort to make sense of variable practices and dispositions in the midst of a common framework focuses on the organizational quality of criminal justice processes (Rossum, 1978; Eisenstein and Jacob, 1977). On this view, it is not the individual case that matters most in explanation, but the working relationships that develop among actors routinely interacting to dispose of criminal problems. Such interactions are a specific response in any jurisdiction to the constraints noted above. The resulting patterns of behavior are not immune to individual idiosyncracies or changes in the relevant substantive or procedural law. They are, however, relatively stable over time, as one would expect in any continuing organization. In the discussion that follows, we focus on the factors that contribute to these patterns, and especially the constraints that underlie them.[5]

A. Policing

The police are the gatekeepers of the criminal justice system (Manning, 1971). Their actions largely determine which cases enter that system, both directly through their own decisions to label incidents as crimes, and indirectly through their influence on citizens to report their own and others' victimizations (Dubow et al., 1979). Furthermore, the evidence the police collect, their methods of doing so, and their actions in dealing with offenders all set significant constraints on the subsequent course of litigation. Finally, with their monopoly on the "legitimate use of force," the police are the preeminent and most visible symbol of the state's interest in repressing allegedly "dangerous," antisocial behavior in society.

There is a tendency to think about and discuss policing as if it were some unidimensional phenomenon. Descriptively, nothing could be further from the truth. There are 19,523 independent law enforcement agencies (U.S. Department of Justice 1979: 42,44). Even more important than sheer numbers, though, are the facts of different working environments (from rural to suburban to urban), different service demands (depending on the local culture and political system), and different functional responsibilities (depending on the level of government served) (Felkenes, 1973). Research on policing has usually focused on large metropolitan departments. This is not entirely inappropriate, because most felony crimes occur within their jurisdictions (Jacob, 1973). Yet small departments deserve attention too, especially in the areas of recruitment, training, resource availability, and the satisfaction of due process requirements. In the end, there are surely generic problems and solutions in policing, but policy must equally be sensitive to the distinctive issues facing the different kinds of enforcement agencies.

Perhaps the central generic problem is the identity crisis in the policing role. The traditional role model is that of law enforcer, which envisions "high priority to vigorous enforcement of all the criminal law by professionally trained officers" (Rhodes, 1977: 77). Yet police actually spend the vast majority of their time performing service and order maintenance activities (Rossum, 1978), the precise distribution across these tasks depending on community values (Wilson, 1968). The operational problem for the police is reconciling the incompatabilities in these demands (Skolnick, 1975). For the policy analyst it is developing performance measures in the face of an ambiguous set of expectations (Ruchelman, 1974).

The performance measure issue deserves special mention. Even if there was agreement on the centrality of crime prevention, certain difficulties would remain. The more efficient the police are in detecting crime, the more ineffective they appear to be, and "whatever amount of crime they actually do prevent by their presence on the street cannot be demonstrated" (Rubenstein, 1973: 368), at least not directly. The ratio of crimes cleared by arrest to crimes known is the most common efficiency measure used, but this measure is easily manipulated (Skolnick, 1975), and in any event it does not speak to the crime incidence problem itself, the focus of policy concern. Should public satisfaction be the measure of police effectiveness, or are task-related measures more appropriate (Ostrom, 1973)? Plainly, further debate is needed.

Discretion is another fundamental problem in policing. Working unsupervised because of geographic isolation, guided by ambiguous laws and rules, confronted by events of immense variety, and expected to act on a moment's notice, the individual patrolman is both forced and expected to use independent judgment in any given situation. A number of factors will influence that judgment, including the patrolman's understanding of the law, peer expectations, personal beliefs, personal fear, supervisor's expectations, offender behavior, citizen demands, and available resources (van Maanen, 1974; LaFave, 1965; Black, 1970; Wilson, 1968). Still, the final decision on both whether and when to act rests with the individual. This tremendous breadth of discretion poses an inevitable constraint on the consistent and systematic implementation of policies. Time and again, programs have been impeded by the unwillingness of those in the street to carry them through (see, e.g., Campbell and Ross, 1968).

Although this individual access to power has always been present, police officers have recently been seeking a more active, collective role in the workplace. This comes in the form of union organizing within major departments across the country (Juris and Feuille, 1973). In the past police organized in fraternal organizations, but their influence was limited by the absence of recourse to job actions to back up their positions. Local police benevolent associations and their national counterpart, the International Association of Chiefs of Police, certainly influenced policy (Bent, 1974; Kranz et al., 1979), but nowhere near the extent that becomes possible once power is concentrated within unions. Opponents express concern that such power may lead to a police state, whereas proponents counter that the movement is really interested only in personnel matters. There is a thin dividing line between operational and personnel issues, however, and it remains to be seen how law enforcement policy will change as unions become further entrenched in the years ahead.

A number of other issues are also on the policy agenda. The use of violence by the police is a perennial concern (Chevigny, 1969; Reiss, 1968), as are police infringements on individual liberties generally (American Friends Service Committee, 1979). Debate on this issue increases and decreases over time as particularly severe incidents attract attention, but a more detailed reading of history will disclose that the problem has endured from place to place over the years (Goldstein, 1978). Similarly enduring is the organizational debate over centralized versus decentralized policing. Those favoring metropolitanization point to economies of scale, policy unity, and better coordinated operations (Berkeley, 1970), whereas opponents focus on evidence of greater citizen satisfaction with smaller departments (Ostrom and Baugh, 1973) and harken to the dangers of concentrated force. Within departments, there is controversy over the desirability of specialized units, proponents again pointing to efficiencies while foes caution against the dangers of vested interests and power concentration (Elliot, 1971; Davis, 1973; Klein et al, 1976; Halper and Ku, 1974). The utilization of trained officers is also an issue, with debate focusing on the proper role of paraprofessionals (Tien and Larsen, 1978), patrol staffing (Larsen, 1976; Boydston et al., 1978), and team policing (Sherman et al., 1973; Bloch and Specht, 1973). Finally, policy makers will always be concerned about the temptations that police face to use their power to serve their own ends (Maas, 1973). Although we can hope that the corruption problem will decline following government inquiry, as with the Knapp Commission study in New York City (1973), hardly anyone can seriously believe that it will really be eradicated (Sherman, 1974). The policy question is how much effort we want to invest in controlling what we can of it.

B. Prosecution

If the police department is the gatekeeper of the criminal justice system, the prosecutor's office is its management center. This may seem an odd portrayal in view of traditional and popular characterizations of the courtroom as the locus of all criminal case activity, with the prosecutor merely one litigant therein. However, with guilty pleas accounting for the vast majority of all case findings (Newman, 1966; Rosett and Cressey, 1976), it is plainly what goes on before the final hearing that matters most. This includes decisions as to which cases will be litigated, what charges will be brought against those arrested, what evidence will be collected and how it will be used, and what dispositions will be sought and accepted (Miller, 1969). The police, defense attorneys, and judges all participate in various aspects of these decisions, but the prosecutor alone is involved throughout. As William McDonald so aptly puts it, these matters comprise the prosecutor's "domain" (1979).

Conduct within that domain naturally varies with the context in which the prosecutor's office is located (Jacoby, 1979). Federal prosecutors, for example, have much less freedom than do their local counterparts because bureaucratic controls exercised in the U.S. Department of Justice are stronger than in most county offices (Rhodes, 1977). Some of this difference may be mitigated in states where the state attorney general exercises control over local prosecution, but such centralization is rare, controversial, and considerably less effective than that found in the federal system (National District Attorneys

Association, 1973). There are similarly great and intuitively understandable differences in style and behavior between small and often part-time rural state's attorney's offices and their large, highly bureaucratized urban counterparts (Revzin, 1976a, 1976b). Sentencing structure also affects the nature of prosecution (Ohlin and Remington, 1958), with prosecutors enjoying considerably more influence in determinate than indeterminate systems (LaGoy et al., 1979). With sentences fixed under determinate laws, the charging decision assumes tremendous importance in the nature of the final disposition upon conviction (Greenberg and Humphries, 1980). The political structure may also affect prosecutorial behavior (Johnson, 1973), although the significance of this factor relative to organizational and task pressures is a matter of debate (Jacob, 1963; Eisenstein and Jacob, 1977).

Although much of the prosecutor's domain has been left unexplored (Cole, 1973; McDonald, 1979), decision processes associated with plea bargaining have been closely examined. Two concerns are at issue: first, the danger of systematic biases in the treatment of particular classes of offenders; and second, the general danger that prosecutors will abuse their authority to invoke the power of the state in order to enhance their bargaining position. Alan Alschuler, in particular, has pointed to the coercive and deceptive aspects of overcharging to ensure an enhanced negotiation position (1968). The reasons for plea bargaining are many, but mainly involve the combined interest of the prosecutor in disposing of cases and of the defendant in minimizing the sanction assigned. There has been speculation that racial factors enter the negotiation process, that rewards are built in for avoiding trial, and that repeat offenders are best able to manipulate the system to their own advantage. Although all of this probably bears some truth, current research suggests that legal criteria and organizational processes better explain the nature and conduct of the plea bargaining process (Eisenstein and Jacob, 1977; Cole, 1979; Heumann, 1978; Skolnick, 1975). More specifically, it is the nature of the evidence and the seriousness of the charges on the one hand, and organizational relationships, especially the socialization of the prosecutor to the organization's efficiency goals, on the other, that matter most. Such findings do not undercut the call for reform aimed either at drawing more interested actors into the plea bargaining process (Kerstetter, 1981), or providing guidelines for plea bargaining (National Advisory Commission on Criminal Justice Standards and Goals, 1973). They do suggest, though, that the policy issue is less one of individual abberations and more a structural matter (Langbein, 1977).

We stand on the verge of a tremendous enhancement of our understanding of the prosecuting function. The main impediment has been the lack of systematic data, not only on plea bargaining, but also on various other aspects of the prosecutor's domain. Recently, a computer-based management system has been instituted that will not only aid the prosecutor in managing office functions, but will also provide researchers with detailed data on those functions. Thus, PROMIS (Prosecutor's Management Information System) will permit exploration of such things as evidence collection and usage, the role and use of witnesses, scheduling to reduce delay, and bail processes (Hamilton, 1979). As the system is placed in more jurisdictions, the opportunity for comparative research on these and other issues will be enhanced as well.

C. Defense

Our notions of justice envision two opposing camps in criminal proceedings, each roughly equal in their capacity to present their claims. Such a view explains the provision in the Sixth Amendment for defense counsel in all federal criminal proceedings, but it was not until *Powell v. Alabama* (1932) that the same principle was explicitly extended to the states. Limited at first in its application, the Supreme Court has subsequently broadened its interpretation of the right to include the indigent, accusations in the police station, and, most recently, even misdemeanor cases where imprisonment is a possible outcome (Barker and Barker, 1978). Providing for such a right is one thing, though, and ensuring its implementation is quite another. For a number of reasons, competent defense representation is a rarity.

Briefly, defense representation involves either privately retained counsel, in which an accused person pays an attorney for representation, or assigned counsel, in which the court provides for representation. Such assignment may be from a pool of private attorneys willing occasionally to represent criminal defendants, from among court house "hangers on" who rely on these referrals for their professional income, or from public defender (PD) offices, supported by the state as separate agencies (Ashman and Ansperk, 1971). Assigned attorneys are available only to indigents, although what this means precisely is not always clear. Some states simply employ the individual's available resources as a measure of indigency, whereas others consider as well the financial burden on defendants who must provide their own representation (Jacob, 1976). Given the increasing unwillingness of states to support social services of any type, it would not be surprising to see increasing use of the more restrictive criterion in the years ahead.

Given a choice, defendants would apparently prefer privately retained counsel. As Jonathan Casper reports from his interviews with prison inmates, the answer to the question, "Did you have a lawyer?" was often "No, I had a public defender" (1972). Distrust grows out of the fact that public defenders are paid by the same state that supports the prosecution, and is enhanced where case loads prevent PDs from spending much time with their clients. When one adds to this the reality that most public defender clients are found guilty or so plead, the poor image they suffer is not difficult to understand. Yet the evidence does not justify this conclusion. Research suggests that when one takes account of the seriousness of the offense and the offender's prior record, public defenders do only slightly worse than private attorneys on convictions and actually do better in the severity of the sentence (Eisenstein and Jacob, 1977).

The explanation for this apparent paradox lies in the nature of private criminal law practice. Although there are some private attorneys for whom such practice is a lucrative venture, in most cases it is a marginal, or at best modestly rewarding career. It represents the lowest step on the profession's status hierarchy, with criminal attorneys in essence judged by the company they keep (Neubauer, 1974). It is financially problematic, first because most clients are unable to pay very much for legal service, and second because collecting the fee can be a chore as well. Those who lose, and most do, will not want to pay, and those who win will be in no great hurry either. Some states have sought to resolve this dilemma by tying the bail refund to the lawyer's payment, and criminal attorneys typically require payment in advance otherwise. Although this may solve the payment problem in one sense, it has the consequent effect of discouraging further effort on be-half of the client beyond that necessary to justify the available sum. This, combined with the small fee, makes it essential for the attorney to turn over cases as quickly as possible. The result is what Abraham Blumberg calls a "confidence game," in which the private attorney tries to win over the client's trust sufficiently to get him or her to go along with whatever strategy and tactics are proposed (1967).

The fee pressure experienced by private counsel is paralleled in the public defender's office by an enormous case load. The resultant pressure is to move cases along as quickly as possible. The public defender cannot ignore the watchful eye of citizen governing boards that monitor his or her activities (Eisenstein and Jacob, 1977), but neither can the mounting case load be ignored. Similarly, the assigned counsel experiences substantial pressure, whether it is from a wholly separate practice that demands attention away from this "atypical" case, or from the need to turn cases over to amass a reasonable income. Overall, assigned attorneys lack the trust and hence the "client control" enjoyed by the private defender (Skolnick, 1967), but must nonetheless work to achieve the same results.

Contrary to defendant perceptions, public defenders are in a better bargaining posi-tion vis-a-vis the prosecutor because they handle more cases than individual private attorneys. As a result, they gain more familiarity with the prosecutor and also have more resources with which to bargain. The available evidence indicates that PDs typically foster this cooperative relationship, with relatively few public defenders indicating that they see themselves as competitors of their prosecuting counterparts (Wice and Pilgrim, 1975). Like prosecutors, they develop a hardened view of their role over time, ultimately losing sight of the individual distinctiveness of their cases, and treating them instead as "normal crimes," with each category to be managed like all the similar ones that pre-ceded it (Sudnow, 1965). The routinized quality of the work and its associated pressure help explain the heavy turnover in the public defender's staff, and hence the relative youth and inexperience in these offices (Eckart and Stover, 1974). Equally frustrating must be the limited support services that are available, especially of investigators to help prepare cases. Still, with these few resources they are better off than most private attorn-eys (Baker and Meyer, 1980).

These several problems—pressure, status, salary, and job frustration—account for the biggest dilemma of the criminal bar, the shortage of attorneys (Wice, 1978). The image problem begins in law school, where criminal law is not a much emphasized part of the curriculum. Also, legal education focuses on doctrinal analysis and drafting skills, not the oral advocacy and client relationship qualities needed by the criminal bar. Greater govern-ment subsidization might increase the attractiveness of criminal law activity, but such support is unlikely in the current period of government service reduction. Reorganization of the public defender's office to allow more attention to individual clients might also help, but, again, resource limitations will probably prevent this. Some might try to justify the present state of affairs by observing that most criminal defendants are guilty anyway. Even if true, this begs the question of the rights of those individuals to a fair and com-petent defense.

D. Judging

With the vast majority of cases disposed of through defense/prosecutor negotiations before trial, what power and influence remains for the criminal court judge (Jones, 1965)? The judge may well be quite passive during such negotiations, although some do inject themselves directly in the discussions. If not, even the passive judge remains an obstacle whose approval will be needed to make the agreement work. When trials are held, the judge oversees the process, especially crucial decisions on the admission of evidence and the charge to the jury. Finally, a more expansive look at the criminal court organization reveals a central role for judges in arraignment, bail hearings, pretrial motion hearings, and sentence rulings (American Bar Association, 1972). In short, organizational tasks still require a great deal of activity, even in plea-dominated systems, and beyond that judges may expand or contract their activities as their role conceptions deem fit (Blumberg, 1979; Gibson, 1978; Heyderbrand, 1977).

Whatever the role specifically entails, the judge's actions are hardly unconstrained (Jacob, 1973). First, the law sets basic guidelines, establishing the framework within which all decisions may be reached. However, the law is necessarily ambiguous, intended to cover a broad array of behaviors (Carter, 1979), and thus leaves the judge with considerable discretion in any given instance. More compelling is the case-load pressure, with the demand for disposition far exceeding what the court's scarce resources can manage effectively (Neubauer, 1977). Judicial behavior is consequently driven throughout by the knowledge that anything other than the quickest possible action will engender personal frustration, defendant suffering, and public criticism (Ash, 1973). Finally, the judge is under considerable pressure from the attorneys, who seek the court's cooperation in return for their assistance in faciliataing the case-load management problem (Smith and Blumberg, 1967).

Reformers concerned about the way in which judges handle these constraints in addressing their role responsibilities have focused on the problem of judicial selection. The historical model is executive appointment, on the assumption that the chief executive of the state is best able to identify the most qualified people for the bench (Chase, 1972). Reformers concerned about political influence in the selection process, and also desiring more direct public accountability, have advocated elections, either through a partisan or a nonpartisan ballot procedure (Nagel, 1973). Yet neither of these approaches (particularly the latter) has produced much public interest, with the consequent charge that either party identification or image ends up mattering more than qualification. Also, because incumbents are usually reelected, and because most incumbents were originally appointed to fill vacancies, the democratic quality of the process is illusory. Thus, so-called merit plans have been strongly pressed in several states, combining in principle the benefits of appointment with public participation (Ashman and Alfini, 1974). Yet here too it is questionable whether merit is the central concern, because nomination commissions are no less free from special interest sentiments than are the other approaches (Watson and Downing, 1969).

Some contend that this debate over selection method is wasted effort, because different plans ultimately produce essentially similar people for the bench. This is not to deny some differences, as with the advantage of politically connected people under the executive appointed and partisan election methods, and of bar association elites under merit plans. However, it is often contended that patterns of decision making actually vary little, perhaps because the role more conditions the occupant than does the occupant the role. Some evidence contradicts this wisdom, though. Most notable is Martin Levin's (1977) finding that recruitment channels help explain the greater severity in sentencing of Minneapolis judges than those in Pittsburgh. The latter come to office through the political machine, developing sympathy along the way for those ultimately facing them as defendants, whereas the reform politics of Minneapolis yields jurists more abstracted from litigants in their courtrooms.

In addition to reasserting the utility of the selection method issue itself, Levin's work also leads us to the prior question of what criteria we should use to evaluate judicial performance (Rosenberg, 1966; Cohen, 1980). Who, for instance, is the preferable jurist, the legalistic and universalistically oriented judges of Minneapolis, or their nonlegalistic and individualistically oriented counterparts in Pittsburgh? Beyond this, is sentencing the only factor we want to take into account? One major aspect of the judge's role, and one rarely considered in detail, is the court management function. It is necessary to ensure that the various administrative staff members perform their responsibilities consistent with the needs of the judge and the litigants. This not only affects present cases, but past ones as well, where, for instance, accurate file information is needed. Unfortunately, judges are to some degree at the mercy of the sponsoring organization that provides the personnel to fill these positions. Similarly in the disposition of cases, judges must make do with whatever quality attorney arrives in the courtroom from the district attorney's or public defender's offices, or the private defense bar.

Looking beyond such management issues, judges also engage in negotiation, legal writing, and legal research. As with the other role tasks, the issues are (1) how to evaluate the performance of these responsibilities, and then (2) what weight to assign them in making a final judgment as to overall competence. Bar polls provide one answer, with lawyers evaluating aspects of the performance of judges before whom they practice (Guterman and Meidinger, 1977; Meidinger, 1977). This is not altogether satisfactory, however, for even though such individuals may be more attentive to legal skills than any other observer, we may reasonably ask whether their perspective is the one we wish to see emphasized in evaluations (Schmidt, 1976). Perhaps the opinions of witnesses, defendants, victims, interest groups, and the public generally should be solicited as well. Judicial review boards (Wheeler and Jackson, 1976) composed of other trial and appellate judges are problematic for the same reason. Still, they have an enforcement dimension that bar polls lack, although the bar polls are much broader in the range of competence issues addressed. The boards consider directly only instances of incompetence, and not adequate or high-quality behavior.

If judges are more than slaves to their role, performance evaluation criteria and methods are essential future policy issues. Given what has already been observed, and the fact that trial decisions are normally final, it is consequential, both to the individual citizen and society generally, who is put on the bench and how well they perform once there. Some standard measures are surely possible, although we must not lose sight of the diversity of working environments already noted. Judges in different contexts (federal or state; urban, suburban, or rural) experience substantially different demands and pressures (Dolbeare, 1967). Some flexibility will therefore be necessary in our assessments.

E. Corrections

The term "corrections" invariably calls forth the popular image of a massive, multitiered maximum security prison, with small cells, towered walls, and an expansive activity yard. These Attica, Stateville, and Soledad-like facilities do exist, but they in fact represent only a small piece of the American correctional picture. Compare the 172 state prisons with the 3921 local jails, and the 118,000 prison inmates with the 1.4 million adults under state parole and probation services (Parisi et al., 1979). Add in federal institutions and supervision functions, juvenile correctional processes, community-based programs and various kinds of special treatment centers. Then, impose multiple goals on the process, including, to greater and lesser degrees at various times, rehabilitation, deterrence, incapacitation, and retribution. The result is a montage well beyond the comprehension or grasp of any single set of policy actors.

This is not to ignore the various themes that have dominated correctional policy at any given time (Rothman, 1971). Until recently, for instance, the theme was "rehabilitation," with institutionalization justified by the belief that offenders could be made law-abiding citizens through psychological, biological, economic, and sociologically based treatment methods. Rehabilitation has fallen from favor of late, though, replaced by calls for deterrence and/or incapacitation. It is charged that rehabilitation has failed, or at best achieved mixed results (Lipton et al., 1975). Without necessarily disputing this, it is nonetheless important to realize that such empirical claims are not by themselves determinative of correctional policy. Rather, they contribute to the more fundamental value debate over what we seek in punishment efforts. Thus, as Robert Martinson has observed, whereas a 50 percent rehabilitation rate might previously have drawn acclaim for so many saved, it is now decried for all those offenders who will return to prey on society (1974). That is, previously the plight and potential reform of offenders was a matter of great public concern, but now the security of the community dominates public interest. Notions of justice and fairness do not permit abandonment of the offender's interest entirely, and certainly rehabilitation would be welcome. However, these matters now take a back seat to control measures, just as the latter did under previous policy incarnations (Cohen and Paris, 1982).

What is the fate of the institution in all this? The 1973 National Advisory Commission Task Force on Corrections offered one answer, deinstitutionalization:

> It is essential to abate use of institutions . . . not . . . out of sympathy for the criminal or disregard of the threat of crime to society. [But] precisely because that threat is too serious to be countered by ineffective methods (1973; see also Coates et al., 1978).

Diminished use is further justified on a variety of grounds: overcrowding (National Advisory Commission, 1973); "prisonization" (the inculcation of deviant values) (Sykes, 1971; Irwin, 1970); violence in prison (Jacobs, 1977); and the generally inhumane quality of the environment, with its boredom and monotony (Keve, 1974). In proposing change, deinstitutionalization advocates begin with a call for more extensive use of community alternatives (McSparren, 1980; Carney, 1977; Carter and Wilkins, 1976), with probation the presumptive sentence (U.S. Department of Justice, 1973). Institutionalization could still be justified for serious offenses or repeat offenders, but sentencing would be fixed by the court rather than left to the discretion of correction officials. This so-called justice model (Fogel, 1975) has been partly implemented through the transition from indeterminate to determinate sentencing procedures. Once in prison, inmates are not to be forced into treatment, but left free to choose their own rehabilitation program, recognizing that doing so will not affect the previously fixed release date. Prisoners are thus expected to take responsibility for, and presumably will get more out of, their own treatment (Morris, 1974).

Opponents contend that the rehabilitation issue has been closed prematurely (Andrews, 1980; Ross and Gendreau, 1980). They allege the absence of a fair test, in light of conflicting goals and counterproductive settings. A recent study disclosing role conflict within and between treatment and custody staffs in prison illustrate this dilemma (Hepburn and Albonetti, 1980). Others question the efficacy of noninstitutional programs when incarceration is not a real threat in the background (Heidjen, 1980). Perhaps most compelling of all for policy makers is the widespread citizen demand to remove potential felons from the community. This creates an impetus to build more, not fewer facilities. Such demands have recently been buoyed by a controversial juvenile corrections study that reported a greater suppression effect of harsh penalties, such as incarceration, than mild ones, such as supervision (Murray and Cox, 1979; but also see McCleary, 1980; Maltz, 1980). A final point is the implication for individual liberty generally of a shift in the control effort from the institution to the community (Mathieson, 1980).

While the deinstitutionalization debate rages, other special issues press the correctional policy agenda. For instance, the death penalty issue has been revived in state legislative action (Schwartz, 1980) from the ashes of *Furman v. Georgia* (1972), with proponents variously lauding its deterrent, retributive, and incapacitative effects (van den Haag, 1975). The cost and quality of incarceration in local jails also demands policy attention (Wayson et al., 1977; Flynn, 1973). The plight of the female inmate is a significant issue too, especially in light of evidence of significantly less resource commitment to them than to their male counterparts (Crites, 1976). Prison riots surfaced in the late 1960s and 1970s as imprisoned activists raised questions about the rights of inmates and the quality of the facilities. An outraged citizenry was torn between the specter of felons running rampant through the prisons and the evidence of brutal retaliation by the state in regaining control. Furthermore, the riots highlighted the often autocratic quality of prison management, and stimulated an infusion of legality principles into prison life (Rudovsky, 1973; Berkman, 1979). Various mechanisms have developed to protect and assert these rights, including grievance panels (McArthur, 1974; Keating and Kolze, 1975), prison unions (Huff, 1974; Browning, 1972), legal service programs (Carderelli and Finkelstein, 1974), and litigation actions under Section 1983 of an early civil rights act. The future of these mechanisms in light of increasing public intolerance of crime remains an open issue.

There can be no doubt that corrections is in the midst of change, even if the scope of that change remains in doubt (Hawkins, 1976). In the meantime, perennial problems plague the practitioner too, such as management and staffing, classification, certification, and pre-service and in-service training. Calls are frequently made for a unified system that would prescribe standards on these and other special substantive matters. Whatever merit such unification may have, it is ultimately encumbered here, as elsewhere in the criminal justice process, by the tremendous diversity of settings in which corrections occurs. This includes variation in terms of urban/rural development, local cultural expectations, available resources, inmate population differences, and the like. The search for standards should hardly be discouraged, but neither should we anticipate very much ease or success in applying standard guidelines either.

III. CRIMINAL JUSTICE AND POLITICS

Although the discussion thus far has been more descriptive than critical, the questions it has raised should leave little doubt about a political element in the criminal justice policy process. This is hardly shocking, as few would contend that the strict neutrality envisioned under the "rule of law" is ever fully or even largely realized. The issue is more often the degree and nature of the deviation from the standard: whether there is some systematic bias which works to the detriment of particular groups or individuals. That is, we are troubled where the law generally and criminal justice policy in particular function as an instrument of power, serving either as a weapon of or as a vehicle for legitimation of some set of interests. The issue must be raised and clarified here not merely as a point of criticism of criminal justice policy, but rather so we can appreciate further the reasons why the criminal justice process assumes the shape it does and what the effective limits are in its reform.

This political dimension is clear in the area of "victimless" crimes, and the associated decriminalization controversy (Schur and Bedau, 1974). Crimes such as prostitution and drug possession are alleged to be victimless because those involved participate by their own choice and inflict relatively little direct harm, if any, on the rest of society (Geis, 1979). Although a number of resource allocation and other economic cost questions enter the controversy, the debate is more fundamentally a normative one. At issue are both the propriety of the behavior in society and also the appropriateness of one segment of society setting behavior standards for everyone. Edwin Schur calls such debates "stigma contests," and cautions that, in seeking to understand them, "we need to keep in mind that deviance struggles always take place within a broader socio-cultural context" (1980: 53; see also Becker, 1963; Erikson, 1962; Goode, 1978; Kitsuse, 1962). Schur would have us ask what there is about society and its underlying value system that produces the particular set of deviance struggles observed.

One could well extend the search for political content in the definition of crime beyond that obviously present in victimless or "moral" offenses. Stephen Schafer observes that "it may be argued that all crimes are political crimes in as much as all prohibitions with penal sanctions represent the defense of a given value system, or morality, in which the prevailing power system believes" (1973: 19; see also Parmelee, 1918). Is Schafer contending that class or other elites manipulate the conduct of the criminal justice process to serve their own ends (Quinney, 1973, 1977)? If so, the standard for evaluation is the neutrality principle, and the focus of our attention is the specific biases that underlie deviations from that principle. Amelioration of the problem depends on personnel changes to remove these elites from influential positions or institutional changes that expand the base of meaningful participation in the political process. Thus, in this view, political surveillance by the Federal Bureau of Investigation can be explained in terms of the power interests of people such as Hoover and his cohorts. Current efforts by the American Civil Liberties Union and others to write a charter for the FBI would diminish the chances for similar abuses in the future. Similarly insightful are Pamela Roby's analysis of the evolution of New York's prostitution laws, with their sexist bias toward sanctioning the prostitute and not the client (1972; see more generally Fitzpatrick, 1974), John Conklin's observation that street crime offenders do less material harm but are punished much more severely than business crime perpetrators (1977), and Susan Brownmiller's attack on the sexist orientation of rape laws in their treatment of victims relative to offenders (1975).

Schafer's observation permits a second and more troubling interpretation of the relationship between law and politics. In this view it is the neutrality principle itself that is problematic. Given an unequal society, that quality in the law which acts as if all citizens were equal simply legitimates and perpetuates the prevailing inequality in society. Isaac Balbus has identified an economic basis in capitalism for this inimical transformation of unequals into equals (1977). Richard Abel's discussion of legal service delivery to the disadvantaged demonstrates the practical limitations on reform so long as we adhere to the "rule of law" ideology. He distinguishes those advantaged by wealth, status, and education from those who are disadvantaged on these grounds. Under the market system, the former can further enhance their relative position by purchasing legal assistance inaccessible to the latter. Reform efforts limited by procedural equality can only assist the disadvantaged to the point of providing analogous, even if lower-quality, legal assistance, or removing legal assistance from both parties. It cannot take a step toward substantive equality by withdrawing legal assistance from the advantaged and giving it to the disadvantaged. Thus, merely idiosyncratic biases in the design and application of criminal justice policy are an acknowledged problem, but not the fundamental issue here. The rule of law standard for evaluating the problem is of no help, because that standard itself lies at the base of the more fundamental political quality of criminal justice policy. In an important sense, it would require suspension of that rule and action guided by a conception of a more equal, less repressive society to overcome this policy dilemma.

The precise impact of these political attributes in the design and execution of criminal justice policy is not always easy to trace. Although space does not permit further exploration here, it is sufficient for the present discussion to note, in conclusion, how constraints are imposed on criminal justice policy at the very earliest stages when implicit or explicit decisions are reached as to what shall count as crimes and toward what ends resources shall be committed. Such constraints are prior to the very real technical problems imposed by the nature of criminal behavior, the availability of resources, and consensus on the best tactics to follow to achieve desired ends. It is these prior decisions, and the values they represent, that one must address if there is to be any hope of changing the basic nature of the criminal justice process.

ACKNOWLEDGMENTS

Comments by Ike Balbus, John Gardiner, Alan Gitelson, Joe Peterson, Doug Thomson, and Charles Williams on an earlier draft of this manuscript are greatly appreciated.

NOTES

1. A number of bibliographic sources are available, including *Crime and Delinquency Abstracts,* the Public Affairs Information Service, and the *Social Science Index.* Additionally, the federal government has sponsored the National Criminal Justice Reference Service, which publishes annotated bibliographies on a wide variety of subjects. The service will also provide researchers with bibliographic printouts on "key word" topics.
2. The *Uniform Crime Reports* Serious Crime Index consists of murder, rape, assault, robbery, burglary, larceny, and auto theft.
3. This disjunction can be illustrated by the following diagram:

		Law Defines Event A as Criminal Event	
		Yes	No
Victim Defines			
Event A	Yes	a	b
as Criminal			
Event			
	No	c	d

   Cells b and c should be especially significant to social and policy analysis. How do individuals come to be located in either of these cells? Is their presence in these cells random or systematic? What is the relative distribtuion of all events across these cells? The idea for this table comes from research by Dr. Paulene Bart about issues in the identification of rape victims.
4. Some specific comparisons have been made between the estimates in these two measures. The findings to date have not been conclusive (Booth et al., 1979; Cohen and Lichbach, 1982; Decker, 1977; Maltz, 1975; Skogan, 1974).
5. Some policy analysts have sought to formalize these processes in models/simulations for purposes of basic research, and also to assess the impact of policy changes in the system (Bohigian, 1977). JUSSIM (Blumstein, 1975) is the prototype simulation/ model in the field, although there are a number of other simulations in use now as well (Chaiken et al., 1975). Stuart Nagel has also played a leading role, especially in the application of deductive optimization models (Nagel, 1977; Nagel and Neef, 1976, 1977, 1979). The chief advantage of these representations is their ability to indicate the likely impact of proposed changes in the system. Of course, the projections are ultimately only as good as the assumptions that underlie the model, and the approach has generally been criticized for its inaccessibility to the fundamental value questions that beset policy making in this area (Reich, 1977). Still, within these constraints, the models surely can be useful tools in policy planning and analysis, especially to the extent that they can be altered to account for the local variation we have been describing.

REFERENCES

Abel, R. L. (1980). Socializing the legal profession: Can redistributing lawyer's services achieve social justics? *Law and Policy Quarterly 1*: 5-52.

Alschuler, A. W. (1968). The prosecutor's role in plea bargaining. *University of Chicago Law Review 36*: 50-112.

American Bar Association (1968). *Advisory Commission on the Criminal Trial: Standards Relating to Pleas of Guilty.* American Bar Association, Chicago.

—— (1972). *Project on Standards for Criminal Justice: Standards Relating to the Function of the Trial Judge.* American Bar Association, Chicago.

American Friends Service Committee (1979). *The Police Threat to Political Liberty.* American Friends Service Committee, Philadelphia.

Andenaes, J. (1974). *Punishment and Deterrence.* University of Michigan Press, Ann Arbor.

Andrews, D. (1980). Some experimental investigations of the principles of differential association through deliberate manipulations of the structure of social systems. *American Sociological Review 45*: 448-462.

Ash, M. (1973). Court delay, crime control and the neglect of the interest of the witnesses. In *Reducing Court Delay.* U.S. Department of Justice, Washington, DC, pp. 1-34.

Ashman, A., and Alfini, J. (1974). *The Key to Judicial Merit Selection: The Nominating Process.* American Judicature Society, Chicago.

Ashman, A., and Asperk, T. (1971). The defense function. In Allan Ashman and Tina Asperk, eds. *Selected Readings in Prosecution,* A. Ashman and T. Asperk (Eds.) American Judicature Society, Chicago

Atkins, B., and Pogrebin, M. (Eds.) (1978). *The Invisible Justice System: Discretion and the Law.* Anderson, Cincinnatti, OH.

Auerbach, J. S. (1976). *Unequal Justice: Lawyers and Social Change in Modern America.* Oxford University Press, New York.

Baker, R., and Meyer, F. A., Jr. (1980). *The Criminal Justice Game: Politics and Players.* Duxbury, North Scituate, MA.

Balbus, I. D. (1977). Commodity form and legal form: An essay on the relative autonomy of the law. *Law and Society Review 11* (Winter): 571-588.

Balch, G., Gardiner, J., and Cohen, L. (1978). Incentives and disincentives to crime prevention behavior: An analysis of the literature and agenda for future research. National Institute of Law Enforcement and Criminal Justice, Washington, DC.

Balkin, S. (1978). Crime control as energy policy. *Policy Analysis 5*: 119-122.

Barker, L. J., and Barker, T. W. (1978). *Civil Liberties and the Constitution: Cases and Commentary.* Prentice-Hall, Englewood Cliffs, NJ.

Barkus, J. L. (1978). *Victims.* Scribner's, New York.

Barnes, H. E. (1926). *The Repression of Crime: Studies in Historical Penology.* George H. Doran, New York.

—— (1931). *Battling the Crime Wave: Applying Sense and Science to the Repression of Crime.* Stratford, Boston.

Beattie, R. H. (1960). Criminal statistics in the United States. *Journal of Criminal Law, Criminology and Police Science 51* (May/June): 49-65.

Becker, H. S. (1963). *Outsiders.* Free Press, New York.

Becker, T. (1974). Place of private police in society: An area of research for the social sciences. *Social Problems 21*: 438-453.

Bent, A. E. (1974). *The Politics of Local Law Enforcement.* Lexington Books, Lexington, MA.

Bequai, A. (1978). *Computer Crime.* Lexington Books, Lexington, MA.

Berkeley, G. E. (1970). Centralization, decentralization and the police. *Journal of Criminal Law, Criminology and Police Science 61*: 309-312.

Berkeley, G. E., Giles, M. W., Hackett, J. F., and Kasoff, N. C. (1976). *Introduction to Criminal Justice.* Holbrook Press, Boston.

Berkman, R. (1979). *Opening the Gates: The Rise of the Prisoner's Movement.* Lexington Books, Lexington, MA.

Black, D. (1970). The production of crime rates. *American Sociological Review 35* (February): 733-747.

Bloch, P. B., and Bell, J. (1976). *Managing Investigations: The Rochester System.* Police Foundation, Washington, DC.

Bloch, P. B., and Specht, D. (1973). *Neighborhood Team Policing.* U.S. Department of Justice, Washington, DC.

Block, R. (1977). *Violent Crime: Interaction and Death.* Lexington Books, Lexington, MA.

Blumberg, A. S. (1967). The practice of law as a confidence game: Organized cooptation of a profession. *Law and Society Review 1* (June): 15-39.

—— (1979). *Criminal Justice: Issues and Ironies.* New Viewpoints, New York.

Blumberg, M. (1979). Injury to victims of personal crimes: Nature and extent. In *Perspectives on Victimology,* W. H. Parsonage (Ed.). Sage, Beverly Hills, CA, pp. 133-147.

Blumstein, A. (1975). A model to aid in planning for the total criminal justice system. In *Quantitative Tools for Criminal Justice Planning,* L. Oberlander (Ed.). U.S. Department of Justice, Washington, DC.

—— (1978). Research on deterrent and incapacitative effects of criminal sanctions. *Journal of Criminal Justice 6* (Spring): 1-10.

Blumstein, A., Cohen, J., and Nagin, D. (Eds.) (1974). *Deterrence and Incapacitation: Estimating the Effects of Criminal Sanctions on Crime Rates.* National Academy of Sciences, Washington, DC.

Bohigan, H. (1977). What is a model? In *Modeling the Criminal Justice System,* S. S. Nagel (Ed.). Sage, Beverly Hills, CA, pp. 15-28.

Boone, A. (1872). *The Increase of Crime and Its Causes.* Anne Boone, Boston.

Booth, A., Johnson, D. R., and Choldin, H. S. (1977). Correlates of city crime rates: Victimization surveys versus official statistics. *Social Proglems 25*: 187-197.

Boydstun, J. E., Sherry, M. E., and Moelter, N. (1978). Patrol staffing in San Diego: One or two officer units. In *Evaluation Studies Review Annual,* vol. 3, T. Cook et al. (Eds.). Sage, Beverly Hills, CA, pp. 456-472.

Browning, F. (1972). Organizing behind bars. In *Prisons, Protest and Politics,* B. Atkins and H. Glick (Eds.). Prentice-Hall, Englewood Cliffs, NJ.

Brownmiller, S. (1975). *Against Our Will: Men, Women and Rape.* Simon and Schuster, New York.

Campbell, D. T., and Ross, H. (1968). The Connecticut crackdown on speeding: Time-series data in quasi experimental analysis. *Law and Society Review 3* (August): 33-76.

Carderelli, A. P., and Finkelstein, M. M. (1974). Correctional administrators assess the adequacy and impact of prison legal service programs in the United States. *Journal of Criminal Law and Criminology 65* (March): 91-102.

Carney, L. P. (1977). *Corrections and the Community.* Prentice-Hall, Englewood Cliffs, NJ.

—— (1980). *Corrections: Treatment and Philosophy.* Prentice-Hall, Englewood Cliffs, NJ.

Carter, L. (1979). *Reason in Law.* Little, Brown, Boston.

Carter, R. F., and Wilkins, L. T. (Eds.). (1976). *Probation, Parole and Community Corrections.* Wiley, New York.

Casper, J. (1972). *American Criminal Justice: The Defendant's Perspective.* Prentice-Hall, Englewood Cliffs, NJ.

Chaiken, J., Crabll, T., Holliday, L. P., Jacquette, D. L., Lawless, M., and Quade, E. A. (1975). *Criminal Justice Models: An Overview.* Rand Corporation, Santa Monica, CA.

Chappel, D., Geis, R., and Geis, G. (1977). *Forcible Rape: The Crime, the Victim and the Offender.* Columbia University Press, New York.

Chase, H. W. (1972). *Federal Judges: The Appointing Process.* University of Minnesota Press, Minneapolis.

Chevigny, P. (1969). *Police Power: Police Abuses in New York City.* Pantheon, New York.

Cho, Y. H. (1974). *Public Policy and Urban Crime.* Ballinger, Cambridge, MA.

Clark, R. (1969). *Crime in America: Observations on Its Nature, Causes, Prevention and Control.* Simon and Schuster, New York.

Clinard, M., and Abbott, D. J. (1973). *Crime in Developing Countries: A Comparative Perspective.* Wiley, New York.

Coates, R. B., Miller, A., and Ohlin, L. (1978). *Diversity in a Youth Correctional System.* Ballinger, Cambridge, MA.

Cohen, L. E., Felson, M., and Land, K. C. (1980). Property crime rates in the United States: A macrodynamic analysis, 1943-1977; with ex ante forecasts for the mid 1980's. *American Sociological Review 86* (July): 90-118.

Cohen, L. J. (1977). Obedience and sanctions: An examination of legal social control policy. Ph.D. thesis, Syracuse University, Syracuse, NY.

—— (1978). Problems of perception in deterrence research. In *Quantitative Studies in Criminal Justice,* C. Wellford (Ed.). Sage, Beverly Hills, CA, pp. 84-99.

—— (1979a). The federal impact on local law enforcement policy: Reevaluating expectations. In *Determinants of Law Enforcement Policies,* F. A. Meyer and R. Baker (Eds.). Heath, Lexington, MA, pp. 193-206.

—— (1980). Judicial competence at the trial bench: A conceptual inventory. Unpublished manuscript.

Cohen, L. J., and Lichbach, M. I. (1982). Evaluating crime reporting policy: An econometric approach to alternative measurement procedures. *Sociological Quarter,* (in press).

Cohen, L. J., and Paris, D. C. (1982). Ethical issues in goal conflict: A continuing problem for policy analysis. *Western Political Quarterly,* (in press).

Cole, G. F. (1973). *Politics and the Administration of Justice.* Sage, Beverly Hills, CA.

—— (1980). *Criminal Justice: Law and Politics.* Duxbury Press, North Scituate, MA.

Conklin, J. E. (1975). *The Impact of Crime.* Macmillan, New York.

—— (1977). *Illegal but Not Criminal: Business Crimes in America.* Prentice-Hall, Englewood Cliffs, NJ.

Crawford, R. (1977). You are dangerous to your health: The ideology and politics of victim blaming. *International Journal of Health Services 7:* 664-680.

Crites, L. (1976). *The Female Offender.* Heath, Lexington, MA.

Danzig, R., and Lowy, M. J. (1975). Everyday disputes and mediation in the United States: A reply to Professor Felstiner. *Law and Society Review 9* (Summer): 675-694.

Davis, E. M. (1973). Neighborhood team policing: Implementing the territorial imperative. *Crime Prevention Review 1* (October): 11-19.

Davis, K. C. (1974). Approach to legal control of the police. *Texas Law Review 52* (April): 703-725.

Decker, S. (1977). Official crime rates and victim surveys: An empirical comparison. *Journal of Criminal Justice 5* (Spring): 47-54.

Dolbeare, K. M. (1967). *Trial Courts in Urban Politics.* Wiley, New York.

Douglas, J. D. (1970). Deviance and responsibility: The social construction of moral meanings. In *Deviance and Respectability,* J. D. Douglas (Ed.). Basic Books, New York, pp. 3-30.

DuBow, F., McCabe, E., and Kaplan, G. (1979). *Reactions to Crime: A Critical Review of the Literature.* U.S. Department of Justice, Washington, DC.

Duncan, R. B. (1973). The climate for change in three police departments: Some implications for action. In *Innovations in Law Enforcement.* U.S. Government Printing Office, Washington, DC.

Eckart, D. R., and Stover, R. (1974). Public defenders and routinized criminal defense processes. *Journal of Urban Law 51*: 254.

Edelherz, H. (1975). *Nature, Impact and Prosecution of White Collar Crime.* U.S. Government Printing Office, Washington, DC.

Eisenstein, J. (1978). *Counsel for the United States: U.S. Attorneys in the Political and Legal Systems.* Johns Hopkins University Press, Baltimore.

Eisenstein, J., and Jacob, H. (1977). *Felony Justice: An Organizational Analysis of Criminal Courts.* Little, Brown, Boston.

Elliot, J. F. (1971). *Crime Control Team: An Experiment in Municipal Police Department Management and Operations.* Charles C. Thomas, Springfield, IL.

Erikson, K. T. (1962). Notes on the sociology of deviance. *Social Problems 9* (Spring): 307-314.

Ermann, M. D., and Lundman, R. J. (Eds.) (1978). *Corporate and Governmental Deviance.* Oxford University Press, New York.

Farr, R. (1975). *The Electronic Criminality.* McGraw-Hill, New York.

Federal Bureau of Investigation (1930-1980). *Uniform Crime Reports for the United States.* U.S. Government Printing Office, Washington, DC.

Feeley, M. (1979). *The Process Is the Punishment: Handling Cases in Lower Criminal Courts.* Russell Sage Foundation, New York.

Feeley, M., Sarat, A., and White, S. O. (1977). The role of state planning in the development of criminal justice federalism. In *Public Law and Public Policy*, J. A. Gardiner (Ed.) Praeger, New York, pp. 204-234.

Felkenes, G. T. (1973). *The Criminal Justice System: Its Functions and Personnel.* Prentice-Hall, Englewood Cliffs, NJ.

Fielding, H. (1751). *An Inquiry into the Causes of the Late Increase of Robbers, with Some Proposals for Remedying this Growing Evil.* A. Millar, London.

Fitzpatrick, J. J. (1974). Cultural difference, not criminal offenses: A redefinition of types of social behavior. In *Politics and Crime.* F. Sylvester and E. Sagarini (Eds). Praeger, New York.

Flynn, E. E. (1973). Jails and criminal justice. In *Prisoners in America*, L. E. Ohlin (Ed.). Prentice-Hall, Englewood Cliffs, NJ.

Fogel, D. (1975). . . . *We Are the Living Proof.* . . . Anderson, Cincinnati, OH.

Fogelson, R. M. (1977). *Big-City Police.* Harvard University Press, Cambridge, MA.

Foote, C. (1956). Vagrancy-type law and its administration. *University of Pennsylvania Law Review 104*: 603.

Foucault, M. (1977). *Discipline and Punish: The Birth of the Prison.* Pantheon, New York.

Fox, J. A. (1978). *Forecasting Crime Data: An Economic Analysis.* Lexington Books, Lexington, MA.

Galaway, B., and Hudson, J. (Eds.). (1977). *Offender Restitution in Theory and Action.* Heath, Lexington, MA.

Gardiner, J., and Lyman, T. (1978). *Decisions for Sale: Corruption and Reform in Land Use and Building Regulation.* Praeger, New York.

Gardiner, J., and Olson, D. J. (Eds.) (1974). *Theft of the City.* Indiana University Press, Bloomington.

Garofalo, J. (1979). Victimization and the fear of crime. *Journal of Research in Crime and Delinquency* (January): 80-97.

Geis, G. (1979). *Not the Law's Business: An Examination of Homosexuality, Abortion, Prostitution, Narcotics and Gambling in the United States.* Schocken, New York.

Gibson, J. L. (1978). Judges' role orientations, attitudes and decisions: An interactive model. *American Political Science Review 72* (September): 911-924.

Glaser, D. (1978). *Crime in Our Changing Society.* Holt, Rinehart and Winston, New York.

Gleason, S. (1978). Hustling: The inside economy of a prison. *Federal Probation 42* (June): 32-40.

Goldstein, J. (1972). Police discretion not to invoke the criminal process—Low visibility decisions in the administration of justice. In *Criminal Justice: Law and Politics,* G. F. Cole (Ed.). Wadsworth, Belmont, CA.

Goldstein, R. J. (1978). *Political Repression in Modern America.* Schenkman, Cambridge, MA.

Goode, E. (1978). *Deviant Behavior: An Interactionist Perspective.* Prentice-Hall, Englewood Cliffs, NJ.

Gould, L. C., and Namenwirth, J. Z. (1971). Contrary objectives: Crime control and the rehabilitation of criminals. In *Crime and Justice in American Society,* J. D. Douglas (Ed.). Bobbs Merrill, Indianapolis, IN, 195-236.

Gray, C. M. (Ed.) (1979). *The Costs of Crime.* Sage, Beverly Hills, CA.

Greenberg, D. F., and Humphries, D. (1980). The cooptation of fixed sentencing reform. *Crime and Delinquency 26* (April): 206-225.

Grimes, J. A. (1975). Police, the union and the productivity imperative. In *Readings on Productivity in Policing.* J. C. Wolfe and J. F. Heaphy (Eds.). Police Foundation, Washington, DC.

Gurr, T. R., Grabosky, P., and Hula, R. C. (1977). *The Politics of Crime and Conflict: A Comparative History of Four Cities.* Sage, Beverly Hills, CA.

Guterman, J. H., and Meidinger, E. E. (1977). *In the Opinion of the Bar: A National Survey of Bar Polling Practices.* American Judicature Society, Chicago.

Hagan, J. (1977). Criminal justice in rural and urban communities: A study of the bureaucratization of justice. *Social Forces 55* (March): 597-612.

Hahn, P. H. (1976). *Crimes Against the Elderly: A Study in Victimology.* Davis, Santa Cruz, CA.

Halper, A., and Ku, R. (1974). *New York Police Department Street Crime Unit: An Exemplary Project.* U.S. Department of Justice, Washington, DC.

Hamilton, W. (1979). Highlights of PROMIS research. In *The Prosecutor,* W. McDonald (Ed.). Sage, Beverly Hills, CA.

Harring, S. L. (1977). Class conflict and the suppression of tramps in Buffalo, 1892-1894. *Law and Society Review 11* (Summer): 873-911.

Harris, R. (1969). *The Fear of Crime.* Praeger, New York.

Hawkins, G. (1976). *The Prison: Policy and Practice.* University of Chicago Press, Chicago.

Heijden, A. (1980). Can we cope with alternatives? *Crime and Delinquency 26* (January): 1-9.

Hepburn, J. P., and Albonetti, C. (1980). Role conflict in correctional institutions. *Criminology 17* (February): 445-459.

Hepburn, J. P., and Monti, D. J. (1979). Victimization, fear of crime and adaptive responses among high school students. In *Perspectives on Victimology,* W. H. Parsonage (Ed.). Sage, Beverly Hills, CA, pp. 121-132.

Herlihy, E. D., and Levine, T. A. (1976). Corporate crime: The overseas payment problem. *Law and Policy in International Business 18*: 547-568.

Heumann, M. (1978). *Plea Bargaining*. Sage, Beverly Hills, CA.

Heydebrand, W. V. (1977). The context of public bureaucracies: An organizational analysis of federal district courts. *Law and Society Review 11* (Summer): 759-822.

Hilberman, E. (1976). *The Rape Victim*. Basic Books, New York.

Hindelang, M. J. (1974). *An Analysis of Victimization Survey Results from the Eight Impact Cities: Summary Report*. U.S. Government Printing Office, Washington, DC.

Hindelang, M. J., Gottfredson, M. J., and Garofalo, J. (1978). *Victims of Personal Crime: An Empirical Foundation for a Theory of Victimization*. Ballinger, Cambridge, MA.

Holtzer, M. (1973). Police productivity: A conceptual framework for measurement and improvement. *Journal of Police Science and Administration 1* (December): 459-469.

Huff, R. C. (1974). Unionization behind the walls. *Criminology 12* (August): 175-194.

Hursch, C. (1977). *The Trouble with Rape*. Nelson Hall, Chicago.

Inciardi, J. (Ed.) (1980). *Radical Criminology: The Coming Crisis*. Sage, Beverly Hills, CA.

Irwin, J. (1970). *The Felon*. Prentice-Hall, Englewood Cliffs, NJ.

Jacob, H. (1963). Politics and criminal prosecution in New Orleans. *Tulane Studies in Political Science 8*: 77-98.

—— (1973). *Urban Justice: Law and Order in American Cities*. Prentice-Hall, Englewood Cliffs, NJ.

—— (1978). *Justice in America: Courts, Lawyers and the Judicial Process*. Little, Brown, Boston.

Jacobs, J. B. (1977). *Stateville: The Penetentiary in Mass Society*. University of Chicago Press, Chicago.

Jacobs, J. B., and O'Meara, V. A. (1979). Toward a maximum security environment: Private police forces in the United States. Unpublished manuscript, Cornell University, Ithaca, NY.

Jacoby, J. (1979). The changing policies of prosecutors. In *The Prosecutor*, W. McDonald (Ed.). Sage, Beverly Hills, CA, pp. 75-97.

Johnson, J. H. (1973). The influence of politics upon the office of the American prosecutor. *American Journal of Criminal Law 2*: 3.

Jones, H. W. (1965). The trial judge: Role analysis and profile. In *The Courts, The Public, and the Law Explosion*, H. Jones (Ed.). Prentice-Hall, Englewood Cliffs, NJ, pp. 124-145.

Juris, H. A., and Feuille, P. (1973a). *Police Unionism: Power and Impact in Public Sector Bargaining*. Lexington-Heath, Lexington, MA.

—— (1973b). The impact of police unions. U.S. Department of Justice, Washington, DC.

Kadish, M. R., and Kadish, S. K. (1973). *Discretion to Disobey: A Study of Lawful Departures from Legal Rules*. Stanford University Press, Stanford, CA.

Kakalik, J. S., and Wildhorn, S. (1972). *Private Police Industry: Findings and Recommendations*. Rand Corporation, Santa Monica, CA.

Katz, J. (1980). The social movement against white collar crime. In *Criminology Review Yearbook*, vol. 2, E. Bittner and S. Messinger (Eds.). Sage, Beverly Hills, CA, pp. 161-184.

Keating, J. M., Jr., and Kolze, R. C. (1975). An inmate grievance mechanism: From deisgn to practice. *Federal Probation 39* (September): 42-47.

Kelling, G. L., Dieckman, P. D., and Brown, C. E. (1974). *Kansas City Preventive Patrol Experiment*. Police Foundation, Washington, DC.

Kerstetter, W. A. (1981). Police perception of influence in the criminal case disposition process. *Law and Police Quarterly,* 3: January.

Keve, P. W. (1974). *Prison Life and Human Worth.* University of Minneapolis Press, Minneapolis, MN.

Kitsuse, J. I. (1962). Societal reactions to deviant behavior. *Social Problems 9* (Winter): 247-256.

Klein, M. W., et al. (1976). The explosion of police diversion programs: Evaluating the structural dimensions of a fad. In *The Juvenile Justice System,* M. Klein (Ed.). Sage, Beverly Hills, CA, pp. 101-119.

Knapp Commission (1973). *Report on Police Corruption.* G. Braziller, New York.

Koeppell, T. W., and Girard, C. M. (1979). *Small Police Agency Consolidation: Suggested Approaches.* U.S. Government Printing Office, Washington, DC.

Kranz, S., Gilnau, B., Bends, C. B., Hallstrom, C. R., Nadwary, E. (1979). *Police Policy-making: The Boston Experience.* Lexington Books, Lexington, MA.

Lafave, W. R. (1965). *Arrest–The Decision to Take a Suspect into Custody.* Little, Brown, Boston.

Lafave, W. R., and Scott, A. W. (1972). *Handbook on Criminal Law.* West Publishing Company, St. Paul, MN.

LaGoy, S. P., Hussey, F. A., and Kramer, J. H. (1979). The prosecutorial function and its relation to determinate sentencing. In *The Prosecutor,* W. McDonald (Ed.). Sage, Beverly Hills, CA, pp. 209-237.

Langbein, J. H. (1977). *Torture and the Law of Proof: Europe and England in the Ancient Regime.* University of Chicago Press, Chicago.

Larsen, R. C. (1976). What happened to patrol operations in Kansas City? *Evaluation Quarterly 3:* 117-123.

Levin, M. (1977). *Urban Politics and the Criminal Courts.* University of Chicago Press, Chicago.

Levine, J. R., Musheno, M. C., Palumbo, D. J. (1973). *The Criminal Justice System: Its Function and Personnel.* Prentice-Hall, Englewood Cliffs, NJ.

Lipton, D., Martinson, R., and Wilks, J. (1975). *The Effectiveness of Correctional Treatment.* Praeger, New York.

Lydston, G. F. (1908). *The Disease of Society.* Lippincott, Philadelphia.

Maas, P. (1973). *Serpico.* Viking Press, New York.

MacDougall, E. (1976). Corrections has not been tried. *Criminal Justice Review 1* (Spring): 73.

Maltz, M. D. (1975). Crime statistics: A mathematical perspective. *Journal of Criminal Justice 3:* 177-193.

—— (1980). Beyond probation: More strum and drang on the correctional front. *Crime and Delinquency 28* (July): 389-397.

Manning, P. K. (1971). The police: Mandate, strategies and appearances. In *Crime and Justice in American Society,* J. D. Douglas (Ed.). Bobbs-Merrill, Indianapolis, IN, pp. 149-194.

Martinson, R. (1974). What works? Questions and answers about penal reform. *Public Interest 35* (Spring): 22-54.

Mathiesen, T. (1980). The future of control systems—The case of Norway. *International Journal of the Sociology of Law 8:* 146-164.

McArthur, V. (1974). Inmate grievance mechanisms: A survey of 209 American prisons. *Federal Probation 38* (December): 41-47.

McCleary, R. (1980). *Beyond Probation:* Book review. *Crime and Delinquency 28* (July): 387-389.

McDonald, W. (1979a). The prosecutor's domain. In *The Prosecutor,* W. McDonald (Ed.). Sage, Beverly Hills, CA, pp. 15-51.

—— (1979b). *The Prosecutor.* Sage, Beverly Hills, CA.

McGillis, D., and Mullen, J. (1977). *Neighborhood Justice Centers: An Analysis of Potential Models.* U.S. Department of Justice, Washington, DC.

McSparren, J. (1980). Community corrections and diversion: Costs and benefits, subsidy modes and start-up recommendations. *Crime and Delinquency 26* (April): 226-247.

Meidinger, E. I. (1977). Bar polls: What they measure what they mean. *Judicature 60* (May): 469.

Mendenhall, W., Ott, L., and Scheaffer, R. L. (1971). *Elementary Survey Sampling.* Duxbury Press, North Scituate, MA.

Miller, F. (1969). *Prosecution: The Decision to Charge a Suspect with a Crime.* Little, Brown, Boston.

Milton, C. (1972). *Women in Policing.* Police Foundation, Washington, DC.

Monkonnen, E. (1977). Toward a dynamic theory of crime and the police. *Historical Methods Newsletter 10* (Fall): 157-165.

—— (1979). Systematic criminal justice history: Some suggestions. *Journal of Inter disciplinary History 9*: 451-464.

Morris, N. (1974). *The Future of Imprisonment.* University of Chicago Press, Chicago.

Murray, C. A., and Cox, L. A., Jr. (1979). *Beyond Probation: Juvenile Corrections and the Chronic Delinquent.* Sage, Beverly Hills, CA.

Nagel, S. S. (1973). *Comparing Elected and Appointed Judicial Systems.* Sage, Beverly Hills, CA.

—— (Ed.) (1977). *Modeling the Criminal Justice System.* Sage, Beverly Hills, CA.

Nagel, S. S., and Neef, M. G. (1976). *The Legal Process: Modeling the System.* Sage, Beverly Hills, CA.

—— (1977). *Legal Policy Analysis: Finding an Optimum Level or Mix.* Lexington Books, Lexington, MA.

—— (1979). *Decision Theory and the Legal Process.* Lexington Books, Lexington, MA.

Nardulli, P. (1978). Plea bargaining: An organizational perspective. *Journal of Criminal Justice 6*: 217-231.

National Advisory Commission on Criminal Justice Standards and Goals (1973). *Task Force Report: Corrections.* U.S. Government Printing Office, Washington, DC.

National District Attorneys Association (1973). *Role of the Local Prosecutor in a Changing Society: A Confrontation with the Major Issues of the Seventies.* National District Attorneys Association, Chicago.

Nettler, G. (1974). *Explaining Crime.* McGraw-Hill, New York.

Neubauer, D. W. (1974). *Criminal Justice in Middle America.* General Learning Press, Morristown, NJ.

—— (1977). Judicial role and case management. *Justice System Journal 3* (Winter): 223-232.

—— (1979). *America's Courts and the Criminal Justice System.* Duxbury Press, North Scituate, MA.

Neumann, G. R. (1976). *Comparative Deviance: Perception and Law in Six Cultures.* Elsevier, New York.

Newman, D. J. (1966). *Conviction: The Determination of Guilt or Innocence Without Trial.* Little, Brown, Boston.

Niederhoffer, A. (1969). *Behind the Shield: The Police in Urban Society.* Doubleday, Garden City, NY.

Oba, S. (1908). *Unverbesserliche Verbrechen und Ihre Behandlung.* Berlin.

Ohlin, L. E., and Remington, F. J. (1958). Sentencing structure: Its effect upon systems for the administration of justice. *Law and Contemporary Problems 23*: 495-507.

Ostrom, E. (1973). On the meaning and measurement of output and efficiency in the provision of urban police services. *Journal of Criminal Justice 1*: 93-112.

Ostrom, E., and Bough, W. H. (1975). *Community Organization and the Provision of Police Services.* Sage, Beverly Hills, CA.

Ostrom, E., Parks, R. B., and Whitaker, P. (1978). *Patterns of Metropolitan Policing.* Ballinger, Cambridge, MA.

O'Toole, G. (1978). *The Private Sector: Private Spies, Rent-A-Cops and the Police Industrial Complex.* Norton, New York.

Parisi, N., Gottfriedson, M. R., Hindelang, M. J., and Flanagan, T. J. (Eds.) (1979). *Sourcebook of Criminal Justice Statistics–1978.* U.S. Department of Justice, Washington, DC.

Parker, D. B. (1976). *Crime by Computer.* Scribner's, New York.

Parmelee, M. F. (1918). *Criminology.* Macmillan, New York.

Performance Measurement and the Criminal Justice System: Four Conceptual Approaches (1976). U.S. Department of Justice, Washington, DC.

Perry, D. C. (1973). *Police in the Metropolis.* Charles E. Merrill, Columbus, OH.

Pope, C. E. (1979). Victimization rates and neighborhood characteristics: Some preliminary findings. *Perspectives on Victimology,* W. H. Parsonage (Ed.). Sage, Beverly Hills, CA, pp. 48-57.

Powell v. Alabama (1932). 287 US 45.

President's Commission on Law Enforcement and Administration of Justice (1967). *Challenge of Crime in a Free Society.* U.S. Government Printing Office, Washington, DC.

Quinney, R. (1973). *Critique of Legal Order.* Little, Brown, Boston.

—— (1977). *Class, State and Crime.* David McKay, New York.

Radzinowicz, Sir L., and King, J. (1977). *The Growth of Crime: The International Experience.* Basic Books, New York.

Reckless, W. C. (1967). *The Crime Problem.* Appleton-Century-Crofts, New York.

Reich, R. B. (1977). Can justice be optimized? In *Modeling the Criminal Justice System,* S. S. Nagel (Ed.). Sage, Beverly Hills, CA.

Reiman, J. H. (1979). *The Rich Get Richer and the Poor Get Prison.* Wiley, New York.

Reisman, W. M. (1979). *Folded Lies: Bribery, Crusades and Reform.* Free Press, New York.

Reiss, A. J. (1968). How common is police brutality? *Transaction 5* (July/August): 10-19.

—— (1971). *The Police and the Public.* Yale University Press, New Haven, CT.

Revzin, P. (1976a). For the people: Prosecutor Rodgers speeds justice along in busy Akron courts. *Wall Street Journal,* (May), p. 1.

—— (1976b). For the people: Richard McQuade has prestige, little crime as a rural prosecutor. *Wall Street Journal,* May 6, p. 1.

Rhodes, R. H. (1977). *The Insoluble Problems of Crime.* Wiley, New York.

Roby, P. A. (1972). Politics and prostitution: A case study of the revision, enforcement and administration of the New York State penal laws on prostitution. *Criminology 9*: 425-447.

Rose-Ackerman, S. (1978). *Corruption: A Study in Political Economy.* Academic Press, New York.

Rosenberg, M. (1966). The qualities of justice: Are they strainable? *Texas Law Review 44* (June): 1063-1080.

Rosenthal, D. E. (1976). Evaluating the competence of lawyers. *Law and Society Review* *11*: 257-286.

Rosett, A. (1979). Connotations of discretion. In *Criminology Review Yearbook,* S. Messinger and E. Bittner (Eds.). Sage, Beverly Hills, CA, pp. 377-401.

Rosett, A., and Cressey, D. R. (1976). *Justice by Consent: Plea Bargains in the American Courthouse.* Lippincott, Philadelphia.

Ross, H. L. (1976). The neturalization of severe penalties: Some traffic law studies. *Law and Society Review 10*: 403-413.

Ross, R. R., and Gendreau, P. (1980). *Effective Correctional Treatment.* Butterworths, Toronto.

Rossum, R. A. (1978). *The Politics of the Criminal Justice System: An Organizational Analysis.* Marcel Dekker, New York.

Rothman, D. (1971). *Discovery of the Asylum.* Little, Brown, Boston.

Rubinstein, J. (1973). *City Police.* Farrar, Straus and Giroux, New York.

Ruchelman, L. (Ed.) (1973). *Who Rules the Police.* New York University Press, New York.

Ruchelman, L. (1974). Police Policy. *Policy Studies Journal 3* (Autumn): 48-53.

Rudovsky, D. (1973). *The Rights of Prisoners.* Avon, New York.

Ruth, H. S., Jr. (1971). To dust ye shall return? In *The Challenge of Crime in a Free Society: Perspectives on the Report of the President's Commission on Law Enforcement and Administration of Justice.* DeCapo, New York.

—— (1977). *Research Priorities for Crime Reduction Efforts.* Urban Institute, Washington, DC.

Ryan, W. (1971). *Blaming the Victim.* Pantheon, New York.

Schafer, S. (1973). *The Political Criminal: The Problems of Morality and Crime.* Free Press, New York.

—— (1974). Compensation and victims of criminal offenses. *Criminal Law Bulletin 10* (September): 605-636.

Schmidt, J. R. (1976). Lawyers and judges: Competence and selection. In *Verdicts on Lawyers.* R. Nader and M. Green (Eds.). Thomas Y. Crowell, New York, pp. 285-294.

Schur, E. M. (1980). *The Politics of Deviance: Stigma Contests and the Uses of Power.* Prentice-Hall, Englewood Cliffs, NJ.

Schur, E., and Bedau, H. A. (1974). *Victimless Crime: Two Sides of a Controversy.* Prentice-Hall, Englewood Cliffs, NJ.

Schwartz, A. I., Vaughn, A. M., Waller, J. D., Wholey, J. S. (1975). *Employing Citizens for Police Work.* U.S. Government Printing Office, Washington, DC.

Schwartz, R. D. (1979). The Supreme Court and capital punishment: A quest for a balance between legal and societal morality. *Law and Policy Quarterly 1* (July): 285-335.

Scull, A. (1977). *Decarceration: Community Treatment and the Deviant—A Radical View.* Prentice-Hall, Englewood Cliffs, NJ.

Sheldon, J. A., and G. J. Zweibel (1975). Historical developments of consumer fraud. In *Survey of Consumer Fraud Law.* U.S. Department of Justice, Washington, DC, pp. 1-17.

Sherman, L. W. (Ed.) (1974). *Police Corruption: A Sociological Perspective.* Anchor, Garden City, NY.

Sherman, L. W. (1978). *Scandal and Reform: Controlling Police Corruption.* University of California Press, Berkeley.

Sherman, L., Milton, C. H., and Kelly, T. V. (1973). *Team Policing: Seven Case Studies*. Police Foundation, Washington, DC.

Shover, N. (1979). *A Sociology of American Corrections*. Dorsey Press, Homewood, IL.

Silberman, C. E. (1978). *Criminal Violence, Criminal Justice*. Random House, New York.

Skogan, W. G. (1974). *The validity of official crime statistics: An empirical investigation*. Social Science Quarterly 55 (June): 25-38.

—— (1977). Public policy and the year of crime in large American cities. In *Public Law and Public Policy*, J. Gardiner (Ed.). Praeger, New York.

Skogan, W. G., and Antunes, G. E. (1979). Information, apprehension and deterrence: Exploring the limits of police productivity. *Journal of Criminal Justice 7*: 217-241.

Skogan, W. G., and Klecka, W. (1977). *The Fear of Crime*. American Political Science Association, Washington, DC.

Skoler, D. L. (1977). *Organizing the Non-System: Governmental Structuring of Criminal Justice Systems*. Lexington Books, Lexington, MA.

Skolnick, J. H. (1967). Social control in an adversary system. *Journal of Conflict Resolution 11*: 52-70.

—— (1975). *Justice Without Trial: Law Enforcement in Democratic Society*. Wiley, New York.

Smith, A., and Blumberg, A. (1967). The problems of objectivity in judicial decision making. *Social Forces 45*: 96-105.

Sparks, R. F., Genn, H., and Dodd, D. J. (1977). *Surveying Victims*. Wiley, New York.

Stone, C. H. (1971). Controlling corporate misconduct. *Public Interest 48* (Summer): 55-71.

Sudnow, D. (1965). Normal crimes: Sociological features of the penal code in a public defencer's office. *Social Problems 12*: 255-276.

Sykes, G. (1971). *The Society of Captives*. Princeton University Press, Princeton, NJ.

Tien, J., and Larsen, R. (1978). Police service aides: Paraprofessionals for police. *Journal of Criminal Justice 6*: 117-131.

University of Pennsylvania Law Review (1966). Guilty plea bargaining: Compromise to secure guilty pleas. *University of Pennsylvania Law Review 112*: 845-895.

van den Haag, E. (1975). *Punishing Criminals: Concerning a Very Old and Painful Question*. Basic Books, New York.

van Maanen, J. (1974). Working the street: A developmental view of police behavior. In *The Potential for Reform in Criminal Justice*, H. Jacob (Ed.)., Sage, Beverly Hills, CA.

Walker, L. E. (1979). *The Battered Woman*. Harper & Row, New York.

Walker, M., and Brodsky, S. (1976). *Sexual Assault: The Victim and the Rapist*. Lexington Books, Lexington, MA.

Watson, R. A., and Downing, R. G. (1969). *The Politics of the Bench and the Bar*. Wiley, New York.

Wayson, B. L., Funka, G. S., Familton, S. F., and Meyer, P. B. (1977). *Local Jails: The New Correctional Dilemma*. Lexington Books, Lexington, MA.

Weaver, S. (1977). *Decision to Prosecute*. M.I.T. Press, Cambridge, MA.

Wheeler, R. R., and Jackson, D. W. (1976). Judicial councils and policy planning: Continuous study and discontinuous institutions. *Justice System Journal 2* (Winter): 121-140.

White, S. O., and Krislov, S. (Eds.) (1977). *Understanding Crime: An Evaluation of the National Institute of Law Enforcement and Criminal Justice*. National Academy of Sciences, Washington, DC.

Wice, P. B. (1978). *Criminal Lawyers: An Endangered Species*. Sage, Beverly Hills, CA.

Wice, P., and Pilgrim, M. (1975). Meeting the Gideon mandate: A survey of public defender programs. *Judicature 58* (March): 400-409.

Wilson, J. Q. (1968). *Varieties of Police Behavior: The Management of Law and Order in Eight Communities.* Atheneum, New York.

—— (1975). *Thinking About Crime.* Basic Books, New York.

Wolfgang, M. (1963). Uniform Crime Reports: A critical appraisal. *University of Pennsylvania Law Review 11*: 708-738.

Zemans, F. K. (1977). Civil or criminal litigation of disputes: A rose by any other name. . . . Midwest Political Science Association, Chicago, Illinois.

25

Education Policy

Fred S. Coombs / University of Illinois, Urbana-Champaign, Illinois

In the 1979–1980 school year about $166 billion (7 percent of our gross national product) was spent on some 3.3 million teachers, 300,000 school administrators, and 100,000 school buildings, as well as books, equipment, and transportation, all committed to the education of our nation's youth. Those teachers taught 58.4 million youngsters; many of the administrators served in one or another of the 16,211 local public school districts, which comprise a unique and fascinating part of our national political culture. In all, almost three of every 10 Americans are engaged in a direct way with the U.S. educational system (Grant and Eiden, 1980). This chapter is about the policy side of that huge enterprise: how the resources are sought and allocated and how the interests of the many people involved are expressed in, and shaped by, education policy.

The declaration that there exists a politics of education worthy of systematic study by political scientists came in Thomas Eliot's (1959) article in the *American Political Science Review*. In what Sroufe (1980) has recently characterized as a "modest article, modestly titled," Eliot called attention to the apolitical mystique that had served to render education immune from political inquiry. He then went on to identify several inviting lines of research, including resource procurement, the coping strategies of school administrators, and the tension between lay and professional control of the curriculum.

Two decades later, despite the presence of a growing band of scholars who specialize in the politics of education, one may still question whether there is anything so distinctive about their work as to warrant the designation of a separate field. P. E. Peterson (1974) identifies the central tenet of much of the politics of education literature ("School policy-formation is conducted autonomously by specialists in the field who are virtually impervious to pressures from external forces.") and suggests that the appeal of this field for many political scientists is the very isolation and autonomy that seems to make it different (p. 350). He goes on, however, to argue that education policymaking, when compared with other policy areas, is probably no more autonomous than many others. "In fact," he concludes, "there is no convincing theoretical reason for claiming that educational politics have such a distinctive character that their study requires special analytical, conceptual, and/or methodological tools" (p. 349).

Although it is still difficult to cite compelling theoretical reasons for the emergence of the field, there are more practical incentives for specialization, some of which ultimately may affect the development of theory. First, educational policy making is an extraordinarily *complex* subject, with thousands of participants working in a staggering array of structural settings. It is laden with its own cultural history, its own legal precedents, its own financial and political arrangements, and its own jargon. It is, in short, a field so vast and varied that attempting to develop some understanding of its nature taxes the abilities of most scholars.

Second, the educational system is relatively *exposed.* By virtue of the simple fact that almost everyone is or has been in school, and many have children in school, most citizens believe they have a special kind of acquaintance with one or another aspect of the system. Whereas large segments of the population escape direct contact with the national defense establishment or the public welfare system, relatively few avoid public schooling at some point. Their exposure to schools, and that of their progeny, heightens their awareness of educational issues (though in most cases their knowledge remains limited), and their own experiences color their orientations toward educational policy. The adage in educational circles is that everyone is an "expert" about school policy. There is an underlying distrust of any professional expertise that contradicts common sense and a possessiveness about the operation of public schools that obtains in few other policy sectors.

Third, education, perhaps more than any other policy field, is marked by a *dispersion of authority* (Halperin, 1978). Policy is not only formulated and implemented at multiple levels, but there is also an intricate distribution of authority within levels. U.S. elementary and secondary education policy is, of course, made and carried out in a system remarkably disjoint from the policy system for postsecondary education. Different local administrators and boards, different state bureaucracies, and different legislative committees typically govern the two realms.[1] But even within the elementary and secondary system one may identify and study educational policy at the classroom, school building, local district, county or regional, state, and federal levels. Each of these strata find well-socialized actors often counterposed in complex relationship to one another. Whether we examine the interaction of students, parents, teachers and principals at the building level; superintendents, members of the board of education, and teacher organization leaders at the local school district level; members of the state school board, the governor, legislators, and judges at the state level; or members of congress, Supreme Court justices, the Secretary of Education, and White House staff at the federal level; authority is diffuse and decentralized, and accountability is difficult. There is frequent overlap of function both within and between levels of government and duplication of programs is not uncommon.

The study of education policy is further complicated by the fact that the educational process itself is marked by multiple objectives and *ambiguity about goals* in most institutional settings. This state of affairs, coupled with our primitive knowledge of how to reach even clearly stated goals and the inherent difficulty of evaluating educational outcomes, has kept the study of education policy more descriptive, more historical, and more normative than policy study in some other areas such as health care, agriculture, or public transit.

Fifth, education is a *labor-intensive* process. Outlays for school buildings, bus trans-portation, and textbooks are not insignificant expenditures, but personnel costs—for teachers, administrators, and support staff—account for approximately 70 percent of the budget of most school districts (Grant and Eiden, 1980). One result of this (reinforced by negotiated reduction-in-force clauses in teacher contracts, which protect faculty with seniority, and by legal constraints in terminating tenured teachers and administrators) is that fixed costs are relatively high. Whereas a governor may contemplate cutting highway construction by 40 percent in a lean fiscal year, cuts of that magnitude are seldom polit-ically feasible in education. Rapidly expanding school enrollments in the 1960s and cor-responding enrollment decline in the 1970s and 1980s have strongly affected the char-acter of education policymaking, but school budgets have not, in general, declined pro-portionately to enrollment (Odden, 1976: 25-27).

I. EMERGENCE OF THE FIELD OF EDUCATION POLICY STUDIES

In attempting to explain the emergence of the politics of education as a field, Schribner and Englert (1977: 6) trace the development of political science through stages of moral philosophy, legalism, realism, and behavioralism. As they suggest, behavioralism, with its emphasis on theory building, comparison across political systems, and integration among the social sciences, set the stage nicely for the advent of the politics of education as a field of study. By 1980, however, the erstwhile enthusiasm for exploring individual ori-entation and behavior had turned sharply toward a reexamination of the policy process itself.[2]

The theoretical lineage of educational policy studies is made up of several distinct bloodlines. Before political science discovered the field, students of educational admin-istration were doing occasional work that today would qualify as politics of education (Counts, 1927; Charters, 1953; Carter, 1960). The scientific management orientation of the early 1900s, with its emphasis on finding the "one best way" (Taylor, 1911; Bobbitt, 1913), had yielded to bureaucratic models stressing efficiency (Weber, 1946; Callahan, 1962), then to human relations approaches (Baldridge, 1971), and modern organization theory assuming limited rationality (Simon, 1945; March and Simon, 1958; Weick, 1969; Cohen et al., 1972). A major component of work in politics of education is still devoted to the analysis of organizations (e.g., schools, classrooms, local districts, state agencies, or even legislatures) using concepts and propositions from organization theory.

Political scientists, on the other hand, have for the most part eschewed organization theory in favor of theoretical approaches that emphasize the interplay of interests in the allocation process. Among the patron saints, Harold Lasswell (1936) receives more acknowledgments than any other political scientist, but his work is most often cited simply to frame the key question: "Who gets what, when, how?" Two other aspects of Lasswell's work, the value configuration approach (Lasswell and Kaplan, 1950) and his description of political man rationalizing private motives in terms of the public interest (Lasswell, 1930) have seldom found their way into the politics of education literature. Robert Dahl's pluralist democracy also resonates with much of the research in politics of education. Some scholars conclude that their observations fit a pluralist model, whereas others lament the existence of an alleged monolithic professional elite that does not.

Although the section of *Who Governs* (1961) that deals with the education issue area is somewhat at variance with most other case studies (P. E. Peterson, 1974), the framework established by Dahl, with shifting coalitions of competing elites in each area, is still a congenial one for many studying the politics of education. The incrementalists (Lindblom, 1959; 1965; Braybrooke and Lindblom, 1963; Wildavsky, 1964) have also been well represented in the politics of education literature, particularly when attention turns to analysis of budgetary processes.

In the background, although now infrequently cited, one can detect the influence of Arthur Bentley (1908) in his path-breaking volume, which called attention to the role of groups in governmental process, and of David Truman (1951), who led the resurgence of group theory in the postwar era. The analysis of the action of interest groups in the development of education policy has served as the basic organizing rubric for scores of case studies (Munger and Fenno, 1962; Gittel, 1968; Iannaccone and Lutz, 1970; Bailey and Mosher, 1968; Thomas, 1975). The relative influence various interest groups exercised, the strategies they employed, the coalitions they formed, and the manner in which they attempted to maintain their own vitality in the process are the topics to which most politics of education researchers turned in their attempts to explain why some proposals become policy and others do not.

There has been, however, a loyal opposition. Gabriel Almond and James Coleman's *The Politics of the Developing Areas* (1960) provided the discipline a functional perspective that ultimately influenced much more than comparative politics. Of their functional categories of behavior, interest aggregation and interest articulation still frequently appear in treatises on politics of education. In the same vein, David Easton's development of systems analysis (1965), building on the work of sociologist Talcott Parsons (1961; 1969), provided a perspective quite different from the group theorists. Attention was drawn to the demands being placed on the educational system, the level and source of diffuse support, the conversion process by which inputs (demands and support) become outputs (usually conceived of as policies), feedback from outputs to inputs, and the relationship of the educational system to its environment.

One almost immediate consequence of systems analysis was the rapid accumulation of studies of political socialization during the 1960s. In the early, generally positive socializing experiences of children, political scientists found the source of the diffuse support for the political system that enables it to withstand the particularistic demands of various interests. Attempts to link that socialization process to the policy process through the mediating concept of participation have appeared in political science (Milbrath, 1965; Verba and Nie, 1972). We still know very little, however, about how individuals develop their basic beliefs and values about education, and even less about how those basic orientations relate to policy preferences or participation in the formation of education policy.

We should not leave David Easton's name without acknowledging one additional contribution: In *The Political System* (1953) he offered a definition of politics ("the authoritative allocation of values") around which most political scientists could rally. Given such an expansive charge, it was only a matter of time until some of Easton's colleagues began to seek out nonconventional arenas where values are allocated authoritatively. The educational system was almost virgin territory.

The most explicit use of systems analysis in educational policy studies appears in a volume by Wirt and Kirst (1972). Chapter headings ("Schools and System Support," "The Origins and Agents of Demand Inputs," and "The Local Conversion Process: Boards and Subsystems") indicate the manner in which these authors used the framework of systems analysis to organize their survey of the field. With the exception of political socialization research, however, few researchers have gone beyond using the language of systems theory as a means of classifying actions and identifying processes. To date there has been little work that generates hypotheses suggested by a systems viewpoint or attempts to test them. As Wirt (1977b: 401) acknowledges: "Quite frankly, the best theory we now have is only descriptive, i.e., the heuristic framework of 'systems analysis'." Using school policy as a case in point, Wirt provides what he hopes will be a "more dynamic aspect to research" with his observation that "policy originates in the gap between two differing distributions in the society, that of existing resources and that of existing needs" (p. 403). Focus on the disjunction between needs and resources in American schools might, in Wirt's view, illuminate many aspects of the policy-making process.

Policy output analyses (where "output" is defined as per-pupil expenditures by state or local governments) using multiple regression techniques have been well represented in the educational politics literature (Dye, 1966; 1967; Sharkansky, 1968; Zeigler and Johnson, 1972). The most prevalent finding from these studies is that "political" variables (e.g., interparty competition, voter turnout, degree of malapportionment of the state legislature, or partisan control of the legislature) has little or no effect on expenditures when compared with certain "economic" variables, such as state per capita income, urbanization, or industrialization.[3] A less discussed finding is that wealthier communities and states tend to spend a smaller portion of their resources for education than their less fortunate counterparts (Bloomberg and Sunshine, 1963; Dye, 1966; 1967).

Two other styles of recent research in political science have scarcely intruded into the politics of education field. Few researchers have attempted to represent any aspect of the educational policy system by formal models or even by tightly reasoned economic theory such as Anthony Downs (1957) provided the field of electoral politics. Equally lacking is a strong Marxist or neo-Marxist tradition. The educational system has had its radical critics, to be sure, but their most persistent theme—that public schooling has tended to reinforce the existing social order—has come largely from sociology (Bourdieu and Passeron, 1970) or economics (Bowles and Gintis, 1976; Carnoy and Levin, 1976) rather than political science.

Even more diverse than the theoretical legacy of policy analysis are the methodologies employed. Information gained from traditional case studies, ethnographies, participant observation, cross-sectional surveys, census data, government reports, depth interviewing, and experiments has contributed to what we know about education policy, and analysis has ranged from historical interpretation to statistical testing of hypotheses, multiple regression techniques, and, on occasion, time-series analysis, and causal modeling. Although a growing band of scholars from both political science and education has converged on education policy in recent years, an interesting contrast exists in the modal research style in each field. Most political scientists, after witnessing decades of case studies that yielded little in the way of cumulative theory, have turned to more systematic, more theoretical studies of the policy process. Many educational researchers, sometimes charged with having provided too little practical help for schools despite decades of testing and experimenting, have abandoned that tradition in favor of ethnographic approaches. In their studies they attempt to impart an intuitive understanding of observed phenomena by describing events in a way the reader can relate to his or her own experience. Exceptions exist, of course, on both sides.

II. FOCUS ON POLICY ANALYSIS

After years of relative neglect, the renewal of attention to *policy* within the discipline of political science has strongly affected work in the politics of education over the last decade. In fact, P. E. Peterson's (1974) identification of *policy analysis* as the unifying theme in a disparate literature may have been prescient. Yet policy analysis means different things in different contexts. For most political scientists, policy analysis is any analysis of the process by which policy is made or implemented. In their quest to understand better the policy process, analysis that leads to generalizations, then theory, about that process is the goal.

For educational policy makers in the U.S. Department of Education, however, policy analysis is likely to mean identification of the major problems and needs in education that require corrective action—and the establishment of priorities in addressing those problems within the limits of available resources. For a policy analyst working in a state education agency, or on the staff of a legislative committee, policy analysis more probably means analysis of a specific policy alternative that has been proposed (perhaps in draft bill form), identifying other viable alternatives and attempting to foresee the consequences of those alternatives. Although these three kinds of endeavors require some of the same skills and perspectives, they are not the same thing. The unseemly confusion about just what policy analysis is stems from three quite legitimate but different uses of the term.

Note that in the first interpretation, where the primary objective is explanation of the policy process, policy is often viewed as a dependent variable and the search will be for independent variables that bring it about. Thus, findings that variation in per-pupil expenditures by state and local governments (viewed as "policy") is best accounted for by such variables as per-capita income, urbanization, or industrialization (Dye, 1966; 1967) help us better understand the process by which policy is generated, even though educational policy makers are virtually powerless to change any of the independent variables. In the second and third kinds of policy analysis, however, policy makers are searching for ways to change policy that will, in turn, affect the dependent "outcome" variables in desirable ways. If, for example, a state legislator wants to know how to raise the reading comprehension scores of graduating seniors in an inner-city district, it may help in understanding the problem to know that economically disadvantaged children generally score lower in reading comprehension, but it won't resolve the problem. He or she still needs to know what can be changed through legislation or school policy that will raise reading scores in that district. Changes in teacher certification laws? Continual assessment programs? More money for remedial programs? Better reading materials and facilities? Changes in grade promotion policy? These are the kinds of variables that can be changed through the policy process, and someone will have to estimate the costs and benefits of each.

Better assessment of the extent to which policy at any level affects the amount and nature of student learning is badly needed. As Hawley (1977: 320) puts it, we need more attention "to issues that go beyond questions of who governs and how governors behave to the straightforward question, 'So what?'" There is substantial evidence that, in general, the nature of the school one attends has less effect on many educational outcomes, including academic achievement, than the nature of the family one grows up in (Coleman et al., 1966). This is not to suggest that schools don't matter, but it does suggest that the kind of school one attends (at least within the range of those available) may not make as much difference as once thought. Most available studies of the impact of variables such as class size, school facilities, the experience, academic qualifications, or salary of teachers, racial desegregation, or per pupil expenditures, provide no strong reassurance that those things have major effect on academic achievement or other desired educational outcomes.

Although many of these studies are flawed, the difficulty of conducting valid impact studies is considerable, in part because they inherently require the attribution of the cause of an observed effect to a policy. With outcomes as difficult to measure as some educational outcomes, all of the familiar problems of causal inference are compounded. Yet the importance of impact studies to the policy analysis enterprise is clear, and they represent one of the most promising areas of research over the next few years.

Educational policy analysis has a strong ally in this imposing task. The field of educational evaluation is a relatively mature, sophisticated area, which can contribute measurably to the work of the policy analyst. Program evaluation in education has profited from years of experience in the extremely difficult task of measuring educational outcomes. Yet, in his list of 11 factors influencing federal education legislation, based on the judgment of congressional staff members in education, Robert Andringa (1976a) ranks program analysis eleventh, two placed behind policy research studies and reports. Evaluations may be heeded more often as their authors become better aware of the political context of their assessments. By the same token, it is difficult to imagine any very informative policy analysis that does not address the predicted effects of proposed courses of action on such educational outcomes as academic achievement, school leaving, self-esteem, or employability. Educational program evaluators can contribute in major ways to policy analysis on the impact side.

III. TYPES OF EDUCATION ISSUES

One indication that theory has been slow to develop in education policy studies is the absence of any widely accepted comprehensive typology of education issues. With emerging awareness of the importance of better understanding the kinds of issues likely to arise under specific conditions (Bachrach and Baratz, 1962), and the likelihood that the nature of the political game changes from one type of issue to another (Dahl, 1961), the value of such a typology becomes apparent. Short of attempting an exhaustive classification, the categories of financial, curricular, access, personnel, school organization, and governance issues suggest themselves.

Most prevalent among research in education policy are studies of *financial* issues that attempt to answer the question: "Who pays, how much, for what?" A challenge to the inequities of the real property tax as a major revenue component in funding elementary and secondary education, based on the "equal protection" clause of the Fourteenth Amendment, is one such issue (Wise, 1967; *Serrano v. Priest,* 1971; *Rodriguez v. San Antonio,* 1971). Proposals for tuition tax credits, aimed at reducing the financial burden for families of youngsters attending private schools, constitute another. Studies of budgeting, referenda, tax and expenditure limitations, and collective bargaining are other examples of research bearing on financial issues.

A second category, *curricular* issues, revolves around the question "What should be taught?" Classic among these confrontations over content has been the still-continuing battle between creationists and the scientific community over the treatment of evolution in biology textbooks (Nelkin, 1977). But the genre is broad enough to include skirmishes in many local school districts over the appropriateness of sex education, driver training, or so-called frills such as art, music, and drama. School boards contemplating graduation requirements or debating the wisdom of adding more vocational courses at the expense of foreign languages are further examples of curriculum decisions. Widely reported episodes, such as the Kanawha County (West Virginia) violence over which books should be included on library reading lists, have received much of the attention, but studies are now beginning to appear that explore the manner in which curricula are established, and the role various institutions such as educational foundations and the commercial textbook industry, have played in shaping it.

The fuller form of the question might well read "What should be taught to whom?" and those last two words point toward a set of what we shall call *access* issues. As industrialized countries have moved inexorably toward universal education, compulsory education laws (usually through age 16) have become the norm. Yet even these educational systems are faced with selecting certain students for certain kinds of educational experiences.[4] How severe this selection should be, at what age it should take place, and on what basis it should be made are inescapable policy issues in the U.S. system as well as others. Some systems defer selection as long as possible and permit substantial student or parental choice in the matter. Others select students for certain tracks or programs relatively early and base the decision on "objective" criteria, such as examinations or grades, rather than the interest or self-assessment of the students. Tracking, ability grouping or streaming, grade repeating, and bilingual programs at the elementary and secondary level, as well as admission requirements at the postsecondary level, typify issues arising from questions of access.

The question "Who should teach and administer the system?" constitutes yet another class of *personnel* issues that have spawned complex certification requirements and tenure laws in every state. Even the manner in which teachers and administrators are recruited from among qualified candidates and the criteria used in their selection have major potential bearing on the effectiveness of the system.

A cluster of *organizational* issues arise from the question: "How should schools be organized and run?" Which schools need to be built, and where? Which ones can be closed? Should there be separate middle schools? How can students and faculty be racially integrated? These and a raft of other organizational problems, including school prayer, suspension policies, dress codes, corporal punishment, daily schedules, school calendar, and strict consolidation may become public issues to be resolved by the policy process.

Finally, *governance* issues address the question: "Who should make policy and who is accountable for the performance of the educational system?" Demands for "local control" of schools reached their peak in the late 1960s and early 1970s (Gittell, 1968), but authorities at each level of policy making tend to try to maximize their own discretion and resent incursions by officials at higher levels. A fair amount of attention has been given to questions of this order (Cronin, 1976; Hill, 1976), including proposals for new and stronger governance responsibilities for the school site (Guthrie, 1978). Other recurring governance issues have included the question of whether or not state boards of education or chief state school officers (CSSOs) should be appointed or elected, and the legitimacy of teacher strikes during negotiation.

Governance also includes the manner in which public officials seek to reassure their constituents that the system is operating efficiently. Demands for accountability are increasing in response to rising costs and apparently declining academic achievement, at least at the secondary level. Minimum competency testing has been one of the major issues at the state level in recent years and is, in large part, an effort to mandate an accounting scheme for student achievement. Students, under these plans, will be tested to ascertain whether they are competent at some stipulated minimal level. Variations on this theme and the motivations of supporters are numerous, but it seems clear that the rash of competency testing legislation has been precipitated by deteriorating public confidence in the performance of schools.

Some issues defy easy classification. For example, comprehensive proposals for a voucher plan are principally financial in nature, but also imply changes in curriculum, personnel, access, school organization, and governance (Coons and Sugarman, 1978).

IV. THE STRUCTURE OF INTERESTS IN EDUCATION

One way or another, almost everyone is involved in education. Students, teachers, and school administrators are engaged daily in the schooling process. Compulsory education commits most children to at least 10 or 11 years of interaction with teachers and other children—approximately six hours a day for 180 days—in a school setting. Many others, including parents, employees, realtors, and taxpayers, have less direct but still important interests in the way that schooling is conducted.

At the root of the erstwhile fiction that education is nonpolitical was the assumption that all actors in the enterprise have the same basic interest: the proper education and welfare of children (Tyack, 1974). Student protests, teacher strikes, and a sharp upturn in voter rejections of school tax increases have disabused us of this notion. We also recognize today that differences among youngsters in their interests, ability, experience, motivation, and needs make it likely that a proper education for one will be improper for another. By its very nature, public education is a series of guesses about what would be optimal for a given student and compromises as that student's claim on scarce resources competes with the claims of other students. Teachers, administrators, parents, and taxpayers, to name just a few, also have their legitimate claims on the system. The political task, performed at many levels by many people, is to identify these competing claims as accurately as possible and resolve them in ways which leave no significant interest alienated.

If we adopt the simplifying expedient of assuming the people's preferences on issues are identical to their interests,[5] it is not difficult to identify several more or less coherent interest groups in the education realm. Some of these interests are not politically effective, because they lack either consensus, organizational talent, or other political resources.

Parents, for example, act like an interest group on only a few kinds of issues, such as expansion or cutting of student aid programs at the college level. On most educational questions they are hopelessly divided. Parent-teacher organizations have waged effective campaigns at the national level against sex and violence in television programming and have generally been among the advocates of increased funding of education at the state level. When general support for schools, administrators, or funds is needed, the local Parent Teacher Association (PTA) can be counted upon, but many controversial issues find members of the PTA on both sides in about equal numbers. It has not been an organization that took the lead in demanding changes in school policy (Campbell et al., 1970; Wirt and Kirst, 1972; Ziegler et al., 1974). Recently parent advocacy groups—most notably the National Committee for Citizens in Education—have organized parents to bring pressure to bear on the education establishment in somewhat more specific ways. It is still too early to assess the ultimate impact of such groups on education policy.

One area where parents have demonstrated their effectiveness beyond all doubt is in special education programs. Parents of the handicapped have the incentive to commit necessary time and resources to bring about improvements in special education programs and make them more accessible. In most states, the special education lobby is a force to be reckoned with.

Students, of course, have even more severe problems than parents in operating as an effective interest. There are few issues on which students have strong agreement, and in cases where consensus does exist, lack of resources hampers effective political action. Even in postsecondary institutions, the experience, political expertise, and resource base of students is in such short supply that long-term influence on institutional policy is rare.

Teachers are a different matter. Their two major organizations, the National Education Association (NEA) and the American Federation of Teachers (AFT), possess all of the attributes of effective interest groups. They enjoy a large, committed membership, organizational talent, ample financial resources, and a clear sense of purpose across a wide range of issues. They have the ability to shape public opinion on some questions and the power to invoke a variety of sanctions, including the strike, when demands are not met. The emergence of these organizations as influential advocates of the interests of teachers at the local, state, and federal levels is one of the most consequential shifts that has taken place in the interest structure of American education since World War II.

To be sure, teachers had some liabilities that historically dampened their impact on education policy. The NEA, heavily influenced by school administrators then in its ranks, ignored many issues that might have benefited teachers in favor of broader professional issues (Iannaccone, 1967; Masters et al., 1964). And the prevailing myth that education was beyond politics weakened the commitment of both men and women teachers to pursue vigorously their own welfare (Rosenthal, 1969; Ziegler and Peak, 1970).

A host of other school-related interests bear upon the policy process as well. School administrators formulate and implement policy, but they also have their own interests, which are articulated by several professional associations.[6] Similarly, school board members have their own associations at the state and federal levels, which advise members how to bargain more effectively with teachers on the one hand, even while lobbying hard on numerous issues in legislative circles on the other. Textbook publishers, teacher colleges, athletic booster clubs, and education research foundations are examples of other parts of the diverse education establishment with discernable interests of their own.

The local community has its own interest in school policy. Growth-oriented business interests look to the salutary reputation of local schools, coupled with low tax rates, to attract new residents and corporate investments. The construction industry profits from new school building programs, and realtors have long recognized the intimate relationship between school location and residential housing patterns, including the social class and racial composition of neighborhoods.

Finally, we must acknowledge the broadest interest of all in terms of numbers of people affected. Schools cost money, and the revenues slated for education are a significant proportion of that paid by taxpayers in most states. Taxpayers have an undeniable interest in the education budget. They may mobilize episodically, during bond or tax increase referenda, or perhaps in support of particularly frugal candidates for the school board. Taxpayer associations are among the most potent lobbying groups in many state capitals and can be counted on to challenge major new educational programs on grounds of fiscal responsibility.

V. COMPETING EDUCATIONAL VALUES: QUALITY, EQUITY, AND EFFICIENCY

One objective of policy studies is to elucidate the relationship between policy alternatives and underlying values (Wirt, 1977b). The values served by education policies are many and varied, but in political discourse that attempts to justify a preference for one alternative over another, three values stand out among the others.

The first value perceived to be at stake in many educational issues is *quality* or excellence. Of course quality is even harder to define and measure in education than in many other policy fields, because a quality program for one student may not be a quality program for another. The term is not entirely devoid of meaning, however. In general usage, "quality" connotes programs that emphasize high academic achievement, highly trained, competent, professional teachers and administrators, and restricted access to weed out students ill suited to a course or program while allowing the most able to realize their full potential.

Other education policies, including many introduced at the state and federal level in the 1960s, are justified primarily on the basis of *equity*. American educators have always prided themselves on the existence of "equality of educational opportunity" in this society. It is clear, however, that geographic disparities—between states, and between local districts within states—in the kind of education provided are greater in American education than in many of the industrialized nations of the world. A major part of these discrepancies is traceable to the reliance of elementary and secondary education on the real property tax, which may yield many times the revenue per pupil in the wealthiest districts as in the poorest districts (Wise, 1967). State (and, to a lesser extent, federal) contributions have gone some appreciable distance toward equalizing revenue per pupil, but the gap between the amounts spent on pupils in wealthy districts and pupils in poor districts is still alarming.

A large number of educational programs and policies have been devised to alleviate such inequities in educational opportunity. School aid formulas in most states provide proportionately more assistance to poorer districts. By far the largest federal education program, in terms of dollars expended, has been Title I of the *Elementary and Secondary Education Act* (ESEA), which provides supplemental assistance to schools with a high proportion of economically and educationally disadvantaged pupils. Head Start, Follow Through, the Education for All Handicapped Children Act, school desegregation, and the Bilingual Education Act are just a few of the other major programs that have been justified primarily on ground of equity. In higher education, Pell grants (formerly Basic Educational Opportunity Grants) and the guaranteed student loan program have provided an opportunity for postsecondary education for many students who might otherwise have been denied the chance.

The value of *efficiency* injects the element of cost into policy considerations. This, it should be pointed out, is a step that runs against the grain for a good part of the education community. Teachers, administrators, and parents often take the position that if a program has been shown to be good for the education of children, it should be pursued, irrespective of the cost. Yet the implementation of most education policies requires money, and there are trade-offs to be considered both within local districts, where the allocation of finite resources requires a judgment about which programs will yield greater benefits for the money, and at the state and federal levels, where education competes with other sectors, such as public health, social welfare, and energy conservation, for a larger share of expected revenue.

A precise definition of efficiency would focus on the ratio of a program's benefits to its costs (McMahon, 1980; Nagel, 1980). Interests that invoke the value of efficiency, however, tend to emphasize the costs. The usual instinct of efficiency-minded individuals is to "cut the fat out" of education budgets, rather than to attempt to improve efficiency by increasing the output at little or no additional cost.

One could easily suggest other values—"community" (Peshkin, 1978), "liberty" (Guthrie, 1980), or "local control" (Wirt, 1977a)—for our list, but for many issues it appears that "quality," "equity," and "efficiency" vie with one another. Court desegregation orders, based on the principle of "equity," are attacked for lowering the "quality" of education provided or raising its costs through expensive (i.e., "inefficient") busing plans (Orfield, 1978; Crain, 1968). School closings, proposed by boards and administrators as a way to increase "efficiency" in a period of enrollment decline, are opposed for the alleged damage wrought on "quality" programs in existing neighborhood schools. Minimum competency testing programs, proposed with an eye toward improving standards ("quality"), are criticized on "equity" grounds for holding back minority and poor students without affecting the economically and socially advantaged, and on "efficiency" grounds for the potential costliness of remediation that may be required. Why and how these three values, or others, are used in the justification of policy positions in education has received very little empirical attention. There are indications that policy research, in education as in other fields, will be moving to clarify and elaborate the linkages between values and policy (Wirt, 1977b; Guthrie, 1980; McMahon, 1980; Merritt and Coombs, 1977).

VI. LOCAL EDUCATION POLICY

By dint of omission, the U.S. Constitution leaves education to the states. State legislatures, however, have typically passed much of their constitutional authority on to local school boards, and there are few places in the American political system where the norm of local control has been as strong. School officials in local school districts continue to make a wide range of policy decisions affecting in important ways the nature and quality of a child's educational experience as he or she moves through that community's public schools. Although it is true that the discretion of local education authorities is increasingly narrowed by state and federal intervention, it is also the case that local boards and administrators continue to exercise substantial control over the nature of the teaching staff, the number, size, and location of schools, the list of courses offered, textbooks used in those courses, extracurricular activities made available, student discipline, grading, graduation and promotion requirements, and a host of other policy concerns (Sergiovanni et al., 1980).

The typical structural arrangement is a local school district, delegated authority by the state, and governed by an elective lay board of education.[7] That board appoints a superintendent of schools to provide leadership in the day-to-day operation of the district. In point of fact, many superintendents exercise substantial policy influence simply by bringing certain policy issues to the board while skirting other potential issues.

Much of the policy studies literature in education at the local level addresses the "who governs" question. Particularly intriguing to scholars in this area has been the relationship between school boards and superintendents. Zeigler et al. (1974) list an assortment of useful political resources available to each camp but find a general tendency for boards to remain overly passive, even on clearly political questions, when confronted with the professional expertise of the superintendent. "School boards should govern or be abolished," they contend, in a system that cherishes lay control but often supports a professional elite characterized as relatively impervious to outside pressures (p. 254).

Iannaccone and Lutz (1970) point to a mechanism that, over time, gives the community some measure of control even though the policy process may appear to be closed at any given point in time. The pattern, which has become known as *incumbent defeat*, begins with some significant change in the socioeconomic composition of the community, which leads to heightened conflict in school board elections, and finally to defeat of an incumbent board member. A change in the control of the board follows, followed by the resignation or dismissal of the superintendent and replacement by a new one better attuned to the values of the new board. Such a process reintroduces the possibility of system responsiveness to strong public dissatisfaction, even without citizens monitoring the board's every move and providing input before each meeting.

Another useful concept in assessing the relative influence of boards, superintendents, and publics is what McGivney and Moynihan (1972) call the *zone of tolerance*. This is a range of activity that will be tolerated by the dominant elements of the public. It is possible that both boards and superintendents jockey for position within this zone (or their perception of the zone) but attempt not to stray outside it to avoid loss of public confidence and, perhaps, the incumbent defeat syndrome.

Closely related to the zone of tolerance notion is another concept that political scientists may recognize as one introduced by Carl Friedrich (1946) some years ago—*the law of anticipated reaction*. This dictum, when applied to education, says that boards and superintendents attempt to anticipate the reactions of the lay public to contemplated policy alternatives, pursuing only those for which the anticipated reaction is favorable, or at least not too threatening. Similarly, superintendents may attempt to anticipate the reactions of board members before structuring agendas or making recommendations to the board. The significance of this is that publics may exercise power over boards, and boards over superintendents, simply by virtue of their reputations, and in a manner that a researcher attempting to observe influence attempts might miss entirely (Boyd, 1976).

Although some researchers believe the school system is capable of responding (albeit in rather ponderous fashion) to shifts in majority sentiment of the laity, less can be said about its responsiveness to minority interests (Boyd, 1976). The demand for local control of schools, pressed most strenuously by blacks during the late 1960s and early 1970s, has met resistance from entrenched administrators, incumbent board members, and teacher organizations alike (Fantini et al., 1970; Gittell and Hollander, 1968). The irony is that minority interests historically have been best served in U.S. education by higher levels of authority. Local school districts have seldom placed equity concerns at the top of their list, and recent advances in school desegregation, compensatory education for the disadvantaged, bilingual education, and special education have all come at the instigation of federal or state government.

When one incorporates the public into our consideration of "who governs," still other questions are raised. Mann (1977: 71) points out that citizens may control either through participation or through representation. But how representative are school boards (usually elected in low-information, low-turnout, and often uncontested elections) of their constituents? To what extent do school board members agree with constituents on their role as trustee or delegate, the importance of issues, or on preferred resolutions to those issues (Ziegler et al., 1974)? Although a community unhappy with the performance of its public schools can still bring about policy changes, Wirt (1975b) suggests several trends that have reduced the responsiveness of local school boards to public demand, including increased state and federal intervention, increased competition among interest groups, greater differentiation of political cultures, and the intensification of professionalism. But how can elected board members in ever larger school districts know what is valued by constituents? In recent years we have begun to accumulate more systematic data bearing on the public's educational values, their beliefs about education, and their preferences on certain current issues (Gallup, 1978). Our understanding of how these citizen orientations develop, change, relate to each other, and ultimately affect the policy process is still inadequate.

One special case of citizen input that has received sustained scholarly attention is the school referendum. Historically, the American school system has relied heavily on a locally assessed real property tax for revenue. The importance to school districts of passing tax increases and bond referenda has made the maintenance of general public support for school programs a high priority for both professional administrators and school board members. Research on the question of why referenda pass or fail has yielded somewhat mixed findings (Drachler, 1977: 205-209). Voters of low socioeconomic status are less likely to vote in school referenda but, in general, the poor, less educated, older voter, and the voter with no children in public school, is less likely to support the referendum when they do vote (Elam, 1973). Furthermore, school referenda are seldom pure tests of public support for local schools. The specifics of the proposal, prevailing economic conditions, and the public mood with respect to the overall tax burden are inextricably entwined with general support for schools.

The most prominent change in the power structure of many districts has been the emergence of teacher organizations as effective political forces. Much of their influence is exercised through the medium of collective bargaining, which provides a means of pressing their demands across an array of perenial issues, including salary and fringe benefits, class size, working conditions, and discipline policy. The rapid growth of the AFT and its success in organizing new districts forced the NEA to adopt a more militant posture with respect to collective bargaining and work actions. In those districts that bargain collectively, the power equation now finds board members and other administrators on one side of the bargaining table and teachers on the other.

Precisely who has benefited more from the advent of collective bargaining is still a matter of some dispute (Odden et al., 1976). Whereas older studies showed that collective bargaining had minimal influence on teachers' salaries, a more recent report by Chambers (1976) indicates that collective bargaining can increase mean teacher salaries by as much as 15 percent. The traditional discretion of superintendents and board members has been reduced in certain key policy areas. School board associations, including the parent National School Board Association (NSBA), have strenuously opposed collective bargaining. The role of superintendent in many districts that have adopted collective bargaining has changed from advocate of the rights and interests of teachers before the board of education to representative of the board in day-to-day contacts with teachers. Although it seems reasonable to assume that collective bargaining may have brought about subtle shifts in the way teachers are perceived by the public, there has not as yet been adequate assessment of the manner in which bargaining has affected diffuse public support for teachers, schools, or the character of the policy process at the local level.

VII. EDUCATION POLICY AT THE STATE LEVEL

Nowhere in the entire spectrum of education policy are things changing more rapidly than at the state level. Not only are most states assuming a larger share of the funding burden from local districts, but federal aid is increasingly channeled to schools through the state administrative apparatus. "Flow-through" funds of this sort offer little additional discretion to state officials, but have bolstered the state education bureaucracy significantly.

State legislatures are center stage in the formulation of education policy at this level, and the transformation in the composition and operation of the legislative branch of state government since World War II has been profound. Even as reapportionment during the 1960s made them more representative, the workload expanded in many states to make legislating a more-or-less full-time job. As the number of bills each session increased, specialization was fostered, some legislators becoming education specialists. Professional staff support for major education committees and political parties became available in many states.

On the executive side, governorships have moved toward four-year terms and more authority in fiscal matters. The education bureaucracy has expanded several-fold. Chief state school officers are inceasingly appointed from the ranks of the profession rather than elected, and the agencies they administer have been among the fastest growing in many state capitals. State boards of education, elected in some states but more generally appointed, initiate more legislation and exercise control over a wide range of lesser policy matters that do not require legislative action.

Iannaccone (1967) drew upon the works of Bailey (1962), Masters et al. (1964), and Usdan (1963) to construct a typology of prevailing linkages between education structures at the state level. Looking specifically at the political activities of school administrators, professional education groups, and school board associations as they influenced the decision making of legislatures in 11 previously studied states, Iannaccone concluded that four types of relationship were observable. The first pattern, found in New England and labeled "disparate," was characterized by provincialism, localism, and defense of the home district against outsiders and central government. The second pattern, "statewide monolithic," was found in New York, New Jersey, and Rhode Island. This product of closed-system politics, presumed to be the modal type, finds compromise taking place among the education interest groups, rather than in the legislature. When cracks occur within the education establishment, as happened in Michigan and California, a "fragmented" pattern may emerge, with education interest groups forming coalitions and aligning with kindred political parties while the legislature assumes a more critical stance. The "syndical" pattern, found only in Illinois, employs a special governmental body, with legislators among its members, to plan, sift, compromise, and recommend education policy to the legislature (Iannoccone, 1967: 41).

The dominant education issue at the state level is the amount of funding to be made available for education in the next fiscal year and the way that sum is to be divided among the education establishment. Education issues involving money get the most attention, and those who hold the purse strings tend to make the decisions on education in the states (Rosenthal and Fuhrman, 1980). Particularly important in recent years have been controversies over the shape of the school aid formula, the division of funds between elementary and secondary schools, on the one hand, and higher educational institutions, on the other, and the extent of state support for private education. Meanwhile, legislators in many states, alarmed by sharp increases in property taxes at the local level and sales and income taxes at the state level, have considered and sometimes imposed tax limitations designed to check the burgeoning costs of education. California led the movement some have characterized as a tax revolt with Proposition 13, and numerous other states have followed suit. More recently, attention has turned to expenditure limitations where constitutional or statutory provisions are passed that cap education budgets.

Aside from performing the function of resource allocation, state governments also perform a regulatory function (deciding the standards by which teachers may be certified, for example) and provide numerous services to local districts. In the larger states each major area of the curriculum is represented by consultants and other service people at the state level available to provide support to local teachers and administrators.

Fiscal issues have not been the only ones surfacing at the state level. For several decades there has been a consolidation of local districts, stimulated by the desire for greater efficiency and the provision of higher-quality education in larger schools that could assemble a critical mass of students, facilities and staff. Only recently has a case been made for the latent functions of the small rural school in the community it serves

(Peshkin, 1978). The most visible current issue in many states is minimum competency testing of students, related to increasing demands for accountability in the educational process. Proposals for competency testing range from systematic assessment of student progress for local guidance counselors, to standardized state-imposed graduation tests that must be passed by a student before he or she can graduate from high school.

Momentum presently seems to be moving towards the states in the interplay of local, state, and federal authorities. This is so for several reasons. Local dissatisfaction with high taxes has already had the effect of increasing the state's contribution in some states. One consequence of that trend has been the assumption of more control for those states over new facets of education policy. At the same time, federal programs are being severely cut in the battle against inflation and the new philosophy in Washington favors block grants, with their increased discretion for state authorities as to their use, over categorical programs targeted for specific uses or populations. Several social changes, including increased within-state and between-state migration and communication, argue for an augmented state role in the educational enterprise.

VIII. THE FEDERAL ROLE

Although the quantum leap in federal education activity did not come until the mid-1960s, several pieces of legislation prior to World War II served as a major stimulus to the development of state and local efforts (Thomas, 1975). The passage of the Lanham Act in 1940, authorizing the construction, maintenance, and operation of schools in federally "impacted" areas, and the Serviceman's Readjustment Act (GI Bill of Rights) in 1944 both signaled a new federal willingness to aid education as a means of attacking other problems. The soaring birth rates following the end of the war, coupled with the precedent of 7.8 million veterans being directly assisted by the federal government, placed a strain on the educational system from preschool through graduate school and virtually guaranteed the continued involvement of the federal government in what had previously been an almost exclusively state and local preserve (Thomas, 1975: 20).

The National Science Foundation Act (1950) established a precedent for federal support for educational research, whereas PL 81-815 (for school construction) and PL 81-874 (for operating expenses) extended categorical aid to impacted areas in a continuation of the principle of the Lanham Act. The U.S. Supreme Court ruling in *Brown v. The Board of Education* (1954) was destined to involve the federal courts and the Department of Justice in hundreds of local school desegregation cases across the country. By 1958 the national preoccupation was with Sputnik I, and Congress responded with the National Defense Education Act (PL 85-864), designed to enhance the national security through better education. The Cooperative Research Act (PL 83-531) of 1954, the Higher Education Facilities Act (1958), the Vocational Education Act (1963), and the Library Construction and Services Act (1964) were other instances of legislation that set the stage for the massive Elementary and Secondary Education Act (ESEA) and the Higher Education Act (HEA) in 1965.

In an insightful paper summarizing a number of characteristics of educational policy making at the federal level, Samuel Halperin (1978) points out that federal initiatives in education are almost never justified as aid to improve education, per se, but are usually attempts to accomplish some noneducation goal through educational means. Most federal programs, in fact, are the consequence of external social forces rather than the efforts of educators, and many of the most influential programs have come from noneducation congressional committees and noneducation agencies in the executive branch.

For the most part, education policy in Washington is arrived at in nonpartisan fashion; in fact, most members of Congress pay relatively little attention to it, and only a handful have emerged as specialists in this policy area. More than 500 educational programs are scattered so widely that no one speaks for education. One could defend the claim, in fact, that there is no education policy, in the broader sense, emerging from the federal level, but rather hundreds of uncoordinated programs and policies.

Education interests are well represented in Washington, and much of the lobbying centers around the quest for more munificent funding of programs rather than questions of educational philosophy. A loosely structured coalition of interests called the *Committee for Full Funding of Education* meets periodically to coordinate their individual assaults on Congress and the national Treasury.

Mention of the role of the courts is, of course, most appropriate when discussing federal policy, although judicial intervention in education has also taken place at the state and local levels. A series of cases, including *Brown v. The Board of Education* (racial desegregation), *Lau v. Nichols* (bilingual education), and *Pennsylvania Association for Retarded Children* (special education), have dramatically shaped the educational issues of our lifetimes. In education, as in other areas, the U.S. Supreme Court has given new meaning to the term judicial activism. It remains to be seen whether an era of judicial restraint is on the horizon (Van Geel, 1977).

The relationship between federal education programs and their state counterparts is not always an easy one. At the time of the passage of the Elementary and Secondary Education Act in 1965, there was general acknowledgment that most states did not have the administrative where-with-all to implement large new federal programs. As a consequence, much federal aid was channeled directly to local districts, even while an attempt was made to bolster the capacity of states to administer such programs in the future. At present it appears that the tide may have turned. State-initiated reform, especially in school finance and special education domains, has been the rule rather than the exception over the past decade (Odden et al., 1976: 27-28). This shift has created a compelling need for greater attention to intergovernmental relationships to assure that categorical aid from the federal government complements the various forms of equalizing formula enacted by the states. Unless careful attention is given to the manner in which state and federal programs mesh, such federal initiatives as impact aid (P.L. 874), Title I of ESEA, and The Education of All Handicapped Children Act (P.L. 94-142), may have unintended disequalizing effects (Odden et al., 1976: 28-29) and may, in fact, serve as a disincentive to states to build equity considerations into their own programs.

IX.   THE ROAD AHEAD IN EDUCATION POLICY STUDIES

As of this writing, the U.S. education system is experiencing sharp discontinuities, which may significantly alter the nature of education policy making and even public schooling itself. Without exception, these changes are responses by the education system to broader changes in the social and economic order.

Most apparent has been the rapid decline in the birth rate during the mid-1960s, which, by 1973, had begun to reverse a growth trend in school enrollments that had been in progress since World War II. Suddenly the teacher shortage became a teacher surplus. Almost as quickly, school boards were faced with closing buildings proudly built a mere decade before. School districts whose local tax sources were supplemented by enrollment-sensitive state formulas found state aid declining. Scholars of school finance who had assumed that growth was the normal condition turned to studies of retrenchment. Business managers accustomed to thinking in terms of incremental budgeting now worried about budget decrements. Legislatures and school boards who had been practicing distributive politics now were faced with the more difficult task of redistributive politics (Lowi, 1964).

Nor is the dramatic change brought about by enrollment declines merely transitory. Whatever the future may hold for birth rates, the demographic certainty is that the U.S. population in the 1990s will be proportionately older. This shift will have implications for the structure of the educational establishment, with relatively more resources going to education beyond the traditional schooling years. It may also portend an increasingly difficult competition with other policy sectors for local, state, and federal dollars. The demands of older citizens will be for more security, better health care, and an assortment of services other than education. Their greater numbers may translate fairly readily into greater political influence.

Enrollments were not the only thing that had grown during the boom years since World War II. Even after discounting inflation, educational expenditures *per pupil* increased fivefold between 1950 and 1975 (Guthrie, 1980: 46). Class size has been reduced, and many educational programs and specializations have been added. Tens of thousands of school buildings were constructed. Yet one can document no dramatic improvement in educational outcomes over this period; in fact, if one accepts standardized test scores as valid indicators of school performance, we may have lost ground (Flanagan, 1976; Munday, 1980).

The combination of demographic shifts, skyrocketing costs, and meager evidence of improving quality of education in our schools has created a volatile political climate for education. The costs of certain equity-based policies of the 1960s, including busing for racial desegregation and the development of state equalization formulas, has been high in terms of the support of many middle-class citizens. Similarly, school closings, one of the most explosive local issues of the 1980s, have stirred the ire of many long-time supporters of public schools. The most genuinely conservative Republican administration since the Great Depression has pledged to return much of the discretion assumed by the federal government to the states and local districts. A public increasingly disenchanted with the performance of their public schools is casting about for alternatives.

Several policy projections are possible. In the near term, at least, states will probably assume an increasingly larger portion of the fiscal responsibility and discretion for public education. There will be calls for more and more accountability, resulting in attempts to document the quality of the work teachers are performing and the effects of schooling on youngsters. Minimum competency testing and teacher competency testing will remain in demand among legislators and interest groups monitoring the performance of schools in terms of quality. The Congress is posed to entertain seriously tuition tax credits as a way of providing an alternative to financially beleagured parents unhappy with the public schools. The private schools, currently expanding especially in the fundamentalist area, would be the principal benefactors of such a law. Voucher plans such as the Coons and Sugarman (1978) proposal may be contemplated much more seriously in an effort to stimulate a greater variety of schooling options at reasonable cost.

One last change in the environment in which educational policy change takes place should be noted. Over much of our national history, we have looked to education as the solution to all social and economic and political problems. As noted earlier, federal programs have almost always been instrumental in character—attempting to use education to eradicate poverty, banish racial prejudice, or develop a better space program. Repeated disillusionments have led to a more guarded, and doubtless more realistic, assessment of the role of education in creating basic social and economic reform (Carnoy and Levin, 1976).

The implications of all of this for the study of educational policy are several. First, if things change so rapidly, it is doubtful that much that we think we know about how education policy is formulated will be true 30 years from now. Tensions between the profession and the lay public will change in character as both the profession and the orientations of the public change. Relationships between the various levels of educational policy making are certain to change rather dramatically. It is difficult to identify laws, propositions, or even common knowledge that we confidently believe will survive these changes.

The need, first of all, is for more basic research on education policy. Impatience with the limited payoff of basic research in education to date has prompted some to suggest that research efforts should be redirected toward applied research that would yield immediate dividends in the improvement of schools. There is, however, no shortcut to improving educational outcomes without improving our knowledge of the policy process. The problem is not that we have had too little basic research, but that it has not usually been policy-relevant. Basic research probing the linkages between the preferences of constituents and the policy process (Tucker and Zeigler, 1980) is needed, as is research that better establishes the link between educational policy and changes in educational outcomes (Hawley, 1977).

For basic research to be policy-relevant, it is necessary to identify variables that are alterable through policy change and that will also bring about the kind of educational outcomes we seek. Until we have a much better idea of how interventions are going to affect academic achievement, student conduct, school leaving, or access to continued schooling, for example, policy analysis is likely to continue to be a sometimes futile exercise.

A concentration of research effort at the state level would seem appropriate at this point. Even before a Republican President who campaigned on a plank advocating a reduced federal role, the growth of education funding from Washington appeared stemmed (Grant and Eiden, 1980: 71). The share of total revenue made available to public elementary and secondary schools by the federal government increased less than 1 percent between 1968 and 1978; the share provided by the states increased 4½ percent over the same period. If present plans to provide more block grants to states materialize, that change, coupled with continued tax revolt at the local level, will almost inevitably throw a greater funding burden on the states. Although the transition from funding to influence is not automatic, the vastly larger and more sophisticated education agencies and legislative staffs in state capitals bespeak a capacity to absorb a part of any responsibility abdicated by the federal or local levels.

There is also a need for research that is more theoretical if we are to better understand the conditions under which certain of our findings no longer obtain (Burlingame and Geske, 1979). Given rapidly shifting wants and changing resources, perhaps Wirt's focus on the intersection of wants and resources is well advised (Wirt, 1977b).

Methodologically, there is a lacunae between shelves of single-case studies on the one hand, and a smaller number of policy output studies using all 50 states to determine the correlates of educational expenditures. Multiple-case studies (Burlingame and Geske, 1978) and even larger studies comparing schools, districts, or states on selected policy-relevant variables are badly needed at this point to elaborate and test our proto-theory.

One implication of these observations is that students of educational policy will probably not be able to do the job alone. Attention to the demographic, social, or economic changes that precipitate changes in education policy will require expertise from specialists in those areas. Closer examination of the impact of education policy on students will require a methodological sophistication and intuition about schooling more likely to be found among educational researchers. Knowledge of the policy process alone leaves us far short of the capability to foresee changes in the environment that will stimulate new policy proposals, to predict the educational outcomes of proposed alternatives with confidence, and to make timely adjustments. Education policy analysis will have come of age when its theories and its methods are equal to that task.

ACKNOWLEDGMENTS

This research was conducted using the library and resources of the Office for the Analysis of State Educational Systems (OASES) at the University of Illinois, Urbana-Champaign. The author is indebted to Marcia K. Chicoine for bibliographic assistance and constructive comments on a preliminary draft.

NOTES

1. See M. W. Peterson (1974) for an excellent discussion of the political aspects of higher education.
2. We should note that the behavior movement was largely directed at explaining relatively discreet behavior, such as voting, by invoking other individual attributes (e.g., demographic variables) or psychological orientations (e.g., attitudes, beliefs, or values). Ironically, the conceptual elaboration of these "explanatory" variables far outstripped our still rudimentary classificatory schemes for political behavior itself (Milbrath, 1965). More useful ways of conceptualizing political behavior are still needed before we can proceed very far in our current attempts to explain policy output.
3. See P. E. Peterson (1974) for a thoughtful critique of examples of comparative policy output analysis in education.
4. Selection in Europe historically has been earlier and more severe than in the United States, but reforms in many countries have virtually eliminated the "11 plus" exam

and its functional equivalents in other countries. Access issues also include the existence of courses or curricula to which some students are not admitted for reason of
ability, age, or sex.

5. Although David Truman (1951) defined interests as attitudes, it would seem more
    straightforward in relating them to the policy process if we focused on specific pref-
    erence on a given issue; i.e., all individuals who favor granting tuition tax credits share
    an interest on that issue. This notion of subjective interest will be of greater utility in
    policy studies than the concept of objective interest.

6. The American Association of School Administrators (AASA) is the most influential,
    with some 18,000 members, many of them superintendents. Other groups are the
    National Association of Secondary School Principals (NASSP) and the National Ele-
    mentary School Principals Association (NESPA).

7. School boards in a number of our largest cities are appointed by the mayor. In many
    of these cities, the separation of city governance and educational governance typical
    of most localities is much less absolute.

BIBLIOGRAPHY

Allison, G. T. (1969). Conceptual models and the Cuban missile crisis. *The American Political Science Review 63*: 689-718.

Almond, G. A., and Coleman, J. S. (Eds.) (1960). *The Politics of the Developing Areas.*
Princeton University Press, Princeton, NJ.

Andringa, R. C. (1976a). Eleven factors influencing federal education legislation. In
Federalism at the Crossroads: Improving Educational Policymaking. George Washington University, Washington, DC, pp. 79-80.

—— (1976b). The view from the hill. In *Federalism at the Crossroads: Improving Educational Policymaking.* George Washington University, Washington, DC, pp. 71-78.

Bachrach, P., and Baratz, M. S. (1962). Two faces of power. *American Political Science
Review 56*: December, 947-952.

Bailey, S. K., and Mosher, E. K. (1968). *ESEA: The Office of Education Act of 1965.*
Inter-University Case Program #100. Bobbs-Merrill, Indianapolis, IN.

Bailey, S. K., Frost, R. T., Marsh, P. E., and Wood, R. C. (1962). *Schoolmen and Politics:
A Study of State Aid to Education in the Northeast.* Syracuse University Press,
Syracuse, NY.

Baldridge, J. V. (1971). The analysis of organizational change: A human relations
strategy versus a political system strategy. R&D memo #75, Stanford Center for
R&D in Teaching, Stanford University, Stanford, CA.

Bentley, A. R. (1908). *The Process of Government.* University of Chicago Press, Chicago.

Berke, J. S., and Kirst, M. W. (1972). *Federal Aid to Education.* Lexington Books, Lexington, MA.

Bloomberg, W., Jr., and Sunshine, M. (1963). *Suburban Power Structures and Public
Education.* Syracuse University Press, Syracuse, NY.

Bobbitt, F., Hall, J. W., and Wolcott, J. D. (Eds.). *The Supervision of City Schools: The
Twelfth Yearbook of the National Society for the Study of Education,* part I.
National Society for the Study of Education, Bloomington, IL.

Bourdieu, P., and Passeron, J. C. (1970). *La reproduction: éléments pour une théorie du
système d'enseignement.* Minuit, Paris.

Bowles, S., and Gintis, H. (1976). *Schooling Capitalist America: Educational Reform and the Contradictions of Economic Life.* Basic Books, New York.

Boyd, W. L. (1976). The public, the professionals, and educational policy making: Who governs? *Teachers College Record 77*: 539-577.

Braybrooke, D., and Lindbloom, C. E. (1963). *A Strategy of Decision.* Free Press, New York.

Broudy, H. S. (1965). Conflict in values. In *Educational Administration–Philosophy in Action,* R. Ohm and W. Monohan (Eds.). University of Oklahoma, College of Education, Norman.

Burlingame, M., and Geske, T. G. (1979). State politics and education: An examination of selected multiple-state case studies. *Educational Administration Quarterly 15*: (Spring) 50-75.

Burnsed, B., (1980). Higher education: Legislative issues in the 80's. *State Legislatures 6*: (September) 21-25.

Callahan, R. (1962). *Education and the Cult of Efficiency.* University of Chicago Press, Chicago.

Campbell, R., Cunningham, L., McPhee, R. F., and Nystrand, R. (1970). *The Organization and Control of American Schools.* Charles A. Merrill, Columbus, OH.

Campbell, R. F., and Mazzoni, T. L., Jr. (1976). *State Policy Making for the Public Schools.* McCutchen, Berkeley, CA.

Carnoy, M., and Levin, H. M. (1976). *The Limits of Educational Reform.* McKay, New York.

Carter, R. F. (1960). *Voters and Their Schools.* Institute for Communication Research, Stanford, CA.

Chambers, J. G. (1976). The impact of bargaining on the earnings of teachers: A report on California and Missouri. Paper presented to the U.K.–U.S. Conference on Teacher Markets, University of Chicago, December.

Charters, W. W. (1953). Social class analysis and the control of public education. *Harvard Educational Review 23*: 268-283.

Cobb, R. W., and Elder, C. D. (1972). *Participation in American Politics: The Dynamics of Agenda-Building.* Allyn & Bacon, Boston.

Cohen, D. M., March, J. G., and Olsen, J. P. (1972). A garbage can model of organizational choice. *Administrative Science Quarterly 17.*

Coleman, J. S., Campbell, E. Q., Jobson, C. J., McPartland, J., Mood, A. M., Weinfield, F. D., and York, R. L. (1966). *Equality of Educational Opportunity.* U.S. Government Printing Office, Washington, DC.

Coombs, F. S. (1977). Who participates in educational change—How? In *Reorganizing Education: Management and Participation for Change,* vol. I. Sage, London.

—— (1980a). Bases of non-compliance with policy. *Policy Studies Journal 8* (Summer): 885-891.

—— (1980b). Opportunities in the comparison of state education policy systems. Stanford University, Institute for Research on Educational Finance and Governance, Project Report No. 80-A16.

Coons, J. E., and Sugarman, S. D. (1978). *Education by Choice: A Case for Family Control.* University of California Press, Berkeley.

Counts, G. S. (1972). The social composition of boards of education: A study in the social control of public education. *Supplementary Education Monographs 30.* University of Chicago Press, Chicago, IL.

Crain, R. (1968). *The Politics of School Desegregation.* Aldine, Chicago.

Cronin, J. M. (1976). The federal takeover: Should the junior partner run the firm? In *Federalism at the Crossroads: Improving Educational Policymaking.* George Washington University, Washington, DC, pp. 1-5.

Dahl, R. (1961). *Who Governs?: Democracy and Power in an American City.* Yale University Press, New Haven, CT.

Dearman, N. B., and Plisko, V. W. (1980). *The Condition of Education,* 1980 ed. National Center for Education Statistics, Washington, DC.

Downs, A. (1957). *An Economic Theory of Democracy.* Harper & Row, New York.

Drachler, N. (1977). Education and politics in large cities, 1950-1970. In *The Politics of Education: The Seventy-Sixth Yearbook of the National Society for the Study of Education,* part II, S. D. Scribner (Ed.). National Society for the Study of Education, Chicago.

Dye, T. R. (1966). *Politics, Economics, and the Public: Policy Outcomes in the American States.* Rand McNally, Chicago.

—— (1967). Governmental structure, urban environment, and educational policy. *Midwest Journal of Political Science 11*: 353-380.

Easton, D. (1953). *The Political System: An Inquiry into the State of Political Science.* Knopf, New York.

—— (1965). *A System Analysis of Political Life.* Wiley, New York.

Easton, D., and Dennis, J. (1965). *Children in the Political System.* Wiley, New York.

Elam, S. (Ed.) (1973). *The Gallup Polls of Attitudes Toward Education, 1969–1973.* Phi Delta Kappa, Bloomington, IN.

Eliot, T. H. (1959). Toward an understanding of public school politics. *American Political Science Review 53*: 1032-1051.

Fantini, M. M., Gittell, M., and Magat, R. (1970). Community Control and the Urban School, Praeger, New York.

Flanagan, J. C. (1976). Changes in school levels of achievement: Project TALENT ten and fifteen year retest. *Educational Researcher 5*: 9-11.

Friedrich, C. J. (1946). *Constitutional Government and Democracy.* Ginn, Boston.

Froman, L. A. (1968). The categorization of policy contents. In *Political Science and Public Policy,* A. Ranney (Ed.). Markham, Chicago, pp. 41-52.

Gallup, G. H. (1978). The 10th annual Gallup poll of the public attitudes toward the public schools. *Phi Delta Kappan,* September, p. 35.

Garms, W. I., Guthrie, J. W., and Pierce, L. C. (1978). *School Finance: The Economics and Politics of Public Education.* Prentice-Hall, Englewood Cliffs, NJ.

Gittell, M. (1968). *Participants and Participation: A Study of School Policy in New York City.* Praeger, New York.

Gittell, M., and Hollander, T. E. (1968). *Six Urban School Districts: A Comparative Study of Institutional Response.* Praeger, New York.

Grant, W. V., and Eiden, L. J. (1980). *Digest of Education Statistics 1980.* National Center for Education Statistics, Washington, DC.

Grimshaw, W. J. (1979). *Union Rule in the Schools: Big-City Politics in Transformation.* Lexington Books, Lexington, MA.

Grumm, J. G., and Wasby, S. L. (Eds.) (1981). *The Analysis of Policy Impact.* Lexington-Heath, Lexington, MA.

Guthrie, J. (1978). Proposition 13 and the future of California's schools. *Phi Delta Kappan,* September, p. 12.

—— (1980). An assessment of educational policy research. *Educational Evaluation and Policy Analysis, 2* (September–October): 41-55.

Halperin, S. (1976a). Block grants or categorical aids? What do we really want—Consolidation, simplification, decentralization? In *Federalism at the Crossroads: Improving*

Educational Policymaking. George Washington University, Washington, DC, pp. 67-70.

—— (1976b). Federal takeover, state default, or a family problem? In *Federalism at the Crossroads: Improving Educational Policymaking.* George Washington University, Washington, DC, pp. 19-22.

—— (1976c). Is the federal government taking over education? *Compact,* Summer, pp. 2-4.

—— (1978). The political world of Washington policymakers in education. Institute for Educational Leadership, Washington, DC, unpublished manuscript.

Hawley, W. D. (1977). If schools are for learning, the study of the politics of education is just beginning. In *The Politics of Education: The Seventy-Sixth Yearbook of the National Society for the Study of Education,* part II, J. D. Scribner (Ed.). National Society for the Study of Education, Chicago.

Hess, R. D., and Torney, J. V. (1967). *The Development of Political Attitudes in Children.* Aldine, Chicago.

Hill, W. G. (1976). The role of the state in education. In *Federalism at the Crossroads: Improving Educational Policymaking.* George Washington University, Washington, DC, pp. 27-34.

Iannaccone, L. (1967). *Politics in Education.* Center for Applied Research in Education, New York.

Iannaccone, L., and Cistone, P. J. (1974). *The Politics of Education.* ERIC Clearinghouse on Educational Management, University of Oregon, Eugene.

Iannaccone, L., and Lutz, F. (1970). *Politics, Power and Policy: The Governing of Local School Districts.* Charles E. Merrill, Columbus, OH.

Institute for Educational Leadership (1976). *Federalism at the Crossroads: Improving Educational Policymaking.* George Washington University, Washington, DC.

Kirst, M. (1979). The new politics of state education finance. *Phi Delta Kappan,* February, p. 427.

Kirst, M. W., and Garms, W. I. (1980). The demographic, fiscal, and political environment of public school finance in the 1980s. Paper delivered at the annual meeting of the American Educational Finance Association (AEFA), San Diego, March.

Kirst, M. W., and Mosher, E. K. (1969). Politics of education. *Review of Educational Research 39* (December): pp. 623-640.

Kissick, S. (1980). The changing look of school finance reform. *State Legislatures 6* (September): pp. 15-19.

Knickman, J. R., and Reschovsky, A. (1980). The implementation of school finance reform. *Policy Sciences 12* (October): 301-314.

Lanone, G. R., and Smith, B. L. R. (1973). *The Politics of School Decentralization.* Heath, Lexington, MA.

Lasswell, H. D. (1930). *Psychopathology and Politics.* Viking Press, New York, pp. 261-262.

—— (1936). *Politics: Who Gets What, When and How?* McGraw-Hill, New York

Lasswell, H. D., and Kaplan, A. (1950). *Power and Society: A Framework for Political Inquiry.* Yale University Press, New Haven, CT.

Lehne, R. (1978). *The Quest for Justice: The Politics of School Finance Reform.* Longman, New York.

Levin, H. M. (Ed.) (1972). *Community Control of Schools.* Brookings Institution, Washington, DC.

Lindblom, C. E. (1959). The science of "muddling through." *Public Administration Review 18:* 79-88.

—— (1965). *The Intelligence of Democracy.* Free Press, New York.

Lowi, T. (1964). American business, public policy, case-studies, and political theory. *World Politics 6*: 677-715.

Lutz, F. W. and Iannaccone, L. (Eds.) (1978). *Public Participation in Local School Districts.* Lexington Books, Lexington, MA.

Mann, D. (1976). *The Politics of Administrative Representation: School Administration and Local Democracy.* Heath, Lexington, MA.

—— (1977). Participation, representation, and control. In *The Politics of Education: The Seventy-Sixth Yearbook of the National Society for the Study of Education,* part II, J. D. Scribner (Ed.). National Society for the Study of Education, Chicago.

March, J., and Simon, H. (1958). *Organizations.* Wiley, New York.

Masters, N. A., Salisbury, R., and Eliot, T. H. (1964). *State Politics and the Public Schools.* Knopf, New York.

Mazzoni, T. L., and Campbell, R. F. (1976). Influentials in state policy-making for the public schools. *Educational Administration Quarterly 12* (Winter): 1-26.

McGivney, J. H., and Moynihan, W. (1972). School and community. *Teachers College Record 74* (December): 317-356.

McMahon, W. W. (1980). Efficiency and equity criteria for educational budgeting and finance. College of Commerce and Business Administration, University of Illinois at Urbana-Champaign, Faculty Working Paper #733.

Merritt, R. L., and Coombs, F. S. (1977). Politics and educational reform. *Comparative Education Review 21* (June/October): 247-273.

Milbrath, L. (1965). *Political Participation: How and Why Do People Get Involved in Politics?* Rand McNally, Chicago.

Minar, D. (1966). Community basis of conflict in school system politics. *American Sociologic Review 31*: 822-835.

Mitchell, D. E., and Iannaccone, L. (1979). The impact of legislative policy on the performance of public school organization. Paper prepared for the California Policy Seminar, University of California, January 1979.

Munday, L. A. (1980). Changing test scores: Basic skills development in 1977 compared with 1970. *Phi Delta Kappan 60*: 670-671.

Munger, F. J., and Fenno, R. F. (1962). *National Politics and Federal Aid to Education.* Syracuse University Press, Syracuse, NY.

Murphy, J. T. (1974). *State Education Agencies and Discretionary Funds. Lexington Books,* Lexington, MA.

—— (Ed.) (1980). *State Leadership in Education: On Being a Chief State School Officer.* Institute for Educational Leadership, George Washington University, Washington, DC.

Nagel, S. S. (1981). What is efficiency in policy evaluation? In *Evaluating and Optimizing Public Policy,* D. Palumbo, S. Fawcett, and P. Wright (Eds.). Lexington Books, Lexington, MA.

Nelkin, D. (1977). *Science Textbook Controversies and the Politics of Equal Time.* M.I.T. Press, Cambridge, MA.

Odden, A., Augenblick, J., and Vincent, P. E. (1976). *School Finance Reform in the States, 1976-1977: An Overview of Legislative Actions, Judicial Decisions and Public Policy Research.* Education Commission of the States, Denver, CO.

Orfield, G. (1969). *The Reconstruction of Southern Education.* Wiley, New York.

—— (1978). *Must We Bus? Segregated Schools and National Policy.* Brookings Institution, Washington, DC.

Parsons, T. (1951). *The Social System.* Free Press, New York.

—— (1969). *Politics and Social Structure.* Free Press, New York.

Peshkin, A. (1978). *Growing up American: Schooling and the Survival of Community.* University of Chicago Press, Chicago.

Peterson, M. W. (1974). Administration in higher education: Sociological and social-psychological perspectives. In *Review of Research in Education,* F. Kerlinger and J. B. Carroll (Eds.). Peacock, Itasca, IL.

Peterson, P. E. (1974). The politics of American education. In *Review of Research in Education,* vol. 2, F. N. and J. B. Carroll (Eds.). Peacock, Itasca, IL.

—— (91976). *School Politics, Chicago Style.* University of Chicago Press, Chicago.

Rich, J. M. (1974). *New Directions in Educational Policy.* Professional Educators Publications, Lincoln, NE.

Rodriguez v. San Antonio Independent School District (1971). 337 F. Supp. 280 (W. W. Texas, 1971), rev'd. 411 U.S. 1.

Rosenthal, A. (1969). *Pedagogues and Power.* Syracuse University Press, Syracuse, NY.

Rosenthal, A., and Fuhrman, S. (1980). Education policy: Money is the name of the game. *State Legislatures 6* (September): 7-10.

Salisbury, R. H. (1965). State politics and education. In *Politics in the American States,* H. Jacobs and K. Vines (Eds.). Little, Brown, Boston, pp. 331-370.

—— (1968). The analysis of public policy: A search for theories and roles. In *Political Science and Public Policy,* A. Ranney (Ed.). Markham, Chicago, pp. 151-175.

—— (1980). *Citizen Participation in the Public Schools.* Lexington Books, Lexington, MA.

Scribner, J. D., and Englert, R. M. (1977). The politics of education: An introduction. In *The Politics of Education: The Seventy-Sixth Yearbook of the National Society for the Study of Education,* part II, J. D. Scribner (Ed.). National Society for the Study of Education, Chicago.

Sergiovanni, T. J., Burlingame, M., Coombs, F. S., and Thurston, P. W. (1980). *Educational Governance and Administration.* Prentice-Hall, Englewood Cliffs, NJ.

Serrano v. Priest (1971). 5 Cal. 3rd 584, 487 p. 2nd 1241.

Sharkansky, I. (1968). *Spending in the American States.* Rand McNally, Chicago.

Simon, H. J. (1945). *Administrative Behavior. Macmillan, New York.*

Sroufe, G. E. (1980). The very last word about politics of education research. Politics of Education Bulletin 9 (Fall): 1-6.

Taylor, F. (1911). *The Principles of Scientific Management.* Harper & Row, New York. Reprinted by Harper & Row, New York, 1945.

Thomas, N. C. (1975). *Education in National Politics.* McKay, New York.

Thompson, J. T. (1976). *Policymaking in American Public Education.* Prentice-Hall, Englewood Cliffs, NJ.

Timpone, M. (1976). Into the maw: The uses of policy in Washington. *Phi Delta Kappan,* October, pp. 177-178.

Truman, D. (1951). *The Governmental Process: Political Interests and Public Opinion.* Knopf, New York.

Tucker, H. J., and Zeigler, L. H. (1980). *Professionals Versus the Public: Attitudes, Communication, and Response in School Districts.* Longman, New York.

Tyack, D. (1974). *The One Best System.* Harvard University Press, Cambridge, MA.

Usdan, M. D. (1963). *The Political Power of Education in New York State.* Institute of Administrative Research, Teachers College, Columbia University, New York.

Van Geel, T. (1977). Two models of the supreme court in school politics. In *The Politics of Education: The Seventy-Sixth Yearbook of the National Society for the Study of Education,* part II, J. D. Scribner (Ed.). National Society for the Study of Education, Chicago.

Verba, S., and Nie, N. H. (1972). *Participation in America: Political Democracy and Social Equality.* Harper & Row, New York.

Walter, R. L. (1975). *The Teacher and Collective Bargaining.* Professional Education Publications, Lincoln, NE.

Weber, M. (1946). *Essays in Sociology,* Translated and edited by H. H. Gerth and C. W. Mills. Oxford University Press, New York.

Weick, K. E. (1969). *The Social Psychology of Organizing.* Addision-Wesley, Reading, MA.

Wildavsky, A. (1964). *The Politics of the Budgetary Process.* Little, Brown, Boston.

Wiley, D. K. (1979). State level educational politics: Old problems and new research directions. Paper presented at the 1979 Annual American Education Research Association (AERA) Meeting, San Francisco, April.

Wirt, F. M. (1975a). *The Polity of the School.* Lexington Books, Lexington, MA.

—— (1975b). Social diversity and school board responsiveness in urban schools. In *Understanding School Boards,* P. L. Cistone (Ed.). Heath, Lexington, MA.

—— (1977a). School policy culture and state decentralization. In *The Politics of Education: The Seventy-Sixth Yearbook of the National Society for the Study of Education,* part II, J. D. Scribner (Ed.). National Society for the Study of Education, Chicago.

—— (1977b). Reassessment needs in the study of the politics of education. *Teachers College Record 78* (May): 401-412.

—— (1980a), Comparing educational policies: Theory, units of analysis, and research strategies. *Comparative Education Review 24* (June): 174-191.

—— (1980b). Is the prince listening? Politics of education and the policymaker. Paper delivered at 1980 Annual Meeting of the American Political Science Association (APSA), Washington, D. C., August 28-31.

Wirt, F. M., and Kirst, M. W. (1972). *The Political Web of American Schools.* Little, Brown, Boston.

Wise, A. E. (1967). *Rich Schools, Poor Schools: The Promise of Equal Educational Opportunity.* University of Chicago Press, Chicago.

Wolanin, T. R. (1976). Congress, information and policymaking for postsecondary education: Don't trouble me with the facts. In *Federalism at the Crossroads: Improving Educational Policymaking.* George Washington University, Washington, DC, pp. 81-98.

Yudof, M. G. (1979). Law-and-education research: Past and future. *New York University Education Quarterly,* Fall, pp. 10-15.

Ziegler, H., and Peak, W. (1970). The political functions of the educational system. *Sociology of Education 43*: 115-142.

Zeigler, L. H. and Jennings, M. K., with Peak, G. W. (1974). *Governing American Schools.* Duxbury Press, North Scituate, MA.

Zeigler, H., and Johnson, K. F. (1972). *The Politics of Education in the States.* Bobbs-Merrill, New York.

26

Population Policy

Michael E. Kraft / University of Wisconsin, Green Bay, Wisconsin

Changes in the characteristics of a nation's population usually occur slowly, are little noticed in the short run, and are treated as either insignificant or beyond the reach of governmental policy. But slight changes in the birth rate, death rate, and the rate of growth of a population, or modest changes in its composition or distribution, can have massive effects on the type and level of demands citizens make on government, on the capacity of government to respond to those demands, and on the distribution of political power. Consequently, it is no exaggeration to say that population changes are among the most important factors affecting the nature of public policy and the quality of life in a nation.

The focus of this chapter is mainly on the United States. I examine recent population trends, major policy developments of the last several decades, the politics of population policy, and probable future policy changes. But I am concerned also with the larger context of world populations problems, both in the less developed countries (LDCs) and the developed countries, and U.S. policies as they bear on those problems. The essay is both descriptive and analytical. Most of the chapter provides an overview of population problems and a broad account of recent policy development in the United States; but there are two other concerns as well: assessment of the current policies and the potential contribution of political scientists and policy analysts to our understanding of population problems and to the making of intelligent policy choices.

Because several other chapters in this Encyclopedia deal with selected aspects of population problems in the United States, I shall give relatively little attention to them here. These include internal migration (Snowbelt to Sunbelt, as well as urban-suburban-rural population shifts), land use, housing, and the environmental and energy implications of population changes. Many public policies, of course, have some effect on the kinds of population problems under consideration here, and population changes have a reciprocal effect on a wide variety of public policies. Partly for this reason, most of this chapter focuses on explicit and direct population policies rather than on all policy actions related in some manner to population.

I. POPULATION POLICY: WHAT IS IT?

Population policy is not easily defined or categorized, and not uncommonly, discussions of it lack precision or coherence. To some extent the reasons are not specific to population policy but can be found in the complexity of public policy in general. Lasswell and Kaplan (1950) define policy concisely as a "projected program of goals, values, and practices." But as Charles Jones notes, public policy is used in a variety of ways. It is taken by some to mean goals or ends to be achieved, plans or proposals (means) to achieve them, formal or authorized programs and their effects, or specific decisions or actions taken in setting goals, formulating plans, and implementing programs (Jones, 1977). Moreover, public policy in a given area may not be self-evident, and must be specified by the analyst using the policy makers' stated intentions or goals, the formal language of statutes and administrative regulations, and the observable policy decisions of government officials.

Aside from the general difficulty of defining public policy precisely, there are some problems unique to the subject of population. For our purposes, a rigorous definition of population policy is not essential, nor need we review the full range of definitional issues that students of population policy have raised. But some attention to these problems is warranted. Corsa and Oakley (1979) offer what seems to be the most comprehensive search for clarity of definition. They review the way in which 34 authors, writing between 1940 and 1975, define population policy, concluding that there was some consensus on the following elements: Some demographic effect is intended or is produced, governments participate in some way, indirect as well as direct means or subpolicies are included, and the concern is population-influencing rather than population-responsive policies. Taking into account the varying usage and these common elements, they offer the following definition: Population policy consists of "those actions of government that affect or attempt to affect the balance between births, deaths, and migration of human beings" (Corsa and Oakley, 1979: 156).

Corsa and Oakley's definition is fairly inclusive in that it allows for unintended consequences of government action and indirect policy impact on components of a nation's population, and does not specify how purposive, sustained, or coherent the "actions" of government need be. Miller and Godwin (1977) expand the scope of population policy even more. It should include, they argue, "something a government chooses to do or not to do" about population problems. Thus "nondecisions," decisions not to take action, are considered worthy of the analyst's attention. By not taking action on population, governments allow other influences (e.g., prevailing private practices) to determine population events.

Clearly, such inclusive definitions are needed to capture much of what the United States and other nations have done (and not done) about population problems. At the same time, for many purposes one needs to differentiate between *explicit* population policies having as their major goal the achievement of particular demographic effects (e.g., lower fertility) and other policies, such as the regulation of abortion, that have only indirect and/or unintended population impacts. The United States has never adopted an explicit and comprehensive national population policy, but a variety of more limited public policies affecting population have been enacted in the last several decades. These policies will be reviewed below, as will a number of proposals of recent years that have as their goal the establishment of a more expansive and explicit population policy.

II. WORLD POPULATION TRENDS AND POLICY IMPLICATIONS

Prior to examining American population trends and policy actions, a brief overview of demographic developments on a worldwide basis—in developing as well as developed nations—is useful. The exercise helps put American population policy issues into the broader context in which they must be assessed.

Without doubt the major population problem worldwide is that of a rapid and potentially catastrophic rate of growth. The magnitude and consequences of the problem are easily demonstrated. The extraordinary modern acceleration of growth began around 1750. Prior to that time human history was characterized by a relatively stable or very slowly growing population. By 1800, however, the world population reached 1 billion people, by 1850 it had increased to 1.3 billion, by 1900 to 1.7 billion, and by 1950 to 2.5 billion (Coale, 1974). The world's population in mid-1980 is estimated to be 4.4 billion; and with an estimated 1979 crude birth rate of 28 per 1000 population and a death rate of 11 per 1000 population, world population is growing at an annual rate of 1.7 percent. World fertility rates have been declining for the last decade, and continued decline is expected. But even with a decline in the rate of growth to 1.5 percent by the year 2000, the United Nations estimates a world population of 6.2 billion at that time. Currently the world population is increasing by 74 million per year, or approximately 200,000 per day. Even with the slower rate of growth expected by the year 2000, the annual net increase in that year is projected to be about 93 million people (because of the larger base of population). With a striking difference in the growth rate between the developed nations (0.6 percent) and the developing nations (2.0 percent), most of the growth in the next two decades (90 percent) will occur in the developing world (van der Tak et al., 1979: 18).

Stabilization of the world's population is unlikely this side of 8 to 10 billion, with some estimates considerably higher. Tsui and Bogue (1978) predict a rapid slowdown to a zero rate of growth, and estimate that a peak global population of 8.1 billion will be reached by 2050; however, their estimate assumes that family planning programs in the developing world are vigorously supported and that social and economic development continues to reinforce the tendency toward lower fertility. Other estimates are less optimistic. The United Nations estimates the peak to be about 11 billion in a century and a half, and some scenarios point to an even larger ultimate population.[1] Naturally, all of these projections depend on assumptions of a declining fertility rate and of no massive increase in mortality rates due to famine, exhaustion of key resources, or war. But with nearly one-half of the developing world's population under the age of 15, there is a built-in momentum that will result in continued population growth even if replacement-level fertility is achieved in the next few years, a highly unlikely occurrence. The later replacement-level fertility is reached, the larger the eventual size of the world's population is likely to be.

These aggregate rates obscure important differences among nations and regions of the world. The fertility decline has been greatest in Asia and Latin America, and especially in some of the most populous nations of Asia such as China, Indonesia, South Korea, the Philippines, and Thailand. In contrast, sub-Saharan Africa has shown almost no fertility decline, and some Asian nations seem to be making very little progress toward lower fertility despite national family planning programs of long standing (e.g., Pakistan, Bangladesh, and India). Some African nations (e.g., Nigeria) and some Latin American nations (e.g., Brazil) have either rejected the suggestion that they have a population problem or still view a larger population as desirable for economic, political, or military reasons.

In sharp contrast to the general picture of rapid growth in the LDCs, fertility is at or below replacement level in some 18 developed nations, including the United States, Canada, and most of Western and Northern Europe (Population Reference Bureau, 1980). A number of European countries have already gone below zero growth; their death rates exceed their birth rates each year. These include Austria, East and West Germany, and Luxembourg. The United Kingdom, Sweden, and Belgium are very close. And if current trends continue, Czechoslovakia, Denmark, Hungary, and Norway will reach or fall below zero rates of growth in a few years, with Bulgaria, Finland, Greece, Italy, and Switzerland following by about 1990 (Westoff, 1978). Although population in the developed nations is still growing by an average of 0.6 percent per year, most demographers expect a continuation of present low fertility rates and stabilization at a relatively early date (e.g., in Europe by the year 2000, and in the United States by about 2025).

A range of problems face nations with a slowing rate of growth, most especially those derived from a changing age structure and perceptions of declining national power or possible effects on economic growth (Petersen, 1978; Finkle and McIntosh, 1978); these will be addressed below for the case of the United States. And one needs to consider the impact of even low rates of growth in the developed nations on the world's supplies of food, energy, and natural resources, and on the global environment; for example, with only 5 percent of the world's population, the United States consumes nearly one-third of the world's commercial energy. But the problems faced by the LDCs are massive and more immediate in impact. Those nations with a 2 percent annual rate of growth (the average for the LDCs in 1980) may be expected to double in size in 35 years. To maintain even the present low standard of living in these nations, the supply of food, raw materials, and energy must be doubled in the same 35 years, a monumental task for much of the developing world, even with appreciably higher levels of external economic aid. Because the growth rate in some regions is considerably higher than the 2 percent average (2.9 percent for Africa, 2.6 percent for Latin America, and more than 3 percent in a few nations), the future in some areas may be even more bleak. There are, of course, varying estimates of the possibility of compensating for such rapid population growth with increases in food, natural resources, energy, public services, and employment, but most observers agree that governmental actions within the next several decades will be critical in shaping future prospects not only within the LDCs, but for satisfactory North-South relations (Ridker and Cecelski, 1979; Brown, 1979; Council on Environmental Quality and Department of State, 1980).

Debate continues on the relative importance of population policy (chiefly family planning programs) and economic and social development in reducing fertility rates in the LDCs. Tsui and Bogue (1978) and Mauldin and Berelson (1978), for example, argue that family planning programs have had a significant, independent effect in reducing fertility, whereas Demeny and others dispute the evidence supporting such conclusions (Demeny, 1979). Increasingly there is some consensus that only a combination of population policy and social and economic development will lower fertility sufficiently to allow economic progress in the developing nations. This position (population *and* development) was endorsed in the World Population Plan of Action approved at the World Population Conference in Bucharest in 1974, and it continues to be widely supported if not always implemented (Finkle and Crane, 1975; Miro; 1977; Mauldin et al., 1974). From this per-spective the emphasis is not necessarily on broad economic and social development (which is a strategy suitable only for the very long-range in many LDCs), but on those development policies likely to enhance a couple's motivation to keep family size small [for example, reduction of infant and child mortality rates, expansion of education for girls, enhancement of the economic and social status of women (Demeny, 1974; Rich, 1973)]. Access to the information and means to achieve desired family size is also es-sential, and thus effective family planning programs still play a key role. To judge from the number of nations adopting such policies in recent years, there is some basis for modest optimism. In 1960, only India and Pakistan supported organized family planning programs for the purpose of reducing birth rates, but by 1978, 35 developing nations—with 77 percent of the developing world's population—had such official policies for re-ducing population growth (van der Tak et al., 1979: 29). Needless to say, the type of policies adopted and the politics of policy making and implementation vary widely (God-win, 1975; Norman and Hofstatter, 1978; Corsa and Oakley, 1979).

On a more pessimistic note, a good many studies and arguments point to poor pros-pects for successful economic and social development and population limitation in a world increasingly subject to ecological constraints (Ophuls, 1977; Clinton, 1979; Ehrlich et al., 1977; Council on Environmental Quality and Department of State, 1980). Sig-nificant changes in political institutions and public policies will be necessary to manage the transition to a nongrowing population and sustainable world society, and there are reasons to doubt that such changes will come about in sufficient time to prevent catas-trophic consequences.

III. POPULATION TRENDS IN THE UNITED STATES AND POLICY IMPLICATIONS

In perhaps the most important respect, population trends in the United States are similar to those of other developed nations: The fertility rate has declined appreciably since the "baby boom" years of 1945–1959, and it remains significantly below the so-called re-placement-level total fertility rate of 2.1.[2] But there are some distinctive features of American demographic changes as well, including a high level of legal immigration, a high but uncertain level of illegal immigration, and population redistribution among regions and between metropolitan and nonmetropolitan areas.

According to the 1980 census, the American population in mid-1980 was approxi-mately 226.5 million. With a birth rate of 16 per 1000 population and a death rate of 9 per 1000 population, the current rate of natural increase is 0.7 percent. Even with the low fertility rate of 1.8, the U.S. population is still growing, and will continue to do so for some time even if the fertility rate remains low (because of the large and increasing number of women of child-bearing age, a product of the baby boom years). Estimates of future fertility dramatically affect projections of future population size and the date of arrival of a stable or stationary (nongrowing) population. Some demographers argue, as does Charles Westoff, that "nothing on the horizon suggests that fertility will not remain low. All the recent evidence on trends in marriage and reproductive behavior encourages a presumption that it will remain low" (Westoff, 1978: 54). As a result of later marriages, higher divorce rates, an increase in the number of women in the labor force, the popularity of smaller families and child-free lifestyles, some expect a further decline in the TFR, possibly to 1.5 children per woman. But others, most notably Richard Easterlin, suggest that fertility rates are likely to rise in the next two decades as a consequence of the less restrictive social and economic conditions under which today's younger cohorts are being raised—less competition due to fewer numbers in each cohort in comparison to the baby boom cohorts (Easterlin et al., 1978; Easterlin, 1980).

The U.S. Census Bureau offers a middle-range estimate of future population growth in its Series II projection, which assumes an increase in the TFR to 2.1, and net immigration of 400,000 per year. Under these conditions the population in the year 2000 would number 260 million, but growth would not cease. Series III, with an assumed decrease in the TFR to 1.7, and with the same level of immigration of 400,000 per year, projects a population of 245 million by the year 2000 and a stationary population of 253 million by the year 2020.

Thus these projections point to a period of continued growth for at least another 40 years (with a net annual increase of about 2 million people at present), but with a probable slowing rate of growth and achievement of a stationary population early in the next century. The major uncertainties in these projections are the prevailing fertility rate and the level of net immigration, which accounts for between 25 and 50 percent of current growth. It is difficult to be precise about net immigration because of poor information on the rate of illegal immigration. The Census Bureau estimates legal immigration per year at between 324,000 and 425,000. These figures may fluctuate considerably, depending on the number of refugees admitted in a given year. The large number of Indochinese and Cuban refugees admitted in the last few years is a perfect example. Estimates of illegal immigration are much less reliable; they range from 166,000 to 1 million or more annual net gain (U.S. Congress, 1978a; Zero Population Growth, 1980).

With a continuation of low fertility, and discounting the uncertain effect of immigration, composition of the population will change; in particular, we can expect an aging population. The average age of 28 in 1970 will probably increase by the year 2020 to about 37. The percentage of the population over age 65 will increase from 11 percent currently to between 14 and 22 percent by 2030, depending on precisely what fertility rates prevail; at current fertility levels, those over age 65 will increase to 18 percent of the population. At the same time, the proportion of the population under age 18 will decline. These changes in the age structure have some obvious and much discussed, though not totally predictable, effects on the demand for public services (e.g., education, social security payments, and health care services) and on politics and the economy (Peterson, 1978; Cutler, 1977, 1978). The impact of the baby boom cohort as it moves through the life cycle has also been much discussed; and because its numbers are known, its impact in the future can be projected with considerable confidence (Bouvier, 1980). However, the exact form of future generational conflicts between young and old cohorts, the severity of them, and the actual long-term effects of the population and age structure on economic and social conditions and policies are still matters of some debate.

A review of the aggregate population changes experienced in recent years and projected for the future tends to obscure existing population distribution among regions and between metropolitan and nonmetropolitan areas and trends in redistribution that pose vastly different policy problems for varying regions, states, and cities. During the 1970s, migration from the Northeast and North Central states to the West and South continued; the Northeast experienced a net migration loss to each of the three other regions, and the North Central states experienced net losses to the South and West. The West continued to have the highest growth rate, but the South was catching up quickly. From 1970 to 1975, the volume of net migration to the South increased to more than double that of the West (Berry and Dahmann, 1977; Biggar, 1979).

Central cities continued to lose population to the suburbs during the 1970s. From 1970 to 1975, central cities experienced an absolute loss of almost 2 million people, or 3 percent of their 1970 population. Such a degree of loss was especially characteristic of the older industrial cities of the Northeast and North Central states. Of even greater potential significance for the future of urban areas is the reversal since 1970 of a long-term net inflow of population to metropolitan areas. Since 1970, the metropolitan areas of the United States have grown more slowly than the nation as a whole. During the last decade, about 3 million persons moved from metropolitan to nonmetropolitan areas. Although the highest rates are found in those areas immediately adjacent to metropolitan areas (exurban fringes), the trend goes beyond the further decentralization of people and jobs from cities to the suburbs which dates back to the 1950s. These recent changes represent what may be a deconcentration of the population. The principal factors explaining this shift to nonmetropolitan areas include the decentralization of manufacturing, recreational and retirement developments, improved transportation facilities, changing personal preferences, and a variety of public policies adopted by cities and suburbs that alter the relative attractiveness (e.g., tax advantages) of residential or manufacturing locations (Berry and Dahmann, 1977; Schneider and Logan, 1978).

If we take these trends in growth, immigration, and distribution as constituting the population problem, governments—and others—must deal with the following major policy issues: (1) whether the United States welcomes sustained low fertility and population stabilization—and continues to support programs and practices that will keep fertility low—or attempts at some point to raise fertility and slow the decline in the growth rate through pronatalist policies; (2) whether, when, and how federal, state, and local governments plan for the changes implied in the age structure coincident with lower fertility, and whether, when, and how they plan for internal migration and immigration and/or adopt measures designed to affect population distribution and immigration; and (3) whether any changes are desirable in foreign policy, including economic and population assistance, in an attempt to deal with world population and resource problems.

The rest of this chapter addresses a number of questions related to at least some of these policy issues. How has American government dealt with population problems and issues in the past, especially in the last 10 years? What have been the key features of the policy-making process, and what social, political, and institutional constraints on future population policy making may be anticipated? What additional policy "needs" exist? What can political scientists and policy analysts contribute to the resolution of population problems in the United States over the next two decades? As noted above, I shall give selective attention to population issues covered elsewhere in this Encyclopedia, and in particular will not dwell on issues of population distribution.[3]

IV. THE EVOLUTION OF AMERICAN POPULATION POLICY

A. Population Policy Developments Before 1960

For most of American history, population problems fell into that category now called "nonissues." Certainly there was a great deal of growth and movement of the American population over the years, but national policies develop only when population is perceived as a problem, when it emerges as a major issue on systemic and institutional agendas, and when governmental intervention is considered legitimate. With a few exceptions, population changes throughout American history simply did not translate into a very visible or urgent problem.

In some respects one can say that concern for the composition and distribution of the nation's population dates back to at least 1790, when the first census was taken. But aside from a variety of laws dealing with births, marriages, divorces, contraception, and abortion—adopted for moral or medical rather than demographic purposes—it is difficult to point to much explicit population policy activity on a national scale. The policies that were adopted, at both the state and federal level, were generally pronatalist. For example, the Comstock Act of 1873 defined contraceptives as obscene material, and prohibited interstate distribution of them (and it was not formally repealed until 1971), and abortion was illegal from the middle of the nineteenth century except to save the life of the mother (Stetson, 1973). The first national concern for a broader population policy seems to have developed in 1938, in the context of extremely low fertility rates during the Depression and fears about economic stagnation. In that year, the subcommittee on population problems of the National Resources Committee presented a report to President Roosevelt entitled *Problems of a Changing Population.* The committee concluded that the "transition from an increasing to a stationary or decreasing population may on the whole be beneficial to the life of the Nation," a finding strikingly similar to that of the Commission on Population Growth and the American Future in 1972. The committee also recommended a conservative immigration policy to limit competition from unskilled workers, expressed concern over the relationships between high fertility levels and poverty, urged expanded programs for equality of opportunity in education, health, and cultural development, urged strengthening research agencies concerned with population studies, and urged the institution of a five-year census rather than the constitutionally prescribed decennial census (Westoff, 1974). Sharing the fate of future population commissions, the committee's report did not get much attention from the President or the nation, partly because of the rapidly changing environment of the late 1930s and early 1940s. A concern for low fertility in the mid-1930s would later become a concern over high fertility (in the late 1960s and early 1970s), which in turn faded away with declining fertility rates. As Charles Westoff notes, after World War II, "the main focus of professional interest in population policy turned toward the underdeveloped world." However, political interest was not to be revived for some time.

Even by the late 1950s, with increasing evidence of the implications of a rapidly growing world population, population issues had barely begun to achieve some visibility and legitimacy in American politics. As one measure of the significance of population concerns during this period, *The New York Times* index entries for population and vital statistics increased only from 1 inch in 1950 to a little more than 2 inches in 1958 (Piotrow, 1973). In part for this reason (and in part because of the political sensitivity of birth control), President Eisenhower did not consider population problems to be among those worthy of presidential attention or governmental action. Although he changed his mind a few years later, his comments during a press conference in December 1959 are still a significant indicator of the politics of population in the late 1950s:

> I cannot imagine anything more emphatically a subject that is not a proper political or governmental activity or function or responsibility. . . . This government will not, as long as I am here, have a positive political doctrine in its program that has to do with the problem of birth control. That's not our business (Piotrow, 1973: 45).

The political sensitivity of birth control, both within the United States and in regard to U.S. assistance to the developing world, reflected the influence of the Catholic church. Catholic opposition to governmental efforts on birth control was evident throughout the 1950s and 1960s. For example, the American Catholic bishops had opposed a recommendation in 1959 by the Committee to Study the Military Assistance Program (also called the Draper committee after its chairman, William Draper) that the U.S. government "assist those countries with which it is cooperating in economic aid programs, on request, in the formulation of their plans designed to deal with the problem of rapid population growth" (Westoff, 1974). The Draper committee failed to impress President Eisenhower with its recommendation; and it had little apparent impact outside the White House despite a determined effort to draw attention to population problems and the need for U.S. assistance. The opposition to these proposals and the lack of sustained media coverage, however, were soon to be reversed. In the late 1950s and early 1960s, population activists were organizing and lobbying on the issues, gaining press coverage, and creating a constituency for policy change.

B. Population Policy Developments, 1960-1969

Breaking with Eisenhower's declaration of nonpolicy, although with considerable reluctance at first, President Kennedy supported population activities of the United Nations, and in 1963 established the National Institute of Child Health and Human Development (NICHD) within the Department of Health, Education and Welfare, which included a research program on human reproduction. In 1963, Congress included in the foreign aid bill authorization to use such funds to support population research, and the U.S. Public Health Service contributed $500,000 to the World Health Organization to be used for research on human reproduction. And by 1965, President Johnson completed the transition from the Eisenhower era. In a State of the Union message he said that he would "seek new ways to use our knowledge to help deal with the explosion in world population and the growing scarcity in world resources." Although a few lines in such a message do not necessarily amount to much, the contrast to the earlier period is notable; a consensus was emerging on the importance of the problem and on public policy to deal with it.

In 1966, Congress amended two statutes, the Foreign Assistance Act and the Food for Peace Act, to authorize additional support for foreign population programs. For fiscal 1968, Congress specifically earmarked $35 million of appropriated funds for population assistance, increased to $50 million for fiscal 1969 (Population Reference Bureau, 1971).

And other actions followed in the executive branch. In 1966, the Department of State, AID, the Peace Corps, and the U.S. Information Agency announced jointly their support for programs aimed at limiting population growth in developing nations, and in 1967 AID made funds available for these purposes. By 1967, then, one part of the federal government's population policy was set in place.[4]

Most of the credit for the impressive changes in U.S. population assistance policy during the 1960s must go to Congress rather than to Presidents Kennedy and Johnson.

> Congress—both individual legislators and specific committees—set the agenda for public discussion of the population problem, defined the issue in ever more acceptable terms, reiterated the relevance and feasibility of action, drew up specific proposals to establish priority in funds as well as in words, and enacted these proposals into binding legislation, largely against the opposition of the executive agencies (Piotrow, 1973).

The actions of some individuals on the Hill stand in sharp contrast to presidential timidity during this period. In a classic demonstration of the role of the Senate in policy incubation, for example, Senator Ernest Gruening (D., Alaska) chaired 31 days of hearings on world population problems, with testimony by 120 witnesses over a period of three years, beginning in June 1965.

On the domestic front, President Johnson, in 1968, created a Committee on Population and Family Planning, jointly chaired by John D. Rockefeller, III, and Wilbur Cohen, the Secretary of HEW. The committee recommended rapid expansion of the foreign assistance program; expansion of the Center for Population Research, which was established in the summer of 1968 in NICHD; establishment of a Commission on Population to be appointed by the President; rapid expansion of the federal government's family planning programs for the poor; and expansion of federal support for population studies centers. Perhaps again illustrating the fate of such studies, the Johnson administration released the report in early January, just before the President's departure from office. Johnson also refused to support the committee's recommendations on funding in the fiscal 1970 budget. As far as population issues had come since 1959, then, they remained controversial, held only a tenuous grip on the nation's attention, and received low priority on the government's agenda.

C. Policy Developments, 1969–1974

In a sense, 1969 was a watershed year for population policy. Following a presidential message on population in 1969, Congress in 1970 created the commission that had been advocated by the Johnson committee two years previously, and enacted major legislation on family planning and population research. Despite such impressive actions in 1969 and 1970, however, population still remained something of a nonissue in American politics, and public policy development did not keep pace with the flurry of recommendations handed down by various commissions and select committees.

On July 18, 1969, President Nixon sent to Congress the first presidential message ever on population. It dealt primarily with domestic population growth, and its major recommendation was to establish a Commission on Population Growth and the American Future to study the impact of continued population growth in the United States. The

President also urged an increase in funding levels for population research and establishment of a family planning office in HEW, and called for a national goal of providing "adequate family planning services within the next five years to all who want them but cannot afford them;" the last request was essentially an increase in federal support for family planning assistance rather than a fundamental change in the type of program the government had instituted as early as 1967 (as part of the Economic Opportunity Act and the Child Health Act of 1967).

In light of the history of population issues, the tone of the President's message was especially gratifying to population activists. He referred to population growth as "one of the most serious challenges to human destiny in the last third of this century," and specifically included growth of the American population as his major concern. Congress was asked to authorize inquiry by the commission in three specific areas: (1) the probable course of population growth, internal migration, and related demographic developments through the year 2000; (2) the resources in the public sector required to deal with anticipated growth in population; and (3) ways in which population growth might affect the activities of federal, state, and local governments. Congress added two additional areas of concern: the impact of population growth on resources and the environment, and "the various means appropriate to the ethical values and principles of this society by which our nation can achieve a population level properly suited for its environmental, natural resources, and other needs." This last mandate allowed the commission "to regard its mission as 'interventionist' rather than 'accommodationist' " (Westoff, 1973).

In March 1970, Congress passed legislation creating the commission. After two years of extensive hearings in Washington and around the nation, the commission issued its recommendations in a report entitled *Population and the American Future,* backed up by six sizable volumes of research findings. The major conclusion of the commission was boldly stated.

> [N]o substantial benefits will result from further growth of the Nation's population, rather that the gradual stabilization of our population through voluntary means would contribute significantly to the Nation's ability to solve its problems. We have looked for, and have not found, any convincing economic argument for continued population growth. The health of our country does not depend on it, nor does the vitality of business nor the welfare of the average person.

The commission was the most significant attempt in the recent history of the United States to treat population issues in a comprehensive and systematic manner. Yet its activities and recommendations not only failed to impress the President who had recommended its creation, they drew a very mixed reaction from several quarters. Bachrach and Bergman (1973) attacked the operation of the commission as an "opportunity forfeited" for its failure to address important issues; they argued that the commission's final report remained "within familiar bounds and dealt with issues in a familiar range." Indeed, the commission emphasized the reduction of unwanted fertility, perhaps the most consensual possible policy option for limiting population growth. The executive director of the commission, Charles Westoff, explained the emphasis as "having everything":

> It implied helping people to achieve what they want; it did not imply any radical solutions to the problem of population growth. . . . it was singularly unobjectionable;

it was theoretically easy to do; and its costs were low! It was difficult to imagine a policy with more political promise (Westoff, 1973).

From a different perspective, as staff director for political research for the commission, Nash (1978) argued that the policy actions recommended by the commission can be traced to some pure elements of chance in the appointments process and in the internal deliberations of the commission. In effect, Nash suggested that the recommendations came out of a process falling considerably short of a model of rational policy analysis.

The reaction of the Nixon White House to the final report was perhaps not unexpected given the sharply declining birth rate at the time, a reduced concern for environmental problems, and the upcoming 1972 election. Two months after its release, the President severely criticized recommendations on abortion and on the provision of contraceptive information and services for minors, and pretty much ignored the rest. His statement made no mention at all of the analysis of the costs and benefits of population growth or the conclusion on the desirability of population stabilization in the United States. Such is often the fate of national commissions.

Aside from the commission, the major development of 1970 was enactment by Congress of the Family Planning Services and Population Research Act of 1970, Title X of the Public Health Service Act—also known as the Tydings Act after its sponsor in the Senate, Joseph Tydings. It provided for an Office of Population Affairs in HEW to help coordinate government population activities, and for grants for voluntary family planning projects; to state health departments for family planning services; for research and training in reproduction, contraceptive development, and behavioral sciences related to family planning and population; and for population and family planning education. The major goal of the act was the extension of family planning services to all in need of them, with special attention to the needs of low-income individuals.

As notable as the 1970 act was, in effect it was mainly a consolidation of previously established family planning programs, and some expansion of authorization in that area, as well as in research, training, and education. As such, it represented no break with the dominant American approach to population policy: voluntary family planning unaccompanied by any explicit demographic goals or governmentwide coordination of objectives and programs having some demographic consequences. Preference for the modest policy evident in the Tydings Act may be seen in part as a reflection of the power of what some call a "population establishment"—including, among others, the Population Council, Planned Parenthood/World Population, the Ford Foundation, the Rockefeller Foundation, and certain prominent individuals identified with federal population activities since the early 1960s (Bachrach and Bergman, 1973); the belief in professional demographic circles that elimination of unwanted fertility would be sufficient to deal with American population problems (Westoff, 1973); the limits or constraints imposed by the prevailing American ideology on population issues (Nash, 1972); and the inability of the critics of this policy perspective to build a large enough constituency to change policy direction.

Nearly all proposals of a sharply different nature introduced in the Congress throughout the 1970s failed to move very far along the legislative obstacle course. And as fertility continued to decline, so did enthusiasm for doing anything further along the lines of the recommendations handed down by the Population Commission, such as creation of a National Institute of Population Sciences, an Office of Population Growth and Distribution in the Executive Office of the President, a Joint Committee on Population in Congress, and strengthening of the Office of Population Affairs in HEW (Commission on Population Growth and the American Future, 1972).

One interesting deviation from the usual inattention to these issues was the holding of hearings in the Senate in August 1971 on SJ Res. 108, the Population Stabilization Resolution. The resolution had been endorsed by the Population Commission, and in many respects was politically safe: it authorized no new governmental spending and no changes in government structure, and it referred specifically only to voluntary means to reach that goal. But it did state boldly and for the first time a specific demographic goal for the nation: stabilization of the population. Introduced in both houses of Congress, and sponsored by 36 senators and 25 representatives, the resolution is now a mere historical footnote. It does have the distinction, however, of having progressed at least to the stage of hearings (Spingarn, 1971; U.S. Congress, 1971).

Although it was not, strictly speaking, a population policy, the decision of the U.S. Supreme Court in *Roe v. Wade* (1973) legalizing abortion must stand as one of the more significant policy developments of the early 1970s (Schneider and Vinovskis, 1980). The Court ruled that access to abortion during the first three months of pregnancy was guaranteed by constitutional rights of privacy, but the decision hardly ended public debate on the subject. Indeed, the Roe decision has itself contributed to a continuing public concern for the effect of abortion on welfare policy, civil liberties, race relations, religion, morality, and women's rights—if not especially on demographic developments. And implementation of the several decisions the court made on abortion policy has proven to be a complex and arduous process (Blake, 1977; Hansen, 1980). The causal relationship between abortion and birth rates is not fully understood, but recent restrictions on abortions paid for under the federal Medicaid program [upheld by the Supreme Court in *Harris v. McRae* (1980)] seem likely to push up fertility rates—even if the exact number of "additional births" cannot be predicted.

D. Policy Developments, 1975-1981

The major political issues in the nation in the late 1960s and early 1970s focused on the implications of continued population growth on the quality of life—both within the United States and worldwide. Thus, this set of issues was explored comprehensively, if not exhaustively, in the reports of the Commission on Population Growth and the American Future. But on the whole, little policy change came about as a result of the commission's work and related efforts to study and/or dramatize this set of issues.

More recently, with the arrival of strikingly lower fertility rates in the United States and with a decline in fertility rates in the developing nations, attention has shifted from issues of national growth policy to questions of population distribution, the local impact of variable growth rates, and the social, political, and economic implications of local growth control policies. Other new issues in the late 1970s included renewed concern for immigration policy, especially the problem of illegal immigration, a changing age structure and its effect on public policy, family policy, and the implications of sustained low fertility and population stabilization. Some issues prominent in the early 1970s, most notably abortion, remained high on the nation's agenda. Two major national efforts to study these—and other—population issues deserve special emphasis: the Select Committee on Population in the U.S. House of Representatives, which operated from 1977 to 1978, and the Select Commission on Immigration and Refugee Policy, which was established by Congress in 1978 and began its work in August 1979.

Select Committee on Population: The Select Committee on Population was established by the House of Representatives on September 28, 1977, and authorized to act only during the 95th Congress. As is the case with select committees, it was authorized only to investigate population problems and government activities bearing on them, not to legislate. Much to the disappointment of population scholars and activists, the committee became a victim of jurisdictional politics in the House. Had it been renewed in the 96th Congress, its agenda would have included the policy implications of population trends so thoroughly documented in 1977–1978. Even with its short life, however, the scope of the committee's work during this period was rivaled only by the Population Commission of 1970–1972. House Res. 70, creating the committee, directed it to conduct a full and complete investigation of the following:

1. The causes of changing population conditions and their consequences for the United States and the world
2. National, regional, and global population characteristics relative to the demands on limited resources and the ability of nations to feed, clothe, house, employ, and govern their citizens and otherwise afford them an improved standard of living
3. Various approaches to population planning (including the study of family planning technology, with emphasis on measures to reduce the frequency of conception rather than the termination of pregnancy, and the relationship of improved economic and social opportunities to family size) in order to ascertain those policies and programs, within the United States as well as other nations, that would be most effective in coping with unplanned population change
4. The means by which the U.S. government can most effectively cooperate with and assist nations and international agencies in addressing successfully, in a noncoercive manner, various national, regional, and global population-related issues (U.S. Congress, 1978a).

To undertake this study, the committee assembled a staff of 30 to 40 people and conducted 37 days of hearings between February and August of 1978. Its final reports on those hearings and other professional staff work were released in some 10 volumes in four major areas: population and development, domestic consequences of U.S. population change, legal and illegal immigration to the United States, and fertility and contraception in the United States.

Among the major recommendations of the select committee were the following: that there be substantial increases in funding for and diversification of population research, especially in the social sciences; substantial expansion of funding for family planning services under Title X of the Public Health Service Act—and more aggressive promotion of these programs by HEW; increased attention to adolescent fertility and contraceptive needs of adolescents; increased support for contraceptive research and development; a comprehensive review of the Immigration and Naturalization Act of 1965 and its implementation; expanded research on immigration and its consequences for the United States;

expansion of U.S. foreign assistance programs, and especially a stronger commitment to population activities at the highest levels of government; expanded research on the consequences of the changing composition of the U.S. population (especially aging of the population), and increased attention to methods of planning for the consequences of population change (U.S. Congress, 1978a, 1978b).

Two recommendations, those dealing with planning for the consequences of a changing population and the use of demographic data in policy making, were of special importance because the problems are so often ignored. On the former, the committee called for the Congress to undertake a thorough investigation to identify all population-sensitive programs and policies, to assess their impact on population, and to consider alternative mechanisms for improving the ability of the federal government to:

1. Conduct continuing analysis of the interrelationships of demographic change and federal programs and policies
2. Coordinate programs and policies that will be affected by changes in the size, composition, and geographic distribution of the population or that may affect population
3. Develop alternative policies and programs for planning for future population change and assess the short-term and long-term costs and benefits of each course of action (U.S. Congress, 1978a).

The failure to have developed institutional mechanisms for such population policy analysis and decision making must stand as one of the major omissions in American population policy.

With respect to the use of demographic data in policy making, closely related to the recommendation above, the committee was concerned with (1) the accuracy, timeliness, and policy relevance of the statistical data produced by federal agencies, and (2) its incorporation into all major presidential, executive agency, and congressional reports—for example, the annual report of the Council on Environmental Quality, the Urban Growth Report, and the Economic Report. In particular, the committee pointed to the need to use extensive *demographic* analysis in all such reports, and the need to develop clear guidelines for the preparation and use of population projections for states and local areas in federal funding allocation formulas where they are already used.

Although many of these recommendations merely reflected long-standing concerns among professional demographers and public officials, their restatement by the select committee may have served, as Chairman James Scheuer (D., N.Y.) put it, a "consciousness-raising" function, particularly for the 16 members of the committee who took those concerns back to their respective standing committees. Given those goals, it may be premature to assess the impact of the select committee's work. But it does seem that coverage of the committee's proceedings in the mass media was fairly limited, depending to a great extent on how controversial the particular subject of each hearing was. And it is difficult as of mid-1981 to point to much impact on Congress or the White House. Regrettably, the inability of the committee to gain the approval of the House for a second term of operation meant that further investigation of the long agenda of items listed by the committee in its final report was unlikely. The more policy-oriented inquiries were intentionally deferred until 1978–1980 in an effort to minimize political attacks on the committee in its first year of operation. Its nonrenewal, then, implies that most of those questions will be deferred until some indefinite future date.

Although there may be no direct connection to the committee's misfortune in not being reauthorized, the Population Association of America (the leading professional association of demographers) formed a Committee on Public Affairs in July 1979 to help call attention to the same kinds of population problems and to provide "objective and scientific briefings on population change for policy makers in the Congress and the Executive Branch" (*P.A.A. Affairs,* 1979). In late 1979 and 1980, these included briefings for several congressional committees on the implications of demographic change for welfare programs and the foreign assistance programs of AID, and on legal and illegal immigration. The Public Affairs Committee has worked with the Congressional Research Service (which includes no professional demographers on its staff) and with the Office of Technology Assessment in Congress, which has a major ongoing project on the technology of birth control and possible changes in U.S. policy on contraceptive development, distribution, and financing in the LDCs. The committee has also worked with the Office of Management and the Budget, which in recent years (fiscal 1980 and fiscal 1981) has begun to consider long-term demographic change as it affects the federal budget. Not too surprisingly, the committee has also been interested in increasing funding for population research through the Center for Population Research in NICHD, the major source of federal research funds on population issues.

Select Commission on Immigration and Refugee Policy: The second major national investigation of population issues in the late 1970s was the Select Commission on Immigration and Refugee Policy. By the late 1970s, the impact of both legal and illegal immigration on the nation and the failure of present policies had become acutely evident (North, 1978; Keeley, 1979). The 16-member commission, chaired by the Rev. Theodore M. Hesburgh, was created by Congress in 1978. Its job was to provide the first comprehensive review of immigration policies and laws since 1911, to assess past and present migration and its consequences, and to recommend policy changes. That work was begun in August 1979, and was completed with publication of its final report in late February 1981. Although the commission enjoyed the services of a staff of 25, and held 12 hearings around the country, it did not compile extensive research reports in the fashion of the Population Commission and the House Select Committee on Population. Its final report was, however, equally controversial, and perhaps no more likely to speed resolution of the difficult issues of immigration policy than the earlier study groups were able to foster development of a national population policy.

As is often the case with population policy, there was a good deal more agreement among the commissioners on the scope of the problems of immigration than there was on the most effective and acceptable solutions. Reports by the commission staff, and voting by the commissioners themselves, pointed to the difficulty of building policy consensus in this highly emotional area. Agreement was reached easily on recommendations such as providing additional funds and staff for enforcement of immigration laws—particularly along the United States-Mexican border—and instituting administrative reforms in the Immigration and Naturalization Service. But a deeply divided commission barely reached agreement on a wide range of other issues, including measures to discourage continued illegal immigration. The question of requiring work permits and worker identification cards was especially sensitive (*The New York Times,* 1980). The commission's key proposals, however, included the establishment of civil and criminal penalties against employers who hire illegal aliens; an amnesty for most illegal aliens already in the United States; a sizable increase in the level of "numerically limited" immigration–from 270,000 a year to 350,000 a year (not counting refugees); and the adoption of stricter enforcement methods along U.S. borders (*The New York Times,* 1981; U.S. Congress, 1981a). The commission did not consider immigration within the larger context of population policy, a peculiar stance given that immigration now contributes so heavily to the overall growth of the American population.

Upon receipt of the report, President Reagan created a Cabinet-level committee chaired by Attorney General William French Smith. The Task Force on Immigration and Refugee Policy submitted its report to the President in May, and he announced his administration's position on immigration policy in late July. He endorsed the commission's proposal of an amnesty–with important restrictions on the waiting period (ten years)–and he agreed with its opposition to employment of illegal aliens; however, he favored a two-year experimental program allowing "guest workers" from Mexico. The administration took unexpectedly strong action in some areas, for example, in an executive order on interdiction at sea of ships suspected of carrying illegal aliens, but backed off on other controversial issues; it was, for example, "explicitly opposed" to the creation of a national identity card, suggested by many as the only means to enforce the ban on employment of illegal aliens. At this writing, Senator Alan Simpson (R., Wyo.), chairman of the Senate Subcommittee on Immigration and Refugee Policy is expected to introduce a comprehensive bill more severe and more sweeping than the one prepared by the Reagan administration.

Although it is still too early to predict what Congress will do to bring some order to the chaos of immigration law and to address the challenge of illegal immigration, the contentious nature of the commission's meetings and the sharp criticism that greeted the administration's proposals underscore one of the major reasons for the absence of a coherent national immigration policy: There is insufficient agreement among the public and policy makers on the substance of what that policy ought to be. Until there is a change in this condition, immigration policy will prove to be as difficult to reform as other aspects of population policy in the United States.

E. Population Policies and Politics in the United States: An Overview

As the review of policy development makes clear, policies directed at components of American population problems have evolved slowly over a considerable time, and for varying purposes. To summarize, the federal government has adopted direct and indirect policies on foreign population assistance, domestic family planning information and services, population research, immigration, and distribution, and population agencies have been established in the Department of Health and Human Services (Office of Population Affairs and NICHD's Center for Population Research) and in the State Department (AID and the Office of Population); a National Security Council Ad Hoc Group on Population Policy was established in 1975 to help coordinate foreign policy aspects of the work of 18 U.S. departments and agencies (NSC Ad Hoc Group on Population Policy, 1980).

Programs established by these policies have grown significantly in the last 10 years, although budgetary constraints and inflationary pressures in the late 1970s and early 1980s will limit future growth. For example, U.S. population assistance through AID and international agencies amounted to more than $1.2 billion between 1965 and 1978, which was two-thirds of all external assistance to the LDCs during those years (van der Tak et al., 1979). For fiscal 1979, $185 million was appropriated for international population assistance through AID. And family planning provided through the several programs in the Department of Health and Human Services serves an estimated two-thirds of the 9.2 million low-income women and teenagers at risk of unwanted pregnancy in the United States today at a cost of several hundred million dollars per year (U.S. Congress, 1978a). Yet this collection of public policies falls short of a comprehensive and coordinated national population policy for the United States. Specifically, the United States has no national growth policy, no national distribution policy, and no institutional capacity for planning for population change.

A number of critics have elaborated on the costs of such omissions and have urged adoption of some form of national population policy (Sundquist, 1975; Corsa, 1979; Zero Population Growth, Inc., 1976; Oosterbaan, 1980; and Oakley and Willson, 1979). For example, the Select Committee on Population, in its 1978 report on Domestic Consequences of U.S. Population Change, put it this way:

> The Federal Government has no capacity to plan systematically for population change; yet changes in the size, age, composition and geographical distribution of the population can, and often do, have profound effects on Federal policies and Federal policies and programs often influence the direction of population change unintentionally (U.S. Congress, 1978b).

Although the Commission on Population Growth and the American Future in 1972 and the Select Committee in 1978, among others, have recommended extensive changes in U.S. population policy, there has been relatively little change in recent years.

In the 97th Congress, bills incorporating explicit population policy were introduced in both the House and the Senate, but there would appear to be little chance that either will receive more than modest attention. The House bill, introduced by Richard Ottinger (D., N.Y.) in January 1981, is concerned almost exclusively with population policy. It declares a "national policy of coordinated planning for the Nation's approach to population change, and to establish a goal of eventual stabilization in the United States as the keystone of a national population policy. . . ." It is directed also at the establishment of a capability in the federal government for analysis of long-term trends in the relationships among population, resources, and the environment, and for that purpose establishes an Office of Population Policy in the Executive Office of the President (U.S. Congress, 1981b). The Senate measure, introduced by Mark Hatfield (R., Ore.) in October 1981, and labeled the Global Resources, Environment and Population Act of 1981, is of a similar nature. It declares that there are "economic, social, governmental, and environmental advantages to the attainment of a national population stabilization in the United States." It declares also that the federal government has the responsibility for "coordinating planning for changes in population characteristics" and improving its capability to engage in analysis of long-term trends in population, natural resources, and environmental change.

It establishes a Council on Global Resources, the Environment, and Population, and calls for an annual National Population Change and Planning Report to help achieve these goals (U.S. Congress, 1981c).

Both of these bills are an outgrowth of the *Global 2000 Report to the President* (Council on Environmental Quality and Department of State, 1980), and reflect the energetic work of a coalition of national environmental groups, the Global Tomorrow Coalition, as well as the efforts of individual population groups such as Zero Population Growth. Hearings in the House were held in May 1981, and in March 1982, and hearings are expected in the Senate in 1982. Although the introduction of these measures and the holding of hearings are significant signs of interest in such policy change, it is premature to judge how far Congress is likely to go in the next few years in developing national population policy.

What explains the limited character of present U.S. population policy? The major reasons can be summarized in three categories: (1) the nature of population problems, (2) institutional characteristics of the American political system, and (3) the politics of population policy making.

The impact of problems such as a slowly growing population—or even maldistribution of the population—is often highly uncertain, long-range, and diffuse rather than clearly predictable, immediate, and specific. Thus, except for certain unusual circumstances or in the case of highly controversial issues such as abortion, population problems have not occupied a prominent position on the systemic or institutional agendas. Moreover, neither the American public nor policy makers tend to be well informed about population trends and their consequences (Kraft, 1973; Hetrick et al., 1972). And to the extent that population problems are associated with sensitive issues of human reproduction and freedom of choice, population policies may be viewed as politically dangerous and best avoided (Littlewood, 1977; Bachrach and Bergman, 1973).

Even when population problems do get on governmental agendas, institutional fragmentation tends to inhibit policy development. For example, Sundquist (1978) compared the policy-making capacity of the United States to five European countries on the issue of population distribution and concluded that the pluralistic American political system made the building of consensus and policy adoption inordinately difficult even when agreement existed in the executive branch on desirable policy change. As if presidential-congressional fragmentation were not enough, Congress itself suffers from certain institutional incapacities. Even though Congress rather than the President has generally been the leader on population matters, it is poorly organized to exercise such policy leadership. Michael Teitlebaum, staff director of the select committee in 1977-1978, has calculated that between 30 and 100 committees in Congress deal with population issues (the number depending on how narrowly population issues are defined). Congress, he says, is characterized by "chaos": "Much that happens is accidental or not understood by those that make it happen," and members of Congress tend not to be interested in population issues and accordingly assign them a low priority (Population Reference Bureau, 1979).

The politics of population policy making also helps explain the modest policies to date and the constraints on future policy development. Policy making is most successful when proposals are supported by large, well-organized interest groups, when there is a strong national constituency for policy change, and when leadership in the White House and Congress helps to overcome institutional fragmentation. But there is no such constituency for national population policy and the issue, as noted, has not generally been high enough on the governmental agenda to merit sustained and energetic leadership by more than a few members of the Congress. The arrival of single-issue politics and a conservative reaction to the extension of governmental authority may well limit further policy development, as may the continuing fragmentation of political institutions, the declining public confidence in government, the decline in public trust in political leadership, and a seeming loss of a sense of shared concern over the nation's collective interest and its future (Sundquist, 1980).

Despite some of these obvious reasons for neglect of policy development in the past and what they imply for future policy making on population issues, a number of issues in future policy choices should be explicated. The concluding section does so.

V. POLICY CHOICES AND POPULATION POLICY ANALYSIS

What new population policies are needed in the United States? The answer, of course, depends on how one assesses population trends and their consequences—both worldwide and in the United States, the capacity of current policies to deal satisfactorily with those problems and the effectiveness of additional or altered population policies. It is not the purpose of this chapter to advocate any particular population policies, and it is beyond its scope to address these questions in great detail. But the type of questions that should be asked in several areas of population policy can be noted, as can the potential contribution of political science research and policy analysis to the resolution to those questions. Five areas of population policy are of interest: growth, distribution, population planning, population research, and international assistance.

1. *Growth Policy.*   Should the United States adopt a formal policy on population growth, setting a particular goal for the "optimum" size of the U.S. population or for a rate of growth consistent with other national goals (e.g., on the environment, energy use, economic growth, and human rights)? In particular, should there be a population stabilization policy clearly setting a goal of a stationary or nongrowing population and providing a variety of means to achieve that goal? What role should immigration policy play within this context? Should net immigration (both legal and illegal) be maintained at the present level, allowed to increase, or reduced? What costs, benefits, and risks are associated with each growth policy alternative? How effective are such policies likely to be? What criteria should govern decision making on growth and immigration policies (e.g., concern for individual freedom, justice or equality, the general welfare)?
2. *Distribution Policy.*   Should the United States adopt an explicit national policy to influence the distribution of the population? What type of policy will best minimize the undesirable economic and social effects of migration and changing patterns of regional growth and economic development? How do present federal, state, and local policies influence the distribution of population and economic growth? What costs and benefits are associated with the major policy alternatives?

3. *Population Planning.* Should federal, state, and local governments adopt policies to facilitate demographic data analysis and planning for changes in the size, age composition, and geographic distribution of the population? What improvements in data gathering and analysis are needed? What types of institutional arrangements are best suited for long-range population planning? What new agencies and programs are needed to build a capacity for population planning, and where should they be located for maximum effectiveness? For example, should the role of the Deputy Assistant Secretary for Population Affairs in the Department of Health and Human Services be strengthened, or should another agency assume some of the responsibilities now lodged in that office?

4. *Population Research.* What type of research should receive the highest priority? Should research in health-related aspects of population sciences and in basic demography be emphasized over the more applied social sciences and policy analysis, as has been the case within NICHD? What type of research is most directly relevant to the current and anticipated needs of policy makers? Are the social and policy sciences capable of providing answers to the questions raised in making population policy and in planning for the consequences of population change? If the present state of the art is not sufficient to that task, how might it be improved through a well-designed expansion of funding for population policy research? How should such research be funded? Should the activities of the Center for Population Research in NICHD be significantly expanded? Should population research, especially in the social sciences, be funded through other government agencies as well—such as the Council on Environmental Quality, the Department of Energy, the Department of Housing and Urban Development, and the Department of Education?

5. *International Assistance.* What changes, if any, are desirable in U.S. foreign policy in relation to international economic and population assistance? Should the amount of population assistance as well as economic assistance be substantially increased? Should present emphasis on family planning programs be changed in some manner? Should aid be channeled through multilateral agencies rather than through AID? Should the population assistance programs be more fully integrated with overall U.S. foreign policy objectives, and should they play a greater role in foreign policy decisions?

One need not claim any special ability to define the public interest in population policy to suggest that the nation would profit from development of a clear national policy on all of these issues, setting both short-term and long-term goals and priorities, and establishing any additional programs required to achieve those goals. This is merely another way of stating that the alternative of muddling through without goals and without a coherent policy involves costs that may be unacceptably high in the long run. The political, social, and institutional constraints on the policy-making process outlined above suggest some reasons for pessimism on early achievement of comprehensive policy change. Yet whatever one's assessment of the politics of population policy-making in the past, there should be agreement that the future of population policy depends on three conditions: (1) building an understanding of the determinants and consequences of population change; (2) clarifying the type of population conditions that may be said to represent the public interest; and (3) building public support or consensus sufficient to enact and implement effectively whatever public policies will guide the nation toward the type of population future determined to be in its long-term interest.

Clearly, development of population policy—particularly comprehensive and coordinated policy—will involve analysis of complex and intensely controversial issues such as immigration, family planning, abortion, and restrictions on internal migration. Policy analysis providing information about costs, benefits, and risks associated with particular demographic changes can contribute to the making of policy choices, chiefly by clarifying policy alternatives and their consequences and by explicating criteria of policy evaluation and choice (Miller and Godwin, 1977: chaps 6–7; Godwin and Shepard, 1978; Stetson, 1978).

However, the task of population policy analysis is by no means an easy one. Despite the building of an enormous literature on population (well over 100,000 books and articles have been indexed by *Population Index* since 1950), fertility and migration decision making is complex, and knowledge of causal relationships is limited and imprecise. Knowledge of the consequences of population change is similarly limited. Thus, considerable uncertainty surrounds any population policy analysis, and policy recommendations often lack a firm grounding in scientific knowledge. These limitations flow partly from inherent methodological weaknesses in the study of population dynamics and their effects—including the uncertainty of long-range population projections. But they also reflect the still modest degree of research on policy-relevant population trends and consequences and on policy alternatives. Only 3 to 4 percent of all citations in the *Population Index* deal with policy issues, and many of these are only marginally related to public policy choice. One consequence of such a weak policy literature is the absence of clear guidelines for policy makers, evident, for example, in the conclusions of a National Academy of Sciences conference on population and development in 1974:

> In the absence of hard data on the effectiveness (and on the secondary and tertiary effects) of most population policies, the seminar participants necessarily relied on common sense, empirical observations, philosophical predilections, ideological biases, and practical political considerations (quoted in Stycos, 1977).

The response to these conditions should not be a general call for "more research," but a specific enumeration of the type of policy-relevant inquiries that offer some promise of success and utility. A number of such research agendas have been prepared for social scientists, and perusal of them would be a useful starting point for those entering the field (Berelson, 1976; Ilchman, 1975).

Political scientists who do not engage in policy analysis per se can nevertheless make a significant contribution to the process of policy development by improving our understanding of the political and institutional constraints on population policy making, and the impact of population change on governmental institutions and political processes. There is no shortage of suggestions for additional research in these areas. Several years ago the Center for Population Research in NICHD distributed an extensive list of topics on "Political Aspects of Population, Family Planning, Reproduction Research: Research Problem Areas and Research Ideas." As the major funding arm of the federal government in this area, the center's support of political research is especially important. Other research ideas may be found in many of the volumes published in recent years on population and politics (e.g., Nash, 1972; Clinton, 1973; Godwin, 1975; and Weiner, 1971). Because the literature on population and politics reveals markedly different perspectives on the nature of population problems, their causes and consequences, appropriate policy actions, and even the legitimate roles for the scholar and policy analyst, one might expect future work to be characterized by a continuing diversity of approaches, theories, and methods (McCoy, 1972; Coulter, 1975; Clinton, 1973; Shepard, 1975).

Of course, improvement in our knowledge of the determinants and consequences of population change and of population policy will not necessarily suggest where the "public interest" in policy choice lies. Policy analysis cannot and will not replace politics as the means for determining the desirable mix of population policies for the nation. As long as population policy involves conflicts of values, resolution of those conflicts will necessarily take place in a political process of interaction, bargaining, and compromise. And given the history of policy development reviewed above, it would seem that one prerequisite for policy change, especially on controversial issues, is a much higher level of public concern and support than now evident. In short, future policy development depends on the changing shape of population politics as well as on expansion of our knowledge of the substantive issues in population policy.

SUGGESTED READINGS

I list here a number of key reference sources, journals, and newsletters important to the study of population policy. A fuller list and a bibliography including items not cited in this chapter can be found in Kraft and Schneider (1979).

Bibliographies

Population Index. Office of Population Research, Princeton University, Princeton, NJ. (quarterly annotated bibliography).

Sourcebook on Population: 1970-1976. Population Reference Bureau, Washington, DC, 1976.

Driver, E. D. (1972). *World Population Policies: An Annotated Bibliography*. Lexington Books, Lexington, MA.

U.S. Immigration and Naturalization Service (1979). *Immigration Literature: Abstracts of Demographic, Economic, and Policy Studies*. U.S. Government Printing Office, Washington, DC.

Data Sources, Newsletters, and Periodicals

U.S. Census of Population. U.S. Bureau of the Census, Washington, DC.

Current Population Reports. U.S. Bureau of the Census, Washington, DC.

Demographic Yearbook. United Nations, New York.

Population and Family Planning Programs, 19th ed. (1980). Population Council, New York.

P.A.A. Affairs. Population Association of America, Washington, DC.

Intercom. Population Reference Bureau, Washington, DC (monthly).

Zero Population Growth Reporter. Zero Population Growth, Washington, DC (monthly).

American Demographics. American Demographics, Ithaca, NY (monthly).

Demography. Population Association of America, Washington, DC.

Population and Development Review. Center for Policy Studies, Population Council, New York.

Population Studies. University Press, London.

Journal of Population. Human Sciences Press, New York.

Population Bulletin. Population Reference Bureau, Washington, DC.

Family Planning Perspectives. Planned Parenthood Federation of America, New York.

Population Reports. Population Information Program, Johns Hopkins, Baltimore.

Population Research and Policy Review. Elsevier Scientific Publishing Company, Amsterdam, The Netherlands.

NOTES

1. There are, of course, major uncertainties in estimating present population sizes and in projecting certain rates and sizes for the future. A good review of some of these uncertainties can be found in Kirk (1979), Demeny (1979), and Bogue and Tsui (1979). Demeny sums up the problem:

   > In an age of national planning bureaus, world plans of action, and global targets, predicting future population is apt to be a thriving industry. Indeed, population projections have proliferated in the last decade or two, well beyond the degree that would be reasonably explained by ordinary human curiosity, increased scientific ability to fathom the future, or the requirements of old-fashioned social policymaking. . . . The interested customer nowadays can choose among an impressive variety of population forecasts, national, regional, and global, and the number of such forecasts seems to increase from year to year (p. 141).

2. The total fertility rate (TFR) refers to the average number of children that would be born to each woman in a population if each were to live through her child-bearing years (15-49) bearing children at the same rate as women of those ages actually did in a given year. In simple terms, the TFR answers the question: How many children are women having at present? In developed nations with low mortality rates, a TFR of 2.1 indicates "replacement-level" fertility or the level at which the nation's population would stop growing eventually. Migration is not considered in calculating the TFR.

3. Recent works on population distribution policy include Sly, et al. (1980), National Academy of Sciences (1980) and Sundquist (1975, 1978). Some of the contributions in Bergman et al. (1974) and Gray and Bergman (1974) are also useful, as is the volume of studies prepared for the Commission on Population Growth and the American Future (Mazie, 1972).

4. An extensive review of U.S. international population policy, including a history of population assistance programs, budgetary allocations in recent years, international conferences held, and current policy issues can be found in NSC Ad Hoc Group on Population Policy (1980).

REFERENCES

Bachrach, P., and Bergman, E. (1973). *Power and Choice: The Formulation of American Population Policy.* Lexington Books, Lexington, MA.

Berelson, B. (1976). Social science research on population: A review. *Population and Development Review 2* (June): 219-266.

Bergman, E., Carter, D., Cook, R. J., Tabors, R. D., Weir, D. R., Jr., and Urann, M. E. (Eds.) (1974). *Population Policymaking in the American States.* Lexington Books, Lexington, MA.

Berry, B. J. L., and Dahmann, D. C. (1977). Population redistribution in the United States in the 1970s. *Population and Development Review 3* (December): 443-472.

Biggar, J. C. (1979). The sunning of America: Migration to the Sunbelt. *Population Bulletin 34* (March): 1-41.

Blake, J. (1977). The Supreme Court's abortion decisions and public opinion in the United States. *Population and Development Review 3* (March/June): 45-62.

Bogue, D. J., and Tsui, A. O. (1979). A reply to Paul Demeny's 'On the End of the Population Explosion.' *Population and Development Review 5* (September): 479-493.

Bouvier, L. F. (1980). America's baby boom generation: The fateful bulge. *Population Bulletin 35* (April): 1-35.

Brown, L. R. (1979). *Resource Trends and Population Policy: A Time for Reassessment.* Worldwatch Institute, Washington, DC.

Clinton, R. L. (1973). Population, politics, and political science. In *Population and Politics,* R. L. Clinton (Ed.). Lexington Books, Lexington, MA, pp. 51-57.

—— (1979). Population dynamics and future prospects for development. In *The Global Predicament,* D. W. Orr and M. S. Soroos (Eds.). University of North Carolina Press, Chapel Hill.

Coale, A. J. (1974). The history of the human population. In *The Human Population,* Scientific American (Ed.). Freeman, San Francisco, pp. 15-25.

Commission on Population Growth and the American Future (1972). *Population and the American Future.* U.S. Government Printing Office, Washington, DC.

Corsa, L. (1979). Population policy in the United States. *Sierra,* May/June, pp. 12-13, 62-63.

Corsa, L., and Oakley, D. (1979). *Population Planning.* University of Michigan Press, Ann Arbor.

Coulter, P. (1975). In search of the master science: Population policy in the seventies. *Public Administration Review 34* (July/August): 419-423.

Council on Environmental Quality and Department of State (1980). *The Global 2000 Report to the President: Entering the Twenty-First Century,* U.S. Government Printing Office, Washington, DC.

Cutler, N. E. (1977). Demographic, social psychological, and political factors in the politics of age: A foundation for research in political gerontology. *American Political Science Review 71*: 1011-1025.

—— (1978). The consequences of population dynamics for political gerontology. In *Population Policy Analysis,* M. E. Kraft and M. Schneider (Eds.). Lexington Books, Lexington, MA., pp. 27-36.

Demeny, P. (1974). The populations of the underdeveloped countries. In *The Human Population,* Scientific American (Ed.). Freeman, San Francisco, pp. 105-115.

—— (1979). On the end of the population explosion. *Population and Development Review 5* (March): 141-162.

Easterlin, R. A. (1980). *Birth and Fortune: The Impact of Numbers on Personal Welfare.* Basic Books, New York.

Easterlin, R. A., Wachter, M. L., and Wachter, S. M. (1978). Demographic influences on economic stability: The United States experience. *Population and Development Review 4* (March): 1-22.

Ehrlich, P. R., Ehrlich, A. H., and Holdren, J. P. (1977). *Ecoscience: Population, Resources, Environment.* Freeman, San Francisco.

Finkle, J. L., and Crane, B. A. (1975). The politics of Bucharest: Population, development, and the new international economic order. *Population and Development Review 1* (September): 87-114.

Finkle, J. L., and McIntosh, A. (1978). Toward an understanding of population policy in industrialized societies. In *Population Policy Analysis,* M. E. Kraft and M. Scheider (Eds.). Lexington Books, Lexington, MA., pp. 37-52.

Godwin, R. K. (Ed.) (1975). *Comparative Policy Analysis: The Study of Population Policy Determinants in Developing Countries.* Lexington Books, Lexington, MA.

Godwin, R. K., and Shepard, W. B. (1978). Policies for the resolution of commons dilemmas in population. In *Population Policy Analysis,* M. E. Kraft and M. Schneider (Eds.). Lexington Books, Lexington, MA, pp. 115-131.

Gray, V., and Bergman, E. (Eds.) (1974). *Political Issues in U.S. Population Policy.* Lexington Books, Lexington, MA.

Hansen, S. B. (1980). State implementation of Supreme Court decisions: Abortion rates since *Roe v. Wade. Journal of Politics 42* (May): 372-395.

Harris v. McRae (1980) 448 U.S. 297.

Hetrick, C. C., Nash, A. E. K., and Wyner, A. J. (1972). Population and politics: Information, concern, and policy support among the American public. In *Governance and Population,* A. E. K. Nash (Ed.). U.S. Government Printing Office, Washington, DC, pp. 301-331.

Ilchman, W. F. (1975). Population knowledge and population policies. In *Comparative Policy Analysis,* R. K. Godwin (Ed.). Lexington Books, Lexington, MA, pp. 217-265.

Jones, C. O. (1977). *An Introduction to the Study of Public Policy,* 2nd ed. Duxbury Press, North Scituate, MA.

Keeley, C. B. (1979). *U. S. Immigration: A Policy Analysis.* Population Council, New York.

Kirk, D. (1979). World population and birth rates: Agreements and disagreements. *Population and Development Review 5* (September): 387-403.

Kraft, M. E. (1973). *Congressional Attitudes Toward the Environment: Attention and Issue-Orientation in Ecological Politics.* Unpublished Ph.D. thesis, Yale University, New Haven, CT.

Kraft, M. E., and Schneider, M. (1979). Population and policy analysis: A bibliography. *Policy Studies Journal 8* (Winter): 494-499.

Lasswell, H. D., and Kaplan, A. (1950). *Power and Society.* Yale University Press, New Haven, CT.

Littlewood, T. B. (1977). *The Politics of Population Control.* University of Notre Dame Press, Notre Dame, IN.

Mauldin, W. P., Choucri, N., Notestein, F. W., and Teitelbaum, M. (1974). A report on Bucharest. *Studies in Family Planning 5* (December): 357-395.

Mauldin, W. P., and Berelson, B. (1978). Conditions of fertility decline in developing countries, 1965-1975. *Studies in Family Planning 9* (May): 89-147.

Mazie, S. M. (Ed.) (1972). *Population, Distribution, and Policy.* U.S. Government Printing Office, Washington, DC.

McCoy, T. L. (1972). Political scientists as problem-solvers: The case of population. *Polity 5* (Winter): 250-259.

Miller, W. B., and Godwin, R. K. (1977). *Psyche and Demos: Individual Psychology and the Issues of Population.* Oxford University Press, New York.

Miro, C. A. (1977). The World Population Plan of Action: A political instrument whose potential has not been realized. *Population and Development Review 3* (December): 421-442.

Nash, A. E. K. (Ed.) (1972). *Governance and Population: The Governmental Implications of Population Change.* U.S. Government Printing Offices, Washington, DC.

Nash, A. E. K. (1978). Procedural and substantive unorthodoxies on the Population Commission's agenda. In *Population Policy Analysis,* M. E. Kraft and M. Schneider (Eds.). Lexington Books, Lexington, MA, pp. 55-65.

National Academy of Sciences (1980). *Population Redistribution and Public Policy.* National Academy Press, Washington, DC.

NSC Ad Hoc Group on Population Policy (1980). *U.S. International Population Policy: Fourth Annual Report of the NSC Ad Hoc Group on Population Policy.* U.S. Department of State, Washington, DC.

The New York Times (1980). Federal commission supports amnesty for illegal aliens. December 8, pp. 1, A21.

The New York Times (1981). Panel asks rise in immigration, with tighter law enforcement. February 27, pp. 1, B5.

North, D. S. (1978). The growing importance of immigration to population policy. In *Population Policy Analysis,* M. E. Kraft and M. Schneider (Eds.). Lexington Books, Lexington, MA, pp. 81-91.

Nortman, D. L., and Hofstatter, E. (1978). *Population and Family Planning Programs,* 9th ed. Population Council, New York.

Oakley, D., and Willson, P. (1979). The need for federal reorganization for population affairs. Paper presented at the annual meeting of the American Public Health Association, New York, November 7.

Oosterbaan, J. (1980). *Population Dispersal: A National Imperative.* Lexington Books, Lexington, MA.

Ophuls, W. (1977). *Ecology and the Politics of Scarcity.* Freeman, San Francisco.

P.A.A. Affairs (1979). Population Association of America, Washington, DC. (Summer).

Petersen, W. (1978). Population policy and age structure. In *Population Policy Analysis,* M. E. Kraft and M. Schneider (Eds.). Lexington Books, Lexington, MA, pp. 15-26.

Piotrow, P. T. (1973). *World Population Crisis: The United States Response.* Praeger, New York.

Population Reference Bureau (1971). Population activities of the United States government. *Population Bulletin 27* (August): 2-27.

—— (1979). *Intercom,* May, p. 12.

—— (1980). *1980 World Population Data Sheet.* Population Reference Bureau, Washington, DC.

Rich, W. (1973). *Smaller Families through Social and Economic Progress.* Overseas Development Council, Washington, DC.

Ridker, R. G., and Cecelski, E. W. (1979). Resources, environment, and population: The nature of future limits. *Population Bulletin 34* (August): 1-42.

Roe v. Wade (1973).410 U.S. 113.

Schneider, C. E. and Vinovskis, M. A. (Eds.) (1980). *The Law and Politics of Abortion.* Lexington Books, Lexington, MA.

Schneider, M., and Logan, J. (1978). The ecological and political determinants of suburban development. In *Population Policy Analysis,* M. E. Kraft and M. Schneider (Eds.). Lexington Books, Lexington, MA, pp. 167-179.

Shepard, B. (1975). Studying the determinants of population policies: An assessment. In *Comparative Policy Analysis,* R. K. Godwin (Ed.). Lexington Books, Lexington, MA, pp. 283-302.

Sly, D., Dye, T. R., Serow, W., and Zelinsky, W. (Eds.) (1980). Metropolitan and regional change in the United States. *Social Science Quarterly 61* (December): 369-675.

Spingarn, N. D. (1971). Population report/fertility drop confuses debate over national population growth policy. *National Journal,* November 20, pp. 2288-2301.

Stetson, D. M. (1973). Population policy and the limits of government capability in the United States. In *Population and Politics,* R. L. Clinton (Ed.). Lexington Books, Lexington, MA, pp. 247-271.

―― (1978). Family policy and fertility in the United States. In *Population Policy Analysis,* M. E. Kraft and M. Schneider (Eds.). Lexington Books, Lexington, MA, pp. 103-114.

Stycos, J. M. (1977). Population policy and development. *Population and Development Review 3* (March/June): 103-112.

Sundquist, J. L. (1975). *Dispersing Population: What America Can Learn from Europe.* Brookings Institution, Washington, DC.

―― (1978). A comparison of policy-making capacity in the United States and five European countries: The case of population distribution. In *Population Policy Analysis,* M. E. Kraft and M. Schneider (Eds.). Lexington Books, Lexington, MA, pp. 67-80.

―― (1980). The crisis of competence in government. In *Setting National Priorities: Agenda for the 1980s,* J. A. Pechman (Ed.). Brookings Institution, Washington, DC, pp. 531-563.

Tsui, A. O., and Bogue, D. J. (1978). Declining world fertility: Trends, causes, implications. *Population Bulletin 33* (October): 1-55.

U.S. Congress (1971). *Declaration of U.S. Policy of Population Stabilization by Voluntary Means.* Special Subcommittee on Human Resources of the Committee on Labor and Public Welfare, U.S. Senate, 92nd Cong., 1st Sess.

―― (1978a). *Final Report of the Select Committee on Population.* U.S. House of Representatives, 95th Cong., 2nd Sess.

―― (1978b). *Domestic Consequences of United States Population Change.* Select Committee on Population, U.S. House of Representatives, 95th Cong., 2nd Sess.

―― (1981a). *U.S. Immigration Policy and the National Interest.* Committee on the Judiciary, U. S. House of Representatives and Committee on the Judiciary, U.S. Senate, 97th Cong., 1st Sess.

―― (1981b). A bill to establish a national population policy and to establish an Office of Population Policy. H.R. 907, 97th Cong., 1st Sess.

―― (1981c). A bill to establish in the Federal Government a global foresight capability with respect to natural resources, the environment, and population. S. 1771, 97th Cong., 1st Sess.

van der Tak, J., Haub, C., and Murphy, E. (1979). Our population predicament: A new look. *Population Bulletin 34* (December): 1-41.

Weiner, M. (1971). Political demography: An inquiry into the political consequences of population change. In *Rapid Population Growth: Consequences and Policy Implications,* National Academy of Sciences (Ed.). Johns Hopkins Press, Baltimore, pp. 567-617.

Westoff, C. F. (1973). The Commission on Population Growth and the American Future: Its origins, operations, and aftermath. *Population Index 39*: 491-502.

—— (1974). United States. In *Population Policy in Developed Nations,* B. Berelson (Ed.). McGraw-Hill, New York, pp. 731-759.

—— (1978). Marriage and fertility in the developed countries. *Scientific American 239* (December): 51-57.

Zero Population Growth, Inc. (1976). *A U. S. Population Policy: Z.P.G.'s Recommendations.* Zero Population Growth, Washington, DC.

—— (1980). *U.S. Population Fact Sheet: 1980 Edition.* Zero Population Growth. Washington, DC.

27

Land Use Policy

Norman Wengert / Colorado State University, Fort Collins, Colorado

I. ORIGINS OF U.S. LAND USE POLICY

Questions of land rights, obligations, allocation of both the means of production and the product, and protection against external threats for both cultivator and for the land cultivated were the land use issues that confronted the first white settlers on the East Coast of what ultimately became the United States. As settlement succeeded, some of the basic survival issues were eliminated. But land use issues continued to be important, influenced by complex social and cultural factors as the colonists adopted and adapted many English institutions, traditions, and values.

One issue, however, was new and dominant: What should be done with the tremendous areas of land regarded as vacant (Indian rights were largely ignored)? And after the colonies became independent, the issue of what to do with the public domain continued to be a dominant land use policy issue.

Historians of public land policy, criticizing nineteenth-century decisions, tend to minimize the novelty of these issues and fail to recognize the experimental and pragmatic aspect of much that was proposed as well as of what was actually attempted. The nation had to learn by doing, and the lessons were often costly (U.S. Public Land Law Review Commission, 1968).

Public domain policy was made within the context of widely shared values and beliefs. Dominant was the desire for individual private land ownership. Until the Withdrawal Act of 1891 (26 Stat. 1095), all public domain policy focused on or resulted in the privatization of the public lands, the federal government being regarded as merely an interim custodian.

Although fraught with fraud, the capstone of nineteenth-century public land policy was the Homestead Act of 1862 (12 Stat. 392), which awarded title to a basic 160 acres to those who occupied and farmed the land. Under this act, as amended, approximately 250 million acres (to 1977) were taken from the public domain. Most were ultimately converted to individual family farms. Throughout the nineteenth century there was little objection to the policy of privatization. Differences arose over means, not ends. And clearly, judged by the quantity and quality of the lands in private ownership, the policy of privatization has been a great success. (For data on disposal of the public domain, see U.S. Census Bureau 1976; U.S. Department of the Interior, 1979).

With the establishment of National Parks, National Forests, and other reserved areas, the policy of complete privatization changed. General authority for reserving public lands for forest preserves (i.e., withdrawing them from entry for disposal under other land laws) was first granted in the Withdrawal Act of 1891 (26 Stat. 1095). Other withdrawals for other than forest purposes were ultimately also authorized. Approximately one-third of the nation is still under federal ownership. How to use, manage, and control these lands continues, therefore, to be an issue of substantial importance.

The balance of this chapter, however, deals with land use policy as related to the two-thirds of the nation that is in private ownership and that has in recent decades stimulated more policy discussion and debate at all levels of government and has generated more attempts at controlling use than has the public domain.

II. DIMENSIONS OF LAND USE POLICY

Public policy with respect to planning and control of private lands has characteristics that tend to set it apart from many other policy areas. First, the Constitution gives special attention to property, giving it protection from certain kinds of governmental action. Although this protection applies to all kinds of property, it has been most significant with respect to land.

Second, as a result of judicial interpretation in literally hundreds of land use control cases, constitutional constraints on governmental action have been considerably expanded and refined. Thus the question of constitutionality is the first and major question that must be faced in proposing a planning and control scheme. Third, citizen involvement in land policy issues has been and continues to be extensive and pointed. This reflects widespread ownership of land, its actual or perceived value, the hope of profits from unearned increments, and the highly structured processes of public decision making. Fourth, land use policy is primarily local government policy, with very specific local applications, so that those most directly affected are generally aware of what is being decided and can organize for or against the proposed action. Fifth, population growth and movement has resulted in a tremendous demand for housing and hence land. Since 1945 about 85 million people have been added to the total U.S. population, representing about 25 million new families desiring land for housing. To this demand must be added the construction of replacement units for old and dilapidated housing, and of units to accommodate the relocation of hundreds of thousands of people. Sixth, in a strongly laissez faire land environment, free market forces have given the entrepreneur unusual opportunities and the search for profits has contributed to fragmented, scattered, strip development, and conversion of highly productive farm lands to urban uses. It has often resulted in ugly and shoddy construction, inadequate streets, and poor sewer and water services. The list of deficiencies is often long. Even where homeowners may be satisfied, negative consequences for particular communities can be severe and costly. Finally, land use policy has both urban and rural dimensions, the urban being closely related to housing and city growth and development, often taking land out of farming, and the rural to soil conservation, agricultural production, environmental values, and maintenance of viable farm communities, and the desire for profits from sale of farm land for development.

III. HISTORICAL ROOTS

Four factors have been of historic importance in shaping present-day land use policies. First has been the dominance of English common law real property concepts, terms, and values. One of these was fee simple ownership, which with the abolition of feudal dues meant virtually absolute ownership. During most of the nineteenth century this reliance on English common law was strengthened, because most American frontier lawyers were trained on Blackstone's *Commentary on the Laws of England,* first published in the 1760s. With fee simple ownership dominant, Blackstone's description (Ehrlich, 1959: 113) was accepted. Ownership involved "that sole and despotic dominion which one man claims and exercises over the external things of the world, in total exclusion of the right of any other individual in the universe." This sole and despotic dominion, Blackstone went on to assert, extended down to the center of the earth and up as far as one could see into the sky!

The second factor shaping land use policy, as already discussed, has been the tremendous quantity of vacant land (Indian rights were commonly ignored or purchased for a pittance) available for the taking. Squatting was frequent; timber, minerals, and water were regarded as "common property" to be used by those who took possession. A land monopoly was not feasible.

The third factor was the development of a land survey system based on latitude and longitude, which made privatization of land very simple, permitting descriptions, sales, and incumbrance many miles away from the property.

The fourth factor, part deliberate policy, part physical circumstance, was the predominance of ownership in small tracts. For Jefferson, and others who followed his lead, land ownership by yeoman citizens was essential to democracy. The land frauds and scandals that loom so large in the interpretations of frontier history, real as they were, tend to obscure the fact that actual ownership, whether of government land or of land purchased from speculators, was in small tracts. The average size of farms in 1935 was 155 acres, when the number of farms peaked at 6.8 million on something over 1 billion acres. By 1970 the number had fallen by more than half, but average size was still a modest 373 acres (U.S. Census Bureau, 1976: 457).

A. Property in Land: A Dominant American Value

Throughout U.S. history, land has been readily available, generally inexpensive, and easy to acquire. In no other country has the general population been able to fulfill what seem to be universal aspirations for land ownership.

Some have concluded that the elaborate structure of legal/constitutional protection for property in federal and state constitutions was a scheme of the rich to protect their interests, using the power of the state to this end. Such economic determinist views may be found in some of the literature, but they are inaccurate and misleading, overlooking two ideological factors of substantial importance in shaping the way in which Americans have dealt with the public domain and land in general. The first of these ideological principles concerns the relationship of land ownership to civil liberties and to resistance to autocratic government. The second is the concept that widely held land ownership is essential to effective democracy.

It was not just rhetoric that led the people of Virginia (1776) and Massachusetts (1780) to link property with life and liberty in their respective Bills of Rights. Two hundred years of English history had well established that possession of property was essential to resistance to tyranny. John Locke's justification of the "Glorious Revolution" of 1688 was familiar to many of the Colonial leaders, if not by direct exposure then through Blackstone's *Commentary on the Laws of England,* published just a decade before the American Revolution. The supremacy of Parliament, as well as the grand importance of property in land, come through loud and clear in Blackstone, from whom Jefferson obviously borrowed some of the choice phrases of the Declaration of Independence.

For Jefferson and many of his peers, moreover, the empty continent held the prospect of widespread land ownership, which in turn was regarded as essential to supporting the kind of yeoman farmers felt to be the foundation of democracy. Although Virginia did not adopt Jefferson's recommendation that every male citizen be granted 40 acres, that state led in abolishing primogeniture and feudal dues, ultimately followed by all the states, so that fee simple ownership became the norm.

B. Town and City Planning

As population increased and cities grew, land was converted to urban uses. Any attendant problems were handled largely by market mechanisms. As population moved west into the new land areas, towns and cities were often laid out in anticipation of growth, federal land laws providing for acquisition of town sites by developers (speculators). Overdevelopment was not infrequent, and location of towns in places where the public was ultimately not interested in settling also occurred.

Modes of transportation—first rivers, then railroads and highways, and finally airports —always played an important role in determining settlement and land use patterns.

Most towns and cities tended to follow grid patterns. In state capitals and county seats the capitol or court house square was a frequent variant from the standard grid. As settlement moved west, where land tended to be flat and relatively cheap, broad streets were common, reputedly to permit U turns by wagon trains. In more rugged terrain, and along rivers, town layouts reflected natural physical features, as well as simply unplanned growth. Perhaps the rural patterns of townships and sections established a checkerboard regularity which was readily transferred to most urban situations.

C. The Chicago Experience

Incorporated as a city in 1837 with a population of 4170, Chicago grew sevenfold in 13 years to almost 30,000 in 1850. Twenty years later (1870), its population approached 300,000. The Great Fire of October 7-9, 1871, destroyed a third of the city—17,450 buildings, leaving 100,000 homeless. But within a few years the city was substantially rebuilt. Thirty years later (1900), the population topped 1.6 million, and it reached 3.6 million in 1950, having increased 100 times in 100 years.

No one would say that Chicago was either beautiful or distinctive—except perhaps for the way in which in the 1890s the lake front and the city park system developed. Chicago's lake front development, traditionally associated with the Columbian Exposition of 1893, reflected the impact of the "City Beautiful" movement of the last years of the nineteenth century. This movement reflected a reaction to the ugliness of industry, and the ugliness and commonness evident in cities generally. Ultimately many cities were affected by the desire to improve—one of the major factors in the beginning of American city planning and urban redevelopment as we know it today. But initially little attention was devoted to urban growth, which was regarded as a natural phenomenon. With the development of streetcars, elevated trains, and subways, growth seemed an endless opportunity.

D. Housing Characteristics

Housing before World War I was based on construction of individual units on a custom basis. During World War I the boxlike triplexes of the Boston metropolitan region provided housing for many war workers, and similar mass housing was constructed elsewhere. Lower-priced housing, moreover, was beginning to be built in a uniform style so that whole neighborhoods often consisted of lookalike houses. Narrow lots of 25 or 30 feet were common, because without automobiles walking to streetcars was important.

Suburbanization occurred around major cities, but suburbs prior to the 1920s were more nearly satellites than simply the bedroom communities they were to become in later periods. Although some commuted, rail service and living close enough to the railroad station was necessary in order to permit the daily trip without too much difficulty. Local streetcar lines were an important link. Autobuses were not developed until late in the 1920s.

IV. ZONING

A. Beginnings

General zoning of an urban area was instituted in New York City in 1916, after a great deal of discussion and involvement of many citizen and community groups (Makielski, 1966). Rural zoning was proposed by land economists at the University of Wisconsin about 10 years later and actually adopted by one county in 1931 (Rowlands et al., 1948; U.S. Department of Agriculture, 1952, 1972).

B. Characteristics

As initially structured, zoning was designed to segregate varieties of urban development by type, seeking a kind of neighborhood homogeneity. The basic objective has been to group similar economic activities to protect property values, to minimize neighborhood change and deterioration, and to establish stability in certain amenity values, especially in residential zones.

Initially this meant the establishment of three basic zones: residential, commercial, and industrial. But very soon, as zoning spread, the number of zones increased substantially. Today residential zones may distinguish between single-family and multifamily housing, some ordinances establishing additional subzones. Commercial zones may distinguish between small neighborhood-type ventures, specialized uses such as gasoline service stations, professional offices, and shopping centers. Industrial zones usually are at least of two types; light industry and heavy industry, but may also distinguish other activities such as warehousing, truck terminals, and so on.

Constitutional Challenge.   It was this zoning segregation that was at issue in the first constitutional case on the subject. Justice Sutherland, writing for the court, sustained the use of the "police power" to secure neighborhood homogeneity. Protection of investments as well as securing a variety of amenities was felt to flow from such use zoning (*Village of Euclid v. Ambler Realty Co., 272 U.S. 365–1926*).

The most frequent challenge to zoning and to land use controls generally has been the "taking" issue, given its modern form in a 1922 opinion by Justice Holmes in the case of *Pennsylvania Coal Co. v. Mahon* (260 U.S. 393). In this case, Holmes enunciated the principle that land use regulation under the police power, if it went too far, could be a "taking or property without due process of law," requiring compensation, or more frequently being unconstitutional pursuant to the Fifth and Fourteenth Amendments. On the basis of this doctrine the courts became arbiters of land use regulations. Many landowners were adversely affected by land use regulations, arguing that the regulations deprived them of property. In practice the issue was left to state courts for decision, with thousands of challenges being initiated on "taking" grounds. It is not surprising that a lack of uniformity developed, some courts being more receptive to regulation, others being very restrictive (U.S. Council on Environmental Quality, 1973).

Spread of Urban Zoning.   Zoning spread rapidly during the 1920s, so that by the end of the decade almost all states had authorized zoning by municipalities. This was in part due to very real concerns about the patterns of development that accompanied the land boom of the post World War I era. But it was also due to the active encouragement given to a model zoning law developed by the U.S. Department of Commerce, then under the leadership of Herbert Hoover.

Toward the end of the decade the Department of Commerce also proposed a model planning act, but this act did not receive nearly as full support as did zoning (Hagman, 1971). Planning was considered radical; but in addition, the collapse in 1927 of the land boom contributed a lack of interest in planning. The model zoning act provided that zoning was to be in accordance with a comprehensive plan. But few jurisdictions were in a position to implement such a provision (Haar, 1955). When zoning was challenged as not conforming to nonexistent comprehensive plans, most courts were willing to concede that the zoning ordinance was itself the plan. Thus when a city was totally zoned, it was fully planned.

A Critique of Urban Zoning.   After 50 years, zoning has proved a weak land use planning and control technique. Among criticisms are the following.

1. Zoning has not been used as a dynamic land use control mechanism, and may perhaps not be suited to such use. Houston, Texas, without zoning, presents land use patterns not significantly worse nor better than cities of similar size and economic character (Siegan, 1972).

2. Zoning has come to be regarded as a game, manipulated by developers and financial interests for their gain. Rezoning, variances, and other loopholes, biases favoring growth and development, have allowed powerful interests to achieve the land use changes and profits they seek (Babcock, 1969; Hinds et al., 1979.)
3. Zoning has often been used as a device by which upper-class suburbs or neighborhoods discriminate against low-income families and keep racial minorities and other undesired groups or economic activities out. By indirectly controlling the size of resident families, it has been possible to minimize school costs. In a variety of ways zoning has been used to keep property taxes on residential property low (Babcock and Bosselman, 1973.)
4. Zoning has added to development costs in a variety of ways, including the encouragement of litigation.
5. Once the requirement that it be in accordance with a comprehensive plan was abrogated, zoning encouraged fragmented land use patterns, and discouraged integrated analyses of the total land use situation (Haar, 1955).

C. Rural Zoning

Rural zoning has had some objectives similar to those associated with urban zoning, particularly when applied to urbanizing areas adjacent to cities. But when originally proposed, rural zoning was conceived of as a device by which land use could be controlled to achieve best uses in relation to its use capability and community interests. In fact, however, this dynamic aspect of rural zoning to guide land uses in directions considered publicly desirable was never fully realized.

Many factors contributed to the initial failure of rural zoning, particularly the lack of county planning staffs, the absence of geologic, hydrologic, and soils data, and an inability of counties to make the economic and political goal decisions that must underpin any attempt at rational land use control.

V. SUBDIVISION CONTROL

Subdivision controls did not become significant until after World War II. They remain, after zoning, the major local control. Subdivision control bears such a close relationship to zoning that it seems appropriate to consider it at this point, even though the historical account is disrupted.

Three categories of subdivision control may be distinguished: The first and oldest focuses on roads and streets, on mapping and plat approval, and is primarily reactive rather than dynamic; the second aspires to shape subdivision development in terms of those who will become residents, stressing desired patterns of growth and criteria of environmental concern. This type of subdivision control remains the exception, although in some states and in some communities the trend is in this direction. In many cases this kind of subdivision control is limited by jurisdictional conflict between city governments, which often have rigorous control, and rural-dominated county governments, which are hostile to control and may not understand longer-run consequences of unrestrained growth. The third type of subdivision control, about which much has been written in recent years (Reilly, 1973), seeks to "restore" state jurisdiction over some aspects of land subdivision and thus to shape the growth of urban areas in relation to more generalized state-level goals and objectives. This is discussed more fully later (Healy, 1976).

In most jurisdictions subdivision regulations do not deal with the wisdom of subdivision proposals, with appropriateness of location, nor with community need for additional development. Consideration may be given to some environmental factors (e.g., open space), and lot size, house bulk, set back, and similar physical criteria may be specified. Streets, sewers, water mains, and some other capital facilities, built to community standards, may be required, and many counties as well as municipalities now enforce building codes. But many critical social and economic factors are not considered. Undeveloped lands already platted and subdivided, within existing municipalities or on the fringes of existing municipalities, would be sufficient to provide housing for many millions. Colorado alone is said to have sufficient land platted for a population of 15 million! But at present institutional devices are not adequate to insist on use of lands already designated for urban purposes before permitting new subdivisions.

VI. AFTER WORLD WAR II

A. The Time of Transition

By the 1930s most cities had zoning ordinances, and some had planning commissions. But planning agencies were generally inadequately staffed, and the few comprehensive plans were often unrealistic dreams for romantically idealized developments. It is not surprising, therefore, that many plans were left on shelves to gather dust.

In any case, land control issues became irrelevant as urban growth stopped with collapse in 1927 of the land boom. Where some growth took place, it was largely a result of New Deal programs such as the "green belt" communities, and most important, the innovative financing support of the Federal Housing Administration.

B. A Problem in Political Theory

The fact that zoning was based on ordinances enacted by the city council had significant legal/constitutional consequences that continue to plague the formulation and implementation of rational land use plans, and contribute to both the extent and form of much litigation. The "separation of powers" doctrine in American constitutional law has meant that the legislative function is distinct and shall not encroach upon the executive function, and both are independent of the judicial function.

From the beginning zoning was regarded as a legislative function, and courts deferred to the policy judgments of legislative bodies, including city councils enacting zoning and other land use ordinances. What this meant and still means in most jurisdictions is that the judiciary will not permit substantive challenges to actions that they have decided are based on a "legislative judgment." Thus questions of the relationship of means to ends can generally not be examined in litigation. Nor can questions of bias, of conflict of interest, of fraud, or of basic rationality and reasonableness be raised. The courts often assert that for them to go behind the legislative judgment would be to substitute their views of what is good for the community for those of the legislative body.

In the broad area of administrative law under Federal Administrative Procedures Act and similar state statutes, the courts have generally insisted that administrative due process must include a record supporting the action taken so that reasonable persons examining the action after the fact would be likely to conclude that it was tenable. Similarly, in the developing field of environmental law, especially under the National Environmental Policy Act of 1969 (NEPA), courts have on occasion insisted that actions of federal agencies affecting the environment be supported by a factual record indicating the essential logic of the action proposed or taken (Wengert, 1979b).

The situation is not static, however. The Oregon Supreme Court has held that whereas the initial zoning decision is legislative in character, rezoning is quasi-judicial and must meet procedural and evidentiary requirements of the judicial process (*Fasano v. Board of County Comm. of Washington County*, 507 P 2d 23–Oregon, 1973). And under its state land use control system, Oregon places considerable stress on basing decisions on evidence laid out in a challengeable record. A few other courts are moving in this direction. In his Mount Laurel, New Jersey, opinion (*Southern Burlington County NAACP v. Twp. of Mt. Laurel*, 67 N.J. 151), Justice Hall of the New Jersey Supreme Court stated explicitly that the issue of the discriminatory character of Mount Laurel's master plan was a matter of "substantive due process," under the New Jersey constitution and within the review competence of the courts. Other courts have achieved a somewhat similar substantive result by once again insisting that zoning be consistent with the comprehensive plan.

C. World War II Period

World War II saw construction of various types of emergency housing, some tied directly to specific military activities or industries, others simply adding to housing supply in war-impacted communities.

D. After the War

The postwar era, with pent-up consumer demands backed by substantial personal savings and easy financing, saw the beginnings of a housing boom that with some ups and downs continued through the 1970s. Population growth, particularly as measured by new family formation, plus prosperity and ease of financing, contributed to the continued high demand for housing (Listokin, 1974).

From 1945 to 1980 U.S. population, mostly urban and suburban, grew from approximately 140 million to about 227 million, or about 85 million. This meant 25 million new families requiring housing units.

Despite criticisms of the so-called flight to the suburbs as having been racially motivated, it must be emphasized that by no stretch of the imagination could the central cities have absorbed the population growth of 85 million. Suburban growth was absolutely necessary if the populace was to be housed. The issue of suburban political independence is a different question. Two factors intensified the problems of suburban growth, namely, postwar prosperity and the cheap availability of the automobile and of gasoline. It is often overlooked that the real impact of the automobile on land use was not felt until after World War II because the Depression had brought an end to the automobile boom. Prior to 1928 the automobile, the truck, and the bus were not up to supporting suburban growth. One must have lived at the time to realize fully how primitive automobile technology was until about 1928. And the highways were only beginning to be built as the Depression hit. They were really not completed until the 1956 Interstate program.

Americans owned 23 million automobiles in 1929 and used 14 million gallons of gasoline. In 1941, these figures were 29.6 million cars and 24 million gallons of gas, with 18 million gallons being used in passenger vehicles. By 1950, only five years after the war, the number of vehicles reached 40 million and gas consumption 35.6 million gallons, of which 25 million gallons were used in passenger cars. In 1970 Americans owned 89 million cars and used 92 million gallons of gas, 66.7 million gallons for passenger vehicles. Just incidentally, the decline in mass transit mileage did not begin until 1950, although the peak was reached in 1921.

E. The Pathology of Growth

Beginning in the 1950s, but especially in the 1960s and 1970s, more and more people looked at the growth around them and were appalled. Ticky-tacky construction (*The Crack in the Picture Window*), urban sprawl, strip cities, fragmented development, with massive conversion of farm lands to nonfarm uses and the decay of central city areas, was most disturbing—although the cacophony of complaints did not add up to a remedial program. There seems little doubt that the Interstate Highway Program (1956) hastened unplanned spread of urban areas (often blight) and the destruction of farm lands. Even if they had understood the consequences, few would have been willing to abandon the highway program and return to the pre-1956 situation. At the same time, it is clear that few highway planners saw the problems that would be triggered by massive highway construction. Governments, like people, learn from bitter experience, by mistakes and miscalculations. And cause-and-effect relationships have often been clouded by those with a dollar interest in the results. Just as in the case of river works, so in the case of Interstate Highway system, the sellers of cement, of asphalt, of earth movers, of line paint, had the greatest immediate interest in seeing the program go ahead.

Many, if not most, of the communities in which growth occurred were ill-equipped to deal with growth. Partly this was a matter of knowledge, understanding, perception, and, unfortunately, greed on the part of speculators and developers; partly it was simply the inadequacy of institutions and lack of data for forward-looking land use decisions.

Significant technological changes had also occurred, the implications of which began to emerge as development proceeded. Only after World War II were diesel-powered earth movers available, and the heavy trucks that are now taken for granted. Mobile cement mixers, power hand tools, and new materials such as plywood and chipboard changed the character of construction. These technological changes, together with new and expanded Federal Housing Authority (FHA) programs, made the housing project a reality, more and more developments involving 40, 80, or even several hundreds of acres at one time.

For much of the period after the war, individuals could purchase new housing with little or no down payment, and thanks to FHA and Veterans Administration (VA) financing, mortgages ran for 25, 30, or more years. As a result, the individually built "custom" house became the symbol of the upper class, while middle- and working-class families moved into projects, where individual detached homes still dominated.

For the developer large acreages became necessary, and these were often available only at some distance from existing urbanized areas. Whole farms or even several adjoining farms would be purchased as the base for project development. So sprawl and scatteration, fragmentation and strip development became a characteristic of postwar development.

One important reason for these situations was that the zoning and planning ordinances enacted in the 1920s were applicable primarily within city limits. Only a few states gave minimal extraterritorial authority to their cities, and most counties had not yet developed land use controls and planning agencies. Although some states required counties to have planning commissions and land use plans, many made their authorizations permissive. Even where mandated, plans were weak, ineffective, or nonexistent. To illustrate, Colorado enacted mandatory county planning in the late 1960s, but by 1980 only 25 of the 63 counties in the state had adopted comprehensive plans.

Much project housing was drab, uninteresting, and unimaginative. Even worse, it was often of poor quality, shoddiness in part reflecting the absence of building codes and related controls in the rural areas being converted to urban uses. Water supply and sewage handling facilities were often inadequate.

As this pattern emerged, the ugliness, the drabness, as well as the social and private costs, became the focus of more and more public attention, and directly stimulated efforts to improve land use planning and control, particularly in those states experiencing rapid growth (U.S. Council on Environmental Quality, 1974).

VII. INNOVATIONS IN LAND USE CONTROLS

Although zoning continues to be the predominant technique for land use control, with subdivision regulation second in importance, the 1970s saw new and amended techniques proposed and sometimes tried as devices for more effective realization of public interests in land use (Burchell and Listokin, 1975; Levin et al., 1974; Williams, 1974).

With respect to the variety of innovations, probably not all were as beneficial as claimed. In many cases results were different than anticipated, and in other cases those pressing for action seem to have had hidden agendas pursuant to which they were really seeking personal values. In zoning and subdivision regulation, the "game" was often to use the system to achieve selfish goals. Space does not permit full descriptions or analyses of some of the newer or revised land use control proposals, but perhaps the following discussion suggests the nature of the policy issues involved in the several more frequently discussed innovations (Wengert, 1979a).

A. Growth Management

Most attention to growth management in the United States has focused on the very local town or city, leading some commentators to challenge whether municipal or county governments are competent to deal with growth control issues that, they argue, usually transcend local boundaries and require regional or state decisions (Urban Land Institute, 1975, 1978, 1980).

Growth management in the United States is not so much a single technique as an objective, implemented by a variety of locally applied controls. As a policy objective, moreover, growth management rests on a number of stated and unstated premises. Not infrequently an underlying premise of growth management has been the desire of a community to preserve its present character, seeking, for example, to retain its rural, small-town setting, or in the case of larger cities (e.g., Boulder, Colorado), to protect amenities associated with a particular life style. Population caps fixing maximum population or limiting annual growth to a definite number of new dwelling units are among devices used (Burrows, 1978).

The constitutionality of growth management as a police power purpose has been under some general attack (Godschalk, et al., 1977). In addition, the more specific means to achieve this objective sometimes have been the subject of constitutional litigation. In some jurisdictions, despite obvious exclusionary results, courts have not struck down such controls. Sometimes they have found legitimate public purposes in the controls, such as historic preservation. In other cases, challenges have been rejected on procedural grounds, such as lack of standing on the part of plaintiffs (*Construction Industry of Sonoma County v. City of Petaluma*, 522 F 2d 897–1975). And in still others constitutional challenges have been rejected on grounds that seem to be similar to the views expressed by Justice Douglas in Belle Terre (see below).

But in other jurisdictions (e.g., New Jersey), courts have struck down controls that had exclusionary results, stressing that where population was increasing and housing was in short supply, communities must absorb a "fair share" of the growth, including in such fair share low-income and minority housing, as in the already cited Mount Laurel, New Jersey, case.

Where purposes other than exclusion are sought (e.g., historic preservation, capital investment phasing in relation to the fiscal capacity of the community, containment of growth costs and provision of adequate services, environmental concerns and quality-of-life considerations), many courts have been willing to accept growth controls as a proper exercise of police powers. Development timing and limited moratoria (e.g., on sewer and water line connections) have also been accepted where it is clear in the record that the purpose is not simply to exclude, but to rationalize and systematize growth.

The literature a decade or two ago suggested that refusal to provide necessary urban infrastructure (water, sewer, streets, lighting, etc.) might provide a means for development control. But large-scale developers often themselves have been required to provide infrastructure facilities, and some courts, using public utility law principles, have stressed the obligation of local governments to serve where physically and reasonably feasible.

The simple fact that dollar costs of service may increase for the entire community has been generally rejected as a basis for limiting development. In this context, the developing law with respect to the obligation of states to provide adequate educational opportunities may provide analogies. In California, Texas, New Jersey, and Wyoming, state governments have been charged with the duty of supplementing local school funds in order to equalize educational opportunities throughout the state. By analogy, one can conceive of future courts reaching similar conclusions with respect to other basic services, including those incident to growth.

Closely related to this emphasis on the duty to provide services is the constitutional doctrine of the "right to travel," usually interpreted as the right to live and work where one may choose. Although not fully articulated in growth management control situations, the right to travel may ultimately have a far-reaching impact on such control attempts as are based on the bald purpose of keeping people out.

B. Intervention of State Government

For at least a decade the argument has been advanced that states should take back powers delegated to local governments with respect to land use control (U.S. Council on Environmental Quality, 1971). The scope of this emphasis has been established by the model code proposed by the American Law Institute after many years of study. That code seeks to reassert state responsibilities over topics of state interest. A few states have moved tentatively in this direction, but not without intense political controversy. In almost every case where state responsibility has been taken back, local governments, aligned with developers and farmers, have formed powerful coalitions to resist or qualify the exercise of state power. For some of the opponents the issues have been ideological, for others a simple recognition that their influence and power could be better exercised at the local level (American Law Institute, 1975). Some states have enacted specialized statutes relating to industrial and/or power plant siting. Under federal pressure, states are enacting strip-mining control statutes. Similarly, some 30 states have enacted or will be enacting coastal zone statues in order to receive federal funds for this purpose.

In 1937, states enacted statutes authorizing soil conservation districts providing authority for rural land use ordinances. Many states deleted the ordinance powers in the model statute as proposed by President Roosevelt, but even where land use ordinance authority was retained, it has not been utilized.

Another special type of control is flood plain zoning and, more broadly, control over development in natural hazard areas (e.g., earthquake faults). Flood plain zoning by city and county governments is becoming quite common because of federal pressures resulting from the terms of the Flood Insurance Act.

C. The Federal Government and Land Use Control

When proposed, general federal land use control bills have been vehemently opposed by diverse interests and rejected by Congress. At the same time, as suggested in previous sections, the federal government has had indirect effects on local land use planning and control practices. The federal impact on land use in insuring home mortgages, in providing for urban redevelopment, in rent subsidies for low-income families, in financing housing projects, in supporting capital investments in highways, in financing and regulating sewer and water systems, and in location of federal post offices and general office facilities, and in supporting urban planning studies, has been substantial. Based primarily on the spending power of the Constitution, programs in these many fields have influenced patterns of urban growth and land use, sometimes for good and sometimes for ill. Many of these programs have in fact been narrow in focus, often paying slight attention to the long-range and secondary effects on patterns of land use.

D. Zoning Developments

Zoning has remained the principal land use control in most jurisdictions. In some cases, both the objectives and the techniques of zoning have evolved to meet public needs and aspirations (Marcus and Groves, 1970; Nelson, 1977; Rose and Rothman, 1977; Weaver and Babcock, 1979). *Open-space zoning*—a variant of earlier density controls—has been used to provide scenic vistas, play areas, and similar amenities. Open-space zoning must be reasonable and must leave some value in the owner.

Planned unit development (PUD) has been another device resulting in provision of open space in return for greater densities in certain sections of a development. *Contract zoning,* of which the PUD approach is a special variant, has also resulted in bargains between developers and planners to secure certain amenities, including open space. In some jurisdictions, financial payments (exactions) are required as a condition for approval of development plans as an alternative to land dedication, the money thus received being used for various capital improvements, which may include acquisition of open space.

Some flexibility has been introduced into zoning (in some jurisdictions) by a number of adaptations that reflect the change in purpose behind zoning. In a few jurisdictions "floating zones" are permitted. These serve as a kind of advance notice to a zoned area that when circumstances develop and the need is clear, predetermined zoning changes will be made.

Incentive zoning and *compensatory zoning* are devices by which positive motivations are given to persuade a developer to fulfill comprehensive plan objectives. In a number of European countries various positive incentives, including subsidies, are used to accomplish community goals and direct the pace and location of development. Two variants involving use of incentives should be mentioned. One is the PUD already discussed, under which higher density and housing diversity on one part of a tract is allowed if the remaining area is left in open space for recreation and similar uses.

The second device based on incentives and economic motivation involves the purchase by the government of development rights, leaving in the property owner only those residual rights approved for use of land in a particular area. Purchase of development rights has been much discussed as a means for preserving prime agricultural lands and preventing their conversion to nonagricultural uses.

A variant of the purchase of development rights is the largely untried device of "transferable development rights"—TDRs—where costs of controls limiting certain kinds of development are converted into a kind of scrip that the restricted owner can then transfer (i.e., sell) to developers who are required to secure additional rights to develop their lands to levels deemed economically attractive. Without purchasing TDRs from restricted owners, developers would themselves be prevented from full development. TDR systems seek to compensate owners for development foregone and at the same time to permit transfer of the foregone development to another piece of property, usually in the vicinity. The TDR system assumes marketlike transactions between private parties, with government establishing the rules under which the market would operate. The TDR system was originally proposed for historic preservation (Costonis, 1974; Rose, 1975), but has since been urged in other contexts, including preservation of farm lands.

E. Problems of Exclusionary Zoning

Although in theory courts will strike down as unconstitutional all overt exclusionary zoning, in practice considerable variation may be found in clarity and firmness among state and federal court decisions. In part, the problem is evidentiary, involving proof of facts of deliberate exclusion as a result of zoning or other land use controls. Because most land use controls are negative, the simple fact that an area may be zoned for low-cost housing does not assure that such housing will be built. In the Mount Laurel, New Jersey, case already referred to, while the New Jersey Supreme Court ruled that the town plan was discriminatory in that it did not include a fair share of low-income and minority housing, a new plan providing for such housing by no means guarantees that it will be built. Only if the town itself undertakes such construction will it be assured, and few cities are prepared to assume this responsibility (Babcock and Bosselman, 1973).

The issue of exclusion has been clouded by the decision in which the majority opinion of Justice Douglas asserted that zoning might appropriately seek to establish:

> . . . a quiet place where yards are wide, people few, and motor vehicles restricted. . . . The police power is not confined to elimination of filth, stench, and unhealthy places. It is ample to lay out zones where family values, youth values, and the blessings of quiet seclusion and clean air make the area a sanctuary for People (*Village of Belle Terre v. Boraas,* 416 U.S. 1–1974).

Although it may be possible for planning commissions to reconcile Justice Douglas' idyllic characterization with "fair share" doctrines as expressed in the Mount Laurel case, this may not be an easy task.

In any case, even where the New Jersey "fair share" rule is used, it is difficult at any particular time to delimit the area or region to which the test is to be applied. Boundaries in metropolitan regions that seem to run on endlessly, as in the New York–Philadelphia corridor, are particularly difficult to delimit.

F. Fiscal Zoning

Both law and policy on fiscal zoning is unclear. If the "right to travel" (i.e., the right to live and work where one may choose) is stressed, then the fact that locational choices may increase government costs must, like the costs of school desegregation, be borne by whatever government operates in the area. At the same time, studies have indicated increased community costs resulting from sprawl, leapfrog development, strip cities, and fragmented subdivisions with vacant or farm lands between.

There is good evidence that most growth is not without some additional costs to the community and by inference places a burden on existing residents. To illustrate, 40-year-old water mains (they have a normal life of perhaps 80 years) were laid when costs of pipe and labor were at an all-time low for this century. Clearly, water mains of the same size and quality put in today to serve a new subdivision will cost many times more. But water rates within the boundaries of a particular jurisdiction are generally uniform ("postage stamp rates"). Capital improvements such as new mains are paid for by the entire system. Hence those served by the 40-year-old mains will be absorbing a greater share of the new capital costs than residents served by new mains. The same situation exists with respect to filtration facilities and water supply investments. Construction of new schools to serve new subdivisions will also generally follow similar principles. In fact, most capital facilities, except those charged directly to abutting property owners, will show a similar disproportionate allocation of cost burdens where rates are uniform. Although the costs of new infrastructure facilities will be higher than those for older areas, many such costs are capitalized in the price of housing. The requirement that land (or in lieu payments) be dedicated for parks, schools, and other facilities similarly places the burden directly on the new developments.

Increased operating costs (e.g., a larger police force, more patrol cars, etc.), where economies of scale do not apply, can mean that old residents pay for the costs of growth.

But in some cases they may also get increased economic benefits. These increases in costs may simply reflect that fact that the country as a whole is growing and that the burdens of population increases must be shared. A community may be on shaky constitutional grounds to assert that mobile Americans should stop moving. And we probably do not know enough nor control a sufficient number of the variables to presume to tell people where it would be most efficient for them to locate from the viewpoint of the national economy. If the Russian totalitarian state is unable to keep people out of Moscow, is it realistic to assume that the United States has the ability to identify and control both social and individual advantages in order to tell people to live in particular places?

Finally, any discussion of the costs of sprawl must deal with the fundamental inequities of the property tax system, and particularly the inefficiencies, inequities, and political manipulation in assessment procedures. Many of the complaints about the costs of growth may be minimized through more effective administration of the property tax system.

What then about fiscal zoning; fiscal zoning seeks to prevent developments that are likely to add to the property tax burden and/or more positively are likely to produce additional, perhaps disproportionate tax benefits. Small communities have reaped windfalls in taxes as a result of a power plant within their boundaries. Other communities have welcomed clean industry for property tax benefits, especially where the employees live outside the community. Thus fiscal zoning involves both motives and techniques; it can be both negative and positive with respect to tax revenue results.

Large-lot zoning, control of bedroom space, particularly in apartments, so that families with children cannot be accommodated, and a variety of other devices are used to minimize costs to the local government. Where motives are clearly negative and the evidence of discrimination is unequivocal, many courts will strike down fiscal zoning. But the evidence is not always clear, and as indicated above, some courts accept zoning designed to preserve a quiet, suburban way of life, even when the principal beneficiaries seem to be middle- and upper-class residents.

G. Preservation of Agricultural Lands

A land use policy issue receiving political attention in many states involves the preservation of farming and farm lands. The rhetoric of this movement is reminiscent of that which was associated with reclamation (irrigation) proposals at the turn of the century. Similar to the reclamation situation, the present concern with preserving farm lands is often not based on economic analyses, nor on concerns for costs, benefits, and feasibility.

Land economists and many agricultural specialists are generally quite guarded in their support of farm preservation programs. An exception has been the Soil Conservation Service, which not only has been stressing the seriousness of soil losses from water and wind erosion and poor farming practices, but also the annual losses of farm acreage to urbanization (more than 1 million acres per year). But some agricultural analysts believe that technological developments will add to the productive base for farm production and will minimize acreage losses. This latter group stresses the fact that much of the land converted to urban uses is in fact not highly productive "prime" land.

Support for farm preservation seems to come from urban people with a variety of motives. Some are concerned about world food shortages; others appreciate the economic and political significance of American agricultural production to the economy of a region and to U.S. balance of payments, and in dealing with socialist nations. Still others worry about the U.S. running out of food, like so many countries. Some share a romantic interest in farming as a way of life and also seek to maintain the attractiveness of farm landscapes. No doubt, especially among planners and those who share planning values, preserving farm lands represents rational land use decisions tending to avoid urban sprawl and associated evils.

H. Land Banking

The term "land banking" suggests a variety of techniques with differing goals and objectives. One form of land banking used in Saskatchewan, Canada, assists young farmers in acquiring farms. Another form occurs in Australia and in Sweden and several other European countries, where it is tied closely to land use controls, providing a holding device for keeping lands out of the speculative market and directing their ultimate use to desired ends (Strong, 1979). In all its various forms, land banking involves a government agency or public corporation that acquired land by purchase, gift, or otherwise to consolidate holdings and to establish tracts for particular controlled uses. The policies guiding acquisition may vary from country to country. The modes of financing may similarly vary, and the purposes or manner in which the land is ultimately used is not necessarily identical in each of the countries. In Holland, for example, municipalities have regularly been acquiring land in advance of development. When the land is needed for development, it is sold or leased, with land needed for public purposes being retained. In German new towns, a quasi-public corporation acquires the land needed and then leases or sells parcels back to developers subject to specified controls. In France, land banking is a device for buying land from willing sellers with the objective of dampening the speculative market, the agency in certain growth circumstances having the first option to buy land in the path of planned development. In most of these situations land banking is a vital part of land use plan implementation.

REFERENCES

American Law Institute (1975). *A Model Land Development Code: Complete Text and Commentary.* American Law Institute, Philadelphia.

Babcock, R. F. (1969). *The Zoning Game.* University of Wisconsin Press, Madison.

Babcock, R. F., and Bosselman, F. P. (1973). *Exclusionary Zoning.* Praeger, New York.

Burchell, R. W., and Listokin, D. (1975). *Future Land Use.* Center for Urban Policy Research, Rutgers University, New Brunswick, NJ.

Burrows, L. B. (1978). *Growth Management.* Center for Urban Policy Research, Rutgers University, New Brunswick, NJ.

Costonis, J. J. (1974). *Space Adrift.* University of Illinois Press, Urbana.

Ehrlich, J. W. (1959). *Ehrlich's Blackstone,* 2 vols. Capricorn, New York.

Frieden, B. J. (1979). *The Environmental Protection Hustle.* M.I.T. Press, Cambridge, MA.

Godschalk, D. R., Brower, D. J., McBennett, L. D., and Vestal, B. A. (1977). *Constitutional Issues of Growth Management.* ASPO Press, American Society of Planning Officials, Chicago.

Haar, C. M. (1955). In accordance with a comprehensive plan. *Harvard Law Review 68*: 1154.

Hagman, D. G. (1971). *Urban Planning and Land Development Control Law.* West, St. Paul, MN.

Healy, R. G. (1976). *Land Use and the States.* Johns Hopkins University Press, Baltimore.

Hinds, D. S., Carn, N. G., and Ordway, N. (1979). *Winning at Zoning.* McGraw-Hill, New York.

Levin, M. R., Rose, J. G., and Slavet, J. S. (1974). *New Approaches to State Land-Use Policies.* Lexington-Heath, Lexington, MA.

Listokin, D. (Ed.) (1974). *Land Use Controls: Present Problems and Future Reform.* Center for Urban Policy Research, Rutgers University, New Brunswick, NJ.

Makielski, S. J., Jr. (1966). *The Politics of Zoning: The New York Experience.* Columbia University Press, New York.

Marcus, N., and Groves, M. W. (Eds.) (1970). *The New Zoning.* Praeger, New York.

Nelson, R. H. (1977). *Zoning and Property Rights.* M.I.T. Press, Cambridge, MA.

Reilly, W. K. (Ed.) (1973). *The Use of Land: A Citizen's Guide to Urban Growth, A Task Force Report Sponsored by the Rockefeller Brothers Fund.* Thomas Y. Crowell, New York.

Rose, J. G. (Ed.) (1975). *Transfer of Development Rights.* Center for Urban Policy Research, Rutgers University, New Brunswick, NJ.

Rose, J. G., and Rothman, R. E. (Eds.) (1977). *After Mount Laurel: The New Suburban Zoning.* Center for Urban Policy Research, Rutgers University, New Brunswick, NJ.

Rowlands, W., Trenk, F., and Penn, R. (1948). *Rural Zoning in Wisconsin.* University of Wisconsin, Agricultural Experiment Stateion, Bulletin 479, Madison.

Siegen, B. H. (1972). *Land Use Without Zoning.* Lexington-Heath, Lexington, MA.

Strong, A. L. (1979). *Land Banking: European Reality, American Prospect.* Johns Hopkins University Press, Baltimore.

Urban Land Institute, (1975, 1978, 1980). *Management and Control of Growth,* vols. 1-3 (1975), vol. 4 (1978), vol. 5 (1980) (Various Eds.). Urban Land Institute, Washington, DC.

U.S. Census Bureau (1976). *The Statistical History of the United States.* Basic Books, New York.

U.S. Council on Environmental Quality (1971). *The Quiet Revolution in Land Use Control.* Prepared by F. Bosselman and D. Callies. U.S. Government Printing Office, Washington, DC.

—— (1973). *The Taking Issue.* Prepared by F. Bosselman, D. Callies, and J. Banta. U.S. Government Printing Office, Washington, DC.

—— (1974). *The Costs of Sprawl,* 3 vols. Prepared by Real Estate Research Corporation. U.S. Government Printing Office, Washington, DC.

U.S. Department of Agriculture, Bureau of Agricultural Economics (1952). *Rural Zoning in the United States.* By E. D. Solberg. Agriculture Information Bulletin No. 59. U.S. Government Printing Office, Washington, DC.

U.S. Department of Agriculture, Economic Research Service (1972). *Rural Zoning in the United States: Analysis of Enabling Legislation. Misc.* Pub. No. 1232. U.S. Government Printing Office, Washington, DC.

U.S. Department of the Interior, Bureau of Land Management (1977). *Public Land Statistics, 1977.* U.S. Government Printing Office, Washington, DC.

U.S. Land Law Review Commission (1968). *History of Public Land Law Development.* By Paul W. Gates U.S. Government Printing Office, Washington, DC.

Weaver, C. L., and Babcock, R. F. (1979). *City Zoning: The Once and Future Frontier.* Planners Press, American Planning Association, Chicago.

Wengert, N. (1979a). National and state experiences with land use planning. In *Planning the Uses and Management of Land.* Agronomy Society of America, Crop Science of America, and Soil Science Society of America, Madison, WI, pp. 27-45.

—— (1979b). Constitutional principles applied to land use planning and regulation: A tentative restatement. *Natural Resources Journal 19*: 1-20. University of New Mexico School of Law, Albuquerque.

Williams, N., Jr. (1974, with updates). *American Planning Law: Land Use and the Police Power,* 5 vols. Callaghan, Chicago.

28

Transportation Policy

James A. Dunn, Jr. / Rutgers University–Camden, Camden, New Jersey

I. INTRODUCTION: TRANSPORTATION AS A POLICY AREA

Few would deny that transportation—conceived as an economic sector or a physical activity—is an important subject. Its statistics are impressive: Transportation activities account directly for approximately 22 percent of the gross national product (GNP) (worth $416 billion in 1977), produce more than 2.6 trillion passenger miles and 2.4 trillion freight ton miles of domestic travel annually, use one-third of all energy and more than one-half of all petroleum consumed each year, and directly employ one out of every nine workers in the labor force. Beyond mere numbers, it is obvious that our modern economy and indeed our while civilization would scarcely be possible without a highly developed transportation system. Virtually every individual, corporation, and region is intimately affected by developments within the transportation system.

Yet, curiously, transportation *policy* has received comparatively little attention from political scientists until quite recently. It is safe to say that there are many more political scientists doing research on African politics than on U.S. transportation policy. Even within the subfield of policy studies, transportation has had a low profile, often being covered as an adjunct to topics such as urban studies, land use policy, interest groups, energy policy, and the like. Why should this be?

Part of the answer lies in the characteristics of transportation as a policy area. In the first place, transportation policy, following the transportation system itself, has tended to be fragmented along modal lines. Each mode (railways, airlines, barges, buses, highways, subways, etc.) is based on a different technology, serves different needs, and involves a different set of actors, interests, and institutions. It is difficult for analysts to master the detail in all of these modes, let alone formulate overarching hypotheses or policy principles. What does airline deregulation have in common with an urban freeway revolt? Second, within each modal policy area, issues tend to be formulated in very technical terms. The skills of engineers, economists, and regulatory lawyers often seem better suited to these formulations than those of political scientists. Third, even though governments have always been actively involved in promoting and regulating transportation, until the creation of the U.S. Department of Transportation in 1967 there was no central institution or intellectual focus for transportation policy making and transportation policy studies. Not so long ago critiques of transportation policy used to begin by charging that the United States did not have a transportation policy. Even today transportation policy issues are processed in a bewildering array of bureaucratic, legislative, judicial, independent regulatory, state, and local arenas. Finally, in the past it often seemed that public policy was only a marginal factor influencing transportation system development and performance. Market processes—effective demand, rates of return on investment, the spread of new technology—were perceived as determining transportation outcomes. The overriding goal of the market-dominated transportation system was growth: more, better, cheaper, and faster transportation for everyone.

In recent years all this has been changing. Broad public concern for issues such as energy scarcity, environmental problems, inflation, public financial crises, regional economic difficulties, and unequal access to social services have come to be seen as linked to transportation system characteristics and performance. These broader concerns have focused attention on the defects and drawbacks of public policy in the area of transportation and are gradually attracting more and more political scientists and interdisciplinary policy specialists to transportation as a subject for policy studies.

A. Changing Themes in Transportation Policy Debate

This is not to suggest that a complete and coherent new framework for integrating transportation policy studies has been achieved. But there has been a major shift in the assumptions and criteria used in evaluating old policies and prescribing new ones. The significance of this shift can best be illustrated by a brief summary of the major themes that have characterized policy discussions throughout the nation's history. Broadly speaking, we can divide the history of American transportation policy development into four major periods. In the first period, roughly 1776 to 1876, the primary transportation problem facing the nation was scarcity of transport. The goal of almost all transportation policy actions at all levels of government was the rapid growth of transportation infrastructure and services to facilitate the opening up and exploitation of the continent. The primary policy modality was *promotion,* principally public actions to make investment in and operation of transportation facilities more attractive to investors (e.g., the land grants made to railroads), and occasionally actual public investment in transportation facilities (e.g., the Erie Canal).

The second period began in the last quarter of the nineteenth century. By then transportation growth in the leading mode, railroads, was largely self-sustaining. The problem was the disorganization of transportation markets, some of which were bleeding producers through unbridled competition and some bleeding shippers through monopoly. The goal of public policy in this period was to assure equity to customers and market stability and revenue to producers. The policy modality was *regulation,* carried out at first by state governments; but after the 1887 passage of the Interstate Commerce Act the most important regulatory action took place at the federal level.

A third stage can be seen to have begun in 1920. The Transportation Act of that year reinforced regulation of the railroads, but the new technologies of the road motor vehicle and the airplane once again switched the nation's transportation goal to growth and expansion. Governments at all levels promoted the growth of auto and truck travel through massive investments in highways. Air travel benefited from both infrastructural investments (airports, air traffic control systems) and subsidies given directly and indirectly to the airlines in their early days. Little effort was made to coordinate the impact of the growth of competing modes with the regulatory policies being pursued toward the railroads, or to rationalize the rail system itself to relieve the burden of overcapacity and a declining share of traffic.

Since the early 1970s the nation has clearly entered into a fourth stage of transportation policy. The growth motif has receded in nearly all of the modes. The outputs of the transportation system are generally seen as quantitatively sufficient. It is the increasing scarcity and cost of the inputs such as energy and capital, as well as undesirable side effects such as air pollution, that are seen as problematic. The goal that is emerging in this period is *rationalization*—maximizing the efficiency of the system from a social accounting point of view, getting the freight and passengers moved with the least cost measured in terms of dollars but also in terms of energy consumed, air polluted, passengers killed and injured, and so on. The main policy modalities have been a combination of deregulation in the traditional transportation industries and a new wave of regulation in the area of individual transportation.

The principal policy debates of the 1970s revolved around the simultaneous thrust to narrow the scope of government authority in the economic regulation of the traditional common carrier transportation industries, and to expand public authority in the regulation of individual passenger travel and the industries providing the means for such travel, urban mass transit systems and the automobile industry. This is not as contradictory as it might seem at first glance. Common carrier economic regulation was originally created to remedy perceived market deficiencies. Time, experience, and analysis have shown that the administrative and policy defects of common carrier economic regulation may be even more serious than the market defects they were created to remedy. In the metropolitan transportation system, the perception of market defects is newer, and expansion of public regulation was still seen as part of the solution rather than as part of the problem.

II. ECONOMIC REGULATION OF THE TRADITIONAL TRANSPORTATION INDUSTRIES

The 1970s saw the liveliest debate and the most significant policy changes in economic regulation of the common carrier transportation industries in 50 years. Several of the decade's most salient political and economic trends (rising inflation rates, capital shortages, growing disenchantment with government in general) helped thrust the policy studies-derived prescription for "deregulation" or "regulatory reform" to the top of the transportation policy-making agenda during these years. As the decade opened, the Interstate Commerce Commission (ICC) and the Civil Aeronautics Board (CAB), presided over most transportation policy matters in a routine and time-honored fashion, while Congress limited itself to relatively minor adjustments and the executive sponsored studies. By 1980 the ICC had been stripped of or voluntarily given up many of its economic regulatory powers, a host of new public and quasi-public agencies had been created in the area of rail transportation, and the CAB was happily preparing for its scheduled demise in 1985.

The deregulation movement, while clearly reflecting the temper of the times, was also a tribute to the power of policy analysis. Policy analysts, led by economists, and including public interest advocates, political scientists, and even historians, leveled a withering barrage of criticism at transportation regulation in the late 1960s and early 1970s.[1] They emphasized the fact that existing regulatory policies and practices did not address new policy problems such as energy and inflation, which had moved to the forefront of national concern. Indeed, they charged that regulation was not doing an effective job of addressing the problems for which it was initially created. Their critique of transportation regulation may be summarized as follows: Once thought necessary as a substitute for market competition in monopoly situations, regulation actually tends to suppress competition. Regulatory policy gave too much weight to existing (often inefficient) carriers by restricting entry of competitors into service and by establishing minimum as well as maximum rates. Regulatory procedures were too slow and costly, and tended to prevent mergers and consolidations that could have led to lower transport costs to the public. Regulatory officials and the congressional committees that oversaw their activity had little notion of how to coordinate the serveral modes of transportation to best effect, and attempts to plan coherent long-term strategies foundered because of the conflicting and contradictory goals embodied in the regulatory system. On the one hand, regulation was supposed to protect the public from overcharging and other abuses by the carriers; but on the other hand, it was supposed to ensure the overall economic health of the industry being regulated so that service would continue to be provided. In modes such as airlines and trucking, regulation was apparently failing in the former responsibility, and in railroads it was failing in the latter.

In mid-decade deregulation began to move forward politically. It became a priority item of the Ford administration, with natural appeal to many Republicans who had long preached the need to get the government off the back of business. In Congress, it won support from many liberals such as Senator Edward M. Kennedy (D., Mass.), who could take satisfaction in shaking big business out of a publicly sanctioned situation in which they could overcharge the public. It won support from many staff members of the regulatory commissions, and soon even the commissioners took up the call to Congress for deregulation, even as they pushed administrative deregulation to the limits of their commission's authority.

Beneath the rhetoric of deregulation there were significant variations in the political and economic dynamics of regulatory change in the different modes. Airline and trucking deregulation were aimed at thriving industries and were intended to lower rates to customers by increasing competition among firms in the same mode. In addition, the trucking industry strongly opposed deregulation. The airlines were not as vehement as the truckers but were hardly enthusiastic. Rail deregulation was applied to an industry in serious financial difficulty. It was aimed at raising revenues for the industry by allowing the companies greater pricing freedom, which in most cases meant freedom to raise their rates. It was, of course, strongly favored by the railroads and opposed by their customers. Policy makers tended to view deregulation in all modes as producing overall savings to society. Savings went to people as consumers of transportation in trucking and air travel, and to people as taxpayers in the rail sector. Rate deregulation was thus seen as a way of avoiding becoming endlessly entangled in a program of subsidies and quasi-public ownership schemes such as Conrail.

Domestic air cargo transport (representing less than 1 percent of all freight shipped) was the first and most thoroughly deregulated sector. This was followed by air passenger deregulation authorized by the Airline Deregulation Act of 1978. This allowed much greater price competition through discount fares, made it easier for airlines to get permission to pick up new routes, and provided that the CAB itself would be phased out of existence by 1985.

The trucking industry and the Teamsters Union had more political influence than the airlines. Consequently the Motor Carrier Act of 1980 did not go nearly as far as airline deregulation. Nevertheless, it did ease restrictions on entry into service by shifting the burden of proof from the applicant to those who oppose the application. It also reduced operating restrictions such as those requiring circuitous routing or empty backhauls, granted some rate-making flexibility within a zone of freedom plus or minus 10 percent of existing rates, and set up a commission to study the impact of further liberalization of rate making.

The rail sector's first tentative steps came with the Railroad Revitalization and Regulatory Reform Act of 1976. The major contribution of this legislation was to funnel some $6.5 billion in loans and grants to the industry, but it did introduce a two-year experiment in limited pricing freedom. Opposition from coal companies and utilities, who feared that they would bear the burden of future rate increases, delayed further progress for years. It was not until the fall of 1980 that a second rail deregulation act could be hammered out in Congress.

The impact of these changes on the traditional common carriers can be assessed only in a preliminary fashion.[2] In the air transportation sector the first year of deregulation was a boom year. Passengers and profits reached new heights. But the 1979–1980 recession hurt. Traffic dropped off, fuel costs rose rapidly, competition kept rates and revenues down. 1980 was the first unprofitable year for the industry since 1947, and 1981 saw some major carriers, such as Braniff, hovering on the brink of insolvency. Some analysts worried that too much price competition may hurt the industry's ability to raise the estimated $90 billion in capital that it will need over the decade of the 1980s to replace its fuel-inefficient older planes, such as the Boeing 707, with newer, more economical craft. The competition, however, seems to have hurt the revenues of the major trunk carriers more than the regional airlines. Ticket prices on short-haul, less competitive routes have held up better than on longer, more competitive ones (a passenger bound from New York to Los Angeles can pay as little as 6 cents per mile, whereas one going from Chicago to Flint, Michigan, may pay up to 34 cents per mile.) Thus, in reintroducing price competition deregulation appears to have made airline revenues more sensitive than ever to general economic conditions and reinforced a tendency toward boom or bust in airline profitability.

It is too soon to say anything about trucking deregulation's impact except that, given the limited nature of the 1980 bill, it is not likely to produce the wholesale cessation of service to small communities and the skyrocketing accident rate that the trucking industry was predicting. Whether it will produce any of the benefits claimed by proponents of the bill remains to be seen. The impact of regulatory reform on the rail sector as a whole is likely to be positive. One question is whether the increased revenues will get to where they will do the most good—to the financially troubled lines in the Northeast and Midwest. It is possible that the expected upsurge in coal traffic may go mainly to benefit the already profitable lines of the West and South. This would leave the Eastern lines still in need of regular infusions of public capital. Conrail's freight and passenger lines are in a precarious financial position. The Reagan administration has shown a determination to cut back rail subsidies and return Conrail to the private sector, either by selling the whole coporation to private investors or by selling off those parts which might be profitable and scraping the rest. Deregulation is of little help in this situation.

The progress made toward reintroducing competition in common carrier transportation industries is a monument to the power of policy analysis. It shows that a sustained and detailed criticism of ineffective public policies can, under the right conditions, help bring about policy reform. What were the conditions that enabled the deregulation movement to score its successes? First, there was a shift in the hierarchy of problem priorities. Satisfying organized groups in the transportation sector came to seem less urgent than finding ways of dealing with the highly salient problems of inflation, energy, and rising budget deficits. This led the executive branch to make a strong commitment to deregulation as a policy tool and to push its procompetitive policies strongly in an arena that had usually been dominated by the legislature. Second, the deregulators were able to find allies within the transport sector (such as the railroad companies, independent truckers, and airline passenger groups), who strongly supported policy reform because it was in their interest. This prevented a united front in opposition to the changes and helped in lobbying the bills through. Third, the spillover effects of the early successes helped rally informed public opinion behind the process by giving clear and concrete evidence of its benefits. A 5 percent reduction in trucking costs is not likely to excite the general public about the benefits of deregulation, but a 50 percent reduction in regular air fares is.

The next few years are likely to see a continuation of interest in deregulation. The Reagan administration's commitment to reducing the size and scope of government regulation of business will likely shift the emphasis from initiatives primarily aimed at fostering competition to actions aimed at reducing regulatory costs and burdens. This may give the process a more ideological and less technocratic flavor. But it appears that deregulation has moved from being the province of faintly ivory tower outsiders and insurgents to being part and parcel of the establishment in transportation policy making.

III. ISSUES IN URBAN TRANSPORTATION POLICY

Urban transportation policy has been subjected to even more rapid shifts in policy thinking than policy toward the traditional transportation industries. Problem perceptions and policy prescriptions have gone through at least three major intellectual phases in the past 25 years. In addition, the political, institutional, and interest group environment of urban transportation policy has undergone very significant expansion and development. The federal government, which had very little direct influence on urban transportation policy prior to 1956, has come to possess a leading role in policy development, with states and local governments responding to federal initiatives. Policy specialists, especially political scientists, urbanologists, and many planners, have experienced both intellectual ferment and some frustrating limits on their ability to bring about major shifts in urban transportation system outputs.

A. From the Market Model to the Public Service Paradigm

In 1956 the urban transportation problem was perceived as being one of congestion—too many private autos clogging major arteries at peak hours, too few parking places. This was damaging the central cities. The central business districts were losing jobs and shoppers because it was increasingly inconvenient for people to travel there. In that same year the federal government took its first major policy initiative in the urban transportation field, the National Defense and Interstate Highway Act, which created the highway trust fund and set the federal matching share of urban interstate highway segments at 90 percent. State and local governments were thereby encouraged to rely almost exclusively on highway investments as their policy response to urban transportation problems for the next decade.

During this golden age of highway building, little thought was given to the impact that this would have on urban transit enterprises, most of which were still privately owned in the late 1950s. By and large, planners and policy makers were willing to let the market determine the level of public transit services available in urban areas. If a public transportation service is popular and in demand, it will be profitable for private entrepreneurs to produce that service. When demand declines, so will profits and service. Eventually, when there are too few customers left, the service will not be produced at all. If left to function according to its own laws, the market will make the optimum allocation of resources among different transportation modes. Clearly the people preferred automobiles to streetcars, buses, and subways. It was the task of government to respond to this popular preference. Federal and state highway trust funds were thought of as quasi-market mechanisms whereby public revenues from gasoline and tire taxes could be channeled back into the mode that generated them. Highways were thus virtually self-financing. The more people voted for highways by consuming more gasoline and rubber, the more highways could be built to serve these same motorists.

The effects of an urban transportation system almost totally dominated by automobile travel were not all positive, however. Critics soon began to detail a host of negative impacts brought about by what they charged was an unbalanced transportation system.[3] They said that by making the daily flow of traffic in and out of the city easier, highways were hurting, not helping the central cities. They encouraged middle-class moves to the suburbs. New superhighway construction disrupted neighborhoods and destroyed urban amenity. With the majority of travel now taking place in autos, only very poor public transportation remained for those who did not have access to autos—the poor, the handicapped, minorities, the elderly. These groups were being deprived of their mobility. Moreover, automobiles were increasingly being blamed for a major portion of metropolitan air pollution.

The critics of the car were generally pro-public transportation. They developed and helped publicize a new philosophy of urban transit.[4] This philosophy holds that because of the scale and complexity of modern urban communities, public transportation should be regarded as an essential public service, like fire and police protection or public education. It is too important to the community to be left in the hands of private firms interested merely in making a profit and apt to skimp and cut back just at the time they should be improving service. Public transportation that truly responds to public needs can be an effective tool for achieving a variety of social goals such as regional development and environmental protection. City dwellers should not be forced to rely exclusively on the private automobile for mobility. The public authorities must intervene with subsidies and public ownership to assure that public transit is available to all the citizens of the community, especially those least able to afford or to use automobiles. Good service will attract riders, help preserve the central cities, protect the environment, conserve scarce resources, and help make the city livable again.

This new outlook on public transit was reinforced by several political developments in the late 1960s and early 1970s. Freeway revolts against the disruption and destruction caused by urban highway construction broke out in city after city across the nation. This considerably diminished the highway's claim to be the legitimate people's choice. Big city mayors, urban planners, construction firms, transit equipment manufacturers, and transportation unions combined to form a transit lobby and push for access to highway trust fund monies to restore some balance to urban transportation.

Viewed from a political and programmatic perspective, the proponents of the public service paradigm for mass transportation had a remarkable run of political successes during the 1970s. At the federal level public funding for urban mass transportation grew to a $3 billion program by 1979. It moved from its early funding of a few demonstration projects through a stage in which capital assistance was provided to hundreds of transit systems, to achieving the capacity, in 1975, to provide both capital and operating assistance to local public transportation enterprises. It gained access to a share of revenues from the highway fund and raised the level of federal matching grants to 80 percent. It built showcase rapid rail systems in a number of cities across the country and provided new buses and other equipment to innumerable smaller cities. It reversed the trend toward declining ridership of public transit and won the support of many state and local public officials who saw it as a way of bringing federal dollars and jobs to their communities in a way that was less controversial than welfare or job training programs.

And yet, among some transportation policy analysts, there arose a certain scepticism about the merits and accomplishments of nearly two decades of urban transit policy. In the first place, they worried about the cost of the program and talk about a fiscal crisis of transit. Federal aid to transit increased some 3000 percent between 1970 and 1978. The operating deficit of the nation's transit industries increased from $11 million in 1965 to $1.7 billion in 1975. Projecting these figures into the next two decades was a shock to budget analysts and gave pause to all but the most ardent advocates of transit.

In the second place, the impact of all this transit spending on the total urban transportation system was disappointingly small. Measured in terms of the percentage of total urban trips taken, transit's share is slightly less than 7 percent. Measured in terms of its percent of total urban passenger miles it is even lower, less than 3 percent. Most studies did not project significant increases in these figures for the year 2000, even under the most favorable assumptions about continued transit financing and ridership growth. Such a small proportion of total urban travel could hardly be expected to bring about major improvement in the ills of the auto-dominated urban transportation system.

Third, as a number of critical studies have pointed out, much of the spending for transit actually seemed to make matters worse in a number of key areas such as energy and equity. Massive amounts of energy are required to construct new transit systems such as BART. The energy saved in operating the system tends to be rather small. The time required before the energy investment is paid back can be quite long. Some studies have suggested payback periods of several centuries. Moreover, expensive new rapid rail systems tend to be used for long-distance commuting more than in-town trips. This in effect constitutes a subsidy to affluent suburbanites rather than to poorer urban inner-city dwellers.[5]

Thus many analysts were beginning to turn a critical eye toward the public service paradigm in urban transportation even before the Reagan administration took office in 1981 with what it perceived as a mandate to slash domestic spending. Urban public transportation was one of the programs targeted for major cuts. The Reagan administration persuaded Congress to phase out transit operating subsidies by 1985 and to significantly reduce federal capital assistance. This sent cities and states scrambling to find ways of continuing to finance their transit systems and to improve productivity to stretch public dollars as far as possible.

The halcyon days of the 1970s appear to be gone for good. One consequence may well be the loss of many of the ridership and service gains produced by massive federal aid. Another less onerous result may be a return to a more realistic set of expectations about what public transportation can and cannot do to achieve energy, air quality and amenity goals in urban communities. Barring an energy catastrophe, public transportation will make only a relatively small contribution to these goals. It will continue to be a major means of downtown mobility in the very largest U.S. cities, and a supplemental means in some other areas. But it will not be a substitute for automobility on any significant scale. Therefore policy makers who wish to address the real or perceived defects of the automobile transportation system will have to target policy changes directly at the undesirable characteristics of the auto system itself.

B. Regulating the Automobile

Historically, states and local governments had performed what minimal regulation was necessary to keep the auto highway system operating smoothly. They had directed virtually all their efforts at the individuals who operated motor vehicles. It was thus the states, not the federal government, that determined who could drive, how far, how fast, where cars could be parked, and the like. But the fact is that there was little political incentive and many political penalties attached to state and local efforts to "crack down" on their drivers for speeding, excess air pollution, or energy overconsumption. With authority over the users of automobiles thus preempted by other levels of government, federal policy makers were obliged to turn to actions regulating the producers of automobiles in order to have a significant impact on the undesirable side effects of the automobile transportation system. By setting standards for vehicle performance in areas such as safety, emissions, and energy, Washington acted directly on Detroit, thereby avoiding jurisdictional clashes with the states and unpopularity with the voters. The auto manufacturing firms were the epitome of successful big business. Despite predictable protests from auto company executives, few in Washington believed that regulation would damage these firms in any significant way.

Federal automobile regulatory efforts began over the question of automobile safety in the mid-1960s. Those years saw rising highway death rates as a result of the influx of new drivers from the postwar "baby boom" generation. A Senate subcommittee was conducting rather dull hearings into the problem when one of its key witnesses, a young lawyer named Ralph Nader, charged that General Motors had hired private investigators to look into his background to discover evidence to discredit his testimony. The highly publicized clash between Nader and GM (which ended with the company president publicly apologizing) was the crucial impetus for the two pieces of legislation that became the foundation for the entire edifice of federal policy on auto safety, the National Traffic and Motor Vehicle Safety Act of 1966 and the Highway Safety Act of the same year. In subsequent years the National Highway Traffic Safety Administration (NHTSA) has taken an extremely active role in pressing Detroit to modify the design and construction of its vehicles to ensure greater occupant safety. NHTSA's experience has taught it to prefer requiring automakers to build safety into vehicles in a hidden or passive fashion, despite higher costs. Active safety devices (such as an ignition interlock safety belt system) or policy (such as a mandatory seat belt law), which might inconvenience motorists, create too much public and congressional opposition. Cost/benefit studies may show that NHTSA has not chosen a least-cost regulatory strategy. Political analysis shows it has followed the line of least public resistance.[6]

The environmental movement gave the next impulse to auto regulation. The Air Quality Act of 1967 preempted states (except California) from acting to establish their own air quality standards, and the Clean Air Act of 1970 set a schedule of strict emissions standards that new motor vehicles would have to meet. All through the 1970s, Detroit and the U.S. Congress went back and forth on enforcement of the standards. Although there has been steady improvement in the emissions levels of new vehicles tested by the environmental protection agency, the full application of the emissions standards was delayed four times between 1970 and 1977. As in the safety area, minimization of producer costs was not the major concern. Strategies such as transportation control plans or stringent inspection and maintenance of pollution control equipment, which would have caused great public inconvenience, were rejected in favor of producer regulation.[7]

A similar path was followed when the 1973 Arab oil embargo thrust energy to the forefront of public concern. After much debate about the merits of "gas guzzler" taxes on energy-inefficient autos, about raising the price of gasoline through taxation, about gasoline rationing, and other auto user strategies, Congress settled once again on a producer regulatory strategy. Embodied in the Energy Policy and Conservation Act of 1975 (EPCA), this strategy involved establishing a schedule of fuel efficiency standards for new cars, rising from an 18 miles per gallon sales-weighted fleet average in 1978, to 27.5 mpg in 1985. Until late 1979 it appeared that Detroit would begin asking for deadline extensions as they had with emissions standards. A dramatic decline in the sales of the larger U.S.-made cars and a surge in sales of fuel-efficient imports in late 1979 and 1980 convinced auto company executives that the American car-buying public had turned irrevocably toward smaller, more fuel-efficient cars. In 1980 all the major U.S. auto manufacturers announced that they planned to produce a product line that would exceed the 1985 fuel economy standards.[8]

If the EPCA energy goals appear to have been fully accepted by motor vehicle makers because of the market switch brought on by the gasoline shortages and price hikes following the Iranian revolution, there is resistance to extending them, e.g., to 35 or 40 mpg, and there is renewed pressure for regulatory rollback in the safety and emissions areas. Detroit argues that it must now spend enormous amounts (up to $80 billion) to retool for a new line of fuel-efficient cars. But at the same time the industry's profits have fallen below zero because of the sales slump and import surge. If the federal government wants to save the U.S. auto industry and the jobs of hundreds of thousands of auto workers, it cannot continue to impose additional regulatory costs on the manufacturers. If Washington will not risk a trade war by imposing strict import quotas on Japanese automakers, the least it can do is relieve Detroit of many of the safety and emissions burdens imposed by past policy. Given the bleak situation of the industry and the political pressures from the auto manufacturers, Washington has been inclined to do what it can in granting some measure of regulatory relief to the auto producers.

C. Urban Transportation Policy Innovation in the 1980s

Innovations in urban transportation policy respond to two different but related sources of change, new technology or new intellectual and social conditions. The great sweeping changes of the past have been based on the introduction of a new technology that has rapidly superceded the existing one. The railroad and the electric streetcar surpassed the horse and buggy and were in their turn supplanted by the automobile. In each case technological change entailed three significant consequences: (1) a sharp increase in the resource inputs into transportation, (2) a dramatic increase in the mobility provided by the system, and (3) a drastic reshaping of land use patterns and population densities.

Such sweeping technological revolutions are rare, however. Most urban transportation policy change is in response to changed perceptions of the societal problems related to the transportation system. Perceptions may change because social conditions have changed or because the values of society have changed or both. This is the kind of problem to which new transportation policy changes will be responding, not rapid technological innovation. There is no new transportation mode that is likely to replace the automobile in the near future. But there is a whole new way of thinking about the automobile and its relationship to the other elements of the urban transportation system that may well alter significantly the way in which policy makers and the public relate to and use the automobile and other forms of urban transport.

An illustration of the implications of this change in viewpoint can be seen by way of analogy to the policy prescriptions recently put forward by Amory B. Lovins (1976, 1977) in the area of energy. Lovins, an Oxford-educated "gadfly scientist," is a critic of the world's increasing reliance on nuclear power. Along with his criticisms, however, he offers an intriguing alternative. His central thesis is that "hard" energy technologies represented by giant centralized power stations (both nuclear and conventional), based on dangerous or depletable resources, should be replaced by "soft" technologies based on decentralized production from renewable energy sources. Such soft technologies use energy more appropriately, more in tune with the second law of thermodynamics. Using a nuclear power plant with temperatures of 10,000 degrees to produce electricity to heat homes to 72 degrees is ridiculously inappropriate. Using a solar collector, a windmill, or the biomass in garbage is appropriate. Moreover, adopting such soft energy paths will have beneficial social effects. They do not require huge concentrated capital investments, which perpetuate economic inequality and social dependence. Soft energy investments can be highly decentralized and made in smaller increments. Individuals and small groups can make such decisions on their own, and they can cooperate with others to make their investments even more effective. The success of soft energy paths depends not on a massive federal crash program and billions of dollars in subsidies but on thousands or millions of individual actions responding to market and marketlike incentives selected and coordinated by public policy.

The notion of hard and soft technologies has clear application to transportation. For example, both superhighways and rail transit systems are hard transportation technologies. They require massive amounts of capital and land; they are environmentally intrusive; they tend to create bureaucratic/interest group constituencies with vested interests in protecting their funding and hence in policy inflexibility. Obviously there must be an important role for such technologies in urban transportation policy. But policies that continue to rely on expansion of such hard transportation paths to extend mobility in our already mobility-intensive society are as inappropriate as policies that rely on atomic power to increase energy in an already energy-intensive economy. Individuals should not have to drive a 4000 pound automobile several miles for a pack of cigarettes, as many suburbanites now have to do. Cities and towns should not be obliged to buy expensive rapid rail transit systems to offer their citizens an alternative to the automobile. Public officials should not feel constrained to plan for future growth only in the context of travel-inducing sprawl on the metropolitan fringe. Innovative methods of community design and transportation organization that minimize the need for new facilities to make long trips by hard transportation modes and that make it easier to substitute shorter trips by softer modes is what the soft technology suggests.

The new soft technologies are not means of locomotion at all but rather means of better utilizing existing modes. They are new developments in management, marketing, and planning. Improving the productivity of the present transportation system will thus be the major focus of creative thinking and policy innovation in the 1980s. The coming decade will not see large new transportation systems built or revolutionary new transportation modes introduced. The older hard technologies will, of course, continue to function. But the "action" in policy making will be in developing the soft technologies that will enable us to achieve better and more satisfactory transportation outputs with fewer resource inputs.

The creative challenge to transportation policy will be to go beyond the categories and conflicts of the past to achieve a new synthesis. It will involve a blending together of the best characteristics of the auto system and the public transportation system. The concept of "paratransit" from public transportation is converging toward the concept of "transportation system management" from the highway transportation field. This convergence promises to overcome the old tendency to think about auto/highway systems versus mass transit as if they were destined to remain sworn enemies.

Paratransit can be broadly construed to cover the whole range of transportation alternatives between the fixed-route, fixed-schedule service of subways and bus lines and the private car. It includes demand-responsive transit—taxicabs, share-a-ride cabs, dial-a-ride buses, and special services for the elderly and handicapped. It also includes ride-sharing modes—carpools, van pools, and subscription bus services.

Ride sharing can be an extremely cost-effective alternative to the automobile for individuals who make regular daily commutation trips. It is also very effective in reducing energy consumption and air pollution per passenger mile. Its promotion requires little public expenditure compared to highways or rapid rail transit. And it makes use of one of the most grossly underutilized transportation resources in the nation, the empty seats that the vast majority of automobile commuters take with them on their daily journeys.

Demand-responsive transit is more costly to provide and usually requires fairly heavy public subsidies. Its great advantage is that it can be targeted at specific groups in the population who are mobility-deprived, especially the elderly and the handicapped. In many instances these groups can be given superior transportation for less cost than by attempting to improve general public transit services for their benefit.

Transportation system management extends to cover productivity-increasing innovations in the highway system and to coordinate these improvements with improvements in transit and paratransit services. It includes policies aimed at improving the passenger throughput of existing roads and highways by traffic improvements (coordinated signals, turning lanes, etc.), preferential treatment for high-occupancy vehicles such as buses and van pools, provisions for bicyclists and pedestrians, controls on parking, changes in work schedules, fare structures, and automobile tolls to reduce peak-period travel and encourage off-peak use of transit facilities, and other similar actions.[9]

Another potential source of soft technological innovation may very well emerge from the automobile production and distribution sector itself. Energy problems, inflation, and international competition have shaken the industry to the point where it must be willing to consider major innovations in products and profit strategies. The industry clearly needs product innovation. For example, it needs to find new specialized vehicles to replace the profits it lost when sales of fuel-inefficient vans, recreational vehicles, dune buggies, and so on, sagged. General Motors recently announced plans to market a commuter car, a tiny, two-passenger minicompact with a gas-saving three-cylinder engine. Beyond new products, Detroit needs to find new markets, new uses for its products, and new ways of discovering and serving the emerging transportation needs of its customers and their communities. Some transportation policy observers have suggested that the automotive industry must soon begin to take its advertising slogan seriously and start thinking of its role as providing transportation to serve people rather than as just building cars. By revising its marketing philosophy and its franchise relationships with its extensive network of 23,000 dealers nationwide, the auto industry could lead the way in creating new modes of using the automobile. These could include ride-sharing programs fostered by private enterprise, neighborhood-based auto leasing systems, community-owned car rental services offering a variety of vehicles for different purposes, and many other innovative ways of permitting people to get the benefits of automobility without many of the drawbacks entailed by the traditional modes of ownership.[10]

D. Planning, Values, and the Shape of the Community

These kinds of innovative transportation policies are emerging because of the need to accommodate disparate trends emerging in future metropolitan area growth. On the one hand, there may well be a new spurt of downtown office growth in many cities, neighborhood revival and gentrification, higher densities in some areas because of new condominium development, and the like. On the other hand, many observers believe that despite rising energy costs the underlying forces that have been pushing toward population dispersion are still strong: rising real family income, strong consumer preference for low-density living, new technologies for industrial and retail activities that are adapted to low-density structures, the desire of people to achieve better schools and less crime in suburban and exurban environments. Given this duality of growth thrusts, transportation policy will have to be designed to respond creatively to higher-density recentralizing trends with improved traditional transit services and to lower-density dispersing trends with improved traffic management and paratransit.[11]

The challenge is to respond projectively in a way that maximizes user satisfaction while minimizing overall social costs rather than attempting to cater post facto to every instance of private growth. Transportation investments—highways, rapid transit lines, airports, etc.—provide a framework around which metropolitan area growth evolves. In the recent past the great bulk of these infrastructural investments have been made by public authorities. Yet it is fair to say that public planning of these investments emphasized the maximization of private benefits (improved accessibility to residential and commercial developments, heightening the utility of and hence the market demand for automobiles, etc.) rather than maximization of public benefits (minimizing consumption of urban land or exhaust emissions, etc.). Recent experience has sensitized transportation planners and policy makers to the desirability of devising engineering solutions and use strategies that also increase the provision of public benefits. This is not to say that transportation policy will become a sharp-edged tool in the hands of a technocratic elite that ignores private interests and preferences. But it does mean that transportation investments and regulations will be subject to more careful scrutiny on a broader range of criteria than in the past.

In practical terms this means that transportation planners will continue to cater to the preference of the majority of Americans for the convenience, comfort, and privacy of automobiles and low-density living. The critics who thought that the energy crisis would force everyone back into transit and apartment houses are most likely mistaken. Some poeple will want to have a higher-density transit-dependent lifestyle, however. Provision will be made for them, but it will be on a more cost-effective basis than during transit investment's boom years of the 1970s, such as express buses in special lanes instead of elevated rapid rail transit. Provision will be made for preserving the automobile as the primary mode of urban mobility as well, but it too will be scaled down—subcompacts on newly designated one-way streets rather than stationwagons on expressways. A more carefully costed out pluralism in transportation policy will emerge to serve the needs of the pluralist values and living patterns of the country's diverse communities. But transportation will still be the key physical means of blending the many diversities of the American scene into a single national community.

NOTES

1. Political scientists who studied regulation had always shown great scepticism about its ability to attain its official aims. See Huntington (1952), Lowi (1969), and Wilson (1971), for example. But whereas political science did contribute a number of important critiques of pluralist or interest group liberal politics and administration, few of its studies focused specifically on the regulated transportation industries. Economists, with their ability to quantify the costs imposed by what they considered arbitrary and inefficient regulatory policies, made a greater contribution. Some of the most notable examples from the late 1960s and early 1970s are

Friedlander (1969), Moore (1972), Hilton (1975), Phillips (1975), Douglas and Miller (1974), and MacAvoy (1979). At the same time a number of more popular "muckraking" books appeared that were critical of transportation regulation. The best-known study of this type was produced by a Ralph Nader study group (Fellmuth, 1970).

2. Airline deregulation has the longest history and thus the most evidence concerning its impact. A recent study of regulatory reform in the air cargo industry suggests great success (Keyes, 1980). Several studies analyzing the political reasons for the success of deregulation are found in Altshuler (1979b) and Miller (1979). Recent articles evaluating the pluses and minuses of airline deregulation from the commercial airlines' point of view are Seneker (1980) and *Business Week* (1980). For an overall evaluation of the impact and the future of deregulation on transportation policy, see Meyer (1980).

3. The critics of the automobile highway complex produced a literature that is as impressive in quantity as it is uneven in quality. Among the most thoughtful of the critical studies are Mumford (1963), Burby (1971), Rothschild (1973), and Flink (1975).

4. A critical elaboration of the assumptions and impact of the social service paradigm of public transit may be found in Dunn (1980a, 1980b). The emergence of the paradigm itself may be traced in the works of Stone (1971), Schaeffer and Sclar (1975), Pushkarev and Zupan (1977), and Taebel and Cornhels (1977).

5. The critics of public transit may usefully be divided into several categories. The first group is composed mainly of economists who are basically convinced of the superiority of the market model of urban transportation. George W. Hilton (1974) is a leading scholarly exponent of this view. B. Bruce-Briggs (1975) is an outspoken critic of public transit and defender of the automobile. A second group of critics focuses on specific failures of transit to deliver what was promised for it. Webber (1976) focuses on a concrete local system, BART. Lave (1978) questions transit's ability to make good in the area of energy savings. The third set of critics may be seen to have begun as predisposed to favor pro-transit policies. But in examining the evidence in the last decade of experience they have become sceptical of the ability of public transit, especially new rail rapid transit systems, to achieve the mobility, energy, and equity goals promised. The preeminent writer of this group is Altshuler (1979a).

6. Ralph Nader's famous *Unsafe at Any Speed* (1965) began the modern policy debate over auto safety. The Nader tradition is carried on outside of government by the work of the Insurance Institute for Highway Safety (Baker and Haddon, 1978). Within the federal bureaucracy the various NHTSA publications (e.g., 1977) also take a very strong position in favor of goverhment-mandated safety measures. B. Bruce-Briggs (1977) and Sam Peltzman (1975) have established themselves as the leading dissenters on the question of the benefits of recent auto safety legislation.

7. Economists have been much quicker to quantify in the environmental area than safety. Some leading studies of costs and benefits are Dewees (1974), Grad et al. (1975), Lave and Seskin (1977), and Gakenheimer (1978). Political scientists have devoted an increasing amount of attention to environmental issues and how they are processed by the political system, e.g., Jones (1975), Enloe (1975), Davies and Davies (1975). Only a small number of political studies focus specifically on the auto case, however. See Margolis (1977) and Altshuler (1979a) for two leading examples. The whole spectrum of public regulation of the automobile is covered by Ginsburg and Abernathy (1980).

8. Several recent studies have put the energy problems of the U.S. automobile in comparative perspective: Brown et al. (1979) and Dunn (1981). The auto sector looms large in most general studies of energy consumption, e.g., Darmstadter et al. (1977), and there are a number of studies devoted specially to energy and the auto: Wildhorn et al. (1976), Harbridge House (1979). Then there are studies of the comparative energy efficiency of different modes of transportation, e.g., Congressional Budget Office (1977).

9. Most of the literature on the various "soft" transportation technolgies of paratransit and transportation systems management has been produced by planners and transportation professionals. See, for example, Kirby et al. (1974), Transportation Research Board (1976), and Urban Mass Transportation Administration (1977). A few attempts have been made to investigate the political aspects of introducing such innovations into the urban transportation system, e.g., Womack (1976) and Teal (1978).

10. The literature on future changes in the social use of the automobile is as ill defined as the future itself. One strand of studies portrays how other societies have created different auto use techniques, e.g., Organization for Economic Cooperation and Development (1979). Another strand seeks to identify possible and likely changes in our own society, e.g., Orski (1980). Still another set of studies are those commissioned by government agencies. These deal with the short- to medium-term future and are usually very conservative in their projections, e.g., Office of Technology Assessment (1979). Perhaps the best hope for a syntheses of the different outlooks will come when the results of the multiyear, multinational project on "The Future of the Automobile" being coordinated at Massachusetts Institute of Technology are made available to the public.

11. The literature on the future shape of cities, land use patterns, densities, and such is too vast to cite here. Several recent works that treat these questions with specific reference to the reciprocal impacts that changing transportation technologies and policies might have on the evolution of metropolitan cityscapes are Wiener et al. (1978), U.S. Department of Transportation (1980), Urban Mass Transit Administration (1980), and Cornehls (1977).

REFERENCES

Altshuler, A. A., with Womack, J. P., and Pucher, J. R. (1979a). *The Urban Transportation System: Politics and Policy Innovation.* M.I.T. Press, Cambridge, MA.

Altshuler, A. A. (Ed.) (1979b). *Current Issues in Transportation Policy.* Lexington Books, Lexington, MA.

Baker, S. P., and Haddon, W., Jr. (1978). *Injury Control.* Insurance Institute for Highway Safety, Washington, DC.

Brown, L. R., Flavin, C., and Norman, C. (1979). *Running on Empty: The Future of the Automobile in an Oil Short World.* Norton, New York.

Bruce-Briggs, B. (1975). Mass transportation and minority transportation. *Public Interest 40*: 43-74.

—— (1977). *The War Against the Automobile.* Dutton, New York.

Burby, J. (1971). *The Great American Motion Sickness: Or Why You Can't Get There from Here.* Little, Brown, Boston.

Business Week (1980). How deregulation increased efficiency and reduced fares. *Business Week,* August 18, 1980, pp. 80-81.

Congressional Budget Office (1977). *Urban Transportation and Energy: The Potential Savings of Different Modes.* U.S. Government Printing Office, Washington, DC.

Cornehls, J. (1977). The automobile society: Urban design and environment. *Traffic Quarterly 31*: 571-590.

Darmstadter, J., Dunkerley, J., and Alterman, J. (1977). *How Industrial Societies Use Energy: A Comparative Analysis.* Johns Hopkins University Press, Baltimore.

Davies, J. C., III, and Davies, B. (1975). *The Politics of Pollution,* 2nd ed. Bobbs-Merrill, Indianapolis, IN.

Dewees, D. N. (1974). *Economics and Public Policy: The Automobile Pollution Case.* M.I.T. Press, Cambridge, MA.

Douglas, G. W., and Miller, J. C., III (1974). *Economic Regulation of Domestic Air Transport: Theory and Policy.* Brookings Institution, Washington, DC.

Dunn, J. A., Jr. (1980a). Urban transportation policy in West Germany and the United States: The limits of subsidy. *Comparative Social Research 3*: 123-143.

—— (1980b). Coordination of urban transit services: The German model. *Transportation 9*: 33-43.

—— (1981). *Miles to Go: European and American Transportation Policies.* M.I.T. Press, Cambridge, MA.

Enloe, C. (1975). *The Politics of Pollution in Comparative Perspective.* McKay, New York.

Fellmuth, R. (1970). *The Interstate Commerce Ommission: The Public Interest and the ICC.* Grossman, New York.

Flink, J. J. (1975). *The Car Culture.* M.I.T. Press, Cambridge, MA.

Friedlander, A. F. (1969). *The Dilemma of Freight Transport Regulation.* Brookings Institution, Washington, DC.

Gakenheimer, R. (Ed.) (1978). *The Automobile and the Environment: An International Perspective.* M.I.T. Press, Cambridge, MA.

Ginsburg, D. H., and Abernathy, W. J. (Eds.) (1980). *Government, Technology and the Future of the Automobile.* McGraw-Hill, New York.

Grad, F. P., Rosenthal, A. J., Rockett, L. R., Fay, J. A., and Heywood, J. *The Automobile and the Regulation of Its Impact on the Environment.* University of Oklahoma Press, Norman.

Harbridge House (1979). *Energy Conservation and the Passenger Car: An Assessment of Public Policy.* Harbridge House, Boston.

Hilton, G. (1974). *Federal Transit Subsidies: The Urban Mass Transportation Assistance Program.* American Enterprise Institute, Washington, DC.

—— (1975). *The Northeast Railroad Problem.* American Enterprise Institute, Washington, DC.

Huntington, S. P. (1952). The marasmus of the ICC: The commission, the railroads, and the public interest. *Yale Law Journal 61*: 467-509.

Jones, C. O. (1975). *Clean Air: The Policies and Politics of Pollution Control.* University of Pittsburgh Press, Pittsburgh, PA.

Keyes, L. S. (1980). *Regulatory Reform in Air Cargo Transportation.* American Enterprise Institute, Washington, DC.

Kirby, R. F., Bhatt, K. U., Kemp, M. A., McGillivray, R. G., and Wohl, M. (1975). *Paratransit: Neglected Options for Urban Mobility.* Urban Institute, Washington, DC.

Lave, C. A. (1978). Transportation and energy: Some current myths. *Policy Analysis 4* (1980): 297-316.

Lave, C. A., and Seskin, E. P. (1977). *Air Pollution and Human Health.* Johns Hopkins University Press, Baltimore.

Lovins, A. B. (1976). Energy strategy: The road is not taken. *Foreign Affairs 55*: 65-96.

—— (1977). *Soft Energy Paths: Toward a Durable Peace.* Harper & Row, New York.

Lowi, T. J. (1969). *The End of Liberalism.* Norton, New York.

MacAvoy, P. W. (1979). *The Regulated Industries and the Economy.* Norton, New York.

Margolis, H. (1977). The politics of auto emissions. *Public Interest 49*: 3-21.

Meyer, J. R. (1980). Transportation deregulation: Possibilities and prospects. *Journal of Contemporary Business 9*: 69-85.

Miller, J. C., III (1979). A perspective on airline regulatory reform. *Journal of Air Law and Commerce 41*: 679-701.

Moore, T. G. (1972). *Freight Transportation Regulation.* American Enterprise Institute, Washington, DC.

Mumford, L. (1963). *The Highway and the City.* Harcourt, Brace, New York.

Nader, R. (1965). *Unsafe at Any Speed.* Grossman, New York, 1965.

National Highway Traffic Safety Administration (1977). *Motor Vehicle Safety 1977.* U.S. Department of Transportation, Washington, DC.

Office of Technology Assessment (1979). *Changes in the Future Use and Characteristics of the Automobile Transportation System,* 2 vols. U.S. Government Printing Office, Washington, DC.

Organization for Economic Cooperation and Development (1979). *Urban Transport and the Environment,* 4 vols. Organization for Economic Cooperation and Development, Paris.

Orski, C. K. (1980). The world automobile industry at a crossroads. Paper presented at the Automotive Suppliers Conference, Cleveland, OH.

Peltzman, S. (1975). *Regulation of Automobile Safety.* American Enterprise Institute, Washington, DC.

Phillips, A. (Ed.) (1975). *Promoting Competition in Regulated Markets.* Brookings Institution, Washington, DC.

Pushkarev, B., and Zupan, J. M. (1977), *Public Transportation and Land Use Policy.* Indiana University Press, Bloomington.

Rothschild, E. (1973). *Paradise Lost: The Decline of the Auto Industrial Age.* Random House, New York.

Schaeffer, K. H., and Sclar, E. (1975). *Access for All.* Penguin, Baltimore.

Seneker, H. (1980). Fare wars. *Forbes,* September 1, 1980, pp. 36-37.

Stone, T. R. (1971). *Beyond the Automobile.* Prentice-Hall, Englewood Cliffs, NJ.

Taebel, D. A., and Cornehls, J. V. (1977). *The Political Economy of Urban Transportation.* Kennikat, Port Washington, NY.

Teal, R. (1978). Para-transit innovation in urban transportation: A political-organizational analysis. Ph.D. dissertation, Tufts University, Medford, MA.

Transportation Research Board (1976). *Paratransit.* National Academy of Sciences, Washington, DC.

Urban Mass Transportation Administration (1980). *The Future Market for Public Transportation; Peak Period Transit Services: Strategies for the 1980s.* U.S. Department of Transportation, Washington, DC.

Urban Mass Transportation Administration and Federal Highway Administration (1977). *Transportation Systems Management: State of the Art.* U.S. Department of Transportation, Washington, DC.

U.S. Department of Transportation (1980). *Profile of the '80s.* U.S. Department of Transportation, Washington, DC.

Webber, M. M. (1976). The BART experience—What have we learned? *Public Interest 45*: 79-108.

Wiener, A. J., Pignataro, L. J., Bloch, A. J., Crowell, W. H., and McShane, W. R. (1978). *Future Directions for Public Transportation: A Basis for Decision.* U.S. Department of Transportation, Washington, DC.

Wildhorn, S., Burright, B. K., Enns, J. H., and Kirkwood, T. F. (1976). *How to Save Gasoline: Public Policy Alternatives for the Automobile.* Ballinger, Cambridge, MA.

Wilson, J. Q. (1971). The dead hand of regulation. *Public Interest 25*: 39-58.

Womack, J. P. (1976). *Overcoming Barriers to Increased Ride Sharing.* Center for Transportation Studies, Massachusetts Institute of Technology, Cambridge, MA.

29

Environmental Protection Policy

Helen M. Ingram* / Utah State University, Logan, Utah
Dean E. Mann / University of California, Santa Barbara, California

I. INTRODUCTION

Environmental policy, while sharing many characteristics with other public policies, is in two ways unique. First is its scope. The aphorism, derived from the ecological perspective, that everything is connected to everything else, while exaggerating the scope of environmental concerns, nevertheless suggests the extensive and pervasive character of environmental policy. Environmental policy is naturally concerned with protection of the natural environment. It is also concerned with aesthetics, human health and safety, food production, energy production and conservation, wilderness and recreation, the survival of biological species, national and international security, scarce renewable and nonrenewable resources, and the political system that endeavors to grapple with these concerns, singly and in their complex and manifold interrelationships.

Second, environmental policy can be set apart from other policies because its ultimate concern is with the survival of humankind and the natural environment as a suitable and rewarding habitat in which to live. In 1980, a well-publicized government publication on the state of the global environment in the year 2000 found that in most ways the world is becoming a worse place in which to live. Without substantial changes in public policy, environmental problems, such as overcrowding, dirty air, contaminated water, widespread exposure to toxic substances, radiation and pesticides, will be aggravated in years to come.[1] Such official reports reinforce a belief some hold that humankind is way out of balance with nature and headed for disaster. Thus, environmental politics takes on an apocalyptic character in which the normal American political strategy of bargaining and coalition formation may have little appeal, and demands may be less negotiable than in other, less volatile policy areas.

Present affiliation: University of Arizona, Tucson, Arizona

Despite extraordinary characteristics, environmental policy encompasses many of the general issues addressed by public policy scholars. The environmental issue is relatively recent, illustrating how issues get on the government agenda.[2] Whereas conservation can be traced to the Progressive Era at the turn of the twentieth century, conservationists were fragmented, focusing separately on discrete issues such as water, forests, or parks. In the 1960s, a number of events occurred and received wide media attention, such as the publication of Rachael Carson's *Silent Spring*, threats to the California redwoods, and the Grand Canyon from developmental interests, the discovery of "dying" Lake Erie, and the Santa Barbara oil spill. By Earth Day, April 1970—a remarkable outpouring of citizen concern—a coherent movement had emerged. The public began to perceive the linkages of economic activity to environmental pollution, developed a sense of ecology, and became upset about specific instances of pollution and environmental degradation in its many manifestations in air and water on the land. This public consciousness invited, some say demanded, governmental action.

Environmental policy provides examples of the usual incremental change, but it also displays less ordinary cases of innovation. Although commentators disagree about the embodied wisdom, they generally recognize that the Clean Air Act of 1970 and the Water Pollution Control Act Amendments of 1972 constituted large changes and dramatic shifts from previous policy. Clearly there was an evolution from an emphasis on research and data gathering, to state responsibility, to holding conferences and negotiation, to strong national regulatory enforcement and shifts to technology-forcing approaches. Twenty years, more or less, were required to make these moves. Yet it may well be argued that the changes in the character of air and water pollution control policy took a dramatic turn during the 1970s with the passage of the Clean Air and Clean Water acts.[3] Technology forcing has been described as highly nonincremental, pushing beyond what anyone could reasonably expect the regulatory system to handle. Even an examination of the budget allocations for municipal waste treatment plants in the 1972 Clean Water Act suggest the nonincremental character of that legislation.[4] Environmental policy presents other major instances of innovative and nonincremental initiatives in a political system dominated by disjointed incremental, pluralistic policy making in the United States.[5] The passage of the Toxic Substances Control Act of 1976, the Noise Pollution Control Act, and the Endangered Species Act all represent major new departures in federal policy making. Perhaps partly because these landmark pieces of legislation were so ambitious in their goals, exacting in their timetables and draconian in their penalties, they encountered great difficulties in the process of implementation. In this respect, environmental protection policy provides an archetype for policy scholars who currently identify the implementation phase of the policy cycle as the most dangerous shoals upon which policies become snagged.

Environmental policy illustrates dramatically how policy choice often involves trade-offs among important values. Kneese and Schultze estimated in 1976 that existing air and water programs will have cost some $375 billion and possibly more between 1972 and 1985.[6] Such sums are bound to have an impact on the economy. At the same time the cost of pollution in terms of human health is also large. It has been estimated that between 60 and 90 percent of all cancers are caused by environmental factors, broadly defined.[7] Other relationships of environmental degradation to human health, including respiratory illnesses and birth defects, are serious. Further, although independence from foreign oil imports would seem to be in our national security interests, every mode of developing further energy resources at home has unfavorable environmental consequences. Similarly, according to the Pentagon, the deployment of a mobile, land-based missile system—the MX—is essential to national defense. Yet wherever such a system is located, the adverse environmental impacts will be very large.

Environmental protection also provides observers with a view of what happens when an established policy area runs afoul of a new administration's priorities. The determination of the Reagan administration to revive the economy, deregulate business, stimulate energy production, and strengthen military defense is often at cross-purposes with environmental legislation, rules and regulations, and government infrastructure built up over a decade.

No encyclopedic overview can hope to cover the field of environmental protection either completely or to any depth. Our aim here, however, is to provide the reader with an accurate picture of the variety of problems and the complexities of policy questions involved. The tasks we have set in the remainder of this chapter are as follows: (1) to illustrate the diverse perspectives that exist on the environment and the type of solutions to which each point; (2) to outline broadly the challenge for environmental policy and describe briefly the evolution and substance of such policies as those affecting air and water pollution; (3) to identify the policy-making process including the structure of policy demands, decision-making arenas, and the character of impacts; (4) to discuss the major contemporary broad theoretical issues in this area such as intergenerational equity and risk assessment; (5) to speculate on the future of environmental policy in what appears to be a less favorable political environment.

II. DIVERSE PERSPECTIVES ON ENVIRONMENTAL PROBLEMS AND APPROPRIATE SOLUTIONS

The first step in classic planning models for problem solving is defining the problem. Yet Aaron Wildavsky has taught that problem definition is an end product rather than the first step in policy analysis. The conception of the problem depends on one's ideas for solving it.[8] Problem definitions, therefore, depend very much on the values, disciplinary orientation, and experiences of whoever is doing the defining. The environmental problem has been subjected to various definitions and accompanying proposed solutions. These conceptions, in turn, have been reflected in the content of public policy. Three of the most common formulations follow.

For some, the environmental problem is a consequence of the failure to hold and follow an environmental ethic. Lynn White traced the philosophical roots of the environmental crisis back to the Christian religion.[9] According to this analysis, Christianity, and thus Western culture, is anthropocentric. Man supposedly is created in the image of God and can and should conquer all of nature, which was planned for man's rule and benefit. Theoretically, man can freely use his ingenuity and technology to exploit the universe without limit. The disasterous consequences of this world view is effectively and dramatically argued by David Brower, who sees man as a biological animal that has gotten out of balance with his natural surroundings.[10] The supporting environment is fragile and changing. The long-term survival of man as a species depends on man's learning to do with less and to assess, to mitigate the effects of, and in some cases to desist from the application of disruptive technology.

The logical consequences of defining the environmental problem as a matter of ethics is the search for a solution in the education of public tastes and values. It follows that environmentalists, especially in the early years of the movement, stressed behavior consistent with the environmental ethic: carrying string bags to and from market, recycling cans and bottles, and husbanding all resources. The basic rationale for the symbolic language often found in environmental legislation is deference to the environmental ethic. For instance, the goal of the National Environmental Policy Act is to bring man and the environment into long-term productive harmony. Similarly, the zero-discharge aim of the 1972 water quality amendments was to make all waters swimmable and safe enough for the propagation of fish and shellfish, a goal more noble than practical.

A second perspective on the environmental problem views it as a failure to bring scientific knowledge and analysis to bear upon governmental action. According to many critics, both physical and social scientists, the environmental problems we encounter are a result of not developing and/or not attending to scientific information. For example, a hydrologist may claim that water shortages and increased levels of salinity in the Colorado River are a result of politicians' blindness to the physical limits of the hydrologic system. An economist may similarly claim that problems on the Colorado River are exacerbated by political actors who do not perform and follow an unbiased benefit-cost analysis in approving water projects. These scientific critics trace many of the barriers to the development and use of scientific information in decision making to the built-in bias of elected officials and governmental agencies that serve particular missions and constituencies. Thus, the Department of Agriculture turned a deaf ear to Rachael Carson's warnings about the long-term adverse consequences of DDT in the food chain because of that agency's dedication to high levels of agricultural production. Similarly, the Atomic Energy Commission deemphasized the dangers of nuclear power because part of its mission was to promote its peaceful uses.

When the problem is defined in terms of availability and use of scientific information, the solution is logically sought in terms of better access of scientists to the decision-making process. For instance, scientists may hold positions on advisory committees, and offices of science advisors may be set up in the executive branch. Some commentators have suggested a science court to arbitrate difficult scientific issues. Formal rules and regulations have been targeted as another means through which to get better scientific information into decision making. For years economists have struggled to introduce more rigor into the benefit/cost analysis performed by federal water resource agencies. The principles and standards that govern analysis of water projects have been continually revised. The objective of Section 102c of the National Environmental Policy Act of 1970 was to require federal agencies to prepare an environmental impact statement in which all adverse consequences of a proposed action on the environment were to be identified. This provision was aimed at forcing agencies to generate scientific information about environmental impacts and, presumably, to modify proposed action accordingly.

A third conception of the environmental problem is the failure of incentives. This perspective is stated most powerfully in Garrett Hardin's "Tragedy of the Commons."[11] Hardin likens the environment to the old English commons on which cattlemen grazed their herds. The commons could not be individually owned, and the consequences of use could not be restricted to particular users. The tragedy was that the social benefit in the use of the commons was not at all the same as the individual benefit. For each cow the herder added to the commons he received the total benefit, but only a fraction of the cost of whatever degradation occurred to the commons as a result of overgrazing. The incentive for the individual was to keep on adding cows despite the social cost of depleted range.

Those who conceive of the environment as a commons problem espouse various solutions. They agree that an appeal to conscience and ethics probably will not work. So long as it is possible that some cattlemen will keep adding cows, it will seem foolish for any individual herder to desist and allow all the benefits to go to others with no resulting improvement of the range. Hardin's own solution to the commons dilemma is mutual coercion, mutually agreed upon. He believes that cattlemen must collectively agree to sanction any user who exceeds a commonly agreed-upon quota. This kind of reasoning underpins the regulatory regime that has been adopted in air, water, pesticides, toxic substances, and most other areas of the environment. Users of common resources such as water and air sheds are prohibited from exceeding certain standards.

While agreeing that failure of incentives is the problem, some analysts, who tend most often to be economists, prefer different solutions. They believe that economic incentives can be used to internalize costs that otherwise are external to the user and must be borne by the commons at large. As we shall explain further along in this chapter, one of the current issues in environmental policy is whether effluent fees and user charges can operate to clean up the environment without the enforcement burdens and inefficiencies of regulations. Although not yet widely adopted, economists' prescriptions of economic incentives were partially included in the 1977 amendments to the Clean Air Act. Still others argue that many resources presently held in common, such as wilderness, forests, and public lands, should be placed in private ownership whether for development or protection or some mixture of both—because private owners would follow appropriate incentives to maintain the long-term values associated with their property. This radical solution, long cherished by private developers in the past, might prove useful in some instances but has serious problems in political feasibility and in ensuring the protection of broad public values in a market economy.[12]

All of the above perspectives on the environmental problem are important, but the definition of most use to a volume on public policy, and the one we shall follow here, is that the environment is a political or policy problem, concerning the authoritative allocation of values, or what government chooses to do or not to do. Pollution is the gap between the objective state of the government and what people—individuals, groups, and interests—want it to be. As J. Clarence and Barbara Davies state:

> Pollutants are those substances which interfere with the use of air, water, or soil for socially desired purposes. If we want to use a particular part of a river for swimming, the water is "polluted" when we cannot swim in it. If we want to remain healthy, the air is "polluted" when it causes disease. Pollution cannot be defined with any scientific or mathematical finality. The definition hinges on the concept of human use, and thus, while we may be able scientifically to define what level of environmental quality is necessary for particular uses, the definition of what constitutes pollution is dependent on the public's decision as to what it wants to make of its environment. It becomes a political decision, a voicing by the community of its concept of the public interest.

   The definition of environmental problems therefore is a political process. In the next section we broadly define some challenges to policy actions and then describe policy responses in particular areas such as air, water, energy, and public lands.

III. ENVIRONMENTAL CHALLENGES AND EVOLUTION OF POLICIES

The United States, together with the rest of the nations of the world, faces major challenges in maintaining the viability of the earth's biosphere as a human habitat. Moreover, the actions taken by individuals, groups, and nations have both direct and indirect impacts on the quality of the environment, the demand structure for resources, and policies adopted in the United States. The image of the earth as a spaceship having finite resources is an appropriate symbol of the present human predicament.

   On a worldwide basis, the environment continues to deteriorate in terms of its capacity to support human population, the per-capita availability of resources, the protection of unique species, and threats to its life-supporting ecological systems.[14] Despite declines in the birth rates in some parts of the world, the growth in the world's population is not likely to decline in the foreseeable future. By the year 2000 it is expected that the world's population will be growing by 100 million per year, in contrast with 75 million per year currently, and that there will be 6 billion people on earth. Most of these additions will occur in the less developed nations of the world. Such vast increases portend serious threats to the worldwide supply of food unless there are major increases in food production and elimination of existing roadblocks to a more equitable distribution of food supplies. Moreover, it is not clear whether such increases can occur at all or whether they would not be accompanied by great devastation of land, water, fish, and forest resources.

   The worldwide pressures on resources have important implications for U.S. policy. Burning of fossil fuels and continued cutting of tropical forests threaten to increase the concentrations of carbon dioxide in the atmosphere and thereby alter world climate patterns and other terrestrial systems such as the levels of the oceans. Continued use of chlorofluorocarbons threatens to deplete the ozone layer and increase ultraviolet radiation reaching the earth, with increasing threats to biological life generally and incidence of cancer in humans as a result. Acid rain resulting from the burning of fossil-fuels—particularly coal—threatens fish life in lakes in the northern hemisphere. Deliberate ocean dumping of toxic substances, radioactive wastes, and chemicals that attack vital elements in the food chain, and accidental spills of other substances such as oil, also threaten basic world resources.

   Current rapid depletion of tropical forests threatens not only overall timber yields but also the productivity of soils, siltation, and flooding, and loss of complex and diverse ecological systems. Demand for wood products and meat in the developed areas has led to clear-cutting as a means of increasing incomes and obtaining foreign exchange in countries having tropical forests. The United States, like other countries, has a stake in protecting ecological diversity and in ensuring long-term economic and social stability in these countries.

   The one bright picture on a global basis concerns nonfuel minerals. The foreseeable future does not suggest major shortages of such minerals, but it is likely that they will increase substantially in cost and that their availability will be subject to changes in the international economic and political systems.

On the other hand, current increases in demand for petroleum threaten to outstrip production and the discovery of new reserves. The next decade may be considered a transition period during which other energy sources must play increasing roles. Nuclear energy production is projected to increase substantially along with energy from coal, particularly in the United States. The United States has coal reserves that will last hundreds of years, but both its mining and use are likely to create significant environmental problems. It is as yet unclear whether radically different technologies, such as fusion energy, will play a significant role as the world leaves the petroleum economy behind.

Within the United States alone, some major environmental problems have corresponded to the global problems indicated above, but others have been more localized but not necessarily less severe.[15] Air and water pollution, toxic waste disposal, disposal of nuclear wastes and environmentally dangerous chemicals, pesticides, land despoilation, and protection of wilderness, unique scenic areas, and endangered species have occupied policy makers during the 1970s when there was a veritable flood of environmentally oriented legislation. Moreover, the United States developed a remarkable procedural requirement—the environmental impact assessment—that led to heightened environmental sensitivity within the national government and to the forging of a political weapon in the hands of environmentalists who were disposed to challenge growth-oriented and environmentally destructive projects.

A. Air Pollution Abatement Policy

Air and water pollution abatement policies followed a similar pattern over the period from the late 1940s and early 1950s to the 1980s. The early phase of policy development concentrated on research and education sponsored by federal funds. The funds appropriated grew apace, but regulatory authority was extremely slow in coming. In the 1960s, federal government encouraged state regulation through subsidies and sponsored conferences to achieve abatement. In 1965 Congress passed its first truly national regulatory act dealing with automobile emissions, and in the late 1960s gave authority to the Secretary of Health, Education and Welfare to establish air quality regions and to require the states to fashion air quality programs.

The real landmark in air quality regulation came in 1970 with the passage of the Clean Air Act.[16] The act required the Environmental Protection Agency (EPA) to set air quality standards for various kinds of pollutants and to require the states to develop programs to achieve those standards. Tight deadlines for achieving air quality goals were set, and authority was granted to impose limitations on effluents by industrial plants. New source performance standards were established by terms of which new polluting plants would be required to install equipment representing the best available or practicable technology. These were the so-called technology-forcing provisions of the act that were designed to improve emission controls drastically in the future. New emission standards for various pollutants were also established for automobiles, with severe penalties for noncompliance. The EPA was required to establish compliance machinery in cooperation with the states. This machinery provided specific targets for individual firms with detailed schedules and steps for achieving full compliance.

Implementation of the Clean Air Act has been difficult owing to the technical problems in achieving the emission standards set under the law by the EPA and the reluctance of industry and motorists to comply with the requirements. The EPA insisted that utilities should install stack scrubbers at the very time that oil shortages led the nation to begin to convert to coal for energy production. Industry argued that the technology was uncertain and expensive and went to court to prove its case. Although not generally successful, many firms were able to delay compliance for several years. The approach to automobile emissions emphasized tinkering with the internal combustion engine rather than any fundamentally new technology. Automobile manufacturers were required to adopt emission control technology such as the catalytic converter with uncertain results owing to the possibility that control of one pollutant resulted in the increase of others and to the lack of maintenance by car owners. Moreover, car owners and their representatives at the state level were reluctant to take serious measures to control emissions by requiring inspections or limiting automobile use through restrictions such as those on downtown parking and bus lanes. The result has been frequent postponement of compliance deadlines for automobile manufacturers.

The EPA was required to set ambient air quality standards for all regions of the country. Primary standards are those designed to protect public health, whereas secondary standards are designed to protect against "any known or anticipated adverse effects" on public welfare. They are based on a notion of threshold effects of pollution, that is, levels below which no adverse effects may be expected. There appears to be no empirical evidence in support of the idea of thresholds. Pollution has a long-term cumulative effect on human health.[17] The 1977 amendments to the Clean Air Act provided for three classes of areas in terms of air quality: (1) those areas of currently clean air where no deterioration would be allowed—these would tend to be national parks where visibility is a crucial asset; (2) areas where larger amounts of pollutants would be permitted to allow moderate growth; and (3) areas where air quality could deteriorate to secondary standards, thus allowing more intensive and concentrated economic development.

By 1979, the EPA had been successful by rigorous monitoring and enforcement actions in bringing 94 percent of major individual polluters into compliance with emission limitations. Especially resistant to their implementation efforts have been power plants, steel mills, and smelters. Firms in these industries claimed financial hardship and doubted the economic benefits of additional improvements. To meet this noncompliance problem, the EPA has been authorized to impose penalties equal to the benefits accruing to the companies in not complying.

Despite the difficulties of implementation, the general trend in air quality continues to be toward improvement. The number of days in which air quality standards for various pollutants (CO, O_3, NO_x, SO_x, and TSP) were exceeded has declined by 18 percent nationally and in most places throughout the country, although serious problems remain in cities such as New York and Los Angeles and worsening conditions have been found in Kansas City and Houston. While improving somewhat, the air quality of Los Angeles and New York can hardly be considered healthful when they averaged, respectively, 242 and 224 "very unhealthful" and "hazardous" days from 1976 to 1978.

The deposition of acids on land and water surfaces—the so-called "acid rain"—owing to the emissions of SO_2 and NO_2 from tall smoke stacks is becoming a more worrisome problem. The tall stacks were increasingly built in the 1970s in order to disperse pollutants to meet local ambient standards. These gases are difficult to measure and they are transported long distances once they have reached considerable heights. Thus the pollutants emitted in the North Central, Central, and South Atlantic regions may create serious problems in regions far removed from their source, namely, in New England and Canada.

B. Water Pollution Abatement Policy

The Federal Water Pollution Control Act Amendment, or the Clean Water Act of 1972, was landmark legislation. It established goals of no discharge of pollutants and all waters to become swimmable and fishable by the mid-1980s. The means to achieve these goals were a permit system for polluters and requirements of the best practicable and later the best available control technology by industry. In addition, the act authorized a major expansion in the construction grant program for municipalities that were required to upgrade their sewage treatment plants at least to secondary treatment. While receiving water standards were continued as a guide to effluent limitations and compliance requirements, they were no longer used as a basis for evaluating the obligation of each polluter. The act recognized that water quality was affected by nonpoint sources as well (agricultural and building site runoff, for example), and provided authority for area-wide planning to achieve reduction in these kinds of polluting sources. Like the Clean Air Act, early deadlines were set.

Implementation has been slow and difficult for many of the same reasons that afflicted the air quality program. The task was of staggering proportions. Industry actively opposed the effluent standards, often in court; the technology was sometimes controversial as to its technical and economic efficiency; and the planning for nonpoint pollution control—estimated to account for a full 50 percent of surface water pollution—was inadequately funded and difficult to make effective in practice. The result was frequent delays, postponements of deadlines, and nonachievement of goals in a timely fashion. The 1977 amendments to the Clean Water Act, while adding to the list of pollutants on which the EPA would exercise such control, granted authority to postpone deadlines. It further reinforced the authority of states to manage their own water pollution programs with approval of the EPA (30 were doing so in 1978). As in the case of air quality control, the EPA has embarked on a policy of imposing economic penalties on delinquent firms, equal to the amount of savings achieved by noncompliance.

The overall record for water pollution abatement shows marked improvement in some rivers and lakes and some improvements along some dimensions of pollution, but in general, water quality has not improved significantly during the past decade. The principal pollution problems are high coliform counts, phosphorous, toxic substances, oxygen-demanding materials, and heavy metals. In virtually none of these categories has there been improvement, and there is growing realization of the seriousness of the pollution from toxic substances and metals. Conditions have not changed markedly in the Great Lakes and in bays and estuaries. Despite reductions in phosphorous loads entering Lake Erie, for example, concentrations have not declined.

There is increasing concern in two related areas of water quality: ground water and drinking water. Pursuant to the Safe Drinking Water Act, the EPA has embarked on a program of monitoring for conformity with three standards: microbiological turbidity, and chemical-radiological. Owing to the uncertainty of the data, the extent of the problem is not yet known, although it appears that the microbiological standard is violated in as many as 10 percent of the drinking water systems.

Ground water is relied on increasingly for drinking water supply, agriculture, and industry; it accounts for 25 percent of all water use in the United States. Nationally, withdrawals exceed recharge by an order of magnitude, and in some areas they exceed recharge by far larger amounts. There is increasing evidence of serious contamination of ground water and in some specific locations where ground water was relied on for drinking water purposes, extractions from ground-water basins have been prohibited for reasons of public health. The sources of pollution are varied: inadequate septic tanks, landfills, industrial lagoons, and mining operations. Protection and management of ground water has historically been a responsibility of state and local government. The federal government clearly has legal authority to play an important role in this area under the Clean Water Act, the Safe Drinking Water, and other acts dealing with hazardous wastes and toxic substances, but to this point it has largely deferred to the states.

A major element of the water pollution abatement program has been the sewage treatment plant construction program, one of the largest public works programs in the history of the United States. By 1980, the EPA had obligated nearly $25 billion, and more than 5000 projects were either under construction or in operation. Nevertheless, a majority of cities did not meet the standard of best practicable technology, which largely meant secondary treatment. With 75 percent of the total construction cost borne by the federal government, one might have expected greater progress, but a number of problems impede the achievement of statutory goals. Probably as many as 50 percent of the plants operate inefficiently and below design specification for lack of labor or other resources. Municipalities wait in line for federal money rather than moving ahead on their own. Industry fails to pretreat its discharges into municipal waste treatment systems, and toxic substances not treated in the waste treatment plants pass through to waterways or sludge. New regulations are designed to impose pretreatment obligations on industry.

In both fields—air pollution and water pollution abatement—critics point out that technology-based regulation and enforcement programs are not likely to be economically efficient or as effective as alternative arrangements, particularly effluent charges. The construction grant program for water pollution abatement provides incentives for capital-intensive approaches and building excess capacity in place of cheaper alternatives. By a variety of devices, polluters are able to delay enforcement, thus saving money and not contributing to enhanced environmental quality. Requirements for adoption of standardized technology lead to costs that may not be balanced by achieved benefits. The critics—mostly economists—argue that effluent charges would be more readily enforceable, collectable at the outset, and would permit industry to adopt whatever approach and whatever level of abatement found appropriate by its managers in terms of economic efficiency.[18] Seen as a cost of production, managers would reduce pollution to the level that was economically efficient.

Congress has yet to be persuaded of the virtue of this concept, though certain market-oriented ideas have begun to appear in the implementation programs. Charges for violations are one approximation of this effluent fee approach. The "bubble" concept is air quality—allowing industry to offset its own pollution by discovering and presumably paying for reductions in emissions elsewhere—provides the basis for a market in pollution rights that may prove economically salutary.

C. Toxic Substances

Americans have become increasingly concerned about the incidence of diseases and deaths that appear to be associated with various chemicals in common use in agriculture, industry, commerce, and in households. Some, such as caffeine or saccharin, are used so extensively that any curtailment of their use leads to widespread public opposition despite evidence of their detrimental effects on human health. Other chemicals used extensively in industry and commerce, such as asbestos, have clearly been identified with serious maladies including asbestosis and cancer, and their use and handling have been severely restricted in places of public gathering and in industry. For still other chemicals or elements, such as lead, there is an awareness of the relationship of concentrations to human health, but uncertainty with respect to the standards that should apply to protect against health effects. Finally, the chemical industry continues to produce new chemicals at a very great rate—as many as 3000 per year—and it is not yet clear that adequate political or scientific machinery has been created to protect the public against chemicals whose toxic effects may not be felt for decades.[19]

Major legislation to deal with toxic substances are the Toxic Substances Control Act (TSCA), passed by Congress in 1976, and the Resource Conservation and Recovery Act of 1976. The TSCA is designed to regulate chemical substances during their entire life cycle—from prior to their manufacture until their disposal. The EPA is required to inventory existing chemicals, to require premanufacture notice of testing, and to report to the EPA on the relative risks of all new chemicals. The administration of this act has been fraught with conflict and uncertainty and charges that the EPA has been both too slow and conservative and too fast and too radical. By mid-1980, only five chemicals—PCBs, chlorofluorocarbons, phthalate esters, chlorinated benzene, and chloromethane—had been subject to any regulations at all. The EPA encountered numerous problems, especially the recruitment and training of new personnel, resistance from industry, and development of appropriate test procedures and standards. Industry frequently failed to provide adequate information with respect to tests on the effects of the chemicals. The EPA has had difficulty deciding on the character of the tests, the basis on which tests would be conducted—on individual substances that are staggering in number or on entire categories of substances sharing similar chemical characteristics—and whether to concentrate on a few chemicals known to have dangerous properties or on the large number of chemicals whose effects are yet unknown. Moreover, there have been serious issues raised with respect to the revelation of trade secrets by firms that are required to submit information on new chemicals they intend to manufacture and purvey.

The Resource Conservation and Recovery Act was designed to deal with hazardous wastes by a system that regulated them "from cradle to grave." The act imposes on generators, transporters, and disposers of hazardous wastes an obligation to handle and dispose of them in a way that does not endanger human health or the environment. The EPA is obligated to set standards and enforce them through requirements of reports and permits. The key element in the regulatory system is the manifest system through which (1) generators must identify hazardous wastes, label and package them appropriately, (2) transporters must deliver the wastes to designated disposal sites, and (3) disposers are required to dispose of the wastes in an acceptable manner.

As with toxic substances, the task imposed on the EPA is staggering. The EPA has estimated that 77 billion pounds of hazardous waste are generated each year but only

10 percent is disposed of in an environmentally sound way. Moreover, there are major legacies of unsound practices in the past: Love Canal, the Valley of the Drums, the Pine Barrens in southern New Jersey, and Sullee landfill in Arkansas, and Pine River, Michigan, are all sites of waste dumpings that have caused serious threats to life, both present and future. Injured parties, the EPA, and Congress have moved in several ways to deal with these past actions. In 1979, the EPA sued several companies for $125 million to compensate for clean-up of the various sites in the Love Canal area. Individuals who contracted illness from asbestos have sued asbestos companies and the federal government. Congress in 1980 passed a superfund program establishing a $1.6 billion fund to pay for clean-up of spills of hazardous substances and inactive waste disposal sites.

Effective means of protecting the public against hazardous materials is still in the development stage. The management system has yet to demonstrate its effectiveness. Its costs may be significant (although seldom equaling the costs to society and specific individuals of not managing them), and those who are subject to regulation may seek alternative solutions having high social costs, such as illicit dumping or exportation to developing countries willing to take the risk for economic benefits. Tort liability has not proven an effective recovery approach because of the difficulty of proving causation between the substances and harm. The United States has not adopted arrangements such as those in Japan in which polluters pay an emission tax from which victims of pollution are compensated.

D. Energy Management

The development and use of various energy sources has an impact on human health and the environment. The burning of fossil fuels results in particulate matter, carbon, nitrogen, and sulfuric oxides in the atmosphere, causing reductions in visibility, eye irritation, respiratory problems, and acid rain, and possible changes in climate. Nuclear energy production threatens the environment through accidents and the problem of disposal of nuclear waste. Large-scale strip mining of coal has devastating effects on the land surface and may lead to degradation of water supplies. Synthetic fuels such as oil shale and tar sands may lead to the same consequences. There may be significant environmental consequences related to the use of more benign energy sources such as biomass or geothermal.

Energy-related policies that have environmental consequences range from pricing to direct regulations and incentives. Policies that result in higher prices for energy lead to more efficient fuel use and therefore conserve energy. (Some price decisions, of course, are out of policy makers' control, notably the price decisions of OPEC with respect to oil.) Recent congressional and presidential decisions to remove price controls on oil, gasoline, and natural gas have reduced demand, in the case of gasoline by as much as 5 percent in 1979. The federal government and some states have also offered tax and financial incentives to industry and homeowners to promote energy efficiency. The overall result has been a marked reduction in the rate of increase in energy consumption, in the energy required per unit of national economic output, and a significant lowering of expected energy demand in the future. Estimates of energy use in the year 2000 made in the early 1970s were in the 180 to 200 quad range; at the end of the decade these estimates were in the 100 quad range.

Energy policy is multifaceted and, in terms of the environment, inconsistent, reflecting the multiple values, interests, and uncertainties involved. Government policy to encourage conversion of electrical utilities to coal leads to increased strip mining and reclamation problems and possible increases in acid rain and exacerbation of the carbon dioxide problem. Nuclear energy, the clean fuel, has an excellent safety and health record despite the accident at Three Mile Island. The Carter administration opposed further development of the breeder reactor, thus slowing down movement toward the next phase in nuclear development. Reduced demand, inflation, and public opposition, sometimes supported by official state policies, significantly reduced interest in nuclear plants, such that it is impossible to predict the role that nuclear energy will play in the nation's future. With respect to nuclear wastes, government policy has failed to find a solution that is both technically and politically adequate, although disposal in mined geologic structures appears to be the consensus solution. Obtaining agreement of states and localities to have such deposits in their environments may prove more difficult than finding suitable geologic structures.

Government policy has encouraged efforts to increase domestic supplies of energy. Congressional approval of the Alaska pipeline, new leases for oil exploration on the outer continental shelf, requirement of utilities to convert to coal, and legislation to subsidize the development of synthetic fuels are all evidence of government support. In some cases these developments are in environmentally sensitive or valued scenic areas and thus stir up much opposition. In the West, in particular, energy development raises the specter of making those areas a "national sacrifice" area or "colony" of the nation.

E. Public Lands and Resources

To deal with the nation's public lands, increasingly the focus of conflict between those who wish to accelerate resource development and those who prefer to protect scenic, recreational, and esthetic qualities, Congress has formalized its long-term multiple-use management approach through legislation. It also has segregated certain areas having unique qualities as park, wilderness, seashore, wild river, or wildlife refuge, thus preventing further development and often occasioning a storm of controversy, such as the "Sagebrush rebellion." As of 1979, approximately 16.4 percent of federal land enjoyed protected status. With the passage of an Alaskan lands bill in 1980, the protected areas grew by 102 million acres but represented about one-half of what conservationists wished to include.

Lands not set aside for special purposes are largely managed by the principle of multiple use: timber harvesting, range land, recreation, mining, water supply. This principle has long guided the Forest Service, albeit the service has been criticized for favoring some users—principally the lumbering interests—over others. It has now been applied formally to the Bureau of Land Management through passage of the Federal Land Policy and Management Act of 1976. Both agencies were forced to undertake controversial studies of the wilderness potentiality of the lands under their jurisdictions, and the Forest Service was attacked from all sides for its Roadless Area Review and Evaluation, the result of which was a recommendation that an additional 15 million acres (8 percent of the forested lands) be set aside for wilderness. A far more pressing problem for the Bureau of Land Management is the poor condition of its range lands. Its policy options—reduced use, and greater investment to restore these lands—are likely to encounter determined opposition from its present users.

Critical to federal land management is the rate, place, and extent of energy development thereon. After a virtual moratorium of coal leasing of nearly a decade and passage

of the Surface Mining Control and Reclamation Act of 1977 the Department of the Interior again once began leasing of coal-bearing lands in 1981. The outer continental shelf
provides about 9 percent of the oil and 23 percent of the gas produced in the United
States, and it is estimated that 60 percent of the undiscovered recoverable oil and gas may
be found in these submerged lands. Government policy under Carter and even more so
under Reagan has been to expedite the coal-bearing and the offshore leasing program.
Although consideration is to be given to environmental dangers and to local sentiment,
it seems clear that national energy priorities are to take precedence over other values.

Other difficult issues face public land managers and to some extent private landowners as well. Much Western land is semi-arid to arid and is undergoing a process known
worldwide as desertification. The characteristics of this process are dropping ground-
water tables, soil depletion, loss of vegetation, urbanization, and general loss of ecological
resilience. This process threatens the basic capacity of these regions to support a productive society. For managers of national parks, the problem is growth of demand: too many
people, too few resources, ecological damage, and inappropriate use. Without additional
labor and money, it is inevitable that the quality of the experience will decline for those
who visit the national parks.

IV. THE POLICY-MAKING PROCESS

The content of environmental policy is the product of and is shaped by the characteristics
of the policy-making process. It is our premise that types of environmental policies actually adopted respond to such important political variables as the structure of demand, the
structure of decision making, and the structure of impacts.[20] The structure of demand
refers to the degree of integration or unity of the interests concerned with policy. The
structure of decision making refers to the extent to which the decision-making system is
fragmented or integrated. The structures of impacts refers to the structure of society that
feels the impacts of the decisions. Clearly related to the decision-making variable is the
variable of cost: the cost of reaching decisions. The complex relationship of these variables determines the kinds of policies produced by the political system. Thus, it may be
argued that the National Environmental Policy Act was a structural as opposed to allocative decision—altering the decision rules that governed the manner in which policies
affecting the environment were arrived at. There were diverse and conflicting interests at
work; the costs of arriving at decisions were high because of the uncertainties involved
and the difficulty in achieving additional certainty; and the decision-making system was
fragmented, involving a host of actors, both legislative and administrative. The decision
was to avoid making a substantive decision that allocated costs and benefits and instead
to make a decision that altered the rules themselves.

In contrast, there are situations—such as public works projects—in which there is a
strong, stable and integrated demand structure, an integrated decision-making structure,
and relatively low decision-making costs, which lead to an allocative and distributive decision. This is the classic "iron triangle" of local interest groups—including public entities—
federal agencies, and congressional committees working effectively to promote water
development projects whose costs are diffused among the general taxpayers.[21]

The vast expansion of regulation in the field of environmental policy results from the configuration of these variables. The purposes are diverse and often conflicting, reflecting not only environmental but also economic concerns; the demand structure contains numerous, varied, and often conflicting groups whose interests must be reconciled; the costs of decision making are high, both in making the transactions that result in policy and in the acquisition of an adequate scientific base on which to make a decision. Moreover, the costs are often direct and cannot be disguised although they might be, and often are, ameliorated by side payments in the form of grants from the federal treasury to reduce the impact on any given economic sector.

By any measure of integration, the American political structure must be considered among the most fragmented in the world. There are innumerable decision points and a host of groups, both public and private, that ordinarily are involved in public decision making. We have made a fetish of participation through the adoption of the initiative and referendum and various devices for participation in bureaucratic decision making. Those enamored of rational decision making despair that this system can produce intelligent solutions that incorporate all of the important values and facts that must be considered in making policy in the public interest. Their preferences run strongly toward centralized planning, the rational ordering of the alternatives, and a ready source of financial and bureaucratic power to ensure the achievement of the goals laid down by the planners.

Yet the environmental record of the United States does not appear to be less notable than other democratic or authoritarian polities, and certainly the accomplishments do not seem to be less for lack of centralized structure of decision making. Indeed, many of the accomplishments may reflect the advantages of decentralized or fragmented structures. Ingram and Ullery have argued, for example, that the federal water pollution control policy innovations of 1970s were achieved *because* of a fragmented structure.[22] Generalizing, they argue that decentralized structures allow for policy entrepreneurship by individuals who could not otherwise gain a purchase on a policy system; that costs of innovation are lowered because subunits can make changes without trying to alter the entire system; that competition fosters change as each competing unit seeks its own advantage; and that the legitimacy of the result is enhanced by the accommodation of diverse interests.

This is a persuasive argument that fragmentation is not necessarily an impediment to innovation or nonincremental decision making. But it is hardly a demonstration that centralized policy making systems are detrimental to innovation. A decision on this matter seems largely to depend on whose ox is being gored. A president who wants a synthetic fuels bill, and is willing to pay the political price, can get it despite its economic and environmental costs. A president who is willing to challenge the water policy establishment with respect to uneconomic and environmentally damaging water projects may also be successful if he is willing to pay the price. Similarly, the head of the Environmental Protection Agency can be hardnosed with respect to delays in the implementation of an air pollution control program, depending on his reading of the environmental damage and/or the economic damage that such tough policy might engender.

Though the structure of demands, the structure of decision making, and the structure of impacts are interlocked in the policy-making process, each of these major variables will be dealt with individually in the sections that follow.

A. Structure of Demand

The demand structure in environmental policy making is the function of a variety of phenomenan, including the nature of public concern about the environment, the relationship of attitudes about the environment to ideology and to other values and attitudes, and the expression of opinion through interest group activity.

Public Opinion: Available data indicate that public opinion about the environment exhibited some dramatic changes around 1970. In 1965, Gallup conducted a poll in which people were presented with a list of 10 national problems and were asked which three should get the most attention from government over the next two years. Reducing pollution of air and water was chosen by only 17 percent of the sample—placing it ninth behind improving highway safety and a little ahead of beautifying America. A Gallup Poll asking the same question in April 1970 resulted in 53 percent choosing the antipollution option—third behind reducing crime. Confirmation of the dramatic shift came in a CBS poll conducted one week after Earth Day. One-fifth of Americans considered pollution to be the most important problem facing the nation.[23]

It has sometimes been argued that the environmental consciousness that arose in the early 1970s was transient, and reflected a poor understanding of the costs of environmental quality. According to this theory, concern with the environment would peak out and fade as soon as it became obvious that achieving environmental quality would not be easy and would come only at the cost of other important values. Yet a government-funded Resources for the Future study released in 1980 found differently. Judging by their answers to questions, most of the population was still willing to pay for environmental protection.[24] For instance, 50 percent of respondents to a survey said spending on environmental problems was too little, and only 15 percent answered that the amount was too much. Given three options on a trade-off between growth and environment, only one in five respondents chose the statement, "We must relax environmental standards in order to achieve economic growth." The study concluded that although the public no longer views the environment as a crisis issue, strong support for environmental protection continues.[25] The Opinion Research Corporation reached the same conclusions in a 1980 study undertaken for the EPA. It reported that:

> the opinions of the people of all levels of society indicate that environmental protection has become a relentless, institutionalized, mass movement with the potential to change the future course of industrial history.[26]

At the same time it can be argued that the public may be willing to accept certain risks and a relaxation of certain pollution control standards to achieve other values: jobs or lessened dependence on foreign oil. Not even the Three Mile Island accident altered the distribution of opinions on nuclear energy substantially. Mitchell concluded that the public "is still wishing to accept the Faustian bargain offered by this technology, albeit by a narrower margin than before."[27]

The strength of the environmental movement is often associated with its leadership, who clearly tend to be middle- and upper middle-class people who have the education, skills, and resources to become active in various causes. But the evidence from polls and voting behavior suggests that environmentalism is not a class movement, that it has appeal beyond those upper-class individuals who are concerned about suitable places to enjoy their leisure time. To some extent, environmentalism is generational, that is, it is more strongly espoused by the younger members of the population.[28] Some researchers have found that it also correlates with ideology, in this case largely with political liberalism. Environmentalism also correlates with Democratic party identification among voters and particularly among members of legislative bodies.[29]

The studies of the relationships between and among various demographic and attitudinal variables and environmental concern and preferences have displayed some inconsistencies and some contradictions. They have also suggested that some more sophisticated conceptualization of linkages is necessary to understand the relationship of environmental concern and other public attitudes. It appears that demographic and political variables explain only a modest proportion of the variance in environmentalism, thus leading to the conclusion that environmental concern is spread sufficiently broadly throughout the American population that such variables as age, education, and political ideology—the most important ones—are only loosely coupled to it. Place of residence, occupational prestige, and party identification were only weekly or inconsistently related to environmental concern.

Using multivariate analysis and National Opinion Research Center Social Survey samples of the adult population for the years 1973–1978, Honnold examined demographic variables with respect to both relative and absolute environmental concern, particularly evaluating the meaning of concern in the context of other policy concerns held by the respondents.[30] She suggests, for example, that the importance of race, sex, and residential background as explanatory variables would lead to a further examination of childhood socialization factors as influences on environmental attitudes. The importance of examining environmental values in the context of other values is suggested by the factor of race: Nonwhites have higher environmental values on an absolute scale but lower on a relative scale, reflecting the intrusion of other policy issues. Over time, absolute values are more predictable than relative values, suggesting both the strength of environmental concerns and also the fluctuations of the strength with such exogenous events as the fuel shortages during the 1970s.

In terms of future research, the overall low explanatory power of these demographic variables might be improved by a greater degree of specification of the dependent variables: specific problems; critical levels; preferred solutions. "Environmental concerns" may be too broad a quality, and the analysis might be sharpened by differentiating environmental issues or problems and providing a sharper focus to the relationship of environmental values to other values held by members of society.

Environmental Ideology: It is not entirely clear that the existing ideological constructs serve our society adequately in the development of a consistent and logical approach to environmental protection in terms of the social and political consequences. The contemporary meaning of liberalism and conservatism and the ideological basis of partisanship in American were forged during the New Deal era in circumstances very different from today. These constructs predate environmentalism, and fit issues that dealt with the age of technological growth. The age of environmentalism clearly is concerned with growth, but also with far more. Conservatism embraces growth and places emphasis on science, technology, and the free market; liberalism relies on state regulation to overcome the ills of growth while continuing to espouse it; and radicalism espouses state ownership of the means of production and a drastic reorientation of values. None of these ideologies is particularly helpful in dealing with the environment, but all are relevant.[31] At the same time they may in specific cases impede rather than facilitate correct courses of action. State regulation may be helpful or damaging, depending on the issue and the circumstance; the market may be useful in some cases but disastrous in others. State ownership may be the answer in some instances, but there is no evidence that social ownership necessarily improves overall environmental quality. Regardless of relationships to appropriate action, however, ideology and party continue to serve as the dominant cues to legislators about how to vote on environmental as on many other issues. Studying the voting records of members of Congress during much of the 1970s, Henry and Margaret Kenski found that liberalism and conservatism were in fact the most powerful predictors of how members of Congress will vote.[32]

Paradigm Shift? Many writers find in the environmental movement a paradigmatic shift, a rejection of the dominant paradigm of the 200 to 300 years of the industrial revolution. The dominant paradigm is "human exemptionalist," with a focus on freedom of human beings to dominate rather than to live with nature. It is argued that the predominant sociological and political thought of this era is one that stresses the exceptional nature of human beings ignoring the natural environment, considering it a "given," and looking on social conditions as the principal constraints on human behavior.[33] In political terms, the dominant paradigm shed the classical emphasis on virtue and internalized limits on behavior in achieving such virtue and adopted freedom to dominate nature as its paramount value. As the constraints of resource limitations were removed, so were the intellectual and moral constraints that limited the quest for power and wealth.[34]

The new paradigm that is associated with environmental movement places human beings back into their natural environment, recognizes ecological limits on their behavior, particularly with respect to the tendency to believe in unlimited growth and the capacity to overcome natural constraints either by social organization or by technology.[35] Environmentalism is the "new religion of self-restraint."[36] Having surveyed elite groups and the general public in the United States, the United Kingdom, and Germany, Milbrath finds strong support for the evolution from the dominant social paradigm to what he calls the new environmental paradigm. The values of the new environmental paradigm emphasize love of nature, public goods, conservation for future generations, cooperation, minimum standards of living, economic planning, and environmental protection over jobs and growth in contrast to the materialist emphasis on economic growth and individualism. There is, however, a broad distribution of values along a large number of dimensions, suggesting that governments during the transition—if it is a transition that Western democratic governments are going through—will have a difficult time discovering or carrying out their mandates—in effect, governing—because about one-half of the public and important segments of elites groups will reject the direction in which they are going.[37]

The diversity and the conflicts they portend lead some environmentalists to stress centralized authoritarian solutions to ecological problems, leaving aside the need for internalized constraints and thus the return to the classical conception of virtuous human beings in society.[38]

Others see the possibility of a paradigmatic shift, relating the favorable disposition toward the environment to a more fundamental and sweeping shift in values, which they label postmaterialist. These postmaterialists tend to emphasize the values of freedom and participation in political and economic decision making, in contrast to the materialists, who have demonstrated principal concern for economic, military, and strategic security.[39] The postmaterialists have become cynical about the likelihood that existing institutional structures can accommodate the necessary changes in society generally and find that the environmental movements and their goals are convenient vehicles for the achievement of their economic and social goals. The Citizen's party, led by Barry Commoner in the 1980 election in the United States, would appear to unite these two strands of values. However, its failure to achieve even 1 percent of the vote does not augur well for the future of such movements, at least for the early 1980s.

Environmental Groups: Because many voters see environmental problems as separate from and unrelated to social and economic issues, it is not surprising that specialized interest groups have served as the institutions linking public opinion and government and aggregating and expressing environmental interests.[40] The environmental movement has not, however, had a single-minded set of interest groups to convey opinions. Rather, the environmental movement had at least three strands with distinct histories and ideas.[41]

One of the earliest roots of current environmental groups can be traced to the progressive era of 1900 to 1910. The conservationists of this era were basically utilitarian.[42] Gifford Pinchot, an early proponent of conservation, held that the first and second principles of conservation were wise use and prevention of waste. Natural resources were to be developed for the greatest use by the greatest number for the longest time. The good was balanced use, reflecting the long-term and often conflicting demands of many users. This approach to the environment was inculcated in resource agencies such as the Forest Service ("land of many uses"), and is articulated today by numbers of user groups such as rod-and-gun clubs, recreationists, and users who are finding use difficult, such as drivers of off-road vehicles.

A second, historic element of the environmental movement is the preservationists, who often take sharp issue with the utilitarians. The basis of preservationist philosophy can be found in the writings of John Muir and George Perkins Marsh. To preservationists, the greatest good to the greatest number is a poor test by which to allocate resources, because some purposes, such as wilderness, represent higher user. It is the preservationists' obligation to defend undisturbed nature. As we have already discussed, preservationists tend to define the environmental problem as an ethical issue. Though modified by time, the ideals of John Muir are today upheld by organizations such as the Sierra Club, the National Audubon Society, and the Wilderness Society.

The third and most recent strand of environmentalism was spawned during the explosion of environmental consciousness in the late 1960s and early 1970s. This perspective is ecological, adopting a unified or "holistic" view of the ecosystem and humanity's position in it. Its focus is less on parks and wilderness or management of resources, such as water or timber, and more on pollution and changing patterns of resource demands and uses. They partake of some features of their predecessors but put them together differently. They desire balance, but in an ecological sense of ensuring protection of food chains and survival of species, including human beings. They employ science more explicitly to defend their values, which often are found to be compatible with those of the preservationists. Among the new environmental groups are such organizations as

Environmental Action, the League of Conservation Voters, the Environmental Defense Fund, and the National Resources Defense Council.

Another classification divides environmentalists between the activist/reformist groups and individuals and those who are part of the "deep" ecology movement, the latter being a revolutionary intellectual assault on the dominant social paradigm with an emphasis on a "new metaphysics, epistomology, cosmology, and environmental ethics."[43] The deep ecology people tend to be thinkers, not reformers. Their emphasis is on criticism of the dominant social paradigm of growth and centralized power, the propagation of a vision of the ecologically satisfactory future, and a demonstration of ecologically sound living by personal examples.

The membership of environmental groups grew enormously in the early 1970s, leveling off by the end of the decade. In relation to the public, the number of active participants in environmental groups was quite small, only 7 percent in 1980.[44] Such numbers may be poor indicators of influence, however, as environmental groups, despite their basic divisions, were able to form power coalitions and lobby effectively on some issues, such as the setting aside of public lands in Alaska and protection of air quality in the regions of national parks. Some environmentally conscious members of Congress achieved positions of influence on legislative committees, and during the Carter administration a number of former officials of environmental organizations held high government offices.

If one assumes that environmentalists themselves are the cutting edge or the harbinger of the future holders of an environmentalist paradigm, the attitudes of members of several environmental organizations do not suggest that radical alteration of society is a major or even important goal. Environmentalists, for the most part white and middle-class, adopt the stance of liberalism and are associated with other familiar "liberal" causes: civil rights, women's rights, antiwar movements, and consumerism. They share an emphasis on income redistribution with the new left but reject the latter's emphasis on decentralization of society and broad public participation. With impending scarcities, divisions within the environmental movement are likely to occur precisely over whether a system that engages in trade-offs should be replaced by a system that has a clear vision of an ecologically oriented society.[45]

B. Structure of Decision Making

There are multiple arenas for environmental policy making, and the interests that find themselves thwarted in one setting tend to gravitate toward others. Consequently, environment policy has not been the product of any particular arena, but rather is hammered out in the conflict and bargaining among arenas.

Congress and the courts have been important foci of activity to protect the environment on the federal level. The Senate Public Works Subcommittees on Environment and Pollution, under the leadership of Senator Edmund Muskie fashioned a number of landmark pieces of legislation including air and water pollution acts. Senator Henry Jackson's Interior Committee, later Energy and Natural Resources, was the source of the National Environmental Policy Act. The vitality of the latter piece of legislation, however, was more the product of judiciary than of Congress. Through the courts, the vague language of the statute was given meaning and force, and a number of important projects were stalled and redesigned through a court finding of an inadequate environmental impact statement. Further, the courts have had an important role in interpreting the requirements of air and water pollution legislation in the process of implementation. In the view of one commentator, the court has in at least one case performed this role well. According to Richard B. Stewart, "The record with respect to judicial review under the Clean Air Act demonstrates that the courts have discharged this role with considerable success. They have devised novel procedural mechanisms to ensure that the agency [EPA] has rationally weighed all of the relevant considerations that the statute and the practicalities of the situation reasonably admit."[46]

Whereas the executive branch has been the source of policy initiatives in a number of policy areas, this is not often the case with environmental policy. Two reasons particularly stand out. First, the Environmental Protection Agency was created out of a reorganization in 1970 that brought together numbers of disparate administrative fragments from various nooks and crannies of the federal establishment. In the words of the first administrator, William Rucklehaus, making the reorganized agency work in the first few years, in the face of a continuous flow of new environmental legislation, was like "performing an appendectomy while running the hundred yard dash."[46a] Second, for most of the decade of the 1970s, control over Congress and the administration was split between parties. Democrats in the Congress were loathe to give Republican administrations credit for a strong role in environmental policy. Executive influence has often been of the negative sort: Nixon refused the Clean Water Act of 1972 on fiscal grounds and killed the Florida barge canal; Carter challenged water policy through his so-called hit list and opposition to new nuclear developments such as the breeder reactor.

The Federal System and Decision-Making Structure: One manifestation of this fragmented character of the environmental policy-making structure is the intergovernmental nature of many environmental programs that developed during the decades of the 1960s and 1970s. This character continues, despite the dramatic shift in the overall locus of decision making toward the federal government. Federal legislation has become the prime mover behind most environmental programs, with the states playing subsidiary roles in their administration and implementation. The functions that the states perform are extremely important, but these functions are within the framework of federal law and policy.

The constitutional basis for state actions dealing with the environment are essentially two: their police powers, that is, those powers to protect the health, welfare, safety, and morals of the citizens within their jurisdictions. The second is the residual powers under the U.S. Constitution, which reserves to the states all powers not granted the federal government. Thus, there is a broad sweep of state authority that can be exercised to protect the environment.

The reluctance of the states to enter into this field without prodding from the national government is explained by several factors. First, the problems frequently are interstate in nature: River systems and lakes often are located within several state jurisdictions and require cooperative efforts that are not forthcoming. The lack of cooperation can be explained, at least in part, because of the competitive nature of the states; states are reluctant to impose burdens on their economies that are not shared generally because of the fear that they will lose industry and jobs to states where burdens are less onerous. Moreover, industrial interests are often more influential at the state level and follow a strategy that emphasizes state responsibility for environmental programs. The state programs they favor are usually anemic and ineffective. Finally, states have different interests because of the balance of values within them. The conflict between the states of California and Nevada over measures to protect Lake Tahoe display this divergence of values, with Nevada pushing for greater shoreline development and showing less concern for the pollution of the lake and California urging limitations of development and stringent measures to restore the lake to its pristine condition. Similarly, the states in the Colorado River Basin have been notoriously divided over the issue of water management, leaving the U.S. Bureau of Reclamation to take the rap if not the lead.

The record of states on specific policy issues varies substantially. In some areas, such a land use planning, some states have taken advanced positions, ignoring the lack of federal support for such planning. Vermont has perhaps gone the furthest with a comprehensive land use statute that establishes a statewide planning board and eight district boards and requires the acquisition of a permit for any major action that will alter the environment—specifically, impose undue burdens on water supply and quality, soil, highways in terms of congestion, the educational system, and esthetic quality. Some states have taken steps to control development along their coastlines: California is the most notable example, with its act passed by voters through an initiative.

Based on data from a study of four states in the Southwest, a group of researchers concluded that the greatest barrier to positive action on environmental problems at the state level was a failure of leadership incentives. Public reluctance to bear the costs of environmental action, thus depriving politicians of constituency support, combined with structural problems of citizen legislatures and constitutionally weak governors, created a policy vacuum. Insufficient rewards existed for political actors to tackle knotty environmental problems on the state level.[47]

Structure of Impact: The actual impact of environmental policies is often very different from stated policy intent. Policy analysts have come increasingly to believe that unwanted and unintended impacts are the results of difficulties encountered during policy implementation. Lofty goals have not been achieved for myriad reasons: lack of resources, lack of personnel, political opposition, difficulties of coordination, technical uncertainties and limitations, lack of authority and leadership, conflicting objectives, and various permutations and combinations of all these factors. It may be argued that in some instances the establishment of lofty goals was a *substitute* for their achievement.

The Clean Air Act Amendments of 1970 are illustrative of the implementation problems that some environmental legislation has encountered. Ten full years after the passage of the act, only modest progress has been made in reducing emissions and improving ambient air quality. Repeated postponements of deadlines affecting auto emissions were experienced. Finally, in 1977, a year after the Clean Air Act dictated that 90 percent reductions in auto emissions should have been achieved, the act was amended to extend the timetable and to reduce the standard for NO_x. Thus, automotive pollution control is a classic example of redefining objectives in the implementation process to match what turned out to be achievable.[48] There are many reasons why the Clean Air Act was not implemented as written, including the Arab oil embargo of 1973, rapid increases in gasoline prices, and political pressure by U.S. automobile companies beleaguered by foreign competition. However, among the most telling reasons is that the strategy of the act was based on fundamentally changing the American motorists' transportation behavior, which turned out to be politically infeasible. The Environmental Protection Agency could not force—indeed, Congress prevented it from forcing—states to adopt bus lanes, parking surcharges, and gasoline rationing.

The limitations on the achievement of environmental goals leads one to conclude that all parties, particularly environmentalists themselves, must have realistic notions of the timetables and the completeness with which environmental objectives may be achieved. The record of accomplishment also suggests the need for a strategy for acheiving goals: a recognition that obstacles must be overcome, competing groups must be challenged or dealt with through negotiation and bargaining, and uncertainties must be removed. This is especially true in periods of contracting budgets and political administrations that emphasize limiting the scope of government authority.

The strategy adopted must reflect the substantive issue with which one is dealing and the political circumstances that surround the debate over a given implementation issue. In some cases the emphasis must be on science—the development of a technical base that will withstand attack from commercial interests. This is clearly the case with toxic substances: without additional scientific evidence, it will be difficult to establish the toxicity of various new chemicals and the host of old chemicals that already pervade modern industrial society. But the strategy also may involve the adoption of certain procedures or standards to simplify the tasks. In the field of chemicals, the EPA opted for classifying chemicals by their properties rather than relying on tests of each individual chemical. Nevertheless, the General Accounting Office, with agreement by the EPA, concluded four years after passage of the Toxic Substances Control Act in 1976 that "neither the public nor the environment are [sic] much better protected."[49]

Some economists have long argued that the fundamental strategy of implementation for clear air and water programs is misguided, largely on the grounds of efficiency but also on the grounds of ease of achievement. They argue that large economic interests are able to bargain, delay, and otherwise avoid the strictures of the law and legitimate penalties because the strategy is one of regulation, that is, standard setting, technological re-requirements and enforcement through orders. They pose the counter strategy of effluent charges, which would be imposed on target firms for every unit of polluting substances they emitted. There would be no escape from the immediate imposition of the penalties, and thus there would be an inducement for the managers to comply.

The implementation of environmental policy is an especially thorny task because of the inevitable implications of some but not all policies for other sectors of society and the economy. Limitations on discharge of pollutants into the atmosphere and water courses of the nation have broad implications for all kinds of industry, the well-being of entire communities, and the behavior of a large number of diverse groups. Coordination of policies that constrain or facilitate economic activity is an especially difficult task.

In an era of inflation and reduced supplies and therefore higher real costs for commodities the consumer must purchase, it is tempting to blame regulation—and particularly environmental regulation—for a major share of those higher costs and lowered productivity. Available evidence does not suggest, however, that environmental controls play a major role in reducing gross national product. In 1975, it was estimated that environmental protection requirements led to the expenditure of $37 billion or 1.5 percent of the gross national product. During much of the period of increasing environmental controls, the rate of growth in the economy slowed substantially, but many factors totally unrelated to environmental protection figured in the decline. Environmental protection probably accounted for no more than 5 to 15 percent of the slowdown of the economy and no more than two-tenths of 1 percent of the annual inflation rate. Moreover, seldom are the benefits of environmental protection—improved health, fewer accidents, more pleasant surroundings—included as positive contributions to national welfare. Air pollution controls alone were predicted to provide $20 billion in health benefits in 1979. Although pollution control costs are real, toward the end of the 1970s it appeared that their effect on productivity was declining.[50]

By far the largest costs associated with environmental protection are for abatement of air and water pollution. At least 95 percent of the total of $36.9 billion went for those purposes, with the next largest fraction—$1.4 billion—devoted to land reclamation. These proportions are not projected to change significantly in the near future, although the absolute amounts for some pollution controls—solid waste, toxic substances, noise pollution, and land reclamation—will likely increase substantially. The EPA has begun to adopt policies providing economic incentives for producers to comply with environmental regulations more efficiently—through bubble and offset policies, for example; further experimentation with charges for pollution may reduce the nation's total cost for protecting the environment.

Another complication is the reliance on intergovernmental structures for achieving environmental goals. The usual pattern is for federal agencies to certify state agencies to carry out the programs authorized by federal statutes. Authorization is granted those agencies that demonstrate the capacity to implement programs and that have adopted standards meeting federal requirements. The relationship between state and federal agencies is always a delicate matter owing to local sensitivities over federal domination and preferences for the protection of unique local interests. Moreover, whatever federal law may provide, local interests have powerful political support from their elected and bureaucratic officials both in their own states and in Washington, D.C.

Finally, the impact of programs may vary when the intended targets are few rather than many. The few, as in the case of automobile companies and emission controls, may be powerful economically and politically and frustrate the efforts of the administrative agency because of technical objections, judicial obstacles, and appeals to the public and elected politicians. On the other hand, when the targets are numerous and diverse, as in the enforcement of the 55 mile per hour speed limit, massive voluntary compliance or resistance may spell the difference in terms of satisfactory achievement of programmatic goals. There is no doubt that more enforcement steps could be taken, but budget limitations, personnel shortages, and prudence make such a rigid posture impractical.[51]

V. CONTEMPORARY THEORETICAL ISSUES IN ENVIRONMENTAL PROTECTION

Underlying existing environmental policies are certain assumptions or implicit positions on a number of theoretical issues. Currently the theoretical underpinnings of environmental policy are under reexamination, and we explore the dimensions of the argument in this section. One such issue is the relative roles of public (collective) or private action. Although most environmental laws seek to enforce a regulatory regime, critics, especially conservatives, argue for a larger role for the market place. We shall discuss the merits and the implications of this debate. A second contemporary issue to be addressed is the evaluation of uncertainty. What degree of protection or compensation should society guarantee, and how? Newspapers and magazines frequently decry the scarcity of a given resource, or declare that we are about to run out of some other commodity. We shall adopt the more useful and precise meaning that economists give to the concept of scarcity in our discussion of that issue. The economists make clear that most cases of scarcity are cases of goods mispriced; yet, as we shall explore, an argument can be made that ultimately goods are exhaustible.

The examination of the issue of scarcity sets the stage for a discussion of the topic of intergenerational equity. If resources are in an ultimate sense exhaustible, is there a way in which the present generation may be fair to those who follow? The final theoretical issue addressed returns very much to the here and now. The achievement of the goals of environmental policies depend on whether the behavioral assumptions on which they are built are correct. We noted that in certain cases there may be reason for doubt.

A. Environmental Policy and the Logic of Collective Action

Environmental policy, by its very nature, invites collective action. Such policy making need not be exclusively collective, but it is inconceivable that some collective action would not be required to deal with environmental problems. Individual action and the behavior of firms inevitably reflects self-interested motivation for the satisfaction of individual wants or the maximization of profits. The efficiency of the marketplace in allocating resources of labor, capital, and natural resources is clearly demonstrated, but equally demonstrated is the failure of individuals and private firms to consider external effects of their choices. These spillover effects (called externalities) take various forms: the pollution of commonly held resources such as the atmosphere, the oceans, watercourses and lakes, and unappropriated land. Individuals and firms use such resources as waste sinks, reducing significantly the values of such resources to the owners of these common properties: the public collectively. Polluters may alter the character of ecological or human biological or genetic structures, causing harm to individuals and threatening the chain of life for many biological species. Individual human beings may make decisions with respect to numbers of their own species or artifacts such as automobiles that impose excessive burdens on ecological systems.

The lack of clearly definable and enforceable property rights makes collective action necessary. The multiple interests in common property resources such as the oceans, the atmosphere, and flowing water make the determination of individual rights difficult if not impossible. Navigation, recreation, municipal water supply, and instream uses all place their demands on a given watercourse. Some social mechanism is required to balance these values or ensure that a minimum quality or standard is respected. Some efforts have been made, however, to assign certain "rights" to common property resources such as the atmosphere: Given firms would be able to pollute up to a certain level or sell their rights to pollute to others. Although not precisely private rights of ownership, such rights permit the creation of a market within an overall collective system of decision making.

Private action to ensure protection of broader collective values is not only possible but to some extent is demonstrated by the performance of some environmental groups that survive as membership organizations and engage in private as well as legislative, judicial, and administrative struggles to protect the environment. Organizations such as the Nature Conservancy actually obtain ownership of environmentally sensitive or unique properties. However, the material resources of such organizations are not especially impressive, whereas their entrepreneurial skills are often notable and their capacity to rally their membership to political action relatively great.

Governmental mechanisms for decision making and management of resources may or may not be effective. "Government failure" may be as common as "market failure." We have noted the barriers to successful implementation and achievement of policy impacts matching goals. Further, legislative bodies are at times given to the passage of legislation establishing high-sounding but impractical goals and providing few resources. Moreover, just as the incentives for private entrepreneurs tend to ignore externalities or collective values, public entrepreneurs or managers may function according to perverse incentives. Their goals may be larger agency budgets, personal advancement, or implementation of some traditional and narrow value of an agency without recognition of the broader implications of their actions.

Not all so-called commons dilemmas are the same, and therefore the institutional solutions chosen to deal with them must reflect the major differences in the circumstances of the resources. One dimension concerns whether the resource is stationary or fugitive: wind, solar radiation, and river water are fugitive, whereas timber and land are stationary. Some are relatively ubiquitous, such as wind; whereas others are scarce, such as land and migrating wildlife. Some situations require even-handed regulations; others differential treatment; others may be solved by government ownership and management, thus removing the resource from the classical commons definition.[52]

The choice of decision-making mechanisms, the market or the public sector, have profound distributional consequences. The market clearly accepts a given distribution of income and makes no effort to alter it except as tastes and technology change. Public-sector decision making unquestionably alters the distribution of income. Relying for the most part on general revenues to maintain parks, to enforce pollution control regulations, or to construct sewage treatment plants, the distributional consequences depend on the progressivity of the tax system and actual use of other direct benefits obtained by various classes of citizens. The construction of a sewage treatment plant, for example, may be of benefit to citizens of all classes within a given urban place. But if citizens elsewhere are required to pay for that plant, their incomes have obviously been diminished without benefit to them. The protection of a wilderness area and thus the failure to develop and use its resources, or the prohibition of logging a redwood forest, has clear distributional consequences; the relatively affluent enjoy the wilderness far more than the working class; those who are hurt most directly and keenly are the individuals whose jobs are lost because of the protection of the forest.

B. Risks and Uncertainty

Modern technology has increased enormously the uncertainties and risks to which human beings are subjected. Science has opened a Pandora's box of new chemicals that promise health and prosperity but that also threaten to destroy those same conditions. Despite enormous investments in research, uncertainty remains a large factor in environmental decision making. Seldom are tests of chemical compounds exhaustive; there is always room for debate over the adequacy of tests, the appropriateness of test populations, and the conditions of experiments. Beyond specific substances, there is great uncertainty with respect to the synergistic relationships among them. There is uncertainty with respect to the impact of a given set of conditions that are considered environmentally unfavorable—such as concentrations of photochemical smog—and health problems of affected populations. Finally, there are uncertainties regarding the impact and the effectiveness of the measures taken to control or mitigate the environmental threat. The sheer number and the profoundly complex relationships among elements in an ecological system make a thorough appreciation of the risks that are being taken extraordinarily difficult.

Most human beings are averse to risk, especially when that risk is imposed on them by others. But that resistance to risk taking is tempered by the awareness of the cost of its avoidance. Moreover, the willingness to take risks may be greatly enhanced by the realization that insistence on risk avoidance may endanger one's employment. There are various approaches to risk analysis and avoidance. One is to set standards based on some societally approved value, which may range from total risk avoidance to some acceptable level of risk measured in probabilistic terms. Cost is often an important factor in the determination of the levels of acceptable risk. A second approach is that any risk is unacceptable, leading to a prohibition of the activity creating the risk. Finally, there is the compensatory approach, whereby society pays those who take additional risks either in the form of additional compensation or awards for damages as they are suffered.

In environmental policy making, it is often necessary to evaluate alternative risk structures in the achievement of social goals. Nowhere is this risk analysis more controversial or more relevant than in the risks associated with nuclear energy and alternative sources of energy production. Risk analysis endeavors to determine the probability of various kinds of accidents occurring at a nuclear facility and the likelihood of deaths and contamination resulting from such accidents. The risk analysis itself is often controversial: The Rasmussen report on accident risks of commercial nuclear plants was severely criticized as excessively optimistic, underestimating risks possibly by a factor of 500.[53] Equally important are estimates of the probability of accidents, death, and pollution resulting from the developing of alternative sources such as coal-fired steam plants. Defenders of nuclear energy development point out the excellent safety record of nuclear plants, despite the major accident at Three Mile Island, while noting the high rates of accidents, lung disease, and pollution resulting from coal plants.

Risk analysis is imperative at still a broader level. There are those who reject the Faustian bargain of nuclear energy while posing the alternatives of "soft energy paths" plus conservation. Estimates of risks associated with complete commitment to the soft paths undoubtedly tempers the enthusiasms of decision makers in that direction. Economic failure owing to shortages of electrical energy leads them to hedge their bets and to seek orderly and gradual transitions to whatever energy economy the future holds for the United States and the world.

Efforts to deal with uncertainty and risk have led to attempts at modeling (1) ecological systems, (2) the impacts of pollutants or hazardous substances on the environment, (3) the consequences of controls imposed on the polluter, and (4) mitigation efforts in behalf of the polluted environment itself. Aided by computers, these models provide decision makers with simplified but reasonably valid approximations of real-world events. These events having to do with environmental and pollution control problems must be examined, of course, in the context of other trends and events in the economy. The EPA has developed such models in its Strategic Environmental Assessment System (SEAS) (for short-term forecasting) and State of the System model (for long-term forecasting). As described by House and Williams, the SEAS model produces a forecast at the national level of the following issues:

> The economy, impact of pollution control regulations on the general economy and of specific industries; detailed interindustry and consumer sales by industry; labor and capital requirements by industry for economic processes and pollution control processes; transportation demand for passengers and freight by mode of travel; energy demand budgets by industrial and consumer type and by fuel type; levels of production of environmental pollutants, before and after pollution control, for a family of about 100 pollutants which are summarized and given a source; the level for recycling of pre- and post-consumer scrap for a set of secondary materials; amounts of primary ore consumed, domestically extracted, levels imported and exported, price of extraction, reserve availability and capital investment costs for a set of raw materials.[54]

These models naturally are subject to challenge by those whose interests might be adversely affected by decisions based on the models and on the basis of additional scientific evidence. The real political issue, of course, is not so much the quantification of risks but the decision of who should bear them.

In risk and uncertainty the main area of contention is the question of who shall bear the burden of proof in establishing that a given substance is environmentally unsafe or a given practice environmentally unsound. Should an industry be required to demonstrate through its research and experimentation that a chemical is safe to human health and to the environment? Or should a public entity assume that burden? In actuality, the United States has it both ways: Thousands of chemicals remain on the market and will remain on the market until the government can demonstrate that they are dangerous; new substances, however, may be marketed only after their developers and producers can demonstrate to the satisfaction of the EPA that they are safe. It is fair to say that the burden of proof in general has shifted to those who wish to promote new development and new substances or products. The National Environmental Policy Act (NEPA) is a clear demonstration of this shift, requiring those who take what can be considered "major federal action" that will affect the environment significantly to file an environmental impact report. Although not requiring any substantive decisions in favor of the environment, such reports clearly place the developers on the defensive in justifying their products.

C. Scarcity and Its Significance

In an economic sense, all goods are scarce except those available in sufficient abundance and accessibility that they are essentially "free." The atmosphere as a waste sink was historically the best example of such a free good. All other commodities are scarce and therefore costly in that they require work to make them available for use and to protect their intrinsic value. The measurement of scarcity has one essential property: It should summarize the sacrifices, direct and indirect, made to obtain a unit of the resource. A resource is scarce if the quantity demanded exceeds the quantity supplied at some benchmark price, such as the prevailing one, so that in a competitive market there is an upward pressure on the price.[55]

The demand, and therefore the price, of resources on a worldwide basis increased markedly in the decade of the 1970s. Dramatic increases in the price of oil, reductions in the number of days of food in reserve on a worldwide basis, the gap between demand for electricity and the available supply in some regions, and the increasing threats from toxic substances and the lack of suitable sites for their deposit or treatment all attest to increasing scarcity and in some cases absolute shortfalls between supplies and that which is necessary to meet all existing human demands. Various worldwide models—of the demand for food, of increases in pollution, of demands for minerals and renewable resources such as fish and forest products—project dramatic increases in levels of scarcity. Some models project mass starvation, especially in the less developed nations, and drastically reduced levels of well-being in most places on the planet. To be sure, these models are to some extent extrapolations of existing trends, without adequate recognition of learning behavior, which suggests adaptations that may prevent the worst results from occurring. But more recent and interactive models are less subject to such criticism, and they similarly project disaster on a worldwide basis in the early part of the twenty-first century.

The classical economists maintain that resource scarcity in the broadest sense is a misconception. They rely on product substitution and technological development as the processes by which even scarce, nonrenewable resources may be replaced by other resources that maintain existing and even enhanced levels of well-being. In a classic statement of this position, Barnett and Morse argue that environmental consequences should be separated from the question of resource availability.[56] They anticipate a highly elastic rate of substitution between exhaustible natural resources and other factors of production such as capital, and are confident that technology will respond to rapid increases in the costs of existing known resources. For the most part, the market may be relied on to provide responses to increasing scarcity of essentially private goods such as exhaustible resources. Separate decisions can be made regarding despoilation of the environment in terms of the costs and benefits of controlling this evil.

Others reject this position, basing their argument ultimately on the laws of entropy: that low-entropy mineral and energy resources (highly concentrated and therefore useful) are eventually degraded (highly diffused and therefore less susceptible to recovery and use) and that this irreversible process means that there is an ultimate exhaustibility of resources for which no technology or substitution will suffice. Price simply cannot provide the signals indicating this entropy-created scarcity, given the inexhaustible and often fabricated wants of the existing generation. Thus, exponents of this position are led to a moral argument that society must reject continued growth and ask questions about ultimate ends: For what benefits will the resources be used, and how will those benefits be distributed? Resource use and management is in their view a profoundly moral question directed toward the meaning and value of human life and modes of living.[57]

The differing perceptions and definitions of scarcity inevitably lead to different prescriptions with respect to the role of the state. Those who argue that society must make decisions that are ultimately moral about the use and distribution of resources obviously perceive a far more expansive role for government. Given that the future steady-state society could no longer be based on the satisfaction of wants, even those determined democratically and not in the marketplace, Ophuls sees the necessity of a more authoritarian state with leaders infused with the values of ecology. He argues that this does not necessarily imply the rejection of some features of the liberal society such as civil rights, but that it does imply a far more authoritarian disposition on the part of the state with respect to property rights and individual behavior with respect to the natural environment.[58] Nor does it necessarily mean the rejection of marketlike decisions by individual entrepreneurs. Daly suggests the use of resource quotas, which might be auctioned off by the state to the private sector, and freely transferable rights to propagate children through a system enforced by the state.[59]

D. Intergenerational Equity

Natural resource use and protection of the environment are under the "dictatorship" of the present generation. What are the appropriate rules to govern decisions? Can one rely on the altruism of the present generation? Can market forces be relied on to protect the interests of future generations? Under conditions of increasing scarcity, what decision rule will relate equitably the enjoyment of existing resources by the current generation with the desire of future generations that they enjoy equal or increased benefits.

In principle, the market appears to be intertemporally efficient: With increasing scarcity, prices rise; as prices rise, there are incentives for technological development and substitution. Scarcity values are reflected in the interest rates, which discount future benefits and at the same time ensure the appropriate formation of capital that will benefit future generations. On the other hand, it may be argued that the market imposes burdens on future generations that they might not wish to accept had they the means of expressing their preferences: (1) The necessary technological development may not occur in a timely fashion, either to provide adequate resources or to protect the environment against pollution; (2) whereas current resource use may increase future capital stocks, it may not because the current resource use is devoted to short-lived consumer goods.[60]

For some, particularly those who espouse the steady-state economy, intergenerational equity is a matter of ethics, not the marketplace. Given their emphasis on the laws of entropy, the absolute exhaustibility of the earth's resources, they would impose quotas or other limiting devices that ration use in an absolute sense, thus ensuring that future generations have at their command a stock that is not substantially depleted.[61]

Questions of intertemporal equity are particularly serious when they concern decisions that are essentially irreversible, such as adoption of nuclear power, ozone depletion, fossil fuel combustion, the so-called greenhouse effect and chemical carcinogens.[62] Equity must be built in at the outset or not at all. Affirmative decisions benefit present generations, whereas future generations bear most of the risk. It may be argued that future generations may unanimously prefer a more conservative approach even if it can be shown that discounted net benefits are positive. A simple discounting analysis may not be satisfactory. One suggestion that retains the marketplace and the discount rate for micro decision making is the adoption of a depletion tax, which would be adjusted over time to ensure that the real price of natural resources would remain constant.[63]

E. Behavioral Assumptions

The achievement of the goals of environmental protection and enhancement depend on sound assumptions about the behavior of individuals, groups—including firms—and public institutions. Like public policy in general, environmental policy may fall short of its goals if the premises about how motivations, incentives, and constraints are improperly structured into the decision-making system.

Environmental policies make a number of implicit assumptions about how individuals will behave when faced with such incentives as the opportunity to participate in a public hearing, exhortations to save, or fees, fines, or penalties. More profoundly, pluralist political thought makes a number of judgments about the adequacy of the governmental system based on citizens' willingness to become active.

Individuals are likely to behave generally in terms of maximizing their own benefits and reducing costs. Private individuals in dealing with environmental conditions usually find that the costs—information and transaction costs—exceed any benefits they might hope to receive by active involvement in the decision-making system. As individuals, few are prepared to invest much time or money in reducing air and water pollution. Clearly, it is a question of intensity of concern and impact. Those living next to the Love Canal and under the flight path of jet airplanes have an intense interest and therefore heightened levels of activity. But their very costs in terms of health and annoyance may be much greater than the costs of others who are farther removed.

A few, usually with some entrepreneurial skills, leisure time, and personal resources, do become activists. They can galvanize a movement, which may be successful in posing alternative formulations of public projects or opposition to any project at all. Mobilizing volunteers, at the local level in particular, often can have a telling effect.

Individual activity depends very much on the access provided by public institutions. The courts are always available, but barring major threats to individual welfare, citizens are unlikely to use the judicial process because of its expense. When public institutions provide access through hearings, advisory boards, open planning, and so on, public involvement may rise substantially.

Finally, individual citizens may respond to crisis situations in a remarkably positive way. Through exhortations, at least on a short-term basis, individuals will conserve water, drive less, save and recycle newspapers, and accept rationing of commodities and services with good grace. It is not clear how well they will respond on a permanent basis. Clearly, the legitimacy of the cause and the credibility of those doing the exhorting are crucial factors in the effectiveness of this approach.

For most analysts, price is considered the principal motivating factor in changed behavior. Conservation is most likely to occur when the price of gasoline, water, lumber, or use of waste sinks increases. Individuals are allowed to make the appropriate adjustments in demand in accordance with their tastes and needs, but the general trend is toward lowered demand, the development of substitutes, and more careful use of what one does buy. The equity of price as a device for dampening demand for environmental amenities remains controversial.

The enforcement of much environmental legislation depends on the presence of a watchdog that insists on laws being strictly interpreted and applied. Presumably, this means that pollution interests and environmentalist organizations are fairly evenly matched. But there are few observers who would not admit that the pluralist system has a bias toward producer groups, which are well organized and have financial, professional, and leadership resources with which to do battle. Moreover, they are highly specialized, each producer interest focusing on the specific issues related directly to their activity. In contrast, consumer and environmental groups tend to be membership organizations, dependent on dues and contributions. Though specialized to some extent, as are the Audubon and the Wilderness Societies, they must cover a much broader territory than producer organizations. Environmental organizations must struggle to maintain membership while developing a strategy that maximizes their impact. This means careful selection of issues and arenas in which to do battle. They have been aided to a considerable extent by grants from philanthropic organizations. Ford Foundation funding was crucial to the establishment of a number of environmental law groups that have had profound impact on judicial involvement in environmental policy. In some restricted instances, government agencies have provided financial assistance to environmental groups in making their cases before administrative hearings.

The political realities faced by environmental groups at times insert some perverse incentives for their behavior in the policy-making process. Scarce resources and competition for membership may lead environmental groups to target highly symbolic media issues for action rather than more mundane questions that may be substantively more important. Further, the psychic benefits that attract members and activists to environmental groups may incline groups toward unwillingness to compromise and bargain. The positions taken by environmental groups on the building of new water projects, for instance, is usually intransigent opposition. The appointment of numbers of environmentalists to high posts in the Carter administration altered incentives somewhat. Environmental groups found it easier to bargain with bureaucrats who were trusted friends. Further, public agency efforts to include these organizations—albeit considered a political necessity—has brought a greatly enhanced role for environmentalist organizations.

The incentives that operate on the environmental movement may change in character over time as environmentalism becomes an accepted element in the economic system. There is, for example, a solar lobby, a trade association consisting of principal manufacturers and distributors of solar heating equipment. Manufacturers of pollution control equipment may figure more predominantly in the pressure system because of their stakes in public decisions regarding pollution policy.

Private firms exist to make profit and therefore are cost minimizers, especially in a competitive market. They have traditionally avoided certain social costs—their external effects on the environment—by treating them as "commons" for which payment was never charged. With the passage of environmental control legislation, these private firms face paying the cost of these side effects in a variety of forms: installation of new technology to control emissions; payment of charges for treatment of their effluent through waste treatment systems; payment for transportation and disposal of solid wastes; taxes in the form of effluent charges for discharges of wastes into streams and atmosphere; higher costs for land owing to the elimination of certain lands for development because of environmental sensitivity. For the United States as a whole, these increased costs are relatively modest, about 1 percent of total GNP, but for individual firms these costs may be substantial indeed. In most instances, of course, these charges may be passed on to the consumer.

As a class of actors in the environmental policy arena, private profit-making firms inevitably resist government regulation because of its direct costs and the interference that it constitutes in management. With respect to nearly all policy proposals, they are to be found on the side of less effective action for protecting the natural environment.

Polluters of air and rivers point to the cost of installing pollution control equipment. They are found on the side of doubters about the effectiveness of a given control approach. They point to the cost of rehabilitating land that has been strip mined. They object to "locking up" of public lands because of their value as natural habitats for wildlife, as scenic wonders, as geologic spectacles, as wilderness.

On the other hand, actors from the private sector may be environmental protectionists under the appropriate incentives. It may be argued that private forestry management companies have a vital stake in renewing their resource because of its potential for producing profits on a cyclical basis. Similarly, oil and mining companies are likely to respond to price increases by enhanced levels of recovery of minerals from ores of low concentration. New firms enter the market to recycle materials that formerly were discarded. Recovery of methane gas from waste deposits becomes a profitable enterprise.

Environmental protection policy has not always been correct in its' assumptions about the incentives to which industry will respond. Under the belief that the automobile companies could do much more than they were then doing to control pollution, the Clean Air Act set close deadlines and imposed large penalties. In the view of close observers, the law served only to stifle long-range systems research and drive the automobile companies into quick, inefficient, short-term, end-of-the-pipe solutions, and stall tactics.[64]

Government regulations suffer from the relative ignorance of bureaucrats of the intricacies of the technology of a given enterprise. Managers of firms often find the requirements for installation of pollution control equipment, for example, illogical, excessive, and overly expensive. The logic of these objections leads in the direction of the adoption of effluent charges based on the quantities of polluting substances emitted by a given plant. These charges would raise the cost of doing business but would allow the managers to decide the manner in which the firm would adjust to the charges. Most economists believe that such a system would increase efficiency and enhance the likelihood of compliance with environmental standards. Industry, however, has not shown great interest in the charges approach, partly because of their acceptance of the regulatory approach but to a considerable extent because they are able to avoid compliance with regulatory orders by litigation, by appeals to the Congress for delays in the compliance schedule, and by long negotiations with the regulatory agency.[65] They appear to prefer the system that permits greater involvement by the regulatory body in their affairs because they are confident that they can postpone the full application of the agency's requirements for lengthy periods of time. On the other hand, it should be pointed out that many environmentalists are equally opposed to the effluent charge approach because of its vulnerability to the charge that firms are granted a "license to pollute."

Environmental protection policies are necessarily constructed on the assumption that government agencies will actively pursue the goals of the legislation under which they operate. This is not to say that congressional sponsors of legislation have assumed a compliant bureaucracy. Indeed the action forcing provisions of the National Environmental Policy Act were designed to make development agencies consider environmental impacts they might otherwise ignore. The length and complexity of air and water pollution legislation in the early 1970s can be traced to congressional distrust of administrative agencies that in the past were insufficiently zealous in imposing regulations.

In fact, the historical role of federal agencies has been mixed. On the one hand, bureaucratic agencies have been in the forefront of economic development, and this has placed them in the vanguard of those who would disturb fragile and unique environments. They have sponsored the construction of canals, the straightening of river channels, the damming of rivers, the draining of marshes, the increase in automobile traffic, the installation of power plants, all of which have had detrimental effects on the natural environment and to some extent on the health of human beings. Such patronage has been in the name of progress, settling a nation, and the productive use of resources.

On the other hand, other public agencies have taken responsibility for husbanding of resources: reservation of public lands, especially those valued for their timber, water production, recreation, and wildlife. They have regulated private activities to ensure compliance with environmental standards with respect to air and water pollution, radiation, pesticides, and other hazardous substances. They have imposed often costly and onerous burdens on those who would develop projects that had significant effects on the environment. Their mandates were established by Congress, both for and in restraint of development, thus their incentives were created by the legal structure itself.

Like other individuals and private firms, however, bureaucrats and their agencies tend to respond to incentives that lead to growth of their roles, their budgets, and their numbers. Lacking standards of efficiency supplied by a private market and depending on appropriations that reflect political considerations, government agencies seek to expand budgets and authority. Stimulated by members of Congress who live by the same political laws, bureaucrats respond by more and bigger projects, often without economic justification. Moreover, bureaucrats may fall victim to ideology—a commitment to values that may not reflect current knowledge or societal values. The ideology leads to doctrinaire norms that govern individual behavior. Being monopolists, their decisions may be less susceptible to attack because consumers have few means of challenging them.

Bureaucracies often suffer, however, from burdens that far outstrip their capacities. They seldom are provided the money, talent, or time to accomplish their tasks in a satisfactory manner: too few inspectors, scientists, and enforcement officials; too little talent because society has failed to produce them or they have been siphoned off into the private sector because of higher salaries; too little time because Congress makes assumptions about deadlines that cannot possibly be kept. The result is loss of credibility among its clientele and loss of stature with the general public.

The varying and often conflicting impulses that propel government agencies toward their policy goals impose a premium on coordination of their manifold efforts. Such coordination is difficult to achieve because there are few in the hierarchical chain of command who are willing to make hard decisions and still fewer who are willing to accept them when they contravene their views on policy. The result is likely to be patchwork policy, with each agency moving haltingly in its chosen direction, negotiating differences where conflicts are severe and progress toward their goals is impeded by the stances of other agencies.

The conflicting values and missions of agencies make comprehensive planning of environmental policy very difficult, if not impossible. For this reason organization for environmental policy making tends to be decentralized in the federal government. Efforts to create a Department of Natural Resources and the Environment founder on these internal conflicts. And for many environmentalists, the existing decentralized system may be preferable, especially as it concerns the role of the Environmental Protection Agency, because the EPA is able to provide a counterpoise to other agencies that may have a more developmental orientation. Lumping all agencies concerned with natural resources and the environment in a single department might result in greater unity and coordination, but the result might also be the suppression of dissent that could be highly protective of environmental values and the development of a concerted position moving in an antienvironmental direction.

Finally, the intergovernmental arrangements in the United States create major incentives for the national government to play the role of environmental regulator and financier of environmental improvements. State and local governments are reluctant to take on costly burdens or lay them on local polluters without assurance that such burdens or lay them on local polluters without assurance that such burdens are being imposed elsewhere. Once the federal government undertakes a mandatory environmental improvement program, it is natural for local governments to expect and to wait for financial assistance from the national government. There is also a strong tendency for both levels of government to emphasize public works projects that are financed by the federal government with only modest contributions by local governments rather than to undertake regulatory or charges approaches that might drastically reduce the cost of public outlays. Engineering approaches seem almost always to be preferred over social remedies.

VI. CONCLUSION AND PROGNOSIS FOR THE FUTURE

Environmental policy has come of age.[66] Public opinion seems to be committed to environmental protection, even in the face of some sacrifices to other values such as jobs, the economy, prices, and energy. Environmental protection is an established part of the government agenda, and the issue is built into governmental routine. Government agencies have accommodated themselves to the task of writing environmental impact statements, and sizable appropriations for environmental protection have become a routine part of budget. There are indications that environmental groups are maturing as political actors. Although the growth of these groups has declined, membership is sizable and stable. Groups are becoming more comfortable with negotiation rather than confrontation strategies.

Legislation passed in a number of fields reviewed here represents large, and in some cases innovative policy change. Protection of air and water quality and regulation of toxic substances are dramatically more forceful than a decade and a half ago. Laws in these and other areas have been accompanied by the growth of large bureaucracies with continuing interest in strong environmental action.

Given the acceptance, legitimacy, and maturity of environmental policy, it is natural that greater attention should be currently focused on implementation and the consequences flowing from policies. Here we are dealing with questions of effectiveness and efficiency and the distributional impacts of policies. Analysts have noted that in the past environmental policies may have produced some perverse incentives. Environmental impact statement requirements may have been met more with a view toward avoiding litigation than using information about environmental damage to modify projects. Some regulations have caused industry to install controls that are costly to consumers but have little impact on environmental quality. At times, environmental regulations may have been used by narrow parochial interests to delay or cancel projects that are in the broader societal interest.

Environmental protection policy is likely to be challenged in the 1980s. Clearly the Reagan administration places a lower priority on this area than its predecessor. Environmental groups may have less access to administration officials than previously, and some of the movement's most ardent supporters have already departed from Congress. Several outcomes are possible. Environmentalists may decide to do battle from their entrenched positions in the established environmental bureaucracy and ongoing law. Despite presidential powers of appointment, reorganization, and influence over the budget, environmentalists are in a strong position. Past policy experience shows how difficult it is for presidents to turn around established programs that have strong political support. Alternatively, the current political situation may provide an opportunity to make some needed improvements in environmental laws. Fine tuning of incentives could result in more efficient and effective environmental protection. The roles of state and local governments and private enterprise could be enhanced in ways to serve better the overall objective of environmental quality.

However policy makers choose to respond, the environmental challenge is not likely to become less pressing. Physical evidence suggests that little headway is being made on recognized problems, while newly discovered problems mount. The consequences of environmental degradation are likely to be too obvious and costly for environment to be pushed off the agenda. An understanding of environmental policy is likely, therefore, to to be of enduring value.

NOTES

1. U.S. Council on Environmental Quality and Department of State, *Global Two Thousand Report*, (U.S. Government Printing Office, Washington, DC, 1980).
2. See, for instance A. Downs, "Up and down with ecology, the issue attention cycle," *Public Interest*, Summer 1972, pp. 38–50.
3. H. M. Ingram and D. E. Mann, "Environmental policy: From innovation to implementation," in *Nationalizing Government: Public Policies in America*, T. J. Lowi and A. Stone, Eds. (Sage, Beverly Hills, CA, 1979).
4. D. E. Mann, "Political incentives in U.S. water policy: Relationships between distribution and regulatory politics," in *What Government Does*, M. Holden, Jr., and D. C. Dresang, Eds. (Sage, Beverly Hills, CA, 1975).
5. P. K. Schulman, "Non-incremental decision-making: Notes toward an alternative paradigm," *American Political Science Review 64*, 4 (December 1975): 1354–1370.
6. A. V. Kneese and C. L. Schultze, *Pollution, Prices, and Public Policy* (Brookings Institution, Washington, DC, 1975), p. 70.
7. World Health Organization, *Prevention of Cancer*, Technical Report, Series 276, (WHO, Geneva, 1974).
8. A. Wildavsky, *Speaking Truth to Power: The Art and Craft of Policy Analysis* (Little, Brown, Boston, 1979).
9. L. White, "The historical roots of our ecological crisis," *Science 155* (March 1967): 1203–1207.

10. J. McPhee, *Encounters with the Archdruid*, (Farrar, Straus, and Giroux, New York, 1971).
11. G. Hardin, "Tragedy of the commons," *Science 162* (December 13, 1968): 243–48.
12. J. Baden and R. Stroup, "Externality, property rights and the management of our national forests," *Journal of Law and Economics 16* (1973): 303-312.
13. J. C. Davies, III and B. Davies, *The Politics of Pollution* (Pegasus, Indianapolis, IN, 1974).
14. Much of the description of the global state of the environment comes from G. O. Barney (Study Director), *The Global 2000 Report to the President of the U.S.: Entering the 21st Century, vol. 1, The Summary Report* (Pergamon, New York, 1980).
15. Sources for the description of U.S. environment and policy include the following: Council on Environmental Quality, *Environmental Quality–1978*, the ninth annual report of the Council on Environmental Quality (U.S. Government Printing Office, Washington, DC, December 1978); Council on Environmental Quality, *Environmental Quality–1980*, the eleventh annual report of the Council on Environmental Quality (U.S. Government Printing Office, Washington, DC, December 1980); Environmental Protection Agency, Office of Research and Development, *Environmental Outlook 1980* (U.S. Government Printing Office, Washington, DC, August 1980).
16. Descriptions of air and water policy come largely from H. Ingram and D. Mann, op. cit.
17. P. Portney, Ed., *Current Issues in U.S. Environmental Policy*, (Johns Hopkins University Press, Baltimore, 1978).
18. Ibid.
19. Ibid., Chap. 4.
20. R. Salisbury and J. Heinz, "A theory of policy analysis and some preliminary applications," in *Policy Analysis in Political Science*, Ira Sharkansky, Ed. (Markham, Chicago, 1970).
21. T. S. Lowi, "Four systems of policy, politics and choice," *Public Administration Review 32* (July/August 1972): 298-310. D. E. Mann, "Political incentives in U.S. water policy: Relationships between distributive and regulatory politics," in Holden and Dresang, op. cit., pp. 94-123.
22. H. M. Ingram and S. Ullery, "Policy innovation and institutional fragmentation," *Policy Studies Journal 8*, 5 (Spring 1980): 664-682.
23. A. Downs, "Up and down with ecology–the issue attention cycle," *Public Interest*, 28 (Spring 1972), 38-50.
24. Council on Environmental Quality, *Public Opinion on Environmental Issues*, (U.S. Government Printing Office, Washington, DC, 1980.
25. Ibid., p. 46.
26. U.S. Environmental Protection Agency, Office of Research and Development, op. cit., p. 30.
27. R. C. Mitchell, "How 'soft,' 'deep,' or 'left?': Present constituencies in the environmental movement for certain world views," *Natural Resources Journal 20*, 2 (April 1980): 7.
28. F. Buttel and W. E. Flinn, "Social class and mass environmental beliefs: A reconsideration," *Environmental Behavior 10*, 3 (September 1978): 433-450.
29. R. E. Dunlap, "The impact of political orientation on environmental attitudes and actions," *Environment and Behavior 7*, 4 (December 1975).
30. J. A. Honnold, "Predictors of public environmental concern in the 1970s," in *Environmental Policy Formation*, D. E. Mann, Ed. (Lexington Books, Lexington, MA, 1981).

31. C. R. Humphrey and F. Buttel, "The sociology of the growth/no growth debate," *Policy Studies Journal 9*, 3 (Winter 1980): pp. 336–345.
32. H. C. Kenski and M. C. Kenski, "Partisanship, ideology, and constituency differences on environmental issues in the U.S. House of Representatives: 1973–78," *Policy Studies Journal 9*, 3 (Winter 1980): 325–335.
33. W. R. Catton, Jr., and R. Z. Dunlap, "New ecological paradigm for post-exuberant society," *American Behavioral Scientist 24*, 1 (September/October 1980): 15–47.
34. J. Rodman, "Paradigm change in political science," *American Behavioral Scientist 24*, 1 (September/October 1980): 49–78.
35. Catton and Dunlap, op. cit.
36. S. L. Hart, "The environmental movement: Fulfillment of Renaissance prophecy?" *Natural Resources Journal 20*, 3 (July 1980): 501–522.
37. L. W. Milbrath, "Environmental values and beliefs of the general public and leaders in the United States, England, and Germany," in Mann, *Environmental Policy Formation*.
38. Rodman, op. cit.
39. N. Watts and G. W. Smith, "Post material values and environmental policy change," *Policy Studies Journal 9*, 3 (Winter 1980): 346–359.
40. H. M. Ingram, N. K. Laney, and J. R. McCain, *A Policy Approach to Political Representation: Lessons from the Four Corners States*, (Johns Hopkins Press, Baltimore, 1980), pp. 166–181.
41. G. McConnell, "The environmental movement past and present," *Western Political Quarterly 7* (1954): 463–478.
42. S. P. Hays, *Conservation and the Gospel of Efficiency* (Harvard University Press, Cambridge, MA, 1959).
43. B. Devall, "The deep ecology movement," *Natural Resources Journal 20*, 2 (April 1980): 299–322.
44. Council on Environmental Quality, Government Printing Office, Washi
45. Mitchell, op. cit.
46. R. B. Stewart, "Judging the imponderables of environmental policy: Judicial review under the Clean Air Act," in *Approaches to Controlling Air Pollution*, A. F. Friedlaender, Ed. (M.I.T. Press, Cambridge, MA, 1978), p. 110.
46a. Quoted in J. Quarles, *Cleaning Up America* Houghton Mifflin, Boston, MA, (1976), p. 32.
47. Ingram, Laney, and McCain, op. cit.
48. Wildavsky, op. cit., Chap. 2.
49. Comptroller General, *EPA Is Slow to Carry out Its Responsibilities to Control Harmful Chemicals*, General Accounting Office, CED 81-1, October 28, 1980, p. i.
50. Paul Portney, op. cit., p. 111.
51. C. T. Clotfelter and J. C. Hahn, "Assessment of the national 55 M.P.H. speed limit," in *The Practice of Policy Evaluation*, David Nachmiss, Ed., (St. Martin's, New York, 1980), pp. 396–411.
52. R. K. Godwin and W. B. Shepard, "Forcing squares, triangles and ellipses in a circular paradigm: The use of commons dilemma in examining the allocation of common resources," *Western Political Quarterly 33* 3 (September 1979): 265–277.
53. National Academy of Sciences, *Energy in Transition 1985–2010*, Final Report of the Committee on Nuclear Energy and Alternate Energy Systems, National Research Council, (Freeman, San Francisco, 1980), pp. 53–55, 60–61.

54. P. W. House and E. R. Williams, *Planning and Conservation: The Emergence of a Frugal Society* (Praeger, New York, 1977), pp. 25–26.
55. A. C. Fisher, "Measures of natural resources scarcity," in *Scarcity and Growth Reconsidered*, V. Kerry Smith, Ed. (Johns Hopkins University Press, Baltimore, 1980), pp. 249–252.
56. H. Barnett and C. Morse, *Scarcity and Growth: The Economics of Natural Resource Availability*, (Johns Hopkins University Press, Baltimore, 1963).
57. See H. Daly, "Entropy, growth and the political economy of scarcity," in Kerry Smith, op. cit., pp. 67–94; also W. Ophuls, *Ecology and the Politics of Scarcity* (Freeman, San Francisco, 1977).
58. Ophuls, op. cit.
59. Daly, "Entropy, growth and the political economy of scarcity," op. cit.
60. T. Page, "Equitable use of the resource base," (Resources for the Future, Washington, DC, 1977), reprint 144.
61. See Daly, op. cit.
62. J. Ferejohn and T. Page, "On the foundations of intertemporal choice," in *Contemporary Issues in Natural Resource Economics*, Emery N. Castle, Ed. (Resources for the Future, Washington, DC, 1978), reprint 152, pp. 15–21.
63. Page, op. cit.
64. H. D. Jacoby and J. D. Steinbruner, *Clearing the Air*, (Ballinger, Cambridge, MA, 1973).
65. F. Anderson, A. V. Kneese, P. D. Reed, S. Taylor, and R. B. Stevenson, *Environmental Improvement Through Economic Incentives* (Johns Hopkins University Press, Baltimore, 1979).
66. D. E. Mann, "Introduction of symposium editor," *Policy Studies Journal 9* 3 (Winter 1980):322.

30

Technological Innovation and Its Assessment

Alan L. Porter and Frederick A. Rossini / Georgia Institute of Technology, Atlanta, Georgia

I. A QUICK PERSPECTIVE

Policy studies can be categorized in many ways. One of the more important ways distinguishes between what we might label "decision-aiding" and "academic" types of studies. These differ in purpose, methods, and practitioners. Decision-aiding policy studies are those conducted for the direct intent of providing assistance to a policy maker. Possibly their most critical attribute is that they are future-oriented. The punch line of such studies is a response to queries such as "What is likely to happen if we do _____?" Such studies would typically be conducted by persons closely affiliated with the policy maker in question. In contrast, academic policy studies are performed primarily for the purpose of advancing knowledge and understanding. They typically focus on a question such as "What happened as a result of _____?" Such retrospective studies have the great advantage of hindsight. Often conducted by scholars in academic settings, such analyses may be found in scholarly journals.

A second distinction can be drawn according to the focus of policy studies. The distinction of interest presently is whether or not that focus is *technological* in nature. Many policy studies emphasize nontechnological content. Upon reflection, the pervasiveness of technology in current policy issues may be somewhat surprising, for instance:

In foreign policy—development concerns of the lesser developed countries, undersea mining as a keystone of the law of the sea

In defense policy—new armament technologies (cruise missile, neutron bombs) and disarmament issues (surveillance)

In labor policy—productivity concerns weighing automation and job intensiveness

In criminal justice—information-retrieval systems and crime-fighting technologies (helicopter patrols, automated fingerprint identification)

And in quite obvious fashions—birth control technologies in population policy, new materials and techniques for construction, energy-conserving innovations in transportation, and the cascade of innovations from the biomedical complex.

What difference does a technological focus make? Although no simple answer can be reli-
ably given, technology-intensive issues often entail greater difficulty in reversing policies,
greater reliance on technical expertise in formulating policy, and a need to consider a
complex innovation process.

The simplest version of an innovation process that results in the development and application of a new technology might be stated as follows. New research leads to an effective development that is diffused through public or private institutions and causes consequences for society. Although we spend some time in the following section exposing the
oversimplicity of such a model, it is nonetheless helpful in drawing an immediate distinction. Policy concerns arise with respect to both the effects *on* the development in question and the effects *of* that development. Public policies can significantly affect a technology in terms of research and development subsidies, tax incentives for capital investment,
or regulations that constrain development. However, policy issues also arise with respect
to the implications of the technology in question—in particular, with respect to the distribution of associated direct and indirect costs and benefits.

Until recent decades, Western civilization has generally promoted technology with
scarcely a second glance at any implications beyond direct economic gains. New highways, new steel mills, and new airplanes were obvious goods to be sought by all. Today's
policy maker cannot subscribe to such illusions of technological beneficence. The litany
of concerns about technology need not be repeated here, but it ranges broadly across issues such as nuclear proliferation and waste disposal, DDT and ecological disruptions,
urban highways and community disruption, cultural homogenization through the mass
media, and population explosion as an unintended effect of improved nutrition and medical care. Society cannot afford to ignore the possible costs attendant on technological development, even as it continues to seek the bounties.

In this chapter we present a brief survey of the innovation process, focusing on
knowledge useful from a policy perspective. The intent is to elucidate the variety of possible governmental policy actions relevant to technological development, the inherent
complexity of the underlying processes, and the place for technology assessment in the
policy processes. Turning then to impact assessment, we briefly sketch its history and
variants, describe how it is done, and address some of the concerns in doing it. Finally, we
step back to look at some broader implications of technology for policy makers and
analysts.

II. TECHNOLOGICAL INNOVATION

This section presents an overview of the process of technological innovation to give the
reader a perspective on the "front end" of innovation, its development, and diffusion. It
emphasizes background for generic policy issues relating to innovation. The treatment follows Kelly et al. (1978) and Rossini and Bozeman (1977).

A technological innovation is the development of a new technology or the substantial modification of an existing technology. There are many extant definitions of a technology, ranging from a physical device to definitions that include almost anything. For our purposes, perhaps the most useful characterization of technology is Gendron's (1977):

> A technology is any systemized practical knowledge, based on experimentation and/or scientific theory, which is embodied in productive skills, organization, or machinery.

This definition has the virtue of including processes, biological techniques, and forms of social organization, as well as physical devices. Yet it excludes unproductive knowledge such as religious dogma.

Technological innovation is the primary response of contemporary industrialized societies to meet the problems that confront them. A caricature of this response is the "technological fix" by which undesirable consequences of one innovation are dealt with by another innovation, and so on, creating an unbroken chain of innovation.

From the public policy perspective, the greatest external leverage on innovation consists of developing favorable societal conditions for it. This implies first making it desirable for organizations with the capability for innovation to do so in socially beneficial ways and to foster favorable conditions for the creation of innovating organizations (even to the extent of creating them, as the National Aeronautics and Space Administration). Second, it involves incentives for the diffusion of innovations for broad societal use. Automotive pollution control devices leap to mind as a case of both encouraging an innovation and its diffusion. Consideration of policy incentives requires a knowledge of the
rocess into its external environment, the
ation (Kelly et al., 1978; Rossini and

A. The External Environment of Innovation

The external environment of innovation can be conveniently divided into values, endowments, and institutions. Values are the least concrete of the three. These preferences and dispositions of individuals vary throughout society. During the 1970s the overwhelmingly positive reaction to technology was tempered by the public realization that some technologies also have undesirable consequences that should be minimized (for some data on public perception of technological innovations, see LaPorte and Metlay 1974; Metlay 1972).

Technological innovation consumes relatively little capital, labor, energy, and materials compared to the more mundane tasks of production and distribution. However, it consumes the lion's share of one major endowment—knowledge.

There is a rhetorical view of innovation as a linear series of more or less clearly defined phases from idea generation to invention to development through broad diffusion. Some studies of the innovation process are structured according to this model (Sherwin and Isenson, 1967; TRACES, 1968; Battelle-Columbus Laboratories, 1973). A linear, directly causal relationship between scientific knowledge and technological innovation has been claimed for the transistor (Jewkes et al., 1969; Nelson, 1962) and nylon (Jewkes et al., 1969; Mueller, 1962). This notion is the basis of providing support for basic science because of its future "payoff" in innovation.

However, and this is crucial to understanding the role of basic scientific knowledge in innovation, the elements in innovation are usually related in a complex, nonlinear manner. Scientific knowledge, if it enters the innovation process at all, may play a variety of roles. In classical Greece there was a deep interest in the development of scientific knowledge without a corresponding concern for using that knowledge to develop innovations (Farrington, 1946). At the other extreme, many innovations in textile machinery during the early industrial revolution were made by tinkers with no scientific background. Reversing the usual direction of information flow presents examples such as the stimulation of the science of thermodynamics by the interest in the relationships among heat, work, and energy aroused by Watt's steam engine (Cardwell, 1971) and the effects on physics of the development of the cyclotron (Jewkes et al., 1969). More complex patterns involve using basic science to fill knowledge gaps in a technological investigation and the confluence of technological and scientific knowledge to produce an innovation (such as the nuclear reactor). Understanding the roles of science in innovation is a determining factor in the level and direction of societal support for science.

Institutions involved in the innovation process include the firm and industry as well as governmental institutions that control, regulate, and develop innovations. We shall recapitulate the role of some key institutions in innovation.

An analysis of the literature on the relationship between firm size and research and development (R&D) activity level (as a surrogate measure for innovation) reached the following conclusions (Kelly et al., 1978: chap. 2):

1. There is a minimum size in terms of sales needed to engage effectively in organized research.
2. There is a generally positive relationship between firm size and R&D activity.
3. There is a point beyond which increases in sales do not bring forth proportional increases in either R&D activity or patents.
4. There is a great deal of variation among industries.

Differences among firms within the same industry are complemented by interindustry differences. Two variables that have been studied are industry concentration and ease of entry. Concentration of an industry is usually measured by the N firm concentration ratio, which is the ratio of the output of the largest N firms in the industry to total industry output. Scherer (1967) and Comanor (1967) found a significantly greater ratio of scientists and engineers to total employment (again a surrogate measure of innovation) in industries with high concentration than in industries with low concentration. It is relatively easy to argue that in a weakly concentrated industry the size of most firms is below that necessary to maintain an R&D establishment; whereas, at the other extreme, a monopoly has no incentive to innovate at all. Yet, in opposition to this position, AT&T, despite its near monopoly, has been a consistent innovator and owns Bell Labs, one of the world's leading industrial R&D organizations. Also, small firms in the electronics, computer, and, now, the genetic engineering industries have been extraordinarily innovative. Comanor (1967) found that moderate barriers to entry produced higher percentages of R&D employment relative to size than high or low barriers. Excessively high barriers insulate the industry against outsiders entering, whereas very low barriers give no firm an advantage. Despite these indications, the understanding of how innovation in an industry is affected by concentration and ease of entry is far from clear.

Governmental institutions have been involved directly in innovation. They follow three organizational patterns. The first is the exclusive in-house performance of R&D, such as is done by the National Bureau of Standards. Second, there is the agency that funds scientific and technological work without itself performing research, such as the National Science Foundation. Third, some agencies, such as the National Aeronautics and Space Administration (NASA), both fund external R&D and perform work in house. With the government share of total R&D expenses in the United States running on the order of one-half for the past two decades, these contributions are a significant determinant of areas where innovation will take place.

As well as being an innovator, the government is responsible for the diffusion of innovations. The Agricultural Extension Service is a prime example of a diffuser of innovations with a channel for feedback from the user (Baker et al., 1963; Knoblauch et al., 1962). Another federal attempt at diffusing innovations, NASA's Technology Utilization Program, simply attempted to apply technologies developed by NASA to other sectors of the economy without considering user needs (Doctors, 1969).

Governmental institutions are also involved in the regulation and control of innovations. Perhaps the oldest example is the Patent Office, which grants multiyear monopolies to inventors of significantly novel entities. This monopoly is sometimes in conflict with the government's antitrust policy, which often requires the compulsory licensing or outright assignment of patents (Oppenheim, 1957). Taxation is another device that can be used to stimulate or impede innovation (see, e.g., Charpie, 1967).

Over the years the government has established a number of bodies, beginning with the Interstate Commerce Commission in the nineteenth century, and extending to the Environmental Protection Agency, which regulate various aspects of the economy. There is a significant body of opinion and fact which contends that the innovative performance of regulated industries is below what could be reasonably expected (Capron, 1971; Gellman Research Associates, 1974). Some useful questions to be asked about the effect of regulation on innovation include the following (Capron, 1971):

1. Are regulators more effective in fostering innovation by regulating profits, prices, or qualitative performances?
2. How is regulation affected by the organization and technological characteristics of the industry being regulated?
3. Does the behavior of the regulatory body toward innovations differ according to its size and composition?
4. Does the innovative performance of the industry affect the goals and policies of the regulatory agency? If so, do interactions between industry and agency also vary systematically with the structure of the regulatory system?

Finally, it is important to note that government regulations and controls affecting innovation are complex, overlapping, and sometimes in conflict with one another. To understand their effects it is often helpful to "map" them for the area of innovation in question.

B. Innovation Within R&D Organizations

Although these "external" institutions, endowments, and values are significant determinants of innovation, the actual innovations usually take place today in R&D organizations. From the policy perspective there is little input to the specific intellectual processes of innovation. However, in selecting general areas of interest and encouraging specific organizational forms, this external influence can be felt significantly, but indirectly, in the development of innovation. Thus, understanding the organizational dynamics of innovation is quite useful.

We use the analysis by Baker (Kelly et al., 1978: chap. 3) of the information flow and process phase models of innovation in the R&D organization. These two models represent the two leading reconstructions of organized innovation.

The information flow model originated in the management science literature (Myers and Marquis, 1969; Utterback, 1973; Rubenstein, 1964). Its steps are typically idea generation, idea submission, proposal review and project selection, and R&D activity—including scheduling and control leading to innovative results.

The process phase model has its origins in the economic literature (Hamberg, 1966; Mansfield, 1971). The phases of this model are typically basic research, applied research, development, and engineering. The two models represent contributions coming from different disciplinary orientations and interests. Although they are usually discussed as linear and unidirectional, considerable feedback occurs from stage to stage. These models should be viewed as complementary rather than competing. This complementarity may be usefully exhibited by combining the models so that organized R&D may be seen simultaneously from both the economic and management science perspectives. The two hybrid models developed by Baker and his colleagues (Kelly et al., 1978: chap. 3) are the phase-dominant model and the project-dominant model.

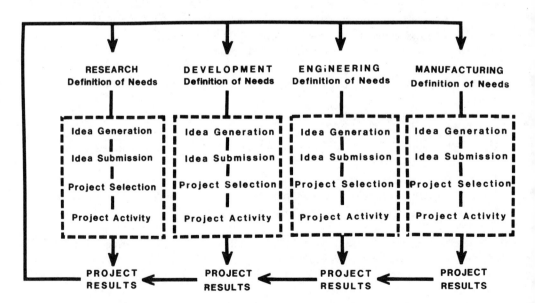

Figure 1. Phase-dominant model of the R&D process. (From Kelly et al., 1978.)

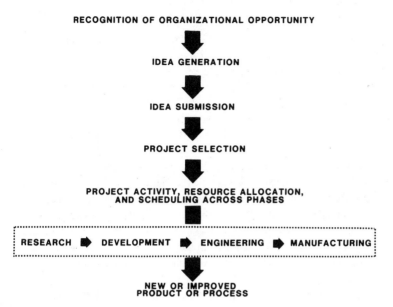

Figure 2. Project-dominant model of the R&D process. (From Kelly et al., 1978.)

The phase-dominant model (Figure 1) retains the process phases as the discrete units of R&D. Within the phases, information flow occurs in accordance with the information flow model. Thus the project moves from basic research to applied research to development to engineering. Within each of these phases idea generation, idea submission, project selection, and project activity occur.

In the project-dominant model (Figure 2), idea generation, idea submission, and project selection are followed by project activity including resource allocation, and scheduling. Project activity takes place across the phases of basic research, applied research, development, and engineering.

Each of these composite models suggests a different dominant organizational form. The phase-dominant model seems to favor a hierarchial organization, emphasizing separate divisions for each phase of the project, requiring the transfer of the project, as it matures, from division to division within the host organization. The project-dominant model implies a matrix organization with overall control at the project level crossing the divisional boundaries of the organization.

Pursuing the composite models further, we now consider the types of R&D projects leading to innovations that may be accommodated within these models. Three types of projects can be usefully distinguished (for similar distinctions, see Hollander, 1965; Rubenstein, 1964; Schwartz, 1973). The first is the *incremental improvement* of existing products or processes. Such projects tend to be relatively small, single-phase projects, involving a limited number of R&D personnel from closely related disciplines. Then there are two types of discontinuous projects, or projects concerned with the development of significant new entities or technological and scientific breakthroughs. One type consists of the cumulation of a number of incremental projects in which some final technical problem is overcome or some new insight is developed—the *cumulative discontinuous* project. Also included here are major advances that result from the efforts of a single individual or small team. Examples include hybrid corn, oral contraceptives, and input-output economic analysis. The final type of project is *disruptive discontinuous.* It can be characterized as a large, multiyear, multiphase project that cuts across organizational and disciplinary boundaries and requires substantial resources to complete. Because of their complexity, such projects require the attention of top-level management. Examples include the Manhattan Project, NASA's manned space effort, and the instant pocket camera.

It is interesting to consider the congruence between the phase-dominant model and the incremental or cumulative discontinuous project on one hand, and the project-dominant model and the disruptive discontinuous project on the other. Indeed, it seems that the hierarchical organization is in line with the phase-dominant model and its concomitant projects, which can be handled within a single division or loosely coordinated across divisions. It is the disruptive discontinuous project that can wreak havoc with such a structure by requiring a project management with cross-division, cross-function authority, and hence demands a matrix organization.

Indeed, it is arguable that the types of centralization, the degree of formalization of the roles of participants, and the complexity of these roles varies dramatically among these types of organizations and projects. The hierarchical organization with its accompanying R&D mode favors divisional control, high formalization of rules, and low complexity of activities, whereas the matrix organization and its concomitant R&D mode favors project control, low formalization, and high complexity.

Although this analysis remains speculative, it suggests the kinds of questions that need to be asked and answered in order systematically to stimulate innovation and, ultimately, productivity.

C. The Diffusion of Innovation

Despite the existence of an innovation, there is little effect on the world at large until it is spread or diffused to its user community. Like the development of innovation in the R&D context, the understanding of diffusion arises from diverse intellectual traditions. The three central perspectives are the geographic, economic, and social-psychological.

The geographic tradition emphasizes spatial considerations, whether simply proximity (Hagerstrand, 1968) or constrained by the information flow within an urban area (Brown, 1968, 1969). The role of propagators within an urban system raises such market-related considerations as economic advantage and societal factors such as the social systems through which information about the innovation flows. Indeed, despite their initial isolation from one another, the economic analysis of diffusion (e.g., Griliches, 1957; Mansfield, 1961, 1966; Nabseth and Ray, 1974) and the social-psychological analysis (Rogers and Shoemaker, 1971) have many points of correspondence.

Such a correspondence has been noted by Kelly et al. (1978: chap. 4). The factors that Mansfield (1966) considers important—economic advantage, initial uncertainty of using the new innovation, amount of commitment required to try the innovation, and rate of reduction of initial uncertainty—can be brought into correspondence with a set of factors due to Rogers and Shoemaker (1971). These are relative advantage (broader than, but inclusive of, economic advantage), compatibility of the innovation with existing conditions (corresponding to initial uncertainty), complexity (corresponding to amount of commitment), and observability and testability (corresponding to the rate of reduction of initial uncertainty).

The closeness and complementarity of the various traditions suggest that any comprehensive understanding of diffusion should include geographic, economic, and social-psychological variables. The suggestion of grouping these variables into four categories to deal comprehensively with innovation has been advanced by Kelly (Kelly et al., 1978: chap. 4). These categories are the characteristics of the adopting sector, the characteristics of the adopters themselves, the characteristics of the innovation, and the propagation mechanisms used.

Policy for encouraging or discouraging adoption may be as simple as legal compulsion, as with innovations for controlling automotive air pollution, or as complex as using further adaptation to end-users' needs to stimulate adoption. Whatever be the situation, however, a generic understanding of diffusion is a first step toward intelligently encouraging adoption.

In sum, innovation is an integral part of modern industrial society. Understanding the process by which innovation occurs is central to formulating policy in many traditional areas such as health, education, defense, and taxation, as well as in national efforts to increase productivity. Innovation is a complex phenomenon that belies simplistic treatments. It may usefully be viewed as an ecological system made up of three subsystems: external environment, R&D context, and the diffusion subsystem. Assessing the consequences of innovation is the subject of the next section.

III. IMPACT ASSESSMENT

The efforts to assess the implications of technological developments in the United States saw their genesis a little more than a decade ago on Capitol Hill. Their development has proceeded along two rather parallel, but separate, paths under the labels technology assessment (TA) and environmental impact assessment (EIA).

Technology assessment has been defined as a class of policy studies that systematically examine the effects on society that may occur when a technology is introduced, extended, or modified. It emphasizes those consequences that are unintended, indirect, or delayed (J. F. Coates, 1976). Concerned about the relative sparsity of technical information for the Congress vis-a-vis the federal executive branch, Congressman Emilio Q. Daddario promoted the development of an Office of Technology Assessment (Daddario, 1967). TA was intended to provide policy makers with a new and powerful tool for coping with the dynamic and pervasive impacts of technology on the fabric of society. It would identify the positive payoffs of technological innovations and foster their transfer into practice. At the same time it would isolate potential negative consequences, thus serving as an early warning system. Daddario felt that policy makers needed to have social, economic, and legal implications taken into consideration along with the strictly technical parameters. Public Law No. 92-484 established the Office of Technology Assessment in 1972 as a staff arm of the Congress. It was set up with a bipartisan governing board consisting of three majority and three minority members of each house. The Office has produced a number of policy studies of technological developments and has generated a good measure of controversy (c.f. Casper, 1978; U.S. Congress, House Subcommittee on Science, Research, and Technology, 1978). It has certainly brought attention to the notion of technology assessment, which has also been institutionalized in the federal executive in many different agencies (V. T. Coates, 1979). Industry has quietly begun to undertake impact assessment as well (U.S. Congress, Office of Technology Assessment, 1976; Maloney, in press). In other nations, TA has usually been viewed as part of existing planning activities (Hahn, 1977).

In a developmental sequence contemporary to that for TA, environmental impact assessment (EIA) was spawned by the National Environmental Policy Act of 1969. An important provision of NEPA requires the preparation of environmental impact statements. As stated in Section 102(c) of the act:

> All agencies of the Federal Government shall include in every recommendation or report on proposals for legislation and other major Federal actions significantly affecting the quality of the human environment, a detailed statement by the responsible official on
>
> (i)   the environmental impact of the proposed action,
> (ii) any adverse environmental effects which cannot be avoided should the proposal be implemented,
> (iii) alternatives to the proposed action,
> (iv) the relationship between local short-term uses of man's environment and the maintenance and enhancement of long-term productivity, and
> (v)   any irreversible and irretrievable commitments of resources which would be involved in the proposed action should it be implemented.

Environmental impact assessment is generally taken as the analytical activity that leads to the environmental impact statement itself. Although the emphasis of this form of impact assessment has been on the natural environment, interpretation has been broadening over the years to emphasize the "human environment," as phrased in the original act. The resulting activities have ranged markedly in their breadth and depth of analysis. Most EIA is oriented to analyzing the likely impacts of a particular project (e.g., a dam or highway). However, generic environmental impact statements have been prepared with a scope as broad as that implied by TA, as in the statement on plutonium recycling (U.S. Nuclear Regulatory Commission, 1976).

The requirements to prepare and the opportunities to comment on environmental impact statements have brought the notion of impact assessment into realistic practice in a variety of locations. Under the overall guidance of the U.S. Council on Environmental Quality (1978), many federal agencies have entered the impact assessment business. Like a wave expanding outward, the ripple effects of these requirements are broad. Private corporations involved in such projects draft the basic environmental report on which the environmental impact statement is based. Many states have adopted statutory requirements for environmental impact assessment modeled on NEPA. Other developed nations and international organizations have adopted some form of environmental impact assessment as a planning aid (Porter et al., 1980).

The notion of impact assessment—that is, the attempt to anticipate the direct and indirect consequences of major policy actions—is inherently logical and attractive. In addition to the variants just introduced, a variety of other kindred forms are emerging. Social impact assessment deals specifically with consequences on human beings. Risk assessment emphasizes the intricacies in evaluating outcomes resulting from certain innovations with a low probability of occurrence but large-magnitude implications. Its greatest emphasis to date has been in the assessment of nuclear power options. In addition, there are community impact assessments, arms control impact assessments, mental health impact assessments, inflation impact assessments, regulatory impact assessments, and so on. All share the basic problematique of trying to anticipate the future in complex socio-technological systems. All are intended to be decision-aiding policy analyses.

A. The Performance of Impact Assessment

To reiterate, impact assessments in their various forms are focused on the potential *effects* of technological developments. They are *future-oriented*, attempting to advance insights into the likely results of alternative policy actions. This, in turn, mandates that they be interdisciplinary (at least in principle) in that the interacting chains of causes and effects know no neat disciplinary boundaries. For instance, the economic consequences of a hypothetical highway development might include major economic gains in the form of the location of new industries in a given area. One must have a good sense of those economic impacts to anticipate the social impacts on existing or new communities apt to be affected. New industries might imply immigration of culturally different workers and their families. The increased community population, in turn, could place new burdens on the ecosystems by increased water usage and effluent generation or by increased usage of local recreational facilities. Restrictions on such usage might increase tension among teenagers in the community, leading to an increase in crime rates. Clearly, understanding indirect cause-and-effect linkages is a difficult undertaking whose complexity belies this oversimplified example.

Serious impact assessment involves a number of component tasks. We like to distinguish 10 such components; naturally, emphases vary according to the type of study, the scale of effort, and the major policy interest. The term "components" is used because these activities do not follow a neat, sequential order. Table 1 lists these components, which we now discuss briefly (Porter et al., 1980: 54-60; Porter and Rossini, 1980).

Problem Definition. The first activity of an assessment is to determine the nature of the study. This qualitative activity, sometimes referred to as "scoping," is now required in the preparation of environmental impact statements (U.S. Council on Environmental Quality, 1978). The policy objectives and available study resources must be matched with the problem in question to determine the coverage that is appropriate. Assessors must decide on who constitute the intended study users and what their needs are (Berg, et al., 1978). Berg (1975) has usefully delineated six areas that deserve consideration: time horizons, spatial extent, institutional interests, technology and range of applications to be considered, impact sectors, and policy options. Though bounding the domain of an impact assessment study is critical, it should be anticipated that findings over the course of a study may alter some study boundaries.

Table 1. Impact Assessment Component Tasks

	1. Problem Definition	
2. Technology description		4. Social description
3. Technology forecast		5. Social forecast
	6. Impact identification	
	7. Impact analysis	
	8. Impact evaluation	
	9. Policy analysis	
	10. Communication of results	

Technology Description. Technology description and forecast and social description and forecast are inherently grouped together (Table 1). Description is an empirical, descriptive task that sometimes uses expert opinion. Appropriate characterization of the subject matter is obviously critical. If one is studying a relatively routine technology, considerable expertise should be available in helping to define and describe that technology (e.g., construction of a dam). For novel technologies, description is perhaps best begun by specifying the level of emergence of that technology. If one is dealing with a technology that is barely beyond the point of scientific insight, not yet on realistic drawing boards, description is apt to be highly uncertain and essentially blends into forecasting (e.g., describing permanent space colonies in 1981). As a technology makes its way through the innovation process, expertise is likely to become more widespread, although stakeholding in the technology may produce colored descriptions. This is particularly troublesome in the case of "high" technologies with strong proprietary interests involved (e.g., microprocessors). The complexity of the technology under study will influence the assessment team membership (i.e., whether physical scientists and engineers with specific expertise are needed) and the conduct of the study (i.e., whether the whole team can grasp the intricacies of the technology involved or whether work must be parceled out). Technology description should go beyond functional description (Jones, 1971) to consider alternative implementations, related technologies, critical socioeconomic influences, and potential end-users.

Technology Forecast. Technology forecasting attempts to anticipate the character, intensity, and timing of changes in technologies (Bright, 1978). This task obviously rests heavily on the technology description, but it also relies on the social description and forecast. For instance, the future evolution of the space shuttle program probably depends more on continued social and political acceptance than on technical feasibility. High-quality forecasts require the synthesis of documented data, relationships, and assumptions. Ascher (1978) has offered three general principles of forecasting: methodological sophistication contributes little; the core assumptions are critical (e.g., will we have a world war during the time span in question?); and a short time frame is strongly associated with increased accuracy. Taken together, these imply that forecasts should be current and well thought out, even if relatively simple. Short-term forecasts can use such relatively quantitative techniques as trend extrapolation and modeling, whereas long-term forecasts rely more on expert opinion and scenarios.

Social Description. Those aspects of the state of society that interact with the techno-logical innovation in question must be described accurately. The notion of a technological delivery system (Wenk and Kuehn, 1977) can help in identifying institutional involve-ments, parties at interest, and social values that may affect, or be affected by, a particular technological development. Both quantitative social indicators (U.S. Office of Manage-ment and Budget, 1974) and qualitative social description can prove useful in this inquiry.

Social Forecast. Social forecasting attempts to depict the plausibe future configurations of relevant dimensions of the society likely to interact with the technological develop-ment in question (Henschel, 1976). It is probably the least developed and least credible component of the impact assessment process. A typical approach is to provide a range of qualitative alternative futures in the form of scenarios based, in part, on expert opinion.

Impact Identification. "Impacts" refer to the products of the interaction between a de-velopment and its societal context. Note in Table 1 that the assessment tasks associated with impacts can be logically distinguished from the prior effort to define technology and its social context. In practice, however, these aspects may become complexly intertwined. In particular, if one is trying to assess the impacts of a long-range technological develop-ment of grand scope, the technology is apt to so affect its context that social and tech-nological forecasting will be closely linked with impact assessment. For instance, shifting the United States to a hydrogen-based economy in the next century would likely affect technological and institutional arrangements so deeply that social forecasting would have to be built around the impact projections. In general, a helpful logical distinction can be drawn between direct impacts (those effects resulting from the development per se) and higher-order impacts (the product of direct and indirect effects). Recall that impact as-sessment is greatly concerned with such indirect impacts.

One strategy of classifying impacts follows disciplinary lines, such as the "EPISTLE" categorization, which distinguishes environmental, psychological, institutional/political, social, technological, legal, and economic impact areas (Porter et al., 1980). An alterna-tive classification scheme is to identify impacts according to the parties affected. Simple organizing techniques such as checklists and matrices may prove helpful. The amount of available study resources will largely dictate the extent of this component. Selection of the most important impacts for further analysis is essential. In the early 1970s, many environmental impact statements identified exhaustive lists of impacts without providing effective discrimination. Too often the result was a document of little or no policy value. Impact identification often is aided by obtaining perspectives from outside experts, stake-holders, and policy makers as to what impacts are of greatest concern and most subject to effective policy action. Indeed, it is often valuable to begin to identify policy options by the time that impacts are identified.

Impact Analysis. Impact analysis links the identification of significant impacts to their evaluation in the formulation of effective policy to deal with them. It is here that the assessors must estimate the likelihood of occurrence and magnitude of potential effects. Disciplinary expertise and quantitative skills play an important role in such areas as environmental modeling and cost-benefit analysis. Social and institutional impact analyses are typically more qualitative, using scenarios and opinion measurement. These are most common areas of primary data generation in impact analysis. Impact analysis has more in common with the judgmental skills of any policy analyst than with elaborate, "frontier-of-knowledge" work of the academic scholar.

Impact Evaluation. Impact evaluation integrates the impact analyses to enable comparison of alternatives and to assist in policy analysis. It and, subsequently, policy analysis grapple with basic issues of value. Techniques such as decision analysis and policy capture are occasionally helpful. Evaluation criteria should encompass utility measures, equity concerns, and nonmaterialistic values (Porter et al., 1980). These may be applied by the assessment team alone or with stakeholder representation in some form. Issues in public participation will be touched upon later in this chapter. In any event, evaluation processes should be explicit and clear to study users.

Policy Analysis. In one of those intriguing little quirks designed to confuse everyone, policy analysis can be seen both as the overarching activity within which impact assessment is one form, and as a specific component of an impact assessment. We obviously are focusing on the latter at this point. Within the context of an impact assessment, policy analysis compares alternatives for implementing innovations and for dealing with desirable or undesirable consequences of these. It is qualitative and heavily value-laden. Beginning early in the assessment process, policy makers and the possible options must be identified. Participation by policy makers and the potentially impacted parties is usually an asset. Unless study sponsors oppose, explicit policy recommendations are usually desirable if the assessors can convince the study users of their credibility and balance. Unfortunately, policy analysis has too often been conducted as an afterthought in impact assessments, truncated because of lack of time and resources.

Communication of Results. Effective communication requires significant efforts at information exchange with study users. Potential users who regard the assessment subject as important do long-range planning, face decisions pertaining to the issues addressed, and are receptive to externally produced information, and are most apt to be influenced. Study usefulness can be increased by early identification of the intended audience, interaction over the course of the study, attention to user perceptions of what constitutes a believable assessment, and dissemination through a variety of means (Berg et al., 1978). Having discussed what needs to be done, we turn now to how to do it.

Not surprisingly, the present state of the art is limited. The lack of usable predictive theories of sociotechnical change forces assessors to rely on their wits augmented by techniques. Rossini et al. (1978) found that the methodological literature that develops techniques usable in impact assessment has been largely ignored by technology assessors. The majority of assessors felt that the techniques made no substantive improvements and were excessively formal. We feel that the techniques noted in Table 2 can sometimes help to develop and present analyses efficiently; we suggest that they deserve serious, but not slavish, consideration.

The selection of techniques to use in various component activities of an impact assessment demands good judgment, in particular, regarding the extent to which quantification is appropriate. This is a function of the resources required versus those available, as well as the usefulness of formal techniques for particular tasks. Quantification requires considerably more expenditure of scarce resources; sometimes it is worth the cost. To be used, many of the techniques listed in Table 2 require data in hand and some assumptions to be met. This is not the place for their detailed examination. Suffice it to say that the techniques we have selected are those that tend to be relatively robust, providing useful structuring and outputs at manageable costs. For instance, input-output analysis might be of great interest in exploring the indirect economic impacts of a regional development; however, in general, export-base models will prove more workable within the confines of an assessment study. The credibility of techniques among assessment users is certainly a factor. Berg et al. (1978) report striking differences in the credibility of techniques among users of impact assessments. Statistical analyses, case studies, cost-benefit analysis, survey research, market analysis, environmental impact analysis, trend analysis, relevance trees, and decision analysis were rated at least moderately credible (in descending order as listed) by the 181 users surveyed. Brainstorming, cross-impact analysis, delphi techniques, systems-dynamics models, technological forecasting and scenario generation, and games and simulation models were less credible (in ascending order from brainstorming at the bottom, with 36 percent rating it moderately credible or better). As assessment practice matures, its systematization involving the use of techniques will remain a very live issue in our judgment.

B. Issues in the Conduct of Impact Assessment

We would like to touch unevenly upon six key areas of concern in this section: use of techniques, project management, interdisciplinarity, valuation, participation, and utilization.

Impact assessment is about a decade old. The decade has been a fruitful one for developing a general sense of what constitutes competent technology assessment, environmental impact assessment, and social impact assessment. For example, one is less apt to see elaborate quantitative gimmickry today in a technology assessment or endless listings of meaningless impacts in an environmental impact statement. However, systematic validation of particular techniques has seldom been undertaken to any significant extent, and it is badly needed. One might even assume a touch of "catch 22" in operation in such policy studies—illumination of a potential negative impact should result in modification of the technology to ameliorate the condition before it occurs. Impact assessments are typically decision-aiding policy studies intended to increase the available information for a particular pending issue: they are not academic reflections. As a result one usually does not find either time or budget available to design evaluative exercises so that one could determine what techniques work best in particular contexts. Comparative assessments conducted at the same time on the same topic could be highly informative as to how one should go about impact assessments (or for that matter, other forms of policy studies) (Rossini et al., 1976).

Project management and participation in impact assessments can be a perilous assignment. One technology assessment coincided with five divorces among the core team (the central participants over most of the project's life). Impact assessments are inherently difficult to bound. Technologies tend to relate to other technologies, and impacts tend to cascade one into another. Where does one draw the line? How does one achieve valid, yet timely, results? Typically, impact assessments involve the formation of an ad hoc study team based on the characteristics of the topic under investigation. Learning to work with

Table 2. Assessment Techniques

Technique/Description	Uses	References
Brainstorming: a group of individuals generate ideas with no criticism allowed	Problem definition Generating lists of potential impacts, affected parties, sectors, etc.	Ayres (1969: chap. 8) Sage (1977: chap. 5)
Interpretive structural modeling: directed graph representation of a particular relationship among all pairs of elements in a set to aid in structuring a complex issue area	Developing preliminary models of issue areas Impact evaluation	Malone (1975a, 1975b) Sage (1977: chap. 4) Watson (1978)
Trend extrapolation: a family of techniques to project time-series data using specified rules	Technology forecasting, both parameter changes and rates of substitution Social forecasting	Hencley and Yates (1974) Mitchell et al. (1975) Ayres (1969: chap. 6) Bright (1978)
Opinion measurement: a variety of techniques (including survey, panels, and Delphi) to accumulate inputs from a number of persons, often experts in an area of interest	Technology forecasting and description Social forecasting and description Impact identification Impact analysis, especially social	Linstone and Turoff (1975)–on Delphi Warwick and Lininger (1975)–on survey
Scenarios: composite descriptions of possible future states incorporating a number of characteristics	Social forecasting Technology forecasting Impact analysis Policy analysis Communication of results	Hencley and Yates (1974) Bright (1978) Mitchell et al. (1975)
Checklists: lists of factors to consider in a particular area of inquiry	Impact identification Policy sector identification	Leopold et al. (1971) Warner and Preston (1974)
Relevance trees: network displays that sequentially identify chains of cause-effect (or other) relationships	Impact identification and analysis	Hencley and Yates (1974) Bright (1978) The Futures Group (1975)–an example

Technique	Application	References
Cross-effect matrices: two-dimensional matrix representation to indicate interactions between two sets of elements	Impact identification and analysis; Analyzing the consequences of policy options	Bright (1978); Kruzic (1974)—on KSIM; Linstone and Turoff (1975); Sage (1977: chap. 5)
Simulation models: simplified representation of a real system used to explain dynamic relationships of the system	Technology forecasting; Impact analysis	J. F. Coates (1976); Wakeland (1976)—compares KSIM, QSIM, and Dynamo[a]; Sage (1977: chap. 6)
Sensitivity analysis: a general means to ascertain the sensitivity of system (model) parameters by making changes in important variables and observing their effects	Impact analysis; Policy analysis	Leininger et al. (1975)
Probabilistic techniques: stochastic properties are emphasized in understanding and predicting system behaviors	Technology forecasting; Impact analysis; Impact evaluation	Gordon and Stover (1976); Gohagen (1975)
Cost-benefit analysis: a set of techniques employed to determine the assets and liabilities accrued over the lifetime of a development	Economic impact analysis; Environmental impact analysis	Sassone and Schaffer (1978)
Export base models: estimates regional changes through a multiplier applied to the development in question	Economic impact analysis	Tiebout (1962); Isard (1960); Richardson (1969); Sage (1977: chap. 6)—on input-output analysis
Decision analysis: formal aid to compare alternatives by weighing the probabilities of occurrences and the magnitudes of their impacts	Impact evaluation; Policy analysis	Bross (1965); Howard et al. (1972)—an example; Sage (1977: chap. 7)
Policy capture: a technique for uncovering the decision rules by which individuals operate	Impact evaluation; Policy analysis	Hammond and Adelman (1976)

Source: Reprinted by permission of the publisher, from A. L. Porter, F. A. Rossini, S. R. Carpenter, and A. T. Roper, *A Guidebook for Technology Assessment and Impact Analysis*, chap. 5, Copyright 1980 by Elsevier North Holland, Inc.
[a]KSIM and QSIM are different cross-impact computer programs to perform cross-impact analysis; Dynamo is a program used for system dynamics.

each other within a confined time span while stretching one's limits of expertise to their fullest is a challenge. The inherently interdisciplinary nature of most assessments is a major feature to be considered. Based on a study of 24 technology assessment projects, we have compiled some observations that may be interesting to those who encounter impact assessments (Rossini et al., 1978).

Boundary conditions on a study are worth some initial reflection. As noted, the resources budgeted to accomplish a study markedly affect the way that study is conducted. The organization in which the assessment is carried out can affect the availability of the appropriate mix of expertise, the extent to which successful impact assessment work is rewarded, and the flexibility of personnel, time, and other resources to meet contingencies as the project unfolds. Small, relatively unstructured organizations tend to be most supportive of the interdisciplinary work involved in technology assessments. In contrast, status and rewards in academic departments traditionally go to disciplinary research, and divisional barriers and rigid accounting reduce operating flexibility in some large contract research organizations.

Characteristics of project leaders and research participants also seem to affect the conduct of impact assessment. Participatory, group-centered leadership style seems to be more effective than either a nondirective, permissive style or an authoritarian, directive style. Interestingly, the size of the core team seems to be an important factor. Review of the technology assessment experiences indicates that a core team size of three to five professionals is desirable to produce a well-integrated output from studies ranging up to about six person-years of effort. Such a team appears large enough for effective division of labor and small enough for good communication.

The interdisciplinary nature of the research brings forth some interesting problems in its own right. For example,

Data versus speculation.   Some researchers find it difficult to project into the future, preferring to have data in hand to support any conclusions drawn. This can cause serious problems for an impact assessment team, particularly when studying long-range implications and issues of high uncertainty.

Social impact assessment.   Some physical scientists and engineers see social impacts as "soft" and hence suitably addressed at the level of common sense. They sometimes clash with data-oriented social scientists whose disciplines indicate rigorous approaches toward social impact assessment. Differences among "hard" and "soft" scientists may be exacerbated by the scholarly pecking order, which favors quantification (Chubin et al., 1979).

Use of assessment techniques.   Many assessors ignore the formal techniques, perceiving them as recasting existing information with a false impression of precision. Others feel that techniques, such as cross-impact matrices, aid in focusing analyses and generating new insights—although the outputs are never more than "guesstimates." A small minority of practitioners value quantitative results of any sort as adding precision to the study.

Economists.   Curiously, economists appear to stand out as difficult colleagues in interdisciplinary impact assessment collaboration because of their specialized jargon, methodological preoccupations, unrealistic data demands, and disregard for the worth of the contributions of other disciplines. However, economics is essential to technology assessment. It is important, therefore, to have economists engaged in such studies who are attuned to the broader institutional and behavioral aspects as well as the policy implications of economic issues. Some assessment teams successfully employ surrogate economists, such as management scientists.

As with other policy studies, impact assessments are inherently value-laden. Special difficulties emerge, however, when assessors delude themselves into believing that they are performing purely scientific studies in which it is possible to maintain a truly neutral stance. We believe that to be impossible and, instead, see two viable alternative stances— adversarial assessment and explicit, "balanced" assessment. Adversarial impact assessment, as the name implies, entails separate analyses being prepared by the stakeholders in a given topic. Despite the consistency of such an approach with many of our policy processes, it has not become popular. The viable alternative is for the assessment team to attempt to present a balanced portrayal of the likely consequences of a given development. This entails explicit attention to value issues, both internal to the assessment and external to it.

At least five value concerns internal to the impact assessment can be identified. First of all, determination of the scope of the assessment must be made. For instance, a technology assessment on the automobile produced by Grad et al. (1975) narrowed its focus to the analysis of automobile air pollution problems using current technologies, thereby excluding energy-consumption issues from consideration and thus eliminating end-states that later proved embarassingly important. Selection of evaluation criteria is often in the hands of the assessors themselves. For instance, assessors addressing a proposed new highway facility might choose to ignore the issue of neighborhood integrity, define neighborhood in different ways, or come up with differing measures for "integrity." Methodological choices may seem innocuous, but they can color results. For example, the more assessors weigh quantifiable impacts, the more likely they are to emphasize technological and economic impacts more highly than the social impacts that are more difficult to quantify. Disciplinary approach preferences can also pervade an impact assessment. To refine an old tale, one might imagine an engineer, a sociologist, and an economist shipwrecked on a desert island with only canned food. The engineer addresses their problem by banging cans open on a rock; the sociologist waits to survey his two colleagues on the best approach. Meanwhile, the economist has a more perfect methodology: He simply assumes the existence of a can opener. Less facetiously, an impact assessment on a given topic directed by a physical scientist could well differ in approach taken and resultant conclusions from one directed by a social scientist. We should not overstate the importance of disciplinary differences among impact assessors. Rather, Rokeach (1973) has documented the value and cultural homogeniety one finds in the scientific community. One might therefore ask whether an impact assessment conducted by professionals is adequate to reflect the values of the wider society.

External value issues arise from the societal context for the impact assessment in question. Costs and benefits are weighed in terms of values, and societal values are not monolithic. In general, it seems advisable to consider alternative value sets representative of the different primary stakeholder groups (Carpenter and Rossini, 1977). Along another dimension, one can ponder whether impact assessments should be based on current or future societal values as the basis for evaluation. To the extent that one can forecast value shifts, these provide an alternative to present values against which to gauge future projected impacts. A third sort of external value issue concerns the acceptance of current technologies. Assessors should beware overstatement of the case for present technological approaches vis-a-vis less familiar alternatives. Particularly in the case of imminent technological changes, one is apt to find staunchly defended stakes in the current technologies.

Given the value sensitivity of impact assessments, what should be the proper extent of participation by outside interests? One stance holds that outside involvement should be minimized to reduce the appearance of bias. For example, Ford Motor Company supported a study of automobile propulsion alternatives by the Jet Propulsion Lab on which Ford and other outside interests were kept at a distance to take full advantage of the lab's scientific credentials. A second approach attempts to represent a full range of values by providing for participation by stakeholder representatives. Environmental impact statement procedural requirements specify hearings and reviews to provide opportunity for such participation. In fact, in a number of environmental impact assessments, commentary received or court actions (a sort of post hoc participation) have markedly altered the scope and findings of the assessments. Should one desire a participatory stance, a number of options are conceivable:

Role playing by the assessment team members to represent viewpoints of critical constituencies

Opportunities for interested parties to comment on the assessment during the course of its conduct

Conferences during the course of the impact assessment to inform potentially interested parties of the possible consequences, then to solicit their opinions

Interviews with selected parties-at-interest during the assessment process

Direct stakeholder participation in the impact assessment itself; for instance, a six-member public interest group was formed in association with an assessment of solar energy to provide nontechnical judgments on relevant political and socioeconomic consequences (Arnstein, 1975)

Adversary assessments in which stakeholder groups perform their own assessments (Rossini et al., 1976).

Attaining a proper and workable balance between professional analysis and public participation is a major current concern in the impact assessment community.

Given that impact assessment is a decision-aiding form of policy analysis, one should appropriately ask how it is being used. The findings of a utilization study of TAs by Berg et al. (1978) are highly informative. The 280 potential TA users surveyed indicated that the assessments were most useful as background information and least useful for decision making. In a parallel set of measures, technology assessments most influenced organizations by bringing issues to the attention of decision makers, and least in selecting policy options. The results indicate that TAs are no more than moderately influential; environmental impact statements seem to share a similar record. Only rarely do impact assessments lead directly to policy actions.

The study by Berg and his colleagues, buttressed by some additional observations (Porter et al., 1980), indicates some potentially effective courses of action to enhance the utilization of impact assessments. For one, the communication process should not await completion of the study. Before the study is undertaken, it should be oriented to the potential target users. For instance, some user audiences have strong technical capabilities; others do not. The study should be formulated accordingly. During the course of the study, several actions appear to increase the utilization of the study's results. Berg and his colleagues found that involvement of the potential users as active participants in the study, as reviewers of drafts of the impact assessment, and as recipients of specific pieces of information through individual contacts all enhanced utilization. Interaction between assessors and potential users in conferences and briefings, or provision of input data to the assessors, were only moderate enhancers of eventual utilization. Surprisingly, involvement on advisory or oversight committees did not seem to increase utilization of the study by those so involved. Berg and his colleagues also report that use of an impact assessment is unlikely unless users view the methods employed in the study as credible. The content of greatest interest to the potential users was

Identification of key areas of uncertainty
Identification of key assumptions in the analysis
Identification and analysis of technological alternatives
Identification and analysis of direct impacts
Identification of external factors or omitted variables that could affect results

It must be noted, however, that interaction with potential users does incur costs in terms of time and study resources, as well as risks to the maintenance of assessment integrity and credibility. Following completion of the study, it appears that, as appropriate from study context, widespread dissemination efforts through a variety of media should be considered.

IV. CONCLUSIONS AND IMPLICATIONS FOR THE POLICY PROCESS

Technology is a dominant force in our society. It is therefore not surprising to observe that most policies of consequence today address issues with significant technological content. Technological policies are often less reversible than others because of the magnitude of investments, intricate linkages with other technologies, and widespreading implications. Serious national and international problems, including the needs to increase productivity and develop energy sources, yet protect the natural and human environments, confront us. Thus, understanding of the innovation process and assessment of its implications in advance of implementation are obvious needs.

From our perspective, however, there has been increased knowledge of innovation and remarkable progress in performing impact assessment during the 1970s. Yet these tasks are so inherently difficult that one can see how some could assert that they are impossible. How do you understand and harness human creativity, and how can you project the implications of large-scale developments that involve compounding guesstimates of future societal values, economic conditions, and alternative technological developments as well? We are striving to understand complex sociotechnical systems, yet we lack decent theory to guide our impact projections. Our knowledge is fragmented and our methodologies are intriguing, but largely unproven. Is this cause for despair? We think not.

Rather, the situation appears quite promising if one considers any increase in useful information as helpful in formulating modestly better policy decisions on such crucial issues. Indeed, the simple asking of broader and more far-reaching questions appears to have expanded the perspectives of our policy making dramatically over the past decade. Possibly of the greatest long-term importance, the increasing availability of information on technological prospects can serve to open up the policy processes. An ill-intentioned policy maker is less apt to act rashly if an informed opposition lurks with telling information.

REFERENCES

Arnstein, S. R. (1975). A working model for public participation. *Public Administration Review 35*: 70–73.

Ascher, W. (1978). *Forecasting: An Appraisal for Policy Makers and Planners*. Johns Hopkins University Press, Baltimore.

Ayres, R. U. (1969). *Technological Forecasting and Long-Range Planning*. McGraw-Hill, New York, chaps. 6, 8.

Baker, G. L., et al. (1963). *A Century of Service: The First 100 Years of the United States Department of Agriculture*. U.S. Department of Agriculture, Washington, DC.

Battelle-Columbus Laboratories (1973). *Interactions of Science and Technology in the Innovative Process: Some Case Studies*. Report for the National Science Foundation NSF-C667, Columbus, OH.

Berg, M. R. (1975). Methodology. In *Perspectives on Technology Assessment*, S. Arnstein and A. Christakis (Eds.). Science and Technology Publishers, Jerusalem, pp. 63–72.

Berg, M. R., Brudney, J. L., Fuller, T. D., Michael, D. N., and Roth, B. K. (1978). Factors affecting utilization of technology assessment studies in policy-making. University of Michigan, Center for Research on Utilization of Scientific Knowledge, , Institute for Social Research, Ann Arbor, MI.

Bright, J. R. (1978). *Practical Technology Forecasting: Concepts and Exercises*. Industrial Management Center, Austin, TX.

Bross, I. D. (1965). *Design for Decision*. Free Press, New York.

Brown, L. A. (1968). *Diffusion Dynamics: A Review and Revision of the Quantitative Theory of the Spatial Diffusion of Innovation*. Lund, Sweden.

––– (1969). Diffusion of innovation: A macro view. *Economic Development and Cultural Change 17*: 89–209.

Capron, W. F. (Ed.) (1971). *Technological Change in Regulated Industries*. Brookings Institution, Washington, DC.

Cardwell, D. S. L. (1971). *From Watt to Clausis: Thermodynamics in the Early Industrial Age*, Cornell University Press, Ithaca, NY.

Carpenter, S. R., and Rossini, F. A. (1977). Value dimensions of technology assessment. In *The General Systems Paradigm: Science of Change and Change of Science*. The Society for General Systems Research, Washington, DC, pp. 463–469.

Casper, B. M. (1978). The rhetoric and reality of congressional technology assessment. *Bulletin of the Atomic Scientists 34* (February): 20–31.

Charpie, R. L. (1967). *Technological Innovation: Its Environment and Management*. U.S. Department of Commerce Report, GPO 0-242-736. U.S. Department of Commerce, Washington, DC.

Chubin, D. E., Rossini, F. A., Porter, A. L., and Mitroff, I. I. (1979). Experimental technology assessment: Explorations in processes of interdisciplinary team research. *Technological Forecasting and Social Change 15*: 87–94.

Coates, J. F. (1976). Technology assessment–A tool kit. *Chemtech*, June, 1976, pp. 372–383.

Coates, V. T. (1979). Technology assessment in federal agencies, 1971–1976. George Washington University, Washington, DC. (Available from NTIS #PB-295969).

Comanor, W. S. (1967). Market structure, product differentiation and industrial research. *Quarterly Journal of Economics 81*: 639–651.

Daddario, E. Q. (1967). Technology assessment: Statement of Chairman, Subcommittee on Science, Research, and Development. 90th Congress, 1st Session.

Doctors, S. I. (1969). *The Role of the Federal Agencies in Technology Transfer.* M.I.T. Press, Cambridge, MA.

Farrington, B. (1946). *Greek Science.* Penguin, Harmondsworth, England.

Futures Group (1975). Technology assessment of geothermal energy resource development. Futures Group, Glastonbury, CT.

Gellman Research Associates (1974). *Economic Regulation and Technological Innovation: A Cross-National Survey of Literature and Analysis.* Prepared for the National R&D Assessment Program, National Science Foundation, Gellman Research Associates, Philadelphia.

Gendron, B. (1977). *Technology and the Human Condition.* St. Martin's, New York.

Gohagan, J. K. (1975). A practical bayesian methodology for program planning and evaluation. ORSA/TIMS Meeting, Law Vegas, 17–19 November.

Gordon, T. J., and Stover, J. (1976). Using perceptions and data about the future to improve the simulation of complex systems. *Technological Forecasting and Social Change 9*: 191–211.

Grad, F. P., Rosenthal, A. J., Rockett, L. R., Fay, J. A., Heywood, J., Kain, J. F., Ingram, G. K., Harrison, D., and Tietenberg, T. (1975). *The Automobile.* University of Oklahoma Press, Norman.

Griliches, Zvi (1957). Hybrid corn: An exploration in the economics of technological change. *Econometrica 25*: 501–22.

Hagerstrand, T. (1968). Diffusion of innovations. In *The International Encyclopedia of the Social Sciences*, D. L. Sills (Ed.). Macmillan, New York, pp. 174–177.

Hahn, W. (1977). Technology assessment: Some alternative perceptions and its implications outside the United States. Testimony before the Subcommittee on Science, Research, and Technology of the House Committee on Science and Technology, August 3. Mimeo, 56 pp.

Hamberg, D. (1966). *R&D: Essays on the Economics of Research and Development.* Random House, New York.

Hammond, K. R., and Adelman, L. (1976). Science, values, and human judgment. *Science 194* (October 22): 389–396.

Hencley, S., and Yates, J. R. (Eds.) (1974). *Futures in Education: Methodologies.* McCutchan, Berkeley, CA.

Henschel, R. L. (1976). *On the Future of Social Prediction.* Bobbs-Merrill, Indianapolis, IN.

Hollander, S. (1965). *The Sources of Increased Efficiency: A Study of Dupont Rayon Plants.* M.I.T. Press, Cambridge, MA.

Howard, R. A., Matheson, J. E., and North, D. W. (1972). The decision to seed hurricanes. *Science 176* (June 16): 1191–1202.

Isard, W. (1960). *Methods of Regional Analysis: An Introduction to Regional Science.* Wiley, New York, chap. 6.

Jewkes, J., Sawyers, D., and Stillerman, R. (1965). *The Sources of Invention.* Norton, New York.

Jones, M. V. (1971). A technology assessment methodology: Some basic propositions. Report MTR6009, Vol. 1, (June) for the Office of Science and Technology, Mitre Corporation, Washington, DC.

Kelly, P., Kranzberg, M., Rossini, F. A., Baker, N. R., Tarpley, F. A., and Mitzner, M. (1978). *Technological Innovation: A Critical Review of Current Knowledge, Volume I, The Ecology of Innovation.* San Francisco Press, San Francisco.

Knoblauch, H. C., et al. (1962). *State Agricultural Experiment Stations: A History of Research Policy and Procedure.* USDA Miscellaneous Publication Number 904. U.S. Department of Agriculture, Washington, DC.

Kruzic, P. G. (1974). Cross-Impact Simulation in Water Resources Planning. Report 74-12 to U.S. Army Engineer Institute for Water Resources. SRI, Fort Belvior, VA, Palo Alto, CA.

LaPorte, T., and Metlay, D. (1974). *Technology Observed: Attitudes of a Wary Publc.* Working Paper No. 9, Institute of Governmental Studies, University of California, Berkeley.

Leininger, G., Jutila, S., King, J., Muraco, W., and Hansell, J. (1975). *The Total Assessment Profile.* University of Toledo, Toledo, OH (NTIS No. N75-31919/4).

Leopold, L. B., Clarke, F. E., Henshaw, B. B., and Balsley, J. R. (1971). *A Procedure for Evaluating Environmental Impact.* U.S. Geological Survey, Washington, DC, Circulation 645.

Linstone, H. A., and Turoff, M. (Eds.) 1975). *The Delphi Method: Techniques and Applications.* Addison-Wesley Advanced Books Program, Reading, MA.

Malone, D. W. (1975a). An overview of interpretitive structural modeling. In *Perspective on Technology Assessment*, S. Arnstein and A. Christakis (Eds.). Science and Technology Publishers, Jerusalem, pp. 229–233.

––– (1975b). An introduction to the application of interpretive structural modeling. In *Portraits of Complexity.* Battelle Monograph No. 9, Columbus, OH.

Maloney, J. D., Jr. (in press). Impact assessment in the private sector: The state of the art. In *Integrated Impact Assessment*, F. A. Rossini, A. L. Porter, and C. P. Wolf (Eds.).

Mansfield, E. (1961). Technical change and rate of innovation. *Econometrica 29*: 741–66.

––– (1966). *Technological Change: Measurement, Determinants and Diffusion.* Report to the President, National Committee on Technology, Automation, and Economic Progress, Washington, DC.

––– (1971). *Technological Change.* Norton, New York.

Metlay, D. (1972). Public attributes toward technology: A preliminary report. In *Social Change, Public Response, and the Regulation of Large Scale Technology*, T. A. LaPorte, et al. (Eds.). Institute for Governmental Studies, University of California, Berkeley, pp. 71–123.

Mitchell, A., Dodge, B. H., Kruzic, P. G., Miller, D. C., Schwartz, P., and Suta, B. E. (1975). *Handbook of Forecasting Techniques.* Stanford Research Institute Report to U.S. Army Corps of Engineers Institute for Water Resources, AD-A019 280. Available from NTIS, Springfield, VA.

Mueller, W. F. (1962). The origins of the basic inventions underlying duPont's major product and process innovations, 1920–1950. In *The Rate and Direction of Inventive Activity*, R. R. Nelson (Ed.). Princeton University Press, Princeton, NJ.

Myers, S., and Marquis, D. G. (1969). Successful industrial innovations. NSF 69-17, National Science Foundation, Washington, DC.

Nabseth, L., and Ray, G. F. (1974). *The Diffusion of New Industrial Processes*, Cambridge University Press, Cambridge.

Nelson, R. R. (1962). The link between science and invention: The case of the transistor. In *The Rate and Direction of Inventive Activity*, R. R. Nelson (Ed.). Princeton University Press, Princeton, NJ, pp. 549–583.

Oppenheim, S. C. (1957). Comments. *Patent, Trademark, and Copyright Journal 52*: 135–136.

Porter, A. L., and Rossini, F. A. (1980). Technology assessment/environmental impact assessment: Toward integrated impact assessment. *IEEE Transactions on Systems, Man, and Cybernetics SMC-10*: 417–424.

Porter, A. L., Rossini, F. A., Carpenter, S. R., and Roper, A. T. (1980). *A Guidebook for Technology Assessment and Impact Analysis*. Elsevier North Holland, New York.

Richardson, H. W. (1969). *Elements of Regional Economics*. Praeger, New York.

Rogers, E. M., and Shoemaker, F. F. (1971). *Communication of Innovations: A Cross Cultural Approach*. Free Press, New York.

Rokeach, M. (1973). *The Nature of Human Values*. Free Press, New York.

Rossini, F. A., and Bozeman, B. (1977). National strategies for technological innovation. *Administration and Society 9*: 81–110.

Rossini, F. A., Porter, A. L., Kelly, P., and Chubin, D. E. (1978). *Frameworks and Factors Affecting Integration Within Technology Assessments*. Report to the National Science Foundation, Grant ERS 76-04474. Georgia Institute of Technology, Atlanta.

Rossini, F. A., Porter, A. L., and Zucker, E. (1976). Multiple technology assessments. *Journal of the International Society for Technology Assessment 2*: 21–28.

Rubenstein, A. H. (1964). Organizational factors affecting research and development decision-making in large decentralized companies. *Management Science 10*: 618–634.

Sage, A. P. (1977). *Methodology for Large Scale Systems*. McGraw-Hill, New York.

Sassone, P. G., and Schaffer, W. A. (1978). *Cost-Benefit Analysis: A Handbook*. Academic Press, New York.

Scherer, F. M. (1967). Research and development resource allocation under rivalry. *Quarterly Journal of Economics 81*: 359–394.

Schwartz, J. J. (1973). The decision to innovate. D.B.A. dissertation, Harvard University, Cambridge, MA.

Sherwin, C. W., and Isenson, R. S. (1967). Project hindsight: A Defense Department study of the utility of research. *Science 156*: 1571–1577.

Tiebout, C. M. (1962). *The Community Economic Base Study*. Committee for Economic Development, Washington, DC.

TRACES (Technology in Retrospect and Critical Events *in Science*) (1968). Report NSF-C535, Illinois Institute of Technology Research Institute, Chicago.

U.S. Congress, House Subcommittee on Science, Research, and Technology (1978). Review of the Office of Technology Assessment and its Organic Act. U.S. Government Printing Office, Washington, DC.

U.S. Congress, Office of Technology Assessment (1976). Hearings before Technology Assessment Board: Technology assessment activities in the industrial, academic, and governmental communities, June 8, 9, 10, 14. U.S. Government Printing Office, Washington, DC.

U.S. Council on Environmental Quality (1978). National Environmental Policy Act—regulations for implementation of procedural provisions. *Federal Register 36* (November 29): Part 6, 55978–56007.

U.S. Nuclear Regulatory Commission (1976). Final generic environmental statement of the use of recycled plutonium in mixed oxide fuel in light water cooled reactors (PB 256 452). NTIS, Washington, DC.)

U.S. Office of Management and Budget (1974). *Social Indicators, 1973*. Office of Management and Budget, Washington, DC.

Utterback, J. M. (1973). Innovation in industry and diffusion of technology. Working Paper, Graduate School of Business, University of Indiana, Bloomington.

Wakeland, W. (1976). QSIM 2: A low budget heuristic approach to modeling and forecasting. *Technological Forecasting and Social Change 9*: 213-229.

Warner, M. L., and Preston, E. H. (1974). *A Review of Environmental Impact Assessment Methodologies*. Prepared for EPA, Office of Research and Development, U.S. Government Printing Office, Washington, DC.

Warwick, D. P., and Lininger, C. A. (1975). *The Sample Survey: Theory and Practice*. McGraw-Hill, New York.

Watson, R. H. (1978). Interpretive structural modeling: A useful tool for technology assessment. *Technological Forecasting and Social Change 11*(2): 165-185.

Wenk, E., Jr., and Kuehn, T. J. (1977). Interinstitutional networks in technological delivery systems. In *Science and Technology Policy*, J. Haberer (Ed.). Lexington Books, Lexington, MA, pp. 153-175.

31

Health Policy

David J. Falcone / Duke University Medical Center, Durham, North Carolina

I. INTRODUCTION

This chapter reviews major issues in health policy and ways of analyzing them. After some definitional questions are aired, the evolution of health policy in the United States is summarized. Following this is a discussion of the state of the art of health policy analysis and an examination of its influence—in the form of its principal disciplinary basis, health services research—on policy formation.

The field is multidimensional and, partly because it is interdisciplinary, dynamic, and relatively new, it has not undergone much of the self-examination that it will have to endure as it matures. Therefore, there probably will be some disagreement about where the boundaries of the field should be located. This is not the place to entertain a methodological discussion on whether one can conduct political analysis that is not policy analysis. (The French handle this semantically by using policy and politics interchangeably; elsewhere the issue is not resolved so neatly.) In order to reflect the state of the art, and not impose an artificial order on the field, it must be recognized that there can be studies of health politics, economics, sociology, and administration that would not style themselves as health policy analyses. By way of illustration, probably the leading journal in the field, *The Journal of Health Politics, Policy and Law*, by its very title implies that political and policy analyses can be distinguished. In fact, this journal regularly carries articles focusing on the policy process or medical care issues (e.g., death and dying) that would require tenuous inference to relate to policy—at least their policy relevance would be no less subtle than anything written on areas where governments have an expressed involvement.

Thus, the following discussion attempts to survey the field with a caveat that the parameters, so to speak, are very difficult to estimate. One conclusion to be drawn from this survey is that the progression of health policy and the state of the art of health policy analysis are closely related, with the former likely to exert more influence in their reciprocal development.

II. HEALTH POLICY

Several types of policy directly affect or seek to affect health. Those that come readily to mind are primarily legislative, but also judicial and public administrative decisions dealing with the rates of production, geographic and specialty distribution of health manpower; health care financing; assurance of the quality of health personnel, institutions, and services; occupational safety and environmental protection; and attempts to limit the consumption of presumably destructive substances such as alcohol, tobacco, and synthetic carcinogens. In some instances, the indirect effects on health of housing, income maintenance, or other welfare policies may be even more consequential than the direct effects of policies that deal patently with health. Nevertheless, it is useful to limit the conception of health policy to the conventional notion of public decisions that seek primarily to affect health or principal actors—professional and institutional—in their roles in the health arena. Indeed, employing this restriction allows one to make statements such as the one above positing that some other policies may ultimately have a more telling impact on health than more strictly health policies, or that there is a need for integrating different policy areas (health and welfare are perhaps those most frequently cited).[1]

III. POLICY

The problem of deriving a useful definition of health policy obviously requires some specification of the meaning of policy. This is an imposing task, not because of the scarcity of meanings with some currency, but because of the lack of commonly accepted conceptions. If they have an underlying dimension, it would be that of an *orientation* that forms the basis for decision rules, whether the decisions are what Amatai Etzioni has called "bit" or "contextuating."[2] In this view, a given policy may virtually preordain that all legislative, bureaucratic, judicial, and administrative actions would be regarded as of the "bit" variety—that is, serially incremental, but part of a shifting policy context. The evolution of the welfare state—at least up until the mid 1970s—is an example of this pattern. The policy toward societal (via government) responsibility for the equality of opportunity and maintenance of a minimally acceptable standard of living has been loosely formulated so as not to collide with the shibboleths of classic liberalism. Therefore, U.S. health policies, such as the Maternal and Child Health/Crippled Children Services Program under the Social Security Act, the Kerr-Mills federal-state conditional granting to provide care for the elderly poor, and the Comprehensive Health Planning Program, Regional Medical Program, Medicare, and Medicaid have been targeted to specific beneficiaries or problem areas as resources have permitted and groups have "demanded."[3]

When we think of policy as an orientation, however, we usually think of a "contextuating" government action, viz., one that explicitly initiates a new government strategy for attacking a problem and sets the stage for further predictable actions. The Social Security Act is a prime example, although even its original set of provisions can be viewed as a pragmatic, episodic response to a perceived crisis. The distinction between contextuating and bit policy is drawn here not so much to set forth a rudimentary typology as to indicate that what we really are distinguishing are explicit and implicit policies. There has been little in the way of distinctively contextuating policy in the United States dealing with health, although some have so regarded the 1946 Hospital Survey and Construction (Hill-Burton) Act, because it marked the legitimacy of at least a measure of government-induced health planning, and Medicare, because it was a "health" as opposed to welfare (i.e., not a means-tested) program.[4]

For this reason, there is a reigning claim that we have no national health policy. (Related to this is the claim that we have no health system but rather a collage of modes of health services delivery.) In the perspective suggested in the foregoing discussion, this claim turns into one that holds that the financing and organization of health care is not yet a government priority, that the United States has not decided to launch an articulated, coordinated movement toward the assumption of societal responsibility for health and the attempt to make health services universally available and accessible.

IV. HEALTH AND HEALTH CARE

If health policy analysis is bounded by its subject matter, then the question arises as to what is meant by health and health care. That there is no dearth of literature on this topic is understandable in light of the fact that the societal meaning of health at any given time obviously has profound consequences for policy. For the Greeks, health was a state of harmony, and some commentators such as Henry Sigerist think that "this is still the best general explanation we have."[5] To some extent this conception is beginning to be institutionalized in the form of the holistic health movement.[6]

A less romantic view is that health is freedom from disease. In either conception, however, as David Banta has put it, "health care could become a tyranny"[7] if defined too broadly, particularly in the case of mental illness and chronic disease (e.g., in some ways, aging at a certain point could be viewed as an illness). Currently, the most widely cited definition of health, that posited by the World Health Organization, if implemented, might invite the tyranny that concerns Banta. According to this definition, health is a "state of complete physical, mental and social well-being and not merely the absence of disease or infirmity."[8] When one takes into consideration the perceptual (e.g., what is "pain") and social (e.g., what is "disability") factors involved in the determination of what constitutes health and disease, there is almost no limit to the scope of health care.

A new issue has been raised by the quantification of health status indices, incorporating social as well as biological factors, which would seem to require some decision about composite cutoff points to designate a threshold of health.[9] The activism of one's orientation then would determine where one would make the cut.

Related to the activism-passivism continuum on which health, and thus health care, can be conceived is the differentiation between personal health and public health services.[10] This distinction is more marked in the United States than in other countries, but it is ubiquitous. Briefly, the public health perspective envisions health in terms of populations or groups, whereas, in the extreme, personal health services are delivered in a mythically unique doctor (or presumably some other health professional)–patient relationship. This distinction is shaded in particular instances (e.g., family practitioners supposedly view their patients in the context of their families and communities, and the public health service does deliver health care to individuals), but it exists in reality and motivates profound differences in attitudes toward policy. For example, the American

Public Health Association has traditionally supported comprehensive universal and publicly administered national health insurance programs in opposition to representatives of the personal health care sector, such as the American Medical Association and, to a lesser extent, the American Hospital Association.[11]

Generally speaking, those with a public health orientation also tend to take a relatively more active stance on sumptuary policies such as those relating to tobacco and alcohol. With some reservations, one could say that when the inevitable clashes between individual liberty and perceived public good occur, the public health persuasion tends to emphasize the latter.

Health and health care obviously are portmanteau terms, as illustrated by the foregoing catalog of conceptions. They all are within the ambit of health policy analysis and often underlie scholarly and public debate—for example, whether the "health" care of the elderly is becoming "overmedicalized." This point will be elaborated in the discussion below on the evolution of U.S. health policy.

V. THE HISTORY OF U.S. HEALTH POLICY: AN OVERVIEW

The evolution of health policy in the United States can be divided into three stages. Vestiges of the past and primordia of the future are evident in each, but the developments seem to follow a historical pattern that has paralleled the relative dominance of classic versus social or reform liberalism in American political culture. In fact, with a tolerable degree of oversimplification, milestones in health policy can be seen as "caused" by different shades of emphasis in the liberal tradition.[12] This is not to say that the underlying factors in the shaping of health policy were not primarily economic or episodic—no one would discount the effects of the Depression, for example—only that the justification for them has been couched in rubrics drawn from two major strains in liberalism: on that stresses the policy goal of equality of opportunity versus another that pursues absolute equalitarianism.

The three stages, the last of which is still emerging and may be regarded as a synthesis of (or compromise between) the first two, can be delineated according to the prevailing societal conception of health in each, that is, whether health care is viewed as (1) a public good, (2) a basic right, or (3) a limited resource.

A. Health Care as a Public Good

This is not the place, and it is probably unnecessary to outline the construct of a public good. In the context of this discussion, suffice it to say that from the late nineteenth century until the Great Depression, the dominant view was that society at large derived a collective benefit from the provision of a minimum level of health care to all, that it was in each *individual's* best interest for government to *impose* a measure of health care. As Jaeger has put it, the primary basis for early U.S. health policy was "economic protectionism."[13] Therefore, quarantine policy was enforced because of the severe economic consequences stemming from the spread of communicable diseases, a threat exacerbated by the urbanization accompanying the Industrial Revolution. Similarly, marine hospitals were established to limit the potential harm to the community from the disease-carrying,

often homeless derelicts who plied the sea trade on which America was heavily dependent. Later, in a decidedly more positive vein, the Progressives argued that our industry,
productivity, and national security was undermined by illness, absenteeism, and disability
and that these losses were unnecessarily left largely to chance. Variations on this theme
were echoed by Theodore and Franklin Roosevelt,[14] Harry Truman,[15] and Dwight Eisenhower,[16] among others.

At first, even some of the most limited, essentially negative, or defensive policies
were criticized by extreme market determinists such as Herbert Spencer; for example,
public provision of care for the insane was not consonant with "social Darwinism."[17]
Although this stance was not necessarily characteristic of the climate of opinion about
health policy (or any other type of policy, for that matter) during the late nineteenth
century, it was sufficiently legitimate to be the explicit basis for President Pierce's veto of
a bill authorizing federal land grants for mental hosptials.[18]

Coupled with economic protectionism in the development of U.S. policy, but certainly not as important and less distinctive to this country, has been a limited paternalism,
as reflected in Herbert Hoover's contention that social and health insurance should rest
on the notion "that the responsibility of the people as a whole is to provide only a
reasonable subsistence . . . and not destroy private institutions and efforts."[19] It is safe to
say that paternalism never has been as pronounced in the United States as has been the
poor-law mentality in the United Kingdom. However, it was a necessary concession to the
decline of philanthropy and to the emergence of reform liberalism with a stress on derived as well as natural rights. The American compromise resulting from the tension between classic liberalism's focus on the preservation of individual autonomy and the expression of free choice and reform liberalism's (including pragmatism's) emphasis on the
need to alter social conditions so as to lessen the impact of adversity, was the view that
the state could take steps to encourage equality of opportunity, that is, to provide individuals the chance to manifest their inherent or acquired inequalities.

Partly as a result of the prevalence of this view, relative to other nations, the assumption of governmental responsibility for the provision of health services in the United
States has lagged behind public education but, in some respects, has outpaced more direct
welfare measures.[20] The first policies of this type were targeted at the blind and disabled,
the elderly poor, needy mothers and children, and crippled children.

B. The Right to Health

Gradually, the legitimacy of government activity to ameliorate misfortune that was
largely beyond the control of the afflicted began to be expanded to include a duty to provide—or ensure the provision—of health care because of individuals' social "right to
health." This notion has not been embodied in policy, but it has been mentioned in the
rhetoric supporting authoritative proposals dating at least as far back as a 1929 address by
Franklin Roosevelt. In 1944 this right became a keystone of national policy, FDR's
"Second Bill of Rights." It was enunciated in his State of the Union message as:[21]

> regardless of station, race or creed . . .
> The right to adequate medical care and the opportunity to achieve and enjoy
> good health;
> The right to adequate protection from the economic fears of old age, sickness,
> unemployment. . . .

Jaeger notes that by 1952 this statement of rights had been expanded by a presidential commission "to include more than just freedom from disease, pain and untimely death, for health now was interpreted to mean 'optional physical, mental and social efficiency and well-being.'"[22]

The right to health has been reasserted by succeeding Presidents and has become a rallying phrase in congressional debate on a variety of national health insurance proposals. It also was a force in the office of Economic Opportunity Neighborhood Health Centers movement of the 1960s. However, as a rationale for policy, the right to health has been overshadowed somewhat by a preoccupation with cost control and by the perceived need to restructure the health care delivery system in order to achieve a higher overall marginal productivity of resources. In short, one could say that the focus now is on the optimum mentioned in the 1952 commission's statement, and that term is being used in its economic sense.

C. Health Care as a Limited Resource

The shift in emphasis can be attributed to trends outside the ideological mainstream highlighted in the foregoing discussion. Of course, even the most politically voluntaristic observer would concede that traditional ideological concerns fluctuate with varying economic circumstances or, at least, that the availability of resources is an enabling factor in the translation of proposals into policy. Another significant conditioning factor in the development of health (as well as other) policy has been the shifting power of the federal versus subnational governments which, in turn, has been the result of cataclysmic environmental changes such as those surrounding World War II and the Great Depression. The former gave rise to titles dealing with health in the Social Security Act, which has been the framework for subsequent redistributive policy such as Titles XVIII (Medicare), XIX (Medicaid), and XX (special services). Although it was not the first legislation to do so, the Social Security Act used the conditional grant to obviate possible constitutional impediments. By 1937 the Supreme Court acknowledged that federal spending power sanctioned this device.

Some portray the New Deal as the thin edge of the wedge in government intrusion into the personal health services sector. Others point in this regard to what was first seen as a more benign conditional grant program to encourage "planned" hospital construction and renovation, the Hill-Burton Act of 1946. The act was an amendment to the Public Health Service Act, as have been other major manpower and planning acts. Hill-Burton was part of the federal program that used "displaced" wartime expenditures in an attempt to revive the hospital industry and reduce the geographic maldistribution of services. In part it accomplished this, but it also established (what now seem to be) limited controls (e.g., the requirement that a recipient hospital render a given portion of free care) and legitimized large-scale government activity at the core of the health system.

By the late 1970s, the government's role, particularly that of the federal government, had expanded greatly (some would say hypertrophically). In 1965, 25 percent of all national health expenditures were public; the corresponding figure for 1980 is 41.1 percent. Of all public expenditures, 70 percent were made by the federal government in 1980, versus 52 percent in 1965.[23] Not only had programs covering specific segments of the population grown in number and scope, the numbers of beneficiaries had increased and health costs had spiraled. This made the health care industry oligopsonistic at least, and some components (e.g. nursing homes) in most states are near monopsonies. As suggested by cross-national comparisons as well as by common sense, this concentration of resources has resulted in a sharpened, if somewhat ineffectual, cost consciousness.[24] The concentration has been heightened by the federalization of financing and, because a significant proportion of state and local expenditures are federally stimulated (e.g., Medicaid and Title XX are conditional grant programs), the effect has perhaps been even more marked than the intergovernmental shift in expenditures would lead one to expect.

Cost consciousness has been expressed at the federal level in the form of what has been termed, some would say euphemistically, planning policy. Initially, "representative" advisory agencies (comprehensive health planning agencies) were formed at the state and local levels to review the purchase of facilities and equipment and new construction. Probably the summary verdict on the effectiveness of these agencies in restraining "unneeded" expansion of the health services delivery network would be that they failed from a process evaluation perspective in providing effective consumer representation and, with respect to outputs, they did not really prevent an unnecessary proliferation of services.[25] To correct these deficiencies, health systems agencies (HSAs) were set up under the legislative authority of Public Law 93-641 with more specific representation mandates and more substantial enforcement powers over resource allocation decisions. Criticism of the functioning of CHPs and HSAs (along with agencies such as PSROs, which are charged with, in effect, cost-benefit review of health professionals decisions) has centered on the fact that (although this might not have been the way the indictments were explicitly phrased) they have been charged with pursuing regulation in lieu of policy. The combined activities of these agencies have been described as constituting a patchwork quilt of regulatory decisions that do not add up to a basic framework for resource allocation. This has caused some influential policy actors to look to national health insurance as a mechanism for regulating resource allocations and delivery modes, thus vindicating the claims of the medical establishment that government financing implies government control.

The emphasis on "rationalization" of the allocation of health resources—reorganization; substitution of paramedical personnel for physicians, ambulatory for inpatient care, family practice for specialist and subspecialist care; shared services versus pure competition among hospitals; an emphasis on prevention or, at least, palliation versus curative strategies; foreshortened versus prolonged, heroic treatment of the terminally ill—has not been solely the result of more starkly visible economic factors, although in specific instances (e.g., euthanasia), financial constraints have been viewed as the prime motivating factors behind the new emphasis in health policy.[26] Rather, the shrinking of resources has been accompanied by demonstrations that the benefit-to-cost ratios of medical care modalities are not particularly impressive, especially in the case of technologically advanced care with frequently undesirable side effects.[27] The fact that accelerated expenditures have been accompanied by virtually constant (or time linear) morbidity and mortality rates has engendered suspicion or cynicism about the efficacy of medical care. When these doubts are combined with an increasing sensitivity to iatrogenesis (treatment-induced illness), the result is a general attitude downplaying the efficacy of medical services in health and, at the extreme, an anti-interventionist stance that regards therapeutic modalities as not only ineffective but despiritualizing or dependency-inducing. The seminal works expressing this view predated modern supertechnology,[28] but their vogue has been enhanced by recent popularist authors such as Ivan Illich.[29] The "antimedicalists" are a decided minority among health care activists (if that is an appropriate term in this particular instance), but they definitely have had a leavening influence on expectations about the susceptibility to medical care of leading causes of morbidity and mortality.

The rising costs and dampened expectations about the efficacy of health care have diminished the force of the right-to-health movement, if only because it is difficult to posit that one has a right to something essentially beyond human control, and because it is clear that, even if it were feasible, government assurance of a right to health care would preclude public attention to other priorities. In the wake of this realization, there have been several attempts to avert a tempting nihilism. One such attempt has been health promotion. An institutionalization of the promotion strategy that has been the object of unusually favorable federal attention in a period of restricted budgets has been the health maintenance organization (HMO).[30] This model can be seen as an effort on the part of decision makers to avoid a trade-off between cost and quality because it promises an optimum by making it economically advantageous for these providers (thus, their salaried physicians) to forego hospitalizing their patients whenever possible. Because HMO enrollees prepay a fixed sum for the entire spectrum of health services, it also is in the institution's best interest to prevent catastrophic illness among its patient population, thus fending off the potential criticism that HMOs have built-in incentives toward undercare.

As appealing as the HMO or other models with similar incentive structures may be in concept, however, their ability to side-step quality-cost trade-offs rests ultimately on the effectiveness of health promotion, if quality is conceived of as encompassing more than the bare essentials of mortality prevention. Such effectiveness has not been demonstrated;[31] therefore, implicit decisions about how much the demand or need for health care can be accommodated may have to be explicated, as uncomfortable as this may be in this patently vital policy-making area. This pessimism, if it is that, could also be extended to planning efforts. If the experience of other countries is instructive, it seems that some kind of rationing of health care services must be resorted to if costs are to be contained.[32]

Before leaving the topic of health care as a limited resource, it should be noted that, for policy purposes, we may have come full circle back to the conception of health care as a public good. That is, because Americans already have collectivized risk largely through not-for-profit third parties and, therefore, most individuals can derive a high (albeit only preceived) marginal benefit from the consumption of health care while incurring a fraction of the marginal cost, it may be appropriate/economical for government to provide a certain minimal level of services that add up to what amounts to the public good, and leave the remainder of demand to be satisfied by the private market. This is the "rational" solution that was proposed by James Buchanan in his observations on the British National Health Service in 1965.[33] However, the attractiveness of this and other rational solutions to problems in the provision of health care is mitigated by the fact that government policies (such as the requirement that providers obtain a certificate-of-need for the acquisition of facilities and equipment) now directly exert controls on the private sector, whereas previously such regulatory policy affected only that portion of the "market" that engaged in manifestly public exchanges (e.g., Medicare or Medicaid reimbursement could be denied a facility for unapproved capital expenditures). In a sense, then, the pursuit of regulation in lieu of policy leaves the American consumer of health services potentially more limited in purchase discretion that his supposedly choice-bereft British counterpart.

VI. THE DISTINCTIVENESS OF HEALTH POLICY: HEALTH POLICY ANALYSIS AS AN AREA STUDY

Up until now health policy has been discussed in such a way that another substantive policy area such as welfare could have been the target for government action; that is, it has not been demonstrated that health policy is at all distinctive, notwithstanding that the division of labor in compiling this encyclopedia rests on the assumption that there is some utility in categorizing policy studies by subject matter area, institutions and actors, with which they are chiefly concerned. Health policy formation and implementation excite a number of interrelated issues involving principal actors and institutions that warrant differentiating it from other area studies, if only because of pedagogical and information management considerations.

The major issues in health policy to some extent coincide with those that form the basis of traditional ideological divisions regarding the allocation, regulation, and distribution of resources, but they can be isolated for analytic purposes and, in fact, are often contested by advocates whose socioeconomic political and "health" positions might appear inconsistent or, at least, multidimensional. For example, a prototypical conservative (classic liberal), who would normally oppose government intervention in the private sector might nevertheless hold that market aberrations in the delivery of health services justify an unusual degree of public regulation in this area. The issues overlap with themselves as well as with general questions regarding individual liberty versus social welfare, equality of opportunity versus equalitarianism. Their relationship with such broader questions need only be remarked once the issues are explicated. The prototypical *health* issues are characterized by differential emphases on:

1. Public versus personal health services
2. Health versus medical care
3. Prevention versus cure
4. Social versus individual responsibility for health

If there is anything approaching a left-right continuum in health policy, the above contrasting positions would probably form the chief components and would be, for the most part, properly arrayed. At one pole would be the advocate of close regulation of "demerit" goods (which probably now include energy along with the traditional items such as tobacco, alcohol, and inappropriately used drugs); promotion of health education; less reliance on medical care and more attention to such factors in health as environmental hazards and housing. At the opposite end of the continuum would be arguments with a ring familiar to students of other policy areas—that is, an equation of "need" with "demand"[34] and, in general, the view that government should treat most health services as it should any other good that can be divisibly consumed. In between these extremes, scaleability would be frustrated by the same variations in salience and inherent noncardinality that characterize other social, psychological, economic, and political policy cleavage patterns. For example, it is tenable that proponents of seatbelt requirements might oppose increases in taxes on the sale of manufactured tobacco products because of perceptions about the price or income elasticity of cigarette consumption or sentiments against regressive taxation. Or, self-interest aside, proponents of a compulsory universal and comprehensive national health insurance might take issue with attempts to increase the supply of physicians on the grounds that the latter would unduly generate demand whereas the former would meet demand with existing resources and, through the concentration of financing, enable effective cost containment. In short, issues in the health policy arena, no less than in others, are multidimensional. As Phillip Converse observed some time ago of left-right "belief systems" in general, positions on health policy tend to cluster more among the "elite" than the "mass public."[35] In health policy, even among those who are most constrained ideologically, there likely are strong cross-currents of opinion. Systematic explanations of these attitudinal questions has scarcely begun.

With regard to process variables, there obviously also are institutional actors distinctive to the health field—the four health subcommittees of Congress, for example, or health agencies of the Department of Health and Human Services. In addition, there are myriad interest groups with an overriding interest in health policy—such as the American Medical Association, the American Hospital Association, the Federation of American Hospitals (representing proprietary hospitals), the American Health Care Association (representing proprietary nursing homes), the American Nursing Association, the National League for Nursing, and the Association of American Medical Colleges—which can be expected to exert influence on all major issues. However, this is a relatively trivial distinction because, as was the case with major issues, the same could be said for any policy area. In fact, focusing health policy analysis on characteristics of such institutions because they are putatively health policy-centered might obscure generalizations about administrative behavior. In short, health policy studies are open to the same criticisms as those leveled against area studies in comparative politics.

Area studies have been defended in this regard on the basis of the special knowledge that accrues from an intensive interdisciplinary understanding of a country or region. The same grounds could be used to justify health policy analysis if a *lietmotiv* for health policy can be demonstrated. One may be found in that, until recently, health policy has been unique in defying the liberal democratic tradition that has been the mainstream of development for other types of policy. The specific form this has taken has been the appropriation of the authority of the state to sanction medical, professional dominance and autonomy. It is true that the presence of disproportionate power relations characterizes political struggles in all policy areas. Nevertheless, the degree to which this is the case in the health field and the fact that it has been explicit marks a deviation from the norm. Granted that this is a distinctive trait, does it justify a policy area approach? Not logically, because, in fact, it is a trans-area perspective that highlights it. However, taking a trans-area policy approach toward health without the intensified focus might not let us see that what we have termed professional dominance is a significant aberration that touches the roots of American democracy.

In a functionalist vein, we would expect professional dominance to wane because it is anomalous and, indeed, as the above discussion of the evolution of American health policy has indicated, it shows signs of doing so. It seems that the United States is attempting to inject into the system a dram of classical liberal democratic spirit (which has resurged in other policy areas, displacing reform liberalism, in the past few years) via regulations such as certificates-of-need and peer and utilization review.

If one accepts that the primary reason for segregating health policy analysis is the marked deviance of health policy with respect to the balance of power of interested parties and relatedly, the relatively low salience of health issues for the general public, then it would seem that this facet of the field would be the most exploited by research. This may be true of medical sociology,[36] but except for a few outstanding studies (such as Robert Alford's *Health Care Politics: Dynamics Without Change*, which won the Woodrow Wilson award in 1976),[37] political scientists and economists have ignored this phenomenon and devoted their attention to aspects of the political process in which a health focus could be viewed as almost incidental. This is not to discount the utility of these studies: Much can be learned about the policy process generally from health policies that span all aspects of policy: regulation, (e.g., PL 93-641, the Health Planning and Resource Development Act, or state licensure and limitation of practice acts), distribution (the Hill-Burton, Hospital Survey and Construction Act of 1946), redistribution (Medicare-Medicaid, Title XX of the Social Security Act), and constituent (e.g., whether the federal conditional grant device is in fact an encroachment on state constitutional authority or a legitimate extension of federal taxing and spending power). Health policies are rarely examined in this functional view; instead they are the subject of descriptive studies that heretofore have been acceptable as such because of the primitive state of the art, the intrinsic interest of the topic, and the dynamism of the field.

A. The State of the Art

One way to categorize the body of health policy analysis, which permits some contrasts to be drawn with other policy area studies and points up needed research, is according to whether the relationships stressed (if this is done with any measure of explicitness) are input-process, process-output, output-outcome, or whether the systems approach is employed wherein input-process-output-outcome linkages (or the first two of them) are assessed simultaneously. There are probaby fewer of the latter in health policy than in education and welfare, and those studies that have been "systemic" seem to be primarily disciplinary (i.e., in the policy analysis "of" health mode, which will be discussed in the ensuing section).

There hardly is a voluminous literature in health policy analysis, but relative to other policy areas, with the possible exception of education, a disproportionate amount of it seems to focus on the determinants of outcomes. A substantial body of program evaluation research has been conducted. Unfortunately, the resulting store of verifiable generalizations does not strike much optimism for those other policy areas with an, as yet, scarce amount of such research. For one thing, the debate noted earlier about what constitutes health clouds the definitiveness of outcome evaluation. For another, outcome evaluation in health shares the problems of multicollinearity that plague similar research in other areas. For example, although screening programs are thought to have been efficacious in reducing cervical-uterine mortality, the disease already was declining as a linear function of time.[38] Or, because so many diseases are self-limiting or of unknown etiology, it is difficult to attribute reduction in morbidity to programs with this intention. Nevertheless, these studies have utility, if only because they raise such questions, forcing implicit assumptions into the open.

Perhaps as surprising as the comparatively large amount of attention devoted to outcomes in health policy analysis is the relative lack of process-output studies. The legislative process in health policy has been the subject of some research—for example, Ted

Marmor's *Politics of Medicare*,[39] Richard Redman's *Dance of Legislation*,[40] and David Price's "Policy Making in Congressional Committees"[41] —but major pieces of legislation, or the fact that there has been a lack of them, have gone largely unexplored. And, returning to the issue discussed earlier about the distinctiveness of this area, it is not the "health" aspects of the policies that are highlighted for their roles in the legislative process, but expected redistributive impact (Marmor), degree of salience and conflict (Price), and personalities and characteristics of the congressional process (Redman). Whether this is true generally of health legislation is problematic but, so far, the burden of proof would seem to be on those who would argue that variables intrinsic to the health field are significant determinants of the legislative process regarding health issues.

The bureaucratic/administrative process in health policy remains a largely unchartered domain. Studies such as Judy Feder's *Medicare*,[42] which attempts to show that the implementation of this policy was affected in large part by the fact it was administered by insurance rather than health-oriented officials, are rare. There even is a paucity of descriptive literature in this area, notwithstanding the number of government publications of this nature.

The courts and health law have been studied more extensively but, again, there is very little that is specific to the health field that would distinguish this literature. Possible exceptions, in light of our earlier discussion, are those works that deal with the incongruity of professional dominance.

Health systems agencies (HSAs) (quasi-governmental in the sense that they have delegated review powers that are subject to administrative appeal and that they are expected to work with local and regional government entities) seem to have been studied more extensively—if nowhere near adequately—than the legislature or the bureaucracy for their role in health policy determination. This may signal that their actions are more significant in the policy process or, simply, that they (and their forerunners, the comprehensive health planning agencies) are more accessible research sites. Research on HSAs has been concerned largely with the relations among state, local, and federal agencies, and board representativeness and degree of consumer participation. Therefore, the focus has been on processes that have, at least implicitly, a *presumed* effect on outputs and outcomes.[43]

Inputs and processes have been the subject of considerable research, characterized generally by a more or less explicit "group" approach. Consonant with what was said earlier about the distinctiveness of certain groups to policy fields (i.e., excluding the business, labor, civic action, partisan-ideological, and consumer groups that can be expected to air views on any or all issues), the health policy process has been dominated by certain group sentiments and interests. The policy relevance of these studies depends on one's judgment about the importance for outputs and outcomes of the group interests have affected policies, but whether the effects have been determining still seems a matter of speculation.

Some have argued that the dominance of the group (or elite) approach in health policy analysis has exaggerated their significance and obscured health (versus traditional) ideological concerns.[44] The first part of this claim has the same weight as do all contentions that the approach selected will, to some extent, prefigure what the analysis yields—the venerable theory-data problem. The second part of the argument is less persuasive. First, it certainly is not improbable that the group approach has been fashionable because it fits the dynamics—or lack of them—of the health policy process. Second, groups have been the purveyors of health ideology, even if Paul Fieldstein is correct in his observation that they always act either in error or to maximize their self-interest (income for professionals, growth for not-for-profit third parties and hospitals, and prestige for teaching hospitals).[45] Finally, the ideological approach has the same major shortcoming it (in this case) ascribes to the group approach but, perhaps, with less face validity.

VII. HEALTH SERVICES RESEARCH, PLANNING, AND ADMINISTRATION

Health policy analysis may or may not fall under the general heading of health services research, depending on the expansiveness of one's conception of the latter term. But health services research, perhaps more than any other pursuit, lays the groundwork for health policy analysis. Health services research has been defined as:

> ... concerned with problems in the organization, staffing, financing, utilization, and evaluation of health services. This is in contrast to biomedical research which is oriented to the etiology, diagnosis and treatment of disease. Health services research subsumes both medical care and patient care research.[46]

The field is by now advanced enough to be recognized by an acronym, HSR, and an entire volume[47] and other literature have been devoted to its meaning.[48] This chapter clearly cannot do justice to the field. However, some of the major subissues involved in its development can be cursorily identified—that is, whether HSR should be "applied" or "basic," discipline-rewarding or policy-oriented, "in" health (with the health field as the principal focus) or "of" health (with disciplinary exploitation of topics in the health area as a primary motivating factor).[49] These largely coincident distinctions can be consequential for research funding (applied research, by and large, is more attractive to dollars). However, whether research is applied is fundamentally an empirical question and thus must, a priori, pose an impressive challenge to a grantor to divine the motives of the researcher. Otherwise, one does not know whether research was basic or applied until its consequences have been evaluated.

One aspect of the basic-applied distinction that surfaces in policy studies is in the form of policy advocacy versus analysis. Perhaps this is a more frank and useful dichotomy than that used in HSR because generally, it self-consciously recognizes motives as its basis: Basic becomes "objective" (or, at least, intersubjective) in orientation; applied can be termed "adversarial" or *explicitly* value-laden.[50]

HSR and health policy analysis dovetail in their focus; possibly the distinguishing trait of the latter is a more macroscopic and government program-centered purview. And here it should be reaffirmed that if policy is to have any meaning, it must be reserved to government (or, to invoke a term commonly used in the health field to denote private agencies with some government sanctioning power, "subgovernmental") decisions.

With respect to the distinguishing features of health policy analysis, planning, and administration, John Kralewski, as chairman of a task force (of the Accrediting Commission for Graduate Education in Health Services Administration) on special accreditation for policy analysis, planning and administration programs, has attempted to, as he prudently puts it, place some sign posts to delimit the boundaries of each field.[51] What emerges from his efforts is a vision of boundaries that are hazy but discernible, with health administration occupying the acreage characterized by management skills and an institutional focus, planning sharing this turf but emphasizing different skills and outlooks (less institutionally defensive, for example), and policy analysis nomadically covering these areas but moving toward a separate area sparsely populated by traditional academic disciplines and increasingly inhabited by a new breed of hybrid health administration (or public health)-discipline educated researcher. Kralewski's work is in an initial state; it is cited here as representative of an effort, grounded in pragmatic considerations, to delimit fields of education that reflect areas of inquiry and practice. His preliminary writing suggests that the most problematic field to isolate may be health policy analysis.

VIII. HEALTH POLICY ANALYSIS AND HEALTH POLICY

With regard to the distinction in health services research between a disciplinary—politics, economics, or sociology, and so on—"of health" versus "in health" orientation, it would seem that health policy analysis, so styled, would lean toward the latter, applied posture. (A political scientist taking the "of health" perspective, for example, probably would consider himself to be primarily a political scientist, at least when doing "basic" research.) Thus it is pertinent to raise the question of whether health policy analysis has influenced health policy. This is a subset of the issue of whether there is any link between HSR and policy. Logical and methodological limitations rule out a definitive answer, but raising the question points up the influence of "political" variables in such a relationship and the utility of a cross-national perspective in this and other policy areas.

The verdict of the majority of the literature on the topic seems to be that HSR either has been entirely ineffectual in influencing policy or it has been epiphenomenal; that is, the conditions that have called for analysis in a given area also have preordained the general nature of the policy adopted to deal with them.[52] This conclusion can be challenged in that the information used to argue that HSR is a relatively insignificant factor in the policy process is suspect. For one thing, the literature has relied on statements of researchers' frustrations that may be exaggerated by the heroic expectations they have had, expectations that are not unique to HSR. For another, the argument may stem from decision makers' laments about the climate of uncertainty in which they must operate. As with researchers' frustrations, decisions makers' complaints may be representative of an existential dilemma rather than reflective of the peculiar inadequacies of HSR.

Most important, however, is that, aside from passing remarks about contextual matters, inferences about the effects of HSR have been made on the basis of process variables almost exclusively. It has been typical to *assert* that HSR has had little additive impact on policy and then to adduce characteristics of HSR and health policy that support the assertion. Nevertheless, it is clear that the "rational" model does not apply in the case of health policy, even though there is some evidence that this policy arena is more insulated from public opinion, at least to the extent that this takes the form of effectively articulated demands, than are others such as social welfare. For example, legislatures appear to be relatively responsibe to the "needs" of their constituencies, despite the fact that the commonly used political indicators of special-interest group demands and socioeconomic status are comparatively insignificant predictors of health policy.[53] The units of analysis in the research that yields these findings are Canadian provincial parliaments, thus complicating attempts to import generalizations based on them. It is probably safe to say, however, that health policy is not highly "politicized," in the usual sense of the word, at the level of the general public. This apolitical atmosphere would seem to provide a favorable climate for rational—that is, research-informed—policy making.

On the other hand, at the elite (activist) level, where ideological constraint is high and health issues interfere with questions about the proper scope of governmental action, there clearly is nothing resembling political quiescence. Perhaps this accounts for King's finding that variations in political culture are associated with differences in state involvement in health (as well as other policy areas) among several developed nations.[54] In a similarly broad perspective and speculative vein, Heidenheimer posits varying "perceptions of the authority of civil servants" and the cohesiveness of providers of health care as explanations of the comparatively "non-progressive" nature of U.S. health policy versus its public education policy.[55] Although her research design is not nearly as methodical as the one employed in the foregoing studies, Altenstetter's comparison between the health policies of West Germany and the United States suggests that several indicators of structures, objectives, and processes affect health policy.[56]

Furthermore, the strength of the relationship between health policy and HSR seems to vary internationally. The impression of the Scandinavian Study Group of the Health Services Study Section Committee that "in a very high proportion of research programs visited, the results had been translated into public policy and did not merely grace the pages of scientific journals or fill library shelves"[57] clearly contrasts with Myers' summary of opinions that in the United States HSR has had very little direct impact on, or even input into, the formulation of national health care policies.[58] Continuing in this impressionistic vein, one could cite the importance of the Hall Commission's recommendations in the development of Medicare in Canada.[59] Also, it could be argued that the concern over recent trends toward the bureaucratization of research in Britain testifies to the presumed consequences of HSR for policy.[60]

Insofar as the characteristics of HSR (quality, quantity, auspices, and other unmeasured, if not ultimately unmeasurable, factors) and policy covary to a lesser degree than do the political variables (structures, processes, and traditions) and policy—and this is likely to be the case, given the international transmissibility of information—then political conditions would appear to be more influential. This hardly constitutes the outline for a pure design, if only because it leaves out the "demonstration effects" of policies, and the conclusions drawn would obviously obtain only at a macroscopic level. Notwithstanding this caveat, international comparisons do seem to attest to the validity of the fact that political considerations interfere with an independent HSR-policy relationship. The international variations in the strength of this relationship alone indicate the mediative role of specific factors in the political system. It is well to remember, however, that the direction of causation may be primarily from policy to research (e.g., the determination of a policy priority such as programs to ameliorate the plight of the frail elderly tends to stimulate research in this area), rather than from research to policy, although the two links are so intertwined as to make a differentiation of this sort virtually impossible.

The reason for even entertaining these notions goes beyond strictly academic concerns. No one would deny that political variables intervene in the HSR-policy relationship. But if the relationship is more tenuous in some contexts because of the relative lack of crystallization of health policies, this detracts from the poignancy of suggested "reforms" of HSR. (As a corallary, it possibly enhances arguments that a complete restructuring of society would be required to effect significant changes in health care.)

Another factor to consider in the argument that policy analysis should inform policy making is the question of the desirability of the policy that might result under conditions that would render research more "productive." The underlying assumption (sometimes explicit to varying degrees) appears to be that a little policy in a given direction on a given topic is better than nothing. Of course, where the research involves multiplicative relationships, a little is frequently tantamount to nothing. For example, a recent article uses research by the American Rehabilitation Foundation on prepaid group practice as an illustration of "effective policy research and analysis."[61] Only the strictest quasi-experimenter would doubt that this research led to the legislative embodiment of the health maintenance organization (HMO) concept. However, there are several articulate exponents of prepaid group practice who would insist that, for HMOs to achieve their aims, they must operate in a market-oriented delivery system. They would thus contend that the apparent policy victory of HMO advocates was hollow, that the consequent legislation has not been conducive to the vitality of the HMO concept.[62] This is hardly the forum for the debate that this subject deserves. However, even this cursory treatment of it should show that "policy effectiveness" is not necessarily synonymous with policy usefulness.

Another explanation for the common supposition that HSR is inefficacious with respect to policy could be that assessments of the state of the art have tended to share a conceptualization of policy that is at once too global and too restrictive. It is too global in that policy seems to be envisioned in its most architectonic sense, as what earlier was referred to as contextuating. As one might expect, the bit policies that emerge under the umbrella of contextuating ones tend to escape observation, although in many cases they are probably easy to trace to specific pieces of health services research. Perhaps the clearest illustration of the relationship between bit policies and HSR are the privately funded research and development projects, such as the child health services and rural local health demonstration programs supported by the Commonwealth Fund that were subsequently adopted by the government. Together, these bit policies may equal or even surpass the significance of the original, contextuating ones.

This reaffirms that, to be recognized as such, a policy does not have to be in the form of a definitive piece of legislation or a specific program. It is a common occurrence that as the positive state has evolved, along with technological and related socioeconomic development, formal law-making bodies have relinquished a good deal of authority to functionally specific organizations.[63] The extreme interpretation of this phenomenon has been found in eulogies for representative democracy (albeit they have perhaps been more plaintive in parliamentary systems, where expertise is more concentrated in the executive function than it is in the United States, where the staffs of individual legislators and, especially, congressional committees still pose a formidable counterweight to the bureaucracy as sources of technical information and analysis).

It seems inconceivable that these new, bureaucratic policy institutions would function without policy analysis. For example, HSA decisions obviously have been influenced by the judgments of the professional staffs. Granted, the translation of HSR into policy has not been direct, but it is safe to predict that the influence of the "representative" board members has been less than overwhelming.

Once the concept of policy is expanded to include more than legislative decision making, it is not necessary to rely on empirical evidence to posit a relationship between policy analysis and policy making. If such evidence were required, it could be readily gleaned from Rich's study of the use of Continuous National Survey data by federal policy makers, although the focus of his analysis was not the existence of an HSR-policy relationship.[64] Shifting attention from the dramatic episodes in the history of health legislation to routine, but perhaps no less consequential, policy making makes it difficult to deny the influence of HSR. At the same time, of course, it complicates causal influence in that the tenuousness of the HSR-policy relationship has often been attributed to the fractionalization of HSR when, as pointed out in the above discussion, the development of American health policy has been along parallel lines. These trends, thus, could be used to hypothesize an association between HSR and policy rather than to emphasize the absence of a unidirectional causal relationship. The fragmentation of HSR, which Flook and Sanazaro note "make it literally impossible to aggregate the research results into a coherent empirical characterization of the existing health services delivery system,"[65] may find its expression in the policies that have guided the system, or it may simply reflect the lack of health policy integration, or both.

Odin Anderson has suggested that the latter interpretation would be most apt. In his overview of the history of HSR and policy until 1966 he concludes that:

> Systematic data gathering and research do not appear until a public policy consensus emerges providing the framework for social and economic research bearing on policy. Such a framework quite unconsciously establishes the guidelines for the selection of data and research problems within the feasibilities of time, resources and research methods. Social research relating to public policy is then largely *instrumental*, serving to analyze the context in which public policy decisions are made, to implement to such decisions, and to evaluate alternatives and their consequences in terms of the objectives sought.[66]

In sum, there seems to be no compelling reason to believe that HSR needs to be reoriented because it has not influenced policy, because the premise of this argument is suspect. Rather, HSR and health policy analysis reflect, or at least are reciprocally related to, the variables underlying the evolution of American health policy. The dynamic interrelatedness of HSR and policy was explicitly recognized by the National Center for Health Services Research and Development in the definition of its task as "accelerating improvements in health services planning and management, more efficient resources development and distribution while operating within a pluralistic system during a period of shifting public policy in health services."[67]

IX. CONCLUSION

Having reviewed the evolution of health policy and its interrelationship with research, there does not appear to be an obvious inner direction to trends in this area on which to base speculation about the future. Another source of portents could be the experiences of other countries where stages along U.S. trend lines, if there were any, would already have been reached. If we could rule out demonstration effects and assume equifinality (i.e., that all nations are converging toward the same end point), the picture would be clearer: One could expect government to assume increased responsibility for the financing of health care, with attendant public controls, followed by a period of attempted reprivitization. However, these assumptions obviously are very shaky, and it could be that the acceleration of government financing has reached an apogee and that the United States will respond to the same pressures for the curtailment of public programs (e.g., diminished resource capacity, perceived inefficacy of welfare statism), as have several other Western nations. This does not mean that government involvement will stabilize at its present level; not only has it been shown that the existing government portion of the health dollar is large enough virtually to control segments of this industry (although certainly not in a coordinated fashion), but certificate-of-need and peer review demonstrate that government influence does not have to be exerted through the relatively indirect method of granting or withholding funds.

The central policy dilemma is that the provision of health care is generally regarded as too important to be left to the competitive market, but society does not now have the resources to effectively restructure the system. It is generally agreed that, so far, the piecemeal policy solutions have not eased the problem, nor are they likely to be successful in the long run. Meanwhile, health policy analysis has no scarcity of research topics but little direction as to what lines of inquiry would be most fruitful to pursue in terms of their policy effectiveness.

NOTES

1. See, for example, G. DeJong, "Interfacing national health insurance and income maintenance: Why health policy and welfare reform go together," *Journal of Health Politics, Policy and Law 1* (Winter 1977): 405–432.
2. "Mixed scanning: A 'third' approach to decision-making," *Public Administration Review 27* (December 1967): 385–1392.
3. The qualification implied by the quotation marks is to indicate that groups need not have been initiators of demand; e.g., in the case of Medicare, the elderly were mobilized by the Democratic party elite.
4. With respect to Medicare, this is the view of T. Marmor, *The Politics of Medicare* (Aldine, Chicago, 1973). On the other hand, J. Feder, in *Medicare* (Heath, Lexington, MA, 1977) argues that whatever its legislative intent, Medicare was implemented as a social insurance rather than as a health program.
5. *Medicine and Human Welfare* (McGrath, College Park, MD, 1970), p. 46, cited in D. Banta, "What is health care?" in *Health Care Delivery in the United States*, Steven Jonas (Ed.) (Springer, New York), p. 14.
6. For a discussion of this movement, see J. W. Salmon and H. Berliner, "Health policy implications of the holistic health movement," *Journal of Health Politics, Policy and Law 5* (Fall 1980).
7. Banta, op. cit., p. 21.
8. World Health Organization, "The constitution of the World Health Organization," *WHO Chronicle 1* (1944).
9. See W. Balinsky and R. Berger, "A review of research on general health status indexes," *Medical Care 13* (1975).

10. The distinction is highlighted in an exchange in the *Journal of Health Politics, Policy Law 2* (Spring 1977): S. Jain, "Whither education in public health?" and C. Sheps, "Reply to Jain," ibid.

11. See I. S. Falk, "Medical care in the U.S.A., 1932–1973: Proposals from the Committee on the Costs of Medical Care to the Committee for National Health Insurance," *Milbank Memorial Fund Quarterly 51*(1973): 1–32.

12. The milestones have been marked by E. E. Flook and P. Sanazaro, "Health services research: Origins and milestones," in *Health Services Research and Research and Development in Perspective*, E. E. Flook and P. Sanzaro (Eds.), (Health Administration Press, Ann Arbor, MI, 1973). The linkages between the liberal tradition and health policy have been drawn by B. J. Jaeger, "The normative bases of American health policy," unpublished paper, 1974.

13. Ibid.

14. "Special message to Congress, January 23, 1939," *The Public Papers and Addresses of Franklin D. Roosevelt, 1939* (Macmillan, New York, 1941), pp. 97ff., cited in Jaeger.

15. The President's Commission on the Health Needs of the Nation, *Findings and Recomendations*, Vol. I, *Building American's Health* (Washington: Government Printing Office, 1952), p. 1, cited in Jaeger, op. cit.

16. "Special message to the Congress on the health needs of the American people, January 18, 1954," in *Public Papers of the Presidents of the United States: Dwight D. Eisenhower, 1954* (Office of the *Federal Register*, National Archives and Records Service, Washington, DC, 1960), p. 77, cited in Jaeger, op. cit.

17. See H. K. Girvetz, *From Wealth to Welfare* (Stanford University Press, Stanford, CA, 1950), pp. 53–54.

18. See J. D. Richardson (Ed.), *A Compilation of the Messages and Papers of Presidents, 1789–1897* Bureau of National Literature, New York, 1897, vol. VI, pp. 2782–2784), cited in Jaeger, op. cit.

19. H. Hoover, *Addresses on the American Road: World War II, 1941–1945* (Van Nostrand, New York, 1946), p. 225, cited in Jaeger, *op. cit.*

20. See A. Heidenheimer, "The politics of public education, health and welfare in the U.S.A. and Western Europe: How growth and reform potentials have differed," *British Journal of Political Science 3* (1973): 315–340.

21. *Congressional Record*, 78th Cong., 2nd Sess., XC (January 11, 1944), cited in Jaeger, op. cit.

22. Jaeger, op. cit., p. 25.

23. M. Freeland, G. Caht, and C. E. Schendler, "Projections of national health expenditures: 1985–1990," *Health Care Financing Review 1* (Winter 1980).

24. For amplification on the relationship between cost consciousness and centralization (or concentration) of financing, see T. Marmor, D. Wittman, and T. Heagy, "The politics of medical inflation," *Journal of Health Politics, Policy and Law 1* (Spring 1976).

25. See D. Altman, "The politics of health care regulation," *Journal of Health Politics, Policy and Law 4* (Winter 1978).

26. See, for example, A. E. Slaby and L. Tancredi, "The politics of moral values: Policy implications," *Journal of Health Politics, Policy and Law 2* (Spring 1977).

27. See, for example, A. Cochrane, *Effectiveness and Efficiency: Random Reflections on Health Services* (Nuffield Provincial Hospitals Trust, London, 1972).

28. See, for example, J. H. Beard, "The contribution of cholera to public health," *Scientific Monthly 43* (November 1936), and Rene Dubos, *Mirage of Health* (Doubleday, Garden City, NY, 1959).

29. *Medical Nemisis* (Pantheon, New York, 1976).
30. For edification on this concept, see J. L. Falkson, *HMOs and the Politics of Health System Reform* (American Hospital Association, Chicago, 1980).
31. See Cochrane, *op. cit.*
32. D. Falcone and R. J. Van Loon, "Health policy and devolution," paper delivered at the Canadian American Conference on Devolution, Ottawa, July 1979.
33. "The inconsistencies of the British National Health Service," in *Theory of Public Choice*, J. Buchanan and R. Tollison (Eds.) (University of Michigan Press, Ann Arbor, 1972).
34. On this distinction, see J. Jeffers, M. F. Bognanno, and J. C. Bartlett, "On the demand vs. need for medical services and the concept of shortages," *American Journal of Public Health 61* (January 1971): 46-57.
35. "The nature of belief systems in mass publics," in *Public Opinion and Public Policy*, N. Luttbeg (Ed.) (Dorsey Press, Homewood, IL, 1968).
36. See, for example, E. Friedson, *Professional Dominance* (Atherton, New York, 1970).
37. (University of Chicago Press, Chicago, 1975).
38. U.S. National Center for Health Statistics, "Age adjusted cancer death rates for selected sites, 1930-1975."
39. Marmor, op. cit.
40. (Simon and Schuster, New York, 1973).
41. *American Political Science Review 72* (June 1978): 548-1574.
42. Feder, op. cit.
43. See K. Ittig, "Consumer participation in health planning and service delivery: A selected review and proposed research agenda," discussion draft, National Center for Health Services Research, Rockville, MD, June 1976.
44. See, for example, G. R. Weller, "The determinants of Canadian health policy," *Journal of Health Politics, Policy and Law 5* (Fall 1980).
45. *Health Associations and the Demand for Legislation* (Ballinger, Cambridge, MA, 1977).
46. Flook and Sanazaro, *Health Services Research*, p. 1.
47. Ibid.
48. Some of it is reviewed in D. Falcone and B. J. Jaeger, "The policy effectiveness of health services research: A reconsideration," *Journal of Community Health 2* (Fall 1976): 36-51, from which this section draws heavily.
49. For amplification of these issues, see R. Eichorn and T. Bice, "Academic disciplines and health services research," in Flook and Sanazaro, pp. 136-149.
50. The emphasis is to recognize that values permeate all inquiry. See D. Falcone, "Michael Polanyi's logic of discovery and the status of values in the study of man," *Carleton University Occasional Papers 2* (December 1972).
51. "The health administration domain." Paper delivered at the 1980 Meeting of the Association of University Programs in Health Administration, Washington, DC, May 10.
52. Falcone and Jaeger, "Policy effectiveness."
53. D. Falcone and W. Mishler, "Legislative determinants of provincial health policy in Canada: A diachronic analysis," *Journal of Politics 39* (May 1977).
54. A. King, "Ideas, institutions and the policies of governments: A comparative analysis: Parts I and II," *British Journal of Political Science 3* (1973): 291-314, 409-424.
55. "The Politics of Public Education."
56. C. Attenstetter, "Health policy-making and administration in West Germany and the United States," in *Sage Professional Papers in Administrative and Policy Studies*, H. Frederickson (Ed.) (Sage, Beverly Hills, CA, 1974).

57. D. W. Clark, et al. "Health services research in Scandinavia," *Milbank Memorial Fund Quarterly/Health Society 44* (1966): 229–261.
58. B. Myers, "HSR and health policy: Interactions," *Medical Care 2* (1973): 353–358.
59. Royal Commission on Health Services, *Report* (Queen's Printer, Ottawa, 1964).
60. P. Draper and T. Smart, "Social science and health policy in the United Kingdom," *International Journal of Health Services 4* (1974): 453–470.
61. L. S. Roberson, et al., "Toward changing the medical care system: Report of an experiment: 1964–68," (National Technical Information Services, Springfield, VA, U.S. Department of Commerce, Report No. P. B. 220–941, 1973).
62. See the Committee of the Institute of Medicine, *Health Maintenance Organizations: Toward a Fair Market Test* (National Academy of Sciences, Washington, DC, 1974).
63. See, among others, J. Ellul, *Technological Society* (Knopf, New York, 1970); and V. Thompson, *Bureaucracy and Innovation* (University of Alabama Press, University, 1969).
64. R. Rich, "Selective utilization of social science research by federal policy makers," *Inquiry 12* (1975): 239–245.
65. Flook and Sanazaro, *Health Services Research*.
66. "Influence of social and economic research on public policy in the health field," in *Politics and Law in Health Care Policy*, J. McKinlay (Ed.) (Prodist, New York, 1973), pp. 45–92.
67. P. Sanazaro, "Federal health services R&D under the auspices of the National Center for Health Services Research and Development," in Flook and Sanazaro, *Health Services Research*, pp. 150–184.

32

Energy Policy

Robert M. Lawrence / Colorado State University, Fort Collins, Colorado

I. INTRODUCTION

Occasionally in the first half of this century someone would issue a warning that the energy utilized to build industrial America would not always be cheap and abundant. These gloomy pronouncements would be followed in due time by discoveries of vast new natural gas and oil fields, and the subject would be forgotten for a while. Despite the discovery of some new natural gas and oil fields, and renewed interest in existing coal deposits, which often were ignored, events occurred in the 1970s that appeared to add substance to the earlier warnings. In response the federal government began work on a national energy plan. The purpose of this chapter is to set forth the context out of which came the decisions to develop a national energy plan, and to analyze the factors that are shaping the growth and implementation of national energy policy.

II. EMERGENCE OF ENERGY AS A POLICY ISSUE IN THE 1970s

President Richard Nixon was the first occupant of the White House to send a national energy message to the Congress. In it the President pinpointed a major reason for the energy problem then emerging as a nationally significant issue. His explanation was that while Americans were using ever more energy to sustain their life style, they were starting to encounter a decreasing amount of easily obtained energy supplies. President Nixon noted the American people were compounding their problem by often being energy wastrels as they pursued their affluent life. This of course was a time when gasoline sold for 25 cents a gallon, and there were price-cutting "gas wars" among filling stations competing for the familiar command from the driver of a "gas guzzler"—"fill'er up."

In retrospect one might justifiably wonder whether things would have been different if the United States had developed mass transportation systems similar to the Europeans and the Japanese. They have sacrificed personal comfort and convenience for the capacity to move large numbers of people at relatively less expenditures of energy. But for a few subway systems, and the Elevated in Chicago, Americans typically did not sacrifice comfort and convenience as they sought the good material life after the privations of World War II. In fact the "American dream" could hardly have been more demanding upon energy. Remember what it was, and still is for some? An air-conditioned five-bedroom home equipped with an all-electric kitchen, located in the suburbs miles from the places of employment. All driving members of the family would have their own car, in which they would drive singly to work or play.

This kind of life style enjoyed by millions, coupled with the energy demands of a military establishment, which fought two wars to contain communism and otherwise was spread about the globe, and the demands of industry committed to providing more to the consumers did not encounter energy supply trouble until several decades after World War II. Then, for a while, the decrease in easily available domestic oil was compensated for by importing cheap oil from those foreign nations amenable to the low price structure of the American and other Western oil companies.

Noting the growing need for the United States to import oil from abroad, President Nixon called for implementation of what he termed Project Independence. In what may today be called an extreme example of technological exuberance, the President stated his intent to direct the nation toward a 10-year program of increasing production of energy, together with reduced consumption, so that by the early 1980s the country would be free of concern about the need to import oil from an unstable region such as the Middle East.

Two years after the Nixon energy message to Congress, the fourth war erupted between Israel and various Arab states. Concomitant to the struggle was the initiation of a partial oil embargo by some of the Arab oil-producing nations as a means to pressure Western consuming states to reduce, or to stop altogether, their support of Israel. The United States refused to cease support of Israel and continued supplying Israel with military equipment, even in the face of possible Soviet entry into the war on the side of Egypt. As a result of the oil embargo, gasoline became scarce in the United States, and tempers flared as impatient motorists waited in line for an allotment of gasoline. Some states inaugurated distribution systems based on whether a driver's car had odd- or even-numbered license plates.

Despite the inconvenience suffered by motorists, and later by some users of home heating oil, one may argue that the oil embargo of 1973 was a blessing in disguise. It served to bring home to Americans that energy supply and consumption were indeed problems deserving of national attention.

There were other reasons for the deteriorating energy situation faced by the United States in the 1970s. One was the quadrupling of world oil prices as a result of decisions taken by the Organization of Petroleum Exporting Countries (OPEC). At times OPEC nations appear to act as a monopoly is expected to act; that is, they take advantage of the fact that they control a commodity the world wants in order to raise its price.

The pricing action of OPEC, however, cannot be understood simply in terms of monopolistic theory. For example, part of the rationale for the OPEC pricing structure, or for the prices charged by non-OPEC members such as Mexico, is the belief that planning must be undertaken to provide for the time when a nation's easily exploited oil supply is diminished. One such action is to charge high prices in order to acquire money that can be placed into a trust fund to be utilized as a source of income when oil revenues fall. A related activity is for an oil-producing nation to employ part of its oil profits to construct an industrial infrastructure not based on oil, which will provide jobs and income long after depletion of cheap oil. Generally the infrastructure building process involves using oil revenues to purchase technology transfer from the West in the form of human expertise and equipment. An example of this is the effort of several Middle East oil-exporting nations to acquire from the West a nuclear power industry. The stated objective of such action is to establish an alternative source of energy before oil becomes too expensive simply to burn for energy.

Another explanation for the high OPEC prices that concerned the United States was well articulated by the late Shah or Iran. His point was that for years the Western industrialized world has been exporting its inflation to the less well-developed nations. This was accomplished, he argued, by selling manufactured goods at an inflated price, and inflating the salaries of Westerners who were employed in technology transfer activities. The Shah held that fairness demanded that such Western inflation be offset by higher oil prices charged to the industrialized nations.

A related, but more grandiose concept, that supported increased prices for oil was found in association with the view that a new economic order should be established between the Western nations and those countries from which raw materials are exported. According to this perspective, Western nations extracted raw materials from the less developed countries (LDCs) at the unfair prices during the imperial era. Now, it is contended, the increasing economic power of the LDCs should be used to increase prices to the West so that the capital lost in the past can be recaptured. This view is closely associated with some of the more militant nations that have gained independence from imperial rule since the end of World War II.

Still another reason for ever higher oil prices among Arab oil-producing states hostile to Israel is the practice of diverting some oil revenues to help finance the effort to destroy Israel.

Another cause of the current energy problems facing the United States is the shortfall in electricity produced by nuclear power plants. At a time when many believed that nuclear energy would start significantly to replace the electricity from fossil fuel plants, there are only 70-odd nuclear plants in the nation. Yet 20 years ago nuclear enthusiasts were predicting that by this time nuclear electricity would by "too cheap to meter."

What happened to the promise of nuclear power? One explanation is that the American people have never fully embraced nuclear power. In fact, there has been considerable organized opposition to the building of commercial nuclear power plants. Much of the opposition can be traced to the manner in which the United States entered the nuclear age—with the atomic destruction of the Japanese cities of Hiroshima and Nagasaki in August 1945. Despite repeated assurances by the nuclear industry and government authorities, some of the public perceive a nuclear power plant as having the potential for a nuclear explosion. Much of the opposition to nuclear power is based on the contention by environmental groups that any more introduction of radioactive materials into the environment should be avoided. Specifically, this argument is directed against the problem of highly radioactive wastes produced by the operation of nuclear power plants, and how such wastes should be disposed of over the very long time it takes for them to decay to nonhazardous levels.

Overall the basic concern about radiation is rooted in the mystery, and lack of full understanding, of the relationship between radiation and genetic damage to living matter, generation after generation.

The accident at the Three Mile Island nuclear power station in Pennsylvania late in the 1970s was highlighted by antinuclear groups as evidence nuclear power plants are dangerous. That accident, in which there was no loss of life, was not the death knell for nuclear power in America that some environmentalists had hoped it would be. However, the accident, together with other events discussed below, have combined to cause the cancellation of a number of nuclear power plants about the nation.

In addition to popular reservations concerning civil nuclear power, the industry has been slowed by rising costs for nuclear plant construction, and the delaying tactics of antinuclear groups, which have been partially successful in their efforts to halt new nuclear plant construction by resort to the courts. The latter activity occurs typically in the form of a class action suit in which it is charged that construction of a nuclear plant will harm the health and safety of nearby residents. A further difficulty encountered by the nuclear power industry has been technical and engineering problems associated with the unusually high performance standards required by law for nuclear power plants.

A frequently heard charge against civil nuclear power is that had it not been for powerful political forces there might not have been a civil nuclear industry. This claim is based on the proposition that the nuclear power industry represented by the pressure group known as the Atomic Industrial Forum has generally received preferential treatment from the federal government. This is particularly true, it is claimed, of the old Atomic Energy Commission in the executive branch, and the Joint Committee on Atomic Energy in the legislative branch. Gregory Daneke (1979) claims that the preferential treatment includes the depletion allowance of 22 percent on uranium mining, government investment in basic research and development, which led to the civil power reactors now in use, government establishment of upper limits of liability for a nuclear accident, and government subsidization of the uranium fuel cycle.

The energy problems for the United States, and more particularly for American allies such as the NATO countries and Japan, were made more difficult by three violent disruptions of the power structure in the Middle East. First came the overthrow of the Iranian government headed by the late Shah by the conservative Muslim leader, the Ayatollah Khomeini. The Ayatollah combined a fundamental brand of Islam with firey Iranian nationalism to produce one of the most virulent forms of anti-Americanism. A causality of the anti-American feeling in Teheran was stoppage of oil shipments from Iran to the United States. Next, late in 1980, Iran and Iraq began a war at the head of the Persian Gulf that threatened the oil production of both Iraq and Iran for the allies of the United States.

Fortunately for the Western oil-using nations, Saudi Arabia led several smaller oil-exporting nations in expanded production during the period of shortfall from the two warring nations.

Third, the assassination of Egyptian President Anwar Sadat removed a central figure from the search for a Middle East peace between the Arabs and the Israelis.

Yet another factor leading to the recognition by the United States of its difficult energy problems was the deep and persistent fear of the Soviet Union, which has influenced so much public policy in the United States since 1947. As the United States and its allies increased their importation of oil from the Middle East and elsewhere, the fear grew in Washington that the Soviet Union would seek to profit from the dependent relations that were forming. One form these fears took was concern that the Soviets might come to control Middle Eastern oil to the extent that Moscow could then ration out oil in accord with the degree of separateness an oil-hungry nation would be willing to put between itself and the United States in terms of alliances and trade. Such a fear was intensified late in 1979 with the Soviet invasion of Afghanistan. The resulting Soviet presence on the border of Iran was perceived by some as constituting the eastern terminus of a pincher movement around the Middle East. The western point of the pincher was seen to be the Soviet presence at the Ethiopian port of Assab, on the Red Sea, and the Soviet forces in the once-British naval base at Aden on the tip of the Arabian peninsula.

Accentuating American concern about Soviet intentions in the Middle East were Central Intelligence Agency (CIA) reports issued in 1979 to the effect that Moscow might be forced to enter competition with the United States and its allies for oil as the easily exploited Soviet oil fields were depleted. No one suggested that the Soviets were absolutely running out of oil. What the CIA analysts did suggest was that the Soviet Union would be more likely to compete for Middle East oil than to undertake the very arduous and expensive extraction of oil from the areas of Siberia and arctic Russia where large quantities of oil and natural gas are thought to be located.

In the 1970s there had been some preliminary discussion, as part of efforts to establish detente with the Soviets, about American capital and technology being used to assist the Soviets with their difficult-to-exploit Siberian and arctic potential. In exchange for U.S. assistance, the Soviets were to have supplied liquefied natural gas to the United States. With the deterioration in U.S.–U.S.S.R. relations, particularly after the invasion of Afghanistan, talk of such a deal ceased, and speculation mounted regarding where the Soviets would obtain oil for the 1980s and 1990s.

Fortunately for the United States and particularly its allies, some NATO nations, most notably Great Britain, are becoming substantially free of dependence on the Middle East. This situation results from the maturation of the North Sea oil and natural gas explorations begun a decade ago. Other NATO allies of the United States have not been so fortunate regarding new energy supplies. For example West Germany took action in late 1981 which caused considerable consternation in Washington. The event was the announcement by the West German government that it was working out a deal with the Soviets which would result in the construction of a large natural gas pipeline from the U.S.S.R. to central Europe. The official American concern was that such a pipeline would dangerously increase the dependence of West Germany and nearby nations on Moscow.

III. IS THE UNITED STATES RUNNING OUT OF ENERGY?

For an American accustomed to reading and hearing of the energy crisis, it may come as a surprise to read here that the crisis is not one of overall supply; it is a crisis of access, development, and distribution. In other words, neither the United States nor the world is running out of energy, as is often popularly stated. Instead, energy shortages result from the fact that natural and human-induced barriers exist that prevent or reduce the flow of energy from where it is to where it is needed. Put most vividly, it may be safely stated that there is far more energy on earth than can possibly be utilized by a much larger population, living at a higher standard of living. As will be noted below, a considerable portion of the energy policy debate centers on ways to remove or to mitigate the barriers that currently separate those who believe they need the energy from the energy itself.

A major barrier that separates civilization from immense amounts of energy on earth, and in the universe, is a technological one. There simply is no technology at this time with which to make certain forms of energy available. At times the technological barrier may be overcome, but the presence of an economic barrier still prevents the utilization of the energy source. In such a situation technology exists for utilizing an energy source, but the cost in dollars is prohibitive for normal use. A brief review of major energy sources that cannot be utilized because technology does not exist for their development, or because existing technology is too expensive, will serve to underscore the point that the crisis is one of supply being tapped, not one of supply not being there.

For example, there is a large amount of heat energy found in the core of the earth. A tiny hint of this geothermal energy is seen in the periodic eruptions of volcanos, and in the thermal activity evident in areas such as Yellowstone National Park. Here and there steam escaping from the earth has been captured to turn a generator in an electric power plant, but generally the technical demands, and the expense, make geothermal energy at this time unusable.

Two-thirds of the earth's surface is covered with water. As any school child knows, the formula for water is H_2O, meaning that for every part of oxygen there are two parts of hydrogen. Hydrogen combusts readily and can be burned in automobile engines that have been modified, and it can be used for space heating. For hydrogen it is not a matter of technology, but cost that is the problem. It is a simple laboratory procedure to separate hydrogen from oxygen in water by using the procedure known as electrolysis, or the running of an electric current through water. However, a vast amount of hydrogen is not available for commercial use because of the cost of electrolysis. Should a means be found to lower the cost of electrolysis considerably, then hydrogen extraction from water would be much more attractive.

Another possible means to use the abundant hydrogen is to replicate on earth the process that powers the sun. That would involve the fusion of light atoms such as isotopes of hydrogen. Work on this process, called the fusion reactor, is underway in many advanced nations. To date success has not been achieved because of very difficult technical problems that remain to be resolved. The main technical problem is the requirement to come close to duplicating the temperatures and pressures found on the sun in order to induce fusion. Currently the only means to achieve those parameters is to detonate an atomic bomb. This, incidentally, is the means by which a hydrogen bomb is detonated. Obviously means other than an atomic explosion must be found if commercial fusion reactors are to become a reality.

Should the technological barriers to fusion be removed, it appears that very large amounts of electricity will be made available. Some believe that relatively cheap electricity from fusion reactors could then be used to separate hydrogen from water for use in transportation and space heating.

Huge amounts of solar energy travel toward the earth from the sun each day. However, much solar energy does not reach the earth because of clouds, and half of the earth is always in darkness. Although the solar energy that does reach the earth is clearly appropriate for utilization by growing plants, it is generally too diffuse for conversion to other forms of energy. Capturing and concentrating the sun's energy can technically be done at this time, but given current interest rates, and the cost of labor and materials, many would prefer to utilize more conventional heating sources such as natural gas. The sun's energy can technically be converted directly into electrical energy, but the cost of a photovoltaic cell is such that it can be justified only when no other source of electricity is available, as is the case on a space satellite.

Coal is one of the most abundant of the fossil fuels. For about $75 a barrel, coal can be converted into synthetic gasoline, which enables a solid energy source to be used as a fuel for automobiles. However, at a time when the world market price of gasoline is in the range of $30 for a barrel of oil, there is little economic incentive to use coal conversion technologies.

It is generally agreed that there is more potential for synthetic gasoline locked up in the oil shales of Colorado, Utah, and Wyoming than there is oil in the Middle East. Industrial processes have been developed to extract a substance similar to petroleum from oil shale and then to refine it to produce synthetic gasoline. A basic problem with oil shale development is that synthetic gasoline from this source currently costs more than that refined from conventional oil. Should OPEC prices rise faster than the inflation of oil shale production, the time may be reached when it will cost about the same to retort oil shale as to import Middle East crude. Judging from federal efforts to spur oil shale development, that time could come in this century. The time will come sooner if the federal government decides to subsidize oil shale because of national security considerations relative to imported oil.

At this time the vast percentage of uranium found in the earth's crust is not utilized as an energy source. The explanation is that less than 1 percent of the uranium is the isotope U-235, which is needed for the fuel of most currently operating nuclear power plants. The remaining uranium is U-238, which is not suitable for reactor fuel unless one is operating an uncommon kind of reactor known as a CANDU reactor.

If a means could be found to utilize the plentiful U-238, then large supplies of currently nonutilizable uranium would become valuable as a new energy source. The search for just this means of using U-238 is found in the efforts to develop a new nuclear reactor known as a breeder reactor. This is a complex device wherein U-238 is bombarded with neutrons in a way that transforms part of the uranium into the artificial element plutonium. Plutonium-239, unlike U-238 from which it is produced, can be used as the fuel for a nuclear power plant. Unfortunately, U-239 can also be used to fabricate nuclear weapons.

Those who support the development of the breeder reactor concept argue that by this means the bulk of currently nonusable uranium can be converted into usable plutonium with which to fuel more reactors, which can convert more U-238 to plutonium as they also produce electricity. Moving to a plutonium fuel cycle would clearly provide much more nuclear energy than is currently available. However, as will be noted in a later section, there are reasons, at least in the United States, why the breeder may not be developed.

Thorium is an element that can be subjected to neutron bombardment and thus converted to U-233, which can in turn be fissioned in a reactor. The process is complex and has not yet been attempted on a commercial scale. However, there are those who call attention to the fact that throium is found about the world, most notably in India, and that it constitutes a source of fission energy that has not as yet been tapped.

It is generally believed by geologists that vast new pools of oil and natural gas await discovery and exploitation when the profit associated with the need to drill deeper and explore inhospitable areas is sufficient to justify the effort. This perspective reflects the view that society will not soon run out of energy, in this case fossil fuel, but that the fuel will merely cost more. In addition to energy companies responding to market inducement and thus finding more fossil fuel, there is in operation the continued improvement in energy detection technology. It is widely believed in the oil and gas industry that such improvement will also substantially contribute to new finds in the future. An example of both higher prices stimulating exploration and development and the contribution being made by improved technology is the recent new finds in what is called the overthrust belt. This is a geologic formation found along the western edge of the Rocky Mountains in Utah and Wyoming particularly. Potentially higher prices and better exploration technology also promise new oil and natural gas discoveries in places such as the Arctic, under the Antarctic icecap, and in the ocean depths beyond current development levels.

If one considers the energy present beyond the earth in our solar system, and beyond that in the entire universe, there seem to be no limits to the total energy available to earthlings. In fact there appear to be sources of energy in deep space, currently detectable by advanced technology, for which there is no known physical explanation. These sources of energy are thought to be extremely large in reference to known and understood energy supplies. Obviously there exist at this time seemingly insurmountable technical and economic barriers to the utilization of such energy sources. However, these barriers may fall in time as science and technology continue to expand.

Thus, if one takes a long-range perspective, it can be strongly argued that truly difficult-to-imagine amounts of energy exist, on earth and beyond. Those who exhibit technological optimism are convinced that the current energy crisis will be resolved through the twin forces of the market and advanced technology.

There is, however, another side of the coin regarding the removal of technical and economic barriers to new energy sources. Part of this concern relates to the immediate physical harm to the environment associated with the extraction and utilization of new energy sources. For example, there would be the environmental damage should extensive mining for coal be done in the Antarctic regions. Perhaps an even greater concern is that unlocking vast amounts of new energy will encourage an ever-increasing population to live at an expanding standard of living. This would not be, as some believe, a good thing, according to many environmentalists. They contend that the resulting demands by a much larger population, using much more of everything, would place very severe demands on the carrying capacity of the earth. Such demands would include, it is contended, the capacity of the earth's atmosphere to absorb the waste heat from additional use of energy, and the capacity of the earth's atmosphere to absorb mounting amounts of energy-generated pollution. To persons with this perspective, the removal of technical and economic barriers to new energy sources should be done with extreme care as to the probable environmental consequences. Those taking this perspective are generally in favor of an intellectual exercise known as technology assessment (TA).

Briefly stated, technology assessment is a structured analysis of the potential impacts should a particular activity be undertaken. In general, TA analysis is designed to provide the answers to three standard questions concerning the potential impact of new technology. These are (1) what impact on the ecosystem, including human society, is likely to result; (2) what barriers to future growth is the new technology likely to remove; and (3) what will be the next barrier to growth that will be subject to future removal? Answers to these questions can be weighed and evaluated against whatever benefits are claimed for the new technology.

Currently the opposition in the United States to the breeder reactor reflects, in part, concern over the environmental impact that could result from the production of large amounts of Pu-239, which is both extremely toxic in a chemical sense and long-lived in terms of the period during with it is radioactive.

The successful efforts in Congress to place areas of Alaska off limits to energy exploration and development constitute another example of an environmental barrier that exists between potential users of new energy and the energy itself.

It should be noted here that President Reagan's Secretary of the Interior, James Watt created considerable uproar in 1981 when he announced plans to open up federally owned lands in the western United States and offshore areas under salt water to increased energy exploration and possible development. Environmental groups formed loose coalitions to oppose what they claimed was a giveaway of energy resources without appropriate environmental safeguards. The interior secretary responded by stating that it would be wrongheaded public policy to "lock up" natural resources at a time when they are required by a nation grown overly dependent on foreign supplies, and needing economic growth stimuli. Secretary Watt's assurance that energy exploration and development would be accomplished in concert with a proper concern for environmental standards did not satisfy many environmentalists. The arguments over theories of how energy resources under federally owned lands should be handled will no doubt continue for some time.

In addition to technical, economic, and environmental barriers to energy sources, there exist geographic and political barriers. Both may be demonstrated by a reference to the contemporary Middle East. A glance at a map that shows the Persian Gulf at one end of the supertanker route to an oil-importing nation such as Japan will make the point. From the Persian Gulf, through the Straits of Hormuz, across the Indian Ocean, through the choke points near the islands comprising Indonesia, and on across the China Sea comprises an arduous geographic journey. Should any nation wish to block Japan's access to Persian Gulf oil by the application of sea power on the tanker route, the Japanese could encounter serious energy supply problems.

Generally thought to be a more serious barrier to Middle East oil utilization than geography is the political barrier represented by the use of the oil weapon on the part of Arab states hostile to the continued existence of Israel. At other times and in other places the enmity between the Soviet Union and the United States may constitute another form of political barrier to the free movement of energy supplies.

To repeat what was noted at the beginning of this section, and what will be examined in greater detail in the sections on government energy organization and policy, and the risks and costs of alternative energy sources, much of the national energy policy currently being implemented by the federal government is designed in various ways to remove the technical, economic, and political barriers to greater supplies of energy in the future. Whether or not such barrier removal policy is sound from an environmental perspective will continue to be much debated.

IV. THE RISKS AND COSTS OF ALTERNATIVE ENERGY SOURCES

Another way to understand the past and the future of U.S. energy policy is to assess the incentives and disincentives to use or not to use different energy sources. Such an analysis, which has as its focus one risk and two costs of contemporary energy sources, will yield a view of the general parameters within which American energy policy planning has begun, and within which policy is likely to be conducted for some time into the future. Therefore, in this section a number of energy sources will be analyzed and compared with each other in terms of the risk to the security of supply and the dollar cost of the energy source, and lastly the anticipated environmental cost of each energy source.

A. Oil

The Security of Supply Risk: In the late 1970s a milestone of sorts was passed by the United States. It was then that approximately half of the petroleum used in the United States each day (nearly 8.5 million barrels out of a total of 17 million barrels) had to be imported from abroad. Some of this imported oil came from nearby and relatively stable nations such as Mexico and Canada, some came from faraway and unstable nations such as Iran and Libya. As the volitility of the Middle East oil region increased, and as the Soviet presence in the area appeared to grow, many agreed with the policy goal suggested by President Nixon when he called for an effort to make the United States independent of imported oil—thus reducing to zero the risk that oil supplies would be cut off.

   The risk to the economy is so great in the case of a Middle East oil cutoff that the Carter administration was committed to alternative fuels that can be produced domestically and so have the security of supply guaranteed. However, the Carter administration appeared more realistic than the Nixon group in that the announced goal was not independence, but lessened dependence. The Reagan administration is much closer to the Carter position than to the Nixon perspective.

Dollar Costs: Of the various sources of conventional energy, it is particularly oil that has undergone the most dramatic increase in cost during the past decade. Before 1973 a barrel of crude from the Middle East sold on the world market for about $3.00. By 1980 the same barrel from the same area sold from between $30 and $40 a barrel, depending on whether it was purchased as part of a regular contract or on the spot oil market. Rarely has the price of such a needed commodity increased to that extent over less than 10 years. How much higher world market prices will rise is a complex matter of supply, demand, domestic and international politics.

   As the price of oil on the world market increased, considerable concern was expressed in the United States over the wealth that was being drained from the nation and the increases in prices of everything made from oil or transported by use of oil. For many months at a time the nation suffered from a negative balance of trade due in large measure to the price of imported oil. "Public enemy number one," that is, inflation, is caused in part by escalating oil prices.

Environmental Costs: Although significant, the environmental costs of oil usage are not generally perceived as so serious a lever on policy decisions as are the security of supply risk and the dollar costs.

A major environmental impact of oil use is the smog with which Americans are so familiar. It results from the burning of gasoline in internal combustion engines, and the burning of diesel fuel in diesel engines, plus inputs of other combustion products from a metropolitan area. Some engine combustion products interact with sunlight, which makes the problem worse at higher altitudes such as Denver, Colorado.

Technical responses to the smog problem have been partially successful. They include the development of cleaner-burning engines, better gasoline, and the mandating by some states of periodic engine tuneups, which result in more efficient combustion with less combustion products entering the air. The smog problem was ameliorated somewhat because people drove less, car- and vanpooled, or took public transportation, mostly as a result of the higher price of gasoline. Here and there communities investigated the advantages of installing a light rail transport system similar to European systems. Some claimed that they could see as a result of these responses a leveling off in the increase of metropolitan smog pollution.

The other major environmental problem with oil—tanker spills and oil rig explosions and spills—both of which polluted portions of the oceans, remains a problem. Some success has been reported with regard to the management of oil spills and their cleanup.

Although it may be too early to assess long-term effects, the Alaska pipeline seems not to be the environmental disaster some were predicting at the time of its construction.

Assessment: Overall, due mainly to the risk that supply will be interrupted, and to the drain of dollars out of the country, imported oil was thought by the policy makers of the Nixon, Ford, Carter and Reagan administrations to be unacceptable as a very large, long-term component of U.S. energy supplies. Understanding this perspective enables one to understand much of the emphasis on fuels that in time are to serve as alternatives to oil, particularly oil from unstable areas.

B. Natural Gas

The Security of Supply Risk: To the extent that natural gas must be imported from unstable foreign areas, it suffers from the same security of supply problem as does oil. However, at the present time, domestic use does not require much importation beyond what can probably be supplied by Mexico, and possibly Canada in the near future. With considerable natural gas being discovered in the lower 48 states, and also in Alaska, it appears that the security of supply risk of natural gas is not particularly high at this point.

Dollar Costs: For many years it was the objective of the federal government to keep the price of domestic natural gas artificially low as a means to encourage its use in domestic and industrial areas. After long and at times bitter debate, the Carter administration accepted the proposition that only higher prices would stimulate greater exploration for new gas fields. Currently, therefore, the price of natural gas is undergoing a phased decontrol. Increased drilling activity in the first year of the 1980s was cited by industry spokespersons as being confirmation of the philosophy that higher remuneration will spur more production.

Environmental Costs: Natural gas combustion results in the least pollution of any of the fossil fuels, and it does not have the radiation problems associated with nuclear power. When natural gas spills or leaks into the atmosphere, it quickly dissipates into the surrounding air. Thus it may be stated that from an environmental perspective natural gas is a premier fuel. From that standpoint it is unfortunate that we cannot draw all of our energy from the burning of natural gas.

Assessment: Compared to imported oil, the security of supply risk for natural gas is small. Although the price is increasing through decontrol, natural gas is still an attractive buy compared to many energy alternatives, especially for space heating. The environmental costs of natural gas are low compared with many other energy alternatives. For these reasons, as long as the supply is adequate, natural gas will continue to be a major component of U.S. energy consumption.

C. Coal

The Security of Supply Risk: The dominant fact regarding coal is that there *are no* security of supply risks because the United States is abundantly supplied with both lignite and anthracite, possibly better endowed with coal than are most nations. Understanding this situation will enable one to understand the central place coal is intended to play in U.S. energy policy.

Because of its importance, some elaboration should be made of the supplies of coal available in the United States. For example, it is estimated that the United States possesses more coal than it does any other type of fossil fuel. Many believe that at current consumption rates there is some 200 years' worth of coal obtainable using contemporary technology. So large in fact are U.S. coal reserves that talk is heard regarding America becoming the OPEC of the 1990s based on export of coal to Western Europe and to Japan.

Substantially enhancing the attractiveness of coal in the context of lessening the security of supply risks associated with imported oil is the fact that coal can be converted to synthetic gasoline, or to synthetic natural gas. Presently the conversion processes are technically difficult and expensive. Both constraints may yield, however, in time, meaning that eventually coal could supplant oil directly in its converted form.

Dollar Costs: Coal prices, unlike those for oil and natural gas, have not been regulated by the federal government. This means, of course, that they cannot increase as a result of decontrol. Further, the domestic price of coal is not related to the world market price because the United States does not import coal. Therefore coal costs will not escalate for the same reasons that natural gas and oil prices will increase. Nevertheless, coal prices will rise. One reason is inflation. Another reason is the cost of bringing new deep mines and strip mines into production. Still another reason for increasing coal costs is what economists term internalizing the externalities. This bit of economic jargon means that some of the environmental costs of coal use, formerly spared the consumer and borne by the environment, will increasingly be charged against those who use the final energy end product of coal combustion. Two examples of internalizing the externalities will suggest how the procedure operates. Federal air quality standards require that technology be bought and applied to the effort to clean up stack gases from coal combustion. The cost is passed on to the consumer of the resultant electricity. Federal strip mine legislation requires that mining companies return, to the extent that it is possible, the mined areas to the original condition. Here again, cost is passed on to the consumer of the coal.

Environmental Costs: The environmental costs for coal use are substantial in terms of what is known. They may be worse in terms of what is only suspected, not yet proved. Still, given the concern over the security of supply for imported oil, the environmental problems with expanded coal use are perceived by government policy makers as being tolerable.

Eastern coal, which is frequently deep mined, is associated with several particular problems. Men who spend their working lives in the mines are subject to a disease of the respiratory system termed black lung disease. This condition results from the gradual accumulation of minute particles of coal on the linings of the lungs. Eastern deep-mined coal is also associated with mine cave-ins and explosions in which human lives are lost. Less direct effects on living matter from Eastern coal mining include the seepage of acid water from mines and tailings into waterways and underground water supplies.

Much Western coal is strip mined. This process involves pealing off the top layers of earth to expose the coal seams below. When the coal has been removed, a depression results which scars the landscape.

When coal is burned in a power plant, combustion products are injected into the atmosphere. These include tiny particles of ash called particulates, and various noxious gases such as carbon monoxide, sulfur dioxide, and the oxides of nitrogen. The precise long-term effects of particulates and the noxious gases are not fully understood, but the matter is receiving increased study. Several potential problems may exist, however. One is called acid rain. Evidence exists that the oxides of sulfur and nitrogen combine with water vapor and precipitate earthward in the form of very weak acid solutions. The resulting accumulation of acid may be beneficial to certain soils and harmful to others. Clear evidence does exist that acid rain is quite harmful to aquatic life. The acid rain phenomenon has been observed in areas downwind from the coal-burning sections of industrialized Europe, and in the Eastern United States. Some studies suggest that the problem is now to be found in the Western United States. In 1980 the federal government launched an acid rain assessment project to determine the causes of acid rain, its disbursement over the nation, and its effects on living matter.

Another environmental concern associated with the burning of coal, indeed of other fossil fuels as well, is the production of carbon dioxide which enters the earth's atmosphere. It is generally agreed among atmospheric scientists that carbon dioxide in the atmosphere traps heat from the sun; the more carbon dioxide the more heat is kept from radiating back into space. The resulting situation is termed the greenhouse effect for obvious reasons. Exactly how much the world's temperature will increase due to increased coal burning is not known, nor are the specific consequences of the warming on climate and agriculture.

Where coal is burned, water is required for cooling. In the Eastern U.S. this is not so much a problem as in the more arid Western portions of the nation. Whether the warmed water is returned to a lake or river, or whether it is evaporated in cooling towers, environmentalists argue that the environment is altered in a negative fashion.

Assessment: Because coal has no security of supply problems associated with it, coal is being heavily emphasized as the replacement, until more exotic fuels become available, for imported oil. The rationale is that the advantages regarding security of supply and the dollar costs of coal far outweigh the environmental costs. Environmentalists are not likely to accept such a perspective in the near term, so considerable skirmishing is to be expected between energy decision makers favoring coal, and environmentalists.

D. Nuclear Energy: Fission

The Security of Supply Risks: As long as American nuclear reactors use as fuel domestically produced U-235, there will be no security of supply problems with nuclear energy. However, because of a physical characteristic of reactors employing the fission process, particularly of the breeder reactor, a unique problem is associated with nuclear energy production. This is a by-product of fission, the artificial element plutonium. Plutonium can be easily separated from spent fuel rods by chemical means and then used as reactor fuel, or for the fabrication of atomic bombs. It is this latter use that has caused the United States considerable difficulty as Washington, as well as Moscow, struggle with how best to preclude Pu-239 from diversion to nuclear weapons production. Plutonium produced in reactor operation is much easier to obtain than is the other element from which nuclear weapons can be manufactured, U-235. To date the expense and technical difficulty of producing weapons-grade U-235 have been so great that only the most advanced nations have done it—the United States, the Soviet Union, England, France, and the Peoples' Republic of China.

On the other hand India has detonated a nuclear explosion from plutonium, and Israel is generally believed to have hidden away some number of plutonium weapons against the day when the Arab threat cannot be answered by other means. Other nations may follow suit.

In response to the dangers associated with the possible proliferation of plutonium about the world, as well as the much slower spread of U-235 separation technology, the United States, England, and the Soviet Union joined forces late in the 1960s to urge the world to adopt a treaty that bans the diversion of fissionable materials to nuclear weapons development. Known as the Nonproliferation Treaty (NPT) the arrangement has been ratified by a majority of states. A number of states, however, that are technically capable of producing plutonium in their reactors, and subsequently manufacturing atomic weapons, have not accepted the NPT.

Because of the plutonium-to-weapons problem, and because of environmental concerns regarding plutonium, President Carter refused to support the American version of the breeder reactor. Despite some support from the Reagan administration the demonstration program, at one time scheduled to be built at Clinch River, Tennessee, is currently in a kind of governmental limbo. Unfortunately, from the perspective of those opposing development of breeder reactors, other advanced nations have not accepted the self-imposed ban on development suggested by President Carter. Therefore it appears that the Western European nations, the Japanese, and the Soviet Union may continue their research on breeders, and later presumably put them into commercial use.

Dollar Costs: The exact dollar costs of currently operating nuclear power plants is a difficult figure to establish with precision. This is because much of the research and development was funded by the Atomic Energy Commission, and thus are not costs that need to be amortized by the industry. Looking toward the future, costs remain hard to estimate because it is not clear how much "downtime" contemporary reactors will undergo as safety regulations require lowering output for the purpose of safety checks and maintenance. Nor is it clear the extent to which the federal government will subsidize the nuclear industry with regard to production of reactor fuel. Further, it appears that the original estimates regarding the normal efficiency of nuclear power plants, that they would operate at 80 percent of their maximum output, were overly optimistic. Gregory Daneke has compiled many of the conflicting economic claims for and against nuclear power (1979).

Environmental Costs: Of all the existing energy sources, nuclear power has created the most vigorous and persistent opposition to its development. As mentioned in the first section, part of this response is due to the mystery surrounding the unknowns of nuclear radiation, and the sinister possibilities with regard to the passing of genetic damage from one generation to another.

Environmental opposition to civil nuclear power centers on four contentions: first, that any increase in the natural background level of radiation found in nature is harmful to living things, and that even minute release of radioactive gas from power plants is therefore unacceptable; second, that water used in cooling nuclear power plants that is dumped back into rivers and lakes changes the temperature of the receiving water bodies to the detriment of aquatic life; third, that whereas the chance of a nuclear explosion at a reactor is very slight, there could be a steam explosion, a meltdown of the reactor core caused by a malfunction of the cooling system, or sabotage intended to produce an explosion; fourth, that there is not a truly safe means to dispose permanently of nuclear wastes from the operation of reactors.

To these propositions the nuclear power industry and government entities involved in nuclear research and safety regulation have replies. First, it is pointed out that many persons voluntarily subject themselves to greater levels of radiation by having a dental x-ray, or by moving to a higher elevation (where radiation from the sun passes through less filtering atmosphere) than is caused by the operation of nuclear power plants. Second, it is pointed out that the warming of water bodies by the discharge of cooling water is slight. Third, it is pointed out that the safety record of the nuclear industry to date is far better than most industrial activities. Fourth, it is pointed out that radioactive wastes can be safely stored on a permanent basis in stable underground locations such as salt strata, which are not exposed to the leaching of underground water or to earthquake activity.

Assessment: A problem for the politician regarding the hazards of civil nuclear power is that impressive arrays of experts are found on both sides of the question. Some argue from impeccable scholarly backgrounds that such power is safe. Others, with equally good academic credentials, state flatly that civil nuclear power is not sufficiently safe. What does the decision maker charged with developing public policy do?

E. Nuclear Energy: Fusion

The Security of Supply Risk: Because the fuel for a fusion reactor will be an isotope of hydrogen, there does not appear to be any security of supply risk associated with this source of energy.

Dollar Costs: At this time it is probably not realistic to attempt to estimate the ultimate costs for fusion power because too much still must be researched and developed.

Environmental Costs: At the present time it appears that there will be much less radio-active wastes from fusion processes than from fission processes. Further, the danger of explosion from whatever source appears less in regard to the fusion reactor as compared to a fission reactor. These preliminary perspectives are based, however, on only fragmentary knowledge as to what a fusion reactor will actually be.

Unlike fission reactors, a fusion reactor is not expected to produce as a by-product an artificial element suitable for fabrication into atomic weapons.

Assessment: Pie in the sky, or a real possibility for awesome amounts of electricity—it could go either way. What is safe to say about fusion is that if it is developed, the world will never be the same.

F. Solar Energy

The Security of Supply Risk: There is obviously no risk to the continued supply of sunlight. Should the United States build solar collectors as earth-orbiting satellites, the possibility would then exist that the satellites could be destroyed by enemy action. But this kind of threat exists with regard to the bombing of installations associated with all other forms of energy, and this is not what is meant by the security of supply risk.

Dollars Costs: Although sunlight itself is free, the collecting of it, the concentrating of it, and the storing of it does incur substantial costs. It is primarily for this reason that so little solar energy is used for residential or for commercial purposes. An example will make the point about the expense of solar power. Would the reader prefer to continue paying the increasing cost of using natural gas to heat his or her home, or to take out a second mortgage at 15 percent for 10 years, and to use the borrowed money to replace the current roof with solar collectors, install plumbing to transport the heated water from the roof to the basement, and construct in the basement a 1000-gallon tank to retain the heated water so that a heat exchanger can transfer the warmth to air which is then circulated through the existing heating system?

Solar proponents correctly point out that should the price for natural gas and other heating alternatives increase dramatically, solar will become correspondingly more attractive. Government can, of course, subsidize solar energy adoption by increasing the tax breaks that now exist for solar construction.

Currently the direct conversion of solar energy into electricity is far too expensive, except for unusual situations where almost any price will be paid for energy, such as in satellites.

Environmental Costs: Solar energy is the darling of the environmentalists. This is because solar as it is currently conceived has very little environmental impact. What impact there is would be associated with the extraction of the materials necessary to construct solar collectors—copper mining, for example, which must be done to supply the material for the hot water pipes.

Looking toward a future when there may be earth satellites collecting solar energy and beaming it down in a form convertible directly to electricity, one could expect some environmental problems. The most obvious would be from the higher standard of living for more people that cheap solar electricity would permit. A more sophisticated concern is about the possible negative alterations in the earth's albedo (the amount of incident light that is reflected back into space), which could have climatic consequences. Altering the earth's albedo would not seemingly be a problem unless very large amounts of sunlight were to be captured.

Assessment: Of the more futuristic sources of energy, solar is most attractive because of the low environmental costs and the absence of security of supply risks. If and when the economic costs become more competitive with alternative energy sources, solar will become widespread in its adoption.

G. Hydro Power

The Security of Supply Risk: Dependent only on nature's supply of annual rain and snow melt, hydroelectric power carries no risk of being interrupted by events in foreign lands.

Dollar Costs: The cost of building hydroelectric dams on major rivers suffers as does everything else from annual inflation. However, there are no special cost escalators affecting hydroelectric price, as is the case with many other forms of energy.

Environmental Costs: When the large hydro power dams such as Grand Coulee, Hoover, and those in the TVA system were built, there was little environmental opposition. This situation is quite changed today. It is hard to imagine either a government entity or a private utility being able to overcome the environmental opposition that would surely form to oppose any proposed large dam now. For example, can anyone believe that it would be politically possible to dam the Grand Canyon? The point here is that the good dam sites that remain untouched are likely to be fiercely defended from being changed in the future.

Assessment: Primarily because of the paucity of good dam sites, and the stern environmentalist defense of the sites that remain, hydro power is not likely to constitute much additional new energy. There is one exception to this statement. That is the activity in the Northeast where old dams are being renovated so that hydroelectric power can be generated.

H. Oil Shale

The Security of Supply Risk: Like coal, the dominant fact regarding oil shale is that there *are no* security of supply risks associated with utilization of shale located in Colorado, Utah, and Wyoming.

Dollar Costs: By 1980 the often-quoted cost for oil shale produced in the Western United States was $35 a barrel. This compared rather favorably with the OPEC price of $30 a barrel for long-term contracted oil. It is not entirely clear what the price for a barrel of oil shale will be in the future, because it is not entirely clear to what degree the federal government will subsidize oil shale development, nor is it entirely clear how much cost will be added to oil shale because of the expense of ameliorating the environmental impact of oil shale development.

Assuming that dollar costs of oil shale will drop as mass production is developed, and assuming that OPEC does not dramatically lower the world price it charges, it appears that oil shale development could become more economically attractive within the next decade.

Environmental Costs: As is the case with Western coal, development of oil shale in the arid regions of the Rocky Mountain West carries with it considerable environmental costs. These costs include use of water in the retorting processes, and use of water to support re-growth of vegetation on the dumps of oil shale residue to prevent erosion. As is the case with Western coal combustion or conversion to synthetic gasoline, the water can be bought from current agricultural uses. Using the in situ process of retorting, where the oil shale is left in the ground and subjected to the 900° temperatures necessary to sepa-rate the petroleum-like substance from the shale rock, would reduce the need to dispose of the oil shale residue on the surface. It is not yet certain, however, whether the in situ process will be viable.

If above-ground retorting is the method of processing, the residue must be disposed of above ground because upon processing it increases in volume and thus will not fit back into the mine from whence it came. Oil shale companies claim that residue dumps can be so stabilized that wind erosion will not occur, and that harmful salts will not be leached out into local ground water supplies, nor into the drainage of the Colorado River. Envi-ronmentalists express doubts about such claims.

As with coal, the impact of the new population needed to operate a large-scale oil shale production operation will fall on the local environment. This means more sewage will need to be treated, more four-wheel-drive vehicles will be operated on nearby lands, more hunters and fishermen will be afield, and so on. Oil shale development also means more demands for social services to support the extra population.

Assessment: As mentioned earlier, the dominant fact about oil shale is that there are no security of supply risks associated with its use. Therefore, despite somewhat higher eco-nomic costs than for imported oil, and some substantial environmental costs, oil shale was emphasized by the Carter administration in its synthetic fuels program. The Reagan ad-ministration is also emphasizing synthetic fuel development, but in a somewhat different fashion. True to his preference for market solutions to production problems, and to his opposition to large governmental activity in the economic sphere, President Reagan voiced the hope that private capital would become more involved in oil shale develop-ment so that federal participation would be less. Therefore the federal role in oil shale de-velopment has been reduced under the Reagan administration.

I. Hydrogen

The Security of Supply Risk: Being ubiquitous, there is no need to import hydrogen, thus there is no security of supply risk to this potential energy source.

Dollar Costs: Currently the cost for hydrogen is prohibitive for its use a fuel. Cheap sources of electricity that can be used in the separation of hydrogen from oxygen in water would change the costs substantially. But until fusion power is at hand, cheap elec-tricity does not appear likely.

Environmental Costs: The combustion of hydrogen does not produce air pollution, nor is there radioactive waste. Nor does the production of hydrogen create environmental problems as does the extraction of coal and oil shale.

Assessment: Until costs can be dramatically reduced, hydrogen has little future as an alternative fuel source.

J. Geothermal Energy

The Security of Supply Risk: There is no security of supply risk associated with geothermal energy.

Dollar Costs: Typically the economic costs of exploiting the heat in the center of the earth is prohibitive. The only exceptions to this observation are the occasional geographic anomalies where geothermal heat is sufficiently near the earth's surface to be captured for energy purposes. An example would be the hot water heating system of Iceland's capital city, Reykjavik.

Environmental Costs: The primary environmental cost is disposal of the often heavily mineralized water which is drawn from the earth. In optimal situations it can be reinjected into the earth.

Assessment: The problem with geothermal energy as an alternative to currently used fuels is the high economic cost.

K. Wind Energy

The Security of Supply Cost: There is no security of supply cost associated with wind power.

Dollar Costs: Although the wind carries no cost, building wind generators to capture the wind's energy and convert it to electricity is expensive. And the supply of wind is not normally dependable, so means are required to store the electricity that can be collected when the wind is blowing. In most situations these costs of wind power in relation to conventional sources of energy make wind energy less than attractive.

Environmental Costs: Except for the esthetic costs of marring the skyline with some type of windmill, there is little environmental cost to wind energy.

Assessment: Wind power will be used here and there under unusual circumstances, but the dollar costs will prevent wind power from being widespread unless the costs of alternative fuels rise very substantially.

L. Biomass

The Security of Supply Risk: Because biomass is comprised of human and animal wastes, and in some instances crops grown for the purpose of converting them into a natural gas-like product, there are no security of supply costs to this type of energy.

Dollar Costs: Human and animal wastes are obviously cheap, but collecting them and converting them to usable energy is not cheap. Growing corn to be converted to gasohol is not cheap either. Therefore the price of energy from biomass will be a factor in constraining its use unless alternative fuels become very expensive.

Environmental Costs: Combustion of biomass gas, like the burning of natural gas, leaves little environmental pollution, and no radioactive wastes.

Assessment: Here and there, at large municipal garbage dumps and where certain crops are not needed for food, some biomass energy will be developed. But it is not likely to form a substantial portion of the nation's energy supplies.

V. GOVERNMENT ENERGY ORGANIZATION AND POLICY

As one would expect in a federal system, the federal government of the United States has shouldered most of the responsibility for organizing to meet the nation's energy problems, and has created most of the national energy policy. However, many state governments have established state energy offices. The responsibilities of such offices are typically related to preparing emergency response plans for fuel allocation situations, and to educating the public regarding energy conservation and efficiency measures.

For many years prior to the energy crisis of the 1970s the most obvious of the federal entities engaged in energy policy was the Atomic Energy Commission (AEC) which was established following the World War II development of nuclear weapons. A primary responsibility of the AEC was to move nuclear energy from military to civilian applications, particularly the development of nuclear power reactors for the production of electricity. A second responsibility of the AEC was the promulgation and enforcement of safety standards for the civil nuclear power industry. During the period of this dual responsibility, some questioned whether an agency charged with promoting civil nuclear power could realistically be expected simultaneously to regulate the industry to achieve maximum safety.

Before the AEC was created, several other federal agencies were involved during the interwar years with bits and pieces of national energy policy development. For example, the Tennessee Valley Authority, and the Department of the Interior (Bonneville Power Administration, Southwest Power Administration, etc.) were engaged in the development of hydropower in the drainages of the Tennessee, Columbia, and Colorado Rivers. The Department of the Interior distributed electricity from its hydroelectric dams by giving preference according to the law to public consumers such as other governmental bodies. The Federal Power Commission and the Interstate Commerce Commission regulated rates for energy shipped across state borders. The Rural Electrification Administration loaned out money to construct electric lines to outlying farm homes, and later built some power plants to supply electricity to farm families. It was not until the 1970s energy crisis that efforts were made in earnest to consolidate the disparate fragments of federal energy activity into a consolidated whole.

Much institutional change occurred in the 1970s. This was a period of experimentation with various federal entities as the Nixon, Ford, and Carter administrations struggled with the task of putting together a coordinated institutional response to the energy problems facing the nation. After delivering the first presidential message to Congress on June 4, 1971, President Nixon tried unsuccessfully to convince Congress to create a Department of National Resources, or a Department of Energy and National Resources. Congress did eventually create another Nixon suggestion, the Energy Research and Development Administration. Into the new entity were combined the research and development functions of the AEC, together with other federal research and development activities such as the Office of Coal Research, then located in the Department of the Interior. The regulatory functions of the Atomic Energy Commission were transferred to the new Nuclear Regulatory Commission, thus satisfying the long-standing criticism of the AEC that promotion of nuclear power and the safe regulation of nuclear power should not be lodged in the same agency. President Nixon also established within the White House staff an Energy Policy Office to coordinate policy at the presidential level.

The Carter administration energy policy generally emphasized the same broad objectives as were originally set forth in the first Nixon energy message. For purposes of review, these efforts may be divided among those designed to provide a better institutional response to energy problems, those intended to increase the supply of energy, and those meant to reduce demand for energy. The latter two objectives would, if accomplished, materially assist in achieving still another national energy goal—reducing dependence of the nation on oil imported from abroad, particularly oil from the Middle East.

With regard to institutional arrangements, the most notable to date has been the creation of the Department of Energy. On the supply side of the energy equation a number of actions have been, or are being, taken. Perhaps the most dramatic is the establishment in 1980 of the Synthetic Fuels Corporation. The objective of the Corporation is to use some $20 billion in federal monies to assist private development of nonpetroleum energy sources. Such sources include synthetic natural gas and synthetic gasoline from oil shale and coal, gas from biomass such as animal manure and organic materials found in plants. The government corporation will also stimulate solar energy development and conservation projects by providing grant money. The production goal of the program thus launched is to provide enough synthetic fuel to offset 8 percent of the current oil imports by the year 1987, with more impressive achievements in the longer-term future.

During its first year in office the Reagan administration indicated skepticism as to the continued value of both the Department of Energy and the Synthetic Fuels Corporation in the form that they were inherited from the Carter administration. Such a perspective was consistent with President Reagan's stated intent to reduce the size and scope of the federal government.

An addition to the Synthetic Fuels Corporation Act, not requested by President Carter, but added by a Senate-House conference committee that prepared the final version of the legislation, provides for the completion of the National Strategic Petroleum Reserve program. The objective of this program is to store 750 million barrels of oil in caves located in east Texas and Louisiana. The purpose of the program is to provide enough oil to fuel the nation's critical needs for a four-month period should external sources be cut off.

A supply-side initiative proposed by the Carter administration that did not pass Congress in 1980 was the Energy Mobilization Board (EMB). The purpose of the EMB was to facilitate the construction of high-priority energy projects by providing the authority to gain quick approval for such projects at the local, state, and federal levels. The Energy Mobilization Board was defeated by a coalition of interests that feared the federal government energy proponents would have used the new authority to override local and state reservations regarding the siting of energy projects, including environmental objections. Although the EMB was defeated in 1980, the proposal could be back before the Congress should severe threats to Middle Eastern oil develop in the future, and the idea thus constitutes a long-term point of dispute regarding the priority that energy projects should take over other considerations.

A precursor argument to that about the Energy Mobilization Board has for a decade been played out in some of the states. The concept is termed "one-stop siting," as contrasted to multistop siting. In a one-stop siting state, all the permits necessary for the construction and operation of an energy facility are considered and rejected or approved at one time and in one place by one responsible body. In a multisite state, requests for different permits (land use, water, air quality, etc.,) are considered at different times by different state entities. The proponents of one-stop siting argue that such a procedure cuts time and reduces costs by permitting the energy developer to make one comprehensive preparation for one body rather than reiterating its proposals before a number of disparate government groups. Those favoring the multisite procedure note that multisiting also means multiple review by various institutions of state government, which could mean a more complete review of the proposed energy development. Multisiting also may give to opposition groups a greater opportunity to veto the project at any one of the siting hearings.

The Carter administration, as did the Nixon and Ford administrations, engaged in efforts to employ market forces to both stimulate supply and dampen demand. One such strategy is the gradual deregulation of natural gas and petroleum prices so that the price can rise to what is called the true replacement cost. The true replacement cost is the price that must be paid at any given time to replace a barrel of oil or a million cubic feet of natural gas. Industry generally favors deregulation of prices on the grounds that higher prices will stimulate greater efforts to find and bring into production new energy reserves. Some conservationists support deregulation because the resulting higher prices are believed to reduce consumption. Economists favor true replacement pricing because, from an economic perspective, goods that are used up ought to be priced at the cost of replacement.

Not all political forces, however, favor price decontrol. Groups representing the poor and the elderly cite the increased hardship on such persons that results from increases in energy prices as an argument against deregulation. Many Democratic members of Congress have this type of person as constituents, which helps to explain the luke-warm reception that price deregulation has received from some in the Congress. The compromise reached by the Carter administration regarding price deregulation has been to incrementally phase in the deregulation over time to lessen the impact, and to provide assistance to hard-hit groups that find it particularly difficult to pay the higher energy costs. Although initially favorable to faster price decontrol, the Reagan administration has adopted a slower decontrol policy, probably due to political pressures.

At least with regard to gasoline consumption, higher prices, from whatever cause (OPEC increases, taxes, deregulation), seem to be reflected in the lessening of gasoline use by 1980; and the associated lessening of the amount of imported oil brought into the United States. According to Department of Commerce data, the average daily imports of oil in July 1980 were substantially lower than the preceding January. By early 1982 the reduced consumption of gasoline had forced prices down to levels not seen for 18 months. Some voiced concern at this point that the national effort to find new energy sources and to conserve might be undercut by a public feeling that the problem was solved as suggested by the lower prices.

It should be noted that declining use of gasoline was not entirely traceable to increased prices. The economic downturn of 1980 and 1981 was also thought to have played a part. Further, changes in gasoline-buying habits were a mixed blessing. This was because part of the gasoline savings was accomplished as a result of the purchase of small foreign cars, which in turn had adverse effects on domestic car manufacturing employment and profits.

An often-used means to stimulate supply and dampen demand is to employ the taxing power of the government in various ways. Thus, higher taxes on energy products, and on devices that are thought to use extreme amounts of energy, such as the so-called gas-guzzler car, are used to curtail consumption and encourage economies. On the other hand, tax credits and subsidies can be used to reward the development of new sources of supply.

Perhaps the most hotly debated of recent tax actions has been the windfall profits tax. The objective of the windfall profits tax is to tax the extra income that oil companies realize as a result of raising their prices to the levels of the world market set by OPEC. Monies collected from the windfall profits tax are to be used to develop alternative energy sources and to assist those most burdened by high energy prices. Whether or not the windfall profits tax will operate in a way to retard new oil discovery and development, as critics of the tax have claimed will be the case, has yet to be determined. The point made by the critics is that the greater profits before the new tax were needed as a stimulus to new oil activity.

No matter which presidential administration is in power, national energy policy must of necessity be worked out within the parameters of the federal system of government, where political power is divided between Washington and the states. The most important ramification of federalism for energy policy is found in the Western United States. Here, because of the pattern of settlement by early pioneers, and the way the states entered the Union, much of the land is owned and managed by the federal government. The largest land management entities are the Bureau of Land Management and the U.S. Forest Service. Other forms of federal land are national parks and monuments, wild and scenic rivers, national grasslands, and extensive military reservations and weapons testing grounds. Indian reservations also dot the Western United States. The extreme case of federal landownership is found in Nevada, where more than 90 percent of the state is in some form of federal ownership. This overwhelming federal presence would be of no particular interest in terms of energy policy development except for the fact that much of the nation's remaining coal, oil shale, uranium, oil, natural gas, and geothermal reserves are found under the federal lands, including those in Alaska.

How this wealth of federally owned energy resources, situated within a number of individual states, will be utilized is a matter not yet fully determined. A brief history of the federal government-Western states interface on energy policy will, however, be instructive in regard to future development.

In the early 1970s, when it became obvious that the nation would increasingly turn to Western energy sources as a means to decrease dependence on high-priced and uncertain foreign oil, an early response heard in the West was "let's keep 'em out." Environmentalists particularly decried what they feared would be the "rape of the Western land," and a number of threats were perceived by Westerners as the nation geared up to develop Western energy.

An often-expressed concern was of boom-and-bust energy development. The Western United States is still dotted with ghost towns near abandoned mines and gouged-out stream beds, relics of the gold and silver mining days when miners scarred the earth, took their treasure, and left. What was, and is, asked in the West is what will become of the boom-towns resulting from coal and oil shale development when the coal and oil shale are depleted? Will they and the new generation of abandoned mines simply be left as another iteration of boom-and-bust exploitation?

The most immediate concern over boomtowns is how will social services such as schools, hospitals, sanitation facilities, recreation opportunities, fire and police protec-tion be provided at the beginning of the growth resulting from the influx of energy workers and those providing support services? Typically the rapidly growing energy boomtown does not receive new tax revenues from the energy development early on when the workers arrive. Taxes flow after the mine, the power plant, the oil shale opera-tion have been in operation for some time. In an effort to compensate for the lag time be-tween when social services are needed and when tax monies are available, Western politi-cians have been active in pursuing federal financial help termed impact assistance. Whether such impact assistance is really needed by the growing energy boomtowns of the West, and is in the public interest, or whether impact assistance is just the latest example of the familiar political ploy of getting monies for one's constituency from some other segment of the population, can be debated. The subject of impact assistance has been crit-ically analyzed by Norman Wengert (1979).

Another concern voiced in the Western United States with regard to the impending energy development is how water will be allocated in the future among the traditional users, of which the largest by far is agriculture, and the new energy requirements. For Eastern readers who have not traveled in the West, it should be emphasized that the cen-tral fact of life in the area from the 100th meridian in central Kansas to the narrow band of wetness along the Pacific coast is the constant, pervasive, aridity. Early explorers scrawled across their maps of the West, "Great American Desert." It still is. However, life flourishes in many places because water has been collected, diverted, and directed to cities and irrigated lands.

One answer to the question of how water will be allocated between the previous uses and energy development is to note that in the West water runs up hill when there is money on the top. In other words, the market can be used to allocate water from farming to energy if the energy companies have the money, which most observers believe they do, to buy up water rights. The resultant decline in some agricultural areas may thus be the price to be paid for extensive energy development in the West.

Another problem arising from the scarcity of water is the increased difficulty and cost of restoring strip-mined areas and oil shale residue dumps with vegetation for both esthetic and dirt stabilization purposes. Revegetation requires water, and it costs money. In the Eastern United States, with abundant rainfull, revegetation is a much more easily accomplished objective, with less cost being added to the price of energy to the consumer.

Gradually during the 1970s, Western attitudes toward energy development changed to reflect the realization that it was constitutionally impossible to preserve all the scenic and environmental values of the West, together with preenergy-crisis life styles. If the rest of the nation wanted the energy under federally owned land, the political and legal muscle existed to support the mining of coal and retorting of oil shale. By the 1980s the political concensus in the West had evolved to accepting energy development but with the strong proviso that the Western states should be involved in the decision making for the new energy development. In this way it was thought that at least the worst aspects of energy development could be mitigated with the acceptance of Western inputs to policy formulation and implementation. An example of how the relationship between the federal agencies and the states was supposed to operate is the current cooperation between federal coal-leasing teams and representatives of states wherein federal coal will be mined.

One means whereby Western states can financially ameliorate the environmental and social costs of energy development is to pass on some of the costs to the consumer, most of whom live out of state because of the sparsely settled character of energy-rich states such as Montana, Wyoming, Utah, New Mexico, and Colorado. The primary way of achieving this objective is through the medium of the severance tax. This is a tax levied when a mineral—for example, coal— is severed from the earth.

A major federal-state problem is emerging with regard to the effect of severance taxes on Western energy resources. The legal and political difficulty is that at some level of taxation any severance tax will become a burden on interstate commerce within the context of the constitutional prohibition of such activity. Whether or not the current severance taxes on coal in Montana and Wyoming (30 percent and 17 percent, respectively) are at the point of becoming a burden to interstate commerce is a matter of much debate. For example, in 1980 the Supreme Court of Montana, citing *Mid-northern Oil Co. v. Montana* (1925, 263 U.S. 45, 45 S.Ct. 440, 69 L.Ed. 841) and *Mid-northern Oil Co. v. Walker* (1922, 65 Mont. 414 211, P. 353) upheld the right of Montana to impose the 30 percent severance tax on coal taken from federal land. There is little doubt that the dispute about what constitutes a burden on interstate commerce will eventually find its way to the U.S. Supreme Court.

As the argument over the amount of severance tax a state can collect worked its way through the court system, the matter was also being considered by Congress. The thrust of several bills introduced in 1980 was to limit severance taxes on coal removed from federal or Indian lands, and which was shipped in interstate commerce, to 12.5 percent of the value of the coal at the site of mining. The severance tax limitation measure was broadly supported in bipartisan fashion by representatives and senators from coal-consuming states. Proponents of the limitation proposals argued that high severance taxes do constitute a burden on interstate commerce, and that such rates are counter to the coal production goals of the nation. During hearings on the severance tax measures, talk was heard referring to the states with the highest rates, Montana and Wyoming, as "blue-eyed Arabs" charging whatever the market would bear.

Western politicians who opposed the severance tax limitation countered that the 12.5 percent limitation represented federal preemption of the states' police power to protect the health, safety, and welfare of their citizens. These responsibilities are viewed by opponents of the limitation move as including environmental protection, and the provision of the social infrastructure needed to support the influx of persons engaged in energy development. Late in 1980 the severance tax limitation measure died in committee. This was not seen, however, as the permanent resolution of the controversy.

Concern in the Western United States over federal energy policy was combined with unhappiness by ranching interests over rules limiting livestock grazing on federal lands, to produce an organized political hostility to the federal presence in the West known as the Sagebrush Rebellion. Emanating from the state with the greatest percent of federal ownership, Nevada, the publicaly stated objective of the Sagebrush Rebellion was the deeding of much of the federal land to the Western states. Sagebrush Rebellion leaders claimed that the states would follow policies more congruent with the interests of Westerners than would the federal government.

The most recent concern of Westerners about federal activity in their region is in regard to the proposed construction of the MX intercontinental ballistic missile (ICBM) in portions of Utah and Nevada, and possibly other Western states. The MX program could involve the building of 4600 to 13,800 sites among which 200 ICBMs would be moved in order to provide prelaunch invulnerability for the missiles, assuming that Soviet targeting ability would be unable to determine in which of the sites the ICBMs are hidden. Regardless of the strategic merits of the MX deployment program, Western politicians, and others, fear the impact of the MX construction program, on top of the new energy construction programs, as constituting unacceptable social and environmental impacts.

There is a substantial external dimension to the federal government's national energy policy. It is comprised of the varied efforts to protect and enhance the security of supply for Middle Eastern oil, and the efforts to find more stable oil-exporting nations, until such time as American dependence on foreign oil can be reduced, or if one is very optimistic, eliminated. In this effort the United States has become entangled in the hostility between the Arab states and Israel, the enmity between the forces of modernization represented by the late Shah of Iran and the conservative religious element personified by the Ayatollah Khomeini, and more recently the competition between Arab and Persian.

During the Nixon and Ford administrations, Henry A. Kissinger, as national security advisor to the President and later secretary of state, used shuttle diplomacy between Egypt and Israel to consolidate a peaceful relationship between the largest Arab state and the Jewish nation. In the Persian Gulf region, where 40 percent of the Western world's oil originates, Kissinger continued U.S. support for the pro-Washington Shah as the dominant military force bordering on the Gulf. Simultaneously the United States continued to cultivate the Saudi royal family, whose authoritarian rule extends over the richest oil nation in the world. Part of the U.S. support was in the form of the sale of military equipment, which greatly upset the Israelis. American influence on both sides of the Persian Gulf was in marked contrast to the Soviet presence in Iraq, the oil-producing nation at the head of the Gulf, and the traditional rival of the Persians who today call themselves Iranians.

The balancing act the United States must pursue to prevent violence and politically motivated restrictions from cutting the flow of Middle East oil became even more complicated in 1979 with the disintegration of the Shah's rule and his replacement by the leader of a religious minority in the Islamic world, the Ayatollah Khomeini of the Shi'ite Muslim faction. Matters soon worsened for the United States in Teheran as the new Iranian government condoned the seizure of people in the American embassy. The price for the release of the hostages was the return of the Shah and his assets taken from the country, plus a public American apology for Washington's support of the Shah's regime.

When war broke out late in 1980 between Iran and Iraq, it further highlighted the continued instability of the Persian Gulf region. Fortunately for the United States, the immediate threat of an oil cutoff from the two belligerents was negligible, but this was not true for American allies in Europe and Japan, which consume much of the production from Iraq and Iran.

The Nixon and Ford years were also a time when Dr. Kissinger laid the groundwork for what evolved into an international agreement between 21 nations that import oil to assist each other in time of emergency. Specifically, the members of the International Energy Agency have agreed that when one member loses 7 percent of its oil imports, other members will enter into an oil-sharing arrangement. The analogy is to an insurance company that pools the risks of individuals and thus spreads the risks among many purchasers of insurance. During the war between Iran and Iraq, several of the larger members of the International Energy Agency cooperated to provide a naval force to be used in case the narrow mouth of the Persian Gulf, the Straits of Hormuz, was threatened with forceful closure by either of the belligerents.

In response to the instability of the Middle East, the Carter administration created out of military units in the United States a rapid deployment force with which it was boldly asserted that the United States could deal with threats of violence that might develop to stop the flow of oil. Scenarios for the use of the American force included protecting the Saudi royal family from religious zealots or leftist revolutionaries; protecting Saudi Arabia from either Iraq or Iran as the three nations contest for the dominant power position in the Persian Gulf; and as a counter to Soviet penetration of the region.

Critics of the rapid deployment force, noting what they perceived as the overall decline in U.S. military capacity, said the force was too little, too late, and it was no substitute for a strong U.S. military presence solidly entrenched in the Middle East. President Reagan kept the rapid deployment force and implemented actions designed to enhance American presence in the Middle East.

An evaluation of the comparative merits of American foreign policy designed to secure Middle Eastern oil as against domestic efforts to increase production illuminates a cruel dilemma facing energy policy decision makers. Eventually they may have to choose between the potential use of force in the Middle East, continuing to live with the possibility of oil cutoffs, or the potential damage to the Western environment if new substitutes to oil are sought there. To many in Washington the difficulties of expanding domestic energy production, plus attempting to dampen demand for energy, appeared as more likely to be overcome than the objective of ensuring continuous oil flow from the Middle East. Another way of putting it is that the federal government was prepared to make some environmental sacrifices in order to reduce the dependence on undependable Middle East oil, and in order to avoid the need to prepare to use force to keep the oil flowing to the United States.

Even if the United States could reduce its dependence on Middle Eastern oil, there would remain the problem of the NATO allies, plus Japan, continuing to be dependent on Middle East oil. Thus, even if Washington could cut its dependence on the Middle East, the Departments of State and Defense would continue to be involved in seeking peace if possible, and being prepared for war if necessary, in the area between Libya and Iran.

Nearer to home, the federal government tried to guarantee that the very substantial oil and natural gas reserves of Mexico and Canada would be available to the United States during the rest of the century. In response the Canadians were careful not to overcommit their oil and natural gas as they worried about their own needs in the future. The Mexican government was careful not to expand production so rapidly that the profits would be inflationary and difficult for the economy to absorb. There was also arguing between Washington and Mexico City as to what constituted a fair price for natural gas.

Americans who worried about the tide of illegal immigrants flowing into the United States from Mexico saw in Mexican oil revenues an answer to the problem. Their point was that the Mexican government could use the oil and natural gas monies to so improve the quality of life that those contemplating leaving for the more attractive economic promise of America would reconsider and remain in Mexico. For the immediate future this seems an unlikely possibility.

VI. DOUBTS AND QUESTIONS

U.S. energy policy is now firmly set along the lines of increasing supply by resorting to market rewards to those who find more, and by using government assistance to support research and development that is supposed to lead to nonconventional sources of energy. Both efforts are designed to reduce dependence on oil from the volatile Middle East. Differences discernible between the Carter administration and the Reagan administration are not so much over the long-run objective, expanding energy supplies, as they are about the precise means of achieving that objective. For example President Carter favored greater use of government funding to advance new energy technologies toward commercial utilization, while President Reagan favors reaching the same goal with more emphasis upon the incentives for development supplied by the market. President Carter would not have opened up various categories of federally owned land to energy exploration and development to the extent that is supported by his successor. Efforts are also being made to dampen demand for energy. Thus, by 1981 the basic structure of contemporary U.S. energy policy is largely in place, and it is not likely that much change will be made in the near term.

Even though change of major proportions in the national energy policy is not likely, this chapter would be incomplete if several voices critical of various parts of the policy were not mentioned at least briefly.

Critical of the emphasis on large-scale energy projects would be the late E. F. Schumacher (1975). He argued that ever greater aggregations of capital, power, and control over the lives of others by large organizations serves to diminish the dignity and individuality of human beings. In his book *Small Is Beautiful,* Schumacher expressed admiration for what he termed Buddhist economics. By this term he meant a life style that does not require resources from afar, which is careful in the use of nonrenewable resources, and which seeks to enhance a person's spiritual well-being more than his or her materialistic acquisitions. Specifically with regard to energy policy, Schumacher warned against using up what he termed capital stocks of energy resources, that is, nonrenewable ones, and urged the switch to what he called income fuels that are renewable, such as solar. For these reasons Schumacher, if living, would probably express doubt about much in U.S. energy policy, although not about the efforts to conserve and dampen consumption.

Critical of what he terms the "hard paths" toward energy is Amory Lovins (1975). Writing and speaking prolifically in the 1970s and early 1980s, Lovins warns of the dangers inherent in permanent attachment to those energy resources whose use result in a "hard" impact on the environment, such as nuclear power of the fission type. He urges adoption of those energy sources whose use leaves a "soft" impact on the environment, such as solar, biomass, and wind. However, Lovins notes that modern societies will need to use fossil fuel for a while as a bridge to the soft and renewable technologies he champions, but that fossil fuels should not be viewed as an end in themselves.

Critical of massive efforts to increase the supply side of the energy equation are the philosophical disciples of Donella H. Meadows, Dennis L. Meadows, Jorgen Randers, and William Behrens, III, and their intellectual mentor Professor Jay Forrester of M.I.T. (1972). Their view, expressed in *The Limits to Growth*, is that policies designed to remove some barrier to growth should be thought through very carefully before implementation. Their point with regard to energy policy is that steps to increase supply not only add to pollution, but will enable more people to live at a higher standard of living, which at some point may push the population up against the carrying capacity of the planet. Those with a *Limits to Growth* perspective suggest as an alternative to constant growth a condition they call global equilibrium. In such a state pollution would be held steady, and the emphasis would be placed on renewable rather than nonrenewable energy sources.

Critical of the technological optimism, and the attendent expectation of a continuing high standard of living, found in association with the U.S. national energy policy is William Ophuls (1977). Ophuls is concerned over a bleak future that he characterizes with the title to his book—*Ecology and the Politics of Scarcity*. As the population grows, and as nonrenewable resources are consumed, Ophuls foresees the replacement of the age of capitalism and democracy with much more somber arrangements. The age of scarcity would feature an authoritarian government employing coercion to make allocations of scarce resources. Borrowing from the writings of Thomas Hobbes (1651) and a contemporary writer, Garrett Hardin, (1968), Ophuls reminds his readers of the lesson to be learned from the tragedy of the commons. This is the story of the common grazing area that was worn down to the bare ground because each livestock owner tried to maximize his self-interest by placing more cattle on the free grazing area than it could support. To prevent the tragedy of the commons from happening with regard to such common property as air and water will require strong governmental action, according to Ophuls.

VII. CONCLUSION

Contemporary U.S. energy policy is rather what one would expect of America. It emphasizes independence from foreign influence; it relies heavily on technology and native ingenuity; it places confidence in both government action and the market to produce what society needs; to some extent it reflects the American concern of late about the environment; and it assumes a continuation of the affluent life style so many Americans have come to believe is normal.

Thus American energy policy is a continuation of the bold political and economic experiment begun 206 years ago. And we contemporary Americans are left with a question —Is boldness, reliance on technology, and a willingness to experiment sufficient for the future?

REFERENCES

Daneke, G. A. (1979). Toward an alternative energy future. In *New Dimensions to Energy Policy*, R. M. Lawrence (Ed.). Lexington Books, Lexington, MA, pp. 103–113.

Hardin, G. (1968). The tragedy of the commons. *Science 162*: 1243–1248.

Hobbes, T.)1651) *Leviathan, or the Matter, Form and Power of a Commonwealth, Ecclesiastical and Civil*, H. W. Schneider (Ed.). Bobbs-Merrill, Indianapolis, IN.

Lovins, A. B. (1975). *World Energy Strategies: Facts, Issues, and Opinions*. Friends of the Earth/Ballinger, Boston.

Meadows, D. H., Meadows, D. L., Randers, J., and Behrens, W., III (1972). *The Limits to Growth*. Universe Books, New York.

Ophuls, W. (1977). *Ecology and the Politics of Scarcity*. Freeman, San Francisco.

Schumacher, E. F. (1975). *Small Is Beautiful*. Harper & Row, New York.

Wengert, N. I. (1979). The energy Boomtown: An analysis of the politics of getting. In *New Dimensions to Energy Policy*, R. M. Lawrence (Ed.). Lexington Books, Lexington, MA, pp. 17–24.

33

Biomedical Policy

Robert H. Blank / University of Idaho, Moscow, Idaho

I. EMERGING ISSUES IN BIOMEDICINE

This chapter provides an overview of the policy issues created by the rapid emergence of a broad assortment of biomedical technologies, which according to Etzioni (1973: 10) represent a "new revolution." It is clear that the intensity and scope of the issues in human genetic intervention (e.g., eugenics, sex selection, genetic counseling, genetic screening), reproductive technology (e.g., abortion, sterilization, prenatal diagnosis, artificial insemination, in vitro fertilization, fetal research), and biomedical intervention in the human life process (e.g., psychosurgery, electrical brain stimulation, drug therapy, organ transplants, euthanasia) will challenge traditional values and social structures at an accelerating rate. Together these issues present a formidable set of policy concerns. In addition to summarizing the major political issues raised by current biomedical research and application, this chapter analyzes the present institutional framework for making biomedical policy and reviews government response to date. It also describes the current state of biomedical policy studies and notes the developing literature on biomedical policy.

Although the biomedical technologies now available pale in comparison to what is promised for the future (Rosen, 1976; Maxmen, 1976), they represent an impressive array of methods for human intervention. The possibility of indefinite artificial maintenance of life, new methods of creating as well as aborting life, drug therapy, and new applications of psychosurgery are but a few of the rapidly advancing techniques that will help reshape our destiny. While offering new hope for many persons, however, these innovations are creating ethical and political dilemmas unparalleled in the past. Changes in technology have always demanded redefinition of issues and policies, but the new discoveries and applications in genetics and medicine represent perhaps the greatest challenge our species has yet faced—the alteration of our most basic definitions of humanhood. Although each innovation raises a unique set of opportunities and problems, they share broader social and political ramifications.

A. Individual Rights

A concern central to all biomedical technology is informed consent (Fletcher, 1967; Annas et al., 1977). Although the guarantee of free choice with knowledge of the options is difficult in any clinical or research situation, it is magnified when patients or subjects are deemed incapable of granting informed consent. Prisoners, the mentally retarded, and children represent very difficult cases indeed. Although some argue that these groups cannot therefore be used in nontherapeutic research (Ramsey, 1970; Mitford, 1972), others would make exceptions (Cohen, 1978; McCormick, 1974) or accept proxy consent by parents or guardians. Informed consent is further complicated in genetic and fetal research where the subjects are fetuses, embryos, or even hypothetical unborn persons (Murphy et al., 1978).

Other issues surrounding biomedical applications center on potential intrusions on individual rights of privacy, procreation, self-determination, and in some cases life. The traditional need to balance the rights of individuals with a broader societal good is heightened by the availability of techniques that draw out conflicts in these rights and call for substantial refinements of accompanying responsibilities. Whether physically manipulating the brain, allocating scarce life-saving resources, or screening for carrier status, traditional rights to privacy, confidentiality, and autonomy are challenged. Many biomedical interventions magnify conflicts among individual rights, for instance, between parents, their offspring, and others in society who often must pay the cost for the actions of the parents. Genetic and reproductive applications are especially difficult because they introduce the added dimension of responsibility to future generations and the rights of the yet unborn.

Stigmatization is a very real problem generated by these technologies, and any biomedical decision must be sensitive of this. Sickle-cell screening programs, no matter how noble in intent, produced a stigma to carriers of the sickle-cell trait, which resulted in them being barred from certain occupations, dropped from insurance programs, and labeled as having a "disease" (Bowman, 1978; Murray, 1978). Stigmatization through any compulsory program, whether it be drug therapy for "hyperactive" children (Schrag and Divoky, 1975), screening for those with an XYY gene complement (Beckwith and King, 1974), or sterilization for eugenic purposes (Robitscher, 1973), must be included as a genuine social cost. Kass (1976: 317) expresses concern for those abnormals who are viewed as having escaped the "net of detection and abortion," and sees attitudes toward such individuals as "progressively eroded."

B. Societal Implications

At the societal level, biomedical applications raise issues of discrimination against minorities as well as social groupings such as the mentally retarded, prisoners, and the poor. Although much controversy over abortion, euthanasia, and reproductive technologies centers on questions of how human life is defined (Tooley, 1972; Swinyard, 1977), when it begins (Fletcher, 1979), and under what conditions it might be terminated (Kamisar, 1976; Russell, 1975; Robertson, 1975), another dimension is the fear by blacks and others that abortion, sterilization (Gray, 1976), genetic screening (Bowman, 1977), and so forth will further oppress, stigmatize, and eventually deplete their numbers.

These social issues also emerge in questions of human experimentation, as dramatized by the Tuskeegee syphilis study and other cases of abuse of subjects (Barber, 1973; Gray, 1975), in the use of psychosurgery and electronic brain stimulation (Valenstein, 1973; Scheflin and Upton, 1978), and in the use of drugs for behavior control (Wells, 1973). Revelations that up to 20 percent of black children in Watts are prescribed Ritalin by the schools for hyperactivity (Kieffer, 1975: 158) do little to allay fears of social control. Conversely, the defenders of these biomedical applications (Mark and Ervin, 1970; Visscher, 1975; Fletcher, 1974) contend that the potential benefits of such research and experimentation outweigh the risks and that society has an obligation to pursue these techniques within reasonable boundaries and exercise of caution.

Other social implications of biomedical technologies relate to their impact on social structures. As technologies become available that provide for gender preselection, surrogate motherhood, behavior modification, a slowing of the aging process, and so forth, social patterns will be affected. Some observers question the impact of such opportunities on the size and dimensions of the family (Martin, 1978), demographic patterns (Etzioni, 1973), and the structure and size of the population (Hardin, 1972). Policy planners will have to account for these potential impacts on the basic structures and patterns of society and decide if provision of such choices is desirable (Blank and Ostheimer, 1979).

Eventually, concerns raised by biomedical innovations are global in scope. Prohibition of research and/or application in one country will most likely shift development of similar technologies elsewhere. At the international level, emerging problems have substantial implications for human rights when blood plasma is transported from one country to another, drugs are tested in poorer nations for the benefit of the richer nations, fetuses are imported for research purposes, and organs are obtained for transplant. Also, while some nations are struggling to control population, others are oblivious to prospects for the future of the globe. Obviously, the moral dilemmas that exist within the United States generated by biomedicine are bound to be amplified across cultures.

At their base, all biomedical technologies focus on the question of the extent to which we ought to intervene directly in the human condition. They differ only in the level of intervention (gametes, fertilized egg, developing embryo, fetus, newborn, within life cycle, end of life) and in the means of accomplishing the intervention, which range from legal restrictions on marriage for genetic reasons to sophisticated biomedical procedures such as gene surgery. Although some observers argue that it is irreverent and ethically dangerous to violate or bypass fundamental human biology (Martin, 1978), others contend that the benefits of such research greatly outweigh the dangers (Fletcher, 1974).

Although all biomedical decisions reduce to moral questions, many concerning quality-of-life versus sanctity-of-life assumptions or the extent to which people ought to tamper with nature or "play God" (Goodfield, 1977), emphasis here is on more direct policy considerations. These relate to the proper role of the government in making biomedical policy. In other words, who makes the difficult decisions raised by biomedicine: scientists, interest groups, the general public, or governmental officials? In the government, what agencies are responsible for setting the agenda, formulating alternatives, and making and implementing biomedical policy?

C. Defining the Role of Government in Biomedical Issues

Although there has always been a reciprocal relationship between technology and society, and technology has always produced conflict as it clashed with traditional social values and established institutions, biomedical technology is unique because it acts directly on humans instead of on the environment. The potential impact on the human condition and possibly on human nature itself is enough to demand serious attention. This, along with the uncertainty of long-range consequences and the potential irreversibility of certain biomedical techniques, either to individuals or future generations, reinforces the need to evaluate each technology carefully before its widespread application. As more advanced biomedical technologies emerge, tensions among the varied elements in society are certain to be accentuated. Questions regarding the equity and efficiency of biomedical research and applications will surface as critical policy issues. According to Coates (1972: 26):

> Biomedical technologies . . . are producing or are likely to produce some of the most profound effects on social mores and behavior of the future. It is likely that public policy issues will soon arise from this area in great numbers, and . . . will be profoundly interwoven with religious, social, economic, cultural and ideological factors.

Although biomedical issues are not at present the nation's "most important problems," they are emerging as major political issues and are of growing significance in the public consciousness (Ostheimer and Ritt, 1976: 283). As stated in a current national commission report (U.S. Department of Health, Education and Welfare, 1978: 105):

> . . . it should be clear that all such decisions finally rest on a political basis and that the entire American electorate has a legitimate stake both in the procedures by which the decisions are made, and in the steps that are taken to monitor and control the consequences.

In addition to balancing out the interests of various individuals and groups, including society itself, hard decisions must be made concerning the just distribution of scarce resources. Increasingly difficult questions concerning the nature of justice, the community good, and fundamental rights are at the forefront of attempts to utilize the various available or potential technologies. Vigilance also is needed in order to curb abuses of power that arise when any method of potential social control becomes available, although these fears alone should not justify elimination of what might be highly beneficial biomedical interventions.

Decisions concerning the use and priorities of biomedical research and technology will continue to be made within a highly politicized context. The politically sensitive nature of these technologies, as well as recent trends in the political arena and increased public awareness, implies that technical decisions will no longer be made independently of politics. One major trend in the 1970s was the growing public role in biomedical research. Hanft (1977: 19) sees this emergence into the public debate as a result of a combination of inflation, multiplying health care costs, and the general freedom-of-information climate. This trend also indicates that as the costs of research and application increase, public debate over priorities will expand. Because a large proportion of the funding comes from public monies, decision makers will scrutinize biomedical expenditures closely, producing an even greater dependence on the public sector.

Another tendency in the political system is that of postponing action until the situation reaches crisis proportions. Although it is doubtful that biomedical technology at present represents a crisis (Green, 1973), it is clear that we cannot afford to wait until such a situation develops, because at that point it might be too late to establish a groundwork for the rational discussion and deliberation of the issues. The extent to which the political institutions deal with these issues now, when the technology is relatively limited, will determine their ability to react to future innovations, which are bound to be even more controversial.

II. THE PUBLIC AND BIOMEDICAL ISSUES

Because biomedical issues increasingly are considered within the realm of public concern, it is not surprising that an often-expressed theme is the need for public participation in the decision-making process. Comroe (1978: 937) notes that in the long run a well-educated and informed public will more often than not make the correct decision. Kaplan (1975) argues that in solving questions of human values raised by biomedical technologies we must rely on the experience of the ordinary citizen, not the experts. Schoenberg (1979: 92) concludes that a public debate is needed to "quickly bring to the surface the moral issues and ethical issues that confront science."

A. Public Opinion

At this stage, research is needed to assess the public's perceptions of biomedical technology and its conception of what constitutes a meaningful human existence. Additional research must be conducted to elucidate the interaction between culture and technology. To what extent are advances in biomedical technology altering values concerning the individual's role in society, the role of the state in such matters, and the human condition? Conversely, what impact do political values and beliefs have on the acceptance or rejection of these technologies?

To date, the most substantial data on a biomedical issue is that concerning abortion. The National Opinion Research Center and other national pollsters frequently include questions on support for abortion under a variety of situations. Harris (1975: 67), in summarizing these data, states that the "rapidity with which moral views about abortion in general have changed swept aside much of the resistance that might have been expected to develop against prenatal diagnosis and selective abortion." Ostheimer (1979) has analyzed similar, though less complete, data on euthanasia. Survey data concerning other biomedical applications and issues, however, are less adequate. There are scattered data on public reaction to various biomedical technologies, including artificial insemination (Miller, 1974), *in vitro* fertilization (U.S. Department of Health, Education and Welfare, 1979), and gender selection (U.S. Department of Health, Education and Welfare, 1978). There are also limited comparative data on attitudes toward prenatal diagnosis and genetic screening (McIntosh and Alston, 1977). Together, these data imply substantial variation in levels of public support across the range of disparate biomedical applications. They also demonstrate that whereas the public is aware of the more sensational aspects of biomedicine, they are less aware of the implications of biomedical research (Etzioni and Nunn, 1974) and fail to display a clear sense of desired priorities for medical research

(U.S. Department of Health, Education and Welfare, 1978: 173). Education at all levels from grade school to adult population is essential. The most impressive efforts in this area to date have come from the Biological Sciences Curriculum Study in Boulder, Colorado (see *BSCS Journal*).

B. Proliferation of Interest Groups

Although groups concerned with biomedical issues are recent in origin, the technical specialization emerging from genetic technology has quickly multiplied the number and scope of such organizations. Because biomedical intervention enhances or challenges strongly held values of many individuals, interest group activity surrounding these issues will continue to expand, especially in this period of heightened competition for scarce resources. The advocacy climate of the 1970s has encouraged the creation of groups, while the mass media has provided a forum and given them saliency. Grobstein (1979: 103), contends that public interest groups in the recombinant DNA (rDNA) debate represent their own view of the public good, and he decries their dependence on "worst-case scenarios" to gain public attention. Conversely, Fanning (1978) contends that genetic screening and counseling have been dominated by an elite composed of scientists, physicians, family planning professionals, and medical directors of life insurance companies, and concludes that these interests have assumed the role of "biomedical engineers" with the hope of reshaping social policies.

Biomedical policy, as it exists, has been influenced greatly by lobbying efforts of a number of groups in favor of governmental action. To a large extent the National Sickle Cell Anemia Control Act (1972), the National Cooley's Anemia Control Act (1972), the Huntington's Chorea and Hemophilia Act (1975), and the various kidney dialysis statutes reflect the lobbying efforts of individuals and groups concerned with each particular disease. Although the National Academy of Sciences (NAS) Committee for the Study of Inborn Errors (1975: 47) rejects Swazey's (1971: 883) contention that the DHEW Children's Bureau engineered the national lobbying effort that resulted in PKU legislation in most states, it admits that the major forces behind such laws were the state associations for retarded children. Reilly (1977: 45), however, cautions that although the NAS report makes it clear that these associations lobbied heavily in many states, "it does not offer convincing proof that the legislation owes its existence to these efforts." At the least, the advocacy for mandatory PKU screening by the National Association for Retarded Children provided credible support to the proponents of such legislation.

One of the more interesting developments in the debate over genetic and reproductive issues, in that it traverses traditional liberal-conservative political lines, is the new alliance evolving against these technologies. These issues have created cleavages among traditional allies and, more important, link unlikely groups together only in their opposition to particular technologies. On the right are those groups who tend to oppose reproductive intervention on moral grounds, most clearly represented by the "pro-life" coalition of Catholics and fundamentalist Protestants. Until now, these "conservative" groups have been the most salient opponents of biomedical technology. Recently, however, these interests have been joined by liberal elements who fear repression, stigmatization, or invasion of privacy. Minority group leaders have criticized publicly various biomedical technologies as counter to the interests of their communities. Also, the presence of a "concerned scientists" lobby (e.g., Science for the People) has added the dimension of largely liberal scientists expressing concern over the effects of technology on society. ·

Most recently, feminists representing the National Organization for Women (NOW) and other groups called for a moratorium on the use of in vitro fertilization, sex pre-selection techniques, and birth control methods designed only for women (Kotulak, 1980). They contend that women not only bear increased health risks for these tech-nologies but that their role in society is threatened by them. Hubbard (1980) argues that in vitro fertilization will "distort our health priorities and funnel scarce resources into a questionable effort."

Interest group activity in biomedical issues will continue to cut across traditional social and political cleavage lines in American society. Because of the complexity of the problems raised by these technologies and the value conflicts they produce, future align-ments of groups will differ substantially from those on other political issues. This makes it highly unlikely that either political party will be able to adopt a strong policy stand on many biomedical technologies without risking loss of substantial bases of support. At the same time, the high stakes involved in policy decisions concerning intervention in the human condition will accentuate group activity and magnify conflict among the interests.

C. The Mass Media and Biomedical Issues

These groups are aware of the "power of the press" and, increasingly, are using the mass media effectively to publicize their concerns and provide the public with information about technological developments. Because the media finds biomedical "breakthroughs" extremely newsworthy, dramatic and widespread coverage is common. Front-page head-lines of the first "test tube" baby, the wide coverage given Rorvik's (1978) contention of the first human clone, and media attention to the controversy over rDNA research exem-plify the type and scope of coverage these issues attract.

In his critique of the rDNA debate, Grobstein (1979: 104) contends that the press it-self is an interest group of consequence that "finds grist for its own mill in emphasizing the more spectacular alternative scenarios and the clash of the more charismatic person-alities." He asserts that in its own version of the public interest, the media exaggerates confrontation but ignores the duller details of the resolution of such conflicts. In spite of these limitations and inherent biases of the media toward sensationalism and simplifica-tion of the issues, it remains for most citizens the single source of information concerning these issues.

III. THE GOVERNMENTAL RESPONSE TO BIOMEDICAL ISSUES

A major factor contributing to the confusion and fueling the controversy over govern-ment involvement in biomedical technology is the inability or unwillingness to define clearly what such involvement entails. Many observers emphasize the dangers of the form of state control they most fear without clarifying distinctions among the various types of governmental action. While supporters of biomedical technologies (Fletcher, 1974; Ingle, 1973) deplore the imposition of public controls over biomedical research and use, oppo-nents (Howard and Rifkin, 1977; Restak, 1975; Lappé, 1979) often point to potential coercive uses of these techniques for social control. In actuality, governmental response to biomedical issues can take any one of four types or combinations thereof, including prohibition, regulation, encouragement, or mandate. Furthermore, government intervention can occur anytime from the earliest stages of research to the application of specific techniques.

Some have proposed that the government actively preclude certain types of genetic research and application (Ramsey, 1975). The 1974 Massachusetts moratorium on fetal research (Curran, 1975) and current attempts to prohibit reproductive research where human embryos are destroyed such as in vitro and cloning research are examples of this form of social control. Although there are many calls for the imposition of governmental prohibitions on biomedical research, most recently in recombinant DNA research (see Cohen, 1977), it seems unlikely that the government will be able to ban permanently specific areas of technology in the near future.

A more likely government activity is the regulation of biomedical technology. The establishment of safety regulations, research priorities, and proper procedures, which until recently were viewed as problems of self-regulation by the scientific community, are increasingly coming under the purview of a variety of public institutions. Despite criticisms from the scientific community (see Stine, 1977) that such action results in cumbersome and unnecessary bureaucratic impediments to research, regulation is bound to increase as these technologies become more salient and opposition groups are mobilized.

In addition to controlling technology, government intervention could be designed to encourage development and application of biomedical technologies, through use of discretionary measures intended to facilitate research and/or application of specific technologies. Because continued federal funding of research is crucial to the expansion of future biomedicine, the government could through increased funding make current technologies available to all citizens on a voluntary compliance basis. Tax credits and other incentive programs could also be implemented to encourage public use.

A final form of governmental action, most feared by those opposed to various human interventions (Snodgrass, 1973), is the establishment of compulsory screening or eugenic policies, generally defended on public health or economic grounds. The compulsory sickle cell legislation of the 1970s in some states and compulsory PKU testing programs are examples of such public intervention. Eugenic sterilization laws still on the books in some states represent a direct intervention in procreation (Ludmerer, 1972). Recent actions, such as the Chicago Bar Association's 1974 attempt to require all applicants for marriage licenses to be tested for carrier status, indicate that state involvement of a compulsory nature cannot be ruled out and that it is attractive to many segments of society (see Beckwith, 1976: 53).

Despite the varied implications of each of these types of action, seldom is the role of government defined clearly. Frequently public involvement is attacked without clarifying exactly what it entails. Those opposed to government intervention usually view it as "intrusion" and emphasize either (1) government prohibition or (2) mandated eugenic policy. Those supporting government involvement (Reilly, 1977; Ellison, 1978) usually refer to the more moderate forms of control represented by regulation and/or encouragement. Despite the warnings of those fearful of government intervention at either extreme, most activity appears to be directed toward these latter two types.

Another factor contributing to the confusion over governmental intervention is the failure to distinguish between the technologies themselves and the uses to which they are put. Often the debate becomes garbled because the participants fail to clarify that they are in fact discussing uses of the technology rather than the techniques. Those opposing biomedical technologies often focus on potential coercive uses (involuntary sterilization, compulsory genetic screening, active euthanasia) or political abuses (human experimentation, psychosurgery, eugenics programs) of specific techniques, whereas those who support them deal exclusively with clinically indicated applications and minimize the possibility of coercive applications. Although the controversy over these technologies would not be eliminated if this distinction was clearly defined, it is unfortunate that at least a part of the debate centers on this lack of conceptual clarity. Despite increasing attention to these issues by the government, however, biomedical policy continues to be a culmination of fragmented, uncoordinated, and often contradictory actions across a myriad of agencies and committees.

A. Congress

The legislative process as now constituted is not designed to handle the kind of issues raised by biomedical technology. As a deliberative body, Congress is extremely slow both in recognizing policy problems and in acting upon them. According to Shick (1977: 10), the "legislative process is weighted against quick and comprehensive responses" and encourages bargaining and compromise to build majorities at each stage. The issues raised by biomedical technology are qualitatively different than traditional public issues revolving around expenditures of funds. Although biomedical issues include that dimension, they also comprise difficult ethical and moral aspects, which political institutions have normally avoided. Reliance on current political procedures results in failure to recognize the richness and complexity of these issues. As Coates (1978: 33) asserts, "cut and fit accommodation and incremental change, the traditional strategies of government, are increasingly ineffective, if not sterile modes of operation." Reinforcing this inherent congressional bias against quick and comprehensive response to problems is the tendency of legislatures to "refrain from enacting regulatory laws until there is an obvious need for legislation" (Green, 1973: 388).

Congress also illustrates how fragmentation of power presents problems in approaching biomedical problems. Although the rationale behind the committee system is to divide labor in order to maximize skill and minimize the overall workload, Tribe (1973: 609) concludes that "the existing system of specialized committees, riddled with rivalries and fragmented by jurisdictional division, cannot be relied upon to provide the focus without which public concern is just so much undirected energy." The present committee system fails to reflect cross-cutting issues and increases duplication as numerous committees stake claims to jurisdiction on important issues, further slowing the process without assuring that relevant policy interdependencies will be considered (Shick, 1977: 14). Because biomedical issues tend to combine what in the past were perceived to be separate issues and have multiplied the number of interests that must be considered, the process is further frustrated.[1]

While these problems persist, Congress has made limited attempts to alleviate them. The establishment of the Congressional Budget Office and the expansion of the function of the General Accounting Office to conduct program audits have given Congress a more adequate oversight capacity in evaluating administrative compliance to congressional intent and a limited role in policy formulation. Congress created the Office of Technology Assessment (OTA) in 1972 to increase its analytical capabilities relating to technological developments.[2] Despite this intention, the OTA was criticized by the Advisory Council in 1976 for dissipating its energies on routine tasks for congressional committees while failing in its ostensible goal of providing "an early warning system for Congress" (Boffey, 1976: 213). This assessment reinforces the perception that the congressional process is dominated by short-run parochial concerns and that it is difficult to establish a prospective orientation in that body.

Although Congress has yet to produce comprehensive biomedical policy, it did pass several pieces of legislation during the 1970s that dealt with biomedical research. In reaction to disclosures of widespread misuse of human subjects in research, Public Law 93-348 (June 1974) created the National Commission for the Protection of Human Subjects of Biomedical and Behavioral Research. The commission was to establish guidelines for the use of human subjects in biomedical testing, directing special attention to research involving children, prisoners, and institutionalized mentally infirm. This commission was to be followed in July 1976 by the creation of a permanent National Advisory Council for the Protection of Subjects of Biomedical and Behavioral Research to advise the Secretary of Health, Education and Welfare (HEW) Department policies.[3] The 1974 legislation also *prohibited* HEW from funding any research using live human fetuses (Maynard-Moody, 1979) or psychosurgery until the commission made recommendations, at which time the moratorium might be lifted. Finally, this law required that all entities seeking HEW funds for research establish institutional review boards to monitor research involving human subjects.

Biomedical legislation in 1975-1976 primarily extended funding for a number of research programs. It authorized a total of $752 million for research to combat heart, lung, and blood diseases and $350 million for the National Research Service Awards program. The National Genetic Disease Act of 1976 authorized the expenditure of $90 million over a three-year period to "establish a national program to provide for basic and applied research, research training, testing, counseling, and information and education programs with respect to genetic disease." This statute reflects a concern that the disease-specific approach used previously for genetic programs was irrational from a planning perspective despite its political attractiveness (Culliton, 1972: 590), and provides the first omnibus genetic bill by including a variety of genetic diseases. As such it superseded the Sickle Cell Disease Control Act and the National Cooley's Anemia Control Act, both of 1972.

Since 1978 biomedical legislation has focused on kidney dialysis, regulation of recombinant DNA research, and a reassessment of the role of Congress in National Institutes of Health (NIH) research. In June 1978, the President signed into law legislation (PL 95-292) designed to encourage persons with kidney failure to conduct home or self-dialysis and provided additional funding of this dialysis through Medicare.[4] In November 1978 the President signed PL 95-622 establishing the Commission for the Study of Ethical Problems in Medicine and Biomedical and Behavioral Research. Unlike past advisory bodies, it was given jurisdiction over all federal agencies. Although its specific recommendations to an agency are not binding, they are to be published in the *Federal Register* and responded to by the agency within six months.[5] This act also added new emphasis on disease-prevention measures and mandated the annual publication of a list of substances known or suspected to be carcinogenic.

The most salient of the biomedical issues during the mid-1970s was debate over the risks of recombinant DNA research (Jackson and Stich, 1979). After two years of consideration, Congress in 1978 shelved efforts to enact legislation to regulate this research (Krimsky, 1979). This resulted largely from the strong lobbying efforts of academic and commercial DNA researchers and officials, who argued that early fears of potential hazards from DNA research were groundless and that federal regulation would constitute unwarranted intrusion into continued research. As a product of this inaction, in January 1979, the NIH relaxed the safety regulations for federally funded DNA research and exempted about one-third of the experiments from federal containment requirements (Congressional Quarterly, 1980: 69A). In May 1980, the Senate Committee on Commerce, Science and Transportation began hearings on industrial applications of recombinant DNA techniques in anticipation one month later of the *Chakrabarty* decision, in which the Supreme Court ruled that new life forms produced by recombinant methods could be patented under existing law.

B. The Courts

The debate over whether or not courts ought to or are able to have a policy-making role has existed as long as the courts themselves. Recently, critics have argued that inherent limitations on judicial policy making preclude its involvement in policy realm of biomedical research (Schoenberg, 1979). Anything with as few legal precedents and as politically controversial as the definition of "life" and "death" should be left for the elected representatives of the people to determine. More specifically, because the judicial process is a passive, retrospective one, it is too slow to react to rapid technological progress. Courts deal with past disputes and usually cannot prevent the development of "dangerous" biomedical technology.

Furthermore, because courts do not have independent investigatory capabilities, they must depend on expert testimony in technical matters. In the biomedical policy area, there are "experts" willing to testify on all sides of an issue, and judges do not have the technical expertise to mediate. This pattern suggests a danger that judicial decisions might be determined by which side employs the most eloquent and convincing testimony. Also, because it is imperative that individual cases be decided on evidence produced by the parties to each case and not on the basis of public policy considerations, decisions are episodic, unpredictable, and often inconsistent. Case-by-case adjudication by a wide variety of state and federal courts adds confusion.[6] Because of the unique process of adjudication and the traditional role of courts, Green (1976: 120) argues that "it is doubtful that the courts will contribute very much to the resolution" of issues raised by biomedical technology.

Proponents of an active role of the courts argue that even in this policy area the courts do have a role to play. The same constraints alleged to prevent the courts from making policy in biomedical research were present in civil rights, and yet courts initiated great policy changes in those areas. The common law American legal tradition allows for judicial innovation. Biomedical engineering involves legal questions such as due process, fundamental rights, and privacy. One need only look at the broad impact of *Roe v. Wade* or at the recent "wrongful life" torts and the pressures they exert on physicians to utilize prenatal diagnostic techniques (Powledge, 1979) to see social consequences extending beyond the original litigation. The concept of fundamental rights, especially as it relates to privacy and self-determination in reproductive matters, and the notion of "compelling state interest," clearly demonstrate the influence of the courts on the application of biomedical technology.

Proponents of an active judicial policy role contend that courts are part of the political process and that, in certain policy areas, courts have the needed expertise and should make policy. Tribe (1973b: 98) suggests that at the expressive and symbolic levels, the law has a potential role as a catalyst for needed changes in the system. The law dramatizes injustices and channels executive as well as legislative attention toward areas that need more systematic reform or comprehensive regulation. While the law reflects public values, it also induces cultural and moral change through alterations in legal doctrine. Despite the fragmented, oblique, and at times contradictory policy implications produced by the court system, it is expected that the most sensitive biomedical issues ultimately will be tested in the Supreme Court.

C. The Bureaucracy

The very size and complexity of the federal bureaucracy, combined with a splintered distribution of jurisdictional boundaries, result in overlapping lines of authority. Given the historical development of the various agencies and the competitiveness of these agencies for power and influence, there is nothing approaching a single locus of power for biomedical policy making. There is no one coordinating mechanism to ensure that policy is consistent or to eliminate duplication and confusion that results when more than one agency makes policy in the same general area. Another unfortunate byproduct of these overlapping jurisdictions is that agencies do not always cooperate fully with each other (Funke, 1979). Comprehensive and future-oriented policy is unlikely to be produced as long as this competition exists.

A final problem inherent to bureaucracies, which minimizes their objectivity and causes them to lose sight of broader public responsibilities, is their dependence on special interest group support. If the government is to make objective and comprehensive biomedical policy, an agency must be created that is free from dominance by interest groups yet allows for widespread public access. This seems unlikely within the current institutional context, where the growth and survival of a public agency depends on its success in establishing routinized relationships with its clients. The bureaucracy, at least as it now operates, appears incapable of dealing with complex and controversial problems raised by biomedical technologies (Breyer and Zeckhauser, 1974: 141).

Some recent developments in the executive branch have moved toward a more active government involvement in biomedical issues. Within the Department of Health, Education and Welfare, an Office of Health Technology was established to coordinate analysis and testing by agencies to determine safety, efficacy, and cost effectiveness of new and existing biomedical technologies, and to assist in determining which mechanisms should be used to promote, inhibit, or control the use of these technologies. In response to the growing ethical implications of these technologies, the Ethics Advisory Board was created in 1978, to make recommendations concerning the ethical appropriateness of research in these areas. During that year, the board held public hearings throughout the United States and took testimony from scholars in many fields while considering whether to lift the moratorium on federal funding of research involving in vitro fertilization of humans.[7]

Also within DHEW, the National Institutes of Health (NIH) created an Office for the Medical Applications of Technology and has attempted to broaden the roles of its various national advisory councils in an effort to enlarge the contribution of public representatives to the development of research policies and priorities. The NIH has continued to come under criticism, however, for its medical elite-dominated decision-making process (Marston, 1978). Despite the reintroduction (1976) of science policy advisors into the Executive Office of the President with the creation of the Office of Science and Technology Policy, it is doubtful that it will offer much consideration of biomedical technologies.

D. Adaptation of Policy Mechanisms to Biomedical Problems

In spite of the difficulties in making biomedical policy, decisions as to whether or not to allocate public funds for each area of biomedical research and technology must be made within a broader political context. As medical costs have risen dramatically as a result of inflation, expensive mid-level technologies, and duplication and waste resulting from poor planning and improper administration, the government has assumed a larger proportion of these costs. Federal funding of research, Medicare and Medicaid coverage, and genetic screening and diagnostic programs has become crucial. Not surprisingly, federal expenditures for biomedical research increased from $110 million in 1950 to $3.35 billion in 1978, a rate of increase of more than 100 percent per year. Furthermore, this increased dependence on public funding comes at a time when public resources are constrained. The result is more emphasis on assessment of technology, cost effectiveness of programs, and the creation of cost-benefit formulas for distributing limited public resources. Accompanying these trends is the demand for increased accountability as to how public funds are spent, leading to further centralization of these programs.

Cost-Benefit Analysis: Given these patterns, emphasis in policy making is shifting to the establishment of criteria for judging the effectiveness of specific programs. Presently, these criteria center on cost-benefit or risk-benefit formulas designed to maximize the return to society per unit of cost. Although cost-benefit analysis (CBA) was developed originally as an aid to the allocation of public monies for irrigation projects, mandatory cost-effectiveness analyses are now applied in most areas of public policy evaluation (Congressional Quarterly, 1980: 124). Despite its expanded use, it is most applicable to programs in which the costs and benefits are tangible, unambiguous, and easily translated into standardized units. Attempts to apply this type of analysis to biomedical programs, where costs and benefits cannot be measured adequately in monetary terms and where intangibles often outweigh those values that can be operationalized effectively, however, are risky.

There is much disagreement surrounding the role of CBA in biomedical policy making. Twiss (1976: 37) sees CBA as being of limited value in setting priorities in biomedical policy and contends that the norm of equity is of greater importance. According to Twiss, CBA cannot solve issues of health policy, determine the social validity of health programs, or provide proof of the social value of any health program. Neuhauser (1977) argues that the application of CBA to medical decision making is callous, and notes that the assumptions of CBA are clearly at odds with those of a traditional doctor-patient approach, where no expense is spared for the patient. Until now, new biomedical technologies have been introduced when clinicians believed that they would benefit the patient, irrespective of cost (Altman and Blendon, 1979: 1). The emphasis on cost effectiveness is altering this traditional mode of operation.[8]

Conversely, Pliskin and Taylor (1977: 6) suggest that although CBA cannot make value judgments for society, it frequently can "clarify the issues by identifying advantages and disadvantages, quantifying effects, and measuring the resources involved." Grosse (1972: 89), too, describes the usefulness of CBA in "framing the right questions," although he notes limitations for its application to health programs. Leach (1970: 292) argues strongly for establishing cost-benefit ratios for screening programs and concludes that "mass prevention campaigns against disease" are generally not efficient investments. Recent applications of CBA to biomedical applications include Bunker, Barnes, and Mosteller (1977); Conley (1973); Swint et al. (1979); Thompson and Milunsky (1979).

In order for CBA to contribute meaningfully to biomedical policy making, (1) measuring instruments must be refined, (2) renewed emphasis must be placed on quantifying major social and psychological costs and benefits, (3) assumptions and their implications must be explicated, and (4) new efforts must be made to anticipate second-order costs and benefits. Even then, the final decision in each case ought to reflect the actual needs, values, and preferences of the people affected by a program and include consideration of other decision-making principles such as equity, justice, and fairness.

Biomedical Technology Assessment: Although the need for assessment of future alternatives has long been recognized, only recently has an effort been made to include future considerations as a crucial dimension in policy making. Still, the short-term, pragmatic emphasis of policy making continues to dominate and as yet no political mechanism has been established to assess continuously the consequences of most biomedical technologies. In practice, technology assessment (TA) has been applied to studies that vary considerably in purpose and methodology. A basic distinction appears to be between what might be termed a narrowly technical assessment and a broader assessment that details the interplay of the technology, values, and society.[9]

Despite the need for narrow TA to explicate the technical benefits and risks inherent in each procedure,[10] TA must include the social, ethical, and political dimensions as well, along the lines of Coates' (1971: 225) definition as "the systematic study of the effects on society that may occur when a technology is introduced, extended, or modified, with special emphasis on the impacts that are unintended, indirect, and delayed." According to the National Academy of Science (1975: 2), little thorough and systematic investigation of biomedical technologies has been conducted. To date most of the major technology assessments have been in nonbiological fields such as energy, transportation, and natural resources (Coates, 1975: 6). According to Walters (1978: 224), one reason for the lack of TA for biomedical technology is that because two-thirds of funding for such research comes from the federal government, "advances in biomedical technology already reflect public-policy decisions to a much greater extent than do technical advances in the field of physics and physical engineering." Among the limited efforts in assessing biomedical technologies to date are a general discussion of future biomedical developments and their potential social impact (Gordon and Ament, 1969), an assessment of four biomedical techniques (National Academy of Sciences, 1975), an overview of nine biomedical candidates for further assessment (Office of Technology Assessment, 1976), and an assessment of life-extending technologies (Gordon et al., 1977).

While recognizing major differences between biological and physical technologies as they affect humans, Walters (1978: 225) hypothesizes that the "same methodology, with minor adjustments is applicable to the biomedical field." The National Academy of Sciences (1975: 3) suggests that modification is necessary to consider better the "deeply ingrained feelings" about the nature of humans, their freedom, dignity, and beliefs, which are much more clearly operative in biomedical areas. Hanft (1977: 23) agrees that too little attention has been paid to the consequences of the introduction of new biomedical technologies and warns: "Once given the *Good Housekeeping* seal of the community, it is very difficult to withhold introduction of a new technology into the health services system, even when efficacy and costs have not been established." Rising expectations of the public, fueled by press reports of miracle advances in biomedical technology, might very easily create a route of no return if adequate assessment is not conducted early in the development process.

Still, in its assessment of four relatively straightforward biomedical technologies, the NAS (1975: 4) concludes that: "The breadth and complexity of the subject matter posed serious obstacles to developing a uniform mode of analysis . . . different technologies presented different kinds of problems for analysis and assessment." While it found assessment of biomedical technology helpful in illuminating important public policy questions and identifying stages in the use of a given technology at which decisions and value choices can be made, NAS is skeptical of the desirability and feasibility of TA for making the final decision. Tribe (1973: 624) adds that, given the rapid advances in biomedical technology, we can no longer depend solely on expanding the instrumental method by simply broadening the range of factors considered. At the least, Tribe (1973: 659) requires increased attempts to enrich policy analysis by adding a constitutive dimension that will deal with these crucial value problems.

Huddle (1972: 155) reiterates the need for a more comprehensive, integrative function, which includes (1) forecasting of technology, (2) the development of social indicators, and (3) the identification of national goals as well as the TA itself. According to Ferkiss (1978: 4), the difficulties involved with TA are compounded when technology is judged within the context of "political and social goals which are themselves subject to controversy." Certainly, biomedical technologies fall in this category.

Although technology assessment serves to bring anticipatory control over technology one step closer to reality, it cannot resolve two critical questions regarding biomedical policy: (1) What criteria ought to be used to establish societal priorities, and (2) who makes the final decision concerning the disposition of each technological innovation? Based on the limited efforts to assess biomedical innovations and the apparent inability of existing political institutions to face the policy issues created as these technologies expand, efforts in the 1980s must be directed toward establishment of procedures and mechanisms for integrating biomedical issues into every stage of the policy process.

IV. BIOMEDICAL POLICY: NEEDS AND DIRECTIONS

Although adequate biomedical policy can emerge only through concentrated effort at every stage of the policy process, including implementation, continuous evaluation of ongoing programs and termination of programs deemed unsatisfactory, immediate attention must focus on agenda setting and the formulation of policy alternatives. If biomedical issues are to receive the necessary public consideration, they first must be viewed as a legitimate element of the public agenda. Once that occurs, it is crucial that feasible and comprehensive policy options be formulated. Concurrently, however, it is critical that mechanisms designed to make and implement policy decisions be developed. In light of the actual and potential political controversies surrounding these technologies, success at each of these stages will be difficult.

A. Agenda Setting

Nelkin (1977a: 413) contends that the policy importance of a technological innovation depends on the degree to which it provokes a public response and its relationship to organized political and economic interests. Political demands focus on issues that are highly visible or dramatic, especially if their potential impact on public health or safety is clear. The resulting interest in these issues is followed by (1) a proliferation of interest groups, (2) protests confronting the technological development, and (3) governmental committees, conferences, and so forth (Nelkin, 1977a: 408). Certainly biomedical issues meet these criteria.

Two tasks appear vital if biomedical issues are to be placed on the public agenda. First, national health goals must be defined clearly and consistently. To date, little success is apparent in setting national objectives regarding preventive health care, including most potential biomedical technologies. Furthermore, health policy continues to be fragmented among the 50 states and the many federal health-related agencies. For Spilhaus (1972: 714), "now is the time to revive ideas of how to plan for large national objectives that transcend local and state interests and that look far beyond present immediacies." Clarifying the goal orientation toward public health is crucial, especially in the context of constrained public resources.

A second task is to determine where biomedical programs fit into these national health objectives in a manner that accounts for the complex moral context of biomedical technology. Only by delineating broader social goals can the direction of biomedical research and development and the priority attached to each potential application be ascertained. Attention must be directed toward setting national goals and establishing a future-oriented public agenda for achieving these goals.

One question of goals centers on the current tendency of American society to expend energies searching out more technical solutions rather than make changes in life styles. Although malnutrition, smoking, a sedentary life style, drug and alcohol misuse, and so forth, are substantially more debilitating to society than genetic disease and other targets of biomedical technologies, we seem to find it more attractive to develop new biomedical technologies than to alter our life style. These priorities must be reevaluated within a framework of meaningful national goals.

B. Formulation of Policy Alternatives

Robbins (1979: 174) notes that we must "improve our capacity to assess technologies during the developmental stage and to encourage those projects which have the greatest promise for yielding effective outcomes." Coates (1978: 36) stresses the necessity of forecasting, feedback, and flexibility in designing public policies. Nowhere is the need for intense evaluation of alternatives prior to the development of the innovations more crucial than in biomedical technology.

At one level, each potential biomedical innovation must be analyzed separately. Included in this assessment are an evaluation of the technical considerations and an inventory of the social impact of each application of the technique on values such as privacy and individualism and on social institutions and patterns of behavior. Although the social consequences of biomedical technologies overlap, many nuances among specific applications remain and should be explicated. A second essential level of formulation is more comprehensive and thus more difficult. Here all biomedical technologies must be appraised as to their contribution toward achieving the national goals delineated during agenda setting. Because of the interconnectedness of biomedical technologies, it is critical that priorities be set. The achievement of one technology might serve as the means through which other, perhaps less desirable and unanticipated, developments occur.[11] The formulation of policy alternatives must take into consideration these ties between technologies and anticipate second- and third-order consequences of each application.

C. New Mechanisms for Biomedical Issues

As in other areas of science policy, there is continuing debate over the extent to which biomedical policy ought to be influenced by scientists and the general public. New policy mechanisms have been suggested in order to facilitate such influence. On the one hand are those who argue that the public must have more input on these crucial issues (Kaplan, 1975; Veatch, 1975). The Science for Citizens Program (Culliton, 1976); expanded use of open meetings, conferences, and public hearings by biomedical commissions (U.S. Department of Health, Education and Welfare, 1978); and the inclusion of lay persons on review boards reflect this viewpoint. Despite these attempts to expand public involvement in developing priorities and providing needed lay public input, Funke (1979: 19) concludes that "we have not yet found wholly appropriate mechanisms for allowing, much less facilitating, public input in the policy process."

Similarly, there have been proposals for mechanisms to ensure continuous and balanced scientific input. The "science court" (Task Force, 1976), designed to clarify questions of technical fact in an adversary setting with final judgment coming from "disinterested" judges, has been criticized from several directions (Nelkin, 1977b). Other options would restructure congressional hearings into an adversary format and televise public forums where experts would debate the social and political as well as the technical implications.

Spilhaus (1972: 715) recommends a permanent U.S. planning board to formulate long-range societal goals. Similarly, Rosenfeld (1977) calls for establishment of a permanent "early alert task force," whose mission it would be to warn all interested publics of the benefits and hazards of biomedical research. Pancheri (1978), taking a different approach, asserts that policy decisions in genetic technology should be made by "value specialists" who are trained in "one or several aspects of value theory and its application," not by the scientific community or the public. She would restrict the exercise of democratic methods to the election of the adversary groups of value theorists who "would assist the decision-makers in learning public values."

In discussing the role of the public, scientists, or value theorists in biomedical decision making, it is crucial to make a distinction between (1) making technical decisions requiring substantial expertise and (2) establishing broad priorities based on social values. Although it is difficult to distinguish clearly between the two in light of the interface between social values and the technology, it seems reasonable that most emphasis should be placed on the latter. Although lay participation on technical review committees might provide useful input, debate must shift toward creation of mechanisms for effective representation on the broader concerns regarding the direction of scientific research and application in a number of areas. Although it is of some urgency that effective mechanisms be established to increase public participation and accountability, set social priorities, assess and monitor technologies, and define and evaluate risks and benefits associated with each technology, effort first must be directed toward adapting current institutions where possible to deal with emerging biomedical issues.

Ultimately, if such a mechanism is to have an impact on policy, it must be established as a permanent, autonomous commission with the authority to make policy decisions similar to the Maryland Commission on Hereditary Disorders.[12] Although recent activities by presidential commissions and advisory boards are encouraging signs of interest in biomedical issues, these ad hoc mechanisms have no policy-making authority. Furthermore, although these bodies provide important contributions by raising issues, demonstrating complex interrelationships, and setting the boundaries for debate, they seldom offer continued scrutiny of the issues. Because biomedical technology continues to advance at a rapid rate, even the definitions of problems are temporary and subject to change with the next technological development. Although commissions often give the impression of producing final, comprehensive studies of a problem, truly effective control of biomedical capabilities must come from permanent bodies that have policy-making authority.

V. CURRENT STATE OF BIOMEDICAL POLICY STUDIES

The current state of policy studies dealing with biomedical issues is primitive. Because of the scope and complexity of biomedicine, analysis of the policy aspects of these issues is rudimentary, fragmentary, and tentative. Although there is a substantial literature on bioethics and a growing interest in the policy dimension, only a small portion of this analysis is written by persons trained in the social or policy sciences. Until now, most attention to biomedical policy has come from the biomedical research community (Conley, Kass, Lappé, Milunsky, Sinsheimer) or from ethicists (Beauchamp, Callahan, Fletcher, McCormick, Ramsey). *The Bibliography of Society, Ethics and the Life Sciences*; *The Encyclopedia of Bioethics*; and *Bibliography of Bioethics* are invaluable resource volumes for this vast literature.

Despite Caldwell's (1964: 2) early call for a "policy synthesis of scientific knowledge and ethical values" to deal with public policy questions raised by the "explosion of biomedical knowledge and technology," Somit and Peterson (1979) conclude that political scientists have yet to give adequate attention to the policy implications of biological issues. There are, however, encouraging signs that this lack of focused attention on biomedicine is changing.

Frankel (1973, 1975) has contributed a series of seminal works on various genetic technologies and human experimentation. Stephens' (1975) investigation of the policy aspects of human experimentation and Ostheimer's (1979) work on euthanasia and other life-death issues both illustrate vividly the types of analysis essential to biomedical policy. White's (1972) work on genetic diversity and democracy and the recent literature in sociobiology clearly supplement these explorations of biomedical policy. Works by Ellison (1978), Reilly (1977), Blank and Ostheimer (1979), and Blank (1979, 1981) provide possible frameworks for biomedical policy studies, but also indicate the prodigious scope of the problems to be faced.

What emerges from this scattered literature is the certain need to view biomedical policy as a genuine interdisciplinary endeavor, not only among bioethicists, policy scientists, and the biomedical community, but also among those familiar with developments in computer applications, health policy, and environmental policy. Interaction among these fields must reflect the intricate interconnections among the technologies, the value system, and biomedical policy. Most of the policy-related materials to date have come from a number of institutes, most notably the Hastings Center through its *Report*.[13] The Center for Biopolitical Research is presently redirecting more energy into the biomedical policy area and serves as a valuable communication link for those interested in politics and the life sciences through its *Journal of Politics and the Life Sciences*.

The next decade will be crucial to the development of an overdue policy emphasis on these rapidly emerging issues. Works of this sort, which attempt to demonstrate the scope of biomedical issues and their policy implications, should have a positive impact on this development and provide something other than despondency over the tasks facing us.

NOTES

1. This process is further fragmented because states retain primary responsibility for making health policy and Congress has shown little propensity to preempt this responsibility as it has in other areas. As a result, biomedical programs vary substantially from state to state, both in quality and format.

2. The Office of Technology Assessment (1978) conducted a series of inquiries into the impact of innovations in biomedical technology and services.

3. Before ending its statutory existence in 1978, the commission issued a series of final reports on psychosurgery and on research involving children, prisoners, the mentally infirm, and fetuses. It also prepared a special study on the "Implications of Advances in Biomedical and Behavioral Research," which reasserted the need to "create new institutions to monitor the development and introduction of new technologies in the biomedical and behavioral fields, and to draw the attention of legislatures and the public to social problems arising from the use of these new technologies." The report called for an independent national agency that would: (1) formulate national policy and facilitate coordination of those agencies that implement policy, (2) monitor and evaluate agencies charged with implementing policy, (3) review and evaluate

the implications of research and technology, and (4) inform the public and scientific community and facilitate public participation in policy decision making (U.S. Department of Health, Education and Welfare, 1978: 35).

4. See Ellison (1978) for a discussion of the issues surrounding the dialysis program.
5. It will be interesting to see how active a role this commission takes in leading the debate over biomedical issues, especially its impact or lack of impact on permanent agency decisions. Given the normal operation of political institutions, however, it is unlikely that the commission will exert substantial influence over the policy process.
6. Contradictory decisions in criminal cases involving defendants with an XYY gene complement demonstrate the importance of technical experts in such court action.
7. The board was not included in the 1981 budget because the Administration decided to request funding only for the new presidential ethics commission. For additional discussion on the role of the Ethics Advisory Board, see Yesley (1980).
8. Blumstein (1976: 233) points out the great inconsistency in the way we deal with costs as they relate to the value of life. Although most persons are willing to spend unlimited funds to maintain the life of a particular individual, we consciously make decisions on a cost-benefit basis that result in the probability of death to x number of individuals. He suggests that whereas CBA might work when the immediate human consequences are not apparent, it breaks down and appears cruel when hypothetical cases become concrete.
9. Other distinctions relate to the prospective or retrospective nature of the study and the extent to which the assessment is evaluative or descriptive.
10. An example of the narrow type of TA is the appraisal of the efficacy and safety of 17 medical procedures conducted by the Office of Technology Assessment (1978).
11. For instance, the technique of in vitro fertilization, although distinct from its potential use in surrogate motherhood and possibly human cloning, is a necessary means through which these extensions might be conducted.
12. Etzioni's (1973: 55) two-tiered approach, which consists of a permanent national commission "charged with formulating alternative guidelines for public policy" to be supplemented by a "myriad of local review boards" to review individual decisions, has merit. Etzioni (1973) and Sinsheimer (1973) contend that international bodies must be established, especially in the field of genetic technology.
13. Other sources of information especially relating to biomedical education are the Biological Sciences Curriculum Study and the National Clearinghouse for Human Genetic Diseases.

REFERENCES

Altman, S. H., and Blendon, R. (Eds.) (1979). *Medical Technology: The Culprit Behind Health Care Costs?* U.S. Department of Health, Education and Welfare, Washington, DC.

Annas, G. J., Glantz, L. H., and Katz, B. F. (1977). *Informed Consent to Human Experimentation: The Subject's Dilemma.* Ballinger, Cambridge, MA.

Barber, B. (1973). *Research on Human Subjects: Problems of Social Control in Medical Experimentation.* Russell Sage Foundation, New York.

Beckwith, J. (1976). Social and political uses of genetics in the United States: Past and present. *Annals of the New York Academy of Sciences 265*: 46–58.

Beckwith, J., and King, J. (1974). The XYY syndrome: A dangerous myth. *New Scientist 64*: 474–476.

Blank, R. H. (1979). Human genetic technology: Some political implications. *Social Science Journal 16*(3): 1-19.

——. (1981). *The Political Implications of Human Genetic Technology*. Westview Press, Boulder, CO.

Blank, R. H., and Ostheimer, J. M. (1979). An overview of biomedical policy: Life and death issues. *Policy Studies Journal 8* (Winter): 470-479.

Blumstein, J. F. (1976). Constitutional perspectives on governmental decisions affecting human life and health. *Law and Contemporary Problems 40* (4): 231-305.

Boffey, P. M. (1976). Office of Technology Assessment: Bad marks on its first report card. *Science 193*: 213-215.

Bowman, J. E. (1977). Genetic screening programs and public policy. *Phylon 38*: 117-142.

———. (1978). Social, legal and economic issues in sickle cell programs. In *Genetics Now: Ethical Issues in Genetic Research*, J. J. Buckley (Ed.). University Press of America, Washington, DC.

Breyer, S., and Zeckhauser, R. (1974). The regulation of genetic engineering. In *Genetic Responsibility: On Choosing Our Children's Genes*, M. Lipkin and P. Rowley, (Eds.). Plenum, New York.

Bunker, J. P., Barnes, B. A., and Mosteller, F. (Eds.) (1977). *Costs, Risks, and Benefits in Surgery*. Oxford University Press, New York.

Caldwell, L. K. (1964). Biopolitics: Science, ethics and public policy. *Yale Review 54* (1): 1-16.

Coates, J. F. (1971). Technology assessment: The benefits . . . the costs . . . the consequences. *Futurist 5*: 225-231.

——. (1975). Technology assessment and public wisdom. *Journal of the Washington Academy of Sciences 65*: 3-12.

——. (1978). What is a public policy issue? In *Judgement and Decision in Public Policy Formation*, K. R. Hammond (Ed.). Westview Press, Boulder, CO.

Coates, V. T. (1972). *Technology and Public Policy: The Process of Technology Assessment in the Federal Government, Vol. 1*. Program of Policy Studies in Science and Technology, George Washington University, Washington, DC.

Cohen, C. (1978). Medical experimentation on prisoners. *Perspectives in Biology and Medicine 21* (3): 357-372.

Cohen, S. N. (1977). Recombinant DNA: Fact and fiction. *Science 195*: 647-654.

Comroe, J. H. (1978). The road from research to new diagnosis and therapy. *Science 200*: 931-937.

Congressional Quarterly (1980). *Health Policy: The Legislative Agenda*. Congressional Quarterly Service, Washington, DC.

Conley, R. W. (1973). *The Economics of Mental Retardation*. Johns Hopkins University Press, Baltimore.

Culliton, B. J. (1972). Cooley's anemia: Special treatment for another ethnic disease. *Science 178*: 590.

——. (1976). N.S.F.: Trying to cope with congressional pressure for public participation. *Science 191*: 274-318.

Curran, W. J. (1975). Experimentation becomes a crime: Fetal research in Massachusetts. *New England Journal of Medicine 292* (February): 300-301.

Ellison, D. L. (1978). *The Biomedical Fix*. Greenwood Press, Westport, CT.

Etzioni, A. (1973). *Genetic Fix: The Next Technological Revolution*. Harper & Row, New York.

Etzioni, A., and Nunn, C. (1974). Public appreciation of science in contemporary America. *Daedalus 103*: 191–206.

Fanning, T. R. (1978). Political genetics: The case of genetic screening and counseling. Unpublished Ph.D. dissertation, SUNY-Binghampton.

Ferkiss, V. (1978). Technology assessment and appropriate technology: The political and moral dimensions. *National Forum*, Fall, pp. 3–7.

Fletcher, J. C. (1967). Human experimentation: Ethics in the consent situation. *Law and Contemporary Problems 32*: 620–649.

Fletcher, J. F. (1974). *The Ethics of Genetic Control: Ending Reproductive Roulette.* Doubleday, Garden City, NY.

—— (1979). *Humanhood.* Prometheus, Buffalo, NY.

Frankel, M. S. (1973). *Genetic Technology: Promises and Problems.* Program of Policy Studies in Science and Technology, George Washington University, Washington, DC.

—— (1975). The development of policy guidelines governing human experimentation in the United States: A case study of public policy making for science and technology. *Ethics in Science and Medicine 2*: 43–59.

Funke, O. (1979). Governing basic science research: Public policy and the recombinant-DNA controversy. Paper presented at annual meeting of the American Political Science Association, Washington, DC, August.

Goodfield, J. (1977). *Playing God: Genetic Engineering and the Manipulation of Life.* Random House, New York.

Gordon, T. J., and Ament, R. H. (1969). *Forecasts of Some Technological Developments and Their Societal Consequences.* Institute for the Future, Middletown, CT.

Gordon, T. J., Gerjuoy, H., and Anderson, M. (1977). *Life Extending Technologies: A Technology Assessment.* Pergamon, New York.

Gray, B. H. (1975). *Human Subjects in Medical Experimentation.* Wiley, New York.

Gray, J. C. (1976). Compulsory sterilization in a free society: Choices and dilemmas. In *Life or Death: Who Controls?* N. C. Ostheimer and J. C. Ostheimer (Eds.). Springer, New York.

Green, H. P. (1973). Mechanisms for public policy decision-making. In *Ethical Issues in Human Genetics*, B. Hilton, D. Callahan, M. Harris, P. Condliffe, and B. Berkley (Eds.). Plenum, New York.

—— (1976). Law and genetic control: Public policy questions. *Annals of the New York Academy of Sciences 265* (January): 170–177.

Grobstein, C. (1979). *A Double Image of the Double Helix: The Recombinant DNA Debate.* Freeman, San Francisco.

Grosse, R. N. (1972). Cost-benefit analysis of health service. *Annals of the American Academy of Sciences 339*: 89–99.

Hanft, R. (1977). Testimony to Senate Subcommittee on Health and Scientific Research. In *Biomedical Research and the Public*, T. Powledge and L. Dach (Eds.). U.S. Government Printing Office, Washington, DC.

Hardin, G. (1972). Genetic consequences of cultural decisions in the realm of population. *Social Biology 19*: 350–361.

Harris, H. (1975). *Prenatal Diagnosis and Selective Abortion.* Harvard University Press, Cambridge, MA.

Howard, T., and Rifkin, J. (1977). *Who Should Play God?* Dell, New York.

Hubbard, R. (1980). Test-tube babies: Solution or problem?" *Technology Review*, March/April, pp. 10–12.

Huddle, F. P. (1972). The social function of technology assessment. In *Technology Assessment: Understanding the Social Consequences of Technological Applications*, R. G. Kasper (Ed.). Praeger, New York.

Ingle, D. (1973). *Who Should Have Children?* Bobbs-Merrill, Indianapolis, IN.

Jackson, D. A., and Stich, S. P. (Eds.) (1979). *The Recombinant DNA Debate*. Prentice-Hall, Englewood Cliffs, NJ.

Kamisar, Y. (1976). Some non-religious views against proposed 'mercy-killing' legislation. *The Human Life Review 2* (Spring): 71–114.

Kaplan, M. B. (1975). The case of the artificial heart panel. *Hastings Center Report 5* (5): 41–48.

Kass, L. R. (1976). Implications of prenatal diagnosis for the human right to life. In *Biomedical Ethics and the Law*, J. M. Humber and R. F. Almeder (Eds.). Plenum, New York.

Kieffer, G. H. (1975). *Ethical Issues in the Life Sciences*. American Association for the Advancement of Science, New York.

Kotulak, R. (1980). Scientific gains being used against women, panel says. *Chicago Tribune*, January 7, p. 3.

Krimsky, S. (1979). Regulating recombinant DNA research. In *Controversy: Practice of Technical Decision*, D. Nelkin (Ed.). Sage, Beverly Hills, CA.

Lappé, M. (1979). *Genetic Politics: The Limits of Biological Control*. Simon and Schuster, New York.

Leach, G. (1970). *The Biocrats*. McGraw-Hill, New York.

Ludmerer, K. M. (1972). *Genetics and American Society*. Johns Hopkins University Press, Baltimore.

Mark, V. H., and Ervin, F. R. (1970). *Violence and the Brain*. Harper & Row, New York.

Marston, R. Q. (1978). Influence of NIH policy past and present on the university health education complex. In *Biomedical Scientists and Public Policy*, H. H. Fudenberg and V. L. Melnik (Eds.). Plenum, New York.

Martin, M. B. (1978). Test-tube morality. *National Review*, October 13, p. 1285.

Maxmen, J. S. (1976). *The Post-Physician Era*. Wiley, New York.

Maynard-Moody, S. (1979). The fetal research dispute. In *Controversy: Practice of Technical Decision*, D. Nelkin (Ed.). Sage Beverly Hills, CA.

McCormick, R. A. (1974). Proxy consent in the experimentation situation. *Perspectives in Biology and Medicine 18*: 2–20.

McIntosh, W., and Alston, H. (1977). Review of the polls: Acceptance of abortion among white Catholics and Protestants, 1962 and 1975. *Journal of the Scientific Study of Religion 16*: 295.

Miller, W. B. (1974). Reproduction, technology and the behavioral sciences. *Science 183*: 149.

Mitford, J. (1972). *Kind and Unusual Punishment: The Prison Business*. Knopf, New York.

Murphy, E. A., Chase, G., and Rodriguez, A. (1978). Genetic intervention: Some social, psychological, and philosophical aspects. In *Genetic Issues in Public Health and Medicine*, B. H. Cohen, A. M. Lilienfeld, and P. C. Huang (Eds.). Charles C Thomas, Springfield, IL.

Murray, R. F. (1978). Public health perspectives on screening and problems in counseling in sickle cell anemia. In *Genetic Issues in Public Health and Medicine*, B. H. Cohen, A. M. Lilienfeld, and P. C. Huang (Eds.). Charles C Thomas, Springfield, IL.

National Academy of Sciences (1975). *Assessing Biomedical Technologies: An Inquiry into the Nature of the Process*. National Science Foundation, Washington, DC.

Nelkin, D. (1977a). Technology and public policy. In *Science, Technology and Society*, Sage, Beverly Hills, CA.

——— (1977b). Thoughts on the proposed science court. *Newsletter on Science, Technology and Human Values 19* (January): 20–31.

Neuhauser, D. (1977). Cost-effective clinical decision-making: Implications for delivery of health services. In *Costs, Risks, and Benefits of Surgery*, J. P. Bunker, B. A. Barnes, and F. Mosteller (Eds.). Oxford University Press, New York.

Office of Technology Assessment (1976). *Development of Medical Technology: Opportunities for Assessment*. U.S. Government Printing Office, Washington, DC.

——— (1978). *Assessing the Efficacy and Safety of Medical Technologies*. U.S. Congress, OTA, Washington, DC.

Ostheimer, J. M. (1979). Euthanasia: Dimensions of a growing political issue. Paper presented at Western Political Science Association meeting, March 29–31, Portland, Oregon.

Ostheimer, J. M., and Ritt, L. G. (1976). Life and death: Current public attitudes. In *Life or Death: Who Controls?*, N. Ostheimer and J. M. Ostheimer (Eds.). Springer, New York.

Pancheri, L. U. (1978). Genetic technology: Policy decisions and democratic principles. In *Genetics Now: Ethical Issues in Genetic Research*, J. J. Buckley (Ed.). University Press of America, Washington, DC.

Pliskin, N., and Taylor, A. K. (1977). General principles: Cost-benefit and decision analysis. In *Costs, Risks, and Benefits of Surgery*, J. P. Bunker, B. A. Barnes, and F. Mosteller (Eds.). Oxford University Press, New York.

Powledge, T. M. (1979). Prenatal diagnosis: New techniques, new questions. *Hastings Center Report 9* (3): 16–17.

Ramsey, P. (1970). *The Patient as a Person*. Yale University Press, New Haven, CT.

——— (1975). *The Ethics of Fetal Research*. Yale University Press, New Haven, CT.

Reilly, P. (1977). *Genetics, Law and Social Policy*. Harvard University Press, Cambridge, MA.

Restak, R. M. (1975). *Premeditated Man: Bioethics and the Control of Future Human Life*. Penguin, New York.

Robbins, F. C. (1979). Assessing the consequences of biomedical research. In *Medical Technology: The Culprit Behind Health Care Costs?* S. H. Altman and R. Blendon (Eds.). U.S. Department of Health, Education and Welfare, Washington, DC.

Robertson, J. A. (1975). Involuntary euthanasia of defective newborns: A legal analysis. *Stanford Law Review 27* (January): 213–267.

Robitscher, J. (Ed). (1973). *Eugenic Sterilization*. Charles C Thomas, Springfield, IL.

Rorvik, D. (1978). *In His Image: The Cloning of a Man*. Lippincott, Philadelphia.

Rosen, S. (1976). *Future Facts*. Simon and Schuster, New York.

Rosenfeld, A. (1977). An early-alert task force for the public. In *Biomedical Research and the Public*, T. M. Powledge and L. Dach (Eds.). U.S. Government Printing Office, Washington, DC, pp. 151–154.

Russell, O. R. (1975). *Freedom to Die: Moral and Legal Aspects of Euthanasia*. Dell, New York.

Scheflin, A. W., and Upton E. M. (1978). *The Mind Manipulators*. Padington, New York.

Schoenberg, B. (1979). Science and anti-science in confrontation. *Man and Medicine 4* (2): 79–102.

Schrag, P., and Divoky D. (1975). *The Myth of the Hyperactive Child and Other Means of Child Control*. Pantheon, New York.

Shick, A. (1977). Complex policymaking in the United States Senate. In *Policy Analyses on Major Issues*, prepared for the Commission on the Operation of the Senate. U.S. Government Printing Office, Washington, DC.

Sinsheimer, R. L. (1973). Prospects for future scientific development: Ambush or opportunity. In *Ethical Issues in Human Genetics*, B. Hilton, D. Callahan, M. Harris, P. Condliffe, and B. Berkley (Eds.). Plenum, New York.

Snodgrass, V. (1973). Political overtones could obscure clinical issues in psychosurgery. *Journal of the American Medical Association 225* (9): 140-164.

Somit, A., and Peterson, S. (1979). Biopolitics: 1978. *Center for Biopolitical Research Notes*, October.

Spilhaus, A. (1972). Ecolibrium. *Science 175*: 711-715.

Stephens, J. (1975). Medical experimentation on humans and the need for public policy. *What Government Does*, M. Holden, Jr. (Ed.). Sage, Beverly Hills, CA.

Stine, G. J. (1977). *Biosocial Genetics: Human Heredity and Social Issues*. Macmillan, New York.

Swazey, J. P. (1971). Phenylketonuria: A case study in biomedical legislation. *Journal of Urban Law 48*: 883.

Swint, J. M., Shapiro, J. J., Corson, V. L., Reynolds, L. W., Thomas, G. H. and Kazazian, H. H. Jr. (1979). The economic returns to community and hospital screening programs for a genetic disease. *Preventive Medicine 8*: 463-470.

Swinyard, C. A. (Ed.) (1977). *Decision Making and the Defective Newborn*. Charles C Thomas, Springfield, IL.

Task Force of the Presidential Advisory Group on Anticipated Advances in Science and Technology (1976). The science court experiment: An interim report. *Science 193*: 653-656.

Thompson, M., and Milunsky, A. (1979). Policy analysis for prenatal genetic diagnosis. *Public Policy 27* (1): 25-48.

Tooley, M. (1972). Abortion and infanticide. *Philosophy and Public Affairs 2* (1): 37-65.

Tribe, L. H. (1973a). Technology assessment and the fourth discontinuity: The limits of instrumental rationality. *Southern California Law Review 46* (June): 617-660.

—— (1973b). *Channeling Technology Through Law*. Bracton, Chicago.

Twiss, S. B. (1976). Ethical issues in priority-setting for utilization of genetic technologies. *Annals of the New York Academy of Sciences 265* (January): 22-45, 166-167.

U.S. Department of Health, Education and Welfare (1978). *Special Study: Implications of Advances in Biomedical and Behavioral Research*, Report to the National Commission for the Protection of Human Subjects of Biomedical and Behavioral Research. U.S. Department of Health, Education and Welfare, Washington, DC.

U.S. Department of Health, Education and Welfare, Ethics Advisory Board (1979). *HEW Support of Research Involving Human in Vitro Fertilization and Embryo Transfer*. U.S. Department of Health, Education and Welfare, Washington, DC.

Valenstein, E. S. (1973). *Brain Control: A Critical Examination of Brain Stimulation and Psychosurgery*. Wiley-Interscience, New York.

Veatch, R. M. (1975). Human experimentation committees. *Hastings Center Report 5* (5): 31-40.

Visscher, M. B. (1975). *Ethical Constraints and Imperatives in Medical Research*. Charles C Thomas, Springfield, IL.

Walters, L. (1978). Technology assessment and genetics. In *Biomedical Scientists and the Public*, H. H. Fudenberg and V. L. Melnik (Eds.). Plenum, New York.

Wells, W. W. (1973). Drug control of school children: The child's right to choose. *Southern California Law Review 46*: 585-616.

White, E. (1972). Genetic diversity and political life: Toward a population-interaction paradigm. *Journal of Politics 34*: 1203-1242.

Yesley, M. S. (1980). The Ethics Advisory Board and the right to know. *Hastings Center Report 10* (5): 5-9.

34

Values, Ethics, and Standards in Policy Analysis

William N. Dunn / University of Pittsburgh, Pittsburgh, Pennsylvania

I. INTRODUCTION

As an applied social science discipline, policy analysis employs multiple methods of inquiry and argument to produce and transform policy-relevant information (Dunn, 1981a). The scope and methods of policy analysis are partly descriptive, aiming at the production of information about causes and consequences of public policies (see, e.g., Dye, 1978; Cook and Campbell, 1979). Yet policy analysis is also normative; an additional key aim is the production of information about the value of such consequences for past, present, and future generations (see, e.g., MacRae, 1976). For this reason policy analysis provides answers to questions that are designative (What are the causes and consequences of public policies?), evaluative (Of what value is the policy?), and advocative (What should be done?). The aims of policy analysis therefore include but go beyond the production of "facts"; policy analysts also seek to produce information about "values" and their realization through planned action.

To fulfill this broad multidisciplinary charter, policy analysts can and must draw from disciplines and fields that specialize in the study of three types of subject matter: *values,* whose attainment is the main test of whether a policy problem has been alleviated or resolved; *facts,* whose existence may enhance or limit the attainment of values; and *actions,* whose considered adoption, based in part on factual information about policy constraints and opportunities, may result in the attainment of values and the alleviation or resolution of problems.

Policy analysis, to the degree that it addresses this complex domain satisfactorily, frequently borrows from disciplines within the social, behavioral, and management sciences—especially political science, public administration, economics, and operations research—disciplines that are chiefly concerned with discovering and generalizing factual constraints and opportunities surrounding action (see, e.g., Lerner and Lasswell, 1951; Frederickson and Wise, 1977; Quade, 1975). Yet policy analysis also draws, if less heavily and directly, from political philosophy, jurisprudence, and ethics (see, e.g., Beauchamp, 1975; Dallmayr, 1981; Callahan and Jennings, 1982). The primary subject matter of these fields, in contrast to that of the social, behavioral, and management sciences, is values and their relation to moral action.

This broad multidisciplinary perspective of policy analysis, because it expands conventionally accepted boundaries of the social, behavioral, and management sciences, imposes a wide range of new and unfamiliar analytic responsibilities. For this and other reasons discussed throughout this chapter, many contributors to the methodology and practice of policy analysis have been reluctant to move the boundaries of the discipline beyond the scientific study of causes and consequences of policies. Thus, for example, the authors of a widely used text on policy analysis (Stokey and Zeckhauser, 1978: 261) argue that policy analysis "should concentrate on differences in prediction as opposed to differences in values." To support their claim that policy disagreements would diminish or disappear if policy analysts could predict with certainty, the authors turn to Milton Friedman's *Essays in Positive Economics* (1953):

> Differences in economic policy among disinterested citizens derive predominantly from different predictions about the economic consequences of taking action— differences that in principle can be eliminated by the progress of positive economics —rather than from fundamental differences in basic values, differences about which men can ultimately only fight (Friedman, 1953: 5; quoted by Stokey and Zeckhauser, 1978: 261).

This positivistic perspective of policy analysis—a perspective according to which the systematic study of values is peripheral, unnecessary, or undesirable—is by no means confined to economists. Political scientists frequently argue that, whereas scientific explanation and prediction represent legitimate aims of policy analysis, "policy advocacy" and other forms of value judgment, prescription, and command do not (see Anderson, 1975; 8; Dye, 1978: 7-8; Wildvasky, 1979). These authors not only affirm that normative statements purporting to provide sound solutions for practical problems are equivalent to commands, pronouncements, and emotional appeals; they also caution policy analysts to keep science and values strictly apart. A concise illustration of this fact-value split may be found in a recent textbook on policy evaluation. Observing that the activity of evaluation and questions of ethics are as old as human history, political scientist David Nachmias argues that contemporary policy evaluation

> departs from earlier evaluation attempts in the social sciences. . . . Its primary concern is with explanation and prediction; it relies on empirical evidence and analysis; it emphasizes middle-range theory building and testing; and it is concerned with being useful to policymakers. The chief concern is with evaluation as a scientific research activity (Nachmias, 1980: 2).

Disputes surrounding the proper domain of policy analysis, as these illustrations suggest, are intimately tied to philosophical questions about the role of values and ethics in science. For every serious argument affirming that facts and values are and should be kept strictly apart, that policy analysis properly deals with questions of "is" rather than those of "ought," one can supply an equally serious argument affirming that facts and values are analytically inseparable. Because the scope of this introductory section is limited to establishing the main contours of this dispute, it is appropriate here merely to outline in general terms the nature and range of issues treated more fully in the rest of the chapter.

Section II reviews definitions of key terms, specifies their relations, and provides examples from contemporary policy analysis. The central purpose of this section is to show how terminological disputes may lead observers to expand or contract, as the case may be, the aims, subject matter, and boundaries of policy analysis. Section III describes three major types of theories about values and ethics (descriptive theories, normative theories, and meta-ethical theories) and provides illustrations from the works of contributors to the methodology and practice of policy analysis. This section, by illustrating the diversity and richness of available theories of values and ethics, suggests that the boundaries of policy analysis are and should remain open to a range of competing perspectives. Section IV contrasts two major strategies for investigating values, ethics, and standards, outlines the role of descriptive, ethical, and meta-ethical hypotheses, and describes a range of appropriate research procedures available for their investigation. This section shows how choices among hypotheses and research procedures are affected by an investigator's underlying philosophical assumptions. Finally, Sec. V provides a summary appraisal of past and recent trends and suggests opportunities for enlarging present capacities to investigate and consciously justify values, ethics, and standards in policy analysis.

II. VALUES, ETHICS, AND STANDARDS

The meanings attached to the key concepts of a discipline reflect its most basic assumptions. Students of policy analysis have yet to agree on the meaning of such key concepts as values and ethics; nor have relations among key concepts (e.g., social values and norms of professional conduct) been satisfactorily specified. Conflicts surrounding the meaning of basic terms and their relations contribute to the highly variable and fragmented nature of the discipline.

A. The Concept of Values

The term "values" may be defined in a comprehensive or restricted manner. If we wish to be comprehensive, the term may be extended to include desires, wants, likes, pleasures, needs, interests, preferences, duties, and perceived moral obligations (Pepper, 1958). Here values represent an extraordinarily broad domain of modalities of selective behavior (Williams, 1968: 283). Because values are anything of interest to human subjects who make evaluations (Perry, 1954), policy analysis may address an enormous variety of public objects judged to be good and bad, right and wrong, just and unjust. In this broad sense, for example, policy may be defined as "the authoritative allocation of values" (Easton, 1953: 129).

A second and more restricted meaning of the term is that which Williams (1960: 401) terms value-as-criterion. Here we are concerned not only with how an object is rated, ranked, or otherwise appraised, but with the criteria employed to make such evaluations. This second meaning of values incorporates assumptions, decision rules, and other standards of assessment in terms of which evaluative and advocative claims are made (Dunn, 1981a: 87-91). Whereas a broad definition of values may include statements to the effect that "policymakers desire, want, like, and prefer locally financed schools," a more restricted definition typically specifies the criterion in terms of which such evaluative claims are made: "Policy makers prefer locally financed education because it promotes economic efficiency."

These two usages of the term "values" call attention to the several contexts in which values may be investigated. These contexts, as Kaplan (1964: 387-397) observes, are personal, standard, and ideal. In the personal context we find that values are *expressed* in the form of preferences, desires, or tastes. By contrast, the standard context involves *statements* about particular (standard) situations in which a typical individual or group is described as holding certain values. For example, a value statement in the standard context is "School busing is a bad policy in the eyes of middle-class citizens." Finally, the ideal context involves *judgments* that are not reducible to value expressions offered in the personal context, or to value statements that arise in the standard context. Value judgmets are based on criteria that warrant or justify claims about the rightness or wrongness, goodness or badness, and justice or injustice of policies. Thus, for example, "School busing is good because it fosters social equality" is a value judgment based on criteria that go much beyond personal preferences or the values of a typical group. In short, although there is usually some basis for explaining values in the personal or standard contexts, we may also supply grounds for their justification (Kaplan, 1964: 387-389).

Divergent meanings of the term values are evident in disciplines that today constitute the broad multidisciplinary domain of policy analysis. Economics continues to employ a specialized definition of value as preference (see, e.g., Arrow, 1963), as do such hybrid fields and disciplinary offshoots as public choice (Mueller, 1979) and political economy (Frohlich and Oppenheimer, 1978). The use of the term by political scientists and sociologists has been more inclusive, emphasizing valued roles and institutions that contribute to civic order (e.g., Lasswell, 1971) or collective social norms that facilitate consensus through an evolving social contract (e.g., Coleman, 1974). Psychologists and social psychologists often define values in terms of individual and collective learning (see Etheredge, 1982) or a developing capacity for reflective moral reasoning (see Piaget, 1948; Kohlberg, 1961). Finally, decision theory has emphasized capacities for revising subjective expected utilities (e.g., Raiffa, 1968), for obtaining greater consistency among subjective preferences (e.g., Saaty, 1981), or for externalizing judgments as part of a debate among policymakers (e.g., Adelman et al., 1975).

Despite these diverse or conflicting meanings, it is nevertheless possible to draw several key distinctions that should be kept in view when considering alternative usages of the concept.

Value Versus Values: Because people express values that we are able to describe, we are not thereby warranted in concluding that such values refer to properties of objects that are necessarily desirable, good, or just. Thus, the meaning of value cannot be established on the basis of observation alone, because it is always possible to ask: "Is this value good?" Consider, for example, a statement attributed to Oscar Wilde: "An economist is a man who knows the price of everything and the value of nothing." Consider as well an economists's retort: "But, Mr. Wilde, prices *are* values" (Dorfman, 1976: 153).

Values Versus Needs: Although values may be a source of needs, as when the value of public enlightenment prompts the analyst to satisfy unmet needs for increased communication with client groups, values are not identical to needs. Conversely, the degree of perceived deficiency that gives rise to a need (e.g., nutrition as a material need) may be relatively independent of such values as security, order, justice, and equality. Complex relationships between needs and values have created many conceptual and methodological tangles for analysts who conduct "needs assessments" in the course of policy-program evaluations.

Values Versus Norms: Whereas norms are more or less specific rules of conduct applicable in particular contexts, values are standards of achievement that may be applied in many or all conceivable contexts. "The same value may be a point of reference for a great many specific norms; a particular norm may represent the simultaneous application of several separable values" (Williams, 1968: 284). For example, values of power, respect, rectitude, affection, well-being, wealth, skill, and enlightenment (Lasswell and Kaplan, 1950) may each result in the establishment of separate sets of norms intended to regulate relationships between analyst and politician, analyst and analyst, analyst and journalist, analyst and client, or analyst and the public at large. Conversely, the norm of public accountability may involve power, respect, well-being, and other values. Although values provide grounds for justifying norms, the more general the norm, the more difficult it is to distinguish it from a value. Codes of conduct for regulating the behavior of professional planners and policy analysts contain many norms that are virtually indistinguishable from values (see Howe and Kaufman, 1981).

Valuation Versus Evaluation: The distinction between valuation and evaluation, borrowed from Dewey (1939), punctuates contrasts among the contexts (personal, standard, ideal) in which values may be investigated. Evaluation as a general social process involving many forms of appraisal should be distinguished from valuation, a process involving attempts to establish the grounds on which particular appraisals are made. Many disputes surrounding the aims and nature of evaluation research turn on the distinction between valuation and evaluation (see Scriven, 1967; House, 1980; Dunn et al., 1982).

Valuation Versus Prescription: Many contributors to the methodology of policy analysis erroneously equate the process of valuation, including value judgments resulting from this process, with emotional appeals, ideological exhortations, and policy advocacy (e.g., Quade, 1975: 21). This misunderstanding is closely related to the claim that policy analysis is and must be value-neutral (Stokey and Zeckhauser, 1978: 4-5). Thus, much of contemporary policy analysis has failed to recognize, in Baier's words, that value judgments are not "commands, prescriptions, or other forms of telling people to do things . . . telling people what they should do is not telling or exhorting them to do it . . . it is purporting to give them sound solutions to their practical problems" (Baier, 1969: 53).

B. Ethics and Metaethics

The term "ethics" refers both to the reflective study of moral action and to the subject matter of that study. The words "ethics" and "ethical" are frequently applied to certain classes of habitual or customary behavior (e.g., in references to "the ethics of policy makers"), as are the terms "morality" and "moral" (e.g., in statements about "morality in government"). Such everyday usages are linked etymologically to the Greek and Latin words *ethos* and *mores*, both of which mean habits or customs. Although it is primarily this meaning that underlies attempts to develop professional standards and ethics for public managers and policy analysts (see Mertins, 1979), these efforts at professional standard setting and regulation contain implicit ethical and moral judgments. "Even when 'customary morality' is spoken of, the reference of the term is not merely to the customs as such—in the sense of regular, repeated sequences of behavior—but also to the view, at least implicitly held by the participants, that what they regularly do is in some way right; it is not merely what is done, it is also what is to be done" (Gewirth, 1978a: 977).

Thus, the term ethics has two different but related meanings. The term descriptive ethics, which incorporates the analysis of descriptive statements about customary morality, is often juxtaposed to the term normative ethics. Normative ethics is concerned with the analysis, evaluation, and development of normative statements, that is, "statements purporting to give guidance to those trying to solve practical problems" (Baier, 1969: 53). In public policy analysis, normative statements are sometimes based on such criteria as Pareto optimality: One social state is better than another if at least one person is better off and no one is worse off. This particular criterion, when subjected to normative ethical analysis, may be questioned on grounds that those who gain (even though none lose) may do so through corruption, fraud, and discrimination (see Brown, 1975).

Normative ethics, therefore, is centrally concerned with the presentation and appraisal of criteria for justifying normative statements. The central questions of normative ethics are of the form: What criteria justify claims about the rightness, goodness, or justice of public actions? By contrast, meta-ethics is concerned primarily with the nature and meaning of normative statements in general. Questions of meta-ethics are of the form: What (meta-ethical) criteria warrant the choice of (ethical) criteria employed to justify claims about the rightness, goodness, or justice of public actions? In this case, as in others that are more familiar to policy analysts, the term "meta" signifies something that is "about" or "of" something else. Meta-policy, for example, is the policy of policy (Dror, 1968); and meta-evaluation is the evaluation of evaluation, because it develops and applies criteria to evaluate evaluation research (Cook and Gruder, 1978). An important original application of meta-ethics to the normative ethics of policy analysis may be found in MacRae (1976).

Distinctions among descriptive ethics, normative ethics, and meta-ethics punctuate important differences among levels of moral discourse. For example, Steinfels (1977) reports what appears to be a primary orientation toward descriptive ethics in the curricula of schools of public policy and management. Students were generally "disappointed with the extent and depth of ethical analysis"; a majority of faculty, while committed to the idea of rigorous ethical analysis, felt incapable of extending their own analyses beyond the level of "consciousness raising" and "hoping some of the anguish will rub off" (Steinfels, 1977: 3-4; Kren, 1978). In short, although faculty and students reportedly discuss ethical issues, they rarely engage in the systematic investigation of criteria employed to justify competing claims about the rightness, goodness, or justice of public actions.

The descriptive-ethical orientation evident in schools of public policy and management may be contrasted with an emphasis on normative ethics in reform-minded writings about the teaching of values and ethics. Fleishman and Payne (1980), for example, focus on normative ethics as a vehicle for addressing ethical dilemmas confronting public policy makers, whereas the Hastings Center has emphasized the teaching of normative ethics in higher education generally (Hastings Center, 1980). In each case we find a concern not merely with developing curricula that acknowledge questions of value and sensitize students to ethical issues (descriptive ethics), but with the acquisition of conceptual and analytic skills required for the systematic investigation of criteria advanced to justify competing ethical claims (normative ethics).

An evident growing concern with the role of normative ethics in public policy analysis has been accompanied by increased attention to questions of meta-ethics. An emphasis on the reflective evaluation of underlying criteria employed to justify normative statements may be found in the general literature on policy analysis (e.g., Tribe, 1972; MacRae, 1976; Fischer, 1980) and in more specialized attempts to examine policy-relevant questions that are ontological (Does ethical knowledge exist?), epistemological (What criteria, if any, govern the truth or falsity of ethical claims?), and practical (What is the relation between ethics and moral action?). Michalos (1981), for example, argues that widely accepted but mistaken ontological assumptions about the existence of two mutually exclusive realms of experience ("facts" and "values") may lead policy analysts to conclude that ethical claims are "scientifically incorrigible." Dallmayr (1981), drawing from critical theory and the work of Jurgen Habermas (1970, 1975), argues that "policy evaluation requires a critically reflective 'practical discourse' open not only to experts or policy analysts but to the public at large . . . recovery of a fully non-instrumental 'practical' judgment presupposes an evaluation not only of concrete policies but of the status of 'policy' itself" (p. 523). Finally, Daneke (1982) makes a general case for the introduction of meta-ethics into the curricula of schools of public policy and management.

As a concluding illustration of distinctions among descriptive ethics, normative ethics, and meta-ethics, let us consider competing approaches to issues of social equity and justice. At the level of descriptive ethics, textbooks on policy analysis (e.g., Stokey and Zeckhauser, 1978) often address issues surrounding distributive justice and social welfare by describing the consequences of adopting neo-utilitarian criteria of net efficiency improvement (maximize total benefits minus total costs), Pareto improvement (maximize total benefits minus total costs up to that point where it is not possible to make any person better off without also making another person worse off), and Kaldor-Hicks improvement (maximize total benefits minus total costs, provided that winners may in principle compensate losers). At the level of normative ethics, these issues of social equity and justice may be addressed in terms of normative theories of justice. For example, we might consider the argument that a pre-civil society where discrepancies in power, wealth, and privilege have not yet evolved—that is, a society characterized by a "veil of ignorance"—would be one where citizens commonly accept the criterion that one social state is better than another if it results in a gain in welfare for members of society who are worst off (see Rawls, 1971). Nevertheless, these same issues may also be addressed at a third, meta-ethical level, one where the underlying meanings and implications of a given normative ethical theory are subjected to further reflective evaluation. Thus, although we may judge Rawls' theory to be superior to neo-utilitarian formulations, meta-ethcial analysis may reveal underlying assumptions that lead us to question our original assessment. In this context, the Rawlsian theory has been challenged on meta-ethical grounds that it presupposes an individualistic conception of human nature where normative statements are no longer products of reasoned social discourse but are

> the contractual composite of arbitrary (even if comprehensible) values individually held and either biologically or socially shaped. . . . The structure of the Rawlsian argument thus corresponds closely to that of instrumental rationality; ends are exogenous, and the exclusive office of thought in the world is to ensure their maximum realization. . . . [Rawl's premises] reduce all thought to the combined operations of formal reason and instrumental prudence in the service of desire (Tribe, 1976: 77).

In summary, the term ethics carries meanings that are normative as well as descriptive; and normative ethics must itself be distinguished from meta-ethics. Although these three modes of ethical analysis are interrelated and interdependent, each performs a different function in policy analysis. Section III elaborates further on these differences.

C. Standards of Conduct

The standards that today guide the behavior of professional policy analysts—that is, the operating norms that constitute the "customary morality" of practitioners—display enormous variability. In part, this variability may be attributed to the diverse and frequently conflicting approaches to the teaching of ethics and values in schools of public policy and management (Fleishman and Payne, 1980; Cahill and Overman, 1982). In addition, the discipline as a whole is conceptually and methodologically tangled: "attempts to develop an interdisciplinary policy science premised on the supposed unifying force of a common methodological core have resulted in fragmentation, not theoretical integration" (Garson, 1981: 535). One manifestation of this fragmentation is disputes about the role of normative theory in policy analysis; another is the present stalemated debate between proponents of the two major "traditions" of policy analysis, the synoptic/empirico-analytic (see, e.g., Stokey and Zeckhauser, 1978) and the antisynoptic/neopluralist (see, e.g., Lindblom, 1980; Wildavsky, 1979). Finally, disputes among university-based policy analysts are not the sole or even most important source of the present variability in professional conduct, because there is mounting evidence that government policy analysts and planners are themselves divided along methodological as well as ethical lines (see Meltsner, 1976; Howe and Kaufman, 1979, 1981).

The present-day variability of professional behavior attests to the wide gap that now separates the normative ethics and meta-ethics of policy analysis, on the one hand, and the everyday ethics or "customary morality" of academic and government practitioners. Efforts to reduce or close this gap (assuming that this is a worthwhile goal) may draw on several sources of standards: (1) social values and norms, including equity, honesty, and fairness, which may guide the actions of policy analysts as well as citizens at large; (2) scientific values and norms, including objectivity, neutrality, and institutionalized self-criticism; (3) professional codes of conduct, including formally stated obligations, duties, and prescriptions; and (4) legal and administrative procedures, including mechanisms for securing informed consent by seeking the formal approval of institutional review boards.

Each source of standards has been more or less accessible to different groups. The communication and critique of social values and norms are central to the research and teaching activities of individual scholars, whereas the communication and revision of scientific and professional norms has occurred largely through the institutionalized curriculum development, review, and evaluation efforts of the National Association of Schools of Public Affairs and Administration (NASPAA) and through the traditional conference and publications activities of the Policy Studies Organization (PSO), the Association for Public Policy and Management (APPAM), and the American Society for Public Administration (ASPA). In addressing the need for a code of professional conduct, but stopping short of the formal codification of standards, ASPA has published and disseminated a pamphlet titled *Professional Standards and Ethics: A Workbook for Public Administrators* (Mertins, 1979). By contrast, legal and administrative procedures to regulate the conduct of research involving human subjects are products of government initiatives rather than those of professional associations or their individual members (see Castellani, 1982). As we shall see in the next section, different standards of conduct are based, explicitly or implicitly, on particular ethical and meta-ethical assumptions.

III. NATURE AND TYPES OF VALUE THEORY

A consideration of divergent meanings of the term values, together with distinctions among descriptive ethics, normative ethics, and meta-ethics, provides a basis for examining different theories of ethics and values. These theories may be conveniently classified according to their principal functions, which include the description, classification, measurement, and generalization of ethics and values (descriptive theories); the development and application of criteria to assess ethical claims (normative theories); and the development and application of additional criteria to assess normative ethical criteria and claims themselves (meta-ethical theories). This classification has important subdivisions —for example, teleological versus deontological normative theories, or cognitivist versus noncognitivist meta-ethical theories—which reflect important differences within classes.

A. Descriptive Theories

Over the past 50 years and more there has been a steady growth in efforts to develop and apply descriptive theories of values and ethics. Prior to the 1920s, as Williams (1968: 284) observes, much of sociology tended to regard values as somehow "subjective," as different in kind from the "hard facts" that were believed to constitute the proper domain of Science. Following the publication of Thomas and Znaniecki's *The Polish Peasant in Europe and America* (1918), especially in the period from 1930 onward, the empirical study of values became a major activity of sociologists, political scientists, anthropologists, and psychologists. Landmark contributions include Allport et al., *A Study of Values* (1931), Kohler's *The Place of Value in a World of Facts* (1938), Mukerjee's *The Social Structure of Values* (1949), Merriam's *Systematic Politics* (1945), Lerner and Lasswell's *The Policy Sciences* (1951), White's *Value Analysis: The Nature and Use of Method* (1951), Williams' *American Society: A Sociological Interpretation* (1951), Kluckhohn and Strodtbeck's *Variations in Value Orientation* (1961), Smith's *Social Psychology and Human Values* (1969), and Rokeach's *The Nature of Human Values* (1973). Because a detailed review of these and other contributions is beyond the scope of this chapter (see bibliographies in Williams, 1968; Baier and Rescher, 1969; Rokeach, 1973; Dunn,

Table 1 Rokeach's Basic Value Typology: Terminal and Instrumental Values

Terminal Value	Instrumental Value
A comfortable life	Ambitious
An exciting life	Broadminded
A sense of accomplishment	Capable
A world at peace	Cheerful
A world of beauty	Clean
Equality	Courageous
Family security	Forgiving
Freedom	Helpful
Happiness	Honest
Inner harmony	Imaginative
Mature love	Independent
National security	Intellectual
Pleasure	Logical
Salvation	Loving
Self-respect	Obedient
Social recognition	Polite
True friendship	Responsible
Wisdom	Self-controlled

Source: Rokeach (1973), Table 2.1, p. 28. Test-retest reliability coefficients and parenthetical quali-
fiers have been omitted.

1978), we shall concentrate on three aspects of descriptive theories: basic value typologies; complex value typologies; and developmental typologies.

Basic Value Typologies: The work of Rokeach (1968, 1973) represents a major synthesis of empirical theories of values undertaken since the 1930s. The scope and depth of
his concern is evident in the claim that

> the concept of values, more than any other, is the core concept across all the social
> sciences. It is the main dependent variable in the study of culture, society, and per-
> sonality, and the main independent variable in the study of social attitudes and be-
> havior. It is difficult for me to conceive of any problem social scientists might be
> interested in that would not deeply implicate human values (Rokeach, 1973: ix).

One of Rokeach's contributions is the development of a basic typology or classification scheme for developing and testing particular empirical theories, for example, theories
of socialization, institutionalization, personality development, self-actualization, and induced personal and social change. The basic typology, which incorporates distinctions
and variations found in many preceding empirical studies, has two major dimensions:
terminal and instrumental values. Terminal values, which are both personal and social,
are beliefs about "desirable end-states of existence"; instrumental values, which include
moral as well as competence or self-actualization values, are beliefs about "desirable
modes of conduct" (Rokeach, 1973: 7). Rokeach's list of 18 terminal and 18 instrumental values is presented in Table 1.

A similar typology of basic values has been employed by Howe and Kaufman (1979, 1981) in their study of the ethics of professional planners. Distinguishing between "ends-oriented" and "means-oriented" ethical principles, Howe and Kaufman seek to investigate the relative impact of commitments to ends on the selection of means (1981: 586). In contrast to Rokeach (1973), who developed his typology chiefly on the basis of intuitive judgments about the importance of a large number of values reported in existing literature, Howe and Kaufman draw their two classes of ethical principles from the 1962 *Code of Professional Responsibility and Rules of Procedure* of the American Institute of Planners. Among the major findings of the study are conclusions that professional and personal ethical norms are often inconsistent; and that a commitment to certain ends (e.g., social equity) affects ethical judgments about the use of particular means (e.g., leaking information to low income groups). Although this study is essentially exploratory, it addresses competing teleological and deontological claims (see Sec. III.B) that good ends justify the selection of means (see Alinsky, 1971) and that means should be justified in their own terms (see Bok, 1978).

Complex Value Typologies: Basic value typologies reduce to orderly terms the enormous range and complexity of human values. Basic typologies embody distinctions that direct the focus of empirical studies by supplying theoretical constructs and suggesting procedures for acquiring needed data. Yet the basic typologies reviewed above rest on a simple ends-means distinction that fails to capture many important dimensions of value. Thus, it is quite incorrect to suppose that when one describes particular types of values (e.g., terminal or instrumental values), one "is talking about the same sort of thing—just so many different ways of classing values with respect to a long but homogeneous list of distinguishing labels" (Rescher, 1969: 19).

A complex value typology based on seven major classificational principles has been developed by Rescher (1969: 13-19) as a means for representing "some of the most urgent requisites for a systematic survey of values that is to be precise in articulation on the one hand and fruitfully applicable on the other." The seven major principles permit us to classify values according to:

Subscribership: Taking the content of values as given, this principle permits the classification of values according to the persons or groups that hold them—personal values, community values, regional values, professional values, national values, etc.

Object: Values may be classified according to the object of evaluation—substance or animal ("thing") values, environmental values, individual values, group values, societal values, global values, etc.

Benefit: Values may be classified according to the benefits expected to occur upon their realization—material or physical values, economic values, moral values, political values, social values, aesthetic values, spiritual values, intellectual values, sentimental values, professional values, etc.

Purpose: Values may be classified according to the type of purpose served by the realization of a benefit—exchange value, bargaining value, deterrent value, persuasive value, truth value, etc.

Subscriber-Beneficiary Relationship: Values may be classified according to the relationship (or lack thereof) between the person who holds a value and some presumed beneficiary—e.g., self-oriented (egocentric) values and other-oriented (alocentric) values, with the latter category including ingroup-oriented (parochial, ethnocentric) values as well as mankind-oriented (humanitarian) values.

Intervalue Relationship: Values may be classified according to the relationship (or lack thereof) they bear to other values—e.g., instrumental (extrinsic, enabling, means) values and terminal (intrinsic, consummatory, end) values.

Temporal Proximity: Values may be classified according to their temporal proximity to the expected realization of benefits—e.g., immediate values, short-term values, medium-term values, long-term values, etc.

A major advantage of this complex typology is that it brings out the diversity and scope of values, but in a systematic and reasonably uncomplicated manner. Thus, we can readily differentiate and specify additional dimensions of the terminal and instrumental values as listed in Table 1. For example, social recognition may be classified as a terminal value that is superordinate to instrumental values of capability, honesty, and imagination (principle of intervalue relationship); a long-term value whose realization may take many years (principle of temporal proximity); an other-oriented value when the beneficiary is a profession (principle of subscriber-beneficiary relationship); an exchange value when the purpose of social recognition is to increase the income of professionals (principle of purpose); a political value when the expected benefit of social recognition is increased access to government policy makers (principle of benefit); a group value when the object is a profession whose social recognition is being evaluated (principle of object); and a personal value when we ourselves hold social recognition as a value (principle of subscribership). Observe that there is no inconsistency or contradiction in classifying this same value in seven different ways. Note also that the cross-classification of these seven principles or dimensions, including illustrative but nonexhaustive subcategories, yields a typology with 36,000 cells.

The message of this illustration is *not* that values are too complex to be investigated systematically; it is rather that we should exercise care in defining and classifying values, because to do otherwise is to risk confusing and misunderstanding a domain with which we have had little direct or systematic experience, but which is no more complex than other more familiar domains. Most people experience no difficulty in accurately describing their friends in terms of age, sex, marital status, occupation, income, education, physical characteristics, place of residence, length of acquaintance, closeness of relationship, and so on, even though it is unnecessary to construct a typology with the 60,000-some cells required, at a minimum, to locate everyone on each dimension simultaneously. In studying values we can employ much the same procedure, provided that we keep firmly in mind the major dimensions according to which values, like friends, may be differentiated.

Developmental Value Typologies: Basic and complex typologies can serve as a basis for examining theories of individual and collective value change and development. Rokeach (1973: 215-234), for example, develops and tests a theory of cognitive inconsistency with data organized according to his typology of terminal and instrumental values. Using the basic typology, he also identifies a variety of developmental patterns based on age differences: "value changes take place not only during adolescence but throughout life" (Rokeach, 1973: 81). These patterns are related to the stages of moral development postulated by Kohlberg (1961) and investigated, largely with school-age populations, in numerous settings in the United States and abroad (see, e.g., Kohlberg and Turiel, 1971; Kohlberg, 1978). Kohlberg's developmental typology distinguishes three levels in the development of moral judgment (preconventional; conventional; and postconventional, autonomous, or principled). Because each level incorporates two stages, the developmental typology yields six stages in all: stage 1 (punishment and obedience orientation); stage 2 (instrumental relativist orientation); stage 3 (interpersonal concordance orientation); stage 4 law-and-order orientation); stage 5 (social-contract legalistic orientation); and stage 6 (universal ethical principle orientation).

Kohlberg's developmental typology is of great potential importance for investigating in greater depth the role of ethical norms and principles in policy analysis. The six stages are claimed to represent an invariant sequence whereby individuals progress in their *capacity* for moral judgment. Because the sequence is invariant and sequential, developmental transitions can occur only between adjacent stages. On the basis of these assumptions, Kohlberg (1971: 226) claims that individuals cannot be expected to move from an egocentric market society (stage 2) to a society based on universal ethical principles (stage 6), for example, principles of the type outlined by Rawls (1971) and others who have challenged the instrumentalist, technocratic, or utilitarian premises of much contemporary policy analysis (e.g., Habermas, 1975; MacRae, 1976; Dallmayr, 1981; Garson, 1981).

The six stages of moral development, because they have been established on comparatively firm empirical grounds, represent an important contribution to discussions surrounding the capacity for normative ethical discourses in contemporary society. In Kohlberg's words: "any conception of what moral judgment ought to be must rest on an adequate conception of what is. The fact that our conception of the moral 'works' empirically is important for its philosophic adequacy" (Kohlberg, 1971: 222).

B. Normative Theories

Normative theories of value, or normative ethics, may be divided into four main types that differ in terms of the respective criteria supplied to evaluate moral actions (see Gewirth, 1978a). Deontological normative theories typically claim that certain kinds of actions are inherently right or obligatory (the Greek *deontos* means "of the obligatory"), or right because they conform to some formal principle. Teleological normative theories, by contrast, hold that certain actions are right because they result in good or valuable ends (the Greek *teleios* means "brought to its end or purpose"). Closely related are axiological normative theories, which claim that certain actions are right because of their inherent value or goodness (the Greek *axios* means "valuable or worthy"), not merely because they result in good or valuable ends. Finally, practical normative theories hold that certain actions are right because they conform to principles, or result in consequences, whose rightness or goodness have been establishedthrough reasoned transactions (the Greek *praktikos* means "to experience, negotiate, or transact") among those who affect and are affected by the creation and application of moral rules. Normative theories of each of these four types may be found in contemporary policy analysis.

Deontological Theories: Deontological theories, in supplying criteria to evaluate action, do not invoke value considerations; normative claims are confined to those based on deontic concepts and principles, as distinguished from claims resting on the value or goodness of consequences. Theories of justice such as that offered by Rawls (1971) are deontological because they employ formal principles of obligation (a pre-civil social contract executed under a "veil of ignorance") to justify arguments about distributive justice ("justice as fairness") and a just society (a society that maximizes the welfare of those who are worst off).

Some deontological theories are material, because they hold that criteria of obligatory or right action (e.g., honesty, accountability, empathy for others) are self-validating features of the actions themselves, thus requiring no further justification. Codes of professional conduct are often based, at least implicitly, on a material deontology. By contrast, formal deontological theories claim that criteria of obligatory or right action (e.g., keeping promises) consist in some logically necessary relation between the rules or principles according to which actions are performed. Theories that ground normative ethical claims on one or another principle of universalizability—that is, a principle that affirms that what is right (or wrong) for one person might be right (or wrong) for any similar person in similar circumstances—are formal deontological theories (see Gewirth, 1978b). Prominent examples of formal deontological theories may be found in core literature on policy analysis.

Perhaps the best-known formal deontological theory is that of Rawls (1971), who has had immense impact on the reassessment of teleological theories that underlie modern cost-benefit analysis and such related forms of utilitarianism as public choice (see Mueller, 1979: 227-260). Equally prominent but less known among students of policy analysis is the formal deontological theory of Gewirth (1978b), which has been applied to problems of social policy and social work by Reamer (1979). The importance of Gewirth's theory is not only that it supplies answers to key meta-ethical questions (Can we establish the truth or falsity of ethical principles?), but that it provides a formal justification (the principle of generic consistency) for the protection of fundamental or "generic" rights of freedom and well-being. In Reamer's words:

> Gewirth's formulation helps establish broad guidelines for and limits on practitioners' interventions. While Gewirth's principle does not provide absolute criteria for reaching conclusions in all cases where there is an ethical dilemma . . . the Principle of Generic Consistency does make the major contribution of identifying and attempting to justify the values—freedom and well-being—which practitioners should consider as primary and according to which their decisions should be made (Reamer, 1979: 241-242).

Formal deontological theories such as those advanced by Rawls and Gewirth have an important bearing on the justification of long-standing values of public administration, including honesty in government, public accountability, and procedural fairness. Whereas others have attempted to base deontological theories on material criteria—that is, criteria that are purportedly self-validating due to their origins in intuitive judgment, practitioner experience, or ordinary knowledge—formalists employ canons of deductive and/or inductive logic to justify fundamental values. Formal theories thus may be contrasted with essentially material arguments offered to justify codes of professional conduct (Mertins, 1979), procedural goals (Nagel, 1981), and incremental policy making (Wildavsky, 1979; Lindblom, 1980).

Teleological Theories: Teleological theories evaluate actions according to the goodness of their consequences. A prominent form of teleological theory, one that has deeply affected policy analysis via modern welfare economics, is utilitarianism. The classical utilitarian theories of Jeremy Bentham and John Stuart Mill held that right actions are those that promote the maximum or greatest good for everyone, that is, the general good. Policy analysts who use cost-benefit analysis are neo-utilitarians to the degree that they base policy recommendations on the criterion of maximizing net income benefits, a criterion presumed to reflect the aggregate satisfaction experienced by members of society (see Stokey and Zeckhauser, 1978). An alternative to this simple aggregative conception of the good is one based on locus-aggregative criteria (e.g., Pareto optimality) for distributing the good among as many persons as possible.

The main properties of teleological theories, including modern neoutilitarian theories, are most easily visualized by comparing them with deontological theories (Gewirth, 1978a: 990). (1) Teleological theories advocate actions because of their consequences (e.g., maximization of net income benefits), whereas deontological theories advocate actions because they conform to some material or formal principle (e.g., protection of the well-being of clients or citizens) or because they are deemed to be inherently right (e.g., employee participation). (2) Teleological theories set forth conditional obligations (e.g., freedom might be compromised in the interests of national security), whereas deontological theories set forth absolute obligations (e.g., freedom is a generic right that cannot be justified in terms of any superordinate principle). (3) Teleological theories advance material or substantive criteria (e.g., pleasure, happiness, or satisfaction), whereas deontological theories advance formal or relational criteria (e.g., social equity or administrative impartiality). (4) Teleological theories supply aggregate criteria (e.g., social welfare as the total satisfaction experienced by members of a community), whereas deontological theories supply distributive criteria regulating the allocation of goods (e.g., municipal services and educational opportunities) or evils (e.g., exposure to toxic wastes and carcinogens). (5) Teleological theories provide a unitary criterion (e.g., income maximization), whereas deontological theories provide criteria which are plural (e.g., justice, freedom, well-being) as well as unitary.

Two major problems of utilitarianism, as may be evident from the above contrasts, pertain to distributive justice and the opportunistic violation of fundamental rights. Utilitarianism makes no specific provision for distributive justice and the allocation of goods and evils in society; nor does it prohibit the abandonment of moral rules when the consequences of violating such rules outweigh obeying them. Several modifications of utilitarianism have been put forth as responses to these problems. Rescher (1966), for example, has advanced the concept of "effective average"—defined as the average number of shares held by a population minus one-half the standard deviation from the average—as a way to choose between two or more distributions. Whereas this modification is intended as a response to problems of distributive justice, other formulations attempt to deal with the violation of moral rules on utilitarian grounds. For example, "rule" utilitarianism has been advanced as an improvement of "act" utilitarianism (Rawls, 1955). Whereas the latter provides that actions in general may be evaluated in terms of their overall consequences, rule utilitarianism provides for the evaluation of rules of action according to their consequences. The problem, as MacRae (1976) observes, is whether expected consequences should indeed be the only criterion of the rightness of acts. These criticisms [of act utilitarianism] have led some to reject ethical systems based solely on consequences. But another response has been to compromise, retaining a concern for consequences by applying it (in unqualified form) only to rules, or classes of acts, rather than to acts in general (MacRae, 1976: 266).

Rule utilitarianism thus seeks to reconcile positive features of teleological and deontological theories. Related efforts at reconciliation have been made by Gauthier (1974), who develops common principles of cooperative action to justify utilitarian outcomes, and by those who have combined a deontological concern with rules of impartiality and unanimity and a teleological concern with the consequences of action (see Buchanan and Tullock, 1962; Harsanyi, 1977). As Mueller (1979: 247) notes, these latter contributions to the theory of utilitarian contracts "form a bridge between John Rawls' contribution to moral philosophy, and the welfare economics and public choice literatures."

Axiological Theories: Axiological theories evaluate actions on the basis of their inherent goodness or value. Whereas teleological theories focus on valued consequences of action, thus viewing actions in terms of their extrinsic value, axiological theories focus on the intrinsic value of action. Whereas material deontological theories claim that certain actions are inherently right or obligatory because of some purportedly self-evident property of the actions themselves, axiological theories make goodness or value the standard of rightness. For example, axiological theories may focus on the inherent value of experiencing pleasure, exerting power, achieving self-actualization, or apprehending beauty.

Axiology, or the theory of value, was introduced by Wilbur Marshall Urban (*Valuation: Its Nature and Laws,* 1909) and subsequently developed in Perry's *General Theory of Value* (1926) and Pepper's *The Sources of Value* (1958). Axiologists have generally held that a value is anything of interest to human subjects who make evaluations in domains of politics, law, economics, science, art, religion, morality, and custom. Axiological theories may be found, at least implicitly, in the works of political scientists who set forth modes for experiencing or exercising control over such valued resources as respect, rectitude, affection, well-being, wealth, power, skill, and enlightenment (Lasswell and Kaplan, 1950). Axiological premises also underlie contributions to the methodology of problem solving in policy analysis:

> There is at least as much satisfaction to be derived from the pursuit of objectives as in attaining them. Therefore, in an ideal state . . . man would not be problem free, but he would be capable of solving a continual flow of increasingly challenging problems. . . . Thus, to make problem solving creative (inspiring) and fun (recreative) is to put art in it. To do so is to reunite work, play, and learning and therefore to reunify man, at least in his problem-solving activities (Ackoff, 1978: 16-17).

Axiological theories, as this example suggests, may be of a mixed or synthetic type. Strictly speaking, these theories are neither deontological, because they provide no specific formal or material criteria of obligation; nor are they teleological, because they supply no specific utilitarian criteria. Noteworthy in this context are works of John Dewey, including *Human Nature and Conduct* (1922) and *Theory of Valuation* (1939), in which he challenged the popular dichotomy between instrumental and intrinsic values. The

simple axiological equation of intrinsic value with any object of interest ignores differences between the enjoyed and the enjoyable, the desired and the desirable, the valued
and the valuable. To answer normative questions about what is valuable, as distinguished
from what is merely valued, Dewey advocated defining value as "enjoyments which are
the consequences of intelligent action."

This position, while it may be criticized on grounds that it permits unethical consequences based on intelligent action (e.g., usury and sadism), must be understood in light
of a broad view of science according to which "scientific values, like moral ones, are interpersonal and subjective: the scientist must put his opinions to the test of scrutiny through
free inquiry by other scientists using methods whose application and results are available
to all" (Gewirth, 1978a: 986). This view of science, intimately related to norms and
values of democracy, represents a synthesis that may not be reduced either to an ethic
of intrinsic value (axiology) or to an ethic of consequences (teleology); it is a dialectical
synthesis, a view that represents more than both. This pragmatic vision of science and
ethics, according to which truth and value are determined by the consequences of intelligent, reflective, or deliberative action, has guided many important conceptual and
methodological contributions to disciplines that today comprise policy analysis, including
planning theory (Ackoff, 1974), operations research (Churchman, 1961), systems thinking (Sutherland, 1973), and political science (Jones, 1977).

Practical Theories: Practical normative theories are in some respects an extension of this
pragmatic view of science and ethics. Whereas Dewey emphasized intelligent action as a
process for discovering the criteria on which value may be known, more recent theories
have stressed reasoned discourse as a process for creating and evaluating ethical and scientific knowledge (see Toulmin, 1950, 1958; Toulmin et al., 1979; Taylor, 1961; Baier,
1965). Sometimes called "good reasons" theories, these theories may also be labeled
"practical" to the extent that certain actions are deemed right or valuable because they
conform to principles, or result in consequences, that have been established on the basis
of reasoned transactions (Greek *praktikos*: "to experience, negotiate, or transact") among
persons who affect and are affected by the development and application of moral rules.

An illuminating example of practical normative theory in contemporary policy analysis is Tribe's attempt to develop a nonteleological and nondeontological basis for defining an environmental ethic, that is, a set of criteria for making environmental choices that
is neither based on the neo-utilarian assumptions of cost-benefit analysis nor on the contractarian assumptions of Rawls' theory of justice. In seeking to provide a rational ground
for limiting the utilitarian domination, exploitation, and depletion of the natural environment, Tribe proposes a synthesis of

> *evolving processes of interaction and change*—processes of action and choice that are
> valued for themselves, for the conceptions of being that they embody, at the same
> time that they are valued as means to the progressive evolution of the conceptions,
> experiences, and ends that characterize the human community in nature at any
> given point in its history. . . . The "way of acting" to which we commit ourselves
> must therefore be a process valued in large part for its intrinsic qualities rather than
> for its likely results alone (Tribe, 1976: 80. Emphasis original.).

Practical normative theories have also been advanced in other domains of policy
analysis. Fischer (1980), for example, has attempted to develop and apply to public policy

evaluation concepts and rules of practical normative discourse drawn from Taylor (1961). Habermas (1970, 1975) seeking to outline the foundations of an evolving rational society, bases his case for "universal pragmatics" on the practical normative theories of Piaget, Kohlberg, and Toulmin. The growth of ethical and scientific knowledge occurs through the rationally motivating force of substantial arguments, that is, arguments that go beyond criteria of conclusiveness, certainty, and universal validity and rely, instead, on rational standards of achievement that enhance the persuasiveness of claims in particular contexts of practice (see Toulmin, 1958: 234). In contrast to the analytic arguments employed by teleologists and deontologists alike, substantial arguments

> are not exhausted in deductive systems of statements. Substantial arguments serve to redeem or to criticize validity claims, whether the claims to truth implicit in assertions or the claims to correctness connected with norms (of action or evaluation) or implied in recommendations and warnings . . . [Substantial arguments] have the force to convince the participants in a discourse of a validity claim, that is, *to provide rational grounds* for the recognition of validity claims (Habermas, 1975: 107. Emphasis original.)

Elements of practical normative theories may also be found in Mason and Mitroff (1981b), who outlines a methodology for strategic planning and policy analysis that is based partly on theories of practical discourse and argument. Relatedly, Dunn (1982b) attempts to develop on similar foundations a transactional model of argument that permits the reflective examination and investigation of competing ethical and nonethical hypotheses. This model extends the concept of "threats to validity" (Cook and Campbell, 1979) to ethical as well as causal inferences, thus enlarging the applied social sciences and policy analysis to a point where social experiments are but one important form of argumentation and social discourse (see Campbell, 1982). A similar movement toward the development of practical normative theory is evident in efforts to enlarge the scope of contemporary political discourse:

> The merit of humanistic discourse is self-evident: it facilitates and extends public thinking about political issues. There are no clearly established rules or limits on the possibilities to be explored by the humanities. . . . Our willingness to discuss—indeed our feeling that we must discuss—political objectives from this expanded vision of ethics-in-use serves as evidence that the cultural foundations of public life support our political institutions (Graham, 1981: 167).

C. Meta-Ethical Theories

The function of normative ethical theories in policy analysis is to answer the question: According to what criteria can we determine whether public actions are right or wrong? Answers to this question, as we saw in the last section, may be based on one or more types of normative ethical criteria: teleological, deontological, axiological, practical. The function of meta-ethical theories, by contrast, is to answer questions about normative ethical claims themselves: Can we determine the truth and falsity of normative ethical claims? Does normative ethics produce a kind of knowledge and, if so, what kind of knowledge is it? If normative ethics is not capable of being true and false, what kinds of

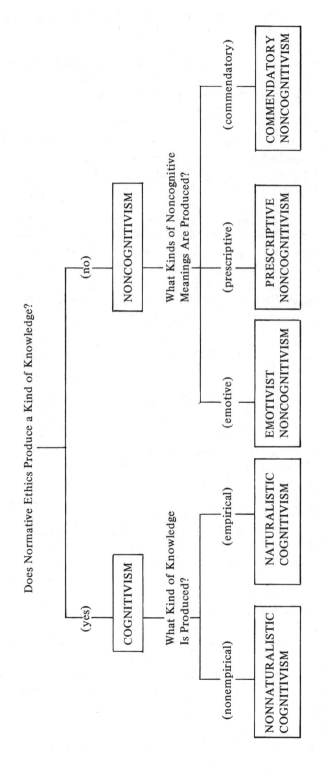

Figure 1 Types of Meta-Ethical Theory.

noncognitive results are produced? Answers to the questions yield two major classes of meta-ethical theories—cognitivism and noncognitivism—each with internal subdivisions (Figure 1).

Meta-ethical theories differ in terms of their assumptions about the epistemological status of normative ethical theories—for example, cognitivism affirms and noncognitivism denies that normative ethical theories are capable of being true or false and of constituting a kind of knowledge. Meta-ethical theories are closely but imperfectly associated with normative ethical theories. Thus, for example, the growth of logical positivism in the social sciences has contributed to noncognitivist meta-ethical doctrines which, in turn, have resulted in the devaluation of normative ethical discourse and a trained incapacity to recognize that putative empirical theories (welfare economics) and analytic routines (cost-benefit analysis) are based on controversial ethical premises. In this case a particular meta-ethical doctrine (noncognitivism) has exerted a direct and logically constraining effect on normative ethics by preempting opportunities for reflective normative discourse and the development of new ethical knowledge. Nevertheless, the relation between meta-ethics and normative ethics is not always so direct or logically compelling. For example, utilitarian, deontological, and practical normative claims offered by Harsanyi (1977), Gewirth (1978b), and Dallmayr (1981), respectively, are logically compatible with naturalistic forms of cognitivism. Hence, normative ethical theories are not fully determined by meta-ethical doctrines.

Nonnaturalistic Cognitivism: Cognitivism holds that normative ethical theories, and moral judgments in general, are a kind of knowledge. What this means is that a particular normative ethical claim—for example, "Honesty in government is good"—contains terms that denote qualities in the world and a moral judgment that may be shown to be true or false. Yet there are two main types of cognitivism: naturalism and nonnaturalism. Nonnaturalistic cognitivism denies that moral terms and judgments are reducible to the kind of knowledge produced in the physical and social sciences, reserving for ethics a special place among the varieties of human knowledge. By contrast, naturalistic cognitivism generally affirms that normative ethics and science share a common methodological platform on the basis of which the truth or falsity of knowledge claims may be assessed. Thus, each doctrine affirms the possibility of ethical knowledge, even as they depart in their respective assumptions about the nature of that knowledge.

Nonnaturalists (frequently labeled intuitionists) contend that basic moral terms such as "good" and "ought" refer to essentially indefinable nonnatural properties of objects. Nonnaturalistic meta-ethical doctrines may be linked with axiological and deontological normative ethical theories that emphasize "good" and "ought," respectively, as basic moral concepts. A prominent example of nonnaturalistic cognitivism, one with an important bearing on contemporary policy analysis, is G. E. Moore's *Principia Ethica* (1903). As an axiologist, Moore sought to provide answers to three related questions surrounding the meaning of "good": What is the nature of the property goodness? What things are intrinsically good? What things are instrumentally good? Focusing on the first of these questions, Moore argued that the property of goodness is simple, undefinable, and unanalyzable, a nonnatural property that may not be investigated with the methods of science.

To confuse nonnatural objects such as "good" with empirically observable natural objects is to commit what Moore called the "naturalistic fallacy." Although there are several closely related versions of this fallacy, the main argument may be stated as follows (Gewirth, 1978a: 981). Consider any proposed definition of good (*G*) in terms of some property (*P*) such that

$$G = dfP$$

where *df* means "is defined in terms of." Given this definition, it is always possible to ask: Is *P G*? This question, however, does not mean the same as: Is *P P*? Because the first question (Is *P G*?) does not mean the same as the second (Is *P P*?), the original definition (*G = dfP*) is not a genuine or correct one—that is, according to Moore, one where the definition has exactly the same meaning as that which it defines. Because this is not the case, it is always possible to query whether *P* is *G*, leading to what Moore called the "open question test."

The open question test and the naturalistic fallacy, although they evolved out of technical disputes within philosophy, have had an important influence on work within the applied social sciences and policy analysis. The open question test, for example, may be asked of any and all arguments that supply benefit-cost data to support claims that "good" policies are those that maximize social welfare, defined as the aggregate satisfaction experienced by members of a community. One version of the "naturalistic fallacy" has been employed by Campbell (1979) to challenge and reject the view, prevalent among sociobiologists, ethologists, and many social scientists, that what is biologically natural is normatively good.

> So widespread has become the acceptance of normative biologism and of its accompanying normative individualism that even when sociobiology intends no such message it is taken as such. Thus, on the U.S. political scene, to tell even the devout Catholic race rioters in South Boston that such rioting is biologically natural is to justify such rioting, giving it a positive moral value (Campbell, 1979: 39).

Disputes surrounding the development of capacities for moral judgment (Kohlberg, 1961) have also turned on the naturalistic fallacy, as is evident from the title of an important contribution: "From Is to Ought: How to Commit the Naturalistic Fallacy and Get Away with It in the Study of Moral Development" (Kohlberg, 1971). Arguing that research on stages of moral development tells us what morality ought to be, Kohlberg denies that two forms of the naturalistic fallacy are appropriately applied to his theory, even as he acknowledges that he commits a third:

> . . . there are two forms of the "naturalistic fallacy" we are not committing. The first is that of deriving moral judgments from psychological, cognitive-predictive judgments or pleasure-pain statements, as is done by naturalistic notions of moral judgment. Our analysis of moral judgment does not assume that moral judgments are really something else, but insists that they are prescriptive and *sui generis*. The second naturalistic fallacy we are not committing is that of assuming that morality or moral maturity is part of man's biological nature, or that the biologically older is

the better. The third form of the "naturalistic fallacy" which we *are* committing is that of asserting that any conception of what moral development ought to be must rest on an adequate conception of what it is . . . any conception of what adequate or ideal moral judgment *should be* rests on an adequate definition of what moral development *is* in the minds of men (Kohlberg, 1971: 222).

Examples such as these involve the rejection of some aspects or versions of the naturalistic fallacy and the acceptance of others. Campbell and Kohlberg, for example, reject the simple equation of is with ought, but nevertheless stop short of accepting the kind of nonnaturalist (intuitionist) doctrines put forth by Moore and others. Indeed, their effort to discriminate among different features of the naturalistic fallacy points to several limitations of nonnaturalist cognitivism. First, the argument that basic moral terms such as "good" and "ought" are not fully definable does not preclude the adoption of a naturalistic or quasi-naturalistic form of cognitivism, because the same problems of complete definition and underdetermination confront the natural and social sciences (see, e.g., Laudan, 1977; Hesse, 1979). Second, and relatedly, it is difficult to maintain that moral concepts and judgments occupy a special ontological domain constituted by nonempirical intuitions and nonnatural properties requiring a special kind of cognition to ascertain them (Gewirth, 1978a: 983).

Naturalistic Cognitivism: Naturalistic cognitivism, while it shares with nonnaturalism the view that normative ethical theories yield a kind of knowledge, nevertheless avoids the nonnaturalists' appeal to nonempirical intuitions as the basis for defining moral qualities. Naturalism seeks to establish the meanings of moral terms on the basis of empirical statements obtained by the methods of science and other observational procedures. Accordingly, ethical knowledge is not distinct from empirical knowledge, as nonnaturalists hold; nor does ethical knowledge require special methods that are altogether different from those employed in the natural and social sciences.

Leading examples of metaethical naturalism are Dewey (1939), Perry (1954), and Pepper (1958). These naturalists, more than any others, have profoundly affected the empirical study of values and ethics in the social, behavioral, and management sciences, including sociology (Williams, 1968), social psychology (Rokeach, 1968, 1973), and operations research (Churchman, 1961). Nevertheless, naturalism is not a unitary doctrine. It has at least four major variants constituted by relations among two dimensions: the source of natural ethical knowledge; and the types of procedures employed to establish relational ethical knowledge (see Figure 2). Additional variants have been elaborated by Gewirth (1978a) and Michalos (1981).

Objectivism Versus Subjectivism: Objective naturalism holds that goodness or value inheres in certain objects simply by virtue of their nature, regardless of whether such objects (e.g., capitalism, socialism, democracy) are known or desired. Subjectivism, by contrast, holds that goodness or value consists in a relation between a knowing or valuing subject and an object. In this context the term "subjective" does not mean that ethical knowledge is unreal or illusory; it means simply that ethical knowledge is not possible without a knowing or valuing subject. Many debates in evaluation research turn on the distinction between objective and subjective sources of ethical knowledge (see, e.g., Patton, 1978).

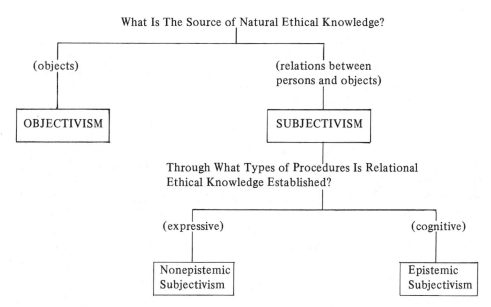

Figure 2 Major variants of naturalism.

Nonepistemic Versus Epistemic Subjectivism: Nonepistemic subjectivism holds that relational ethical knowledge is established through procedures that involve the expression of interests, desires, and preferences. By contrast, epistemic subjectivism holds that relational ethical knowledge is established through cognitive procedures, that is, procedures that involve the reflective evaluation of interests, desires, and preferences. The definition of value as "any object of interest" (Perry, 1954) is an illustration of nonepistemic subjectivism as found in ethics of demands and interests. Epistemic subjectivism, by contrast, is best illustrated by Dewey: "Without the intervention of thought, enjoyments are not values but problematic goods . . . enjoyment becomes a value when we discover the relations upon which its presence depends" (quoted by Gewirth, 1978a: 984). Epistemic subjectivism in contemporary policy analysis is characteristic of contributions by Churchman (1971), Fischer (1980), and Mason and Mitroff (1981), while nonepistemic subjectivism is characteristic of major empirical studies of values (Rokeach, 1968, 1973) and of most applications of decision theory to problems of policy analysis and evaluation (e.g., Raiffa, 1968; Edwards et al., 1975; Saaty, 1981). Each of these latter illustrations of nonepistemic subjectivism are noteworthy for their neglect or avoidance of assumptions, criteria, or standards of assessment that underlie the process of evaluating policies and programs (see Dunn et al., 1981).

Noncognitivism: Noncognitivists, in contrast to nonnaturalists and naturalists alike, deny that normative ethics can provide a kind of knowledge, because moral terms lack descriptive meaning. Normative ethical claims do not state facts about the world; nor can reason provide specific or general justifications for such normative claims. Noncognitivists (e.g., Ayer, 1946; Stevenson, 1944; Hare, 1952) hold that several kinds of meanings are produced by normative ethical theories, the most important of which (see Figure 1) are emotive, prescriptive, and commendatory.

Emotivism, as the term suggests, holds that the meanings generated by normative ethical claims are emotive—that is, they merely express the feelings of those who make them and have no cognitive meaning. By contrast, prescriptivism holds that the meanings of normative ethical claims are in the nature of commands telling people what to do, rather than descriptive statements proper. The commendatory variant of noncognitivism also denies that normative ethical claims describe anything, because their function is merely to commend some object to another person. All three types of meaning—emotive, prescriptive, and commendatory—are distinguished from cognitive meaning by advancing the principle of verifiability. This principle, embraced by early logical positivists, provides that there are only two kinds of cognitively meaningful sentences: analytic sentences whose cognitive meaning is verified merely by formal relations among terms; and synthetic sentences whose cognitive meaning is verified by empirical observations. Ethical sentences, because they do not conform to either procedure, are neither verifiable nor cognitively meaningful.

Noncognitivist metatheories continue to exert an important influence on the applied social sciences and policy analysis. Many of the most important and widely used frameworks for studying public policy, as Dallmayr (1981: 525) observes, "are beset by the positivist 'fact-value' dichotomy and its implications, especially the unresolved query whether choices and decisions are amenable not only to empirical testing and prediction but also to normative evaluation and judgment." MacRae (1976), whose scope of critical concern is not limited to political science, argues that the widespread commitment to noncognitivism in the social and behavioral sciences has resulted in the rejection of normative ethical discourse in economics, sociology, psychology, and political science:

> This rejection derives not only from the model of natural science, but also from the influence of logical positivism—a philosophic doctrine claiming to interpret natural science, which has pronounced valuative discourse to be "meaningless" other than as an expression of personal emotions. The effect of this doctrine has gone far beyond the justifiable *distinction* between factual and valuative statements to eliminate reasoned valuative discourse from almost all of social science . . . the dismissal of ethical principles from the recognized discourse of the social sciences has left these disciplines without sufficient guidance in dealing with the valuative problems of policy choice (MacRae, 1976: 55. Emphasis original.).

IV. NATURE AND TYPES OF RESEARCH

The uneven commitment to particular types of descriptive, normative, and meta-ethical theories reviewed in the last section has profoundly affected the nature and direction of research on values and ethics in the applied social sciences and policy analysis. The bulk of available research has been devoted to the development and testing of descriptive theories (see Sec. III.A), with little explicit attention to problems of normative ethics and meta-ethics that lie at the core of contemporary policy analysis.

A. Normative and Empirical Inquiry

Empirical studies of values and ethics far outnumber normative investigations. Apart from scattered and essentially ad hoc critiques of the discipline, works by Tribe (1972), Rein (1976), MacRae (1976), and Fischer (1980) are among the few systematic and genuine contributions to normative and meta-ethical inquiry in policy analysis. Of particular importance is MacRae's *The Social Function of Social Science* (1976), a landmark study that supplies unusual insight into problems of normative ethics and meta-ethics in the applied social sciences. The significance of this major work does not lie in its critique of logical positivism, a project that by now is hardly new or unique; it is rather the development of a methodology for conducting normative discourse in policy analysis that distinguishes this work from others in the field.

A central concept is that of "ethical hypotheses," that is, systems of normative conjectures about the rightness, goodness, or value of public actions. To investigate competing ethical hypotheses, MacRae (1976: 92-93) proposes three metaethical rules:

1. *Specification of Ethical Hypotheses*: Systems of ethical hypotheses put forth by two or more proponents shall be specified in writing in advance. "This specification is intended to support the norm of clarity and can include definitions specified in ways other than those of ordinary usage, statements of principles set off from context, and logical or mathematical symbols" (p. 92).
2. *Application of Common Standards of Assessment*: Proponents of competing systems of ethical hypotheses shall apply common standards for assessing normative disputes. Common standards of assessment include generality (scope of application), internal consistency (absence of contradictions within a system of ethical hypotheses), and external consistency (absence of contradictions between a system of ethical hypotheses and other convictions about morally justifiable actions). "It is expected that an internally consistent ethical system, specified in this way, will not be consistent with all the particular moral convictions of its proponents; the aim of this procedure is to test whether the system must be modified, or whether particular convictions must be suppressed, as a basis for further argument" (p. 93).
3. *Assessment of Situational Adequacy*: Proponents of competing systems of ethical hypotheses shall suggest different "conflict situations" designed to elicit inconsistencies in opposing arguments. "After each such opportunity to present conflict situations, the proponent of the ethical system under criticism shall decide whether he wishes to alter his ethical system or make the choice dictated by it" (p. 93).

This framework of rules for normative inquiry in policy analysis, which constitutes a "normative meta-ethics" (MacRae, 1976: 92), represents a notable advance over other available procedures. The framework is "about" normative ethical discourse in policy analysis; it does not constitute a system of ethical judgment per se. For this reason, MacRae's work must be sharply distinguished from others that offer specific moral judgments about the technocratic role of contemporary policy analysis (e.g., Horowitz and Katz, 1975), the desirability of distributive justice (e.g., DeGregori, 1974), the utilitarian advantages of decentralized democratic administration (e.g., Ostrom, 1974), or about dishonesty in public and private life (e.g., Bok, 1978). Significantly, MacRae's meta-ethical framework for investigating competing ethical hypotheses parallels meta-empirical frameworks designed to investigate competing empirical hypotheses (e.g., Campbell and Stanley, 1963). While each framework is designed for different purposes, both employ procedures that are "meta" to particular (ethical or empirical) hypotheses. The development of both frameworks is heavily indebted to a critical rationalist philosophy of science (Popper, 1968), which holds that the growth of knowledge occurs through deliberate attempts to falsify, rather than confirm, established hypotheses (see MacRae, 1976: 90-91; Campbell, 1974; Cook and Campbell, 1979).

Contrasts between normative and empirical inquiry raise important questions about the appropriateness of available procedures for conducting research on ethics and values. If we wish to investigate hypotheses about the existence of values and ethics, including their relations, origins, and consequences, a large and useful repertoire of research procedures is readily available (see, e.g., Robinson et al., 1968, 1969; Robinson and Shaver, 1969; Shaw and Wright, 1967; Lake et al., 1973; Miller, 1979). Yet these procedures are not appropriate for investigating normative ethical hypotheses, as these have been defined above, because they supply no means for assessing competing claims about the goodness or rightness of public actions. Although we may agree that "any conception of what moral judgment ought to be must rest on an adequate concpetion of what is" (Kohlberg, 1971: 222), normative ethical and meta-ethical research clearly require procedures that supplement those available in the social and behavioral sciences. One way to visualize these procedures is to return to the three major levels at which questions about values and ethics may be posed: meta-ethics, normative ethics, and descriptive ethics (see Sec. III).

B. Meta-Ethical Research

At the level of meta-ethics we may investigate hypotheses about the existence and nature of ethical knowledge (ontology) and the standards available for assessing its truth and falsity (epistemology). Here we shall want to consider arguments and counterarguments supplied in connection with noncognitivism and cognitivism, including distinctions among cognitivist arguments that are naturalistic versus nonnaturalistic, subjectivist versus objectivist, and epistemic versus nonepistemic (see Figure 2). Research procedures relevant to questions posed at this level include the reflective examination and critique of presuppositions of knowledge, for example, the presupposition that science merely states "facts" about the world. This presupposition, when treated as a conjecture, may be challenged with the alternate hypothesis that "all scientific theories are *underdetermined* by facts . . . this being the case, there are further criteria for scientific theories that have to be rationally discussed, and that these may include considerations of value" (Hesse, 1978: 1. Emphasis original.).

Conclusions reached at the meta-ethical level constrain the types of normative ethical hypotheses formulated at the next level. A particular meta-ethical conclusion—for example, that normative judgments are cognitively meaningless and may not be true or false—may preclude the formulation and investigation of normative ethical hypotheses about the rational defensibility of freedom, well-being, or distributive justice. Meta-ethical hypotheses, it should be stressed, are themselves often based on extrascientific criteria that include value judgments. In the history of the natural, social, and behavioral sciences, value judgments have assumed the form of "*assertions* that it is desirable that the universe be of such and such a kind *and* that it is or is not broadly as it is desired to be" (Hesse, 1978: 2. Emphasis original.). Examples include assertions that men ought to be and therefore are at the center of the physical universe; that the human mind is devalued when viewed as a natural entity and, therefore, that mind cannot be reduced to matter; and that the human and material environment ought to be controllable and, therefore, that it is stable, regular, and predictable.

C. Normative Ethical Research

At the level of normative ethics we may investigate competing hypotheses about moral actions justified in terms of consequences (teleological hypotheses), material or formal principles (deontological hypotheses), intrinsic value (axiological hypotheses), or reasoned discourse (practical hypotheses). Normative ethical hypotheses, while they depend in part on relevant facts surrounding an object of moral concern, are not empirical or causal conjectures. They are, rather, conjectures about the goodness, rightness, or value of certain actions. Research procedures relevant at this level include the application of standards or rules that govern reasoned discourse in the examination of normative ethical hypotheses. Because many or most analysts do not always think systematically or critically about normative ethical questions, the aim of these procedures is to facilitate the process of rational normative discourse, where "rational" means that we are aware both of how we are reasoning and of the full implications of accepting competing ethical hypotheses (see Taylor, 1961).

Procedures for conducting normative ethical research are of two main types: substantive and heuristic. Substantive procedures involve the application of rules such as the "principle of generic consistency" (Gewirth, 1978b) or the "difference principle" (Rawls, 1971), each of which supplies a standard for assessing the rational content or substance of ethical hypotheses. By contrast, heuristic procedures involve the application of rules that "make explicit the ideal of rationality implicit in our use of value language" (Coombs, 1971: 5). A justification for the use of such heuristic procedures may be found in Toulmin (1958), Baier (1965), Taylor (1961), and Dunn (1982). Specific heuristic procedures for conducting normative ethical research, generally and in public policy analysis, are available in MacRae's *The Social Function of Social Science* (1976), Smith's *A Practical Guide to Value Clarification* (1977), Toulmin et al.'s *An Introduction to Reasoning* (1979), and Fischer's *Politics, Values, and Public Policy: The Problem of Methodology* (1980).

Conclusions reached at the level of normative ethical research constrain the types of descriptive ethical hypotheses formulated at the next level. A particular normative ethical conclusion—for example, that good public policies are those that maximize the aggregate satisfaction experienced by members of a community—may preclude the investigation of descriptive hypotheses about individual capacities for moral judgment. If utilitarian ethical judgments are accepted without qualification, there is little point in investigating theories which hypothesize that the instrumental satisfaction of individual needs is characteristic of persons at an early stage of moral development who have a limited capacity for moral judgment (Kohlberg, 1961).

D. Descriptive Ethical Research

At the level of descriptive ethics—or, more generally, the empirical study of values—we may investigate competing hypotheses about the existence, relations, sources, and consequences of individual, professional, and social values. Research procedures relevant at this level include the full range of methods available in the social and behavioral sciences, from survey research, interviews, and projective tests to secondary analysis, content analysis, and direct observations of behavior (see, e.g., Kerlinger, 1973; Webb et al., 1981). These procedures, as we have seen (Secs. II and III), yield descriptive data on ethics, values, and standards, or what may be called the "ethos" or "conventional morality" of a population. Nevertheless, the use of these procedures reflects implicit or explicit commitments to particular normative ethical and metaethical theories. For example, research on stages of moral judgment (Kohlberg, 1971) is based on a deontological theory of moral obligation, whereas research on human values in general (Rokeach, 1973) has been deeply affected by axiological theories. Similarly, research conducted within the framework of public choice (Mueller, 1979) is based on explicit or implicit teleological theories, including modern forms of utilitarianism and welfare economics.

Descriptive studies of values, ethics, and standards are also based, even if implicitly, on the several different types of meta-ethical theories discussed in the last section (see Figures 1 and 2). The noncognitivist meta-ethical doctrines of early logical postivism, including emotivism and prescriptivism, continue to exert a strong influence on the applied social sciences and policy analysis, as is evident in such recent statements that reform-minded policy analysts who disseminate the results of their research create

> a mask for policy advocacy. Under the guise of spreading knowledge, disseminators try to make changes which policymakers perceive as unnecessary or . . . to promote their own policy to the exclusion of others. Here dissemination becomes equivalent to command . . . an effort to tell policymakers what should be done. . . . Advocacy is not exactly objectivity (Knott and Wildavsky, 1980: 540).

This prescriptive variant of noncognitivism may be found in many of the most widely used textbooks in public policy analysis (e.g., Anderson, 1975; Dye, 1978; Wildavsky, 1979).

Research on descriptive ethics, including studies of individual, professional, and social values, has been conducted largely on the basis of cognitivist meta-theories. Yet the internal divisions of cognitivism (see Figure 2) have been reproduced in contemporary empirical research. The nonnaturalistic (or intuitionist) variant of cognitivism would appear to characterize the meta-ethical assumptions of Quade (1975: 4), who stresses that much of policy analysis rests on the selective employment of "intuition" and "judgment." By contrast, many concepts of modern economics—including "consumer demand," "willingness to pay," and "revealed preference"—reflect strong tendencies toward an objectivist form of naturalistic cognitivism. Alternatively, much of modern measurement theory in the social and behavioral sciences (see Handy, 1970) is based on the subjectivistic naturalism of L. L. Thurstone:

> Human values are essentially subjective. They can certainly not be adequately represented by physical objects. Their intensities or magnitudes cannot be represented by

physical measurement. At the very start we are faced with the problem of establishing a subjective metric. This is the central theme in modern psychophysics in its many applications to the measurement of social values, moral values, and esthetic values. Exactly the same problem reappears in the measurement of utility in economics (Thurstone, 1954: 47).

Finally, the distinction between epistemic and nonepistemic forms of subjectivistic naturalism also helps to compare and contrast research on values, ethics, and standards. Research by Rokeach (1968, 1973) reflects nonepistemic premises, as does the bulk of contributions to multiattribute decision theory in policy analysis and evaluation, including multiattribute utility analysis (Edwards et al., 1975), social judgment theory (Hammond, 1977), and the analytic hierarchy process (Saaty, 1981). In each case investigators conduct research on values, interests, and preferences, but without attempting to elicit the underlying assumptions or criteria employed by respondents to justify value judgments. By contrast, there is a small and perhaps growing body of research based on epistemic meta-ethical premises, particularly those of Dewey (1939) and the works of "good reasons" philosophers (e.g., Toulmin, 1958; Baier, 1965; Taylor, 1961). In policy analysis and evaluation contributions by Kohlberg (1961), Ackoff (1974), MacRae (1976), Fischer (1980), Mason and Mitroff (1981b), Graham (1981), Dunn (1982a), and Campbell (1982) have already been cited in this connection. Nevertheless, it should be clearly understood that each variant of naturalism—that is, objective and subjective, epistemic and nonepistemic—is based on cognitivist metaethical premises according to which ethics and values represent a form of knowledge whose truth or falsity may be assessed through systematic research procedures. For this reason it is somewhat beside the point to attribute contemporary disputes surrounding the role of values and ethics in policy analysis to the doctrine of verificationism and, relatedly, the fact-value dichotomy. Many of the most important present-day divisions in the applied social sciences and policy analysis may not be reduced to these now outmoded tenets of early logical positivism.

V. AN OVERALL ASSESSMENT

Preceding sections have drawn attention to a central unresolved problem of policy analysis: If policy analysts are expected to produce ethical as well as empirico-analytic knowledge, what methods should be employed to assess competing knowledge claims? Answers to this difficult question, as we have seen, may assume a rich variety of forms, which depend not only on available descriptive theories, but also on prior commitments to particular normative ethical and meta-ethical premises. This concluding section attempts to identify and evaluate broad contemporary trends among those who seek answers to this question.

A. Metaethics of Value Neutrality

The dominant orientation of contemporary policy analysis remains one of value neutrality. This orientation is expressed clearly and succinctly by the authors of a leading text on policy analysis:

Most of the materials in this book are equally applicable to a socialist, capitalist, or mixed-enterprise society, to a democracy or a dictatorship. . . . Questions of values are, nevertheless, a critical and inevitable part of policy analysis. . . . Still, the very nature of [policy analysis] reflects a philosophical bias and a particular set of ethical concerns. [Policy analysis] is a discipline for working within the political and economic system, not for changing it . . . the predominant Western intellectual tradition of recent centuries . . . regards the well-being of individuals as the ultimate objective of public policy (Stokey and Zeckhauser, 1978: 4).

One may accept, reject, or seek to qualify this widely accepted position. Nevertheless, it is important to recognize that it rests on particular ethical and meta-ethical premises. To the extent that policy analysis is or can be value-neutral, fully adaptable to any political or economic system, policy analysis is also likely to proceed from a noncognitivist meta-ethical platform: The truth or falsity of normative ethical claims cannot be assessed with the methods available in the applied social sciences and policy analysis. This platform, apart from the fact that it rests on implicit value judgments similar in kind to those of the natural sciences (Hesse, 1978), is not the only one available to policy analysts who wish to investigate ethical and meta-ethical hypotheses. Normative ethical and metaethical theories reviewed in Sec. III provide many potential alternatives.

B. The Quest for Ethical Certainty

A countertrend in policy analysis is represented by those who, passing from despair to dogma (Dallmayr, 1976), seek to replace value neutrality with absolute and universally justifiable moral principles. Regrettably, the commitment to such principles often reflects a questionable search for ethical certainty. As Baier observes,

the means-end model has dominated philosophical thinking in this field. It has led some philosophers, maintaining (rightly) that we can ask which is the best thing to aim at in these circumstances, to conclude (wrongly) that there must be an ultimate aim or end, a summum bonum, to which all ordinary aims or ends are merely means. Hence, they claim, whether this or that is the better end to aim at must be judged by its serving the ultimate end or summum bonum. Other philosophers, maintaining (rightly) that there can be no such ultimate end or summum bonum, have concluded (wrongly) that we cannot ask which is the better end to aim at. They have claimed that reason can tell us only about what are the best means to given ends, but that ends themselves cannot be determined or judged by reason (Baier, 1963: 278).

These observations on philosophy are equally relevant to the applied social sciences and policy analysis, where value neutrality and relativism seem easily to give way to a quest for ultimate ethical truths.

C. Practical Discourse

Another countertrend, but one that seeks to avoid both value neutrality and the quest for ethical certainty, is evident in efforts to explore the informal logic of practical discourse (e.g., MacRae, 1976; Rein, 1976; Fisher, 1980) and "ethics in use" (Graham, 1981). Although specific features of practical discourse vary from one author to the next—for example, MacRae (1976) derives rules for practical discourse from the natural sciences whereas others do not—each of these efforts is motivated, in Fischer's words, "by the recognition that . . . in practical affairs people do, in fact, reason about values, even if the kind of rigor found in science is not employed, and . . . value judgments cannot be justified in some ultimate fashion" (Fischer, 1980: 90).

D. Need for Methodological Innovation

One of the main purposes of this chapter has been to document the diversity and richness of available theories and procedures in terms of which we may investigate ethics, values, and standards in policy analysis. There is no one best way to address normative issues; nor is there common agreement on the standards that properly should regulate the behavior of policy analysts. Nevertheless, there have been relatively few systematic attempts to investigate descriptive, normative, and meta-ethical questions surrounding the role of values, ethics, and standards in policy analysis. Apart from a few empirical studies, there is little substantive information about the "ethics in use" of policy analysts. While the discipline has become increasingly sensitive to normative ethical and meta-ethical questions, the bulk of standard policy-analytic procedures do not permit the systematic and reflective appraisal of competing ethical hypotheses. Needed are methodological innovations that enlarge present capacities to investigate the full range of questions that lie within the broad multidisciplinary domain of policy analysis: What are the causes and consequences of public policies? Of what value are these policies? What should be done?

REFERENCES

Ackoff, R. (1974). *Redesigning the Future.* Wiley, New York.
—— (1978). *The Art of Problem Solving.* Wiley Interscience, Chicago.
Adelman, L., Stewart, T. R., and Hammond, K. R. (1975). A case history of the application of social judgment theory to policy formulation. *Policy Sciences* 6:137-159.
Alinsky, S., (1971). *Rules for Radicals.* Random House, New York.
Allport, G. W., Vernon, P. E., and Lindzey, G. (1931, 1960). *A Study of Values.* Houghton Mifflin, Boston.
Anderson, J. E. (1975). *Public Policy-Making.* Praeger, New York.
Arrow, K. (1963). *Social Choice and Individual Values,* 2nd ed. Yale University Press, New Haven, CT.
Ayer, A. J. (1946). *Language, Truth, and Logic,* 2nd ed. Gollancz, London.
Baier, K. (1963). Reasonings in practical deliberation. In *The Moral Judgment,* P. W. Taylor (Ed.). Prentice-Hall, Englewood Cliffs, NJ.
—— (1965). *The Moral Point of View,* rev. ed. Cornell University Press, Ithaca, NY.
—— (1969). What is value? An analysis of the concept. In *Values and the Future: The Impact of Technological Change on American Values,* K. Baier and N. Rescher (Eds.). Free Press, New York.
Baier, K., and Rescher, N. (Eds.) (1969). *Values and the Future: The Impact of Technological Change on American Values.* Free Press, New York.
Beauchamp, T. L. (1975). *Ethics and Public Policy.* Prentice-Hall, Englewood Cliffs, NJ.
Bok, S. (1978). *Lying: Moral Choice in Public and Private Life.* Pantheon, New York

Brown, P. G. (1975). Ethics and Policy Research. *Policy Analysis 2*: 325-340.

Buchanan, J. M., and Tullock, G. (1962). *The Calculus of Consent.* University of Michigan Press, Ann Arbor.

Cahill, A. G., and Overman, E. S. (1982). The teaching of ethics in schools of public affairs. Unpublished manuscript. University of Pittsburgh, Graduate School of Public and International Affairs, Pittsburgh.

Callahan, D., and Jennings, B. (1982). *Ethics, the Social Sciences, and Policy Analysis.* Plenum, New York.

Campbell, D. T. (1974). Evolutionary epistemology. In *The Philosophy of Karl Popper,* P. A. Schilpp (Ed.). Open Court Press, LaSalle, IL, pp. 413-463.

—— (1979). Comments on the sociobiology of ethics and moralizing. *Behavioral Science 24*: 37-45.

—— (1982). Experiments as arguments. *Knowledge: Creation-Diffusion-Utilization 3*, 3.

Campbell, D. T., and Stanley, J. C. (1963). *Experimental and Quasi-Experimental Designs for Research.* Rand McNally, Chicago.

Castellani, P. (1982). Ethics and public policy: The regulation of research involving human subjects. In *Ethics, Values and the Practice of Policy Analysis,* W. N. Dunn (Ed.). Heath, Lexington, MA.

Churchman, C. W. (1961). *Prediction and Optimal Decision: Philosophical Issues of a Science of Values.* Prentice-Hall, Englewood Cliffs, NJ.

—— (1968). *The Systems Approach.* Delacorte, New York.

—— (1971). *The Design of Inquiring Systems.* Basic Books, New York.

—— (1979). *The Systems Approach and Its Enemies.* Basic Books, New York.

Coleman, J. S. (1974). Inequality, sociology, and moral philosophy. *American Journal of Sociology 80*, 3: 739-764.

Cook, T. D., and Campbell, D. T. (1979). *Quasi-Experimentation.* Rand McNally, Chicago.

Cook, T. D., and Gruder, C. (1978). Metaevaluation research. *Evaluation Quarterly 2*: 5-51.

Coombs, J. E. (1971). Rational strategies and procedures. *National Council for the Social Studies Yearbook 41*: 1-28.

Dallmayr, F. R. (1976). Beyond dogma and despair: Toward a critical theory of politics. *American Political Science Review 70*: 64-79.

—— (1981). Critical theory and public policy. In Symposium on Social Values and Public Policy, W. N. Dunn (Ed.). *Policy Studies Journal 9*, 3: 522-535 (Special Issue No. 2).

Daneke, G. (1982). Beyond ethical reductionism in public policy education. In *Ethics, Values and the Practice of Policy Analysis,* W. N. Dunn (Ed.). Heath, Lexington, MA.

DeGregori, T. R. (1974). Caveat emptor: A critique of the emerging paradigm of public choice. *Administration and Society,* August: 205-228.

Dewey, J. (1922). *Human Nature and Conduct.* Knopf, New York.

—— (1939). *Theory of Valuation. International Encyclopedia of Unified Science ,* vol. no. *11,* 4.

Dorfman, R. (1976). An afterword: Humane values and environmental decisions. In *When Values Conflict,* L. Tribe, C. S. Schelling, and J. Voss (Eds.). Ballinger, Cambridge, MA.

Dror, Y. (1968). *Public Policy-Making Re-examined.* Chandler, San Francisco.

—— (1971). *Design for Policy Sciences.* American Elsevier, New York.

Dunn, W. N. (1978). Social values and public policy: A selected bibliography. *Policy Studies Journal 7*: 328-335.

—— (1981a). *Public Policy Analysis: An Introduction.* Prentice-Hall, Englewood Cliffs, NJ.

—— (Ed.) (1981b). Symposium on social values and public policy. *Policy Studies Journal* 9, 4: 517-636 (Special Issue No. 2).

—— (1982a). Reforms as arguments. *Knowledge: Creation-Diffusion-Utilization 3*, 3.

—— (1982b) (ed.) *Values, Ethics, and the Practice of Policy Analysis.* Heath, Lexington, MA.

Dunn, W. N., and Fozouni, B. (1976). *Towards a critical administrative theory. Sage Professional Papers in Administrative and Policy Studies,* vol 3, series no. 03-026. Sage, Beverly Hills, CA, and London.

Dunn, W. N., Mitroff, I. I., and Deutsch, S. J. (1981). The obsolescence of evaluation research. *Evaluation and Program Planning 4*, 3: 207-218.

Dye, T. R. (1978). *Understanding Public Policy,* 3rd ed. Prentice-Hall, Englewood Cliffs, NJ.

Easton, D. (1953). *The Political System.* Knopf, Chicago.

Edwards, W., Guttentag, M., and Snapper, K. (1975). A decision theoretic approach to evaluation research. In *Handbook of Evaluation Research,* vol. 1, E. Streuning and M. Guttentag (Eds.), pp. 139-182, Sage, Beverly Hills, CA.

Etheredge, L. (1982). Government learning: An overview. In *Handbook of Politiaal Behavior,* S. Long (Ed.). Plenum, New York.

Fischer, F. (1980). *Politics, Values, and Public Policy: The Problem of Methodology.* Westview, Boulder, CO.

Fleishman, J. L., and Payne, B. L. (1980). *Ethical Dilemmas and the Education of Policymakers.* Hastings Center, Hastings-on-Hudson, NY.

Frederickson, H. G., and Wise, C. (Eds.) (1977). *Public Administration and Public Policy.* Heath, Lexington, MA.

Friedman, M. (1953). *Essays in Positive Economics.* University of Chicago Press, Chicago.

Frohlich, N., and Oppenheimer, J. A. (1978). *Modern Political Economy.* Prentice-Hall, Englewood Cliffs, NJ.

Garson, G. D. (1981). From policy science to policy analysis: A quarter century of progress. In Symposium on Social Values and Public Policy, W. N. Dunn (Ed.). *Policy Studies Journal 9,* 4: 535-544 (Special Issue No. 2).

Gauthier, D. (1974). Rational cooperation. *NOUS 8*: 53-65.

Gewirth, A. (1960). Positive ethics and normative science. *Philosophical Review 69*: 311-330.

—— (1978a). Ethics. In *Encyclopedia Britannica,* 15th ed. Encyclopedia Britannica, Chicago, pp. 976-998.

—— (1978b). *Reason and Morality.* University of Chicago Press, Chicago.

Graham, G. J., Jr. (1981). The role of the humanities in public policy evaluation. *Soundings 64*, 2: 150-169.

Habermas, J. (1970). *Toward a Rational Society.* Beacon, Boston.

—— (1975). *Legitimation Crisis.* Beacon, Chicago.

Hammond, K. R. (1977). *Judgment and Decision in Public Policy Formation.* Westview, Boulder, CO.

Handy, R. (1970). *The Measurement of Values: Behavioral Science and Philosophical Approaches.* Green, St. Louis.

Hare, R. M. (1952). *The Language of Morals.* Cambridge University Press, Cambridge.

—— (1963). *Freedom and Reason.* Oxford University Press, New York.

Harsanyi, J. C. (1977). *Rational Behavior and Bargaining Equilibrium in Games and Social Situations.* Cambridge University Press, Cambridge.

Hastings Center (1980). *Teaching of Ethics in Higher Education.* Hastings Center, Hastings-on-Hudson, NY.

Hesse, M. (1978). Theory and value in the social sciences. In *Action and Interpretation: Studies in the Philosophy of the Social Sciences.* C. Hookway and P. Pettit (Eds.). Cambridge University Press, Cambridge, pp. 1-16.

—— (1979). *Revolutions and Reconstructions in the Philosophy of Science.* Indiana University Press, Bloomington.

Horowitz, I. L., and Katz, J. (1975). *Social Science and Public Policy in the United States.* Praeger, New York.

House, E. R. (1980). *Evaluating with Validity.* Sage, Beverly Hills, CA.

Howe, E., and Kaufman, J. (1979). The ethics of contemporary American planners. *Journal of the American Planning Association 45*: 243-255.

—— (1981). Ethics and professional practice in planning and related policy professions. In Symposium on Social Values and Public Policy, W. N. Dunn (Ed.). *Policy Studies Journal 9*, 4: 585-594 (Special Issue No. 2).

Jones, C. O. (1977). *An Introduction to the Study of Public Policy,* 2nd ed. Duxbury, North Scituate, MA.

Kaplan, A. (1964). *The Conduct of Inquiry.* Chandler, San Francisco.

Kerlinger, F. (1973). *Foundations of Behavioral Research,* 2nd ed. Holt, Rinehart and Winston, New York.

Kern, J. (1979). Ethics and values in schools of public policy. *Journal of Public and International Affairs 1*, 1: 41-46.

Kluckhohn, F. R., and Strodtbeck, F. L. (1961). *Variations in Value Orientation.* Row, Peterson, Evanston, IL.

Knott, J., and Wildavsky, A. (1980). If dissemination is the solution, what is the problem? *Knowledge: Creation-Diffusion-Utilization 1*, 4.

Kohlberg, L. (1961). *Stages in the Development of Moral Thought and Action.* Holt, Rinehart and Winston, New York.

—— (1971). From is to ought: How to commit the naturalistic fallacy and get away with it in the study of moral development. In *Cognitive Development and Epistemology,* T. Mischel (Ed.). Academic Press, New York, pp. 151-235.

—— (1978). Cognitive-developmental approach to behavior disorders: Study of the development of moral reasoning in delinquents. In *Cognitive Defects in the Development of Mental Illness,* G. Serbian (Ed.). Brimner-Mazel, New York, pp. 207-219.

Kohlberg, L., and Turiel, E. (1971). *Recent Research in Moral Development.* Holt, Rinehart and Winston, New York.

Kohler, W. (1938). *The Place of Value in a World of Facts.* Liveright, New York.

Lake, D. G., Miles, M. B., and Earle, R. B., Jr. (1973). *Measuring Human Behavior.* Teachers College Press, Columbia University, New York.

Lasswell, H. D. (1963). *The Future of Political Science.* Atherton, New York.

—— (1971). *A Preview of Policy Sciences.* Elsevier, New York.

Lasswell, H. D., and Kaplan, A. (1950). *Power and Society.* Yale University Press, New Haven, CT.

Laudan, L. (1977). *Progress and Its Problems: Towards a Theory of Scientific Growth.* University of California Press, Berkeley and Los Angeles.

Lerner, D., and Lasswell, H. D. (1951). *The Policy Sciences.* Stanford University Press, Stanford, CA.

Lindblom, C. E. (1980). *The Policy-Making Process.* Prentice-Hall, Englewood Cliffs, NJ.

Little, I. M. D. (1950). *A Critique of Welfare Economics.* Clarendon Press, Oxford.

MacRae, D., Jr. (1976). *The Social Function of Social Science.* Yale University Press, New Haven, CT.

Mason, R. O., and Mitroff, I. I. (1981a). *Challenging Strategic Planning Assumptions.* Wiley, Chicago.

—— (1981b). Policy analysis as argument. In Symposium on Social Values and Public Policy, W. N. Dunn (Ed.). *Policy Studies Journal 9*, 4: 579-584 (Special Issue No. 2).

Meltsner, A. J. (1976). *Policy Analysts in the Bureaucracy.* Basic Books, New York.

Merriam, C. (1945). *Systematic Politics.* University of Chicago Press, Chicago.

Mertins, H. (1979). *Professional Standards and Ethics: A Workbook for Public Administrators.* American Society for Public Administration, Washington, DC.

Michalos, A. C. (1981). Facts, values, and rational decision making. In Symposium on Social Values and Public Policy, W. N. Dunn (Ed.). *Policy Studies Journal 9*, 4: 544-551 (Special Issue No. 2).

Miller, D. C. (1979). *Handbook of Research Design and Social Measurement,* 3rd ed. David McKay, Chicago.

Moore, G. E. (1903). *Principia Ethica.* Cambridge University Press, Cambridge.

Mueller, D. C. (1979). *Public Choice.* Cambridge University Press, Cambridge.

Mukerjee, R. (1949). *The Social Structure of Values.* Macmillan, London.

Nachmias, D. (1980). *Public Policy Evaluation.* St. Martin's, New York.

Nagel, S. S. (1981). The means may be a goal. In Symposium on Social Values and Public Policy, W. N. Dunn (Ed.). *Policy Studies Journal 9*, 4: 567-579 (Special Issue No. 2).

Ostrom, V. (1974). *The Intellectual Crisis in American Public Administration,* rev. ed. University of Alabama Press, 1974.

Patton, M. Q. (1978). *Utilization-Focused Evaluation.* Sage, Beverly Hills, CA.

Pepper, S. C. (1958). *The Sources of Value.* University of California Press, Berkeley.

Perry, R. B. (1926). *General Theory of Value.* Harvard University Press, Cambridge, MA.

—— (1954). *Realms of Value.* Harvard University Press, Cambridge, MA.

Piaget, J. (1948). *The Moral Judgment of the Child.* Free Press, Glencoe, IL.

Popper, K. R. (1968). *The Logic of Scientific Discovery.* Harper & Row, New York.

Quade, E. S. (1975). *Analysis for Public Decisions.* American Elsevier, New York.

Raiffa, H. (1968). *Decision Analysis: Pure and Applied.* Addison-Wesley, Reading, MA.

Rawls, J. (1955). Two concepts of rules. *Philosophical Review 44*, 1: 3-32.

—— (1971). *A Theory of Justice.* Harvard University Press, Cambridge, MA.

Reamer, F. G. (1979). Fundamental ethical issues in social work: An essay review. *Social Service Review* June: 229-243.

Reid, H. G., and Yanarella, E. J. (1975). Political science and the postmodern critique of science and domination. *Review of Politics 37*, 3: 286-316.

Rein, M. (1976). *Social Science and Public Policy.* Penguin, Baltimore.

Rescher, N. (1966). *Distributive Justice: A Constructive Critique of the Utilitarian Theory of Justice.* Bobbs-Merrill, Indianapolis, IN.

—— (1969). *Introduction to Value Theory.* Prentice-Hall, Englewood Cliffs, NJ.

Robinson, J. P., Athanasiou, R., and Head, K. B. (1969). *Measures of Occupational Attitudes and Occupational Characteristics.* Institute for Social Research, University of Michigan, Ann Arbor.

Robinson, J. P., Rusk, J. G., and Head, K. B. (1968). *Measures of Political Attitudes.* Institute for Social Research, University of Michigan, Ann Arbor.

Robinson, J. P., and Shaver, P. R. (1969). *Measures of Social Psychological Attitudes,* Institute for Social Research, University of Michigan, Ann Arbor.

Rokeach, M. (1968). *Beliefs, Attitudes, and Values.* Jossey-Bass, San Francisco.

—— (1973). *The Nature of Human Values.* Free Press, New York.

Saaty, T. (1981). *The Analytic Hierarchy Process.* McGraw-Hill, New York.

Scriven, M. (1967). The methodology of evaluation. In *Perspecitves of Curriculum Evaluation.* Rand McNally, Chicago.

Shaw, M. E., and Wright, J. W. (1967). *Scales for the Measurement of Attitudes.* McGraw-Hill, New York.

Smith, M. (1977). *A Practical Guide to Value Clarification.* University Associates, LaJolla, CA.

Smith, M. B. (1969). *Social Psychology and Human Values.* Aldine, Chicago.

Steinfels, P. (1977). The place of ethics in schools of public policy: A report from the Hastings Center, Institute of Society, Ethics, and the Life Science to the Ford Foundation. Hastings Center, Hastings-on-Hudson, NY. Mimeo.

Stevenson, C. L. (1944). *Ethics and Language.* Cambridge University Press, Cambridge.

Stokey, E., and Zeckhauser, R. (1978). *A Primer for Policy Analysis.* Norton, New York.

Sutherland, J. W. (1973). *A General Systems Philosophy for the Social and Behavioral Sciences.* Braziller, New York.

—— (1974). Axiological predicates of scientific enterprise. *General Systems 19*: 3-13.

Taylor, P. (1961). *Normative Discourse.* Prentice-Hall, Englewood Cliffs, NJ.

Thomas, W. I., and Znaniecki, F. (1918). *The Polish Peasant in Europe and America.* University of Chicago Press, Chicago.

Thurstone, L. L. (1954). The measurement of values. *Psychological Review 61.*

Toulmin, S. (1950). *The Place of Reason in Ethics.* Oxford University Press, Oxford.

—— (1958). *The Uses of Argument.* Cambridge University Press, Cambridge.

Toulmin, S., Rieke, R., and Janik, A. (1979). *An Introduction to Reasoning.* Macmillan, New York.

Tribe, L. (1972). Policy science: Analysis or ideology. *Philosophy and Public Affairs 2,* 1: 66-110.

—— (1976). Ways not to think about plastic trees. In *When Values Conflict.* L. H. Tribe, C. S. Schelling, and J. Voss (Eds.). Ballinger, Cambridge, MA, pp. 61-91.

Tribe, L. H., Schelling, C. S., and Voss, J. (Eds.) (1976). *When Values Conflict: Essays on Environmental Analysis, Discourse, and Decision.* Ballinger, Cambridge, MA.

Webb, E. J., Campbell, D. T., Schwartz, R. D., and Sechrest, L. B. (1981). *Unobtrusive Measures.* Rand McNally, Chicago.

White, R. K. (1951). *Value Analysis: The Nature and Use of Method.* Society for the Psychological Study of Social Issues, Glen Gardner, NJ.

Wildavsky, A. (1979). *Speaking Truth to Power: The Art and Craft of Policy Analysis.* Little, Brown, Boston.

Williams, R. M., Jr. (1951, 1960). *American Society: A Sociological Interpretation,* 2nd ed. Knopf, New York.

—— (1968). The concept of values. In *Encyclopedia of Social Sciences,* pp. 283-287.

Author Index

Numbers in parentheses are reference numbers and indicate that an author's work is re-ferred to although the name may not be cited in the text. Numbers in brackets give the page on which the complete reference is listed.

A

Aaron, H., [262], 487, [498]
Abbott, D. J., 560, [578]
Abel, R. L., 557, [575]
Aberbach, J. D., 365, [386]
Abernathy, W. T., 681, [683]
Ackoff, R. L., 19, 23, 37, [38], 846, 847, 859, [861]
Adamany, D. W., 351, [355]
Adams, B., 538, [539]
Adams, C. F., 163, [168]
Adams, C. T., 171, [197], 545, 546, [554]
Adams, G., 184, [195]
Adelman, L., 743, [74], 834, [861]
Agarwala-Rogers, R., 95, [111]
Agarwall, R. K., 312(54), [328]
Albonetti, C., 572, [580]
Alchian, A. A., [461]
Alexander, C., 50, [61]
Alexander, H. E., 351, [355], 369, 378, 384, [386]
Alexis, M., 544, [554]
Alfini, J., 568, [576]
Alford, R. A., [264]
Alinky, S., 841, [861]
Alkin, M. C., 105, [111]
Allardt, E., 173, [195]
Allen, R. L., 247, [261]
Alleyne, R. H., [460]
Allison, G. T., 98, [111], 184, [195], 272, 277, 287, 290, [291], 323(95), [330, 610]

Allport, G. W., [861]
Almond, G. A., 172, 185, [196], 271, 280, [291]
Alschuler, A. W., 557, 566, [575]
Alschuler, L. R., 284, [291]
Alston, H., 809, [827]
Altenstetter, C., 152, [165]
Altenstittic, C., 757(56), [772]
Alterman, T., 682, [683]
Altman, D., 147, [165], 759(25), [771]
Altman, S. H., 818, [824]
Altschuler, A. A., 681, [682]
Amacher, R., 212, [218], 490, [498]
Ament, R. H., [826]
Ames, B., 489, [498]
Andenaes, T., [576]
Anderson, F., 720(65), [726]
Anderson, J., [460]
Anderson, J. E., 119, 123, [140], 832, 858, [861]
Anderson, M., 818, 819, [826]
Ando, A., 487, [498]
Andrews, D., 572, [576]
Andringa, R. C., 595, [610]
Andriole, S. J., 283, 287, 289, [298]
Annas, G. J., 806, [824]
Ansio, T., 32, [38]
Anton, T. J., 192, [196]
Antunes, G. E., 561, [586]
Aperk, T., 567, [576]
Apter, D. E., 185, [196]
Arcelus, F., 490, [498]
Archibald, G. C., [461]
Argyris, C., 102, [111]

867

Subject Index